UNITED NATIONS PEACEKEEPING

1946–1967

DOCUMENTS AND COMMENTARY

The Royal Institute of International Affairs is an unofficial body which promotes the scientific study of international questions and does not express opinions of its own. The opinions expressed in this publication are the responsibility of the author.

The Institute gratefully acknowledges the comments and suggestions of the following who read the manuscript on behalf of the Research Committee: Professor Geoffrey Goodwin, Eli Lauterpacht, and H. G. Nicholas.

UNITED NATIONS PEACEKEEPING

1946–1967

DOCUMENTS AND COMMENTARY

I

The Middle East

ROSALYN HIGGINS

M.A., LL.B. (Cantab.), J.S.D. (Yale)

Issued under the auspices of the
Royal Institute of International Affairs

OXFORD UNIVERSITY PRESS

LONDON   NEW YORK   TORONTO

1969

Oxford University Press, Ely House, London W.1

GLASGOW NEW YORK TORONTO MELBOURNE WELLINGTON
CAPE TOWN SALISBURY IBADAN NAIROBI LUSAKA ADDIS ABABA
BOMBAY CALCUTTA MADRAS KARACHI LAHORE DACCA
KUALA LUMPUR SINGAPORE HONG KONG TOKYO

JX
1981
P7
H5
Vol. 1

57776

PRINTED IN GREAT BRITAIN BY
EBENEZER BAYLIS AND SON, LIMITED,
THE TRINITY PRESS, WORCESTER, AND LONDON

CONTENTS

Abbreviations   viii
Preface and Acknowledgements   ix

Part 1

THE UNITED NATIONS TRUCE SUPERVISION ORGANIZATION (UNTSO), 1949–

1   Introduction   5
2   Enabling Resolutions and Voting   16
3   Functions and Mandate   18
4   Constitutional Basis   60
5   Political Control   63
6   Administrative and Military Control   64
7   Composition and Size   66
8   Relations with Contributing States   72
9   Relations with Host States   72
10   Relations with Other States Involved   132
11   Finance   133
12   Implementation   137
13   Annexes   212
     A. Checklist of Documents   212
     B. Bibliography   216

Part 2

THE UNITED NATIONS EMERGENCY FORCE (UNEF), 1956–67

1   Introduction   221
2   Enabling Resolutions and Voting   227
3   Functions and Mandate   241
4   Constitutional Basis   260
5   Political Control   273
6   Administrative and Military Control   278
7   Composition and Size   300
8   Relations with Contributing States   324
9   Relations with Host States   335
10   Relations with Other States Involved   385
11   Finance   415
12   Implementation   456
13   Annexes   526
     A. Checklist of Documents   526
     B. Bibliography   528

Part 3

THE UNITED NATIONS OBSERVER GROUP IN LEBANON (UNOGIL), 1958

1	Introduction	535
2	Enabling Resolution and Voting	546
3	Functions and Mandate	547
4	Constitutional Basis	549
5	Political Control	551
6	Administrative and Military Control	553
7	Composition and Size	555
8	Relations with Contributing States	558
9	Relations with Host States	558
10	Relations with Other States Involved	565
11	Finance	566
12	Implementation	568
13	Annexes	602
	A. Checklist of Documents	602
	B. Bibliography	603

Part 4

THE UNITED NATIONS YEMEN OBSERVATION MISSION (UNYOM), 1963-4

1	Introduction	609
2	Enabling Resolution and Voting	620
3	Functions and Mandate	622
4	Constitutional Basis	625
5	Political Control	635
6	Administrative and Military Control	637
7	Composition and Size	638
8	Relations with Contributing States	641
9	Relations with Host States	641
10	Relations with Other States Involved	645
11	Finance	645
12	Implementation	653
13	Annexes	669
	A. Checklist of Documents	669
	B. Bibliography	669
	Index	671

MAPS

1   The Middle East, showing the 1949 Armistice Agreements between Israel
    and Lebanon, Syria, Jordan and Egypt   4

2   Deployment of UNEF in May 1967   218

3   Operations of the UN Observation Group in Lebanon, 1958   534

4   Yemen showing Demilitarized Zone   608

ABBREVIATIONS

a.i.	Agenda item
ann.	annex
AJIL	*American Journal of International Law*
B.	*Bulletin*
BYIL	*British Yearbook of International Law*
ECOSOC	Economic and Social Council
FDLs	Forward Defensive Lines
GAOR	*General Assembly Official Records*
ICJ Rep.	*International Court of Justice Reports*
ICLQ	*International and Comparative Law Quarterly*
Int. Org.	*International Organization*
J.	*Journal*
MAC	Mixed Armistice Commission
ONUC	Organisation des Nations Unies au Congo
plen.	plenary
R.	*Review*
Res.	Resolution
s.	section
SCOR	*Security Council Official Records*
SCUA	Suez Canal Users' Association
sess.	session
suppl.	supplement
UNEF	UN Emergency Force
UNOGIL	UN Observation Group in Lebanon
UNSCOP	UN Special Committee on Palestine
UNTS	UN Treaty Series
UNTSO	UN Truce Supervision Organization
UNYOM	UN Yemen Observation Mission

PREFACE AND ACKNOWLEDGEMENTS

THIS is the first of three projected volumes of documents and commentary on United Nations peacekeeping operations. It deals with UN actions in the Middle East, covering specifically the Palestine Truce Supervision Organization, the Emergency Force in Egypt, and the observer groups in Lebanon and Yemen. The second volume will cover UN operations in Asia—the enforcement action in Korea, observers in Indonesia, the Security Force in West Irian, and the two distinct military observer groups in Kashmir and India and Pakistan. The final volume will be concerned with peacekeeping in the Balkans, Cyprus, and the Congo.

The concept of 'peacekeeping' is open to a variety of definitions, and it has been used in several ways by different persons writing on the subject. To some, peacekeeping is a broad concept, referring to the entire role of the UN in maintaining, or restoring, international peace. According to this definition, any book on peacekeeping must refer not only to UN Forces, but to investigation committees, special representatives of the Secretary-General, and diplomacy within the UN system. Others have suggested that peacekeeping is a term which has come to refer to UN Forces and observer groups which are operational on a territory with the consent of its government. Yet others have insisted that the term peacekeeping cannot include UN observers. There is, of course, no one 'correct' definition. All of these definitions, and some others besides, may be permissible according to the purpose of the particular study. In these three volumes UN peacekeeping has been taken to refer to operations in which personnel owing allegiance to the UN are engaged in military or para-military duties; and/or are carrying weapons for their own defence in the pursuit of duties designated by the UN as necessary for the maintenance or restoration of peace. These criteria have been taken as the relevant ones, whether or not the operation depends upon the consent of the government on whose territory it is taking place. Accordingly, this study deals with para-military actions such as ONUC in the Congo and UNEF in Egypt; with military operations such as the UN action against North Korea; and with the military observer groups which have served in the Lebanon, Kashmir, the Middle East, and elsewhere. It does not include separate examination of the diplomatic role of the Secretary-General, or of the various contributions to peace which have been made by his personal representatives or by special fact-finding commissions.

In view of the existing literature on UN peacekeeping, it may be appropriate to set out the reasons why it has been felt necessary to compile these volumes.

The existing literature may roughly be grouped in three categories. First, studies of particular operations—Korea, the Emergency Force in Egypt, the Congo operation—of which the studies by Burns and Heathcote, Poirier, Goodrich, and Gabriella Rosner are excellent examples. Second, studies such as those by Wainhouse or Ruth Russell, which seek to touch on all the UN's peacekeeping activities, if only briefly. And finally, studies by internationa lawyers such as Bowett and Seyersted drawing attention to the complex legal problems involved. The detailed studies of the first category are, by definition, limited to one or two operations; the broader-ranging studies of the second group are necessarily limited in depth; and the legal studies again either emphasize the better-known operations or concentrate upon a particular cluster of legal problems.

Moreover, though each of these studies is an extremely important contribution to the subject, none of them makes much use of primary source materials. There are references to, and occasionally brief quotations from, UN documents, but these are to support the author's text. There is no one single place to which the student of peacekeeping can turn for ready access to all the documentation. He has been obliged to flounder among the voluminous and unsifted UN documentation—with which he may not be familiar—and has had no guarantee that he has discovered all the relevant materials or that he has fully appreciated their implications. The events of May–June 1967 in the Middle East clearly illustrate the need that is felt for readily available documentation on UN peacekeeping. The public debates of these weeks also show the dangers of familiarity with only isolated documents, rather than the entire range of documentary evidence presented within its proper historical, political, and legal context.

For this reason, my aim in these volumes has been to provide a study of all the UN peacekeeping operations, giving the least known the same close attention as the best known, so that the reader who wishes to study the Balkans in 1949 or Kashmir in 1965 will, I trust, find as much pertinent material as the reader who may seek information on the Middle East or the Congo. I have also tried to ensure that the user of these volumes should be enabled to familiarize himself not only with the details of the UN's role in each country concerned, but also to pursue any interest he might have in, for example, the financing of UN peacekeeping, or the problems of command structure, in all the operations.

The arrangement has been devised to facilitate both comparative analysis and understanding of the significance of particular documents. While the volumes are broadly regional in scope, in each the main order is the order in time at which each operation started. But the documents comprising any one operation are not presented purely chronologically but are divided by categories which are common to all operations, such as the functions of the force, financing, relations between the UN and the host states, etc.

The main aim of the commentaries is to link the documents so as to present the entire story of each operation and to clarify points which are not wholly apparent in the UN texts. I have endeavoured to avoid using the commentaries as a vehicle for editorial opinion: the object is to clarify the differing viewpoints of the protagonists, not to pronounce in favour of any viewpoint. Only in two circumstances does the commentary go beyond this role. The first is in the historical introduction which prefaces each operation, demonstrating how the UN became involved. The second is to analyse points at issue in the case of documents which touch on problems of international law, and to refer the reader to relevant published work.

The materials themselves are limited to official UN documents and records of UN organs. I have been well aware of the dangers of limiting the source materials in this way, but the decision has been dictated by two compelling reasons. In the first place, if the aim were to provide a comprehensive survey of UN documentation on peacekeeping, the size of the endeavour would leave little space for government documents or quotations from books or articles. Second, language is inevitably a limiting factor: translation of documents from, for example, Russian or Arabic, would be a task of considerable magnitude, and would in any event entail an initial process of selection which I am not competent to conduct. However, all nations have the opportunity of presenting their viewpoint within the UN in one of the five major working languages. I have sought to offset any shortcomings of this decision by several means. Great pains have been taken to present all the different arguments raised, though I have relied on statements issued at the UN for this purpose. I have also endeavoured to give information which is relevant to an understanding of the documents, whether Attlee's celebrated flight to Washington in 1950, Eshkol's domestic position in early 1967, or Shastri's death in 1966. Reference is also made in footnotes to some of the more important national documents, and to various secondary sources. Finally, a bibliography of major books and articles is given at the end of each Part.

These bibliographies necessarily refer to particular operations. However, there are certain basic books, which do not fall readily within any one operation, to which any student of UN peacekeeping must refer, and I have made great use of the following: Lincoln Bloomfield and others, *International Military Forces* (1964); Derek Bowett, *United Nations Forces* (1964); Arthur Burns and Nina Heathcote, *Peacekeeping by UN Forces* (1963); Jack Citrin, *United Nations Peacekeeping Activities: a Case Study in Organizational Task Expansion* (Denver, Col., 1965, mimeo.); Arthur Cox, *Prospects for Peacekeeping* (1967); Per Frydenberg, *Peacekeeping: Experience and Evaluation* (1964); Ruth Russell, *United Nations Experience with Military Forces: Political and Legal Aspects* (1964); Finn Seyersted, *United Nations Forces in the Law of Peace and War* (1966); John Stoessinger, *Financing the United Nations System* (1964); David Wainhouse, *International Peace Observation* (1966); and Oran Young, *Trends in International Peacekeeping* (Princeton, N.J., Jan. 1966).

A word needs to be said about my method of using the documents. Although I have avoided brief quotations, many documents are not reproduced in their entirety. This is because UN documents are frequently repetitive, and once the decision had been taken to present them under subject headings, rather than chronologically, it became apparent that not everything in a document was relevant to the particular heading. I can here only rely on the conventions of scholarship. All omissions are indicated in the customary manner. My selection has been made solely for the purpose of placing materials within the categories to which they logically belong. The reader may at all times confirm this by means of citations which appear at the end of every document and of the checklist of documents which appears in an appendix at the end of each Part. It remains to add that a few documents of major importance, which one has come to think of as an integral whole—such as the Secretary-General's report in 1958 of the experience of UNEF—are reproduced in their entirety, though small extracts from them may also appear under other headings where they naturally belong. Numbered footnotes are those of the Editor; footnotes bearing symbols are quoted from the document concerned. When the printed version of any UN document was not available at the time of writing, it was necessary to rely on the provisional or mimeographed versions, as has been indicated in citing the sources. These versions differ in minor respects from the ultimate, authorized record.

As the Contents page shows, the documents and accompanying commentary are divided throughout into twelve sections. Inevitably, there are certain difficult choices that have had to be made as to the section to which a particular document belongs. The effectiveness of a UN operation may in part depend upon whether satisfactory relations exist between the UN and the host country. Thus sometimes materials seem relevant both to section 9 and section 12. Equally, an operation may be hampered by lack of financial support, and the documentary materials again relate both to section 11 and to section 12. There are many other examples which could be given. I have sought, when faced with these choices, to place documents within those sections where their centre of gravity seems to fall. In each case, the text makes the position clear. In the final analysis, the detailed synopsis at the beginning of each Part, or the index, should lead the reader to them, but I have followed certain guidelines. In each Part section 12 on Implementation covers matters which have not fallen under the previous sections, though cross-references are provided to these where they are relevant. The great bulk of field reports to the UN (Chief of Command reports, etc.) fall within this section, except in so far as they dealt with matters specifically enumerated in sections 5–11. Agreements made between the UN and the nations providing forces or observers will always be found in section 8, as will treatment of claims for compensation for death or injury. Directives and instructions issued by the UN to its observers or forces fall under section 6, as does the question of jurisdiction over offences by UN para-military personnel. Status of Forces Agreements are examined within the framework of section 9.

It remains to explain that throughout I have sought to do more than merely provide the formal documents. Thus the examination of relations between the UN and a host state is by no means confined to a reproduction of the relevant Status of Forces Agreement; other documents and the commentary trace the ups and downs of the relationship. I have attempted to illustrate and explain what really happened, what difficulties arose, and what understandings were reached.

In these endeavours I have been greatly aided by many people, to whom I would here like to express my thanks. This study has been financed by the Carnegie Endowment for International Peace, for whose generosity and patience as this project expanded—and expanded still further—I am most grateful. The support of the Carnegie Endowment has been far more than financial: the great personal interest which Joe Johnson and Anne Winslow have shown in this venture, and their readiness to join in seeking the answers to particularly knotty points, has been a constant source of encouragement to me. Various officials in the UN Secretariat have given me generous assistance. I have had the advantage of long conversations with Ralph Bunche in the autumn of 1966, and his total recall on matters concerning the UN role in the Middle East has benefited me greatly. Brian Urquhart has been extraordinarily kind in clarifying matters for me on which the documents were obscure, and in responding to queries to which no answers could be found in London. I am very grateful that he and Ralph Bunche should have found time to help me when they have had so many pressing and important duties. Blaine Sloan and Oscar Schachter have helped me greatly with information relating to legal points which have arisen, and the readiness with which they have answered my questions has been most helpful. And Bruce Turner has patiently explained to me some of the more baffling aspects of UN accounting procedure.

Nor can I allow the debt which I owe the London UN Information Centre to go unacknowledged. It is to Margaret McAfee that I have gone with my most intractable problems, with demands for the most recondite documents. I thank her for her efficient and good-humoured assistance, and also William Henson for his help.

James Knott, of the International Information Center on Peacekeeping Operations, has been a constant source of information on the size, national composition, and logistics of UN Forces. Arthur Hillis, formerly of the United Kingdom Mission to the UN, has advised me on technical questions relating to the financing of certain UN operations. And Donald Watt has cast a historian's critical eye over the historical introduction to each Part.

The entire manuscript has been read by Eli Lauterpacht of Trinity College, Cambridge; Geoffrey Goodwin of the London School of Economics; and Herbert Nicholas of New College, Oxford. The extraordinary care with which they have read this work and their comments and proposals have been invaluable. I have adopted many of their suggestions and am deeply grateful for the care they have taken and the interest they have shown.

In Chatham House many people have lent their labours to this venture. The members of the Library staff have all been immensely helpful, and June Wells and Angela Williams have, successively, borne the brunt of my insatiable appetite for UN documents. Their efficiency and enthusiasm are much appreciated. To Bridget Martyn, who did the initial editorial work on this manuscript, I extend my thanks. She constantly directed my attention, in presenting this vast mass of material, to the needs of the reader. I am greatly indebted to Hermia Oliver for her editorial expertise, and for the meticulous and scholarly manner with which she has handled this volume. I have relied on her editorial experience and judgement, and have benefited greatly from her considerable labours. A special expression of appreciation is due to my secretary, Rene Landman: she has coped valiantly with the many secretarial problems that arise in preparing a study of this sort, and has somehow transformed a myriad of instructions, clippings, references, and comments into a coherent manuscript. Above all, she has helped to keep both of our heads (just) above the sea of documents. Nor should the contribution of Maggie Lim be underestimated, for she has, with speed and good humour, done all the photocopying which this volume has entailed.

Finally, I must thank my husband, Terence Higgins, whose tolerance, forebearance, and encouragement has contributed so much to this work.

While I am in the debt of all these persons, none of them is of course in any way responsible for any shortcomings or errors in this book, nor do they necessarily share the views expressed therein.

R.H.

London, February 1968

Part 1

THE UNITED NATIONS
TRUCE SUPERVISION ORGANIZATION
(UNTSO), 1949–

1. INTRODUCTION (p. 5)

THE British mandate in Palestine; the Balfour Declaration and the Palestine White Paper of May 1939; the situation at the end of World War II; foreign policy of the British Labour government; Truman's reaction to the proposals of the Anglo-American Committee of Enquiry; civil violence in Palestine; the issue goes to the General Assembly; the UN Special Committee on Palestine (UNSCOP); a Plan of Partition; response of the Arabs and Jews; the Security Council orders two truces and appoints a Mediator; Special Session of the General Assembly; Britain terminates the mandate; birth of the State of Israel and war with the Arabs.

2. ENABLING RESOLUTIONS AND VOTING (p. 16)

The establishment of a Truce Commission; reaction of designated members; affirmation by the Security Council of the Armistice Agreements; Soviet attitudes to the United Nations Truce Supervision Organization (UNTSO).

3. FUNCTIONS AND MANDATE (p. 18)

(a) *Functions of the Truce Commission in relation to the Truces of 1948:* compliance with the cease-fire order, negotiation and maintenance of a truce; investigation of incidents; instructions issued to observers.

(b) *Functions of UNTSO under Armistice Agreements:* reasons for retention of UN observers; duties under each Armistice Agreement; tasks of the mixed Armistice Commissions; assignment of additional duties to UNTSO by subsequent Security Council resolutions; quasi-judicial functions of Chief of Staff of UNTSO; texts of all four agreements.

(c) *Functions of UNTSO after November 1956:* UNTSO on the Egyptian–Israel frontier; relationship of UNEF to UNTSO;

(d) *Functions of UNTSO after June 1967:* UNTSO during the six-day war; functions in respect of achieving, mapping, and observing the cease-fires; establishment of UN observers along the Suez Canal.

4. CONSTITUTIONAL BASIS (p. 60)

Basis of action of 1948; and of UNTSO under the Armistice Agreements; and of the placing of observers along the Suez Canal in 1967; Charter authority and the consent of the parties; the 'informal consensus' of July and December 1967.

5. POLITICAL CONTROL (p. 63)

Role of Secretary-General; relationship to both Security Council and Chief of Staff.

6. ADMINISTRATIVE AND MILITARY CONTROL (p. 64)

(a) *Under the 1948 Resolutions:* role of Mediator, Truce Supervision Boards, observers;

(b) *Under the 1949 Armistice Agreements:* particular arrangements in each agreement; attachment of observers to MACs (Mixed Armistice Commissions); role of Chairmen of MACs.

7. COMPOSITION AND SIZE (p. 66)
Number and nationalities of observers on Truce Commission; nations contributing to UNTSO under Armistice Agreements; reductions in number; various Chiefs of Staff; enlargement of numbers of observers, and nations represented, after war of June 1967.

8. RELATIONS WITH CONTRIBUTING STATES (p. 72)
Method of hiring UNTSO personnel; claims for reparation for injuries or death.

9. RELATIONS WITH HOST STATES (p. 72)
(a) *During the 1948 Truces:* relations with the Mediator; agreements concerning Jerusalem and Mount Scopus; problem of irregulars; assassination of Count Bernadotte; claims for reparation made in respect of UN personnel; Security Council calls for a cease-fire.
(b) *Under the 1949 Armistice Agreements*
  i. *The Syria–Israel Armistice*
     Relations 1949–56: Problems of Article V of the Agreement; disputes over the role of the MAC in the demilitarized zone; the Chief of Staff attempts quasi-judicial tasks; incidents on Lake Huleh; Security Council resolution of May 1951; breakdown of MAC meetings.
     Relations 1956–67: Continuing problems over the demilitarized zone.
  ii. *The Egypt–Israel Armistice*
     Relations 1949–56: Impediments to regular meetings of the MAC; UN suggestions for Gaza patrolling.
     Relations 1956–67: Israel's attitude to UNTSO after the intervention of 1956; claim that Armistice abrogated; Egyptian claims to belligerency under the armistice regime; views of Dag Hammarskjöld.
  iii. *The Jordan–Israel Armistice*
     Relations 1949–56: Problems concerning the demilitarization of Mount Scopus; the Scorpion Pass incident, and Israel's withdrawal from the MAC.
     Relations 1956–67: Civilian activity in the demilitarized zone; UN claims for reparation against Jordan.
  iv. *The Lebanon–Israel Armistice*
     Relations 1949–67
(c) *Under the June 1967 Cease-Fire Orders* Government House falls to Israeli control; and is eventually returned to UNTSO; Syria and Israel co-operate with UNTSO in mapping the cease-fire.

10. RELATIONS WITH OTHER STATES INVOLVED (p. 132)
Materials all dealt with under s. 9.

11. FINANCE (p. 133)
Expenditures on UNTSO between 1949 and 1967; method of apportioning them.

12. IMPLEMENTATION (p. 137)
(a) *1949–56*
  i. *Syria–Israel Armistice 1949–56*
     Problem of the demilitarized zone and reclamation of Huleh Marshes; disputes about role of Israeli police; incidents on Lake Tiberias; Security Council resolutions of 1956; report of Secretary-General on problems underlying Israel–Syrian relations.
  ii. *Egypt–Israel Armistice 1949–56*
     UNTSO's role in respect of refugees; decisions of the MAC; *fedayeen* raids from Gaza strip; Security Council resolutions of 1955; freedom of movement for UN observers;

breaches of Article VIII of Armistice Agreement; freedom of passage through the Suez Canal; and in the Gulf of Aqaba.

iii. *Jordan–Israel Armistice 1949–56*

Demarcation line incidents; civilian incursions; the boycotting of the MAC; General Bennike reports to the Security Council; Security Council resolution of 1953; local measures taken; Scorpion Pass and Beit Liqya incidents; special committee established under Article VIII.

iv. *Lebanon–Israel Armistice 1949–56*

Successful meetings of MAC; minor incidents only.

(*b*) *Observations common to all 4 Armistices, 1956*

Security Council resolution of April 1956; Secretary-General's reports; the question of reprisals and self defence.

(*c*) *1957–67*

i. *Syria–Israel Armistice 1956–67*

Continuing problems over demilitarized zone; failure of Colonel Leary's suggestions; project for diverting River Jordan; serious breakdown of the Armistice in Lake Tiberias region; incursions and reprisals in 1966; six-power resolution vetoed; U Thant reports on obstacles to UNTSO's work.

ii. *Egypt–Israel Armistice 1956–67*

Israel's denunciation; role of UNEF; the Armistice Agreement and the question of freedom of shipping through the Straits of Tiran, 1967.

iii. *Jordan–Israel Armistice 1956–67*

Jordan's role in 1966; reprisals by Israel; condemnation by Security Council.

iv. *Lebanon–Israel Armistice 1956–67*

Continuing efficacy.

(*d*) *After June 1967*

UNTSO's role in establishing the cease-fires; Security Council resolutions; the carrying out of new tasks in the Suez Canal zone; the question of movement of boats on the Canal; General Bull secures agreement.

13. ANNEXES (p. 212)

A. Checklist of Documents (p. 212)

B. Bibliography (p. 216)

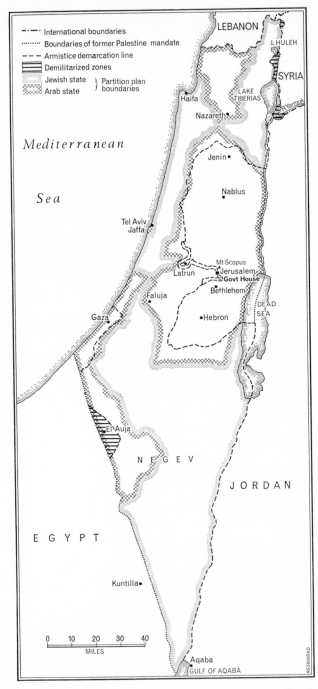

1. The Middle East, showing the 1949 Armistice Agreements between Israel and Lebanon, Syria, Jordan, and Egypt

I

INTRODUCTION

BRITAIN held a mandate over Palestine of the 'A' class—that is to say, a mandate which applied to 'certain communities belonging to the Turkish Empire' which had 'reached a stage of development where their existence as independent nations' could 'be provisionally recognised'. At the time the mandate was granted the majority of the population was composed of Palestinian Arabs. None the less, the mandate also contained provision for the establishment in Palestine of a national home for the Jews; and the Balfour Declaration also pledged a national home for the Jewish people. The differing interpretations which could stem from these various commitments need no emphasis here. However, the Palestine White Paper of May 1939 had severely limited Jewish immigration to Palestine, at a time when hundreds of thousands of Jews were seeking an escape from Nazi Europe. At the end of World War II the appalling plight of Jewish survivors of the concentration camps was yet another humanitarian reason for pressure for immediate large-scale immigration into Palestine. An active World Zionist Movement urged the establishment of a Jewish state in Palestine, and immediately upon the end of the war the Zionists presented the outgoing British government with a series of radical demands.[1] The demands were repeated to the new Labour government. The chief Zionist underground military organization, the Haganah, became very active in Palestine in smuggling in illegal immigrants and forcibly releasing illegal immigrants who were held by the British. Organized terrorist activities among other Jewish groups now became widespread, and as time went by Haganah became less and less concerned to dissociate itself from these acts. Violence in Palestine, and intense diplomatic activity abroad, marked the background to an Anglo-American Committee of Enquiry, established at the invitation of the British Labour government's foreign secretary, Ernest Bevin. Although two members of the Committee personally favoured the partition of Palestine, they joined the majority of the Committee which 'having regard to the economic interdependence of the two politically rival communities (and also, no doubt, to the Soviet pressure on the northern edge of the Middle East) clung to the hope, against all the experience of the previous ten years, that somehow the two communities might be induced to live together in peace'.[2] The Committee made many detailed proposals, including the rejection of the idea of either a

---

[1] For an excellent survey of these critical months see George Kirk, *The Middle East, 1945–50* (1953; RIIA, *Survey of International Affairs 1939–46*), pp. 187–98.
[2] Kirk, *The Middle East, 1945–50*, p. 213.

Jewish or an Arab state in favour of a trusteeship, and the recommendation of the immediate issue of 100,000 immigration certificates for Jewish refugees.[3] President Truman indicated that he accepted those parts of the report that favoured the Zionists, but said of the pro-Arab parts that they required careful study which he would take 'under advisement'.[4] Bevin was fairly widely regarded as unsympathetic to the Jewish cause, and refused to discuss the matter with Richard Crossman, the Labour MP who had been on the Anglo-American Committee. He obtained the support of Attlee for the view that the proposed 100,000 immigration certificates should be issued only when the illegal Jewish military organizations in Palestine had been disbanded and their arms handed in. Violence continued, however, and it soon became evident that Britain was not to have the support of the United States in implementing the report of the Committee. And Bevin now indicated that to allow 100,000 Jews into Palestine would necessitate the sending of another division of British troops there, which Britain could not afford financially.

British troops already in Palestine became increasingly engaged in fighting with members of various Jewish military organizations, and a period of violence and counter-violence culminated in the blowing up of the King David Hotel in Jerusalem, certain parts of which were the British Palestine government's headquarters. The explosion caused the death of 91 persons and wounded 45 others. Vigorous punitive counter-measures were taken by the British.

The British government soon after announced a new plan—the Provincial Autonomy Plan—but once again could obtain little American support. The plan was also rejected by the Jewish Agency Executive. However, the appointment of a new Colonial Secretary—Creech Jones—allowed a breathing space, for he introduced a series of measures designed to lower the temperature between the Jews and the British, and to indicate a measure of goodwill,[5] in spite of the continuing violence.

In January 1947 the Arab states had begun talks with the British government, and separate talks began between the British and the Jewish Agency. A compromise offer was made by Bevin, but was rejected by both sides. The immigration restrictions remained unrelaxed, and terrorism in Palestine continued unabated.

The British government now decided to place the issue before the United Nations. On 2 April 1947 the United Kingdom asked the Acting Secretary-General to place the question of Palestine on the agenda of the next regular session of the General Assembly. It further requested that a special session of the General Assembly be convened as soon as possible, for the purpose of setting up a special committee which would prepare for the consideration of the question at the next regular Assembly session. The letter also indicated that the United Kingdom government would submit an account of its administration of the Palestine mandate to the General Assembly, and would ask the Assembly to

[3] US Dept. State, Anglo-American Committee of Enquiry, *Report* (1946).
[4] US, 79th Congress, 2nd sess., Senate Doc. 182, p. iii.
[5] For the measures which Creech Jones introduced, see Kirk, *The Middle East, 1945–50*, p. 230.

make recommendations under Article 10 of the Charter, for the future government of Palestine. It was at this juncture that Sir Alexander Cadogan made his celebrated statement that Britain 'should not have the sole responsibility for enforcing a solution which is not accepted by both parties and which we cannot reconcile with our conscience'.[6]

Accordingly, the First Committee of the General Assembly devoted some twelve meetings to the question of constituting and instructing a Special Committee on Palestine (UNSCOP). It was readily agreed that the Special Committee should be given broad competence to investigate and report on the facts; discussion on composition took rather longer, and revolved mainly around the inclusion or non-inclusion of the five permanent members of the Security Council. Eventually agreement was reached—in the face of Russian opposition—on an Australian proposal whereby UNSCOP would consist of eleven members, not including the five permanent members of the Security Council. The General Assembly approved the recommendations of its First Committee, and when the first special session of the Assembly came to be held the following resolution was carried by 47 to 7, with 1 abstention:

Whereas the General Assembly of the United Nations has been called into special session for the purpose of constituting and instructing a special committee to prepare for consideration at the next regular session of the Assembly, a report on the question of Palestine,

The General Assembly
Resolves that:
1. A Special Committee be created for the above-mentioned purpose consisting of the representatives of Australia, Canada, Czechoslovakia, Guatemala, India, Iran, Netherlands, Peru, Sweden, Uruguay and Yugoslavia;
2. The Special Committee shall have the widest powers to ascertain and record facts, and to investigate all questions and issues relevant to the problem of Palestine;
3. The Special Committee shall determine its own procedure;
4. The Special Committee shall conduct investigations in Palestine and wherever it may deem useful, receive and examine written or oral testimony, whichever it may consider appropriate in each case, from the mandatory Power, from representatives of the population of Palestine, from Governments and from such organizations and individuals as it may deem necessary;
5. The Special Committee shall give most careful consideration to the religious interests in Palestine of Islam, Judaism and Christianity;
6. The Special Committee shall prepare a report to the General Assembly and shall submit such proposals as it may consider appropriate for the solution of the problem of Palestine;
7. The Special Committee's report shall be communicated to the Secretary-General not later than 1 September 1947, in order that it may be circulated to the Members of the United Nations in time for consideration by the second regular session of the General Assembly;

The General Assembly
8. *Requests* the Secretary-General to enter into suitable arrangements with the proper authorities of any State in whose territory the Special Committee may wish to sit or to travel, to provide necessary facilities, and to assign appropriate staff to the Special Committee;
9. *Authorizes* the Secretary-General to reimburse travel and subsistence expenses of a representative and an alternate representative from each Government represented on the Special Committee on such basis and in such form as he may determine most appropriate in the circumstances. [*106 (S–1), 15 May, 1947*.]

[6] *GAOR*, 1st spec. sess., iii. 184.

The Communist countries, including those represented on UNSCOP, were in favour of the immediate termination of the British mandate and the proclamation of the independence of Palestine. Gromyko appeared to part company from the Arab states, however, in letting it be known that a partition of Palestine between the Zionists and Arabs would be acceptable if a single independent state could not be attained. The Guatemalan member of UNSCOP, on the other hand, was a known supporter of Zionism, and the Uruguayan representative was also sympathetic to the Jewish case. By the time UNSCOP arrived in Palestine, the Arab community had decided to boycott it. During the period of the Committee's inquiry the Zionists succeeded in a variety of ways in demonstrating their independence of action and in embarrassing the British government.[7]

UNSCOP, considerably divided within itself, retired in August 1947 to Geneva to draw up the recommendations which it was due to present to the General Assembly by 1 September. Although there was general agreement that the mandate had proved unworkable, only the Yugoslav, Iranian, and Indian representatives recommended a bi-national federal state. The other eight members of UNSCOP drew up a plan for partition with economic union.[8] Basically, the country was to be divided longitudinally, with Jerusalem and Bethlehem forming an internationalized enclave. The detailed proposals were submitted to the General Assembly,[9] which referred it to an *ad hoc* committee for consideration. The *ad hoc* committee approved, with certain minor alterations, the proposals of UNSCOP, and its own recommendations (A/516) were accepted by the Assembly, when on 29 November 1947 it adopted Resolution A 181(11) on the Future Government of Palestine. The plan of partition contained in this resolution provided *inter alia*, that the British mandate over Palestine should be terminated and British armed forces should leave the country by 1 August 1948; that the Arab State, the Jewish State, and the International Régime for Jerusalem were to come into being two months after the departure of the British armed forces; and that a UN Palestine Commission was to be established in order to implement the resolution. The resolution also called upon the Security Council to assist in the implementation of the plan, to determine whether the situation in Palestine constituted a threat to peace, and to take the necessary measures to preserve the peace. The provisions for the setting up of a Palestine Commission—one of a long line of institutional antecedents of UNTSO—were as follows:

B. STEPS PREPARATORY TO INDEPENDENCE

1. A Commission shall be set up consisting of one representative of each of five Member States. The Members represented on the Commission shall be elected by the General Assembly on as broad a basis, geographically and otherwise, as possible.

[7] Among the incidents occurring during this period was the arrival of the *Exodus*. The recounting of this incident, together with a detailed analysis of events in Palestine from 1945–8, may be found in Kirk, *The Middle East, 1945–50*, pp. 187–319. The Editor has relied heavily upon this volume.

[8] The factors, geographical and otherwise, which led to the recommendation of this particular compromise, are recounted ibid. pp. 245–6.

[9] Report of UNSCOP to the General Assembly, A/364, *GAOR*, 3rd sess., suppl. 11.

2. The administration of Palestine shall, as the mandatory Power withdraws its armed forces, be progressively turned over to the Commission, which shall act in conformity with the recommendations of the General Assembly, under the guidance of the Security Council. The mandatory Power shall to the fullest possible extent co-ordinate its plans for withdrawal with the plans of the Commission to take over and administer areas which have been evacuated.

In the discharge of this administrative responsibility the Commission shall have authority to issue necessary regulations and take other measures as required.

The mandatory Power shall not take any action to prevent, obstruct or delay the implementation by the Commission of the measures recommended by the General Assembly.

3. On its arrival in Palestine the Commission shall proceed to carry out measures for the establishment of the frontiers of the Arab and Jewish States and the City of Jerusalem in accordance with the general lines of the recommendations of the General Assembly on the partition of Palestine. Nevertheless, the boundaries as described in part II of this plan are to be modified in such a way that village areas as a rule will not be divided by state boundaries unless pressing reasons make that necessary.

4. The Commission, after consultation with the democratic parties and other public organizations of the Arab and Jewish States, shall select and establish in each State as rapidly as possible a Provisional Council of Government. The activities of both the Arab and Jewish Provisional Councils of Government shall be carried out under the general direction of the Commission.

If by 1 April 1948 a Provisional Council of Government cannot be selected for either of the States, or, if selected, cannot carry out its functions, the Commission shall communicate that fact to the Security Council for such action with respect to that State as the Security Council may deem proper, and to the Secretary-General for communication to the Members of the United Nations.

5. Subject to the provisions of these recommendations, during the transitional period the Provisional Councils of Government, acting under the Commission, shall have full authority in the areas under their control, including authority over matters of immigration and land regulation.

6. The Provisional Council of Government of each State, acting under the Commission, shall progressively receive from the Commission full responsibility for the administration of that State in the period between the termination of the Mandate and the establishment of the State's independence.

7. The Commission shall instruct the Provisional Councils of Government of both the Arab and Jewish States, after their formation, to proceed to the establishment of administrative organs of government, central and local.

8. The Provisional Council of Government of each State shall, within the shortest time possible, recruit an armed militia from the residents of that State, sufficient in number to maintain internal order and to prevent frontier clashes.

This armed militia in each State shall, for operational purposes, be under the command of Jewish or Arab officers resident in that State, but general political and military control, including the choice of the militia's High Command, shall be exercised by the Commission.

9. The Provisional Council of Government of each State shall, not later than two months after the withdrawal of the armed forces of the mandatory Power, hold elections to the Constituent Assembly which shall be conducted on democratic lines.

The election regulations in each State shall be drawn up by the Provisional Council of Government and approved by the Commission. . . .

11. The Commission shall appoint a preparatory economic commission of three members to make whatever arrangements are possible for economic co-operation, with a view to establishing, as soon as practicable, the Economic Union and the Joint Economic Board, as provided in section D below.

12. During the period between the adoption of the recommendations on the question of Palestine by the General Assembly and the termination of the Mandate, the mandatory

Power in Palestine shall maintain full responsibility for administration in areas from which it has not withdrawn its armed forces. The Commission shall assist the mandatory Power in the carrying out of these functions. Similarly the mandatory Power shall co-operate with the Commission in the execution of its functions.

13. With a view to ensuring that there shall be continuity in the functioning of administrative services and that, on the withdrawal of the armed forces of the mandatory Power, the whole administration shall be in the charge of the Provisional Councils and the Joint Economic Board, respectively, acting under the Commission, there shall be a progressive transfer, from the mandatory Power to the Commission, of responsibility for all the functions of government, including that of maintaining law and order in the areas from which the forces of the mandatory Power have been withdrawn.

14. The Commission shall be guided in its activities by the recommendations of the General Assembly and by such instructions as the Security Council may consider necessary to issue.

The measures taken by the Commission, within the recommendations of the General Assembly, shall become immediately effective unless the Commission has previously received contrary instructions from the Security Council.

The Commission shall render periodic monthly progress reports, or more frequently if desirable, to the Security Council.

15. The Commission shall make its final report to the next regular session of the General Assembly and to the Security Council simultaneously. [*GA Res. 181(11)A, 29 Nov. 1947.*]

The passing of this resolution by no means represented a common front by the UN. The Muslim countries had continued to press for a unitary state, and there were deep divisions between the United Kingdom and the United States. (Both the United States and the Soviet Union supported the partition proposals, though each had reservations about the precise drawing of the frontiers.) The British government, now firmly committed to a rapid withdrawal from its responsibilities, announced once more that British troops and administration could not be used to uphold any decision on Palestine that was not acceptable to both parties. The United States let it be known that she thought the British attitude unco-operative. For their part, the Arabs made it clear that their attitude was still one of uncompromising opposition to the Assembly's proposals; while the Jewish Agency declared its willingness to work within the framework of the proposals.[10]

Sporadic fighting had been going on in Palestine during the four months that had passed since UNSCOP left; the UN resolution now occasioned further outbreaks of violence. Both the Arab and Jewish communities suffered serious loss of life. In the meantime the UN Palestine Commission was set up, composed of Bolivia, Czechoslovakia, Denmark, Panama, and the Philippines. In January 1948, the Palestine Commission invited the United Kingdom, the Jewish Agency, and the Arab Higher Committee to designate representatives to assist it. The first two appointed representatives, but the Arab Higher Committee refused in the strongest terms. Troops from neighbouring Arab states began to enter Palestine and open fighting developed. On 16 February 1948 the

---

[10] The drama of the vote-counting in the Assembly has been told elsewhere. Many states had abstained from voting in the *ad hoc* committee and, a two-thirds vote being needed in the Assembly, their votes were of crucial importance. See Kirk, *The Middle East, 1945–50*, pp. 248–51; Sumner Welles, *We Need Not Fail* (1948), p. 63; J. García Granados, *The Birth of Israel* (1948), p. 269. Many small states were later to complain that the United States—in a pre-electoral period, and with an important Jewish population—had exercised undue pressure upon them.

Commission made a special report (S/676) to the Security Council stating that the conditions prevailing in Palestine made it impossible for it to implement the Assembly's Resolution 181 (II) without the assistance of adequate armed forces. Shortly after this, the Secretariat of the UN, at the request of the Commission, produced a paper on the powers of the Palestine Commission and the Security Council; this paper included a discussion of the conditions under which the Commission or the Security Council could employ an international armed force.[11]

Finally, on 10 April, the Palestine Commission submitted a report to the General Assembly in which it stated:

The Commission, therefore, has the duty to report to the General Assembly that the armed hostility of both Palestinian and non-Palestinian Arab elements, the lack of co-operation from the mandatory Power, the disintegrating security situation in Palestine, and the fact that the Security Council did not furnish the Commission with the necessary armed assistance, are the factors which have made it impossible for the Commission to implement the Assembly's resolution. [*A/532, GAOR, 2nd spec. sess., suppl. 1*, p. 36, para. 5.][12]

The United Kingdom had informed the Commission that she had decided to terminate the mandatory administration of Palestine on 15 May 1948 and that there would be no transfer of any authority to the Commission before that date. The Commission was, therefore, never permitted by the United Kingdom government to enter Palestine.

Meanwhile, on 24 February 1948, the Security Council had begun discussions on Palestine (it will be noted that an interval of three months had elapsed since the Assembly had asked, in Resolution 181 (II), the Council to address itself to the peace and security aspects of the problem). On 1 April 1948 the Security Council called for a truce to the fighting and also for the convening of another special session of the Assembly on Palestine:

I

The Security Council,

In the exercise of its primary responsibility for the maintenance of international peace and security,

Notes the increasing violence and disorder in Palestine and believes it is of the utmost urgency that an immediate truce be effected in Palestine,

Calls upon the Jewish Agency for Palestine and the Arab Higher Committee to make representatives available to the Security Council for the purpose of arranging a truce between the Arab and Jewish communities of Palestine; and emphasizes the heavy responsibility which would fall upon any party failing to observe such a truce;

Calls upon the Arab and Jewish armed groups in Palestine to cease acts of violence immediately.

---

[11] A/AC.21/13, 9 Feb. 1948.
[12] For a résumé of the UN role in events of this period, see *YBUN, 1947–8*. The Editor wishes to acknowledge the assistance she has received from work done by Mrs Margaret Garrard in establishing the chronology of events in Palestine between 1947 and 1949.

II

The Security Council,

Having received, on 9 December 1947, the resolution of the General Assembly concerning Palestine dated 29 November 1947;

Having taken note of the United Nations Palestine Commission's first and second Monthly Progress Reports and the First Special Report on the problems of security,

Having called, on 5 March 1948, on the permanent members of the Council to consult;

Having taken note of the reports made concerning these consultations;

Requests the Secretary-General in accordance with Article 20 of the United Nations Charter, to invoke a special session of the General Assembly to consider further the question of the future Government of Palestine. [*SC Res. S/714, 1 Apr. 1948.*]

Another resolution was adopted just over two weeks later, in mandatory language, calling for specific measures to be taken towards the implementation of a truce:

Considering the Council's resolution of 1 April 1948 and the conversations held by its President with the representatives of the Jewish Agency for Palestine and the Arab Higher Committee with a view to arranging a truce between Arabs and Jews in Palestine;

Considering that, as stated in that resolution, it is of the utmost urgency to bring about the immediate cessation of acts of violence in Palestine, and to establish conditions of peace and order in that country;

Considering that the United Kingdom Government, so long as it remains the Mandatory Power, is responsible for the maintenance of peace and order in Palestine and should continue to take all steps necessary to that end; and that, in so doing, it should receive the co-operation and support of the Security Council in particular as well as of all the Members of the United Nations;

The Security Council:

1. *Calls upon* all persons and organizations in Palestine and especially upon the Arab Higher Committee and the Jewish Agency to take immediately, without prejudice to their rights, claims, or positions, and as a contribution to the well-being and permanent interest of Palestine, the following measures:

(*a*) Cease all activities of a military or para-military nature, as well as acts of violence, terrorism and sabotage;

(*b*) Refrain from bringing and from assisting and encouraging the entry into Palestine of armed bands and fighting personnel, groups and individuals, whatever their origin;

(*c*) Refrain from importing or acquiring or assisting or encouraging the importation or acquisition of weapons and war materials;

(*d*) Refrain, pending further consideration of the future government of Palestine by the General Assembly, from any political activity which might prejudice the rights, claims, or positions of either community;

(*e*) Co-operate with the Mandatory authorities for the effective maintenance of law and order and of essential services, particularly those relating to transportation, communications, health, and food and water supplies;

(*f*) Refrain from any action which will endanger the safety of the Holy Places in Palestine and from any action which would interfere with access to all shrines and sanctuaries for the purpose of worship by those who have an established right to visit and worship at them.

2. *Requests* the United Kingdom Government, for so long as it remains the Mandatory Power, to use its best efforts to bring all those concerned in Palestine to accept the measures set forth under paragraph 1 above and, subject to retaining the freedom of action of its own forces, to supervise the execution of these measures by all those concerned, and to keep the Security Council and the General Assembly currently informed on the situation in Palestine.

3. *Calls upon* all Governments and particularly those of the countries neighbouring Palestine to take all possible steps to assist in the implementation of the measures set out under paragraph 1 above, and particularly those referring to the entry into Palestine of armed bands and fighting personnel, groups and individuals and weapons and war materials. [*SC Res. S/723, 16 Apr. 1948.*]

A few days later a further resolution was passed by the Security Council establishing a Truce Commission, and it is from the concept of truce observance in this resolution that UNTSO eventually sprang:

The Security Council
Referring to its resolution of 17 April 1948 calling upon all parties concerned to comply with specific terms for a truce in Palestine,
Establishes a truce commission for Palestine composed of representatives of those members of the Security Council which have career consular officers in Jerusalem, noting, however, that the representative of Syria has indicated that his Government is not prepared to serve on the Commission. The function of the Commission shall be to assist the Security Council in supervising the implementation by the parties of the resolution of the Security Council of 17 April 1948;
Requests the Commission to report to the President of the Security Council within four days regarding its activities and the development of the situation, and subsequently to keep the Security Council currently informed with respect thereto.
The Commission, its members, their assistants and its personnel shall be entitled to travel, separately or together, wherever the Commission deems necessary to carry out its tasks.
The Secretary-General of the United Nations shall furnish the Commission with such personnel and assistance as it may require, taking into account the special urgency of the situation with respect to Palestine. [*SC Res. S/727, 23 Apr. 1948.*]

The members of the Security Council who had career consular offices in Jerusalem were Belgium, France, and the United States. Accordingly, these countries were invited to form the Truce Commisson. The urgency of the matter at this stage was acute—not least because of the United Kingdom's insistence that she would lay down her mandate on 15 May, and would not thereafter be responsible for law and order.

The General Assembly, now meeting in its second special session, took parallel action: there being no prospect of implementing the plan for partition, it terminated the existence of the UN Palestine Commission, and decided to appoint a Mediator in Palestine:

The General Assembly,
Taking account of the present situation in regard to Palestine,

I

Strongly affirms its support of the efforts of the Security Council to secure a truce in Palestine and calls upon all Governments, organizations and persons to co-operate in making effective such a truce;

II

1. *Empowers* a United Nations Mediator in Palestine, to be chosen by a committee of the General Assembly composed of representatives of China, France, the Union of Soviet Socialist Republics, the United Kingdom and the United States of America to exercise, the following functions:

(*a*) To use his good offices with the local and community authorities in Palestine to:

(i) Arrange for the operation of common services necessary to the safety and well-being of the population of Palestine;

(ii) Assure the protection of the Holy Places, religious buildings and sites in Palestine;

(iii) Promote a peaceful adjustment of the future situation of Palestine;

(*b*) To co-operate with the Truce Commission for Palestine appointed by the Security Council in its resolution of 23 April 1948;

(*c*) To invite, as seems to him advisable, with a view to the promotion of the welfare of the inhabitants of Palestine, the assistance and co-operation of appropriate specialized agencies of the United Nations, such as the World Health Organization, of the International Red Cross, and of other governmental or non-governmental organizations of a humanitarian and non-political character;

2. *Instructs* the United Nations Mediator to render progress reports monthly, or more frequently as he deems necessary, to the Security Council and to the Secretary-General for transmission to the Members of the United Nations;

3. *Directs* the United Nations Mediator to conform in his activities with the provisions of this resolution, and with such instructions as the General Assembly or the Security Council may issue;

4. *Authorizes* the Secretary-General to pay the United Nations Mediator an emolument equal to that paid to the President of the International Court of Justice, and to provide the Mediator with the necessary staff to assist in carrying out the functions assigned to the Mediator by the General Assembly;

III

Relieves the Palestine Commission from the further exercise of responsibilities under resolution 181 (II) of 29 November 1947   [*GA Res. 186 (ES–11), 14 May 1948.*]

The ground was thus laid for co-operation between the Mediator and the Truce Commission. Count Bernadotte was appointed Mediator.

On 15 May 1948 the United Kingdom mandate for Palestine came to an end, and the State of Israel was at once proclaimed within the boundaries recommended by the General Assembly partition plan. The armed forces of Egypt, Iraq, Transjordan, Syria, and Lebanon crossed the frontier, and widespread and intense fighting broke out. The Security Council again called for an immediate cease-fire:

The Security Council,

Taking into consideration that previous resolutions of the Security Council in respect to Palestine have not been complied with and that military operations are taking place in Palestine;

Calls upon all Governments and authorities, without prejudice to the rights, claims or position of the parties concerned, to abstain from any hostile military action in Palestine and to that end to issue a cease-fire order to their military and para-military forces to become effective within thirty-six hours after midnight New York Standard Time, 22 May 1948;

Calls upon the Truce Commission and upon all parties concerned to give the highest priority to the negotiation and maintenance of a truce in the City of Jerusalem;

Directs the Truce Commission established by the Security Council by its resolution of 23 April 1948 to report to the Security Council on the compliance with the two preceding paragraphs of this resolution;

Calls upon all parties concerned to facilitate by all means in their power the task of the United Nations Mediator appointed in execution of the resolution of the General Assembly of 14 May 1948. [*SC Res. S/773, 22 May 1948.*]

The Chairman of the Truce Commission informed the President of the Security Council that in order to be able to carry out its allotted tasks the Commission would need military advisers and observers.[13] When the Security Council succeeded, on 29 May 1948, in getting a four-week cease-fire accepted, this request was duly incorporated into the arrangements.

The Security Council,

Desiring to bring about a cessation of hostilities in Palestine without prejudice to the rights, claims and position of either Arabs or Jews,

Calls upon all Governments and authorities concerned to order a cessation of all acts of armed force for a period of four weeks;

Calls upon all Governments and authorities concerned to undertake that they will not introduce fighting personnel into Palestine, Egypt, Iraq, Lebanon, Saudi Arabia, Syria, Transjordan and Yemen during the cease-fire and

Calls upon all Governments and authorities concerned, should men of military age be introduced into countries or territories under their control, to undertake not to mobilize or submit them to military training during the cease-fire;

Calls upon all Governments and authorities concerned to refrain from importing war material into or to Palestine, Egypt, Iraq, Lebanon, Saudi Arabia, Syria, Transjordan and Yemen during the cease-fire;

Urges all Governments and authorities concerned to take every possible precaution for the protection of the Holy Places and of the City of Jerusalem, including access to all shrines and sanctuaries for the purpose of worship by those who have an established right to visit and worship at them;

Instructs the United Nations Mediator for Palestine in concert with the Truce Commission to supervise the observance of the above provisions, and decides that they shall be provided with a sufficient number of military observers;

Instructs the United Nations Mediator to make contact with all parties as soon as the cease-fire is in force with a view to carrying out his functions as determined by the General Assembly;

Calls upon all concerned to give the greatest possible assistance to the United Nations Mediator;

Instructs the United Nations Mediator to make a weekly report to the Security Council during the cease-fire;

Invites the States members of the Arab League and the Jewish and Arab authorities in Palestine to communicate their acceptance of this resolution to the Security Council not later than 6 p.m. New York Standard Time on 1 June 1948;

Decides that if the present resolution is rejected by either party or by both, or if, having been accepted, it is subsequently repudiated or violated, the situation in Palestine will be reconsidered with a view to action under Chapter VII of the Charter.

Calls upon all Governments to take all possible steps to assist in the implementation of this resolution. [*SC Res. S/801, 29 May 1948.*]

There was thus a clear decision that the Mediator would act in concert with the Truce Commission in supervising the truce. Under a private arrangement between the Mediator and the Truce Commission, the latter's authority was limited to Jerusalem.[14] Count Bernadotte, the UN Mediator, embarked upon a week of intense diplomatic activity, and succeeded in gaining the acceptance of all parties to the conditions of the truce which he had formulated and to its effective date of 11 June.

[13] S/778, 23 May 1948. It may be noted that the Truce Commission had already on previous occasions asked for military observers, but without success: S/741 and S/762.

[14] E. L. M. Burns, *Between Arab and Israeli* (1962), p. 24.

On 7, 10, and 15 June there were discussions in the Security Council as to how the Mediator should obtain the military observer personnel that he needed; no decision was reached, however, and it was left to the Mediator to proceed as he saw fit.[15]

This point may be said to mark the birth of a body for UN Truce Supervision. The precise functions and responsibilities of UNTSO, as we shall see, changed to a considerable degree through time. The role of UNTSO may be seen in four main phases—relating to the truce in 1948-9; to the Armistice Agreements in 1949-56; to the post-Suez era from 1956 to 1967; and to the period following the six-day war of June 1967. Even within these four phases UNTSO was sometimes given additional duties by Security Council resolutions directed towards particular aspects of Arab–Israeli relations. These shifting functions are examined below (pp. 18–59). It remains true, however, that UNTSO has performed, in differing circumstances and under a variety of commanders, delicate tasks concerned with supervising a minimum order in the Middle East for some eighteen years.

2

ENABLING RESOLUTIONS AND VOTING

As EXPLAINED above, there was never any resolution expressly establishing a 'Truce Supervision Organization' though a Truce Commission was set up. The following resolutions and voting records are relevant to the establishment of the body that developed into UNTSO:

The Security Council,
Referring to its resolution 46 (1948) of 17 April 1948[1] calling upon all parties concerned to comply with specific terms for a truce in Palestine;
Establishes a Truce Commission for Palestine composed of representatives of those members of the Security Council which have career consular offices in Jerusalem, noting, however, that the representative of Syria has indicated that his Government is not prepared to serve on the Commission. The function of the Commission shall be to assist the Security Council in supervising the implementation by the parties of its resolution 46 (1948);
Requests the Commission to report to the President of the Security Council within four days regarding its activities and the development of the situation, and subsequently to keep the Security Council currently informed with respect thereto.
The Commission, its members, their assistants and its personnel shall be entitled to travel, separately or together, wherever the Commission deems necessary to carry out its tasks.

[15] For details as to the means which he employed, see below, pp. 67–68. Burns (p. 24), in a curious error, asserts that 'Under the terms of the Security Council resolution (of 29 May), the members of the Truce Commission—i.e. Belgium, France, and the United States—were to supply 63 military observers, as well as military and naval equipment and auxiliary technical personnel as required for the supervision of the truce'. There was no such provision in the resolution.
[1] i.e. S/723, on pp. 12–13 above.

The Secretary-General shall furnish the Commission with such personnel and assistance as it may require, taking into account the special urgency of the situation with respect to Palestine. [*SC Res. S/727, 23 Apr. 1948.*]

Voting: For: Argentina, Belgium, Canada, China, France, Syria, UK, USA.
    Against: nil
    Abstaining Colombia, Ukrainian SSR, USSR.

Syria's vote, in spite of her refusal to participate in the Truce Commission, may be explained by the fact that her decision was motivated by a belief that this was in the best interest of the negotiations. In other words, there was a wish to utilize the people on the spot—the consular officers in Jerusalem—and although Syria thus qualified for membership, she shared a common feeling that her participation could be politically embarrassing to the Truce Commission.[2] Her decision not to participate in the Commission in no way stemmed from hostility to that body, and was quite consistent with an affirmative vote on its establishment.

The Ukraine, however, abstained for very different reasons. Her representative claimed to see in the proposal to establish a Truce Commission a proposal whereby the United States and the United Kingdom could establish the need for a trusteeship:

The United Kingdom as mandatory Power should have taken effective steps to ensure the implementation of the truce. Has this been done? No, the facts point to the contrary . . .
  . . . The United States representative has now again raised the question of a truce, but in order to have yet another resolution to use in his own political interests, in the interests of the Government of the United States, which have no relation to an actual and real truce. The United States Government apparently wants yet another resolution so that it can then say that it is obvious that all the measures which are being taken, even those for a temporary truce, are of no avail; that only one course remains: trusteeship. This is a political preparation for the attempt to gain such a decision on trusteeship or to struggle for it. [*SCOR, 3rd yr, pt 2, 287th mtg*, pp. 18, 19.]

This theme was also evident in the speech of Mr Gromyko.[3] In addition, the Soviet Union thought that the failure to adopt her proposals submitted on 16 April to give 'teeth' to the truce showed lack of serious intent by the Council. Moreover, the proposed Truce Commission would consist of the United States, Belgium, and France, and 'the attitude of these three Powers stood out clearly, in the case of Indonesia where their policy was to force on the Indonesian Republic a one-sided agreement designed to crush the Indonesian national movement for freedom'.[4] In other words, Mr Gromyko thought that 'the United States proposal for a commission is a logical sequence of the United States Government's attitude towards the Palestine question, and a step designed to allow it to take over the whole question, including control over the truce . . .'[5] No explanation of his vote was given by the representative of Colombia (who happened at that time to be President of the Security Council). Mr Lopez had played a very active part in the drawing up of the actual terms of the truce, and in finding a common basis for the resolution of 17 April.

[2] See *SCOR*, 3rd yr, pt 2, 287th mtg, pp. 17–18.   [3] Ibid. p. 22 .   [4] Ibid. p. 23.
[5] Ibid. p. 24.

The adoption of Resolution (S/1376) of 11 August 1949,[6] by which the Security Council affirmed the Armistice Agreements and specified certain tasks for the UNTSO Chief of Staff and the Secretary-General, was carried by 9 votes to nil, with the Ukraine and the USSR abstaining. The Soviet Union wished to see an end to the presence of a Mediator in Palestine (and pt I of Resolution 1376 did, in fact, terminate the services of the Mediator); it was also contended that the Armistice Agreements showed a willingness on the part of the parties involved to co-operate voluntarily, and hence 'there is no need to maintain United Nations observers in Palestine; indeed, in the opinion of the USSR delegation, they should be recalled and the staff which has been established there should be disbanded'.[7] The Soviet Union introduced an amendment to this effect (S/1368) which would have recalled all UN observers from Palestine and disbanded UNTSO. However, she was unwilling to veto a resolution which had the approval of the parties directly concerned. The Russian abstention on the resolution may thus be explained. Her proposal to disband UNTSO and recall all observers was defeated by 2 (Ukraine, USSR) to 2 against (USA, UK), with Argentina, Canada, China, Cuba, Egypt, France, and Norway abstaining. (Egypt was entitled to vote by virtue of her membership at that time of the Security Council; Israel, though she was invited to take part in the debates, was not entitled to vote.)

Certain 'decisions' about the placing of UNTSO personnel along the Suez Canal in July 1967, and enlarging their number in December 1967, were taken without any formal resolutions being submitted or voted on. For details of the 'consensus' method employed, see section 4, pp. 62–63 below.

3

FUNCTIONS AND MANDATE

THE need for UNTSO, and hence its purpose, is to be found in the protracted history of institutions established to resolve the Palestine dispute. Their failure —and the inability to find a formula—led to fighting of such intensity that it could only be halted by the Security Council using its full authority under Chapter VII of the Charter to demand a truce; and the basic function of the Truce Commission was to supervise that truce. With the signing of the Armistice Agreements the Truce Supervision Organization—now properly so called, but built upon the already existing Truce Commission—came into existence. However, the details of UNTSO's tasks have changed and developed through time, and are best considered in three phases.

---

[6] For text, see below, pp.29–30.   [7] *SCOR*, 4th yr, pt 2, 435th mtg., p. 6.

(a) The Functions of the Truce Commission in Relation to the Truces of 1948

By its Resolution S/727 of 23 April 1948 the Security Council established a Truce Commission, and noted:

. . . The function of the Commission shall be to assist the Security Council in supervising the implementation by the parties of the resolution of the Security Council of 17 April 1948.

[The Security Council] requests the Commission to report to the President of the Security Council within four days regarding its activities and the development of the situation, and subsequently to keep the Security Council currently informed with respect thereto.

The Commission, its members, their assistants and its personnel shall be entitled to travel, separately or together, wherever the Commission deems necessary to carry out its tasks.

Resolution S/723 of 17 April, which is referred to, is quoted in full on pp. 12–13 above. In it, the Security Council laid down what actions by the Arab Higher Committee and the Jewish Agency it deemed necessary for a cease-fire. The Truce Commission was thus instructed to assist the Security Council in achieving the implementation of these measures.

The General Assembly effectively clarified the Truce Commission's role by instructing a Mediator 'to co-operate with the Truce Commission in carrying out his own tasks': and these have been quoted above in full (pp. 13–14).

When major hostilities broke out upon the proclamation of the State of Israel, the Truce Commission's task was elaborated further—shifting to meet new circumstances.

The Security Council. . . .

Calls upon all Governments and authorities, without prejudice to the rights, claims or positions of the parties concerned, to abstain from any hostile military action in Palestine and to that end to issue a cease-fire order to their military and para-military forces to become effective within 36 hours after midnight, New York Standard Time, 22 May 1948;

Calls upon the Truce Commission and upon all parties concerned to give the highest priority to the negotiation and maintenance of a truce in the City of Jerusalem;

Directs the Truce Commission established by the Security Council by its resolution of 23 April 1948 to report to the Security Council on the compliance with the two preceding paragraphs of this resolution. . . . [*SC Res. S/773, 22 May 1948.*]

Thus the Truce Commission was to observe compliance with the cease-fire order, negotiate and maintain a truce, and report on both to the Security Council.

A week later the Security Council called for a four-week truce, instructing (in operative paragraph 6) the Mediator 'in concert with the Truce Commission to supervise the observance' of the truce provisions there elaborated, and granting them for that purpose 'a sufficient number of military observers':

The Security Council,

Desiring to bring about a cessation of hostilities in Palestine without prejudice to the rights, claims and position of either Arabs or Jews,

Calls upon all Governments and authorities concerned to order a cessation of all acts of armed force for a period of four weeks;

Calls upon all Governments and authorities concerned to undertake that they will not introduce fighting personnel into Palestine, Egypt, Iraq, Lebanon, Saudi Arabia, Syria, Transjordan and Yemen during the cease-fire

2

Calls upon all Governments and authorities concerned, should men of military age be introduced into countries or territories under their control, to undertake not to mobilize or submit them to military training during the cease-fire;

Calls upon all Governments and authorities concerned to refrain from importing or exporting war material into or to Palestine, Egypt, Iraq, Lebanon, Saudi Arabia, Syria, Transjordan and Yemen during the cease-fire;

Urges all Governments and authorities concerned to take every possible precaution for the protection of the Holy Places and of the city of Jerusalem, including access to all shrines and sanctuaries for the purpose of worship by those who have an established right to visit and worship at them,

Instructs the United Nations Mediator for Palestine in concert with the Truce Commission to supervise the observance of the above provisions, and decides that they shall be provided with a sufficient number of military observers; . . . [*SC Res. S/801, 29 May 1948.*]

The Mediator expressly recognized in his report to the Security Council that a four-week truce could never be maintained unless a 'system of supervision could be effectively applied from the very beginning'.[1] In the event, a skeleton observer staff had been assembled by the time the truce entered into effect. The Truce Commission inevitably found that truce supervision entailed a number of functions which could not have been foreseen: '. . . When it developed that for reasons of internal policy the International Committee of the Red Cross could not assume responsibility for supervising the relief convoys to Jerusalem, the Truce Commission also discharged that function.'[2] This function was in addition to the duties of air, ground, and sea observation of coasts, ports, airfields, frontiers, strategic road points, and front lines.[3] Inevitably, the precise division of functions as between the Mediator and the Truce Commission evolved in a somewhat pragmatic fashion.

5. In connexion with the City of Jerusalem it was agreed between the Truce Commission and myself that the Commission would be responsible for the supervision of the cease-fire and truce in the city and that the observers would assist them and deal with incidents and breaches. Our respective spheres of authority were somewhat vague and were never clearly defined; but I received the fullest co-operation at all times from the members of the Truce Commission. 6. The observers were given detailed instructions on their role. In addition to investigating alleged breaches of the truce, they were charged with the task of carrying on routine observation and with dealing with incidents and complaints on the spot. They had no power to prevent a violation of the truce or to enforce their decisions. In the case of any complaint or incident where they could not achieve a settlement between the parties on the spot, their only recourse was to report the matter to their superiors or to me. Complaints by local civilians or troops were dealt with by observers on the spot, those by military commanders were dealt with by the Chief of Staff or an area commander, and those by governments were dealt with by myself. In cases requiring investigation, the inquiries were carried out by observers on the spot wherever possible. [*A/648, Progress Report of the Mediator to the General Assembly, GAOR, 3rd sess., suppl. 11,* p. 33.]

The first four-week truce came to an end on 9 June, and in spite of intense efforts by the Mediator, hostilities were resumed. The Security Council was once again called upon to fulfil its task of providing for peace, and, on 15 July, ordered a cease-fire.

---

[1] Report of the Mediator to the Security Council, S/888, 12 July 1948, para. 13.
[2] Ibid. para. 15.
[3] Ibid. para 14.

The Security Council,

Taking into consideration that the Provisional Government of Israel has indicated its accept-ance in principle of a prolongation of the truce in Palestine; that the States members of the Arab League have rejected successive appeals of the United Nations Mediator, and of the Security Council in its resolution of 7 July 1948, for the prolongation of the truce in Palestine; and that there has consequently developed a renewal of hostilities in Palestine:

Determines that the situation in Palestine constitutes a threat to the peace within the meaning of Article 39 of the Charter·

Orders the Governments and authorities concerned, pursuant to Article 40 of the Charter of the United Nations, to desist from further military action and to this end to issue cease-fire orders to their military and para-military forces, to take effect at a time to be determined by the Mediator, but in any event not later than three days from the date of the adoption of this resolution;

Declares that failure by any of the Governments or authorities concerned to comply with the preceding paragraph of this resolution would demonstrate the existence of a breach of the peace within the meaning of Article 39 of the Charter requiring immediate consideration by the Security Council with a view to such further action under Chapter VII of the Charter as may be decided upon by the Council;

Calls upon all Governments and authorities concerned to continue to co-operate with the Mediator with a view to the maintenance of peace in Palestine in conformity with the reso-lution adopted by the Security Council on 29 May 1948;

Orders as a matter of special and urgent necessity an immediate and unconditional cease-fire in the City of Jerusalem to take effect 24 hours from the time of the adoption of this reso-lution, and instructs the Truce Commission to take any necessary steps to make this cease-fire effective;

Instructs the Mediator to continue his efforts to bring about the demilitarization of the City of Jerusalem, without prejudice to the future political status of Jerusalem, and to assure the protection of and access to the Holy Places, religious buildings and sites in Palestine;

Instructs the Mediator to supervise the observance of the truce and to establish procedures for examining alleged breaches of the truce since 11 June 1948, authorizes him to deal with breaches so far as it is within his capacity to do so by appropriate local action, and requests him to keep the Security Council currently informed concerning the operation of the truce and when necessary to take appropriate action;

Decides that, subject to further decision by the Security Council or the General Assembly, the truce shall remain in force, in accordance with the present resolution and with that of 29 May 1948, until a peaceful adjustment of the future situation of Palestine is reached;

Reiterates the appeal to the parties contained in the last paragraph of its resolution of 22 May and urges upon the parties that they continue conversations with the Mediator in a spirit of conciliation and mutual concession in order that all points under dispute may be settled peacefully:

Requests the Secretary-General to provide the Mediator with the necessary staff and faci-lities to assist in carrying out the functions assigned to him under the resolution of the General Assembly of 14 May, and under this resolution; and

Requests that the Secretary-General make appropriate arrangements to provide necessary funds to meet the obligations arising from this resolution. [*SC Res. S/902, 15 July 1948.*]

No time-limit was fixed by this resolution for the expiry of the truce. It will be noted that the resolution is in mandatory terms, and that the Truce Commission was by implication granted wide powers under the instruction 'to take any necessary steps to make this cease-fire effective'. The Mediator was instructed to supervise the observance of the truce and, moreover, to establish procedures to examine alleged breaches and to deal with them at a local level. By implica-tion these tasks fell to UNTSO and with the second truce its tasks increased.

This increase in duties 'had mainly to do with the attempt to prevent arms and munitions from coming into the country'.[4]

Under the terms of this resolution the Mediator, Count Bernadotte, fixed 18 July 1948 as the date for the entry into effect of this truce: and the Security Council's orders were obeyed by both parties.

The role of the Truce Commission Observers for the handling of complaints under this second truce was as follows:

8. All complaints are submitted to investigation by observers in the field and, where necessary, by a special investigation team. In cases where they cannot be settled by observers on the spot, they are referred, together with the observer's report to, Haifa Headquarters for disposal. The less serious cases are referred to the Chief of Staff, and the more serious ones' to the Central Truce Supervision Board.[5] Decisions by both the Chief of Staff and the Central Truce Supervision Board are transmitted to me for review and are then dispatched to the Governments concerned. Major violations, if not immediately rectified by the parties, are reported to the Security Council. [*A/648, Progress Report of the UN Mediator to the General Assembly, GAOR, 3rd sess., suppl. 11*, p. 38.]

During the second truce it was decided that the Chief of Military Staff should be assisted by a Central Truce Supervision Board, and it was this body which carried out the function authorized in the Security Council's resolution of 15 July 1948, namely the examination of alleged breaches of the truce. The interplay of the Board, the observers, and the Mediator is illustrated by the following incident:

The Central Truce Supervision Board decided on 27 August that the Israeli forces had committed two flagrant violations of the terms of the truce in launching the attack and in retaining troops in the Red Cross zones and ordered them to withdraw by 29 August. At the same time the Board decided to create a neutral zone, supervised by United Nations observers around the Red Cross zone, and ordered all troops to be withdrawn from both areas. On the same day I sent a report on the matter to the Security Council. [*Ibid*. p. 40.]

18. In addition to their investigation of complaints . . . the observers deal with many incidents on the spot. In a number of cases they have succeeded in settling minor complaints or in preventing incidents and violations of the truce by their presence and prompt action. . . .
19. Another important function of the observation organization is in carrying on constant reconnaissance and patrolling by land, sea and air for incoming ships and planes, to prevent the introduction of war material and fighting personnel into the truce area and to keep a check on the immigration of men of military age. This work is performed mainly by the two observer groups in charge of coasts and ports and of airports. . . .

23. During the second truce, the Truce Commission again collaborated with me and my representatives in supervising the truce in Jerusalem. . . . [*Ibid*. p. 41.]

The instructions given to UN observers[6] engaged in truce supervision further clarify the functions assigned to them:

1. *The Role of the Observer*
   (i) Primary function of observer is to discharge observance of terms of truce in area to

---

[4] Burns, p. 25.
[5] On the organization of the Truce Commission during the second truce, see below, p. 65.
[6] The instructions are fully dealt with in relation to the political administration and military control exercised over the Truce Commission. See below, pp. 64–65.

which he is assigned. To discharge this function properly observer must be completely objective in his attitudes and judgments and must maintain a thorough neutrality as regards political issues in the Palestine situation. Fundamental objective of terms of truce is to ensure to fullest extent possible that no military advantage will accrue to either side as result of application of truce. Observer is entitled to demand that acts contrary to terms of truce be not committed or be rectified but he has no power to enforce such demands and must rely largely upon his ability to settle disputes locally by direct approaches to local commanders and authorities and where possible by bringing the commanders and authorities together. It is responsibility of the observer to call promptly to attention of appropriate local commanders and authorities every act which in his opinion is contrary to letter and spirit of truce. . . .

2. *Operational Instructions*

(ii) Each observer will report daily as instructed and on forms prescribed. Reports should cover each incident in particular locality relating to application of truce and should include other information pertinent to function of Mediator.

(iii) Any failure to comply with conditions of truce on part of either party shall immediately be reported by observer. Report to extent possible shall fully explain each such failure and shall clearly fix responsibility therefor. . . .

(iv) Observer shall investigate and report on as instructed all complaints of alleged violations of truce occurring within area to which he is assigned. . . .

(viii) Observers assigned to coastal areas where landing of immigrants and war material can be expected shall maintain effective observation involving reconnaissance by air, land and sea and securing fullest possible information about any violations suspected or alleged of truce conditions. All fighting personnel which shall include persons identified as belonging to organized military units and all persons bearing arms shall be denied entry.

(ix) Men of military age (i.e. in the age group 18 to 45) among immigrants shall be permitted entry during truce only in such limited numbers as the Mediator in the exercise of his discretion may determine . . . No men of military age shall be disembarked until they have been registered by local authorities . . . Such men are not [*sic?*] to be assigned to particular area or areas which shall be approved by observers who shall periodically check on whereabouts and activities of such men. [*S/928, Instructions given by UN Mediator to UN observers engaged in supervision of the Truce in Palestine, 28 July 1948.*]

The Mediator's instructions also clarify the functions of the Truce Supervision Board. The Mediator's Chief of Military Staff was to:

(*a*) organize a detailed plan for land, sea and air observation with the greatest possible dispatch

(*b*) assign the observers to their posts and direct their activities

(*c*) on the basis of field observations to define on a map the position of the respective armed forces in the several fighting sectors at the beginning of the truce . . .

Questions of principle relating to the interpretation of the terms of the truce shall be referred to the Mediator for decision. . . .

The Central Truce Supervision Board shall advise the Chief of Military Staff on all questions relating to the administration of the truce. [*Ibid.* pp. 5–6.]

These instructions also indicate (p. 8) that it was originally intended that there should also be regional truce supervision 'but this was found to be impractical and in their place special investigating teams were established, as required, and attached to the Truce Supervision Headquarters'.[7] Count Bernadotte also issued some general instructions on the observance of the second truce:

[7] A/648, Progress Report of UN Mediator to General Assembly, para. 6, p. 38.

3. The resolution of the Security Council, besides ordering the truce, entrusted the supervision of its observance to the Mediator, who is instructed to establish procedures for examining alleged breaches of the truce. Such procedures are intended to prevent breaches of the truces, and should they occur, to facilitate appropriate action.

4. If one party finds itself under unprovoked attack, it should limit its self-defence to operations necessary to repulse such attack pending action by United Nations observers. Such observers shall recall to the parties concerned the terms of the truce. Any refusal to comply with these terms, particularly by refusing to issue a cease-fire order or to take the necessary measures indicated by the observers for putting an end to the breach of the truce, shall be reported by the observers. Whatever the result of operations undertaken in self-defence, the *status quo ante* shall be restored. [*S/955, Cablegram from Mediator to Secretary-General, 7 Aug. 1948.*]

Although serious breaches of both truces occurred, there was now some control over the hostilities. The Mediator, in his Progress Report to the General Assembly (A/648), suggested that a critical point had been reached at which it was essential to move forward to something more permanent if the UN were not to slip backwards altogether in Palestine. He recommended, *inter alia*, the establishment of a Conciliation Commission. The next day, his tragic death occurred at the hands of Israeli assassins.[8] Dr Ralph Bunche, of the UN Secretariat, was authorized temporarily to take over Count Bernadotte's duties. Subsequently Dr Bunche became UN Acting Mediator in Palestine.

On 11 December 1948 the General Assembly accepted the suggestion of the late Count Bernadotte, and adopted a resolution establishing a UN Palestine Conciliation Commission. This three-state Commission had some bearing upon the functions of the Truce Commission in that, in addition to being instructed to 'take steps to assist the governments and authorities concerned to achieve a final settlement of all questions outstanding between them', it was also directed:

2 (*c*) To undertake, upon the request of the Security Council, any of the functions now assigned to the United Nations Mediator on Palestine or to the United Nations Truce Supervision Commission by resolutions of the Security Council; upon such request to the Conciliation Commission by the Security Council with respect to all the remaining functions of the United Nations Mediator on Palestine under Security Council resolutions, the office of the Mediator shall be terminated. [*GA Res. 194 (III), 11 Dec. 1948.*]

From this time the Truce Commission thus became inactive, though no formal resolution was ever passed terminating its existence. The Acting Mediator spent the first half of 1949 conducting separate armistice negotiations between the provisional government of Israel, on the one hand, and the governments of Egypt, Lebanon, Jordan, and Syria, on the other. By the end of July all such agreements had been concluded, and the Acting Mediator declared that his mission had now been completed, and recommended that the UN Conciliation Commission, with the assistance of UNTSO, should be entrusted with all future steps towards a permanent settlement.[9]

---

[8] See below, pp. 77–86.
[9] S/1357, Report to Security Council by Acting Mediator for Palestine, 21 June 1949, *SCOR*, 4th yr, suppl. for Aug. 1949.

(b) The Functions of UNTSO under the Armistice Agreements

The four Armistice Agreements[10] refer to functions to be carried out by 'The United Nations Truce Supervision Organization'—the first time this phrase is explicitly used. At this juncture semantic confusion all but clouds the picture, for the term 'UN Truce Supervision Organization' was now being used—for the very first time—at the precise moment at which it had been agreed in debates that UNTSO was being eliminated under the Armistice Agreements. In other words, what had been the Truce Commission and its observers is now referred to as UNTSO; while many nations believed that although UNTSO's Chief of Staff, and new MACs had functions under the Armistice Agreements, UNTSO itself had not. Russia's objections to the continued existence of truce supervision machinery elicited this response from the Israeli delegate:

Under the Armistice Agreements the Parties themselves have established Mixed Armistice Commissions and have invited the United Nations to provide chairmen for those Commissions. The Parties have also agreed that there may be circumstances in which observers may exercise useful functions in specific questions arising from the Armistice Agreements. On the other hand, it is our understanding that the Truce Supervision Organization proper is to be dissolved. . . . [SCOR, 4th yr, pt 2, 435th mtg, p. 11.]

This understanding—which was to a large degree shared by the Arabs and the French representative—does not appear to be correct. The correct view seems to be that UNTSO continued in existence, though considerably diminished, and that it now performed the functions allocated by the Armistice Agreements. The remnants of UNTSO—specifically, the Chief of Staff, his agents, and observers—remained in Palestine: but their task was no longer truce supervision, but rather—together with the MACs—armistice supervision. This being said, it should be added that this cluster of UN personnel, performing those functions allotted under the Armistice Agreements, remains known as UNTSO to this day.

The reasons for the retention of a limited number of UNTSO personnel were explained by Dr Bunche:

First of all, as in article 7 of the Israeli–Syrian Armistice Agreement, each of those four Agreements provides that the fifth member of the Commission shall be the United Nations Chief of Staff of the Truce Supervision Organization or an officer from the personnel of that organization designated by him. In other words, the Mixed Armistice Commissions themselves could not operate without some personnel of this kind being out there, for the simple reason that they provide the fifth man in the Commissions.

Secondly, each of the Agreements also provides that the Commission shall call upon, for supervising the implementation of the Agreement, observers from their own ranks—Arab or Jewish—or from the ranks of the United Nations observers, and that when these United Nations observers are called upon, they remain under the command of the Chief of Staff. This was written into the Agreement because both sides recognized the fact that in certain types of missions in connection with the supervision of the Armistice Agreements, it would be preferable to have neutral personnel rather than the personnel belonging to one side or the other, particularly when some question of crossing a border was involved.

Then, thirdly, there are specific provisions in each of these Agreements dealing with special

[10] See below, pp. 32–52.

situations. In the Egyptian–Israeli Agreement, for example, there is a neutral zone, the Elauja Zone, which calls for United Nations personnel to be there until the final disposition of the area involved is made, and not having military observers for placement there would be to nullify that provision of the Agreement. The Elauja provision of the Agreement was the last provision agreed upon and the most difficult one arrived at at the Egyptian–Israeli negotiations. In the Israeli–Jordanian Agreement, there is the provision for the demilitarized zones at Mt. Scopus and Government House, which, until the representatives of Israel and the Hashemite Kingdom of Jordan reach further agreement, remain demilitarized zones, with United Nations observer personnel in control. If we did not have that personnel, this very vital part of the Agreement would be wiped out, and that would inevitably lead to trouble, because these are the most vital zones in Jerusalem. And in the Israeli–Syrian Agreement, which has just been concluded, the most difficult subject on which agreement was finally reached after long negotiation, was a demilitarized zone between the Israeli and Syrian forces, which involved the employment of United Nations observers.

Therefore, in each of these three Agreements, in addition to the ordinary function of assisting the Parties and supervising the implementation of the Agreements, there is a special provision calling for the employment of United Nations observer personnel. Thus, while the principle of withdrawal of truce supervision personnel is entirely sound—and, in general, withdrawal has already taken place—a nucleus of such observers must be kept on the spot until the final peace settlements are made or until the Parties themselves agree to changes in the Armistice Agreements which would no longer make necessary the employment or the presence of such United Nations staff. [*SCOR, 4th yr, pt 2, 435th mtg*, pp. 8–9.]

It should be mentioned that although the Chief of Staff of UNTSO was to remain: 'that officer will in future perform completely different functions from those previously assigned to him. Those functions will be the functions of the chairman of mixed armistice commissions . . .'[11] UNTSO is by implication granted the authority to establish subsidiary bodies, for the Armistice Agreements refer to the setting up of MACs to operate within the UNTSO framework. The Armistice Agreements are in fact remarkably unspecific as to the tasks to be carried out by UNTSO and its observers, though considerably more detailed as to the duties of the MACs and their observers. The implication seems to be that, apart from the duties explicitly mentioned, UNTSO is to carry on with observer tasks similar to those entrusted to it under the two truces of 1948. UNTSO and the MACs were assigned the following functions under the Israeli–Egyptian Armistice.

Article VII
2. The areas comprising the western and eastern fronts shall be defined by the United Nations Chief of Staff of the Truce Supervision Organization, on the basis of the deployment of forces against each other and past military activity or the future possibility thereof in the area. This definition of the western and eastern fronts is set forth in Annex II of this Agreement. . . .

Article VIII
1. The area comprising the village of El Auja and vicinity, as defined in paragraph 2 of this Article, shall be demilitarized, and both Egyptian and Israeli armed forces shall be totally excluded therefrom. The Chairman of the Mixed Armistice Commission established in Article X of this Agreement and United Nations Observers attached to the Commission shall be responsible for ensuring the full implementation of this provision. . . .

[11] Per the representative of France, *SCOR*, 4th yr, pt 2, 437th mtg, p. 4.

Article IX

All prisoners of war detained by either Party to this Agreement and belonging to the armed forces, regular or irregular, of the other Party shall be exchanged as follows:

1. The exchange of prisoners of war shall be under United Nations supervision and control throughout. The exchange shall begin within ten days after the signing of this Agreement and shall be completed not later than twenty-one days following. Upon the signing of this Agreement, the Chairman of the Mixed Armistice Commission established in Article X of this Agreement, in consultation with the appropriate military authorities of the Parties, shall formulate a plan for the exchange of prisoners of war within the above period, defining the date and places of exchange and all other relevant details. . . .

5. The Mixed Armistice Commission established in Article X of this Agreement shall assume responsibility for locating missing persons, whether military or civilian, within the areas controlled by each Party to facilitate their expeditious exchange. Each Party undertakes to extend to the Commission full co-operation and assistance in the discharge of this function.

Article X

1. The execution of the provisions of this Agreement shall be supervised by a Mixed Armistice Commission composed of seven members. . . .

7. Claims or complaints presented by either Party relating to the application of this Agreement shall be referred immediately to the Mixed Armistice Commission through its Chairman. The Commission shall take such action on all such claims or complaints by means of its observation and investigation machinery as it may deem appropriate, with a view to equitable and mutually satisfactory settlement.

8. Where interpretation of the meaning of a particular provision of this Agreement is at issue, the Commission's interpretation shall prevail, subject to the right of appeal as provided in paragraph 4. The Commission, in its discretion and as the need arises, may from time to time recommend to the Parties modifications in the provisions of this Agreement.

9. The Mixed Armistice Commission shall submit to both parties reports on its activities as frequently as it may consider necessary. A copy of each such report shall be presented to the Secretary-General of the United Nations for transmission to the appropriate organ or agency of the United Nations. . . .

Annex I

Plan of withdrawal from Al Faluja

The withdrawal of Egyptian troops with all of their military impedimenta from the Al Faluja areas to points beyond the Egypt–Palestine frontier shall be executed in accordance with the following plan:

1. The withdrawal operation shall begin on 26 February 1949 at 0500 hours GMT and shall be under United Nations supervision and control throughout.

2. In view of the substantial number of troops involved and in the interest of minimizing the possibility of friction and incidents and ensuring effective United Nations supervision during the operation, the execution of the withdrawal shall be completed within a period of five days from the effective date of the plan of withdrawal.

3. The road Al Faluja–Iraq–Suweidan–Bureir–Gaza–Rafah shall be used as the route of withdrawal; provided that if this route proves impassable on the date of withdrawal the United Nations Chief of Staff of the Truce Supervision Organization shall select an alternative route in consultation with both Parties.

4. At least forty-eight hours prior to the scheduled time of withdrawal the General Officer Commanding the Egyptian Forces in Palestine shall submit to the United Nations Chief of Staff (or his representative), for his approval, a detailed plan for the withdrawal of the Egyptian garrison at Al Faluja, to include: the number of troops and amount and type of material to be

2*

withdrawn each day, the number and type of vehicles to be used each day in the withdraw a movement, and the number of trips necessary to complete each day's movement.

5. The detailed plan referred to in paragraph 4 above shall be based on an order of priority in the withdrawal operation defined by the United Nations Chief of Staff of the Truce Supervision which shall provide *inter alia* that following the evacuation of sick and wounded already accounted for, infantry forces together with their personal arms and possessions shall be first evacuated, and . . . the evacuation of heavy equipment shall be to a point in Egyptian territory to be designated by the United Nations Chief of Staff and there, as Egyptian property, to be placed and kept under custody, guard and seal of the United Nations until such time as the Chief of Staff is satisfied that the Armistice has become effective, whereupon this equipment will be handed over to the appropriate Egyptian authorities.

6. The Israeli authorities and officers in the Al Faluja–Gaza area shall extend their full co-operation to the operation and shall be responsible for ensuring that during the withdrawal movements the route to be followed shall be free of obstructions of all kinds and that during the operation Israeli troops shall be kept away from the roads over which the withdrawal will take place.

7. United Nations Military Observers shall be stationed with both the Egyptian and Israeli forces to ensure that this plan of withdrawal, and such subsequent instructions relating to its execution as may be issued by the United Nations Chief of Staff, are fully complied with by both Parties. Such inspections as may be necessary in the conduct of the withdrawal shall be made exclusively by United Nations Military Observers, and their decisions in all such cases shall be accepted as final.

Annex II

Demarcation of the western and eastern fronts in Palestine

On the sole basis of military consideration involving the forces of the two Parties to this Agreement as well as third party forces in the area not covered by this Agreement, the demarcation of the western and eastern fronts in Palestine is to be understood as follows:

a. Western Front:

The area south and west of the line delineated in paragraph 2.A of the Memorandum of 13 November 1948 on the implementation of the resolution of the Security Council of 4 November 1948, from its point of origin on the west to the point at MR 12581196, thence south along the road to Hatta–Al Faluja–RJ at MR 12140823–Beersheba and ending north of Bir Asluj at point 402.

b. Eastern Front:

The area east of the line described in paragraph *a*. above, and from point 402 down to the southernmost tip of Palestine, by a straight line marking half the distance between the Egypt–Palestine and Transjordan–Palestine frontiers.

Annex V

Letter from Ralph J. Bunche, Acting Mediator, to Dr Walter Eytan, Head of the Israeli Delegation at Rhodes

In connexion with the Egyptian–Israeli General Armistice Agreement, your confirmation is desired of the understanding that at any time following the signing of this Agreement, the Egyptian Forces now in the Bethlehem–Hebron area, together with all of their arms, equipment, personal possessions and vehicles, may be withdrawn across the Egyptian frontier exclusively under United Nations supervision and escort, and by a direct route to be determined by the United Nations Chief of Staff of the Truce Supervision in consultation with the appropriate Israeli authorities. [*Egyptian–Israel General Armistice Agreement, signed 24 Feb. 1949, 42 UNTS 252.*]

Similar functions were assigned under the three other Armistice Agreements: see Articles VI(1), VI(5), VII(1), VII (7), VII (9) of the Israel–Lebanon General

Armistice, signed 23 March 1949, 42 UNTS 288; Articles VIII, XI (1), XI(7), XI (8), XI (9), of the Israel–Jordan General Armistice, signed 3 April 1949, 42 UNTS 304; and Articles V (3), V (5) (c) and (e), VI, VII (1), VII (7), VII (8), VII (9) of the Israel–Syria General Armistice, 20 July 1949, 42 *UNTS* 327. For the full texts of these articles see below, pp. 32–52. It may be noted that under the Israel–Jordan Agreement a Special Committee was set up in addition to the MAC. The general execution of the provisions of the Agreement was the duty of the MAC, with the exception of those matters which fell within the exclusive competence of the Special Committee under Article VIII. The Special Committee was required to formulate agreed plans and arrangements designed to enlarge the scope of the Agreement and effect improvements in its application, and a list of items for its attention in this respect appear in Article VIII(2). In Article V of the Israel–Syria Agreement, moreover, the Chairman of the MAC was given responsibility for the general supervision of the demilitarized zone.

In summary, it may be said that the four MACs were thus assigned the following main tasks:

... to avoid any resumption of hostilities; to arrange for the exchange of prisoners of war; to establish permanent armistice demarcation lines in accordance with the principles laid down in the agreements; and to carry out specific provisions made in those agreements with a view to facilitating the transition to a permanent peace in Palestine. [*A/1287, Annual Report of the Secretary-General, 1 July 1949–30 June 1950, GAOR, 5th sess. suppl. 1*, p. 2.]

These functions were approved by a Security Council resolution of 11 August 1949, passed after the conclusion of all the Armistice Agreements:

The Security Council,

Having noted with satisfaction the several Armistice Agreements concluded by means of negotiations between the Parties involved in the conflict in Palestine in pursuance of its resolution of 16 November 1948 (S/1080);

Expresses the hope that the Governments and authorities concerned, having undertaken by means of the negotiations now being conducted by the Palestine Conciliation Commission, to fulfil the request of the General Assembly in its resolution of 11 December 1948 to extend the scope of the armistice negotiations and to seek agreement by negotiations conducted either with the Conciliation Commission or directly, will at an early date achieve agreement on the final settlement of all questions outstanding between them;

Finds that the Armistice Agreements constitute an important step toward the establishment of permanent peace in Palestine and considers that these Agreements supersede the truce provided for in the resolutions of the Security Council of 29 May and 15 July 1948;

Reaffirms, pending the final peace settlement, the order contained in its resolution of 15 July 1948 to the Governments and authorities concerned, pursuant to Article 40 of the Charter of the United Nations, to observe an unconditional cease-fire and, bearing in mind that the several Armistice Agreements include firm pledges against any further acts of hostility between the Parties and also provide for their supervision by the Parties themselves, relies upon the Parties to ensure the continued application and observance of these Agreements;

Decides that all functions assigned to the United Nations Mediator on Palestine having been discharged, the Acting Mediator is relieved of any further responsibility under Security Council resolutions;

Notes that the Armistice Agreements provide that the execution of those Agreements shall be supervised by Mixed Armistice Commissions whose Chairman in each case shall be the

United Nations Chief of Staff of the Truce Supervision Organization or a senior officer from the observer personnel of that organization designated by him following consultation with the Parties to the Agreements;

Requests the Secretary-General to arrange for the continued service of such of the personnel of the present Truce Supervision Organization as may be required in observing and maintaining the cease-fire, and as may be necessary in assisting the Parties to the Armistice Agreements in the supervision of the application and observance of the terms of those Agreements, with particular regard to the desires of the Parties as expressed in the relevant articles of the Agreements;

Requests the Chief of Staff mentioned above to report to the Security Council on the observance of the cease-fire in Palestine in accordance with the terms of this resolution; and to keep the Palestine Conciliation Commission informed of matters affecting the Commission's work under the General Assembly resolution of 11 December 1948. [*S/1376 (II) 11 Aug. 1949*].

This resolution, which refers to 'the continued service of . . . the present Truce Supervision Organisation' is in fact the first to use this term. Clearly however, UNTSO sprang from the observers provided by members of the Truce Commission, and this resolution provides guidance as to its role under the Armistice Agreements, together with the newly established MACs. Basically, therefore, the MACs were to supervise the execution of the Agreements, while UNTSO itself was to observe and report on their implementation.

On 9 November 1953, replying to a question put to him by the representative of France on the Security Council, the Chief of Staff of UNTSO had said:

. . . the personnel of the Truce Supervision Organization performs two functions. The first is 'observing and maintaining the cease-fire' ordered by the Security Council on 15 July 1948 . . . The second function is 'assisting the parties to the armistice agreements in the supervision of the application and observance of the terms of those agreements'. With regard to the observance and maintenance of the cease-fire, the powers of the Chief of Staff of the Truce Supervision Organization are derived directly from the Security Council resolution, and United Nations observers acting under my instructions may take measures to observe and maintain the cease-fire. Should an incident involving a breach of the cease-fire occur, observers will be sent immediately to the spot, the authorities of the respective parties will be contacted, and every effort made to bring an end to the incident. [*SCOR, 9th yr, 635th mtg, ann.*, pp. 23–24.]

In subsequent resolutions which the Security Council passed—largely to meet those grave breaches of the Armistice which occurred from time to time—additional tasks were given to UNTSO. Subsequent resolutions also clarified the authority granted under the initial resolutions. Thus additional diplomatic authority was granted to the Chief of Staff of UNTSO in respect of the refugee problem:

The Security Council. . . .

3. *Requests* the Egyptian–Israel Mixed Armistice Commission to give urgent attention to the Egyptian complaint of expulsion of thousands of Palestine Arabs;

4. *Calls upon* both parties to give effect to any finding of the Egyptian–Israel Mixed Armistice Commission regarding the repatriation of any such Arabs who in the Commission's opinion are entitled to return;

5. *Authorizes* the Chief of Staff of the Truce Supervision Organization, with regard to the movement of nomadic Arabs, to recommend to Israel, Egypt and such other Arab states as may be appropriate such steps as he may consider necessary to control the movement of such nomadic Arabs across international frontiers or armistice lines by mutual agreement;

6. *Calls upon* the Governments concerned to take in the future no action involving the transfer of persons across international frontiers or armistice lines without prior consultation through the Mixed Armistice Commissions . . . [*SC Res. S/1907, 17 Nov. 1950.*]

The Security Council also had occasion to request the Chief of Staff to undertake certain specific steps in order to reduce tension along the Armistice lines:

The Security Council . . .

Anxious that all possible steps shall be taken to preserve security [along the Egyptian–Israel armistice line] . . .

1. *Requests* the Chief of Staff to continue his consultations with the Governments of Egypt and Israel with a view to the introduction of practical measures to that end . . . [*SC Res., S/3379, 30 Mar. 1955.*]

The Security Council. . . .

7. Requests the Chief of Staff to pursue his suggestions for improving the situation in the area of Lake Tiberias without prejudice to the rights, claims and positions of the parties and to report to the Council as appropriate on the success of his efforts . . . [*SC Res. S/3538, 19 Jan. 1956.*]

In addition to his specific functions as Chairman of the MACs, it is clear that the Chief of Staff of UNTSO assumed certain other quasi-judicial functions.[12]

---

[12] 'Examples can be found in his decision that attempts to harvest crops made by civilians in no-man's land should be permitted only up to the halfway line and no nearer to the Israeli positions (A/648, pp. 43–34), or in the decisions taken to determine the truce lines (S/2833, and Add. 1) . . . Even individual observers occasionally assumed such functions: under the withdrawal plan for Al Faluja inspections of the withdrawal were to "be made exclusively by UN Military Observers, and their decisions in all such cases shall be accepted as final" [S/1264, rev. 1, ann. 1, para. 7]. By resolution of 22 January 1958 the Security Council directed the chief of Staff to conduct a survey of property records in the area surrounding Government House, Jerusalem, "with a view to determining property ownership in the zone" (S/3942). The supervisory functions of UNTSO in relation to the convoys to Mount Scopus, whereby the observers determined whether items in the cargo manifest were properly to be included in the convoy are, similarly, quasi-judicial functions' (D. W. Bowett, *UN Forces* (1964), pp. 78–79).

THE ARAB ARMISTICE AGREEMENTS

1. ISRAEL–JORDAN

Preamble

The Parties to the present Agreement,

Responding to the Security Council resolution of 16 November 1948, calling upon them, as a further provisional measure under Article 40 of the Charter of the United Nations and in order to facilitate the transition from the present truce to permanent peace in Palestine, to negotiate an armistice;

Having decided to enter into negotiations under United Nations chairmanship concerning the implementation of the Security Council resolution of 16 November 1948; and having appointed representatives empowered to negotiate and conclude an Armistice Agreement;

The undersigned representatives of their respective Governments, having exchanged their full powers found to be in good and proper form, have agreed upon the following provisions:

Article I

With a view to promoting the return of permanent peace in Palestine and in recognition of the importance in this regard of mutual assurances concerning the future military operations of the Parties, the following principles, which shall be fully observed by both Parties during the armistice, are hereby affirmed:

1. The injunction of the Security Council against resort to military force in the settlement of the Palestine question shall henceforth be scrupulously respected by both Parties;

2. No aggressive action by the armed forces—land, sea, or air—of either Party shall be undertaken, planned, or threatened against the people or the armed forces of the other; it being understood that the use of the term *planned* in this context has no bearing on normal staff planning as generally practised in military organizations;

3. The right of each Party to its security and freedom from fear of attack by the armed forces of the other shall be fully respected;

4. The establishment of an armistice between the armed forces of the two Parties is accepted as an indispensable step toward the liquidation of armed conflict and the restoration of peace in Palestine.

Article II

With a specific view to the implementation of the resolution of the Security Council of 16 November 1948, the following principles and purposes are affirmed:

1. The principle that no military or political advantage should be gained under the truce ordered by the Security Council is recognized;

2. It is also recognized that no provision of this Agreement shall in any way prejudice the

rights, claims and positions of either Party hereto in the ultimate peaceful settlement of the Palestine question, the provisions of this Agreement being dictated exclusively by military considerations.

Article III

1. In pursuance of the foregoing principles and of the resolution of the Security Council of 16 November 1948, a general armistice between the armed forces of the two Parties—land, sea and air—is hereby established.

2. No element of the land, sea or air, military or para-military forces of either Party, including non-regular forces, shall commit any warlike or hostile act against the military or para-military forces of the other Party, or against civilians in territory under the control of that Party; or shall advance beyond or pass over for any purpose whatsoever the Armistice Demarcation Lines set forth in articles V and VI of this Agreement; or enter into or pass through the air space of the other Party.

3. No warlike act or act of hostility shall be conducted from territory controlled by one of the Parties to this Agreement against the other party.

Article IV

1. The lines described in articles V and VI of this Agreement shall be designated as the Armistice Demarcation Lines and are delineated in pursuance of the purpose and intent of the resolution of the Security Council of 16 November 1948.

2. The basic purpose of the Armistice Demarcation Lines is to delineate the lines beyond which the armed forces of the respective Parties shall not move.

3. Rules and regulations of the armed forces of the Parties, which prohibit civilians from crossing the fighting lines or entering the area between the lines, shall remain in effect after the signing of this Agreement with application to the Armistice Demarcation Lines defined in articles V and VI.

Article V

1. The Armistice Demarcation Lines for all sectors other than the sector now held by Iraqi forces shall be as delineated on the maps[1] in annex I to this Agreement, and shall be defined as follows:

(*a*) In the sector Kh Deir Arab (MR 1510–1574) to the northern terminus of the lines defined in the 30 November 1948 Cease-Fire Agreement for the Jerusalem area, the Armistice Demarcation Lines shall follow the truce lines as certified by the United Nations Truce Supervision Organization;

(*b*) In the Jerusalem sector, the Armistice Demarcation Lines shall correspond to the lines defined in the 30 November 1948 Cease-Fire Agreement for the Jerusalem area;

(*c*) In the Hebron–Dead Sea sector, the Armistice Demarcation Line shall be as delineated on Map 1 and marked B in annex I to this Agreement;

(*d*) In the sector from a point on the Dead Sea (MR 1925–0958) to the southernmost tip of Palestine, the Armistice Demarcation Line shall be determined by existing military positions as surveyed in March 1949 by United Nations observers, and shall run from north to south as delineated on map 1 in annex I to this Agreement.

[1] Not reproduced here because of their large size and small scale.

Article VI

1. It is agreed that the forces of the Hashemite Jordan Kingdom shall replace the forces of Iraq in the sector now held by the latter forces, the intention of the Government of Iraq in this regard having been communicated to the Acting Mediator in the message of 20 March from the Foreign Minister of Iraq authorizing the delegation of the Hashemite Jordan Kingdom to negotiate for the Iraqi forces and stating that those forces would be withdrawn.

2. The Armistice Demarcation Line for the sector now held by Iraqi forces shall be as delineated on map 1 in annex I to this Agreement and marked A.

3. The Armistice Demarcation Line provided for in paragraph 2 of this article shall be established in stages as follows, pending which the existing military lines may be maintained:

(*a*) In the area west of the road from Baqa to Jaljulia, and thence to the east of Kafr Qasim; within five weeks of the date on which this Armistice Agreement is signed;
(*b*) In the area of Wadi Ara north of the line from Baqa to Zubeiba: within seven weeks of the date on which this Armistice Agreement is signed;
(*c*) In all other areas of the Iraqi sector: within fifteen weeks of the date on which this Armistice Agreement is signed.

4. The Armistice Demarcation Line in the Hebron–Dead Sea sector, referred to in paragraph (c) of article V of this Agreement and marked B on map 1 in annex I, which involves substantial deviation from the existing military lines in favour of the forces of the Hashemite Jordan Kingdom, is designated to offset the modifications of the existing military lines in the Iraqi sector set forth in paragraph 3 of this article.

5. In compensation for the road acquired between Tulkarem and Qalqiliya, the Government of Israel agrees to pay to the Government of the Hashemite Jordan Kingdom the cost of constructing twenty kilometres of first-class new road.

6. Wherever villages may be affected by the establishment of the Armistice Demarcation Line provided for in paragraph 2 of this article, the inhabitants of such villages shall be entitled to maintain, and shall be protected in, their full rights of residence, property and freedom. In the event any of the inhabitants should decide to leave their villages, they shall be entitled to take with them their livestock and other movable property, and to receive without delay full compensation for the land which they have left. It shall be prohibited for Israeli forces to enter or to be stationed in such villages, in which locally recruited Arab police shall be organized and stationed for internal security purposes.

7. The Hashemite Jordan Kingdom accepts responsibility for all Iraqi forces in Palestine.

8. The provisions of this article shall not be interpreted as prejudicing, in any sense, an ultimate political settlement between the Parties to this Agreement.

9. The Armistice Demarcation Lines defined in articles V and VI of this Agreement are agreed upon by the Parties without prejudice to future territorial settlements or boundary lines or to claims of either Party relating thereto.

10. Except where otherwise provided, the Armistice Demarcation Lines shall be established, including such withdrawal of forces as may be necessary for this purpose, within ten days from the date on which this Agreement is signed.

11. The Armistice Demarcation Lines defined in this article and in article V shall be subject to such rectification as may be agreed upon by the Parties to this Agreement, and all such

rectifications shall have the same force and effect as if they had been incorporated in full in this General Armistice Agreement.

Article VII

1. The military forces of the Parties to this Agreement shall be limited to defensive forces only in the areas extending ten kilometres from each side of the Armistice Demarcation Lines, except where geographical considerations make this impractical. as at the southernmost tip of Palestine and the coastal strip. Defensive forces permissible in each sector shall be as defined in annex II to this Agreement. In the sector now held [by] Iraqi forces, calculations on the reduction of forces shall include the number of Iraqi forces in this sector.

2. Reduction of forces to defensive strength in accordance with the preceding paragraph shall be completed within ten days of the establishment of the Armistice Demarcation Lines defined in this Agreement. In the same way the removal of mines from mined roads and areas evacuated by either Party, and the transmission of plans showing the location of such minefields to the other Party, shall be completed within the same period.

3. The strength of the forces which may be maintained by the Parties on each side of the Armistice Demarcation Lines shall be subject to periodical review with a view toward further reduction of such forces by mutual agreement of the Parties.

Article VIII

1. A Special Committee, composed of two representatives of each Party designated by the respective Governments, shall be established for the purpose of formulating agreed plans and arrangements designed to enlarge the scope of this Agreement and to effect improvements in its application.

2. The Special Committee shall be organized immediately following the coming into effect of this Agreement and shall direct its attention to the formulation of agreed plans and arrangements for such matters as either Party may submit to it, which, in any case, shall include the following, on which agreement in principle already exists: free movement of traffic on vital roads, including the Bethlehem and Latrun-Jerusalem roads; resumption of the normal functioning of the cultural and humanitarian institutions on Mount Scopus and free access thereto; free access to the Holy Places and cultural institutions and use of the cemetery on the Mount of Olives; resumption of operation of the Latrun pumping station; provision of electricity for the Old City; and resumption of operation of the railroad to Jerusalem.

3. The Special Committee shall have exclusive competence over such matters as may be referred to it. Agreed plans and arrangements formulated by it may provide for the exercise of supervisory functions by the Mixed Armistice Commission established in article XI.

Article IX

Agreements reached between the Parties subsequent to the signing of this Armistice Agreement relating to such matters as further reduction of forces as contemplated in paragraph 3 of article VII, future adjustments of the Armistice Demarcation Lines, and plans and arrangements formulated by the Special Committee established in article VIII, shall have the same force and effect as the provisions of this Agreement and shall be equally binding upon the Parties.

Article X

An exchange of prisoners of war having been effected by special arrangement between the Parties prior to the signing of this Agreement, no further arrangements on this matter are required except that the Mixed Armistice Commission shall undertake to re-examine whether there may be any prisoners of war belonging to either Party which were not included in the previous exchange. In the event that prisoners of war shall be found to exist, the Mixed Armistice Commission shall arrange for an early exchange of such prisoners. The Parties to this Agreement undertake to afford full co-operation to the Mixed Armistice Commission in its discharge of this responsibility.

Article XI

1. The execution of the provisions of this Agreement, with the exception of such matters as fall within the exclusive competence of the Special Committee established in article VIII, shall be supervised by a Mixed Armistice Commission composed of five members, of whom each Party to this Agreement shall designate two, and whose Chairman shall be the United Nations Chief of Staff of the Truce Supervision Organization or a senior officer from the observer personnel of that organization designated by him following consultation with both Parties to this Agreement.

2. The Mixed Armistice Commission shall maintain its headquarters at Jerusalem and shall hold its meeting at such places and at such times as is it may deem necessary for the effective conduct conduct of its work.

3. The Mixed Armistice Commission shall be convened in its first meeting by the United Nations Chief of Staff of the Truce Supervision Organization not later than one week following the signing of this Agreement.

4. Decisions of the Mixed Armistice Commission, to the extent possible, shall be based on the principle of unanimity. In the absence of unanimity, decisions shall be taken by a majority vote of the members of the Commission present and voting.

5. The Mixed Armistice Commission shall formulate its own rules of procedure. Meetings shall be held only after due notice to the members by the Chairman. The quorum for its meetings shall be a majority of its members.

6. The Commission shall be empowered to employ observers, who may be from among the military organizations of the Parties or from the military personnel of the United Nations Truce Supervision Organization, or from both, in such numbers as may be considered essential to the performance of its functions. In the event United Nations observers should be so employed, they shall remain under the command of the United Nations Chief of Staff of the Truce Supervision Organization. Assignments of a general or special nature given to United Nations observers attached to the Mixed Armistice Commission shall be subject to approval by the United Nations Chief of Staff or his designated representative on the Commission, whichever is serving as Chairman.

7. Claims or complaints presented by either Party relating to the application of this Agreement shall be referred immediately to the Mixed Armistice Commission through its Chairman. The Commission shall take such action on all such claims or complaints by means of its observation and investigation machinery as it may deem appropriate, with a view to equitable and mutually satisfactory settlement.

8. Where interpretation of the meaning of a particular provision of this Agreement, other than the preamble and articles I and II, is at issue, the Commission's interpretation shall prevail. The Commission, in its discretion and as the need arises, may from time to time recommend to the Parties modifications in the provisions of this Agreement.

9. The Mixed Armistice Commission shall submit to both Parties reports on its activities as frequently as it may consider necessary. A copy of each such report shall be presented to the Secretary-General of the United Nations for transmission to the appropriate organ or agency of the United Nations.

10. Members of the Commission and its observers shall be accorded such freedom of movement and access in the area covered by this Agreement as the Commission may determine to be necessary, provided that when such decisions of the Commission are reached by a majority vote United Nations observers only shall be employed.

11. The expenses of the Commission, other than those relating to United Nations observers, shall be apportioned in equal shares between the two Parties to this Agreement.

Article XII

1. The present Agreement is not subject to ratification and shall come into force immediately upon being signed.

2. This Agreement, having been negotiated and concluded in pursuance of the resolution of the Security Council of 16 November 1948 calling for the establishment of an armistice in order to eliminate the threat to the peace in Palestine and to facilitate the transition from the present truce to permanent peace in Palestine, shall remain in force until a peaceful settlement between the Parties is achieved, except as provided in paragraph 3 of this article.

3. The Parties to this Agreement, may, by mutual consent, revise this Agreement or any of its provisions, or may suspend its application, other than articles I and III, at any time. In the absence of mutual agreement and after this Agreement has been in effect for one year from the date of its signing, either of the Parties may call upon the Secretary-General of the United Nations to convoke a conference of representatives of the two Parties for the purpose of reviewing, revising, or suspending any of the provisions of this Agreement other than articles I and III. Participation in such conference shall be obligatory upon the Parties.

4. If the conference provided for in paragraph 3 of this article does not result in an agreed solution of a point in dispute, either Party may bring the matter before the Security Council of the United Nations for the relief sought on the grounds that this Agreement has been concluded in pursuance of Security Council action toward the end of achieving peace in Palestine.

5. This Agreement is signed in quintuplicate, of which one copy shall be retained by each Party, two copies communicated to the Secretary-General of the United Nations for transmission to the Security Council and to the United Nations Conciliation Commission on Palestine, and one copy to the United Nations Acting Mediator on Palestine.

DONE at Rhodes, Island of Rhodes, Greece, on the third of April one thousand nine hundred and forty-nine in the presence of the United Nations Acting Mediator on Palestine and the United Nations Chief of Staff of the Truce Supervision Organization.

For and on behalf of the Government of the Hashemite Jordan Kingdom:	For and on behalf of the Government of Israel:
(*Signed*)	(*Signed*
Colonel Ahmed Sudki EL-JUNDI	Reuven SHILOAH
Lieutenant-Colonel Mohamed MAAYTE	Lieutenant-Colonel Moshe DAYAN

2. ISRAEL–SYRIA

Preamble

The Parties to the present Agreement,

Responding to the Security Council resolution of 16 November 1948, calling upon them, as a further provisional measure under Article 40 of the Charter of the United Nations and in order to facilitate the transition from the present truce to permanent peace in Palestine, to negotiate an armistice;

Having decided to enter into negotiations under United Nations Chairmanship concerning the implementation of the Security Council resolution of 16 November 1948; and having appointed representatives empowered to negotiate and conclude an Armistice Agreement;

The undersigned representatives, having exchanged their full powers found to be in good and proper form, have agreed upon the following provisions:

Article I

With a view to promoting the return of permanent peace in Palestine and in recognition of the importance in this regard of mutual assurances concerning the future military operations of the Parties, the following principles, which shall be fully observed by both Parties during the armistice, are hereby affirmed:

1. The injunction of the Security Council against resort to military force in the settlement of the Palestine question shall henceforth be scrupulously respected by both Parties. The establishment of an armistice between their armed forces is accepted as an indispensable step toward the liquidation of armed conflict and the restoration of peace in Palestine.

2. No aggressive action by the armed forces—land, sea or air—of either Party shall be undertaken, planned, or threatened against the people or the armed forces of the other; it being understood that the use of the term *planned* in this context has no bearing on normal staff planning as generally practised in military organizations.

3. The right of each Party to its security and freedom from fear of attack by the armed forces of the other shall be fully respected.

Article II

With a specific view to the implementation of the resolution of the Security Council of 16 November 1948, the following principles and purposes are affirmed:

1. The principle that no military or political advantage should be gained under the truce ordered by the Security Council is recognized.

2. It is also recognized that no provision of this Agreement shall in any way prejudice the rights, claims and positions of either Party hereto in the ultimate peaceful settlement of the Palestine question, the provisions of this Agreement being dictated exclusively by military, and not by political, considerations.

Article III

1. In pursuance of the foregoing principles and of the resolution of the Security Council of of 16 November 1948, a general armistice between the armed forces of the two Parties—land, sea and air—is hereby established.

2. No element of the land, sea or air, military or para-military, forces of either Party, including non-regular forces, shall commit any warlike or hostile act against the military or para-military forces of the other Party, or against civilians in territory under the control of that Party; or shall advance beyond or pass over for any purpose whatsoever the Armistice Demarcation Line set forth in article V of this Agreement; or enter into or pass through the air space of the other Party or through the waters within three miles of the coastline of the other Party.

3. No warlike act or act of hostility shall be conducted from territory controlled by one of the Parties to this Agreement against the other Party or against civilians in territory under control of that Party.

Article IV

1. The line described in article V of this Agreement shall be designated as the Armistice Demarcation Line and is delineated in pursuance of the purpose and intent of the resolution of the Security Council of 16 November 1948.

2. The basic purpose of the Armistice Demarcation Line is to delineate the line beyond which the armed forces of the respective Parties shall not move.

3. Rules and regulations of the armed forces of the Parties, which prohibit civilians from crossing the fighting lines or entering the area between the lines, shall remain in effect after the signing of this Agreement, with application to the Armistice Demarcation Line defined in article V, subject to the provisions of paragraph 5 of that article.

Article V

1. It is emphasized that the following arrangements for the Armistice Demarcation Line between the Israeli and Syrian armed forces and for the Demilitarized Zone are not to be interpreted as having any relation whatsoever to ultimate territorial arrangements affecting the two Parties to this Agreement.

2. In pursuance of the spirit of the Security Council resolution of 16 November 1948, the Armistice Demarcation Line and the Demilitarized Zone have been defined with a view toward separating the armed forces of the two Parties in such manner as to minimize the possibility of friction and incident, while providing for the gradual restoration of normal civilian life in the area of the Demilitarized Zone, without prejudice to the ultimate settlement.

3. The Armistice Demarcation Line shall be as delineated on the map attached to this Agreement as annex I. The Armistice Demarcation Line shall follow a line midway between the existing truce lines, as certified by the United Nations Truce Supervision Organization for the Israeli and Syrian forces. Where the existing truce lines run along the international boundary between Syria and Palestine, the Armistice Demarcation Line shall follow the boundary line.

4. The armed forces of the two Parties shall nowhere advance beyond the Armistice Demarcation Line.

5. (*a*) Where the Armistice Demarcation Line does not correspond to the international

boundary between Syria and Palestine, the area between the Armistice Demarcation Line and the boundary, pending final territorial settlement between the Parties, shall be established as a Demilitarized Zone from which the armed forces of both Parties shall be totally excluded, and in which no activities by military or para-military forces shall be permitted. This provision applies to the Ein Gev and Dardara sectors which shall form part of the Demilitarized Zone.

(*b*) Any advance by the armed forces, military or para-military, of either Party into any part of the Demilitarized Zone, when confirmed by the United Nations representatives referred to in the following sub-paragraph, shall constitute a flagrant violation of this Agreement.

(*c*) The Chairman of the Mixed Armistice Commission established in article VII of this Agreement and United Nations observers attached to the Commission shall be responsible for ensuring the full implementation of this article.

(*d*) The withdrawal of such armed forces as are now found in the Demilitarized Zone shall be in accordance with the schedule of withdrawal annexed to this Agreement (annex II).

(*e*) The Chairman of the Mixed Armistice Commission shall be empowered to authorize the return of civilians to villages and settlements in the Demilitarized Zone and the employment of limited numbers of locally recruited civilian police in the zone for internal security purposes, and shall be guided in this regard by the schedule of withdrawal referred to in sub-paragraph (*d*) of this article.

6. On each side of the Demilitarized Zone there shall be areas, as defined in annex III to this Agreement, in which defensive forces only shall be maintained, in accordance with the definition of defensive forces set forth in annex IV to this Agreement.

Article VI

All prisoners of war detained by either Party to this Agreement and belonging to the armed forces, regular or irregular, of the other Party, shall be exchanged as follows:

1. The exchange of prisoners of war shall be under United Nations supervision and control throughout. The exchange shall take place at the site of the Armistice Conference within twenty-four hours of the signing of this Agreement.

2. Prisoners of war against whom a penal prosecution may be pending, as well as those sentenced for crime or other offence, shall be included in this exchange of prisoners.

3. All articles of personal use, valuables, letters, documents, identification marks, and other personal effects of whatever nature, belonging to prisoners of war who are being exchanged, shall be returned to them, or, if they have escaped or died, to the Party to whose armed forces they belonged.

4. All matters not specifically regulated in this Agreement shall be decided in accordance with the principles laid down in the International Convention relating to the Treatment of Prisoners of War, signed at Geneva on 27 July 1929.

5. The Mixed Armistice Commission established in article VII of this Agreement shall assume responsibility for locating missing persons, whether military or civilian, within the areas controlled by each Party, to facilitate their expeditious exchange. Each Party undertakes to extend to the Commission full co-operation and assistance in the discharge of this function.

Article VII

1. The execution of the provisions of this Agreement shall be supervised by a Mixed

Armistice Commission composed of five members, of whom each Party to this Agreement shall designate two, and whose Chairman shall be the United Nations Chief of Staff of the Truce Supervision Organization or a senior officer from the observer personnel of that organization designated by him following consultation with both Parties to this Agreement.

2. The Mixed Armistice Commission shall maintain its headquarters at the Customs House near Jisr Banat Ya'qub and at Mahanayim, and shall hold its meetings at such places and at such times as it may deem necessary for the effective conduct of its work.

3. The Mixed Armistice Commission shall be convened in its first meeting by the United Nations Chief of Staff of the Truce Supervision Organization not later than one week following the signing of this Agreement.

4. Decisions of the Mixed Armistice Commission, to the extent possible, shall be based on the principle of unanimity. In the absence of unanimity, decisions shall be taken by majority vote of the members of the Commission present and voting.

5. The Mixed Armistice Commission shall formulate its own rules of procedure. Meetings shall be held only after due notice to the members by the Chairman. The quorum for its meetings shall be a majority of its members.

6. The Commission shall be empowered to employ observers, who may be from among the military organizations of the Parties or from the military personnel of the United Nations Truce Supervision Organization, or from both, in such numbers as may be considered essential to the performance of its functions. In the event United Nations observers should be so employed, they shall remain under the command of the United Nations Chief of Staff of the Truce Supervision Organization. Assignments of a general or special nature given to United Nations observers attached to the Mixed Armistice Commission shall be subject to approval by the United Nations Chief of Staff or his designated representative on the Commission, whichever is serving as Chairman.

7. Claims or complaints presented by either Party relating to the application of this Agreement shall be referred immediately to the Mixed Armistice Commission through its Chairman. The Commission shall take such action on all such claims or complaints by means of its observation and investigation machinery as it may deem appropriate, with a view to equitable and mutually satisfactory settlement.

8. Where interpretation of the meaning of a particular provision of this Agreement, other than the preamble and article I and II, is at issue, the Commission's interpretation shall prevail. The Commission, in its discretion and as the need arises, may from time to time recommend to the Parties modifications in the provisions of this Agreement.

9. The Mixed Armistice Commission shall submit to both Parties reports on its activities as frequently as it may consider necessary. A copy of each such report shall be presented to the Secretary-General of the United Nations for transmission to the appropriate organ or agency of the United Nations.

10. Members of the Commission and its observers shall be accorded such freedom of movement and access in the area covered by this Agreement as the Commission may determine to be necessary, provided that when such decisions of the Commission are reached by a majority vote United Nations observers only shall be employed.

11. The expenses of the Commission, other than those relating to United Nations observers, shall be apportioned in equal shares between the two Parties to this Agreement.

Article VIII

1. The present Agreement is not subject to ratification and shall come into force immediately upon being signed.

2. This Agreement, having been negotiated and concluded in pursuance of the resolution of the Security Council of 16 November 1948, calling for the establishment of an armistice in order to eliminate the threat to the peace in Palestine and to facilitate the transition from the present truce to permanent peace in Palestine, shall remain in force until a peaceful settlement between the Parties is achieved, except as provided in paragraph 3 of this article.

3. The Parties to this Agreement may, by mutual consent, revise this agreement or any of its provisions, or may suspend its application, other than articles I and III, at any time. In the absence of mutual agreement and after this Agreement has been in effect for one year from the date of its signing either of the Parties may call upon the Secretary-General of the United Nations to convoke a conference of representatives of the two Parties for the purpose of reviewing, revising, or suspending any of the provisions of this Agreement other than articles I and III. Participation in such conferences shall be obligatory upon the Parties.

4. If the conference provided for in paragraph 3 of this article does not result in an agreed solution of a point in dispute, either Party may bring the matter before the Security Council of the United Nations for the relief sought on the grounds that this Agreement has been concluded in pursuance of Security Council action toward the end of achieving peace in Palestine.

5. This Agreement, of which the English and French texts are equally authentic, is signed in quintuplicate. One copy shall be retained by each Party, two copies communicated to the Secretary-General of the United Nations for transmission to the Security Council and the United Nations Conciliation Commission on Palestine, and one copy to the Acting Mediator on Palestine.

DONE at Hill 232 near Mahanayim on the twentieth of July nineteen forty-nine, in the presence of the personal deputy of the United Nations Acting Mediator on Palestine and the United Nations Chief of Staff of the Truce Supervision Organization.

For and on behalf of the Israeli Government:	For and on behalf of the Syrian Government:
(*Signed*)	(*Signed*)
Lieutenant-Colonel Mordechai MAKLEFF	Colonel Fozi SELO
Yehoshua PELMAN	Lieutenant-Colonel Mohamed NASSER
Shabtai ROSENNE	Captain Afif SIZRI

3. ISRAEL–EGYPT

Preamble

The Parties to the present Agreement, responding to the Security Council resolution of 16 November 1948 calling upon them, as a further provisional measure under Article 40 of the Charter of the United Nations and in order to facilitate the transition from the present truce to permanent peace in Palestine, to negotiate an Armistice; having decided to enter into negotiations under United Nations Chairmanship concerning the implementation of the Security Council resolutions of 4 and 16 November 1948 ; and having appointed representatives empowered to negotiate and conclude an Armistice Agreement;

The undersigned representatives, in the full authority entrusted to them by their respective Governments, have agreed upon the following provisions:

Article I

With a view to promoting the return to permanent peace in Palestine and in recognition of the importance in this regard of mutual assurances concerning the future military operations of the Parties, the following principles, which shall be fully observed by both Parties during the Armistice, are hereby affirmed:

1. The injunction of the Security Council against resort to military force in the settlement of the Palestine question shall henceforth be scrupulously respected by both Parties.

2. No aggressive action by the armed forces—land, sea, or air—of either Party shall be undertaken, planned, or threatened against the people or the armed forces of the other; it being understood that the use of the term 'planned' in this context has no bearing on normal staff planning as generally practised in military organizations.

3. The right of each Party to its security and freedom from fear of attack by the armed forces of the other shall be fully respected.

4. The establishment of an armistice between the armed forces of the two Parties is accepted as an indispensable step toward the liquidation of armed conflict and the restoration of peace in Palestine.

Article II

1. In pursuance of the foregoing principles and of the resolutions of the Security Council of 4 and 16 November 1948, a general armistice between the armed forces of the two Parties— land, sea and air—is hereby established.

2. No element of the land, sea or air military or para-military forces of either Party, including non-regular forces, shall commit any warlike or hostile act against the military or para-military forces of the other Party, or against civilians in territory under the control of that Party; or shall advance beyond or pass over for any purpose whatsoever the Armistice Demarcation Line set forth in Article VI of this Agreement except as provided in Article III of this Agreement; and elsewhere shall not violate the international frontier; or enter into or pass through the air space of the other Party or through the waters within three miles of the coastline of the other Party.

Article III

1. In pursuance of the Security Council's resolution of 4 November 1948, and with a view

43

to the implementation of the Security Council's resolution of 16 November 1948, the Egyptian Military Forces in the AL FALUJA area shall be withdrawn.

2. This withdrawal shall begin on the day after that which follows the signing of this Agreement, at 0500 hours GMT, and shall be beyond the Egypt–Palestine frontier.

3. The withdrawal shall be under the supervision of the United Nations and in accordance with the Plan of Withdrawal set forth in Annex I to this Agreement.

Article IV

With specific reference to the implementation of the resolutions of the Security Council of 4 and 16 November 1948, the following principles and purposes are affirmed:

1. The principle that no military or political advantage should be gained under the truce ordered by the Security Council is recognized.

2. It is also recognized that the basic purposes and spirit of the Armistice would not be served by the restoration of previously held military positions, changes from those now held other than as specifically provided for in this Agreement, or by the advance of the military forces of either side beyond positions held at the time this Armistice Agreement is signed.

3. It is further recognized that rights, claims or interests of a non-military character in the area of Palestine covered by this Agreement may be asserted by either Party, and that these, by mutual agreement being excluded from the Armistice negotiations, shall be, at the discretion of the Parties, the subject of later settlement. It is emphasized that it is not the purpose of this Agreement to establish, to recognize, to strengthen, or to weaken or nullify, in any way, any territorial, custodial or other rights, claims or interests which may be asserted by either Party in the area of Palestine or any part or locality thereof covered by this Agreement, whether such asserted rights, claims or interests derive from Security Council resolutions, including the resolution of 4 November 1948 and the Memorandum of 13 November 1948 for its implementation, or from any other source. The provisions of this Agreement are dictated exclusively by military considerations and are valid only for the period of the Armistice.

Article V

1. The line described in Article VI of this Agreement shall be designated as the Armistice Demarcation Line and is delineated in pursuance of the purpose and intent of the resolutions of the Security Council of 4 and 16 November 1948.

2. The Armistice Demarcation Line is not to be construed in any sense as a political or territorial boundary, and is delineated without prejudice to rights, claims and positions of either Party to the Armistice as regards ultimate settlement of the Palestine question.

3. The basic purpose of the Armistice Demarcation Line is to delineate the line beyond which the armed forces of the respective Parties shall not move except as provided in Article III of this Agreement.

4. Rules and regulations of the armed forces of the Parties, which prohibit civilians from crossing the fighting lines or entering the area between the lines, shall remain in effect after the signing of this Agreement with application to the Armistice Demarcation Line defined in Article VI.

Article VI

1. In the GAZA-RAFAH area the Armistice Demarcation Line shall be as delineated in para-

graph 2.B (i) of the Memorandum of 13 November 1948 on the implementation of the Security Council resolution of 4 November 1948, namely by a line from the coast at the mouth of the Wadi Hasi in an easterly direction through Deir Suneid and across the Gaza-Al Majdal Highway to a point 3 kilometres east of the Highway, then in a southerly direction parallel to the Gaza-Al Madjal Highway, and continuing thus to the Egyptian frontier.

2. Within this line Egyptian forces shall nowhere advance beyond their present positions, and this shall include Beit Hanun and its surrounding area from which Israeli forces shall be withdrawn to north of the Armistice Demarcation Line, and any other positions within the line delineated in paragraph 1 which shall be evacuated by Israeli forces as set forth in paragraph 3.

3. Israeli outposts, each limited to platoon strength, may be maintained in this area at the following points: Deir Suneid, on the north side of the Wadi (MR 10751090); 700 SW of Sa'ad (MR 10500982); Sulphur Quarries (MR 09870924); Tall-Jamma (MR 09720887); and KH AL Ma'in (MR 09320821). The Israeli outpost maintained at the Cemetery (MR 08160723) shall be evacuated on the day after that which follows the signing of this Agreement. The Israeli outpost at Hill 79 (MR 10451017) shall be evacuated not later than four weeks following the day on which this Agreement is signed. Following the evacuation of the above outposts, new Israeli outposts may be established at MR 08360700, and at a point due east of Hill 79 east of the Armistice Demarcation Line.

4. In the BETHLEHEM-HEBRON area, wherever positions are held by Egyptian forces, the provisions of this Agreement shall apply to the forces of both Parties in each such locality, except that the demarcation of the Armistice Line and reciprocal arrangements for withdrawal and reduction of forces shall be undertaken in such manner as may be decided by the Parties, at such time as an Armistice Agreement may be concluded covering military forces in that area other than those of the Parties to this Agreement, or sooner at the will of the Parties.

Article VII

1. It is recognized by the Parties to this Agreement that in certain sectors of the total area involved, the proximity of the forces of a third party not covered by this Agreement makes impractical the full application of all provisions of the Agreement to such sectors. For this reason alone, therefore, and pending the conclusion of an Armistice Agreement in place of the existing truce with that third party, the provisions of this Agreement relating to reciprocal reduction and withdrawal of forces shall apply only to the western front and not to the eastern front.

2. The areas comprising the western and eastern fronts shall be as defined by the United Nations Chief of Staff of the Truce Supervision Organization, on the basis of the deployment of forces against each other and past military activity or the future possibility thereof in the area. This definition of the western and eastern fronts is set forth in Annex II of this Agreement.

3. In the area of the western front under Egyptian control, Egyptian defensive forces only may be maintained. All other Egyptian forces shall be withdrawn from this area to a point or points no further east than El Arish-Abou Aoueigila.

4. In the area of the western front under Israeli control, Israeli defensive forces only, which shall be based on the settlements, may be maintained. All other Israeli forces shall be withdrawn from this area to a point or points north of the line delineated in paragraph 2.A of the Memorandum of 13 November 1948 on the implementation of the resolution of the Security Council of 4 November 1948.

5. The defensive forces referred to in paragraphs 3 and 4 above shall be as defined in Annex III to this Agreement.

Article VIII

1. The area comprising the village of El Auja and vicinity, as defined in paragraph 2 of this Article, shall be demilitarized, and both Egyptian and Israeli armed forces shall be totally excluded therefrom. The Chairman of the Mixed Armistice Commission established in Article X of this Agreement and United Nations Observers attached to the Commission shall be responsible for ensuring the full implementation of this provision.

2. The area thus demilitarized shall be as follows: From a point on the Egypt–Palestine frontier five (5) kilometres north-west of the intersection of the Rafah–El Auja road and the frontier (MR 08750468), south-east to Khashm El Mamdud (MR 09650414), thence south-east to Hill 405 (MR 10780285), thence south-west to a point on the Egypt–Palestine frontier five (5) kilometres south-east of the intersection of the old railway tracks and the frontier (MR 09950145), thence returning north-west along the Egypt–Palestine frontier to the point of origin.

3. On the Egyptian side of the frontier, facing the El Auja area, no Egyptian defensive positions shall be closer to El Auja than El Qouseima and Abou Aoueigila.

4. The road Taba–Qouseima–Auja shall not be employed by any military forces whatsoever for the purpose of entering Palestine.

5. The movement of armed forces of either Party to this Agreement into any part of the area defined in paragraph 2 of this Article, for any purpose, or failure by either Party to respect or fulfil any of the other provisions of this Article, when confirmed by the United Nations representatives, shall constitute a flagrant violation of this Agreement.

Article IX

All prisoners of war detained by either Party to this Agreement and belonging to the armed forces, regular or irregular, of the other Party shall be exchanged as follows:

1. The exchange of prisoners of war shall be under United Nations supervision and control throughout. The exchange shall begin within ten days after the signing of this Agreement and shall be completed not later than twenty-one days following. Upon the signing of this Agreement, the Chairman of the Mixed Armistice Commission established in Article X of this Agreement, in consultation with the appropriate military authorities of the Parties, shall formulate a plan for the exchange of prisoners of war within the above period, defining the date and places of exchange and all other relevant details.

2. Prisoners of war against whom a penal prosecution may be pending, as well as those sentenced for crime or other offence, shall be included in this exchange of prisoners.

3. All articles of personal use, valuables, letters, documents, identification marks, and other personal effects of whatever nature, belonging to prisoners of war who are being exchanged, shall be returned to them, or, if they have escaped or died, to the Party to whose armed forces they belonged.

4. All matters not specifically regulated in this Agreement shall be decided in accordance with the principles laid down in the International Convention relating to the Treatment of Prisoners of War, signed at Geneva on 27 July 1929.

5. The Mixed Armistice Commission established in Article X of this Agreement shall

assume responsibility for locating missing persons, whether military or civilian, within the areas controlled by each Party, to facilitate their expeditious exchange. Each Party undertakes to extend to the Commission full co-operation and assistance in the discharge of this function.

Article X

1. The execution of the provisions of this Agreement shall be supervised by a Mixed Armistice Commission composed of seven members, of whom each Party to this Agreement shall designate three, and whose Chairman shall be the United Nations Chief of Staff of the Truce Supervision Organization or a senior officer from the Observer personnel of that Organization designated by him following consultation with both Parties to this Agreement.

2. The Mixed Armistice Commission shall maintain its headquarters at El Auja, and shall hold its meetings at such places and at such times as it may deem necessary for the effective conduct of its work.

3. The Mixed Armistice Commission shall be convened in its first meeting by the United Nations Chief of Staff of the Truce Supervision Organization not later than one week following the signing of this Agreement.

4. Decisions of the Mixed Armistice Commission, to the extent possible, shall be based on the principle of unanimity. In the absence of unanimity, decisions shall be taken by a majority vote of the members of the Commission present and voting. On questions of principle, appeal shall lie to a Special Committee, composed of the United Nations Chief of Staff of the Truce Supervision Organization and one member each of the Egyptian and Israeli Delegations to the Armistice Conference at Rhodes or some other senior officer, whose decisions on all such questions shall be final. If no appeal against a decision of the Commission is filed within one week from the date of said decision, that decision shall be taken as final. Appeals to the Special Committee shall be presented to the United Nations Chief of Staff of the Truce Supervision Organization, who shall convene the Committee at the earliest possible date.

5. The Mixed Armistice Commission shall formulate its own rules of procedure. Meetings shall be held only after due notice to the members by the Chairman. The quorum for its meetings shall be a majority of its members.

6. The Commission shall be empowered to employ Observers, who may be from among the military organizations of the Parties or from the military personnel of the United Nations Truce Supervision Organization, or from both, in such numbers as may be considered essential to the performance of its functions. In the event United Nations Observers should be so employed, they shall remain under the command of the United Nations Chief of Staff of the Truce Supervision Organization. Assignments of a general or special nature given to United Nations Observers attached to the Mixed Armistice Commission shall be subject to approval by the United Nations Chief of Staff or his designated representative on the Commission, whichever is serving as Chairman.

7. Claims or complaints presented by either Party relating to the application of this Agreement shall be referred immediately to the Mixed Armistice Commission through its Chairman. The Commission shall take such action on all such claims or complaints by means of its observation and investigation machinery as it may deem appropriate, with a view to equitable and mutually satisfactory settlement.

8. Where interpretation of the meaning of a particular provision of this Agreement is at issue, the Commission's interpretation shall prevail, subject to the right of appeal as provided in paragraph 4. The Commission, in its discretion and as the need arises, may from time to time recommend to the Parties modifications in the provisions of this Agreement.

9. The Mixed Armistice Commission shall submit to both Parties reports on its activities as frequently as it may consider necessary. A copy of each such report shall be presented to the Secretary-General of the United Nations for transmission to the appropriate organ or agency of the United Nations.

10. Members of the Commission and its Observers shall be accorded such freedom of movement and access in the areas covered by this Agreement as the Commission may determine to be necessary, provided that when such decisions of the Commission are reached by a majority vote United Nations Observers only shall be employed.

11. The expenses of the Commission, other than those relating to United Nations Observers, shall be apportioned in equal shares between the two Parties to this Agreement.

Article XI

No provision of this Agreement shall in any way prejudice the rights, claims and positions of either Party hereto in the ultimate peaceful settlement of the Palestine question.

Article XII

1. The present Agreement is not subject to ratification and shall come into force immediately upon being signed.

2. This Agreement, having been negotiated and concluded in pursuance of the resolution of the Security Council of 16 November 1948 calling for the establishment of an armistice in order to eliminate the threat to the peace in Palestine and to facilitate the transition from the present truce to permanent peace in Palestine, shall remain in force until a peaceful settlement between the Parties is achieved, except as provided in paragraph 3 of this Article.

3. The Parties to this Agreement may, by mutual consent, revise this Agreement or any of its provisions, or may suspend its application, other than Articles I and II, at any time. In the absence of mutual agreement and after this Agreement has been in effect for one year from the date of its signing, either of the Parties may call upon the Secretary-General of the United Nations to convoke a conference of representatives of the two Parties for the purpose of reviewing, revising or suspending any of the provisions of this Agreement other than Articles I and II. Participation in such conference shall be obligatory upon the Parties.

4. If the conference provided for in paragraph 3 of this Article does not result in an agreed solution of a point in dispute, either Party may bring the matter before the Security Council of the United Nations for the relief sought on the grounds that this Agreement has been concluded in pursuance of Security Council action toward the end of achieving peace in Palestine.

5. This Agreement supersedes the Egyptian-Israeli General Cease-Fire Agreement entered into by the Parties on 24 January 1949.

6. This Agreement is signed in quintuplicate, of which one copy shall be retained by each Party, two copies communicated to the Secretary-General of the United Nations for transmission to the Security Council and to the United Nations Conciliation Commission on Palestine, and one copy to the Acting Mediator on Palestine.

4. ISRAEL–LEBANON

Preamble

The Parties to the present Agreement,

Responding to the Security Council resolution of 16 November 1948, calling upon them, as a further provisional measure under Article 40 of the Charter of the United Nations and in order to facilitate the transition from the present truce to permanent peace in Palestine, to negotiate an armistice;

Having decided to enter into negotiations under United Nations Chairmanship concerning the implementation of the Security Council resolution of 16 November 1948; and having appointed representatives empowered to negotiate and conclude an Armistice Agreement;

The undersigned representatives, having exchanged their full powers found to be in good and proper form, have agreed upon the following provisions:

Article I

With a view to promoting the return of permanent peace in Palestine and in recognition of the importance in this regard of mutual assurances concerning the future military operations of the Parties, the following principles, which shall be fully observed by both Parties during the armistice, are hereby affirmed:

1. The injunction of the Security Council against resort to military force in the settlement of the Palestine question shall henceforth be scrupulously respected by both Parties.

2. No aggressive action by the armed forces—land, sea, or air—of either Party shall be undertaken, planned, or threatened against the people or the armed forces of the other; it being understood that the use of the term 'planned' in this context has no bearing on normal staff planning as generally practised in military organizations.

3. The right of each Party to its security and freedom from fear of attack by the armed forces of the other shall be fully respected.

4. The establishment of an armistice between the armed forces of the two Parties is accepted as an indispensable step toward the liquidation of armed conflict and the restoration of peace in Palestine.

Article II

With a specific view to the implementation of the resolution of the Security Council of 16 November 1948, the following principles and purposes are affirmed:

1. The principle that no military or political advantage should be gained under the truce ordered by the Security Council is recognized.

2. It is also recognized that no provision of this Agreement shall in any way prejudice the rights, claims and positions of either Party hereto in the ultimate peaceful settlement of the Palestine question, the provisions of this agreement being dictated exclusively by military considerations.

Article III

1. In pursuance of the foregoing principles and of the resolution of the Security Council

of 16 November 1948 a general armistice between the armed forces of the two Parties—land, sea and air—is hereby established.

2. No element of the land, sea or air military or para-military forces of either Party, including non-regular forces, shall commit any warlike or hostile act against the military or para-military forces of the other Party, or against civilians in territory under the control of that Party; or shall advance beyond or pass over for any purpose whatsoever the Armistice Demarcation Line set forth in Article V of this Agreement; or enter into or pass through the air space of the other Party or through the waters within three miles of the coastline of the other Party.

3. No warlike act or act of hostility shall be conducted from territory controlled by one of the Parties to this Agreement against the other Party.

Article IV

1. The line described in Article V of this Agreement shall be designated as the Armistice Demarcation Line and is delineated in pursuance of the purpose and intent of the resolutions of the Security Council of 16 November 1948.

2. The basic purpose of the Armistice Demarcation Line is to delineate the line beyond which the armed forces of the respective Parties shall not move.

3. Rules and regulations of the armed forces of the Parties, which prohibit civilians from crossing the fighting lines or entering the area between the lines, shall remain in effect after the signing of this Agreement with application to the Armistice Demarcation Line defined in article V.

Article V

1. The Armistice Demarcation Line shall follow the international boundary between the Lebanon and Palestine.

2. In the region of the Armistice Demarcation Line the military forces of the Parties shall consist of defensive forces only as is defined in the Annex to this Agreement.

3. Withdrawal of forces to the Armistice Demarcation Line and their reduction to defensive strength in accordance with the preceding paragraph shall be completed within ten days of the signing of this Agreement. In the same way the removal of mines from mined roads and areas evacuated by either Party, and the transmission of plans showing the location of such minefields to the other Party shall be completed within the same period.

Article VI

All prisoners of war detained by either Party to this Agreement and belonging to the armed forces, regular or irregular, of the other Party, shall be exchanged as follows:

1. The exchange of prisoners of war shall be under United Nations supervision and control throughout. The exchange shall take place at Ras En Naqoura within twenty-four hours of the signing of this Agreement.

2. Prisoners of war against whom a penal prosecution may be pending, as well as those sentenced for crime or other offence, shall be included in this exchange of prisoners.

3. All articles of personal use, valuables, letters, documents, identification marks, and other personal effects of whatever nature, belonging to prisoners of war who are being exchanged,

shall be returned to them, or, if they have escaped or died, to the Party to whose armed forces they belonged.

4. All matters not specifically regulated in this Agreement shall be decided in accordance with the principles laid down in the International Convention relating to the Treatment of Prisoners of War, signed at Geneva on 27 July 1929.

5. The Mixed Armistice Commission established in Article VII of this Agreement shall assume responsibility for locating missing persons, whether military or civilian, within the areas controlled by each Party, to facilitate their expeditious exchange. Each Party undertakes to extend to the Commission full co-operation and assistance in the discharge of this function.

Article VII

1. The execution of the provisions of this Agreement shall be supervised by a Mixed Armistice Commission composed of five members, of whom each Party to this Agreement shall designate two, and whose Chairman shall be the United Nations Chief of Staff of the Truce Supervision Organization or a senior officer from the Observer personnel of that Organization designated by him following consultation with both Parties to this Agreement.

2. The Mixed Armistice Commission shall maintain its headquarters at the Frontier Post north of Metulla and at the Lebanese Frontier Post at En Naqoura, and shall hold its meetings at such places and at such times as it may deem necessary for the effective conduct of its work.

3. The Mixed Armistice Commission shall be convened in its first meeting by the United Nations Chief of Staff of the Truce Supervision Organization not later than one week following the signing of this Agreement.

4. Decisions of the Mixed Armistice Commission, to the extent possible, shall be based on the principle of unanimity. In the absence of unanimity, decisions shall be taken by majority vote of the members of the Commission present and voting.

5. The Mixed Armistice Commission shall formulate its own rules of procedure. Meetings shall be held only after due notice to the members by the Chairman. The quorum for its meetings shall be a majority of its members.

6. The Commission shall be empowered to employ Observers, who may be from among the military organizations of the Parties or from the military personnel of the United Nations Truce Supervision Organization, or from both, in such numbers as may be considered essential to the performance of its functions. In the event United Nations Observers should be so employed, they shall remain under the command of the United Nations Chief of Staff of the Truce Supervision Organization. Assignments of a general or special nature given to United Nations Observers attached to the Mixed Armistice Commission shall be subject to approval by the United Nations Chief of Staff or his designated representative on the Commission, whichever is serving as Chairman.

7. Claims or complaints presented by either Party relating to the application of this Agreement shall be referred immediately to the Mixed Armistice Commission through its Chairman. The Commission shall take such action on all such claims or complaints by means of its observation and investigation machinery as it may deem appropriate, with a view to equitable and mutually satisfactory settlement.

8. Where interpretation of the meaning of a particular provision of this Agreement, other than the Preamble and Articles I and II, is at issue, the Commission's interpretation shall

3

prevail. The Commission, in its discretion and as the need arises, may from time to time recommend to the Parties modifications in the provisions of this Agreement.

9. The Mixed Armistice Commission shall submit to both Parties reports on its activities as frequently as it may consider necessary. A copy of each such report shall be presented to the Secretary-General of the United Nations for transmission to the appropriate organ or agency of the United Nations.

10. Members of the Commission and its Observers shall be accorded such freedom of movement and access in the areas covered by this Agreement as the Commission may determine to be necessary, provided that when such decisions of the Commission are reached by a majority vote United Nations Observers only shall be employed.

11. The expenses of the Commission, other than those relating to United Nations Observers, shall be apportioned in equal shares between the two Parties to this Agreement.

Article VIII

1. The present Agreement is not subject to ratification and shall come into force immediately upon being signed.

2. This Agreement, having been negotiated and concluded in pursuance of the resolution of the Security Council of 16 November 1948 calling for the establishment of an armistice in order to eliminate the threat to the peace in Palestine and to facilitate the transition from the present truce to permanent peace in Palestine, shall remain in force until a peaceful settlement between the Parties is achieved, except as provided in paragraph 3 of this Article.

3. The Parties to this Agreement may, by mutual consent, revise this Agreement or any of its provisions, or may suspend its application, other than Articles I and III, at any time. In the absence of mutual agreement and after this Agreement has been in effect for one year from the date of its signing, either of the Parties may call upon the Secretary-General of the United Nations to convoke a conference of representatives of the two Parties for the purpose of reviewing, revising, or suspending any of the provisions of this Agreement other than Articles I and III. Participation in such conference shall be obligatory upon the Parties.

4. If the conference provided for in paragraph 3 of this Article does not result in an agreed solution of a point in dispute, either Party may bring the matter before the Security Council of the United Nations for the relief sought on the grounds that this Agreement has been concluded in pursuance of Security Council action toward the end of achieving peace in Palestine.

5. This Agreement is signed in quintuplicate, of which one copy shall be retained by each Party, two copies communicated to the Secretary-General of the United Nations for transmission to the Security Council and to the United Nations Conciliation Commission on Palestine, and one copy to the Acting Mediator on Palestine.

DONE at Ras En Naqoura on the twenty-third of March nineteen forty-nine, in the presence of the Personal Deputy of the United Nations Acting Mediator on Palestine and the United Nations Chief of Staff of the Truce Supervision Organization.

For and on behalf of the Government of Israel:	For and on behalf of the Government of the Lebanon:
(Signed)	*(Signed)*
Lieutenant-Colonel Mordechai MAKLEFF	Lieutenant-Colonel Toufic SALEM
Yenoshua PELMAN	Commandant J. HARB
Shabtai ROSENNE	

(c) The Functions of UNTSO after November 1956

After the Israeli entry into Egyptian territory, and the Anglo-French intervention of 1956, a new United Nations organ—the UN Emergency Force (UNEF)—was established. The task of UNEF was to secure and supervise the cessation of hostilities; UNTSO remained in existence to implement, observe, and supervise the Armistice structure set up in 1949. The details of the establishment and role of UNEF are examined elsewhere (pp. 242–60) but it will readily be appreciated that its existence, and the events of 1956, inevitably affected to a certain degree the scope of UNTSO's duties.

The resolution establishing UNEF (General Assembly Res. 1000 (ES–1)) transferred the Chief of Staff of UNTSO to the post of Chief of Command of UNEF; and it also authorized recruitment from UNTSO to UNEF. Although UNEF and UNTSO had different functions, they were linked, and close co-ordination was essential. Ultimately, for operational reasons, the duties of UNTSO in the Gaza area were placed under the operational control of UNEF:

The United Nations Truce Supervision Organization established under the armistice agreements assists, as one of its main duties, in the prevention of incursions and raids. It is in accord with the call for scrupulous observance of the armistice agreements for the parties to take all appropriate measures to give UNTSO the support necessary to render it fully effective. It is a primary duty of the United Nations Emergency Force to supervise and enforce the cease-fire to which the parties committed themselves in response to the request of the General Assembly in the resolution of 2 November. Appropriate liaison should be established between these two United Nations auxiliary organizations. Further consideration may have to be given to the question of the extent to which the Force might assume responsibilities so far carried by the Truce Supervision Organization. [*A/3500, Report by Secretary-General on compliance with General Assembly Resolutions, 15 Jan. 1957*, p. 43.]

The United Nations Emergency Force is deployed at the dividing line between the forces of Israel and Egypt. The General Assembly concurred in paragraph 12 of the Secretary-General's second and final report (A/3302) which specifically referred to the deployment of the Force on only one side of the armistice line. On this basis, the Force would have units in the Gaza areas as well as opposite El Auja. With demilitarization of the El Auja zone in accordance with the Armistice Agreement, it might be indicated that the Force should have units stationed also on the Israel side of the armistice demarcation line, at least, in that zone. Such deployment, which would require a new decision by the General Assembly, would have the advantage of the Force being in a position to assume the supervisory duties of the Truce Supervision Organization in all the territory where that Organization now functions under the Armistice Agreement between Egypt and Israel In both Gaza and El Auja, the functions of the Truce Supervision Organization and the Force would somewhat overlap if such an arrangement were not to be made. As an arrangement of this kind was not foreseen by the Armistice Agreement, it obviously would require the consent of the two parties to that Agreement. Such mutual consent might be given to the United Nations directly, especially since the arrangement would be on an *ad hoc* basis. (*A/3512, Secretary-General's Report in pursuance of General Assembly Res. 1123 (XI), 24 Jan. 1957*, p. 49.]

The Secretary-General finally wishes to inform the General Assembly that arrangements will be made through which, without any change of the legal structure or status of the United Nations Truce Supervision Organization, functions of UNTSO in the Gaza area will be placed under the operational control of the Force. A close co-operation between UNTSO and UNEF will be maintained. (*A/3568, 2nd Report of Secretary-General in pursuance of General Assembly Res. 1124 (XI) and 1125 (XII), 8 Mar. 1957*.]

Further guidance on UNTSO's duties after the establishment of UNEF may be found in the Secretary-General's study of the experience derived from the establishment and operation of UNEF:

8 . . . Resolution 997 ES–1 of 2 November [envisaged a force to secure and supervise] . . . the withdrawal of non-Egyptian forces from Egyptian territory and the restoration of observance of the provisions of the General Armistice Agreement between Egypt and Israel. These objectives could not be achieved through an organ similar in kind to UNTSO or to the Egyptian–Israel Mixed Armistice Commission, which had been established in other and different circumstances and were designed to meet different and narrower needs. The role of UNTSO is to observe and maintain the cease-fire in Palestine ordered by the Security Council. The Mixed Armistice Commission, serviced by UNTSO, is the bilateral machinery established under the Egyptian–Israeli General Armistice Agreement in connexion with the execution of the provisions of that Agreement, exercising such functions as the investigation of incidents and complaints. . . .

72. The deployment of UNEF along the armistice demarcation line and the line south of Gaza raised the question of the respective responsibilities of UNEF and UNTSO. The governments of Israel took the position that the Egyptian–Israel General Armistice Agreement was no longer in effect. The UN, however, could not accept a unilateral decision on the Armistice Agreement, and therefore the Chairman of the Egyptian–Israel Mixed Armistice Commission and the UNTSO military observers have continued at their posts throughout the Israel occupation of the Gaza strip, and since. . . .

73. Upon the withdrawal of the Israel forces, arrangements were made which, without any change in its legal status, placed the Egyptian–Israel Mixed Armistice Commission under the operational control of the Commander of UNEF. Upon the appointment in March 1958 of a new Chief of Staff for UNTSO, the Secretary-General confirmed to the representatives of Egypt and Israel that the Commander of the Force would continue to exercise his functions as Chief of Staff in respect of the Egyptian–Israel General Armistice Agreement, i.e. as Chairman *ex officio* of the Mixed Armistice Commission, in accordance with Article X of that Agreement.

74. In view of its position with respect to the Armistice Agreement, the Government of Israel has preferred to lodge its complaints with UNEF, but UNEF representatives have consistently maintained that official investigations of incidents can be carried out only through the Mixed Armistice Commissions.[13] [*A/3943, Summary Study prepared by the*

___

[13] A most useful comparison of the functions of UNEF and UNTSO is to be found in Gabriella Rosner, *The United Nations Emergency Force* (1963). She notes, *inter alia,* that: 'The function of the Truce Supervision Organization is not only to observe and maintain the cease-fire in Palestine which the Security Council had ordered, but to service the Mixed Armistice Commission (MAC)—bilateral machinery established under the Egyptian–Israel General Armistice Agreement of 1949. The MAC helps to execute the terms of the Agreement and is entrusted with such functions as the investigation of incidents and complaints. UNEF, on the contrary, is obliged to direct and administer the cessation of hostilities brought about by the Israeli–British–French invasion of Egypt in November 1956, secure and supervise the withdrawal of forces, and seek observance of the provisions of the General Armistice Agreement between Egypt and Israel. As a result, UNEF has a wider and different role to play in the Middle East than has the Truce Supervision Organization. It is a police and patrol force rather than an observer corps . . .' (pp. 70–71). Further, in relation to the Armistice functions, Miss Rosner writes: 'Although a useful institution for observation and a practical mechanism for the airing of complaints, the Egypt–Israel armistice machinery—comprising UNTSO and MAC—has been unable to prevent skirmishes, theft, and smuggling along the border, or guerrilla raids across the demarcation lines. Therefore, in February 1957, the prevention of these incidents was designated as UNEF'S task. While members of the Truce Supervision Organization and the MAC, unarmed and small in number, were mainly authorized to engage in activities of observation and investigation, UNEF soldiers were, in addition, competent to establish observation posts, patrol the demarcation lines, and actively prevent movement across the frontiers. To prevent duplication in their tasks, however, arrangements were made for the Egypt–Israel Mixed Armistice Commission to be placed under the operational control of UNEF's commander' (p.98).

Secretary-General of the experience derived from the establishment and operation of UNEF, GAOR, 13th sess., anns., a.i. 65.]

(d) Functions of UNTSO after June 1967

In June 1967 there occurred the astonishing six-day war between Israel and her Arab neighbours.[14] During the actual fighting UNTSO played an invaluable role in providing information, and it rapidly assumed, in the early stages of the cease-fire, an observer role in several crucial areas. UNTSO, having its headquarters at Government House in Jerusalem, was directly in the line of fighting. The war broke out on 5 June, and on that day the Secretary-General reported that communications with General Odd Bull had been cut off. Even in these circumstances, and at this early stage, UNTSO sought to organize cease-fires on the ground. As the Secretary-General puts it:

We understand, however, that heavy firing is taking place in and around the Government House compound in Jerusalem. A cease-fire in the area was called for at 1500 hours LT but was not respected, although both delegates to the Israel-Jordan Mixed Armistice Commission agreed to the arrangement. [*S/7930, 5 June 1967*, para. 2, *Supplemental Information received by the Secretary-General.*

The chairman of the Hashemite Kingdom of Jordan–Israel Mixed Armistice Commission had been informed by the Israel delegate that Jordan was shelling Tel Aviv and Lydda and by the Jordanian delegate that Israel was shelling Jenin. He was further informed by the Israel delegate that Israel would bomb Ramallah and Amman if Jordan did not stop shelling Tel Aviv and Lydda. The Chairman of the Mixed Armistice Commission approached both sides in an effort to stop Jordanian shelling and the threatened retaliation by Israel. [*S/7930/Add.1, 6 June 1967.*]

UNTSO could not, of course, contain a fully-fledged war of this sort: but it performed a dual function during the fighting—acting as a channel of communication between the belligerents, and a source of information for the UN. As soon as the fighting halted, UNTSO contributed to securing the cease-fire agreed upon especially on the Jordanian and Syrian fronts:

The following information from General Bull was received at United Nations Headquarters in the early afternoon of 10 June 1967:

'1. Afternoon 10 June I proposed to both parties following practical arrangements to make implementation of cease-fire demand effective:

'(a) cessation of all firing and troop movement at 1630 10 June;

'(b) Chairman ISMAC to re-establish control centre Kuneitra by 1715 10 June. Observers will be positioned on Syrian side with representatives of local command morning 11 June;

'(c) Officer-in-Charge, Tiberias Control Centre getting in touch with SID Tiberias in order to prepare positioning of observers on Israel side in liaison with representatives of local command morning 11 June.

'2. Both sides have now notified acceptance of proposed arrangements.

'3. I shall advise both parties that cease-fire should be complete and absolute.'

[*S/7930/Add.2, 10 June 1967.*]

General Bull deployed Damascus-based UN military observers on the

---

[14] See below, pp. 203-12.

morning of 11 June. Tiberias teams were delayed owing to lack of agreement with Israel on the proposal to re-establish the Kuneitra Control Centre.[15] However, the cease-fire went into effect, and U Thant sent the following message to General Odd Bull:

I convey to you my great appreciation of the initiative and skill you have demonstrated in your cease-fire arrangement in implementation of the Security Council's demand for a cease-fire between Israel and Syria. It is rare, indeed, that a cease-fire can be self-executing. You have provided the intermediary, co-ordination and observance which were essential to bring the cease-fire into reality. U Thant. [*S/7930/Add. 3, 11 June 1967.*]

On 12 June the Security Council passed a resolution relating exclusively to the cease-fire between Syria and Israel and in its final paragraph expressly invoked the assistance of UNTSO and its military observers 'in implementing the cease-fire, including freedom of movement and adequate communications facilities'.[16]

By 12 June General Bull had established nine observer teams on the Israel side of the Israel–Syria CFL, operated from Tiberias Control Centre.[17] The Israel Foreign Office now requested UNTSO to carry out a specific task relating to the cease-fire:

we request that observer teams should start immediately with mapping the positions of the forces on the ground so that the cease-fire can be effectively ensured along the entire front. The Government of Israel would like to see the cease-fire strictly complied with by the parties and shall extend co-operation to you in the work to that end. . . . [*S/7930/Add 4, 12 June 1967*, para. 7.]

General Bull made clear that the carrying out of this function depended to a large degree on co-operation with the parties:[18]

8. General Bull comments on Mr Tekoah's message that the mapping of the positions of the forces on the ground has been the first and highest priority task for observers and it is indeed their first objective. General Bull notes that apart from the many difficulties encountered in the field, achievement of this first objective will be impossible without adequate communications between him and his observers. He emphasized that adequate communications can only be ensured when General Bull is again in his Headquarters in Government House and can re-establish communication from that locality and not from any other locality in the Israel–Syria area.

9. General Bull further comments that the necessity of mapping positions of the forces was first referred to by him at his meeting with General Dayan on 10 June, and it was also implicit in the guidance given by him to the Chairman of the ISMAC. He will also endeavour to obtain similar assurances from the Syrian authorities so that the mapping of the positions of the forces can start as soon as possible. [*Ibid.*]

The mapping function was soon under way—even ahead of the return of Government House to UNTSO. A working document embodying the map references of Israel's foremost defended localities as occupied at 16.30 hrs GMT on 10 June 1967 was signed by the representative of the Chief of Staff of UNTSO and the representative of the Israel Defence Forces on 15 June 1967.[19]

[15] See below, pp. 128–9. [16] S/236, 12 June 1967; for full text see below, pp. 204–5.
[17] S/7930/Add. 4. [18] On Israel–UNTSO relations during this period, see pp.127–8.
[19] S/7930/Add. 17.

An agreement embodying the map references of the foremost defended localities on the Syrian side was signed by the representative of the Chief of Staff of UNTSO and the representatives of the Syrian Armed Forces on 26 June 1967.[20]

UNTSO also played a part in providing facilities for the exchange of prisoners of war:

6. General Bull also raised the question of the exchange of war prisoners which has been suggested by Mr Sasson.[21] General Bull stated that it was his intention with the full support of the Secretary-General to make his good offices available for the exchange of war prisoners. Mr Sasson informed General Bull that the Israel authorities had got in touch with the Red Cross also for this purpose. General Bull remarked that in the past UNTSO's good offices for the exchange of prisoners had been exercised in full co-operation with the Red Cross and that his good offices were available at all times if and when necessary. [*S/7930/Add. 5, 12 June 1967.*]

There were none the less physical limits to the task which UNTSO could undertake during the period following hostilities:

4. General Bull has advised United Nations Headquarters that the existing resources of UNTSO do not make it possible for him to investigate allegations about the treatment of civilian population in the area of the recent hostilities, in view of UNTSO's commitments in observing and securing the implementation of the cease-fire. He has, however, used his good offices wherever possible in such cases in drawing the attention of the authorities concerned to the allegations made, and will continue to do so. [*S/7930/Add. 14, 23 June 1967.*]

The value of UNTSO and its observers on the Syria–Israel cease-fire line was so manifest that the Secretary-General explored the possibility of extending its functions to the Suez Canal. He noted that Resolution 236 (1967) had expressly called for UNTSO's assistance in relation to the Israel–Syria cease-fire:

. . . However, the Security Council's general cease-fire resolutions of 6 and 7 June 1967, resolutions 233 (1967) and 234 (1967), which are applicable to the cease-fire between Israel and the United Arab Republic, request the Secretary-General to keep the Council informed about the situation, but make no provision for any assistance with regard to implementation of the cease-fire.

Realizing that I could not discharge my reporting responsibility under these latter two resolutions without any means of obtaining reliable information, and, more important, that a cease-fire without any observation or policing assistance in its implementation is inevitably vulnerable, I decided on 4 July to take an initiative towards a possible alleviation of this situation. On that date I undertook two exploratory talks. In an afternoon meeting with Dr Mahmoud Fawzi, Deputy Prime Minister of the United Arab Republic, I inquired of him what the reaction of his Government would likely be to a suggestion from me that United Nations Military Observers might be stationed in the sector of the Suez Canal where there is now confrontation between the armed forces of the United Arab Republic and those of Israel. Such Observers, of course, would have to be stationed on both sides, as has been done in the sector where the forces of Israel and Syria are in confrontation. This, I explained, would be especially necessary if the Secretary-General is to be enabled to fulfil his reporting responsibilities under the Security Council resolutions of 6 and 7 June 1967. Dr Fawzi advised me that he would bring this idea to the attention of his Government and obtain their reaction to it. Immediately following the meeting with Dr Fawzi I had a similar discussion with Foreign Minister Abba Eban of Israel and advanced the same suggestion to him. The Foreign Minister also assured me that he would seek his Government's reaction to this idea.

---

[20] Ibid, For details of this demarcation procedure, see below, pp. 206–8.   [21] See s. 9, pp. 128–32.

As of now, I have had no word about the reaction of either Government to this suggestion, which I consider to be constructive and helpful in the light of the prevailing circumstances and in the reporting context of the relevant Security Council resolutions.

If it should be agreed that United Nations Observers should proceed to Sinai and the Suez sector, this could be quickly done, according to information from the Chief of Staff, General Bull, within his present Observer strength, but it would be necessary to increase the number of Observers available to him at a very early date thereafter.

II. *Statement at the 1366th meeting on 9 July 1967*

Members of the Council will recall that in my statement to the Council at its meeting of yesterday, 8 July, I pointed out that if there should be agreement on the stationing of United Nations Observers to observe the cease-fire in the Suez sector, additional Observers would have to be made available to the Chief of Staff, General Bull.

I have since consulted General Bull and he has informed me that for the Suez sector his estimated need would be for an additional twenty-five Observers who should be made available to him as soon as possible. Pending the arrival of these additional Observers, the Chief of Staff, if called upon to do so, can dispatch a small team of Observers now on his staff to the Suez Canal area. They could institute patrols on both United Arab Republic and Israel sides of the front.

The Observers operating in this area, of course, would have to have logistical support to be provided by Field Service, including radio operators, transport and transport mechanics, supply, security and secretarial personnel. For immediate purposes, this could be provided from UNTSO's existing establishment.

United Nations Observers have been serving in the Near East since 1948, when there were well over 700 as against the 133 now serving in the area. Wherever United Nations Military Observers have been employed, it has been established practice to have the approval of the Governments directly concerned—in the present case, the Governments of Israel and the United Arab Republic—regarding the countries from which Military Observers for the particular operation may be drawn. That practice continues.

The financial implications of such an increase can be made available to the Council later. It can be said now, however, that they would not be excessive.   [*S/8046, Statements of the Secretary-General at the 1365th and 1366th mtgs of the Security Council*, 9 *July 1967*, mimeo.]

The Security Council discussed the matter, and the Soviet Union bitterly attacked the failure of the UN to compel Israel to withdraw. None the less, Russia agreed to the statement of consensus permitting UNTSO to extend its functions to the Suez Canal area:

Recalling Security Council resolutions 233, 234, 235 and 236 (1967), and emphasizing the need for all parties to observe scrupulously the provisions of these resolutions, having heard the statements made by the Secretary-General and the suggestions he has addressed to the parties concerned, I believe that I am reflecting the view of the Council that the Secretary-General should proceed, as he has suggested in his statements before the Council on 8 and 9 July 1967, to request the Chief of Staff of the United Nations Truce Supervision Organization in Palestine, General Odd Bull, to work out with the Governments of the United Arab Republic and Israel, as speedily as possible, the necessary arrangements to station United Nations Military Observers in the Suez Canal sector under the Chief of Staff of UNTSO. [*S/8047, Consensus expressed by the President and approved by the Security Council at the 1366th mtg on 9–10 July 1967*, mimeo.]

On 11 July the Secretary-General was able to report:

2. Both the Government of the United Arab Republic and the Government of Israel have now informed the Secretary-General of their acceptance of the proposed stationing of United

Nations Military Observers in the Suez Canal sector (see letters attached in annexes I and II). The Secretary-General has, therefore, requested the Chief of Staff of UNTSO, General Odd Bull, to work out with the local authorities on both sides a plan for the actual stationing of Military Observers and to send as many Military Observers as possible from his present establishment without delay to the Suez Canal sector.

3. The Secretary-General is also, after consultation with the parties, undertaking the recruitment of the needed twenty-five additional Military Observers, as reported to the Council in his statement of 9 July 1967.

Annex I

Letter dated 10 July 1967 from the Permanent Representative of the United Arab Republic addressed to the Secretary-General

I have the honour to confirm the consent of my Government as to your proposal made in the Security Council regarding the placing on both sides, as a temporary measure, of United Nations Observers in the Canal sector.

I take it that Major General Odd Bull, UNTSO Chief of Staff, in implementing the consensus agreed upon by the Security Council at the end of its meeting held on 9 June 1967, will contact the United Arab Republic authorities regarding the modalities of recruiting, placing and deployment of the Observers. . . .

(*Signed*) Mohamed Awad EL KONY

Annex II

Letter dated 11 July 1967 from the Permanent Representative of Israel addressed to the Secretary-General

I have the honour to convey to you the reply of the Government of Israel on the proposal to station United Nations observers, under the Chief of Staff, General Odd Bull, in the Suez Canal sector.

The Government of Israel again reaffirms its policy of strict observance of the cease-fire and shares the desire of the Security Council that the cease-fire instituted by the Security Council should be effective.

The Government of Israel accepts to discuss with General Bull arrangements to station United Nations observers in observation posts in the Suez Canal sector to observe the cease-fire agreement, it being understood that such observation posts will, on the basis of reciprocity, be set up on both sides of the line.

(*Signed*) Gideon RAFAEL

[*S/8053 and anns, Report of the Secretary-General on the stationing of UN military observers in the Suez Canal sector, 11 July 1967*, mimeo.]

Thus, in 1967, UNTSO extended its operations to (1) providing information on the hostilities waged in the week of 5 June, (2) providing good offices to seek to contain those hostilities, (3) mapping the agreed cease-fire positions on the Syria–Israel front, (4) carrying out specific observer-and communications functions in respect of the Syria–Israel cease-fire, (5) facilitating the exchange of prisoners of war, (6) channelling complaints about the treatment of civilians, (7) providing observers to supervise the cease-fire in the Suez Canal sector.[22] The withdrawal of UNEF had occasioned a great deal of publicity, and much criticism of the UN; the quiet and competent way in which UNTSO adapted itself to the needs of June 1967 deserves recognition and is worthy of much credit.

[22] For the particular problems faced by the military observers in respect of this function see s.12, pp. 208–11 below.

3*

4

CONSTITUTIONAL BASIS

ON 1 April 1948 the Security Council had called for a truce (S/704) and on 23 April had established a Truce Commission.[1] It will be recalled that the Commission itself requested the United Nations to send out the personnel necessary for supervising the truce. On 22 May 1948 the Security Council called for a cease-fire (S/773), and although no article of the Charter is specifically mentioned, it would appear to be based on Article 40. On 29 May the Council instructed the Mediator, in concert with the Truce Commission, to supervise the provisions; and decided that they should be provided with a sufficient number of military advisers (S/801). Thus UNTSO was initially created by the Mediator (acting within the tacit framework of Article 40) and the Truce Commission.[2]

After the death of Count Bernadotte, and upon the conclusion of the first Armistice Agreement in February 1949, the Acting Mediator was relieved of further functions; but UNTSO was specifically retained.[3] At this juncture, therefore, UNTSO, whilst originally developed by the Mediator, acting in consultation with the Secretary-General,[4] became a subsidiary organ of the Security Council engaged in functions covered by Article 40 of the Charter. This constitutional basis had its own practical significance in terms of the legal privileges and immunities that flowed from it.[5]

The constitutional basis of UNTSO after 1949 is somewhat ambiguous, because the nature of its functions changed and became two-fold. On the one hand—despite its name—it was no longer supervising a 'truce', though a core of its personnel was to be retained to assist in maintaining the cease-fire. On the other hand, the Chief of Staff and his observers were given specific tasks under the Armistice Agreements. Dr Bunche was at pains to point out to the Security Council that UNTSO's role under these Agreements was

United Nations assistance which the parties themselves request in the Armistice Agreements, and which the United Nations should of course grant. It must, however, be emphasized that the parties themselves have devised their own agreements for joint supervision of the terms of the voluntary agreements, and the United Nations therefore, has no general responsibility for the supervision of the Armistice Agreements. [Per Bunche, SCOR, 4th yr, pt 2, 433rd mtg, p. 7.]

Later he elaborated that

there are actually two functions envisaged . . . maintaining the cease-fire . . . [and also] the provision of such staff 'as may be necessary in assisting the Parties to the Armistice Agreements in the supervision of the application and observance of the terms of those Agreements'. That was to be done by the Secretary-General, and he would obviously do that in consultation

---

[1] S/727, and above, pp. 16–17.
[2] Res. S/902 of 13 July 1948 specifically based itself on Arts 39 and 40.
[3] S/1376; see above, p. pp. 24–25.   [4] See Bowett, p. 63.   [5] See below, p. 82.

with the Chief of Staff who would be the Chairman of the Mixed Armistice Commission and under whose command the United Nations observers would serve, even when they were assisting the Parties in the implementation of the Armistice Agreements; for throughout these negotiations, it was kept in mind that the United Nations would not wish to provide observers to the Parties to the Armistice Agreements who would be exclusively under the command of the Parties; that, in some way, these observers must be kept under the command of the United Nations and made available to the Parties. The formula that was worked out to achieve this purpose in the Armistice Agreements was that observers would be made available to the Parties, under the direction of the Chief of Staff of the Truce Supervision Organization. [*Ibid. 434th mtg*, p. 39.]

The constitutional basis for this second function would therefore seem to be somewhat different from the joint cease-fire function. The maintenance of the cease-fire presumably still falls under Article 40, for the resolution which the Council adopted (S/1376) specifically reaffirms 'the order . . . pursuant to Article 40 . . . to observe an unconditional cease-fire'.

This dual aspect subsequently required further clarification: and it also became necessary to assert that observers sent by the Chief of Staff (or his representative) in the capacity of Chairman of a MAC should have the same rights as observers sent by the Chief of Staff to maintain the cease-fire ordered by the Security Council:

With regard to the observance and maintenance of the cease-fire, the powers of the Chief of Staff of the Truce Supervision Organization are derived directly from the Security Council resolution, and United Nations observers acting under my instructions may take measures to observe and maintain the cease-fire. Should an incident involving a breach of the cease-fire occur, observers will be sent immediately to the spot, the authorities of the respective parties will be contacted, and every effort made to bring an end to the incident.

I should like to add that United Nations observers sent by the Chief of Staff of the Truce Supervision Organization to observe and maintain the cease-fire ordered by the Security Council should, in my opinion be granted the same co-operation and the same freedom of movement as observers sent by the Chairman of a mixed armistice commission to investigate a complaint according to the provisions of a general armistice agreement. [*S/3252, 25 June 1954, Report of Chief of Staff to the Secretary-General*, p. 16.]

An interesting exchange occurred at this same time over the relationship of the Chief of Staff to the Security Council. The Soviet Union wished—in spite of Dr Bunche's explanation of the vital role which the Chief of Staff and his observers had been given in the Agreements, and in spite of the approval of the parties thereto—to disband UNTSO totally. The underlying motive was revealed in a speech by the Ukrainian representative, who said:

. . . Why then should all possible conflicts be referred to one State—the United States—as represented by the United Nations Chief of Staff? . . . The Security Council has achieved some results. Why now abandon this position and change to a totally new course by handing over all these questions to a single State?[6]

The Israel representative, seeking to meet these fears, said: 'He [the UNTSO Chief of Staff] appears to us as a representative not of any particular country but of the Security Council itself, and presumably the Security Council is qualified to appoint anyone it sees fit to assume those functions.'[7]

The main gist of this was no doubt correct, and the point was well made that

---

[6] *SCOR*, 435th mtg, pp. 9–10. [7] Ibid. p. 12.

although the present Chief of Staff happened to be American, he could in the future be of *any* nationality. However, the correctness of the assumption that the appointment lay in the hands of the Security Council was much more questionable. No Chief of Staff, before or since, has ever been appointed by the Security Council. His appointment has been at the discretion of the Secretary-General—indeed, the Security Council has usually not even been specifically notified of changes of appointments. Further, as the representative of the United States pointed out:

Neither the Mediator nor the Truce Supervision Organization was named by this Council. We have to bear that constantly in mind. The post of Mediator was created by the General Assembly. He built the Truce Supervision Organization from the staff of the Palestine Truce Commission and from staff assembled by the Secretary-General in accordance with the request of the Council. [*SCOR, 436th mtg.* p. 7.]

A word may be said about the constitutional basis of the functions given to UNTSO in the Suez Canal sector after the six-day war of June 1967.[8] Where did authority lie for placing UNTSO personnel along either side of the Canal? Whether or not Israeli consent was legally required for the stationing of UN observers on the eastern side of the Canal, it was obviously essential politically that it be obtained. Both Egypt and Israel gave their consent. One may note, however, that Israel had denounced the Egypt–Israel armistice in 1956, and in logic this must have been from her perspective a UN operation *de novo*. The United Kingdom and United States regarded the stationing of personnel along the Canal as a mere extension of UNTSO's present functions, and within the discretion of the Secretary-General if he had the agreement of the directly interested parties. The Soviet Union was opposed, not to the idea of stationing such observers in the Canal zone, but rather to the notion that this lay within the competence of the Secretary-General. A vote on the issue was avoided by the unusual means of having the President of the Security Council issue a 'statement of consensus' which no member of the Council opposed:

. . . I believe that I am reflecting the view of the Council that the Secretary-General should proceed, as he has suggested in his statements before the Council on 8 and 9 July 1967, to request the Chief of Staff of the United Nations Truce Supervision Organization in Palestine, General Odd Bull, to work out with the Governments of the United Arab Republic and Israel, as speedily as possible, the necessary arrangements to station United Nations Military Observers in the Suez Canal sector under the Chief of Staff of UNTSO. [*S/8047, 10 July 1967*, mimeo.]

After the sinking by Egypt of the Israeli ship *Eilat* on 21 October 1967, and the Israeli retaliatory shelling of the refineries of Port Suez, the Secretary-General wished to enlarge the observer group in the Canal sector. Here again there was disagreement between the Soviet Union on the one hand, and Britain and America on the other, as to whether this fell within the Secretary-General's authority. The Secretary-General stated to the Council on 25 October 1967[9] that the enlargement of the group was necessary if the Security Council's consensus of 9–10 July were to be given proper effect. The Soviet Union introduced a draft resolution seeking to make this request subject to the specific

[8] See s. 3, pp. 57–59. above.   [9] S/PV. 1371, pp. 6–11.

authorization of the Security Council; but this was resisted by those nations which argued that the original resolutions establishing UNTSO had charged the Secretary-General with ensuring the availability of adequate personnel. In resolving this dilemma, this time even a meeting of the Council was avoided. Instead, the President—Chief Adebo of Nigeria—talked to all the members on the terms of a possible consensus, which he then circulated. The Secretary-General acted on the authority of this, without any meeting of the Security Council being called:

STATEMENT BY THE PRESIDENT OF THE SECURITY COUNCIL

The following statement is circulated in connexion with the report by the Secretary-General on the observation of the cease-fire line in the Suez Canal sector (S/8053/Add 3). After consultations I have had with the representatives, I understand there is no objection to my transmittal of this statement as reflecting the views of the members of the Council:

As regards document S/8053/Add. 3, brought to the attention of the Security Council, the members, recalling the consensus reached at its 1366th meeting of 9 July 1967, recognize the necessity of the enlargement by the Secretary-General of the number of observers in the Suez Canal zone and the provision of additional technical material and means of transportation. [*S/8289, 8 Dec. 1967,* mimeo.]

5

POLITICAL CONTROL

THE Chief of Staff of UNTSO is directly responsible to the Secretary-General, who in turn is responsible to the Security Council. The Security Council's authority lies both in the fact that its Resolutions S/773, S/801, and S/902 confirmed the order for a cease-fire, and in that the Armistice Agreements proclaim, in their preambles, that they are in response to the Security Council's call under Article 40. It is to the Secretary-General, however, that the Chief of Staff reports (though his reports are circulated as Security Council documents), and his appointment and dismissal are in the hands of the Secretary-General. Although the Chief of Staff's powers concerning the observance of the 1948 cease-fire stem from the Security Council Resolutions S/773 and S/801, his powers concerning the armistices stem from the Armistice Agreements themselves. Further, in respect of these he owed a direct responsibility to the parties.

Accordingly, it was not felt appropriate that the Chief of Staff should report directly to, or be directly questioned by, the Security Council—though this did happen on one occasion.[1] The experiment was not regarded as successful—at least by the Secretary-General's office—and it was not repeated.

While a wide range of discretion is granted to the Chief of Staff in day-to-day matters, it is the Secretary-General's office which has always formulated the

[1] See below, pp. 68–69.

overall policy guidelines. The Secretary-General himself will, when a special report is requested by the Security Council, base himself closely on the observations of the Chief of Staff;[2] and in 1956 he visited the various countries concerned, at the request of the Security Council, for the purpose of making recommendations to that organ.[3] The Chief of Staff takes the oath of international allegiance required of a Secretariat member.[4]

6

ADMINISTRATIVE AND MILITARY CONTROL

(a) Under Resolutions S/727 of 23 April 1948 and S/773 of 22 May 1948, calling for a truce

THE Truce Commission was required both to supervise and to examine alleged breaches of the truce. To these ends Count Bernadotte, the UN Mediator, devised a scheme

covering both the supervision of the observation of that truce and the establishment of procedure for examining alleged breaches of the truce.

A. Supervision
(i) *Chief of Military Staff, Central Truce Supervision Board*
The system of observation will be administered on behalf of the Mediator by the Mediator's Chief of Military Staff assisted by an Advisory Board to be known as the 'Central Truce Supervision Board'. Particularly it will be the duty of the Chief of Military Staff to:
(a) organize a detailed plan for land, sea and air observation with the greatest possible dispatch;
(b) assign the observers to their posts and direct their activities;
(c) on the basis of field observations to define on a map the positions of the respective armed forces in the several fighting sectors at the beginning of the truce. Alterations of such position should be only in connection with local agreements negotiated concerning no-man's land. Questions of principle relating to the interpretation of the terms of the truce shall be referred to the Mediator for decision.
(ii) *Composition and Functions of the Central Truce Supervision Board*
The Central Truce Supervision Board shall function under the chairmanship of the Chief of Military Staff and shall consist of one American, one Belgian, and one French Senior Officer to be designated by the Mediator and the political advisor to the Chief of Military Staff. The Chief of Military Staff may designate a member of the Board to act as vice-chairman. The Central Truce Supervision Board shall advise the Chief of Military Staff on all questions relating to the administration of the truce.
(iii) *Regional Truce Supervision Boards*
... the areas affected by the truce will be divided into zones in each of which there will be a 'Regional Truce Supervision Board', the members of which will be designated by the Central Truce Supervision Board. Each regional board will be responsible to the Central Supervision Board for the system of observation to be established in that region.[1]

---

[2] See e.g. S/7553.   [3] See below, pp. 178–84.   [4] See Burns, p. 9.
[1] The plan for Regional Truce Supervision Boards was abortive; see above, p. 22.

B. Establishment of procedures for examining alleged breaches of the truce

(i) Requests by Governments for investigation of alleged breaches of the truce which have not been settled by observers on the spot shall be submitted to the Central Truce Supervision Board, which shall refer them for investigation and report to the appropriate Regional Truce Supervision Board, or to an observer or a special investigation team designated for this specific purpose.

(ii) As circumstances permit, each of the parties may appoint military experts to act as liaison officers with observers in the field, with Regional Truce Supervision Boards, or with the Special Investigation teams.

(iii) Investigations of alleged breaches shall be undertaken on the spot . . . The special investigation teams and the Regional Truce Supervision Boards should normally indicate the measures which ought to be taken to preserve the respective rights of either party. The findings of such bodies shall be submitted to the Central Truce Supervision Board . . . [*S/928, Instructions given by UN Mediator to UN observers engaged in supervision of the truce in Palestine, 28 July 1948.*]

The instructions also indicate that the observers were to be provided with *per diem* advances of $15 per day, to meet meals, laundry, lodging, and incidental expenses. Additional expenditures could be authorized by the administrative officer, but prior request should be sought save in case of clear emergency. 'When emergencies require such action without prior approval, the Chief Administrative Officer must be notified at once.'[2]

Under the first truce this had meant:

. . . In addition to investigating alleged breaches of the truce, they were charged with the task of carrying on routine observation and with dealing with incidents and complaints on the spot. They had no power to prevent a violation of the truce or to enforce their decisions. In the case of any complaint or incident where they could not achieve a settlement between the parties on the spot, their only recourse was to report the matter to their superiors or to me. Complaints by local officers or troops were dealt with by the observers on the spot, those by military commanders were dealt with by the Chief of Staff or an area commander, and those by Governments were dealt with by myself. In cases requiring investigation, the inquiries were carried out by observers on the spot wherever possible. [*A/648, Progress Report of Mediator to General Assembly, GAOR, 3rd sess., suppl. 11, p. 33.*]

Under the second truce

8. All complaints are submitted to investigation by observers in the field and, where necessary, by a special investigation team. In cases where they cannot be settled by observers on the spot, they are referred, together with the observer's report, to Haifa Headquarters for disposal. The less serious cases are referred to the Chief of Staff, and the more serious ones to the Central Truce Supervision Board. Decisions by both the Chief of Staff and the Central Truce Supervision Board are transmitted to me for review and are then dispatched to the Governments concerned. Major violations, if not immediately rectified by the parties, are reported to the Security Council. [*Ibid.* p. 38.]

(*b*) Under the Armistice Agreements

The line of administrative command was dependent upon the arrangements specified in the Armistice Agreements. The authority of the Chief of Staff, and his relationship both with the MAC and the UN observers, are laid down in the Armistice Agreements: Israel–Jordan, Article XI; Israel–Syria, Article VII; Israel–Egypt, Article X; and Israel–Lebanon, Article VII.[3]

[2] S/928, Instructions given by Mediator, p. 3.   [3] For texts, see above, pp. 36, 41, 47, 51.

In each case the Chief of Staff, or a senior officer of UNTSO chosen by him after consultation with the parties, was to be Chairman. The choice of an officer for this function lies completely with the Chief of Staff so long as he consults with the parties. Neither in theory nor in practice has he needed to inform, or secure the permission of, the Secretary-General. Observers were to be used by the MACs, and they could be drawn from the military organizations of the parties or from the military personnel of UNTSO or both. When UNTSO observers are employed, they are attached to the MAC, but remain under the command of the Chief of Staff rather than that of the MAC. UNTSO observers are employed by a MAC according to its rules and its practice, which vary in the different commissions.[4] Further, assignments of either a general or special nature given to UNTSO observers attached to a MAC are subject to approval by the Chairman of the MAC, i.e. by the Chief of Staff himself or by his representative. Thus a distinction is made between the Chief of Staff, on the one hand, and the personnel of UNTSO under his command on the other.

So far as the observance and maintenance of the cease-fire are concerned, the authority of the Chief of Staff is derived directly from Security Council Resolution S/1376, and UN observers act under his sole instructions.[5]

7

COMPOSITION AND SIZE

THE Truce Commission—from which the Mediator was subsequently to forge a Truce Supervision Organization, including observer personnel—was composed in principle of 'representatives of those members of the Security Council which have career consular offices in Jerusalem . . .'[1] In practice this meant Belgium, France, the United States, and Syria. Syria, however, decided not to participate.[2] The reason was tactfully given by the French representative:

If we establish a body to assist in the implementation of the truce, that body must, like Caesar's wife, be above suspicion. And although we may be absolutely certain that a commission consisting of four consuls, including the Syrian consul, would be perfectly impartial, it is preferable that no-one should be able to entertain any doubt regarding the impartiality of the commission. . . .' [SCOR, 3rd yr, pt 2, 387th mtg, p. 17.]

The military observers were drawn from the nations represented on the Truce Commission, and numbered some 500 at the height of the truce supervision operation. The mounting of the observer organization had to be done from scratch, and with the greatest speed as the truce had already entered into effect:

---

[4] SCOR, 8th yr, 635 mtg, ann., p. 24.
[5] For the complete listing of UNTSO Chiefs of Staff, and their nationalities, see below, p.70.
[1] Res. S/727, 23 Apr. 1948.   [2] See above, p. 17.

I requested the services of five colonels of the Swedish Army to act as my personal representatives to assist in supervising the truce, and I appointed one of these, Colonel Thord Bonde, as my Chief of Staff for the truce supervision. I also requested the member States of the Truce Commission—Belgium, France and the United States of America—each to furnish 21 officers from their armed forces to act as military observers. These 63 observers arrived in Cairo between 11 and 14 June and were immediately despatched to Palestine and some of the Arab States. I also obtained from the Secretary-General of the United Nations on 21 June the services of 51 guards recruited from the Secretariat to assist the military observers, and subsequently requested Belgium, France and the United States of America each to send 10 more officers to act as observers. These 30 additional officers arrived during the period 27 June to 5 July. I also obtained from the United States armed forces some 10 auxiliary technical personnel such as aircraft pilots and maintenance men, radio operators, motor-vehicle drivers and maintenance men, and medical personnel. . . .

. . . I obtained some used vehicles, planes and radio equipment from the Governments of the United States of America and the United Kingdom, a naval corvette from France and three destroyers from the United States. This equipment was obtained between 12 and 14 June. It was not sufficient for the immense task involved, and some of the equipment, particularly the motor-vehicles and radio sets, soon became unserviceable due to the lack of repairs and spare parts. [*A/648, Progress Report of UN Mediator to General Assembly, GAOR, 3rd sess. suppl. 11*, pp. 32–33.]

When the first truce ended, fighting recommenced[3] on a very large scale. As the second truce was to be of indefinite duration, it was felt that a more elaborate system of truce supervision was necessary. Once again, however, the observation group had to be built up from scratch.[4]

4. Before leaving Lake Success on 16 July to return to Rhodes, I had approached the member States of the Truce Commission and they had agreed to furnish 300 officer observers, apportioned as follows: Belgium, 50; France, 125; and the United States of America, 125. By 1 August 1948, 137 of these observers had arrived (47 Belgian, 50 French and 40 United States) and had been despatched to Palestine. I appointed as my Chief of Military Staff and personal representative, Major-General Lundstrom of the Swedish Air Force. He and nine Swedish officer observers attached to my personal staff, arrived on 29 July. By the middle of August practically all of the 300 officer observers had arrived, and it became evident that even this number would not be sufficient to discharge fully the task of observation. I accordingly requested the services of 300 enlisted men (50 Belgian, 125 French and 125 United States) to act as observers and to assist the officer observers in their work. Of this additional 300 observers, 84 United States enlisted men had arrived at the time of writing this report. I also obtained 4 French and 78 United States enlisted men to serve the observers as auxiliary technical personnel. These included aircrewmen, clerks, communications and motor transport personnel and medical assistants.

5. In order to carry out its tasks the observation organization required facilities for communications, reconnaissance and transportation, for which radio equipment, planes, ships and motor vehicles were needed. The work of supervision during the first truce had been severely hampered by the shortage of such equipment. During the second truce, although equipment was difficult to obtain and was slow in arriving, the facilities were greatly improved. At the present time sufficient planes and ships are available, but there is still an urgent need for more motor vehicles, particularly spare parts for repairs, and some special radio equipment. The following equipment has been made available:

Radio equipment. A considerable amount of radio equipment has been supplied by the United Nations and the United States of America, and some by the United Kingdom. . . .

Aircraft. The United Nations has contracted for 14 small planes, and the United States of America has furnished 4 C-47 Dakotas.

[3] See above, p. 20.   [4] Progress Report of UN Mediator to General Assembly, A/648, p. 37.

Ships. France furnished one naval corvette and the United States of America 3 destroyers.

Motor vehicles. The United Kingdom supplied 50 jeeps, 20 jeep trailers and 2 automobiles, and the United States of America 12 jeeps and 5 trucks.

In addition certain aircraft and vehicle spare parts, and field rations and medical supplies were received from the United Kingdom and the United States of America. The Secretary-General of the United Nations continued to make available to me a chartered aircraft for covering the truce area and trips to the capitals of the various Governments.

6. Haifa was again chosen as the headquarters of the observation organization. The Chief of Military Staff was assisted by a Central Truce Supervision Board of which he was the Chairman and the senior American, Belgian and French officer observers were members. . . . The observers were divided into a number of groups, of which one was assigned to each Arab army and to each Israeli army group. One group was assigned to Jerusalem, one to cover the coast and ports of the truce area, and one to control convoys between Tel-Aviv and Jerusalem. At the end of August another group was created to cover airports in the truce area. . . .

7. By 1 August, observers were stationed as follows:
Israel: Haifa, 49; Tel-Aviv, 26; Tiberias, 8.
Jerusalem: 10.
Arab areas of Palestine: Gaza, 7; Nablus, 8; Ramallah, 1.
Lebanon: Beirut, 8.
Syria: Damascus, 7.
Transjordan: Amman, 7.

The Provisional Government of Israel had complained that, during both the first and second truces, the truce supervision work was confined almost exclusively to Palestine, and that it was inadequate in the Arab States. There was some force in this complaint, and I endeavoured, while recognizing that the primary task must be discharged in Palestine to extend the scope of the observation organization to cover the entire truce area. On 8 September, the distribution and location of observers was as follows:

Israel: Haifa, 76; Aqir, 2; Natanya, 4; Rama David, 4; Tel Aviv, 28; Tiberias, 13.
Jerusalem: 79.
Arab areas of Palestine: Hebron, 4; Gaza, 14; Nablus, 15; Ramallah, 7.
Egypt: Alexandria, 5; Cairo, 5; El Arish, 3; Port-Said, 1.
Iraq: Baghdad, 3; Basra, 3.
Lebanon: Beirut, 17.
Syria: Damascus, 14.
Transjordan: Aqaba, 2; Amman, 16. [*Ibid*. pp. 37–38.]

Under the Armistice Agreements, which were signed in 1949, the Truce Supervision Organization acquired new functions, and its size and composition were altered accordingly. Speaking at the Security Council meeting which considered the Agreements, Acting Mediator Bunche indicated that in the light of this changed role he envisaged a reduction of UNTSO personnel to 70. In fact, though the numbers for a time dropped lower still, they have now settled at around 130. No trace of regularly presented figures is to be found in the official records. However, in October of 1953, after incidents at Libya, the Acting Chief of Staff of UNTSO, General Bennike, was invited to attend meetings of the Security Council, and gave replies to questions put to him by Security Council members and by the interested parties. He answered the following question from the representative of the United Kingdom:

7. Would General Bennike explain exactly how the observer corps at his disposal works? Does he believe that there are enough observers? Have they adequate transport and com-

munication? Are they based in Jerusalem or do they cover the whole frontier? Could the Chief of Staff say whether in his view the observer corps could be strengthened and, if so, how?

Answer. At the present time, I have nineteen military observers at my disposal. Four of them are serving as Chairmen of the Mixed Armistice Commissions. One observer works as my military assistant; another is in charge of the Mount Scopus demilitarized area. The others are assigned, according to the work load, to the armistice commissions. At the present time, two observers are assigned to the Israel–Lebanon Commission, four to the Egyptian–Israel Commission, six to the Israel–Syrian Commission, and five to the Hashemite Jordan Kingdom–Israel Commission. These figures include the chairmen.

We will take, for example, the workings of the Jordan–Israel Mixed Armistice Commission. The five observers assigned to it are based in Jerusalem, which is the headquarters of the Commission. They have a border approximately 620 kilometres in length to cover. Each observer attends from two to three local commanders' meetings per week, in addition to the investigation of complaints assigned him by the Chairman.

It is not, moreover, uncommon for military observers to be called into quick action to obtain a cease-fire. In this, they have been very effective on several occasions.

With 620 kilometres of demarcation lines between Israel and Jordan to cover, and the fact that 345 complaints have been handed in so far this year, many of which have been investigated, it is easy to see that the observers' task is not an easy one.

About one month after I assumed my duties as Chief of Staff of the Truce Supervision Organization, I was invited by the Secretary-General to come to Headquarters in order to review the functioning of the Truce Supervision Organization, and in particular, to consider such recommendations as one month's experience in the field might have enabled me to make with a view to strengthening the effectiveness of the Truce Supervision Organization. During that visit to Headquarters, which lasted from 9 to 28 August, I had very full consultations with the Secretary-General and with the members of the Missions Co-ordination Committee, consisting of senior officials of the Secretariat who have various responsibilities in connection with the work of United Nations missions in the field. These consultations were very fruitful and resulted in the acceptance of my recommendation that the number of observers be increased by seven and that additional observers be drawn from Sweden, Denmark and New Zealand. The Secretary-General has requested the Governments of New Zealand and Sweden to second two officers each and the Government of Denmark to second three officers for this assignment. My intention is to station four officers on the Israeli side of the Jordan–Israel demarcation line, and three officers on the Jordan side of the line. I believe that with this increase I shall have enough observers at my disposal, unless, of course, the situation should deteriorate, in which case I may request the Secretary-General to provide more observers.

I also requested the Secretary-General to increase my civilian secretariat staff by the addition of a political affairs officer and a legal adviser; this has already been done. I have examined in detail the question of transport and communications, and I believe that I shall have sufficient equipment to meet the needs of the work. [*SCOR, 8th yr, 635th mtg, annex,* pp. 19–20.]

Further, when replying to a Jordanian question, he said:

No reinforcement of the Truce Supervision Organization can in itself ensure respect of the Armistice Agreements. Such respect must come from the parties themselves. However, it is my opinion that the present tense situation might be improved, particularly with regard to the observance of the cease-fire, if the observer group were strengthened to enable the Truce Supervision Organization to maintain observers at critical points along the armistice demarcation lines. [*Ibid.* p. 42.]

The first Chief of Staff, Colonel Bonde had, of course, been appointed personally by the Mediator, Count Bernadotte. When Dr Bunche became Acting

Mediator, he selected Lt.-General Riley. All subsequent appointments have been made by the Secretary-General.

Major-General Burns served with great distinction, and left UNTSO when appointed as Commander of UNEF. Major-General von Horn left to command the UN Observation Mission in the Yemen. Lt.-General Riley's departure came after five full years of energetic service; and Colonel Leary's appointment was only intended to be temporary. The Acting Mediator is believed to have felt that General Lundstrom's protection of UNTSO's independence after Bernadotte's murder was insufficient; and it is commonly thought that Major-General Bennike gave the impression of pro-Arab sympathies.

There have been several changes in the appointment of Chief of Staff of UNTSO. These are not published in any systematic way in official documents, but may be learned by noting the varying signatures at the end of the Commander-in-Chief's periodic reports to the Security Council and Secretary-General. It may be noted that the Security Council was at no time formally required to give its approval to any such appointment.

Name	Designation	Nationality	Dates	Document (if any) from which appointment may be deduced
Col. Bonde	Chief of Staff	Sweden	1948 (during the 2 truces)	
Maj.-Gen. Lundstrom	Chief of Staff	Sweden	July–Sept. 1948	
Maj.-Gen. Riley	Chief of Staff	USA	Sept. 1948–July 1953	S/1152 25 Dec. 1948 S/2194 13 June 1951
Col. de Ridder	Acting Chief of Staff during Riley's absence	Belgium	Apr.–June 1951	S/2067 4 Apr. 1951
Maj.-Gen. Bennike	Chief of Staff	Denmark	July 1953–Sept. 1954	S/3122 23 Oct. 1953
Maj.-Gen. Burns	Chief of Staff	Canada	Sept. 1954–Oct. 1956	S/3319 16 Nov. 1954
Col. Byron Leary	Acting Chief of Staff (NB. however, Gen. Burns retained his duties as Chief of Staff in relation to the Demarcation lines between Israel & Egypt (*YBUN 1957*, p. 515.)	USA	Nov. 1956–Mar. 1958	
Maj.-Gen. von Horn	Chief of Staff	Sweden	Mar. 1958–June 1963	S/4036 17 June 1958
Lt.-Gen. Odd Bull		Norway	1963–	S/5401 24 Aug. 1963

The strength and representation of UNTSO as at 6 July 1966 was as follows:

Observers

Australia	4	Italy	9	
Belgium	7	Netherlands	15	
Canada	20	New Zealand	5	
Denmark	12	Norway	12 + General Odd Bull	
France	5	Sweden	20	
Iceland	10	USA	14	

133

In 1965 there had been 140 observers,[5] and a total staff of 401 persons.

In May 1967 the number of observers stood at 132. After the war of June 1967 the list of UNTSO contributors was enlarged to include Argentina, Austria, Burma, Chile, and Finland. This was largely to meet the needs of the new, additional task of observation along the Suez Canal. This began on 17 July 1967 with 9 observers—5 on the UAR side and 4 on the Israel side. On 10 August the Secretary-General indicated that the Chief of Staff had requested some 50 observers in the Suez Canal sector.[6] After the hostilities which flared again in October 1967 with the sinking of the Israeli ship *Eilat*, and the retaliation against Port Suez, the number was increased to 90.[7] Certain other information on UNTSO's composition is available from secondary, though not primary, sources.[8]

---

[5] A/6005, p. 148.   [6] S/8053/Add. 1, para. 8.   [7] S/8182/Add. 1, 1 Dec. 1967.

[8] Prof. N. Bar-Yaacov, in his excellent and impartial study, *The Israel–Syrian Armistice* (1967), p. 308 n. 36, provides the following information:

'UNTSO headquarters, located in the former Mandatory Government House in Jerusalem, comprise two main offices: the Office of the Chief of Staff, and the Office of the Chief Administrative Officer.

The following personnel, amongst others, are assigned to the Office of the Chief of Staff: Assistant Chief of Staff, Chief Operation Officer, Military Personnel Officer, Special Adviser to the Chief of Staff, Chief Administrative Officer, Senior Legal Adviser, Information Officer and Reports Officer.

The Office of the Chief Administrative Officer includes Communications, Security and Transport Sections.

At 15 April 1964 the distribution of UNTSO military personnel in the Mixed Armistice Commission was as follows:

ISRAEL–SYRIAN MIXED ARMISTICE COMMISSION: On the Syrian side—Chairman, Deputy Chairman, Senior Operation Officer, Assistant Operation Officer, Operation Officer and twenty-eight military observers; on the Israel side—OIC Tiberias, Operation Officer, Assistant Operation Officer and twenty military observers.

ISRAEL–JORDANIAN MIXED ARMISTICE COMMISSION: Chairman, Chief of Staff representative for Mount Scopus, Operation Officer, Assistant Operation Officer and thirty-two military observers.

ISRAEL–LEBANESE MIXED ARMISTICE COMMISSION: Chairman, Operation Officer, OIC Naqura and three military observers.

ISRAEL–EGYPTIAN MIXED ARMISTICE COMMISSION: Chairman, Operation Officer and five military observers.'

Prof. Bar-Yaacov states that he obtained this information from UNTSO Headquarters.

8

RELATIONS WITH CONTRIBUTING STATES

To TALK of 'contributing states' in the context of UNTSO is misleading in so far as all the observers were hired as *individuals*, albeit by secondment from their own armed services.

No problems arose in terms of the relations between the states concerned and the UN.

No formal agreements were ever entered into between the UN and these governments partly because it was felt inappropriate in the case of individual secondments, and partly because, in terms of the UN's own history, it was simply too early.

So far as claims for reparation for injury or death to UN personnel were concerned, the Secretary-General was advised by the International Court that the UN had legal capacity to present a claim against a sovereign government, and that the 'host' government owed it certain duties.[1] The UN thus claimed compensation from Israel for the death of Count Bernadotte and Colonel Sérot, who were assassinated by Jewish terrorists.[2] It also presented claims to Jordan and Egypt in respect of other UNTSO personnel.[3] The practice became established —in this and other UN peacekeeping operations—of claims for reparation being entered by the UN, both for its own loss and on behalf of the family of the injured or deceased. The UN would first clear with the government of the observer killed or injured that it did not intend to pursue a claim of its own against the Arab or Israel government concerned.[4] (In certain UN operations, such as UNEF, rather more complex arrangements were made as between the UN, its forces, their families, and their governments, in which commercial insurance coverage played an important part.)[5]

9

RELATIONS WITH HOST STATES

(*a*) **During the period of the truces established by Resolutions S/727 of 23 April 1948 and S/773 of 22 May 1948**

DURING this period the two truces sought to control fighting which was occurring in Palestine, and to which the Jews on the one hand, and Egypt, Iraq,

---

[1] *Reparation for Injuries* case, *ICJ Rep. 1949*, p. 188; and below, s. 9, pp. 77–78.
[2] See below, s. 9, pp. 78–79.   [3] See below, pp. 79–81.
[4] See the responses of Norway and France, pp. 79, 80 below.
[5] See pp. 329–35 below.

Lebanon, Saudi Arabia, Syria, Transjordan, and the Yemen, on the other, were parties. Until 14 May Britain, as the Mandatory, was officially responsible for Palestine: on 15 May the State of Israel was declared, and the provisional government of Israel came into existence.

It is convenient, in the context of this period, to examine under one heading relations between the United Nations and all these various parties; though as we shall see, an examination of relations under the Armistice provisions will require the drawing of distinctions between each of the Arab states which signed the agreements.

The Truce Commission for Palestine was set up[1] at a time when the United Kingdom was still the Mandatory. In law it was thus the United Kingdom who was responsible[2] for carrying out that part of the resolution which stated: 'The Commission, its members, their assistants and its personnel shall be entitled to travel, separately or together, whenever the Commission deems necessary to carry out its task.' When fighting broke out upon the termination of the mandate and the declaration of the State of Israel 'all the parties concerned'[3] were called upon to order a cease-fire and to give the highest priority to the negotiation and maintenance of a truce in Jerusalem. Equally, 'all parties' were called upon to facilitate by all means in their power the tasks of the United Nations Mediator.

On 29 May, in Resolution S/801, the Security Council called for a cessation of hostilities for four weeks, and specifically urged three provisions—the non-introduction of fighting personnel into Palestine, Egypt, Iraq, Lebanon, Saudi Arabia, Syria, Transjordan, and the Yemen; the prohibition by all governments and authorities on the import or export of war materials in the above countries; and the protection of the Holy Places and the City of Jerusalem. It was left to the Mediator, however, to work out in detail the provisions of such a cease-fire with all the parties, and he was subsequently also authorized to fix the date for the entry into effect of the truce. He fixed the date at 11 June 1948. The details of the truce agreed between the parties and the Mediator—and which were to govern relations during the ensuing weeks between the UN and the authorities concerned—were based upon an agreed interpretation of the Security Council resolution of 29 May:

(1) No fighting personnel, which shall include persons identified as belonging to organized military units as well as all persons bearing arms, shall be introduced into any of the Arab States or into any part of Palestine.

(2) As regards men of military age, the Mediator shall exercise his discretion during the period of the truce in determining whether men of military age are represented among immigrants in such numbers as to give one side a military advantage if their entry is permitted, and in such event shall refuse them entry. Should men of military age be introduced in numbers necessarily limited by the application of the foregoing principle, they are to be kept in camps during the period of the truce under the surveillance of observers of the Mediator, and shall not be mobilized in the armed forces or given military or para-military training during such period.

[1] Res. S/727, 23 Apr. 1948.
[2] See also Res. S/723 which explicitly affirms the continuing responsibility of the UK.
[3] S/773, para. 2, 22 May 1948.

(3) The Mediator shall exercise, to the fullest extent practicable, a check on all immigration at the ports of embarkation and debarkation, and shall place United Nations observers in ships bearing immigrants, and, to this end, shall be notified well in advance as to the port of embarkation of any ship bearing immigrants.

(4) During the first week following the truce, in consideration of the time required for setting up the controls essential to effective application of the resolution, the Mediator shall exercise his discretion as regards the entry of any immigrants irrespective of age or sex.

(5) Movement of troops or war materials from one interested country to another, or closer to the borders of Palestine or to the fighting fronts in Palestine are prohibited during the period of the truce.

(6) All fighting fronts and lines shall remain stabilized during the period of the truce, and there shall be no increase in the fighting strength deployed along the fronts and lines, nor in the war materials on hand. Routine replacement of personnel may be undertaken.

(7) War materials shall not be imported into the country or territory of any interested party.

(8) Relief to populations of both sides in municipal areas which have suffered severely from the conflict, as in Jerusalem and Jaffa, shall be administered by an International Red Cross Committee in such a manner as to ensure that reserves of stocks of essential supplies shall not be substantially greater or less at the end of the truce than they were at its beginning.

(9) All warlike acts, whether on land, sea or air, shall be prohibited during the truce.

I recognize fully that both the effectiveness of the truce and its fairness depend in large measure on the manner in which it is supervised and applied. A detailed plan for its application is in preparation and will be put into operation when the truce begins. No doubt numerous questions will arise in connection with the details of supervising the truce. Consultations on such matters of detail may be undertaken when the truce is in effect.

I am deeply appreciative of the spirit of co-operation manifested by both sides in the difficult negotiations over the truce. I trust that this same spirit will continue in order that the truce may be achieved and the larger work of mediation may proceed constructively in an atmosphere of peace in Palestine. [*S/829, Cablegram of 7 June 1948 from Mediator to Secretary-General*, pp. 82–83.]

The effectiveness of this first truce is discussed elsewhere (see above, pp. 20–24). Both the Arab states and Israel submitted many complaints to the Mediator. Only occasionally did the protests concern the Mediator's interpretation of the truce provisions, rather than the behaviour of the other parties:

The Israeli authorities protested against the refusal of the United Kingdom to permit Jewish men of military age who were interned in Cyprus to leave for Palestine. I informed them that this was a unilateral decision of the United Kingdom, for which I was not responsible and that, so far as I was concerned, the same rules applied to immigration from Cyprus as from other places. [*A/648, Progress Report of the UN Mediator to the General Assembly*, p. 34.]

Difficulties did arise, however, over irregular forces in both Arab and Jewish occupied territories:

13. These irregulars in many cases considered themselves as not bound by the provisions of the ceasefire and truce agreement and were responsible for breaches of the truce on both sides. The only course of dealing with the problem was for me to insist that the Arab and Israeli forces and their respective Governments accept full responsibility for all activities occurring in the areas occupied by them. [*Ibid.* p. 34.]

The Mediator was upheld on this by the Security Council, which in a subsequent resolution both confirmed this point and sought to answer other objections which the parties had been making to the UN about the working of the truce:

The Security Council . . .

Decides . . .
(*a*) Each party is responsible for the actions of both regular and irregular forces operating under its authority or in territory under its control;
(*b*) Each party has the obligation to use all means at its disposal to prevent action violating the truce by individuals or groups who are subject to its authority or who are in territory under its control;
(*c*) Each party has the obligation to bring to speedy trial, and in case of conviction to punishment, any and all persons within their jurisdiction who are involved in a breach of the truce;
(*d*) No party is permitted to violate the truce on the ground that it is undertaking reprisals or retaliations against the other party;
(*e*) No party is entitled to gain military or political advantage through violations of the truce. [*S/983, 19 Aug. 1948.*]

Relations between the UN and the interested parties were further clarified by two additional agreements which they entered into, in respect of Jerusalem and of the Mount Scopus area. These were drawn up on the initiative of the Mediator, for pressing reasons, and are of particular interest as they survived beyond the truce period.

16. The opposing forces in Jerusalem confronted each other across lines that were very close—in some places opposite sides of the same street. Feeling was tense and there was frequent sniping and occasional firing of machine guns, mortars and artillery, as well as attempts by both sides to improve their lines and strengthen their positions. As it was, Jerusalem accounted for nearly half the total of complaints and incidents during the entire truce. As a result of successful negotiations by the Truce Commission and the United Nations observers, an agreement, commonly referred to as the 'No man's land Agreement', was arrived at on 16 June, whereby each of the opposing parties withdrew its forces to an agreed line, and a no man's land was established between the two lines, the houses and buildings in the no man's land being evacuated. Although this agreement did not eliminate all incidents, it was on the whole generally accepted and adhered to, and reduced both the possibilities of friction and the number of incidents.

18. At the beginning of the truce Mount Scopus had remained as an island of Jewish occupation behind the Arab lines in Jerusalem. Israeli forces were in possession of the Hadassah Hospital and the Hebrew University and controlled the Arab village of Issawiya, while the Arab Legion was in possession of the Augusta Victoria Hospice. It was evident that this area would become the scene of violent battle in case the truce terminated. Accordingly, on 7 July, the Arab and Israeli military commanders in Jerusalem executed an agreement with the Truce Commission and the senior United Nations observer in Jerusalem for the demilitarization of the Mount Scopus area, and the United Nations accepted responsibility for the security of the area and for providing food and water supplies. This agreement, despite the shortage of United Nations personnel to enforce it, was carried into effect and was also observed by both sides during the period of hostilities between the two truces. [*A/648, Mediator's Progress Report to General Assembly*, p. 35.]

The precise meaning to be given to certain points of the agreement on Mount Scopus was later to be the subject of fierce controversy,[4] and it is thus useful to reproduce the agreement in full at this point:

---

[4] See below, pp. 120–4.

Agreement of 7 July 1948 for the de-militarization of the Mount Scopus Area

It is hereby jointly agreed that

1. The area as delineated on the attached map will be assigned to United Nations protection until hostilities cease or a new agreement is entered upon. It shall include the areas designated as Hadassah Hospital, Hebrew University, Augusta Victoria and the Arab village of Issawiya. The United Nations agree to become a signatory to this document by representation through the Senior Observer in the Jerusalem area and the Chairman of the Truce Commission. It therefore accepts responsibility for the security of this area as described herewith.

2. There shall be a no-mans-land location extending for approximately 200 yards along the main road between the Augusta Victoria and the Hebrew University Buildings, with suitable checkposts established at each end. Other checkposts will be established on the Perimeter of the zone under protection, and all parties agree that access desired should be along the main road via the United Nations checkposts as established by the United Nations Commander. All other attempts at entry will be considered as unlawful invasion and treated accordingly.

3. In their respective areas armed Arab and Jewish civilian police will be placed on duty under the United Nations Commander. The United Nations flag will fly on the main buildings. All military personnel of both sides will be withdrawn this day, together with their equipment and such other supplies as are not required by the United Nations Commander.

4. The United Nations will arrange that both parties receive adequate supplies of food and water. Replacements of necessary personnel in residence on Mount Scopus will be scheduled by the United Nations Commander. Visits of properly accredited individuals will also be arranged by the United Nations Commander in consultation with each party in respect of its area. The United Nations undertakes to limit the population on Mount Scopus to those individuals needed for its operation, plus the present population of the village of Issawiya. No addition will be made to the village population except by agreement of both parties. The initial personnel roster of civilian police in the Jewish section shall not exceed a total of 85. The civilian personnel attached thereto shall not exceed a total of 53. The Arab civilian population at Augusta Victoria shall not exceed a total of 50.

5. It is hereby agreed by both parties that the area is not to be used as a base for military operations, nor will it be attacked or unlawfully entered upon.

6. In the event that the Arab Legion withdraws from the area, the United Nations Commander is to be given sufficient advanced notice in writing in order that satisfactory arrangements may be made to substitute for this protocol another agreement.

> *(Signed)* LASH (Arab Military Commander)
> SHALTIEL (Jewish Military Commander)
> NIEUWENHUYS (Chairman, UN Truce Commission)
> BRUNSSON (Senior Observer, Mediator's Jerusalem Group)
> [*S/3015, 25 May 1953*.][5]

As the end of the first four-week truce approached, the parties began intense preparations for a resumption of hostilities. The UN Mediator was engaged upon urgent negotiations for a renewal of the truce, but encountered objections from each of the parties, who contended that a truce operated against their interests. With every indication that a widespread renewal of hostilities was to be expected, the Security Council used its authority under Chapter VII of the Charter to *order* a new truce, irrespective of the wishes of the parties. The acceptance by the parties of this command, where they had previously refused

---

[5] This pattern of supplementary local agreements was to continue under the Armistice system. For the local commanders' agreements established subsequent to the Israel–Jordan agreement, see below, pp. 162–7.

voluntary compliance,[6] is a telling example of the authority of the Security Council in the field of peace and security, where the major Powers are in agreement and it is minor Powers to whom the directives are issued.[7] This new truce was to be for an indefinite duration, and, because of its mandatory nature, there was no question of the details of its terms being negotiated with the parties. Once again, while difficulties remained, the new truce was successful in containing large-scale hostilities: but at the same time there began to appear an

unco-operative attitude displayed by some local commanders, troops and irregulars on both sides. This has been expressed in some instances in a tendency to take matters into their own hands, and to defy the authority of the observers. This attitude has sometimes been encouraged by official public pronouncements of responsible leaders. [*A/648, Progress Report of UN Mediator to General Assembly*, p. 39.]

The Mediator endeavoured to meet this challenge by securing a clear statement from the Security Council.[8] Moreover, the Mediator decided to enlarge the neutral zone in Jerusalem:

The [Central Truce Supervision] Board decided to create a neutral zone, supervised by United Nations Observers around the Red Cross Zone, and ordered all troops to be withdrawn from the neutral zone by 29 August. The parties delayed in accepting the two decisions but, as a result of persistent negotiations by the observers, all three forces finally accepted, and on 4 September all troops were withdrawn from both areas. [*Ibid.* p. 40.]

Although both sides continued to have confidence in the impartiality of the UN observers and Mediator, tension still ran extremely high, and several UN observers—unarmed, and with no power to enforce the rights and duties under the truce—were killed. Considerably more were wounded.

This fact leads us on to a particular aspect of UN-Israeli relations, which merits separate treatment. Very shortly after indicating to the Assembly that a crucial stage had been reached in Palestine, and that it was essential to move forward beyond the truce to some settlement if all that had been achieved was not to be lost, the UN Mediator was killed by Jewish terrorists. This action was immediately disowned and deplored by the provisional government of Israel, which informed the Secretary-General that it would at once seek to apprehend and bring to justice those involved.[9] In fact, this was never done. Ralph Bunche was immediately sent to Palestine as the personal representative of the Secretary-General, and subsequently the Council approved the Secretary-General's request that Bunche be empowered to assume full authority of the Palestine mission. The General Assembly now sought to discover—by means of requesting an Advisory Opinion from the International Court of Justice—whether the UN could sue the State of Israel for damages for the loss

[6] There is evidence, however, that at least one of the Arab states *wanted* a mandatory resolution, rather than a further truce by agreement; for in this way fighting could be halted without laying the government open to the charge from its own public that it had 'voluntarily conceded' the fight in Palestine.

[7] See also SC res. concerning Kashmir 209, 4 Sept. 1965.

[8] It has already been mentioned (pp. 75–76) that the Security Council adopted a resolution directed to the question of irregulars and reprisals.

[9] S/1005, 17 Sept. 1948.

of Count Bernadotte and Colonel Sérot, who was killed with him. The Court answered in the affirmative. This judicial pronouncement, and the concomitant clarification of underlying issues,[10] were to shape the claims procedure of the UN in subsequent peacekeeping operations.

The legal issues concerning claims in respect of the Palestine question itself are of sufficient importance to merit separate treatment here.

Claims for reparations for injuries suffered in the service of the UN

The Secretary-General, in conformity with General Assembly Resolution 258 (III) of 3 December 1948, submitted a set of proposals for action to be taken by the UN in the light of the Court's Advisory Opinion. Accordingly, the General Assembly, by Resolution 365 (IV) of 1 December 1949, authorized the Secretary-General to present an international claim against the government of a state, whether member or non-member of the UN, alleged to be responsible for damage caused to the victim, persons entitled through him, and the UN. The resolution authorized agreement to arbitration if such claims could not be settled by negotiation; and further entitled the Secretary-General 'to take the steps and to negotiate in each particular case the agreements necessary to reconcile action by the United Nations with such rights as may be possessed by the state of which the victim is a national'.

The Secretary-General accordingly addressed communications to France, Norway, Sweden, and the United States, each of whom had had nationals killed and wounded in Palestine in circumstances which seemed to involve the legal responsibility of states.

On 21 April 1950, the Secretary-General, after having received assurances from the Swedish Government, as provided under the resolution, addressed a letter to the Minister for Foreign Affairs of Israel requesting a formal apology to the United Nations for the murder of Count Bernadotte, in territory under the control of the Israeli Government, the continuation and intensification of that Government's efforts to apprehend and bring to justice the perpetrators of the crime, and the payment to the United Nations of the sum of $54,628 as reparation for the monetary damage borne by the United Nations.

It was stated in the letter that, in view of the decision of the widow of the late Mediator not to present a claim for pecuniary redress with regard to the damage suffered by her on account of the death of Count Bernadotte, the monetary reparation demanded was limited to the pecuniary damage suffered by the United Nations in connexion with the murder of the Mediator.

The claim by the United Nations was based upon three elements of responsibility: failure to exercise due diligence and to take all reasonable measures for the prevention of the murder; liability of the Government for actions committed by irregular forces in territory under the control of the Israeli authorities; and failure to take all measures required by international law and by the Security Council resolution of 19 October 1948 to bring the culprits to justice.

In his reply, dated 14 June 1950, to the Secretary-General's letter of 21 April 1950, the Minister for Foreign Affairs of Israel stated that the Government of Israel had decided,

---

[10] The points at issue in this Opinion were complex, and of considerable significance for the future development of the UN. The UN sought to learn whether it had capacity at law to present a claim against a sovereign government; whether that government was in law responsible for the acts of terrorists within its territory; and whether it owed legal responsibility to the UN from which damages could flow, for injury and death to a servant of the UN who remained a national of a particular third country. For the Opinion of the Court, see *Reparation for Injuries* case, *ICJ Rep. 1949*, p. 188.

without admitting the validity of all the legal contentions put forward on behalf of the United Nations, to take the action requested in the Secretary-General's letter, and accordingly a remittance of $54,628 was enclosed as reparation for the damage borne by the United Nations. The Government of Israel expressed 'its most sincere regret that this dastardly assassination took place on Israeli territory, and that despite all its efforts the criminals have gone undetected', and added that 'these facts are deeply deplored'. With regard to the continuation and intensification of the Government's efforts to apprehend the culprits, the Minister for Foreign Affairs stated that 'the Government is forced to the conclusion that nothing fresh is likely to emerge from a re-examination of the crime, carried out on the basis of the existing material, both that on the police file and that assembled by the army. This does not, however, imply that the Government regards the case as closed, but that the course of further investigation would depend on the nature and value of any fresh evidence that may come to light.'

On 22 June 1950, the Secretary-General replied to the Government of Israel. After expressing his regret that the efforts so far made by that Government had not resulted in the apprehension and trial of the perpetrators of the crime, the Secretary-General stated that the payment of indemnity, the expression of regret and the report on the steps taken to date, which were included in the letter of the Israeli Government, constituted substantial compliance with the claim submitted in the Secretary-General's letter of 21 April 1950. The letter from the Israeli Government and the Secretary-General's reply were brought to the notice of the Security Council. [*A/1287, Annual Report of the Secretary-General on the work of the Organization, 1 July 1949–30 July 1950, p. 125.*]

Though Israel may have been lax in apprehending the criminals, her payment of the indemnity contrasted favourably with the response of Arab states to questions of reparation. The next year, the Secretary-General reported:

Claim for the death of Mr Ole Helge Bakke

Mr Bakke, a United Nations guard of Norwegian nationality who was serving with the Mediator's staff in Palestine, was killed on 13 July 1948, in territory under the control of the Government of the Hashemite Kingdom of Jordan, by members of the Jordan armed forces. Before presenting a claim for reparation the Secretary-General obtained assurance from the Governments of Norway and of the United States of America, the countries of nationality of the victim and of his widow respectively, that neither of the two Governments intended to bring a separate claim in connexion with Mr Bakke's death. Similar assurances were obtained from the victim's widow and from the daughter of a first marriage. On the other hand, the Norwegian Government transmitted to the Secretary-General a request from the mother of the deceased to present on her behalf a claim for loss of contribution in the amount of 22,000 Norwegian kroner.

On 25 May 1951, the Secretary-General addressed a letter to the Minister for Foreign Affairs of the Hashemite Kingdom of Jordan requesting a formal apology to the United Nations, a report on the measures taken in connexion with the incident, and the payment of the sum of $US 36,803.76 as reparation for the monetary damage suffered by the Organization, and of the sum of 22,000 Norwegian kroner (or $US 3,080) for the damage suffered by Mr Bakke's mother.

The United Nations claim was based upon the following elements of responsibility: violation of the Agreement of 7 July 1948 regarding the demilitarization of Mount Scopus; violation of obligations owed by Jordan to the United Nations to facilitate the carrying out of the Mediator's mandate, and to furnish adequate protection to the Mediator and his staff; and failure to take the necessary measures to bring the culprits to justice. [*A/1844, Annual Report of the Secretary-General on the work of the Organization, 1 July 1950–30 June 1951, p. 189.*]

On 9 January 1952 the Secretary-General proposed that the controversy should be submitted to arbitration in accordance with General Assembly Resolution 365 (IV). Jordan, however, maintained her position, claiming that the bullet which had killed Mr Bakke was not fired by a member of the Arab League. She requested that the Secretary-General release the government from all financial liability. The Secretary-General felt unable to do this, and pointed out that an arbitration would in fact determine whether or not Jordan had international responsibility.[11] No progress was subsequently made on this claim in spite of further urging by the Assembly in Resolution 690 (VII). The Secretary-General sought other means to settle the matter, and proposed the setting up of a board of inquiry, to establish the facts and submit recommendations. Jordan would only agree to a fact-finding committee, but not a commitee with recommendatory powers.[12] The Secretary-General then agreed to a fact-finding committee, and authorized the Legal Adviser to the Chief of Staff of UNTSO to act as his representative in setting up the committee in consultation with Jordan. At this stage the Jordan government withdrew its agreement to the fact-finding committee.[13]

In so far as the Secretary-General's letter to the French government was concerned, that government agreed on 23 October 1951 to the presentation of international claims by the UN, and stated that it would refrain from bringing any claim against the responsible state.[14] Accordingly the Secretary-General entered the following claims:

Injuries to and death of French military observers

Having received the necessary assurances from the French Government required by General Assembly resolution 365 (IV), the Secretary-General, during the year under review, took the following steps in connection with the reparation claims for the deaths of four French military observers and for the injuries suffered by another in Palestine:

Colonel André Sérot. On 11 September 1952, the Secretary-General wrote to the Government of Israel requesting payment to the United Nations of the sum of $US 25,233.00 as reparation for the monetary damage borne by the Organization as a consequence of the death of the United Nations military observer Colonel André Sérot, who was assassinated with the United Nations Mediator Count Folke Bernadotte in Jerusalem on 17 September 1948. Subsequently, the Secretary-General was requested by Colonel Sérot's father to present a claim on his behalf for the payment of 200,000 French francs for the monetary damage caused to him by the death of Colonel Sérot. The Secretary-General, by a letter of 9 December 1952, submitted the additional claim to the Government of Israel.

In reply to the Secretary-General's communications, the Permanent Representative of Israel to the United Nations, by a *note verbale* dated 2 April 1953, remitted the sum of $US 25,233.00 in payment of the claim for damage to the United Nations, and $575.00 (equivalent to 200,000 French francs) in payment of the claim for damage to Colonel Sérot's father.

Lt.-Colonel Joseph Queru and Captain Pierre Jeannel. On 5 September 1952, the Secretary-General addressed a letter to the Government of Egypt presenting a claim in the amount of $US 52,874.20 as reparation for the damage caused to the United Nations as a consequence of the deaths of Lt.-Colonel Queru and Captain Jeannel, United Nations military observers who were killed in Palestine on 28 August 1948. The Secretary-General recalled that the two officers had been attacked and killed by Saudi Arabian troops under Egyptian command after leaving their plane with United Nations markings, which had landed at the Gaza airfield. The

---

[11] A/2141, pp. 160–1.   [12] A/2663, p. 102.   [13] A/2911, p. 109.   [14] Ibid., p. 161.

Secretary-General stated that the United Nations claim was based upon the failure by the Government of Egypt fully to discharge its duty to furnish the Mediator and his staff with appropriate protection, and its failure to take the necessary steps to bring the responsible persons to justice. While acknowledging that the Egyptian authorities had not received notice of the arrival of the United Nations plane and that the aircraft had apparently flown over a forbidden zone, the Secretary-General did not agree with the position previously taken by the Egyptian Government to the effect that the incident did not involve the responsibility of Egypt. The Secretary-General proposed that, if the Government declined to make payment, the question of the responsibility for the deaths of the two United Nations observers should be submitted to arbitration.

No reply has yet been received to the Secretary-General's letter of 5 September 1952.

Commander René de Labarrière and Commander Étienne de Canchy. Having examined in detail the circumstances of the death of Commander de Labarrière and the injuries to Commander de Canchy, which occurred on 6 July 1948 in the Nazareth region, the Secretary-General came to the conclusion that the incident was attributable to the explosion of land mines accidentally set off by two members of the observers' party. The Secretary-General, on the basis of the information available to him, has therefore determined that the incident does not involve the international responsibility of any government, and does not intend to take any further action in the matter. [*A/2404, Annual Report of the Secretary-General on the work of the Organization, 1 July 1952–30 June 1953*, p. 145.]

The Egyptian authorities did not even do the Secretary-General the courtesy of replying, and after eleven months had elapsed the Secretary-General

wrote again on 4 August 1953 indicating that, in addition to arbitration, he would be prepared to consider any other means of settling the matter that might be suggested by the Egyptian Government. By a letter dated 12 November 1953, the Egyptian Government advised the Secretary-General that the claim was being examined by the competent authorities. [*A/2663, Annual Report of the Secretary-General on the work of the Organization, 1 July 1953–30 June 1954*, p. 102.]

But a further silence ensued, and the Secretary-General had to write once again on 14 June 1954. One full year—and another letter—later, still no reply had been received from Egypt.[15] No satisfaction has been received for any claims addressed to the Arab states,[16] and only Israel has responded in a cooperative and responsible manner.

The assassinations of 1948, at once shocking and tragic, reflected a general deterioration in respect for the UN presence in Palestine, and in addition to pursuing claims against the responsible parties, immediate political action by the UN was obviously necessary:

For President Security Council:

One. The assassinations of Count Bernadotte and Colonel Sérot have thrown a tragic light on an increasingly serious situation in Palestine as regards the authority, prestige and even the safety of the personnel engaged in the truce supervision work.

Two. During the truce ordered by the Security Council in its resolution of 15 July 1948 (S/902), there has been a disturbing tendency on the part of both Arabs and Jews to withhold co-operation from the Truce Supervision Organization and to place obstacles in the way of its effective operation.

[15] A/2911, p. 109.

[16] A further controversy between the UN and Jordan, in respect of reparations, occurred in the period 1956–67. See below, p. 126.

Three. The following may be cited as illustrative of current practices and attitudes which greatly hamper the conduct of the Truce Supervision: (A) Requiring advance clearance of twenty-four hours or longer for flights of United Nations aircraft, all of which are painted white with highly visible United Nations markings; (B) Imposing conditions for access of United Nations observers to airfields or to be stationed there, which in practice have proved tantamount to refusal of access; (C) Refusal to allow observers free access to certain ports and strategic areas; (D) Reluctance and delay in extending essential co-operation to observers engaged in investigations of specific incidents, particularly as regards witnesses and vital testimony; (E) Failure to implement, by issue of necessary orders to commanders in the field, agreements reached at the governmental level through the good offices of the Mediator and observers.

Four. The evidences of disregard for the authority of the United Nations, its personnel, credentials, flag and markings on vehicles, find most serious reflection in actual assaults upon Truce Supervision personnel. To date, six lives have been lost in the truce supervision work including that of the Mediator himself, and seven men have been wounded. The unarmed United Nations personnel engaged in this work and their aircraft and vehicles have been frequently subjected to sniper and other types of fire, particularly in the Jerusalem area, and on two recent occasions individual observers have been waylaid and have had their cars and personal funds taken from them at gun-point. There is little evidence that up to now the authorities on either side have regarded incidents involving attacks on United Nations personnel as demanding any extraordinary effort toward apprehending and disciplining the guilty individuals. That the Truce Supervision personnel, civilian and military alike, all of whom are unarmed, carry on their hazardous work under these circumstances is eloquent testimony to their high sense of duty.

Five. The current attitudes of both parties toward the truce supervision involve a serious tendency to disregard the provisions of the resolution of the Security Council of 29 May (S/801) and 15 July (S/902). The resolution of 29 May 'Calls upon all concerned to give the greatest possible assistance to the United Nations Mediator' while the resolution of 15 July 'Calls upon all Governments and authorities concerned to continue to co-operate with the Mediator with a view to the maintenance of peace in Palestine in conformity with the resolution adopted by the Security Council on 29 May 1948.'

Seven. In particular it would seem desirable to give special emphasis to the following obligations and liabilities of the parties with regard to the Truce Supervision: (A) The obligation to allow duly accredited United Nations observers and other Truce Supervision personnel bearing proper credentials, on official notification from Central Truce Supervision Board, ready access to all places where their duties require them to go including airfields, ports, truce lines and strategic points and areas; (B) The obligation to facilitate the freedom of movement of Truce Supervision personnel and transport by alleviation of burdensome flight clearance restrictions on United Nations aircraft now in effect, and by assurance of safe conduct for all United Nations aircraft and other means of transport; (C) The obligation to co-operate fully with the Truce Supervision personnel in their conduct of investigations into incidents involving alleged breaches of the truce, including the making available of witnesses, testimony and other evidence on request; (D) The obligation to implement fully by appropriate and prompt instructions to the commanders in the field all agreements entered into through the good offices of the Mediator or his representatives; (E) The obligation of each party to take all reasonable measures to ensure the safety and safeconduct of the Truce Supervision personnel and the representatives of the Mediator, their aircraft and vehicles, while in territory under its control; (F) The liability of each party for any assault upon or other aggressive act against the Truce Supervision personnel or the representatives of the Mediator in territory under its control, including the obligation to make every effort to apprehend and promptly punish the guilty.

Six. There can be little doubt that appropriate action by the Security Council at this time would be helpful to the effort to ensure the maintenance and the effective supervision of the truce in Palestine. In this regard it might well be called to the attention of the disputing parties that the Security Council resolutions of 15 July and 19 August (S/902 and S/983) remain firm, and that all of the obligations on the parties therein set forth with regard to the maintenance of peace in Palestine are to be fully discharged. [*S/1022, Cablegram of 30 Sept. 1948 from Acting UN Mediator to Secretary-General.*]

On the same date an urgent cable was dispatched by the Chairman of the Truce Commission to the Security Council.

Deliberate Jewish campaign led by Military Governor, Dr. Bernard Joseph, to discredit Truce Commission and Acting Mediator, Dr. Bunche, now apparent developing along lines of attack launched against late Count Bernadotte prior to his assassination and marked by such deliberate discourtesies as release to Press of communications sent to United Nations organizations before their receipt by addressees. Obviously undertaken in effort to destroy public confidence in and arouse public animosity towards the two bodies. [*S/1023, 30 Sept. 1948.*]

Serious fighting broke out again in the Negev section of Palestine. The UN Chief of Staff demanded a truce, and an exchange of complaints occurred between Israel and the Acting Mediator.

Background of the outbreak

9. The present outbreak of fighting in the Negeb is largely due to the failure of both sides to accept the decision of the Central Truce Supervision Board approved by the late Mediator regarding the passing of supply convoys in the Karatiya area. This decision (case no. 12), attached hereto as annex 1, stipulated that within defined periods each day and subject to the conditions set forth in the decision, both parties should use the crossroads lying between Hatta and Karatiya for the passage of such supplies as were permitted under the conditions of the truce. The convoys were to be subject to United Nations supervision. An integral part of the decision precluded the Provisional Government of Israel from supplying its forces in outlying settlements by air except in the case of settlements without road communications and then only under United Nations supervision. Reference to this vital part of the decision, with which the Israeli authorities have thus far failed to comply, was omitted from paragraph 2 of the letter dated 8 October addressed to the Secretary-General by the representative of the Provisional Government of Israel concerning alleged violations of the truce by Arab forces, and circulated to the Security Council as document S/1030.

10. Persistent efforts by the United Nations Truce Supervision Organization to implement this decision, communicated by the late Mediator to the two Governments on 15 September 1948, have failed. The Egyptian Government refused to permit the Israeli convoys to pass until the supplying of Jewish settlements by air was stopped, while the Provisional Government of Israel refused to stop the aerial convoys or submit them to United Nations supervision until the Egyptians permitted the land convoys through. Thus an unreasonable impasse was created. [*S/1042, Report of 18 Oct. 1948 from the Acting Mediator to the Secretary-General.*]

Similar difficulties were also occurring in the Lebanese sector:

7. On 28 October, following urgent advice received from the United Nations observer headquarters at Tiberias, the chief of staff of the truce supervision addressed a warning to Israeli headquarters against any retaliatory action in Galilee and against the denial of freedom of movement to United Nations observers. [*S/1071, Report of 6 Nov. 1948 from Acting Mediator to the Secretary-General.*]

On 22 December I received a message from Haifa signed by the Chief of Staff of the Truce Supervision, General Riley, informing me that on the morning of 21 December a note had been received from Israeli military authorities as follows:

4

'In the light of the present situation in the country, the Chief of General Staff Baruch considers that the moment is opportune for reviewing the routines of truce supervision with a view to their simplification and to increasing the usefulness and efficiency of the liaison staff attached to the observers in the service of the Chief of Staff.

'I am accordingly instructed to suggest to you to appoint an officer to discuss new methods and routines of supervision with myself and to inform you that in the meantime the Chief of General Staff Baruch has decided to suspend temporarily all current arrangements for observers' tours.

'The Chief of General Staff Baruch would be grateful if you could inform this headquarters at your convenience of the name of the officer appointed, so that an initial meeting can be arranged without delay.

'General Riley stated in reply to this message that the suspension of United Nations observer operations would be contrary to the provisions of paragraph A of the Security Council resolution of 19 October 1948 (*S/1045*) and that the suggestion was unacceptable.

'On 21 December the senior United Nations observer at Tel Aviv reported that he had been informed by Israeli authorities that they would not provide liaison officers for routine observation trips until the meeting they desired had been held, and that liaison officers would be provided only for unusual incidents or complaints. On 22 December General Riley received a second message in same vein, but adding that Israeli authorities "did not intend to suspend observer operations indefinitely" ' . . . [*S/1152, Cablegram of 25 Dec. 1948 from Acting Mediator to President of the Security Council.*]

These events were matched by attempts by the Security Council, in a series of resolutions between September and December 1948, to come to grips with the situation and to secure the UN a more acceptable position in Palestine. The movement of events in these resolutions speaks for itself:

The Security Council,

Having in mind the report of the Acting Mediator concerning the assassinations on 17 September of the United Nations Mediator Count Folke Bernadotte and United Nations Observer Colonel André Sérot (S/1018), the report of the Acting Mediator concerning difficulties encountered in the supervision of the truce (S/1022), and the report of the Truce Commission for Palestine concerning the situation in Jerusalem (S/1023),

Notes with concern that the Provisional Government of Israel has to date submitted no report to the Security Council or to the Acting Mediator regarding the progress of the investigation into the assassinations;

Requests that Government to submit to the Security Council at an early date an account of the progress made in the investigation and to indicate therein the measures taken with regard to negligence on the part of officials or other factors affecting the crime;

Reminds the Governments and authorities concerned that all the obligations and responsibilities of the parties set forth in its resolution of 15 July (S/902) and 19 August 1948 (S/983) are to be discharged fully and in good faith;

Reminds the Mediator of the desirability of an equitable distribution of the United Nations observers for the purpose of observing the truce on the territories of both parties;

Determines, pursuant to its resolutions of 15 July and 19 August 1948, that the Governments and authorities have the duty:

(*a*) To allow duly accredited United Nations observers and other Truce Supervision personnel bearing proper credentials, on official notification, ready access to all places where their duties require them to go including airfields, ports, truce lines and strategic points and areas;

(*b*) To facilitate the freedom of movement of Truce Supervision personnel and transport by simplifying procedures on United Nations aircraft now in effect, and by assurance of safe-conduct for all United Nations aircraft and other means of transport;

(*c*) To co-operate fully with the Truce Supervision personnel in their conduct of investigations into incidents involving alleged breaches of the truce, including the making available of witnesses, testimony and other evidence on request;

(*d*) To implement fully by appropriate and prompt instructions to the commanders in the field all agreements entered into through the good offices of the Mediator or his representatives;

(*e*) To take all reasonable measures to ensure the safety and safe-conduct of the Truce Supervision personnel and the representatives of the Mediator, their aircraft and vehicles, while in territory under their control;

(*f*) To make every effort to apprehend and promptly punish any and all persons within their jurisdictions guilty of any assault upon or other aggressive act against the Truce Supervision personnel of the representatives of the Mediator. [*SC Res. S/1045, 19 Oct. 1948.*]

The Security Council,

Having decided on 15 July that, subject to further decision by the Security Council or the General Assembly, the truce shall remain in force in accordance with the resolution of that date and with that of 29 May 1948 until a peaceful adjustment of the future situation of Palestine is reached;

Having decided on 19 August that no party is permitted to violate the truce on the ground that it is undertaking reprisals or retaliations against the other party, and that no party is entitled to gain military or political advantage through violation of the truce; and

Having decided on 29 May that, if the truce was subsequently repudiated or violated by either party or by both, the situation in Palestine could be reconsidered with a view to action under Chapter VII of the Charter,

Takes note of the request communicated to the Government of Egypt and the Provisional Government of Israel by the Acting Mediator on 26 October (S/1058) following upon the resolution adopted by the Security Council on 19 October 1948; and

Calls upon the interested Governments, without prejudice to their rights, claims or position with regard to a peaceful adjustment of the future situation of Palestine or to the position which the Members of the United Nations may wish to take in the General Assembly on such peaceful adjustment:

(1) To withdraw those of their forces which have advanced beyond the positions held on 14 October, the Acting Mediator being authorized to establish provisional lines beyond which no movement of troops shall take place;

(2) To establish, through negotiations conducted directly between the parties, or failing that, through the intermediaries in the service of the United Nations, permanent truce lines and such neutral or demilitarized zones as may appear advantageous, in order to ensure henceforth the full observance of the truce in that area. Failing an agreement, the permanent lines and neutral zones shall be established by decision of the Acting Mediator; and

Appoints a Committee of the Council, consisting of the five permanent members together with Belgium and Colombia, to give such advice as the Acting Mediator may require with regard to his responsibilities under this resolution and, in the event that either party or both should fail to comply with sub-paragraphs (1) and (2) of the preceding paragraph of this resolution within whatever time-limits the Acting Mediator may think it desirable to fix, to study as a matter of urgency and to report to the Council on further measures it would be appropriate to take under Chapter VII of the Charter. [*SC Res. S/1070, 4 Nov. 1948.*]

The Security Council,

Reaffirming its previous resolutions concerning the establishment and implementation of the truce in Palestine and, recalling particularly its resolution of 15 July 1948 which determined that the situation in Palestine constitutes a threat to the peace within the meaning of Article 39 of the Charter;

Taking note that the General Assembly is continuing its consideration of the future government of Palestine in response to the request of the Security Council of 1 April 1948 (S/714):

Without prejudice to the actions of the Acting Mediator regarding the implementation of the resolution of the Security Council of 4 November 1948,

Decides that, in order to eliminate the threat to the peace in Palestine and to facilitate the transition from the present truce to permanent peace in Palestine, an armistice shall be established in all sectors of Palestine;

Calls upon the parties directly involved in the conflict in Palestine, as a further provisional measure under Article 40 of the Charter, to seek agreement forthwith, by negotiations conducted either directly or through the Acting Mediator on Palestine, with a view to the immediate establishment of the armistice including:

(*a*) The delineation of permanent armistice demarcation lines beyond which the armed forces of the respective parties shall not move;

(*b*) Such withdrawal and reduction of their armed forces as will ensure the maintenance of the armistice during the transition to permanent peace in Palestine. [*SC Res. S/1075, 9 Nov. 1948*].

The Security Council,

Having considered the report of the Acting Mediator on the hostilities which broke out in Southern Palestine on 22 December 1948,

Calls upon the Governments concerned:

(i) To order an immediate cease-fire;

(ii) To implement without further delay resolution of 4 November 1948 and the instructions issued by the Acting Mediator in accordance with sub-paragraph 1 of the fifth paragraph of that resolution;

(iii) To allow and facilitate the complete supervision of the truce by the United Nations observers . . . [*SC Res. S/1169, 29 Dec. 1948.*]

As we have seen elsewhere (p. 24), Count Bernadotte's insistence that the precarious truce must move forward towards something more permanent was achieved—albeit after his death. And in 1949 the Armistice Agreements were signed. The relations between the UN and the signatories under these Agreements requires separate treatment.

(*b*) Under the 1949 Armistice Agreements

In each of the four Armistice Agreements certain obligations were undertaken by the parties, and certain tasks for the fulfilment thereof were assigned to the various UN organs set up under the Agreements. There were to arise a series of controversies as to the interpretations and, occasionally, on the scope of the authority of UNTSO to settle these controversies. The MAC came to perform a quasi-judicial function.

i. *The Syria–Israel Armistice*

Relations 1949–56

Article V of the Syria–Israel Armistice Agreement (pp. 39–40) created a demilitarized zone in that area 'where the Armistice Demarcation Line does not correspond to the international boundary between Syria and Palestine'. Under the same Article, (1) the armed forces of both parties were excluded (Article V (a)); (2) the Chairman of the MAC and the UN observers were designated as responsible for ensuring the full implementation of the provisions on the demilitarized zone (Article V (c)); (3) the Chairman of the MAC was empowered to authorize the return of civilians to villages and settlements in the demilitarized zone (Article V(e)). Article II (1) provided—as in all the Armistice Agreements—that 'no military or political advantage should be gained under the truce ordered by the Security Council'.

Each of these clauses was to give rise to difficulties in practice, and as they involved the role of the Chairman of the MAC, they inevitably affected relations between each of the parties on the one hand, and the UN on the other.

First, there was disagreement about the legal nature of the zone. Israel claimed that it was still under Israeli sovereignty, the exercise of which that nation had voluntarily limited. Israel therefore claimed that Syria had no *locus standi* to complain to the MAC about matters relating to sovereignty in the demilitarized zone, but only about those military and political matters governed by the Armistice Agreement. On non-military matters Israel regarded the proper course of procedure as discussion between the Chairman and the party concerned, on the grounds that under Article V the Chairman alone (and not the MAC) was responsible for implementing the relevant provisions. Syria, on the other hand, rejected Israeli sovereignty over the zone, regarding her status as *sui generis*; denied that she had no *locus standi*; and equally rejected the view that complaints could not be dealt with by the MAC. Syria contended that although the Chairman was responsible for implementation, this did not prevent the submission of complaints to the MAC by both parties.

These differences of view emerged specifically in the context of an Israeli project for draining Lake Huleh,[17] in order to reclaim the marshes. The lake and marshes were outside the demilitarized zone, but preliminary work would need to take place within the zone. Was Israel required to obtain the consent of Syria to such work? And was she entitled to expropriate, even for full compensation, Arab lands in the demilitarized zone? Syria claimed that not only was her consent required, but that it could of necessity not be forthcoming, because a topographical change would ensue in the demilitarized zone, which would be an advantage to Israel, which was forbidden by Article II(1). Israel countered by referring to Dr Bunche's celebrated statement that it was not intended that the demilitarized zone should become or remain a wasteland. The project would reclaim for cultivation 15,000 acres of swamp or flooded land, and eliminate malaria. The work was to be carried out by the Palestine Land Development Company under a concession which had been confirmed by a Mandatory Ordinance of 1938, which had become part of the law of Israel.[18]

When work began on the project on 12 February 1951, Syria protested to the MAC. A meeting was held on 21 February 1951, when Syria stated that she would refuse any compensation offered, as the work was in contravention to the 'no advantage' clause of Article 11(i). Syria also contended that Israel had no legal authority in the zone to carry out expropriations of land. Israel contended that the MAC could not deal with matters relating to sovereignty within the

[17] An admirable account of this dispute appears in Bar-Yaacov, pp. 66–113. The book provides a thorough and scholarly review of all the problems of implementation that came within the scope of this Armistice from 1949 to 1966.

[18] Ibid. p. 69.

zone, though the Chairman and Israel could discuss the issue. Israel and Syria both agreed to ask Major-General Riley, the Chief of Staff (and *ex-officio* Chairman of the MAC) to offer an opinion on whether or not the work was contrary to Article II(1). Major-General Riley came to the following conclusions:

1. The main concern of the Israel–Syrian Mixed Armistice Commission has been the administration of demilitarized zones and the problems arising therefrom. The Israel project for straightening and deepening the bed of the Jordan River at the southern end of Lake Huleh has led to complaints to the Israel–Syrian Mixed Armistice Commission by the Syrian delegation. The aim of this project is to lower the water level of Lake Huleh and to dry the marshes north thereto. The Syrian delegation has contended that the carrying out of this project would remove a natural military obstacle, in contravention of article II, paragraph 1 of the Israel–Syrian General Armistice Agreement, which states:

'The principle that no military or political advantage should be gained under the truce ordered by the Security Council is recognized. . . .

'It is concluded that:

'(i) In draining Lake Huleh, the Israelis will not enjoy any military advantages not equally applicable to the Syrians;

'(ii) The demilitarized zone was *not* created where natural obstacles to the movement of armed forces were non-existent. . . .

'The demilitarized zone created by the Armistice Agreement was defined with a view toward separating the armed forces of both parties while providing for the *gradual restoration of normal civilian life in the area of the demilitarized zone*. The Chairman of the Mixed Armistice Commission was charged with the responsibility of ensuring that the provisions of the Armistice Agreement with respect to the demilitarized zone were implemented. It follows that neither party to the Armistice Agreement therefore enjoys rights of sovereignty within the demilitarized zone. Any laws, regulations or ordinances in force prior to the Armistice Agreement which affected any areas included in the demilitarized zone are null and void. Therefore, the concessionaires do not enjoy the right to expropriate lands or buildings, to occupy lands temporarily or to force the owners of lands to accept compensation. There is no law of expropriation within the demilitarized zone. Any occupancy of lands either temporary or permanent, without the full consent of the landowners, is a hindrance to the restoration of normal civilian life in the demilitarized zone, and a violation of article V, paragraph 2, of the Armistice Agreement.

'B. Until such time as a mutual agreement is reached between the Governments of Syria and Israel, with respect to the work now being conducted in the demilitarized zone in connection with the drainage of the Lake Huleh marshes, the Palestine Land Development Company or any successors are, in the opinion of the Chief of Staff, not justified in continuing such work.

'C. In the opinion of the Chief of Staff, the Palestine Land Development Company, Limited, should be instructed forthwith to cease all operations within the demilitarized zone, until such time as a mutual agreement is arranged through the Chairman between Syria and Israel for continuing this project.

'(*Signed*) W. E. RILEY,
Major-General, USMC.'

(*Note:* The United Nations Chief of Staff now believes that his memorandum should have stated that any laws, regulations or ordinances in force prior to the Armistice Agreement which affected any areas included in the demilitarized zone 'are held in abeyance' instead of 'are null and void'.) [*S/2049, Report of UN Chief of Staff to Secretary-General, 21 Mar. 1951.*]

The appended note to the above document indicates the difficulties facing a non-judicial body in having to pronounce upon matters involving complicated legal rights and duties. Initially the Chief of Staff declared prior regulations null; and then merely in abeyance; later, however, he accepted that the Palestine Land Development Company was entitled to execute a concession in the zone which was valid under Israeli law, so long as there was no question of forcible expropriation of Arab lands (p. 99 below). The Israeli delegation, while gratified that the Chief of Staff found that the proposed works were not contrary to Article II(1), objected that he had gone beyond his mandate in recommending that work should cease pending Syrian agreement:

4. At the meeting, of 7 March 1951, the Israel delegation contended that the Israel–Syrian Mixed Armistice Commission had invited the United Nations Chief of Staff to express an opinion whether or not the work being done by Israel was a contravention of article II of the General Armistice Agreement. It was not in order for him to go outside the scope of the request as he had done in his memorandum. The Israel delegation charged the United Nations Chief of Staff with assuming prerogatives in the demilitarized zones which were not given him under the General Armistice Agreement. The Israel delegation maintained that Israel was determined to uphold its sovereignty in the demilitarized zone except in so far as it was limited by the terms of the General Armistice Agreement.

5. The Syrian delegation stressed that it would have been improper for the United Nations Chief of Staff to express an opinion on one aspect of the problem only. He was within his rights to advise the Israel–Syrian Mixed Armistice Commission on all aspects of the problem. [Ibid.]

The Israelis refused to attend the scheduled meeting of the MAC and did not cease work on the projects within the demilitarized zone.[19] Subsequently, the Israelis indicated that they would stop the work on the Huleh drainage scheme between 15 and 23 March 1951. The ensuing controversy centred on the authority allocated to the Commission and Chairman respectively:

. . . the Israel delegation proposed that all complaints of a civilian nature originating in the demilitarized zone be stricken from the agenda of the Israel–Syrian Mixed Armistice Commission, stating that the Commission should not consider complaints which were within the competence of the Chairman. The Syrian delegation could not acquiesce to an arrangement whereby the Israel authorities acted in the demilitarized zone as if the area was Israel territory. He referred to the question of Israel police in the demilitarized zone and the cultivation of lands by Israelis against the will of the Arab owners. . . .

12. The Israel delegation stressed that Israel officials had never exercised any authority in the demilitarized zone which was not permitted under the General Armistice Agreement, and added that the Government of Israel considered the Huleh works as a purely civilian project which would permit the return to normal civilian life under the General Armistice Agreement. Further, under article V of the General Armistice Agreement, the Chairman could act in matters of a civilian nature with the consent and co-operation of the people of the demilitarized aone. [S/2067, Report of Acting Chief of Staff of UNTSO to Secretary-General, 4 Apr. 1951.]

The Chairman of the MAC indicated that under Article V of the Armistice Agreement, he was establishing an investigation, and ordered cessation of work in the demilitarized zone during this period.[20] The Israelis would only agree to suspend work until 26 March, and when bulldozers were brought up to resume

[19] S/2049, para 8.   [20] S/2067, para. 20.

work, they were fired upon by Arabs. Firing ceased only upon the intervention of UN observers.[21] Violence of this nature was repeated on 27 March, and the Acting Chief of Staff formally informed Israel that it was in violation of Articles I, III, and V of the Armistice Agreement.[22] After protracted efforts by the Acting Chief of Staff, Israeli forces which had been brought into the demilitarized zone during these incidents were withdrawn.[23] When other minor incidents occurred in this area, the Israeli delegation stuck to its earlier position that

it was not prepared to discuss civilian matters pertaining to the demilitarized zone before the Mixed Armistice Commission, but it was prepared to discuss these matters with the Chairman only. The Syrian delegation replied that the Israelis . . . had repeatedly failed to recognize the Chairman's authority under article V of the General Armistice Agreement. [*S/2084*, *10 Apr. 1951*, para. 10.]

After further incidents in the area between Tiberias and El Hamma, the following correspondence was sent by the Israelis to the Acting Chief of Staff:

The Israel delegation to the Israel–Syrian Mixed Armistice Commission has been instructed to attend no further meetings with the Syrian delegation while Syrian forces are firing on United Nations observers and on the police responsible for the security of the demilitarized zones.[24]

The Acting Chief of Staff indicated that as this was not the first time that the personal safety of UN observers had been endangered: 'I am at a loss to understand why the Israel delegation should cite this as a reason for its refusal to attend any further meetings of the Mixed Armistice Commission.'[25] The Israelis, however, also let it be known that the Israel delegation to the Israel–Syrian MAC had been forbidden

. . . to take any part in meetings to be presided over by Colonel Georges Bossavy,[26] or to have any further official contact with him. . . . The fact is that a *crise de confiance* has arisen in our relations with Colonel Georges Bossavy, and that under the circumstances I consider it would be in the interests of all concerned that he should no longer function as the Chairman. . . . [*S/2084*, paras 25 and 36.]

In an endeavour to get the meetings going again, without appearing to lose the right to nominate his own personnel, the Acting Chief of Staff of UNTSO announced: 'Colonel Georges Bossavy will continue to be Chairman of the Israel–Syrian Mixed Armistice Commission, and the acting Chief of Staff will preside at meetings of the Commission at which incidents of the past four weeks will be discussed'.[27]

Israel now made a full statement on the major points of the dispute over the Huleh area:

1. The Israel project for the drainage of the marshes at Lake Huleh is part of a major drainage and irrigation scheme initiated a number of years ago by Jewish public bodies under a

---

[21] Ibid. paras 32, 33. For a detailed account, see Bar-Yaacov, pp. 77–78.
[22] Ibid. paras 42, 44.   [23] S/2084, 12 Apr. 1951, para. 8.   [24] Ibid. para. 25, p. 48.
[25] Ibid. para. 26.   [26] The Chairman of the MAC.
[27] S/2088, cablegram from Acting Chief of Staff of UNTSO to the President of the Security Council, 13 Apr. 1951.

concession granted in 1934 by the British Mandatory Government to the Palestine Land Development Company. In execution of this project, works have been in progress in the Huleh area, with the full knowledge of the Syrian and United Nations authorities, since October 1950. Not until 14 February 1951, did the Syrian Government lodge any complaint with the Israel–Syrian Mixed Armistice Commission. Thereupon, on 21 February 1951, it was mutually agreed by both delegations that an opinion be sought of the United Nations Chief of Staff whether or not the drainage activities undertaken by the Israel authorities constituted a contravention of article II (Military advantage) of the General Armistice Agreement (S/2049, section IV, para 2).

2. It will be noted from the final sentence of the above paragraph that:

(*a*) The request for the opinion of the Chief of Staff of the Truce Supervision Organization was based not on any provision of the General Armistice Agreement, but on the voluntary consent of the two parties.

(*b*) The delegations did not commit themselves to acceptance of the opinion of the Chief of Staff.

(*c*) The terms of reference for this opinion were clearly defined and were limited exclusively to the problem of conformity or non-conformity with article II, paragraph 2 of the Israel–Syrian General Armistice Agreement.

3. The reply of the Chief of Staff, within his terms of reference, is clear and unequivocal, namely (*S/2049, section IV*, para. 3).

'It is concluded that

'(i) In draining Lake Huleh, the Israelis will not enjoy any military advantage not equally applicable to the Syrians. . . .'

The Government of Israel is glad to state that it concurs with this conclusion, and notes that this finding fully vindicates the legality of its activities within the Huleh area.

4. The Chief of Staff did not, however, limit his opinion to the mutually agreed terms of reference, but also embarked on matters *ultra vires* those terms, namely, the discussion of certain other aspects of the Huleh undertaking. Thus, he proceeded to establish a distinction between 'control' and 'sovereignty'; to rule on the legal force of the Huleh Concession (Boundaries) Ordinance of 17 March 1938 (Supplement No. 1 to the Palestine Gazette No. 770 of 24 March 1938); and to declare 'null and void' (later corrected to read 'held in abeyance'), the legislation concerning the Huleh concession. As a result of this diversion into intricate problems of international law affecting so vital an issue as the continuing validity of concessions, it was implied by the Chief of Staff that Syria commanded a right to decide whether Israel might or might not continue with the work of drainage. . . .

7. The Government of Israel wishes to draw attention to the singular interpretation given in document S/2049 to the expression 'demilitarized zone'. Only two distinctions characterize the demilitarized zone from the rest of Israel territory; first, that no activities of a military character are permitted in the former, while no such restriction affects the latter; secondly, that in regard to the latter the Chairman of the Israel–Syrian Mixed Armistice Commission possesses the authority explicitly defined in article V, sub-paragraph 5 (*e*). The interpretation given by the Chief of Staff to the meaning of 'demilitarized zone' and to article V of the Israel–Syrian Armistice Agreement contradicts the terms of article V, sub-paragraph 5 (*e*) and the interpretation of that article given by Mr Bunche in the substantially identical letters he addressed to the Israel and Syrian Ministers for Foreign Affairs and in his explanatory note dated 26 June 1949, included in the summary record of the 11th plenary meeting of the Armistice Conference held on 3 July 1949. It will be recalled that this note was, by agreement between the parties, to form an authoritative commentary on article V of the Armistice Agreement. (See Mr Vigier's statement at the 11th plenary meeting (S/11, page 2) and at the 12th plenary meeting on 18 July 1949 (S/12, page 10)).

One paragraph of Mr Bunche's letter may usefully be quoted here:

'I may also assure both parties that the United Nations, through the chairman of the
4*

proposed Israel–Syrian mixed armistice commission, will also ensure that the demilitarized zone will not be a vacuum or wasteland, and that normal civilian life under normal local civilian administration and policing will be operative in the zone.'

8. It was on this basis that the Government of Israel agreed to sign the General Armistice Agreement. The Government of Israel first satisfied itself by a close scrutiny of the text and the associated documents that the Agreement contained nothing which would give authority to the Syrian Government or to the Chairman of the Mixed Armistice Commission to impede or suspend non-military activities in the area concerned.

. . . The situation would be different only if the Armistice Agreement included within the competence of the United Nations Chairman of the Mixed Armistice Commission a specific authorization to rule or pronounce on the legality or legitimacy of this work or of other civilian activities. But this is not the case. The Armistice Agreement contains no such provision.

11. According to the opinion of the Chief of Staff, 'any laws, regulations or ordinances in force prior to the Armistice Agreement which affected any areas included in the demilitarized zone are null and void (are held in abeyance).' This produces the absurdity that the area and its inhabitants would be in a legal vacuum, immune from the incidence of the laws, obligations, rights and restraints of government, which have, incidentally, applied with the full knowledge of all parties for nearly two years. It is inconceivable that the United Nations can desire to uphold the doctrine that this territory, described by General Riley 'as territory under Israel control', is instead an island of anarchy dedicated to the maintenance of a swamp. All the legal criteria, separately and together—both those derived from the Palestine Mandate, later confirmed by Israel legislation, and those based on the Armistice Agreement—establish the full legality of the Huleh concession and of Israel control, limited only by the specific reservations of the Armistice Agreement, which, in its turn, makes no reference or implied reference, to any impediment to the carrying out of this work.   [*Ibid. ann.*]

This dispute over the demilitarized zone continued, with intermittent outbreaks of violence between Syrians and Israelis involving injury and death to UN observers who endeavoured to patrol the area. Meanwhile Syria prepared her own statement on the major points at issue:

2. The Israel representative contested the right of the Chief of Staff of the Truce Supervision Organization to study and make recommendations on certain other aspects of the Huleh undertaking, and, as a result, he emphasized that the views of the Chief of Staff on those matters which he discussed in his report do not fall within his powers, and are null and void. Such allegation is groundless for the following reasons:

(*a*) The Chief of Staff discussed and expressed an opinion on the construction of a dam at the south end of Lake Huleh and the effect of this work on the lands owned by the Arab local inhabitants which will be flooded because of the dam. He concluded by asserting that (*S/2049, sect. IV*, para. 3): '. . . This flooding, therefore, is an obstacle in the return to normal civilian life of the inhabitants of the demilitarized zone,' and '. . . is a violation of article V, paragraph 2 of the Armistice Agreement'. As the Chief of Staff is responsible for insuring the full implementation of article V of the Agreement by virtue of sub-paragraph 5 (*c*) of that article, we cannot but reject as utterly false and groundless Mr Eban's contention that the Chief of Staff of the Truce Supervision Organization has no authority to embark on this matter.

(*b*) The second point dealt with by the Chief of Staff is the work within the demilitarized zone where the whole of the Huleh undertaking is to be performed. This zone was created by the Israel–Syrian General Armistice Agreement, the implementation of which is to be supervised and ensured by the Chief of Staff and the United Nations observers attached to the Mixed Armistice Commission. His primary duties are to safeguard the status of this zone and prohibit any activities therein which are likely to affect the relations between the parties concerned or to cause any change in the *status quo*. Therefore, Israel's claim that the Chief of

Staff's intervention in this matter is *ultra vires* his terms of reference is groundless and completely absurd. . . .

(*c*) The third point discussed by the Chief of Staff is the position of the Arab inhabitants who own lands within the demilitarized zone, and the forceful occupation of their lands by Israelis against their wishes. These peasants complained to the Chief of Staff in his capacity as the United Nations representative charged with the task of redressing the wrongs done to them. The Chief of Staff responded to their call and expressed his view that the concessionnaires, that is, the Palestine Land Development Company, do not possess the right to expropriate or occupy lands or buildings or to force the owners of lands to accept compensation. He further affirmed that there is no law of expropriation, within the demilitarized zone, and that any occupancy of lands either temporary or permanent, without the full consent of the landowners, is a hindrance to the restoration of normal civilian life in the demilitarized zone, and constitutes a violation of article V, paragraph 2 of the armistice agreement. . . .

(*e*) The fifth point examined by the United Nations Chief of Staff is the question of sovereignty over the demilitarized zone. He declared (*S/2049, sect. IV*, para 3):

'Neither party to the Armistice Agreement therefore enjoys rights of sovereignty within the demilitarized zone. Any laws, regulations or ordinances in force prior to the Armistice Agreement which affect any areas included in the demilitarized zone are held in abeyance.'

This decision does not mean that the demilitarized zone is to be a vacuum or waste land. It means that its inhabitants are to return and enjoy a peaceful and normal life under the provisions of the Armistice Agreement which should prevail over any previous regulations. The Chief of Staff based his opinion on the Security Council resolution of 16 November, 1948 (*S/1079*), and on the Armistice Agreement concluded between Syria and Israel. Article V, paragraph 2 of the Armistice Agreement clearly stipulates that the demilitarized zone was established with a view toward separating the armed forces of both parties while providing for the gradual restoration of normal civilian life in the area of the demilitarized zone. Moreover, article V, sub-paragraph 5 (*c*), charges the Chairman of the Mixed Armistice Commission with the responsibility of ensuring the full implementation of the provisions of the Armistice Agreement with respect to the demilitarized zone. Under these conditions the Chief of Staff is the sole judge of the existence of a conflict between anterior regulations and the present Armistice Agreement. The Chief of Staff declared that he considered the draining works conducted in the demilitarized zone as contrary to the provisions of the Armistice Agreement and ordered:

'The Palestine Land Development Company should be instructed forthwith to cease all operations within the demilitarized zone, until such time as a mutual agreement is arranged through the Chairman between Syria and Israel for continuing this project.' (*S/2049, sect. IV*, para 3.)

But the Israel Government has hitherto shown no sincere desire of obeying the orders of the Chief of Staff.

3. As to the letter of Mr Ralph Bunche, quoted in part by Mr Eban in his above-mentioned memorandum, it is not legally binding on the signatory parties because it is not part of the Armistice Agreement. Nor can it in any wise be interpreted in such a manner as to contradict the provisions of the Armistice Agreement or to infringe the rights of the landowners and the rights of Syria. Furthermore, the passage quoted from Mr Bunche's letter does not deal with the right of sovereignty over the demilitarized zone, nor does it claim to give such a right to one of the two parties. Finally, the above-mentioned passage quoted by Mr Eban does not exist in the letter addressed to the Syrian Government by Mr Bunche. In fact, the Syrian Government received from Mr Bunche one note subsequent to questions addressed to him on 21 June 1949, and a letter dated 26 June 1949, addressed to the Syrian Government. Both of these documents do not contain the passage quoted by Mr Eban. [*S/2105, Memo. of 24 Apr. 1951 submitted by Syria to the President of the Security Council.*]

Parenthetically, it is of interest to note the nature of the directives which the Chief of Staff of UNTSO issued to Israel and Syria in an attempt to restore order:

(1) All military and para-military forces in the respective defensive zones adjoining the central sector of the demilitarized zone to be withdrawn to a distance of 500 meters from the closest limit of the demilitarized zone. Only those check points authorized by the United Nations Chairman of the Israel–Syrian Mixed Armistice Commission will be permitted within the areas concerned. Minor adjustments to this arrangement to be effected by the United Nations Chairman of the Israel–Syrian Mixed Armistice Commission following acceptance by both parties of the requirements set forth on this document. The provisions of this paragraph to be effected by 0900 hours GMT on 9 May 1951.

(2) All military and para-military forces to be withdrawn from the northern and southern sectors of the demilitarized zone, permitting return to the status envisaged in the Israel–Syrian General Armistice Agreement. The provisions of this paragraph to be effected by 0900 hours GMT on 9 May 1951.

(3) United Nations observers to be attached to the respective headquarters in defensive zones, with the authority to move anywhere at any time within the defensive zone, accompanied when requested by an officer of equal rank from the party concerned. Movements of United Nations observers to be made only upon the decision of United Nations Chairman of the Israel–Syrian Mixed Armistice Commission. The provisions of this paragraph to be effected by 0900 hours GMT on 9 May 1951.

(4) In the areas specified where no military or para-military forces are to be maintained (see paragraph 1 above), the respective civilian authorities to be required to ensure the collecting of weapons from all civilians in the area by 0900 hours GMT on 9 May 1951.

(5) United Nations observers to be authorized to supervise collection of arms from all civilians in the demilitarized zone. Observers may call upon local civilian authorities to assist them in this task if required. United Nations Chairman to organize at his discretion mixed patrols of local residents in the demilitarized zone to ensure the complete disarming of civilians. The provisions of this paragraph to be effected as soon as arrangements can be made by the United Nations Chairman of the Israel–Syrian Mixed Armistice Commission. [*S/2127, Report of Chief of Staff of UNTSO, 8 May 1951.*]

The authority which the Chief of Staff defined for his observers *vis-à-vis* individuals (see para. 5) is particularly interesting. One of the recurring problems under the Armistice Agreements was the lack of any direct UN authority over civilians. The control of civilians (who frequently posed a threat to the security of the armistice by wandering across frontiers) was a matter for the civil police of the parties, and in spite of occasional attempts to acquire some minimal authority over them—as in paragraph 5 referred to above—this remained a very real difficulty.[28]

After a further deterioration in the situation the Security Council acted, passing Resolution S/2157, 10 May 1951:

[28] See on this point Bowett, p. 83, who notes that Article V (4) of the Egypt–Israel Armistice recognized the duty of the parties to control civilians. He adds: 'As late as 1957 the Acting Chief of Staff of UNTSO was reporting difficulties in the areas of Government House and Mount Scopus due to civilian activities and arising from the lack of any specific authority over civilian activities. Indeed, the control of civilian activities was one of the problems specifically referred to the Mixed Armistice Commission by the Security Council (S/3942, para. 3a, 22 Jan. 1958). The principle seems clear, that the parties bound either by Resolutions of the Security Council or by the terms of the Truce or Armistice Agreements are under a duty to ensure that all persons within the areas subject to their control so conduct themselves as to maintain the validity of the Resolutions or Agreements.'

The Security Council . . .
Noting that the Chief of Staff of the Truce Supervision Organization in a memorandum of
7 March 1951 [S/2049, sect. IV, para. 3] and the Chairman of the Syrian–Israel Mixed
Armistice Commission on a number of occasions have requested the Israel Delegation to the
Mixed Armistice Commission to ensure that the Palestine Land Development Company,
Limited, is instructed to cease all operations in the demilitarized zone until such time as an
agreement is arranged through the Chairman of the Mixed Armistice Commission for con-
tinuing this project;
Noting further that Article V of the General Armistice Agreement and between Israel and
Syria gives to the Chairman the responsibility for the general supervision of the demilitarized
zone;
Endorses the requests of the Chief of Staff and the Chairman of the Mixed Armistice Commission on this matter and calls upon the Government of Israel to comply with them;
Declares that in order to promote the return of permanent peace in Palestine, it is essential
that the Governments of Israel and Syria observe faithfully the General Armistice Agreement
of 20 July 1949;
Notes that under Article VII, paragraph 8, of the Armistice Agreement, where interpretation
of the meaning of a particular provision of the agreement, other than the preamble and
Articles 1 and 11, is at issue, the Mixed Armistice Commission's interpretation shall prevail;
Calls upon the Governments of Israel and Syria to bring before the Mixed Armistice Commission or its Chairman, whichever has the pertinent responsibility under the Armistice
Agreement, their complaints and to abide by the decisions resulting therefrom;
Considers that it is inconsistent with the objectives and intent of the Armistice Agreement to
refuse to participate in meetings of the Mixed Armistice Commission or to fail to respect
requests of the Chairman of the Mixed Armistice Commission as they relate to his obligations
under Article V and calls upon the parties to be represented at all meetings called by the
Chairman. . . . [*SC Res. S/2157, 18 May 1951.*]

The resolution also called upon the parties to give effect to Dr Bunche's
authoritative interpretation of Article V;[29] to allow Arab civilians to return to
their homes in the demilitarized zone; and to accord full freedom of movement
of UNTSO observers. The sponsors of the resolution (France, Turkey, the
United Kingdom, and the United States) did, however, make it clear that they
did not wish the resolution to mean that the Huleh project should be abandoned;
rather, there would be a renewed effort at agreement on the project between
Israel and Syria. The United Kingdom delegate went so far as to say that if
there was failure to reach agreement with Syria, then Israel might report back
to the Security Council to ask for permission to buy land and to proceed with
the work.[30]

Although both parties indicated that they would obey the resolution

a difference of opinion does exist between the parties relative to interpretation of the 'intent'
of the Security Council resolution in regard to the third and fourth paragraphs of the resolution which deal with the operations of the Palestine Land Development Company in the
demilitarized zone.

3. On the one hand, Israel understands that the point at issue is the 'safeguarding of the
legitimate rights and interests of the Arab owners of land in the demilitarized zone affected
by the Huleh drainage operations'. Israel does not consider that the Security Council envisaged indefinite suspension of work on the project. Israel has made it clear that 'in complying
with the Security Council's directions, it reserves fully what it holds to be Israel's inalienable

---

[29] See above, pp. 91–92.
[30] *SCOR*, 547th mtg, 18 May 1951; also, for details of the debates, Bar-Yaacov, pp. 79–93.

right to bring the Huleh drainage project to a successful close in the interests of Israel and of the inhabitants of the region.'

4. On the other hand, Syria holds the view that its request to the Security Council took into consideration not only the interests of Arabs whose land was involved in the drainage project, but was also intended to prevent the creation of military or political advantages in the area. This is why Syria must maintain its point of view and make the strongest reservations if the Israelis continue their work.

5. My views, which have been expressed to officials of both Governments in my talks, are in general accord with those of Israel as regards the 'intent' of the Security Council. I believe that at no time did members of Security Council entertain the idea that the Huleh project, as a project, was to be stopped indefinitely. However, the Security Council resolution did endorse the requests of the Chief of Staff and the Chairman of the Mixed Armistice Commission to the Israel representative on the Commission to 'ensure that the Palestine Land Development Company, Limited, is instructed to cease all operations in the demilitarized zone until such time as an agreement is arranged through the Chairman of the Mixed Armistice Commission for continuing their project' . . .

10 . . . Israel has expressed its willingness to permit the return of those Arabs who desire to do so. Before this can be accomplished, I must of necessity have the agreement of the Government of Israel to allow United Nations observers to interview the Arabs of the demilitarized zone, who are now in Israel, without Israel army or police officers being present, in order to determine desires of these individuals. Such agreement has not been received to date. [*S/2173*, *Report of Chief of Staff of UNTSO to Secretary-General, 29 May 1951.*][31]

Permission was, however, given, and the Chairman interviewed the Arab land-owners, who indicated that there was no sum of compensation for which they were prepared to sell their lands.

Israel now sought to devise ways whereby she could proceed with the project (which the Chief of Staff had not found to be contrary to Article II(1)) without having to work on any of the Arab lands in the demilitarized zone; and this the Chief of Staff agreed to on 9 June 1951. Syria objected, saying that this was contrary to the Security Council resolution.

General Riley, the Chief of Staff of UNTSO at this time[32] (who had recently replaced Colonel de Ridder, the Acting Chief of Staff noted) that he had

authorized, early in June 1951, the Palestine Land Development Company Ltd. to continue to work on lands within the demilitarized zone which were considered by me to be lands not in dispute. The Government of Israel and the Government of Syria criticized my decision. The Government of Syria claimed that it was not consistent with the Security Council resolution. The Government of Israel maintained that under the terms of the Armistice Agreement and the explanatory note of 26 June 1949, the Chairman or myself could authorize work not only on 'lands not in dispute' but on Arab lands as well without the necessity of obtaining the concurrence of the individual landowners. [*S/2300*, *Report from Chief of Staff of UNTSO to Secretary-General, 17 Aug. 1951.*]

Neither party would attend meetings of the Israel–Syria MAC because an agenda agreeable to both could not be found.[33] The Chief of Staff had to report

---

[31] At this point, Gen. Riley had resumed as Chief of Staff, taking over from Col. B. de Ridder.

[32] For chronology of Chiefs of Staff, see above, p. 70.

[33] S/2300, para. 30. Syria declared that by virtue of Art. VII (I), the MAC could deal with all matters relating to the demilitarized zone; and she would not attend MAC meetings if these matters were not discussed; Israel claimed that under Art. V, 5(c), only the chairman had competence in either civilian or military matters relating to the zone; and would not attend the MAC if these matters were discussed. Bar-Yaacov gives a full account, pp. 95–97.

in November that it still had not been possible to secure a resumption of the MAC.[34] Individual discussions were held with both the Israeli and the Syrian delegations, however, in an attempt to find some common ground. A continuing source of friction between Israel and UNTSO were the rights and duties of each in the demilitarized zone:

14. The problem of Israel police in the demilitarized zone has been made particularly difficult by the position taken by the Government of Israel on the status of the demilitarized zone. It holds that the zone, except the small section to the east of the international boundary between Syria and Palestine, is under Israel control, subject only to the limitations contained in the General Armistice Agreement. This legal position has been expressed or assumed by Israel representatives in many discussions concerning the police problem and other problems of civil administration in the demilitarized zone. In my view, Mr Bunche's authoritative comment, quoted in the Security Council resolution of 18 May 1951, provides the basis for the discussion of such problems. Paragraph 1 of this comment reads:

'The question of civil administration in villages and settlements in the demilitarized zone is provided for, within the framework of an Armistice Agreement, in sub-paragraphs 5 (b) and 5 (f) of the draft article. Such civil administration including policing, will be on a local basis, *without raising general questions of administration, jurisdiction, citizenship, and sovereignty.*'

(I have given emphasis to these last words which, in my opinion, should be kept in mind when civilian problems in the demilitarized zone are discussed.)

15. Article V, sub-paragraph 5 (e) of the General Armistice Agreement provides that 'the Chairman of the Mixed Armistice Commission shall be empowered to authorize . . . the employment of limited numbers of locally recruited civilian police in the zone for internal security purposes'. The authoritative comment provides that 'where Israel civilians return to or remain in an Israel village or settlement, the civil administration and policing of the village or settlement will be by Israelis. Similarly, were Arab civilians return to or remain in an Arab village, a local Arab administration and police unit will be authorized'. In view of these provisions, I and the Chairman of the Mixed Armistice Commission had taken objection to various activities of the Israel police. We had *inter alia* objected to the establishment of an Israel police post at the Arab Khoury Farm south of Lake Huleh. On 7 September, I was informed that the Israel police would be removed from Khoury Farm, together with the Palestine Land Development Company's equipment which it guarded. The Israel police post was withdrawn on 11 September. However, the Chairman continues to report that Israel police are making routine check-up in Khoury Farm.

16. I have referred in paragraph 9 of document S/2300 to other activities of the Israel police in the demilitarized zone. This police, wearing the uniform of State of Israel police and subject to Israel orders from without the zone, has controlled the movements of Arabs and interfered with the freedom of movement of the Chairman of the Mixed Armistice Commission and United Nations observers (see penultimate paragraph of my letter to Mr Eban of 4 August set forth in document S/2309). The representatives of the Israel Government and I have endeavoured to agree on certain directives which should assist the Chairman of the Mixed Armistice Commission and the Israel representatives in working out a practical arrangement. Mr Bunche's authoritative comment refers to the Chairman's 'general supervision' and excludes his 'assuming responsibility for direct administration of the zone'. It was agreed that the Chairman, while he is empowered to authorize the employment of limited numbers of locally recruited Israel and Arab police, is not himself entitled to employ or command them. Police units are to be at the disposal of the local authorities. The police—Arab and Israel—are employed in the zone for internal security purposes. They should not be tied down exclusively to any one settlement or village. They should have

---

[34] S/2389, 8 Nov. 1951.

freedom of movement within the zone in the execution of their duties. There should, however, be certain limits to this freedom: I received the assurance that Israel police would not
enter or act directly in Arab villages except in emergency cases when the local Arab police
could not cope with the situation, and then only after agreement had first been sought with
the Chairman of the Mixed Armistice Commission. My point of view is that in the absence
of arrangements authorized by the Chairman, Israel police must not enter the area of an Arab
village and vice versa. The Chairman and the representative of Israel, in working out practicable arrangements, should endeavour to reach an agreement on the problem of emergency
cases and of the action to be taken in such cases by Israel and Arab police. [*S/2389, Report
of Chief of Staff of UNTSO to the Secretary-General, 8 Nov. 1951.*]

Although both informal and emergency meetings continued to be held
periodically, no formal meetings of the MAC could be held and it remained in a
'state of semi-paralysis'.[35]

General Riley's report on this state of affairs[36] met with great disapproval on
the part of Syria, which entered a detailed objection both to the report, which
she termed 'ambiguous' for merely explaining the controversies without starting
where the rights and wrongs lay.[37] Among many complaints directed at General
Riley's report was the following:

Article V, paragraph 5 (*c*), stipulated that the Chairman of the Mixed Armistice Commission and the United Nations observers attached to the Commission shall be responsible
for ensuring the full implementation of article V. But the Israel delegation insists that civil
matters concerning the Demilitarized Zone must be settled directly between them and the
Chairman of the Commission; the Mixed Armistice Commission otherwise has nothing to
say on these matters; and, consequently, the Syrian delegation also. General Riley at first
approved the Israel interpretation, but, after meeting with strong opposition from the Syrian
delegation, left to the Chairman the freedom to decide the issue.
The attitude of the Syrian delegation has been and is still the following:

'Article VII, paragraph 7, stated that "claims and complaints presented by either party
relating to the application of this agreement shall be referred immediately to the Mixed
Armistice Commission through its Chairman. The Commission shall take such action on
all such claims or complaints by means of its observation and investigation machinery as
it may deem appropriate, with a view to equitable and mutually satisfactory settlement".'

Accordingly, the interpretation of article V of the Armistice Agreement would fall under
the jurisdiction of the Mixed Armistice Commission. Israel as well as Syria have the equal right
to discuss all civil matters relating to the Demilitarized Zone within the Armistice Commission. There is no clause whatsoever which gives the Israelis a right or a competence that
was not given to Syria. The Chairman of the Commission approves this interpretation and
considers himself a representative of the Syrians and Israelis alike within the Demilitarized
Zone.
As General Riley does not give an opinion on this issue and leaves the responsibility to the
Chairman of the Commission, it is the view of the Syrian Government that the only way
out of this difficulty is to have an official interpretation emanating from the Mixed Armistice
Commission. [*S/2956, Letter from Minister of Foreign Affairs of Syria to the Secretary-
General, 12 Mar. 1953.*]

General Riley had tried to bide a middle course, and stated on 28 May 1951
that as Chairman he, and not the MAC, had general supervision over the
demilitarized zone and thus over the Huleh works; but that Syria might submit

---

[35] S/2833, para. 47.   [36] Ibid.   [37] S/2956, 12 Mar. 1953.

complaints to the MAC concerning the interpretation of Article V of the Armistice and its applicability to the work project.[38]

When General Bennike replaced General Riley shortly thereafter, he was called upon, in his capacity as Chairman of the Israel–Syrian MAC, to decide the legality of certain work begun by Israel on the banks of the Jordan, in the demilitarized zone, which raised many of the same issues. He reported:

3. It has been explained on the Israeli side that the work in question, begun in the central sector of the demilitarized zone, is preliminary to the digging of a canal between the Jordan River and Lake Tiberias. By far the greater part of the canal would be to the west of the demilitarized zone. A reservoir would be constructed at approximately MR 2040–2568 at a height of 40 metres above sea level. A power station would be erected about 2 kilometres west of the mouth of the Jordan, at a height of 200 metres below sea level. The water drop of 240 metres from the reservoir to the power station would generate electric power of '24,000 kilowatts per hour'. The project is sponsored by the Israeli Government Water Planning Authority. I was told that the project was being carried out within the framework of the concession granted on 5 March 1926 to the Palestine Electric Corporation for the utilization of the waters of the Jordan and the Yarmuk for generating and supplying electrical energy.

4. According to article V, paragraph 2, of the General Armistice Agreement, 'the armistice demarcation line and the demilitarized zone have been defined with a view toward separating the armed forces of the two parties in such manner as to minimize the possibility of friction and incident, while providing for the gradual restoration of normal civilian life in the area of the demilitarized zone . . .'

5. In considering the work undertaken in the demilitarized zone with a view to the construction of the projected canal, I have endeavoured to determine:

(a) Whether the work so far performed in the demilitarized zone has interfered with the normal civilian life referred to in article V, paragraph 2, of the General Armistice Agreement, and in the Acting Mediator's statement agreed to by the parties as an authoritative comment on article V;

(b) Whether the construction of the projected canal was likely to interfere with normal civilian life in the demilitarized zone;

(c) Whether the first object of the definition of the demilitarized zone according to article V, paragraph 2, of the General Armistice Agreement, viz., 'separating the armed forces of the two parties in such manner as to minimize the possibility of friction and incident', would be affected by work aimed at diverting a considerable quantity of water from the river-bed in the demilitarized zone.

6. Before making my decision, I have visited both banks of the Jordan, viz., the site of the present Israeli work on the west bank on 12 September, and the east bank on 14 September. I have also carefully considered the views of the two parties to the General Armistice Agreement.

7. The following is the result of my enquiry:

(a) Work has been started on the west bank of the Jordan allegedly on no lands other than Israeli lands, but this is now being disputed. If the investigation by United Nations observers of land titles in the possession of Arabs or in the Land Office at Safad in Israel proves Arab ownership, work started on Arab lands without the consent of the owners would be contrary to the provision relating to normal civilian life. Moreover, work in the bed of the river has resulted in flooding partially the small island at MR 2088–2675. In this case also the question of ownership is in dispute.

(b) On 14 September, I was shown on the east bank two Arab water-mills which had ceased to work owing to lack of water and an Arab land which had ceased to be irrigated. Though

---

[38] S/4270, 23 Feb. 1960. In practice, the general tendency of ensuing Chairmen of the MAC has been to treat the Chairman alone as competent for civilian matters in the demilitarized zone; while allowing some authority to the MAC in respect of armed disputes in the zone. For detailed examples see Bar-Yaacov, pp. 98–100.

I was not present when the mills ceased to work and the land to be irrigated, the explanation given, that lack of water resulted from Israeli work in the bed of the river, appeared to me, after a rapid investigation, plausible.

(c) As regards the likelihood of interference with normal civilian life in the demilitarized zone resulting from the construction of the projected canal, the lowering of the waters of the Jordan will affect the life of the Arab villagers depending on the river. It will, in particular, interfere with the working of the water-mills (nine at present) which they use.

(d) In this connection, the question of the irrigation of lands belonging to Syrian land-owners is of particular importance. The Israeli Government is aware of this problem. The rich lands of Buteiha Farm, with their three annual crops, depend on an elaborate irrigation system. In October 1951, during a two-day test by the Israelis of checking-gates south of Lake Huleh, that irrigation system lost 70 per cent of its water. In April 1952, after emergency repairs to Banat Ya'coub Bridge, during which the checking-gates had been operated with the agreement of both Parties, the Chairman of the Mixed Armistice Commission, in view of strong representations from the owners of Buteiha Farm, withdrew his concurrence to further use of the checking-gates until another agreement was reached by the two Parties. The Government of Israel has stated that the full volume of Jordan water now being used by Arab landowners for irrigation purposes would be assured. The Syrians object to the irriga-tion of their lands depending in the future on Israeli good will. Irrespective of that Syrian point of view, it may be said that the waters in the bed of the river are already very low during the dry season and it is probable that, unless special arrangements are made, the pro-jected canal and power station would sometimes leave the Jordan with very little, if any, water.

(e) As regards the military aspect of the question, the Jordan, in its deep valley, is a serious obstacle for any troops, particularly motorized troops, which would attempt to cross it. A party to the General Armistice Agreement which, by means of a canal, could control the flow of the Jordan in the demilitarized zone, changing it or possibly even drying it up at will, could alter the value to the other party of the demilitarized zone, which has been 'defined with a view towards separating the armed forces of the two Parties in such manner as to minimize the possibility of friction and incident . . .'

8. In view of the above, both on the basis of the protection of normal civilian life in the area of the demilitarized zone and of the value of the zone to both parties for the separation of their armed forces, I do not consider that a party should, in the absence of an agreement, carry out in the demilitarized zone work prejudicing the objects of the demilitarized zone, as stated in article V, paragraph 2, of the General Armistice Agreement.

9. Acting under the provisions of article V of the General Armistice Agreement, the only provisions which, as Chairman of the Mixed Armistice Commission, I am called upon to consider in this case, I request the Israeli Government to ensure that the authority which started work in the demilitarized zone on 2 September 1953 is instructed to cease working in the zone so long as an agreement is not arranged.   [S/3122, Report of Chief of Staff of UNTSO to Secretary-General, 23 Oct. 1953.]

Israel informed General Bennike that she thought this decision was 'at marked variance with the position so far maintained by the competent organs of the United Nations as regards works of this nature in the demilitarized zone'.[39] The Israeli Foreign Minister referred once again to Ralph Bunche's oft-quoted comment of 26 June 1949 that 'the demilitarized zone will not be a vacuum or wasteland'. General Bennike replied[40] that his fear was that the water project might interfere with some Arab lands 'which for many years have depended on the water of the Jordan for irrigation, [and now] might become, in the Acting Mediator's words 'a vacuum or wasteland'. An exchange now occurred between

[39] S/3122, 23 Oct. 1953, ann. II, para. 2.   [40] Ibid. ann. III, para. 2.

Israel and General Bennike as to the degree of legal authority which attached to the latter's decision. Israel stated:

10. It remains the firm policy of the Government of Israel to adhere strictly to its obligations under the Armistice Agreement.

In stating its views on the issue which has arisen, the Government of Israel does not depart from its conception of the powers and functions of the Chairman of the Mixed Armistice Commission under the terms of the Israel–Syria General Armistice Agreement. The Israel Government's understanding in this regard was formulated by its representative, Ambassador A. Eban, at the 547th meeting of the Security Council on 18 May 1951 in the following terms:

'. . . the Chairman of the Mixed Armistice Commission is not an authority appointed by the United Nations and imposed over the signatories of the Agreement. He is an organ established as a result of their agreement and his functions are precisely those which they have defined. If either party had not wished the Chairman to have certain functions, then he would not have had them. This fact, together with the specific provision that he may not exercise administrative responsibilities anywhere, rules out any idea that he should operate by mandatory requests directed to the very Governments which have defined his functions and which are presumably, therefore, in a position to know what powers they have conceded to him.'

11. I am confident that you will give the considerations set forth in this letter your very serious attention and shall be glad to receive your comments on them.
Jerusalem, 24 September 1953

> (*Signed*) Moshe SHARETT
> *Minister for Foreign Affairs*

[*Ibid. ann.* II.]

The Chief of Staff rejoined:

10. I welcome the statement that 'it remains the firm policy of the Government of Israel to adhere strictly to its obligations under the Armistice Agreement'. You refer at the same time to your Government's conception of the powers and functions of the Chairman of the Mixed Armistice Commission under the terms of the Armistice Agreement. You quote, in this connection, a passage from the Israel representative's statement at the 547th meeting of the Security Council on 18 May 1951. I quite agree that, as stated by Ambassador A. Eban, 'if either party had not wished the Chairman to have certain functions, then he would not have had them'. I am sure, however, that this cannot be taken to imply that it remains for either party to decide whether the Chairman acts in conformity or not with the functions conferred upon him by both parties. That would mean anarchy in the demilitarized zone, in which both Parties have agreed to confer special powers upon the Chairman under the provisions of article V of the Armistice Agreement. If there is a difference in the interpretation of these provisions, the two Parties have provided a remedy. Article V is not one of the articles which the Mixed Armistice Commission may not interpret, since article VII, paragraph 8, reads as follows:

'8. Where interpretation of the meaning of a particular provision of this Agreement, other than the preamble and article I and II, is at issue, the Commission's interpretation shall prevail. The Commission, in its discretion and as the need arises, may from time to time recommend to the parties modifications in the provisions of this Agreement.'

With regard to the idea, ruled out by your representative, that the Chairman of the Mixed Armistice Commission should operate by 'mandatory requests' directed to the very Governments which have defined his functions, I should like to point out that the Chairman has been operating by 'requests' in the past and that, apart from the objection raised by your representative in the passage you have quoted, there has been neither on the Israeli side nor on the Syrian side any objection in principle to such procedure. My predecessor, in his reports to the Security Council, has mentioned that such requests have been made from time to time. I shall give only two instances, which refer to the period following Ambassador A. Eban's statement. On 7 August 1951, General Riley wrote a letter to Your Excellency which is reproduced in his report to the Security Council dated 16 August 1951 (S/2300, para. 7). At that time, the Palestine Land Development Company, in the course of the execution of the Huleh drainage scheme, was contemplating the employing of a survey team on the east bank of the Jordan, south of Lake Huleh, and the emplacing between the two banks of a dam which, according to information received, would stop the flow of the river between Lake Huleh and Lake Tiberias about five days a week for a considerable period of time. The last paragraph of the letter which my predecessor wrote in this connection to Your Excellency reads as follows:

'Therefore, in view of the responsibility given to the Chairman of the Mixed Armistice Commission by article V of the General Armistice Agreement and in accordance with instructions contained in the Security Council resolution S/2157 dated 18 May 1951, which authorizes the Chief of Staff to take such measures to restore peace in the area and to make such representation to the Governments of Israel and Syria as he may deem necessary, and further, in view of the consultations on outstanding problems envisaged in Mr Eban's letter to me of 4 August 1951, I urge strongly that the Palestine Land Development Company be restrained from dispatching a survey team to the east bank of the Jordan and from proceeding with the proposed emplacing of the dam across the Jordan.'

There was, it seems, no objection to his issuing such request. It was apparently complied with, since the following paragraph of his report (para. 8) states:

'I have just been informed that the Palestine Land Development Company has submitted a project which, it is claimed, can be carried out without encroaching on the east bank of the Jordan and interfering with normal irrigation.'

I will give another instance, that of the test of the checking-gates south of Lake Huleh, on 8 and 9 October 1951. In this connection, General Riley has reported to the Security Council as follows (para. 22 of his report dated 6 November 1951 (S/2389)):

'The water loss in the irrigation system of Buteiha Farm (in Syrian territory) was estimated by United Nations observers to have been as much as 70 per cent. The test was terminated and the project to reduce the flow by means of the checking-gate abandoned. It is a matter of satisfaction that, in this case, requests to cease the operations made by the Chairman were immediately complied with.'

11. The above are the comments you had requested on the considerations you have set forth. I apologize for their length. I have, however, thought it necessary to explain as fully as possible the motives of my decision, especially in view of the fact that the issue has been submitted to the Security Council.

> (*Signed*) Vagn BENNIKE
> *Chief of Staff*

Jerusalem, 20 October 1953

[*Ibid. ann. III.*]

The matter was taken to the Security Council. Various views were expressed there,[41] and Israel agreed to stop work pending the Council's investigation (S/3128). The three major Western Powers on the Council would have been content to allow the Chief of Staff to permit continuation of the work after examination by experts of all the data. The Soviet Union insisted that agreement by Syria was necessary. Israel contended that the Huleh project was a clear precedent.[42] Whether the Huleh case was indeed quite parallel turned, in large

---

[41] *SCOR*, mtgs in Oct., Nov., and Dec. 1953; and Jan. 1954.
[42] 'Mr Eban claimed . . . If Syria's objections to work in the demilitarized zone were rejected in 1951, then equally they could not be accepted with regard to work in the demilitarized zone leading to power and irrigation development outside the zone' (Bar-Yaacov, p. 124).

part, upon whether the Chief of Staff's assessment was correct that in this case the matter *could* have military advantages for Israel. Israel urged that under a permanent Armistice, when she was committed to peace, this should not be the pivotal point; and the French delegate declared that it would be an unfortunate thing 'if a region's future and economic development were to be decided by theoretical military exercises carried out on maps'.[43] On 22 January 1954 voting took place upon a resolution drafted by the Western Powers: for the first time on the Arab–Israel question the Soviet Union cast her veto. This may be said to mark a turning point, in so far as from that time forward Syria has been guaranteed Soviet protection in the Security Council both in cases such as this —where there was much merit in both sides of the argument—and on occasions when the great majority of the Council have felt a clear breach of the Armistice to have been caused by Syria.

During 1954 and 1955 there was no change in the situation, and relations between the UN and the two parties remained much the same. The disputes over the activities of the Israeli police in the demilitarized zone, the competence of the MAC in respect of that zone, and about the Huleh and Jordan Canal projects continued: and the MAC was unable to hold regular meetings since June 1951. Both sides continued to inscribe complaints for discussion at 'the next formal meeting of the Mixed Armistice Commission'—well knowing that the inflexibility of their positions was preventing any meetings from being called. Thus by December 1955 there were outstanding for the next 'formal meeting' 568 Syrian and 401 Israeli complaints. And by 1956 even 'emergency meetings' were no longer resorted to. To a considerable extent 'the traditional Mixed Armistice Commission procedure of formal discussion has broken down. It has been replaced with more or less success by informal conversations. . . .'[44]

Relations 1956–7

In July 1957 Colonel Leary, the then Acting Chief of Staff, found it necessary to enter a detailed report on the problems being presented by the parties to UN observers

5. While . . . United Nations observers' movements in the demilitarized zone have been restricted from time to time in the past, it can be said that generally until June 1956 observers circulated freely in the zone either on routine visits or for investigation purposes.

6. In the early part of June 1956, difficulties were experienced in connection with the investigation of a Syrian complaint regarding the erection of fortifications in the Israel settlement of Hagovrim in the central sector of the demilitarized zone and at Susita in the southern sector. Observers were first refused entrance to Hagovrim and Susita and were allowed to proceed with the investigations only after a delay of several days. Since then, United Nations observers have been prevented from carrying out investigations in these two areas (see para. 13 below).

7. On 30 October 1956, when the Israel military action in Egypt had started, the Chairman of the Israel–Syrian Mixed Armistice Commission was advised by the Israel delegation that the demilitarized zones, including the western approach of the Banat Ya'coub bridge, had been mined. From that date on, for the most part requests to enter the central demilitarized

---

[43] *SCOR*, 648th mtg.

[44] S/3516, Report of Chief of Staff of UNTSO to Secretary-General, 20 Dec. 1955.

zone were refused and attempts to proceed with routine visits or investigations were stopped by Israel police, who prevented United Nations observers from entering the central demilitarized zone except on the road from Rosh Pina in Israel-controlled territory to the Israel police post at Mishmar Hayarden in the demilitarized zone. Exceptions to this restriction have occurred, in particular recently, in connection with visits to the new Huleh bridge—during which United Nations observers meet now with no difficulties—and the investigation of one incident on 16 June 1957 (the death of an Israel engineer, shot on the western bank of the Jordan, allegedly by a Syrian sniper). Besides Hagovrim and Susita, access to Dardara in the central sector of the demilitarized zone has continued to be denied to the observers and to the Acting Chief of Staff of the United Nations Truce Supervision Organization. In the southern sector, observers were not able to proceed with an investigation in Ein Gev on 28 May 1957.

8. On 2 November 1956, the Syrian delegation to the Israel–Syrian Mixed Armistice Commission submitted a complaint alleging that on 30 October 1956, 103 inhabitants of Baqqara and Channame villages in the central sector of the demilitarized zone were forced by the Israel authorities to take refuge in Syria; that they were forced at gun point to leave their homes and lands; that their houses were burned and that some of them were taken to Sha'b in Israel territory. The Chief of Staff of Truce Supervision Organization was requested to intervene in order to permit the return of the inhabitants to their villages. United Nations observers were unable to carry out an investigation on the spot owing to the refusal of the Israel authorities to let them enter the central sector of the demilitarized zone.

9. The Syrian authorities do not refuse to let United Nations observers enter the demilitarized zone for investigations or routine visits after their identity has been checked on the Syrian side of the boundary. Occasionally, however, an investigation or a routine visit may be delayed. The investigation of five Israel complaints alleging the existence of fortifications and the presence of a Syrian Army unit in the Al Hamma portion of the southern sector of the demilitarized zone in violation of the General Armistice Agreement was deferred several days, owing to delay in securing a Syrian liaison officer to accompany United Nations military observers in the area along the international boundary where circulation is controlled.

10. In a conversation in Damascus on 12 June 1957, the Syrian Army Chief of Staff assured the Acting Chief of Staff of the Truce Supervision Organization that action would be taken to eliminate delays in securing Syrian liaison officers to accompany United Nations observers in the area along the international boundary. [S/3844, Report of Acting Chief of Staff to Secretary-General, 1 July 1957.]

At this time the Acting Chief of Staff made certain suggestions for the more effective implementation of the Armistice.[45] These included the posting of some observers on a 24-hour basis in certain portions of the demilitarized zone:

2. On 25 July 1957, the Acting Chief of Staff advised the Government of Israel through the Director of Armistice Affairs, Israel Foreign Ministry, of the Truce Supervision Organization's intention to establish an observation post near the newly erected bridge at the outlet of Lake Huleh (MR 20915–27175), in the central sector of the demilitarized zone. The Acting Chief of Staff considers that such an observation post would be desirable to reduce the risks of incidents especially during the final stages of the Huleh reclamation project. Tension had in particular been created on 23 July 1957 when Israel workmen, without prior notice to the Truce Supervision Organization, reduced temporarily the flow of the Jordan river by an estimated 50 to 66 per cent, by erecting a dam just north of the Huleh bridge. (According to an Israel engineer, it has been necessary to raise the water level of Lake Huleh in order to operate a floating dredge.) Also, United Nations military observers reported on 21 and 22 July 1957 the presence of Israel soldiers and military equipment within the demilitarized zone. Furthermore, Syria alleged that military activity had been observed on 23 July 1957 in the vicinity of the Huleh bridge.

[45] See below, pp. 186–7.

3. On 26 July, the Acting Chief of Staff was informed by the Director of Armistice Affairs Israel Foreign Ministry, that in Israel's view the terms of the General Armistice Agreement did not entitle the Truce Supervision Organization to act in the demilitarized zone without Israel's consent and that the Truce Supervision Organization's announcement of its intention to establish an observation post near Huleh bridge—without requesting permission from the Israel Government—was not in conformity with the General Armistice Agreement. Consequently, the Israel Government would not consider the announcement. In addition to these legal considerations, the Director of Armistice Affairs stated that in the view of the Government of Israel there was no present need for an observation post near the Huleh bridge since that area was visited twice a day by United Nations military observers.

4. It is apparent that the position of the Israel Government in this matter is closely linked to her claim to sovereignty over the demilitarized zone. (See in this connection paragraphs 6 and following of Major-General Burns' report of 11 January 1955 (S/3343).)

5. The Acting Chief of Staff, UNTSO, believes that the establishment of an observation post, operating on a twenty-four-hour basis, in the vicinity of the newly erected Huleh bridge would contribute to the maintenance of tranquillity in that area by rendering surveillance more effective, and that it would facilitate the implementation of article V of the General Armistice Agreement for which the Chairman of the Israel–Syrian Mixed Armistice Commission and the military observers are responsible. Such a post would complement advantageously the planned observation post in the Mishmar Hayarden area mentioned in paragraph 23, the report of the Chief of Staff (S/3844). To date no reply has been received to request of the Truce Supervision Organization for lodging and facilities in the latter area.

6. In view of Israel's opposition to the establishment of the observation post in the area of the new Huleh bridge, the Acting Chief of Staff, in a further effort to improve surveillance in that area and as a practical measure, directed, on 27 July 1957, United Nations military observers through the Chairman of the Israel–Syrian Mixed Armistice Commission, to extend the duration of their stay in that area during their twice-a-day visits. The observers were unable to carry out these instructions because of objections on the part of the Israel authorities who stated that they could see no present need for such a measure. [S/3844/Add 1, Addendum to Acting Chief of Staff's Report, 7 Aug. 1957.]

ii. The Egypt–Israel Armistice

Relations 1949–56

Although no difficulties in UN–host state relations occurred in the early phase of the Egypt–Israel Armistice Agreement, the familiar pattern of non-participation in armistice organs began gradually to appear:

4. The emergency meeting, held on 4 May 1952, was convened by the Chairman of the Mixed Armistice Commission in order to discuss ways for improving the general situation along the Armistice Demarcation Line which had deteriorated seriously during the previous months. The Mixed Armistice Commission had not functioned since its 38th formal meeting held on 3 October 1951. Although contact was maintained through weekly meetings of a sub-committee composed of delegates of each party and a United Nations representative, the failure to hold formal meetings was one of the causes of deterioration in the situation.

5. At the emergency meeting on 4 May 1952, proposals for action to be taken by both parties to prevent the recurrence of incidents were considered. An understanding was also concluded on the principle of reinstating mixed patrols along the Armistice Demarcation Line. The manner in which this last agreement should be carried out was referred to the sub-committee for discussion. Up to the present date, however, no practical arrangement has been reached for its implementation.

6. The 39th formal meeting was held in two sessions, on 26 August and 9 September, 1952. Three hundred and fourteen complaints had accumulated on the agenda of this first formal meeting held by the Mixed Armistice Commission in over ten months. After discussion

at the first session of the meeting of a proposal made by the Israel delegation that all complaints on the agenda should be filed without further deliberations, it was agreed unanimously at the second session that all complaints on the agenda, which by then totalled 324, were 'to be considered as acted upon by the Mixed Armistice Commission and to be filed'. These included all the complaints mentioned in paragraph 1 which the parties had desired to place on the agenda (295), together with twenty-nine outstanding complaints submitted prior to 1 November 1951.

7. An informal agreement was also concluded that no further complaints would be brought before the Mixed Armistice Commission by either party and that direct and frequent contacts between representatives of both sides would be established. . . . [S/2833, *Report of Chief of Staff, 4 Nov. 1952.*]

The Egyptian delegation now appealed against certain decisions, and the appeal was placed on the draft agenda of the Special Committee. But though 'Repeated efforts have been made to convene a meeting of the Special Committee to consider these appeals, which are from decisions taken by the Mixed Armistice Commission between May and October 1951 . . . no date has been found mutually acceptable to the parties'.[46] The MAC did continue to function, however.

In 1954 the Chief of Staff suggested:

(*a*) Patrolling sensitive sections of the demarcation line by joint patrols consisting of military vehicles from each party and from the United Nations;

(*b*) Negotiation of a local commanders' agreement, generally along the lines of the Israel–Jordan Local Commanders Agreement in force prior to 1 June 1954. . . . [S/3319, *Report of Chief of Staff, 11 Nov. 1954.*]

Shortly after, the MAC prepared a draft of methods which would improve the situation.

Annex VIII

Egyptian–Israeli Mixed Armistice Commission
Arrangements for the Purpose of Preventing Incidents in the Gaza Area

1 February 1955

Draft

1. The purpose of these arrangements is to prevent, to the greatest extent possible, the unauthorized crossing of the demarcation line between Egyptian-controlled territory and Israel-controlled territory and breaches of the General Armistice Agreement.

2. Both parties shall issue strict orders to the responsible local authorities, both police and military, to suppress illegal crossing of the demarcation line.

3. The authorities of both parties, on information submitted by either party, shall investigate and take action against infiltrators and their accomplices according to their national laws.

4. The parties agree that only well trained and disciplined regular military or police personnel will be employed in a zone one kilometre wide on either side of the demarcation line.

5. Each party shall nominate a senior officer to represent it at meetings with the other party in furtherance of these arrangements. This representative shall be vested with authority to ensure the required action on the part of the military and police forces who are responsible

[46] S/2833, 4 Nov. 1952.

for the security of the areas adjoining the demarcation line and for preventing unauthorized crossing of the demarcation line.

6. (*a*) Periodic meetings shall take place between representatives of both parties at kilometre 95 or at a mutually agreed point to co-ordinate their efforts to combat infiltration and to co-operate on all matters regarding border relations. By mutual agreement, the representatives can meet at other places than the usual place or proceed to such other places as their respective duties require.

(*b*) Persons who cross the demarcation line between Egyptian-controlled territory and Israel-controlled territory, and who commit an offence against the laws of the party into whose territory they have penetrated and are convicted by due legal powers, shall be handed back to the authorities of their own country at a representatives' meeting, after they have served their sentences.

(*c*) Persons who cross the demarcation line, but who are not charged with committing any offence, shall be handed back to the authorities of their own country at representatives' meetings.

(*d*) Members of the security forces or civilians who cross the demarcation line in error shall be returned immediately.

(*e*) Recovered stolen property shall be handed back to the party from whose territory it was stolen within 48 hours.

7. Complaints shall be handed in to the Mixed Armistice Commission by either party according to normal procedure; however, both parties agree to keep complaints at a minimum by attempting to settle minor incidents at the local representatives' level.

8. When a local representatives' meeting is scheduled and one local representative cannot attend, he will make every effort to give the Mixed Armistice Commission notice 24 hours prior to the scheduled time of the meeting.

9. These arrangements, upon signature of the parties concerned, are valid for a period of one year from the date of signature, but either party may withdraw on giving one month's notice. Discussions on the extension of these arrangements will begin one month prior to their expiration.

10. Additions and amendments to these arrangements may be made before their expiry by unanimous consent of the two parties if above-mentioned additions or amendments are placed in an official document signed by both parties.

....
Senior Egyptian delegate   *Senior Israel delegate*
    Witnessed by: ....

Chairman,
Egyptian–Israeli Mixed
Armistice Commission

[*S/3373, Report of Chief of Staff of UNTSO, 17 Mar. 1955.*]

The Chief of Staff later reported that, so far as his own suggestion of the institution of joint patrols was concerned 'Egypt is prepared in principle to set these up; I have not yet received the final reply from the Israel authorities.'[47]

Relations 1956–67

Although UNTSO retains a separate identity from UNEF, the issues affecting these two bodies became so closely intertwined after the Suez intervention that much of the relevant material is subsumed under Part II on UNEF (below, pp. 219–529).

Even prior to Suez Israel's attitude towards Egyptian implementation of

[47] S/3390, Report of Chief of Staff, 14 Apr. 1955.

Article 1 of the Armistice Agreement was having repercussions upon the convening of the MAC:

2. On 5 July 1956 the Chairman of the Egypt–Israel Mixed Armistice Commission was informed by the Senior Israel Delegate that movement of United Nations military observers in the El Auja demilitarized zone would be restricted to the use of the road from Beersheba, through the demilitarized zone, to the Mixed Armistice Commission Headquarters; and that no movement on other roads would be allowed in the demilitarized zone, and radio messages sent would be restricted to administrative reports.

3. The Chief of Staff protested against this decision to the Minister for Foreign Affairs, pointing out that 'in its resolution of 4 June 1956 (*S/3605*), the Security Council has declared "that full freedom of movement of United Nations observers must be respected along the armistice demarcation lines, in the demilitarized zones and in the defensive areas, as defined in the armistice agreements, to enable them to fulfil their functions"'. The Chief of Staff requested the Israel Government to reconsider its decision, as an action of this kind would constitute a further step in the process of non-compliance with the provisions of article VIII relating to the demilitarized zone and the duties of United Nations military observers in that zone.

4. On 17 July 1956, the Chief of Staff received a reply from the Ministry for Foreign Affairs of Israel contending that in their conversations with the Secretary-General (in the month of April) it was recognized that articles VII and VIII of the General Armistice Agreement were not operative as long as Egypt did not implement article I in all four of its sections, and that in default of such implementation, Israel did not regard itself as bound by article VIII. Therefore, the presence of United Nations observers in the Nitzana (El Auja) area was, in the view of the Israel Government, altogether superfluous.

5. The letter also referred to the refusal of the Egyptian authorities to allow United Nations military observers to investigate complaints of the infringement of article VIII paragraph 3 in the area between the line El Qusaima—Abu'Aweig'ila and the International Frontier, implying that the restrictions imposed by the two Parties were on a par. In fact, article VIII paragraph 1 gives the Chairman and observers of the Egyptian–Israel Mixed Armistice Commission a responsibility in regard to the demilitarized zone which they do not have in regard to the area on the other side of the international frontier.

6. The view was further expressed that 'Israel cannot be regarded as an "extra-territorial" area where United Nations observers are not subject to the laws of the State. Outside of the duties they are required to discharge under the armistice agreement, they should not claim any special rights'. This presumably refers to paragraph 5 of the Security Council resolution of 4 June 1956 (*S/3605*).

7. The matter was discussed during the talks between the Prime Minister and Foreign Minister of Israel and the Secretary-General and the Chief of Staff on 20 July 1956. Finally, at a meeting with the Chief of Staff on 3 September 1956, the Prime Minister of Israel maintained the viewpoints set forth above. He indicated that since the demilitarized zone was now occupied by Israel military forces, it served no purpose to have United Nations military observers there.

8. In the view of the Chief of Staff, irrespective of the lack of compliance with articles VII and VIII of the General Armistice Agreement by both Egypt and Israel (see annex 5 to the Secretary-General's report of 9 May 1956 (*S/3596*)), the maintenance of observers in the El Auja demilitarized zone, with freedom of movement and to transmit messages to the Chairman of the Egypt–Israel Mixed Armistice Commission and the United Nations Truce Supervision Organization by the speediest means, is essential in order to fulfil the duties imposed on the United Nations Truce Supervision Organization by paragraphs 3 and 5 of the Security Council resolution of 4 June 1956 (*S/3605*). The strategic importance of the roads radiating from El Auja is such that if one side or the other should contemplate aggression on a large scale against the territory of the other, primary or secondary lines of operations would

certainly be established through the demilitarized zone. If either side entered the demilitarized zone with forces on an offensive scale, this would be *prima facie* evidence of aggression. The presence of United Nations military observers, therefore, is a deterrent against aggression and their withdrawal from the area would be a removal of this deterrent.

9. El Auja is not only the centre of the demilitarized zone, as defined in paragraph 2, article VIII of the armistice agreement. It is also, under article X, paragraph 2, the headquarters of the Mixed Armistice Commission. Because of her military occupation of the demilitarized zone, Israel refuses access to El Auja to the Egyptian members of the Mixed Armistice Commission. Article X, paragraph 2, also stipulates that the Mixed Armistice Commission shall hold its meetings at such places and such times as it may deem necessary for the effective conduct of its work. The Egyptian Authorities have not accepted the Israel refusal to allow the Mixed Armistice Commission to hold meetings at its headquarters. They have proposed that the Mixed Armistice Commission should hold every other meeting at El Auja. Meetings of the Mixed Armistice Commission—ordinary or emergency—have not been resumed. Complaints by either party are being investigated when an investigation is requested. The fact that the complaints are no longer considered in the Mixed Armistice Commission greatly increases the responsibility of the United Nations Truce Supervision Organization Chief of Staff and his representative, the Chairman of the Mixed Armistice Commission, for observing the maintenance of the cease-fire by the two parties.

10. At his meeting with the Chief of Staff on 3 September 1956, Mr Ben-Gurion repeated his refusal to allow meetings of the Mixed Armistice Commission at El Auja, stating that article VIII of the General Armistice Agreement and the provision in article X paragraph 2 relating to the headquarters of the Mixed Armistice Commission, were in suspension owing to Egypt's non-compliance with article I and the Security Council resolution of 1 September 1951 concerning interference with the passage through the Suez Canal of shipping bound for Israel. No Egyptians could now be allowed in the El Auja area for security reasons. He was willing, however, to have the Mixed Armistice Commission meet at other places. [*S/3659, Report of 12 Sept. 1956 by the Secretary-General to the Security Council pursuant to the resolutions of 4 Apr. 1956 and 4 June 1956*, pp. 59–60.]

After the Anglo-French–Israeli intervention in Suez in 1956, Israel declared that she no longer regarded herself as bound by the Israel–Egypt Armistice Agreement. This denunciation of the Armistice Agreement inevitably posed very acute problems for the UN. Although the latter did not accept Israel's denunciation, it nevertheless became politic for the UN to deal with Israel as much as possible via UNEF,[48] rather than UNTSO, on the Egyptian frontier. Mr Abba Eban explained the Israeli position:

171. Egypt, by its repeated assertions over the years that a state of war exists between it and Israel, has distorted the motive and purpose of the General Armistice Agreement, which, as stated in the agreement itself five times, is the restoration of permanent peace. Egypt has used this agreement, conceived as a transition to permanent peace, as a cover for murderous attacks against the population of Israel and for a relentless siege of the country by land, sea and air. Week after week and month after month, specially trained units of the Egyptian army known as *fedayeen* have entered Israel territory for murder and sabotage. Egypt has organized and directed similar gangs in other Arab countries for action against Israel. Egypt has closed the Gulf of Elath and the Suez Canal to Israel shipping. Egypt maintains a complete economic boycott against Israel, and by threat and intimidation presses commercial interests throughout the world to abstain from legitimate trade with Israel.

172. Moreover, in preparation for an all-out attempt to eliminate Israel by force, Egypt has concluded military alliances with Israel's neighbours. Egypt has contravened her solemn obligation under the United Nations Charter, under the Constantinople Convention of 1888,

[48] For the details of UN–Israel relations in respect of UNEF, see below, pp. 385–406.

and under the Security Council's resolutions of 1 September 1951 (*S/2322*) and 13 October 1956 (*S/3675*) with reference to the Suez Canal. By this and other hostile acts, Egypt has undermined the peace and deprived the armistice agreement of all its functions. The armistice agreement has, under this policy, become a fiction to which Egypt still pays lip-service in so far as it thinks this may serve a destructive design. Thus, a return to the armistice agreement would be a return to a system which has served as a cover for the victimization, the boycott and the blockade of Israel and for a policy aimed at Israel's ultimate annihilation. Moreover, Egypt interprets that agreement in terms of belligerency.

173. Egypt having thus destroyed the armistice agreement, the Government of Israel suggests that paragraph 2 of the General Assembly resolution adopted on 2 November (*997 (ES-I)*) does not serve the basic purpose of the United Nations as expressed in its Charter, to maintain international peace and security, to develop friendly relations amongst nations and to achieve international co-operation in solving international problems. Moreover, Egypt interprets the armistice as a state of war, and it cannot be the function of the General Assembly to promote or to foster a system of war.

174. Accordingly, the Government of Israel feels that the only answer to this situation is the establishment of peace between Israel and Egypt by direct negotiations between the two countries, and it notifies the General Assembly that it would welcome the immediate opening of negotiations to that end, for which it is prepared forthwith to send representatives for discussions with Egypt. Israel would also welcome similar negotiations with the Governments of other Arab States.

175. The crucial question with which, in the interests of all the world's peoples, the Egyptian Government must be confronted is: does it want peace or war? Israel appeals to the United Nations to lend its entire authority to the establishment of a freely negotiated peace between the Governments and peoples of the Middle East. [*GAOR, 1st emerg. spec. sess., 563rd mtg.*][49]

On 7 November Mr Krishna Menon informed the special session of the Assembly that a memorandum had come into his hands, which read:

'United Nations Secretary-General Dag Hammarskjold today received a cablegram from Major-General E. L. M. Burns, Chief of Staff of the United Nations Truce Supervision Organization, stating that Israel military units this morning were expected to make "a raid" on the Truce Supervision Organization Headquarters in Gaza. General Burns reported that Colonel R. F. Bayard, Chairman of the Israel–Egyptian Mixed Armistice Commission, had sent messages stating that the Israelis were reported intending to seize his radio transmitter but leave the receiver and to restrict all observers and jeeps to the Mixed Armistice Commission compound; also, that food purchases may be restricted.

'General Burns reported that the last transmission received from Colonel Bayard indicated that he did not expect to be able to re-establish connexions. He added that it is presumed that the Israelis forced their way into the Mixed Armistice Commission House to accomplish their mission. He did not expect UNTSO personnel would be harmed. When this information was conveyed to the foreign press, General Burns reported that it was held up by the Israel censor.

'Secretary-General Hammarskjold made an immediate strong *démarche* to the representative of Israel for prompt transmittal to his Government.

'Previously, on 3 November, the Israel Government requested the withdrawal of the personnel of UNTSO from Gaza and Beersheba.'

'The memorandum goes on to say':

'In a reply of 4 November, the Israel Foreign Ministry referred to the statement by the Israel representative before the General Assembly . . . to the effect that the General Armistice Agreement had become a fiction and was no longer valid. . . .

[49] Confirmed in A/3279, *aide-mémoire* to Secretary-General, 4 Nov. 1956.

'On 6 November, Colonel Nursella of the Israel Ministry of Foreign Affairs, informed General Burns that the Government of Israel "required" the withdrawal of UNTSO personnel from the Gaza and Beersheba areas and that instructions to this effect had been issued to the army commanders concerned. When General Burns asked for clarification of these statements, Colonel Nursella replied that Israel had not intended to imply that force would be used relative to the withdrawal of UNTSO personnel from Gaza and Beersheba. Colonel Nursella added that the UNTSO would have to abide by the regulations of the Israel military governor and would be asked not to use the United Nations radio station, and so on.' [*GAOR, 1st emerg. spec. sess, 567th mtg,* para. 209.]

The Secretary-General immediately replied that, 'I think the matter is better handled in regular diplomatic and administrative forms'.[50] Further, General Burns had now reported:

The representative of the Israel Government called and tendered apologies on behalf of the Government for the action taken in the forcible closing of the radio station at Gaza. He stated that, through a misunderstanding of his instructions, the officer in Gaza had exceeded his authority and taken action which was not intended. The forcible closing of the radio station in Gaza was never the intention of the military authorities. He informed me that orders had been given by General Dayan that the radio transmitter will be replaced at once, and that the station can continue to be used. [*Ibid.*]

The Secretary-General had already reported that General Burns had informed him that the Ministry of Foreign Affairs in Egypt had notified him that the

General Armistice Agreement had become a fiction and no longer had validity. The Government did not intend to return to the General Armistice Agreement with Egypt. United Nations Truce Supervision Organization personnel had no function to perform in Gaza or Beersheba and I was asked to give orders for their withdrawal. In his reply dated 4 November, General Burns referred to the instructions of the Secretary-General (see A/3267, para. 7), and stated that in view of his instructions he was unable to accede to the demand for withdrawal. General Burns added that if the Government of Israel disagreed with his decision their representative might be instructed to take up the matter with the Secretary-General. General Burns also informed the Secretary-General that the Israel prohibition of United Nations military observers entering the Gaza area was put into effect on 4 November, when two military observers were refused entrance. A convoy of the United Nations Relief and Works Agency for Palestine Refugees in the Near East over the road from Lydda arrived at Gaza at 16.00 GMT. [*A/3284, 2nd Report of Secretary-General submitted in pursuance of Res. 997 (ES-1),* para. 5, *4 Nov. 1956.*]

(It is interesting to note that Israel was in 1967 to repeat, in virtually identical terms, arguments for the denunciation of the Armistice Agreements—though on this latter occasion Israel declared dead not only the Agreement with Egypt but also those with her other Arab neighbours. As in 1956, Israel contended that the Arab countries were seeking the benefits of the Armistice while totally rejecting their own duties thereunder; and that it was necessary to move on to a permanent peace in the Middle East. In 1956 the Secretary-General indicated that, from the UN perspective, the Armistice Agreement continued in force. After the June war of 1967 the UN itself was very cautious about pronouncing on the continued validity of the Armistice Agreements: and a case can be made for asserting that they are no longer in effect.)

[50] *GAOR,* 1st emerg. spec. sess., 567th mtg, para. 214.

In January 1957 the Secretary-General presented a detailed report which dealt with this question, among others:

15. In its first article, the Armistice Agreement between Egypt and Israel provides that no aggressive action by the armed forces—land, sea, or air—of either party shall be undertaken, planned or threatened against the people or the armed forces of the other. The same article establishes the right of each party to its security and freedom from fear of attack by the armed forces of the other. This article assimilates the Armistice Agreement to a non-aggression pact, providing for mutual and full abstention from belligerent acts. A restoration of relations between the parties, more stable than those now prevailing, can therefore be based on a reaffirmation of this article of the Armistice Agreement. It is natural to envisage that such a reaffirmation should extend also to other clauses of the Armistice Agreement, especially to those in which the substance has an immediate bearing on the state of tension prevailing at the outbreak of the crisis. The Secretary-General, in this context, wishes to draw attention specifically to articles VII and VIII, which provide for restrictions on the deployment of the military forces of the parties along both sides of the Armistice Demarcation Line. The provisions of articles VII and VIII have been undermined progressively by the developments in recent years, and, at the beginning of the crisis, were not being fulfilled. There is universal recognition that the condition of affairs of which this deterioration formed a part should not be permitted to return. Renewed full implementation of the clauses of the Armistice Agreement obviously presumes such an attitude on the part of the Governments concerned, and such supporting measures as would guarantee a return to the state of affairs envisaged in the Armistice Agreement, and avoidance of the state of affairs into which conditions, due to a lack of compliance with the Agreement, had progressively deteriorated.

16. Whatever the state of non-compliance with the Armistice Agreement in general before the crisis, it would seem apparent that a by-passing of that Agreement now would seriously impede efforts to lay the foundation for progress toward solutions of pending problems. A return to full implementation of articles VII and VIII would be a valuable step toward reduction of tension and the establishment of peaceful conditions in the region. The provisions in these articles were the result of careful analysis of the military situation, and the objectives defined in the course of the armistice negotiations should still have validity as steps in the desired direction. If the military clauses of the Armistice Agreement were again to be fully implemented, this would have important positive bearing on other problems in the region.

17. According to article VII, Egyptian 'defensive forces' only may be maintained in the area of the western front under Egyptian control. All other Egyptian forces shall be withdrawn from this area to a point or points no further east than El Arish-Abou Aoueigila. According to the same article, Israel 'defensive forces' only, which shall be based on the settlements, may be maintained in the area of the western front under Israel control. All other Israel forces shall be withdrawn from this area to a point or points north of the line delineated in the special memorandum of 13 November 1948 on the implementation of the resolution of the Security Council of 4 November 1948. The definition of 'defensive forces' is given in an annex to the Agreement.

18. Article VIII of the Agreement provides that an area comprising the village of El Auja and vicinity, as defined in the article, shall be demilitarized, and that both Egyptian and Israel armed forces shall be totally excluded therefrom. The article further provides that on the Egyptian side of the frontier, facing the El Auja area, no Egyptian defensive positions shall be closer to El Auja than El Qouseima and Abou Aoueigila. It also states that the road Taba–Qouseima–Auja shall not be employed by any military forces whatsoever 'for the purpose of entering Palestine'.

19. The Agreement provides that the execution of its provisions shall be supervised by the Mixed Armistice Commission, established under it, and that the headquarters of the Commission shall be maintained in El Auja. . . .

21. The implementation of articles VII and VIII of the Agreement would at present be

facilitated by the fact that there are no Egyptian military positions in the area under consideration and that, therefore, implementation by Israel does not require a simultaneous withdrawal of military units on the Egyptian side. The condition which must be fulfilled in order to establish reciprocity, would be Egyptian assurance that Egyptian forces will not take up positions in the area in contravention of articles VII and VIII. Up to now Egypt has moved into Sinai only small police units which have been considered necessary in support of the re-established local civil administrations. . . .

D

23. In connexion with the question of Israel withdrawal from the Sharm el-Sheikh area, attention has been directed to the situation in the Gulf of Aqaba and the Straits of Tiran. This matter is of longer duration and not directly related to the present crisis. The concern now evinced in it, however, calls for consideration of the legal aspects of the matter as a problem in its own right. It follows from principles guiding the United Nations that the Israel military action and its consequences should not be elements influencing the solution.

24. As stated in the previous report (A/3500 and Add.1), the international significance of the Gulf of Aqaba may be considered to justify the right of innocent passage through the Straits of Tiran and the Gulf in accordance with recognized rules of international law. However, in its commentary to article 17 of the articles of the law of the sea (A/3159, page 20), the International Law Commission reserved consideration of the question 'what would be the legal position of straits forming part of the territorial sea of one or more States and constituting the sole means of access to the port of another State'. This description applies to the Gulf of Aqaba and the Straits of Tiran. A legal controversy exists as to the extent of the right of innocent passage through these waters.

25. Under these circumstances, it is indicated that whatever rights there may be in relation to the Gulf and the Straits, such rights be exercised with restraint on all sides. Any possible claims of belligerent rights should take into account the international interests involved and, therefore, if asserted, should be limited to clearly non-controversial situations.

26. The Security Council, in its resolution of 1 September 1951 concerning passage of international commercial shipping and goods through the Suez Canal, considered 'that since the armistice régime, which has been in existence for nearly two and a half years, is of a permanent character, neither party can reasonably assert that it actively is a belligerent or requires to exercise the right of visit, search and seizure for any legitimate purpose of self defence', a basis on which the Council called upon Egypt to terminate the restrictions on the passage of international commercial shipping and goods through the Suez Canal. This general finding of the Security Council has a direct bearing on the question here under consideration. It remains valid and warrants corresponding conclusions as long as the assumptions defined by the Council remain correct. However in later years, an ever-widening non-compliance with the Armistice Agreement has developed, ending in the Israel military action of 29 October 1956, as a result of which Israel still has military forces on Egyptian territory contrary to the Armistice Agreement. It may be further noted that Israel, in its communication of 23 January 1957, makes proposals concerning the Gaza Strip which cannot be reconciled with maintaining the validity of the Armistice Agreement.

27. The armistice régime may be considered as operative, at least in part, provided forces are withdrawn behind the armistice lines, even if non-compliance were to continue in relation to other substantive clauses of the Armistice Agreement. It follows from the finding of the Security Council in 1951 that under such circumstances the parties to the Armistice Agreement may be considered as not entitled to claim any belligerent rights. Were the substantive clauses of the Armistice Agreement, especially articles VII and VIII, again to be implemented, the case against all acts of belligerency, which is based on the existence of the armistice régime, would gain full cogency. With such a broader implementation of the Armistice Agreement, the parties should be asked to give assurances that, on the basis established, they will not assert any belligerent rights (including, of course, such rights in the Gulf of Aqaba and the Straits of Tiran).

28. As a conclusion from paragraphs 24–27, it may be held that, in a situation where the armistice régime is partly operative by observance of the provisions of the Armistice Agreement concerning the armistice lines, possible claims to rights of belligerency would be at least so much in doubt that, having regard for the general international interest at stake, no such claim should be exercised in the Gulf of Aqaba and the Straits of Tiran. Such a *de facto* position, if taken, obviously would be a part of efforts to re-establish as complete an armistice régime as possible and, as such, would be detached from the policy of implementation of the unconditional General Assembly request for withdrawal behind the armistice lines. The situation resulting from such a position should be stabilized when the Armistice Agreement is more fully implemented. [*A/3512, Report of the Secretary-General in pursuance of Res. 1123 (XI), 24 Jan. 1957*, ss. C and D.]

Referring to this report, the representative of Israel indicated that the Armistice Agreement must be fully operative, or not at all:

41. The report deals in detail with the 1949 Armistice Agreement. It is important that we frankly analyse the status of that agreement today. It is important that we ask ourselves the question which the report raises: does this agreement really offer a framework in which peaceful relations between Egypt and Israel can be established?

42. The report admits that the General Armistice Agreement has 'deteriorated' (paragraph 15); that it has been 'undermined progressively by developments in recent years' (paragraph 15); that 'ever-widening non-compliance' with it has developed (paragraph 26); and, by implication, that it has ceased to be operative at all, to the extent that, even after withdrawal behind the armistice lines, it could be considered as operative only in part, since non-compliance would still continue in other substantive clauses. That is the judgement in paragraph 27.

43. The Israel delegation has addressed the Security Council and the General Assembly many times on the events which led to the breakdown of the 1949 Armistice Agreement with Egypt. By the time we had reached the point of explosion in October 1956, Israel was enjoying practically none of its rights under that agreement.

44. We had no 'security and freedom from fear of attack'. We had no recognition by Egypt of the character of the agreement as a condition leading to permanent peace. The demarcation line offered us no protection against raids, assaults and *fedayeen* incursions. We had no freedom of navigation in the Gulf of Aqaba. We had no free use of the Suez Canal. We had no acceptance by Egypt of our very sovereignty, although this is inherent in the existence of a contract between two Member States of the United Nations. We had direct reason to know that Egypt would refuse to negotiate any agreement for the revision, suspension or replacement of the Agreement in favour of permanent peace.

45. Thus, as armed gangs roamed across our countryside and our commerce was strangled in both international waterways, we realized that every single right, every amenity, every advantage which Israel had a claim to enjoy under the 1949 Agreement was effectively denied to us. At the same time Egypt claimed, and sometimes received, international support in its efforts to secure respect of the agreement by Israel.

46. The rock on which the Armistice Agreement foundered was that of belligerency. For eight years an effort was made to keep this agreement alive in conditions quite incompatible with its existence. These conditions were the doctrine and the practice of 'a state of war'; the claim of belligerent rights; non-recognition of Israel's independence and integrity as a state; and the refusal by Egypt to respect the dynamic and fowardlooking character of the Armistice Agreement as a transition to the negotiation of permanent peace. . . .

53. My Government feels that reliance on a partially operative 1949 agreement is not necessary in order to secure the objectives of withdrawal and permanent non-belligerency in the Gulf of Aqaba and in Gaza. These questions can be solved on their merits and in conformity with United Nations objectives. But we think that there is little value in the partial restoration of an agreement which was meant to be an integrated whole, and which in any case was to be followed by an early transition to peace.

54. In its commendable desire for realism, the report admits that a full restoration is impossible. It says:

'The armistice régime may be considered as operative at least in part, provided forces are withdrawn behind the armistice lines, even if non-compliance were to continue in relation to other substantive clauses of the Armistice Agreement.' (*A/3512*, para. 27.)

55. But, on examination, this thesis of the partial operativeness of the Agreement becomes difficult to sustain. It could, in the strict sense of language, be interpreted to mean that the armistice would be operative if respected by Israel, even if it were violated by Egypt in essential points. That is what the words could mean—certainly not what the intention can be. This idea of a partial recognition of the Agreement would conflict with the principle of the integrality, mutuality and equilibrium of treaties. No State has a duty to respect an agreement which is not totally respected on the other side.

56. For these reasons we strongly doubt whether any system of relations can be established, by rebuilding this collapsed structure on the basis of some of its less significant provisions such as articles VII and VIII. But one truth does emerge from the central thinking of the report. The report admits that fresh agreements are required in any case between Egypt and Israel. Would it not, then, be wise to use such agreements for a serious and stable solution of outstanding security problems, rather than to revive an agreement which has collapsed beyond repair? Since the report admits that many provisions of the armistice agreements now have to be replaced or modified, surely efforts should be directed towards the establishment of a peaceful relationship between Israel and Egypt, rather than towards the restoration of a framework in which belligerency and hostility have flourished. [*GAOR, 11th sess., plen. mtgs, vol. 2, 645th mtg.*]

In the ensuing debate the representative of Uruguay contributed a thoughtful legal analysis of the status of the partially-effective Armistice which merits reproduction:

53. It is clear that many of the provisions of the Armistice Agreement have not been complied with. But what legal instrument of international law becomes a dead letter simply because the parties do not comply with it? However, the Armistice Agreement has a special legal character. It is not a bilateral legal instrument which is binding solely upon Egypt and Israel. It arose out of the intervention of the Security Council and the General Assembly during the period of misunderstanding and hostilities between Israel and Egypt. The Security Council ordered the truce and then subsequently summoned the parties to sign the Armistice Agreement.

54. What is the nature of the Agreement? It is a bilateral instrument of public international law implementing a provisional measure taken under Article 40 of the Charter. It had to be submitted for approval to the Security Council, which remained responsible for ensuring its implementation. This bilateral instrument therefore derives from a provisional measure and is intended to implement a provisional measure, which gives it the legal character of an integral part of a measure taken by the United Nations. This is specifically stated in the preamble to the Agreement.

55. However, it also has the following additional characteristics: by mutual consent, Israel and Egypt can revise the Agreement during the first year it is in force and they can subsequently revise it by calling a reviewing conference, but the revision of articles I and II is specifically excluded. The Armistice Agreement therefore contains a certain element which does not depend on the will of the parties, but which depends on a heteronomous will functioning independently of the parties.

56. The terms of articles I and II of the Armistice Agreement give its full significance to the second draft resolution. In the first place, that draft takes account of the preoccupations that moved us, together with several other States, to broaden the terms of the last resolution adopted on this subject by recalling expressly that it is the duty of both parties to observe the armistice. Furthermore, the draft resolution leaves no room for doubt—I consider it a

5

legal conclusion beyond all dispute—that the Armistice Agreement is now in force and that it is the inescapable duty of the parties and the United Nations to respect it as positive international law.

57. Thus these articles I and II, which the parties cannot revise, not only forbid both parties to engage not only in any military operation, but also in any act of hostility. The intention of these articles of the Armistice Agreement, which followed the truce and constitutes a step towards final peace, is to assure both parties that they may live free from fear, free from threats, and without involving themselves in reciprocal hostile acts.

58. If the Armistice Agreement did not exist, we would be obliged by the Charter to maintain that, since no war had been waged by the Organization, and since our *prima facie* study of the situation had not shown that there had been any war of individual or collective self-defence, the proper course was to return to the *status quo ante bellum*—which itself was a provisional situation produced by a variety of circumstances which would exist until the parties concluded a definitive peace, with substantive solutions for the problems in dispute.

59. With respect to this Armistice Agreement, I wish to refute one argument which seems to recur with a certain consistency in the Secretary-General's report. I think that one who reasons with such logic and circumspection and who stands so far above the surge of events could not have wished to advance this argument against the validity of the Armistice Agreement.

60. It has been said by one of the parties to the dispute that, if certain provisions are not complied with, the Armistice Agreement will no longer be valid. I think that two things have been confused here which in law ought to be carefully distinguished: problems of validity and problems of effectiveness.

61. As far as I am concerned, the validity of the Armistice Agreement is unquestionable. The Agreement was concluded as part of a provisional measure taken by the Security Council, and its text contains the procedure prescribed for its own revision. The parties at the reviewing conference can decide to delete or amend any provisions they consider inappropriate or objectionable, with the exception of articles I and II. In my opinion, Egypt and Israel should respect the world's desire for peace and make use of this procedure. If they consider any provisions of the armistice objectionable, they can revise them—except for that part which is sacred dogma and not subject to the will of the parties—and adapt them to resolve the points currently at issue between them.

62. Thus there can be no question concerning the validity of the Armistice Agreement. The validity of a legal instrument is determined in accordance with the legal system to which it belongs. It is a very simple problem of legal geometry. The problem posed by the Armistice Agreement is that of its effectiveness; but its effectiveness does not affect its validity unless there is a general lack of compliance with the legal system by the entire community. By effectiveness we mean the capacity for moulding conduct possessed by the system of legal rules. In this case, both parties have constantly stressed the importance they attach to the Armistice Agreement, although they have been unable to agree on the interpretation of its provisions.

63. The Armistice Agreement, in the light of the interpretation I have previously given of the United Nations legal system, is absolutely clear. It is not an agreement between two belligerent forces; it is the fulfilment of an international command. It embodies the substance of a provisional measure adopted by the United Nations. The preamble of the Armistice Agreement refers to Article 40 of the Charter, so that non-observance makes our attention to the matter even more mandatory, especially in view of the possibility of revising those parts of it to which I have referred; and articles I and II provide that threats and hostile acts of any kind are forbidden. This means that it was not a truce, a period of calm between two armies encamped opposite each other. The Security Council approved it as abolishing the truce, as establishing a definitive cessation of hostilities. And the Security Council unequivocally gave this interpretation which I have just defended in the resolution which it adopted on 1 September 1951 (*S/2322*), and the same interpretation was put forward in the debate on the New Zealand draft resolution (*S/3188 and Corr.1*) in March 1954, and again in February 1955.

64. Since the United Nations Charter came into force, it is no longer possible, in public international law, to speak of any right of belligerency apart from the use of armed force which the Charter considers legitimate, i.e., warfare engaged in by the Organization or military action taken as a means of individual or collective self-defence. That is what is said in the Charter, and the Armistice Agreement does not allow of any right of belligerency. It regards the state of war between Egypt and Israel as terminated, and calls upon both countries, expressly, directly, immediately, effectively, and without ambiguity whatsoever, to refrain from any hostile act. Such acts under international law specifically include reprisals and blockades, no matter what fancy adjectives may be applied to them.

65. I therefore believe that it is eminently appropriate that the two parties to the dispute should be reminded that they are subject to a legal system which they must respect. We think that it would be a step forward if the Armistice Agreement were not presented merely as a geographical handbook for the purpose of defining the area to be occupied by the United Nations Emergency Force, but rather as a legal system which the two parties must scrupulously observe. [*Ibid. 651st mtg.*]

The Assembly, by implication at least, did not accept the Israel view, for on 2 February 1957, in Resolution 1125 (XI) it called upon the governments concerned scrupulously to observe the Armistice Agreements.

However, Israel nevertheless withdrew from participation in all work of the MAC: 'This came about as a result of Egypt's persistent exercise, contrary to the Armistice Agreement and the United Nations Charter of alleged rights of war against Israel, including the obstruction of Israel's lawful commerce and shipping in the Suez Canal.'[51] Thus Egypt has during this period been able to command an automatic majority in the MAC, and has reported to the Security Council all decisions of the MAC, for they have condemned Israel.[52]

iii. *The Jordan–Israel Armistice*

Relations 1949–56

Israel and Jordan have each on occasions expressed dissatisfaction with the operation of the MAC, for reasons that have been outlined elsewhere. Brief withdrawals of co-operation by Jordan have occurred, and rather more prolonged indications of no-confidence have been shown by Israel. Both the scope of authority of the UN under the Armistice Agreement, and decisions in particular cases, have been at issue:

1. In view of the letter addressed to the Secretary-General of the United Nations by the Prime Minister and Minister of Foreign Affairs of the Hashemite Kingdom of the Jordan, dated 16 December 1952, in which he demanded that the United Nations Organization which 'is responsible for the general management and peaceful running of the Mount Scopus demilitarized zone carries out a thorough search of the area', and in view of additional letters addressed to the Chief of Staff by the Senior Member of the delegation of the Hashemite Kingdom of the Jordan to the Jordan–Israel Mixed Armistice Commission on the same subject, I have the honour to report the results of the inspection which was held on 28–30 April 1953.

2. In each of the above-mentioned communications, the representatives of the Hashemite Kingdom of the Jordan had made additional requests concerning the way in which the search should be carried out. These additional requests were not in accord with the terms of the

---

[51] S/4231, Letter from the representative of Israel to the Secretary-General, 22 Oct. 1959, para. 2.
[52] See S/4155, S/4160, S/4167, S/4226, S/4240, for such communications.

Mount Scopus Agreement. It was not until 13 March 1953 that the Senior Jordan Representative to the Jordan–Israel Mixed Armistice Commission requested that an inspection be made as the Chief of Staff saw fit. He further stated that he was primarily interested in a report on the results of the investigation.

3. Under the terms of the agreement entered into by the parties on 7 July 1948 (see annex), the Mount Scopus area is divided into three sections: (1) the 'Jewish section', (2) the Arab village of Issawiya, and (3) the Augusta Victoria Hospital area.

4. In the 'Jewish section' which, according to the 7 July 1948 Agreement, includes the Hadassah Hospital and the Hebrew University, the investigating team consisting of two United Nations observers checked the number of Israeli personnel and found that it was not in excess of that authorized by the 7 July 1948 Agreement. An inspection of the area was also made for the purpose of determining whether or not the Israeli police had in their possession arms or ammunition in excess of, or of a type different from, those authorized in November 1948.

5. The investigating team moved freely throughout the 'Jewish section' and received the co-operation and assistance of the Israeli police inspector in charge of the Israeli detachment. The only grounds which it did not enter were those suspected of being mined. It entered all the buildings, and all rooms, with the exception of six located in the Ratnoff building, were inspected. The six rooms in question could not be opened due to lack of keys. No arms or ammunition were found in excess of those which were authorized in 1948.

6. With reference to the grounds suspected of being mined, which include the British Memorial War Cemetery, I invite your attention to paragraph 38 of my last report to the Security Council dated 30 October 1952 (*S/2833 and Add.1*), in which it is stated that the Israelis were 'ready to co-operate with my representative for the detection and destruction of mines which may remain in the area'.

7. In order to effect the removal or destruction of the suspected mines in the 'Jewish section', I requested the Jordan representative to authorize a de-mining team of ten Israeli soldiers to proceed to Mount Scopus. The Jordan representative refused to agree and offered in turn a de-mining team from Jordan. To date no de-mining team has proceeded to Mount Scopus.

8. As to the second section of the demilitarized area, Issawiya village, a check was made by the investigating team with regard to the population of that village. According to paragraph 4 of the 7 July 1948 Agreement, '. . . the United Nations undertakes to limit the population on Mount Scopus to those individuals needed for its operation, plus the present population of the village of Issawiya . . .'.

9. The interpretation of the words 'present population of the village of Issawiya' has given rise to difficulties. No census was taken either before or after the 7 July Agreement was signed (two days later, the first truce arranged under United Nations auspices came to an end and hostilities were resumed—they were not resumed on Mount Scopus, thanks to the Agreement). As a matter of fact the population of Issawiya—estimated at 650 in the *Gazetteer* published in 1940 by the Mandate authorities and reported to have reached 950 in May 1948 —sought refuge in safer places at the end of May or beginning of June 1948, when clashes increased on Mount Scopus. Consequently nobody was probably residing in the village when the 7 July Agreement was signed, though male inhabitants were said to be continuously visiting it, especially at night, to check their properties. According to the Government of Israel, the words 'present population of the village of Issawiya' means the inhabitants who were allowed to re-enter the village shortly after the signing of the Agreement, *viz.*, 150. Whether this figure represented the total number of inhabitants who were permitted to re-enter, or male inhabitants, who were allowed to take their families with them, has been a moot point. When Israel representatives have brought it up, I have taken the position that, in the absence of any authoritative contemporary record proving that the first alternative was right, I accepted the second alternative. One hundred and fifty male inhabitants, plus their families, brings the population of Issawiya to a figure closer to that of May 1948.

10. The investigating team has reported that the inhabitants of Issawiya are today 1,000

Many of the villagers work their farms, while others are employed in the Old City of Jerusalem. They have not been carried on the rolls of UNRWA for relief. A decision to reduce their number would result in increasing the number of Arab refugees.

11. According to the 7 July 1948 Agreement, 'the Arab civilian police population at Augusta Victoria shall not exceed a total of 40'. The investigating team has reported that the present Arab police population is considerably below the authorized total.

12. Inspection of the area discloses further that a hospital is being operated at Augusta Victoria by UNRWA for the care of Arab refugees. It has a staff of about 290, 90 per cent of whom are refugees. The daily average of beds occupied is 316. Although the Agreement of 7 July 1948 would preclude the operation of the hospital, it is in fact performing a most valuable service for Arab refugees in the Jerusalem area, particularly in view of the shortage of badly needed medical services.

(*Signed*) W. E. RILEY,

Lieut. General, USMC Ret.

Chief of Staff

ANNEX

7 JULY 1948 AGREEMENT FOR THE DEMILITARIZATION OF MOUNT SCOPUS AREA

It is hereby jointly agreed that

1. The area as delineated on the attached map will be assigned to United Nations protection until hostilities cease or a new agreement is entered upon. It shall include the areas designated as Hadassah Hospital, Hebrew University, Augusta Victoria and the Arab village of Issawiya. The United Nations agrees to become a signatory to this document by representation through the Senior Observer in the Jerusalem area and the Chairman of the Truce Commission. It therefore accepts responsibility for the security of this area as described herewith.

2. There shall be a no-man's-land location extending for approximately 200 yards along the main road between the Augusta Victoria and Hebrew University buildings, with suitable check-posts established at each end. Other check-posts will be established on the perimeter of the zone under protection, and all parties agree that access desired should be sought along the main road via the United Nations check-posts as established by the United Nations Commander. All other attempts at entry will be considered as unlawful invasion and treated accordingly.

3. In their respective areas armed Arab and Jewish civilian police will be placed on duty under the United Nations Commander. The United Nations flag will fly on the main buildings. All military personnel of both sides will be withdrawn this day, together with their equipment and such other supplies as are not required by the United Nations Commander.

4. The United Nations will arrange that both parties receive adequate supplies of food and water. Replacements of necessary personnel in residence on Mount Scopus will be scheduled by the United Nations Commander. Visits of properly accredited individuals will also be arranged by the United Nations Commander in consultation with each party in respect of its area. The United Nations undertakes to limit the population on Mount Scopus to those individuals needed for its operation, plus the present population of the village of Issawiya. No additions will be made to the village population except by agreement of both parties. The initial personnel roster of civilian police in the Jewish section shall not exceed a total of 85. The civilian personnel attached thereto shall not exceed a total of 33. The Arab civilian police population at Augusta Victoria shall not exceed a total of 40.

5. It is hereby agreed by both parties that the area is not to be used as a base for military operations, nor will it be attacked or unlawfully entered upon.

6. In the event that the Arab Legion withdraws from the area, the United Nations Com-

mander is to be given sufficient advanced notice in writing in order that satisfactory arrangements may be made to substitute for this protocol another agreement.

(*Signed*) LASH
Arab Military Commander

SHALTIEL
Jewish Military Commander, for Provisional Government,
State of Israel

JEAN NIEUWENHUYS
Chairman, Truce Commission, United Nations

Nils BRUNSSON
Senior Observer, Mediator's
Jerusalem Group, United Nations

7th of July 1948.
[*S/3007 and Corr.1, Report of the Chief of Staff of UNTSO, 8 May 1953.*]

The problems which the Chief of Staff faced in connection with the Mount Scopus agreement were later elaborated by General Bennike, when he answered questions put to him by the Security Council:

We must rely upon the governments of the countries in which we carry out our functions to take the necessary measures to safeguard the lives of the agents of the United Nations. I am satisfied that the governments concerned are aware of their responsibilities in this respect. About a month ago, the Israeli authorities felt that in discharge of this responsibility, they must insist on my being accompanied by a police escort in Israel territory. Shortly afterwards, the Jordan authorities requested my permission to patrol the grounds of my house at night, because of its location a short distance away from the demarcation line. I have not the means to evaluate the factual data, if any, which may have prompted the two Governments to take these precautions; that is a matter for the appropriate authorities of each State. In both cases, therefore, I gave my concurrence, and I shall always be glad to co-operate with the authorities of any of the parties in the discharge of their responsibilities for the safety of United Nations personnel, provided that any measures they take do not interfere with my freedom of movement or that of the observers. . . .

2. Have General Bennike and his organization been prevented from performing their functions? If so, when, how and by whom?

Answer. In the course of their duties, United Nations military observers have met with some obstruction on the part of Israeli civilians and some over-zealous Israeli officials in the two demilitarized zones created by the Israel–Egyptian and Israel–Syrian Armistice Agreements and in the Mount Scopus demilitarized zone. In the first two demilitarized zones, an appeal to higher authorities has removed the obstruction. The situation, however, has not been improved on Mount Scopus, which I attempted to inspect on 25 September 1953, in discharge of the responsibility for the security of this area placed upon the United Nations by the agreement dated 7 July 1948 (S/3015, annex).

On 23 September, two days prior to the intended inspection, a letter was sent to the general staff officer in charge of the Israeli delegations to the Mixed Armistice Commissions and to the officer in charge of the Jordan delegation, informing them of my intentions.

At approximately 6.30 a.m., I arrived at the area with several United Nations observers. The senior Israeli police inspector in charge informed me that he had received specific orders not to allow anyone to enter the buildings in the Jewish sector. I inquired as to who had issued this order and was told that his superiors in Jerusalem were responsible. He refused to divulge the name of the superior who had issued the order. At about 11.20 a.m., after many difficulties and after an Israeli police inspector had been brought to the spot from the Israeli section of Jerusalem, we were allowed to start the inspection, but the observers met with minimum co-operation. Keys to locked doors could not be found, and the operation of mine detectors was not allowed. At approximately 12.40, the Israeli police inspector announced that he had received orders to stop the inspection. I then withdrew from the area.

Subsequently, I received a letter dated 26 September from the general staff officer in charge of the Israeli delegations to the Mixed Armistice Commissions, explaining that he had received my letter of 23 September only after the time set for the inspection, and objecting to searches by the United Nations Truce Supervision Organization in the Jewish sector of Mount Scopus demilitarized area. Before the receipt of this communication, I had addressed a letter, on 27 September, to the Minister for Foreign Affairs of Israel, drawing his attention to the difficulties I had encountered in connexion with the inspection of Mount Scopus and to the responsibility of the Chief of Staff for the security of the area. I stated that such responsibility implied the right of United Nations representatives, when the chief of staff so decides, to inspect the area as he thinks fit. I added that I did not consider that statements made by police officers stationed on Mount Scopus expressed the opinion of the Israel Government on the matter, and I requested his Government's views as early as possible. To this date I have not received a reply.

On the night of 1 November 1953, a water line in Jordan-controlled territory north-east of Jerusalem was destroyed by explosives. Jordan entered a complaint and an investigating team was sent to the scene on the morning of 2 November. A United Nations observer, three Jordanian officers and an experienced tracker followed tracks from the scene of the incident to within seven metres of the fence around the Jewish sector of Mount Scopus. Here the investigating party was stopped by an Israeli police inspector. Even though the United Nations observer was satisfied that the tracks he saw at the point near the Scopus fence were the same as those seen at the site of the explosion, the Israeli inspector refused to let the tracker or the United Nations observer come nearer the fence. The United Nations observer, who is my representative for Mount Scopus, was at that time with the Israeli inspector inside the Mount Scopus area and was not allowed to continue the investigation inside the area.

On the morning of 2 November, my representative for Mount Scopus wanted to investigate another explosion alleged to have taken place a few hours earlier in the Jewish sector of the demilitarized zone, in the vicinity of the amphitheatre. The Israeli inspector stated that his instructions were to prohibit United Nations personnel from inspecting the Jewish sector unless they had permission from Israeli police headquarters in Jerusalem. My representative was, however, allowed to visit the ground near the amphitheatre. On returning the same afternoon, he was told by the Israeli inspector that, according to instructions just received, he could not be permitted to inspect anywhere without permission from police headquarters. On 3 November, however, the general staff officer in charge of the Israeli delegations to the Mixed Armistice Commissions informed the headquarters of the Truce Supervision Organization in Jerusalem that the police inspector on Mount Scopus would be immediately instructed to permit my representative freedom of movement.

I must emphasize that the government concerned should take all necessary steps to ensure that all its officials who come in contact with United Nations military observers are properly instructed as to the privileges, immunities and authority of the observers in carrying out their functions. Should any Government in the area place any obstacles in the way of military observers carrying out their lawful duties, or should a government endorse any obstructive action by a subordinate official, I shall feel bound to place the matter before the Security Council. [*SCOR, 8th yr, 635th mtg, ann.*]

The Scorpion Pass incident in 1954, briefly described elsewhere (s. 12, p. 172), triggered off Israel's withdrawal from the work of the MAC.

The Israel delegation submitted the following draft resolution:

'1. *The Mixed Armistice Commission*

'*Deeply deplores* the loss of innocent lives incurred as a result of the attack on an Israel bus carried out by a Jordanian armed and organized gang, near Ma'ale Akrabim (Scorpion Pass), on 17 March 1954.

'2. The unprovoked attack from an ambush on a passenger bus on the main highway from Eilat to Beersheba, carried out on 17 March 1954 by an organized and armed Jordanian gang, which had crossed the demarcation line into Israel, resulting in the cold-blooded murder of 9 men and 2 women passengers, and the serious wounding of 2 other passengers—a young woman and a nine-year-old boy—constitutes a most flagrant violation by Jordan of the General Armistice Agreement, in particular of article III, paragraph 2, thereof.

'3. *The Mixed Armistice Commission*

'*Finds* Jordan responsible for this outrage, condemns in the strongest terms this latest Jordanian aggression, and calls on the Jordanian authorities:

'(*a*) To terminate all warlike or hostile acts of any type whatsoever against Israel;

'(*b*) To take the most effective measures to terminate all incursions from Jordan across the demarcation line and to prevent any other violation of the General Armistice Agreement in the future;

'(*c*) To apprehend the culprits; and,

'(*d*) To mete out the severest punishment to the perpetrators of this crime and to those responsible for its non prevention.'

The voting on the above draft resolution was as follows:

> *Paragraph 1:*
>
> Israel .... 2 votes in favour.
>
> Jordan .... 2 votes against.
>
> Chairman .... 1 abstention.
>
> *Paragraph 2:*
>
> Israel .... 2 votes in favour.
>
> Jordan .... 2 votes against.
>
> Chairman .... 1 abstention.

The draft resolution was not adopted.

XII. THE CHAIRMAN'S STATEMENT AFTER THE VOTE

The Chairman made the following statement:

'On Wednesday of last week, the Mixed Armistice Commission was shocked by the news of an attack on an Israel bus near Ma'ale Akrabim (Scorpion Pass). United Nations military observers were sent immediately to the scene of the incident, and their initial reports were graphic in describing this horrible crime. Since that first day, most of the military observers assigned to the Jordan-Israel Mixed Armistice Commission have been working on this case. These observers, working with members of the Israel delegation to the Mixed Armistice Commission, Israel police and army officials, dog handlers with highly trained tracking hounds, expert Israel trackers, joined later by experienced Bedouin trackers from Jordan, have worked almost beyond endurance to establish the guilt for this crime. At no time during the years since the conclusion of the armistice agreement has a more intensive investigation been carried out. Even so, the evidence brought out is far from being conclusive. I do regret the Israel delegation's refusal to allow the Mixed Armistice Commission the opportunity completely to investigate Israel's claim of knowledge concerning the actual perpetrators of this crime. The possibility of Jordanians being responsible for this crime still exists; however, persons from outside Jordan could also be guilty of this outrage. True, tracks were found, perhaps connected to this crime, but they were lost approximately 10 kilometres in a straight line from the demarcation line. The empty cartridges found at the scene of the incident do not point conclusively to any one group. The testimony of the witnesses indicates that Arabs were involved; however, the description of the two men who allegedly entered the bus leaves a doubt as to whether they were all Arabs. And the establishment of the fact that Arabs were involved does not in the least connect this crime to the inhabitants of any one country. This Mixed Armistice Commission will always avoid condemning a government on inconclusive evidence.

'My abstention, in this case, must not be construed as a lack of sympathy for those who suffered by this crime. On the contrary, those many people have my deepest sympathy. I firmly believe that this Mixed Armistice Commission should consider itself obligated to continue relentlessly its efforts to have those responsible for this crime brought to justice. I will expect the Jordan and Israel delegations to keep this Commission informed of any further developments in this case.

'It is quite important at this time for the parties to guard against any inflammatory actions or statements that will only aggravate an already tense situation. You should realize that the perpetrators of this crime are enemies, not only of both countries, but of all humanity. You should co-operate in your efforts to ferret out these killers.'

XIII. WITHDRAWAL OF THE ISRAEL DELEGATION FROM THE MIXED ARMISTICE COMMISSION

After the Chairman's statement, the Israel delegation announced its withdrawal from the Mixed Armistice Commission in the following terms:

'I have to express my extreme regret and concern over the vote taken just now by Jordan and the Chairman. Such a vote is contrary to the evidence produced before the Mixed Armistice Commission and to the nature of the case, as well as any other information produced by the observers during the investigation.

'The decision should have actually served to assure no further incidents of this nature, but the vote taken is actually or will actually encourage further Jordanian aggressions and attacks.

'The Israel delegation is not in a position, under the present circumstances, to continue its participation in the Israel–Jordan Mixed Armistice Commission.'

Since 23 March 1954, the Israel Government has severed all connections with the Mixed Armistice Commission. It has also discontinued attendance at the local commanders' meetings provided for under a separate Israel–Jordan agreement. Israel communications referring to alleged violations by Jordan of the General Armistice Agreement have been addressed to the Secretary-General of the United Nations, with the request that they should be circulated to the members of the Security Council. The Chief of Staff of the Truce Supervision Organization in Jerusalem has been informed of such alleged violations of the General Armistice Agreement only on receiving from New York a copy of the Security Council document. The non-co-operation of the Israel Government has prevented the investigation of such alleged violations in conformity with the provisions of the General Armistice Agreement.

Emergency meetings of the Mixed Armistice Commission have been held in the absence of the Israel delegation to deal with Jordanian complaints about incidents whose gravity had been ascertained by United Nations observers.

In a communication which I addressed to the Prime Minister of Israel on 20 April 1954 I expressed the hope that the Israel Government would instruct its delegation to return to the Israel–Jordan Mixed Armistice Commission. So far, my hope has not been fulfilled.

I should like to add that United Nations observers sent by the Chief of Staff of the Truce Supervision Organization to observe and maintain the cease-fire ordered by the Security Council should, in my opinion, be granted the same co-operation and the same freedom of movement as observers sent by the Chairman of a mixed armistice commission to investigate a complaint according to the provisions of a general armistice agreement. [*S/3252, Report of the Chief of Staff of UNTSO to the Secretary-General, 25 June 1954.*]

Relations 1956–67

Israel's non-participation in the MAC, and non-use of UN observers, continued to present the Chief of Staff with a major obstacle during this period. (Israel did attend some sub-committee meetings, however.)

As I informed the Foreign Ministry on 5 October 1956, I considered that an emergency meeting should be called in connection with Israel complaint No. 364 filed on the same day

5*

with the Hashemite Jordan Kingdom–Israel Mixed Armistice Commission. In this connexion, it might be pointed out that under the Commission's rules of procedure, of 2 July 1953 (as amended), the Chairman has the sole right to decide whether a complaint lodged by either party calls for an emergency meeting. I requested specifically your Government's co-operation for an investigation of the incident by United Nations military observers, because under the rules of procedure a party's prior agreement is required before a United Nations military observer investigation pursuant to the General Armistice Agreement can take place on that party's side of the demarcation line. In your letter, you also refer to article XI, paragraph 6 of the General Armistice Agreement. Article VI of the Hashemite Jordan Kingdom–Israel Mixed Armistice Commission rules of procedure refers to this article and stipulates, *inter alia*, that the unanimous vote of the Commission is necessary for an investigation of an incident to be carried out by observers from among the military organizations of the parties, either alone or together with the United Nations military observers. In regard to the incident near Sedom no such decision was taken by the Mixed Armistice Commission and an investigation carried out by the Israel authorities, without a previous decision of the Commission, cannot, therefore, be considered as valid under the General Armistice Agreement.

I should like to express again my regret that your Government has found it necessary to discontinue its participation in the examination of incidents in the Hashemite Jordan Kingdom–Israel Mixed Armistice Commission and to forego the investigation by United Nations military observers of incidents occurring on the Israel side of the demarcation line. . . . [*S/3670, ann. IV, Report of 11 Oct. 1956 by Chief of Staff to Secretary-General*, p. 18.]

Dag Hammarskjöld noted a week later, in a letter to the President of the Security Council, that the Chief of Staff had stated that:

One of the parties to the General Armistice Agreement makes its own investigations, which are not—and cannot be made—subject to check or confirmation by the United Nations observers, publishes the results of such investigations, draws its own conclusions from them and undertakes actions by its military forces on that basis. I endorse the view of the Chief of Staff that this is a dangerous negation of vital elements of the Armistice Agreement. It represents a further step in the direction of a limitation of the functions of the United Nations Truce Supervision Organization. [*S/3685, Letter transmitting report from Chief of Staff, 17 Oct. 1956.*]

The UN continued to disagree with the parties over surveillance of the demilitarized zone. Complaints of infringements of the demilitarized character were dealt with initially by the MAC; and later also by the Chief of Staff of UNTSO, specifically in 1955 and again in 1956 when Major-General Burns ordered an inspection of the whole area by UN military observers, and drew the attention of both parties to infringements revealed by the inspection.[53]

6. As has been shown above, the United Nations Truce Supervision Organization considers itself competent to exercise surveillance over the Zone in order to maintain its demilitarized status. The Truce Supervision Organization does not, however, possess any specific authority or terms of reference with respect to the civilian activities in this area. General W. E. Riley, first Chief of Staff of the Truce Supervision Organization, made the following statement at the 9th Mixed Armistice Commission meeting on 12 June 1949:

'I realize full well that the question of withdrawal of military forces from this area is not a solution of the problem. I am keenly interested in this area as I was involved initially in setting up the demilitarized area around Government House and grounds which is now part of the area between the demarcation lines as set forth in the Armistice Agreement.

[53] S/3892. para, 4.

Initially, or during the period of the truce, it was possible for the Truce Supervision Organization to control the civilian situation within this area. Upon the signing of the Armistice Agreement between the two States, the truce supervision control was withdrawn. We still have civilians in this area. I consider that it is essential that some corrective action be taken in this regard.'

In this connexion, it might be pointed out that the same year a Jordanian representative suggested that this Zone be placed under United Nations control. This suggestion was, however, not further discussed.

7. In view of the absence of any provisions in the General Armistice Agreement regarding the status of the Zone and the lack of any terms of reference, the Truce Supervision Organization cannot express any authoritative opinion as to the merits of the arguments advanced by the respective parties in the present dispute. It is evident from a reading of the records that the civilian matters of the Zone have been left regrettably vague for many years. A review of the records would furthermore appear to indicate that although some arguments advanced by the parties have merit and should be given due consideration, other arguments do not apoear to be fully supported. . . .

8. The Truce Supervision Organization has from the outset of the present controversy taken active steps in an effort to assist the parties in finding a solution to the controversy. First, it endeavoured to arrange a meeting between the parties to discuss the dispute. Unfortunately, such a meeting could not be arranged. Since October 1956 Israel has not participated in emergency Mixed Armistice Commission meetings (see document *S/3670*). An Israel delegation attends Sub-Committee meetings of the Mixed Armistice Commission. Israel declined to participate in an emergency meeting to discuss the Jordanian complaints on the present work in the Zone but expressed willingness to attend any other type of meeting, including a Sub-Committee meeting of the Mixed Armistice Commission. Jordan refused to attend any meetings except an emergency meeting on this matter. In recent years sub-committee meetings have normally dealt with questions relating to civilian activities in the Zone. On 25 July 1957, the Truce Supervision Organization commenced a fact-finding investigation concerning the Zone which was completed on 22 August. Several meetings were held with representatives of the Jordan and Israel Governments. The Acting Chief of Staff and his representatives also urged Israel on several occasions, particularly on 21 July and on 2, 12 and 25 August, to suspend the work for the sake of maintaining the tranquillity which had prevailed in the area for many months. Israel indicated that it did not feel justified in suspending the work which it claimed was a permissible civilian activity on its side of the so-called civilian line. The work, it emphasized, was of a purely civilian nature and would be strictly limited to this afforestation project; in particular, no buildings would be erected. [*S/3892, Report by Acting Chief of Staff of UNTSO to Secretary-General, 23 Sept. 1957.*]

In 1958, after the sniping on Mount Scopus—almost certainly from Jordanian territory—which resulted in the deaths of four Israelis and a UN observer, the Chief of Staff, in carrying out his investigation, sought

complete freedom of movement on Mount Scopus for the fulfilment of its task. The Director-General of the Ministry of Foreign Affairs of Israel replied immediately that he considered it 'essential, in order to avoid an aggravation of the situation, that United Nations observers should co-operate with our police and in particular use only the accepted entrances and routes in our area'. [*S/4030, 17 June 1958*, para. 58.]

Difficulties were also made concerning interrogation, for the Israelis wished interrogation of witnesses to occur only on the site of the incident, and in the presence of an Israel armed patrol. This position was later modified, and interviews were conducted in the Hadassah hospital. Negotiation was also pursued as to the desire of the Chief of Staff to carry out investigations on the spot without the presence of an Israeli armed patrol.[54]

Difficulties arose between Jordan and the UN in respect of a claim by the latter for reparation for the death of its observer during the Mount Scopus incident.

At the time of the incident an investigation was carried out, and General von Horn, the UNTSO Chief of Staff, reported that the evidence showed that Lt.-Colonel Flint 'was probably shot by a bullet fired from Jordanian-controlled territory to the north north-east. The element of doubt which subsists in this respect relates to the possibility, which may be considered as remote, that the bullet may have made a ricochet on a solid object.'[55] A ballistic examination was held to consider this possibility and General von Horn then reported: '2. The examination has revealed that the bullet which killed Lt.-Colonel Flint was a direct shot. It is thus to be considered as established that Lt.-Colonel Flint was shot by a bullet fired from Jordanian-controlled territory.'[56] No progress was made in the UN's claim on behalf of the Canadian government, and nine years later U Thant was still pressing the case. It now became tied up with the change of fortunes which had occurred in General von Horn's relationship with the UN. General von Horn had resigned, while leading the UN's observer mission in the Yemen in 1963, from UN service, and subsequently wrote a book largely critical of the UN Secretariat. He also showed in it a considerable sympathy for the Arab cause. In describing the Scopus affair in his book,[57] he clearly felt that Israel had done much to provoke the fighting which had broken out in the area. As to whether it was none the less a Jordanian bullet which killed Lt.-Colonel Flint, General von Horn did not commit himself, but rather emphasized the obstacles which the Israelis placed in the way of an efficient investigation of the whole incident, and complained that the Israeli version of events was distorted.

The Jordan government now cited these passages in support of its refusal to pay compensation (S/7867); while U Thant insisted that he must rely on General von Horn's official reports submitted at the time in his capacity as Chief of Staff of UNTSO 'rather than upon the personal views expressed by him very much later in a book which is, presumably, based on recollection and in which personal views and opinions are liberally intertwined with facts with all the interpretive freedom which memory and hindsight so often afford.'[58] In spite of further exchanges,[59] no progress has been made, although Jordan and U Thant agreed to have discussions.

---

[54] S/4030, paras 59–64.   [55] Ibid. para. 57.   [56] Ibid. Add. 1, 28 July 1958, para. 2
[57] Carl von Horn, *Soldiering for Peace* (1965), pp. 83–85.   [58] S/7873 4 May 1967.
[59] S/7867, S/7976, S/7882, S/7886.

iv. *The Lebanon–Israel Armistice*

Relations 1949–67

No problems arose in respect of this Armistice Agreement.

(c) Relations under the June 1967 cease-fire orders

In Resolutions 233–7 the Security Council issued a series of cease-fire orders aimed at halting the war of June 1967 between Israel and her Arab neighbours.[60]

UNTSO was now faced with a new situation—that of dealing with Israel not only within its 1949 Armistice Agreement limits, but also in the very considerable tracts of territory which she now held under military occupation. As of June 1967, the situation was that measures had been taken by Israel for the unification of Jerusalem (contrary to the wishes of the General Assembly, which had called in Resolution GA 2253 (ES-IV) for no alternation to the status of Jerusalem); the rest of the Arab territories were however in principle negotiable, and were being held until the Arabs could be persuaded to participate in peace talks.

UNTSO managed to retain cordial relations with Israel and the Arabs in these changed circumstances, though inevitably there were particular difficulties that had to be overcome. Most important of these was the fact that during the fighting Israel had taken over UNTSO headquarters in Jerusalem. As the Secretary-General replied:

12. A later report received through a non-United Nations channel, sent by the Chief of Staff UNTSO indicates that heavy firing broke out in the Government House area in Jerusalem at about 1130 hours GMT on 5 June and all communications were cut shortly thereafter. Jordanian soldiers in the compound were attacked and later driven out by Israel troops. The Israel troops then forced their way into Government House at about 1230 hours GMT. When the firing subsided temporarily at about 1400 hours GMT, the Chief of Staff UNTSO and his staff were ordered out of the Government House by the Israel troops and escorted into Israel. Government House itself was heavily damaged but there were no casualties among UNTSO personnel. General Bull reported that firing was still going on in Jerusalem at 1410 hours GMT. The Chairman of the Israel–Jordan Mixed Armistice Commisson and his staff are continuing to function, and General Bull is attempting to establish a temporary Headquarters.

13. In view of these developments, I have sent the following cable to the Prime Minister of Israel, Mr Levi Eshkol:

'I understand that Israel forces have now displaced the forces of Jordan in the Government House Compound in Jerusalem. Whatever the circumstances leading to the Israel occupation of Government House and its grounds, its continued occupation by Israel troops is a most serious breach of the undertaking to respect its inviolability.

'I therefore request the Government of Israel to restore the grounds and buildings of the Government House Compound urgently to exclusive United Nations control. When this has been done I propose to seek a formal undertaking from both sides to respect UNTSO's occupation of Government House in the future.'

[*S/7930, Suppl. Information received by the Secretary-General, 5 June 1967.*]

The Secretary-General, on 11 June, ordered the Chief of Staff to

3. Stand firm on your demand for prompt return your Government House Headquarters.

[60] For details, see pp. 204–5 below.

We consider continuing delay in facilitating this to be unjustified, unco-operative and un-friendly to the U.N.

4. Full information on developments sent in this and earlier cables on 11 June is greatly appreciated this end.

Despite the strong appeals that have been made on the matter of the return of UNTSO to its Government House Headquarters, UNTSO continues to be greatly handicapped through its lack of facilities, and particularly its communications set-up and its deprival of access to its records. This is a great handicap to me also since there is no longer any channel for confidential communication between United Nations Headquarters and the Chief of Staff. There is now an effective cease-fire between Israel and Jordan, there has not been any fighting in the Government House area for days and, indeed, no reason at all is now given for the refusal to permit the Chief of Staff and his colleagues to return to Government House. I regard this as a highly serious matter. [*S/7930/Add.3, 11 June 1967*, para. 4.]

The Secretary-General reported:

4. I have already mentioned on several occasions in the Council the serious handicap which continued lack of access to UNTSO Headquarters in Government House imposes upon General Bull and his observers. On the afternoon of 12 June I received from General Bull the following message on the subject:

'(i) A whole week after our eviction we are still being denied return to Government House despite my repeated requests and appeals from Secretary-General and President of the Security Council.

'(ii) This question becomes evermore urgent because of Security Council Resolution of 12 June (res. 236 (1967)). We cannot work in proper conditions at temporary makeshift Headquarters. In particular, we have no adequate communication facilities and no access to our maps and documents. In those circumstances I do not feel I can provide Secre-tary-General and Security Council with information required.

'(iii) I plan to approach Sasson again tomorrow 13 June and if reply should be negative or still delayed I would recommend that you raise this question in a report to the Security Council, informing it that because we are prevented from returning to Government House Chief of Staff UNTSO considered it impossible to discharge properly the re-sponsibilities placed upon him by the Security Council resolution of 12 June for im-plementation of the cease-fire.' [*S/7930/Add.5, 12 June 1967.*]

On 13 June the Secretary-General sent the following cable to the Prime Minister of Israel:

I have the honour to refer to my cabled message to you of 5 June about facilitating the return of UNTSO to its headquarters at Government House. I have had as yet no word from your Government about this matter although the very great importance which I attach to this has been communicated to your representative at the United Nations, both directly and by the several statements to this effect which I have made to the Security Council. In this regard I would call to your attention that the President of the Security Council, Mr Tabor, represen-tative of Denmark, at the Council's meeting Friday night, 9 June . . . made the following statement: 'It appears that we all agree . . . that we should request the Government of Israel to restore the use of Government House to General Odd Bull.' I would very much hope for a favourable reply from you without further delay. [*S/7930/Add.6, 13 June 1967.*]

The UN at this time was in great disfavour in Israel, where the withdrawal of UNEF was regarded as a betrayal. The view that Israel must henceforth rely solely on herself had the support of the great majority of the Israeli popu-lation. Further, Government House—UNTSO's headquarters—was in Jerusalem, which Israel had declared would now remain united. All of these factors, therefore, operated against a speedy return of Government House to UNTSO. On 4 July the Israeli government suggested that UNTSO's Armistice functions were over:

2. On 28 June 1967 I addressed the following note to the Permanent Representative of Israel:

'The Secretary-General of the United Nations presents his compliments to the Permanent Representative of Israel to the United Nations and has the honour to refer once again to the urgent matter of the return of UNTSO to its Headquarters at Government House in Jerusalem.

'The Permanent Representative will recall that the Foreign Minister of Israel during his discussion with the Secretary-General on the evening of Thursday, 22 June, assured the Secretary-General that a reply from his Government on the question of UNTSO's return to Government House would be presented to the Secretary-General "in a day or two". It was also indicated by the Foreign Minister at that time that it was thought that the matter could be dealt with by an exchange of letters in which the Government of Israel would make clear its position that UNTSO's sole concern and function now should be with the recent cease-fire resolutions of the Security Council and no longer with the Armistice Agreements and the now obsolete arrangements of the past. The Secretary-General, it will also be recalled, responded that he could and would take note of these views of Israel but clearly he could not take a position which would be prejudicial to any Security Council resolution, past or present.

'In view of the fact that the functioning of UNTSO continues to be handicapped by being deprived of its long-established Headquarters, the Secretary-General must regard this is as a matter of real urgency. He is obliged, therefore, to ask the Government of Israel to expedite its reply to his several appeals on this matter, particularly since the outcome is of concern to the Security Council to which the Secretary-General is obliged to report about it.

'The Secretary-General takes this opportunity to renew to the Permanent Representative of Israel the assurances of his highest consideration.'

3. Ensuing consultations have led to an exchange of letters by which UNTSO and its Chief of Staff will now be enabled to regain their Headquarters for their exclusive use without further delay. These letters from the Permanent Representative of Israel to the Secretary-General and from the Secretary-General to the Permanent Representative of Israel are dated 29 June 1967 and 1 July 1967 respectively, and were exchanged on the morning of 4 July 1967. Their texts are as follows:

Letter from the Permanent Representative of Israel to the
Secretary-General, dated 29 June 1967:

'Excellency,

'I have the honour to refer to your telegram to the Prime Minister of 13 June 1967 in connection with Government House, Jerusalem, and to transmit you the following reply.

'As you reported to the 1347th meeting of the Security Council on 5 June, the Government House area, in which the UNTSO was accommodated, was first attacked and occupied by Jordanian troops as part of the Jordanian aggression against Israel, when they commenced their hostilities in Jerusalem on 5 June. This produced an extremely disturbing security situation in Jerusalem and compelled the Government of Israel to take counter-measures to dislodge the Jordanian troops from the Government House area and to ensure that they would not return there.

'In the course of the fighting, the building was severely damaged. While the area was still under heavy Jordanian fire, the Israel Forces helped to evacuate General Bull and his staff to a place of safety in Jerusalem. After the cease-fire between Israel and Jordan became effective, Israeli authorities in Jerusalem undertook the necessary work to clear away the debris and to repair the damage.

'Subsequently, the Government of Israel, as you are aware, did its utmost in the difficult circumstances prevailing in the aftermath of the fighting to make adequate facilities available to General Bull and his staff to enable him to discharge the functions placed upon him following the Security Council resolutions 233, 234, 235 and 236 of 1967. These included housing and office accommodation and facilities for communications. It remains the policy of the Government of Israel to continue to make these facilities available to General Bull for that purpose.

'However, since you believe that the facilities now available to General Bull are inadequate for him to carry out his functions under the recent cease-fire resolutions, the Government of Israel agrees to enable him and his staff to use Government House in the performance of their duties.

'It is understood that in the view of the Government of Israel, the sole function and concern of General Bull and his staff is with those cease-fire resolutions of the Security Council and no longer with the General Armistice Agreements and the now obsolete arrangements of the past.

'Please accept, Excellency, the assurances of my highest consideration.

(Signed) Gideon RAFAEL'

Letter from the Secretary-General to the Permanent
Representative of Israel, dated 1 July 1967:

'Sir,

'I have the honour to acknowledge receipt of your letter of 29 June 1967, replying to my message to the Prime Minister of Israel of 13 June, asking him to facilitate the return of UNTSO and its Chief of Staff to their Headquarters at Government House, Jerusalem.

'As you are aware, I have attached great urgency to this matter because the functioning of this important United Nations operation continues to be handicapped through being deprived of the facilities essential to the performance of its duties which are fully available only at its Government House Headquarters. It is reassuring, therefore, to have your Government's favourable response to the request made in my message to the Prime Minister of 13 June, a message which also reiterated my original request in my approach of 5 June. This is especially so in the light of the vital work being required of this United Nations operation in connection with the current cease-fire as set forth in paragraph 5 of the Security Council resolution of 12 June 1967, and the reporting responsibility required of the Secretary-General in the Council's resolutions of 6, 7 and 9 June. I take it that the return of the Chief of Staff, General Bull, and his staff to the exclusive use on behalf of the United Nations of their Headquarters at Government House will now take place without further delay.

'The specific views of your Government as set forth in the last paragraph of your letter, have been noted.

'Solely from a practical standpoint, of course, it may be said that UNTSO's primary purpose in the area at this time is to do and to be enabled to do all that it can toward maintaining quiet and averting any resumption of hostilities in the region.

'The subject of this correspondence being a matter of concern to the Security Council, it is my intention to inform the Council at an early date of your favourable response to my request and I assume that you would have no objection to the inclusion in that report of the full text of your letter to me of 29 June as well as of this reply.

'Accept, Sir, the assurances of my highest consideration.

U THANT'

4. As indicated in the Secretary-General's letter to the Permanent Representative of Israel, the specific views of the Government of Israel with regard to the functions and status of UNTSO have been noted only without any appraisal or expression of opinion on them by the Secretary-General.

5. The return of UNTSO to its Headquarters will greatly facilitate its work, although in the Government House compound the main building and other structures suffered considerable

damage during the fighting and there was subsequent damage to and loss of United Nations records, vehicles, equipment and other property as well as personal belongings of staff members through looting and acts of vandalism. General Bull has been advised of the accord and it is assumed that he will return promptly to his Headquarters. [*S/7930/Add.20, 4 July 1967.*]

On 23 August UNTSO was allowed to return to Government House.

Related problems arose concerning the freedom of movement of UN observers, but these were dealt with in a co-operative manner:

4. On the morning of 11 June I also received from General Bull the following messages:

'I will see Mr. Sasson at 1130 11 June to discuss the following:

'a. Israel authorities' slowness in allowing deployment of UNMO teams from Tiberias. Israel authorities have not provided an adequate number of LOs (liaison officers) to properly cover cease-fire line.

'b. Complete freedom of movement for these teams has not been granted by Israel authorities.

'c. The taking of a Syrian Liaison Officeer prisoner who was with one of the UNMO teams from Damascus.

'Incident was reported by Tiberias Control Centre as follows:

'At 1005 11 June UNMO-203 one of the teams deployed from Damascus is at OP Echo checkpoint which is now an Israeli position. The Israelis have taken the UNMO's Syrian Liaison Officer prisoner.'

'I saw Sasson 11 June and discussed following matters:

'1. Sasson agreed with me that everything should be done to expedite the deployment of UNMOs. To that effect I requested that IDF make available seven more Liaison Officers immediately so that we could have nine UNMO teams on Israel side. He agreed to this suggestion subject to concurrence by Dayan.

'2. Regarding freedom of movement of UNMO teams he agreed that such movement should be granted in IDF battle areas on the understanding that movement should be co-ordinated with local unit commanders in view of military necessities.

'3. In order to ensure greater co-ordination between United Nations and Israel authorities Sasson informed that Col. Gath had been designated as the officer responsible for liaison with United Nations in Tiberias for implementation of Secco cease-fire demand. [*S/7930/Add.3, 11 June 1967.*]

4. Only way of ascertaining time at which Israel troops entered Kuneitra 10 June would be to question Sasson. I questioned Sasson on subject evening 10 June and he replied it was before time fixed for cease-fire, but did not give me further details. I shall question him again soonest. . . .

5. General Bull met with Mr. Sasson of the Israel Foreign Office on the afternoon of 12 June to discuss this and other matters. These included the implementation of the Security Council resolution 236 (1967) of 12 June. General Bull also raised with Mr. Sasson the question of mapping the position of the forces and made it clear that the positions to be mapped should be those occupied as of the time of the cease-fire, i.e., 1630 hours GMT 10 June, Mr. Sasson agreed with this position and promised that full co-operation would be given to United Nations Military Observers for this purpose.

6. General Bull also raised the question of the exchange of war prisoners which had been suggested by Mr. Sasson. General Bull stated that it was his intention with the full support of the Secretary-General to make his good offices available for the exchange of war prisoners. Mr. Sasson informed General Bull that the Israel authorities had got in touch with the Red Cross also for this purpose. General Bull remarked that in the past UNTSO's good offices for the exchange of prisoners had been exercised in full co-operation with the Red Cross and that his good offices were available at all times if and when necessary.

7. General Bull also raised the question of freedom of movement of United Nations personnel which was not at present adequate. He pointed out that United Nations Military Observers had now to be accompanied by Israel liaison officers in their movements. Mr. Sasson observed that the present situation was an emergency one and that the Government of Israel would consider establishing freedom of movement for observers as soon as possible. [*S/7930/ Add.5, 12 June 1967.*]

1. No serious incidents have been reported from the cease-fire area.
2. General Bull reports that in a meeting with Mr. Sasson of the Israeli Foreign Office on the evening of 12 June 1967 Mr. Sasson stated, in reply to a question put to him earlier, that Kuneitra had been taken at 1400 hours GMT on 10 June.
3. Mr. Sasson assured General Bull that UNTSO's Observers would have complete freedom of movement in Israel, as distinct from occupied territory, from the morning of 13 June 1967 and that United Nations personnel would be able to travel unaccompanied by Liaison Officers. Passes would be issued to allow UN Observers to travel between the Israel sector of Jerusalem and the old city. [*S/7930/Add.6, 13 June 1967.*]

General Odd Bull also showed considerable skill in his handling of relations with Egypt and Israel in respect of the stationing of UNTSO observers in the Suez Canal zone. After the Security Council had reached a consensus on 9–10 July to place UN observers along either side of the Canal, the Chief of Staff held discussions with both the Israeli and the Egyptian authorities.

6. In the initial discussions with the parties various limitations on the observation operation were suggested which would, in the opinion of the Chief of Staff, seriously hamper its effectiveness. These related mainly to movement of observers, and to communications. The problem of the movement of observers has been resolved and the communications problems partially resolved. . . .
10. United Nations Observers are patrolling from and between the established [operation posts] during daylight hours. UAR and Israel military Liaison Officers are available to United Nations Military Observers on their respective sides. [*S/8053/Add.1, 10 Aug. 1967,* mimeo.][61]

10

RELATIONS WITH OTHER STATES INVOLVED

Israel was not a 'host state' because she declined to accept the presence of UNTSO personnel on her territory. Quite obviously, she was still a party 'directly involved' in the operating of UNTSO. However, given the existence of four parallel Armistice Agreements it has been thought that reasons of clarity militate against dealing separately with UN-Israeli relations. Instead, all the relevant materials are subsumed under Section 9 above.

[61] For details of the arrangements made by General Bull concerning ships on the Canal, and the Egyptian and Israeli positions on this, see below, s. 12, pp. 209–11.

II

FINANCE

UNTSO has always been financed out of the regular budget of the United Nations, and assessed among UN members in accordance with their scale of contributions. It has been treated, for budgetary purposes, as a 'special mission', provision for which falls quite normally within the regular budget.[1] Until 1963 there were no major controversies over the financing of UNTSO, though a nominal objection was customarily made, by the Communist nations, to the inclusion in the regular budget of all UN 'presences' or 'observers'. In May 1963, with the UN membership deeply divided on the question of peacekeeping expenses, and following the Opinion of the International Court on that matter, the Communist nations announced that they would not pay those parts of their regular budget assessments which were for UNTSO or UNCURK. They also refused to pay for the 200-man Field Service, some 75 per cent of which was assigned to UNTSO in 1963.[2]

The method of presenting the figures has undergone several major changes during the period of UNTSO's existence. From 1949 to 1951 no separate figures are provided for UNTSO; instead, one must look to the UN Conciliation Commission for Palestine, item (iii) of which refers to 'Travel and subsistence of observers and military technical staff'. Thereafter, UNTSO appears as a separately listed item. In 1952 it included the expenditures of the UN Conciliation Commission for Palestine, and the breaking down of the figures for this year is in a form not subsequently repeated. Two further variables must be noted: (1) from the eighth to the eleventh sessions, the breakdown of UNTSO expenses appears in the Detailed Schedule to the Budget Estimates; (2) after 1956, the estimates no longer contain a detailed schedule; accordingly, the methods by which the figures were broken down again change.

---

[1] Finding one's way around the UN budget is no easy matter. The item 'Special Mission and Inquiries' covers all UN peacekeeping operations save for ONUC and UNEF, for which finances were raised in *ad hoc* and special accounts; the UN Force in Korea, which was financed outside of the UN budget; UNYOM and UNSF, which were financed by the parties involved; and UNFICYP, which was financed by voluntary contributions, with the parties most directly involved paying the major share. From 1945–60 the item 'Special Missions' appears as Sect. 4 (or occasionally, 5) in the Annual Budget Estimates; from 1960–4 it appears as Sect. 18; and after 1965 as Sect. 16. The Budget Estimates not only provide the estimates for the forthcoming financial year; they also refer back to the expenditures of the previous year (from 1946–52), or of the previous two years (1952–67). Where information is provided as to the expenditures of the previous two years, the earlier will be final and accurate, while the most recent year's figures are still 'round' at the stage that they appear, by way of reference back in the ensuing year's Budget Estimates. Thus, to find out what was spent on UNTSO in 1958, one should look in the Official Records for the 14th session (1959), seeking out the Budget Estimates (always suppl. 5 of the Assembly records) for 1960.

[2] J. Stoessinger, *Financing the United Nations System* (1964), p. 106.

I. 1949–51 EXPENDITURES*

UNTSO total (appearing as item (iii) of Expenses for UN Commission for Palestine)

	$	Source
1949:	1,154,374	A/1267
1950:	188,276	A/1812
1951:	167,154	A/2125

II. 1952 EXPENDITURES*

	$
Temporary assistance	162,700
Travel & subsistence of observers	131,989
Travel & subsistence of staff	184,936
Communications services	4,266
Rental & maintenance of premises & equipment	12,158
Stationery & office supplies	3,428
Local transportation	451
Operation & maintenance of transportation equipment	35,856
Freight, cartage & express	7,891
Insurance	9,069
Miscellaneous supplies & services	12,302
Contractual & support services	157,226
Purchase of motor vehicles	11,656
Miscellaneous equipment	1,100
Travel & subsistence of members	1,783
Furniture & fixtures	920
Hospitality	10
Total:	$737,742

* *including expenditures for UN Conciliation Commission for Palestine*
Source: A/2383

III. 1952–5 EXPENDITURES*

	1953	1954
Temporary assistance	76,108	95,652
Travel & subsistence of observers	110,311	160,864
Travel & subsistence of staff	152,076	167,371
Communications services	4,801	5,413
Rental & maintenance of premises & equipment	16,648	13,253
Stationery & office supplies	3,263	4,737
Local transportation	372	1,145
Operation & maintenance of transportation & equipment	34,161	30,609
Freight, cartage & express	7,019	15,896
Insurance	3,608	5,259
Misc. supplies & services	3,688	5,069
Transportation equipment	39,833	45,847
Misc. equipment	3,953	16,707
Contractual support services	799	—
Hospitality	290	290
Rental of aircraft		23,000
Total: $	456,921	591,112

* The Budget Estimates of the session of the Assembly give no breakdown for 1955—for individual UN missions. Only a total is given for the overall item 'Special Missions', together with a breakdown for the UN Advisory Council for Somaliland under Italian Administration. Thus no figures are available for UNTSO for that year.

Sources: A/2647, A/2904

IV 1956–8 EXPENDITURES

	1956	1957	1958
Salaries & wages	107,882	129,456	136,481
Travel & subsistence of observers	267,079	309,963	389,897
Transport & subsistence of staff	251,437	299,012	320,772
Transport equipment	125,939		
Misc. equipment	83,853		
Misc. supplies & services	253,445	291,096	330,645
Permanent equipment		147,692	112,240
Total: $	1,089,635	1,177,221	1,290,035

Sources: A/3600, A/3825, A/4110.

V. 1959–66 EXPENDITURES

	1959	1960	1961	1962	1963	1964	1965	1966 391,378*
Salaries and wages	138,733	136,536	153,354	175,529	190,331	189,442	195,355	1,087,577
Subsistence and travel of observers	458,087	477,650	460,188	481,778	488,778	521,073	546,767	582,862
Subsistence and travel of staff	357,113	335,576	356,380	355,201	360,688	347,987	367,575	534,09
Communications, freight and supply services	86,703	89,425	110,326	145,904	130,618	117,875	117,834	136,67
Maintenance of premises and equipment	122,079	92,995	77,790	92,440	136,973	134,803	108,575	97,310
Maintenance of vehicles	122,331	132,739	124,996	116,932	120,253	117,976	115,366	93,25
Purchase of vehicles	110,609	79,290	85,769	177,474	111,014	61,894	163,203	111,63
Rental of aircraft	72,617	79,290	75,000	65,000	98,731	79,638	80,000	80,40
Furniture and fixtures	64,599	144,102	14,743	47,786	25,583	46,620	73,548	20,31
Total	$1,532,871	1,561,253	1,458,546	1,657,332	1,669,969	1,617,308	1,768,223	3,135,49

*Common staff costs
    Sources: A/4370,   A/4770 A/5205, A/5505, A/5805, A/6005, A/6305, A/67c

Note: None of the above tables is, as such, an official UN document. The tables have, however, been compiled, for the sake of brevity, clarity, and comparability, from the official records, the sources of which are given.

On 25 October 1967 the Secretary-General indicated that if the Security Council's consensus of 9–10 July 1967 (following the six-day war) were to be put into effect, additional observers would be needed in the Suez Canal sector.[3] These requirements were elaborated on 31 October 1967.[4] Some 47 additional observers were obtained and on 1 December 1967 the Secretary-General reported that the total additional expenditure was expected to be $315,820, broken down as follows:

VI. 1967 EXPENDITURE

Travel and subsistence of 47 military observers	87,370
Rental and maintenance of premises & equipment	12,560
Operation and maintenance of vehicles	5,000
Communications, freight, supplies and services	30,890
Purchase of furniture and equipment	24,000
Purchase of vehicles	156,000
Total:	$315,820

Source: S/8126/Add.1.

He also noted that 'should the Observer operation in the Suez Canal sector be continued in 1968, the estimated cost of the operation for that year', on the basis of a continuing observers strength of ninety, would be $873,000'.

[3] See pp. 55–59, s. 3 above, and s. 7 above, p. 71.   [4] S/8053/Add. 3, and Corr. 1. See s. 4, pp. 62–63.

12

IMPLEMENTATION

(a) 1949–56

i. *Syria–Israel Armistice, 1949–56*

ALTHOUGH major violence was fairly successfully contained in the 1949–56 period, the Syria–Israel Armistice Agreement ran into certain major difficulties. Certain of these difficulties related to genuine differences in the interpretation of particular aspects of the Agreement. The respective authority of the Chairman and of the Commission under Article V of the Agreement; the compatibility of the draining of the Huleh marshes with the 'no-military advantage' clause; the employment of Israeli police in the demilitarized zone; and the controversial building of the canal to the Jordan are all cases in point. These have been documented elsewhere (pp. 86–107), as they were questions which influenced greatly not only the implementation of the Agreement, but also the relations of Syria and Israel with the UN.

The refusal of the parties on certain occasions to accept the ruling of either the Chairman or of the Commission inevitably led to direct clashes with each other, and to breaches of the Agreement. For example:

33. On the morning of 26 March, two bulldozers belonging to the Palestine Land Development Company were brought up to the western bank of the Jordan River near the Banat Yakub bridge and were immediately fired upon by Arab civilians. Upon the intervention of United Nations observers, firing ceased.

34. The Chairman reported that the Israel civilians had emplaced two 3.5″ mortars approximately 200 metres northwest of Mishmar Hay Yarden in the central sector of the demilitarized zone. These mortars were served by civilians from a nearby settlement. Orders given by the Chairman to withdraw these weapons were disregarded by Israel police officers and members of the Israel delegation to the Israel–Syrian Mixed Armistice Commission.

35. This action prompted the acting Chief of Staff to send the following message to the Chief of Staff, Israel Defence Forces:

'I am informed by the Chairman of the Israel–Syrian Mixed Armistice Commission that Israel civilians have emplaced two 3.5″ mortars in the central sector of the demilitarized zone, 200 metres northwest of Mishmar Hay Yarden.

'I consider these civilians to constitute an Israel para-military force within the demilitarized zone. This action, having been confirmed by the United Nations representative, constitutes a flagrant violation of the General Armistice Agreement between Israel and Syria.

'You are requested to issue the necessary orders to effect the immediate withdrawal of this force together with their weapons.'

36. Later the same day, the Syrian delegation alleged that Israel troops had moved into the demilitarized zone in the vicinity of Khoury Farm. Investigation by United Nations observers showed that no Israel military forces were in the area mentioned in the Syrian complaint. [*S/2067, Report of Acting Chief of Staff of UNTSO to Secretary-General, 4 Apr. 1951.*]

At the same time, the very existence of the Armistice machinery, including UNTSO, provided contacts for informal talks between the parties: 'On 26 March 1951, the Deputy Chief of Staff, Israel Defence Forces and the Deputy Chief of Staff of the Syrian Army met for five hours and discussed the question of the Huleh works.'[1] The reports of 1951 and 1952 reveal an almost continuous series of violations of the Armistice, usually in respect of the demilitarized zone. Ensuring the carrying out of the Armistice was made even more difficult by the obstacles placed in the way of the UN observers. One may cite examples:

29. On 6 April 1951 . . . the commander of the local police of [the Syrian outpost of] El Hamma was not prepared to guarantee the safety of the United Nations observers in El Hamma as the local population was very excited and armed. . . .

31. On the afternoon of 6 April, three United Nations observers were stopped on the track leading from Baqqara village . . . by a group of armed Israelis who surrounded them and threatened them with death. . . . The observers returned to the main road at gunpoint. The United Nations observers then requested assurances from the Israeli delegation that they would be permitted to operate freely in the demilitarized zone in areas inhabitated by Israelis. . . . [*S/2084, Report of Acting Chief of Staff to Secretary-General, 10 Apr. 1951.*]

In May 1951 the breaches of the Armistice became so marked that it was found necessary to refer the issue to the Security Council, resulting in Resolution S/2157.[2] Compliance with this resolution was good, however, and matters now began to be brought under control.

I have the honour to submit for transmission to the President of the Security Council a further interim report on steps taken to give effect to the Security Council resolution of 18 May 1951 (*S/2157*).

1. On 23 May 1951, the Palestine Land Development Company ceased operation in connection with the Huleh concession project on all Arab-owned land in the demilitarized zone, which land had been the subject of dispute since 12 February 1951.

2. The Chairman of the Israel–Syrian Mixed Armistice Commission then initiated an enquiry amongst Arabs whose lands lie along the Jordan River or contiguous thereto to determine if agreement were possible whereby acceptance of fair compensation or exchange of land within the demilitarized zone could be arranged to avoid jeopardizing restoration of normal civilian life. [*S/2213, Report of Chief of Staff of UNTSO to Secretary-General, 26 June 1951.*]

It was the device of proceeding with work in the demilitarized zone without having to requisition Arab property there that led the way out of the Huleh impasse. The return of Arab civilians to the demilitarized zone presented particular problems:

1. On 30 June 1951, arrangements were made with the Government of Israel for the return of Arab civilians who had been removed from the demilitarized zone. It was agreed that the Chairman and United Nations observers would interview the heads of Arab families [in order to ascertain their wishes] . . .

3. The heads of families interviewed by the Chairman on 2 and 3 July 1951 represented 632 Arab civilians out of 785 evacuated from the demilitarized zone. Of this number, approximately 250 to 260 elected to return to the demilitarized zone.

4. The Chairman also visited four Arabs who were confined in jail at Shafaamr charged with violation of the Israel emergency regulations, to wit 'communicating with the enemy'.

[1] S/2067, 4 Apr. 1951, para. 37.   [2] See above, p. 94.

One of them was the Mukhtar of Baqqara. They were released and allowed to return to the demilitarized zone on 5 July.

5. As there was a discrepancy of some 153 Arabs between the number represented by the heads of families interviewed and the number evacuated from the demilitarized zone, the Chairman requested that he be permitted to return to Sha'ab and to have announced publicly that any heads of families who had not been interviewed could come forward at once and state their desires. The request was refused. He then requested permission to revisit Sha'ab on 4 July to complete the interviews. This request was tentatively agreed to but later rejected by the senior Israel representative.

6. The Chairman insisted that United Nations observers should be present at Sha'ab on 5 July, the date on which the convoy was to embark the Arab civilians who elected to return to the demilitarized zone, so that individuals who elected to return or who desired to change their previous declaration might have the opportunity to make their wishes known, but this request was rejected by the senior Israel representative. The Chairman is now scheduled to return to Sha'ab on 9 July 1951 to interrogate additional Arab civilians.

7. On 4 July, the Chairman informed the senior Israel representative that he would return to the demilitarized zone the 115 Arab civilians, former inhabitants of Baqqara and Ghanname who had fled to the Syrian side on the outbreak of disturbances. The senior Israel representative replied that only eleven individuals of the group would be allowed to return to the zone. In addition, the owner of considerable property in the demilitarized zone, especially Khoury Farm, was denied permission to return to the zone.

'*From Chairman of Israel–Syrian Mixed Armistice Commission to senior Israel representative, 4 July 1951:* This is to confirm our conversation of today 4 July and to make my position as Chairman Israel–Syrian Mixed Armistice Commission absolutely clear regarding demilitarized zone Arabs. I consider that all demilitarized zone Arabs evacuated or who fled from Baqqara, Ghanname, Khoury Farm regardless of whether they went to Israel, Syria or other parts of demilitarized zone, must be permitted to return forthwith to their village. My position is similar with regard to Arabs from other parts of demilitarized zone. . . .'

9. Arab civilians who were returned to the demilitarized zone on 5 July are now installed in tents in the Baqqara village area and are receiving food supplies from the United Nations Relief and Works Agency. These Arab civilians, as well as others who may be returned, must of necessity be housed in tents until the villages destroyed are replaced.

General RILEY

[*S/2234, Report of Chief of Staff of UNTSO to Secretary-General, 9 July 1951.*]

The report of 17 August 1951 (S/2300) indicated that the Chief of Staff had still not been successful in securing adequate co-operation in this particular matter.

A particular difficulty had been whether Syria was correct in claiming that Israel should not be permitted to build settlements for the returning civilians on the ground that this would violate Article II (1) and Article V (2) of the Armistice, and give Israel military and political gains. The Chairman of the MAC held that building such settlements gave no military advantage to Israel; and Israel then developed a cluster of settlements in the demilitarized zone. The settlement of all problems concerning the demilitarized zone was plagued by the impossibility of convening regular meetings of the MAC, due to this failure of the parties to agree on what would be an acceptable agenda.[3]

31. The Chairman of the Mixed Armistice Commission has continued to exert his influence on the parties, looking to a resumption of meetings of the Commission. To date he has not been successful.

[3] S/2300, para. 9.

32. In conference, on 2 August, the senior Syrian representative informed the Chairman that his 'Government approves all measures aiming at the return of normal civilian life in the demilitarized zone'. He also added that if the Chairman considered that resumption of Mixed Armistice Commission meetings would lead to a settlement of the violations of the General Armistice Agreement, the Syrian representative was ready to help. However, on 3 August 1951, he informed the Chairman that he, personally, could see no point in holding a meeting of the Mixed Armistice Commission unless fundamental issues were considered first. He listed as fundamental issues:

(*a*) Resumption of the interrogation, with no Israeli present, of the Arabs removed to the Sha'ab area;

(*b*) Cessation of all Huleh drainage works until governmental agreement was reached;

(*c*) The question of the local police in the demilitarized zone;

(*d*) No exercise of sovereignty by either Israel or Syria within the demilitarized zone.

33. The permanent representative of Israel to the United Nations in a communication addressed to me on 4 August also raised the question of the non-functioning of the Mixed Armistice Commission. He stated that between 18 May and 30 June 1951 Israel had submitted eighteen complaints to the Chairman of the Mixed Armistice Commission in accordance with paragraph 7 of article VII of the General Armistice Agreement. These complaints had not been brought up for discussion. The representative of Israel added that 'In view of the many items requiring urgent decision it is hoped this paralysis of the armistice machinery will not be prolonged any further.'   [*Ibid.*]

Israel continued to insist that under paragraph 5 (c) of Article 5, it was the Chairman of the Commission (or the Chief of Staff), and not the Commission, who had responsibility for all activities in the zone. Israel claimed that Syria was trying to create an unwarranted *locus standi* for herself in respect of the demilitarized zone, by reference to the MAC, of which she was a member.[4] Syria on the other hand continued to insist that

. . . the Mixed Armistice Commission being competent to supervise the execution of the provisions of the General Armistice Agreement, including article V, relating to the demilitarized zone, is empowered to deal with complaints submitted by the parties relating to the implementation of article V. Paragraph 5 (*c*) of article V of the armistice agreement refers to the responsibility of the Chairman of the Mixed Armistice Commision and United Nations observers for ensuring 'the full implementation' of the article, whereas the first paragraph of article VII provides that the Mixed Armistice Commission shall supervise the execution of the provisions of the agreement.   [*S/3345, 11 Jan. 1955*, para. 21.]

The outcome of this conflict of views was the failure of the MAC to hold regular meetings, since 20 June 1951. Although emergency meetings were periodically called, occasionally one party would fail to attend them.[5] These meetings, too, began to lapse.

Little progress could be made, and in November 1951 General Riley reported:

4. The Security Council resolution of 18 May directs the Chief of Staff 'to take the necessary steps to give effect to this resolution for the purpose of restoring peace in the area, and authorizes him to take such measures to restore peace in the area and to make such representations to the Governments of Israel and Syria as he may deem necessary'. The continuing paralysis of the Mixed Armistice Commission has imposed on the Chief of Staff heavier

[4] See above, pp. 87–88; and the detailed statements by Israel and Syria in Ann. A. and B to S/3343, 11 Jan. 1955.
[5] S/3345, para. 24.

duties as regards the implementation of the Security Council resolution. The responsibility 'for ensuring the full implementation' of article V of the Armistice Agreement has become much greater for the Chairman of the Mixed Armistice Commission since he has had to work without benefit of direction from the Commission. There are differences of opinion between the parties to the Armistice Agreement on the meaning of various provisions of article V, including those which relate to the Chairman's powers, but neither party has requested an interpretation by the Mixed Armistice Commission in the manner established by article VII of the Agreement, and the Chairman has had to rely on his own interpretation, knowing that in many cases it would probably be found unacceptable by one party or by both and that his requests were likely to meet with refusal on the ground that he was exceeding his powers or acting in some other manner contrary to the provisions of the Armistice Agreement.

6. During the conversation held at the Ministry for Foreign Affairs on 6 September, it was reaffirmed to me that the policy of the Government of Israel was to allow full freedom of movement to the United Nations observers in the demilitarized zone, and that nothing would be done by anybody to obstruct the observers or hamper them in the execution of their duty. I, for my part, agreed that normal identity checking at the entrance to the demilitarized zone did not constitute a curtailment of the freedom of movement of the United Nations observers in the zone.

18. The Chairman of the Mixed Armistice Commission and the Israel representative have not yet worked out a practicable arrangement concerning the police question in conformity with the above principles. Up to now there has been progress on one point: in conformity with the assurances given to me by the representatives of the Israel Government (see paragraph 6 above) interference with the freedom of movement of the Chairman and United Nations observers within the demilitarized zone has ceased. It was also stated to me, on 6 September, that the Israelis would do their best to make the lives of the Baqqara and Ghanname villagers as comfortable as possible and would not interfere with them or otherwise create difficulties. I recalled this statement to the representative of the Government of Israel on 2 November.

19. The Chairman of the Mixed Armistice Commission will inform the senior Syrian representative to the Mixed Armistice Commission of any further development in connexion not only with the police question but with any other question concerning the demilitarized zone. The Governments of Israel and Syria have agreed that the Chairman 'and United Nations observers attached to the Commission shall be responsible for ensuring the full implementaton' of article V of the General Armistice Agreement. The Mixed Armistice Commission has been prevented from dealing with questions concerning the implementation of article V. The Chairman's duty is to maintain contact with the two delegations, to receive their information and their requests, and to inform them of developments concerning the implementation of article V. [*S/2389, Report of Chief of Staff of UNTSO to Secretary-General, 8 Nov. 1951.*]

General Riley showed a considerable flexibility at this time in seeking to secure *ad hoc* arrangements. The agreement reached on 'directives'[6] was supplemented by similar formulas. For example, an *impasse* had been reached over the road block erected by the Syrians at El Hamma, which they refused to remove because of suspicions of the intentions of the Israeli police. Israel, for her part, insisted that the right of free movement through the area be acknowledged. A compromise was reached whereby General Riley persuaded the government of Israel

to distinguish between the right of free access and of freedom of movement in the demilitarized zone on the one hand, and the actual exercise of that right on the other. It was further agreed that such a right existed, but that the automatic exercise of that right was, under present circumstances, quite a different thing, though it might be hoped to have even this made

[6] S/2389, paras 6 and 18.

possible once current difficulties had been got out of the way and the present tension had subsided. [*Ibid.* para. 24.]

Arrangements such as these had a lasting importance,[7] though the specific plans which were intended to follow from the agreed formulas[8] on the employment of locally-recruited police never materialized:

It was expected in 1951 that the agreement would be followed by practical arrangements. Such arrangements did not materialize.

18. During 1952 and 1953, there was no change as regards the activities of the Israel police in the demilitarized zone. Police from the State of Israel, acting under orders from police headquarters outside the demilitarized zone, dominated the zone, with the exception of small areas about Nuqeib, El Hamma and Shamalne. The Chairman of the Mixed Armistice Commission was unable to implement the provision of the General Armistice Agreement requiring the employment of 'locally recruited civilian police' in the zone. Repeated requests by the Chairman of the Mixed Armistice Commission to remove the non-local police from the demilitarized zone were rejected. The same situation prevailed throughout 1954. [*S/3343, Report of Chief of Staff of UNTSO to the Secretary-General, 11 Jan. 1955.*]

Israel claimed that it had been impracticable to recruit police entirely from local inhabitants, and that in fact it made little difference as in any event she would still have been the authority responsible for them. There were, essentially, two points at issue concerning the policing of the military zone: first, compliance with the Armistice requirement that the police be locally recruited, and second, the scope of their authority. On 31 January 1951 Israel had agreed to notify the Chairman of the MAC before any action was taken by Israel police in respect of Arab persons or property in the demilitarized zone.[9] This she would do only in cases of emergency. The normal practice would be for local Arab police to seek to deal with the situation.

In 1955 there occurred serious incidents of Syrian shooting at Israeli boats on Lake Tiberias,[10] which occasioned retaliatory action by Israel. Relations between Israel and Syria deteriorated still further, and the official machinery became employed less and less:

27. Relations between the parties were more seriously embittered by their failure to agree to an exchange of prisoners during the current year. Israel public opinion was extremely agitated over the fate of the four soldiers taken prisoner on 8 December 1954, when carrying out an intelligence operation in Syrian territory, as set forth in the resolution of the Israel–Syrian Mixed Armistice Commission adopted on the proposal of the Syrian delegation on 12 January 1955 (annex I to this report). There was originally a fifth prisoner, who committed suicide on the evening of 12 January, when in prison. Investigation disclosed no signs of physical ill-treatment nor any evident reason why he should have taken his life. Subsequent

---

[7] See e.g. S/2833, para. 58, and S/3343 paras 14–15.   [8] S/2389, paras 6 and 18.

[9] See Bar-Yaacov, p. 67 n. 4. He also relates examples of Israel police actions, under the scrutiny of and with the approval of UNTSO observers, in two situations where this proved necessary (pp. 103–4).

[10] Ibid. pp. 214–16 for an account of the underlying causes of resentment. Bar-Yaacov notes that Syria resented the Israel view that licences for fishing had to be acquired from the Israel authorities; that Israel claimed that her police patrol boats were protecting Israel fishermen from Syrian shooting, and preventing the Syrians from crossing the demarcation line to fish, while Syria claimed that they were merely protecting her legitimate fishing rights; and that Israel contended that the Syrians frequently fired, without provocation, from the 10-metre strip on the north-east shore of the lake, which was in fact Israeli territory.

to this, the prisoners have been regularly visited by United Nations military observers and their treatment has been in accordance with the Geneva Convention.

28. The course of the prolonged negotiations to secure the release of these four Israel prisoners was interrupted by the incident of 22 October 1955, during which Israel military raiding parties killed three, wounded six and captured five Syrian military personnel. The press release I issued after this incident is annexed to this report (annex II). It may be noted in this connexion that the Mixed Armistice Commission has not considered the United Nations observers' report on the investigation of this grave incident, since Syria has not requested an emergency meeting. Syria, like Israel, has for several months, filed complaints 'for the next formal meeting of the Mixed Armistice Commission.' On 9 December 1955 there were thus outstanding for the next formal meeting 568 Syrian and 401 Israel complaints. The fact that, after formal meetings which fell into disuse in June 1951 emergency meetings are no longer resorted to (the last one took place in March 1955), indicates the extent to which the traditional Mixed Armistice Commission procedure of formal discussion has broken down. It has been replaced with more or less success by informal conversations. [*S/3516, Report of Chief of Staff of UNTSO to Secretary-General, 20 Dec. 1955.*]

In January 1956 the Security Council discussed draft resolutions on a Syrian complaint that Israel armed forces had attacked Syrian armed forces on Syrian territory east of Lake Tiberias, on the night of 11–12 December 1955. The Israel attack—which was clearly so designated by the UNTSO Chief of Staff in his report—had been preceded by illegal Syrian interference with Israeli activities on Lake Tiberias. The Security Council was thus faced—and not for the last time[11]—with the question of seeking to maintain the continuing legal validity of the Armistice Agreements in the face of illegal action and reprisal by the parties thereto. The following strongly-worded resolution was adopted unanimously on 19 January 1956:

The Security Council,

Recalling its resolutions of 15 July 1948, 11 August 1949, 18 May 1951, 24 November 1953, and 29 March 1955;

Taking into consideration the statements of the representatives of Syria and Israel and the reports of the Chief of Staff of the United Nations Truce Supervision Organization on the Syrian complaint that an attack was committed by Israel regular army forces against Syrian regular army forces on Syrian territory on 11 December 1955,

Noting the report of the Chief of Staff that this Israel action was a deliberate violation of the provisions of the General Armistice Agreement, including those relating to the demilitarized zone, which was crossed by the Israel forces which entered Syria,

Noting also, without prejudice to the ultimate rights, claims and positions of the parties, that according to the reports of the Chief of Staff there has been interference by the Syrian authorities with Israel activities on Lake Tiberias, in contravention of the terms of the General Armistice Agreement between Israel and Syria,

1. *Holds* that this interference in no way justifies the Israel action;

2. *Reminds* the Government of Israel that the Council has already condemned military action in breach of the general armistice agreements, whether or not undertaken by way of retaliation, and has called upon Israel to take effective measures to prevent such actions;

3. *Condemns* the attack of 11 December 1955 as a flagrant violation of the cease-fire provisions of its resolution of 15 July 1948, of the terms of the General Armistice Agreement between Israel and Syria, and of Israel's obligations under the Charter;

4. *Expresses its grave concern* at the failure of the Government of Israel to comply with its obligations;

[11] See below pp. 193–4

5. *Calls upon* the Government of Israel to do so in the future, in default of which the Council will have to consider what further measures under the Charter are required to maintain or restore the peace.

6. *Calls upon* the parties to comply with their obligations under article V of the General Armistice Agreement to respect the armistice demarcation line and the demilitarized zone;

7. *Requests* the Chief of Staff to pursue his suggestions for improving the situation in the area of Lake Tiberias without prejudice to the rights, claims and positions of the parties and to report to the Council as appropriate on the success of his efforts;

8. *Calls upon* the parties to arrange with the Chief of Staff for an immediate exchange of all military prisoners;

9. *Calls upon* both parties to co-operate with the Chief of Staff in this and all other respects, to carry out the provisions of the General Armistice Agreement in good faith, and in particular to make full use of the Mixed Armistice Commission's machinery in the interpretation and application of its provisions.   [*SC Res. S/3538, 19 Jan. 1956.*]

At six meetings held between 28 March and 4 April 1956 the Security Council discussed (at the request of the United States) the broader question of the status of compliance with the Armistice Agreements and recently adopted resolutions of the Security Council.[12] It was decided to request the Secretary-General to undertake a survey on the question of compliance with each of the Armistice Agreements, and to authorize him to arrange with the parties measures for reducing tensions.[13] The Secretary-General was asked to report on compliance not only with the Armistice Agreements themselves, but also with the Security Council's resolutions of 30 March 1955 (S/3379); of 8 September 1955 (S/3435); and 19 January 1956 (S/3538). This last, of course, concerned the Israel–Syria Armistice. Referring to Lake Tiberias, the Secretary-General reported on suggestions which had been made for improving the situation, and which reflected directly on the freedom of movement required for UN observers:

85. In order to facilitate compliance with the General Armistice Agreement and with the special arrangements made in regard to the eastern shore of Lake Tiberias, proposals were made both to Syria and to Israel for the placing of fixed observation posts manned by United Nations observers on the eastern and north-eastern shore of the lake. Approximately two such posts would be on Syrian-controlled territory and one in territory controlled by Israel. In addition observers should have the right to move to these posts and to any point where difficulties requiring their intervention might arise in a special United Nations boat.

86. Syria accepted these proposals and, in regard to the movement of a United Nations boat on the lake, expressed the view that as the greater portion of the lake lies in the defensive zone provided for in article V, paragraph 6, and annex III of the General Armistice Agreement, United Nations observers should have complete freedom of movement thereon.

87. Israel does not agree to the movement of a United Nations military observer boat on Lake Tiberias nor to the establishment of a military observer post on Israel territory, considering these measures uncalled for and as derogating from the rights which she claims over the whole extent of the lake and the territory to the north thereof and as far east as the old Palestine–Syrian boundary. Israel would nevertheless be prepared, after the lapse of a month, to consider a proposal by the Chief of Staff for the establishment of a United Nations military observer post, should he then consider it desirable.

[12] *SCOR*, mtgs 717–28.
[13] For the role given to the Secretary-General in respect of all the Agreements, and his work thereunder, see p. 63. Materials relating to all the Armistice Agreements as a whole are gathered below, pp. 178–84.

88. I have declared that I find it necessary to maintain the proposal both for a police boat and for a post on Israel territory. Short of these arrangements, I can scarcely find that the patrolling arrangements, mentioned below under (d), provide adequate safeguards.

89. It will be recalled that in its resolution of 19 January 1956, the Security Council endorsed five proposals in regard to Lake Tiberias which had been made by the Chief of Staff. The present status of these proposals is as follows:

(a) The request to refrain from firing in contravention of article III, paragraph 2, of the Israel–Syrian General Armistice Agreement is covered by the cease-fire assurances referred to earlier in this report.

(b) The Syrian authorities have agreed to prevent the inhabitants of Syria from fishing in the lake pending a solution of the problem of fishing permits. The Israelis have agreed to grant fishing permits to inhabitants of villages in Syria and the demilitarized zone near the lake. As the Israelis hold that they alone can issue permits to fish in the lake, application must be made through the Syrian representative on the Mixed Armistice Commission to the Israel representative. The Syrian Government, on the other hand, considers that permits should be issued by the Chairman of the Mixed Armistice Commission.

(c) The Israel authorities have agreed not to interfere with the inhabitants of Syria who water their cattle in or draw water from Lake Tiberias, provided that water is drawn for domestic purposes only. The Syrian authorities have agreed not to interfere with Israel fishing in Lake Tiberias.

(d) Israel has agreed to adopt a policy to keep their police boats back from the eastern shore of the lake, except when it is necessary to approach it 'for security purposes'. I understand this latter phrase to refer only to measures for the preservation of order and the protection of Israel fishermen. As to my evaluation of the stated Israel patrolling policy on Lake Tiberias, I refer to my observations on the corresponding problem in the Gaza area. [S/3596, Report of the Secretary-General to the Security-Council pursuant to the Security Council res. of 4 Apr. 1956.]

The following annexes, directly relevant to Syria–Israel relations, were appended to the Secretary-General's report:

Annex 7

MEMORANDUM CONCERNING THE COMPLAINTS OF SYRIA OF NON-COMPLIANCE BY ISRAEL WITH ARTICLE V OF THE GENERAL ARMISTICE AGREEMENT ADDRESSED TO THE SECRETARY-GENERAL BY THE CHIEF OF STAFF

The complaints of the Government of Syria relative to non-compliance by Israel with article V of the General Armistice Agreement, which relates to the demilitarized zone between the two countries, are set forth at length in the report of the Chief of Staff UNTSO to the Secretary-General dated 11 January 1955 and the Aide-Mémoire of the Ministry of Foreign Affairs attached thereto as annex 4. The position has not changed in any essential since then.

The complaints may be briefly summarized as follows:

(a) Syria alleges that Israel violates article V, paragraph 5 b by having a para-military force, viz. the border police, in the demilitarized zone. Only 'locally recruited civilian police' are allowed, vide V (5 e). This complaint is substantiated by the facts.

(b) Syria also complains that Israel military and para-military forces continue to carry on activities within the demilitarized zone in contravention of article V (5 a). It is not considered that this complaint is borne out by the facts as established by United Nations observers, except as regards (a) above.

(c) Syria further complains that the restitution of normal civilian life in certain villages in the demilitarized zone inhabited by Arabs has not taken place. This is true, and the circumstances are described in the Chief of Staff's report referred to above. Since it was written, however, some improvement has been effected in the conditions of the inhabitants of the

Baqqara and Ghannama villages, due to a more liberal policy being followed by the Israel authorities.

The Israel–Syria Mixed Armistice Commission has ceased holding either emergency or ordinary meetings for a considerable period (see Chief of Staff's report to the Security Council dated 15 December 1955). Israel, which refused emergency meetings while certain para-military prisoners were held by the Syrians, has indicated willingness to resume such meetings, now that the prisoners have been released.

The Syrians have lodged complaints regarding the violation of article V which they want the Mixed Armistice Commission to discuss. Israel maintains that violations of article V are a matter between the Israel delegation and the Chairman, and that the Syrians have no right to intervene. Consequent disagreement regarding the agenda has prevented ordinary meetings being held since 1951. It is apparently impossible to resume regular meetings unless Israel agrees to submit to the Mixed Armistice Commission the interpretation of article V for a decision as to its competence in matters concerning the demilitarized zone, a procedure, which according to the legal advice I have received, is in accordance with the terms of the Armistice Agreement.   [*Ibid*. pp. 63–64.]

Annex 8

COMPLIANCE WITH THE SECURITY COUNCIL'S RESOLUTIONS OF 30 MARCH 1955, 8 SEPTEMBER 1955, and 19 JANUARY 1956 . . . .

The suggestions of the Chief of Staff for improving the situation in the area of Lake Tiberias which the Security Council resolution of 19 January 1956 requested him to pursue, were communicated by the Chief of Staff to the two Governments on 21 January 1956. They consisted of the following points:

(*a*) Both parties will give strict orders to their armed forces not to advance beyond or fire across the armistice demarcation line;

(*b*) Pending an arrangement which might be arrived at with the assistance of the Chairman of the Mixed Armistice Commission, the Syrian authorities will prevent the inhabitants of Syria from fishing in Lake Tiberias;

(*c*) The Israelis will not interfere with the inhabitants of Syria who water their cattle in or draw water from Lake Tiberias;

(*d*) The Syrian authorities will not interfere with Israelis fishing in Lake Tiberias;

(*e*) The Israeli police boats will not come closer than 250 metres from the shore of the lake;

(*f*) Acceptance of the above suggestions will in no way prejudice the rights, claims and positions of either party in an ultimate peaceful settlement.

Syria assured the Chief of Staff of its co-operation in putting the above suggestions into effect and of its desire to have the Security Council resolution implemented in its entirety, particularly as it concerned article V of the General Armistice Agreement relating to the demilitarized zone, and as it sought an improvement of the situation not only in the area of Lake Tiberias but along the entire demarcation line.

The Government of Israel indicated that in its view the immediate exchange of prisoners should have priority over the implementation of the Chief of Staff's suggestions, although they were willing to discuss these before any exchange took place. They considered further that negotiations between the Chief of Staff and the parties should be restricted to a consideration of the Chief of Staff's suggestions and to the exchange of military prisoners.

With regard to the suggestions of the Chief of Staff, both parties accepted points (*a*), (*b*) and (*d*). With regard to point (*c*), Israel considered that it would be acceptable if 'drawing water' meant drawing water for domestic purposes only, excluding irrigation. Syria agreed that 'drawing water' meant drawing water for domestic purposes and did not refer to irrigation.

Israel considered point (*e*) as unacceptable if there were any implication that the 250 metres were related to Syria as territorial waters or in some other way. Syria denied that any implica-tion that 250 metres from the shore of the Lake would be considered as 'territorial waters' was involved.

Israel also indicated that it regarded the implementation of points (*c*) and (*e*) as necessitating revision of the Armistice Agreement and that such revision would have to be effected under the procedures laid down in article VIII of the Agreement. At that time, Israel would probably wish to put forward some other subjects for discussion. Syria considered that points (*c*) and (*e*) be discussed at a meeting of the Mixed Armistice Commission.

The paragraph of the Security Council resolution relating to the exchange of prisoners was implemented on 29 March 1956. [*Ibid*. pp. 65–66.]

ii. *Egypt–Israel Armistice Agreement, 1949–56*

Early problems over the withdrawal of troops to lines laid down in the Armistice Agreements, and the status of refugees, were referred to the Security Council. In its resolution of 17 November 1950 the Security Council:

noted that the various Armistice Agreements provided that the execution of the Agreements would be supervised by mixed armistice commissions whose chairman in each case would be the Chief of Staff of the United Nations Truce Supervision Organization in Palestine or his designated representative....

3. *Requests* the Egyptian–Israel Mixed Armistice Commission to give urgent attention to the Egyptian complaint of expulsion of thousands of Palestine Arabs;

4. *Calls upon* both parties to give effect to any finding of the Egyptian–Israel Mixed Armistice Commission regarding the repatriation of any such Arabs who in the Commission's opinion are entitled to return;

5. *Authorizes* the Chief of Staff of the Truce Supervision Organization, with regard to the movement of nomadic Arabs, to recommend to Israel, Egypt and such other Arab States as may be appropriate such steps as he may consider necessary to control the movement of such nomadic Arabs across international frontiers or armistice lines by mutual agreement;

6. *Calls upon* the Governments concerned to take in the future no action involving the transfer of persons across international frontiers or armistice lines without prior consultation through the Mixed Armistice Commissions;

7. *Takes note* of the statement of the Government of Israel that Israel armed forces will evacuate Bir Qattar pursuant to the 20 March 1950 decision of the Special Committee provided for in article X, paragraph 4, of the Egyptian–Israel General Armistice Agreement, and that the Israel armed forces will withdraw to positions authorized by the Armistice Agreement ... [*S/1907, 17 Nov. 1950.*]

In December Egypt requested investigation of Israel's compliance, and UN observers visiting Bir Qattar 'found no evidence of military positions there, and former defence works had been filled in'.[14] Apart from isolated incidents, the directive of the Special Committee was fulfilled.

The problem of Arab refugees was to prove much more intractable: while the recommendations of the Security Council were accepted in principle, difficulties arose over specific cases. For example, there was considerable controversy as to whether the Azazme bedouin tribe fell within the category of those entitled to repatriation in Israel:

8. On the question of members of the Azazme bedouin tribe, the Israel delegation stated that its position remained unchanged. The Azazme bedouins, the Israel delegation maintained, had fled into the Sinai during military operations and were not in Israel territory at the time of the signing of the General Armistice Agreement. Following the signing of the Agree-

6

[14] S/2049, para. 1.

ment, Israel had registered all bedouins under Israel control. The members of the Azazme tribe were not among those bedouins registered at the time; they had returned to Israel-controlled territory at a later date. Therefore they were infiltrators and would be treated as such. . . .

10. The Chairman proposed that both delegations explore informally the possibility of arriving at a mutually acceptable solution of the problem of the Azazme tribe. The Israel delegation rejected this suggestion, stating that a compromise solution to this problem would be a dangerous precedent for Israel. Should a compromise be found on this matter, all other questions would similarly be resolved by compromise. The Egyptian delegation, however agreed to an informal discussion. [*S/2049, Report of Chief of Staff to UNTSO, 21 Mar. 1951.*]

The parties themselves were unable to reach agreement and the Chairman of the MAC had to use his casting vote. An unhappy pattern of incidents along the Gaza Strip also began to develop:

2. The first efforts of the Chairman of the Mixed Armistice Commission to assist the Parties in reaching mutually acceptable solutions of the above questions have been described in document S/2049; those efforts were continued without success and, in the absence of unanimity, the following decisions were taken on 30 May 1951 by a majority vote of the members of the Mixed Armistice Commission (Egyptian delegation and Chairman in favour; Israel delegation against):

(*a*) '*The Mixed Armistice Commission,*

'*Having examined* the case of expulsion of about 2,000 Arabs from El Majdal by the Israel authorities to the Gaza strip,

'*Decides* that those who in its opinion deserve to return, be repatriated as soon as possible, and restored in their rights and properties, in accordance with the resolution of the Security Council adopted at its 524th meeting on 17 November 1950 (*S/1907 and Corr.1*).

(*b*) '*The Mixed Armistice Commission,*

'*Recalling* the resolution concerning the Palestine question adopted at the 524th meeting of the Security Council on 17 November 1950,

'*Having discussed and considered* the two Egyptian complaints submitted to the Mixed Armistice Commission on 5 and 11 September 1950, related to the expulsion of some sub-tribes of the Azazme Bedouins by the Israel authorities across the international border to the Egyptian territory, and

'*Having considered* the Israel point of view,

'*Decides:*

'1) That a number of Bedouins estimated at between 6,000 to 7,000 appertaining to the following sub-tribes of the Azazme tribe have been expelled from the area under Israel control and from the demilitarized zone across the international border, into Egyptian territory: (*a*) Subheyeen, (*b*) Mohammadeen, (*c*) Isbaihat, (*d*) Sawakneh, (*e*) Imrea'at, (*f*) El Assayat;

'2) That these Arabs be repatriated to the Israel-controlled area;

'3) That this decision will receive immediate effect in conformity with the aforesaid resolution of the Security Council.'

3. The Egyptian–Israel Mixed Armistice Commission further rejected by the same majority vote (Egyptian delegation and Chairman opposed; Israel delegation in favour) the following resolution proposed by the Israel delegation:

'*The Mixed Armistice Commission*

'*Decides* that during October and November 1950, approximately 4,000 Bedouins of the Azazme tribe (Subheyeen, Mohammadeen and Imrea'at) were expelled by the Egyptian authorities into Israel and should now be returned to Egyptian-controlled territory.'

4. On 4 June, Israel appealed against the above three decisions to the Special Committee provided for under article X, paragraph 4, of the Egyptian–Israel General Armistice Agree-

ment. The appeals have been placed on the draft agenda of the Special Committee. It has not been possible so far to arrange for a meeting of the Special Committee on a date which would suit both parties.

5. At its meeting of 30 May 1951, the Egyptian–Israel Mixed Armistice Commission also considered the question, raised by Egypt, of the interpretation of article VII, paragraph 1, of the Egyptian–Israel General Armistice Agreement. The Egyptian Government has contended that 'the parting of the area covered by the Armistice Agreement into two zones, the western zone and the eastern zone, does not stand any more; that it appears clearly from article VII, paragraph 1, that the main reason of this separation was the non-conclusion, at the time, of a general armistice agreement between Israel and Transjordan (Jordan) and the uncertain situation which resulted; that the Armistice Agreement between Israel and Jordan having been concluded since April 1949, the differentiation between eastern and western fronts should have disappeared and all the provisions of the Egyptian–Israel Armistice Agreement of 24 February 1949 should have received, at the time, their full application both and indistinctly in the western and the eastern fronts, and that a right interpretation of the text of article VII, paragraph 1, of the Egyptian–Israel Armistice Agreement leads inevitably to such a conclusion that cannot suffer any changes by the insertion of a provision in the Israel–Jordan Armistice Agreement which remains for Egypt *res inter alios acta*'.

6. The Mixed Armistice Commission, by a majority vote (Israel delegation and Chairman against; Egyptian delegation in favour) disagreed with the Egyptian interpretation of article VII, paragraph 1, and held that there must of necessity be a dividing line to delineate the territory to be governed by the respective armistice agreements.

7. The Egyptian delegation has appealed to the Special Committee against the Mixed Armistice Commission's interpretation of article VII, paragraph 1. The appeal has been placed on the draft agenda of the Special Committee.

8. Most of the complaints received by the Mixed Armistice Commission have referred to incidents along the demarcation line between Israel-controlled territory and the Gaza strip under Egyptian control. A total of 166 complaints, of which 72 per cent came from the Israel delegation, have been received during the last eight and one-half months.

9. During March and April 1951, the Israel complaints generally concerned the crossing of the armistice demarcation line by Arabs from the Gaza strip, in which great number of Palestine Arabs have taken refuge. It was alleged that Arab groups had crossed the line to cut and steal wheat from Israel-controlled territory. The Egyptians, on the other hand, complained that the Israelis had killed six Arabs and wounded five. The United Nations Chairman appealed to the Israel delegation to intervene with the Israel army authorities with a view to preventing the opening of fire on Arab civilians who crossed the armistice demarcation line. He also requested the Egyptian delegation to see that such illegal crossings of the demarcation line were stopped immediately. For a time, effective measures were taken to prevent the crossing of the demarcation line, along which the Egyptian authorities instituted regular mounted police patrol.

10. During the last four months the situation has taken a more serious turn. There has been an increase in the number of complaints alleging armed robbery and attacks on Israel settlements and Israel patrols by Arab bands from the Gaza strip. There have also been complaints alleging the mining of roads in Israel-controlled territory. The Egyptians, on the other hand, have complained of retaliatory raids by Israelis and of boat and plane violations of waters and territory under Egyptian control.

11. Incidents in the Gaza strip area, in so far as they could not be disposed of by a sub-committee of the Mixed Armistice Commission, have been considered by the Mixed Armistice Commission itself. At a meeting held on 23 September 1951, it examined an Egyptian complaint alleging that on 19 September Israelis had shelled the Beit Hanum area in the Gaza strip and that they had blown up a number of houses, killing and injuring some Arabs. The Commission adopted the following resolution by unanimous vote:

'*The Mixed Armistice Commission,*

'*Having examined* the Egyptian complaint dated 19 September 1951 and the report of the investigation carried out by the United Nations observer,

'*Decides* that the action carried out by Israelis on 19 September 1951 is a violation of article II, paragraph 2, of the Egyptian–Israel Armistice Agreement;

"*Calls upon* the Israel delegation to request the Israel authorities to take the necessary steps to put an end to these aggressive actions which do not help the maintenance of peace.'

12. At the same meeting, the Mixed Armistice Commission also considered an Israel complaint. It adopted the following resolution by a majority vote (Israel delegation and the Chairman in favour; Egyptian delegation against):

'*The Mixed Armistice Commission*

'*Decides* that during the night of 5–6 September 1951, Arabs from the Gaza strip crossed the demarcation line and laid two mines inside Israel territory with the result that one tractor and one army car were blown up and one officer and two civilians were wounded;

'*Condemns* this act of violence, as a violation by Egypt of article II, paragraph 2, of the Armistice Agreement;

'*Calls upon* the Egyptian delegation to call upon the Egyptian authorities to put an end to such aggressive actions."

13. The Egyptian delegation had appealed to the Special Committee against this decision. The appeal has been placed on the draft agenda of the Special Committee.

14. At a meeting held on 3 October, the Mixed Armistice Commission considered further complaints concerning the crossing of the armistice demarcation line and other actions in the Gaza strip area. With regard to an Israel complaint according to which five or six Arabs from the Gaza strip had, during the night of 7–8 March 1951, attacked three times the guards of a road-building company near Magen settlement, the Commission took the following decision by a majority vote (Israel delegation and Chairman in favour; Eygptian delegation against):

'*The Mixed Armistice Commission*

'*Decides* that, if such aggressive acts were carried out by Arabs from the Gaza strip during the night of 7–8 March, they constitute a violation of article II, paragraph 2, of the General Armistice Agreement;

'*Calls upon* the Egyptian delegation to request the Egyptian authorities to take all possible steps to prevent the occurrence of such acts.'

15. At the same meeting of the Mixed Armistice Commission, two other majority votes were taken also condemning actions of Arabs from the Gaza strip, if such actions had happened as alleged by the Israel delegation (laying of a land mine in Israel-controlled territory in June; exchange of fire during which an Israeli was wounded in July). In these two cases, as in the case referred to in the preceding paragraph, the Israel allegation had not been proven by investigations carried out by United Nations observers. Neither had the allegations been disproved. . . . [*S/2388, Report of Chief of Staff of UNTSO, 8 Nov. 1951.*]

The incidents along the Gaza Strip continued, but were in the main minor, and concerned individual civilians.[15]

In February 1954 the Chief of Staff had reported that while such incidents continued to be small-scale, they had increased in number in the last few months.[16] This presented the Chief of Staff with an administrative problem:

[15] S/2833, 4 Nov. 1952, para. 2.   [16] S/3183 and Corr. 1, sect. II, para. 3.

7. Faced with an accumulation of complaints, the Chairman of the Mixed Armistice Commission has suggested to the two Parties that future complaints should be handled by a sub-committee of the Mixed Armistice Commission consisting of a representative of each party and a United Nations observer, and attended by police or military officers from both sides. These officers should be the ones responsible for civil and/or military affairs on each side of the line where an incident had occurred and the meetings should take place as quickly as possible after the incident. This should permit the solution of many incidents on a local level. It might also be hoped that co-operation between the local representatives of the parties would result in lessening the number of incidents. Tension along the demarcation line has increased to such an extent that the parties should try to implement the Chairman's suggestion. [*S/3183 and corr . 1, Report of Chief of Staff, 1 March 1954*, sect. ii.]

By October of 1954 however, the incidents had fallen off, both in numbers and in importance.[17] The implementation of the Armistice along the Gaza Strip was during the period of 1949 to early 1955, remarkably successful, though incidents of greater severity did occur in February 1955.[18] This led to an overall deterioration.[19] The nature of the incidents now changed, and a clear pattern was established of well-organized sabotage far within Israeli territory. This was clearly no longer a matter of isolated civilian incidents.

The establishment of fedayeen raids in defiance of the Armistice Agreement was to prove an extremely important factor in the breakdown of the system which was to occur the following year:

2. The period of violence began with the incident of 22 August, in which an Egyptian post at Hill 79, near the demarcation line and five kilometres due east of Gaza, was occupied by Israel forces. This incident, in which one Egyptian officer and two soldiers were killed and three others wounded, started off the chain of violence. It is one more example of the type of incident arising frequently between 28 February and 1 June from the combination of Israel motor patrols along one side of the demarcation line and Egyptian outposts on the other side and close to it. In my view the Mixed Armistice Commission may be unable to determine which of the parties was responsible for beginning the action.

3. The episode of 22 August was soon after followed by an organized series of attacks on vehicles, installations and persons, carried out by gangs of marauders in Israel territory which, according to my information, resulted in the deaths of eleven military and civilian personnel and the injury of nine.

4. The number and nature of these acts of sabotage perpetrated well within Israel territory are such as to suggest that they are the work of organized and well-trained groups. Investigations so far completed by United Nations military observers tend to support this view. The sudden resumption of this type of incident after they had practically ceased for three months is significant. [*S/3430, Report of Chief of Staff, 6 Sept. 1955*.]

At the same time, hostilities were flaring up between Egyptian outposts and Israeli patrols at the border. On 3 September it was necessary for the Chief of Staff to issue a formal cease-fire.[20] The matter assumed such serious proportions that a meeting of the Security Council was held, and the following resolution was adopted:

The Security Council,
Recalling its resolution of 30 March 1955 (*S/3379*).
Having received the report of the Chief of Staff of the Truce Supervision Organization (*S/3430*),

[17] S/3319, 16 Nov. 1954, para. 3.   [18] S/3373, 17 Mar. 1955.
[19] S/3390, 14 Apr. 1955, para. 25.   [20] S/3430, para. 17.

Noting with grave concern the discontinuance of the talks initiated by the Chief of Staff in accordance with the above-mentioned resolution,

Deploring the recent outbreak of violence in the area along the armistice demarcation line established between Egypt and Israel on 24 February 1949,

1. *Notes with approval* the acceptance by both parties of the appeal of the Chief of Staff for an unconditional cease-fire;

2. *Calls upon* both parties forthwith to take all steps necessary to bring about order and tranquillity in the area, and in particular to desist from further acts of violence and to continue the cease-fire in full force and effect;

3. *Endorses* the view of the Chief of Staff that the armed forces of both parties should be clearly and effectively separated by measures such as those which he has proposed;

4. *Declares* that freedom of movement must be afforded to United Nations observers in the area to enable them to fulfil their functions;

5. *Calls upon* both parties to appoint representatives to meet with the Chief of Staff and to co-operate fully with him to these ends;

6. *Requests* the Chief of Staff to report to the Security Council on the action taken to carry out this resolution.   [*SC Res. S/3455, 8 Sept. 1955.*]

The Secretary-General, as we have noted below (pp. 178–9), was charged in early 1956 with examining compliance with the Armistice Agreements and also with certain recently adopted resolutions. Two of three resolutions referred to[21] concerned the Egypt–Israel situation. The resolution of 30 March had requested the Chief of Staff to continue his consultations with the governments of Egypt and Israel with a view to the introduction of practical measures to preserve security in the area of the armistice demarcation line between Egypt and Israel. It also called upon the governments of Egypt and Israel to co-operate with the Chief of Staff with regard to his proposals, bearing in mind that in his opinion infiltration could be reduced to an occasional nuisance if the agreement were effected between the parties along the lines he had proposed. The terms of the resolution of 8 September 1955 have been reproduced above.

The Secretary-General had reason, early in 1956, to feel that some progress was being made, because he had received on 18 April 1956 unconditional assurances by both Governments that they would observe the cease-fire. These assurances were unqualified 'either by requests for compliance by the other party with any other clauses of the Armistice Agreement, or by requests for certain measures by the other party based on the agreements or for compliance with resolutions of the General Assembly or the Security Council relating to the Agreement'.[22]

The Secretary-General also endorsed certain local suggestions made by the Chief of Staff:

The Gaza demarcation line

75. In order to observe and assist compliance with the cease-fire assurances along the Gaza demarcation line, arrangements proposed by the Chief of Staff for the establishment of an equal number of fixed United Nations observer posts on each side of the line have been accepted by the Governments of Egypt and Israel. The activities of United Nations military

[21] S/3379, 30 Mar. 1955, and S/3455, 8 Sept. 1955.
[22] S/3596, Report of the Secretary-General to the Security Council pursuant to the Council's resolution of 4 Apr. 1956, para. 33.

observers covered by these arrangements are, of course, additional to those provided for in the General Armistice Agreement.

76. In accepting this arrangement the Government of Israel set a time limit of six months (until 31 October 1956) for its operation. It is understood, however, that the Government of Israel will consider proposals from the Chief of Staff for the continuance of this arrangement after 31 October, if, in his view, the situation at that time calls for it. The Government of Egypt, for its part, sets no time limit on its adherence to the arrangement.

77. The arrangement as negotiated in the terms set out below will be formally adopted in the Mixed Armistice Commission to meet a request of the Government of Israel that the arrangement be tied in with procedure under the General Armistice Agreement. The arrangement is as follows:

(a) The location and number of the observation posts on the Egyptian side of the demarcation line shall be agreed with Egypt and of those on the Israel side with Israel. There shall be an equal number of observation posts established on each side. It is the intention of the Chief of Staff to arrange for the establishment of six such posts on each side of the line;

(b) United Nations observers shall have free access to those positions at any time;

(c) If so desired by the party concerned, they shall be accompanied on their way to and during their stay at the observation posts by an officer of the party on whose side of the demarcation line the observation post is situated;

(d) Before proceeding to any of the observation posts, the United Nations observer shall notify the senior Israel (senior Egyptian) delegate, or his representative, to arrange that the party's forces allow passage to the posts;

(e) The reports of United Nations observers stationed in observation posts shall cover violations of article II, paragraph 2, of the General Armistice Agreement, shall be directed to the Mixed Armistice Commission, and shall be used in the examination of complaints in the Commission;

(f) The parties shall designate a route which the United Nations observers shall follow to the observation posts;

(g) The United Nations Truce Supervision Organization may send patrols along the demarcation line between the observation posts when required, arrangements being made beforehand with senior delegates to the Mixed Armistice Commission. The aforesaid provisions in (c), (d), (e) and (f) shall apply to the patrols.

78. As regards proposals for local arrangements in the Gaza area, or outside of it, referred to in paragraph 3 (c) of the Security Council resolution of 4 April 1956, their present status and the attitude of the parties towards them is as follows:

(a) *Separation of parties' forces in the field*

79. The proposal that the parties should withdraw their armed forces, especially patrols, observation posts and defensive positions, back from the demarcation line to a distance sufficient to eliminate or greatly reduce provocation which might induce undisciplined individuals to open fire leading to extensive breaches of article II, paragraph 2, of the General Armistice Agreement has been accepted by Egypt without reservations. The intentions of Israel are understood to be that they would refrain from sending patrols up to the demarcation line except when it proved essential to do so in order to protect agricultural operations of their settlers or to prevent incursions by persons from Egyptian controlled territory. If supported by an effective observer arrangement, the line taken by Israel may prove adequate, although it falls short of the firmer arrangements proposed by the Chief of Staff and endorsed by the Security Council and by me. Should the line now taken not meet the needs of the situation, I would find it necessary to bring the matter up for new consideration.

(b) *Erection of a physical obstacle along the demarcation line*

80. Israel is prepared to consider a proposal for the erection of a physical obstacle along the demarcation line by the Truce Supervision Organization when and if such a proposal is submitted by the Chief of Staff. Egypt agrees to the erection of obstacles along selected portions

of the demarcation line, subject to discussion with the Chief of Staff. In the present circumstances and until the situation has remained stable for a reasonable period, the Chief of Staff does not propose to submit any specific proposals to this end.

(c) *Marking of the demarcation line*

81. Both parties have agreed to the placing, by the United Nations Truce Supervision Organization, of conspicuous markers along the demarcation line surrounding the Gaza strip. The Chief of Staff proposes to make a beginning on this work as soon as possible.

(d) *Local commanders' agreement*

82. The negotiations to effect an arrangement including a local commanders' agreement between the parties for maintaining security along the demarcation line of the Gaza strip have been at a standstill since August 1955. After a sufficient period of tranquillity the Chief of Staff proposes to suggest to the parties that these negotiations be resumed.

(e) *Joint patrols*

83. It does not now appear opportune to establish joint patrols nor does it seem likely that they would be accepted by either party. Moreover, the proposal for joint patrols is in effect superseded by the agreement for the separation of the parties' forces and the agreement to allow United Nations military observers to patrol along the demarcation line accompanied by an officer of the party concerned. . . . [*S/3596, Report of the Secretary-General to the Security Council pursuant to the Council's resolution of 4 Apr. 1956.*]

So far as Articles VII and VIII of the Egypt–Israel Armistice were concerned, the Secretary-General found that both parties, to a greater or lesser extent, were in violation of their obligations.[23] Article VIII established the demilitarized zone centred on El Auja:

Israel has had elements of armed forces in the demilitarized zone since the beginning of November 1955, and these at present are of the order of three companies of infantry. The three proposals put forward by the Secretary-General in a letter dated 3 November 1955, which *inter alia* provided for the withdrawal of this force, were accepted in principle by the Government of Israel, but not implemented because Israel took the stand that its national security would be imperilled if it did so while Egypt continued to occupy defensive positions in the area between the line El Quseima–Abu Aweigila and the demilitarized zone in violation of Article VIII, paragraph 3, and also had prohibited arms and an excess of troops in the defensive zone of the western Front established by Article VII.

68. Egypt has refused to permit investigation of Israel complaints to the Mixed Armistice Commission of the violations alleged above; and it may therefore be presumed that the violations in fact exist. In turn, Egypt has complained on several occasions of Israel violations of Article VII, particularly as regards the presence of armoured vehicles and heavy mortars in the defensive zone, which is prohibited. [*Ibid.*]

Accordingly, the following plan was now recommended:

Annex 5

MEMORANDUM ON THE IMPLEMENTATION OF ARTICLES VII AND VIII OF THE GENERAL ARMISTICE AGREEMENT BETWEEN EGYPT AND ISRAEL ADDRESSED TO THE SECRETARY-GENERAL BY THE CHIEF OF STAFF, AND PRESENTED TO THE GOVERNMENTS CONCERNED

The implementation of article VII, paragraphs 3 and 4, should be carried out simultaneously by both parties within an agreed time limit to be fixed in consultation with the Chief of Staff.

[23] S/3596, para. 70.

Upon completion of the operation, the areas referred to in article VII, paragraphs 3 and 4, will be visited by United Nations observers. Subsequently, the areas in question will be visited periodically by United Nations observers as required by the Chief of Staff to ensure that the stipulations of Article VII continue to be complied with.

The implementation of article VIII should be carried out upon completion of the implementation of article VII.

(*a*) The Israel armed forces presently in the demilitarized zone will be evacuated, the existing fortifications will be dismantled and the minefields will be removed within a time limit fixed by the Chief of Staff in consultation with the authorities concerned. Pending a decision by the Security Council, the Kibbutz Ktsiot within the demilitarized zone will be maintained, together with a number of civilian police which in view of the needs of the Kibbutz may be considered normal.

(*b*) The Egyptian armed forces will dismantle any defensive positions established in the area referred to in article VIII, paragraph 3. The Egyptian checkposts as defined by the Chairman of the Mixed Armistice Commission on 22 June 1955, in his statement appended to the MAC resolution of that date, will not be considered as defensive positions within the meaning of article VIII, paragraph 3.

Upon the completion of the operation in (*a*) and (*b*) above, United Nations observers will verify compliance by a visit to the areas referred to in article VIII, and by subsequent periodic visits. [*Ibid.*]

The ensuing report on the effectiveness of the Egypt–Israel Armistice was also attached:

Annex 8

COMPLIANCE WITH THE SECURITY COUNCIL'S RESOLUTIONS OF 30 MARCH 1955, 8 SEPTEMBER 1955, AND 19 JANUARY 1956

The proposals of the Chief of Staff referred to in the resolution of 30 March 1955 were as follows:

(*a*) Joint patrols along sensitive sections of the demarcation line;

(*b*) Negotiation of a local commander's agreement;

(*c*) A barbed wire obstacle along certain portions of the demarcation line;

(*d*) Manning of all outposts and patrols by regular Egyptian and Israel troops.

On 28 June meetings on these proposals were initiated under the chairmanship of the Chief of Staff. Egypt agreed in principle with a detailed plan for joint patrols along sensitive sections of the demarcation line presented by the Chief of Staff.

No progress was made, however, because of a wide difference of views between the parties as to the scope and nature of the proposed joint patrols.

In discussions on a local commanders' agreement the following points were accepted by both parties:

(*a*) Only well-trained and disciplined military personnel would be employed on military duties;

(*b*) Strict measures would be taken to prevent civilians from crossing the demarcation line;

(*c*) The parties would exchange all relevant information concerning civilians who illegally crossed the demarcation line and would investigate suspected crossings;

(*d*) The parties would use their best endeavours to recover livestock and property stolen from the other party.

No agreement, however, was reached on the type and status of the responsible officers on each side, the presence of United Nations observers at local commanders' meetings, the establishment of telephonic communications between the responsible officers on both sides, and the form of signature to be used in concluding the agreement. In consequence of the position taken by the parties on these points it proved impossible to conclude a local commanders' agreement.

6*

With regard to the proposal to erect a barbed wire obstacle along certain portions of the demarcation line, Israel took the position that two physical barriers with a space between them should be erected all along the line. Egypt indicated that it had no objections to the erection by Israel of a continuous obstacle within Israel-controlled territory along the demarcation line. Egypt, however, was opposed to the erection of an obstacle along the demarcation line itself, but was prepared to erect barbed wire fences along certain portions inside the Gaza strip. As a result of lack of progress on other points, the proposal to erect a physical obstacle never came up for formal consideration.

Agreement had been reached in principle that only well-trained and disciplined regular military or police personnel would be employed on security duties in a zone one kilometre wide on either side of the demarcation line, when discussions broke down with the beginning of the series of incidents which culminated in the incident of Khan Yunis on 31 August 1955.

The proposals of the Chief of Staff which the Security Council endorsed in its resolution of 8 September 1955 were:

(*a*) The separation of the armed forces of Egypt and Israel by an effective barrier along the demarcation line;

(*b*) Defensive positions and motorized patrols of both parties to be kept at least 500 metres from the demarcation line.

On the separation of forces, Egypt restated its willingness to keep its forces 500 metres back from the demarcation line. Israel was prepared to consider such an arrangement only after the establishment of a physical barrier along the whole demarcation line.

Freedom of movement of United Nations observers continued to be impeded, principally in the El Auja demilitarized zone and vicinity, from time to time by both parties. Reasons given for such interference included military activities, the presence of mines and the safety of the observers.

On 21 September 1955 the El Auja demilitarized zone was occupied by Israel forces. [*Ibid.*]

In July of 1956 occurred the nationalization of the Suez Canal by President Nasser. It is obvious that materials on the implementation of the Armistice Agreements between July and November of 1956 must be read in the light of the major repercussions which began to flow from that act. The sequence of events triggered off by the nationalization of the Canal forms the background to another UN peacekeeping endeavour—the mounting of UNEF—and is in that context recounted below (pp. 222–30). We may here simply limit ourselves to the comment that the failure of the parties, in the circumstances of the second half of 1956, to put into effect the Secretary-General's recommendations for the implementation of the Armistice Agreements is hardly surprising.

SECTION I

Developments in the El Auja demilitarized zone

1. The Israel Army continues to occupy the El Auja demilitarized zone created by article VIII paragraph 1 of the Egypt–Israel General Armistice Agreement. The Israel settlement of the area which began with the establishment of *kibbutz* Qetsi'ot in September 1953, is also being expanded. Israel has further decided considerably to limit the freedom of movement and access of United Nations military observers in the demilitarized zone. . . .

Meetings of the Egyptian–Israel Mixed Armistice Commission

9. El Auja is not only the centre of the demilitarized zone, as defined in paragraph 2, article VIII of the armistice agreement. It is also, under article X, paragraph 2, the headquarters of the Mixed Armistice Commission. Because of her military occupation of the

demilitarized zone, Israel refuses access to El Auja to the Egyptian members of the Mixed Armistice Commission. Article X, paragraph 2, also stipulates that the Mixed Armistice Commission shall hold its meetings at such places and such times as it may deem necessary for the effective conduct of its work. The Egyptian Authorities have not accepted the Israel refusal to allow the Mixed Armistice Commission to hold meetings at its headquarters. They have proposed that the Mixed Armistice Commission should hold every other meeting at El Auja. Meetings of the Mixed Armistice Commission—ordinary or emergency—have not been resumed. Complaints by either party are being investigated when an investigation is requested. The fact that the complaints are no longer considered in the Mixed Armistice Commission greatly increases the responsibility of the United Nations Truce Supervision Organization Chief of Staff and his representative, the Chairman of the Mixed Armistice Commission, for observing the maintenance of the cease-fire by the two parties.

10. At his meeting with the Chief of Staff on 3 September 1956, Mr Ben-Gurion repeated his refusal to allow meetings of the Mixed Armistice Commission at El Auja, stating that article VIII of the General Armistice Agreement and the provision in article X paragraph 2 relating to the headquarters of the Mixed Armistice Commission, were in suspension owing to Egypt's non-compliance with article I and the Security Council resolution of 1 September 1951 concerning interference with the passage through the Suez Canal of shipping bound for Israel. No Egyptians could now be allowed in the El Auja area for security reasons. He was willing, however, to have the Mixed Armistice Commission meet at other places. [*S/3659, Report of Chief of Staff of UNTSO, incorporated in Secretary-General's report to Security Council, 27 Sept. 1956.*]

The other great controversy affecting the Egypt–Israel Armistice was the question of the passage of goods to Israel through the Suez Canal. Not only were the rights and wrongs of the Egyptian prohibition at issue, but so was the appropriate action for the MAC:

The meeting of the Egyptian–Israel Special Committee reconvened on this date, 12 June 1951, at kilometre 95 for the purpose of completing the discussion which began on 16 January 1951, as reported in document S/2047 of 21 March 1951, on the question as to whether or not the Mixed Armistice Commission has the right to demand from the Egyptian Government not to interfere with the passing of goods to Israel through the Suez Canal.

In explanation of his vote, which was contrary to the stand taken by Israel, the Chief of Staff made the following statement:

'It is quite clear to me that action taken by Egyptian authorities in interfering with passage of goods destined for Israel through the Suez Canal must be considered an aggressive action. However, due to the limitation imposed by the text itself on the words "aggressive action", this action is not necessarily against article I, paragraph 2 of the General Armistice Agreement which states in part, "No aggressive action by armed forces—land, sea, or air—of either party shall be undertaken, planned, or threatened against the people or the armed forces of the other".

'Similarly, I must of necessity consider that interference with the passage of goods destined for Israel through the Suez Canal is a hostile act, but not necessarily against the General Armistice Agreement because of the limitations imposed on the term "hostile act" in the text of article II, paragraph 2 of the General Armistice Agreement, which says, "No element of the land, sea or air military or para-military forces of either party, including non-regular forces, shall commit any warlike or hostile act against the military or para-military forces of the other party . . ."

'It follows, therefore, that I have no other choice but to cast my vote with Egypt that the Mixed Armistice Commission does not have the right to demand from the Egyptian Government that it should not interfere with the passage of goods to Israel through the Suez Canal.

'In my opinion, this interference is an aggressive and hostile action, and if I had certain knowledge that it was being committed by the armed forces of Egypt—land, sea or air, or para-military forces, including non-regular forces—I would most firmly hold that this constituted a violation of article I, paragraph 2, and article II, paragraph 2 of the General Armistice Agreement, and would uphold contention advanced by Israel. Lacking such knowledge, I see no way under the General Armistice Agreement of taking this course, even though I am convinced that the Egyptian action does not foster the objectives of the General Armistice Agreement.

'As Chief of Staff of the United Nations Truce Supervision Organization, I am forced to base my position in this matter on the specific provisions of the General Armistice Agreement signed by Egypt and Israel. I deliberately avoid, therefore, any consideration of the status of the Suez Canal or the rights of any party with regard to it.

'While I feel bound to take this technical position on the basis of the relevant provisions of the General Armistice Agreement, I must also say that the action of the Egyptian authorities in this instance is, in my view, entirely contrary to the spirit of the General Armistice Agreement and does, in fact, jeopardize its effective functioning. It was certainly never contemplated at Rhodes that what is, in effect, an act of blockade or at least an act undertaken in the spirit of a blockade and having the partial effect of one, would be continued by one of the parties to the General Armistice Agreement more than two years after it had been signed.

'Although, in my view, there is no adequate basis for agreeing that the Mixed Armistice Commission has competence to deal with the question, it must be clear, and it certainly is to me, that the question cannot rest here. Either the Egyptian Government must, in the spirit of the General Armistice Agreement, relax the practice of interference with the passage of goods destined for Israel through the Suez Canal, or the question must be referred to some higher competent authority such as the Security Council or the International Court of Justice.

'I have no doubt in my mind that the General Armistice Agreement was never intended to provide a cloak for the commission of acts by either party which in their intent and effects are indeed hostile.

'Because of the effect which such continued action will have on the implementation of the Armistice Agreement and the future operations of the Mixed Armistice Commission, I am compelled to direct a strong request to the Egyptian delegate to intercede with his Government to desist from the present practice of interfering with goods destined for Israel through the Suez Canal, since such acts can only be construed as inconsistent with the spirit of the Armistice Agreement. [*S/2194, Report by Chief of Staff of UNTSO, 13 June 1951.*]

Israel decided to take the matter to the Security Council, and submitted the following comments:

. . . In contravention of international law, of the Suez Canal Convention (1888) and of the Egyptian–Israel General Armistice Agreement, the Government of Egypt continues to detain, visit and search ships seeking to pass through the Suez Canal, on the grounds that their cargoes are destined for Israel. This practice has been carried out for over two years, in defiance of the specific appeals and requests of United Nations representatives charged with the negotiation and implementation of the General Armistice Agreement. Thus, on 4 August 1949, Mr Ralph J. Bunche, who had represented the United Nations in the armistice talks, interpreted the Armistice Agreement as follows (*433rd meeting*):

'There should be free movement for legitimate shipping, and no vestiges of the wartime blockade should be allowed to remain as they are inconsistent with both the letter and the spirit of the Armistice Agreements.'

In the light of this authoritative ruling, the Security Council (*435th meeting*) adopted a resolution on 11 August 1949 (*S/1367*) calling upon the parties to observe the Armistice Agreements and reminding them that these agreements 'include firm pledges against any further acts of hostility between the parties'.

Throughout the ensuing period the Government of Israel has patiently sought redress through the machinery established by the Armistice Agreement. On 17 November 1950, the Security Council (*524th meeting*) referred the matter back to the Chief of Staff of the United Nations Truce Supervision Organization (*S/1907*). These efforts by United Nations organs to reach a solution culminated in a meeting of the Special Committee on the Egyptian–Israel General Armistice Agreement held on 12 June 1951 under the chairmanship of Lieut.-General William E. Riley. . . .

General Riley's observations have been submitted to the Security Council in document S/2194. It will be noted that the United Nations Chief of Staff characterizes the Egyptian blockade as 'an aggressive action', and 'a hostile act'. He concludes: 'that the action of the Egyptian authorities in this instance is, in my view, entirely contrary to the spirit of the General Armistice Agreement and does, in fact, jeopardize its effective functioning'.

Accordingly, the Government of Israel now brings the question before the Security Council as a matter jeopardizing the Armistice Agreement and endangering the peace and security of the Middle East. The Egyptian action also adversely affects the economic life of the region, and particularly its oil-refining capacity. . . .

In the whole record of the armistice system there is no other instance of an aggressive and hostile practice being continued in the face of urgent condemnation by the authorized United Nations representatives. Moreover, the Security Council has never yet failed to endorse and confirm the requests of the Chief of Staff in any case where the effective functioning of the armistice system has been jeopardized. Thus, if the Security Council were not to act, it is apparent that injury would be done to the strength and equity of the armistice system and to the authority of United Nations officers charged with supervising the armistice. [*S/2241, 12 July 1951.*]

It is obviously beyond the purposes of this collection of documents to repeat in full the legal arguments raised by both sides in respect of this question;[24] our focus here is upon the implementation of the Armistice Agreements, and the Security Council stated (8 votes to nil, with China, India, and the USSR abstaining) that:

The Security Council,
Recalling that in its resolution S/1376 of 11 August 1949 relating to the conclusion of Armistice Agreements between Israel and the neighbouring Arab States it drew attention to the pledges in these Agreements 'against any further acts of hostility between the parties',
Recalling further that in its resolution S/1907 of 17 November 1950 it reminded the States concerned that the Armistice Agreements to which they were parties contemplated 'the return of permanent peace in Palestine', and, therefore, urged them and the other States in the area to take all such steps as would lead to the settlement of the issues between them,
Noting the report of the Chief of Staff of the United Nations Truce Supervision Organization in Palestine to the Security Council of 12 June 1951,
Further noting that the Chief of Staff of the Truce Supervision Organization recalled the statement of the senior Egyptian delegate in Rhodes on 13 January 1949, to the effect that his delegation was 'inspired with every spirit of co-operation, conciliation and a sincere desire to restore peace in Palestine', and that the Egyptian Government has not complied with the earnest plea of the Chief of Staff made to the Egyptian delegate on 12 June 1951, that it desist from the present practice of interfering with the passage through the Suez Canal of goods destined for Israel,
Considering that since the armistice régime, which has been in existence for nearly two and a half years, is of a permanent character, neither party can reasonably assert that it is actively a

---

[24] But see Yoram Dinitz, 'The Legal Aspects of the Egyptian Blockade of the Suez Canal', 45 *Georgetown Law R.* (1956–7); M. El Hefnaoui, *Les problèmes contemporains posés par le Canal de Suez* (1951); Leo Gross, 'Passage through the Suez Canal of Israel-bound Cargo and Israel ships', 51 *AJIL* (1957), p. 530; R. Baxter, *The Law of International Waterways* (1964).

belligerent or requires to exercise the right of visit, search and seizure for any legitimate purpose of self defence,

Finds that the maintenance of the practice mentioned in the fourth paragraph of the present resolution is inconsistent with the objectives of a peaceful settlement between the parties and the establishment of a permanent peace in Palestine set forth in the Armistice Agreement between Egypt and Israel;

Finds further that such practice is an abuse of the exercise of the right of visit, search and seizure;

Further finds that that practice cannot in the prevailing circumstances be justified on the ground that it is necessary for self-defence;

And further noting that the restrictions on the passage of goods through the Suez Canal to Israel ports are denying to nations at no time connected with the conflict in Palestine valuable supplies required for their economic reconstruction, and that these restrictions together with sanctions applied by Egypt to certain ships which have visited Israel ports represent unjustified interference with the rights of nations to navigate the seas and to trade freely with one another, including the Arab States and Israel,

Calls upon Egypt to terminate the restrictions on the passage of international commercial shipping and goods through the Suez Canal wherever bound and to cease all interference with such shipping beyond that essential to the safety of shipping in the Canal itself and to the observance of the international conventions in force. [*SC Res. S/2322, 1 Sept. 1951.*]

Egyptian interference with Suez shipping bound to and from Israel did not cease, however, and the Israel government in 1954 returned to the Security Council on this question, and on the question of 'interference by Egypt with shipping proceeding to the Israeli port of Elath on the Gulf of Akaba'. On 29 September 1954 Israel protested to the Security Council over the confiscation of the Israeli ship *Bat Galim* (S/3296). Egypt filed a counter-complaint. The Chief of Staff endeavoured to get a meeting of the MAC, but the parties could not agree, within the existing rules of procedure, to bring the matter forward from the end of the long list of complaints awaiting examination.[25] In spite of the personal efforts of the Secretary-General, compliance with the Armistice régime by Egypt in terms of permitting freedom of shipping remained unachieved.[26] These personal efforts, it may be observed, were made as part of the Secretary-General's diplomatic function, but not as an aspect of his mandate of April 1956 to report on the compliance with the Armistice Agreements. He stated that

93. My attitude has been that the Suez question, as adjudicated by the Security Council, is not a question of compliance with the Armistice Agreement in the sense of my mandate. For that reason I have not, within the framework of my mandate, discussed the issue with the Egyptian Government. . . .

94. My mandate . . . is directly concerned with the state of tension along the armistice demarcation lines and the state of compliance or non-compliance with the armistice agreements as a cause of such tension. In an approach looking beyond the immediate problems which, as I understand the resolution of 4 April 1956, the Security Council had in mind, it is obvious that the question raised by the Government of Israel should come under consideration. . . . [*S/3594, Report of the Secretary-General to the Security Council pursuant to the Council's resolution of 4 Apr. 1956.*]

---

[25] S/3315, 10 Nov. 1954, per the Chief of Staff.   [26] For the legal points at issue, see pp.200–1.

iii. *Jordan–Israel Armistice, 1949–56*

It is on Jordanian territory that the great majority of refugees from Palestine lived after the war of 1948, often within sight of their former lands. The Israelis have been eager to work the land right up to the demarcation lines; and the Jordanian king has faced considerable internal hostility, as well as pressures emanating from Cairo and Damascus. The Jordan–Israel Armistice Agreement has had to operate within the framework of all these factors.

1. On 10 September 1950, the Government of the Hashemite Kingdom of Jordan complained in a telegram to the Security Council that Israel armed forces had violated the northern frontiers of the Hashemite Kingdom of Jordan by occupying a piece of land abutting on the hydro-electric works near Naharayim (*S/1780*).

2. On 7 October 1950, the Israel delegation to the Jordan–Israel Mixed Armistice Commission addressed a letter to the United Nations Chief of Staff of the Truce Supervision Organization on the question of the dispute over the Naharayim area. The Israel delegation requested that an 'emergency meeting be convened to discuss and vote on the question whether the disputed area lies east or west of the demarcation line, or, in other words, did Israel violate the Armistice Agreement by ploughing this area'.

3. The Security Council discussed this complaint in October and the early part of November 1950. In its resolution of 17 November 1950, the Security Council, 'taking into consideration the views expressed and the data given by the representatives of Egypt, Israel and the Hashemite Kingdom of Jordan, and the United Nations Chief of Staff of the Truce Supervision Organization', called upon the parties to the complaints before the Security Council to consent to their being handled according to the procedures established in the General Armistice Agreements.

4. The Israel delegation's request of 7 October 1950 was communicated to the delegation of the Hashemite Kingdom of Jordan, and informal talks are in progress.

5. A major problem settled by the Jordan–Israel Mixed Armistice Commission concerned the location of a diversion of the Beersheba-Elath road in the Wadi Araba. On 22 November 1950, the Jordan delegation complained that a diversion of the Beersheba-Elath road had been constructed by Israel during 1950 on Jordan territory. Following a series of meetings, the Jordan–Israel Mixed Armistice Commission, on 14 February, decided that:

(*a*) The stretch of the road in the Wadi Araba between MR. 165,292–954,700 and map reference 165,562–953,250 is to be considered as being in Jordan-controlled territory.

(*b*) The remainder of the road, between kilometre 74 and kilometre 78, is to be considered as being in Israel-controlled territory, it being recognized that these two decisions shall not in any way prejudice the rights, claims, and positions of either party in an ultimate peace settlement between them.

(*c*) Israel traffic shall cease to use that portion of the Wadi Araba road declared to be in Jordan-controlled territory, from 1200 hours on 25 February 1951.

On 25 February 1951, the portion of the road declared to be in Jordan-controlled territory was blocked and Israel traffic ceased to use it. (The Wadi Araba dispute is discussed fully in a separate report to the Security Council dated 12 March 1951 and set forth in document S/2048).

6. During the period 15 December 1950 to 15 February 1951, a series of incidents along the demarcation lines between the Hashemite Kingdom of Jordan and Israel led to sixteen requests for emergency meetings of the Jordan–Israel Mixed Armistice Commission. At its meeting on 14 February 1951, the Commission adopted a resolution, unanimously, condemning the wanton killings and murders, and drew attention to the imperative need for preventing the recurrence of such acts. It was further resolved that, as high-ranking Jordan and Israel military officers were to meet shortly to discuss the prevention of future incidents,

the sixteen complaints would be considered as having been acted upon by the Jordan–Israel Mixed Armistice Commission. At subsequent sub-committee meetings, a total of 116 complaints were stricken from the agenda of the Jordan–Israel Mixed Armistice Commission. (This subject is discussed fully in the separate report to the Security Council dated 12 March 1951.)

7. At the Mixed Armistice Commission meeting on 14 February 1951, it was also decided unanimously that in the future the Chairman would have the sole right to determine which complaints called for emergency meetings. In the event the Chairman decided that a complaint was of an emergency nature, a meeting of the Jordan–Israel Mixed Armistice Commission would be called within twenty-four hours. [*S/2049, Report of the Chief of Staff of UNTSO to the Secretary-General, 21 Mar. 1951*, p. 15.]

In the period immediately following, these incidents along the demarcation lines did not persist, and there was comparative quiet, with the exception of incidents in the vicinity of Idna in the Hebron area and in the triangle area in western Jordan:

21. The arrangements made early this year at the meeting of the Deputy Chiefs of Staff of the two States, with a view to preventing further incidents, have to a large extent been implemented with satisfactory results. Minor incidents have been dealt with on the spot with the minimum of delay. The task of marking the armistice demarcation lines on the ground, which was suspended a year ago, has been resumed and completed in the more critical areas. The crossing of the demarcation lines by civilians has, however, continued. The Jordan authorities have made arrangements for the trial, in their own courts, of their citizens accused of infiltrating into Israel-controlled territory. They have also, by the Press and wireless, warned their citizens of the dangers of crossing the demarcation lines. The United Nations observers, for their part, have insisted that many incidents could be prevented if the Arabs living close to the demarcation lines had a clear knowledge of the location of the lines, which implied that they should be marked clearly on the ground.

22. The Israel–Jordan Mixed Armistice Commission met in emergency session on 8 and 15 March 1951, to consider complaints made by Jordan regarding the shelling of the village of Idna in the Hebron area on 7 March 1951. The Commission adopted the following resolution:

'*The Hashemite Kingdom of Jordan–Israel Mixed Armistice Commission,*

'1. *Considers* that the shelling of Idna village by Israel forces constituted a technical violation of article III, paragraphs 2 and 3, of the General Armistice Agreement and condemns such violation;

'2. *Considers* that the violation indicated in paragraph 1 above was the result of lesser contraventions of the General Armistice Agreement by residents of the Hashemite Kingdom of Jordan;

'3. *Therefore resolves:*

'(*a*) That the demarcation line in this area be clearly marked on the ground from where the demarcation line meets the Beit Jibrin road to opposite Beit Awwa village;

'(*b*) That direct telephone communications be set up between Beit Jibrin and Tarqumiya villages to facilitate quick contact in case of need between the local commanders, thus enabling them to act promptly.'

23. At a meeting of the Israel–Jordan Mixed Armistice Commission on 19 April 1951, representatives reviewed existing arrangements aimed at preventing incidents along the armistice demarcation lines and decided on the following:

(*a*) Telephone communications to be established between Dhahiriya and Beersheba; Jenin and Afula; Israel and Jordan posts in the Tulkarm area; Israel and Jordan posts in the Latrun area, and between Beit Jibrin and Tarqumiya. These communications to be subject to a daily check for one hour in the morning and one hour in the afternoon;

(*b*) Meetings to take place at specified points on the demarcation line between Israel and Jordan officers to settle minor incidents summarily;

(*c*) Liaison officers of one party to inform their opposite numbers on incidents within three hours of their occurrence;

(*d*) The cost of damage caused by infiltrating flocks and the cost of upkeep of flocks while in custody to be paid by the owner of the flocks. Livestock crossing the demarcation line to be returned promptly, minus 2 per cent of the flock;

(*e*) Shepherds and other civilians who crossed the demarcation line unintentionally to be returned immediately.

Both delegations undertook to fulfil these conditions until 30 June 1951, when a further review would be made. It has been alleged by the Israel authorities that the other side did not show the necessary co-operation, especially in the Hebron area. However, the agreement is still partly observed and it is hoped that it will shortly be renewed.

24. The Jordan–Israel Mixed Armistice Commission met on 26 April 1951 to consider a Jordan complaint alleging that on 11 April 1951 Israelis had again shelled the village of Idna with mortars. The United Nations Chairman summed up the evidence presented in the following terms:

'(*a*) A routine Israel border patrol along the demarcation line had inadvertently entered Jordan-controlled territory;

'(*b*) An armed conflict ensued between the Israel patrol and elements of the Arab Legion, national guards and civilians;

'(*c*) The Israel patrol withdrew with a subsequent crossing of the demarcation line by the Jordan forces:

'(*d*) At the time of the indident the demarcation line in the vicinity of Idna was not marked, this being a contributing factor to the incident.'

After some discussion, the Mixed Armistice Commission decided that:

(*a*) Both parties will take more stringent measures against their respective nationals who illegally cross the demarcation line;

(*b*) Surprise checks for demarcation line violations will be made by both delegations on their respective sides of the demarcation line, accompanied when possible by a United Nations observer.

25. The marking on the ground of the demarcation line has since been completed in the Idna area and incidents have become very rare.

26. On 3 July 1951, the Israel–Jordan Mixed Armistice Commission decided that the buildings occupied by either Israelis or Arabs in the no-man's-land area separating the Jordan-controlled and Israel-controlled parts of Jerusalem would continue to be occupied without prejudice to a future settlement. It was further agreed that no more buildings would be occupied by citizens of either State. Complaints referring to illegal occupation of buildings in no-man's-land have frequently figured on the agenda of the Mixed Armistice Commission meetings. It is expected that this agreement will result in a marked decrease of incidents and complaints regarding the no-man's-land area.

27. During the period under review, the process of eliminating from the Commission's agenda long-standing complaints, which with the passage of time had lost their original purpose, was also continued satisfactorily.

28. Article VIII, paragraph 1, of the Israel–Jordan General Armistice Agreement established a Special Committee composed of 'two representatives of each party for the purpose of formulating agreed plans and arrangements designed to enlarge the scope of this . . . Agreement and to effect improvements in its application'. Paragraph 2 of this article states:

'The Special Committee shall be organized immediately following the coming into effect of this Agreement and shall direct its attention to the formulation of agreed plans and arrangements for such matters as either party may submit to it, which, in any case, shall include the following, on which agreements in principle already exists: free movement of traffic on vital roads, including the Bethlehem and Latrun–Jerusalem roads; resumption of the normal functioning of the cultural and humanitarian institutions on Mount Scopus and free access thereto; free access to the Holy Places and cultural institutions and use of the cemetery on the Mount of Olives; resumption of operation of the Latrun pumping station; provision of electricity for the Old City, and resumption of operation of the railroad to Jerusalem.'

29. The parties to the General Armistice Agreement envisaged direct negotiations by political representatives appointed as members of this Committee without the presence of a United Nations respresentative. This Committee to date has not reached agreement on items that might be discussed before this body.

30. As a result, the Chiefs of Staff, on behalf of the United Nations, continues to administer the agreement of 7 July 1948 entered into by the military commanders of both parties regarding the preservation of buildings and equipment of Hadassah Hospital and Hebrew University and the Augusta Victoria Hospital until the parties to the agreement take action in the Special Committee. Under the terms of the 7 July 1948 agreement, the United Nations continues to arrange for supplies of food and water for the Israel police detachment and a limited number of artisans who are retained as guards and maintenance crew in and about the hospital and university buildings.

31. The United Nations Relief and Works Agency continues to operate the Augusta Victoria Hospital for the care of about 400 Arab refugees. Although the Israel representatives have in the past two years entered complaints against this activity as a violation of the 7 July 1948 agreement, they have not pressed the complaint, due in part to the Chief of Staff's request not to force its closing.   [*S/2388, Report of Chief of Staff UNTSO to the Secretary-General.*]

By September 1952 the unhappy pattern had been set of civilian infiltration by armed Arab groups, clashes with Israel frontier patrols, and in some cases retaliatory raids by Israelis into Jordanian territory. It would seem that at this juncture the Jordanian government was genuinely trying to control civilian infiltration. The Israelis, at that time and ever since, have allowed only official, uniformed personnel to participate in retaliatory raids. The outcome is apparent: evidence against 'unauthorized' civilian incursions is more difficult to gather than evidence against retaliation (illegal under the Armistice Agreement) by uniformed Israelis. The MAC, supported by UNTSO, sought ways to meet this dilemma, for the situation was prone to lead to the boycotting of the official machinery by one side or the other:

11. During the year ending 30 September 1952 a total of 506 complaints were submitted to the Jordan–Israel Mixed Armistice Commission. Of these, 243 were settled individually after investigation; 157 were cleared from the agenda of the Commission after agreement that the passage of time had reduced their original importance; and 106 remained on the agenda.

12. Of the above complaints 152 were submitted by Jordan. One hundred and twenty-three of these alleged military activity along the Demarcation Line, including crossing of the line by patrols or other elements of Israel military forces, firing across the line by Israel military forces, and overflying of the line, while twenty-nine alleged violations involving civilians crossing the Demarcation Line. Of the 354 complaints submitted by Israel, thirty-three alleged military activity on the part of Jordanian military forces and 321 alleged infiltration and other illegal crossing of the Demarcation Line by civilians.

13. The numerous instances of civilian infiltration for smuggling, theft or other purposes have presented a serious problem in the relations between the parties. Clashes between Israel frontier guards or patrols and armed Arab groups have frequently occurred, followed in some cases by retaliatory raids by Israelis into Jordan controlled territory.

14. Efforts to solve this problem of civilian infiltration have continued throughout the period of this report. An agreement on measures to curb infiltration and unauthorized crossing of the Demarcation Line by civilians was concluded by representatives of the two parties on 30 January 1952 and has subsequently been amended and extended for varying periods. On 13 May this agreement was extended in a modified form for an indefinite period, with the proviso that it could be cancelled only after two-weeks advance notice given by either party. The terms of this agreement called for:

(a) Weekly or semi-weekly meetings of Israel and Jordan local commanders at agreed times and places on the Demarcation Line;

(b) The exchange of information in regard to stolen property and other matters leading to unrest along the line;

(c) Incidents to be dealt with, in so far as possible, on a basis of unanimity between local commanders;

(d) Infiltrators to be handed over for trial to their own governments, with the proviso that sentences passed on them will be reported to the party in whose territory they were captured;

(e) Stolen property to be returned immediately, without waiting for equivalent returns from the other side;

(f) All flocks found grazing on the wrong side of the line to be handed back minus a fine of 2 per cent, and immediate payment to be made for any damage caused by the flock. Previously agreed rates for expenses incurred while flocks are held pending return to their owners to be paid by both sides in Jordan currency.

15. The most effective of these measures is the schedule of weekly or semi-weekly conferences of local commanders representing both military and police agencies, to be held at specified points along the Demarcation Line. United Nations military observers usually attend these meetings. Complaints are discussed before being brought to the Mixed Armistice Commission and, whenever possible, settled on the spot by agreement between the local commanders. During the period from 31 January to 4 May after the adoption of this scheme, the majority of complaints were settled on this local level. On 4 May 1952, following the occurrence of a series of particularly serious incidents, it was agreed that complaints would, as heretofore, be referred to the Mixed Armistice Commission for discussion, as well as to the local commanders. The effectiveness of the local commanders' meetings continued, however, as a means of securing increased co-operation on the local enforcement level. Measures so agreed upon have been responsible for a significant drop in both the number and seriousness of cases of infiltration, border crossings and smuggling.

16. Jordan authorities have also reported the following measures in effect from 1 November 1951 to curb infiltration:

(a) National guards and village authorities have been instructed to point out the location of the Demarcation Line to villagers, and to warn them of the danger they face in making illegal crossings; shepherds are instructed to keep their flocks as far as practicable from the line, to prevent accidental crossing and consequent confiscation by Israeli authorities; guards are stationed along the Demarcation Line, and a list of people owning or cultivating lands along the line has been established.

(b) In areas difficult to control (particularly along the Wadi Araba), Bedouin tribes have been ordered to move back from the Demarcation Line to areas deeper inside Jordan.

17. Another cause of frequent incidents along the Demarcation Line is the cultivation of land by residents of one party in the territory controlled by the other or in no-man's-land. As in previous years, the grain harvest months . . . were marked by numerous clashes which resulted in the loss of life in many instances. . . .

20. During the period covered by this report two incidents occurred which momentarily jeopardized the cease-fire between Israel and the Hashemite Jordan Kingdom. The first of these occurred on 4 June 1952, following failure to agree on the application of an informal *status quo* arrangement regarding certain cultivated lands under dispute in the Qalqilya area. Further attempt at settlement by United Nations observers present having failed, an

engagement ensued between the regular forces of the two parties which lasted for several hours. One Israel soldier was killed and a number of Jordanian soldiers and civilians were wounded.

21. A meeting of the Mixed Armistice Commission was called by the Chairman on 7 June 1952 to deal with that incident. The Commission decided by majority vote (the Israel delegation and the Chairman in favour; the Jordan delegation against) that the shooting of an Israel soldier inside Israel territory by Jordan fire from over the armistice line in the Qalqilya area on 4 June was a breach of article III, paragraph 3 of the General Armistice Agreement. The Commission also decided by majority vote (the Jordan delegation and the Chairman in favour; the Israel delegation against) that the shooting from the Israel side by Israel security forces into Jordan territory, which resulted in the wounding of two villagers, was a breach of article III, paragraph 3 of the General Armistice Agreement.

22. In a further series of resolutions relating to this same incident, the Mixed Armistice Commission by majority vote took three decisions against Israel and three decisions against Jordan for violations of article III, paragraph 3 of the General Armistice Agreement. In an effort to prevent further misunderstandings in the area, the parties agreed to mark the Demarcation Line in this sector by a plough furrow.

23. The second incident which threatened the cease-fire occurred on 17 September 1952 when Israel olive pickers were fired on by Jordanians in the Qaffin area. Both sides admitted participation of regular military forces during the ensuing two-day engagement. . . .

31. Coincidental with the difficulties over the Commission headquarters, another series of events contributed to the interruption of meetings. On 9 June 1952, two Israel soldiers were captured by a Jordanian patrol, within Jordan-controlled territory in the vicinity of the Latrun monastery. In a sub-committee meeting held on 12 August, a member of the Jordanian delegation agreed to the return of the two soldiers to Israel within two days. On the following day, however, he informed the Chairman that he had received orders from his superiors that the two men could not be returned until they had been tried by a Jordanian court on charges of infiltration and possession of arms in Jordanian territory. It was explained that a precedent for this action existed in the recent report contained in the Israeli newspapers that two infiltrators from Jordan had been tried by Israel courts and sentenced to ten years in prison for similar offences.

32. The Israel delegation refused to attend any meetings of the Mixed Armistice Commission until the two men had been returned. For a short period after 7 September, Israel representatives also failed to appear for sub-committee and local commanders meetings.

33. On 4 September 1952, the Jordanian delegation submitted a complaint against the kidnapping of two Arab Legionnaires during what it alleged to have been a pre-arranged meeting in Israel-controlled territory in the northern sector (Jisr esh Sheikh Hussein). Because of this incident, and in order to guard against a recurrence, the Jordanian delegation informed the Chairman that from 10 September orders had been issued that no local commander from Jordan would attend scheduled meetings on the demarcation line. However, partial agreement was reached shortly thereafter for a resumption of these meetings.

34. The Chairman brought both delegations together at a formal Mixed Armistice Commission meeting on 17 September 1952 for the express purpose of discussing ways to end the impasse. At this meeting, it was agreed that the prisoners whose detention had brought about the existing deadlock would be exchanged by the local commanders at Mandelbaum Gate, and that a meeting of the Mixed Armistice Commission would be held on 24 September 1952 at which outstanding complaints would be considered.

35. On 18 September, the prisoner exchange was carried out according to agreement, occupation of the new Mixed Armistice Commission offices followed and normal functioning of the Commission has been in effect since that date.

36. As pointed out in my last report (*S/2388, paras. 27–30*), pending action by the parties in the Special Committee provided by article VIII of the General Armistice Agreement, I continue to administer, on behalf of the United Nations, the Agreement of 7 July 1948 for the

demilitarization of Mount Scopus. Jordan has declined thus far to meet in the Special Committee.

37. Several incidents connected with the Mount Scopus agreement have contributed to the embittering of relations between the parties. I have already referred to the incident of 4 June 1952 and to its development (see paragraphs 27 and following). A second incident resulted from the establishment of various installations by the police of the 'Jewish Section' of Mount Scopus, against the express requests of my representative.

38. Under the terms of the agreement of 7 July 1948, the Arab and Jewish civilian police on Mount Scopus are 'placed on duty under the United Nations Commander'. As I considered that the installations in question were not in accordance with the terms of the agreement for the demilitarization of the area, I requested, by memorandum of 17 August 1952 addressed to the Israeli Civilian Police Inspector in charge of the 'Jewish Section' of Mount Scopus, that these installations be removed. I also took the matter up with the office of the Chief of Staff of the Israel Defence Forces and the Ministry for Foreign Affairs. On 20 October 1952, I was officially informed by the Ministry for Foreign Affairs that instructions had been issued to the Israel civilian police inspector to conform with my requests, on the understanding that this action did not prejudice in any manner Israel's rights in the Mount Scopus area, nor did it affect the interpretation to be given to any of the provisions of the 7 July 1948 Agreement, or the validity to be attached to the map annexed thereto or to any other map referring to that area. The requests to which Israel undertook to conform on 20 October 1952 included the withdrawal of the post and shelter located at MR. 173.05–133.28 to which I had objected, the re-establishment of the post at its original position, the filling in of the semi foxholes and slit trenches and the restoration of the area to its state of 4 April 1952. The observation post on the top of one of the hospital buildings was also to be eliminated and the sandbag emplacements removed. Moreover should any mines be found in the area, they should be destroyed on the spot as soon as possible. With the exception of the removal of the post and shelter located at MR. 173.05–133.28, no other action has been taken to date to comply with my request.   [*S/2833, Report of Chief of Staff of UNTSO to Secretary-General, 4 Nov. 1952.*]

12. During last few months the situation has been deteriorating along demarcation line between Israel and Jordan, first in other areas than Jerusalem and later Jerusalem. Israel has complained in particular of an increase in thefts and murders by Arab infiltrators and held the Jordanian authorities responsible for such situations. Jordan delegation has maintained that Jordan authorities were making every effort to combat infiltration which, in their view, was purely a police matter, according to general armistice agreement. Jordan also considers that there is tendency in Israel to attribute without sufficient proof crimes in border areas to Arab infiltrators. Drastic measures announced and taken by Israel to curb infiltration have not (repeat not) eased tension. Public opinion in two countries has been inflamed by incidents in which Arabs or Israelis have been wounded or killed in vicinity of demarcation line. In many cases, even before an investigation could be started through machinery of Mixed Armistice Commission, official or semi-official versions of such incidents were published. They remained the true versions for public opinion, irrespective of any investigation through machinery of Mixed Armistice Commission. This machinery itself did not (repeat not) function properly, since delegates tended to act as lawyers defending a case in court and Chairman consequently appeared as the judge who had to decide between conflicting conclusions, each party moving that the other be condemned for breaking General Armistice Agreement.

13. In such circumstances, machinery of Mixed Armistice Commission becomes inadequate. It is effective only when both parties are ready to use it to settle their difficulties, when they willingly co-operate in an investigation with assistance of Chairman and United Nations observers and when, in absence of agreed decision, they accept a majority decision, as provided in General Armistice Agreement.

14. Such is not (repeat not) atmosphere today in Israel–Jordan Mixed Armistice Commission. Time has arrived for two Governments to review problem of infiltration and perhaps also other problems the solution of which would relieve tension along demarcation line. When

present tension has been eased by agreed measures, machinery of General Armistice Agreement can, pending establishment of peace, assist in dealing with minor incidents and even, it may be hoped, preventing such serious outburst as that which occurred in Jerusalem on 22 April.

15. I have approached the two parties and suggested they should review situation in high-level talks. Favourable reply has been received from Israel Government and I sincerely hope that Government which has just been constituted in Amman will also accept my suggestion.

(*Signed*) RILEY

[*S/3007 and Corr. 1, Cabled Report of Chief of Staff to Secretary-General, 8 May 1953.*]

The tone of irritation in General Riley's final report as UNTSO Chief of Staff comes over clearly. His successor, General Bennike of Denmark, was able to report that the meeting which Riley had worked for

took place in Jerusalem on 29 June. Israel was represented by General Moshe Dayan, Jordan by General Radi Ennab.

3. The results of the meeting may be summed up as follows: Jordan is taking measures against infiltration and will continue to do so. Israel will co-operate by supplying information to Jordan on infiltration. Israel will seek to improve methods of transmitting such information quickly so that Jordan can make effective use of it. Detailed arrangements will be worked out in a meeting of high-ranking police officers of both sides which has been convened for 8 July. No further meeting between the two senior military commanders has been scheduled. However with an improvement of the situation another meeting between them might be arranged with a view to achieving further progress.

(*Signed*) General BENNIKE

[*S/3047, Report from Chief of Staff of UNTSO to Secretary-General, 30 June 1953.*]

General Bennike returned to New York in 1953 to answer questions put to him by members of the Security Council. (This isolated practice of direct contact between the UNTSO Chief of Staff and the Security Council has not been repeated. The Security Council meets when it is convened to act on particular crises in the Middle East; other than that, its interest in the day to day operation of the MAC, and UNTSO, is limited to its receipt of the periodic reports which the Chief of Staff transmits to the Secretary-General.)

II. *Questions put by the representative of France*

1. Can General Bennike tell the Council, with a few details, how the various bodies sub ordinate to the Truce Supervision Organization, in particular the Mixed Armistice Commissions such as the Jordan–Israel Commission, are operating at present?

Answer. To explain with a few details the actual happenings when a complaint is received by the Jordan–Israel Mixed Armistice Commission, I will relate as an example the Mixed Armistice Commission activities during the recent Qibya incident.

On the night of 14–15 October, just after midnight, the Chairman of the Jordan–Israel Mixed Armistice Commission received a call from the Jordan delegate who alleged that a major attack was at that time being carried out against the village of Qibya by Israeli military forces. He asked for a cease-fire, an immediate investigation and an emergency Mixed Armistice Commission meeting to discuss the case. The chairman told the Jordan delegate he would act immediately on his requests for a cease-fire and an investigation, and asked him to make sure that his people did not return the fire. He then went to the Mixed Armistice Commission office in the Jerusalem no man's land, contacted the Israeli delegate, informed him of the Jordan complaint, and requested an immediate cease-fire and permission to send out an investigating team. The Israeli delegate agreed to the investigation and said that he would contact the area for information as to what was happening, and that he would ask for a cease-fire. The Jordan delegate was then told that Israel had agreed to an investigation, and arrangements were made to send out the investigating team. Two observers were called and told to go to the spot and carry out an investigation. The Jordan delegate called shortly after, stating that mortar fire was being directed at the village of Budrus in the same area. This information was forwarded to the Israel delegate, who later reported that he had learned that firing had been heard in that area, but that it had stopped. At about dawn, the Jordan delegate called to say that all firing had ceased. The investigating team had already departed for the area. An observer was then sent with a member of the Israeli delegation to stand by inside Israel territory in case the investigation had to be continued on the Israeli side of the demarcation line.

The chairman, who had withheld his decision to hold the emergency meeting requested by Jordan, then went to Qibya to gain first-hand information. (According to an agreement reached during the 49th meeting of the Mixed Armistice Commission on 14 February 1951, the chairman of the Jordan–Israel Mixed Armistice Commission has the sole right to decide on an emergency meeting; if he decides to call an emergency meeting, he must call it within twenty-four hours of the submission of the complaint.)

On his return from Qibya, the chairman notified the parties that an emergency meeting would be held that afternoon. At the meeting, the Jordan delegation presented its complaint, the report of the United Nations investigating team was read, questions were put to the United Nations observers and, after a discussion, the draft resolution moved by the Jordan delegation was adopted by majority vote.

When the chairman decides that a complaint does not call for an emergency meeting, the complaint is placed, in its chronological order, on the agenda of a regular meeting of the Mixed Armistice Commission.

The rules of procedure of the Jordan–Israel Mixed Armistice Commission also provide for the possibility of referring to a sub-committee any claim or complaint relating to the application of the Armistice Agreement presented by either party. A sub-committee, made up of delegates from both sides and United Nations observers has met from time to time in an attempt to settle minor questions or to agree on the withdrawal or settlement of complaints. All decisions reached by the sub-committee must be unanimous and must be later ratified by the Mixed Armistice Commission during a formal Mixed Armistice Commission meeting.

2. Could General Bennike inform us whether in his opinion there is anything lacking in the operation of the various organs and whether he could make any suggestions with a view to improving their organization?

Answer. The operation of the Mixed Armistice Commissions, and in particular of the Jordan–Israel Mixed Armistice Commission, would be improved if, instead of acting 'as lawyers defending a case in court'—this phrase was recently used by General Riley in a report to the Security Council (S/3007, para. 12)—delegates of the parties acted in conformity with the spirit and the letter of the Armistice Agreements. The Armistice Agreements provide that action by the Mixed Armistice Commissions on claims and complaints shall be taken 'with a view to equitable and mutually satisfactory settlement'. I have presided over emergency meetings of the Israel–Jordan Mixed Armistice Commission, soon after I took over from General Riley. Like him, I found out that one delegate acted as the prosecuting attorney, the other defence, and I had to sit as a judge, without the benefit of a jury.

Another unsatisfactory aspect of the procedure is that the voting is on a draft resolution presented by one side or the other. Although in some respects the chairman's position may be compared to that of a judge, he is at a disadvantage in that he cannot formulate the verdict. He can cast his vote only after both parties have cast theirs. It is, therefore, impossible for the chairman to submit a draft resolution of his own, as this would be tantamount to announcing his vote in advance. This would open him to the accusation of partiality or of prejudging the issue. As the debate on the complaint continues right up to the moment of voting, the chairman is compelled to cast his vote on whatever text has been submitted by one side or the other. Consequently there is a very wide variation in the language of resolutions, particularly with respect to adjectives used to describe the breach of the Agreement. In this situation, the

Chairman's sole concern must be to establish the facts and to determine whether a breach of the Armistice Agreement has in fact occurred.

It would have a generally moderating effect on public opinion if the parties agreed to vote solely on the question whether a breach of the Agreement has taken place, leaving it to the chairman to formulate the verdict in appropriate terms.

When presiding over emergency meetings I also felt—and this impression has been confirmed by experience—that the Mixed Armistice Commission could be compared to a scoreboard, with the parties fighting to stack up decisions, one against the other. If the parties agreed to take action on claims and complaints 'with a view to equitable and mutually satisfactory settlement', the operation of the Mixed Armistice Commissions would be greatly improved.

Failing such fundamental change, the following suggestions might assist in improving the operation of the Mixed Armistice Commissions. I shall refer in particular to the Israel–Jordan Mixed Armistice Commission.

First, there is the question of congestion of work in the Israel–Jordan Mixed Armistice Commission. Many cases, which are not dealt with in emergency meetings, accumulate on the list of items to be considered in future regular meetings. An incident is sometimes long past before it comes up for hearing. If such incident was not investigated immediately or soon after it took place, the decision to enquire into it when the Mixed Armistice Commission begins to consider it several weeks or months later leads in many cases to no results. On 31 August 1953, the Israel and Jordan delegations took a drastic decision in wiping out 338 cases from the Mixed Armistice Commission's agenda. Normally, however, the reference of as many cases as possible to a sub-committee or to meetings of local commanders should greatly reduce congestion of work. Congestion of work would be limited to periods of tension, when practically every incident is either dealt with immediately in an emergency meeting or put on the list of questions to be dealt with later at regular meetings.

In the second place, there is the question of possible improvements in the investigation procedure. In the Israel–Jordan Mixed Armistice Commission observers may not be sent on an investigation unless the commission so decides. (It may take decisions by a majority vote.) In practice, when the consent of both parties is obtained informally by telephone or otherwise, a formal meeting in not required. When the consent of both parties is not obtained informally, an investigation may be considerably delayed and its results rendered worthless. The rules of procedure of the Israel–Egyptian Mixed Armistice Commission are more liberal. An investigation takes place following an agreement of the parties or a request by one of them to the chairman or his representative on either side. If, at the request of either party, the chairman decides to hold an emergency meeting of the Mixed Armistice Commission, he arranges for an investigation to be held within twenty-four hours of the submission of the claim or complaint. The investigation procedure in the Israel–Jordan Mixed Armistice Commission would be improved if its rules of procedure were amended to include similar provisions.

In the third place, it might be useful for the parties to discuss matters from time to time on a higher level than the Mixed Armistice Commission. Such talks might, if desired, be carefully prepared. The United Nations Truce Supervision Organization would lend such assistance as the parties might request. [*SCOR, 8th yr, 635th mtg, ann.*, pp. 19–20.]

On 24 November 1953 the Security Council adopted a resolution,[27] the last paragraph of which requested the Chief of Staff of UNTSO

to report within three months to the Security Council with such recommendations as he may consider appropriate on compliance with and enforcement of the General Armistice Agreements with particular reference to the provisions of this resolution and taking into account any agreement reached in pursuance of the request by the Government of Israel for the convocation of a conference under article XII of the General Armistice Agreement between Israel and Jordan.

[27] S/3139/Rev. 2.

The Chief of Staff submitted a report in March 1954 in compliance with the Security Council's request:

I. The Israel-Jordan General Armistice Agreement

3. Section A of the resolution adopted by the Security Council on 24 November 1953 dealt with 'the retaliatory action at Qibya by armed forces of Israel on 14–15 October 1953'. The Security Council has called upon Israel 'to take effective measures to prevent all such actions in the future'.

4. No incident of major proportions comparable to the incident at Qibya has occurred since the adoption of the Security Council resolution. Acts of violence apparently committed in some cases by groups bent on retaliatory action have, however, not only maintained tension along the demarcation line, but actually increased it. (See paragraph 10 below.)

5. In section B of its resolution of 24 November 1953, the Security Council 'takes note of the fact that there is substantial evidence of crossing of the demarcation line by unauthorized persons often resulting in acts of violence and requests the Government of Jordan to continue and strengthen the measures which they are already taking to prevent such crossing.'

6. The following measures have been taken by the Government of Jordan:

(*a*) Increase of the number of police assigned to the border area;

(*b*) Increase of the number of patrols;

(*c*) Replacement of village mukhtars and area commanders, where laxity of border control was suspected;

(*d*) Removal from the border area of suspected infiltrators and imposing of heavy sentences on known infiltrators;

(*e*) Effective measures, both preventive and punitive, in order to put a stop to incidents resulting from ploughing across the demarcation line. In this connexion, the Israel delegation to the Mixed Armistice Commission has been requested to co-operate by notifying the Mixed Armistice Commission or the Jordan local commander immediately on observing any illegal cultivation.

7. The number of Israeli complaints alleging crossing of the demarcation line has greatly increased during the last few months. (See appendices A and B to this report.) An increase in the number of complaints does not, however, suffice to indicate a deterioration in the local situation on the border. It may indicate an intensification of the cold war between the central authorities. Indeed, since the adoption of the resolution of the Security Council, the total number of complaints of various kinds has substantially increased on both sides. There have been other periods of psychological warfare—not only in the case of Israel and Jordan—when the parties to a General Armistice Agreement have apparently rivalled with one another in piling up complaints which, in quieter times, would not have been submitted to a Mixed Armistice Commission but would have been dealt with in informal talks, or, in the case of Israel and Jordan, at local commanders' meetings.

8. It may be said that, following the measures taken by the Jordan authorities on one side and the improvement and increase of the Israeli border police on the other, infiltration and the loss sustained by Israel as a result of marauding have now decreased.

9. In section B of its resolution, the Security Council has further recalled to the Governments of Israel and Jordan 'their obligations under Security Council resolution and the General Armistice Agreement to prevent all acts of violence on either side of the demarcation line'.

10. During the last three months, several acts of violence have contributed to periods of extreme tension. I shall refer in particular to the serious incidents in the Hebron area in the second half of December 1953 and to the present situation resulting in particular from the killing of an Israeli guard at Mahasyia, on 14 February, followed by the attack of a house in Kharass Village in Jordan, three days later. . . .

These incidents are then reported in detail:

11. If one considers the acts of violence committed in the various areas during the last few weeks, it may be concluded that tension has mounted along the whole Israel–Jordan border, except for the far south. There has been a quick succession of emergency meetings of the Mixed Armistice Commission, in an effort to cope with an explosive situation.

12. In the last paragraph of section B of its resolution, the Security Council has called upon 'the Governments of Israel and Jordan to ensure the effective co-operation of local security forces'.

13. The local commanders' agreement which was signed on 8 June 1953 was renewed on 16 February 1954 for a further period of three months, 1 March to 1 June 1954. There is no indication, at the present time, of the possibility of closer co-operation between the two Governments to ensure greater tranquillity on the border. As indicated above, Jordan has taken measures to prevent illegal crossings of the demarcation line and Israel has re-inforced its border patrol, but no joint effort has yet been attempted.

14. While a joint effort in itself would not suppress all thieving, armed robbery and smuggling, it would reduce them to a minimum. Patrols of local security forces of the parties, if not working jointly, at least in contact with each other, more frequent meetings and better communications between local commanders bestowed with greater police authority, would assist in relieving tension.

15. Today (24 February 1954) the question of the convocation of a conference under article XII of the General Armistice Agreement requested by the Government of Israel still remains unsettled. The Secretary-General of the United Nations has communicated to the Security Council his exchange of correspondence with the Governments of Jordan and Israel on the matter (*S/3180*). The difficulties which have arisen in connexion with the convocation of that conference have not contributed to create a better atmosphere between the two countries. [*S/3183 and Corr. 1, Report by Chief of Staff of UNTSO pursuant to the Security Council's resolution of 24 Nov. 1953.*]

Later in March 1954 there occurred an ambush on the Scorpion Pass which resulted in considerable loss of life among Israeli bus passengers. The MAC (the Chairman voting with Jordan) refused to adopt a resolution condemning Jordan in the strongest possible terms. The Chairman declared that the evidence was insufficient for such a finding. The Israeli delegation withdrew from the MAC, and on 23 March 1954, the Israeli government severed all connections with it.[28]

In September 1954 incidents occurred in the Beit Liqya area. UN observers investigating on the Jordanian side of the demarcation line, found clear evidence of Israeli incursion, including weapons and '. . . the tracks of the Israel force [which] were clearly visible in the areas of action and were easily followed to the demarcation line and on into no-man's land in the direction of Israel. Large bloodstains, Israel ammunition and other items of Israel equipment were found along the track.'[29]

The Israeli government would not allow the UN observer team to carry out investigation on the Israeli side of the demarcation line. The MAC—which the Israeli representatives did not attend—condemned Israel both for this refusal and for the acts concerned.[30]

By the spring of the next year UNTSO had succeeded at least in getting the foundations laid for a local agreement relating to the Jerusalem area.

[28] S/3278. For details of these events, and the ensuing deterioration between UN officials and Israel, see above, pp. 121–3.

[29] S/3290. Report by the Chief of Staff of UNTSO to the Secretary-General, 14 Sept. 1954.

[30] Ibid.

Colonel Abdul Halim al Saket and Aloof Mishne Chaim Herzog, who have respectively been designated by the Hashemite Kingdom of Jordan and the State of Israel as officers in control of military and police in the Jerusalem area, met at the offices of the Mixed Armistice Commission, in no-man's land, near the Mandelbaum Gate, at 10 a.m. on Monday, 18 April 1955.

This first meeting of these officers brought into effect an arrangement between Jordan and Israel to prevent, if possible, or in any case suppress immediately, all outbreaks of firing and hostile acts in the Jerusalem area.

The area covered by the arrangement is a rectangle 7 kilometres east and west and 9 kilometres north and south, centred roughly on the Jerusalem railway station.

While there is no document signed by the parties, they have signified to the United Nations Truce Supervision Organization that they agree to the provisions of the arrangement. These are, besides those referred to above, the following:

That only well trained and disciplined military or police personnel will be employed in the first line of defensive organization in this area;

That sentries, police guards, etc., will have strict orders not to fire unless by orders of an officer or if they are in danger of attack by superior numbers;

That designated senior officers will have direct telephone communication through which they may speak to each other to discuss and settle questions regarding the maintenance of peace in Jerusalem;

That the Chief of Staff of the United Nations Truce Supervision Organization or such other United Nations military observers as he may nominate to act on his behalf, may communicate with the designated officers and call for an informal meeting in case of firing or other disturbances;

That the senior officers responsible, on receiving any report of firing or other hostile acts or threat thereof, will take immediate action to stop firing, or put an end to other distrubances;

That each senior officer, when absent from his command headquarters, will be represented by an officer having full authority to act on his behalf. [*S/3394, Cable from the Chief of Staff of UNTSO to the Secretary-General, 18 Apr. 1955.*]

Negotiations to establish a local commanders' agreement covering the whole of the demarcation line between Jordan and Israel reached an advanced stage in the autumn of 1955, but broke down over whether a UN observer should be present—if requested by either party—at meetings between local commanders and area commanders of the two parties. The Chief of Staff urged resumption of the negotiations.[31]

Any discussion of the implementation of the Israel–Jordan Armistice must also make reference to the work of the Special Committee established in Article VIII of the General Armistice Agreement.[32] This committee first met on 20 April 1949 and settled several questions, including Israel's request for the reopening of the railway of Jerusalem. Two questions which it had not been able to resolve—resumption of operation of Latrun pumping station and provision of electricity for the Old City—lost their major significance with the passage of time. Despite the Security Council's Resolution S/1907 of 17 November 1950, the Special Committee stopped meeting after 1950 (S/3596).

2. The question of the resumption of the work of the Special Committee established in article VIII of the General Armistice Agreement has been raised several times by the Israel Government.

3. In its resolution of 17 November 1950 (S/1907), the Security Council:

[31] S/3596, para. 90   [32] See above, p. 35.

'Notes that with regard to the implementation of article VIII of the Israel–Jordan General Armistice Agreement the Special Committee has been formed and has convened, and hopes that it will proceed expeditiously to carry out the functions contemplated in paragraphs 2 and 3 of that article.'

4. The Security Council's hope has not been fulfilled. In April 1956, when the Secretary-General of the United Nations carried out in the Middle East the mission entrusted to him by the Security Council resolution of 4 April 1956 (S/3575), the Israel Government again raised, *inter alia*, the question of the implementation of article VIII.

5. In his report to the Security Council, the Secretary-General indicated that he had discussed in substance with the Israel and Jordan Governments the matters involved. He further stated:

'However, I do not feel that I should in this report go into the questions to which the article gives rise, as the judgement as to the state of compliance is primarily dependent on the jurisdiction of the Chief of Staff or on negotiations to be conducted by him. A memorandum submitted to me by the Chief of Staff on this subject is annexed to the report.' (S/3596, para. 99.)

6. The Chief of Staff's memorandum (S/3596, annex 6), after mentioning the meetings of the Special Committee in 1949 during which the resumption of the operation of the railroad to Jerusalem desired by Israel was arranged, referred to the other matters listed in paragraph 2 of article VIII and to the Israel request for the formulation by the Special Committee of agreed plans and arrangements for several of these matters. The Chief of Staff's memorandum further stated the position of Jordan, which considered it 'impossible in present circumstances to find practical means of solving these remaining problems because of serious security reasons' and which it 'generally favours maintaining the *status quo* regarding the outstanding specific matters until changes in the general situation remove the security problems involved'.

7. This Jordanian position has been maintained. For example, elaborate security measures are taken by the Jordanian authorities to ensure the safety of the fortnightly convoy which, under United Nations supervision, crosses part of Jordan-controlled Jerusalem to relieve and bring supplies to Israel personnel on Mount Scopus. The problem of the security measures necessary to ensure in present circumstances 'the normal functioning of the cultural and humanitarian institutions on Mount Scopus and free access thereto' would clearly be much more difficult to solve. Any situation involving the possibility of dangerous incidents, particularly in the Jerusalem area, cannot be taken lightly. On the other hand, Israel is entitled to request the implementation of the provisions of article VIII and an agreed solution of problems to which either party attaches great importance would help in relaxing tension between the two countries.

8. In June and July 1956 an exchange of views took place between the Israel Government and the Chief of Staff of the Truce Supervision Organization. The Israel Government stated in the following terms the action it desired to be taken in respect to article VIII:

'We reiterate our request that the Special Committee be convened without delay, and that it discuss first the matters agreed to in article VIII. For our part, we shall be prepared to discuss also such proposals as Jordan may submit "to enlarge the scope of the Agreement and to effect improvements in its applications", as provided by article VIII, paragraph 1. In this connection it is clear that precedence ought to be given to the discussion of the implementation of those agreed matters that Jordan has until now refused to implement.'

9. Israel's request that precedence be given to the 'agreed matters that Jordan has until now refused to implement' illustrates the continuing impasse. As indicated in annex 6 to document S/3596, among the matters on which agreement in principle existed in 1949, the Jordanian authorities have been able to settle by their own means and without resort to the Special Committee two matters which interested Jordan primarily (communications between Jerusalem and Bethlehem, provision of electricity for the Old City of Jerusalem). With the

exception of the question of free access to the Holy Places,* the remaining 'agreed matters' to which Israel wants to give priority over other matters which 'either party may submit' to the Special Committee are of interest primarily to Israel.

10. According to paragraph 1 of article VIII the Special Committee is to be composed of two representatives of each party designated by the respective Governments. No provision is made for any assistance to be rendered to the Committee by representatives of the Truce Supervision Organization or of any other United Nations body. Paragraph 1 of article VIII states that the Committee 'shall be established for the purpose of formulating agreed plans and arrangements designed to enlarge the scope of this Agreement and to effect improvements in its application'. From the point of view of effecting improvements in the application of the Armistice Agreement the main problem is the resumption by the Israel Government of full participation in the meetings of the Mixed Armistice Commission and full co-operation with the observation and investigation machinery of the Truce Supervision Organization. Since October 1956 Israel has refused to co-operate with the observation and investigation machinery of the Mixed Armistice Commission with respect to incidents affecting Israel. Israel has also ceased to attend plenary meetings of the Mixed Armistice Commission convened for the discussion of Jordan complaints because it saw 'no useful purpose in the continuation of routine examination of incidents in the Commission'. The Secretary-General in his report dated 17 October 1956 (S/3685) drew attention to this situation.

11. In view of the constitution of the Special Committee, which is composed of the representatives of the parties alone, a decision to meet must be taken by mutual agreement of the parties. The Acting Chief of Staff of the United Nations Truce Supervision Organization would be glad to extend such assistance in this connexion as the two parties might request.

[*S/3913, Report of the Acting Chief of Staff of UNTSO, 18 Nov. 1957.*]

The extent to which the revival of the Special Committee was bound up with Israel's willingness to participate in the work of the MAC—as well as the limitations upon UNTSO's ability to lend its good offices to the Special Committee—is made clear in paragraph 10 above. A summary of other aspects of Jordan–Israel relations is also included in the report of the Acting Chief of Staff:

12. In his complaint to the Security Council (S/3883), the acting permanent representative of Israel stated that 'other provisions of the General Armistice Agreement (besides article VIII) of which Jordan is in standing violation include her refusal to comply with the four fundamental principles of the Agreement outlined in article I'.

13. The question of compliance with the principles outlined in article I has been raised by the Israel Government on a number of occasions. It has been raised especially in connexion with what the Israel complaint to the Security Council describes as 'the incessant campaign of threat, intimidation and incitement pursued by the leaders of the Jordanian Government against the security and integrity of Israel in violation of articles I and III, as well as of the Charter of the United Nations'. The acting representative of Israel, at the 788th meeting of the Security Council, referred to recent 'threatening statements', which, he said, imply non-compliance 'with the fundamental principles of non-aggression, non-intimidation, and the promotion of peace which are included in article I of the Agreement'.

14. In the Jordan view Israel is considered as having repeatedly violated the basic provisions of the General Armistice Agreement, specifically as regards the retaliatory military actions undertaken by Israel against Jordan civilians or armed forces. . . .

16. The scope for action of the Truce Supervision Organization, besides being often reduced by lack of co-operation, is limited. In particular, it can do little to secure the implementation of article I. The Chairmen of the Mixed Armistice Commissions have generally considered that this article falls outside the competence of the Commission concerned to interpret and apply. They have based themselves on the provisions of the General Armistice Agree-

* Some of the Holy Places—Christian, Jewish and Moslem—are on the Israel side of the demarcation line: a greater number are on the Jordan side.

ments (in the case of the General Armistice Agreement between Israel and Jordan, article XI, para. 8). [*Ibid.*]

Attempts to convene a conference under Article XII of the Jordan–Israel Armistice Agreement may also be raised at this juncture. The Israel government had sought[33] to call a conference for the purpose of reviewing the agreement as envisaged in Article XII, paragraph 3. Jordan refused.

iv. *Lebanon–Israel Armistice, 1949–56*

The implementation of the Israel–Lebanon Armistice has been the most successful, and least difficult, of the four agreements.

III. *Lebanese–Israel Mixed Armistice Commission*

1. The task of marking on the ground the demarcation lines between Israel and Lebanon was completed on 27 January 1951. The purpose of this project, undertaken by a special sub-committee set up by the Lebanese–Israel Mixed Armistice Commission on 16 November 1949, was to reduce incidents arising out of uncertainty as to the exact location of the demarcation line. In general, the work of this sub-committee progressed smoothly. For example, in a number of cases special measures were taken with respect to fields lying astride the demarcation lines, it being understood that such measures would not affect final decisions to be incorporated in an eventual peace treaty. However, with respect to a small portion of the demarcation lines, the Israel and Lebanese delegations were unable to come to an agreement, as a result of differing interpretations of the text of the Anglo-French Agreement of 1923. The sub-committee is now engaged in preparing the final draft of its report and is expected to meet in March 1951 for a final study of the draft report before its submission.

2. On 23 November 1950, the Lebanese–Israel Mixed Armistice Commission considered a complaint submitted by the Lebanese delegation, which alleged that Israel military aircraft had flown across the demarcation lines. The Israel delegation replied that annex I (Definition of defensive forces) of the Lebanese–Israel General Armistice Agreement did not prohibit military aircraft from using the air space above the defensive zone. The Lebanese delegation rejected this interpretation and requested the Lebanese–Israel Mixed Armistice Commission to take a decision on the matter. The Chairman suggested, and both parties agreed, that the Israel position should be studied further before the question was voted upon. At a subsequent meeting, both delegations agreed that the deputy Chiefs of Staff of the Israel and Lebanese armed forces, who had signed the General Armistice Agreement, should meet in order to resolve the question. In the meantime, the Israel delegation agreed to prohibit military aircraft from entering the air space above the defensive zone. To date, the proposed meeting of the deputy Chiefs of Staff has not taken place.

3. In addition, the Lebanese–Israel Mixed Armistice Commission dealt with the following matters:

(*a*) The return of persons from Israel and Lebanon who had made unauthorized crossings of the demarcation lines and were apprehended. In this respect, following an agreement reached in the Lebanese–Israel Mixed Armistice Commission, several hundred Palestine Arab refugees who had infiltrated into Israel from Lebanon were returned to Lebanon through the instrumentality of the Lebanese–Israel Mixed Armistice Commission.

(*b*) The return of herds of livestock and individual domestic animals which had wandered across the demarcation lines and were seized.

(*c*) The return of fishing boats from one State which had entered the waters of the other and were seized.

(*d*) The disposition of cases of smuggling and theft along the demarcation lines.

[33] S/3140, 23 Nov. 1953.

(*e*) The consideration of the repatriation to Israel of Arab refugees who had fled to Lebanon during the hostilities. [*S/2049, Report of Chief of Staff of UNTSO, 21 Mar. 1951.*]

III. *Israel–Lebanese Mixed Armistice Commission*

32. As stated in my previous report (*S/2049, Part III, paragraph 1*), the marking on the ground of the armistice demarcation line was completed on 27 January 1951. The final report of the Israel–Lebanese Mixed Armistice Commission on the staking of the demarcation line is nearing completion. The line is now marked on the ground by piles of white-washed stone, with iron posts and notice boards at intervals. Incidents arising out of uncertainty as to the exact location of the line have shown a marked decrease.

33. Before the harvest a sub-committee of the Israel–Lebanese Mixed Armistice Commission toured the border areas warning inhabitants on both sides against the use of firearms during harvest time. No case of indiscriminate shooting occurred.

34. During the period under review the Israel authorities returned to Lebanon, through the Mixed Armistice Commission, a number of Lebanese fishermen who had entered Israel waters. The Israel authorities also allowed some Palestine families (most of them Armenian) which were in Lebanon to enter Israel. A number of persons who had crossed the demarcation line were returned to their respective countries.

35. Cases of theft and smuggling across the demarcation line have been on the decrease as a result of mixed investigation by the police of both parties in the border areas.

36. The Lebanese delegation has made a number of complaints against Israel aircraft crossing into Lebanese territory. The senior Israel representative explained at meetings of the Mixed Armistice Commission that orders against flying over Lebanese territory had been reissued to the Israel Air Force. He stressed that these instances of over-flying the border were purely accidental and should in no way be construed as being deliberate unfriendly acts against Lebanon.

(*Signed*) W. E. RILEY
Lieutenant General USMC, retired
Chief of Staff, Truce Supervision
Organization in Palestine

[*S/2388, Report of Chief of Staff of UNTSO, 8 Nov. 1951.*]

III. *Lebanon–Israel Mixed Armistice Commission*

39. The Lebanon–Israel Mixed Armistice Commission held twenty-five formal meetings from 1 November 1951 to 15 October 1952. It also held two meetings on the chief of staff level and a number of unofficial or special meetings. In addition there were frequent meetings of the Sub-Committee for Border Incidents and of the Sub-Committee for Staking of the Border. Constabulary officers are now included in the delegations of both parties, and their participation in meetings of the Commission has facilitated the handling of border incidents relating to police matters.

40. With regard to the marking of the Armistice Demarcation Line (*S/2388, para. 31*), the existing markings have been improved by the construction of supplementary markers, the repair of damaged markers, and the correction of errors. The line has been marked on the ground for its entire length, with the exception of one section in the east of approximately five kilometres between boundary pillar 38 and the Hasbani River. The Mixed Armistice Commission is endeavouring to find a temporary solution permitting normal life in this area where the boundary is in dispute. It is proposed that a temporary line referred to as the 'civilian line' should be surveyed following the boundaries of properties owned by nationals of the respective countries. Lands of Palestinian refugees would be included on the Israel side. The Sub-Committee for the Staking of the Border is at present studying documents which would enable the tracing of this civilian line on a large-scale map acceptable to both parties. The line would then be materialized on the ground, and at the same time two other lines corresponding

to the respective interpretations of Israel and of Lebanon concerning the border in this area would also be marked pending final agreement by the parties on a single line.

41. During the period of this report there was one series of events which caused tension between the parties (seizure by the Lebanese customs on 20 January 1952 of a cargo of beans destined for Israel; seizure in retaliation by representatives of the Government of Israel of several flocks of sheep, goats and some cattle). As a result of these actions the functioning of the Mixed Armistice Commission was disrupted for a period of about one month. Meetings of the Commission were only resumed following special meetings of the Chiefs of Staff or their representatives under my chairmanship. Agreement was reached between the parties, the co-operative spirit existing prior to these difficulties was re-established and the Mixed Armistice Commission again began to function. Other incidents involving herds that stray across the demarcation line are now being promptly settled on the basis of the return of the animals against payment of moderate indemnification and the reserve of claims for damage to cultivation.

42. The Commission has continued to effect the repatriation to Israel of some former Palestinian refugees in Lebanon and the crossing of certain persons to Israel on the basis of the principle of the reunion of families. During the period under review, 129 persons crossed to Israel and twenty-five persons crossed to Lebanon. A number of persons who had infiltrated across the demarcation line were returned to their respective countries in accordance with a procedure supervised by the Commission's Sub-Committee for Border Incidents.

43. Complaints concerning overflying of the demarcation line have been received throughout the period of this report on an average of about three per month. Approximately three-fourths of these complaints have come from Lebanon whose delegation continues to express concern (S/2388, para. 35). In one instance an illegal flight was admitted by Israel and the pilot was punished. In all other cases the parties have denied responsibility. No instance of alleged overflying has had the character of a serious incident and efforts are being made to improve the situation.

44. The Commission has also dealt with a large number of matters having a penal, administrative, or civil character. These included smuggling and illegal fishing; crimes and offences in the border region; return of property, documents and money confiscated or abandoned; collaboration of judicial and police authorities in conducting investigations and procuring testimony; requests for information or news concerning relatives and missing persons; and collaboration of the parties in combating locusts. In general, these questions may be considered as having little connexion with the normal work of an armistice commission. They are, however, matters on which co-operation is desirable, and their solution is possible through the instrumentality of the Mixed Armistice Commission, which is the only regular contact available. [S/2833, Report of Chief of Staff, 4 Nov. 1952.]

In March 1954 the Chief of Staff was able to remind the Secretary-General that in his statement to the Security Council of 27 October 1953 he had been able to say that the Israel–Lebanon Armistice had given rise to 'relatively few and minor difficulties. There has been no change in this respect during the last three months' (S/3183 and Corr.1, 1 Mar. 1954). The brevity of the reports on this agreement contrast with the long and detailed submissions of disputes under the other three Armistice Agreements.

(b) Observations on Implementation Common to all the Armistice Agreements, 1956

On 4 April 1956 the Security Council unanimously adopted the following resolution:

The Security Council,

Recalling its resolutions of 30 March 1955. 8 September 1955, and 19 January 1956,

Recalling that in each of these resolutions the Chief of Staff of the United Nations Truce Supervision Organization and the parties to the general armistice agreements concerned were requested by the Council to undertake certain specific steps for the purpose of ensuring that the tensions along the armistice demarcation lines should be reduced,

Noting with grave concern that despite the efforts of the Chief of Staff the proposed steps have not been carried out,

1. *Considers* that the situation now prevailing between the parties concerning the enforcement of the armistice agreements and the compliance given to the above-mentioned resolutions of the Council is such that its continuance is likely to endanger the maintenance of international peace and security;

2. *Requests* the Secretary-General to undertake, as a matter of urgent concern, a survey of the various aspects of enforcement of and compliance with the four general armistice agreements and the Council's resolutions under reference;

3. *Requests* the Secretary-General to arrange with the parties for the adoption of any measures which, after discussion with the parties and with the Chief of Staff, he considers would reduce existing tensions along the armistice demarcation lines, including the following points:

(*a*) Withdrawal of their forces from the armistice demarcation lines;

(*b*) Full freedom of movement for observers along the armistice demarcation lines in the demilitarized zones and in the defensive areas;

(*c*) Establishment of local arrangements for the prevention of incidents and the prompt detection of any violations of the armistice agreements;

4. *Calls upon* the parties to the general armistice agreements to co-operate with the Secretary-General in the implementation of this resolution;

5. *Requests* the Secretary-General to report to the Council in his discretion but not later than one month from this date on the implementation given to this resolution in order to assist the Council in considering what further action may be required. [*S/3575, 4 Apr. 1956.*]

Following a progress report of 2 May (S/3594), the Secretary-General submitted a report on 9 May (S/3596).

9. My talks with the Governments have, without exception, been conducted on the basis of agreement that their purpose was to explore the possibility of re-establishing the full implementation of the armistice agreements. . . .

12. The demarcation lines established by the armistice agreements were based on existing truce lines. They had, in many cases, no basis in history or in the distribution of population or private property. . . .

A chain of actions and reactions was created which, unless broken, is bound finally to constitute a threat to peace and security.

13. The development could have taken another turn, if the Government and citizens of one country had felt able to assume that transgressors from the other country—in violation of the provisions of the armistice agreement—had acted without any instigation or approval by the authorities and that the authorities had taken active counter-measures, including appropriate punishment for transgressions. No reason would then have existed for acts of reprisal which might be considered, by the country taking action, as acts in self-defence; instead a complaint to the other party would have been the natural outlet for reactions.

14. This last pattern is obviously the new state of affairs towards which any effort to re-establish the full and integral implementation of the armistice agreements must aim. . . .

16. . . . From no side has it been said that a breach of an armistice agreement, to whatever clause it may refer, gives the other party a free hand concerning the agreement as a whole; but a tendency to regard the agreements, including the cease-fire clauses, as entities may ex-

7

plain a feeling that in fact, due to infringements of this or that clause, the obligations are no longer in a strict sense fully binding, and specifically that a breach of one of the clauses, other than the cease-fire clause, may justify action in contravention of that clause. . . .

18. The very logic of the armistice agreements shows that infringements of other articles cannot serve as a justification for an infringement of the cease-fire article. If that were not recognized, it would mean that any one of such infringements might not only nullify the armistice régime, but in fact put in jeopardy the cease-fire itself. . . . [*S/3596, Report of the Secretary-General to the Security Council pursuant to the Council's resolution of 4 Apr. 1956, 9 May 1956.*]

When asked by the Secretary-General, through UNTSO's Chief of Staff, for an assurance on this matter, the governments of Israel and Egypt replied in the following way, and received the following rejoinder from the Secretary-General:

REPLY FROM THE PRIME MINISTER OF ISRAEL TO THE CHIEF OF STAFF OF THE UNITED NATIONS TRUCE SUPERVISION ORGANIZATION

Jerusalem, 9 April 1956

Further to our conversation today, the following is the Prime Minister's reply to your letter of 9 April 1956, enclosing the Secretary-General's letter to the Prime Minister, dated 8 April 1956.

'We agree unconditionally to comply fully with the provisions of article II, paragraph 2, of the Israel–Egyptian General Armistice Agreement, it being understood that Egypt will do likewise. As I stated in my conversation with General Burns yesterday, if Egypt does not comply with article II, paragraph 2, and continues her warlike acts against Israel, we must reserve our freedom to act in self-defence.'

(*Signed*) Y. TEKOAH
Director of Armistice Affairs

EXTRACT FROM *Aide-mémoire* FROM THE SECRETARY-GENERAL TO THE PRIME MINISTER OF ISRAEL

Tel Aviv, 10 April 1956

The Secretary-General expresses his gratitude for the reply he has received to his recent message to Mr Ben Gurion. He notes that the Government of Israel reserves its freedom to act in self-defence. He understands that that reservation does in no way detract from the unconditional undertaking to observe article II, paragraph 2, of the General Armistice Agreement, and that, therefore, the words 'in self-defence' have to be interpreted in conformity with the stipulations of the said paragraph.

Aide-mémoire FROM THE GOVERNMENT OF EGYPT TO THE SECRETARY-GENERAL

Cairo, 11 April 1956

The Government of Egypt, while reserving the right of self-defence as stipulated in the Charter of the United Nations, reiterate the expression of their unconditional acceptance of article II, paragraph 2, of the Egyptian–Israel Armistice Agreement.

Aide-mémoire FROM THE SECRETARY-GENERAL TO THE PRIME MINISTER OF EGYPT

Cairo, 11 April 1956

The Secretary-General notes with appreciation the statement of the Government of Egypt. He notes that the Government of Egypt reserves the rights to self-defence as stipulated in the Charter of the United Nations and he understands that that reservation does in no way detract from the unconditional undertaking to observe article II, paragraph 2, of the General Armistice Agreement and that, therefore, the words 'in self-defence' have to be interpreted in conformity with the stipulations of the said paragraph and the Charter of the United Nations. [*S/3584, 12 Apr. 1956*, pp. 16–17.]

The ensuing exchanges on this question subsequently occurred between the Secretary-General and Jordan, Syria, and Lebanon—these last taking the opportunity to raise the question of the proposed Israeli diversion of the Jordan. They reveal materials of some interest on the legal scope of self-defence under the UN Charter and under armistice arrangements:

ANNEX 1

A. Letter from the Prime Minister of the Hashemite Kingdom of the Jordan to the Secretary-General

(Original text: English)
29 April 1956

Our agreement is hereby confirmed. I wish to invite your utmost care and attention to the grave consequences, if the Jordan River diversion works are resumed by Israel. On the strength of your statement to me that the Security Council resolution affecting this problem can only be interpreted by the Security Council alone, it becomes evident that any unilateral action by Israel would mean not only violation of the said resolution but also defiance of the principle indicated by you. . . .

B. Letter from the Secretary-General to the Prime Minister of the Hashemite Kingdom of the Jordan

(Original text: English)
Jerusalem 2 May 1956

I thank you for your letter of 29 April 1956. I note that by that letter you confirm our agreement.

Your confirmation establishes reciprocity with the assurance given to me by the Government of Israel, that they would observe unconditionally their obligations under article II, paragraph 2, of the Jordan–Israel Armistice Agreement, reserving only the right to self-defence. I thus note that your confirmation means that I have from you an unconditional assurance to the same effect, with a reserve only as to your right to self-defence under Article 51 of the Charter.

You will remember that I stated in explanation of the reserve for self-defence, that I understand that this reservation does in no way detract from the unconditional undertaking to observe article III, paragraph 2, of the General Armistice Agreement, and that, therefore, the word 'self-defence' has to be interpreted in conformity with the stipulations of the said paragraph and the Charter of the United Nations.

As our agreement concerning the unconditional assurance was based on a text which I handed you, but as, on the other hand, no minutes were taken of our meetings, I have found it appropriate in this way, in my reply, to put on record the substance of our agreement in this respect.

I avail myself of this opportunity to thank you for our useful talks in Amman.

(Signed) Dag Hammarskjöld

ANNEX 2

A. Letter dated 1 May 1956 from the Foreign Minister of Lebanon to the Secretary-General

(Original text: French)

I have the honour to communicate to you the following declaration:

'The Government of Lebanon, while reserving the right of self-defence recognized by the Charter of the United Nations, reaffirms its unconditional acceptance of the provisions of article III, 2, of the Lebanon–Israel General Armistice Agreement.'

(*Signed*) Salim LAHOUD

B. LETTER FROM THE FOREIGN MINISTER OF LEBANON TO THE SECRETARY-GENERAL

(*Original text: French*)
Beirut, 1 May 1956

I am pleased to send you herewith:

An official declaration by the Government of Lebanon regarding the application of article III, paragraph 2, of the Lebanon–Israel General Armistice Agreement.

A letter repeating the Lebanese Government's point of view expressed during our conversation of 27 April 1956, concerning the need to obtain assurances with regard to the diversion of the Waters of the Jordan.

The Government of Syria has informed me of the contents of your letter of 28 April 1956 and of its reply dated 30 April 1956.

I was glad to note that you expected to receive, within one or two days, from the Israel side, assurances concerning respect for the Security Council's resolutions relating to the putting into force and the implementation of the Syrian–Israel General Armistice Agreement.

It is my firm hope that, when you visit Damascus on Wednesday, 2 May, you will be able to satisfy the Syrian request which we fully support.

(*Signed*) Salim LAHOUD

C. LETTER FROM THE FOREIGN MINISTER OF LEBANON TO THE SECRETARY-GENERAL

(*Original text: French*)
Beirut, 1 May 1956

I have the honour to communicate to you the declaration of the Government of Lebanon with regard to the application of article III, paragraph 2, of the Lebanese–Israel General Armistice Agreement.

Further to our conversation of 27 April 1956, I should like to draw your attention once more to the prime importance, from the point of view of the maintenance of peace, of the question of the diversion of the Waters of the Jordan. You were good enough to inform me in this connexion that, during the conversations you are to have with the Israeli authorities, you will endeavour to obtain from them the assurance that they will not undertake any work in the demilitarized zone with a view to diverting the waters of the Jordan.

I cannot too strongly urge that any such initiative taken by Israel might have extremely serious consequences, and would constitute a manifest breach both of the General Armistice Agreement with Syria and of the resolution adopted by the Security Council in this matter.

I trust that your efforts will be crowned with success. Your mission of peace will then have been accomplished in the most satisfactory manner.

(*Signed*) Salim LAHOUD

D. LETTER FROM THE SECRETARY-GENERAL TO THE FOREIGN MINISTER OF LEBANON

(*Original text: French*)
2 May 1956

I have the honour to acknowledge receipt of your letter of 1 May, and also of the declaration in which you reaffirm your unconditional acceptance of the provisions of article III, paragraph 2, of the Lebanon–Israel General Armistice Agreement.

I appreciate your declaration, of which I take note. I note that the Government of Lebanon reserves the right of self-defence recognized in the Charter of the United Nations. This reservation in no way detracts from the unconditional undertaking to observe the provisions of article III, paragraph 2, of the General Armistice Agreement. The word 'self-defence' should therefore be interpreted in conformity with the stipulations of the aforesaid paragraph and of the Charter on the United Nations.

I have also noted the observations made by you in the covering letter accompanying your declaration. When making public the exchanges of messages, I propose to quote the first and third paragraphs of that letter.

(*Signed*) Dag HAMMARSKJÖLD

ANNEX 3

A. DECLARATION OF THE GOVERNMENT OF SYRIA COMMUNICATED TO THE SECRETARY-GENERAL UNDER COVER OF A LETTER DATED 2 MAY 1956 FROM THE PRESIDENT OF THE COUNCIL AND FOREIGN MINISTER OF SYRIA

(*Original text: French*)

The Government of Syria, while reserving the right of self-defence recognized by the Charter of the United Nations, reaffirms its unconditional acceptance of the provisions of article III, paragraph 2, of the Syrian–Israel General Armistice Agreement.

B. LETTER FROM THE PRESIDENT OF THE COUNCIL AND FOREIGN MINISTER OF SYRIA TO THE SECRETARY-GENERAL

(*Original text: French*)

Damascus, 2 May 1956

I have the honour to communicate to you herewith the declaration concerning article III, paragraph 2, of the Syrian–Israel General Armistice Agreement.

Please note that the aforesaid declaration is made within the framework of the Charter of the United Nations. In this connexion, I should be glad if you would take note of the following declaration:

'Considering that, under the terms of Article 25 of the Charter of the United Nations, "the Members of the United Nations agree to accept and carry out the decisions of the Security Council in accordance with the present Charter",

'The Government of Syria reaffirms its resolve to respect the provisions of the resolutions adopted by the Security Council in connexion with the putting into force and implementation of the Syrian–Israel General Armistice Agreement, including the resolution of 27 October 1953.'

I consider that the Syrian Government's attitude should be shared by the other party to the Armistice Agreement.

(*Signed*) Said EL-GHAZZI

C. LETTER FROM THE SECRETARY-GENERAL TO THE PRESIDENT OF THE COUNCIL AND FOREIGN MINISTER OF SYRIA

(*Original text: French*)

Damascus, 2 May 1959

I have the honour to acknowledge receipt of your note of today's date communicating to me a declaration under which the Government of Syria, while reserving the right of self-defence recognized in the Charter of the United Nations reaffirms its unconditional acceptance of the provisions of article III, paragraph 2, of the Syrian–Israel General Armistice Agreement.

I appreciate this declaration, of which I take note. I note that the Government of Syria reserves the right of self-defence recognized in the United Nations Charter. That reservation in no way detracts from the unconditional undertaking to comply with the provisions of Article III, paragraph 2, of the General Armistice Agreement. The term 'self-defence' should therefore be interpreted in conformity with the stipulations of the said paragraph and with the Charter of the United Nations.

I note your statement regarding the general framework within which the undertaking to comply with the cease-fire instituted by article III, paragraph 2, of the General Armistice Agreement is given. I can confirm that Article 25 of the United Nations Charter enters into the framework of the Secretary-General's conversations during his current mission. [*S/3596, Report of the Secretary-General to the Security Council pursuant to the Council's resolution of 4 Apr. 1956, ann. 3.*]

The Secretary-General reported that while he had to accept reservations as to self-defence, this reservation was necessarily indeterminate, for 'its meaning in a concrete situation can be determined only by the Security Council, as established in the Charter'.[34] The reservation could not derogate from the obligations assumed under Article II, para. 2 of the Egypt–Israel Armistice Agreement, or under Article III, para. 2 of the other Armistice Agreements.[35] Nor did a reservation as to self-defence permit acts of retaliation.[36]

Hammarskjöld decided not to include in his report 'a recapitulation of past failures', preferring instead 'a constructive forward look'.[37] He observed:

64. There is not in all cases an adequate functioning machinery for resolving disputes concerning the interpretation, or implementation of the obligations assumed by the parties under the agreements. Obviously an assurance to comply with the armistice agreements has little practical bearing on the situation to the extent that any party can reserve for itself the right to give to the obligations its own interpretation, which may be different from the one which in good faith is maintained by the other party.

65. A further weakness is that no procedure has been established for the handling of conflicts covered by the general clauses in the armistice agreements. For example, the first article of the several agreements establishes a right to security and freedom from fear of attack. The parties have in many cases complained of actions from the other side as being in conflict with this stipulation. Were diplomatic relations maintained, such complaints would undoubtedly be handled through normal diplomatic channels and might in that way to a large extent be resolved. In cases of this kind which the party may not wish to bring to the Security Council, there is at present no such possibility available within the framework of the armistice régime as applied.

66. . . . The Governments, while taking note of my observations concerning the procedural weaknesses indicated, have not gone further into the matter. [*Ibid.*]

(c) 1956-67

i. *Syria–Israel Armistice, 1956–67*

After the events of October 1956 UNTSO was called upon for a while to check upon rather different sorts of complaints:

Upon receipt of a telegram dated 21 November 1956 from the Minister for Foreign Affairs of Syria and circulated to the General Assembly as document A/3378, the Secretary-General requested the United Nations Truce Supervision Organization for Palestine to investigate the matter referred to therein.

The Secretary-General has the honour to report that he has now received a communication from the acting Chief of Staff of the United Nations Truce Supervision Organization for Palestine to the following effect:

'With reference to the telegram addressed to you by the Syrian Minister for Foreign Affairs on 21 November 1956 (A/3378), I have the honour to report as follows:

'1. Investigations carried out by United Nations observers on 22 and 23 November do not confirm the allegation that "Israel has proceeded to the massing of troops on the Syrian–Israel and Jordan–Israel demarcation lines" and that "French and British forces are participating in this operation in company with Israel troops".

[34] S/3596, para. 44.   [35] Ibid. para. 45.   [36] Ibid. para. 46.   [37] Ibid. para. 62.

'2. On 22 and 23 November, the United Nations observers, with the co-operation of the Israel authorities concerned, visited various sectors of the so-called defensive areas, which extended ten kilometres from the demarcation lines, as well as sectors of the demilitarized zone created by the Israel–Syrian General Armistice Agreement. Traffic on the roads was normal and there was nothing which indicated a military build-up in the Israel settlements which were visited. [*A/3388, Note by the Secretary-General, 23 Nov. 1956.*]

But it was primarily the old cluster of controversies which continued to mar the full implementation of this Armistice Agreement. In March 1957 the Syrians claimed that the Israelis were building a bridge at the outlet of Lake Huleh, and that it was a prohibited military fortification:

3. The Chairman contacted the Israel delegation with a view to an investigation. In conformity with the position adopted by the Israel Government concerning Syrian complaints relating to the demilitarized zone, the senior Israel delegate refused to consider the Syrian complaint. He added that United Nations military observers should not enter the demilitarized zone from Syrian territory and that no investigation would be allowed from the Israel side. [*S/3815, Report of Acting Chief of Staff of UNTSO to the Secretary-General, 23 Apr. 1957.*]

The question also arose as to whether Israel should be required to demolish fortification works at Hagovrim and Susita, which she claimed were necessary for self-defence in the light of Syria's failure to adhere to Article 1 of the Armistice.[38] General Burns now decided, after inspection by UN observers, that certain of those fortifications

went beyond what was required for the protection of civilian life. He accordingly requested the dismantling of the fortifications in question—which was and still is refused by Israel. . . .

Minefields and mines in the demilitarized zone

17. In paragraph 12 of his report of 20 April 1957 (*S/3815*) the Acting Chief of Staff pointed out that an area on the western approaches of the newly erected bridge at the outlet of Lake Huleh, (MR 209150–271750) was marked as being mined in contravention of annex II, paragraph 3, of the General Armistice Agreement; he further indicated that he was taking steps to have any existing mines removed from the area in question. At the Security Council meeting held on 23 May 1957 (*780th meeting*), the representative of Israel informed the Council that 'all mines in this field have been removed and that Colonel Leary has been advised of it'. According to the information received from the Israel authorities, the mines were removed on 22 May.

18. On 30 October 1956, when the Israel military action against Egypt had begun, the Chairman was informed by the Israel delegation to the Israel–Syrian Mixed Armistice Commission that the Banat Ya'coub bridge across the Jordan River in the central sector of the demilitarized zone was mined at its western approach, and that United Nations Military Observers would not be permitted to use it. The Chairman of the Israel–Syrian Mixed Armistice Commission, the Chief of Staff and the Acting Chief of Staff, have protested against the closing of the bridge. Besides being a violation of annex II, paragraph 3, of the General Armistice Agreement, the mining of the approach to Banat Ya'coub bridge—which, *inter alia*, provides the only direct access to the headquarters of the Mixed Armistice Commission, the Customs House, on the Syrian side, and Mahanayim on the Israel side (article VII, paragraph 2, of the General Armistice Agreement)—has restricted the movement of United Nations Military Observers and caused serious inconvenience and delay to the staff of the Truce Supervision Organization in the carrying out of their duties. Following new repre-

---

[38] The last inspection by UN observers in this area had been in June 1956. Since then, they had been prevented from carrying out the inspection (S/3844, para. 13).

sentations made by the Acting Chief of Staff, the Israel authorities have agreed to remove the mines so that the bridge should again be open to Truce Supervision Organization personnel. On 22 June, the Chairman was informed by the senior Israel delegate that the Israelis had completed clearing the mines and checking the area the night before and that the bridge was open for traffic starting that day. The bridge was used again by United Nations military observers on 23 June.

19. With the removal of the mines at the newly erected Huleh bridge and at the Banat Ya'coub bridge there should remain no Israel minefields or mines in the demilitarized zone. In this connexion, the Acting Chief of Staff relies on a statement made to him by the Director of Armistice Affairs, Israel Foreign Ministry, to the effect that any mines which may have been placed in the demilitarized zone at the beginning of the military action against Egypt have now been removed. [*S/3844, Report of Acting Chief of Staff of UNTSO to Secretary-General, 1 July 1957.*]

Colonel Leary then went on to make certain suggestions for the more effective implementation of the Armistice:

Conclusions

20. The matters dealt with in this report raise the question of the ability of the Chairman of the Mixed Armistice Commission and United Nations observers attached to the Commission to ensure the full implementation of article V, paragraph 5 (*c*), for which they are responsible.

21. The first prerequisite for such implementation is that the Chairman and United Nations observers should enjoy unhampered freedom of movement—a question on which the Security Council has already expressed its views, particularly in its resolution of 18 May 1951.

22. This report has shown that the Chairman and United Nations observers have been prevented on various occasions from entering certain areas and localities in the demilitarized zone. The Security Council, in its resolution of 18 May 1951, has noted, *inter alia*, 'that article V of the General Armistice Agreement gives to the Chairman the responsibility for the general supervision of the demilitarized zone'. This responsibility applies not only to the military clauses of the General Armistice Agreement but also to the civilian matters referred to in article V and in Dr Bunche's authoritative comment quoted in the Security Council resolution of 18 May 1951. In order to carry out their duties, the Chairman and the United Nations observers must at all times and without prior authorization have freedom of access to and freedom of movement in the demilitarized zone, whether they are on a routine visit or carrying out an investigation.

23. It may be considered desirable for the purposes of surveillance and more rapid investigation that the Chairman have some observers remain on a 24-hour basis in portions of the demilitarized zone selected by him. Following two recent incidents in the central sector of the demilitarized zone (the wounding of an Israel farmer by a mine on 14 June, and the death on 16 June of an Israel engineer, mortally wounded on the western bank of the Jordan River), the Acting Chief of Staff has requested the Israel authorities to find out if lodging facilities could be provided in the Mishmar Hayarden area for one or two observers.

24. It seems there should be no objection in principle to such an arrangement, which would permit more rapid investigation of incidents. (On 16 June, several hours elapsed between the fatal shooting of the Israel engineer and the arrival of United Nations observers on the spot.)

25. Freedom of movement within the demilitarized zone should meet with no difficulties from the parties to the General Armistice Agreement, or the local authorities in the various sectors. There should be neither refusal to permit access to any area, nor any conditions, such as the presence of military or police officers during a visit. It is for the Chairman to decide whether they would be escorted. An escort may be necessary, for instance, during an investigation when witnesses have to be interrogated or when the local authorities of an area refuse to meet the United Nations observers alone or speak a language which the latter do not sufficiently understand. Once the principle of unconditional freedom of movement is accepted,

there should be no difficulty in settling practical problems in a co-operative spirit. At the meeting of the Security Council held on 23 May 1957, 780th meeting, the representative of Israel stated that he wished to assure the Council that it was Israel's firm policy not to interfere in any way with the movement of military observers in the demilitarized zones, when such movement was necessitated by their official functions. This statement is in conformity with the statement made to the Chief of Staff of the Truce Supervision Organization on 6 September 1951 (see para. 4 above).

26. On 23 May 1957, the representative of Israel claimed that the difficulties encountered by the Chairman and United Nations military observers in connexion with the investigation of the building of the Huleh bridge (*see document S/3815*) proceeded from Israel's refusal to entertain Syrian complaints in the demilitarized zone, but that no difficulty had been encountered in the case of requests for investigations conducted by or on behalf of the Chairman of the Mixed Armistice Commission in pursuance of his functions under article V of the General Armistice Agreement. Mr Kidron's statement is in conformity with what has been explained to me by the Israel Ministry for Foreign Affairs, that is, that Israel's objection was of a purely formal nature. I understand that Israel does not object to any investigation carried out by or on behalf of the Chairman on the basis of his authority under article V.

27. The possibility of carrying out an investigation at any time under article V of the General Armistice Agreement and the enjoyment by United Nations observers of full freedom of movement in the demilitarized zone during an investigation or during routine visits is indispensable to ensure the observance of article V, paragraph 5 (*b*), which prohibits 'any advance by the armed forces, military or para-military, of either party into any part of the demilitarized zone'. From time to time allegations concerning the violation of this provision have been made. Under the Armistice Agreement, an allegation is not a sufficient basis for considering that a violation of the General Armistice Agreement has taken place. United Nations observers must first confirm that there has actually been an advance of armed forces. A prompt investigation may either serve to allay apprehension, if the allegation is shown to be unfounded, or it may serve as the factual basis for an immediate request to evacuate the forces which may have advanced into the demilitarized zone. [*Ibid.*]

But the fact remained that the Israel–Syria MAC had not met in regular session since June 1951, and had held even emergency meetings only rarely. The practice instead had grown up of lodging complaints—and these continued throughout 1958—without a request for a meeting of the MAC, often without a request for an investigation. This led to very real difficulties:

18. As a result of the failure of the Israel–Syrian Mixed Armistice Commission to hold regular sessions since June 1951 and to hold emergency meetings save in very exceptional circumstances, the Chairman of the Commission and the Chief of Staff of the Truce Supervision Organization cannot speak on behalf of the Commission when they ask for the implementation of the General Armistice Agreement. In the case of the demilitarized zone they rely, in some cases successfully, on the special powers conferred on the Chairman under Article V of the General Armistice Agreement. When they cannot invoke article V, the representations and suggestions they are asked by one party to make to the other are usually met by counter complaints. A party which asks the Chairman, or the Chief of Staff, to tell the other party to stop an 'illegal' practice considers him as a more or less useful go-between, if not as the bearer of a more or less disguised ultimatum: 'Tell them to stop this work' or 'Tell them that we always return fire'.

19. The fact that the Mixed Armistice Commission does not meet and that the Chairman and the Chief of Staff are considered as intermediaries who should obtain the stoppage of 'illegal' practices by the other party has created a state of mind contrary to the letter and the spirit of the General Armistice Agreement. This state of mind explains the second phase of the 3 December incident, namely the resort to artillery after a first phase in which small arms were used. The pattern for the 3 December incident was set on 6 November when resort to

7*

artillery followed the use of small arms (on 6 November the use of small arms had resulted in no casualty).

20. It is this pattern: use of artillery after the use of small arms which may endanger the peace, already threatened by the tension which has developed in the growing disrespect for the obligations agreed to in 1949, when the General Armistice Agreement was concluded. [*S/4124, Report of the Chief of Staff of UNTSO to the Security Council, 8 Dec. 1958.*]

The non-functioning of the MAC—and the legal arguments addressed by the parties to support this fact—gravely hampered the work of UNTSO in the ensuing years. In 1960 the Chief of Staff noted:

9. The consequences of some legal positions have been felt since 1951. These positions are based on interpretations of the General Armistice Agreement. Whilst article VII, paragraph 1 stipulates that 'the execution of the provisions of this Agreement shall be supervised by a Mixed Armistice Commission composed of representatives of the two Parties and a United Nations Chairman,' article V, paragraph 5 (*c*) provides that the Chairman and United Nations observers attached to the Commission 'shall be responsible for ensuring the full implementation of this article'.

10. The Security Council considered in May 1951 complaints by Syria and Israel relating to the demilitarized zone. In its resolution of 18 May 1951, after noting *inter alia* 'that article V of the General Armistice Agreement gives to the Chairman the responsibility for general supervision of the demilitarized zone' the Security Council:

'*Notes* that under article VII, paragraph 8 of the Armistice Agreement, where interpretation of the meaning of a particular provision of the Agreement, other than the preamble and articles I and II, is at issue, the Mixed Armistice Commission's interpretation shall prevail;

'*Calls upon* the Governments of Israel and Syria to bring before the Mixed Armistic-Commission or its Chairman, whichever has the pertinent responsibility under the Armistice Agreement, their complaints and to abide by the decisions resulting therefrom;

'*Considers* that it is inconsistent with the objectives and intent of the Armistice Agreement to refuse to participate in meetings of the Mixed Armistice Commission or to fail to respect requests of the Chairman of the Mixed Armistice Commission as they relate to his obligations under article V, and calls upon the Parties to be represented at all meetings called by the Chairman of the Commission and to respect such requests.'

11. The observance of the General Armistice Agreement and of the Security Council resolution of 18 May 1951 should have permitted the settlement of legal disputes, since, when the competence of the Mixed Armistice Commission or the Chairman was challenged, an interpretation of the relevant provisions of the General Armistice Agreement by the Mixed Armistice Commission should have determined whether the Commission or the Chairman had the pertinent responsibility under the General Armistice Agreement.

12. The developments which have taken place since 1951 are however very different from those which the Security Council resolution permitted to envisage. The Government of Israel has denied that the Mixed Armistice Commission was competent to deal with issues pertaining to the demilitarized zone, arguing that these issues should be dealt with by the Chairman and that he should contact the Israel delegation with a view to their settlement. On the other hand, the Government of Syria has argued that there was nothing in the Armistice Agreement which prevented its delegation from being similarly contacted. It has moreover requested that certain of its complaints relating to the demilitarized zone should be considered by the Mixed Armistice Commission in its formal regular meetings. Israel's refusal to attend such meetings has resulted in a suspension, since June 1951, of regular meetings of the Mixed Armistice Commission dealing with any issue whatsoever, whether they related to the demilitarized zone or not. No doubt, it would have been possible, in view of article VII,

paragraph 5, of the General Armistice Agreement, to convoke regular meetings which would have discussed and voted resolutions in the absence of one of the Parties. But experience has proved, also in connexion with other Mixed Armistice Commissions which have been similarly boycotted, that while meetings composed of representatives of one Party and the Chairman are legally possible, the usefulness of such meetings would be very small, if not negative, as their repetition would be liable to detract from the importance of emergency meetings convoked in connexion with incidents or situations of an exceptional gravity, and which should be held, even if a Party refuses to be represented.

13. It has also been considered that, though it would be theoretically possible under article VII, paragraphs 5 and 8 of the General Armistice Agreement, an interpretation of the provisions of the Agreement by the Mixed Armistice Commission in the absence of one of the Parties would have no useful results.

14. The admission that it would be of little use to hold regular meetings of the Mixed Armistice Commission to consider, in the absence of one of the Parties, problems relating to the demilitarized zone has thrown on the Chairman—without any assistance or direction from the Mixed Armistice Commission—the responsibility to ensure respect for the provisions of article V of the General Armistice Agreement. In one of the above-mentioned paragraphs of its resolution of 18 May 1951, the Security Council:

> '*Considers* that it is inconsistent with the objectives and intent of the Armistice Agreement to refuse to participate in meetings of the Mixed Armistice Commission or to fail to respect requests of the Chairman of the Mixed Armistice Commission as they relate to his obligations under Article V. . . .'

When, as indicated above, meetings of the Mixed Armistice Commission are rendered practically impossible, the alternative, as far as matters pertaining to the demilitarized zone are concerned, is a 'request' by the Chairman, issued in the form of a decision or findings relating to a particular issue. The Security Council had expected that such requests would be respected.

15. In September 1953, the Government of Israel objected to a request by the then Chief of Staff of the United Nations Truce Supervision Organization that work started in the demilitarized zone, in connexion with a projected canal between the Jordan River and Lake Tiberias be stopped so long as an agreement was not arranged (*S/3122*). In its reply to this request, the Government of Israel referred *inter alia* to a previous statement by its representative at the United Nations. According to this statement, the Chairman of the Mixed Armistice Commission should not 'operate by mandatory requests directed to the very Governments which have defined his functions and which are presumably, therefore, in a position to know what powers they have conceded to him' (*S/3122, annex II, para. 10*). Major-General Vagn Bennike observed that:

> '. . . this cannot be taken to imply that it remains for either Party to decide whether the Chairman acts in conformity or not with the functions conferred upon him by both Parties. That would mean anarchy in the demilitarized zone, in which both Parties have agreed to confer special powers upon the Chairman under the provisions of Article V of the Armistice Agreement. If there is a difference on the interpretation of these provisions, the two Parties have provided a remedy. Article V is not one of the Articles which the Mixed Armistice Commission may not interpret . . .' (*S/3122, annex III, para. 10*).

16. The above explanations may facilitate understanding of the importance of the obstacles which have so far prevented the success of efforts to put an end to the dangerous situation which has developed in the southern demilitarized zone: informal conversations between the Chairman of the Mixed Armistice Commission and the Israel delegation led nowhere; a proposal for a meeting of representatives of the farmers of Tawafiq and Tel Qatsir was rejected by the Israel delegation; findings which I have issued under article V, as Chairman of the

Mixed Armistice Commission, have not, I understand, been formally rejected, but my right to issue them was questioned, though no attempt was made to bring the matter before the Mixed Armistice Commission and request an interpretation of the General Armistice Agreement, as provided for in article VII, paragraph 8. [*S/4270, Report of Chief of Staff of UNTSO to Secretary-General, 16 Feb. 1960.*]

The Chief of Staff took the position that the steadily deteriorating situation made it necessary for him to make use of the last resort available under Article V of the General Armistice Agreement, viz. the exercise of the power of 'general supervision of the demilitarized zone' given to the Chief of Staff of UNTSO as Chairman *ex officio* of the MAC.[39]

In reply to recommendations on the incidents at Tawafiq and Tel Qatsir made by the Chief of Staff (para. 16, S/4270), Israel agreed to negotiate with the Arabs concerned on this question of 'cultivation in the demilitarized zone'.[40] Syria, however, wanted UNTSO to be present at the negotiations. The point must be made that the Arabs concerned were not necessarily Syrians—many were Arab Israelis.

In April 1962 the Security Council urged that 'all steps necessary for re-activating the Mixed Armistice Commission' be promptly taken,[41] and General Odd Bull, who was then the UNTSO Chief of Staff, made efforts, without success, to do so. The impasse over the regular use of the MAC, with Israel insisting that it has no competence to discuss complaints relating to the demilitarized zone, continued. During 1958 major incidents occurred which contributed to increasing tension not only in the demilitarized zone, but in the whole border area. UN observers were eye-witnesses to an incident in which Syrian fire was opened on Israeli shepherds within Israeli territory, and the ensuing situation became so serious that it was necessary for the Chairman of the MAC to issue a formal cease-fire notice. This cease-fire was broken by sporadic Syrian firing at Israeli patrols.[42] So far as the demilitarized zone was concerned, tensions mounted because of mine clearing operations in the northern sector.

A. *Mine clearing operations in the northern sector of the demilitarized zone.*

22. It will be recalled that mine clearing operations undertaken by the Israelis in January and February 1958 in the northern sector of the demilitarized zone led to incidents which were the object of communications to the Security Council from both Israel (*S/3945 and S/3955*) and Syria (*S/3946, S/3948 and S/3950*). Firing incidents occurred in that area on 23, 24 and 28 January, and on 4 February. On 28 January, two Israel policemen were killed and five wounded during an exchange of fire which lasted approximately 2 hours. Two different versions were given by the parties. According to the Israelis, rifle and automatic fire was opened from Syrian fortified positions at a party of Israeli policemen who were engaged in clearing mines in fields located in the demilitarized zone. A Syrian Army unit then entered the area and attacked the Israel policemen, who were armed with rifles only. The Syrian force withdrew after the arrival of Israel reinforcements, which returned the automatic fire. According to the Syrians, an Israel military detachment and an armoured vehicle which had

---

[39] S/4270, para. 98.

[40] Ibid. para. 103. For details of all the incidents over land cultivation and a commentary thereon, see Bar-Yaacov, pp. 182–214.

[41] S/5111, 9 Apr. 1962.   [42] Ibid. paras. 2–7.

entered the demilitarized zone opened fire on Arab farmers who were working on their lands. An exchange of fire ensued and Israel reinforcements were brought into the area. It should be noted that the Israeli delegation to the Mixed Armistice Commission had given no indication to the Chairman that mine clearing operations would be carried out. Consequently, UN military observers did not accompany the Israel party into the demilitarized zone, the UN observation posts in the area could not be notified, and the incident was not observed. . . .' [*Ibid.*]

The 1958 Report of the Chief of Staff also contained details of violence which had broken out over the determination of the western limit of the demilitarized zone along the former shoreline of Lake Huleh; and also over civilian activities in the eastern Huleh area.[43]

In 1960 a similar problem—Israeli cultivation of lands, which the Arabs regarded as encroachment—had arisen in respect of the southern sector of the demilitarized zone. Following this incident the Chief of Staff (at that time General von Horn) issued findings fixing boundaries concerning the use of lands in that area, without prejudice to the validity of legal claims presented by either party.[44] These boundaries were not at that stage marked on the ground, but none the less greatly alleviated tension, and a sharp decrease in incidents followed. Later, the next Chief of Staff was to propose 'materialization on the ground' of these limits.[45]

As if the disputes which existed over cultivation of the demilitarized zone, and the interpretation of Article V were not crippling enough, in 1962 there also arose the new controversy concerning the projected diversion by Israel of waters from the Jordan:

I have the honour to make the following observations on the letter dated 2 March 1962 from the representative of the Syrian Arab Republic (*S/5084*), concerning water resources:

(*a*) The Syrian Government's complaint is based on its declared premise that Israel has no right to exist—hence its absurd statement that it 'does not consider that Israel can be regarded as a party in matters involving the Jordan waters'.

(*b*) The Syrian Government in its complaint further arrogates to itself the right to intervene in matters which are exclusively within the jurisdiction of the Government of Israel, such as the reclamation of its desert lands and their settlement. Syria has no such right.

(*c*) Contrary to Syrian allegations as contained in document S/5084, particularly in points 3 and 4, the planned development of the water resources within its territory, by the Israel Government, does not in any manner whatsoever prejudice the rights or legitimate interest of any other State.

(*d*) Previous efforts to bring about agreement on an over-all water development project— vital to the area as a whole—met with full co-operation from the Israel Government. After two years of discussion technical experts of Israel, Jordan, Lebanon and Syria agreed upon every important detail of a unified Jordan Valley plan. But in October 1955, it was rejected for political reasons at a meeting of the League of Arab States. Syria objected to the project because it would benefit Israel as well as the Arab countries.

(*e*) In the circumstances Israel obviously could not allow its own vital domestic water development to be deflected by the politically motivated attitude of certain Arab Governments. Syria herself and Jordan have embarked on the execution of water development projects utilizing the waters of the common river system. Similarly, Israel could no longer defer the development of its water resources within its territory.

[43] S/4270, paras. 23–26.   [44] Ibid. ann. V.
[45] S/5401 and Add. 1–4, 24 Aug. 1963, para. 44.

(*f*) These activities are not in violation of the provisions of the Israel–Syrian Armistice Agreement, nor are they contrary to the resolutions of the United Nations Security Council, referred to in point 5 of the Syrian letter. These references are inserted for the sole purpose of confusing the issue.   [*S/5091, Letter of 16 Mar. 1962 from the representative of Israel to the President of the Security Council.*]

This was in reply to a letter from the Syrian representative declaring:

1. Article V of the Israeli–Syrian General Armistice Agreement provides for the maintenance of the *status quo* in the demilitarized zone and forbids either of the parties to take any action giving it an advantage over the other. The works undertaken by the Israeli authorities are irrefutable proof of their intention to continue the operations to divert the waters of the Jordan which they began in the central demilitarized zone and which they suspended in accordance with a Security Council resolution.

2. As soon as the project is completed, Israel will be in a position to settle several million people in the Negev, who will constitute a new force threatening the whole of the Arab world.

3. Furthermore, by diverting part of the waters of the Jordan, an international river, to the Negev, Israel is assuming new rights over the river without the consent of interested parties. That is a violation of the principles of international law regarding the sharing of rights over international rivers. In any case, the Government of the Syrian Arab Republic does not consider that Israel can be regarded as a party in matters involving the Jordan waters.

4. It has been clearly proved that to divert part of the waters of the Jordan from Lake Tiberias will increase the proportion of salt in the lake, with the result that it will not be possible to use its water to irrigate Arab lands, and that considerable harm will be done to those lands.

5. The Syrian authorities opposed the project in question in 1953, after Israel had begun operations to divert the waters in the central demilitarized zone. In September 1953, a complaint to that effect was submitted to the Chief of Staff of the Palestine Truce Supervision Organization, who gave a decision, dated 23 September 1953, calling upon the Israeli authorities to stop the work which they had already begun and which they could not continue without the consent of Syria.

Since Israel refused to comply with that decision, the Syrian Government brought the matter before the Security Council, which, in its resolution adopted on 27 October 1953 (*631st meeting*), decided that the works connected with the diversion of the water should be suspended until a final decision was reached on the matter. The Security Council has not yet given its final decision on the Syrian complaint.

In view of the foregoing, the Government of the Syrian Arab Republic considers it necessary to draw the attention of all States members of the Security Council to the gravity of the situation. The Arab States consider the activities of the Israeli authorities as serious a matter as the establishment of Israel in 1948, which violated the lawful rights of the inhabitants of the country and gave rise to a series of international crises which threatened peace. [*S/5084, 2 Mar. 1962.*]

The argument concerning the diversion of the Jordan largely occurred, of course, in the context of Israel–Jordan relations.[46]

In 1962 a further serious breakdown of the Armistice occurred on Lake Tiberias. The pattern was the now customary one—a series of complaints by Israel of Syrian gunfire at Israeli fishing boats;[47] followed by an attack by the Israeli army at Syrian positions on the north-eastern shore of the lake. Israel

---

[46] In 1954 a plan for the sharing of the Jordan had been devised by Mr Eric Johnston, a special envoy of President Eisenhower. Israel subsequently based her works on using 'the Johnston share' allotted to her. Jordan in turn diverted half the flow of the Yarmuk, a tributary, and thus in effect appropriated part of her 'Johnston share'.

[47] S/5093, 19 Mar. 1962; S/5102, 26 Mar. 1962.

asserted that the purpose of her attack was to silence Syrian gun positions, whose very existence, let alone their use, contravened the provisions of the Armistice conerning the demilitarized zone. Syria denied that she had any such military posts, and stated that the Israeli attack had been upon Arab villages.[48] The examination by the UN observers was unable to reveal the correct state of affairs. The Security Council adopted a resolution[49] which deplored the fighting, determined that the Israeli attack was a flagrant violation of the Armistice Agreement, and urged strict observance of Article V of the Armistice Agreement, which prohibited the presence of armed forces in the demilitarized zone. The resolution did not refer to the prior Syrian actions, and it was because of this that the French representative abstained.

In 1966, after comparatively successful containment for the previous few years, the situation deteriorated rapidly and explosively. A new government in Syria, which had come to power in February 1966, was engaged in contending with Nasser for the leadership of the Arab world. The Soviet Union was also showing some interest in supporting this government,which pursued a militantly anti-Israeli policy. Raids into Israeli territory across the Syrian border occurred with frequency, and the Syrian government, far from attempting to control the al-Fath incursions, encouraged them.[50] The Syrian authorities refused to accept responsibility for these incursions, asserting that they had not been proven, and in any event

Nor is Syria responsible for the rise of Palestinian Arab organizations striving to liberate their conquered and occupied territory. . . . Had the Israel intentions been sincere, Israel would have resorted to the Mixed Armistice Commission, the international organ created for such a purpose. [S/7412, 18 July 1966.]

At the same time, Syria complained of the shelling by Israeli aircraft of sites at the Jordan development scheme. The Secretary-General stated that General Odd Bull had confirmation from the UN military observer that four to six Israel jet aircraft had in fact attacked targets in Syria.[51]

The UNTSO Chief of Staff used all his diplomatic endeavours to obtain an amelioration in the situation.[52] His difficulties were compounded not only by the border raids, but by the flaring up at this moment of the old dispute about cultivation in the demilitarized zone.[53] The matter received the detailed attention of the Security Council.[54] It became apparent that any resolution condemning Syrian activity would have no chance of success in the Security Council. A six-Power draft (sponsored by Argentina, Japan, Netherlands, New Zealand, Nigeria, and Uganda) invited Syria to strengthen her measures for preventing incidents that constituted a violation of the Armistice Agreement; invited Israel to co-operate fully with the MAC; and called upon both Syria and Israel to facilitate the work of UNTSO. The Soviet Union vetoed the resolution. The vote was 10 to 4 (USSR, Bulgaria, Mali, Jordan, with China

[48] S/5102, 26 Mar. 1962.   [49] S/5111, 9 Apr. 1962, 10–0, with France abstaining.
[50] For evidence of the overt encouragement of the Syrian government, see S/7411, 14 July 1966.
[51] S/7432, 26 July 1966, para. 6.   [52] S/7434, 27 July 1966.   [53] Ibid. para. 5.
[54] SCOR, 20th yr, mtgs 1288–95, 1307–10.

abstaining). Public opinion in Israel pressed for action in the face of the Security Council's inability to issue an effective warning against Syrian raids. On 15 August 1966 a Syrian air attack, witnessed by UNTSO observers, took place against Israel fishing boats on Lake Tiberias. A large number of acts of sabotage were reported, ranging from demolition charges in Jerusalem to land mine explosions on Israel patrol routes. Israel took the matter back to the Security Council on 12 October 1966 and a resolution which had the support of Argentina, Japan, Nigeria, Uruguay, and Uganda, as well as the United Kingdom and the United States, was vetoed by the Soviet Union.[55]

At Syrian instigation, but without the approval of King Hussein, Jordanian territory was used as a base for further Arab raids into Israel. Israel now retaliated—but against Jordan rather than Syria. The Security Council was faced with the choice of not condemning this action because it had been unable to pass a resolution condemning the previous Syrian incursions, or of condemning Israel and attempting to prevent a further erosion of the Armistice Agreement. It chose the latter course, and passed Resolution S/7598 condemning Israel.[56]

During the course of the debates in the Security Council, considerable concern was expressed about the apparent inability of UNTSO to prevent conflict across the Israel–Syrian border. The matter arose both in relation to the original Israel complaint against Syria;[57] and the subsequent Jordan complaint against Israel (S/7586). U Thant first presented a report on the inability of the MAC to function (S/7572) and then a note on the effectiveness of UNTSO (S/7603). These documents merit substantial reproduction:

3. Since 1951, Israel has taken the position that the Mixed Armistice Commission is not competent to deal with issues pertaining to the demilitarized zone, asserting that these issues should be dealt with by the Chairman of the Mixed Armistice Commission and that he should contact the Israel delegation with a view to their settlement. As stated in paragraph 20 of the Chief of Staff's report of 6 January 1955 (S/3343), Israel, in explaining its attitude, referred to article V, paragraph 5 (c) of the Israel–Syrian General Armistice Agreement.
referred to article V, paragraph 5 (c) of the Israel–Syrian General Armistice Agreement.

   In this provision Israel found a 'limitation' of the competence of the Israel–Syrian Mixed Armistice Commission and a conclusive demonstration of the absence of any Syrian *locus standi* in the demilitarized zone on a claim for sovereignty, and concluded that it should uphold the 'basic tenet of the armistice agreement—the exclusion of Syria from any rights within the demilitarized zone, even if this sometimes necessitates absenting itself from meetings of the Mixed Armistice Commission at which Syria seeks to intervene in questions affecting the zone'.

4. The Syrian position was summarized as follows in paragraphs 21 and 22 of the report. The Mixed Armistice Commission, being competent to supervise the execution of the provisions of the General Armistice Agreement, including article V, relating to the demilitarized zone, is empowered to deal with complaints submitted by the parties relating to the implementation of article V. Paragraph 5 (c) of article V of the Armistice Agreement refers to the responsibility of the Chairman of the Mixed Armistice Commission and United Nations Observers for ensuring 'the full implementation' of the article, whereas the first paragraph of article VII provides that the Mixed Armistice Commission shall supervise the execution of the provisions of the Agreement.

[55] S/7575/Rev. 1, 3 Nov. 1966.
[56] For the text of the resolution, see Implementation of the Jordan–Israel Armistice, pp. 202–3.
[57] S/7536 and S/7540.

5. It may be recalled that during the current series of meetings of the Security Council on the Palestine question the representatives of Syria and Israel made references—at the 1308th and 1309th meetings respectively—to the positions of their respective Governments regarding co-operation with the Mixed Armistice Commission.

6. Complaints relating to the demilitarized zone were considered by the Israel–Syrian Mixed Armistice Commission before 1951, but subsequent conflicting positions on the competence of the Mixed Armistice Commission in relation to the demilitarized zone have resulted in its inability to hold regular meetings since 1951. The Syrian delegation refuses to withdraw complaints relating to the demilitirized zone from the list of complaints pending before the Mixed Armistice Commission, while the Israel delegation insists that such complaints be deleted. The last regular meeting of the Mixed Armistice Commission was held in 1l951.

7. The total number of accumulated and outstanding complaints as of 14 October 1966 was as follows: Israel 35,485; Syria 30,600; total 66,085. No statistics exist of the total number of such complaints which relate to the demilitarized zone. However, a sample checking of the complaints filed in one week in January, March, June and September 1965 indicates that 96 per cent of the Syrian complaints and 71 per cent of the Israel complaints related to the demilitarized zone. A similar check in February, April, July and October 1966 indicates that 92 per cent of the Syrian complaints and 69 per cent of the Israel complaints related to the demilitarized zone. The resulting average in those two years, therefore would be as follows: 94 per cent of the Syrian complaints and 70 per cent of the Israel complaints relating to the demilitarized zone.

8. Since 1951, seventeen emergency meetings of the Mixed Armistice Commission have been held of which Israel failed to attend two. In connexion with emergency meetings Israel has maintained the same principle as for regular meetings, and stated at the emergency meeting held on 2 June 1954:

'(a) Matters outside of the competence of the Mixed Armistice Commission cannot be discussed by the Commission except when there is agreement on it;
(b) Any matters concerning the demilitarized zone are, according to article V of the General Armistice Agreement, within the competence of the Chairman and not of the Mixed Armistice Commission.'

9. The last emergency meeting of the Mixed Armistice Commission took place on 16 February 1960 at the request of the Syrian delegation, following the attack by Israel on the Arab village of Khirbat at Tawafiq in the southern demilitarized zone. At that meeting, held in the absence of Israel, two resolutions were adopted, the first condemning the Israel attack against the village of Khirbat at Tawafiq during the night of 31 January–1 February 1960, the second the overflight of Syrian territory by the Israel Air Force on 1 February 1960.

10. No other meeting either regular or emergency has taken place since February 1960, and neither party has requested the Chairman to convene a meeting since that time.

11. It is relevant to this report to note that the Security Council has given attention to the functioning of the Israel–Syrian Mixed Armistice Commission on several occasions in the past. For example, in its resolution 93 (1951) of 18 May 1951, the following paragraphs appear:

'Calls upon the Governments of Israel and Syria to bring before the Mixed Armistice Commission or its Chairman, whichever has the pertinent responsibility under the Armistice Agreement, their complaints and to abide by the decisions resulting therefrom;
'Considers that it is inconsistent with the objectives and intent of the Armistice Agreement to refuse to participate in meetings of the Mixed Armistice Commission or to fail to respect requests of the Chairman of the Mixed Armistice Commission as they relate to his obligations under article V, and calls upon the parties to be represented at all meetings called by the Chairman of the Commission and to respect such requests;'

Council resolution 111 (1956) of 19 January 1956 concludes with the following paragraph:

> '*Calls upon* both parties to co-operate with the Chief of Staff in this and all other respects, to carry out the provisions of the General Armistice Agreement in good faith, and in particular to make full use of the Mixed Armistice Commission's machinery in the interpretation and application of its provisions.'

In Council resolution 171 (1962) of 9 April 1962, is included the following paragraph:

> '*Calls upon* the Governments of Israel and Syria to co-operate with the Chief of Staff in carrying out his responsibilities under the General Armistice Agreement and the pertinent resolutions of the Security Council, and urges that all steps necessary for reactivating the Mixed Armistice Commission and for making full use of the Mixed Armistice machinery be promptly taken;'

12. The inability of the Israel–Syrian Mixed Armistice Commission to function undoubtedly weakens the efforts to maintain quiet along the line between Israel and Syria. As a result of this situation, matters which properly should first be considered in the Mixed Armistice Commission and which often might well be disposed of there, are brought instead directly to the attention of the Security Council where they can be considered primarily in a political context and atmosphere. The Mixed Armistice Commission, of course, is the machinery created by the parties and for whose operation they alone are responsible. It is the product of their solemn undertaking in the General Armistice Agreement. Its effectiveness depends upon the willingness of the two parties to abide by the General Armistice Agreement and to participate fully in and co-operate with it. The several appeals of the Security Council to the parties to this effect have thus far been unavailing. Serious consideration might well be given now as to whether there might be some more fruitful approach to the goal of enabling the Israel–Syrian Mixed Armistice Commission to function effectively. [*S/7572, Report by the Secretary-General on the present inability of the Israel–Syrian MAC to function, and the attitudes of the parties thereto, 1 Nov. 1966.*]

It will be recognized, of course, that there is a fundamental limitation on the scope and effectiveness of UNTSO's activities, which is due to the nature of the operation. It is an observation operation whose principal function is to help maintain peace by servicing the armistice machinery established by the parties themselves—Lebanon, Israel, Jordan, Syria and the United Arab Republic—in the four General Armistice Agreements to which they are respectively signatories. As an observation mission, UNTSO has no authority to give orders, to reach judgements, or forcibly to prevent actions. It operates on the territories of sovereign, independent States only with their explicit permission. Everything that it does—its ability to move about freely, to investigate, to find and question witnesses, to negotiate local cease-fires —depends upon the co-operation it receives from the parties directly concerned. It undertakes to investigate incidents when complaints by either or both of the parties are submitted to it. It is not in a position to anticipate incidents nor is it empowered to prevent them by any means other than persuasion. The observers are not deployed along the armistice lines—that would require personnel of a peace-force size instead of the existing total of 133 Observers—and maintain only a few stationary observation posts with the express consent of the parties. The observers carry no arms of any kind. Thus, UNTSO does not, and under its existing mandate cannot, play the buffer and preventive roles undertaken by the peace forces, such as the United Nations Emergency Force in Gaza and the United Nations Peace-keeping Force in Cyprus.

As regards reporting, since the observers rarely are eyewitnesses to an incident at the time it occurs, their investigation of an incident must depend upon their ability to move about freely and to see all that they can on the spot as soon as possible after the incident has occurred, and upon interviewing witnesses on opposite sides of the line, who, especially under the emotional stress of the moment, are, of course, quite likely to be subjective and biased.

In this regard, it may be pointed out that reporting on incidents that have occurred and have been complained about by the parties is not the only and perhaps not the most important role of UNTSO. Over the years, the ability of UNTSO observers to get quickly to the scene of fighting and by operating on both sides of the line to negotiate cease-fires on the spot, has in countless instances stopped fighting and has prevented it from escalating into possibly full-scale warfare.

Despite its inherent limitations, it is possible for UNTSO's effectiveness as an instrument for safeguarding the peace to be strengthened without changing its existing mandate or function. The first requirement, of course, is full co-operation of the parties to the General Armistice Agreements with UNTSO in the performance of its functions and full observance by the parties of the obligations they have freely and solemnly accepted in those agreements. In this regard, the parties should extend to the UNTSO observers engaged in investigations full freedom of movement in the area of the incidents, in the demilitarized zones, along the armistice demarcation lines and across those lines, and in no-man's land between the lines. It should be made possible by the parties for those observers who act as chairman of the Mixed Armistice Commissions to get in touch with responsible authorities on either side at any time of the day or night. The parties should agree to the deployment by UNTSO of mobile observation posts in sensitive sectors or wherever it may be apparent that an UNTSO presence might avert a military confrontation. The parties should give to UNTSO every facility for getting its observers to the scene of an incident as speedily as possible. The parties should also agree to a wider employment by UNTSO of experts in its conduct of investigations, including its trackers with dogs and handlers, surveyors, demolition and explosive specialists and interpreters for both the Arabic and Hebrew languages. Having a helicopter available and a speed boat stationed on Lake Tiberias would, no doubt, greatly facilitate the conduct of UNTSO investigations, although they would, of course, substantially increase the cost of the operation. [*S/7603, Note by the Secretary-General, 29 Nov. 1966.*]

The Secretary-General also reported, at the request of the Security Council, on the status of the demilitarized zones in the Armistice Agreements. Referring to a series of complaints by both Israel and Syria, alleging illegal fortification, the Secretary-General noted:

6. The above-mentioned Israel and Syrian complaints have been submitted daily for several years. Israel authorities have requested no investigation of their complaints alleging encroachment by Syrian fortifications upon the demilitarized zone. Syrian authorities have asked for the investigation of their above-mentioned complaints in respect of Israel fortifications in the demilitarized zone.

7. No investigation of the Syrian complaints has been carried out. In his report dated 27 June 1957, the Acting Chief of Staff of UNTSO referred to the difficulties experienced in connexion with the investigation in June 1956 of a Syrian complaint regarding the erection of fortifications in the Israel settlement of Hagovrim, in the central sector of the demilitarized zone and at Susita, in the southern sector. Investigations were allowed only after a delay of several days. Since June 1956, United Nations military observers have been prevented from carrying out investigations in the Hagovrim and Susita areas. Access to the Dardara area, in the central sector of the demilitarized zone, has also been refused to United Nations military observers. Such restriction on the freedom of movement of United Nations military observers has prevented the investigation of recent Syrian complaints relating to Israel fortifications in the demilitarized zone. Israel contests the right of Syria, which it asserts has no *locus standi* in the demilitarized zone, to forward such complaints to the Chairman of the Mixed Armistice Commission (see paragraph 20 of the report by the UNTSO Chief of Staff of 6 January 1955 (S/3343).

8. The practical result is that the daily complaints lodged with the Chairman of the ISMAC by the delegations of Israel and Syria concerning fortifications are, so to speak, standing complaints in which each party reaffirms its position against an 'illegal' situation which is neither

considered by a Mixed Armistice Commission which does not meet, nor even investigated by United Nations military observers acting according to the Mixed Armistice Commission procedure or under article V, paragraph 5, of the General Armistice Agreement.

9. The simultaneous inspections of the demilitarized zone and of the defensive areas arranged from time to time during periods of tension by the Chief of Staff of UNTSO do not allow an adequate visit to alleged fortifications in the demilitarized zone. Like the previous one, the last inspection carried out on 19 October 1966 dealt exclusively with 'accusations of a build-up of forces and equipment' (see *S/7561/Rev.1*). During the course of this inspection, the United Nations military observers saw a number of Israel and Syrian military positions in the demilitarized zone, although such observations did not come expressly within the purview of their inspection.

11. Although the present extent of Syrian and Israel fortifications in the demilitarized zone has not been investigated, a comparison of the complaints lodged in this respect by the parties in 1956–1957 with the recent complaints mentioned in paragraph 4 of this report tends to show that the number of fortified military positions in the demilitarized zone has probably increased.

B. *Implementation of article V, paragraph 5, of the General Armistice Agreement*

12. The 'return of civilians to villages and settlements in the demilitarized zone and the employment of limited numbers of locally recruited civilian police in the zone for internal security purposes' were provided for in article V, paragraph 5, of the General Armistice Agreement.

13. In October 1952, the then Chief of Staff of UNTSO, General William E. Riley, stated the following in paragraph 58 of his report (S/2833): 'with the exception of Nuqeib, El Hamma and Shamalne (which were under Syrian control) Israel police, acting under orders from police headquarters outside the demilitarized zone exercise control over practically the entire demilitarized zone'. The Syrians continue to complain practically every day about the presence in the demilitarized zone of armed 'soldiers', who Israel states are Israel border police, a force which should not enter the demilitarized zone, according to article V, paragraph 5, of the General Armistice Agreement.

14. The problem of the use of lands in the demilitarized zone still constitutes one of the main preoccupations of the Chief of Staff of UNTSO and of the Chairman of the Mixed Armistice Commission.

15. In a report which was submitted to the Security Council after the Almagor incident of 19 August 1963, reference was made to previous efforts to reduce tension by marking on the ground in the southern sector of the demilitarized zone the limits of a *status quo* of cultivation acceptable to both parties (see S/5401, para. 44). The establishment of agreed limits of cultivation has been sought and continues to be pursued by UNTSO.

16. ... On the western bank, Arab villages have been demolished, their inhabitants evacuated. The inhabitants of the villages of Baqqara and Ghanname returned following Security Council resolution 93 (1951) of 18 May 1951. They were later (on 30 October 1956) forced to cross into Syria where they are still living. Their lands on the western bank of the river, and Khoury Farm in the same area, are cultivated by Israel nationals.

17. With regard to the use of land in the central sector of the D/Zone, the Syrian delegation to the Mixed Armistice Commission has continued to complain that Israelis cultivate 'the Arab lands of Baqqara, Ghanname and Khoury Farm'. The Israel delegation, on the other hand, complains of Syrian cultivation and grazing in Israel, in an area west of the D/Zone, the Kibbutz Almagor area (MR 2085–2590). . . .

18. Claims and counter-claims have been made concerning the exercise of ownership rights in parcels located in this area and which have been used 'in adverse possession' by Arabs or Israelis. UNTSO is endeavouring to find a practical arrangement to cultivation problems in this and other areas in co-operation with Israel and Syria.

19. On 27 July 1966, the Secretary-General communicated to the Security Council a 'note on efforts of UNTSO to relieve tension along the line between Israel and the Syrian Arab Re-

public' (S/7434). This note dealt in particular with the acceptance by both parties of an unconditional cease-fire and with arrangements for an inspection by United Nations Military Observers of the D/Zone and the defensive areas on both sides. Such an inspection took place on 13 June 1966. The unconditional cease-fire and the inspection helped in creating a favourable atmosphere for talks aiming at a settlement of certain cultivation problems, particularly in the area of the D/Zone.

20. The development of the current tension between Israel and Syria has interfered with the progress of the talks relating to cultivation problems conducted by UNTSO in Israel and in Syria. However, the problems to be discussed have been cleared to a certain extent and it is the hope of the Chief of Staff of UNTSO that the conversations can be resumed after the Security Council concludes its present debate. [S/7573, *Report of the Secretary-General on the present status of the demilitarized zone set up by the General Armistice Agreement between Israel and Syria, 2 Nov. 1966.*]

By early 1967 tension between Israel and Syria was extremely high. Israel claimed an almost continuous stream of border raids and sabotage coming from Syria. Prime Minister Eshkol spoke of the need to march on Damascus if this harassment continued unabated. Syria now looked to Nasser for support. Nasser spoke of the need to have access to his borders to go to Syria's defence if she were attacked, and asked for UNEF's withdrawal. The Secretary-General withdrew UNEF, and not only were Israel's borders exposed to the massing Egyptian military, but the control of Sharm el Sheikh passed back to Egypt. Ships could no longer come to the Israel port of Eilat on the Gulf of Aqaba. Thus there occurred the chain of events which led inexorably to the outbreak of war in the Middle East on 5 June 1967. The failure of the Israel–Syrian Armistice, and the militancy of the new Syrian régime of Premier Atassi, were beyond doubt the major contributory factors.

ii. *Egypt–Israel Armistice, 1956–67*

The profound and major breach of the Armistice which occurred in October 1956, when Israeli forces penetrated Egyptian territory, is dealt with in detail in the Part on UNEF. The establishment of UNEF to supervise a cease-fire and withdrawal of foreign troops led to the necessity of co-ordination of UNTSO, and to some alteration in the functions of the latter. This has been examined above.

Incidents still did occur however, and were considered periodically by the Egypt–Israel MAC. However, Israel had not participated in the MAC since 1956 (see above, p. 109). The Suez Canal remained shut to Israeli shipping; but in the post-1956 phase a change took place concerning the Gulf of Aqaba. Israeli shipping had, it will be recalled, been denied passage through the Straits of Tiran into the Gulf of Aqaba. Although the resolutions establishing UNEF did not stipulate the exact positions which UNEF was to occupy, the Secretary-General obtained Israel's withdrawal from Sharm el Sheikh, which she had occupied in the fighting of 1956, in return for an agreement by Egypt that UNEF would be stationed at Sharm el Sheikh. Thus from 1957–67 Israel had access to the Gulf of Aqaba through the Straits of Tiran, and built up a considerable trade with Africa and Asia, based on her port at Eilat. This access was cut by Nasser in May 1967, after he had asked for UNEF's withdrawal from Egypt; but was restored after the war of June 1967, when Israel armed forces occupied Sharm el Sheikh.[58]

In the period after 1956 most of the relevant materials concerning the Israel–Egypt Armistice are subsumed under UNEF. Indeed, the very refusal of Israel to co-operate with the Israel–Egyptian MAC encouraged the UN to operate as much as possible through UNEF rather than UNTSO.

In the post-Suez years the great majority of Arab–Israeli incidents which have found their way into the official documentation in fact concerned Israeli–Syrian relations. On the other three Armistice Agreements there is little documentation—partly a reflection of the success and usefulness of UNTSO during this period, and partly a reflection of the other major issues that came to command the centre of the UN stage. The year 1958 saw the inter-Arab conflicts that led to the formation of UNOGIL.[59] In 1959 the question of Laos was occupying the Security Council, and by 1960 the Eichmann case and, above all, the question of the Congo, and these assumed prior importance. Israel and the Arabs will each have had their reasons for not making claims upon the time of the Security Council—and the priorities of the new African members—at this time.

After 1956 freedom of passage in the Gulf of Aqaba became a major issue in Egypt–Israel relations. Israel had sought to make her withdrawal from Egypt in early 1957 dependent upon a guarantee of her access in the Gulf. The only navigable access is through the narrow Straits of Tiran, a channel flowing through Egyptian territorial waters. While the UN refused to accept any 'conditions' for Israel's withdrawal, it was agreed between Hammarskjöld and Nasser that UNEF forces should be stationed at Sharm el Sheikh, at the entry to the Straits of Tiran. The United States also made a public pronouncement confirming her belief that the Straits were an international waterway, and promising that freedom of passage through them would be upheld. Still denied free passage through the Suez Canal, and relying on the presence of the UN at Sharm el Sheikh, and the United States guarantee, Israel now concentrated on building up the port of Eilat. This port rapidly grew in importance and was used for an expanding trade with Africa and Asia, and by the import of oil.

In May 1967 President Nasser asked for the withdrawal of UNEF,[60] and then closed the Straits of Tiran to all Israeli shipping, or shipping bound to or from Israel. Egypt denied that this was a breach of the Armistice Agreement, stating (1) the Straits were within her territorial waters and Israel had no legal rights therein; (2) Israel held Eilat illegally, as it had not been assigned to her under the Egypt–Israel Armistice Agreement; (3) under that Agreement no Israel ships were allowed within three miles of Egypt's coast; (4) Egypt was in any event entitled to exercise belligerent rights in respect of shipping that aided Israel, with whom she had signed no peace treaty; (5) the Gulf of Aqaba was an internal, Arab bay. On the other hand, Israel responded that (1) the Straits

---

[58] For details see below, pp. 336–49.   [59] See below, p. 535–46.
[60] For full details, see pp. 361–2 below.

were indeed within Egypt's territorial waters, but they were an international waterway, thus subject to the duty of innocent passage; they could not be sealed off by the riparian state; (2) Eilat was within the area allotted *de facto* to Israel under the Jordan–Israel Armistice, and it did not fall within the scope of the Egypt–Israel Armistice; (3) the prohibition in Article 2 of the latter Armistice clearly refers only to military shipping; (4) the existence of the Armistice Agreements precluded the exercise of belligerent rights: these were not traditional armistices, but meant to be a step towards permanent peace, underwritten by the UN, and the Security Council had taken this view with respect to the exercise of belligerent rights in the Suez Canal; (5) to argue that the Gulf of Aqaba is an internal bay is to ignore the very existence of Israel. An internal bay (as opposed to an international waterway) may be shut, but only with the consent of *all* riparians.

Egypt was not a party to the 1958 Convention on the Territorial Seas, Article 15 (8) of which had provided that an international waterway was one which linked high seas with high seas, *or high seas with territorial waters.* Having very much in mind the status of Aqaba, Egypt objected to the italicized formula. It is perhaps open to debate whether this formula represented new law (in that it went beyond the traditional definition of a narrow passage linking high seas with high seas) or whether it merely codified a generally accepted practice. If the former, it could be said that Egypt was not bound by the provisions of Article 15 (8); and if the latter, she was bound by the rule of general customary law, her non-acceptance of the Convention notwithstanding. This Editor is inclined to the view that Article 15 (8) represented new, rather than customary law. Be that as it may, Israel was still correct in her claim to access through the Gulf, because the Gulf is, in the legal sense, a bay; a bay may not, as we have already said, be shut without the consent of *all* the riparian states. This Editor also believes that the Egyptian contentions concerning belligerent rights, Article 2 of the Armistice, and the 'illegal' occupation of Aqaba, were not well founded in law.[61]

iii. *Jordan–Israel Armistice, 1956–67*

The period 1956–66 saw a sharp decline in the output of UN documentation on the Jordan–Israel Armistice.

In September 1957 the Chief of Staff submitted a report concerning activities in the area of Government House at Jerusalem (S/3892). On 22 January 1958 the Security Council adopted a resolution (S/3942) observing that neither Israel nor Jordan could claim sovereignty over the zone, and endorsing the recommendation of the Chief of Staff that the parties should discuss civilian activities in the zone through the MAC. The resolution also recommended that Israel suspend her activities in the zone 'in order to create an atmosphere which would be more conducive to fruitful discussion' (para. 2 (b)).

In May of 1958 however, serious incidents occurred at Mount Scopus (in

[21] See R. Higgins, 'The June War: the UN and legal background', *J. of Contemp. History*, July 1968.

the Israeli sector of the demilitarized zone). Firing from the Jordanian side[62] resulted in the deaths of four Israelis and of Colonel Flint, a Canadian UN observer.[63]

The severe tensions which built up between Israel and Syria in 1966 had direct repercussions on the Israel–Jordan Armistice, for, at Syrian instigation, Jordan-based incursions were made into Israel territory—frequently, it would seem, by Arabs with little sympathy for King Hussein, whom they regarded as too moderate. Israel[64] chose to strike back against Jordan rather than Syria. The alleged incident was investigated by UNTSO, and a report was submitted to the Secretary-General.[65] The Israeli representative disputed the evidence, though—in accordance with the usual Israeli policy—affirming that the action had been carried out by authorized regular troops:

It appears from General Bull's report that the account of the Israel action given in it is based on hearsay—namely, statements made after the event to the UN Military Observers, by Jordanian witnesses. These statements are for the most part exaggerated and inaccurate. . . .

(*a*) The sole objective of the Israel action was to demolish a limited number of empty houses, after their occupants had been evacuated. This was done as a warning against aiding and harbouring saboteur and terrorist groups that had been carrying out a number of raids into Israel in the sector of the border. . . . [*S/7514, Letter of 21 Nov. 1966 from the Permanent Representative of Israel addressed to the President of the Security Council*, mimeo.]

Israel gave the number of casualties as three killed and seventeen injured. Given the clear prohibition against reprisals in the Armistice Agreements, and despite the Council's failure to adopt a resolution on the Syria–Israel hostilities (see p. 193), the Security Council now adopted the following resolution by 14 votes to nil, with New Zealand abstaining:

The Security Council,

Having heard the statements of the representatives of Jordan and Israel concerning the grave Israel military action which took place in the southern Hebron area on 13 November 1966,

Having noted the information provided by the Secretary-General concerning this military action in his statement of 16 November and also in his report of 18 November [S/7593 & Corr. 1 & Add. 1],

Observing that this incident constituted a large-scale and carefully planned military action on the territory of Jordan by the armed forces of Israel,

Reaffirming the previous resolutions of the Security Council condemning past incidents of reprisal in breach of the General Armistice Agreement between Israel and Jordan and of the United Nations Charter,

Recalling the repeated resolutions of the Security Council asking for the cessation of violent incidents across the demarcation line, and not overlooking past incidents of this nature,

Reaffirming the necessity for strict adherence to the General Armistice Agreement,

    1. Deplores the loss of life and heavy damage to property resulting from the action of the Government of Israel on 13 November 1966;

    2. Censures Israel for this large-scale military action in violation of the United Nations Charter and of the General Armistice Agreement between Israel and Jordan;

[62] The Chief of Staff's report does not categorically assert that the incident originated from Jordanian territory, but all the evidence in the report adds up to this conclusion.

[63] S/4011, 29 May 1958, for the Israel statement; S/4030, 17 July 1958 for the report of UNTSO's Chief of Staff.

[64] See p. 194.   [65] S/7593, 18 Nov. 1966.

3. Emphasizes to Israel that actions of military reprisal cannot be tolerated and that, if they are repeated, the Security Council will have to consider further and more effective steps as envisaged in the Charter to ensure against the repetition of such acts;

4. Request the Secretary-General to keep the situation under review and to report to the Security Council as appropriate. (*SC Res. S/7598, 25 Nov. 1966.*]

The more immediate result of the Israeli action was not 'an effective warning against . . . the harbouring [of] saboteurs', but rather the endangering of the position of King Hussein—a consequence hardly desirable to the Israeli government. Hussein was widely condemned by Syria and militant Arab nationalists for having allowed the Israeli reprisals to occur, and it was claimed that it was his 'softness' that encouraged the Israeli authorities. Hussein's position was ultimately retrieved by his entry into a militaty alliance with Nasser, and by his prominent participation in the six-days' war of 1967.

iv. *Lebanon–Israel Armistice, 1956–67*

The MAC, and UNTSO generally, continued to work effectively in this period, and, at least so far as this border was concerned, the Security Council's hopes for the Armistice system were realized.

(d) After June 1967

After the fighting of June 1967, when Israel occupied Sinai, Gaza, the Syrian hills on Tiberias, Jerusalem, and the west bank of Jordan, the legal status of the 1949 Armistice became very doubtful. Israel insisted that the time had come for peace between herself and the Arab states, to be reached in face-to-face talks. There could be no reversion to a mere armistice, under which the Arabs claimed belligerent rights and did not recognize Israel's right to exist.

The war of June 1967 quite clearly marked the total breakdown of the substantive rights and duties of the 1949 Armistice arrangements. At the same time, UNTSO and its observers remained in the field, carrying out their reporting[66] and liaison functions: and the MACs remained in existence. Moreover, UNTSO performed valuable duties during the hostilities, and acquired new functions— by Security Council resolution in respect of the Syrian–Israeli cease-fire, and by consensus of the Security Council in respect of the Suez zone[67]—after the termination of the war.

When the fighting broke out on 5 June the Security Council, though meeting day and night, was unable to reach agreement on a cease-fire demand. The United States wished a simple cease-fire order, while the Soviet Union insisted that it be coupled with a condemnation of Israel and a demand for Israeli withdrawal from Arab territory. By the evening of 6 June the results of the fighting had gone so much in Israel's favour that the Arabs—and thus the Soviet Union—were prepared to accept a cease-fire on whatever terms they could get:

[66] See for example, S/7930, 5 June 1967; S/7930/Add. 1, 6 June 1967.
[67] For details of these extended functions, see pp. 55–59 above.

The Security Council,

Noting the oral report of the Secretary-General in this situation,

Having heard the statements made in the Council,

Concerned at the outbreak of fighting and with the menacing situation in the Near East,

1. *Calls upon* the Governments concerned as a first step to take forthwith all measures for an immediate cease-fire and for a cessation of all military activities in the area;

2. *Requests* the Secretary-General to keep the Council promptly and currently informed on the situation. [*SC Res. S/233, 6 June 1967,* mimeo.]

Israel accepted the order provided the Arab states accepted it;[68] Jordan and Lebanon accepted, but Egypt, Syria, and Algeria initially refused. The fighting continued, with Israel pushing further and further into Arab territory. The next day the Security Council passed a further resolution:

The Security Council,

Noting that, in spite of its appeal to the Governments concerned to take forthwith as a first step all measures for an immediate cease-fire and for a cessation of all military activities in the Near East (resolution 233 (1967)), military activities in the area are continuing,

Concerned that the continuation of military activities may create an even more menacing situation in the area,

1. *Demands* that the Governments concerned should as a first step cease fire and discontinue all military activities at 20.00 hours GMT on 7 June 1967;

2. *Requests* the Secretary-General to keep the Council promptly and currently informed on the situation. [*SC Res. S/234, 7 June 1967,* mimeo.]

On 9 June a resolution was directed specifically at the situation obtaining on the Syria–Israel front:

The Security Council,

Recalling its resolutions 233 (1967) and 234 (1967),

Noting that the Governments of Israel and Syria have announced their mutual acceptance of the Council's demand for a cease-fire,

Noting the statements made by the representatives of Syria and Israel,

1. *Confirms* its previous resolutions about immediate cease-fire and cessation of military action;

2. *Demands* that hostilities should cease forthwith;

3. *Requests* the Secretary-General to make immediate contacts with the Governments of Israel and Syria to arrange immediate compliance with the above-mentioned resolutions, and to report to the Security Council not later than two hours from now. [*SC Res. S/235, 9 June 1967,* mimeo.]

The cease-fire on that front was failing to hold, and a further resolution was passed which envisaged a role for UNTSO and its military observers:

The Security Council,

Taking note of the oral reports of the Secretary-General on the situation between Israel and Syria, made at the 1354th, 1355th, 1356th and 1357th meetings and the supplemental information supplied in documents S/7930 and Add. 1–3,

1. *Condemns* any and all violations of the cease-fire;

2. *Requests* the Secretary-General to continue his investigations and to report to the Council as soon as possible;

---

[68] For details on the response to the cease-fire, see S/7985, 15 June 1967.

3. *Affirms* that its demand for a cease-fire and discontinuance of all military activities includes a prohibition of any forward military movements subsequent to the cease-fire;

4. *Calls for* the prompt return to the cease-fire positions of any troops which may have moved forward subsequent to 16.30 GMT on 10 June 1967;

5. *Calls for* full co-operation with the Chief of Staff of the United Nations Truce Supervision Organization in Palestine and the observers in implementing the cease-fire, including freedom of movement and adequate communications facilities. [*SC Res. S/236, 11 June 1967*, mimeo.]

These extended functions appear,[69] at the moment of writing, to have been very satisfactorily implemented by UNTSO—as has its new observer role in the Suez Canal sector, emanating from the consensus expressed by the Security Council[70] at its meeting. In the initial stages the effectiveness of UNTSO[71] was hampered by the fact that the Chief of Staff was not in possession of his headquarters and communications network in Jerusalem. But UNTSO's work proceeded none the less, and on 23 August Government House was returned by Israel to the use of UNTSO.

2. The cease-fire arrangement as proposed and negotiated by the Chief of Staff, UNTSO and accepted by the parties and which went into effect at 16.30 hours GMT on 10 June is being observed and no serious breaches had been reported in that period up to 15.00 hours EDT on 11 June.

3. As envisaged in General Bull's cease-fire arrangement, United Nations Military Observers on the morning of 11 June were deployed. . . . [*S/7930/Add. 3, 11 June 1967.*]

General Bull reported that UN teams were deployed on Israel–Syrian forward defended lines, and in Gaza. There was a temporary delay in deploying observers at Tiberias due to a lack of agreement with Israel on a proposal to re-establish Kuneitra control centre. All the UNMO teams were accompanied by either Arab or Israeli liaison officers, and they maintained radio communications with the UN control headquarters.[72]

On 14 July General Bull was able to report continuing calm[73] and that the UNMOs were continuing with the mapping of the forward defended localities.[74] From 19 to 23 June various minor infringements by the parties were observed.[75]

---

[69] For details of the tasks entailed, see p. 55 above.   [70] Above, pp. 62–63.

[71] There were, of course, other resolutions passed by the Security Council and by the General Assembly. Security Council Res. 237 called upon Israel to ensure the safety, welfare, and security of inhabitants where military operations had taken place, and recommended to all governments scrupulous respect for humanitarian principles in their treatment of prisoners of war. It was adopted unanimously. The Assembly, in its special session, adopted a resolution calling for aid for refugees by 116 votes to nil, with 2 abstentions (GA Res. 2252 (ES–IV)); and another resolution calling on Israel not to alter the status of Jerusalem (GA Res. 2253 (ES–IV)) was adopted 99–0 ,with 20 abstentions). The Soviet draft resolution, condemning Israel, was heavily defeated (A/L. 519). The American draft resolution, which did not seek to apportion blame, but recommended mutual recognition by the parties, freedom of maritime passage, a just solution to the refugee problem, and limitation and registration on arms shipments, was not put to the vote (A/L. 520). A Latin American resolution (A/L. 523) requesting Israel to withdraw her forces from Arab territory, an international régime for Jerusalem, and the establishment of coexistence between the parties, just failed to get a two-thirds majority: the voting was 57–43, with 20 abstentions. A Yugoslav resolution (A/L. 522/rev. 3), calling for the withdrawal of Israel forces (without either condemnation or mention of Arab–Israel coexistence), the appointment of a special representative of the Secretary-General, also failed by 54–46–19 to get a two-thirds majority. As none of these are directly relevant to the work of UNTSO they have not been reproduced here.

[72] S/7930/Add. 5, para. 2, 12 June 1967.   [73] Ibid. Adds 8–10.   [74] Ibid. Add. 7.
[75] Ibid. Add 11–14.

On 27 June General Bull announced agreement on the detailed mapping of the cease-fire line.

1. General Bull reports that the situation in general remains quiet.
2. The demarcation of the Israel foremost defended localities was completed on 15 June 1967. A working document embodying the map references of the Israel foremost defended localities as occupied at 16.30 hours GMT on 10 June 1967 was signed by the representative of the Chief of Staff of UNTSO and the representative of the Israel Defence Forces.
3. An agreement embodying the map references of the foremost defended localities on the Syrian side was signed by the representative of the Chief of Staff of UNTSO and the representative of the Syrian Armed Forces on 26 June 1967. The Syrian representative signed this agreement with the following reservation:

'The Syrian representative stresses the cease-fire line thus established is a purely practical arrangement for the specific purpose of facilitating the observation by the United Nations of the cease-fire and should not affect or prejudice the claims and positions of the Syrian Government. He emphasizes that the Israel forces are in Syrian territory. The Syrian side asserts the following: "On the morning of 9th June 1967, when both Syria and Israel had announced their acceptance of the cease-fire, the Israelis were not at that time at any point beyond the armistice line established by the armistice agreement of 1949 . . . The Israelis continued their firing on the morning of 9th June and repeated their attacks on Syrian positions. At the end of the day of 9th June, when the Security Council ordered cease-fire at 15.20 GMT, they reached the violet line shown on the map as annex B[76] and they stopped at the line until the morning of 10th June. Then on 10th June, they resumed firing. At 16.30 GMT, the time-limit for the cease-fire ordered for the third time by the Security Council, they reached the orange line indicated also on the map attached as annex B. After that, they used same helicopters with a certain number of soldiers to reach new points well advanced and near from battle lines."' [S/7930/Add. 17, 27 June 1967.]

By the beginning of July UNTSO was able to point to real progress in the carrying out of its tasks, and succeeded sufficiently to obtain a Syria–Israel agreement to a cease-fire demarcation working document:

1. The following report on the demarcation of the cease-fire lines between Israel and Syria is submitted to the Security Council pursuant to its resolutions 235 (1967) of 9 June 1967 and 236 (1967) of 12 June 1967. It is based upon information reported to me by the Chief of Staff of the United Nations Truce Supervision Organization in Palestine (UNTSO).
2. On 10 June 1967 the Chief of Staff of UNTSO proposed to Israel and Syria as a practical arrangement for implementing the cease-fire demanded by the Security Council in its resolutions, of 7 and 9 June 1967, that both sides cease all firing and forward movement at 16.30 hours GMT on 10 June 1967. The Chief of Staff also proposed that United Nations military observers on each side, accompanied by liaison officers appointed by the respective armed forces, be deployed along the front lines as soon as possible in order to observe the implementation of the cease-fire. His proposals were accepted by both sides.
3. Though it was planned that deployment of observers on both sides should commence immediately after the cease-fire became effective, this could not be done prior to darkness on 10 June. First deployment of observers along the front lines began on the morning of 11 June and, for certain areas, was completed a few days later.
4. On 11 June the observers, in co-operation with the representatives of the armed forces on their respective sides, started the demarcation of the limits of the Forward Defended Localities (FDLs) occupied by the armed forces at the time of the cease-fire. These limits would constitute the cease-fire line on each side across which the respective armed forces would not fire or move forward.
5. The observers completed the demarcation of the cease-fire line on the Israel side on

[76] In fact the map was *not* attached as an annex to S/7930/, Add. 17.

15 June and a working document on the subject was signed on the same day, the text of which is reproduced in annex I to this report.

6. As of 18 June the demarcation of the cease-fire line on the Syrian side was not yet completed, although considerable progress had been made. In a meeting with the Chief of Staff on that day in Tel Aviv, the Israel authorities protested against the delay in demarcating the Syrian cease-fire line which they claimed was due to the unco-operative attitude of the Syrian authorities. They asserted that recently the Israel forces had observed some Syrian troop movements advancing towards the Israel lines and expressed the view that the Syrian troops should stay at positions they actually had held at the time of the cease-fire. The Chief of Staff observed that on 10 June the Israel forces were progressing in Syrian territory, while the Syrian forces were retreating from their previously held positions and that the determination of the positions occupied by the respective forces at the time of the cease-fire should be viewed in the light of these facts. The Chief of Staff remarked that, under such conditions, the demarcation of the cease-fire line on the Syrian side was bound to proceed more slowly than that on the Israel side and he assured the Israel authorities that he would continue his efforts to expedite the demarcation of the Syrian cease-fire line.

7. By 19 June the United Nations observers, in co-operation with representatives of the Syrian armed forces, had completed the demarcation of the cease-fire line on the Syrian side except for three areas, concerning which the Syrian authorities made the following reservations:

(a) The Mount Hermon area west of the Israel cease-fire line had been occupied by Israel forces brought there by helicopters after the cease-fire time.

(b) The Syrian forces had continued to occupy the Tell Qle area . . . after the cease-fire became effective.

(c) Point 22 of the Israel cease-fire line . . . at the southernmost tip of the line should be on the west bank and not on the east bank of the wadi.

8. Having ascertained the views of the Syrian authorities, and taking into account the fact that the observers had not been able to observe the positions actually occupied by the respective forces at the time of the cease-fire, the Chief of Staff approached the Israel authorities on 21 June and asked their agreement to some adjustments in their cease-fire line in the Mount Hermon and Tell Qle areas. Their reply was that the positions demarcated by the observers were those actually occupied by Israel forces at the time of the cease-fire and that they saw no reason to modify the Israel line.

9. On 21 June the United Nations observers visited the area of Tell Qle and found that there were no military forces at Tell Qle and no indication of recent occupation there. A United Nations observation post was established as from 22 June. It should be noted that a request had been made by Syrian authorities on 16 June that United Nations observers visit that area; it had not been possible to carry out this visit at that time because of the impossibility for United Nations observers on the Syrian side to cross the Israel cease-fire line and of the delay in transmitting through the inadequate communication system available at the temporary Headquarters of UNTSO this confidential information to United Nations observers on the Israel side.

10. Concerning point 22 of the Israel line, the Syrian authorities stated that during the reconnaissance of 16 June, United Nations observers had found it unmanned. Observers' reports confirm this statement but indicate that, during a reconnaissance carried out on 12 June from the Israel-controlled side in that area, United Nations observers had seen from a vantage point a 'few Israel soldiers' in position at point 22. It was not possible for UNTSO to ascertain whether point 22 was occupied prior to 12 June.

11. On 24 June the Chief of Staff UNTSO saw the Syrian authorities in Damascus and informed them of the developments mentioned above. He again suggested that as a practical arrangement for the implementation of the cease-fire the Syrian authorities should agree to his proposed cease-fire line. They accepted, but with a number of reservations. A document describing the agreed cease-fire line on the Syrian side and setting forth in detail the Syrian reservations was signed on 26 June 1967. . . .

12. The Chief of Staff has informed both sides that any firing across the cease-fire lines thus established, any movement forward of the lines and any flight of aircraft across the lines would be considered as violations of the cease-fire and immediately reported to the Secretary-General.

13. The observation of the cease-fire is being carried out by the observers at observation posts and through patrols organized from these posts. As of 27 June, 110 United Nations observers were deployed on both sides manning a total of sixteen observation posts and a reinforced control centre at Kuneitra. Arrangements are being made to increase the number of observation posts and to relocate certain of them so as to establish a comprehensive network with inter-visibility and radio contact between posts on the same side as well as with those on the opposite side. . . .

The Syrian representative stresses that the cease-fire line [establishing through UN mapping in agreement with the parties] is a purely practical arrangement for the specific purpose of facilitating the observation by the United Nations of the cease-fire and should not affect or prejudice the claims and positions of the Syrian Government. He emphasizes that the Israel forces are in Syrian territory. The Syrian side asserts the following: 'On the morning of 9 June 1967, when both Syria and Israel had announced their acceptance of the cease-fire, the Israelis were not at that time at any point beyond the armistice line established by the Armistice Agreement of 1949 (see green line on map attached as annex B). The Israelis continued their firing on the morning of 9 June and repeated their attacks on Syrian positions. At the end of the day of 9 June, when the Security Council ordered cease-fire at 15.20 hours GMT, they reached the violet line shown on the map attached as annex B and they stopped at the line until the morning of 10 June. Then on 10 June, they resumed firing. At 16.30 GMT, the time-limit for the cease-fire ordered for the third time by the Security Council they reached the orange line indicated also on the map attached as annex B. After that, they used some helicopters with a certain number of soldiers to reach new points well advanced and far from battle lines. These are shown in yellow on the map attached as annex B'.

For and on behalf of the
Chief of Staff of UNTSO

For and on behalf of the
Chief of Staff of the
Syrian Arab Armed Forces

(*Signed*) R. W. BUNWORTH, Lt.-Col.
Irish Army
Chairman ISMAC

(*Signed*) A. ABDALLAH, Captain
Syrian Arab Navy
Senior Syrian Delegate
Damascus,
26 June 1967

[*S/7930/Add. 18, 1 July 1967.*]

On 17 July the functions of the UN military observers were extended to the Suez Canal area,[77] where daily fighting was occurring across the Canal.

2. Advance parties of United Nations military observers, who had arrived in Ismailia and el Kantara respectively on 15 July, were instructed by General Bull to begin observation operations on both sides of the sector at 16.00 hrs. GMT on 17 July. Details of the practical arrangements for this operation will be reported on separately. [*S/7930/Add. 23, 17 July 1967.*]

In fact, the UN observer operation ran into difficulties over demarcation. Egypt insisted that she, and she alone, possessed all of the Canal. The cease-fire line should be along the east bank. Israel wanted the line to run down the middle of the Canal. Israel was seeking, of course, to establish a right to sail on the Canal, which aim Egypt was determined to prevent.

General Bull initiated negotiations to find a formula acceptable to both Parties, under which UNTSO could become operational in the Canal area:

[77] For the events that led to this, see above, p. 62.

The question of movement of boats in the Suez Canal

12. The differences in the positions of the United Arab Republic and Israel in connexion with the presence of boats in the Suez Canal were discussed by the Chief of Staff with Israel authorities on 19 and 25 July and with United Arab Republic authorities during visits to Cairo from 19 to 25 July and from 29 July to 1 August. During these discussions the Chief of Staff expressed his concern that the presence and movement of boats on the Canal could lead to a breach of the cease-fire; his concern was also expressed to both parties through their Liaison Officers by the officers-in-charge at Ismailia and El Quantara.

13. Israel maintained that either the boats of both parties should be allowed to move freely on the appropriate sides of the Canal, or that no boats should be permitted there. Israel also expressed its intention of placing its boats on the Canal.

14. The United Arab Republic stated that the best way to avoid any violation of the cease-fire was for the parties to desist from seeking to change the situation which prevailed on 10 July when the consensus was reached in the Security Council. The United Arab Republic maintained that there had been Egyptian boats on the Canal at that time, but not Israel boats. It stated that it would regard the placing of Israel boats on the Canal as a violation of the cease-fire to which the United Arab Republic would feel obliged to reply by firing on the boats. (The United Arab Republic position was also set forth in a letter to the Secretary-General (document S/8070).)

15. The situation in the Suez Canal sector is further complicated by the presence in the Bitter Lakes of ships which have been stranded there since the beginning of hostilities on 5 June when the Canal was blocked. Arrangements were made with the United Arab Republic authorities by the national authorities whose flag the ships were flying for the reprovisioning of these ships and for measures for their safety.

16. Concerned lest the movement of boats in the Canal should precipitate an incident, the Chief of Staff on 18 July addressed a request to both parties that each should refrain from any action which might impair the quiet in the area.

17. Since, during the week following, the positions of the parties remained unchanged and danger of renewal of hostilities continued, on 27 July 1967 the Chief of Staff addressed an identical message to the parties (see annex I) asking that all military activity in the Canal be stopped, including the movement of boats in or into the Canal, for one month from 27 July, and requesting them to co-operate with the Chief of Staff in establishing the limits of the cease-fire sectors. In his request, he noted that it was understood that the boats of the Suez Canal Authority would continue to revictual and ensure the safety of the ships stranded in the Canal. It was also understood that all such measures were to be considered strictly from the point of view of maintaining the cease-fire without prejudice to the political, legal or other issues involved.

18. The Chief of Staff received a message in reply from the United Arab Republic authorities on the same day, 27 July 1967 (see annex II).

19. The Chief of Staff replied on 27 July (see annex III) noting with satisfaction that the United Arab Republic was not carrying out any military activity in the Canal. The Chief of Staff reiterated his request that for one month all movement of boats be stopped except for those of the Canal authorities for the revictualling and safety of boats stranded in the Canal. On 31 July the United Arab Republic authorities stated that the Chief of Staff's conversations in Cairo on 30 and 31 July 'showed that the contents of your above-mentioned message (27 July) coincide with the contents of my message (27 July) in respect of the movements of our boats in the Suez Canal in response to the Security Council cease-fire decision'.

20. On 1 August, at the conclusion of the conversations with the United Arab Republic authorities in Cairo, the Chief of Staff stated that as a result of these conversations it was understood:

'(*a*) That the United Arab Republic in observance of the cease-fire decisions does not carry out any military activity in the Canal;

(*b*) That the movement of boats and craft in the Suez Canal is confined to the boats of the

Suez Canal Authority which also controls the boats of the commercial firms which provide supplies to the ships stranded in the Canal and those which ensure their safety.'

21. On 28 July the Chief of Staff received a letter (see annex IV) from the Israel authorities in reply to his letter of 27 July.

22. In view of the acceptance by both parties of the measure regarding movement of boats in the Canal, the Chief of Staff addressed to the Israel and United Arab Republic authorities a message dated 1 August as follows:

'In my message of 27 July 1967 I called upon the Governments of Israel and the United Arab Republic to stop all military activities in the Suez Canal, including the movement in or into the Canal of boats and craft for a period of one month, commencing on 27 July 1967 at 0800 hours GMT. I added in this connexion that it is understood that the Canal authorities will continue to revictual and ensure the safety of the ships stranded in the Canal.

'I should like to inform you that the two parties have responded favourably to this call with the understanding on the part of the United Arab Republic that the movement of boats and craft in the Suez Canal includes the boats of the Suez Canal Authority and the boats of the commercial firms which provide supplies to the ships stranded in the Canal and those which ensure their safety, all of which are under the control of the Canal Authority.

'Accordingly, I am instructing the officers in charge of the observation groups to observe and report on the movement of boats in the Suez Canal sector.

'In co-operation with both parties I will continue my efforts in order to adopt all measures which might facilitate the implementation of the decisions of the Security Council on the cease-fire and on the observation of the cease-fire.'

ANNEX I

Message dated 27 July 1967 by General Odd Bull, Chief of Staff
to the Governments of Israel and the United Arab Republic

Having in mind the communications and conversations involving the two Governments on the question of boats in the Suez Canal, as well as other aspects of the implementation of the cease-fire demanded by the Security Council in its resolution of 6 and 7 June 1967, and the consensus of the Security Council of 9/10 July;

As a means of ensuring full observance of the cease-fire, calls upon the Governments of Israel and of the United Arab Republic to stop all military activities in the Suez Canal, including the movement in or into the Canal of boats and craft for a period of one month commencing on 27 July 1967 at 10.00 hours LT;

Requests the parties to co-operate with the Chief of Staff in order to establish the limits of the cease-fire sectors to allow him to discharge properly his duties of observation of the cease-fire. It is understood that the Canal authorities will continue to revictual and ensure the safety of the ships stranded in the Canal.

Further, it is understood that all these measures are considered strictly from the point of view of the cease-fire without prejudice to the political, legal or other issues which the parties involved may consider.

ANNEX II

Message dated 27 July 1967 from the United Arab Republic
Government to General Bull, Chief of Staff

Bull from Ambassador Salah Gohar.

1. With reference to your message dated today July 27, I wish to inform you the following:

2. Any presence of Israeli Forces on any part of the United Arab Republic territory is an aggression and consequently no right of any sort for Israel could result therefrom.

3. No Israeli Forces were present on the East Bank of the Suez Canal at the time when the Security Council took its decision concerning the cease-fire.

4. Any attempt by Israel to move boats into the Canal would constitute a military act aimed at the extension of aggression and is, therefore, a violation of the cease-fire decision.

5. The United Arab Republic, observing the cease-fire decision, does not carry any military activity in the Suez Canal. Its activities in the Canal are confined to the boats of the Suez Canal Authority and the commercial firms which provide supplies to the ships stranded in the Canal, those which ensure it safety, as well as fishing boats.

6. The above-mentioned situation has been prevailing at the time when UNTSO started its operation on July 17th 1967. We consider that the maintenance of that situation would ensure against any threat to the cease-fire decision.

(*Signed*) SALAH GOHAR

ANNEX III

Message dated 27 July 1967 from General Odd Bull, Chief of Staff to Ambassador Salah Gohar of the UAR

Ambassador Salah Gohar from General Bull, Chief of Staff.

1. Thank you for your message, dated 27 July answering mine of the same date.

2. I note with satisfaction your affirmation that the United Arab Republic does not carry out any military activity in the Suez Canal.

3. I note also that the activities in the Canal are confined to the boats of the Suez Canal Authority and the commercial firms which provide supplies to the ships stranded in the Canal, and those which ensure their safety.

4. Further, I note your mention of the question of fishing boats. I know your views concerning the latter and while I appreciate your reasons, I must, however, reiterate my request that for a month all movement of boats be stopped, except for those of the Canal authorities for the revictualling and safety of the boats stranded in the Canal.

5. I hope you will understand also my reasons for this temporary measure and, therefore, that you will be able to give a positive answer to my request.

6. I will appreciate your prompt answer.

7. Concerning the other questions referred to in my message, I am at your disposal to proceed to Cairo in order to discuss them with you.

Please accept, Ambassador Gohar, the assurances of my consideration.

ANNEX IV

Letter from Mr Y. Tekoah, Assistant Director-General, Ministry for Foreign Affairs, Israel, to Lt.-General Odd Bull, Chief of Staff, dated 28 July 1967

I refer to your letter of 27 July 1967 in which you 'call upon the Governments of Israel and of the United Arab Republic to stop all military activity in the Suez Canal, including the movement in or into the Canal of boats and craft for a period of one month commencing on 27 July 1967 at 0800 hours GMT'.

I write to inform you that the Government of Israel accepts your proposal on condition of reciprocity. Appropriate instructions will be issued as soon as we are informed of the UAR's acceptance.

We note your request to the parties to co-operate with you in establishing 'the limits of the cease-fire sectors' to allow you to discharge properly your duties of observation of the cease-fire. We are willing to co-operate in establishing cease-fire lines and would like to receive without delay a map with cease-fire lines clearly marked and signed by the parties (as the one for the Syrian border).

(*Signed*) Y. TEKOAH

[S/8053/Add. 1, 10 Aug. 1967, mimeo.]

At the end of October, after the sinking by Egypt of the Israeli ship *Eilat*, and the retaliatory raid by Israel on the refineries of Port Suez, further measures were taken to make the work of the observers more effective. These included enlarging the UNTSO group stationed on the Canal,[78] and providing patrol craft and helicopters.[79] Agreement was reached with Israel and Egypt both as to the nationality of the additional observers[80] and the positions at which they would be stationed.[81]

13

ANNEXES

A. Checklist of Documents

GENERAL ASSEMBLY

Documents

A/648	3rd sess.	suppl. 11
A/1287	5th sess.	suppl. 1
A/1844	6th sess.	suppl. 1
A/2141	7th sess.	suppl. 1

Resolutions

106 (S–1)　15 May 1947
181 (11)　29 Nov. 1947

186 (S–2)　14 May 1948
194 (III)　11 Dec. 1948

SECURITY COUNCIL

1. REPORTS BY MEDIATOR

S/839	15 June 1948		S/979	19 Aug. 1948
S/846	18 June 1948		S/1022	30 Sept. 1948
S/854	23 June 1948		S/1042	18 Oct. 1948
S/856 & Add.	25 June 1948		S/1071	6 Nov. 1948
S/861 & Add.	1 July 1948		S/1152	25 Dec. 1948
S/865	5 July 1948		S/1269	1 Mar. 1949
S/869	7 July 1948		S/1285	11 Mar. 1949
S/888	12 July 1948		S/1286	13 Mar. 1949
S/955	7 Aug. 1948		S/1295	22 Mar. 1949
S/961	12 Aug. 1948		S/1357	21 July 1949

2. RESOLUTIONS

Introduction

S/714	1 Apr. 1948		S/1045	19 Oct. 1948
S/723	16 Apr. 1948		S/1070	4 Nov. 1948
S/727	23 Apr. 1948		S/1080	16 Nov. 1948
S/773	22 May 1948		S/1169	29 Dec. 1948
S/801	29 May 1948		S/1376	11 Aug. 1949
S/902	15 July 1948			

---

[78] See above, s.7, p. 71.　　　[79] S/8053/Add. 3, 31 Oct. 1967.　　　[80] See above, s.7, p. 71.
[81] S/8053/Add. 4, 1 Dec. 1967.

In respect of all 4 Armistice Agreements
S/3575   4 Apr. 1956   S/3605   4 June 1956

In respect of the Syrian–Israel Armistice
S/1907   17 Nov. 1950   S/3538   19 Jan. 1956
S/2157   18 May 1951   S/5111   9 Apr. 1962

In respect of the Egypt–Israel Armistice
S/3435   8 Sept. 1955

In respect of the Jordan–Israel Armistice
S/3942   22 Jan. 1958   S/7598   25 Nov. 1966

In respect of the 1967 war
SC res. 233, 7 June 1967; SC res. 234, 7 June 1967; SC res. 235, 9 June 1967; SC res. 236, 12 June 1967;

3. REPORTS BY THE CHIEF OF STAFF OF UNTSO
[NOTE: Included here are also reports by the Secretary-General to the Security Council, when they transmit, without addition, information from the Chief of Staff.]

In respect of all 4 Armistice Agreements
S/2049   21 Mar. 1951   S/2833/Add. 1   7 Nov. 1952
S/2300   17 Aug. 1951   S/3183 & Corr. 1 7 Mar. 1954

In respect of the Syrian–Israel Armistice
S/2067   27 Mar. 1951   S/2185   6 June 1951
S/2084   10 Apr. 1951   S/2213   27 June 1951
S/2088   13 Apr. 1951   S/2234   8 July 1951
S/2099   23 Apr. 1951   S/2359   1 Oct. 1951
S/2101   24 Apr. 1951   S/3122   23 Oct. 1953
S/2111   1 May 1951   S/3343   11 Jan. 1955
S/2119   4 May 1951   S/3558   12 Mar. 1956
S/2120   4 May 1951   S/3815   23 Apr. 1957
S/2122   7 May 1951   S/3844 & Add. 1   27 June 1957
S/2123   7 May 1951   S/4124   8 Dec. 1958
S/2124   7 May 1951   S/4154   29 Jan. 1959
S/2127   8 May 1951   S/5102 & Add. 1   26 Mar. 1962
S/2136   8 May 1951   S/5401 & Add. 1–4 24 Aug. 1963
S/2138   8 May 1951   S/6061 & Add. 1   24 Nov. 1964
S/2141   9 May 1951   S/7432   26 July 1966
S/2148   14 May 1951   S/7433   27 July 1966
S/2173   29 May 1951   S/7561   22 Oct. 1966

In respect of the Egypt–Israel Armistice
S/2194   13 June 1951   S/3390   13 Apr. 1955
S/3309   25 Oct. 1954   S/3390 & Add. 1   18 Apr. 1955
S/3319 & Add. 1   11 Nov. 1954   S/3430   6 Sept. 1955
S/3323   25 Nov. 1954   S/3430 & Add. 1   7 Sept. 1955
S/3373   17 Mar. 1955   S/3638   21 Aug. 1956

In respect of the Jordan–Israel Armistice

S/3007 & Corr. 1	8 May 1953	S/3680	26 Sept. 1956
S/3015	25 May 1953	S/3685	18 Oct. 1956
S/3040	19 June 1953	S/3892	28 Sept. 1957
S/3047	30 June 1953	S/3913	18 Nov. 1957
S/3251	25 June 1954	S/4030 & Add. 1	7 June 1958
S/3252	25 June 1954	S/7553	17 Oct. 1966
S/3394	18 April 1955	S/7593	18 Nov. 1966

4. THE ARMISTICE AGREEMENTS

S/1302/rev. 1	3 Apr. 1949	(Jordan–Israel)
S/1353/rev. 1	20 July 1949	(Syria–Israel)
S/1264/rev. 1	23 Feb. 1949	(Egypt–Israel)
S/1296	23 Mar. 1949	(Lebanon–Israel)

5. REPORTS BY THE SECRETARY-GENERAL

S/3561	21 Mar. 1956	S/3659	27 Sept. 1956
S/3669	8 Oct. 1956	S/7572	1 Nov. 1966
S/3584	12 Apr. 1956	S/7573	2 Nov. 1966
S/3586	13 Apr. 1956	S/7603	29 Nov. 1966
S/3587	16 Apr. 1956	S/7930 & Add. 1–23,	5 June 1967
S/3594	2 May 1956	S/8046	9 July 1967
S/3596	9 May 1956	S/8053 & Annexes	11 July 1967
S/3632	3 Aug. 1956		

6. COMPLAINTS BY THE PARTIES

In respect of the Syria–Israel Armistice

S/2061	29 Mar. 1950	S/4123	4 Dec. 1958
S/2065	2 Apr. 1950	S/5091	16 Mar. 1962
S/2072	6 Apr. 1950	S/5092	17 Mar. 1962
S/2074	6 Apr. 1950	S/5093	19 Mar. 1962
S/2085	12 Apr. 1950	S/5096	20 Mar. 1962
S/2089	16 Apr. 1950	S/5098	21 Mar. 1962
S/2105	26 Apr. 1951	S/5100	22 Mar. 1962
S/2117	4 May 1951	S/5258	11 Mar. 1963
S/2125	7 May 1951	S/5261	15 Mar. 1963
S/2126	7 May 1951	S/5329	10 June 1963
S/2168	24 May 1951	S/5332	11 June 1963
S/2309	24 Aug. 1951	S/5394	21 Aug. 1963
S/2596	12 Mar. 1953	S/5395	21 Aug. 1963
S/3106	13 Oct. 1953	S/5396	22 Aug. 1963
S/3107	15 Oct. 1953	S/5801	7 July 1964
S/3108/rev. 1	16 Oct. 1953	S/5805	8 July 1964
S/3554	7 Mar. 1956	S/5854	6 Aug. 1964
S/3555	8 Mar. 1956	S/5874	10 Aug. 1964
S/3634	7 Aug. 1956	S/6044	14 Nov. 1964
S/3827	13 May 1957	S/6045	14 Nov. 1964
S/3945	30 Jan. 1958	S/6046	16 Nov. 1964
S/3946	31 Jan. 1958	S/6051	15 Nov. 1964
S/3948	4 Feb. 1958	S/6243	17 Mar. 1965
S/3950	11 Feb. 1958	S/6248	19 Mar. 1965
S/3985	2 Apr. 1958	S/6382	25 May 1965

In respect of the Syria–Israel Armistice—cont.

S/7411	14 July 1966	S/7540	12 Oct. 1966
S/7412	18 July 1966	S/7656	30 Dec. 1966
S/7536	10 Oct. 1966		

In respect of the Egypt–Israel Armistice

S/1797	18 Sept. 1950	S/3431	6 Sept. 1955
S/2240	11 July 1951	S/3433	7 Sept. 1955
S/2241	12 July 1951	S/3434	8 Sept. 1955
S/3093	10 Sept. 1953	S/3559	14 Mar. 1956
S/3101	2 Oct. 1953	S/3576	5 Apr. 1956
S/3103	7 Oct. 1953	S/3577	6 Apr. 1956
S/3168 & Add. 1	28 Jan. 1954	S/3579/rev. 1	9 Apr. 1956
S/3172	3 Feb. 1954	S/3580	9 Apr. 1956
S/3179	15 Feb. 1954	S/3581	10 Apr. 1956
S/3300	4 Oct. 1954	S/3582	10 Apr. 1956
S/3302	7 Oct. 1954	S/3583	11 Apr. 1956
S/3311	27 Oct. 1954	S/3585	12 Apr. 1956
S/3315	10 Nov. 1954	S/3603	1 June 1956
S/3325	30 Nov. 1954	S/3606	8 June 1956
S/3326	4 Dec. 1954	S/3611	28 June 1956
S/3333	20 Dec. 1954	S/3642	5 Sept. 1956
S/3335	23 Dec. 1954	S/3810	8 Apr. 1957
S/3367	2 Mar. 1955	S/3812	16 Apr. 1957
S/3368	3 Mar. 1955	S/3814	22 Apr. 1957
S/3376	25 Mar. 1955	S/3899	11 Oct. 1957
S/3385	4 Apr. 1955	S/4160	7 Feb. 1959
S/3386	5 Apr. 1955	S/4164	20 Feb. 1959
S/3389	11 Apr. 1955	S/4167	23 Feb. 1959
S/3393	18 Apr. 1955	S/4173	17 Mar. 1959
S/3425	30 Aug. 1955	S/4226	7 Oct. 1959
S/3426	30 Aug. 1955	S/4240	14 Nov. 1959
S/3427	31 Aug. 1955	S/5405	28 Aug. 1963
S/3428	2 Sept. 1955		

In respect of the Jordan–Israel Armistice

S/1780	11 Sept. 1950	S/3914	19 Nov. 1957
S/1792	15 Sept. 1950	S/4011	29 May 1958
S/3113	19 Oct. 1953	S/5144	20 July 1962
S/3116	20 Oct. 1953	S/5152	1 Aug. 1962
S/3140	23 Nov. 1953	S/6077	2 Dec. 1964
S/3180 & Adds. 1–2	19 Feb. 1954	S/6208	1 Mar. 1965
S/3195	1 Apr. 1954	S/6209	2 Mar. 1965
S/3196	5 Apr. 1954	S/6235	15 Mar. 1965
S/3196 & Add. 1	6 Apr. 1954	S/6387	28 May 1965
S/3621	16 July 1956	S/6390	28 May 1965
S/3628	26 July 1956	S/6414	4 June 1965
S/3878	4 Sept. 1957	S/6415	5 June 1965
S/3883	5 Sept. 1957	S/6440	16 June 1965
S/3907	11 Nov. 1957	S/7586	13 Nov. 1966
S/3909	11 Nov. 1957	S/7594	21 Nov. 1966
S/3910	14 Nov. 1957		

In respect of the Lebanon–Israel Armistice
    S/1631   26 July 1950   S/1650   31 July 1950
    S/1648   31 July 1950   S/3741   13 Nov. 1950

7. MEETINGS

General Assembly

1st and 2nd spec. sess.
2nd sess.: Plen. mtgs, 90, 124–48
        Ad Hoc Cttee mtgs, 1–23
3rd Session, Pt I
        Plen. mtgs, 136, 139, 140, 142, 143–8, 163, 184–6
        1st Cttee mtgs, 143, 160–1, 166, 169, 208–28
        3rd Cttee mtgs, 108–9, 117–18, 135–6
4th Session
        Plen. mtgs, 222–3, 225–9, 238, 273–5
        General Cttee mtgs, 65, 68
        Ad Hoc Political Cttee mtgs, 43–55, 57–61

Security Council

    3rd yr, mtgs 243, 253–5, 258, 267, 260–3, 270–7, 283, 287, 302, 309–10 314–17, 320–49, 365–6, 373–81, 393–6
    4th yr, mtgs 413, 433–5, 437
    5th yr, mtgs 502–3, 511, 517, 518, 522, 524
    6th yr, mtgs 541–2, 544–7, 549–53, 555–6, 558
    8th yr, mtgs 627, 629–33, 635, 636–40, 642–3, 645–6, 648–54
    9th yr, mtgs 655–71, 682–6
    10th yr, mtgs 687, 688, 697, 698, 700, 701, 709
    11th yr, mtgs 710–15, 717–28, 744–5
    12th yr, mtgs 780–2, 787–8, 806, 809–10
    13th yr, mtgs 841, 844
    14th yr, mtg 845
    16th yr, mtgs 947–9
    17th yr, mtgs 999–1006
    18th yr, mtgs 1057–63
    19th yr, mtgs 1162, 1164–9, 1179, 1182
    21st yr, mtgs 1288–95, 1305, 1307–10, 1312–14, 1316, 1317, 1319, 1320–28

B. Bibliography

Afifi, Mohammed el-Hadi. *The Arabs and the United Nations*. Ontario, 1964.

Bar-Yaacov, N. *The Israel–Syrian Armistice; Problems of Implementation 1946–66*. Jerusalem, 1967.

Baxter, R. *The Law of International Waterways*. Cambridge, Mass., 1964.

Bentwich, Norman. Israel–Syrian armistice agreement. *Internat. Relations*. 1967.

Bernadotte, Folke. *To Jerusalem*. London, 1951.

Bowett, Derek. *United Nations Forces*. London, 1964.

Brook, David. *Preface to Peace: the United Nations and the Arab–Israel Armistice System*. Washington, 1964.

Burns, E. L. M. *Between Arab and Israeli*. London, 1962.

García Granados, J. *The Birth of Israel*. New York, 1948.

Higgins, Rosalyn. The June War: United Nations and legal background. *J. of Contemp. History*, July 1968.

Hula Development Authority. *The Drainage and Development of the Hula Area* [in Hebrew]. 1960.

Hurewitz, Jacob C. The Israel–Syrian crisis in the light of the Arab–Israel armistice system. *Int. Org.*, Aug. 1951.

Hutchison, E. *Violent Truce: a military observer looks at the Arab–Israeli conflict, 1951–5*. New York, 1956.

Khoury, Fred J. Friction and conflict on the Israeli–Syrian front. *Middle East J.*, Winter/Spring 1963.

Kirk, G. E. *The Middle East, 1945–50*. London, 1954. (RIIA *Survey 1939–46*.)

Leonard, Larry. The United Nations and Palestine. *Int. Conciliation*, Oct. 1949.

Levie, P. The nature and scope of the armistice agreements. 50 *AJIL*, 1956.

Mohn, P. Problems of truce supervision. *Int. Conciliation*, Feb. 1952.

Rosenne, Shabtai. *Israel's Armistice Agreements with the Arab States*. Tel-Aviv, 1951.

Rosner, Gabriella. *The United Nations Emergency Force*. New York, 1963.

Welles, Sumner. *We Need not Fail*. Boston, 1948.

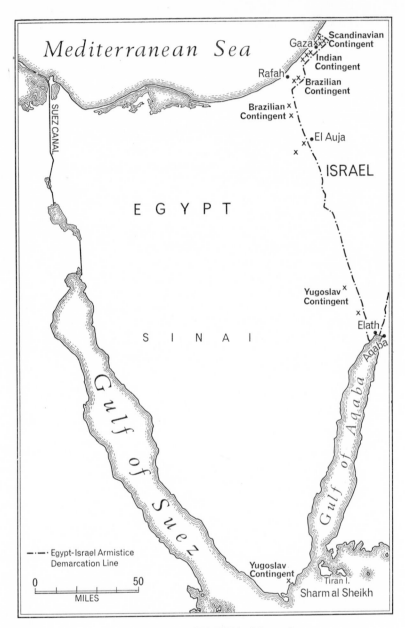

2. Deployment of UNEF in May 1967

Based on maps nos. 1727, 1728, 1729, GAOR, 22nd sess., ann., a.i.21, A/6672 & Add.1.

Part 2

THE UNITED NATIONS
EMERGENCY FORCE (UNEF), 1956–67

1. INTRODUCTION (p. 221)
Deterioration of the Egypt–Israel Armistice; breakdown of the Tripartite Declaration; nationalization of the Suez Canal; British reaction; Conference of Canal Users agrees on proposals, which are rejected by Egypt; second conference in London rejects Egyptian counter-proposals; military plans between Britain and France; Hammarskjöld makes progress on a six-point plan; Ben-Gurion attends a meeting at Sèvres; Israel attacks Egypt on 29 October; Britain and France issue an ultimatum; failure to agree in the Security Council; resolutions pass in the General Assembly 1st emergency special session.

2. ENABLING RESOLUTIONS AND VOTING (p. 227)
The resolutions of the 1st emergency special session and the eleventh regular session; the attitudes of Britain, France, Israel, Egypt, the United States, the Soviet Union, and other countries.

3. FUNCTIONS AND MANDATE (p. 241)
Debate about the purpose of UN Emergency Force (UNEF); cessation of hostilities and withdrawal behind armistice lines; controversy as to UNEF's role in Gaza, on the Gulf of Aqaba, in overseeing the Armistice Agreement; divergent views of certain countries; relevance to events of May 1967.

4. CONSTITUTIONAL BASIS (p. 260)
The Uniting for Peace resolution; the establishment of UNEF by the Assembly; Soviet claims of constitutional illegality; the question of Egypt's consent and the non-enforcement nature of UNEF; the constitutional basis and the question of UN peacekeeping expenses; the 1962 Advisory Opinion of the International Court; Articles 10, 11, 12, and 14 of the Charter; constitutional authority for the termination of UNEF in 1967.

5. POLITICAL CONTROL (p. 273)
Delegation of powers to the Secretary-General; UNEF's Advisory Committee; the orders for UNEF's withdrawal.

6. ADMINISTRATIVE AND MILITARY CONTROL (p. 278)
Role of the Commander and his relationship to Secretary-General and General Assembly; organization and administration in the field; logistics; UNEF's Regulations; administrative and military arrangements on the withdrawal of UNEF; UNEF'S Commanders.

7. COMPOSITION AND SIZE (p. 300)
Authority to determine composition of UNEF; ten nations represented; details of national contingents; size of UNEF; reductions in the face of financial problems.

8*

8. RELATIONS WITH CONTRIBUTING STATES (p. 324)
Statements by certain nations of conditions of service of their contingents; letter from Secretary-General to all contributing states; international legal character of UNEF; arrangements for compensation for death, injury or illness attributable to service.

9. RELATIONS WITH THE HOST STATE (p. 335)
(*a*) *The question of consent:* establishment, stationing and withdrawal. The scope of Egypt's consent to UNEF: the *aide-mémoire* of 20 November 1956; U Thant's views on the 'consent' principle in May 1967; Hammarskjöld's private *aide-mémoire* of August 1957; chronology of events concerning UNEF's withdrawal.
(*b*) *The question of composition:* Egyptian views on the composition of UNEF; treatment of this question by the Secretary-General.
(*c*) *Status of Forces Agreement:* text and commentary.

10. RELATIONS WITH OTHER STATES INVOLVED (p. 385)
(*a*) *Israel:* response of Israel to the demands of the General Assembly concerning withdrawal from Egypt; and the possible stationing of UNEF in Israel; Israel asks the UN to administer Gaza; and to provide guarantees at Sharm el Sheikh; response of the Secretary-General; Israel's relations with UNEF during the fighting of 1967.
(*b*) *The United Kingdom and France:* eventual acceptance of cease-fire; attempts to secure conditions for withdrawal; offers to clear Canal rejected.

11. FINANCE (p. 415)
(*a*) *Apportionment of the costs between the UN and Contributing States:* detailed arrangements formulated by the General Assembly.
(*b*) *Apportionment of the UN's expenses among its members:*
  i. *The method employed for appropriating UNEF expenses:* the Special Account; the Working Capital Fund; arrangements of loans; voluntary contributions.
  ii. *The method of apportioning UNEF expenses:* views of Communist countries; Latin-American attitude; western viewpoint; attempts by Assembly to deal with these divergencies; benefits granted to less developed countries; the Assembly asks for an Advisory Opinion; the problem of arrears and Article 19; the Court's Opinion; subsequent events in the Assembly; the United States withdraws its insistence on the application of Article 19.

12. IMPLEMENTATION (p. 456)
(*a*) *Securing the cease-fire and cessation of hostilities.*
(*b*) *Supervising the withdrawal of foreign troops:* delays in achieving this objective; arrangements by which progress was made; Hammarskjöld's discussions with Israel.
(*c*) *Patrolling the armistice lines:* role of UNEF in respect of the Armistice; effectiveness of UNEF in reducing number and severity of frontier incidents.
(*d*) *Observation of the Armistice Agreement:* the question of passage through the Suez Canal and the Gulf of Aqaba; legal aspects; the demand for UNEF's withdrawal.
  The Secretary-General's study on the experience derived from UNEF; and his final annual report on UNEF.

13. ANNEXES (p. 526)
  A. Checklist of Documents (p. 526)
  B. Bibliography (p. 528)

I

INTRODUCTION

THE background to the establishment of UNEF is, of all the UN peacekeeping operations, the most extensively chronicled.[1] The ensuing editorial note makes no pretence at being comprehensive. Its task is to try to draw together the major strands in the history of 1956 which ended the reliance on UNTSO as the UN presence in Egyptian–Israeli relations, and instead led to the formation of UNEF. In spite of its abrupt and controversial demise in May 1967,[2] UNEF was a brilliant innovation, an extraordinarily imaginative departure in the affairs of the UN, reflecting particularly the inventiveness of its progenitor, Lester Pearson of Canada, and the capabilities of its begetter, Dag Hammarskjöld.

The Armistice Agreement between Israel and Egypt had been rapidly deteriorating. This period of Egyptian–Israeli relations has been covered in Part I, but we may here recall that fedayeen raids were occurring with frequency from Sinai and Gaza, and were the occasion of increasingly severe Israeli retaliation. The Suez Canal remained closed to Israel, with Egypt continuing to assert that she was exercising legitimate belligerent rights, in spite of the Security Council resolution of 1951 which denied the compatibility of the exercise of belligerent rights with the armistice. Egypt also commanded the entrance to the Gulf of Aqaba, at Sharm el Sheikh, which overlooked the Straits of Tiran. Here no international convention governed the waterway. As has been stated (p. 201), Israel claimed that the Gulf could not legally be shut to blockade one riparian; while Egypt again relied on rights of belligerency, and observed that the navigable passage of the Straits fell within her territorial waters.[3]

By April 1956 the Security Council had become so much concerned about matters that it asked the Secretary-General to undertake urgently a survey of the state of compliance with the Armistice Agreements. A detailed report, together with recommendations, was submitted by the Secretary-General on

---

[1] See Anthony Moncrieff, ed., *Suez: Ten Years After* (1967); Hugh Thomas, *The Suez Affair* (1967); Anthony Nutting, *No End of a Lesson* (1967); M. Dayan, *Diary of the Sinai Campaign* (1966); H. Azeau, *Le piège de Suez* (1964); T. Robertson, *Crisis* (1965); L. D. Epstein, *British Politics in the Suez Crisis* (1964); Peter Calvocoressi, 'Suez: Ten Years After', *The Listener*, 14, 21 July, 18 Aug. 1966.

[2] See below, pp. 338–49.

[3] After 1958 it was easier for Israel also to rely on the argument that the Straits constituted an international waterway which should remain open; for the Geneva Convention on Territorial Seas, in spite of opposition by Arab nations, incorporated a provision which characterized as straits a narrow passage of water linking high seas with high seas *or with territorial waters*. Egypt did not become a party to this convention, and how far this provision was in fact declaratory of existing law remains controversial. For further discussion on the question of the Gulf of Aqaba, see above, pp. 200–1.

9 May 1956.[4] On 2 June 1956 the Council unanimously adopted Resolution S/3605, urging the parties to co-operate with the Chief of Staff and the Secretary-General in putting into effect the practical proposals of the latter.

Conditions along the demarcation line surrounding the Gaza Strip had improved since the Security Council's resolution of April, but in the middle of July they began to deteriorate. The El Auja demilitarized zone was also the scene of tension.[5]

Armaments in the Middle East gave some cause for concern too. The control of armaments which the Tripartite Declaration of 1950 (between France, Britain, and the United States) had sought to impose had clearly broken down. The French were, under a secret agreement of 1954, supplying Mystère-2 fighter aircraft to Israel, and President Nasser, having failed to get arms from the West, obtained in July 1955 Russian weapons from Czechoslovakia.[6] An arms race was now on, and Israel secured a revision of her agreement with the French in order to obtain Mystère-4 fighters rather than Mystère-2s.

There had also occurred in 1955 the formation of the Baghdad Pact, which, given the inclusion of Nuri es Said's Iraq, Nasser viewed as an anti-Egyptian rather than an anti-Soviet alliance.[7] Exchanges over this had contributed to a deterioration in British–Egyptian relations. These were exacerbated over the removal of General Glubb from the command of the Jordan army, which was widely viewed as due to pressure from Nasser.[8] On 19 July 1956 the United States announced her decision not to proceed with her financing of the Aswan Dam project.[9]

On 26 July 1956 Nasser announced the nationalization of the Suez Canal Company, and declared that Canal dues would be used to finance the Aswan Dam. The Suez Canal Company was placed in the hands of an Egyptian operating authority. The decree provided for compensation on the basis of the market value of the shares on 25 July, upon receipt of all the assets and property of the

---

[4] See pp. 179–84.   [5] See pp. 154–7.

[6] Nasser's recognition of Peking at this time—a factor which was further to dismay the US Congress —is explained by Peter Calvocoressi: 'Nasser remained nervous about his Russian supplies because he feared that the British might talk the Russians into a new Middle East embargo during the visit of Bulganin and Khrushchev to London; he therefore recognized Peking in case he should need to turn in that direction' ('Suez: Ten Years After', *The Listener*, 14 July 1966, p. 45).

[7] Ibid. p. 46.

[8] Calvocoressi succinctly states: '[This] reinforced [the British] view of Nasser as a man determined to meddle all over the Arab world and unite it under his leadership, with the results of displacing British hegemony, preventing Britain from pursuing its traditional policy of keeping other powers (notably the Russians) out of the Middle East, threatening British communications through and beyond Suez, and endangering Britain's oil supplies' (ibid. p. 46).

[9] Robert Bowie lists the reasons as follows: (1) the conviction that Egypt's purchase of Czech arms would necessarily make it impossible for Egypt to contribute its agreed share to carry out the scheme; (2) that any prodding of Egyptian financiers would be resented; (3) that it was unwise to put into a single project all the money which Congress was likely to appropriate for Egypt for years to come, thus leaving other major projects which the Russians could take up for propaganda advantage; (4) Congress resented Nasser's anti-Israel stance as well as his recognition of Peking; (5) Congress was also very protection-minded over granting American money to build a dam which would contribute to the growth of cotton to compete with American cotton on the world market (Calvocoressi, p. 46).

Canal Company.[10] Nasser indicated that he remained bound by the obligation in the Constantinople Convention of 1888 to keep the Canal open at all times.

The hostility of British reaction was not limited to the Conservative Party. Hugh Gaitskell, Leader of the Opposition, stated 'we deeply deplore this high-handed and totally unjustifiable step by the Egyptian Government', and asked for the blocking of Egyptian balances.[11] The Conservative Party felt that the country's oil supplies were put at risk, that Egypt would be unable to run the Canal competently, that it was essential that Nasser be shown not to have succeeded. There was general feeling that if Britain did not act to redress the situation, she would 'become another Netherlands', instead of remaining a Great Power.[12] Above all, there was the feeling, keenly felt by the Prime Minister, Anthony Eden, and also by the Chancellor, Harold Macmillan, that the situation was 'another Munich'. Within the British government there was now disagreement as to the appropriate course to follow: Eden was not disposed to follow the Foreign Office's inclination to take the matter to the UN—he regarded that line of action as too slow.[13] A special 'inner Cabinet' was set up to examine the question; and a meeting of the British Chiefs of Staff on 27 July revealed that, for logistical reasons, immediate military action would be out of the question.[14]

President Eisenhower made it clear that his administration did not regard the use of force as an appropriate solution to this problem. Secretary of State Dulles, while not at this early stage expressly ruling out United States support for use of force, told Eden that other means could be found of tackling Nasser and the Suez Canal question. Eden apparently believed that, in the last resort, the United States would support military action by the British; while Dulles thought that lack of American support had been made plain. The personal, mutual dislike of the two men made common understanding all the more difficult. Although in the debates in the House of Commons on 2 and 3 August the government appeared to receive considerable support from the Opposition for a 'tougher' line, Gaitskell wrote to Eden after the debate saying that his

---

[10] Calvocoressi states: 'This, as I understand it, put him in the right legally so long as the compensation was adequate and credible; but if the dues were to be used for the dam the company had a pertinent question to ask about where the compensation was to come from' (ibid. p. 46). The international law standard obtaining at that time—whatever its status may be today—required that compensation for expropriation should be 'adequate, prompt and effective'. The decree certainly stipulated adequate compensation; but whether this could be made effective, and promptly met, was another matter. It may also be added that the whole legal question was made very much more complex by the fact that the Canal was an international waterway. Whereas international law clearly permits expropriation of foreign assets if adequate, prompt, and effective compensation is forthcoming, it is much more controversial whether this permissive principle extends to the nationalization of a company operating an international waterway. Non-parties of the Company have legal rights in the Canal by virtue of its status as an international waterway.

[11] H.C. Deb. 557, col. 778, 27 July 1956.

[12] Harold Macmillan to US envoy Robert Murphy (quoted in Thomas, p. 49). See also Eden's cable to Eisenhower: 'If we do not [take action] our influence and yours throughout the Middle East will, we are convinced, be finally destroyed' (ibid. p. 3).

[13] Nutting has also stated that Eden disliked Nasser so much that, even before the nationalization of the Canal Company, he was seeking ways to remove him.

[14] Thomas, pp. 41–43.

position had been misunderstood, and that he would not support any use of force which was not authorized by the UN. Eden, it would seem, saw this as a reversal of Gaitskell's promise of support, and henceforth scarcely consulted him.

The French, too, were affected by the expropriation of the Anglo-French Canal Company, and had other direct interests to consider. They believed that Nasser was the source of considerable support to the rebels in Algeria, and that no solution would be reached on the Algerian problem while Nasser remained in power.

The Canal, however, remained open and operated efficiently, and was to continue to do so even after the departure of the Canal Company employees on 15 September. After talks with France and the United States, the United Kingdom issued an invitation to a conference in London of all the parties to the Constantinople Convention of 1888, and to other nations largely concerned with the use of the Canal. Israel was not invited, nor were the Communist nations. President Nasser was invited. He declined, but proposed instead a conference of the forty-five users of the Canal, including the Communist users, to reconsider the 1888 Convention, and to confirm freedom of navigation through the Canal. The London Suez Conference went ahead, none the less, and 18 of the 22 nations attending agreed on proposals to be presented to Egypt:

The system was to assure: (1) efficient operation and development of the Canal and a free, open and secure international waterway; (2) insulation of that operation from the politics of any nation; (3) an equitable financial return to Egypt, increasing as the Canal was enlarged and used by more shipping; and (4) Canal duties as low as was consistent with the above provisions. To achieve these results, a Suez Canal Board was to operate, maintain and develop the Canal, the Board to include Egypt and to make periodic reports to the United Nations [*YBUN, 1956*, p. 19.]

The Prime Minister of Australia headed a five-nation committee which went to Cairo on 3 September to present this plan. It was rejected by Egypt, which stated that control or management of the operation of the Canal must be in Egyptian hands alone. International control and provisions for sanctions were unacceptable.

A second London Suez Conference was held between 19 and 21 September, where Egyptian counter-proposals were considered, but held by the supporters of the eighteen-Power plan to be too imprecise to afford a basis for further discussion. On 12 September France and the United Kingdom had placed the issue before the Security Council for the first time. Dulles, obviously fearing the imminent use of force, now urged the idea of a Suez Canal Users' Association (SCUA), which would take the form of an international organization with ships at each end of the Canal. Eden reluctantly agreed to promote this idea, though with many misgivings; and the French were very sceptical of it.[15] Military plans between the French and British were already under way, though the extensiveness of the preparations appears to have been known to very few. When parliament reconvened, the Labour Party now demanded that force

[15] Thomas, p. 77.

should only be used with the backing of the UN; and some Conservatives too urged reference to the UN.[16] The majority of the Conservative Party, however, believed that the United States would back the idea of a Users' Association with force if necessary; but Dulles now said, at a press conference, that the United States would not uphold SCUA by force: 'If we are met by force then we intend to send our boats around the Cape.'[17] Relations between Dulles and Eden deteriorated further, the latter feeling that he had been misled and betrayed. From this point on the United States was not kept fully informed by the United Kingdom. On 15 September the Soviet Union transmitted to the Security Council a protest at the formation of SCUA, which she declared to be incompatible with Egypt's sovereignty and a potential threat to peace. On 17 September Egypt informed the Security Council that she viewed SCUA (of which fifteen nations had become members) as a threat to the very independence of Egypt; the more so, as for ten days a full and indeed increased flow of traffic had been passing through the Canal.

On 5 October, without notifying Dulles (who now in turn felt aggrieved), Britain and France asked for a meeting of the UN and the Foreign Minister, Selwyn Lloyd, went to New York to handle the case for Britain.

There is evidence that since the second week of August Israel had been in the closest touch with France,[18] and that France was eager to push ahead with military action, concerted to follow up an Israeli pre-emptive attack. We have already noted that the *fedayeen* raids had been a security problem for Israel since April 1955, and that the Suez Canal and the Gulf of Aqaba were shut to her. Eden was informed of the Franco–Israeli talks, but the British Foreign Office, traditionally pro-Arab, were not told. It is believed[19] that on 3 October Eden for the first time told his full Cabinet that Israel might attack Egypt, thus putting the Anglo-French military arrangements into effect.

Meanwhile, at the UN, Hammarskjöld had lent his good offices to private negotiation between the French Foreign Secretary, Christian Pineau, Selwyn Lloyd, and the Egyptian Foreign Minister, Mahmoud Fawzi. By 12 October matters had progressed sufficiently for Hammarskjöld to prepare six points on which there seemed to be a measure of agreement: (1) free and open passage through the Canal without discrimination, overt or covert; (2) respect for the sovereignty of Egypt; (3) the insulation of the Canal from the politics of any country; (4) the manner of fixing tolls and dues to be settled between Egypt and the users; (5) a fair proportion of the dues to be allotted to development; (6) in the case of disputes, unresolved affairs between the Suez Canal Company and the Egyptian government to be settled by arbitration.[20] These points, comprising part of a draft resolution, were adopted unanimously by the Security Council on 13 October, and it looked for the first time as if prospects existed for progress.

In London and Paris however, policy was moving inexorably towards the use of force, in spite of the progress in New York. Secret arrangements were

[16] Ibid. pp. 81–82. [17] *The Times*, 14 Sept. 1956. [18] See Thomas, p. 86.
[19] Ibid. p. 96. [0] *YBUN, 1956*, p. 23.

proceeded with for an Anglo-French 'police' action following an Israeli attack upon Egypt. At the same time Selwyn Lloyd informed the United States Ambassador that there was some anxiety that Israel might attack Jordan,[21] with whom frontier tension and violence had been increasing. Britain had a defence treaty with Jordan and, after a major Israeli retaliation into Jordanian territory at Qalqilya on 10 October, indicated that she would support Jordan. Iraqi troops had already gone to Jordan's aid.[22]

There now seems ample evidence that a highly secret meeting took place at Sèvres on 23 October between the French, British, and Israelis, when plans for the Israeli attack, and the ensuing[23] 'police action' were co-ordinated, and formally agreed upon. The United States was not informed.

On 29 October Israel attacked Egypt, and the United States immediately asked the Council to determine that a breach of the peace had occurred and to order Israel to withdraw behind the armistice lines. The United States took this firm position in spite of the imminence of an election in which Jewish voters, especially in New York State, could be expected to oppose the administration's position. The Chief of Staff of UNTSO confirmed that Israel troops had violated the armistice and crossed the international frontier. Israel defended her action as security measures to eliminate Egyptian *fedayeen* bases in the Sinai peninsula, and claimed that this action was self-defence under Article 51 of the UN Charter.[24] On 30 October Britain and France sent joint ultimata to Egypt and Israel, calling upon both sides to stop all warlike action and to withdraw to within ten miles of the Canal. As Israel was not within ten miles of the Canal, this in fact allowed her to advance, and was accepted. Egypt rejected the ultimatum, finding it totally inappropriate that she should be told by Britain and France to cease the defence of her own territory. At dusk on 31 October a Franco-British air offensive began (France had already been clandestinely providing an air fighter umbrella to Israeli cities) on Egyptian airfields, and leaflets were dropped warning people to stay away from the air bases. Nasser now withdrew his forces to form a defence around Alexandria and Cairo; and he ordered the Canal to be blocked by sinking ships in it.

By this time there was very considerable political opposition in Britain: the Labour Party was vehemently attacking government policy, and the first questions were being asked about 'collusion' with Israel. Resignations were taking place within the Conservative Party.[25] Israel had by now accomplished her

[21] W. Aldrich, 'The Suez Crisis: A footnote to history', *Foreign Affairs* (1967), p. 541.

[22] Dayan (p. 59) has commented, in respect of these diversions on the Jordan frontier, 'I must confess to the feeling that, save for the Almighty, only the British are capable of complicating affairs to such a degree. At the very moment when they are preparing to topple Nasser . . . they insist on getting the Iraqi army into Jordan even if such action leads to war between Israel and Jordan in which they, the British, will take part against Israel.'

[22] On the Sèvres meeting, see Moncrieff, pp. 83–107; Thomas, p. 112–15; Robertson, pp. 157–74.

[24] For a legal analysis, see Higgins, *The Development of International Law through the Political Organs of the United Nations* (1963).

[25] The resignation of Anthony Nutting, Minister of State at the Foreign Office, was announced on 4 November; Sir Edward Boyle also resigned office, and Sir Walter Monckton sought a change of office. For a group of eleven Conservatives who prepared a letter of protest to Eden, see Thomas, pp. 138–9.

objectives—the removal of the *fedayeen* bases and the securing of Sharm el Sheikh at the entrance to the Gulf of Aqaba—and wished to accept the UN cease-fire, though Britain and France had not yet secured the desired control over the Canal, still less toppled Nasser. Eden announced that if the UN could provide an effective presence to separate the Egyptians and Israelis, Britain and France would withdraw. Not only did the UN take up this challenge of providing an effective UN force, but other pressures, in addition to those of world opinion, were making themselves felt. The position of sterling became very serious, and Macmillan now favoured an early end to the venture. The US was making her influence felt within the weighted voting system of the IMF, and no withdrawal of funds was permitted to the United Kingdom to meet the run on sterling. Eden, who had been ill throughout this period, now agreed to the UN's call for a cease-fire, as did Mollet, the French Premier.

Britain and France had cast negative votes in the Security Council on 30 October, and no resolution was agreed upon. The matter was, upon the suggestion of the Yugoslav delegate, transferred to the General Assembly under the Uniting for Peace procedure (by 7 to 2, with 2 abstentions: under this procedure only a simple majority is needed, with the veto not operative, to transfer a question to the Assembly).

The first emergency special session of the Assembly convened on 1 November and passed a series of resolutions calling for a cease-fire and a withdrawal by Israel, France, and Britain. These received overwhelming support, including the United States and all Commonwealth countries save for Australia and New Zealand. It was against this background that the idea of a UN international force began to emerge. The idea of UNEF came largely from Lester Pearson of Canada,[26] and was moulded and formulated by Hammarskjöld, and formally approved by the Assembly. The establishment of the Force met the interests of all the parties involved, and it remained in being until May 1967.

2

ENABLING RESOLUTIONS AND VOTING

THE draft proposal for the following resolution was submitted by the United States of America.

The General Assembly,

Noting the disregard on many occasions by parties to the Israel–Arab armistice agreements of 1949 of the terms of such agreements, and that the armed forces of Israel have penetrated deeply into Egyptian territory in violation of the General Armistice Agreement between Egypt and Israel of 24 February 1949,

[26] Robertson, esp. pp. 215-28.

Noting that armed forces of France and the United Kingdom of Great Britain and Northern Ireland are conducting military operations against Egyptian territory,

Noting that traffic through the Suez Canal is now interrupted to the serious prejudice of many nations,

Expressing its grave concern over these developments,

1. *Urges* as a matter of priority that all parties now involved in hostilities in the area agree to an immediate cease-fire and, as part thereof, halt the movement of military forces and arms into the area;

2. *Urges* the parties to the armistice agreements promptly to withdraw all forces behind the armistice lines, to desist from raids across the armistice lines into neighbouring territory, and to observe scrupulously the provisions of the armistice agreements;

3. *Recommends* that all Member States refrain from introducing military goods in the area of hostilities and in general refrain from any acts which would delay or prevent the implementation of the present resolution;

4. *Urges* that, upon the cease-fire being effective steps be taken to reopen the Suez Canal and restore secure freedom of navigation;

5. *Requests* the Secretary-General to observe and report promptly on the compliance with the present resolution to the Security Council and to the General Assembly, for such further action as they may deem appropriate in accordance with the Charter;

6. *Decides* to remain in emergency session pending compliance with the present resolution.

[*GA Res. 997* (ES–I), 2 Nov. *1956*.]

VOTING: 64–5, with 6 abstentions.

> *For:* Afghanistan, Albania, Argentina, Austria, Bolivia, Brazil, Bulgaria, Burma, Byelorussian SSR, Cambodia, Ceylon, Chile, China, Colombia, Costa Rica, Cuba, Czechoslovakia, Denmark, Dominican Republic, Ecuador, Egypt, El Salvador, Ethiopia, Finland, Greece, Guatemala, Haiti, Honduras, Hungary, Iceland, India, Indonesia, Iran, Iraq, Ireland, Italy, Jordan, Lebanon, Liberia, Libya, Mexico, Nepal, Nicaragua, Norway, Pakistan, Panama, Paraguay, Peru, Philippines, Poland, Romania, Saudi Arabia, Spain, Sweden, Syria, Thailand, Turkey, Ukrainian SSR, USSR, USA, Uruguay, Venezuela, Yemen, Yugoslavia.

Against: Australia, France, Israel, New Zealand, UK.

Abstaining: Belgium, Canada, Laos, Netherlands, Portugal, South Africa.

Certain representatives availed themselves of the right to explain their vote. The Canadian abstention, given the major role that Prime Minister Pearson was subsequently to play in the establishment of UNEF, merits explanation in full:

296. Mr. PEARSON (Canada): I rise not to take part in this debate, because the debate is over; the vote has been taken. But I do wish to explain the abstention of my delegation on that vote.

297. It is never easy to explain an abstention, and in this case it is particularly difficult, because we are in favour of some parts of this resolution, and also because this resolution deals with such a complicated question.

298. Because we are in favour of some parts of the resolution, we could not vote against it, especially as, in our opinion, it is a moderate proposal couched in reasonable and objective terms, without unfair or unbalanced condemnation; and also, by referring to violations by both sides to the armistice agreements, it puts, I think, recent action by the United Kingdom and France—and rightly—against the background of those repeated violations and provocations.

299. We support the effort being made to bring the fighting to an end. We support it, among other reasons, because we regret that force was used in the circumstances that face us at this time. As my delegation sees it, however, this resolution which the General Assembly has thus

adopted in its present form—and there was very little chance to alter that form—is inadequate to achieve the purposes which we have in mind at this session. Those purposes are defined in the resolution of the General Assembly under which we are meeting—resolution 377 (V), entitled 'Uniting for peace'—and peace is far more than ceasing to fire, although it certainly must include that essential factor.

300. This is the first time that action has been taken under the 'Uniting for peace' resolution, and I confess to a feeling of sadness, indeed even distress, at not being able to support the position taken by two countries whose ties with my country are and will remain close and intimate; two countries which have contributed so much to man's progress and freedom under law; and two countries which are Canada's mother countries.

301. I regret the use of military force in the circumstances which we have been discussing, but I regret also that there was not more time, before a vote was taken, for consideration of the best way to bring about that kind of cease-fire which would have enduring and beneficial results. I think that we were entitled to that time, for this is not only a tragic moment for the countries and peoples immediately affected, but it is an equally difficult time for the United Nations itself. I know, of course, that the situation is of special and, indeed, poignant urgency, a human urgency, and that action could not be postponed by dragging out a discussion, as has been done so often in this Assembly. I do feel, however, that had that time, which has always, to my knowledge, in the past been permitted for adequate examination of even the most critical and urgent resolution, been available on this occasion, the result might have been a better resolution. Such a short delay would not, I think, have done harm but, in the long run, would have helped those in the area who need help most at this time.

302. Why do I say this? In the first place, our resolution, though it has been adopted, is only a recommendation, and its moral effects would have been greater if it could have received a more unanimous vote in this Assembly—which might have been possible if there had been somewhat more delay.

303. Secondly, this recommendation which we have adopted cannot be effective without the compliance of those to whom it is addressed and who have to carry it out. I had ventured to hope that, by a short delay and in informal talks, we might have made some headway, or at least have tried to make some headway, in securing a favourable response, before the vote was taken, from those Governments and delegations which will be responsible for carrying it out.

304. I consider that there is one great omission from this resolution, which has already been pointed out by previous speakers—more particularly by the representative of New Zealand, who has preceded me. This resolution does provide for a cease-fire, and I admit that that is of first importance and urgency. But, alongside a cease-fire and a withdrawal of troops, it does not provide for any steps to be taken by the United Nations for a peace settlement, without which a cease-fire will be only of temporary value at best. Surely we should have used this opportunity to link a cease-fire to the absolute necessity of a political settlement in Palestine and for the Suez, and perhaps we might also have been able to recommend a procedure by which this absolutely essential process might begin.

305. Today we are facing a feeling of almost despairing crisis for the United Nations and for peace. Surely that feeling might have been harnessed to action, or at least for a formal resolve to act at long last and to do. [*GAOR, 1st emerg. spec. sess., 562nd plen. mtg.*]

The South African representative let it be known that he had abstained because, in the few hours since the draft resolution had been available, his government had 'had no time whatsoever to consider it in all its far-reaching implications'.[1] Sir Pierson Dixon, the United Kingdom representative, also had had no time to consult the British government on the resolution, but explained that 'I therefore felt obliged to vote against it, since it seems not consistent with the policy of my Government.'[2] More than this he did not venture

---

[1] 1st emerg. spec. sess., 562nd plen. mtg, para. 310. [2] Ibid. para. 311.

at this stage.[3] Israel did not offer an explanation after the vote was taken, but it was clear from earlier speeches made by Abba Eban that any resolution which fell short of providing certain guarantees to Israel against Egyptian harassment, would be unacceptable. The requirements which Israel stipulated were summarized in Mr Eban's statement:

Israel has no desire or intention to wield arms beyond the limits of its legitimate defensive mission. But whatever is demanded of us by way of restoring Egypt's rights and respecting Egypt's security under international law must surely be accompanied by equally binding Egyptian undertakings to respect Israel's security and Israel's rights under the identical law. Egypt's obligation to abstain from acts of hostility, to liquidate its commando activities, to abolish its illicit discrimination against Israel shipping in the Suez Canal and in the Gulf of Aqaba, is equal and identical in law to Israel's obligation to respect the established armistice lines. Our signpost is not backward to belligerency, but forward to peace. Whatever Israel is now asked to do for Egypt must have its counterpart in Egypt's reciprocal duty to give Israel the plenitude of its rights. [*Ibid.* para. 159.)

The French government based its opposition to the resolution partly on constitutional grounds,[4] and partly because it felt that the draft merely 'singled out one incident' of a much wider problem.[5] The resolution separated the situation in the Sinai peninsula from the Suez question which had led up to it, and indeed from Arab breaches of the armistice with Israel which had been protected by the Russian veto.

New Zealand voted against the resolution not only because she had 'full confidence in the intentions of the United Kingdom in moving forces into the Suez Canal zone . . . [accepting] that its operations are designed solely to protect the Suez Canal and to halt the fighting between Israel and Egyptian forces',[6] but also because the resolution contained certain defects as to the future course of action to be taken:

As I read the draft resolution, it appears to raise more questions than it answers. Who, for example, is to take steps to re-open the Suez Canal and restore secure freedom of navigation? . . . [There is no] proposal for dealing effectively with the situation in the Middle East as a whole, a situation which has been so seriously aggravated by the action of the Egyptian government in seizing the Suez Canal. [*Ibid.* para. 282.]

The other states which did not vote for Assembly Resolution 997 (ES–I), Australia, Portugal, Belgium, Laos, and the Netherlands—did not explain their votes. It may be reasonably assumed that the Australian view was identical with that expressed by Sir Leslie Munro on behalf of New Zealand.

On 3 November 1956 the Assembly adopted two further resolutions, nos 998 (ES–I) and 999 (ES–I). The former, which contained the seed of the idea that was to become UNEF, was sponsored by Canada; and the latter represented a nineteen-Power proposal.

The General Assembly,
Bearing in mind the urgent necessity of facilitating compliance with the resolution 997 (ES–I) of 2 November 1956,

[3] For the reservations of the UK on the constitutional—as opposed to political—issue, see below, p. 261.
[4] See below, p. 261.   [5] 1st emerg. spec. sess., 562nd plen. mtg, para. 216.   [6] Ibid. para. 278.

Requests, as a matter of priority, the Secretary-General to submit to it within forty-eight hours a plan for the setting up, with the consent of the nations concerned, of an emergency international United Nations Force to secure and supervise the cessation of hostilities in accordance with all the terms of the aforementioned resolution. [*GA Res. 998 (ES–I), 4 Nov. 1956.*]

VOTING: 57–0, with 19 abstentions.

    For: Afghanistan, Argentina, Belgium, Bolivia, Brazil, Burma, Cambodia, Canada, Ceylon, Chile, China, Colombia, Costa Rica, Cuba, Denmark, Dominican Republic, Ecuador, El Salvador, Ethiopia, Finland, Greece, Guatemala, Haiti, Honduras, Iceland, India, Indonesia, Iran, Iraq, Ireland, Italy, Jordan, Lebanon, Liberia, Libya, Luxembourg, Mexico, Nepal, Netherlands, Nicaragua, Norway, Pakistan, Panama, Paraguay, Peru, Philippines, Saudi Arabia, Spain, Sweden, Syria, Thailand, Turkey, Uruguay, USA, Venezuela, Yemen, Yugoslavia.

Abstaining: Albania, Australia, Austria, Bulgaria, Byelorussian SSR, Czechoslovakia, Egypt, France, Hungary, Israel, Laos, New Zealand, Poland, Portugal, Romania, Ukrainian SSR, UK, Union of South Africa, USSR.

It will be seen that, in the proposal to establish a UN Force, the USSR and allies found themselves in the same company as the United Kingdom and France—though for greatly differing reasons.

The United Kingdom reason for abstaining was once again somewhat oblique. After declaring that she believed 'that police action of the most urgent kind is called for . . . [and] the sooner the United Nations can take over from us the more we shall welcome that',[7] Sir Pierson Dixon added: 'It does seem to me that in some respects the resolution goes too far and in others not far enough. It was for that reason that I was not able to vote for the resolution, but, equally, I was able to abstain.'[8]

It was apparent that the United Kingdom representative was having difficulties in obtaining precise instructions from London.

The French representative indicated that 'I abstained in the vote on the draft resolution proposed by the Canadian delegation chiefly because of its reference to the resolution adopted by this Assembly[9] which we did not accept'.[10] Equally, Australia pronounced herself in favour of the proposal that the Secretary-General should submit a plan for the setting up of an Emergency Force to secure and supervise the cessation of hostilities—but abstention was necessary because 'this proposal is embodied in a resolution of two days ago, against which we voted'.[11] The same reason for abstention was offered by New Zealand, who, however, not only indicated her support for a UN Force, but also her willingness to contribute troops to it.[12] The Portuguese delegation stated that its abstention was due to lack of time to refer the draft to its government, but that it had 'every reason to believe that the Portuguese Government favours the principle that is embodied in the resolution'.[13]

The Communist reasons for abstention were different, though at this stage they were not fully articulated. The Czechoslovak delegate merely said: 'We abstained from voting on the Canadian draft resolution because we have serious doubts as to its possible implications and effectiveness.'[14] The Romanian dele-

---

[7] 1st emerg. spec. sess., 563rd plen. mtg, para. 292.   [8] Ibid. para. 293.
[9] 997 (ES–1).   [10] Ibid. para. 307.   [11] Ibid. para. 297.   [12] Ibid. para. 354.
[13] Ibid. para. 363.   [14] Ibid. para. 371.

gate limited himself to stating that it was the nineteen-Power draft resolution[15] which met the needs of the situation, and therefore it was that which had his support.[16] He did not explain why he regarded them as incompatible. An identical view was offered by the Ukrainian delegate;[17] somewhat mystifyingly, the Bulgarian delegate observed that, because he believed the UN should take all necessary measures to attain a cease-fire and withdrawal of foreign troops from Egypt, he had 'voted for the resolution which the General Assembly adopted on 2 November and for the resolutions which it adopted today'.[18] But the record clearly shows that Bulgaria did *not* vote for the Canadian resolution, though she did for the nineteen-Power one. The Soviet Union did not avail herself of the opportunity to explain her vote.

The nineteen-Power draft was adopted by the Assembly on the same day:

The General Assembly,

Noting with regret that not all the parties concerned have yet agreed to comply with the provisions of its resolution 997 (ES–I) of 2 November 1956,

Noting the special priority given in that resolution to an immediate cease-fire and, as part thereof, to the halting of the movement of military forces and arms into the area,

Nothing further that the resolution urged the parties to the armistice agreements promptly to withdraw all forces behind the armistice lines, to desist from raids across the armistice lines into neighbouring territory, and to observe scrupulously the provisions of the armistice agreements,

1. *Reaffirms* its resolution 997 (ES–I) and once again calls upon the parties immediately to comply with the provisions of the said resolution;

2. *Authorizes* the Secretary-General immediately to arrange with the parties concerned for the implementation of the cease-fire and the halting of the movement of military forces and arms into the area, and requests him to report compliance forthwith and, in any case, not later than twelve hours from the time of adoption of the present resolution;

3. *Requests* the Secretary-General, with the assistance of the Chief of Staff and the members of the United Nations Truce Supervision Organization, to obtain compliance of the withdrawal of all forces behind the armistice lines;

4. *Decides* to meet again immediately on receipt of the Secretary-General's report referred to in paragraph 2 of the present resolution. [*GA Res. 999 (ES–I), 3 Nov. 1956.*]

VOTING: 59–5, with 12 abstentions.

> *For:* Afghanistan, Albania, Argentina, Austria, Bolivia, Brazil, Bulgaria, Burma, Byelorussian SSR, Cambodia, Canada, Ceylon, Chile, China, Colombia, Costa Rica, Cuba, Czechoslovakia, Ecuador, Egypt, El Salvador, Ethiopia, Greece, Guatemala, Haiti, Honduras, Hungary, India, Indonesia, Iran, Iraq, Ireland, Italy, Jordan, Lebanon, Liberia, Libya, Mexico, Nepal, Nicaragua, Pakistan, Panama, Paraguay, Peru, Philippines, Poland, Romania, Saudi Arabia, Spain, Syria, Thailand, Turkey, Ukrainian SSR, Uruguay, USA, USSR, Venezuela, Yemen, Yugoslavia.

Against: Australia, France, Israel, New Zealand, UK.

The votes require little explanation. Sir Pierson Dixon explained that Resolution 999 was unacceptable simply because

. . . it sets out in a more emphatic form the resolution adopted by the General Assembly

---

[15] Adopted as Res. 999 (ES–I.)   [16] Ibid. para. 348.   [17] Ibid. para. 324.
[18] Ibid. para. 329.

forty-eight hours ago and, in our view, does not go to the root of the problem, as my Government sees it. In our view, if we followed the course of that resolution it would only lead us back to the unhappy and increasingly dangerous state of affairs that has already prevailed for far too long in that part of the world and that has caused the recent tragic outburst of violence by Israel against Egypt. [*1st emerg. spec. sess., 563rd mtg, para. 294.*]

The other nations voting against the resolution took the same view, the Australian representative quoting Prime Minister Menzies' opinion that 'that the author of the Suez Canal confiscation and the promoter of anti-British and anti-Israel activities in the Middle East should now be represented as the innocent victim of unprovoked aggression is, of course, both wrong and absurd'.[19]

So far as abstentions are concerned, it is interesting to compare the list with those abstaining on Resolution 997 (given the argument that Resolution 999 was merely a 'more emphatic form' of that earlier resolution). Canada no longer figures among the abstainers—Mr Pearson explained that if the machinery set up under his draft were approved, then the nineteen-Power resolution would be both compatible and acceptable.[20] Portugal, South Africa, Belgium, Laos, and the Netherlands were now joined by the Nordic countries—Iceland, Finland, Denmark, Norway, and Sweden. Of this group only the representative of Denmark spoke after the vote, and although he was very critical of the United Kingdom and France, he did not explain his abstention on the nineteen-Power resolution.[21]

The Secretary-General, showing extraordinary competence and resilience, met the requests of Resolution 998, and submitted a plan (A/3289). This made it possible for the Assembly to adopt the following resolution in the early hours of 5 November, which had been proposed jointly by Canada, Norway, and Colombia:

The General Assembly,

Having requested the Secretary-General, in its resolution 998 (ES–I) of 4 November 1956, to submit to it a plan for an emergency international United Nations Force, for the purposes stated,

Noting with satisfaction the first report of the Secretary-General on the plan (A/3289), and having in mind particularly paragraph 4 of that report,

1. *Establishes* a United Nations Command for an emergency international Force to secure and supervise the cessation of hostilities in accordance with all the terms of General Assembly resolution 997 (ES–I) of 2 November 1956;

2. *Appoints,* on an emergency basis, the Chief of Staff of the United Nations Truce Supervision Organization, Major-General E. L. M. Burns, as Chief of the Command;

3. *Authorizes* the Chief of the Command immediately to recruit, from the observer corps of the United Nations Truce Supervision Organization, a limited number of officers who shall be nationals of countries other than those having permanent membership in the Security Council, and further authorizes him, in consultation with the Secretary-General, to undertake the recruitment directly, from various Member States other than the permanent members of the Security Council, of the additional number of officers needed;

4. *Invites* the Secretary-General to take such administrative measures as may be necessary for the prompt execution of the actions envisaged in the present resolution. [*GA Res. 1000 (ES–I), 5 Nov. 1956.*]

---

[19] 1st emerg. spec. sess., 563rd mtg, para. 296.   [20] Ibid. para. 105   [21] Ibid. paras. 356–9.

VOTING: 57–0, with 19 abstentions.

    For: Afghanistan, Argentina, Austria, Belgium, Bolivia, Brazil, Burma, Cambodia, Canada, Ceylon, Chile, China, Colombia, Costa Rica, Cuba, Denmark, Dominican Republic, Ecuador, El Salvador, Ethiopia, Finland, Greece, Guatemala, Haiti, Honduras, Iceland, India, Indonesia, Iran, Iraq, Ireland, Italy, Jordan, Lebanon, Liberia, Libya, Luxembourg, Mexico, Nepal, Netherlands, Nicaragua, Norway, Pakistan, Panama, Paraguay, Peru, Philippines, Saudi Arabia, Spain, Sweden, Syria, Thailand, Uruguay, USA, Venezuela, Yemen, Yugoslavia.

    Against: None.

    Abstaining: Albania, Australia, Bulgaria, Byelorussian SSR, Czechoslovakia, Egypt, France, Hungary, Israel, Laos, New Zealand, Poland, Portugal, Romania, Turkey, UK, Ukrainian SSR, Union of South Africa, USSR.

It will be seen that all abstainers and opponents of previous resolutions now abstained—joined by Turkey, and by Egypt herself. Sir Leslie Munro explained that while he approved of everything in the resolution, it had been voted on so hastily that he had had no time to get explicit instructions from his government, and had therefore abstained.[22] The same reason was offered by France and the United Kingdom. The Egyptian representative, too, declared himself 'not at the moment in a position to give his views' on the resolution.[23] Turkey did not explain her vote, but probably the same considerations obtained.

On 7 November two more resolutions were adopted. The text of Resolution 1001 (ES–I) was proposed by Argentina, Burma, Ceylon, Denmark, Ecuador, Ethiopia, and Sweden. Resolution 1002 (ES–I) was proposed by Afghanistan, Burma, Ceylon, Ethiopia, India, Indonesia, Iran, Iraq, Jordan, Lebanon, Liberia, Libya, Nepal, Pakistan, Philippines, Saudi Arabia, Syria, Thailand, and Yemen.

The General Assembly,

Recalling its resolution 997 (ES–I) of 2 November 1956 concerning the cease-fire, withdrawal of troops and other matters related to the military operations in Egyptian territory, as well as its resolution 998 (ES–I) of 4 November 1956 concerning the request to the Secretary-General to submit a plan for an emergency international United Nations Force,

Having established by its resolution 1000 (ES–I) of 5 November 1956 a United Nations Command for an emergency international Force, having appointed the Chief of Staff of the United Nations Truce Supervision Organization as Chief of the Command with authorization to him to begin the recruitment of officers for the Command, and having invited the Secretary-General to take the administrative measures necessary for the prompt execution of that resolution.

Noting with appreciation the second and final report of the Secretary-General (A/3302) on the plan for an emergency international United Nations Force as requested in General Assembly resolution 998 (ES–I), and having examined that plan,

    1. *Expresses its approval* of the guiding principles for the organization and functioning of the emergency international United Nations Force as expounded in paragraphs 6 to 9 of the Secretary-General's report;

    2. *Concurs* in the definition of the functions of the Force as stated in paragraph 12 of the Secretary General's report;

    3. *Invites* the Secretary-General to continue discussions with Governments of Member States concerning offers of participation in the Force, toward the objective of its balanced composition;

---

[22] 1st emerg. spec. sess. 565th ple n. mtg, para. 110.   [23] Ibid. para. 18.

4. *Requests* the Chief of the Command, in consultation with the Secretary-General as regards size and composition, to proceed forthwith with the full organization of the Force;

5. *Approves provisionally* the basic rule concerning the financing of the Force laid down in paragraph 15 of the Secretary-General's report;

6. *Establishes* an Advisory Committee composed of one representative from each of the following countries: Brazil, Canada, Ceylon, Colombia, India, Norway and Pakistan, and requests this Committee, whose Chairman shall be the Secretary-General, to undertake the development of those aspects of the planning for the Force and its operation not already dealt with by the General Assembly and which do not fall within the area of the direct responsibility of the Chief of the Command;

7. *Authorizes* the Secretary-General to issue all regulations and instructions which may be essential to the effective functioning of the Force, following consultation with the Committee aforementioned, and to take all other necessary administrative and executive action;

8. *Determines* that, following the fulfilment of the immediate responsibilities defined for it in operative paragraphs 6 and 7 above, the Advisory Committee shall continue to assist the Secretary-General in the responsibilities falling to him under the present and other relevant resolutions;

9. *Decides* that the Advisory Committee, in the performance of its duties, shall be empowered to request through the usual procedures, the convening of the General Assembly and to report to the Assembly whenever matters arise which, in its opinion, are of such urgency and importance as to require consideration by the General Assembly itself;

10. *Requests* all Member States to afford assistance as necessary to the United Nations Command in the performance of its functioning, including arrangements for passage to and from the area involved.   [*GA Res. 1001 (ES–I), 7 Nov. 1956.*]

VOTING: 64–0, with 12 abstentions.

> *For:* Afghanistan, Argentina, Australia, Austria, Belgium, Bolivia, Brazil, Burma, Cambodia, Canada, Ceylon, Chile, China, Colombia, Costa Rica, Cuba, Denmark, Dominican Republic, Ecuador, El Salvador, Ethiopia, Finland, France, Greece, Guatemala, Haiti, Honduras, Iceland, India, Indonesia, Iran, Iraq, Ireland, Italy, Jordan, Laos, Lebanon, Liberia, Libya, Luxembourg, Mexico, Nepal, Netherlands, New Zealand, Nicaragua, Norway, Pakistan, Panama, Paraguay, Peru, Philippines, Portugal, Saudi Arabia, Spain, Sweden, Syria, Thailand, Turkey, UK, Uruguay, USA, Venezuela, Yemen, Yugoslavia.

Against: None.

Abstaining: Albania, Bulgaria, Byelorussian SSR, Czechoslovakia, Egypt, Hungary, Israel, Poland, Romania, Ukrainian SSR, Union of South Africa, USSR.

It will be seen that South Africa parted company with Britain, Australia, and New Zealand, and abstained, along with Egypt, Israel, and the Communist nations. (Yugoslavia throughout these resolutions voted with the majority.) Poland had indicated that her objection to this resolution lay in the fact that no eastern European country was represented in the Advisory Committee established under paragraph 6. The Polish representative said that if an amendment was carried to allow Czech participation in the Advisory Committee, he would vote for the resolution. His suggestion was rejected by 31 to 23, with 14 abstentions.

The Soviet Union explained her abstention on different grounds, contending that the establishment of the Force under Resolution 1000 (ES–1), and the plan for its implementation in Resolution 1001 (ES–1), were contrary to the Charter.[24] The only reason for abstaining, rather than voting against the pro-

[24] For details of the Soviet view, see the section on the constitutional basis of UNEF, below, pp. 260–4.

posal, lay in the hope of preventing any further extension of the aggression.[25]

The United Kingdom and France indicated that the resolution was acceptable because it provided, as they had urged, for an effective international force in the area. Israel and South Africa did not explain their vote. Nor did Egypt— but her abstention may be taken as a desire to indicate that she was accepting UNEF reluctantly, as one forced into this position because of the Anglo-Israel-French intervention.

The nineteen-Power draft resolution was adopted on the same day:

The General Assembly,

Recalling its resolution 997 (ES–I) of 2 November 1956, 998 (ES–I) and 999 (ES–I) of 4 November 1956 and 1000 (ES–I) of 5 November 1956, adopted by overwhelming majorities,

Noting in particular that the General Assembly, by its resolution 1000 (ES–I), established a United Nations Command for an emergency international Force to secure and supervise the cessation of hostilities in accordance with all the terms of its resolution 997 (ES–I),

1. *Reaffirms* the above-mentioned resolutions;

2. *Calls once again upon* Israel immediately to withdraw all its forces behind the armistice lines established by the General Armistice Agreement between Egypt and Israel of 24 February 1949,

3. *Calls once again upon* the United Kingdom and France immediately to withdraw all their forces from Egyptian territory, consistently with the above-mentioned resolutions;

4. *Urges* the Secretary-General to communicate the present resolution to the parties concerned, and requests him promptly to report to the General Assembly on the compliance with this resolution. [*GA Res. 1002 (ES–I), 7 Nov. 1956.*]

VOTING: 65–1, with 10 abstentions.

For: Afghanistan, Albania, Argentina, Austria, Bolivia, Brazil, Bulgaria, Burma, Byelorussian SSR, Cambodia, Canada, Ceylon, Chile, China, Colombia, Costa Rica, Cuba, Czechoslovakia, Denmark, Dominican Republic, Ecuador, Egypt, El Salvador, Ethiopia, Finland, Greece, Guatemala, Haiti, Honduras, Hungary, Iceland, India, Indonesia, Iran, Iraq, Ireland, Italy, Jordan, Lebanon, Liberia, Libya, Mexico, Nepal, Nicaragua, Norway, Pakistan, Panama, Paraguay, Peru, Philippines, Poland, Romania, Saudi Arabia, Spain, Sweden, Syria, Thailand, Turkey, Ukrainian SSR USA, USSR, Uruguay, Venezuela, Yemen, Yugoslavia.

Against: Israel.

Abstaining: Australia, Belgium, France, Laos, Luxembourg, Netherlands, New Zealand, Portugal, Union of South Africa, UK.

Israel cast the sole negative vote. The Soviet Union and her allies voted affirmatively; France, the United Kingdom, Australia, and New Zealand abstained, and were joined by Belgium, Luxembourg, the Netherlands, Laos, Portugal, and South Africa. The complexity of all the aspects of this problem was revealed in the variations in the voting pattern during these critical days. The Nordic countries, which had abstained on Resolution 999 (ES–I), no longer ranked among the abstainers. With the passage of time, too, certain states preferred to abstain rather than vote against the clear will of the Assembly.

For New Zealand, Sir Leslie Munro explained that:

85. The second draft resolution before us (*A/3309*) calls, *inter alia*, upon the United King-

---

[25] 1st emerg. spec. sess., 567th mtg, para. 297.

dom and France once again 'immediately to withdraw'—I stress the word 'immediately'—'all their forces from Egyptian territory'.

86. In the view of my delegation, the withdrawal of United Kingdom and French forces must be related to the readiness of an effective and suitably constituted United Nations force to establish itself in the area. An immediate withdrawal—construing the word literally—might make it extremely difficult for a United Nations force to take up its position in the area and perform its intended functions. For this reason alone, my delegation cannot support the draft resolution submitted by the nineteen countries.

87. My delegation is also obliged to note, however, that, considered as a whole, the draft resolution is no more than an unconstructive repetition of resolutions adopted in a situation which differed from that which obtains today. Since the Assembly last met, substantial progress has been made towards restoring peace and order in the Middle East. Any resolution we may now adopt should at the very least take account of events. Let us be realistic. [*1st emerg. spec. sess., 567th plen. mtg.*]

Similar observations were made by the Australian representative:

118. The draft resolution ignores the offer made previously by the United Kingdom and France, which has been followed up by the introduction of a cease-fire. More than that, the draft would appear to obstruct, in our view, the operation of setting up the international force which has been proposed in the other draft resolution that is before the Assembly. [*Ibid.*]

France indicated that the problem in supporting the nineteen-Power draft lay in the fact that the words 'immediately to withdraw all their forces from Egyptian territory' could lead to a power vacuum between Egyptian and Israel forces. The withdrawal could only be subsequent to proof of the effective operation of UNEF.[26] Sir Pierson Dixon spoke to the same effect,[27] as did the Belgian representative.[28]

In General Assembly Resolution 1003 (ES–I) it was decided to refer the matter to the eleventh regular session of the Assembly, which was then convening. A cluster of resolutions was adopted during this session. Resolution 1120 (XI) was proposed by Afghanistan, Burma, Cambodia, Ceylon, Ethiopia, India, Indonesia, Iran, Saudi Arabia, Sudan, Syria, Tunisia, and the Yemen, and was adopted at the 594th plenary meeting.

The General Assembly,

Having received the report of the Secretary-General on compliance with General Assembly resolutions 997 (ES–I) and 1002 (ES–I) of 2 and 7 November 1956,

Recalling that its resolution 1002 (ES–I) called upon Israel immediately to withdraw its forces behind the demarcation line established by the General Armistice Agreement between Egypt and Israel of 24 February 1949,

Recalling further that the above-mentioned resolution also called upon France and the United Kingdom of Great Britain and Northern Ireland immediately to withdraw their forces from Egyptian territory, in conformity with previous resolutions,

1. *Notes with regret* that, according to the communications received by the Secretary-General, two-thirds of the French forces remain, all the United Kingdom forces remain although it has been announced that arrangements are being made for the withdrawal of one battalion, and no Israel forces have been withdrawn behind the armistice line although a considerable time has elapsed since the adoption of the relevant General Assembly resolutions;

2. *Reiterates* its call to France, Israel and the United Kingdom of Great Britain and

---

[26] 1st emerg. spec. sess., 567th plen. mtg, paras 129–30.   [27] Ibid. paras 99–100.
[28] Ibid. para 302.

Northern Ireland to comply forthwith with resolutions 997 (ES–I) and 1002 (ES–I) of 2 and 7 November 1956;

3. *Requests* the Secretary-General urgently to communicate the present resolution to the parties concerned, and to report without delay to the General Assembly on the implementation thereof. [*GA Res. 1120 (XI), 24 Nov. 1956.*]

VOTING: 63–5, with 10 abstentions.
   For: Afghanistan, Albania, Argentina, Austria, Bolivia, Brazil, Bulgaria, Burma, Byelorussian SSR, Cambodia, Ceylon, Chile, Colombia, Costa Rica, Czechoslovakia, Denmark, Ecuador, Egypt, El Salvador, Ethiopia, Finland, Greece, Guatemala, Haiti, Honduras, Hungary, Iceland, India, Indonesia, Iran, Iraq, Ireland, Jordan, Laos, Lebanon, Liberia, Libya, Mexico, Morocco, Nepal, Norway, Pakistan, Panama, Paraguay, Peru, Philippines, Poland, Romania, Saudi Arabia, Spain, Sudan, Sweden, Syria, Thailand, Tunisia, Turkey, Ukrainian SSR, USA, USSR, Uruguay, Venezuela, Yemen, Yugoslavia.
   Against: Australia, France, Israel, New Zealand, UK.
   Abstaining: Belgium, Canada, China, Cuba, Dominican Republic, Italy, Luxembourg, Netherlands, Portugal, Union of South Africa.

It will be seen that while Laos now voted in favour of the resolution, Italy, China, Cuba, Canada, and the Dominican Republic abstained for the first time. France and the United Kingdom voted against the resolution because it 'attributes to us ulterior motives which we do not have and—for a calculated effect—casts doubt on our good faith'.[29] Belgium found it necessary to abstain, because although she was in favour of the withdrawal of French, British, and Israeli troops, she felt that the first operative paragraph made no reference to subsequent communications by France, the UK, and Israel as to the announcement of withdrawals.[30] M. Spaak indicated that he was also speaking on behalf of the Netherlands and Luxembourg. The Israeli representative found this in fact reason enough for voting against the resolution: 'Thousands of our armed forces have . . . been withdrawn from Egypt. . . . It is not a matter of opinion here; it is a matter of fact.'[31] South Africa declared that she accepted the assurance of the British Foreign Minister that the British–French forces would be withdrawn as soon as UNEF could carry out the tasks assigned to it, and consequently could not vote for the immediate withdrawal of these forces.[32] Italy, China, Cuba, Canada, and the Dominican Republic did not explain their votes, but their reason must be assumed to lie in support of Belgium's position, as they voted in favour of a Belgian amendment to this effect. (The amendment was rejected, 37 votes to 23, with 18 abstentions.)[33]

Another resolution, proposed by Canada, Colombia, India, Norway, Yugoslavia, and the USA was adopted on the same day:

The General Assembly,

Having received the report of the Secretary-General on basic points for the presence and functioning in Egypt of the United Nations Emergency Force,

Having received also the report of the Secretary-General on arrangements for clearing the Suez Canal,

[29] *GAOR*, 11th sess., 593rd plen. mtg, para. 116.
[30] Ibid. 594th plen. mtg, paras 14–19.
[31] Ibid. paras 46 and 48.   [32] Ibid. para. 59.   [33] Ibid. para. 148.

1. *Notes with approval* the contents of the *aide-mémoire* on the basis for the presence and functioning of the United Nations Emergency Force in Egypt, as annexed to the report of the Secretary-General;

2. *Notes with approval* the progress so far made by the Secretary-General in connexion with arrangements for clearing the Suez Canal, as set forth in his report;

3. *Authorizes* the Secretary-General to proceed with the exploration of practical arrangements and the negotiation of agreements so that the clearing operations may be speedily and effectively undertaken. [*GA Res. 1121 (XI), 24 Nov. 1956.*]

VOTING: 65–0, with 9 abstentions.

The records give no breakdown of the voting on this resolution. By deduction, however, one may assume that the nine abstaining nations were the Communist Powers.[34]

On 26 November the Assembly adopted Resolution 1122 (XI) by 52 to 9 votes, with 13 abstentions. This draft resolution was submitted by the Secretary-General, and concerned the financing of UNEF: details will be found below (p. 431). (All the resolutions concerning finance are collected in Section 11.)

On 19 January 1957 a further resolution was adopted by the Assembly, concerning Israel's withdrawal.[35]

The General Assembly,

Recalling its resolutions 997 (ES–I) of 2 November 1956, 998 (ES–I) and 999 (ES–I) of 4 November 1956, 1002 (ES–I) of 7 November 1956 and 1120 (XI) of 24 November 1956,

Noting the report of the Secretary-General of 15 January 1957,

1. *Notes with regret and concern* the failure of Israel to comply with the terms of the above-mentioned resolutions;

2. *Requests* the Secretary-General to continue his efforts for securing the complete withdrawal of Israel in pursuance of the above-mentioned resolutions, and to report on such completion to the General Assembly, within five days. [*GA Res. 1123 (XI), 642nd plen. mtg, 19 Jan. 1957.*]

VOTING: 74–2, with 2 abstentions.
Against: France, Israel.
Abstaining: Costa Rica, Cuba.

Not only are the two abstaining countries here of interest, but so is the split in voting between the United Kingdom, on the one hand, and Israel and France on the other. Israel stated 'in complete candour . . . that a policy consisting only of withdrawal without simultaneous related measures would lead to results such as war at sea and on land. . . .'[36] France agreed with the view that Israel was entitled to certain guarantees, concerning protection from *fedayeen* raids, and freedom of passage through the Canal, before completing her withdrawal from Egypt.[37] The United Kingdom too felt that Israel's demands were eminently reasonable; but she voted for the resolution because, while she 'considered that the Government of Israel had very serious grievances

[34] France and the UK had indicated that they would vote for the resolution: *GAOR*, 11th sess., 893rd mtg, paras. 116 and 129.
[35] For details of the Israeli position, and reactions thereto, see below, pp. 386–403.
[36] 11th sess. 642nd plen. mtg, para. 113.   [37] Ibid. paras 28–38.

against the Government of Egypt . . . it does not consider, and it never did consider, that this justified the attack on Egypt'.[38]

A further resolution concerning Israel was adopted at the 652nd plenary meeting on 2 February:

The General Assembly,

Recalling its resolutions 997 (ES–I) of 2 November 1956, 998 (ES–I) and 999 (ES–I) of 4 November 1956, 1002 (ES–I) of 7 November 1956, 1120 (XI) of 24 November 1956 and 1123 (XI) of 19 January 1957,

1. *Deplores* the non-compliance of Israel to complete its withdrawal behind the armistice demarcation line despite the repeated requests of the General Assembly;

2. *Calls upon* Israel to complete its withdrawal behind the armistice demarcation line without further delay.   [*GA Res. 1124 (XI), 2 Feb. 1957.*]

VOTING: 74–2, with 2 abstentions.

Those voting against were Israel and France. But the abstainers, instead of being Costa Rica and Cuba, were this time Luxembourg and the Netherlands. Costa Rica and Cuba cast affirmative votes. They offered no explanation for this change of attitude. The Netherlands representative stated: 'That my delegation will also abstain on [this] draft resolution is obvious from the stand which we have consistently taken in previous discussions on this matter.'[39] One may note, however, that the Netherlands did not, despite these remarks, abstain on Resolution 1123 (XI). Luxembourg did not explain her vote.

The same seven Powers who had submitted this resolution (Brazil, Colombia, India, Indonesia, Norway, the United States and Yugoslavia), submitted a further resolution which was also carried, though with a greater number of abstentions:

The General Assembly,

Having received the report of the Secretary-General of 24 January 1957,

Recognizing that withdrawal by Israel must be followed by action which would assure progress towards the creation of peaceful conditions,

1. *Notes with appreciation* the Secretary-General's report and the measures therein to be carried out upon Israel's complete withdrawal;

2. *Calls upon* the Governments of Egypt and Israel scrupulously to observe the provisions of the General Armistice Agreement between Egypt and Israel of 24 February 1949;

3. *Considers* that, after full withdrawal of Israel from the Sharm el Sheikh and Gaza areas, the scrupulous maintenance of the Armistice Agreement requires the placing of the United Nations Emergency Force on the Egyptian–Israel armistice demarcation line and the implementation of other measures as proposed in the Secretary-General's report, with due regard to the considerations set out therein with a view to assist in achieving situations conducive to the maintenance of peaceful conditions in the area;

4. *Requests* the Secretary-General, in consultation with the parties concerned, to take steps to carry out these measures and to report, as appropriate, to the General Assembly. [*GA Res. 1125 (XI), 2 Feb. 1957.*]

VOTING: 56–0, with 22 abstentions.

Against: None.

Abstaining: Albania, Bulgaria, Byelorussian SSR, Czechoslovakia, Egypt, France, Iraq, Israel,

---

[38] Ibid. 640th mtg. para. 108.   [39] *GAOR*, 11th sess., 651st plen. mtg, para. 35.

Jordan, Lebanon, Libya, Morocco, Netherlands, Poland, Romania, Saudi Arabia, Sudan, Syria, Tunisia, Ukrainian SSR, USSR, Yemen.

It will be seen that the core of the abstentions here consisted of the Communist group and the Arab nations, each of whom viewed with suspicion any extended vote for UNEF. Again, Israel and France parted company from the United Kingdom. The Netherlands representative indicated that he was abstaining because the resolution did not provide reliable guarantees for the prevention of further disputes between the parties. The Assembly itself should take responsibility for the cessation of interference with shipping and the prevention of belligerent acts along the demarcation line.[40]

On 22 February the Assembly approved the arrangements which the Secretary-General had made concerning the status of UNEF:

The General Assembly,

Bearing in mind its resolutions 1000 (ES–I) and 1001 (ES–I) of 5 and 7 November 1956 concerning the United Nations Emergency Force,

Having received the report of the Secretary-General of 8 February 1957 on arrangements concerning the status of the United Nations Emergency Force in Egypt,

Notes with approval this report. [*GA Res. 1126 (XI) 22 Feb. 1957.*]

VOTING: 67–0, with 7 abstentions.

The records contain no details of the voting, though the Soviet Union indicated that she would abstain because she believed that UNEF was illegally set up.[41] One may therefore assume that the other six abstentions were eastern European nations—though two who normally number among that group must have broken ranks on this occasion to vote with the majority.

All subsequent resolutions on UNEF[42] concern the financing of the Force, and hence are dealt with under section 11 below, pp. 421–56.

3

FUNCTIONS AND MANDATE

RESOLUTION 998 (ES–I) of 3 November 1956 had requested the Secretary-General to prepare a plan for an Emergency Force which would 'secure and supervise the cessation of hostilities in accordance with all the terms of the aforementioned resolution'. The 'aforementioned resolution' was 997 (ES–I), which had, in addition to the cease-fire, called for the withdrawal of all parties behind the armistice lines.[1] It may be noted, however, that in Resolution 999

[40] *GAOR*, 11th sess., 651st plen. mtg, paras 33–34.
[41] Ibid. 659th plen. mtg, para. 21.
[42] See check list, p. 526 below.
[1] See pp. 227–8.

(ES–I) it was envisaged that overseeing the withdrawal behind the armistice lines was a function for 'the Secretary-General, with the assistance of the Chief of Staff and the members of the United Nations Truce Supervision Organization'.[2] We shall see how the dual objectives of a cease-fire and withdrawal became essentially intermeshed, and how in turn the functions of UNTSO and UNEF became closely related. Resolution 1000 (ES–I), of 5 November 1956, which actually established UNEF, again stated that its function was 'to secure and supervise the cessation of hostilities in accordance with all the terms of General Assembly resolution 997 (ES–I)'.

Further elaboration was provided in the Second and Final Report of the Secretary-General on the plan for UNEF. He stipulated

8. . . . the General Assembly . . . resolution on the matter, indicates that the Assembly intends that the Force should be of a temporary nature, the length of the assignment being determined by the needs arising out of the present conflict . . . It follows from its terms of reference that there is no intent in the establishment of the Force to influence the military balance in the present conflict and, thereby, the political balance affecting efforts to settle the conflict. By the establishment of the Force, therefore, the General Assembly has not taken a stand in relation to aims other than those clearly and fully indicated in its resolution 997 (ES–I) of 2 November 1956. . . .

10. . . . There is an obvious difference between establishing the Force in order to secure the cessation of hostilities, with a withdrawal of forces, and establishing such a Force with a view to enforcing a withdrawal of forces. . . .

12. In the General Assembly resolution 998 (ES–I) the terms of reference are, as already stated, 'to secure . . . the cessation of hostilities in accordance with all the terms' of resolution 997 (ES–I) of 2 November 1956. This resolution urges that 'all parties now involved in hostilities in the area agree to an immediate cease-fire and, as part thereof, halt the movement of military forces and arms into the area;' and also 'urges the parties to the armistice agreements promptly to withdraw all forces behind the armistice lines, to desist from raids across the armistice lines into neighbouring territory, and to observe scrupulously the provisions of the armistice agreements.' These two provisions combined indicate that the functions of the United Nations Force would be, when a cease-fire is being established, to enter Egyptian territory with the consent of the Egyptian Government, in order to help maintain quiet during and after the withdrawal of non-Egyptian troops, and to secure compliance with the other terms established in the resolution of 2 November 1956. The Force obviously should have no rights other than those necessary for the execution of its functions, in co-operation with local authorities. It would be more than an observers' corps, but in no way a military force temporarily controlling the territory in which it is stationed; nor, moreover, should the Force have military functions exceeding those necessary to secure peaceful conditions on the assumption that the parties to the conflict take all necessary steps for compliance with the recommendations of the General Assembly. Its functions can, on this basis, be assumed to cover an area extending roughly from the Suez Canal to the armistice demarcation lines established in the armistice agreement between Egypt and Israel. [*A/3302, 2nd and final Report of the Secretary-General on the plan for an emergency international UN Force, 6 Nov. 1956.*]

This elaboration of UNEF's functions was approved by the General Assembly in paragraph 2 of its Resolution 1001 (ES–I), of 7 November 1956.[3]

The idea of a UN Force was first advanced by Canada, Prime Minister Pearson seeing it as a practical means of carrying out the resolution calling for a

---

[2] See above, p. 232.   [3] See above, pp. 234–5.

cease-fire. Thus the plan for UNEF would have the 'purpose of facilitating and making effective compliance with the resolution which we have already passed on the part of those whose compliance is absolutely essential. It also has the purpose of providing for international supervision of that compliance through the United Nations. . . .'[4]

Agreement on these dual functions to effect a cessation of hostilities and to secure withdrawal behind the armistice lines was thus clear; but there existed considerable controversy as to the interpretation to be given to UNEF's mandate. Basically, the controversy may be summarized by saying that certain nations thought that UNEF should contribute to an improvement of the situation in the Middle East, and a role was envisaged for it in the settlement of outstanding disputes: Aqaba, passage through the Canal itself, and Gaza were the main instances at issue. Other nations, however, thought that UNEF should only restore the *status quo ante* prior to the Suez invasion. The following documents highlight these different views.

212. In the position in which Egypt is placed today, I say that our first duty is to see that Egypt is in a condition to exercise its sovereign rights. When that position has been created, then it will be time to consider how best the Suez Canal dispute should be decided and how best the Israel–Arab dispute should be disposed of. I freely grant that a solution may be found. This cannot go on for long, but at the same time the present moment certainly is not the occasion for the consideration of that problem. The problem before us is simply how we can secure a cease-fire, how we can secure a cessation of hostilities, and how we can put Egypt into a *status quo ante*. That is exactly the position in which we are placed. [*Per the representative of Ceylon, GAOR, 1st emerg. spec. sess., 563rd plen. mtg.*]

106. Furthermore, the emergency international United Nations Force, as its name indicates should be of a temporary nature. The emergency international Force should be limited to the objectives set out in the resolutions of 4 and 5 November, and these do not imply that the Force should remain in the area for an unspecified period of time or pending the solution of the political questions affecting the area. We are in agreement with the conditions stipulated by the Swedish Government in its letter dated 5 November 1956, from its permanent representative (*A/3302, annex 7*). This was equally our understanding when we voted in favour of the establishment of an emergency international Force, as well as the understanding, we believe, of the Secretary-General. We also understand that the emergency international Force will be confined to the Armistice demarcation line, once the withdrawal of foreign troops from Egypt and the withdrawal of Israel forces behind the armistice line are completed. [*Per the representative of Syria, ibid. 566th mtg.*]

The Syrian view—at this juncture at least—was that the withdrawal of Israel forces behind the armistice line, and the total withdrawal of French and British troops from Egyptian territory, must precede the establishment of UNEF.[5]

This was completely incompatible with the British and French insistence that they would only withdraw once an effective United Nations Force had been established. The Syrian position was based on the fact that UNEF was not to be an *enforcement* organ; hence it was essential that Britain, France, and Israel should have heeded the Assembly resolutions *before* UNEF went into Egypt. Should they still remain at the moment UNEF entered Egypt, 'the United

[4] Per Mr Lester Pearson, Canada, *GAOR*, 1st emerg. spec. sess., 563rd plen. mtg, para. 108.
[5] Per the representative of Syria, *GAOR*, 1st emerg. spec. sess., 566th mtg, para. 107.

9

Nations emergency international Force will stand helpless before such a situation. Egypt then will have been presented with a *fait accompli* and will have been deprived of its right under the Charter to defend its independence and sovereignty'.[6]

Other nations, including Indonesia, were willing that UNEF should be established once there was 'clear indication that the three parties concerned are ready and willing to withdraw their forces from Egyptian soil'.[7] After supporting the Secretary-General's statement in his second report that UNEF was not to be used to affect the military, and thus political, balance in the area, the Indonesian representative stated that UNEF had been set up

in order to secure and supervise the enforcement of a cease-fire, the withdrawal of non-Egyptian troops, and compliance with the other provisions of the resolution of 2 November —all these functions being carried out in co-operation with local authorities. And surely this international Force was been set up without prejudice to the question of the Suez Canal. Its task ends as soon as the objectives of this Assembly's resolution are fully achieved. The sovereignty, territorial integrity and security of Egypt can in no way be compromised by the existence of this—even temporary—international Force and by its carrying out of its functions. [*Ibid*. para. 117.]

The Soviet Union took a less temperate view:

288. In the Soviet delegation's opinion, however, the resolution would be more likely to achieve its purpose if it set a definite time-limit for the withdrawal of Israel forces to their own territory and the removal of United Kingdom and French forces from Egypt.

289. The General Assembly has adopted a proposal to set up an international force. It follows from the text of the resolution and the Secretary-General's report on the matter that the United Nations is in effect accepting the United Kingdom and French condition that the armed forces of the two countries should remain on the Egyptian territory they have seized until the United Nations has constituted its own armed force and stationed it at localities designated with Egypt's consent.

290. Surely, there can be no doubt that the draft resolution, providing as it does for the transfer of control over the Suez Canal to an international force, is an undisguised attempt to bring about a settlement of the Suez Canal question favourable to the United Kingdom and France and to endow such a settlement with the authority of the United Nations.

291. The Soviet Union regards the presence of the aggressors' armed forces in the sovereign State of Egypt as inadmissible. . . .

294. But the resolution 1000 (ES–I) of 5 November 1956 and the plan for its implementation, which is contained in the resolution just adopted provide for the use of an international force for quite another purpose than that of repelling aggression against Egypt. The plan provides for the introduction of the international force into Egyptian territory and the transfer of a large part of that territory, including the Suez Canal zone, to its control.

295. No one can fail to see that the occupation of the Suez Canal zone by an international force really means removing the Canal from Egyptian administration—and that, as we all know, was one of the purposes of the United Kingdom and France in launching aggressive operations against Egypt. [*Per the Soviet representative, ibid. 567th mtg.*]

It is, however, the understanding of the Ethiopian delegation . . . that the police force to be created will have limited functions and duties to perform. These functions have been set out in paragraph 12 of the Secretary-General's report as 'to secure the cessation of hostilities in accordance with all the terms of the resolution 997 (ES–I) of 2 November 1956'. Consequently, my delegation finds itself in complete agreement with the representative of

---

[6] Ibid. para. 102.   [7] Ibid. para.115.

Sweden who said at the 566th meeting that the international force would not be sent to the Middle East to take over the functions which the Franco-British forces had set out to accomplish. I will add further that in my delegation's clear understanding the nature and the duties to be assigned to the international police force shall not exceed the objective of securing the cessation of hostilities in accordance with the terms of General Assembly resolution 997 (ES-I), which, of course, includes the supervision of the withdrawal of invading troops from Egyptian territory. [*Per the representative of Ethiopia, ibid. 567th mtg, para. 109.*]

The Indian delegation saw certain difficulties in interpreting the mandate with reference to Resolution 997 (ES-I), because circumstances had somewhat changed in the intervening time

170. . . . Therefore, when votes are cast it should be with the definite understanding that this draft resolution urges, in accordance with the terms of resolution 997 (ES-I), that 'all parties now involved in hostilities in the area agree to an immediate cease-fire and, as part thereof, halt the movement of military forces and arms into the area'. This was at the time when the landings had not taken place in Egypt and invasion was only by way of aerial bombardment. But now we have a new situation and, therefore, the sense of that sentence is not merely to halt the movement of military forces but to reverse the movement of military forces and withdraw them. Therefore, I feel sure that the Secretary-General would agree that this is the implication of this paragraph.

170. Paragraph 12 says further:

'These two provisions combined indicate that the functions of the United Nations Force would be, when a cease-fire is being established, to enter Egyptian territory with the consent of the Egyptian Government, in order to help maintain quiet during and after the withdrawal of non-Egyptian troops.'

'Non-Egyptian troops' now would mean all non-Egyptian troops since, at the time this resolution was passed, the only non-Egyptian troops in Egypt were the Israel troops, and, therefore, it must be meant to include the others.

171. We turn now to a point on which we wish to lay some emphasis. The last sentence of paragraph 12 reads as follows:

'Its functions can, on this basis, be assumed to cover an area extending roughly from the Suez Canal to the armistice demarcation lines, established in the Armistice Agreement between Egypt and Israel.'

It must be clearly understood that when we say 'an area extending roughly from the Suez Canal to the armistice demarcation lines', it is only in the sense that Egypt will permit the use of its territory by the troops in order to perform their functions, which are to keep the Israel invading armies within their own frontiers. It cannot in any sense at any time be construed that this Force has any occupation function in these areas or will in any way infringe the sovereignty of Egypt, but only that it has the right of way wherever necessary. [*Per the representative of India, ibid. 567th mtg.*]

These views, while they were fairly widely held, contrasted with those of certain other nations who saw in UNEF an instrument not for returning to the *status quo ante*, but for achieving a solution to the major Arab–Israel problems on a somewhat new basis:

306. I believe that there is another omission from this resolution,[8] to which attention has also already been directed. The armed forces of Israel and of Egypt are to withdraw or, if you like, to return to the armistice lines, where presumably, if this is done, they will once again face each other in fear and hatred. What then? What then, six months from now? Are we to go

[8] i.e. Res. 997 (ES–I).

through all this again? Are we to return to the *status quo*? Such a return would not be to a position of security, or even a tolerable position, but would be a return to terror, bloodshed, strife, incidents, charges and counter-charges, and ultimately another explosion which the United Nations Truce Supervision Organization would be powerless to prevent and possibly even to investigate.

307. I therefore would have liked to see a provision in this resolution—and this has been mentioned by previous speakers—authorizing the Secretary-General to begin to make arrangements with Member States for a United Nations force large enough to keep these borders at peace while a political settlement is being worked out. I regret exceedingly that time has not been given to follow up this idea, which was mentioned also by the representative of the United Kingdom in his first speech, and I hope that even now, when action on the resolution has been completed, it may not be too late to give consideration to this matter. [*Per the representative of Canada, ibid. 562nd mtg.*]

The United Kingdom and France viewed a UN Force as an essential precondition not only to their withdrawal but also to the cessation of hostilities, and anticipated that it might have an extended 'buffer' role between Egypt and Israel:

As the Assembly is aware, Her Majesty's Government declared yesterday (A/3306) that it would agree to stop further military operations if the Secretary-General could confirm that (*a*) the Egyptian and Israel Governments had accepted an unconditional cease-fire and (*b*) that the international force to be set up would be competent to secure and supervise the attainment of the objectives set out in operative paragraphs of General Assembly resolution 997 (ES–I). As is well known, Her Majesty's Government has already ordered its forces to cease fire unless attacked. The Governments of France and the United Kingdom have stated that all further military operations would be stopped on receipt of confirmation from the Secretary-General regarding the above-mentioned points (*a*) and (*b*). It will, of course, be necessary even then that an effective force should be interpolated as a shield between Israel and Egypt. [*Per the UK representative, ibid. 567th plen. mtg. para. 102.*]
mtg, para. 102.]

For the United Kingdom, therefore, the Force was being established

to prevent the resumption of hostilities between Israel and Egypt and to secure the withdrawal of Israel forces. It is the earnest hope of Her Majesty's Government that the presence of the international Force in the area will help to bring about, among other things, a generally acceptable settlement of the Palestine and Suez Canal problems. In the view of Her Majesty's Government, the international Force should remain in the area until all these problems have been solved, and we think the logic of events will make this clear. [*Ibid.* para. 103.]

These differences in perspective continued to reveal themselves in the eleventh regular session of the Assembly, which was convened immediately pursuant to the emergency special sessions.[9] Israel made clear that she believed it essential for the United Nations to endeavour now to resolve *all* the major Arab–Israel problems, and that UNEF's functions must be seen in this context. Nor, it was argued, must the fact that UNEF required Egyptian consent to be on her territory allow Egypt unilaterally to decide that UNEF's functions had been discharged:

131. If we were to accept . . . that the Force should separate Egyptian and Israel troops for

---

[9] The second emergency special session being on the question of Hungary.

as long as Egypt thought it convenient and should then be withdrawn on Egypt's unilateral request—we would reach a reduction to absurdity. Egypt would then be in a position to build up, behind the screen of this Force, its full military preparations and, when it felt that those military preparations had reached their desired climax, to dismiss the United Nations Emergency Force and to stand again in close contact and proximity with the territory of Israel. . . . [*Per the Israel representative, GAOR, 11th sess., plen. mtgs, vol. 1, 592nd mtg.*]

Even in Sinai, and especially in the eastern part, we believe that the United Nations Emergency Force should so deploy itself as to maintain a broad separation between Egyptian and Israel forces. . . .

93. Now some of those who have been unwilling to look beyond the problem of withdrawal in its narrowest context have said that the results of force must not be recognized, and that a return must first be made to legal situations. But here we have an anomaly. The previous situations were the result of force, the previous situations were illegal. The Gaza occupation was achieved by force in defiance of Security Council decisions and the maintenance of *fedayeen* activities and of bases for guerrilla warfare against Israel was certainly an illegal situation to which general Assembly should not seek a return. Similarly, the *status quo* in the Gulf of Aqaba was not a *status quo* of law, it was a *status quo* of piracy and illegality. To argue here that the *status quo* must be restored is to say that illegal and anti-Charter conditions must be restored as a prelude to the search for legal solutions and for peace-serving solutions·

94. This then is the problem. It is a genuine anomaly. If it thinks only of withdrawal, the General Assembly will be restoring belligerency to Gaza, will be restoring a blockade to the Gulf of Aqaba and the Straits of Tiran, unless in arranging withdrawal it arranges other things also, and arranges them carefully and well. I do not wish to repeat in detail the considerations which have been submitted to the General Assembly on the problem of the Gulf of Aqaba. This is an open waterway—open now—there are no guns to deter free passage through the Straits of Tiran. The right of innocent passage, in conformity with recognized principles of international law, is referred to in the Secretary-General's report (*A/3500 and Add. 1*) and was upheld with gratifying emphasis by many delegations in the course of this debate, especially by those who represent the great seafaring nations of the world. I do not want to go deeply into the juridical problems here involved. Surely the United Nations General Assembly can agree that ships should not be shot at but should be allowed to proceed. The United Nations, with its preference for peace against war and for tranquillity against belligerency, cannot take any other view. This is not an open question. . . .

104. Here then is the interdependence in law as well as in political fact between the question of Israel's occupation of the Straits of Tiran and the Egyptian thesis and doctrine of a blockade. And this is the argument for a simultaneous liquidation both of the provocation and of the reaction, both of the blockade and of whatever the blockade has elicited by way of response. This leaves us really with three courses in an approach to the question of the Straits of Tiran. There are but three alternatives. One is that Israel should go away with no measures and with no related steps to ensure that the blockade will not be renewed. Then by the sequence which I have described we shall return to belligerency and to the danger of active conflict. This is the imprudent course which we think should be rejected.

105. The second course would be for Israel to remain as a response to the Egyptian policy of blockade so long as that is maintained. We fully understand all the grave reasons which operate against such a course. Therefore, we seek the middle course; the withdrawal of troops and simultaneous arrangements and measures to ensure permanent freedom of navigation and, therefore, the absence of belligerent acts in this international waterway. . . .

106. In relation to this problem and to other problems, some representatives have speculated upon the possible utilization of the United Nations Emergency Force. My delegation has already explained that a guarantee for an issue such as freedom of navigation is only of value if it has permanence and continuous duration. Therefore, the mere invitation of the possible functions of the United Nations Emergency Force does not solve this problem until or unless

greater precision and clarity are given to the functions of the United Nations force and the terms and conditions for its tenure.

107. It seems that there are different conceptions within the General Assembly of the functions and objectives of this Force. There are two versions, one which sees it as an instrument of the General Assembly to prevent belligerency in the areas in which it operates, and another, I am afraid, which comes very near to regarding the Force as a temporary facility made available to Egypt to clear the path for a return to whatever Egyptian forces were doing before, and to whatever it is that Egyptian forces plan to do in the future. I fear that if this very lax definition of the United Nations Emergency Force function be accepted, the Force would find itself inadvertently in military alliance with Egypt until Egypt's striking power were restored. I would therefore say that the question whether the United Nations force can be a factor depends upon a definition in terms of clarity and precision of its functions and of the duration of its tenure.

108. To sum up, then, the issue involves great national interests of Israel, great international interests and, above all, it embodies and symbolizes the whole problem of avoiding renewed belligerency and war. We shall carry forward our discussions with the Secretary-General on this matter. In the centre of Israel's approach lies the necessity of implementing the 1951 Security Council resolution, the question of Egypt's reciprocal duties towards Israel and the problem of the precise definition of the functions of the United Nations Emergency Force. . . .

110. We do not believe that an international force can carry out administrative or security functions. We do not think that existing administrative processes should be uprooted. We do believe that the withdrawal of the military forces of Israel from the Gaza Strip is an element in the solution which we should seek. We consider that larger possibilities in the solution of the refugee problem open out here. We seek nothing in fact but provisional *de facto* arrangements which embody some of the ideas which have been mooted here and which perhaps we can evolve with greater clarity in the next stage of the negotiation envisaged. . . . [*Per the Israeli representative, GAOR, 11th sess., 642nd plen. mtg.*]

16. . . . The report[10] considers that the United Nations cannot condone a change of what is called the '*status juris* resulting from military action', and that it 'must, therefore, maintain that the *status juris* existing prior to such military action be re-established by a withdrawal of troops, and by the relinquishment or nullification of rights asserted in territories covered by the military action and depending upon it'. (Ibid., para 5 (*a*).)

17. The term '*status juris*' is unknown in international law. The Latin words signify not a legal situation but a situation in which law finds itself. Israel's apprehension on this point is lest these words be interpreted as implying a duty to re-establish the situation prevailing before the recent hostilities began.

18. Our view is simple. In the three oustanding issues—the Suez Canal, the Gulf of Aqaba and the Gaza Strip—our duty is not to re-establish but to prevent the re-establishment of the previous situation, for in each case the situation on 28 October 1956 was one of illegality and not of law. The blockade in the Suez Canal was illegal. The blockade in the Gulf of Aqaba was illegal. The organization of the *fedayeen* movement from Gaza was illegal. These three illegalities, more than any other factors, brought about the hostilities which we are now seeking to liquidate. In pursuing its policy for the withdrawal of non-Egyptian troops, the United Nations surely has no duty to restore Egypt's blockading and raiding capacity to its former state. . . .

21. In the light of this history, and of other events in Asia and in Europe, the idea that the United Nations cannot function for peace except on the basis of restoring the *status quo* requires some qualification. In this case, my Government must certainly hold that the United Nations may not restore illegal situations, even if it has reservations about the method whereby those illegalities have been removed. We cannot go back to blockades in the Gulf and the Canal or to the terror which raged from Gaza. Neither in national conscience nor in international responsibility should we do this. . . .

[10] A/3512, Report of the Secretary-General.

58. In our discussions recently on withdrawal and related problems, we sought to clarify the functions of the United Nations Emergency Force with some precision. At times we understood that its functions might include the prevention of belligerency and that it would remain in any area as long as necessary to discharge that function. This point is still not clear. It is vital and urgent that it be clarified further, for if the entry of the Force were merely the prelude to Egyptian reoccupation, and if the activities and duration of the Force were subject to Egyptian control, it would be hard to envisage it as an effective barrier against the policies of belligerency and blockade which Egypt has for so long maintained, and has, to the extent of our knowledge, not yet renounced. . . .

68. There is thus a direct relationship, in law and in fact, between Egypt's blockade of the straits and Israel's occupation of the territory commanding them. Both the blockade and the occupation are anomalies which ought to be liquidated simultaneously. If Egypt practises warfare against Israel from those positions, then Israel's reciprocal right to defend itself against that warfare cannot be contested. . . .

71. The best solution of this problem would be for the countries—four of them—bordering on the gulf to sign a treaty safeguarding freedom of navigation for all ships, wherever bound, without distinction of flag. Until such time as a solution of this kind became practicable, the problem would be solved if the General Assembly would decide that the United Nations Emergency Force should assure freedom of passage, and that it should not leave the coastal strip until a final settlement was obtained between Israel and Egypt, or until some special arrangement on permanent freedom of navigation in the Gulf was reached in an agreement between Israel and the other interests concerned. My delegation believes that the General Assembly could take this decision. [*Per the Israeli representative, ibid. 645th mtg.*]

The Israeli position was confirmed and elaborated in an *aide-mémoire* transmitted to the Secretary-General. After speaking of belligerent acts against her shipping in the Straits of Tiran, the Gulf of Aqaba, and the Suez Canal, the *aide-mémoire* declared:

10. The Government of Israel considers that the United Nations Emergency Force could be a factor in the solution of this problem if the following arrangements were confirmed and implemented:

(*a*) On the withdrawal of Israel forces, the positions evacuated along the western coast of the Gulf of Aqaba would be held by the United Nations Emergency Force, as had been the case with other areas from which Israel forces have withdrawn.

(*b*) It would be the function of the United Nations Emergency Force to see to it that freedom of navigation was maintained and belligerent acts avoided in the Gulf of Aqaba and the Straits of Tiran. The prevention of acts of belligerency is definitely within the mandate of the United Nations Emergency Force.

(*c*) The United Nations Emergency Force would remain in the area under discussion so long as it has its function to prevent any renewal of hostilities.

(*d*) In view of the above considerations the United Nations Emergency Force would maintain its position along the western shore of the Gulf of Aqaba until another effective means was agreed upon between the parties concerned for ensuring permanent freedom of navigation and the absence of belligerent acts in the Straits of Tiran and the Gulf of Aqaba.

(*e*) Such effective means would be deemed to have been found when a peace settlement was achieved; or when secure freedom of navigation was guaranteed by other international instruments to which Israel was a party.

C. *The function of the United Nations Emergency Force*

11. All the elements in the above proposals (the withdrawal of forces; the need to guarantee free navigation; the assignment of the United Nations Emergency Force with the function of preventing belligerency; and the need to secure compliance with the Security Council's

resolution of 1 September 1951) were advocated by many delegations in the course of the recent General Assembly debate.

12. It is evident that, if the United Nations Emergency Force is to develop its capacity to help solve this problem, more clarity and precision are needed in defining its character, its functions and, above all, the duration of its tenure and the conditions for the termination of its assignments. The need for such precision is the more urgent in view of the fact that many delegations, including those whose troops compose the Force, have expressed conflicting views on the functions and nature of the Force. [*A/3511, 24 Jan. 1957.*]

The Israeli view received some support, especially in the early part of 1957, when the immediacy of the dangers receded, and the question arose of UNEF's role in the broader context of Arab–Israel relations:

. . . it is essential, in my view, on the withdrawal of Israel forces from the Gaza Strip and the positions in the Gulf of Aqaba, to ensure that those positions are not directly or indirectly occupied by Egyptian forces, thereby creating again a situation of imminent danger.
74. The positions relinquished by Israel troops must, we believe, be occupied effectively by elements of the United Nations Emergency Force, at least for so long as it is necessary to establish procedures for the settlement of the problems existing in those areas. It is my understanding that the functions of the United Nations Emergency Force specifically include the occupation of areas relinquished by opposing parties, and I hope that my understanding in this respect will be confirmed.
75. The second requirement is that procedures should be evolved which would be calculated to lead to permanent solutions. In the case of Gaza, in which the United Nations has a direct interest, particularly having in mind the fate of over 200,000 unfortunate Arab refugees, some machinery should be set in motion to ensure that the area would play its due part in the maintenance of international peace and security. . . .
76. With regard to the Gulf of Aqaba, interim arrangements are also possible. The positions evacuated by Israel forces should be occupied forthwith by United Nations Emergency Force troops, who should, during their occupation, ensure that the status of the gulf as an international waterway was safeguarded and respected. The gulf serves no less than four littoral States—Israel, Egypt, Jordan and Saudi Arabia—all of which should without discrimination be able to use this waterway for their own peaceful purposes.
77. The question of the Gulf of Aqaba, indeed, raises similar issues to those raised by the situation in the Suez Canal, and my Government is concerned to ensure that international waterways should be maintained to serve the interests of all States desiring to use them. It seems to me that safeguards to this end should be studied by the United Nations, and appropriate guarantees, arrived at by convention or in some other convenient way, should be elaborated under the auspices of this Organization. This would surely be to the interest not only of Israel but of all States, including Egypt, whose territories border on the gulf and whose commerce is dependent upon the maintenance of free passage and navigation in the gulf. . . .
82. I am also happy to note that the Secretary-General considers that the basic function of the United Nations Emergency Force gives the Force great value as a background for efforts towards solving the pending problems to which the Secretary-General has referred, those of Gaza and the Gulf of Aqaba. [*Per the Australian representative, GAOR, 11th sess., plen. mtgs, vol. 2, 638th mtg.*]

Thus, while not explicitly suggesting that UNEF's role was concerned with Aqaba and the Gaza Strip, it was suggested that these were immediately relevant for consideration by the Assembly, and that UNEF could provide a 'background' to any proposals. The New Zealand representative suggested, among other things, that '. . . the Force, in the performance of its function of securing and supervising the cessation of hostilities, should remain in the area at least until the Suez and Aqaba issues are settled, and some progress is made towards an over-all settlement.'[11]

Equally, Lester Pearson had suggested that:

While the political climate of the Middle East is maturing towards the time when conditions will be more appropriate for a comprehensive settlement, is is essential, I think, for the countries of the region, and indeed for us all, that there should be no return to the former state of strife and tension and conflict on the borders; that security should be maintained and, indeed, guaranteed. I suggest that for this purpose there will be a continuing need, during the period until a political settlement is achieved, for the stabilizing international influence that the Emergency Force is now exercising. And this essential stabilizing role might well require the continuing presence of a United Nations force along the boundary between Egypt and Israel; perhaps also for a time in the Gaza Strip and, with the consent of the States involved, along the borders between Israel and its other Arab neighbours, though that of course would require further resolution from the United Nations Assembly.

It seems to me that some such United Nations supervision might help to ensure the security of the nations concerned, which is so vital if they are to approach with the necessary confidence negotiations towards a comprehensive solution of their conflicts. [*Ibid.* para 105.]

Other, similar suggestions were also made:

79. The Secretary-General has already indicated, in paragraph 11 of his report, that study might be given, for instance, to 'the question of the extent to which the (United Nations Emergency) Force might assume responsibilities so far carried by the Truce Supervision Organization'. That Truce Supervision Organization certainly has not, in our view, the power, or authority effectively to interpose itself between the forces of the two conflicting parties. The United Nations Emergency Force, however, would now be effective for this purpose, and, following closely the Israel forces, could be deployed in the area of the demarcation line from the Mediterranean to the Gulf of Aqaba, where it could function in order to prevent incidents, to keep the peace and to make secure the cessation of hostilities which has already been brought about by the United Nations. And in so doing, it would facilitate the compliance of the parties concerned with other relevant United Nations recommendations which have been or which may be passed. . . .

82. The withdrawal of Israel forces from Sharm el Sheikh, which is a strategic and important position for controlling the straits leading to the gulf and navigation through them, might be followed by the posting of observers of the United Nations Emergency Force at that point to assist in securing the peace and keeping navigation open, pending the determination of the legal and other issues involved. [*Per the representative of Greece, ibid. 640th mtg.*]

115. The over-all task of the Assembly must be to see that hostilities do not break out again. We must see to it that new attacks across the armistice lines, whether by Israel forces or the Egyptian forces or the *fedayeen* elements, cannot reoccur. This, in our view, makes it imperative that the United Nations Force should be so deployed as to prevent a recurrence of such attacks.

116. The United Nations Force has, of course, been charged with far wider functions than merely supervising the cessation of hostilities and the withdrawal of forces behind the armistice lines. It has, among other things, to secure the cessation of hostilities in accordance with all the terms of the Assembly resolution 997 (ES–I) of 2 November 1956, with which we are all familiar. This means that the United Nations Force has responsibilities for ensuring against a resumption of hostilities in any form. [*Per the representative of the UK, ibid. 640th mtg.*]

Agreement on an enlarged role for UNEF extended to those who had criticized the United Kingdom and France for their intervention in Suez:

[11] Per the New Zealand representative, *GAOR*, 11th sess., plen. mtgs, vol. 2, 639th mtg, para III(*c*).

9*

99. Let me make one observation with respect to what is called 'the residual problem' in connexion with Israel's evacuation of the Sinai peninsula, namely, the problem of the Straits of Tiran and the Gulf of Aqaba. Both as a Member of the United Nations and as a representative of a seafaring nation, I hold strong views on the question of the freedom of navigation in those waters, as in all other waters of importance to world trade and world shipping. We are vitally interested in the establishment of a situation in that area in which warfare will be excluded. It seems to us that the United Nations Emergency Force is the very means by which the United Nations, in co-operation with the parties concerned, should be able to secure a situation in the Straits of Tiran in which there will be no resumption of hostilities to disturb the relations between the parties to the present conflict or to prevent the free flow of traffic through this important waterway. We feel that measures should be taken to this effect in accordance with the procedure hitherto followed in the deployment of the United Nations Emergency Force in connexion with the cease-fire and withdrawal in Egypt. This procedure corresponds strictly to the premises and provisions upon which the United Nations Emergency Force has been assembled and stationed in Egypt. [*Per the Norwegian representative, ibid. 641st mtg.*]

4. We believe it is essential that units of the United Nations Emergency Force be stationed at the Straits of Tiran in order to achieve there the separation of Egyptian and Israel land and sea forces. This separation is essential until it is clear that the non-exercise of any claim to belligerent rights has established in practice the peaceful conditions which must govern navigation in waters having such an international interest. All of this, of course, would be without prejudice to any ultimate determination which might be made of any legal questions concerning the Gulf of Aqaba. [*Per the US representative, ibid. 645th mtg.*]

73. In this connexion, we believe that the deployment of UNEF and its duties in this area and all along the demarcation line must correspond to the need to ensure respect for all the obligations deriving from the Armistice Agreement for as long as may be required, whether those obligations relate to the cease-fire, the cessation of raids, the demilitarization of certain areas or the obligation not to exercise belligerent rights. Moreover, some degree of administrative responsibility in the Gaza area could be assumed by the United Nations in order that the proposed restoration of peace might be carried out more effectively. [*Per the Italian representative, ibid. 651st mtg.*]

The rationale for the legal basis of this view was well expressed by the Australian representative:

83. . . . Paragraph 12 of the Secretary-General's report of 6 November 1956 (*A/3302*) on the establishment of the United Nations Emergency Force—with which the 7 November resolution concurred as regards the definition of the functions of the United Nations Emergency Force—states that those functions would be, 'when a cease-fire is being established, to enter Egyptian territory with the consent of the Egyptian Government, in order to help maintain quiet during and after—and the word 'after' is a vitally important one—'the withdrawal of non-Egyptian troops, and to secure compliance with the other terms established in the resolution (*997 (ES–I)*) of 2 November 1956'.
84. What were those 'other terms' of the resolution of 2 November—a resolution which, by its terms, was directed to all parties involved in the hostilities? These terms were as follows: first, that there should be an immediate cease-fire; second, that the movement of military forces and equipment, and so forth, into the area should be halted; third, that the parties to the armistice agreements should observe scrupulously the provisions of the agreements; and, fourth, that, upon the cease-fire becoming effective—and this event has now occurred—steps should be taken to reopen the Suez Canal and secure freedom of navigation.
85. We think it is important to note that the functions of the United Nations Emergency Force are not directed solely to taking over territory as it is vacated by non-Egyptian forces; rather, the Force is to remain in positions occupied by it after the withdrawal, in order to secure compliance with the terms of the resolution here cited. [*Ibid. 649th mtg.*]

These views were not, however, accepted by the Arab nations, the Communist group, and certain other countries:

30. The Soviet Government supports Egypt's position in this matter. When United Kingdom and French forces have been withdrawn from Port Said, United Nations units should not be assigned any functions either in Port Said or in the Canal zone in general. Units of the international Force that disembarked at Port Said on 21 November should remain there only until the evacuation of the United Kingdom and French forces has been completed. They should then leave Port Said immediately and join the detachments of the international Force to be stationed along the demarcation line separating Egyptian and Israel forces in accordance with the well-known Armistice Agreement. But even in this area their stay should not exceed the period considered necessary by Egypt.

31. It is noteworthy, however, that the ruling circles of those countries that launched the aggression against Egypt are only too ready to place a completely distorted construction on the purpose and functions of the United Nations Force. Thus, for example, an idea has gained currency in these countries that the United Nations Force is a kind of substitute for the occupation forces of the United Kingdom, France and Israel. At the same time, increasingly frequent assertions are being made to the effect that United Kingdom and French forces should remain in those areas of Egyptian territory seized by them until the idea of the so-called 'internationalization of the Canal' has become a reality. Mr Lloyd, in particular, hinted at this today in speaking from this rostrum when he said that the presence of troops on Egyptian territory was connected with the settlement of the question of freedom of navigation in the Suez Canal and other matters.

32. In this light—and I should like to emphasize this point—it was no coincidence that the United Kingdom and French troops who landed on Egyptian territory brought with them in their train a large number of officials of the former Suez Canal Company, apparently in order to resume control of the administration of the Canal.

33. The task of restoring navigation on the Suez Canal is undoubtedly an urgent and pressing matter, now that the cease-fire has been achieved. It is quite obvious, however, that certain people would like to turn even the solution of this technical problem to their own political ends. That is precisely why attempts are now being made to drawn an artificial connexion between this question and that of the presence of United Nations forces in the Canal zone.

34. As Mr Hammarskjöld has informed us, the Egyptian Government considers that the work of clearing the Canal should begin immediately after the withdrawal of non-Egyptian armed forces from Port Said and from the Canal zone and that it is for Egypt to conclude contracts with the appropriate firms. The contribution of the United Nations to the solution of this important problem should be to assist Egypt in the matter. It would be strange, to say the least, if, as is now being proposed in certain quarters, the United Nations itself began to undertake operations in the Suez Canal area, and act almost as if it were its lessee.

35. The attempts to create an artificial link between the question of the presence of the United Nations Emergency Force in Egypt and that of the administration of the Suez Canal reflect the plans of those circles in the United Kingdom and France, which cannot reconcile themselves to the fact that the Canal is the inalienable property of Egypt and are trying to restore the old order.

36. In this connexion, reference must be made to the extensive plans for re-drawing the map of the Arab East now being discussed by circles close to influential imperialist monopolies. The theory advanced in justification of these plans is that in our time a political rearrangement in the Near East has followed upon the heels of every war and that the present time is auspicious for such changes in this area. [*Per the representative of the USSR, ibid. 592nd mtg.*]

86. Then, again, what do the British and French Governments mean by 'effective'? Effective for what? The United Nations Force was never meant to exercise any functions except those of supervising the cease-fire and the withdrawal of the occupying forces. It was never meant

to be a combat force, nor was it destined to secure the withdrawal of foreign occupiers by force. Its presence in the Canal area was to be symbolic, with hardly anything to do if and when the foreign invaders left peacefully and in an orderly manner.

87. Are we to understand by British and French insistence on the effectiveness of the United Nations Force that they had other functions in mind for that Force? If so, then the General Assembly finds itself up against yet another act of defiance on the part of the aggressors, for to use the United Nations Force for any purposes other than to secure the cease-fire and the withdrawal of the invading forces would be contrary to the wishes of the General Assembly as expressed in its resolutions 998 (ES–I) and 1000 (ES–I) of 4 and 5 November respectively. [*Per the Lebanon representative, ibid. 595th mtg.*]

87. Israel's refusal to withdraw its armed forces from the western shore of the Gulf of Aqaba constitutes a further hostile act which creates difficulties for the United Nations. The object of that refusal is clearly to exert pressure on Egypt to make it accept a settlement of the question of navigation in the gulf. If possible, Israel hopes to achieve the same result through the United Nations Emergency Force. Thus, under the conditions laid down by Israel for the withdrawal of its troops, all matters still pending between the two countries must be settled to the satisfaction of Israel under pressure exerted upon Egypt by UNEF which must replace the Israel forces along the western shore of the Gulf of Aqaba.

88. After stressing that the United Nations Emergency Force would be brought into the Sharm el Sheikh area immediately following the evacuation of the Israel army and that it would remain in the area until an effective means was agreed for ensuring Israel permanent freedom of navigation, the *aide-mémoire* continues that 'such effective means would be deemed to have been found when a peace settlement was achieved; or when secure freedom of navigation was guaranteed by other international instruments to which Israel was a party'. (*A/3511, para. 10 (e)*.) The significance of these detailed conditions becomes apparent in the light of paragraph 24 of the last report by the Secretary-General (*A/3512*).

89. The first obvious comment is that Israel wishes, through the presence of the United Nations Emergency Force, to ensure a solution favourable to its own interests in a manner which is a subject of legal controversy. The Assembly should also note that Israel, in requesting UNEF to ensure it effective freedom of navigation, is trying to have the Force stay there until such time as a peace with Egypt, on conditions it finds favourable, has been achieved. If, however, Israel sees fit to impose conditions which Egypt cannot accept, then Egypt will have the alternative of an unfavourable peace treaty or the presence on its territory of an occupying force for an indefinite period.

90. Obviously, in that case, UNEF would play the role of an occupying force. It should be noted, however, that Israel's claims, unacceptable as they may be, have been seconded and supported by the representatives of certain countries both in the Assembly's debate on the previous resolution and during the present discussion.

91. Thus, the representatives of New Zealand, Australia and the United States have stressed, and are still persistently stressing, the need for establishing UNEF in the Middle East as an occupying force to ensure the settlement of questions pending between Israel and the Arab countries. These protagonists of Middle East occupation by UNEF have been joined by Canada, whose representative, on 29 January (*646th meeting*), made the following statement:

'. . . that Force, which is our own creation and which is functioning so effectively in the interest of peace and security already, might assume the supervisory duties of the United Nations Truce Supervision Organization and prevent incursions and raids across the demarcation line . . .'.

92. The Force is now apparently to be given further powers which were not specified in the resolutions by which it was set up. Just because UNEF was established in violation of the Charter, outside the Security Council which alone has the power to decide on the establishment of such a force, does that constitute sufficient justification for the continued non-observance of the Charter by endowing the Force with further powers and again

circumventing the Security Council? Or do those Powers which, through the amendment of the Charter, seek to make the United Nations the tool of their policies, believe that they can accomplish their purpose by attempting to circumvent the Security Council? If that should be the intention of those who wish the General Assembly to decide matters which, under the Charter, are the responsibility of the Security Council, they would be doing a disservice to the Organization by undermining its basic principles. [*Per the representative of Bulgaria, ibid. 651st mtg.*]

It was thus the view of these nations that 'with the withdrawal of Israel forces from Egyptian territory, the functions of UNEF will cease, and this force ought to leave Egyptian territory'.[12]

These views may be contrasted with more moderate views advanced concerning UNEF's proper role; and which came to be accepted:

61. What are the functions of this United Nations Emergency Force? Those functions and the task—and it is a very difficult task indeed which confronts the Force—have been laid down by resolutions of the General Assembly, and they are found also in the Secretary-General's second and final report (*A/3302*), which has been approved by the Assembly. The basic resolution for these purposes is 1000 (*ES-I*), which we adopted on 5 November and which states that the function of this Force is 'to secure and supervise the cessation of hostilities in accordance with all'—and I emphasize the word 'all'—'the terms of General Assembly resolution 997 (*ES-I*) of 2 November 1956'. In the latter resolution, as representatives will remember, provision is made for a cease-fire, for a prompt withdrawal of forces, and also—and this is no time to forget this provision—'that all Member States refrain from introducing military goods in the area of hostilities and in general refrain from any acts which would delay or prevent the implementation of the present resolution'. And in paragraph 4 of that resolution we have the provision that, upon the cease-fire being effective, steps are to be taken 'to reopen the Suez Canal and restore secure freedom of navigation'.
62. Later, by resolution 1001 (*ES-I*) of 7 November, the Assembly approved certain principles for the organization and functioning of the United Nations Emergency Force, and those principles were stated in certain paragraphs of the Secretary-General's report which was linked to the resolution (*A/3302*). [*Per the Canadian representative, ibid. 592nd mtg.*]

117. Basically, we repeat that the Assembly resolutions call for four things: a cease-fire; the cessation of hostilities; abstention from military raids and military incursions; and scrupulous observance of the armistice agreements.
118. The United Nations Emergency Force was created and organized to give effect to the terms of these resolutions. . . . [*Per the representative of the Philippines, ibid. 645th mtg.*]

It was this middle view which prevailed, and it is now possible to see that it entailed two things: first, that UNEF had functions over and above its role in the cease-fire and the withdrawal from hostilities—namely, the prevention of military raids and contribution to the observance of the Armistice Agreements; second, that UNEF's role in any of these tasks was not dependent upon the prior or simultaneous resolving of other continuing problems in the area, such as passage through Suez and the Gulf of Aqaba.

In so far as UNEF's tasks included contributing towards the upholding of the Armistice Agreements, it will be seen that it was necessary to define the

---

[12] Per the representative of the USSR, *GAOR*, 11th sess., 652nd mtg, para. 19.

relationship between UNEF and UNTSO.[13] This was the more so, given the fact that Israel had denounced the continuing validity of the Egypt–Israel Armistice.[14] From the UN viewpoint therefore, while avoiding comment upon Israel's repudiation of the Armistice Agreement and non-participation in UNTSO's work in respect of it, it was prudent to re-allocate some of that work to the new organ, UNEF.

Thus the Norwegian delegation urged that UNEF 'should become one more United Nations auxiliary organ associated with the United Nations Truce Supervision Organization as a supporting organ of the armistice machinery'.[15] Furthermore:

97. . . . the Secretary-General should go further. So far the United Nations Truce Supervision Organization has been the sole United Nations body entrusted with the task of securing the observance of the armistice. Within its terms of reference, the United Nations Truce Supervision Organization has, I am sure, done its best. But we all know that it has not been an adequate and effective instrument for such a vast and complicated task. It has had no machinery for the prevention of raids and incursions. Its task has been to investigate and observe. It seems to us that there now exists an opportunity to remedy this shortcoming of the United Nations Truce Supervision Organization. The United Nations now has a second organization in this area, the United Nations Emergency Force, whose primary function is to supervise and enforce the cease-fire. Geographically this function will be carried out in the same area where parts of the Truce Supervision Organization are functioning, namely along the demarcation line between Egypt and Israel, through Sinai and along the Gaza Strip after the evacuation of Israel forces. This fact alone will make liaison and co-operation necessary between the two United Nations organs in the area since they have essentially the same functions.

98. My delegation notes with great interest the observations which the Secretary-General makes in paragraph 11 of his report (*A/3500 and Add. 1.*) His final remark in this paragraph seems to us to be completely appropriate, and I quote it:

'Further consideration may have to be given to the question of the extent to which the Force might assume responsibilities so far carried by the Truce Supervision Organization.'

As far as my delegation is concerned, we should like to encourage the Secretary-General to give such further consideration to this problem. We find it essential that the means of the United Nations be strengthened in order to enable it to discharge its duties in a more efficient manner than it has had the power to do in the past. The utilization of the United Nations Emergency Force as a peace-ensuring factor in the area may be the turning point in the development towards improved relations, which we all, of course, would welcome. We hope that such a function of the United Nations Emergency Force will be acceptable to all parties concerned and that the stationing of the United Nations Emergency Force will be accepted on both sides of the demarcation line in order that the Force may most effectively discharge its duties in maintaining peaceful conditions in the border areas, and thus allow the people living there to enjoy the feeling of security which, I am sure, they all long for and which is such an indispensable requirement for the transformation of the Armistice into a durable peace. I hope that the Secretary-General will see his way to devote urgent attention to this particular problem and, in due course, enlighten us further on its prospects. [*Ibid. 641st mtg.*]

The Secretary-General advised:

As to the question of the conflict of the functions of the Chief of Staff, it is a matter of course that if the Assembly were to give this new assignment to the Chief of Staff, he would

[13] See pp. 53–54.　　[14] See pp. 110–16.　　[15] *GAOR*, 11th sess. plen. mtgs, vol. 2, p. 1084.

leave his present post. He would change his functions, and other arrangements would be made with the United Nations Truce Supervision Organization. Secondly, the recruitment of officers for the proposed group corresponds to the functions which the Chief of Staff already possesses in relation to the Observer Corps of the Truce Supervision Organization. [*GAOR, 1st emerg. spec. sess., 565th mtg*, para. 47.]

6. The basic resolution of the General Assembly on the Middle East crisis (2 November 1956) urged a prompt withdrawal of the forces of all parties to the armistice agreements behind the armistice lines and requested the Secretary-General 'to observe and report promptly on the compliance' with the resolution, for such further action as may be deemed appropriate in accordance with the Charter. The resolution also covered other points of significance to progress toward improved conditions in the region. Thus, in the same operative paragraph in which the request was made for a withdrawal of forces behind the armistice lines, the parties were urged 'to desist from raids across the armistice lines into neighbouring territory and to observe scrupulously the provisions of the armistice agreements'. The three points in this operative paragraph, while existing simultaneously within the terms of the paragraph, were not linked together conditionally.

7. The request in the resolution of 2 November that the Secretary-General observe and report on compliance was later added to in resolution 999 (ES–I) of 4 November wherein the Secretary-General, with the assistance of the Chief of Staff and the members of the United Nations Truce Supervision Organization, is asked 'to obtain compliance of the withdrawal of all forces behind the armistice lines'. The discussions with representatives of the Government of Israel, the results of which have been noted above, have been conducted on the basis of this mandate to the Secretary-General for taking action to achieve full implementation of the request for withdrawal. The resolution of 4 November, asking the Secretary-General to undertake specific executive responsibilities, covered also the implementation of the cease-fire and the halting of the movement of military forces and arms into the area, but was not extended to the other points in the resolution of 2 November.

8. In consequence of the intended withdrawal announced in the latest communication to the Secretary-General from the Government of Israel on 14 January 1957, the United Nations Emergency Force on 22 January will reach the armistice demarcation line wherever it follows the north-eastern boundary of the Sinai desert. At that stage the last two points in operative paragraph 2 of the resolution of 2 November will assume added importance. . . .

9. One of these points is the request for full observance of the provisions of the armistice agreements. This request makes it clear that the withdrawal of Israel forces must be behind the armistice line as it has been established in the General Armistice Agreement between Egypt and Israel. In this context it is to be noted, therefore, that the Israel communication is silent about withdrawal from the Gaza Strip which, according to this armistice agreement, falls on the Egyptian side of the armistice demarcation line. Further discussions with the representatives of Israel are required on this point. It is assumed that the Government of Israel wishes to make further observations on the question. Thus, when presenting the aforementioned communication on 14 January 1957, the Representative of Israel stated orally that his Government is prepared 'at an early stage' to discuss with the Secretary-General 'proposals for arrangements for the Gaza Strip'.

10. The other point which is mentioned together with the request for withdrawal refers to raids across the armistice demarcation lines into neighbouring territory. Such raids are prohibited also in the armistice agreements. The call for general observance of these agreements reinforces the specific request to the parties to desist from raids. The cease-fire assurances given to the Secretary-General by the parties in April and May 1956 lent further legal solemnity to the relevant articles in the armistice agreements.

11. The United Nations Truce Supervision Organization established under the armistice agreements assists, as one of its main duties, in the prevention of incursions and raids. It is in accord with the call for scrupulous observance of the armistice agreements for the parties to take all appropriate measures to give UNTSO the support necessary to render it fully

effective. It is a primary duty of the United Nations Emergency Force to supervise and enforce the cease-fire to which the parties committed themselves in response to the request of the General Assembly in the resolution of 2 November. Appropriate liaison should be established between these two United Nations auxiliary organizations. Further consideration may have to be given to the question of the extent to which the Force might assume responsibilities so far carried by the Truce Supervision Organization. . . .

14. The international significance of the Gulf of Aqaba may be considered to justify the right of innocent passage through the Straits of Tiran and the Gulf in accordance with recognized rules of international law. The Secretary-General has not considered that a discussion of the various aspects of this matter, and its possible relation to the action requested in the General Assembly resolutions on the Middle East crisis, falls within the mandate established for him in the resolution of 4 November. . . .

16. The Assembly, in taking this position, in no way disregarded all the other aims which must be achieved in order to create more satisfactory conditions than those prevailing during the period preceding the crisis. Some of these aims were mentioned by the Assembly. Others are to be found in previous decisions of the United Nations. All of them call for urgent attention. The basic function of the United Nations Emergency Force, to help maintain quiet, gives the Force great value as a background for efforts toward resolving such pending problems, although it is not in itself a means to that end. . . . [*A/3500, Report of the Secretary-General on compliance with General Assembly Res. 1123 (XI), 15 Jan. 1957.*]

20. The United Nations Emergency Force is deployed at the dividing line between the forces of Israel and Egypt. The General Assembly concurred in paragraph 12 of the Secretary-General's second and final report (A/3302) which specifically referred to the deployment of the Force on only one side of the armistice line. On this basis, the Force would have units in the Gaza area as well as opposite El Auja. With demilitarization of the El Auja zone in accordance with the Armistice Agreement, it might be indicated that the Force should have units stationed also on the Israel side of the armistice demarcation line, at least, in that zone. Such deployment, which would require a new decision by the General Assembly, would have the advantage of the Force being in a position to assume the supervisory duties of the Truce Supervision Organization in all the territory where that Organization now functions under the Armistice Agreement between Egypt and Israel. In both Gaza and El Auja, the functions of the Truce Supervision Organization and the Force would somewhat overlap if such an arrangement were not to be made. As an arrangement of this kind was not foreseen by the Armistice Agreement, it obviously would require the consent of the two parties to that Agreement. Such mutual consent might be given to the United Nations directly, especially since the arrangement would be on an *ad hoc* basis.

22. As indicated in the previous report (A/3500 and Add. 1), the United Nations Emergency Force and the Truce Supervision Organization, with their respective responsibilities for the cease-fire, should co-operate in the prevention of incursions and raids across the armistice demarcation lines. It was further indicated in the same report that, once the withdrawal is ensured, in implementation of the General Assembly resolution of 2 November 1956, formal assurance should be solicited from the parties to desist from raids and to take active measures to prevent incursions. In the course of the discussions which have taken place since the circulation of his last report, the Secretary-General has been informed of the desire of the Government of Egypt that all raids and incursions across the armistice line, in both directions, be brought to an end, and that United Nations auxiliary organs afford effective assistance to that effect. [*A/3512, Report of the Secretary-General in pursuance of General Assembly Res. 1123 (XI), 24 Jan. 1957.*]

The Assembly approved the Secretary-General's recommendations concerning the functions of UNEF (Res. 1121 (XI)); and in Resolution 1125 (X) urged that UNEF should be placed on the Egyptian–Israeli armistice demarcation line, 'after full withdrawal by Israel from the Sharm el Sheikh and Gaza areas . . . with a view to assist in achieving situations conducive to the maintenance of peaceful conditions in the area'.

This resolution was only partly fulfilled, as UNEF was deployed only on the Egyptian side of the armistice demarcation line and the international frontier. But, in very specific terms, the sorts of functions which UNEF carried out may be seen from the following:

(a) *In the Suez area*

The initial activity of UNEF centred in the Suez Canal area, mainly during the period between the arrival of UNEF in Egypt on 12 November and the withdrawal of the Anglo-French forces on 22 December 1956. Within that period it:

(i) Was interposed between the Anglo-French and Egyptian forces through occupation of a buffer zone south of El Cap, extending northwards to Port Said, as the Anglo-French troops moved in that direction;

(ii) Rendered assistance in Port Said and Port Fuad in maintaining calm between the civilian population and the Anglo-French forces, through stationing and patrolling, and also shared responsibility with local authorities for keeping the peace among the civilian population;

(iii) Guarded the power station in Port Fuad;

(iv) Maintained a safety cordon around areas in Port Said and Port Fuad from which Anglo-French forces were embarking in the final stage of their withdrawal;

(v) Assisted, at the request of Egypt, in avoiding sabotage of the oilfields at Sadar and El Balayin;

(vi) Cleared mine fields;

(vii) Arranged and carried out the exchange in the buffer zone of approximately 850 prisoners, detainees and internees, between the Egyptian Government and the Anglo-French Command;

(viii) Provided protection for British and French ships engaged in the Suez Canal salvage operation;

(ix) Conducted investigations of various complaints and inquiries by Egyptian authorities and the Anglo-French Command concerning such matters as violations of cease-fire, smuggling activities and missing personnel;

(x) Guarded the off-loading of stores and vehicles for UNEF from ships at Port Said, and continues to do so.

(b) *In the Sinai Peninsula*

The second period of UNEF activity, from December 1956 to March 1957, centred in the Sinai Peninsula after the Anglo-French withdrawals and the gradual withdrawal of Israel forces. In this stage it:

(i) Took over from the Israel forces in the successive stages of their withdrawal from Sinai, including the Sharm el Sheikh region;

(ii) Took over from Israel forces the Saint Catherine's Monastery in southern Sinai, accompanied, on entry, by a representative of the United Nations Educational, Scientific and Cultural Organization to ascertain the condition of the Monastery's cultural treasures; prior to the Israel withdrawal, a UNEF supply convoy to the Monastery was arranged at the request of Egypt and with the consent of Israel;

(iii) Has been interposed between the forces of Egypt and Israel, east of the Canal, from 3 December 1956 onwards;

(iv) Arranged and carried out the exchange of all prisoners of war between Egypt and Israel;

(v) Cleared many Sinai mine fields;

(vi) Cleared and repaired portions of damaged roads and rough tracks crossing the Sinai;

(vii) Investigated, at the request of Egypt, the Romani railroad station incident.

(c) *In the Gaza Strip*

UNEF's heaviest responsibilities and most difficult duties have been in the Gaza Strip since 8 March. The Force:

(i) On the withdrawal of Israel troops and in the absence of any organized or responsible local administration, took up positions in all centres of population and camps in the area, controlled all entry into and exit from the Strip, and, with the assistance of officials of the United Nations Relief and Works Agency for Palestine Refugees in the Near East (UNRWA), temporarily assumed responsibility for some essential services in the Strip, including internal security functions mainly relating to guard and check post duty and patrolling with a view to preventing mob disorders, violence and looting;

(ii) Assumed temporary control of the prisons;

(iii) Guarded key installations, such as all public utilities;

(iv) Took in safe keeping local vital records which it found;

(v) Manned temporarily the telephone switchboard of the town of Gaza;

(vi) In view of the shortage in Gaza of petroleum products, arranged for loan of diesel oil from UNRWA supply to maintain essential electric service;

(vii) Assisted efforts to determine whereabouts of deportees from Gaza, while it was under Israel's control;

(viii) Through deployment around the perimeter of the Gaza Strip and constant patrolling assisted by orders of the Gaza administration to the people not to cross the line nor, after darkness, to enter a zone extending 500 metres from it, prevents infiltrations and crossings of the demarcation line for any purpose;

(ix) Continues, with regard to UNEF personnel and affairs, to man joint Egyptian–UNEF check posts controlling entry into and exit from the Gaza Strip, from and into Egypt;

(x) Cleared extensive and thickly sown mine fields.

(d) *General*

In addition to the above, UNEF:

(i) Airlifted seventy-two Egyptian prisoners of war from Djibouti (French Somaliland) to Cairo;

(ii) Arranged for repatriation to Egypt of two persons under treatment in a hospital on the Israel side of Jerusalem. [*A/3694 and Add. 1, Report of the Secretary-General, 9 Oct. 1957.*]

4

CONSTITUTIONAL BASIS

THE negative votes of France and the United Kingdom in the Security Council prevented that organ from reaching agreement on a United States draft resolution of the Suez intervention.[1] Still less acceptable was a Russian draft. On 31 October 1956 a resolution was carried calling for an emergency special

[1] S/3710. This draft resolution called upon the parties to 'refrain from the use of force or the threat of force in the area in any manner inconsistent with the principles of the United Nations' and 'to assist the United Nations in ensuring the integrity of the armistice agreement' between Egypt and Israel.

session of the Assembly. France and the United Kingdom voted against this resolution (S/3719), but under the 'Uniting for Peace' procedure established by Resolution 377(V), such a resolution is not subject to the veto. Accordingly, having obtained the seven necessary affirmative votes, the question was transferred to the General Assembly. It will be recalled that the Assembly then passed Resolution 997 (ES–I) on 2 November 1956, which was based on a United States draft. Resolution 997 (ES–I) asked for a plan by the Secretary-General on the setting up of an emergency force; and the Force was established by Resolution 1000 (ES–I), which was based on a draft submitted by Canada, Colombia, and Norway.

Although the United Kingdom and France have never challenged the constitutionality of UNEF, they did argue that the transfer of the matter from the Security Council to the Assembly was an improper use of the Uniting for Peace resolution.[2] These countries took the view that

In the debate on the Egyptian complaint, no draft resolution was submitted. Therefore there was no vote and, consequently, no manifestation of the lack of unanimity of the permanent members. In the circumstances, the Council could not legally bring the Egyptian complaint before the Assembly. The United States complaint, on the other hand, was clearly within the framework of Chapter VI, not Chapter VII, of the Charter. In that case too there was no reason to bring the matter before the Assembly, because, irrespective of whether or not Chapter VII was involved, the second condition laid down by the 'Uniting for peace' resolution was not fulfilled.[3] [*Per the representative of France, GAOR, 1st emerg. spec. sess., 561st mtg, 1 Nov. 1956.*]

The fact that UNEF was established at a special session of the Assembly convened by the Uniting for Peace procedure has led some persons to assume that the constitutional authority for UNEF thus lies in the Uniting for Peace resolution.[4] The Uniting for Peace resolution—originating as it did from the Korean situation, and aiming to guarantee future UN action even when the veto of a permanent member prevents agreement in the Security Council—had always been opposed by the Soviet Union and her allies.[5] Two other possible bases for UNEF existed, however. The first was based on the argument that

[2] See *SCOR*, 11th yr, 751st mtg. The so-called 'Uniting for Peace' resolution provides, *inter alia* 'that if the Security Council, because of lack of unanimity of the permanent members, fails to exercise its primary responsibility for the maintenance of international peace and security in any case where there appears to be a threat to the peace, breach of the peace, or act of aggression, the General Assembly shall consider the matter immediately with a view to making appropriate recommendations to Members for collective measures, including in the case of a breach of the peace or act of aggression the use of armed force when necessary, to maintain or restore international peace and security. If not in session at the time, the General Assembly may meet in emergency special session within twenty-four hours of the request therefor. Such emergency special session shall be called if requested by the Security Council on the vote of any seven members' (General Assembly Res. 377 (V)).

[3] For a criticism of these arguments, see R. St J. Macdonald, 1957, 35 *Canadian Bar R.*, p. 53.

[4] See, for example, the Canadian view in *Certain Expenses of the United Nations, ICJ, Pleadings, 1962*, pp. 216–19.

[5] For a detailed discussion of the Soviet attitude towards this resolution see this writer's, 'The Functions and Constitutional Bases of United Nations Forces', in D. Bowett, *United Nations Forces* (1964), esp. pp. 290–8. While denying that this resolution can provide the legal basis of UN para-military action, Russia has from time to time found it useful to approve the purely *procedural* device in this resolution—namely the transfer of a matter from a veto-ridden Security Council to the General Assembly. And the transfer of the Suez question, under discussion, is a case in point.

everything that is not explicitly prohibited in the Charter is permitted. Accordingly, it has been argued, UNEF must be regarded as legal since there is nothing which formally forbids the General Assembly to establish a peacekeeping force which operates with the consent of the host country. The Soviet Union and other eastern European countries, however, have contended that the provisions of Chapter VII do in effect entail a prohibition to the Assembly in respect of the establishment of UN Forces. The second alternative basis for UNEF has been sought in certain specific articles of the Charter, which have been pointed to as capable of sustaining a force such as UNEF, set up by the Assembly. Again the Soviet Union and her friends, when looking at these same articles—Articles 10, 11, 14, and 22 of the Charter—have denied that they can provide a legal basis for UNEF, the more so as they must be read in conjunction with Chapter VII which, it is claimed, reserves all military action to the sole prerogative of the Security Council. It was only because Egypt consented to UNEF that the Soviet Union abstained on, rather than voted against its creation.

These arguments have proved far from merely academic, for they represent the formal enunciation of the positions which governments have taken on the desirability or wisdom of acknowledging Assembly authority to initiate peacekeeping action. Those who have regarded such action by the Assembly as illegal have shown their disapproval in a variety of ways, which have made an exact repetition of the UNEF model unlikely. Moreover, they have—on these and other grounds—refused to contribute to the financial support of UNEF, which has in the course of time not only presented UNEF with severe financial difficulties, but has also led the UN into the severest political difficulties.[6] The details of the arguments concerning the finance of UNEF are reproduced below, in Section 11. They must, however, be read together with this section, for the dispute over the financing of UNEF has been in reality a dispute over where, within the UN, control over peacekeeping should lie. The opposing views briefly outlined above on the aternative constitutional bases of UNEF were eventually elaborated before the International Court of Justice, and we shall return to them below.

The question of whether the General Assembly could legally establish a peacekeeping force was essentially interwoven with the question of the 'consent' of the host state; for the majority view has been that enforcement action against a state may well be reserved to the Security Council,[7] but UNEF represents 'policing' action which, far from being carried out against a state, depends upon the specific consent of the host government. This, it has been contended, is perfectly appropriate for the Assembly to authorize. Nor, it should be added,

---

[6] For an account of the issues at stake in the financial and political crisis which came to a head in the early 1960s, see Higgins, 'United Nations Peacekeeping; political and financial problems', *World Today*, Aug. 1965, pp. 324–37.

[7] At least in so far as that organ is purporting to *order* such action. The Uniting for Peace resolution provides that where there is a breach of the peace or act of aggression, the Assembly may recommend collective measures. (The Security Council may act under Art. 39 of the Charter, not only when there is a breach of the peace or act of aggression, but also where there is a threat to the peace.)

was UNEF established in order to compel a withdrawal by the British, French, and Israeli forces.

In his second and final report on the plan for setting up of an Emergency Force, the Secretary-General touched on some of these constitutional issues:

QUESTIONS OF PRINCIPLE

4. An emergency international United Nations Force can be developed on the basis of three different concepts:

(a) It can, in the *first* place, be set up on the basis of principles reflected in the constitution of the United Nations itself. This would mean that its chief responsible officer should be appointed by the United Nations, and that he, in his functions, should be responsible ulti-mately to the General Assembly and/or the Security Council. His authority should be so defined as to make him fully independent of the policies of any one nation. His relations to the Secretary-General of the United Nations should correspond to those of the Chief of Staff of the United Nations Truce Supervision Organization;

(b) A *second* possibility is that the United Nations charge a country, or a group of countries, with the responsibility to provide independently for an emergency international Force serving for purposes determined by the United Nations. In this case it would obviously be impossible to achieve the same independence in relation to national policies as would be established through the first approach;

(c) Finally, as a *third* possibility, an emergency international Force may be set up in agree-ment among a group of nations, later to be brought into an appropriate relationship to the United Nations. This approach is open to the same reservation as the second one, and possibly others.

Variations of form, of course, are possible within a wide range, but the three concepts mentioned seem to circumscribe the problem.

5. In the decision on the establishment of the United Nations Command, on an emergency basis, which the General Assembly took on 5 November 1956, the Assembly chose to follow the first of the three types mentioned in paragraph 4 above. The second type was that fol-lowed in the case of the Unified Command in Korea. There is no precedent for the use of the third type, but it would seem to represent one of the possible forms for implementation of the suggestion in the replies of 5 November 1956 of the Governments of France and the United Kingdom (A/3294, A/3293) to my request for a cease-fire. In attempting to work out a plan for setting up an emergency international United Nations Force, I have based my considera-tions on the legal situation created by the decision in principle of the General Assembly, implied in the request of the Assembly to me to submit within forty-eight hours a plan for such a Force, and in its later decision to establish a United Nations Command, in implemen-tation of this first resolution.

9. Functioning, as it would, on the basis of a decision reached under the terms of the reso-lution 337 (V) 'Uniting for Peace', the Force, if established, would be limited in its operations to the extent that consent of the parties concerned is required under generally recognized international law. While the General Assembly is enabled to *establish* the Force with the con-sent of those parties which contribute units to the Force, it could not request the Force to be *stationed* or *operate* on the territory of a given country without the consent of the Government of that country. This does not exclude the possibility that the Security Council could use such a Force within the wider margins provided under Chapter VII of the United Nations Charter. I would not for the present consider it necessary to elaborate this point further, since no use of the Force under Chapter VII, with the rights in relation to Member States that this would entail, has been envisaged.

10. The point just made permits the conclusion that the setting up of the Force should not be guided by the needs which would have existed had the measure been considered as part of an enforcement action directed against a Member country. There is an obvious difference

between establishing the Force in order to secure the cessation of hostilities, with a withdrawal of forces, and establishing such a Force with a view to enforcing a withdrawal of forces. It follows that while the Force is different in that, as in many other respects, from the observers of the United Nations Truce Supervision Organization, it is, although para-military in nature, not a Force with military objectives. [*A/3302, 2nd and final Report of the Secretary-General on the plan for an emergency UN Force, 6 Nov. 1956.*]

The Soviet Union clearly stated her own position, however:

As regards the creation and stationing on Egyptian territory of an international police force, the Soviet delegation is obliged to point out that this Force is being created in violation of the United Nations Charter.

292. The General Assembly resolution on the basis of which it is now proposed to form this Force is inconsistent with the Charter. Chapter VII of the Charter empowers the Security Council, and the Security Council only, not the General Assembly, to set up an international armed force and to take such action as it may deem necessary, including the use of such a force, to maintain or restore international peace and security.

293. The resolution on the creation of an international armed force is also inconsistent with the purposes for which the United Nations Charter permits the creation and use of an international force. The Charter envisages the use of such a force to help a State victim of aggression to repel the aggressor and to defend such a State against the aggressor. [*Per the Russian representative, GAOR, 1st emerg. spec. sess., 567th mtg, 7 Nov. 1956.*]

The Soviet Union later elaborated the implications of this view:

64. As we all know, the creation of an international United Nations force under Chapter VII of the Charter is a matter exclusively within the competence of the Security Council. The General Assembly's decision to establish the United Nations Emergency Force is therefore completely contrary to that chapter of the Charter.

65. For that reason . . . the Soviet delegation reiterates that the Soviet Union will not contribute to meet the expenses of the United Nations Emergency Force, created in violation of the Charter, and that all expenditure arising out of the action taken by the United Nations to put an end to the aggression against Egypt should be borne by the aggressors. [*GAOR, 11th sess., 632nd plen. mtg.*]

While the Secretary-General's report received widespread support, certain nations felt that paragraph 9 went altogether too far in suggesting that UNEF, set up for one purpose by the Assembly, could possibly be subsequently used by the Security Council for action under Chapter VII:[8]

308. Mr SERRANO (Philippines): We abstained on operative paragraph 1 of the draft resolution in document A/3308 because that paragraph approved in its entirety the exposition of principles contained in paragraphs 6 to 9 of the Secretary-General's report. While we are in full agreement with those principles, we cannot subscribe to a sentence contained therein, in so far as it relates to the possibility of using this international police force for collective action under Chapter VII of the Charter. We feel that to open the door to that possibility is rather dangerous and may create serious apprehensions in the minds of contributing Governments. [*GAOR, 1st emerg. spec. sess., 567th plen. mtg.*]

The need for consent was generally accepted, Israel being among those supporting the principle:

92. The first and crucial legal problem which arises is that of the sovereignty of States in the context of the consent required for the implementation of this project. The consent required

---

[8] This criticism of para. 9 is one with which the present Editor concurs.

is not merely or primarily the consent of the States invited to participate in the force, but chiefly the consent of those States upon the territory of which it is proposed to station these forces. It would seem to my delegation to be axiomatic under the law of the Charter that the stationing of any force in a territory under Israel's jurisdiction or control is not possible in law without the Israel Government's sovereign consent and that this principle would of course apply to the territory of any other State under whose jurisdictional control it was proposed to station these forces. Although this matter might be regarded as axiomatic, it would, I think, be helpful if the authors of the draft resolution would clarify this most important point of law. If this question of sovereign consent were not clarified, then a precedent would be created whereby a majority of the General Assembly could decide to station forces in the territory of any State irrespective of its prior consent. . . . [*Ibid. 565th mtg.*]

Furthermore

22. We note the suggestion in the report that 'the Secretary-General, in carrying out the policies of the United Nations, must act with scrupulous regard for the decisions of the General Assembly, the Security Council and the other principal organs'. (*A/3512, para. 5.*) My delegation sees no reason for departing from the text of the Charter which, under Article 25, ascribes the capacity of 'decision' only to the Security Council, and, under other articles, the capacity of 'recommendation' to the General Assembly. This point has relevance to the present case, in view of Israel's claim of legal priority for the Security Council's decision of 1 September 1951 over anything that the General Assembly can recommend, especially in any context affecting maritime freedom. [*GAOR, 11th sess., 645th plen. mtg.*]

This being so, the Secretary-General established contact with the Egyptian government, and arranged for General Burns to fly to Cairo for consultations.

4. The Chief of Command has established direct radio contact with allied forces in Cyprus, which will be necessary for clearance and aircraft passage and, later, for other purposes. Egyptian authorities agreed this morning also, in principle, to accept ten observers at once in Cairo. These observers will need jeeps and radios. Therefore the Chief of Command will try to send these by road to Egypt. The Israel Government has been requested to allow passage. That is the announcement I feel I should make as the first progress report on the setting up of the Force in the area. [*GAOR, 1st emerg. spec. sess., 566th mtg.*]

A year later, the Secretary-General had the following observations to make on the legal basis for UNEF:

30. By mid-September 1957, UNEF will have completed ten months of duty, during which it has been called upon to undertake important responsibilities involving a considerable variety of tasks. The Command for the Force, established by General Assembly resolution 1000 (ES–I), was to 'secure and supervise the cessation of hostilities in accordance with all the terms of General Assembly resolution 997 (ES–I)'. The General Assembly, in resolution 1001 (ES–I), approved guiding principles for the organization and functioning of the Force, as set forth in the Secretary-General's report of 6 November 1956 (A/3302), whereby, as must follow from its status under the Charter, the Force could not be stationed or operate on a country's territory without that country's consent.

31. The Force, which has an international character as a subsidiary organ of the General Assembly, as affirmed in its regulations, was not established to undertake enforcement actions. While UNEF has a military organization, it does not use all normal military methods in achieving the objectives defined for it by the General Assembly. As indicated in the Secretary-General's report mentioned above, the functions foreseen for UNEF, when the cease-fire was being established, were to enter Egyptian territory with the consent of the Egyptian Government, in order 'to help maintain quiet during and after the withdrawal of non-Egyptian troops'. [*A/3694, Report of the Secretary-General, 9 Oct. 1957.*]

He had also said:

19. The Charter has given to the Security Council means of enforcement and the right to take decisions with mandatory effect. No such authority is given to the General Assembly, which can only recommend action to Member Governments, which, in turn, may follow the recommendations or disregard them. This is also true of recommendations adopted by the General Assembly within the framework of the 'Uniting for peace' resolution (*resolution 377 (V)*). However, under that resolution the General Assembly has certain rights otherwise reserved to the Security Council. Thus, it can, under that resolution, recommend collective measures. In this case, also, the recommendation has not compulsory force.

20. It seems, in this context, appropriate to distinguish between recommendations which implement a Charter principle, which in itself is binding on Member States, and recommendations which, although adopted under the Charter, do not implement any such basic provision. A recommendation of the first kind would have behind it the force of the Charter, to which collective measures recommended by the General Assembly could add emphasis, without, however, changing the legal character of the recommendation. A decision on collective measures referring to a recommendation of the second kind, although likewise formally retaining its legal character, would mean that the recommendation is recognized by the General Assembly as being of such significance to the efforts of the United Nations as to assimilate it to a recommendation expressing an obligation established by the Charter. If, in some case, collective measures under the 'Uniting for peace' resolution were to be considered, these and other important questions of principle would require attention; this may also be said of the effect of such steps which, while supporting efforts to achieve peaceful solutions, may perhaps, on the other hand, be introducing new elements of conflict. [*A/3527, Report of the Secretary-General in pursuance of General Assembly Res. 1124 (XI) and 1125 (XI), 11 Feb. 1957.*]

The preparation in 1958 of a summary study on the experience derived from UNEF provided opportunity for further comments on the constitutional position:

15. The first emergency special session of the General Assembly, at which it was decided to establish an emergency force, had been called into session under the terms of the 'Uniting for peace' resolution (resolution 377 (V) of 3 November 1950). Thus, UNEF has been necessarily limited in its operations to the extent that consent of the parties concerned is required under generally recognized international law. It followed that, while the General Assembly could establish the Force, subject only to the concurrence of the States providing contingents, the consent of the Government of the country concerned was required before the Assembly could request the Force to be stationed or to operate on the territory of that country. The Force has no rights other than those necessary for the execution of the functions assigned to it by the General Assembly and agreed to by the country or countries concerned. The Force is paramilitary in character and much more than an observer corps, but it is in no sense a military force exercising, through force of arms, even temporary control over the territory in which it is stationed; nor does it have military objectives, or military functions exceeding those necessary to secure peaceful conditions on the assumption that the parties to the conflict will take all the necessary steps for compliance with the recommendations of the General Assembly. . . .

19. The Regulations for the Force (ST/SGB/UNEF/1) affirm its international character as a subsidiary organ of the General Assembly. The Assembly intended that the Force should be a temporary arrangement, whose duration would be determined by the needs created by the emergency, and whose tasks and legal basis could be defined only by the Assembly. . . . .

127. The Force was recognized as a subsidiary organ of the General Assembly, established under the authority of Article 22 of the Charter of the United Nations (Regulation 6). [*A/3943, Summary Study on the experience of UNEF.*]

In December 1961 the General Assembly, faced with a growing financial and political crisis,[9] decided to ask the International Court whether the expenditures authorized by the Assembly in respect of UNEF and ONUC (the operation in the Congo) were ' "expenses of the Organization" within the meaning of Article 17, paragraph 2, of the Charter of the United Nations'. The constitutionality of UNEF (and ONUC) was thus not directly at issue, although indirectly it was at issue, because the Court had to address itself to the argument that expenditures on illegal operations could not constitute 'expenses of the Organizations' under Article 17 (2). In the event, the Court asserted that if action was taken which was within the scope of the UN, it could give rise to 'expenses of the Organization' even if it was initiated or carried out in a manner not in conformity with the division of functions between the Assembly and the Security Council.[10] Nevertheless, the Court offered a detailed analysis of the legal authority of the UN in respect of peacekeeping, which is directly relevant to the legal basis of UNEF. The Court indicated that the argument on expenses

leads to an examination of the respective functions of the General Assembly and of the Security Council under the Charter, particularly with respect to the maintenance of international peace and security.

Article 24 of the Charter provides:

'In order to ensure prompt and effective action by the United Nations, its Members confer on the Security Council primary responsibility for the maintenance of international peace and security. . . .'

The responsibility conferred is 'primary', not exclusive. This primary responsibility is conferred upon the Security Council, as stated in Article 24, 'in order to ensure prompt and effective action'. To this end, it is the Security Council which is given a power to impose an explicit obligation of compliance if for example it issues an order or command to an aggressor under Chapter VII. It is only the Security Council which can require enforcement by coercive action against an aggressor.

The Charter makes it abundantly clear, however, that the General Assembly is also to be concerned with international peace and security.

Article 14 authorizes the General Assembly to 'recommend measures for the peaceful adjustment of any situation, regardless of origin, which it deems likely to impair the general welfare or friendly relations among nations, including situations resulting from a violation of the provisions of the present Charter setting forth the purposes and principles of the United Nations'. The word 'measures' implies some kind of action, and the only limitation which Article 14 imposes on the General Assembly is the restriction found in Article 12, namely, that the Assembly should not recommend measures while the Security Council is dealing with the same matter unless the Council requests it to do so. Thus while it is the Security Council which, exclusively, may order coercive action, the functions and powers conferred by the Charter on the General Assembly are not confined to discussion, consideration, the initiation of studies and the making of recommendations; they are not merely hortatory. Article 18 deals with '*decisions*' of the General Assembly 'on important questions'. These 'decisions' do indeed include certain recommendations, but others have dispositive force and effect. Among these latter decisions, Article 18 includes suspension of rights and privileges of membership, expulsion of Members, 'and budgetary questions'. In connection with the suspension of rights and privileges of membership and expulsion from membership under Articles 5 and 6,

---

[9] See s. 11, pp. 438ff.

[10] 'Certain Expenses of the UN', Advisory Opinion of 20 July 1962, *ICJ Rep. 1962*, p. 168.

it is the Security Council which has only the power to recommend and it is the General Assembly which decides and whose decision determines status; but there is a close collaboration between the two organs. Moreover, these powers of decision of the General Assembly under Articles 5 and 6 are specifically related to preventive or enforcement measures. . . .

The argument supporting a limitation on the budgetary authority of the General Assembly with respect to the maintenance of international peace and security relies especially on the reference to 'action' in the last sentence of Article 11, paragraph 2. This paragraph reads as follows:

'The General Assembly may discuss any questions relating to the maintenance of international peace and security brought before it by any Member of the United Nations, or by the Security Council, or by a State which is not a Member of the United Nations in accordance with Article 35, paragraph 2, and, except as provided in Article 12, may make recommendations with regard to any such question to the State or States concerned or to the Security Council, or to both. Any such question on which action is necessary shall be referred to the Security Council by the General Assembly either before or after discussion.'

The Court considers that the kind of action referred to in Article 11, paragraph 2, is coercive or enforcement action.

This paragraph, which applies not merely to general questions relating to peace and security, but also to specific cases brought before the General Assembly by a State under Article 35, in its first sentence empowers the General Assembly, by means of recommendations to States or to the Security Council, or to both, to organize peacekeeping operations, at the request, or with the consent, of the States concerned. This power of the General Assembly is a special power which in no way derogates from its general powers under Article 10 or Article 14, except as limited by the last sentence of Article 11, paragraph 2. This last sentence says that when 'action' is necessary the General Assembly shall refer the question to the Security Council. The word 'action' must mean such action as is solely within the province of the Security Council. It cannot refer to recommendations which the Security Council might make, as for instance under Article 38, because the General Assembly under Article 11 has a comparable power. The 'action' which is solely within the province of the Security Council is that which is indicated by the title of Chapter VII of the Charter, namely 'Action with respect to threats to the peace, breaches of the peace, and acts of aggression'. If the word 'action' in Article 11, paragraph 2, were interpreted to mean that the General Assembly could make recommendations only of a general character affecting peace and security in the abstract, and not in relation to specific cases, the paragraph would not have provided that the General Assembly may make recommendations on questions brought before it by States or by the Security Council. Accordingly, the last sentence of Article 11, paragraph 2, has no application where the necessary action is not enforcement action.

The practice of the Organization throughout its history bears out the foregoing elucidation of the term 'action' in the last sentence of Article 11, paragraph 2. Whether the General Assembly proceeds under Article 11 or under Article 14, the implementation of its recommendations for setting up commissions or other bodies involves organizational activity—action—in connection with the maintenance of international peace and security. Such implementation is a normal feature of the functioning of the United Nations. Such committees, commissions or other bodies or individuals, constitute, in some cases, subsidiary organs established under the authority of Article 22 of the Charter. The functions of the General Assembly for which it may establish such subsidiary organs include, for example, investigation, observation and supervision, but the way in which such subsidiary organs are utilized depends on the consent of the State or States concerned.

The Court accordingly finds that the argument which seeks, by reference to Article 11, paragraph 2, to limit the bugetary authority of the General Assembly in respect of the maintenance of international peace and security, is unfounded.

It has further been argued before the Court that Article 43 of the Charter constitutes a particular rule, a *lex specialis*, which derogates from the general rule in Article 17, whenever an expenditure for the maintenance of international peace and security is involved. Article 43 provides that Members shall negotiate agreements with the Security Council on its initiative, stipulating what 'armed forces, assistance and facilities, including rights of passage, necessary for the purpose of maintaining international peace and security', the Member State will make available to the Security Council on its call. According to paragraph 2 of the Article:

'Such agreement or agreements shall govern the numbers and types of forces, their degree of readiness and general location, and the nature of the facilities and assistance to be provided.'

The argument is that such agreements were intended to include specifications concerning the allocation of costs of such enforcement actions as might be taken by direction of the Security Council, and that it is only the Security Council which has the authority to arrange for meeting such costs.

With reference to this argument, the Court will state at the outset that, for reasons fully expounded later in this Opinion, the operations known as UNEF and ONUC were not *enforcement* actions within the compass of Chapter VII of the Charter and that therefore Article 43 could not have any applicability to the cases with which the Court is here concerned. However, even if Article 43 were applicable, the Court could not accept this interpretation of its text. . . .

In considering the operations in the Middle East, the Court must analyze the functions of UNEF as set forth in resolutions of the General Assembly. Resolution 998 (ES–I) of 4 November 1956 requested the Secretary-General to submit a plan 'for the setting up, with the consent of the nations concerned, of an emergency international United Nations Force to secure and supervise the cessation of hostilities in accordance with all the terms of' the General Assembly's previous resolution 997 (ES–I) of 2 November 1956. The verb 'secure' as applied to such matters as halting the movement of military forces and arms into the area and the conclusion of a cease-fire, might suggest measures of enforcement, were it not that the Force was to be set up 'with the consent of the nations concerned'.

In his first report on the plan for an emergency international Force the Secretary-General used the language of resolution 998 (ES–I) in submitting his proposals. The same terms are used in General Assembly resolution 1000 (ES–I) of 5 November in which operative paragraph 1 reads:

'*Establishes* a United Nations Command for an emergency international Force to secure and supervise the cessation of hostilities in accordance with all the terms of General Assembly resolution 997 (ES–I) of 2 November 1956.'

This resolution was adopted without a dissenting vote. In his second and final report on the plan for an emergency international Force of 6 November, the Secretary-General, in paragraphs 9 and 10, stated:

'While the General Assembly is enabled to *establish* the Force with the consent of those parties which contribute units to the Force, it could not request the Force to be *stationed* or *operate* on the territory of a given country without the consent of the Government of that country. This does not exclude the possibility that the Security Council could use such a Force within the wider margins provided under Chapter VII of the United Nations Charter. I would not for the present consider it necessary to elaborate this point further, since no use of the Force under Chapter VII, with the rights in relation to Member States that this would entail, has been envisaged.

10. The point just made permits the conclusion that the setting up of the Force should not be guided by the needs which would have existed had the measure been considered as part of an enforcement action directed against a Member country. There is an obvious difference between establishing the Force in order to secure the cessation of hostilities,

with a withdrawal of forces, and establishing such a Force with a view to enforcing a withdrawal of forces.'

Paragraph 12 of the Report is particularly important because in resolution 1001 (ES–I) the General Assembly, again without a dissenting vote, '*Concurs* in the definition of the functions of the Force as stated in paragraph 12 of the Secretary-General's report'. Paragraph 12 reads in part as follows:

> 'the functions of the United Nations Force would be, when a cease-fire is being established, to enter Egyptian territory with the consent of the Egyptian Government, in order to help maintain quiet during and after the withdrawal of non-Egyptian troops, and to secure compliance with the other terms established in the resolution of 2 November 1956. The Force obviously should have no rights other than those necessary for the execution of its functions, in co-operation with local authorities. It would be more than an observers' corps, but in no way a military force temporarily controlling the territory in which it is stationed; nor, moreover, should the Force have military functions exceeding those necessary to secure peaceful conditions on the assumption that the parties to the conflict take all necessary steps for compliance with the recommendations of the General Assembly.'

It is not possible to find in this description of the functions of UNEF, as outlined by the Secretary-General and concurred in by the General Assembly without a dissenting vote, any evidence that the Force was to be used for purposes of enforcement. Nor can such evidence be found in the subsequent operations of the Force, operations which did not exceed the scope of the functions ascribed to it.

It could not therefore have been patent on the face of the resolution that the establishment of UNEF was in effect 'enforcement action' under Chapter VII which, in accordance with the Charter, could be authorized only by the Security Council.

On the other hand, it is apparent that the operations were undertaken to fulfil a prime purpose of the United Nations, that is, to promote and to maintain a peaceful settlement of the situation. This being true, the Secretary-General properly exercised the authority given him to incur financial obligations of the Organization and expenses resulting from such obligations must be considered 'expenses of the Organization within the meaning of Article 17, paragraph 2'.

Apropos what has already been said about the meaning of the word 'action' in Article 11 of the Charter, attention may be called to the fact that resolution 997 (ES–I), which is chronologically the first of the resolutions concerning the operations in the Middle East mentioned in the request for the advisory opinion, provides in paragraph 5:

> '*Requests* the Secretary-General to observe and report promptly on the compliance with the present resolution to the Security Council *and* to the General Assembly, for such further *action as they may deem appropriate in accordance with the Charter.*'

The italicized words reveal an understanding that either of the two organs might take 'action' in the premises. Actually, as one knows, the 'action' was taken by the General Assembly in adopting two days later without a dissenting vote, resolution 998 (ES–I) and, also without a dissenting vote, within another three days, resolutions 1000 (ES–I) and 1001 (ES–I), all providing for UNEF.

The Court notes that these 'actions' may be considered 'measures' recommended under Article 14, rather than 'action' recommended under Article 11. The powers of the General Assembly stated in Article 14 are not made subject to the provisions of Article 11, but only of Article 12. Furthermore, as the Court has already noted, the word 'measures' implies some kind of action. So far as concerns the nature of the situations in the Middle East in 1956, they could be described as 'likely to impair . . . friendly relations among nations', just as well as they could be considered to involve 'the maintenance of international peace and security'. Since the resolutions of the General Assembly in question do not mention upon which article they are based, and since the language used in most of them might imply reference to either

Article 14 or Article 11, it cannot be excluded that they were based upon the former rather than the latter article. [*Extract from Advisory Opinion on Certain Expenses of the UN*,[11] *ICJ Reports 1962*, pp. 163–4, 170–2.]

It may thus be seen that the Court found that not only was UNEF a subsidiary organ of the Assembly legally constituted under Article 22, but that a more precise basis[12] could be found in other articles of the Charter.[13]

In 1967, when President Nasser requested UNEF's withdrawal, the question arose as to the appropriate organ to consider this request. U Thant in fact himself took the decision to withdraw UNEF. It is open to debate as to whether the Secretary-General has the constitutional authority to terminate a UN peacekeeping operation established by the Security Council or the General Assembly. The Secretary-General did not address himself to this point directly, but rather noted that he had fully consulted the Advisory Committee.[14] He appeared to argue that because UNEF had to withdraw if requested, no decision of the Assembly was needed. But the decision had none the less to be taken, and the question remains: did the Secretary-General have the constitutional authority? The truer reason for not going to the Assembly is revealed in paragraph 41 of the following document, when U Thant pointed to the likely hazards of an Assembly session. But this is hardly a legal reason.[15] The Secretary-General issued the following report:

The Question of Consultations

37. It has been said also that there was not adequate consultation with the organs of the United Nations concerned or with the Members before the decision was taken to withdraw

[11] For a detailed examination of the Court's Opinion, see L. Gross, 'Expenses of the UN peacekeeping operations; the Advisory Opinion of the International Court of Justice', *Int. Org.* (Winter 1963), pp. 1–35; R. Y. Jennings, 11 *Int. & Comp. Law Q* (1962), p. 1170; J. G. Stoessinger, *Financing the UN System* (1964), pp. 140–53.

[12] Art. 22 is limited by the scope of the Assembly's functions as they are defined elsewhere in the Charter, and thus cannot—in the view of this Editor—*of itself* provide the basis of a UN Force.

[13] The Court's 'preference for Article 14 which is stated only obliquely, is perhaps surprising, for that Article refers to the "peaceful adjustment of any situation . . . which it deems likely to impair the general welfare or friendly relations among nations", which seems to err on the side of understatement as a description of the situation following the intervention in Egypt in 1956' (Higgins, 'The Functions and Constitutional Bases of United Nations Forces', in Bowett, p. 289). Further 'The Court seems to be rejecting the popular and long-held view that the essential distinction between the powers of the Assembly and Security Council is that the former—with certain expectations—may only recommend, while the latter may order; in other words, that the Assembly may do by recommendation all that the Security Council can do under Chapter VII. The Court's definition of "action" is "coercive on enforcement action" not because that is the only *mandatory* form of action, but rather because this is the action that is "solely within the province of the Security Council". There is a strong suggestion in the language employed by the Court that coercive action is the sole prerogative of the Security Council, even if mobilized by means of recommendations. This point is very relevant to the constitutional authority to be found in the Uniting for Peace Resolution, which is largely based on the assumption that the Assembly may by means of recommendation do all that the Council can do under Chapter VII. It is perhaps significant that the Court omits completely in its Opinion all reference to this resolution' (pp. 288–9).

[14] For details on the Advisory Committee and on this aspect of UNEF's withdrawal, see below, pp. 274–7.

[15] One may contrast this with the expectations of students of UN peacekeeping. As recently as 1964 it had been said: 'The ultimate strategic and political control over UNEF lies with the General Assembly, which has the ultimate power of dissolution of the Force' (Bowett, p. 117).

the Force. The Secretary-General was, and is, firmly of the opinion that the decision for withdrawal of the Force, on the request of the host Government, rested with the Secretary-General after consultation with the Advisory Committe on UNEF, which is the organ established by the General Assembly for consultation regarding such matters. This was made clear by Secretary-General Hammarskjöld, who took the following position on 26 February 1957 in reply to a question about the withdrawal of the Force from Sharm el Sheikh:

> 'An indicated procedure would be for the Secretary-General to inform the Advisory Committee on the United Nations Emergency Force, which would determine whether the matter should be brought to the attention of the Assembly.'[16]

The Secretary-General consulted the Advisory Committee before replying to the letter of 18 May 1967 from the United Arab Republic requesting withdrawal. This consultation took place within a few hours after receipt of the United Arab Republic request, and the Advisory Committee was thus quickly informed of the decision which the Secretary-General had in mind to convey in his reply to the Foreign Minister of the United Arab Republic. As indicated in the report to the Security Council of 26 May 1967:

> 'The Committee did not move, as it was its right to do under the terms of paragraph 9 of General Assembly resolution 1001 (ES–I) of 7 November 1956, to request the convening of the General Assembly on the situation which had arisen.' (S7906, para. 4)

38. Before consulting the Advisory Committee on UNEF, the Secretary-General had also consulted the Permanent Representatives of the seven countries providing the contingents of UNEF and informed them of his intentions. This, in fact, was more than was formally required of the Secretary-General in the way of consultation.

39. Obviously, many Governments were concerned about the presence and functioning of UNEF and about the general situation in the area, but it would have been physically impossible to consult all of the interested representatives within any reasonable time. This was an emergency situation requiring urgent action. Moreover, it was perfectly clear that such consultations were sure to produce sharply divided counsel, even if they were limited to the permanent members of the Security Council. Such sharply divided advice would have complicated and exacerbated the situation, and, far from relieving the Secretary-General of the responsibility for the decision to be taken, would have made the decision much more difficult to take.

40. It has been said that the final decision on the withdrawal of UNEF should have been taken only after consideration by the General Assembly. This position is not only incorrect but also unrealistic. In resolution 1000 (ES–I) the General Assembly established a United Nations command for an emergency international force. On the basis of that resolution the Force was quickly recruited and its forward elements flown to the staging area at Naples. Thus, though established, it had to await the permission of the Government of Egypt to enter Egyptian territory. That permission was subsequently given by the Government of Egypt as a result of direct discussions between Secretary-General Hammarskjöld and President Nasser of Egypt. There is no official United Nations document on the basis of which any case could be made that there was any limitation on the authority of the Government of Egypt to rescind that consent at its pleasure, or which would indicate that the United Arab Republic had in any way surrendered its right to ask for and obtain at any time the removal of UNEF from its territory. This point is elaborated later in this report. . . .

41. As a practical matter, there would be little point in any case in taking such an issue to the General Assembly unless there would be reasonable certainty that that body could be expected expeditiously to reach a substantive decision. In the prevailing circumstances, the question could have been validly raised as to what decision other than the withdrawal of UNEF could have been reached by the Assembly once United Arab Republic consent for the continued presence of UNEF was withdrawn.

[16] *GAOR*, 11th sess., ann., a.i.66, doc. A/3563, ann. 1B, 2.

42. As regards the practical possibility of the Assembly considering the request for UNEF's withdrawal, it is relevant to observe that the next regular session of the General Assembly was some four months off at the time the withdrawal request was made. The special session of the General Assembly which was meeting at the time could have considered the question, according to rule 19 of the Assembly's rules of procedure, only if two-thirds or eighty-two members voted for the inclusion of the item in the agenda. It is questionable, to say the least, whether the necessary support could have been mustered for such a controversial item. There could have been no emergency special session since the issue was not then before the Security Council, and therefore the condition of lack of unanimity did not exist.

43. As far as consultation with or action by the Security Council was concerned, the Secretary-General reported to the Council on the situation leading up to and created by the withdrawal of UNEF on 19 May 1967 (S/7896). In that report he characterized the situation in the Near East as 'extremely menacing'. The Council met for the first time after this report on 24 May 1967, but took no action.

44. As has already been stated, the Advisory Committee did not make any move to bring the matter before the General Assembly, and no representative of any Member Government requested a meeting of either the Security Council or the General Assembly immediately following the Secretary-General's reports (A/6730 and S/7896). In this situation, the Secretary-General himself did not believe that any useful purpose would be served by his seeking a meeting of either organ, nor did he consider that there was basis for him to do so at that time. Furthermore, the information available to the Secretary-General did not lead him to believe that either the General Assembly or the Security Council would have decided that UNEF should remain on United Arab Republic territory, by force if necessary, despite the request of the Government of the United Arab Republic that it should leave. [*A/6730/Add.3, Report of the Secretary-General on the withdrawal of UNEF, 26 June 1967.*]

5

POLITICAL CONTROL

UNEF was established by the General Assembly, and in that sense the ultimate political control over the Force lay with that organ. It was the Assembly, also, which approved the appointment of the first Commander of UNEF,[1] and which had the authority to dismiss him. In fact, however, the Assembly delegated a very great deal of its powers: the Secretary-General did most of the military planning, including the negotiating with Egypt as to UNEF's geographical position. This may be said to mark the beginning of a four-year period, in which the Assembly embraced the policy of 'leave it to Dag'. In matters of strategic control he was assisted by a committee of military representatives from the contributing nations; and in political matters he was assisted by the Advisory Committee created by Assembly Resolution 1001 (ES–I). When Egypt required UNEF to withdraw, in May 1967, the decision to comply was taken by the Secretary-General, without any reference to the General Assembly.

---

[1] Cf. the Korean experience, where the Commander was designated by the USA and was dismissed by the USA. See the forthcoming Vol. 2 of this study, dealing with Asia.

The General Assembly. . . .

1. *Establishes* a United Nations Command for an emergency international Force. . . .

2. *Appoints*, on an emergency basis, the Chief of Staff of the United Nations Truce Super-vision Organization, Major-General E. L. M. Burns, as Chief of the Command. . . .

4. *Invites* the Secretary-General to take such administrative measures as may be necessary for the prompt execution of the actions envisaged in the present resolution. [*GA Res. 1000 (ES–I), 5 Nov. 1956.*]

The General Assembly. . . .

6. *Establishes* an Advisory Committee composed of one representative from each of the following countries: Brazil, Canada, Ceylon, Colombia, India, Norway and Pakistan, and requests this Committee, whose Chairman shall be the Secretary-General, to undertake the development of those aspects of the planning for the Force and its operation not already dealt with by the General Assembly and which do not fall within the area of the direct respon-sibility of the Chief of the Command;

7. *Authorizes* the Secretary-General to issue all regulations and instructions which may be essential to the effective functioning of the Force, following consultation with the Committee aforementioned, and to take all other necessary administrative and executive actions;

8. *Determines* that, following the fulfilment of the immediate responsibilities defined for it in operative paragraphs 6 and 7 above, the Advisory Committee shall continue to assist the Secretary-General in the responsibilities falling to him under the present and other relevant resolutions;

9. *Decides* that the Advisory Committee, in the performance of its duties, shall be empowered to request, through the usual procedures, the convening of the General Assembly and to report to the Assembly whenever matters arise which, in its opinion, are of such urgency and importance as to require consideration by the General Assembly itself. . . . [*GA Res. 1001 (ES–I), 7 Nov. 1956.*]

The Secretary-General himself had requested the establishment of such an Advisory Committee,[2] The Advisory Committee continued in existence throughout UNEF's stay in Egypt, but played a less important role after the first few months, when most of the major problems were ironed out.

None the less, the advice given, especially during the earlier stages, by the Advisory Committee, was undoubtedly valuable to the Secretary-General. The committee provided a manageable link both to the Assembly at large[3] and to the states contributing troops.

2. The Government of Egypt had, prior to the final decision of the General Assembly, accep-ted the Force in principle by formally accepting the preceding resolution 1000 (ES–I) on the establishment of a United Nations Command. Before consenting to the arrival of the Force, the Government of Egypt wished to have certain points in the resolutions of the General Assembly clarified. An exchange of views took place between the Secretary-General and the Government of Egypt in which the Secretary-General, in reply to questions addressed to him by the Government of Egypt, gave his interpretations of the relevant General Assembly resolutions, in respect of the character and functions of the Force. At the end of the exchange, he gave to the Advisory Committee set up by General Assembly resolution 1001 (ES–I), a full account of the interpretations given. Approving these interpretations, the Advisory Committee recommended that the Secretary-General should proceed to start the transfer of the United Nations Emergency Force. [*A/3375, 20 Nov. 1956, p. 9.*]

[2] A/3302, 2nd and Final Report on the Plan for UNEF, 6 Nov. 1956, para. 18.

[3] There had, nevertheless, been some criticism of the composition of the committee. In particular the omission of an eastern European country was resented in some quarters, and an attempt to secure Czechoslovak participation was made (*GAOR*, 1st emerg. spec. sess., p. 108, per Poland).

This approval, by both Egypt and the Advisory Committee, permitted the speedy dispatch of the first UNEF contingents without waiting for any final agreements. The Advisory Committee was also consulted on the promulgation of the regulations for UNEF. The Advisory Committee also had an important role to play in respect of Gaza—initially the UN assigned civilian administrators to the Gaza Strip,[4] but anti-UN riots occurred. Egypt then accused UNEF—on 12 March 1957—of exceeding its authority, and President Nasser named an Egyptian governor for the region. The Advisory Committee for UNEF met on 18 March, and although some six members urged that the UN retain internal security over Gaza in worder to prevent a resumption of the *fedayeen* raids, there was no further attempt by the UN to 'govern' the Gaza Strip.[5] The Advisory Committee was also consulted when the policy was formulated that UNEF should use force only in self defence.[6] The Assembly further assigned to 'the Secretary-General, in consultation with the Advisory Committee . . . final authority for all administrative and financial operations of the Force'.[7]

Thus the system of political control adopted was the appointment of a Commander by the Assembly, to act under instructions from the Secretary-General (in conformity with purposes stipulated by the Assembly), who was in turn to consult a special committee of the Assembly. In his Summary Study of UNEF, written in 1958, the Secretary-General was to comment:

30. . . . In its advisory capacity, this Committee was to assist the Secretary-General in the planning and operation of the Force. It was empowered to request, through the usual procedures, the convening of the General Assembly and to report to the Assembly, if matters should arise which, in its opinion, were of such urgency and importance as to require consideration by the Assembly itself. It has had no occasion to invoke this authority. Meetings of the Advisory Committee have been held whenever matters have arisen requiring discussion, or whenever the Secretary-General has sought advice, or, at times, only to keep the Committee informed on current developments. The Advisory Committee has been consulted particularly on those questions which the Assembly had indicated should be the subject of consultation between it and the Secretary-General, such as the Regulations for the Force, the policy of the Force with regard to self-defence, and the issue of medals. The effective assistance rendered by the Committee was noted with appreciation by the Assembly at its twelfth session, in resolution 1151 (XII) and the Secretary-General, in the introduction to his annual report to that session (A/3594/Add. 1) paid tribute to the indispensable services performed by the Committee. [*A/3943, 9 Oct. 1958.*]

The Secretary-General himself was assigned by the Assembly the respon-

---

[4] The legal status of the Gaza Štrip was in some doubt. Many nations regarded it as falling under Egyptian administration, by virtue of the 1949 Armistice, but *not* being territory over which Egypt had sovereignty. Mrs Meir, then Foreign Secretary of Israel, said in the General Assembly on 17 January 1957: 'Egypt did not annex the Gaza strip, but treated it as occupied territory provisionally administered by the Egyptian military authorities. In a ruling given by the Cairo court of administrative jurisdiction in September 1955, it was stated that the Gaza Strip was outside Egyptian territory and that the Egyptian authorities were exercising "a kind of control over part of the territory of Palestine" ' (*GAOR*, 11th sess., 638th plen. mtg, p. 890).

[5] See Rosner, pp. 89–92.

[6] Details on the Advisory Committee's work are not available, however: minutes of its meetings were confidential. But see some informed speculation in Maxwell Cohen's 'The United Nations Emergency Force: A preliminary view', 12 *Internat. J.* (Spring 1957), pp. 120–1.

[7] A/3383, para. 2 (*h*).
10

sibility for drawing up the plans for UNEF; arranging the cease-fire; halting the movement of arms; securing, with the Chief of Staff and military observers of UNTSO, the withdrawal behind armistice lines; issuing regulations and instructions; negotiating with all the relevant parties to the dispute; drawing up arrangements with the contributing governments; establishing a Special Financial Account,[8] and deciding on the composition of the Force.[9] There can be no doubt of the brilliance with which he carried out these tasks.

It fell to a later Secretary-General, U Thant, to handle in May 1967 President Nasser's request for the withdrawal of UNEF.[10] At that time U Thant did consult the Advisory Committee, where opinion was divided. Canada, Brazil, and Norway opposed immediate withdrawal of UNEF, whereas India and Pakistan insisted that UNEF must leave Egypt at once. The Advisory Committee made no use of operative paragraph 9 of Resolution 1001 (ES–I) (above, p. 235). The matter was not put to the Assembly,[11] and the decision was in effect taken by the Secretary-General, after consultation with his divided Advisory Committee, and in the light of Egyptian occupation of important UNEF positions, and the Indian and Yugoslav insistence upon the withdrawal of their troops.

Role of the UNEF Advisory Committee

94. General Assembly resolution 1001 (ES–I) of 7 November 1956, by which the Assembly approved the guiding principles for the organization and functioning of UNEF, established an Advisory Committee on UNEF under the chairmanship of the Secretary-General. The Assembly decided that the Advisory Committee, in the performance of its duties, should be empowered to request, through the usual procedures, the convening of the General Assembly and to report to the Assembly whenever matters arose which, in its opinion, were of such urgency and importance as to require consideration by the General Assembly itself.

95. The memorandum of important points in the discussion between the representative of Israel and the Secretary-General on 25 February 1957 recorded the following question raised by the representative of Israel:

'In connexion with the duration of UNEF's deployment in the Sharm el Sheikh area, would the Secretary-General give notice to the General Assembly of the United Nations before UNEF would be withdrawn from the area, with or without Egyptian insistence, or before the Secretary-General would agree to its withdrawal?'[12]

96. The response of the Secretary-General was recorded as follows:

'On the question of notification to the General Assembly, the Secretary-General wanted to state his view at a later meeting. An indicated procedure would be for the Secretary-General to inform the Advisory Committee on the United Nations Emergency Force, which would determine whether the matter should be brought to the attention of the Assembly.'[13]

97. On 1 March 1957 the Foreign Minister of Israel stated at the 666th plenary meeting of the General Assembly:

'My Government has noted the assurance embodied in the Secretary-General's note of 26 February 1957 (A/3363, annex) that any proposal for the withdrawal of the United Nations Emergency Force from the Gulf of Aqaba area would first come to the Advisory

---

[8] See below, p. 431.   [9] A/3383, paras 26–29.
[10] For details on other aspects of this event, see pp. 338–67.
[11] On which see above, p. 271.   [12] A/3563, ann. I.   [13] Ibid. ann. I. B, 2.

Committee on the United Nations Emergency Force, which represents the General Assembly in the implementation of its resolution 997 (ES–I) of 2 November 1956. This procedure will give the General Assembly an opportunity to ensure that no precipitate changes are made which would have the effect of increasing the possibility of belligerent acts.'[14]

98. In fact, the 25 February 1957 memorandum does not go as far as the interpretation given by the Foreign Minister of Israel. In any event, however, it gives no indication of any commitment by Egypt, and so far as the Secretary-General is concerned it only indicates that a procedure would be for the Secretary-General to inform the Advisory Committee which would determine whether the matter should be brought to the attention of the General Assembly. This was also the procedure provided in General Assembly resolution 1001 (ES–I). It was, furthermore, the procedure followed by the Secretary-General on the withdrawal of UNEF. [*A/6730/Add.3, Report of the Secretary-General on the withdrawal of UNEF, 26 June 1967.*]

It was the Secretary-General (in para. 7 of this document) who gave the detailed order for withdrawal to the UNEF Commander (indeed, he had already informed the Egyptians that it was improper for them to have addressed the initial request for a pulling back to the Commander, General Rikhye, rather than to himself).

ANNEX

Cable containing instructions for the withdrawal of UNEF sent by the Secretary-General to the Commander of UNEF on 18 May 1967, at 22.30 hours New York time

The following instructions are to be put in effect by you as of date and time of their receipt and shall remain operative until and unless new instructions are sent by me.

1. UNEF is being withdrawn because the consent of the Government of the United Arab Republic for its continued deployment on United Arab Republic territory and United Arab Republic-controlled territory has been rescinded.

2. Date of the commencement of the withdrawal of UNEF will be 19 May when the Secretary-General's response to the request for withdrawal will be received in Cairo by the Government of the United Arab Republic, when also the General Assembly will be informed of the action taken and the action will become public knowledge.

3. The withdrawal of UNEF is to be orderly and must be carried out with dignity befitting a Force which has contributed greatly to the maintenance of quiet and peace in the area of its deployment and has earned widespread admiration.

4. The Force does not cease to exist or to lose its status or any of its entitlements, privileges and immunities until all of its elements have departed from the area of its operation.

5. It will be a practical fact that must be reckoned with by the Commander that as of the date of the announcement of its withdrawal the Force will no longer be able to carry out its established functions as a buffer and as a deterrent to infiltration. Its duties, therefore, after 19 May and until all elements have been withdrawn, will be entirely nominal and concerned primarily with devising arrangements and implementation of arrangements for withdrawal and the morale of the personnel.

6. The Force, of course, will remain under the exclusive command of its United Nations Commander and is to take no orders from any other source, whether United Arab Republic or national.

7. The Commander, his headquarters staff and the contingent commanders shall take every reasonable precaution to ensure the continuance of good relations with the local authorities and the local population.

[14] 11th sess., plen. mtgs, 666th mtg, para. 8.

8. In this regard, it should be made entirely clear by the Commander to the officers and other ranks in the Force that there is no discredit of the Force in this withdrawal and no humiliation involved for the reason that the Force has operated very successfully and with, on the whole, co-operation from the Government on the territory of an independent sovereign State for over ten years, which is a very long time; and, moreover, the reasons for the termination of the operation are of an overriding political nature, having no relation whatsoever to the performance of the Force in the discharge of its duties.

9. The Commander and subordinate officers must do their utmost to avoid any resort to the use of arms and any clash with the forces of the United Arab Republic or with the local civilian population.

10. A small working team will be sent from Headquarters by the Secretary-General to assist in the arrangements for, and effectuation of, the withdrawal.

11. The Commander shall take all necessary steps to protect United Nations installations, properties and stores during the period of withdrawal.

12. If necessary, a small detail of personnel of the Force or preferably of United Nations security officers will be maintained as long as necessary for the protection of United Nations properties pending their ultimate disposition.

13. UNEF aircraft will continue flights as necessary in connexion with the withdrawal arrangements but observation flights will be discontinued immediately.

14. Elements of the Force now deployed along the Line will be first removed from the Line, the international frontier and armistice demarcation line, including Sharm el Sheikh to their camps and progressively to central staging.

15. The pace of the withdrawal will of course depend upon the availability of transport by air, sea and ground to Port Said. The priority in withdrawal should of course be personnel and their personal arms and equipment first, followed by contingent stores and equipment.

16. We must proceed on the assumption that UNEF will have full co-operation of United Arab Republic authorities on all aspects of evacuation, and to this end a request will be made by me to the United Arab Republic Government through their Mission here.

17. As early as possible the Commander of UNEF should prepare and transmit to the Secretary-General a plan and schedule for the evacuation of troops and their equipment.

18. Preparation of the draft of the sections of the annual report by the Secretary-General to the General Assembly should be undertaken and, to the extent possible, completed during the period of the withdrawal.

19. In the interests of the Force itself and the United Nations, every possible measure should be taken to ensure against public comments or comments likely to become public on the withdrawal, the reasons for it and reactions to it. [*A/6730/Add. 3, 26 June 1967.*]

6

ADMINISTRATIVE AND MILITARY CONTROL

THE command structure for UNEF was necessarily unusual, for a means had to be found of welding units of sovereign states into an international force. UNEF was designated a subsidiary organ of the General Assembly under Article 22 of the Charter; but the national units still remained part of their own national forces, even though on this occasion owing international allegiance.

In Resolution 1000 (ES–I), the General Assembly authorized the appointment of Major-General[1] E. L. M. Burns, of Canada, as Chief of Command of the Force. His title was later altered to Commander of the Force.[2] The Secretary-General stipulated: 'The authority of the Commander should be so defined as to make him fully independent of the policies of any one nation.'[3] It was he, in consultation with the Secretary-General, who was entitled to recruit officers for the Force:

(*a*) All personnel assigned to the Force will be under the direct supervision of the Commander who, in consultation as required with the Secretary-General, will undertake the recruitment from Member Governments of officers for his command. The Commander may hire such local personnel as he requires and arrange with the Secretary-General for such detailment of staff from the United Nations Secretariat as may be necessary.

(*b*) The Commander will have charge of the billeting and the provision of food for all personnel attached to the Force, and may negotiate with Governments and private suppliers for the provision of premises and food.

(*c*) The Commander will arrange for the transportation of personnel and equipment to and from the area of operations; will make provision for local transportation within the area; and will co-ordinate the use of all transportation facilities furnished by Governments.

(*d*) The Commander will be responsible for the procurement, storage and issuance of supplies required by the Force.

(*e*) The Commander will make such arrangements as may be necessary for obtaining equipment required by the Force, other than the standard equipment expected to accompany national contingents.

(*f*) The Commander, in consultation with the Secretary-General, will make appropriate arrangements for the inclusion in the Force of such supporting units as may be necessary to provide for the establishment, operation and maintenance of communications within the area of operations and with United Nations Offices.

(*g*) The Commander, in consultation with the Secretary-General, will also arrange for the necessary supporting units to provide medical, dental and sanitary services for all personnel.

[*A/3383 and Rev. 1, Report of the Secretary-General on administrative and financial arrangements for the UN Emergency Force, 21 Nov. 1956, para. 2.*]

Commanding officers from the contributing countries were placed at the head of their own national units, and were directly responsible to Major-General Burns. They took orders only from him.

2. *Organization*

8. The national contingents are the components of the Force and each of them, under the commanding officer of the unit, who is directly responsible to the Commander of the Force, retains its identity and organizational unity. The demands of service made upon the Force, however, frequently require the deployment of elements of a contingent, whether companies or platoons, in separate sectors. The Danish and Norwegian contingents, by voluntary arrangement between them, constitute a single battalion, commanded in rotation by officers of the two nationalities. The Norwegian medical company, which serves the entire Force, is under exclusively Norwegian command.

9. The 'Chief of the Command', Major-General E. L. M. Burns, who is Commander of the Force, was appointed by action of General Assembly resolution 1000 (ES–I) of 5 November 1956. The chain of command runs directly from the Commander of the Force to the commanding officers of each of the national contingents. The Force is subject to orders and

---

[1] Later Lt.-General.   [2] By virtue of General Assembly Res. 1122 (XI) of 26 Nov. 1956.
[3] A/3302, Secretary-General's 2nd and final Report, para. 4.

instructions only from its Commander and, through him, from the Secretary-General of the United Nations.

10. The headquarters of UNEF is located in the town of Gaza. There is a Chief of Staff, who is also Deputy Commander; a headquarters staff, consisting of personnel, operations and logistics sections, each of which is headed by a Lieutenant-Colonel; and a special staff, consisting of officers responsible for legal, provost, engineer, signals, air staff and medical matters. The Chief Administrative Officer and his staff are civilians, drawn almost entirely from the United Nations Secretariat. In addition, a number of locally recruited civilians are employed.

11. Communications traffic between United Nations Headquarters and UNEF stations in the area, which is of substantial volume, is efficiently handled by experienced United Nations Field Service communications personnel. The UNEF communications network is co-ordinated with the established United Nations communications system. [*A/3694, Report of the Secretary-General, 9 Oct. 1956.*]

Further detailed arrangements were also made in respect of administrative matters:

ADMINISTRATIVE AND FINANCIAL ASPECTS OF THE PROVISIONAL ARRANGEMENTS CONCERNING THE ESTABLISHMENT AND ORGANIZATION OF THE EMERGENCY FORCE

5. The Advisory Committee understands that the following administrative arrangements are provisionally in effect. At Headquarters, New York, supporting administrative services have so far been provided without addition to the staff. At the 'staging' or assembly area at Capodichino, near Naples, such services are being furnished through assignments from established United Nations offices and through the temporary engagement of staff for clerical duties. As regards operations in the field, at Abu Suweir, Port Said and other points, a Chief Finance Officer, a Procurement Officer and other Headquarters officials competent in matters of finance, supplies, etc., are on duty in the area. In addition, an official of the Technical Assistance Board (TAB), at the Director level, has been detailed for service with the Commander of the Force and will be in charge of all administrative matters. The Advisory Committee is not at present in a position to give detailed information on the costs or on the total number of staff involved. This will be included in a subsequent report of the Committee.

6. Most of the troops comprising the Emergency Force have been, or will be, transported to the assembly area by the United States Air Force, without charge either to the United Nations or to the Member State contributing troops. The transport of troops from the assembly area to Abu Suweir was undertaken initially by the Swissair Company, at a cost, under a normal commercial contract, of approximately $500,000, which has been wholly defrayed by the Swiss Federal Government. The Canadian and Italian Governments have now undertaken to assist the United Nations by providing facilities for the transport of troops by air.

7. In one case, a national contingent, together with its heavy equipment, has been carried by ship to Port Said. Information submitted to the Advisory Committee shows that very reasonable charter rates have been obtained.

8. Immediate supplies for the Force, both at Capodichino and in Egypt, are being obtained at this initial stage largely from United States Government sources. The extent of the financial liability of the United Nations in the matter cannot yet be determined. [*A/3402, 22nd Report of the Advisory Committee on Administrative and Budgetary Questions, 30 Nov. 1956.*]

25. Practical arrangements for the establishment of UNEF were facilitated by the presence in the area in which the Force was to operate of the United Nations Truce Supervision Organization and the United Nations Relief and Works Agency for Palestine Refugees in the Near East (UNRWA), which, through their personnel, facilities and extensive experience in the region, were able to give valuable assistance. The immediate availability, for temporary

transfer, of a corps of experienced military officers who had been serving as military observers in UNTSO was especially helpful. Most important, the Chief of Staff of UNTSO was able and willing to assume the post of Commander of the Force. Pending the re-establishment, following the withdrawal of Israel, of naval administrative machinery by the local authorities in the Gaza strip, UNRWA, which exercises important functions among the refugees in that area, also gave substantial assistance through aid to the non-refugee population. . . .

31. Invaluable assistance on military aspects of the initial planning was given by a group of military representatives of the countries contributing troops to UNEF, who sat as an informal military advisory committee at United Nations Headquarters during the early stages of the operation. This group, under the informal chairmanship of a Major-General, appointed temporarily as personal adviser to the Secretary-General on UNEF military matters, provided expert planning and advice on matters of military organization, transport, equipment and logistics, and also greatly expedited the dispatch of contingents by their Governments. . . .

Use of Secretariat Resources

32. At the outset, the Secretary-General directed that United Nations Secretariat personnel, procedures and facilities should be utilized to the maximum in organizing and maintaining the Force. This reduced substantially the degree of improvisation which would otherwise have been required for a project so large and so new in international experience as UNEF. Even so, there was much occasion to improvise in the early stages. The Secretariat, as a result of long and well-tested experience, could provide UNEF with efficient services and personnel in such necessary fields as administration, financial procedures, personnel recruitment, legal and political advice, public information, procurement and supply and communications. High-level responsibility for the organization and direction of the operation was facilitated by the principle of flexibility in the use of senior staff. From the beginning, the Secretary-General designated one of his Under-Secretaries without Department to be responsible for direct supervision of the organization and operation of the Force and the co-ordination of administrative actions relating to it (see A/AC.89/R.1). Most of the major units of the Secretariat were called upon to make their contribution to the total task in one way or another, with the Executive Office of the Secretary-General, the Office of General Services, the Office of the Controller, the Office of Legal Affairs and the Office of Personnel rendering especially important assistance.

33. The experience gained by the Secretariat over the years in the administration of missions in various parts of the world provided many well-tried procedures which were immediately put to good use in meeting the broad requirements of UNEF. Machinery for the necessary administrative co-ordination at United Nations Headquarters already existed and was readily adapted to the new emergency task. Certain mission facilities which had been found essential over a period of years were immediately available in the area: an aircraft permanently assigned to UNTSO provided emergency transportation locally, which was indispensable to the early planning; an independent United Nations network of low-powered radio receivers and transmitters, linking UNTSO offices in Cairo and Gaza with UNTSO headquarters in Jerusalem, gave United Nations personnel in the area an uninterrupted contact of their own with United Nations Headquarters in New York through the United Nations relay station in Geneva; an adequate code system and routine procedures for the handling of United Nations diplomatic pouches ensured security for United Nations communications. Arranging for such needs as identity cards, visas, passports and inoculations, and obtaining clearances for flying over the territory of numerous countries, were routine duties for the Secretariat.

Initial Assessment of Requirements

34. The Commander of UNEF estimated that, in order to perform the tasks assigned by the General Assembly, the Force would require the equivalent of two combat brigades, or

about 6,000 men. The initial concept of military organization, later modified in the light of further clarification of the functions of the Force, was that it should be built around regimental combat teams. It would require an independent signals company expanded to provide all necessary communications facilities for Force headquarters and in the field. In addition, headquarters, engineer, transport, shop repair and medical personnel would be needed. It was decided that the infantry should be equipped with normal regimental weapons, that there should be a transport company sufficient to lift one infantry battalion, and that each battalion should be administratively self-contained. The Commander also stressed the desirability of an armoured car squadron for reconnaissance work, in view of the nature of the terrain and the task of the Force. It was further concluded at an early stage that a light air unit was essential for functions inside the UNEF operations area.

The first phase

35. There was urgent need to assemble a usable force, as rapidly as possible, and to land it in Egypt. While awaiting the conclusion of arrangements with Egypt for the entry of the Force into that country, it was decided that a staging area near the Mediterranean would be necessary, as it would expedite the flow of troops and *matériel* to Egypt. Arrangements were quickly made with the Government of Italy for the use of Capodichino airport, Naples, for this purpose. Most of the troops brought to Egypt by air were sent via Naples, others were flown in via Beirut, while others came by sea to Port Said. The small staff in charge of the staging area at Capodichino took care of the incoming (and later outgoing) contingents, dealt with the several authorities in Europe through whom major logistic support was obtained, supervised the air-lift to Egypt and arranged for the surface transport of heavy stores.

36. The initial movements of troops from their home bases to Italy were arranged through United Nations Headquarters. The problems were mainly transportation and co-ordination. The bulk of the transport to the staging area was provided by the United States Air Force. The representatives of the contributing countries supplied information to United Nations Headquarters concerning the numbers, equipment and state of readiness of their national units, and this was transmitted to the representatives of the United States Air Force designated for this purpose. The latter, in turn, gave notification concerning the precise arrangements for transporting the contingents named, which was transmitted to the appropriate Governments by their military representatives at United Nations Headquarters.

37. A selected group of United Nations military observers, who were detached temporarily from their duties with UNTSO and who commenced planning while still in Jerusalem, served at first as the nucleus of a UNEF headquarters staff. They arrived in Egypt on 12 November 1956, established a temporary headquarters in Cairo and, together with Secretariat officials, arranged for the reception and billeting of the first contingents, and the early procurement, storage and issue of the supplies and equipment required. Through negotiations with the Egyptian Government, an air base at Abu Suweir, near Ismailia, became the arrival depot for the early contingents. As the contingents arrived, their officers took over the duties being performed by the military observers, who were then able to return to their UNTSO duties in Jerusalem.

38. Advance elements of UNEF were moved to Egypt at a time when hostilities had but recently ceased; there were restrictions on the times and lanes of flights, and aircraft transporting contingents had to be of suitable nationalities. The initial air-lift of troops to Abu Suweir was carried out by Swissair. The Naples to Egypt air-lift was subsequently taken over by the Royal Canadian Air Force with some assistance from the Italian Air Force in lifting supplies.

39. Speed was a major reason for initially moving some troops and equipment to Egypt by air, but as ships under some flags could not be used, and as ships proceeding to Port Said at that time were required to be self-sustaining, the immediate possibilities of employing sea transport were in any case severely reduced. The Yugoslav reconnaissance battalion, with all its equipment, was brought to Port Said by sea on 28 November 1956, while the main elements

of the Canadian and Brazilian contingents arrived in national naval vessels on 11 January and 2 February 1957, respectively. All heavy equipment for UNEF was brought in by ship.

40. One consequence of having to rely on air transport for the first units and their equipment was an immediate and severe shortage of transport vehicles. This difficulty was aggravated by the fact that several of the contingents had not contemplated bringing most of their vehicular transport with them in any event because of the desert conditions. The shortage was alleviated by obtaining vehicles from UNRWA, by local purchases and by rental. But, as requirements mounted, these sources became inadequate.

41. A preliminary understanding had been reached in New York on the purchase of vehicles and supplies in Port Said from the British forces as they withdrew, the details of the transaction being worked out on the spot. This procurement was very helpful in facilitating the rapid deployment of UNEF forces in the Sinai Peninsula and in equipping the two transportation platoons used for supplying the forces. Shortly after the formation of the Force, a large order for vehicles was placed with United States military authorities. These vehicles arrived in January 1957 and filled the additional transport requirements.

42. The need to transport UNEF units to positions evacuated by the Anglo-French and Israel forces, to keep them supplied and to provide replacements, required the immediate establishment at Abu Suweir of a dump of petrol, oil and lubricants. The necessary stocks and installations were obtained in the area. Additional storage facilities were obtained in Port Said, and further supply points were established as the operation moved forward.

43. The clear identification of UNEF personnel, beyond the customary United Nations armbands, was an immediate necessity for security and other reasons. Light blue helmet liners with United Nations markings were adopted for this purpose, and were later supplemented by blue berets and desert caps and UNEF badges and insignia. Vehicles and aircraft were painted white with United Nations markings. . . .

CHAPTER IV. ORGANIZATION AND ADMINISTRATION IN THE FIELD

Organizational structure

The Commander

75. The functioning of UNEF in the field is the direct responsibility of the Commander, who serves both as the director of operations and as the supervisor of all other activities of the Force.

76. The Commander holds office through appointment by the General Assembly. He operates under the instructions and guidance of the Secretary-General on the basis of executive responsibility for the operation entrusted to him by the Assembly. In practice, from the inception of the Force, the Commander has functioned as the principal agent of the Secretary-General in the area of operations, within the limits of his post.

77. The position of Commander combines leadership of the Force with the role of representative of the United Nations. Much the same qualities are called for in the Chief of Staff of UNTSO, although the military observers in UNTSO do not form a military organization in the UNEF sense and their functions are quite different. Both operations, however, combine political and administrative with military functions.

Military staff organization

78. The military staff organization of UNEF consists of officers selected from each of the contingents, and is headed by the Chief of Staff. The Chief of Staff acts for the Commander during his absence. The position of Deputy Commander was tried for a while but was found to be unnecessary. The Headquarters Staff comprises three sections—(1) Personnel, (2) Operations, and (3) Logistics—and a Special Staff composed of a number of specialized officers who advise and assist the Commander in particular fields and, in some cases, co-ordinate, supervise or carry out functional activities. The physical separation of UNEF headquarters in Gaza from the maintenance area at Rafah results in some inconvenience and perhaps a mild loss of efficiency, but it is unavoidable and there is no practical alternative.

10*

79. The contingents receive their instructions and direction from the Commander, advised and assisted by his Staff. The commanding officers of the units are held responsible by the Commander for the proper functioning and discipline of their personnel. The contingent commanders are free to communicate with their home Governments on all matters affecting their units.

80. It is the practice of those contingents furnishing units for more than one functional task to designate a contingent commander, in addition to commanders for each functional activity. This contributes to clarification of responsibility in those matters affecting personnel which are subject to national authority.

81. Aside from the battalions with clearly defined missions of a military nature, normally involving patrol duties along the armistice demarcation line and the international frontier as well as guard duties, there are a number of units assigned to UNEF which perform administrative and other support tasks. Supporting elements for any force represent a special problem in co-ordination and control. To weld together elements of several different nationalities having similar functions would be very difficult. For this reason, UNEF has tended to rely mainly upon two countries, Canada and India, for its supporting units other than the medical.

82. Some of the contributing Governments designated 'liaison officers' to represent their interests on the scene of operations of UNEF and to serve as points of contact for them. These liaison officers, not being under the authority of the Commander, are not members of UNEF. Their status, therefore, is rather anomalous. In practice, the liaison officer function has worked best when the officer concerned was one assigned to a UNEF post having important duties in its own right. Those liaison officers not combining functions in this manner have no direct responsibility to the Commander, yet can scarcely avoid becoming involved in matters of Force administration and operations. Moreover, it is difficult for the Commander and his staff, as well as for the commanders of operating units, to decide when and under what circumstances the liaison officers should be consulted and informed. However, in the early days of the organization of the Force, liaison officers for special purposes performed a useful and necessary function.

83. From the beginning of the Force, it was found useful, even essential, to maintain representation in Cairo for liaison with the appropriate authorities in the host Government. UNEF also has liaison representation in Tel Aviv. Military observers have been seconded from the staff of UNTSO for service with UNEF as its liaison officers. UNEF representation is also maintained at places outside the area of operations where UNEF activities and interests are involved, as in Beirut and Pisa (and earlier in Naples) in connexion with the airlift.

The Secretariat

84. Administratively, responsibility for UNEF rests with the Secretary-General, in order to ensure that the operation will be executed in a manner consistent with the established practices and administrative principles of the United Nations. The day-to-day responsibilities of administration are exercised by the Commander of the Force, assisted by the senior Secretariat officials assigned by the Secretary-General to the Force, and such military officers having important administrative functions as the Chiefs of Personnel and Logistics. Experience has demonstrated that, by and large, requirements for the administrative servicing of an operation such as UNEF, both at Headquarters and in the field, can be met through existing Secretariat services, modestly expanded in certain sections to permit the absorption of heavier work-loads, together with such administrative assistance from the military side as may be implicit in the nature of the organization.

85. Three categories of Secretariat staff have served and are serving with the Force:

(*a*) Officers, such as the Chief Administrative Officer, with responsibility for the financial affairs of the Force and for the application of United Nations administrative rules and procedures. The Chief Administrative Officer reports directly to the Commander and works closely with him, but also has a direct reporting link with United Nations Headquarters, as the senior Secretariat official who is designated by the Secretary-General and in that capacity is responsible to him. He is assisted by a Chief Procurement Officer, a Chief Finance Officer and a Personnel Officer;

(b) Officials such as the Legal Adviser and the Public Information Officer, both of whom belong to the staff of the Chief Administrative Officer, but who work directly with the Commander in view of the nature of their duties;

(c) Personnel providing services not readily available from military sources, or requiring special training and knowledge. The Field Operations Service, for example, which assists the operation in many ways, quickly sets up external communications service with skilled personnel, and also provides trained security personnel.

86. The main and most direct impact of staffing and control arrangements is, of course, felt in the field. With the continuing expansion of the administrative responsibilities of the United Nations in connexion with the growing number of operations in widely scattered places, it has become increasingly apparent that qualified administrative personnel within the regular Secretariat do not exist in sufficient numbers adequately to cover all important tasks, particularly in the financial area. The addition of UNEF to existing responsibilities, and the possibility of other such operations in the future, has made it necessary to devise ways and means of augmenting the regular Secretariat in order to assure that financial administration in the field is properly carried out. To service these activities, accountants, auditors, procurement and property control specialists and supporting staff, of high calibre, are required for service in the field in substantial numbers. The fluctuating needs of the Organization argue against expanding the permanent Secretariat staff. Increasing attention, therefore, is being given to the development of additional sources of field assistance including, in particular, arrangements whereby specialist civilian personnel may be made available by Member-Governments on a temporary secondment basis for service with UNEF as part of the Secretariat staff, following brief periods of training or briefing at Headquarters or at another United Nations office prior to taking up their field assignments. . . .

Logistic and administrative problems

90. Unusual and perplexing administrative problems are constantly encountered by UNEF in many fields of activity, and the brief descriptions of some of the broader ones set forth below are intended only as selected examples of the novel difficulties faced.

Procurements

91. In military logistics work, it is customary for supply requirements to be met through requisitions prepared or screened against standard supply tables, and the procurement action is undertaken without further review. The heterogeneous composition of UNEF has precluded thus far the development of detailed and standardized supply tables, although these are in course of preparation. In the meantime, the Chief Procurement Officer must assure himself that each requisition covers only essential supplies for which there are no other alternatives, and differences sometimes tend to arise over the conclusions about paper purchase.

92. An important area of difficulty is the procurement and delivery of supplies and equipment, after agreement is reached on requirements. Four main sources of supply have been drawn upon by UNEF:

(a) A good part of the requirements is furnished by the participating Governments directly to their own troops;

(b) United Nations Headquarters procures and ships those supplies that can be economically secured through its own procurement channels;

(c) The UNEF supply office in Italy procures and ships other supplies from military sources in Europe, when authorized by United Nations Headquarters under standing arrangements with Governments of Member States;

(d) Supplies are purchased locally when the exigencies of the situation so demand or when price comparisons show that this is the most economical course. . . .

93. In the early days of an operation such as UNEF it is imperative to have an assured

source that can produce most of the supplies required by modern troops in the field. Once a 'pipeline' has been established, attention can be given to developing alternative sources that may be cheaper or more satisfactory in other ways. The provision of rations in sufficient quantity and appropriate variety for soldiers of differing nationalities and dietary habits is especially important and often difficult. The question of the most suitable ration scale for UNEF is kept under review. In the early stages, when UNEF was concentrated at Abu Suweir, the quantities of rations brought in by air-lift were inadequate, and procurements through the Egyptian Army was necessary for a brief period. This arrangement ceased when local contractors were able to deal directly with United Nations procurement officers. The necessity of bringing rations in by air greatly reduced the air-lift available for other purposes and caused much difficulty.

Transportation

94. Transportation within the area of operations when public and commercial facilities are limited is a burdensome problem. Major reliance has to be placed on the use of UNEF vehicles and aircraft, with a consequent strain on maintenance and repair facilities and supplies. The periodic movement of troops on rotation to and from the home country creates an administrative challenge, owing largely to the absence of scheduled air or shipping services from that country to the area of operations and the rapidity with which sizeable units of troops must be interchanged. Rotational movements of troops have required intensive planning and complex administrative arrangements. Use has been made of commercial and governmental aircraft and ships, the arrangements varying according to the demands of the particular situation.

95. It is apparent that a force in the circumstances of UNEF must be largely self-sufficient as regards vehicular and aircraft maintenance, for outside facilities are largely unavailable and generally unsuitable when they do exist. The maintenance and repair facilities provided by the Royal Canadian Air Force have kept the UNEF aircraft up to a satisfactory operational standard. The situation has been far more difficult with regard to motor vehicles. The Ordnance Workshop facilities, also provided by Canada, are not designed for the repair of large components and, until contract arrangements were made for such repairs, many vehicles were out of action for long periods. Moreover, it has proved very difficult to obtain the necessary quantities of spare parts for absolete vehicles. . . .

Signals communications

100. Responsibility for UNEF's communications services is divided. The necessity at the outset for instant communications services within the area of operations dictated the use of a military signals system, while the heavy United Nations traffic to and from New York, Geneva and other points made it essential to establish a typical unit, although larger than usual, of United Nations radio officers. Thus, military personnel (largely Canadian, but including a small Indian unit), under the Chief Signals officer, have undertaken most of the communications functions involving operational requirements in the local area, while most traffic going beyond the area is handled by United Nations Field Service personnel. Telephonic service in UNEF has been provided satisfactorily by military signals personnel. Varying standards of performance and quite different types of equipment have made it difficult to achieve a cohesive communications pattern and full effectiveness on the part of available personnel. The entire radio communications service, including the military operational requirements, possibly could be performed satisfactorily by the United Nations Field Service, but only with increased staff resources. A fully integrated and cohesive external and internal communications service would then be possible. . . .

Legal character of UNEF; its Regulations

127. The Force was recognized as a subsidiary organ of the General Assembly, established under the authority of Article 22 of the Charter of the United Nations (regulation 6). A prob-

lem of first importance, therefore, was that of harmonizing the international character of the Force with the fact of its being composed of national contingents. This was accomplished through the chain of command and through definition of the legal status of the Force and of its members. Subject to the resolutions of the General Assembly, the Secretary-General has authority for all executive, administrative and financial matters affecting the Force (regulation 15).* The Commander has direct command authority over the Force and its operations. Acting in consultation with the Secretary-General in the exercise of this authority, he remains operationally responsible for the performance of all functions assigned to the Force by the United Nations, and for the deployment and assignment of troops placed at the disposal of the Force (regulations 11 and 16). By designating the chain of command for the Force, through which he is empowered to delegate his authority, the Commander in turn is able to make use of the commanding officers of the national contingents (regulation 12).

128. This effective marriage of national military service with international function is also reflected in the status of individual members of the Force. Although remaining in their national service, they are, during the period of their assignment with UNEF, international personnel under the authority of the United Nations and subject to the instructions only of the Commander and his chain of command. They discharge exclusively international functions (regulations 6, 29, 31 and 32).† The immunities necessary to assure their international character as members of the Force are developed in detail in the Agreement on the status of the Force, discussed below.

129. As a subsidiary organ, UNEF enjoys the status, privileges and immunities of the Organization as already established by the Convention on the Privileges and Immunities of the United Nations. The independent exercise of the functions of UNEF was thus assured in respect of property supplied by the United Nations, but it was necessary to make provision for supplies and equipment which were the property of the national contingents. It was accordingly established that the relevant terms of the Convention also applied to the property, funds and assets of the participating States used in connexion with UNEF (regulation 10). [*A/3943, Summary Study of the experience of UNEF, 9 Oct. 1958.*]

It will be noted that the Status of Forces Agreement with Egypt provided that the contributing states would undertake to punish their own nationals if necessary,[4] for 'to confer such authority upon the Commander would probably require specific legislation in most participating States'.[5] This was completed by the arrangements laid out in the Regulations issued for UNEF by the Secretary-General, for they confirmed that the national contingents were subject to the disciplinary powers of their own commanders, and each contingent's military police were given powers of arrest. But the Commander himself was also given authority to establish military police, who shared in the power to punish. The complete Regulations (which were agreed to by the contributing governments)[6] are reproduced overleaf:

---

* See also Regulation 4, which provides that Command orders issued by the Commander are subject to review by the Secretary-General.

† See also Regulation 19 (b) which provides that members of the Secretariat detailed to UNEF remain subject to the authority of the Secretary-General.

[4] See below, p. 375.   [5] A/3943, para. 139.   [6] See below, p. 325.

4. Regulations for the United Nations Emergency Force, February 20, 1957[7]
CHAPTER I. GENERAL PROVISIONS

1. *Issuance of Regulations.* The Regulations for the United Nations Emergency Force (UNEF) (hereinafter referred to as the Force) are issued by the Secretary-General, following consultation with the Advisory Committee established under General Assembly resolution 1001 (ES–I) of 7 November 1956 (hereinafter referred to as the Advisory Committee), pursuant to paragraph 7 of that resolution. They shall be effective from 1 March 1957. The Regulations, and supplemental instructions and orders referred to in Regulations 3 and 4, shall be made available to all units of the Force.

2. *Amendments.* These Regulations may be amended or revised by the Secretary-General, following consultation with the Advisory Committee.

3. *Supplemental instructions.* Supplemental instructions consistent with the present Regulations may be issued by the Secretary-General as required with respect to matters not delegated to the Commander of the United Nations Emergency Force (hereinafter referred to as the Commander).

4. *Command Orders.* The Commander may issue Orders not inconsistent with the resolutions of the General Assembly relating to the Force, these Regulations and amendments thereto, and with supplemental instructions referred to in Regulation 3:

(*a*) in the discharge of his duties as Commander of the Force; or

(*b*) in implementation or explanation of these Regulations.

Command Orders shall be subject to review by the Secretary-General.

5. *Definitions.* The following definitions shall apply to the terms used in the present Regulations:

(*a*) The 'Commander of the United Nations Emergency Force (UNEF)' or the 'Commander' is the general officer appointed as 'Chief of the United Nations Command' by the General Assembly.

(*b*) The 'United Nations Command' is the Commander together with his Headquarters Staff.

(*c*) The 'United Nations Emergency Force' or 'Force' is the subsidiary organ of the United Nations described in Regulation 6 below.

(*d*) A 'member of the United Nations Emergency Force' or a 'member of the Force' is the Commander and any person belonging to the military services of a State serving under the Commander either on the United Nations Command or with a national contingent.

(*e*) A 'Participating State' is a State providing national contingents to the Force. A 'Participating Government' is the government of a Participating State.

(*f*) The 'authorities of a Participating State' are those authorities who are empowered by the law of that State to enforce its military or other law with respect to the members of its armed forces.

(*g*) A 'Host State' is a State in which the Force operates. A 'Host Government' is the Government of a Host State.

CHAPTER II. INTERNATIONAL CHARACTER, UNIFORM, INSIGNIA, AND PRIVILEGES AND IMMUNITIES

6. *International character.* The United Nations Emergency Force is a subsidiary organ of the United Nations consisting of the United Nations Command established by General

[7] ST/SGB/UNEF/1. Attached to the Regulations was a note from the Secretary-General stating that they were issued pursuant to Assembly Resolution 1001 (ES–I), following consultation with the Advisory Committee. The Secretary-General observed that the Regulations entered into effect on 1 March 1957, and were in the main intended to continue the orders, instructions, and practices under which UNEF had operated since it came into existence.

Assembly resolution 1000 (ES–I) of 5 November 1956, and all military personnel placed under the United Nations Command by Member States. The members of the Force, although remaining in their national service, are, during the period of their assignment to the Force, international personnel under the authority of the United Nations and subject to the instructions of the Commander through the chain of command. The functions of the Force are exclusively international and members of the Force shall discharge these functions and regulate their conduct with the interest of the United Nations only in view.

7. *Flag.* The Force is authorized to fly the United Nations flag in accordance with the United Nations Flag Code and Regulations. The United Nations Command shall display the United Nations flag and emblem on its Headquarters, posts, vehicles and otherwise as decided by the Commander. Other flags or pennants may be displayed only in exceptional cases and in accordance with conditions prescribed by the Commander.

8. *Uniform and insignia.* Members of the Force shall wear such uniform and distinctive insignia as the Commander, in consultation with the Secretary-General, shall prescribe. Civilian dress may be worn at such times and in accordance with such conditions as may be authorized by the Commander.

9. *Markings.* All means of transportation of the Force, including vehicles, vessels and aircraft, and all other equipment when specifically designated by the Commander shall bear a distinctive United Nations mark and licence.

10. *Privileges and immunities.* The Force, as a subsidiary organ of the United Nations, enjoys the status, privileges and immunities of the Organization provided in the Convention on the Privileges and Immunities of the United Nations. The entry without duty of equipment and supplies of the Force, and of personal effects of members of the Force upon their first arrival shall be effected in accordance with details to be arranged with the Host State concerned. The provisions of article II of the Convention on the Privileges and Immunities of the United Nations shall also apply to the property, funds and assets of Participating States used in a Host State in connexion with the national contingents serving in the Force.

CHAPTER III. AUTHORITY OF THE COMMANDER OF THE UNITED NATIONS EMERGENCY FORCE

11. *Command authority.* The Commander has full command authority over the Force. He is operationally responsible for the performance of all functions assigned to the Force by the United Nations, and for the deployment and assignment of troops placed at the disposal of the Force.

12. *Chain of command and delegation of authority.* The Commander shall designate the chain of command for the Force, making use of the officers of the United Nations Command and the commanders of the national contingents made available by Participating Governments. He may delegate his authority through the chain of command. Changes in commanders of national contingents made available by Participating Governments shall be made in consultation between the Commander of the UNEF and the appropriate authorities of the Participating Government. The Commander of the UNEF may make such provisional emergency assignments as may be required. The Commander of the UNEF has full authority with respect to all assignments of members of the United Nations Command and, through the chain of command, of all members of the Force. Instructions from principal organs of the United Nations shall be channelled by the Secretary-General through the Commander and the chain of command designated by him.

13. *Good order and discipline.* The Commander of the UNEF shall have general responsibility for the good order of the Force. Responsibility for disciplinary action in national contingents provided for the Force rests with the commanders of the national contingents. Reports concerning disciplinary action shall be communicated to the Commander of the UNEF who may consult with the commander of the national contingent and if necessary the authorities of the Participating State concerned.

14. *Military police.* The Commander shall provide for military police for any camps, establishments or other premises which are occupied by the Force in a Host State and for

such areas where the Force is deployed in the performance of its functions. Elsewhere military police of the Force may be employed, in so far as such employment is necessary to maintain discipline and order among members of the Force, subject to arrangements with the authorities of the Host State concerned, and in liaison with those authorities. For the purpose of this Regulation the military police of the Force shall have the power of arrest over members of the Force. Nothing in this Regulation is in derogation of the authority of arrest conferred upon members of a national contingent *vis-à-vis* one another.

CHAPTER IV. GENERAL ADMINISTRATIVE, EXECUTIVE AND FINANCIAL ARRANGEMENTS

15. *Authority of the Secretary-General.* The Secretary-General of the United Nations shall have authority for all administrative, executive and financial matters affecting the Force and shall be responsible for the negotiation and conclusion of agreements with Governments concerning the Force. He shall make provisions for the settlement of claims arising with respect to the Force.

16. *Authority of the Commander.* The Commander shall have direct authority for the operation of the Force and for arrangements for the provision of facilities, supplies and auxiliary services. In the exercise of this authority he shall act in consultation with the Secretary-General and in accordance with the administrative and financial principles contained in Regulations 17–28 following.

17. *United Nations Command Headquarters.* The Commander shall establish the Headquarters for the Force and such other operational centres and liaison offices as may be found necessary.

18. *Finance and accounting.* Financial administration of the Force shall be in accordance with the Financial Rules for the United Nations Emergency Force Special Account, such of the United Nations Financial Regulations and Rules as are not inconsistent with them, and the procedures prescribed by the Secretary-General.

19. *Personnel.*

(*a*) The Commander shall recruit from Member Governments officers for this Command. Such officers are entitled to the privileges and immunities of article VI of the Convention on the Privileges and Immunities of the United Nations. The Commander shall be entitled to the privileges, immunities and facilities of sections 19 and 27 of the Convention on the Privileges and Immunities of the United Nations.

(*b*) The Commander shall arrange with the Secretary-General for such detailment of staff from the United Nations Secretariat to serve with the Force as may be necessary. Staff members of the United Nations detailed by the Secretary-General to serve with the Force shall be responsible to the Commander in the performance of their functions in accordance with the terms of their assignment by the Secretary-General. They remain subject to the Staff Regulations of the United Nations and to the authority of the Secretary-General and remain entitled to the privileges and immunities of articles V and VII of the Convention on the Privileges and Immunities of the United Nations.

(*c*) The Commander may recruit such local personnel as he requires. The terms and conditions of employment for locally recruited personnel shall be prescribed by the Commander and shall generally, to the extent practicable, follow the practice prevailing in the locality. They shall not be subject to or entitled to the benefits of the Staff Regulations of the United Nations, but shall be entitled to the immunity in respect of official acts provided in section 18 (*a*) of the Convention on the Privileges and Immunities of the United Nations. Disputes concerning the terms of employment and conditions of service of locally recruited personnel shall be settled by administrative procedure to be established by the Commander.

20. *Food, accommodations and amenities.* The Commander shall have charge of the billeting and the provision of food for all personnel attached to the Force, and may negotiate with Governments and private suppliers for the provision of premises and food. The Commander may establish, maintain and operate at headquarters, camps and posts, in accordance with such conditions as he may prescribe, service institutes providing amenities for members of the

Force and of the United Nations Secretariat detailed by the Secretary-General to serve with the Force.

21. *Transportation.* The Commander shall arrange for the transportation of personnel and equipment to and from the area of operations; shall make provision for local transportation within the area; and shall co-ordinate the use of all transportation facilities.

22. *Supplies.* The Commander shall be responsible for the procurement, storage and issuance of supplies required by the Force.

23. *Equipment.* The Commander shall make such arrangements as may be necessary for obtaining equipment required by the Force, other than the standard equipment expected to accompany national contingents.

24. *Communications services.* The Commander shall make appropriate arrangements for the inclusion in the Force of such supporting units as may be necessary to provide for the establishment, operation and maintenance of telecommunication and postal services within the area of operations and with the United Nations offices.

25. *Maintenance and other services.* The Commander shall arrange for the necessary supporting units to provide maintenance repairs and other services required for the operation of the Force.

26. *Medical, dental and sanitary services.* The Commander shall arrange for the necessary supporting units to provide medical, dental and sanitary services for all personnel and shall make such other arrangements as may be necessary.

27. *Contracts.* The Commander shall enter into contracts and make commitments for the purpose of carrying out his functions under these Regulations.

28. *Public information.* Public information activities of the Force and relations of the Force with the Press and other information media shall be the responsibility of the Commander acting in accordance with policy defined by the Secretary-General.

CHAPTER V. RIGHTS AND DUTIES OF MEMBERS OF THE FORCE

29. *Respect for local law and conduct befitting international status.* It is the duty of members of the Force to respect the laws and regulations of a Host State and to refrain from any activity of a political character in a Host State or other action incompatible with the international nature of their duties. They shall conduct themselves at all times in a manner befitting their status as members of the United Nations Emergency Force.

30. *United Nations legal protection.* Members of the Force are entitled to the legal protection of the United Nations and shall be regarded as agents of the United Nations for the purpose of such protection.

31. *Instructions.* In the performance of their duties for the Force the members of the Force shall receive their instructions only from the Commander and the chain of command designated by him.

32. *Discretion and non-communication of information.* Members of the Force shall exercise the utmost discretion in regard to all matters relating to their duties and functions. They shall not communicate to any person any information known to them by reason of their position with the Force which has not been made public, except in the course of their duties or by authorization of the Commander. The obligations of this Regulation do not cease upon the termination of their assignment with the Force.

33. *Honours and remuneration from external sources.* No member of the Force may accept any honour, decoration, favour, gift or remuneration incompatible with the individual's status and functions as a member of the Force.

34. *Jurisdiction.*

(*a*) Members of the Force shall be subject to the criminal jurisdiction of their respective national States in accordance with the laws and regulations of those States. They shall not be subject to the criminal jurisdiction of the courts of the Host State. Responsibility for the exercise of criminal jurisdiction shall rest with the authorities of the State concerned, including as appropriate the commanders of the national contingents.

(*b*) Members of the Force shall not be subject to the civil jurisdiction of the courts of the Host State or to other legal process in any matter relating to their official duties.

(*c*) Members of the Force shall remain subject to the military rules and regulations of their respective national States without derogating from their responsibilities as members of the Force as defined in these Regulations and any rules made pursuant thereto.

(*d*) Disputes involving the Force and its members shall be settled in accordance with such procedures provided by the Secretary-General as may be required, including the establishment of a claims commission or commissions. Supplemental instructions defining the jurisdiction of such commissions or other bodies as may be established shall be issued by the Secretary-General in accordance with article 3 of these Regulations.

35. *Customs duties and foreign exchange regulations.* Members of the Force shall comply with such arrangements regarding customs and foreign exchange regulations as may be made between the Host State concerned are the United Nations.

36. *Identity cards.* The Commander, under the authority of the Secretary-General, shall provide for the issuance and use of personal identity cards certifying that the bearer is a member of the United Nations Emergency Force. Members of the Force may be required to present, but not to surrender, their identity cards upon demand of an appropriate authority of a State in which the Force operates.

37. *Driving.* In driving vehicles members of the Force shall exercise the utmost care at all times. Orders concerning driving of service vehicles and permits or licences for such operation shall be issued by the Commander.

38. *Pay.* Responsibility for pay of members of the Force shall rest with their respective national State. They shall be paid in the field in accordance with arrangements to be made between the appropriate pay officer of their respective national State and the Commander.

39. *Overseas service allowance.* The Secretary-General shall fix a scale for a daily overseas service allowance not to exceed one US dollar ($1.00) a day to be paid by the United Nations in the appropriate currency to those members of the Force determined to be eligible for such allowance. Eligibility and entitlement shall be decided by the Commander in accordance with conditions prescribed in rules provided by him in accordance with article 4 of these Regulations.

40. *Service incurred death, injury or illness.* In the event of death, injury or illness of a member of the Force attributable to service with the Force, the respective State from whose military services the member has come will be responsible for such benefits or compensation awards as may be payable under the laws and regulations applicable to service in the armed forces of that State. The Commander shall have responsibility for arrangements concerning the body and personal property of a deceased member of the Force.

41. *Dependants.* Members of the Force may not be accompanied to their duty station by members of their families except where expressly authorized and in accordance with conditions prescribed by the Commander.

42. *Leave.* The Commander shall provide conditions for the granting of passes and leave.

43. *Promotions.* Promotions in rank for members of the Force remain the responsibility of the Participating Government.

CHAPTER VI. APPLICABILITY OF INTERNATIONAL CONVENTIONS

44. *Observance of Conventions.* The Force shall observe the principles and spirit of the general international Conventions applicable to the conduct of military personnel. [*ST/SGB/UNEF/1.*]

Although the basic administrative arrangements, and chain of command, remained the same for UNEF, inevitably there have been changes in personnel:

1. The General Assembly, in its resolution 1000 (ES–I) of 5 November 1956, acting on the suggestion made in the report of the Secretary-General, appointed, on an emergency basis, as Chief of the Command for the emergency international Force, Major-General E. L. M.

Burns of Canada, who was then serving as Chief of Staff of the United Nations Truce Supervision Organization in Jerusalem. The Force has continued until the present day under the command of General Burns, who now has the rank of Lieutenant-General. General Assembly resolution 1122 (XI) of 26 November 1956 provided that henceforth the Force would be known as the 'United Nations Emergency Force' and that the Chief of Command would be its 'Commander'.

2. The Government of Canada for some time has registered a desire to have General Burns return to national service, and General Burns himself, urged by the United Nations, has prolonged his tour of duty mainly in response to a sense of duty. Now, however, because of a new governmental assignment for him of unusual importance and urgency, for which General Burns wishes release, it has become necessary to accede to the request that he be relieved of his command before the end of the year 1959. This conclusion has been reached in the light of the fact that General Burns has served the United Nations in the Middle East for more than five years, having been Chief of Staff of the United Nations Truce Supervision Organization from 9 August 1954 until he assumed the command of the United Nations Emergency Force (UNEF).

3. In these two capacities, and particularly as Commander of UNEF, General Burns has rendered distinguished service to the United Nations and has made a signal contribution of its efforts toward quiet and peace in the area. With devotion to the United Nations and its ideals, he has helped to mould, and has ably led, this unique and pioneering peace force. A considerable debt of gratitude is acknowledged to him for this service and also to the Government of Canada for making him available to the United Nations for a period so extended.

4. The impending loss of the services of General Burns gives rise to the question of a successor. There were good reasons for looking, in the first instance, to India for this purpose, among them being the fact that India provides the largest contingent in UNEF and has given full co-operation to it from the beginning. Consequently, an inquiry about possible candidates for the position of Commander was directed by the Secretary-General to India early in November. In response, the Government of India has submitted the name of an experienced officer with the rank of General who must be considered as thoroughly qualified to undertake the important responsibility involved.

5. The Secretary-General, therefore, acting under the authority vested in him by resolution 1001 (ES-I) of 7 November 1956, submits to the General Assembly for its approval the appointment as Commander of the United Nations Emergency Force of Major-General P. S. Gyani, a senior Major-General of the Indian Army, as successor to Lieutenant-General E. L. M. Burns. This appointment is to be effective as of the date on which General Burns relinquishes command, and is on the same terms as those which have applied to General Burns. The Government of India informs the Secretary-General that General Gyani is in line for promotion to the rank of Lieutenant-General. [*A/4210/Add. 1, 3 Dec. 1959.*]

UNEF COMMANDERS

Name	Nationality	Dates
1. Lt.-Gen. BURNS	Canada	Nov. 1956–Dec. 1959
2. Maj.-Gen. GYANI	India	Dec. 1959–Jan. 1964
3. Maj.-Gen. CHAVES	Brazil	Jan. 1964–Jan. 1965
4. Maj.Gen. SARMENTO	Brazil	Jan. 1965–Jan. 1966
5. Maj.-Gen. RIKHYE	India	Jan. 1966–May 1967

ACTING COMMANDERS

1. Col. E. C. CONDIL	Denmark	Sept. 1963–Nov. 1963
2. Col. MUZICKI	Yugoslavia	Aug. 1964–Jan. 1965

Note: This table is not an official UN document, but has been compiled by the Editor.

Whereas it was the Secretary-General who gave, in May 1967, the order to the Commander to withdraw, and provided the guidelines for this operation,[8] it was for the Commander to carry this out.

VII. WITHDRAWAL OF UNEF

General

61. Developments leading to the withdrawal of UNEF have been reported in the special reports of the Secretary-General on UNEF (A/6730 and Add. 1–3 and Add. 3/Corr. 1).

62. Subsequent to the withdrawal of all observation posts along the Armistice Demarcation Line and the International Frontier, the Commander of UNEF ordered concentration of the contingents in preparation for their final withdrawal from the area. On 19 May 1967, the Yugoslav detachments at El Sabha and at Ras Nasrani were withdrawn to Camp El Qusaima and Camp Sharm el Sheikh, respectively; platoons of the Swedish battalion at Camps Kastellet, Dan and Goeta were withdrawn to their parent company camps. On 20 May, a platoon of the Swedish battalion at Camp Freja was withdrawn to its parent camp; platoons of the Indian battalion at Camps Agra, Bombay, Jaipur, Madras and Poona were withdrawn to their parent company camps; the Yugoslav battalion started withdrawal of its detachments from Camps El Amr, El Qusaima, El Kuntilla and Ras el Naqb; and the Brazilian battalion started withdrawing its detachments from Camps Fort Saunders, Fort Robinson, Rio Grande do Sul, Santa Catarina and Rio de Janeiro and completed these movements by the following day. On 21 May, the Indian battalion withdrew its platoons at Camps Varberg and Falgenberg to its parent company camp. The detachment of the Yugoslav battalion at Sharm el Sheikh was withdrawn on 23 May.

63. The deployment of UNEF on 24 May 1967 was as follows:

Swedish battalion: platoon, Asgard; company, Camp Beit Lahiya; company, Beit Hanun; battalion headquarters, Camp Hill 88.

Indian battalion (1 Sikh Light Infantry): company, Camp David's Field; company, Camp Calcutta; company, Camp Lucknow; company, Camp Chandigarh; battalion headquarters, Camp Delhi.

Brazilian battalion: company, Fort Worthington (within boundary of Camp Rafah); battalion less one company, main Brazilian Camp, Rafah.

Yugoslav battalion: main camp, El Arish.

UNEF Support Group and UNEF Hospital: Camp Rafah.

Air Transport Unit: Marina Camp, El Arish.

64. Orders had been issued to units to return all UNEF stores to the depots at Camp Rafah, to pack their national stores and to prepare for an early departure from the area. All requisitions were reviewed, and those which had not been processed were cancelled.

65. The authorities of the United Arab Republic offered airfield and port facilities at Port Said for the departure of UNEF troops. Accordingly, under a senior headquarters UNEF officer a camp was established at Port Said. Adequate movement control staff, vehicles, supplies, vehicles for loading and unloading, and hotel accommodation for transit personnel were provided. The United Arab Republic authorities also agreed to provide adequate rail rolling stock for the movement of troops and their baggage.

66. There were about 2,800 men and over 1,000 tons of contingent stores to be transported. Besides a large part of the Force's vehicle fleet, engineer and communication equipment, and several tons of specialized items were to be transported to the United Nations stockpile at Livorno near Pisa. Furthermore, since the only exit made available for the withdrawal of the Force was the airfield and port at Port Said, UNEF personnel and stores had first to be brought by train to this point. UNEF trains were permitted only during hours of darkness, and the capacity of the rolling stock was limited. All this entailed a large-scale transportation

[8] For text, see p. 277-8.

problem. The United Nations has no transportation of its own for such needs, and therefore shipping and aircraft had to be obtained on commercial charter. Based on inquiries made from commercial organizations around the world and depending on the availability of transport, withdrawal of the troops from the area was planned as follows:

22 May	Canadian advance party, by air;
22–27 May	All dependants by air to Beirut pending finalization of their further travel;
3–4 June	Half of Yugoslav battalion by air in transport already contracted for routine rotation of half the battalion planned for this time;
5–7 June	Swedish battalion, by air;
19 June	Brazilian battalion, by sea; remainder Yugoslav battalion, by sea; Canadian main party, by air;
20 June	Norwegian hospital, by air;
21 June	Indian contingent, by sea;
30 June	Canadian remaining personnel, by air.

[*A/6672, Annual Report of the Secretary-General on UNEF, 12 July 1967*, mimeo.]

The Commander had also the unenviable task of protecting the remaining[9] contingents of the non-operational UNEF once fighting broke out. Severe casualties were in fact suffered by UN personnel:

Outbreak of hostilities in the area

81. When hostilities broke out on 5 June, the detailed deployment of UNEF was as follows (see also map 2):

Swedish battalion: The battalion was concentrated at Camp Hill 88 in preparation for its departure by train for Port Said that night. An advance party with all the contingent's heavy baggage had left for Port Said by train on the evening of 4 June.

Indian battalion (1 Sikh Light Infantry): The battalion, less three companies and a reinforced platoon, was at Camp Delhi. A company each was at Camps David's Field (including a platoon at Gaza airfield), Chandigarh and Lucknow as adequate accommodation and administrative facilities were not sufficient at the main battalion camp. A reinforced platoon replaced the Swedish guards at UNEF headquarters and Camp Tre Kroner.

Brazilian battalion: The battalion, less two companies, was at the main camp at Rafah. The other two companies had replaced the Canadian guard unit after its withdrawal on 30 May to provide guard duties at UNEF Support Group Camp, Rafah.

Yugoslav battalion: Approximately half the battalion had already departed on 3–4 June for their home country. The remainder was at the main camp at El Arish.

82. When fighting broke out, the Commander ordered immediate concentration of the Indian battalion, less one company, at Camp Delhi. Just before the planned departure of the Swedish battalion, the Indian battalion had taken over guard duties from them in Gaza. The Indian company at David's Field had also assumed responsibilities for the security of Gaza airfield, which had added importance in the withdrawal plan of UNEF. This company was now cut off from its main battalion because of the fighting. Therefore, the Commander ordered the company at Camp David's Field and at Gaza airfield to withdraw to Camp Tre Kroner.

83. The Commander took the following security measures to protect the personnel and installations.

(a) All UNEF movement was stopped except on an emergency basis with the authority of the commanding officers of units and senior headquarters staff.

(b) UNEF military and international staff in Gaza were moved into Camp Tre Kroner by the afternoon of 5 June. A few villas in the immediate vicinity of the Commander's mess provided billets for female staff and key personnel to their maximum capacity. The headquarters mess and all other accommodations were closed down before sundown that day.

---

[9] For the early withdrawal of the Canadians, see S.9, pp. 369–72.

(*c*) All camps were ordered to stock up food and supplies, petrol, oil and lubricants for fifteen days' use.

(*d*) All camps and vehicles would prominently display the United Nations flag and markings so that they would be clearly visible from ground and air.

(*e*) All camps would take necessary precautions against air and ground attack.

(*f*) In the event any camps, vehicles or personnel were involved in actual fighting between the two parties, they would display large white flags and identify themselves. They would also attempt to establish contact with local commanders.

(*g*) In the event of the breakdown of normal radio and telephone communications, commanding officers would use mobile Motorola sets.

(*h*) All units were ordered to prepare for an emergency evacuation at one hour's notice as from 6 June.

84. Details of the events of 5 and 6 June have been reported in the statement of the Secretary-General to the Security Council on the morning of 5 June (S/PV.1374) and in the supplemental information reported by him (S/7930 and Add. 1). After the end of fighting many UNEF personnel who had been missing returned. Some personnel were held by the Israel authorities but were returned by 7 June. A thorough search for the remaining missing personnel was conducted. It was not possible to account for all killed and wounded until the evening of 9 June.

85. Casualties suffered by UNEF contingents were as follows:

> *Brazil*—one killed and one wounded
> *India*—fourteen killed and twenty wounded.

86. Early reports from UNEF were inevitably based on incomplete information. Details could be obtained and verified only after interrogation of the wounded and the missing personnel when they returned. It was also not until 9 June that contact was re-established with the international staff at Camp Rafah. The information given below is based on this more complete picture of the events affecting UNEF. When fighting began on 5 June, UNEF had been withdrawn from the line and was no longer operational. Therefore, it was in no position to report on what actually happened in the area. Its means of observation, investigation and verification were no longer available to it.

87. Fighting in the UNEF area of operations in the Gaza Strip broke out on the morning of 5 June. The first indication of hostilities in the area came at 09.15 hours local time when an Israel Defence Forces jet aircraft was shot down by anti-aircraft fire near the Gaza beach. Fighting then continued in the Gaza Strip for two days.

88. Immediately on the outbreak of hostilities, the Commander addressed personal appeals to Israel and United Arab Republic military authorities to ensure the safety of UNEF personnel and installations. In his appeal to Major-General Yitzhak Rabin, Chief of Staff, Israel Defence Forces, conveyed through Lieutenant-General Odd Bull, Chief of Staff, United Nations Truce Supervision Organization, he requested that safety of UNEF installations be ensured and that Israel forces refrain from firing into those areas. The Israel defence forces were fully acquainted with the detailed deployment of UNEF. General Rabin replied to the Commander's appeal in the affirmative but stated that he could not guarantee 100 per cent safety. In a similar appeal to General Abdul Mohsen Kamul Mortaga, Commander Eastern Front and Commander of Land troops of the United Arab Republic, the Commander of UNEF requested that the United Arab Republic forces in the immediate vicinity of UNEF camps, buildings and installations be removed to prevent Israel counter-fire.

89. On the evening of 5 June, when the Commander of UNEF selected Camp Tre Kroner and the beaches nearby in Gaza as a safe area for the concentration and embarkation of UNEF personnel, at his request the authorities of the United Arab Republic removed their troops from the area, which later proved to be the only UNEF area in Gaza which escaped Israel fire.

90. The effect of the fighting on UNEF troops can best be described in relation to general areas where the troops were located during this period. These areas were:

(*a*) Gaza area, including Hill 88 and David's Field;
(*b*) Deir el Balah and Khan Yunis;
(*c*) Rafah;
(*d*) El Arish;
(*e*) Port Said.

Gaza

91. On 5 June, at 12.00 hours local time, the area near the Swedish battalion at Hill 88 came under artillery fire. Sniping in the area continued up to 16.00 hours, and at 16.22 hours the area again came under artillery fire.

At 18.30 hours, the Swedish battalion was ordered to withdraw to Gaza from Hill 88. The move was completed by 20.15 hours.

92. The company from the Indian battalion at David's Field Camp, which had a platoon at the Gaza airfield, was withdrawn to Gaza at 13.00 hours.

93. At 22.35 hours, Gaza town came under intermittent shelling, and the radio antenna on the UNEF headquarters building was damaged, thereby disrupting communications until 23.30 hours when the antenna was repaired under fire by Field Service technicians. Shelling of Gaza town was resumed on the morning of 6 June, at 04.30 hours, and continued throughout the day. UNEF headquarters building was continuously under artillery fire from 09.00 to 14.30 hours during which period three Indian soldiers were killed and two wounded while on duty at headquarters. There was extensive damage to the buildings, offices and vehicles. At about 11.30 hours, UNEF headquarters received direct hits, and all its radio links were broken. It became necessary to evacuate the remaining personnel under fire and to re-establish the headquarters at Camp Tre Kroner. During the afternoon small arms fire was heard around Gaza town, but by 17.30 hours the situation was stabilized after Gaza had been occupied by the Israel forces. A small Indian guard had been left behind for security of the offices at UNEF headquarters. This unit was disarmed by the Israel soldiers. Later, on the Commander's personal intervention, the weapons were returned to the Indian guard.

Deir el Balah and Khan Yunis

94. On 5 June, at 09.20 hours, UNEF vehicles came under air strafing, small arms and tank fire on the road between Deir el Balah and Rafah. At about this time a supply convoy of the Indian battalion, while returning from Rafah, was fired upon by Israel aircraft, tanks and machine-guns, resulting in the death of five Indian soldiers. One Indian group (one officer and two other ranks) and one Swedish group (one officer and two other ranks), who were also in the area of Khan Yunis at this time, came under fire from both sides. The groups took cover during the fighting until they were escorted back to the Indian battalion headquarters at Camp Delhi on 7 June by Israel military personnel. The Israel military personnel also brought back one Brazilian soldier along with the two groups.

95. On 5 June, at 09.30 hours, the Indian battalion companies located at Camps Chandigarh and Lucknow were ordered to withdraw to Deir el Balah. At this time troops of the United Arab Republic had moved away from their positions in the area, and when the Israel attack came, the Israel tanks directly confronted the Indian soldiers who had taken cover in trenches to protect themselves from the firing from both sides.

96. At 15.25 hours, mortars of the United Arab Republic started firing from a location close to the Indian battalion's Camp Delhi. This drew Israel counter-mortar fire, and as a result the Indian battalion suffered three killed and fourteen wounded.

97. Because of the deteriorating conditions and in order to prevent further casualties to the Indian troops at Camp Delhi, the Commander of UNEF ordered the Indian battalion to withdraw to a safe area on the beach. This withdrawal unfortunately could not take place owing to the continuous heavy shelling and mortaring of the area.

98. On 6 June, at 09.00 hours, an Indian officer evacuating two seriously wounded soldiers in a vehicle to the hospital in Gaza ran over a mine on the Deir el Balah-Gaza road, resulting in the deaths of all three.

Rafah

99. On 5 June, at 11.30 hours, artillery fire was heard two to three kilometres from Rafah Camp. At 11.35 hours Israel Defence Forces aircraft were bombing areas close to the camp, and from 12.05 to 16.00 hours there was an exchange of small arms fire outside the camp. One Brazilian soldier was killed by machine-gun fire in the Brazilian main camp at Rafah during this period. At 16.10 hours the camp came under artillery fire. Between 16.10 and 18.10 hours large concentrations of troops and the landing of helicopters were observed near the camp. At 18.10 hours the camp came under artillery and tank fire, and by 19.00 hours Israel Defence Forces tanks were inside the camp firing on the local UNEF civilian employees. By 20.00 hours fighting in the area had stopped.

100. The Israel forces, on arrival in Camp Rafah, separated the United Nations international and military personnel from the United Nations local civilian staff. An Israel officer ordered the United Nations international and military staff, who had identified themselves as such, to lie on the ground where they remained until the morning of 6 June. Only the personnel of the Norwegian hospital unit and the patients there were unmolested. The commanding officer of the Norwegian hospital unit succeeded in providing blankets to the UNEF group who were forced to spend the night on the sand in the open without food or water. On 6 June, at about 09.00 hours, the Israel officer in charge allowed this group to return to its normal quarters.

El Arish

101. On 5 June, at 15.40 hours, anti-aircraft firing on Israel Defence Forces aircraft started near the Yugoslav camp. At about 17.20 hours the area of the Yugoslav battalion was strafed by Israel Defence Forces aircraft, and thereafter small arms fire was heard around the camp up to 19.30 hours. At 20.30 hours a few shells were fired inside the camp by tanks moving on the road outside, resulting in the blowing up of two water tanks.

102. In order to ensure their safety, the Commander suggested that the Yugoslav battalion withdraw to the beach and bivouac there. However, the Yugoslav battalion encountered certain practical difficulties, and after re-examination of the situation, it was agreed that the battalion should remain in its main camp. Thereafter the situation in the camp was quiet and no incidents were reported during the night.

Port Said

103. UNEF personnel at Port Said reported that the town was under an air raid during the morning of 5 June. Thereafter, for several hours there were no communications with Port Said until later in the afternoon when the UNEF office reported that the advance party of the Swedish battalion, which had left Gaza by train on the night of 4 June, had reached Qantara East. The United Arab Republic authorities had stopped the train there; however, arrangements had been made to move the Swedish personnel and their baggage by train to Port Said. This move was completed late that evening.

104. On 6 June, instructions were received from the Ministry of Foreign Affairs of the United Arab Republic to close down the UNEF radio at Port Said. Contact was maintained, however, through the UNEF liaison office at Cairo. All UNEF personnel, less Swedish contingent stores and two Field Service staff in charge of UNEF stores, were evacuated by sea to Cyprus where they rejoined their national contingents and ultimately returned to their home countries.

Evacuation

105. Immediately after fighting broke out in the area, the Secretary-General received a most urgent request from the Commander of UNEF to arrange for the immediate evacuation of the Force by ship from the Gaza beaches. Immediate action was taken by the Field Operations Service to find shipping in the area for the immediate evacuation of UNEF from Gaza. A Swedish ship was made available to proceed to Gaza on 6 June. This was followed subse-

quently by three more ships under the flags of Greece or Yugoslavia and a Brazilian Navy ship which was already on its way to transport the Brazilian contingent.

106. During the afternoon of 5 June the United Arab Republic liaison staff had agreed to assist with the embarkation of UNEF at Gaza port. Since there were no docking facilities, motor launches, lighters and fishing boats were to be made available for embarkation. The occupation of Gaza by Israel forces, however, made new arrangements necessary.

107. On 6 June, at 19.45 hours, an Israel liaison officer arrived at Camp Tre Kroner and invited the Commander of UNEF to meet the Commander of the Israel forces at his command post in Gaza. At this meeting the UNEF Commander requested (a) permission to reinforce the guard at UNEF headquarters to protect UNEF property and documents; (b) that assistance be provided to him and his staff to return to UNEF headquarters on 7 June; (c) that assistance be given to run a convoy to Camp Rafah to bring food and to contact UNEF personnel there and the Indian and Brazilian battalions situated along the road; and (d) that information be provided, if available, about the missing Indian personnel.

108. The Commander of the Israel forces gave assurances of his co-operation, agreed to the requests in (a) and (b) above, and offered armed escorts as isolated pockets of resistance and snipers remained in the city of Gaza. He also promised to obtain any information available concerning the missing Indian personnel. He was not able at that time, however, to assist UNEF in collecting food from Rafah or in establishing contact with its units elsewhere in the Gaza Strip.

109. On 7 June, the Commander of UNEF with his senior staff returned to UNEF headquarters and was able to retrieve all his and some other official documents. The radio was found only slightly damaged, although there was extensive damage to spare parts and to the vehicles in the car park. All important documents and equipment were removed to Camp Tre Kroner thereafter. As repairs to the communications equipment were not practicable, it was decided to retain Camp Tre Kroner as the location of UNEF headquarters.

110. Later on the morning of 7 June the Commander of UNEF had a meeting with Colonel Itzhak Shany who had been appointed liaison officer to UNEF by the Israel Defence Forces. The Commander was informed that the United Arab Republic Governor-General of the Gaza Strip had signed a surrender document about 17.00 hours on 6 June. He was also informed that Israel forces had not completed clearing the remaining snipers, especially in the northern part of Gaza. Israel authorities believed that there was a large number of small arms in the area. In view of this it would not be possible to authorize the use of Gaza port facilities in time to permit UNEF evacuation from there. Therefore, the Israel authorities had arranged for the Swedish ship to proceed to Ashdod, a newly developed port for cargo ships north of Gaza in Israel. The Israel authorities offered transportation and other assistance for the movement of UNEF troops.

111. The Commander of UNEF was also informed that there were remaining pockets of resistance in the Khan Yunis area. The Israel authorities would, however, permit the use of a bypass through Israel territory to Camp Rafah. The Commander requested assistance to restore the water supply which had been put out during the fighting in the town. The Israel authorities already had measures in hand and expected to restore the water and electric supply in a few days.

112. During the remainder of 7 June, scattered firing was heard in Gaza, and there were reports of Israel activity against isolated pockets of resistance from Deir el Balah and Khan Yunis. At about 19.00 hours, the Commander was invited to meet Israel's Minister of Defence, Major-General Moshe Dayan, at the residence of the former United Arab Republic Governor-General of the Gaza Strip. The Chairman of the Egyptian–Israel Mixed Armistice Commission and the Director of UNRWA in Gaza were also present. The Commander requested the Defence Minister's assistance in the early evacuation of UNEF from Gaza. After discussions with Israel officers, the Minister stated that as it was not practicable to use Gaza, facilities at Ashdod would be made available. At the Commander's request the Minister offered every facility for the speedy evacuation of UNEF from the area.

113. On 9 June, the Israel authorities permitted the Chief Administrative Officer of UNEF

to visit Camp Rafah. The same day contact was established with all the contingents in the Force. On 10 June, the Commander carried out a personal inspection of units in the Force. As indicated above, the Indian battalion at Camp Delhi had suffered a number of casualties. The Commander found, however, that the damage to UNEF and Indian national stores was slight. The Commander also decided to evacuate immediately the Indian wounded, who had by then been collected at the Indian Medical Inspection Room, for proper hospitalization by the United Nations Force in Cyprus. Twelve stretcher and four sitting cases, accompanied by the senior Indian medical officer and nursing assistants, were evacuated by special charter aircraft from Lod Airport for Nicosia on the afternoon of 11 June.

114. While it was preferable for UNEF to embark from Gaza, there were a number of factors militating against it. The Israel Army had yet to clear the northern part of the town, including the embarkation area. It was known that a number of Arab armed personnel, after discarding their uniforms but still retaining their weapons, had disappeared among the local population in the area, including the large refugee camp in the vicinity. All the motor boats and lighters had disappeared, and the fishermen remained in their homes and were inaccessible. The Israel authorities, who had first thought that it might take two or three days to clear this area, stated their inability to do so for about seven to ten days.

115. Meanwhile the situation of UNEF personnel had become most difficult. As already stated, Gaza was without water and electricity. UNEF had been unable to procure any food, and there were only two days' supplies left. Some twenty serious medical cases, including wounded, needed immediate hospitalization. Because of lack of water, sanitation in Camp Tre Kroner had already reached a dangerous stage. It had thus become essential to commence the evacuation of personnel from any point from which embarkation could be effected. Accordingly instructions were issued to ships under charter to proceed to Ashdod, and the Commander was authorized to embark his troops from there if the situation, in his view, demanded it. Israel authorities provided civilian buses for the transportation of UNEF personnel, while the Force made its own arrangements on an *ad hoc* basis for the transportation of unit stores and heavy baggage. UNEF personnel carried their personal weapons and equipment with them and moved under UNEF arrangements with Israel guides only. The evacuation of the Force from Ashdod was completed on 17 June as reported in document A/6730/Add. 2. [*Ibid.*]

7

COMPOSITION AND SIZE

The Secretary-General made it clear that the composition of the Force was a matter for him to decide. This point was disputed by the Soviet Union, who insisted that the Security Council's 'inalienable right to decide in each specific case on the formation of and use of United Nations Forces should be observed'.[1] Although it was desirable that all the contingents should be acceptable to the host state,[2] the international character of the Force meant that the composition was not to be dictated by the other parties involved:

It may in this context be observed that the Franco-British proposal, to which I have already referred, may imply that the question of the composition of the staff and contingents should

---

[1] *GAOR*, 11th sess., 592nd mtg, para. 29.   [2] On which point, see below, pp. 367-8.

be subject to agreement by the parties involved, which it would be difficult to reconcile with the development of the international force along the course already being followed by the General Assembly. [*A/3302*, para. 6.]

The Secretary-General had already enumerated the principle of exclusion of Security Council members from participation in UNEF:[3]

. . . I would try to determine from which countries the necessary troops might be drawn without delay, as well as from which countries recruitment may be possible for a somewhat later stage. For both stages I would endeavour to develop a plan where, as a matter of principle, troops should not be drawn from countries which are permanent members of the Security Council. [*A/3289, 1st Report on an emergency internat. Force, 4 Nov. 1956*, para. 5.]

As this Force was to be set up by the Assembly and not the Security Council under Chapter VII there was no question of states being compelled to participate if they did not wish. In his Second Report on the plan for an Emergency Force the Secretary-General elaborated on some of the underlying principles and the practical questions flowing from them.

6. In its resolution 1000 (ES–I) on the United Nations Command, the General Assembly authorized the Chief of Command, in consultation with the Secretary-General, to recruit officers from the United Nations Truce Supervision Organization, or directly from various Member States other than the permanent members of the Security Council. This recruitment procedure affords an important indication of the character of the Force to be set up. On the one hand, the independence of the Chief of Command in recruiting officers is recognized. On the other hand, the principle is established that the Force should be recruited from Member States other than the permanent members of the Security Council. The first of these elements in the new approach has an important bearing on the interpretation of the status of the Chief of Command. The second point has an equally important bearing on the character of the whole Command. . . .

QUESTIONS OF SIZE AND ORGANIZATION OF THE FORCE

13. Time has so far not permitted the necessary technical studies. It is therefore not yet possible to say what should be the size of the Force. In my first report, I pointed out that the situation is likely to involve two stages: the first one when certain immediate tasks have to be fulfilled, the second one when somewhat different tasks, although within the framework set out in paragraph 12 above, will fall upon the Force. It is likely that the size of the Force will require some adjustment to the development of the tasks. Further study of such matters is required, and I have invited the Chief of the United Nations Command, General Burns, to present his views urgently.

14. It is not possible at this time to make any proposals as to the general organization of the Force beyond those clearly following from resolution 998 (ES–I) of 4 November 1956. General experience seems to indicate that it is desirable that countries participating in the Force should provide self-contained units in order to avoid the loss of time and efficiency which is unavoidable when new units are set up through joining together small groups of different nationalities. The question requires additional study and is obviously closely linked to the condition that various Member States will provide sufficiently large units. The difficulty in presenting a detailed plan of organization need not delay the establishment of the Force. It is likely that during the first period, at all events, the Force would have to be composed of a few units of battalion strength, drawn from countries or groups of countries which can provide such troops without delay. It is my endeavour in the approaches to Governments

---

[3] And one may note how far this principle, readily accepted in respect of an *ad hoc* peacekeeping force such as UNEF, had moved from the original intentions of the Charter in Arts 43-49.

to build up a panel sufficiently broad to permit such a choice of units as would provide for a balanced composition in the Force. Further planning and decisions on organization will to a large extent have to depend on the judgement of the Chief of Command and his staff. . . .

QUESTIONS OF RECRUITMENT

16. Time permitted me to discuss the question of participation in the Force with only a limited number of Member Governments. Offers of assistance in writing so far received are annexed to the present report. In cases other than those covered by the annexed letters, the question of participation is under consideration by the Governments. It is my hope that broader participation will be possible as soon as a plan is approved, so that a more definite judgement may be possible concerning the implications of participation. The reactions so far received lead me to believe that it should be possible to meet quickly at least the most basic need for personnel. The possibilities, as finally established, may call for an adjustment later of the size and organization of the Force in relation to what would in principle be the most satisfactory solution. [*A/3302*.]

Thus the Commander of the Force (appointed by the Assembly) was authorized to recruit his own staff from the officers serving with UNTSO, or from member states. The recruitment of contingents from member states was undertaken by the Secretary-General.

In the event some twenty-four nations offered contingents: Afghanistan, Brazil, Burma, Canada, Ceylon, Chile, Colombia, Czechoslovakia, Denmark, Ecuador, Ethiopia, Finland, Indonesia, Iran, India, Laos, New Zealand, Norway, Pakistan, Peru, Philippines, Romania, Sweden, and Yugoslavia.[4] Egypt found Pakistan and New Zealand unacceptable. In the event, the Secretary-General selected contingents and supporting units from ten nations: Brazil, Canada, Colombia, Denmark, Finland, India, Indonesia, Norway, Sweden, and Yugoslavia.

UNEF Commanders and Acting Commanders have been drawn from five nations to date—Canada, India, Brazil, Denmark and Yugoslavia. For details see above, p. 293.

UNEF CONTINGENTS

	A/3694 9.10.57	A/3839 3.7.58	A/4210 10.9.59	A/4486 1.8.60	A/4857 30.8.61	A/5172 22.8.62	A/5494 12.9.63	A/5736 29.9.64	A/59 27.9
BRAZIL									
Officers	44	41	39	41	40	40	40	41	3
Other ranks	501	594	609	591	585	590	576	588	40
Total	545	635	648	632	625	630	616	629	43
CANADA									
Officers	113	83	86	87	85	82	88	94	8
Other ranks	1,095	892	897	845	851	863	852	877	86
Total	1,172	975	983	932	936	945	940	971	95

[4] The texts of the offers to the Secretary-General of most of these nations are to be found in the annexes to his Second and Final Report on the plan for UNEF (A/3302).

UNEF CONTINGENTS—*continued*

	A/3694 9.10.57	A/3839 3.7.58	A/4210 10.9.59	A/4486 1.8.60	A/4857 30.8.61	A/5172 22.8.62	A/5494 12.9.63	A/5736 29.9.64	A/5919 27.9.65
LOMBIA									
Officers	31	26							
Other ranks	491	466							
Total	522	492*							
NMARK									
Officers	25	32	36	42	47	45	45	35	67
Other ranks	399	427	512	523	515	517	518	393	424
Total	424	459	548	565	562	562	563	428	491
LAND									
Officers	15								
Other ranks	240								
Total	255†								
DIA									
Officers	27	70	69	74	75	80	78	78	67
Other ranks	930	1,097	1,105	1,172	1,176	1,169	1,174	1,187	1,193
Total	957	1,167	1,174	1,246	1,251	1,249	1,252	1,265	1,269
DONESIA									
Officers	37								
Other ranks	545								
Total	582‡								
RWAY									
Officers	71	73	85	66	87	84	57	55	55
Other ranks	427	465	518	515	527	529	437	440	442
Total	498	538	603	601	614	613	494	495	497
DEN									
Officers	27	34	39	36	33	33	57	57	46
Other ranks	322	471	620	620	430	391	472	481	380
Total	349	505	659	650	463	424	529	538	426
GOSLAVIA									
Officers	55	67	75	71	70	68	67	58	52
Other ranks	618	607	644	638	638	642	641	549	454
Total	673	674	719	709	708	710	708	607	506
TAL	5,977	5,445	5,334	5,341	5,159	5,133	5,102	4,933	4,581

* Withdrew 28 Oct. 1958   † Withdrew 5 Dec. 1957   ‡ Withdrew 12 Sept. 1957

Notes: 1. This is not an official document, but has been compiled by the Editor from official UN sources.

2. Basically, Brazil, Denmark, India, Norway, and Sweden all provided infantry. Yugoslavia contributed an infantry reconnaissance battalion. India provided signals and service units as well as infantry. Canada gave a reconnaissance squadron, engineering signals and service units; and an air transport unit.

3. From 1958-9 the figures for Canada include personnel of the Royal Canadian Air Force stationed at El Arish.

4. At the inception of UNEF there was a Canadian-manned hospital at Rafah, and a Norwegian-manned hospital in Gaza town. In November 1957 they were merged into a single unit at Rafah. From March 1959 the hospital was staffed entirely by Norwegian personnel, until May 1963. At that date Norway indicated that it was becoming increasingly difficult to find medical personnel, and Sweden then took over the assignment. In 1965 the task of manning the hospital went to Denmark.

5. In 1965 the Norwegian and Danish units were placed under a single battalion and the structure of command was alternated between Denmark and Norway.

6. The Swedish contingent became considerably reduced in 1961 and 1962 by the dispatch of the equivalent of two companies to serve in the Congo.

INITIAL ASSESSMENT OF REQUIREMENTS

34. The Commander of UNEF estimated that, in order to perform the tasks assigned by the General Assembly, the Force would require the equivalent of two combat brigades, or about 6,000 men. The initial concept of military organization, later modified in the light of further clarification of the functions of the Force, was that it should be built around regimental combat teams. It would require an independent signals company expanded to provide all necessary communications facilities for Force headquarters and in the field. In addition, headquarters, engineer, transport, shop repair and medical personnel would be needed. It was decided that the infantry should be equipped with normal regimental weapons, that there should be a transport company sufficient to lift one infantry battalion, and that each battalion should be administratively self-contained. The Commander also stressed the desirability of an armoured car squadron for reconnaissance work, in view of the nature of the terrain and the task of the Force. It was further concluded at an early stage that a light air unit was essential for functions inside the UNEF operations area.

The first phase

35. There was urgent need to assemble a usable force, as rapidly as possible, and to land it in Egypt. While awaiting the conclusion of arrangements with Egypt for the entry of the Force into that country, it was decided that a staging area near the Mediterranean would be necessary, as it would expedite the flow of troops and *matériel* to Egypt. Arrangements were quickly made with the Government of Italy for the use of Capodichino airport, Naples, for this purpose. Most of the troops brought to Egypt by air were sent via Naples, others were flown in via Beirut, while others came by sea to Port Said. The small staff in charge of the staging area at Capodichino took care of the incoming (and later outgoing) contingents, dealt with the several authorities in Europe through whom major logistic support was obtained, supervised the air-lift to Egypt and arranged for the surface transport of heavy stores.

36. The initial movements of troops from their home bases to Italy were arranged through United Nations Headquarters. The problems were mainly transportation and co-ordination. The bulk of the transport to the staging area was provided by the United States Air Force. The representatives of the contributing countries supplied information to United Nations Headquarters concerning the numbers, equipment and state of readiness of their national units, and this was transmitted to the representatives of the United States Air Force designated for this purpose. The latter, in turn, gave notification concerning the precise arrange-

ments for transporting the contingents named, which was transmitted to the appropriate Governments by their military representatives at United Nations Headquarters.

37. A selected group of United Nations military observers, who were detached temporarily from their duties with UNTSO and who commenced planning while still in Jerusalem, served at first as the nucleus of a UNEF headquarters staff. They arrived in Egypt on 12 November 1956, established a temporary headquarters in Cairo and, together with Secretariat officials, arranged for the reception and billeting of the first contingents, and the early procurement, storage and issue of the supplies and equipment required. Through negotiations with the Egyptian Government, an air base at Abu Suweir, near Ismailia, became the arrival depot for the early contingents. As the contingents arrived, their officers took over the duties being performed by the military observers, who were then able to return to their UNTSO duties in Jerusalem.

38. Advance elements of UNEF were moved to Egypt at a time when hostilities had but recently ceased; there were restrictions on the times and lanes of flights, and aircraft transporting contingents had to be of suitable nationalities. The initial air-lift of troops to Abu Suweir was carried out by Swissair. The Naples to Egypt air-lift was subsequently taken over by the Royal Canadian Air Force with some assistance from the Italian Air Force in lifting supplies.

39. Speed was a major reason for initially moving some troops and equipment to Egypt by air, but as ships under some flags could not be used, and as ships proceeding to Port Said at that time were required to be self-sustaining, the immediate possibilities of employing sea transport were in any case severely reduced. The Yugoslav reconnaissance battalion, with all its equipment, was brought to Port Said by sea on 28 November 1956, while the main elements of the Canadian and Brazilian contingents arrived in national naval vessels on 11 January and 2 February 1957, respectively. All heavy equipment for UNEF was brought in by ship.

40. One consequence of having to rely on air transport for the first units and their equipment was an immediate and severe shortage of transport vehicles. This difficulty was aggravated by the fact that several of the contingents had not contemplated bringing most of their vehicular transport with them in any event because of the desert conditions. The shortage was alleviated by obtaining vehicles from UNRWA, by local purchases and by rental. But, as requirements mounted, these sources became inadequate.

41. A preliminary understanding had been reached in New York on the purchase of vehicles and supplies in Port Said from the British forces as they withdrew, the details of the transaction being worked out on the spot. This procurement was very helpful in facilitating the rapid deployment of UNEF forces in the Sinai Peninsula and in equipping the two transportation platoons used for supplying the forces. Shortly after the formation of the Force, a large order for vehicles was placed with United States military authorities. These vehicles arrived in January 1957 and filled the additional transport requirements.

42. The need to transport UNEF units to positions evacuated by the Anglo-French and Israel forces, to keep them supplied and to provide replacements, required the immediate establishment at Abu Suweir of a dump of petrol, oil and lubricants. The necessary stocks and installations were obtained in the area. Additional storage facilities were obtained in Port Said, and further supply points were established as the operation moved forward.

43. The clear identification of UNEF personnel, beyond the customary United Nations armbands, was an immediate necessity for security and other reasons. Light blue helmet liners with United Nations markings were adopted for this purpose, and were later supplemented by blue berets and desert caps and UNEF badges and insignia. Vehicles and aircraft were painted white with United Nations markings.

National contingents and supporting units

44. On the basis of the position taken in the General Assembly resolutions—which reflects a principle that is both sound and practical—no units from any of the permanent members of the Security Council have been included in the Force. Nor have any been recruited from

countries in the area or from countries which might, for other reasons, be thought to have a special interest in the conflict situation. In selecting contingents, weight was given to such factors as their suitability in terms of the needs of the Force, their size and availability, the extent to which they would be self-contained, the undesirability of too great a variation in ordnance and basic equipment, the problem of transportation, and the goal of balanced composition.

45. In the period November–December 1956, twenty-four Member States offered to provide units (see A/3302 and Add. 1–30). A number of these countries also offered other forms of assistance, as did two other Member States and one non-member. Most of the offers of assistance were of infantry units. The Force, at the peak of its strength totalling about 6,000 officers and men, consisted of contingents from the following countries: Brazil, Canada, Colombia, Denmark, Finland, India, Indonesia, Norway, Sweden and Yugoslavia.

46. The extent of the area to be covered by UNEF called for highly mobile reconnaissance. This need was met by Yugoslavia, which provided a complete reconnaissance battalion, and by Canada, which later provided a fully-equipped light armoured squadron.

47. Supporting units were obtained and assigned with the same urgency as those engaged in patrolling. Experience with the Force soon demonstrated the desirability of limiting the number of countries participating in it, particularly those providing support units, in view of the difficulties in co-ordinating and controlling a number of relatively small units having different arms and equipment, requiring varying diets and speaking different languages. Thus, to simplify the organization in the interest of efficiency, the Indian contingent was given responsibility for the Supply Depot and the Service Institute; Canada and India provided units for Transport, the Provost Marshal and Signals; Norway and Canada covered the medical needs. The Canadian contingent was also made responsible for the Ordnance Depot and Workshop, the Base Post Office, Engineering, the Dental Unit, Movement Control and Air Support.

48. When the contingents were being accepted, it was impossible to determine or to foresee the duration of the UNEF mission. National terms of military service, the nature of the mission, conditions of weather and terrain, and considerations of morale and efficiency, gave strong support to the principle and practice of rather frequent periodic rotation. The exact rotation policies adopted by contributing Governments, however, have varied somewhat, and in some cases the length of the period of service has been shorter than would be dictated exclusively by considerations of efficiency and economy. Full responsibility for the cost of transportation is accepted by the United Nations.

49. The schedules of rotation are fixed by the contributing countries in consultation with the Commander, in such a way as to ensure continuity of national participation in the Force and to protect it from being undermanned.

50. With regard to the withdrawal of contingents from the Force, the contributing Governments agreed with the Secretary-General that, in order to protect the organizational strength of the Force, participating Governments would inform the Secretary-General in advance of a decision to withdraw their contingents. In each of the two cases of withdrawal that have occurred to date, notice was given sufficiently in advance to enable the Force to obtain replacements through increasing the size of one or more of the existing contingents. [*A/3493, Summary Study of the experience of UNEF, 9 Oct. 1958.*]

The size of the Force was, in the early years of UNEF, kept at a fairly constant level—though it was understandably at its highest at the very first phase. From 1960 onwards, however, both political and financial pressures led to the whittling down of the numbers of UNEF personnel.

5. The determination of the numerical strength of the Force and its components is based upon assessments of need by the Commander of the Force, which have been reviewed from time to time. The main considerations weighed in determining the size and composition of the Force have been: the needs of the Force on the basis of its functions and responsibilities, at

first in the Suez Canal region and, later, in the Sinai Peninsula and the Gaza Strip areas; the desirability of balance in the Force with regard to considerations of both geographical distribution and military organization; the comparative utility, in the light of assessed needs, of the troops offered; and the relative availability and economy of transport for the troops offered, together with their essential gear and vehicles.

6. On the basis of the most recent appraisal by the Commander, a reduction before long in the size of the Force by some 400 officers and men may be anticipated. As in any military organization, though perhaps to a lesser degree in UNEF, a substantial part of the personnel is necessarily engaged in vital support functions, such as administration, signals, engineering, supply and transport, workshop, ordnance, medical, dental, postal, pay, provost and movement control. Elements of the Force engaged in such activities, as the Commander has pointed out, are neither suitable nor available for patrol and guard duties. Thus, of the total force on 1 September of nearly 6,000, only seventy-four platoons, each of strength varying from thirty to forty-five all ranks—a total of less than 3,500 officers and men—were at the Commander's disposition for the regular patrol and guard duties of UNEF. The departure of the Indonesian contingent in mid-September reduced the number of platoons for such duty to sixty-five.

7. The Commander has emphasized in his reports, that, for the task it is called upon to perform, UNEF's ground deployment is 'very thin', even with the present numbers. He urges that the Force be maintained at a strength permitting a minimum of seventy-one duty platoons, which takes into account necessary allowances for leave, rotation, sickness, training and essential reserve. Through planned reorganization and adjustments in support units, however, it is expected that a force, reduced from its present total of 5,977 to about 5,600 officers and men, would permit this minimum need for deployment to be satisfied. [*A/3665*, *Report of the Secretary-General, 16 Sept. 1957.*]

Size of Force

10. The Advisory Committee is informed that there is a frequent shift in numbers because of replacement activity, but that the average daily strength of officers and other ranks during 1958 is estimated at 5,400 men, as compared with the actual strength of approximately 6,000 on 1 September 1957 and of 5,407 on 15 May q958. The Commander's basic requirement for adequate deployment, as stated in the Secretary-General's report to the General Assembly at its twelfth session, was that the Force should be maintained at a minimum level of seventy-one duty platoons, representing a total of between 5,500 and 5,600 men. The present strength is, therefore, below this basic requirement. This is mainly due to the fact that the deficiency caused by the withdrawal of the Indonesian and Finnish contingents has not been fully restored. However, the Committee understands that the Force, even at its present reduced strength, continues to meet even the most urgent demands of the situation. [*A/3839*, *2nd Report of the Advisory Committee on Administrative and Budgetary Questions, 3 July 1958.*]

4. The consolidated strength of the Force throughout the period under review has been maintained at approximately 5,400 officers and other ranks, comprising contingents from eight contributing countries: Brazil, Canada, Colombia, Denmark, India, Norway, Sweden and Yugoslavia. This is below the figure anticipated in the previous report (A/3694, paras 6–7). The Commander reports that the present strength of the Force makes sixty-eight platoons available for patrolling and guard duties, the strength of each platoon varying from twenty to forty all ranks. Thus, only approximately 2,500 officers and men are actually available for patrolling and guard duties, the rest of the Force consisting of supporting units. The Commander feels that any reduction of the Force below its present numerical strength would result in loss of effectiveness through inability to cover adequately the long lines involved and lack of the necessary reserves. [*A/3899*, *Report of Secretary-General, 27 Aug. 1958.*]

A moderate reduction in its over-all strength was achieved by replacing only partially the

Colombian contingent which was withdrawn on 28 October 1958, and by a small scaling down in the ordnance and signals detachments.

4. The total strength of the Force, following the withdrawal of the Colombian contingent, was, as at April 1959, approximately 5,000 officers and other ranks. Since then, through partially replacing the Colombians by an icrease of approximately 300 (all ranks) in the Scandinavian contingents, the Force has been maintained at approximately 5,350 officers and other ranks. Brazil, Canada, Denmark, India, Norway, Sweden and Yugoslavia are the countries now participating in the Force.

5. The present strength of the Force makes seventy-one platoons available for patrol and guard duty on the armistice demarcation line (ADL), international frontier (IF) and elsewhere. The strength of each platoon varies from twenty-six to thirty-nine, all ranks. Approximately 2,500 officers and men are thus available for active duty, the rest of the Force consisting of support units.

6. The Commander firmly takes the position, which is endorsed by United Nations Headquarters, that the Force must be maintained at its present level if it is to continue to carry out its mission with the same degree of effectiveness which has characterized the operation thus far, and that to protect its record any further reduction in its numbers should be accompanied by an appropriate redefinition of function and responsibility. The Commander's view is supported by the fact that incidents did increase in those parts of the line where manpower shortage was mainly felt during the period between the withdrawal of the Colombian contingent and its partial replacement by the increased number of Scandinavian troops. [*A/4210, Progress Report of the Secretary-General, 10 Sept. 1959.*]

The UN Force in the Congo drew a considerable part of its strength from UNEF and this inevitably led to administrative and logistic difficulties for the latter:

The equivalent of two companies was dispatched from the Swedish battalion immediately after it had arrived in the area on rotation on 16 April 1961. These two companies are still in the Congo and, since in their absence the Force has had to operate at reduced strength for six months, dispositions have had to be adjusted on a long-term basis. Six observation posts (OP's) formerly in the sector manned by the Swedish battalion, as well as guard duties at Port Said and Marina Camp, have been taken over by the Indian and the Yugoslav reconnaissance battalions, respectively. As a result of this adjustment all reserve platoons of the Indian and Swedish battalions are committed. This situation is quite unsatisfactory, and it is not considered advisable to continue such an arrangement much longer. Another instance of support to ONUC was the transfer of approximately 80,000 lb. of defence stores on short notice during the month of June 1961. Provision of these stores reduced UNEF's reserves below operational requirements and immediate action had to be taken to bring stocks back to the required level.   [*A/4857, Report of Secretary-General, 30 Aug. 1961.*]

The role of the UN in the Yemen meant further strains upon UNEF:

4. During June and July 1963 UNEF was called upon on short notice to provide administrative and logistics support for the United Nations Yemen Observation Mission. This support consisted of personnel, *matériel* and aircraft. In the initial stages, two of the five RCAF aircraft normally assigned to UNEF were placed at the disposal of the mission together with crews, maintenance personnel and equipment. The Force also provided certain key staff officers, together with the bulk of the required equipment and supplies to sustain the advance elements of the mission for a thirty-day period. Both personnel and *matériel* were airlifted to Yemen from the UNEF air base at El Arish. Preceded by a small advance party which was transported by air, one company of approximately 115, all ranks, from the UNEF-based Yugoslav reconnaissance battalion was embarked by ship from Port Said on 28 June under UNEF arrangements. Heavy equipment for this unit was provided by the Government of

Yugoslavia but all pack rations, medical, canteen and miscellaneous stores such as uniforms, bedding, tentage, field cookers, refrigerators, communications equipment and a few vehicles and water trailers were supplied by UNEF.

5. During 1962–1963 there has been no significant change in the operational functions and pattern of deployment of UNEF, the details of which are set forth in section II below. The strength of UNEF has remained very much the same except for minor changes in organization and the elimination of a few specific appointments as a result of reviews made from time to time. It is still a fact that any appreciable reduction in the strength of UNEF, and thereby in its cost, would require a redefinition and review of its role, the area of its deployment and its over-all composition. It is also true that UNEF is well into its seventh year of deployment in Gaza and Sinai at a substantial annual expenditure, and this assumes increasing importance in this period of financial crisis for the Organization. The Force, naturally, was not established as a permanent institution. It has been so effective, however, in restoring and maintaining peace along the Gaza–Sinai line that it has become virtually indispensable, at least until it can be demonstrated that attitudes and relations between the peoples on both sides of the line have improved to the degree that a buffer between them is no longer necessary to prevent daily armed conflict. Still, the time may have arrived when it would be useful to look carefully into the question of whether there may be ways of redefining and limiting the functions of UNEF so as to reduce both its size and cost without unduly increasing the risk of a resumption of warfare along the line. At the wish of the members, I would, of course, undertake such a study and report on its results to the General Assembly. [*A/5494, Report of the Secretary-General, 1963.*]

The study suggested in the last-quoted paragraph was indeed undertaken. (In February 1964 the air unit of the UN Yemen Observation Mission moved to El Arish and the two units were combined with the responsibility of carrying out air support for both missions.)

The pressure mounted for cutting down UNEF, in spite of the clear annual statement by the Commander on the undesirability of any such reductions. The pressure occurred in the context of the severe financial problems facing the UN and thus reference should also be made to Section 11 below. An initial informal survey was carried out by a Secretariat Study Group, led by Lt-General Gyani, then Commander of UNEF:

5. A careful review of the UNEF operation establishes that the present cost of maintenance of the Force is the minimum for its existing strength. Further economies without a simultaneous reduction in strength could only affect adversely the efficiency of the Force.

6. The international and representative nature of UNEF has been from its beginning an important element in its success. From the outset, it has been important to maintain some balance in its composition. In general, the more homogeneous the Force is, the less costly it should tend to be, but only if the troops are drawn from a country whose rates of reimbursable overseas military pay and allowances are not in the higher categories. But that is not practical. This is also, however, a limiting factor in any attempt to cut down or 'streamline' the Force. It is to be remembered, of course, that the several Governments providing contingents for UNEF have made special efforts and sacrifices in making those contingents available year after year. Should any contingent be eliminated from UNEF entirely, it would not be possible, promptly if at all, to get it back again in an emergency. The present composition of UNEF is based on a broad geographical representation. Any change in this basis might well have an unsettling effect upon the situation, the people in the area, and relationships generally, and would thus entail unadvisable risks. For such reasons, a change in the basic national composition of UNEF would not be advisable at the present time.

AREAS WHERE A LIMITING OF FUNCTIONS AND A REDUCTION OF EXPENDITURES MAY BE USEFULLY
CONSIDERED

7. It follows that the main means by which a reduction in strength might be achieved would be by changing the deployment and method of operation of the Force in certain areas, the basic function of UNEF remaining the same.

DEPLOYMENT AND METHOD OF OPERATIONS

8. The Commander of UNEF shares the opinion that it would now be possible, without taking undue risks, to reduce the number of static posts at present manned on the ADL, leaving manned posts to cover only sensitive or critical areas where crossings of the line are most likely to take place. Other parts of the line would then be covered by regular mobile patrols. There would be no change in the present scheme of night patrolling, which is considered vital to the effective execution of UNEF's task. The Commander is of the opinion that changes of this nature would not seriously decrease the effectiveness of UNEF on the line, although he observes that they would leave him little or no reserve for unforeseen contingencies, such as emergency situations which might arise in Gaza or elsewhere.

POSSIBLE REDUCTIONS

9. The Swedish and Norwegian contingents at present consist of a headquarters element and two rifle companies each, and it is considered that no further reduction can be safely made in these two contingents.

10. It is likewise not feasible to reduce the strength of the Canadian Reconnaissance Squadron and the Canadian air unit. The possibility of some pruning in the service units of the Canadian contingent will be thoroughly examined by UNEF, but the over-all reduction that could be expected would be negligible.

11. The possibility of a small reduction in strength of the Indian battalion was examined but rejected on the grounds that this battalion is a regular Indian Army battalion which was not recruited especially for UNEF. Its personnel are permanently posted to it and remain with it throughout their service. The detachment of a group of its personnel while the battalion is serving with UNEF would therefore affect unfavourably the administration and training of the battalion. Moreover, owing to the very low rate of reimbursable overseas pay and allowances applicable to Indian contingents, such a reduction would in any case result only in a saving of little consequence.

12. The suggested curtailment of posts along the ADL should make it possible to effect an over-all reduction of about 500 men. This could be implemented as follows:

(*a*) Reduction of one Danish rifle company of three platoons;
(*b*) Reduction of one Brazilian rifle company of three platoons;
(*c*) Reduction of some 190 men in the Yugoslav battalion.

13. In connexion with the above-mentioned reductions, the following consideration should be noted:

(*a*) The Brazilian battalion commander has recommended that if a decrease in strength must take place in his unit, it should be effected by a reduction of fifty men in each company rather than the elimination of one complete company;
(*b*) It is found that a reduction in strength of the Yugoslav battalion would require a complete reorganization of the battalion on a new establishment, and this would have to be negotiated with the Yugoslav Government;
(*c*) It is to be noted that the method of reduction proposed will unavoidably increase the proportion of administrative personnel to riflemen on the line and will thus produce some imbalance in the organization of units.

14. The foregoing proposals will require the approval of the Governments providing contingents, and therefore it may be possible to implement them only during the next rotation

which, in the case of the Scandinavians and Yugoslavs, is to take place in April/May 1964. The next rotation of the Brazilian contingent is to take place on 30 January 1954, and the relief for the present unit is leaving Brazil on 4 January 1964.

OTHER AREAS WHERE A REDUCTION OF COSTS MIGHT BE CONSIDERED

15. *Rotation.* UNEF is made up of contingents provided by seven countries. These contingents rotate at different intervals. The contingents of Brazil, Canada and India serve for one year. The contingents of Denmark, Norway, Sweden and Yugoslavia serve for six months. The six-months rotation system not only accounts for increased costs to the United Nations but also decreases the efficiency of the Force and greatly increases staff work. This is, admittedly, a difficult and delicate problem on which Governments have strong views and special national problems. It is intended, however, to raise this matter again with the Governments concerned with a view to obtaining agreement on a minimum term of duty, preferably nine months, for future contingents.

16. *Reimbursable overseas pay and allowances.* The variations among the rates of reimbursable overseas pay and allowances paid to the different contingents are one of the anomalies of United Nations para-military peace operations. These reimbursable costs constitute a very large item in part B of the UNEF budget. It is true that this problem has been often tackled. The fact that differences exist in national legislation and practice is, of course, the stubborn obstacle to a solution of the problem.

17. *Logistical and supporting services.* Some relatively small savings might possibly be effected by economies in the logistics support units of UNEF. This, and any reduction of civilian staff, will be examined in detail with UNEF itself.

REDUCTION IN COSTS

18. Implementation of the reductions in strength suggested in the foregoing paragraphs would result in a saving of approximately $1,712,500 per year. For the year 1964, however, as the major reductions could not be effected in advance of planned rotations, the savings in total expenditures would not be anticipated to be more than $832,000.

19. The Study Group confined itself to possibilities which would effect major reductions and economies. Such reductions, no doubt, would effect corresponding economies in other areas, such as in the cost of transport equipment and supplies. There is also a continuing effort at UNEF headquarters, on both military and civilian sides, to achieve economies and to hold staff and expenditure down to a workable minimum.

20. The possible reductions referred to above must be considered, of course, in relation to the cost estimates for the maintenance of the Force in 1964 which the Secretary-General submitted to the General Assembly in his report of 16 September 1963 (A/5495). It will be recalled that those estimates total $18,954,300, of which $10,029,300 represents the estimated operating costs to be incurred directly by the United Nations and $8,925,000 represents the estimated amount required for reimbursements of extra and extraordinary costs incurred by Governments providing contingents to UNEF.

21. There is annexed hereto a table showing by budget chapters and sections the 1964 budget estimates for the Force as originally submitted in document A/5495, and the reductions therein that might be achieved in 1964 and on an annual basis thereafter if the possibilities outlined above can be realized. It will be seen that the major reductions on an annual basis and for 1964 would be effected in the reimbursements of extra and extraordinary costs incurred by Governments providing contingents, and in those chapters and sections of part A of the budget estimates that are directly related and proportionate to the numerical strength of the military Force. These latter include the estimates for daily service allowances for military personnel, purchase of transport equipment, rations, and leave centre costs. Other substantial, although not proportionate, reductions are shown for rotation of military personnel, maintenance and operation of transport equipment, operational supplies and services, freight, cartage and express and the salaries and wages of locally recruited staff.

ANNEX

UNITED NATIONS EMERGENCY FORCE

Revised cost estimates for the period 1 January to 31 December 1964

	1964 budget estimates	Estimated reductions on an annual basis	Estimated reductions in 1964
	United States dollars		
Part A. Operating costs incurred by the United Nations			
SECTION 1. MILITARY PERSONNEL			
Chapter			
I. Allowances	1,590,000	157,000	87,000
II. Rotation of contingents	1,435,000	100,000	—
III. Travel and subsistence	125,000	5,000	—
TOTAL, section 1	3,150,000	262,000	87,000
SECTION 2. OPERATIONAL EXPENSES			
Chapter			
I. Purchase of equipment			
(i) Motor transport and heavy mobile equipment	248,300	21,000	21,000
(ii) Operation of aircraft	86,800	3,500	3,500
II. Maintenance and operation of equipment			
(i) Maintenance and operation of motor transport, heavy mobile equipment and stationary engines	735,000	38,000	19,000
(ii) Operation of aircraft	470,200	—	—
III. Supplies and services			
(i) Stationery and office supplies	50,000	—	—
(ii) Operational supplies and services	850,000	50,000	25,000
IV. Communications services	38,000	—	—
V. Freight, cartage and express	386,000	15,000	5,000
VI. External audit	15,000	—	—
VII. Claims and adjustments	5,000	—	—
TOTAL, section 2	2,884,300	127,500	73,500
SECTION 3. RENTAL OF PREMISES	165,000	—	—
SECTION 4. RATIONS	1,210,000	118,000	65,000
SECTION 5. WELFARE			
Chapter			
I. Leave centre	355,000	36,000	18,000
II. Recreational and sports supplies	27,000	—	—
III. Films	72,000	—	—
IV. Live shows	21,000	—	—
V. Postage for personal mail	68,000	—	—
TOTAL, section 5	543,000	36,000	18,000
SECTION 6. NON-MILITARY PERSONNEL			
Chapter			
I. Salaries of international staff	749,000	—	—
II. Salaries and wages of locally recruited staff	825,000	20,000	10,000
III. Common staff costs	165,000	—	—
IV. Travel and subsistence	238,000	—	—
TOTAL, section 6	1,977,000	20,000	10,000
SECTION 7. CONTINGENCIES	100,000	—	—
TOTAL, PART A	10,029,300	563,500	253,500

ANNEX—*continued*

UNITED NATIONS EMERGENCY FORCE

Revised cost estimates for the period 1 January to 31 December 1964

	1964 budget estimates	*Estimated reductions on an annual basis*	*Estimated reductions in 1964*
	United States dollars		
Part B. Reimbursement of extra and extraordinary costs incurred by Governments providing contingents			
SECTION 8. REIMBURSEMENT IN RESPECT OF EXTRA AND EXTRAORDINARY COSTS RELATING TO PAY AND ALLOWANCES OF CONTINGENTS	8,250,000	1,102,000	560,000
SECTION 9. REIMBURSEMENT IN RESPECT OF EQUIPMENT, MATERIALS AND SUPPLIES FURNISHED BY GOVERNMENTS TO THEIR CONTINGENTS	600,000	47,000	18,500
SECTION 10. REIMBURSEMENT IN RESPECT OF DEATH AND DISABILITY AWARDS ON BEHALF OF MEMBERS OF CONTINGENTS	75,000	—	—
TOTAL, PART B	8,925,000	1,149,000	578,500
GRAND TOTAL	18,954,300	1,712,500	832,000

[*A/C.5/1001, Report of the Secretary-General, 2 Dec. 1963.*]

The special study on UNEF was carried out by a team appointed by the Secretary-General, and its findings were published in December 1965:

I. PREFACE

1. In November 1965 the Secretary-General decided to appoint a Survey Team to make a new survey of the United Nations Emergency Force in Gaza and Sinai with particular reference to its functioning and cost, in view of 'the acute and uncertain financial situation affecting UNEF'. The composition of the Team was the following:

Lt.-General Sean McKeown (Chief of Staff of the Irish Army and former Commander of ONUC);
Mr Jiří Nosek, Under-Secretary of Conference Services;
Mr Carey Seward, Deputy Director of General Services;
Mr Brian Urquhart, Principal Officer in the Offices of the Under-Secretaries for Special Political Affairs;
Mr John Birckhead, Special Assistant, Office of the Controller;
Mr Alain Dangeard, First Officer of the Executive Officer of the Secretary-General.

General McKeown and Mr Nosek served as Co-Chairmen of the Team. The Team was requested to report to the Secretary-General not later than 10 December 1965. Its specific terms of reference are attached as annex A.

2. The Survey Team left New York on 24 November and arrived at Gaza on 26 November. It immediately embarked on an intensive and comprehensive visit to the units and installations of UNEF and thereafter engaged in a round of consultations at UNEF Headquarters in Gaza. The Team was briefed in detail on the ground by the commander of each contingent and thereafter surveyed the functioning of the contingent in its allotted area. In this way it visited the DANOR Battalion, the Swedish Battalion, the Indian Battalion and the Brazilian

Battalion on the Armistice Demarcation Line (ADL) and the Yugoslav Battalion and the Canadian Reconnaissance Squadron on the International Frontier (IF) and the Swedish detachment at Sharm-el-Sheikh. It spent the better part of a day visiting and being briefed on the maintenance base and UNEF Hospital at Rafah. It was also briefed by the Commander of 115 Air Transport Unit.

3. At UNEF Headquarters, and indeed throughout its mission, the Team had the advantage of the presence and advice of the Commander, the Chief of Staff, the Chief Administrative Officer and senior staff officers, with all of whom it later held detailed consultations. The members of the Team wish to take this opportunity of expressing their appreciation to the Commander, the Chief of Staff, the Chief Administrative Officer and all contingent commanders for the thoroughness and efficiency of the arrangements made and the very useful briefings which were given on the tasks, problems and organization of UNEF.

4. The Team left Gaza on 3 December to complete its report in New York.

II. Introduction

Assessment of prevailing circumstances on the Line

5. The original mandate of UNEF was laid down by the General Assembly in resolution 1001 (ES–I), when United Kingdom, French and Israeli forces were still on the territory of the United Arab Republic. Following on an earlier resolution calling on Egypt, France, Israel and the United Kingdom for an immediate cease-fire, UNEF was asked to 'secure and supervise the cessation of hostilities' and, according to resolution 997 (ES–I) of 2 November 1956, this cessation of hostilities included not only withdrawal of all forces behind the Armistice Demarcation Line, but also the stopping of 'raids across the armistice lines into neighbouring territory' and, more generally, 'any acts which would delay or prevent the implementation of the present resolution'. The mandate is spelled out in paragraph 12 of the report of the Secretary-General [A/3302] endorsed by the General Assembly which states, *inter alia*, that UNEF 'would be more than observers' corps, but in no way a military force temporarily controlling the territory in which it is stationed', and that it should not have 'military functions exceeding those necessary to secure peaceful conditions on the assumption that the parties to the conflict take all necessary steps for compliance with the recommendations of the General Assembly'. These two quotations spell out the upper and lower limits of UNEF and still account for its present organization and method of functioning. UNEF's mandate has never been formally changed or updated by the General Assembly itself. Rather its basic functions have been established by practice over the years, and its organization and functioning have been reported on annually to the General Assembly by the Secretary-General.

6. The strength of UNEF as at 15 November 1965 was 4,579 all ranks, comprising contingents supplied by seven countries. The Force observes and patrols the ADL in the Gaza Strip, a line 59 km long, running through populated and highly cultivated country, and the IF, approximately 209 km long, running for the most part through rugged and unpopulated country or sparsely populated desert; it also mans the outpost of Sharm-el-Sheikh on the Straits of Tiran. UNEF's basic functions, as established by practice over the years, are described in the Survey Team's terms of reference as follows:

> To act as an informal buffer between the armed forces of Israel and the United Arab Republic along the Armistice Demarcation Line and the International Frontiers;
> To prevent, in order to avert incidents, illegal crossings of these lines by civilians of either side, for whatever purpose;
> To observe and report on all violations of the lines whether on land, sea, or in the air.

7. UNEF carries out these functions by various means. On the ADL by day it mans a system of fixed posts and watch-towers backed up by standby patrols. By night, the fixed posts are not manned, but there is an intensive pattern of night patrolling of planned irregularity.

8. On the IF the method of operation is different. In the northern sector, the Canadian

Reconnaissance Squadron runs regular jeep patrols along the IF and the 500-metre zone road and also maintains a camp at each end of its area.

9. In the Yugoslav Battalion sector of the IF, the terrain is so rugged as to preclude regular patrols of the IF itself. The troops from the three Yugoslav camps behind the IF do extended patrols of the tracks in the area and this is supplemented by regular air reconnaissance.

10. There is, by agreement with the UAR authorities, a 500-metre zone on the UAR side along the ADL which is barred to armed personnel at all times, and only local residents are allowed to come within 50 metres of the ADL. On the IF, armed personnel are not allowed within 2 km of the Line by day and 5 km by night. No civilians are allowed within 500 metres of the Line. Immediately behind these zones, however, there are military presences of various kinds. On the ADL a network of observation posts is maintained by Gaza police and the Palestine Liberation Army, while on the IF the United Arab Republic Army has a number of posts visible behind the restricted zone. On the Israel-controlled side, where UNEF is not present and where there is no restricted zone, a patrol track runs the whole length of the ADL and is constantly in use by Israel Army personnel. There is also a patrol track along the northern portion of the IF and on some parts of the extreme southern portion. There are a number of kibbutzim along the ADL on the Israel side which are reported to have a military or para-military function.

11. At Sharm-el-Sheikh a Swedish detachment mans an observation post in the former coastal battery position at Ras Nasrani and observes and reports on all shipping going through the Straits of Tiran.

12. It is the impression of the Survey Team that throughout the Force, although some stations are much more rigorous than others, the officers and men are on duty for as long periods of time as is desirable. It is estimated that the average soldier is on duty between ten and twelve hours a day. This, of course, includes troops on standby duty for special patrols and for local defence. It should be remembered also that many of the men are out on frequent night patrols and that the Yugoslav detachments in the Sinai serve for forty-five days in isolated camps in very hot and arid terrain. It is not considered justifiable to ask more of the individual soldier than is at present required of him. Reductions will, therefore, have to be made by means other than giving additional duties under the present system.

13. The Team's findings indicate that UNEF's capacity is absorbed in the fulfilment of its tasks. It has organized itself so that it could be in a position at all times to observe effectively, report immediately, and try to deal speedily with any violations of the restricted areas established in agreement with the local authorities from the United Arab Republic side or any violations of the Line from Israel-controlled territory.

14. Some indications of the prevalence and types of incidents which UNEF deals with are given in annex B to this report, but perhaps the most important aspect of its functions lies in what does not happen on the Line and in the deterrent to violations and the grounds for peace which the Force affords.

15. The Survey Team received a detailed briefing from the Commander of UNEF and his subordinate commanders and surveyed the work of UNEF on the ADL and IF and the prevailing circumstances along the Line. As a result of what it heard and saw, the Team concluded that a continued United Nations presence of the UNEF type is an important element in the maintenance of peace and security in the area, since its withdrawal at this time might well give rise to a sharp increase in the frequency of incidents and violations, probably with serious consequences. The Survey Team therefore, does not feel justified in recommending a change in the existing functions and responsibilities of the Force, since it is not possible to say that such a change would not increase the risk of trouble in the area. The degree of UNEF's success, despite the prevailing situation in the area, can be measured by the atmosphere of peace and quiet all along the Line, by the growing prosperity of the Gaza Strip and, on the ADL, by the intensive cultivation which now goes on right up to the marker ditch on both sides of the Line.

Possibility of a change in UNEF's mandate

16. Its observation of the current situation in the area of operations has led the Survey Team to conclude that little purpose would be served by a redefinition of the mandate of the Force at this time, since UNEF's functioning, as developed in practice over the years, clearly fulfils a still pressing need in acting as an informal buffer between the armed forces of Israel and the United Arab Republic, and the situation on the Line has not in recent years changed in a way which would justify a formal change in the mandate.

Limitations of the Survey Team

17. In carrying out its task the Survey Team has been keenly aware that there are severe limitations to the practicability of some courses of action which common sense or military efficiency would seem to indicate as providing good prospects of economy and reduction in costs. Obviously there are overriding political considerations which rule out a number of simple solutions. For example, it is desirable and necessary to maintain a broad geographical basis for the Force, even though this undoubtedly complicates its structure and adds to its expense. Similarly, the different conditions under which Governments make contingents available both complicate the administration of the Force and inevitably give rise to greater costs than would a more standardized system which provided for yearly rotations and standard rates of overseas allowances throughout the Force.

18. The Team has also been careful to avoid conclusions which would result in the Force continuing to be responsible for the discharge of its present functions while being reduced by economies and cuts to a state in which it could not possibly discharge those functions effectively. This is not to say that economies are not possible even in the present reduced establishment, but rather that there is a minimum establishment below which the Force cannot be expected to perform effectively.

19. The team is convinced that the basic organization of UNEF is correct and that the Force is and has been well-managed. While the cost of UNEF is very modest by comparison with that of an active fighting force of comparable size, there are certain circumstances which contribute heavily to its overhead expenses. Such factors include the length of the line to be surveyed, the distance from any shipping port, the distance between the airport and the units, the limited resources of the economy of the Gaza area, and the conditions in the desert of the Sinai.

20. The Survey Team has therefore concentrated its attention on measures which, by gradually improving certain aspects of the operation, would permit, after a period of time, certain savings or prevent increases which would be otherwise inevitable.

III. DISCHARGE OF UNEF's FUNCTIONS

Possible reductions in present strength

21. UNEF's present strength of 4,579 is the level reached after a progressive reduction in numbers over the nine years of its existence from a maximum original strength of 6,615 all ranks, comprising ten contingents. Its task on the ADL and IF cannot be effectively executed without a sizable number of troops actually stationed on and patrolling the Line. The present number of troops actually on the Line at any given time is 2,100, the total number of operational troops in the Force being 3,389. Any drastic reduction in this number could be made only if the mandate were changed or the responsibilities of UNEF diminished.

22. If UNEF is to be expected to continue to discharge successfully its present mandate, it must have a certain minimum military capacity to prevent violations of the Line by civilians or small military parties from escalating into more serious affairs. But, on the other hand, since under the best of circumstances UNEF could not, and should not, try to achieve a real military significance in relation to the opposing forces, there is no compelling argument, for attempting to improve on its present military effectiveness and its equipment. The use of

more sophisticated equipment for observation or interception could even prove a disadvantage if it were to arouse the suspicions of either side.

23. The problem of a more effective use of the troops available and a reorganization both of the Force itself and the methods it uses has been going on for some time within UNEF itself. This study has already resulted in the use of watch-towers on the ADL which allow for a reduction in static manned posts, in an increased and more flexible system of patrolling and in a more rational deployment of units along the ADL.

24. However, there is no doubt that the present composition of the Force does not allow either for the maximum proportion of its strength to be used on the Line nor for the most efficient and effective deployment of the troops available. For example, owing to previous reductions in strength, the battalion organization of the Brazilian Battalion (two companies of two platoons each), the Yugoslav Battalion (three companies of 100 all ranks each) or of the DANOR Battalion (one company with seven officers, and one company with twelve officers) are not militarily sound or economical, since they are top-heavy with Headquarters and administrative personnel and have a high ratio of officers to other ranks. Similarly, the actual deployment of troops is for various reasons inefficient to some extent—for example, the DANOR Battalion provides guards for Rafah 30 km away, the Swedish Battalion on the ADL has a post in Sharm-el-Sheikh and the Indian Battalion on the ADL provides guards for 115 Air Transport Unit at El Arish airport. The Canadian Reconnaissance Squadron, a very highly trained and efficient unit, has a vehicle and radio scale out of all proportion to the rest of the Force and, though it covers a vast mileage per month, in fact, is only responsible for 44 km of the Line and can only operate effectively in daylight.

25. Without for the moment going into the possibilities of a more sophisticated and mobile force using more aircraft, equipment and vehicles, the best force would, on the basis of present methods of operation, consist of three full and coherent battalions on the ADL and one full battalion on the IF including Sharm-el-Sheikh. As an example, such a Force might include one Scandinavian Battalion—perhaps alternating each rotation between the three countries—one Indian Battalion, one Brazilian and one Yugoslav Battalion. The Canadian Reconnaissance Squadron might be eliminated. Canada would be well represented in the service units and the Air Unit. The hospital might be provided by a Scandinavian country other than the country or countries providing the Scandinavian contingent.

26. The Commander and Headquarters staff of UNEF, after detailed study, have reached the conclusion that it is possible and desirable to streamline the administrative element of the Force centred on Rafah. If agreement can be obtained from Governments providing contingents, considerable savings could be made by giving responsibility for signal and transport operations to one country only—Canada. The division of responsibility between the Canadian and Indian contingents is also impracticable from the point of view of command and control and causes duplication and uneven functioning.

27. Reductions have already been made in UNEF Headquarters, and some reductions in international and local civilian staff are also already under way.

28. The present organization of 115 Air Transport Unit appears to be the minimum necessary for adequate functioning of the Force.

29. The UNEF Hospital has a total strength of fifty-seven all ranks, which shows a reduction as compared with April 1965. Experience has shown that this reduction was excessive and an increase of twelve all ranks is recommended.

30. The above proposals would result in greater operational efficiency. They would also result in a reduction in strength of UNEF to a total of 3,959. Should all parts of these proposals be adopted, the geographical composition of the Force at any given time would be approximately as follows:

Brazilian Battalion	600
Scandinavian Battalion	600
Indian Battalion (plus service personnel: 126)	1,010
Yugoslav Battalion	700

Canadian contingent	692
Headquarters and outstations	73
Hospital (provided by another Scandinavian country)	69
Air unit (Canadian)	89

There would be a net reduction in the strength of the Force of 622 from the figure of 4,581 on which the 1966 cost estimates are based.

31. The over-all savings which could be made if all of the above proposals were adopted are estimated at $775,000 in the operational expenses under part A of the UNEF cost estimates, and $2,725,000 in part B, or an approximate total of $3.5 million. The details regarding the calculation of the possible savings outlined above are obtainable from the Survey Team. An indication of the savings which might be effected in the 1966 budget and on a longer-term basis is given in annex C.

Possible alternative means of discharging functions

32. UNEF has now been operating on roughly the same lines for nearly nine years. During that time the possibility of alternative means of functioning has been considered periodically by United Nations Headquarters as well as by the Commander and his staff. Until now no alternative has been found which would combine increased efficiency with decreased costs. The fact of the matter is that UNEF, by normal standards, is a relatively primitive force in terms of vehicles and equipment, and can therefore operate on a financial level which is low in comparison with the cost of a normal fighting unit operating overseas. The fact that UNEF is not expected, in any circumstances, to engage in conventional military operations makes it possible for it to operate on this relatively primitive military basis.

33. The Survey Team has considered possible alternative military means of discharging the functions of UNEF, starting from the premise that on most, if not all, of the Line there is no satisfactory substitute for the presence of troops on the ground. In particular, it examined possibilities of increased mechanization and mobility both by land and by air which might make possible a sizable reduction in the strength of the Force. For example, the use of one or two air cavalry squadrons for patrolling and immediate concentration on the ADL and the remoter parts of the IF was considered. Both the expense and complication of supporting and operating these units, which are normally designed for offensive purposes, and the fact that they would not, in the opinion of the Team, be an adequate and complete substitute for the regular presence of troops on the ADL, led the Team to conclude that the addition of air cavalry units to UNEF would not be warranted. Helicopters were also considered as a means of making the work of troops on the more rugged parts of the IF both easier and more effective. While there is certainly room for improvement in both the quantity and quality of the present types of vehicles available to UNEF, the terrain and the task are such that it was felt that a major change in the vehicle establishment might make for increased operational effectiveness, but it would not result in a reduction in strength. The desirability of increased military effectiveness is dealt with in paragraph 22 above.

34. There is no doubt that the addition of helicopters would facilitate the work of troops on the IF. This is a possibility which has been considered periodically in the past and rejected on the basis of cost and operating difficulties. The Survey Team believes that here again such a change at this time would be liable to increase expenditures with no corresponding saving in manpower, although the possibility should be kept under review. Air patrols and observation are carried out regularly along the IF and are a useful part of UNEF's surveillance activity, but they are a supplement to, and not a substitute for, the presence of troops on the ground. They could only possibly reduce the necessity of having troops on the ground if they were used in combination with air cavalry elements, which have been mentioned above. Thus, though extra light aircraft for air observation might to some extent increase the intensity and effectiveness of UNEF's surveillance, they would increase rather than decrease costs and are therefore not recommended, since the present establishment of two light aircraft would seem to be adequate and efficient.

35. Various suggestions have been made as to the utility of special devices, especially in relation to the saving of manpower. In particular, short- and medium-range radar and infra-red devices have been mentioned as methods of improving night surveillance. Such devices would undoubtedly increase to some extent the effectiveness of UNEF's night patrolling, but are not a substitute for it. Nor is it believed that the slight reductions which such devices would make possible in night patrol patterns would compensate for the extra expense and complication involved.

36. The Team gave special consideration to the possibilities of increasing observation tasks in relation to patrols and fixed posts within the present plan of operation of the Force. Observation has already been greatly improved by the programme, which is continuing, of building watch-towers on the ADL. These towers have made it possible to decrease the number of manned posts on the ADL by day and to increase the efficiency of surveillance. The Team examined the possibility of reducing the number of troops on the IF by the increased use of observation methods. The difficulty on the IF is that the terrain is so rugged that some stretches of the Line are virtually inaccessible, and the maintenance of static observation posts in such country would be neither practicable nor useful. Air observation is already used on the IF in conjunction with ground patrols, and the Team reluctantly concluded that increased observation would not lessen the need for troops on the ground based on the camps at present located behind the IF. The further possibilities of observation methods should, however, be a matter of continuing study.

37. In considering such possibilities, which are at first sight attractive from the point of view of economy, it is necessary to bear in mind the experience of the United Nations with other observation missions, notably the United Nations Truce Supervision Organization in Palestine and the United Nations Military Observers Group in India and Pakistan. The nature of these missions gives them no responsibility for actually preventing incidents and violations. In their task of preventing the escalation of incidents, these missions have largely relied on observation, reporting and a procedure of joint investigation and the awarding of violations which is agreed on and accepted by both sides. It should also be remembered that the Gaza–Sinai Line is covered by the Armistice Agreements and is theoretically in the sphere of responsibility of the Truce Supervision Organization. The machinery of the Egyptian–Israel Mixed Armistice Commission still exists but has been unable to function effectively in the area since 1956 owing to the denunciation of the Armistice Agreement between Israel and the United Arab Republic by one of the parties to it. Furthermore, the effectiveness of an observer operation requires the presence of observers on both sides of the Line and the observance of a demilitarized zone along the Line by both sides. These considerations have caused the Survey Team to consider that a predominantly observer operation would be inadequate to the fulfilment of the mandate of UNEF at the present time.

38. The increased use of animals to assist patrols might be considered. The experience of the DANOR and Swedish Battalions, which use dogs on foot patrols, has been reportedly quite successful. The Team found that horses and camels are presently being used for patrols by the Gaza police. The Team believes that it would be useful to explore further whether some savings might be obtained by using horses for transporting men on patrols on the ADL or part of it.

IV. PROBLEMS ARISING FROM THE COMPOSITION OF THE FORCE

39. The cost of reimbursing Governments in respect of the extraordinary expenses incurred by them relating to pay and allowances of the contingents they provide represents in the 1966 cost estimates $8·6 million out of the $18·5 million total. These reimbursements are unequally divided between the contingents, the largest share of the $8·6 million total being absorbed by three or four contingents. It is therefore obvious that if the Secretary-General were able to change the composition of the Force either by retaining only those contingents whose Governments' claims are relatively low, or by replacing 'expensive contingents' by less costly ones, very substantial savings could be made.

40. The Survey Team is well aware of the numerous political and other problems involved in this situation. The Team, therefore, feels that it is not in a position to recommend to the Secretary-General a drastic change in the composition of UNEF based on the complete elimination of one or two contingents, or the replacement of the more expensive contingents, although, theoretically, a reorganization of UNEF on this basis would be the surest way of rapidly obtaining important reductions in expenditure. Nevertheless, these considerations should be borne in mind in considering the proposal for streamlining the Force outlined in section III above, where a change in the present composition of the Force is suggested without actually eliminating any of the present contingents, but rather by arranging for the presence of some of them in rotation. The success of this proposal in reducing expenditure, while at the same time maintaining UNEF at the necessary strength, will be dependent in some measure upon the extent to which Governments providing contingents are prepared to agree to the changes suggested.

V. Main conclusions

41. The Team did not find itself in a position to suggest more important cuts in the UNEF cost estimates than those put forward in this report, since these would inevitably affect the Force's capacity to discharge its present functions and would possibly result in an increase of incidents and violations along the Line. The Survey Team consequently does not believe that any radical reorganization or reduction of UNEF would be advisable unless it were decided to alter and limit the mandate of the Force. In the light of its observations in the area, the Team also concluded that a change in the mandate of the Force is not feasible in the prevailing conditions.

42. The Team proposes a streamlining of the Force along the lines suggested in paragraphs 25–31 above.

43. In view of the proposed reduction in strength of the Force and considering the large United Nations investment which the Rafah Base represents, the Team recommends that the Base should be surveyed in detail by independent experts with a view to possible consequent savings in this area also.

44. The Team suggests that the problems of establishing a uniform system of rotation, based on one year's service with UNEF, should again be explored with the Governments concerned.

ANNEXES

ANNEX A

Terms of reference for the team to undertake the new survey of the United Nations Emergency Force

The terms of reference of the survey team are the following:

(a) The main purpose of the survey shall be to undertake a searching examination of functioning of UNEF with a view to determining whether and where economies may be reasonably made without adversely affecting the basic functions of the Force as they now exist.

(b) The basic functions of UNEF, as established by practice over the years, are the following:

To act as an informal buffer between the armed forces of Israel and the United Arab Republic along the Armistice Demarcation Line and the International Frontiers;

To prevent, in order to avert incidents, illegal crossings of these lines by civilians of either side, for whatever purpose; and

To observe and report on all violations of the lines whether on land, sea, or in the air.

(c) The Survey Team should determine whether those basic functions could, in fact, be discharged by a Force substantially reduced in numbers from its present strength, whether there are means of discharging those functions effectively other than those now employed and which might require fewer men and cost less, and whether there is any declining need with regard to any of those functions.

(*d*) The Survey Team should consider, in the light of prevailing circumstances along the lines, whether it would be feasible to consider changing the mandate of the Force by reducing its existing functions and responsibilities without increasing the risk of trouble along the lines.

(*e*) The Survey Team should examine whether increased mechanization and mobility and greater use of aerial patrols could make possible a reduction in the Force without loss of effectiveness in the discharge of its current responsibilities.

(*f*) The Survey Team should give some attention to the question whether military observers in place of a peace force could be expected to be able to meet the needs of the existing situation.

(*g*) Attention should be given also to the question of what would be the likely result if UNEF were to be withdrawn altogether without any substitute United Nations presence.

ANNEX B

Analysis of violations and incidents in the area of operations of the United Nations Emergency Force

1. The record of violations of the ADL and the IF and the Restricted Zone over the last four years from 1 August 1961 to 1 August 1965 is shown in the table following this annex. A broad analysis of the incidents and violations is given in the following paragraphs.

GENERAL OBSERVATIONS

2. There has, throughout the period, been approximately one ground incident during every four days. Further, it has been noticed that firing across the ADL and the IF from ICT to UARCT and *vice versa* has occurred approximately 5 to 10 times every year in spite of the deployment and patrolling of UNEF in the area. During this period there have been thirteen cases in which firing was directed on UNEF observation posts and patrols. In five of these cases the firing was accidental. Only in one case was a UNEF soldier wounded.

CROSSINGS OF THE ADL OR THE IF

3. A study of the crossings of the ADL and the IF shows that there have been between 72 to 120 crossings per year in both directions. As an example, we have taken the comparative figures for the period 1 January to 31 October 1964 and 1 January to 31 October 1965, in order that conclusions may be drawn as to the number and type of violations in the successive years 1964 and 1965.

Crossings of the ADL or the IF from ICT to UARCT

4. (a) *1 January to 31 October 1964*
During this period there was a total of 101 crossings, of which 36 were by military patrols involving 242 armed personnel. These crossings by military patrols have usually been 10 to 30 metres in depth on the IF and 5 to 20 metres in depth on the ADL. Of these incidents, 7 to 10 violations were of a more serious nature, military patrols having come inside UARCT for a distance of 60 to 2,000 metres. In such cases, UNEF patrols stopped the IDF patrols and asked them to go back, which in most cases they did. In two cases several shots were fired on the IDF patrols from UARCT.

(b) *1 January to 31 October 1965*
During the corresponding period in 1965 only 65 crossings took place, of which 47 were by IDF patrols involving a total of 599 armed personnel. The number of crossings in 1965 was reduced to some extent, owing in the opinion of UNEF Headquarters to more intensive day

and night patrolling by UNEF units deployed on the ADL and the IF. However, the nature of the violations in 1965 was more serious than in 1964. For example, in the DANOR Battalion sector there were, during a two-month period, three serious violations by IDF patrols. These violations were intentional and deliberate, although undertaken perhaps more in a spirit of adventure and bravado, and possibly due to decisions taken at a junior commander level by IDF troops. If UNEF were not deployed in the area, such adventurous but deliberate violations might have resulted in a clash between the IDF patrols and PLA posts deployed just behind the Restricted Zone on the ADL.

Comparison of violations from ICT on ADL and IF

5. A study has also been made of the proportion of crossings of the IF in relation to those of the ADL. During the period from August 1964 to August 1965 there was a total of 63 crossings by armed patrols. Of these, 51 were on the IF and 12 on the ADL. In the opinion of UNEF Headquarters, the high proportion of crossings on the IF is due to two factors. Firstly, the UNEF posts on the IF are widely dispersed, and patrolling and observation of the IF is not so intensive and thorough as on the ADL. Second, the IDF's purpose in sending these patrols across the IF is possibly to obtain information about the UAR Army which is deployed in the Sinai behind the UNEF posts. It is also likely that, owing to the wide dispersal of the posts, some violations by IDF patrols may have gone unnoticed by UNEF.

Crossings of the ADL or the IF from UARCT to ICT

6. In 1964 (January–October) there was a total of 51 violations of the ADL and the IF from the UAR, but only two were by military patrols, involving three men. In 1965 (January–October) 21 crossings were observed, of which one was by a military patrol.

7. In the opinion of UNEF Headquarters, the crossings from UARCT to ICT have been fewer, compared with the number from ICT to UARCT, because of the 'Restricted Zone' on the ADL and the IF. If a similar zone existed on the Israel side of the ADL and the IF, the number of crossings from the Israel side would probably be reduced. However, there have been a number of violations of the Restricted Zone from the UAR side, and the details of these have been analysed in the succeeding paragraph.

Violations of the Restricted Zone by UAR forces

8. In 1964 (January–October) there were 76 violations of the Restricted Zone, of which 25 were by military patrols involving a total of 65 military personnel. In 1965 (January–October) there were 84 violations of the Restricted Zone, of which 56 were by military patrols involving a total of 106 armed personnel.

9. In the opinion of UNEF Headquarters, the violations of the Restricted Zone during 1965 have not only shown an increase but have been more deliberate, owing to the increased activity of the Palestine Liberation Army in the Gaza Strip.

AIR VIOLATIONS

10. On an average there have been 1 to 2 air violations per day and approximately 300 to 400 violations during any one year. Approximately 95 per cent of the air violations have been from ICT to UARCT. Fifty per cent of such violations can be ascribed either to navigational errors or to peculiar flying conditions arising because of the location of air strips—for example, violations of the north-east sector of the DANOR Battalion. 25 to 35 per cent of the above violations were serious and were committed either by adventurous pilots or for reconnaissance purposes.

SEA VIOLATIONS

11. Violations of the seaward extension of the ADL have, generally speaking, been of a non-serious nature. Crossings are usually made by fishing boats or commercial ships.

SUMMARY OF INCIDENTS AND VIOLATIONS DURING THE PAST FOUR YEARS

			Years			
No.	Description	1961/1962	1962/1963	1963/1964	1964/1965	Remarks
1. Ground incidents:						
	Firing across the ADL or the IF	4	8	8	5	
	Firing on UNEF	—	6	3	4	
	Crossing the ADL or the IF	122	114	71	74	
	TOTAL	126	128	82	83	1 incident in 3 to 4 days
2. Handovers:						
	Dead bodies	—	16	18	9	
	Prisoners	—	47	70	40	
	TOTAL	—	63	88	49	
3. Air violations:						
	By UAR aircraft	4	1	5	4	
	By IDF aircraft	394	318	250	382	
	By unidentified aircraft	24	57	41	33	
	TOTAL	422	376	296	419	1 to 2 violations per day
4. Sea violations:						
	Violations of ICW	63	72	91	64	
	Violations of UARCW	66	30	73	49	
	TOTAL	129	102	164	113	0·6 violations per day

[A/C.5/1049, Survey of UNEF: Report of the Secretary-General,[5] 13 Dec. 1965.]

The following documentation indicates the composition of UNEF at the time of its withdrawal in May 1967: since 31 July 1966 the Force had been reduced by a further 581 men. On 19 May the numerical strength stood at 3,378.

[5] Secretary-General's Introductory Comments and ann. C omitted.

Country	Contingent	All Ranks	Total
Brazil	Infantry battalion Military police and HQ Staff	423 10	433
Canada	Service units and HQ Staff Air transport unit	702 93	795
Denmark	HQ Staff	3	3
India	Infantry battalion Service troops, HQ Indian contingent, and HQ Staff	923 55	978
Sweden	Infantry battalion Military police and HQ Staff	521 9	530
Yugoslavia	Reconnaissance battalion Military police and HQ Staff	562 17	579
	GRAND TOTAL		3,378

[*A/6672, Annual Report of the Secretary-General on UNEF, 12 July 1967.*]

8

RELATIONS WITH CONTRIBUTING STATES

IN HIS second report on UNEF the Secretary-General had observed that the Force 'would be limited in its operations to the extent that consent of the parties concerned is required under generally recognized international law'.[1] It became clear from the discussions that the principle of consent was relevant not only to Egypt, the host state, but also the participating states. The Assembly could

---

[1] A/3302, p. 20.

recommend that UN members participate in UNEF, but it could not compel them to do so. In Resolution 1001 (ES–I) the Assembly had asked the Secretary-General 'to continue discussions with Governments of Member States concerning offers of participation in the Force'. Some twenty-four countries made offers to the Secretary-General, and offers were accepted[2] from Sweden, Denmark, Norway, Finland, Indonesia, Colombia, India, Brazil, Canada, and Yugoslavia.

UNEF was an international force, and the fact that it was composed of national contingents necessitated arrangements to meet problems both of principle and of practice. The question of principle concerned the need of the national contingents to serve the UN, and not the interests of any one state; the practical questions included the need for the UN to provide its troops with adequate protection, and to evolve command, liaison, and financial arrangements to cover all nationalities.

When certain nations offered to participate in UNEF, they attached certain conditions. Thus the Finnish permanent representative wished confirmation

that the Finnish unit will not be stationed in foreign territory without the permission of the State concerned, that the question of costs for the unit will be subject to an agreement between the Finnish Government and the United Nations.

My Government also understands that the assignment of the Finnish unit will be for a limited time only and therefore determined exclusively by the needs arising out of the present conflict in the area in question. [A/3302/Add. 21, 14 Nov. 1956.]

In the event, the Finnish unit was one of three which did ask to be released at an early stage of UNEF's stay in Egypt.[3] The government of Sweden wrote:

The Swedish Government presume that the task of the Force should be limited to the objective set out in the above-mentioned resolutions of 4 and 5 November [Resolutions 998 (ES–I) and 1000 (ES–I)], and that it should not imply that the Force should remain on watch duty in the area for an unspecified period of time, or pending the solution of the political questions affecting that area.

Further, the Swedish Government presume that the Swedish unit shall not be stationed in foreign territory without the consent of the State concerned, and that the costs involved will, to a considerable extent, be borne by the United Nations in accordance with a specific agreement to be concluded for that purpose with the United Nations. [A/3302, ann. 7, p. 23.]

The Indian government also spelt out its understanding of the conditions within which an Indian contingent would serve:

1. The emergency Force is set up in the context of the withdrawal of Anglo-French forces from Egypt and on the basis of the call to Israel to withdraw behind the armistice lines.
2. The Force is not in any sense a successor to the invading Anglo-French forces, or [is] in any sense to take over its functions.
3. It is understood the Force may have to function through Egyptian territory. Therefore, there must be Egyptian consent for its establishment.
4. The Force is a temporary one for an emergency. Its purpose is to separate the combatants, namely Egypt and Israel, with the latter withdrawing as required by the resolution.
5. The Force must be a balanced one in its composition.
6. The agreement would be in principle and the position in regard to actual participation is reserved until the full plan is before us.

[2]See above, pp. 302–3.   [3] See above, p. 303.

It is also understood that transport, including airlift and all facilities, will be provided by or through the United Nations. [*A/3302/Add. 4/Rev. 1*, pp. 23–24.]

It was for the Secretary-General to decide whether these conditions were compatible with the international character of UNEF, and the mandate authorized by the Assembly. None of the above-quoted reservations presented any difficulties. It should be pointed out, however, that these attitudes were to prove very important in May 1967, when President Nasser asked for UNEF to withdraw from Egypt. India and Yugoslavia insisted that their troops were to be withdrawn, and that Egypt's request should be complied with forthwith. Although Sweden and Canada took a different view—namely, that the legal need for Nasser's consent did not mean that he could demand UNEF's withdrawal without further reference to the General Assembly—the practical considerations which flowed from the Indian and Yugoslav attitude made withdrawal necessary.[4]. The relationship between the UN and the contributing states was further formalized, however, by agreements entered into on 21 June 1957. The Secretary-General addressed a letter to each of the contributing nations, and, together with the replies thereto, this constituted a legal agreement between the UN and the countries concerned:

Annex 1

TEXT OF LETTER DATED 21 JUNE 1957 FROM THE SECRETARY-GENERAL TO THE STATES PROVIDING CONTINGENTS

1. I have the honour to refer to the resolutions of the General Assembly relating to the United Nations Emergency Force (UNEF) and particularly to resolution 1000 (ES–I) of 5 November 1956 and resolution 1001 (ES–I) of 7 November 1956. I also have the honour to refer to our previous communications concerning the national contingent provided by your Government for service with UNEF.

2. It will be recalled that the guiding principles for the organization and functioning of the Force were set out in paragraphs 6 to 9 of the 'Second and final report of the Secretary-General on the plan for an emergency international United Nations Force' (A/3302). They were approved by the General Assembly in paragraph 1 of resolution 1001 (ES–I). By paragraph 2 of the same resolution the General Assembly concurred in the definition of the functions of the Force as stated in paragraph 12 of the Secretary-General's report.

3. Paragraph 7 of resolution 1001 (ES–I) authorized the Secretary-General to issue regulations and instructions which may be essential to the effective functioning of the Force, following consultation with the Advisory Committee established by the same resolution, and to take all other necessary administrative and executive actions. Pursuant to this resolution I have, on 8 February 1957, concluded by exchange of letters an Agreement between the United Nations and the Government of Egypt concerning the status of UNEF in Egypt. On the same date I submitted a report (A/3526) on this Agreement to the General Assembly which was noted with approval by resolution 1126(XI)adopted on 22 February 1957. Following consulttation with the Advisory Committee, the participating States, and the Commander of the Force, I have also issued Regulations for the United Nations Emergency Force (ST/SGB/UNEF/1) on 20 February 1957. Copies of these documents are attached as annexes I and II respectively.

4. The Regulations referred to above affirm the international character of the Force as a subsidiary organ of the General Assembly and define the conditions of service for the mem-

---

[4] For details on the withdrawal of UNEF, see pp. 338–49.

bers of the Force. National contingents provided for UNEF serve under these Regulations.

5. The Regulations and the Agreement referred to in paragraph 3 of this letter also secure to the Force and its individual members the privileges and immunities necessary for the independent exercise of its functions. I should like to direct your attention to the provisions of the Regulations and of the Agreement which provide these privileges and immunities and particularly to article 34 of the Regulations and to paragraphs 10, 11 and 12 of my letter to the Minister of Foreign Affairs of Egypt of 8 February 1957 (A/3526). It will be noted that paragraph 11 of this letter states that 'Members of the Force shall be subject to the exclusive jurisdiction of their respective national States in respect of any criminal offences which may be committed by them in Egypt'. This immunity from the jurisdiction of Egypt is based on the understanding that the authorities of the participating States would exercise such jurisdiction as might be necessary with respect to crimes or offences committed in Egypt by any members of the Force provided from their own military services. It is assumed that the participating States will act accordingly.

6. I should also like to direct your attention to article 13 of the UNEF Regulations concerning 'Good order and discipline'. This article provides:

'The Commander of the UNEF shall have general responsibility for the good order of the Force. Responsibility for disciplinary action in national contingents provided for the Force rests with the commanders of the national contingents. Reports concerning disciplinary action shall be communicated to the Commander of the UNEF who may consult with the commander of the national contingent and if necessary the authorities of the Participating State concerned.'

7. In view of the considerations set out in paragraphs 5 and 6 above, I should appreciate your assurance that the commander of the national contingent provided by your Government will be in a position to exercise the necessary disciplinary authority. I should also appreciate your assurance that your Government will be prepared to exercise jurisdiction with respect to any crime or offence which might be committed by a Member of such national contingent.

8. The effective functioning of the United Nations Emergency Force requires that some continuity of service of units with the Force be ensured in order that the UNEF Commander may be in a position to plan his operations with knowledge of what units will be available. I should, therefore, appreciate your assurance that the national contingent provided by your Government will not be withdrawn without adequate prior notification to the Secretary-General, so as to avoid the impairment of the ability of the Force to discharge its functions. Likewise, should circumstances render the service of your national contingent with the Force no longer necessary, the Secretary-General undertakes to consult with your Government and to give adequate prior notification concerning its withdrawal.

9. Reference is also made to articles 11 and 12 of the UNEF Regulations which deal with 'Command authority' and 'Chain of command and delegation of authority'. Article 12 provides, *inter alia*, that changes in commanders of national contingents which have been made available by participating Governments should be made in consultation between the Commander of the United Nations Emergency Force and the appropriate authorities of the participating Government.

10. Finally, I suggest that questions involving the allocation of expenses should be dealt with, in the light of relevant resolutions of the General Assembly, in a supplemental agreement. Such other supplementary arrangements concerning the service of your national contingents with the Force may be made as occasion requires.

11. It is the intention that this letter together with your reply accepting the proposals set forth herein shall constitute an agreement between the United Nations and . . ., and shall be deemed to have taken effect from the date that the national contingent provided by your Government departed from its home country to assume duties with UNEF. It is also intended that it shall remain in force until such time as your national contingent may be withdrawn from the Force either in accordance with the terms of paragraph 8 above or in the light of developments affecting the functioning of the Force which may render its service no

longer necessary. The provisions of paragraph 12 relating to the settlement of disputes should remain in force until all outstanding claims have been settled.

12. It is also proposed that all disputes between the United Nations and your Government concerning the interpretation or application of this agreement which are not settled by negotiation or other agreed mode of settlement shall be referred for final settlement to a tribunal of three arbitrators. One of the arbitrators shall be appointed by the Secretary-General of the United Nations, one by your Government, and the umpire shall be chosen jointly by the Secretary-General and your Government. If the two parties fail to agree on the appointment of the umpire within one month of the proposal of arbitration by one of the parties, the President of the International Court of Justice shall be asked by either party to appoint the umpire. Should a vacancy occur for any reason, the vacancy shall be filled within thirty days by the method laid down in this paragraph for the original appointment. The tribunal shall come into existence upon the appointment of the umpire and at least one of the other members of the tribunal. Two members of the tribunal shall constitute a quorum for the performance of its functions, and for all deliberations and decisions of the tribunal a favourable vote of two members shall be sufficient.

(*Signed*) Dag HAMMARSKJÖLD

[*A/3943, ann. 1, Summary Study of the experience of UNEF.*]

It will be seen that the letter refers to the guiding principles and the policies adopted by the General Assembly, as well as to the relevant provisions of the Agreement reached with Egypt on 8 February 1957 on the status of the Force.[5] The Secretary-General also enclosed the texts of the Regulations issued for UNEF, and of the Status of Forces Agreement: thus acceptance of the Secretary-General's letter must be taken to include approval in these two documents.[6] Colombia and Indonesia sent no reply to the Secretary-General, and later withdrew their contingents.[7]

Particular emphasis was placed, in the agreement between the UN and the contributing states, on those aspects of the regulations and Status of Forces Agreement which affirmed the international character of UNEF. Thus the agreement stresses the immunity of the contingents from the criminal jurisdiction of Egypt[8] and the concomitant duty on contributing states to exercise that jurisdiction over their own forces; and the provision of the national commanders with the necessary disciplinary powers. The agreement also alludes to the need for supplementary financial arrangements, and provides that any change in the national commanders of contingents should be made in consultation with the UNEF commander. The other major point concerns the withdrawal of national units: such withdrawal is permissible, so long as adequate prior notification is given. By not relying excessively on the services of any one state, the Secretary-General avoided putting UNEF in a position where pressure in respect of its policies could be brought to bear by a contributing state

---

[5] See below, pp. 373–82.   [6] Bowett, p. 112.
[7] See above, p. 303. For the replies, see 274 UNTS 199 (Brazil); ibid. p. 41 (Canada); ibid. p. 81 (Denmark); ibid. p. 233 (India); 271 UNTS 135 (Finland); ibid. p. 223 (Norway); ibid. p. 187 (Sweden); 277 UNTS 191 (Yugoslavia).
[8] For the text and commentary on the Status of Forces Agreement, see below, pp. 374–5. For detailed analysis, see Bowett, pp. 110–14, 126–36; Rosner, ch. 6; UNEF Regulation 13 confirms that disciplinary action is in the hands of the contingent commander.

threatening to withdraw.[9] Paragraph 12 of the UN Status of Forces Agreement provides for an arbitration procedure in respect of any dispute between the parties. And Regulation 6, being among the regulations agreed to by the contributing states, stipulates that 'members of the Force, although remaining in their national service, are, during the period of their assignment to the Force, international personnel under the authority of the United Nations'.[10]

In addition to these broad questions, there were a cluster of financial arrangements which needed to be resolved as between the UN and the contributing states. They related to compensation for death or injury to UNEF personnel, and to the allocation of costs between the UN and the participating nations.

Compensation for death, injury or illness attributable to service with the Force

12. For staff members detailed for service with the Force, the normal staff rules relating to service-incurred death, injury or illness would apply. The Organization has reinsured itself by commercial coverage at relatively nominal cost against possible major loss.

13. With regard to troops of the United Nations Emergency Force, it has been assumed that in case of death, injury or illness attributable to service with the Force, such personnel or their dependants would qualify for benefits under their own national service pension or compensation regulations, and that they would not receive such benefits directly from the United Nations. However, in order to meet possible claims from Governments for reimbursement of pensions and compensation paid by them, it has been deemed expedient for the Organization to take out commercial insurance covering death and dismemberment of members of the Force. Such coverage has been obtained on a temporary (one month minimum) basis in the unit amount of $25,000 for death or dismemberment, at a cost of $25 per month per member, commencing with initial travel (from the home country) in each case.

14. In view of the costs involved in providing such insurance, the Secretary-General believes that the General Assembly may wish to consider whether the existing commercial coverage should be continued or, alternatively, whether the Organization should assume the risks on a non-insured basis. [*A/3383 and Rev. 1, Report of the Secretary-General on administrative and financial arrangements for UNEF, 21 Nov. 1956.*]

The Advisory Committee on Administrative and Budgetary Questions considered the matter raised by the Secretary-General:

24. The present policy, which has been written on a temporary basis for a minimum of one month from 12 November 1956, limits compensation in respect of any one member of the Force to $25,000, with the following further provisions:

(*a*) The aggregate amount that may be paid in respect of claims arising out of any one accident will be limited to a maximum of $2 million;

(*b*) The aggregate amount in respect of claims arising in any one month will be limited to $5 million.

25. By the earliest date for cancellation of the policy, 4,100 troops will have been transported to bases in Egypt, with a consequent substantial reduction in one of the principal risks. It would therefore be sufficient, in the Advisory Committee's opinion, if commercial coverage were limited thereafter to catastrophe risks arising out of the transport by air of any large groups. For staff members of the United Nations serving with the Force in an administrative

---

[9] F. Seyersted, *United Nations Forces in the Law of Peace and War* (1967), p. 53; Bowett, p. 113.

[10] For the complete text of the regulations, see s. 6 above. Seyersted has pointed out that the major implication of the provision that UNEF contingents remain in their national service is that 'their Government is responsible for providing their uniforms and for all questions of promotion and in large measure pays and equips them . . .' (p. 59).

capacity, the normal provisions for compensation in case of disability or death apply; no special insurance arrangements are called for. [*A/3402, 22nd Report of the Advisory Committee on Administrative and Budgetary Questions, 30 Nov. 1956.*]

The matter of possible claims by member states for injury or death to their personnel was now examined in further detail:

1. At its 541st meeting on 3 December 1956, the Fifth Committee decided to refer to the Advisory Committee on Administrative and Budgetary Questions, for further study and report, the question of possible claims by Member States in respect of death or disability attributable to service with the United Nations Emergency Force. This question was the subject of comment in paragraphs 23 to 25 of a previous report of the Committee (A/3402) on administrative and financial matters relating to the Force. Those matters did not include the method of allocating to Member States the costs of the Force which are to be financed by the United Nations.

2. In making the present detailed study the Advisory Committee has had regard to the report of the Secretary-General (A/3383 and Rev. 1, paras 12 to 14) as well as to the views expressed by members of the Fifth Committee at its 541st meeting. In addition, consultations have been held with representatives of the Secretary-General.

3. The Secretary-General has assumed (A/3383 and Rev. 1, para 13) with regard to troops of the Emergency Force, that in the event of death, injury or illness attributable to service with the Force, such personnel or their dependants would qualify for pension benefits or compensation under their own national service schemes, and that they would not receive such benefits directly from the United Nations. Payments would be made to beneficiaries, at any rate in the first instance, by the Governments concerned.

4. This appears to be a valid assumption and one consistent with the existing practice in respect of military officers seconded as military observers to United Nations missions such as the Truce Supervision Organization in Palestine.

5. The question therefore arises whether, and—if so—to what extent, the United Nations should accept liability in respect of claims from Governments for the reimbursement of pensions and compensation paid by them. Although the acceptance of such a liability appears to be implicit in the Secretary-General's report (A/3383 and Rev. 1, para. 13), on which previous discussion of this matter has been based, there would be advantage in the Fifth Committee's taking a firm decision on the point.

6. Should the Fifth Committee and the General Assembly decide in favour of assuming liability for any such claims that may be submitted by Governments furnishing troops, a further question would arise; whether the United Nations should itself carry the risk attaching to this liability or seek, through commercial insurance, full or partial protection. In the Advisory Committee's opinion, the cost of commercial insurance in relation to the potential risk must be the major factor determining this question.

7. At least three distinct elements of risk are involved:

(*a*) Accidents during the transport of troops to and from the area, and within the area, particularly in the case of air transport;

(*b*) Various accidental and other risks in the area, other than those resulting from actual fighting or acts of war; and

(*c*) Risks arising from actual fighting or acts of war.

As regards point (*a*), a major portion of this risk has already lapsed with the movement into the area of most of the Force. The risk may, however, again arise in the event of any large-scale air-lift of troops into or within the area and, at a later stage, upon their repatriation.

8. The Secretary-General has reported (A/3383, and Rev. 1, para. 13) that commercial insurance, covering death and dismemberment of members of the Force from all causes, has been obtained on a temporary basis for a minimum period of one month from 12 November 1956 to provide benefits limited as follows:

(*a*) The compensation in respect of any one member of the Force is limited to $25,000;

(*b*) The aggregate amount that may be paid in respect of claims arising out of any one accident or occurrence is limited to a maximum of $2 million; and

(*c*) The aggregate amount in respect of all claims arising in any one month is limited to $5 million.

This comprehensive coverage, which is due to expire in any event on 21 December 1956, costs $1 per month per $1,000, or $25 per month for every member of the Force. Based on a strength of 4,000 men, the monthly cost of the insurance would be $100,000.

9. The Advisory Committee understands that, according to informal advices from underwriters, the present coverage, if continued beyond 21 December 1956, would carry a rate of between $2.50 and $3.00 per month per $1,000, representing, for like conditions and a like number of troops, a monthly cost of $250,000–$300,000. In other words, the monthly cost would be equal to the maximum benefit payable in respect of the death of ten to twelve members of the Force.

10. In the face of the prohibitive cost of commercial insurance for comprehensive coverage, the Secretary-General has studied the possibility of securing commercial coverage on a limited scale. Available information indicates that the cost of commercial insurance on the limited 'excess risk' bases described below would be approximately as follows:

Type of coverage	*Approximate cost*
I. Coverage $25,000 per man, the underwriters to be liable only for benefits in respect of losses exceeding $250,000 from any one occurrence (i.e., ten men); aggregate benefit in any one occurrence limited to $1.5 million; cumulative aggregate of all claims in any one month limited to $3 million.	$1.50 per month per $1,000, i.e., $37.50 per month per man. For 4,000 men, monthly cost: $150,000.
II. Coverage $15,000 per man, the underwriters to be liable only for benefits in respect of losses exceeding $150,000 from any one occurrence (i.e., ten men); aggregate benefit in any one occurrence limited to $1 million; cumulative aggregate of all claims in any one month limited to $2 million.	$1.50 per month per $1,000, i.e., $22.50 per month per man. For 4,000 men, monthly cost; $90,000.
III. Coverage as under either I or II above but limited to risks arising solely from transport by air and no other cause.	Very tentative indication: roughly 65 per cent of the corresponding cost under I or II above.

11. In the Secretary-General's opinion, with which the Advisory Committee agrees, the cost of commercial insurance, even on a limited 'excess risk' basis, is unduly high in relation to the potential risk. Furthermore, there are indications that some at least of the Governments providing troops may waive, in whole or in part, claims that may arise in respect of their troops. Consequently, on the basis of the evidence so far available, the Advisory Committee believes that, subject to a decision on the basic question of policy (see para. 5 above), the Organization itself should carry the related risks, without commercial insurance. The Committee suggests, however, that should it subsequently prove possible to obtain commercial coverage, even on a limited basis, at a reasonable cost, the matter might be the subject of a full review.

12. Independently of the arrangements for covering whatever liability may rest with the Organization in this matter, it will clearly be desirable to ensure that the administrative procedures for dealing with claims from Member States are simplified. It may be possible, for instance, to agree, on the one hand, to exclude claims involving minor amounts and, on the other, to develop some uniform and easily applicable method of determining the commuted value of annual pensions.

13. The Advisory Committee proposes to review at intervals whatever arrangements are

approved by the General Assembly for the settlement of possible claims from Governments. The Committee will at the same time examine related problems that may arise. *[A/3456, 35th Report of the Advisory Committee on Admin. and Budgetary Questions, 14 Dec. 1956.]*

The Fifth (Budgetary) Committee of the Assembly approved by 46 votes to 7, with 5 abstentions, the proposals in paragraph 11 of its Advisory Committee's report, reproduced above.[11]

In October 1957 the Secretary-General reported:

95. Following upon such consultations, the Secretary-General advised Governments participating in the Force that the possibility could be explored of arranging an adequate system for compensation by the United Nations in the case of death, injury or illness as a result of service with UNEF; and that, until such a system was established and pending its confirmation by the General Assembly, the United Nations would reimburse indemnities paid by a participating Government based on national regulations.

96. According to the records available to the United Nations, a total of thirteen members of the Force have died or been killed to date: others have sustained injuries of lesser or greater degree. No claims for compensation payment have, however, yet been formally transmitted to the United Nations by the Governments concerned.

97. It is the considered view of the Secretary-General, upon further reflection, that the initially stated principle should be adhered to, namely, that, in the event of death or injury attributable to service with the Force, such personnel or their dependants would qualify for pension benefits or compensation under their own national service schemes; payments to beneficiaries would be made by the Governments concerned, which would in turn lodge claims with the United Nations. In the view of the Secretary-General, this plan is likely to prove the most feasible administratively, and the most equitable for all parties.

98. The Secretary-General would also recommend in regard to such compensation that:

(i) Claims of participating Governments should normally be restricted to cases of death or serious disability involving a material cost to the Government for medical costs and/or pension benefits;

(ii) No formal rules should be established at this time; but, until some experience is gained of the problems likely to arise, such claims should be dealt with as presented, based on the circumstances of each case;

(iii) So far as possible, administration of monthly or other periodic payments should rest with the participating Government; consideration would be given, as and when appropriate, to the working out between the United Nations and the Government concerned of an arrangement whereby the United Nations liability would be commuted to a lump sum payment. *[A/3694, Report of the Secretary-General, 9 Oct. 1957.]*

These became the established principles. Payments to beneficiaries were made by the government concerned, which, in turn, lodged claims with the UN.

The question of compensation arose not only in respect of possible claims by contributing nations for death or injury to their nationals in UNEF, but in respect of equipment, material, and supplies furnished by governments to their contingents. It was decided to set aside a reserve for this purpose.[12] The total estimated value of the equipment and material involved ran, between November 1957 and December 1958, at about $12 million.

A formula for cost sharing as between the UN and the participating states had been adopted by the General Assembly on 22 November 1957[13] based on proposals submitted by the Secretary-General,

---

[11] A/3560 and Add. 1, para. 20, 25 Feb. 1957.   [12] A/4002, para. 18.
[13] Res. 1151 (XII). See s. 11, p. 420. For the details of the negotiations with the contributing states, see A/3694, paras 81–91.

as a result of many difficulties which had earlier arisen in arriving at equitable and uniform reimbursement arrangements:

(*a*) For the first six months (i.e., during what might reasonably be regarded as the initial emergency period), the United Nations would reimburse to participating Governments any special allowances, as distinct from basic salaries, paid to members of their contingents as a direct result of their service with UNEF in its area of operations, provided that such allowances could be considered as reasonable.

(*b*) In the event of a contingent serving beyond the initial six-month period, or of a replacement contingent being made available, the United Nations would assume financial responsibility for all extra and extraordinary costs which a Government was obliged to incur in making such forces available for UNEF service. Apart from the costs of equipment referred to below, this means, in effect, reimbursement by the United Nations of expenditure incurred in respect of pay and allowances over and above those costs which the Government concerned would have been obliged to meet in any event.

118. These principles were designed to provide a generally equitable basis upon which a collective United Nations responsibility could be discharged and to avoid the possibility of a few Member States assuming a disproportionately heavy financial burden beyond a limited emergency period. But their application in practice has proved difficult. For example, in the case of the formula in sub-paragraph (*a*) of the preceding paragraph, it has been extremely difficult, in view of widely differing national practices, to define what may be reasonably regarded as a 'special allowance'. Furthermore, although it had been assumed that national contingents would be composed of regular army personnel who would, in any event, have been in the service of their country, certain Governments organized special volunteer units to serve with UNEF. This was done because national laws precluded the assignment of members of the regular armed forces to service overseas other than in defence of the homeland. In other cases, new units had to be organized within the contributing States to replace regular units dispatched for UNEF duty. In these circumstances, some Governments from the outset assumed additional financial liabilities which they believed should be compensated for by the United Nations. Experience indicates the validity of the view that the most equitable collective arrangement is one which distributes among the membership as a whole those costs which a participating Government would not otherwise have incurred.

119. According to the formula adopted by the General Assembly in resolution 1151 (XII), the United Nations would assume financial responsibility for the replacement of equipment destroyed or worn out and for such deterioration beyond that provided for under normal depreciation schedules as could be assessed at the conclusion of the total period of service of a Government's contingent. It is not specified, however, whether or not the word 'equipment' should be interpreted in the wider sense of 'equipment, *matériel* or supplies', and no qualification is made as to the terms under which the items had been made available, i.e., it is not indicated either that they should have been normal and necessary in the circumstances or that they should have saved the United Nations expenditure which it otherwise would have had to incur. Consequently, decisions must be based on interpretations of the formula in the light of the actual circumstances of each particular case.

Expenses borne by the United Nations directly

120. On the basis of the relevant decisions of the General Assembly, the United Nations assumes the following direct costs, when they are not otherwise provided for:

(*a*) Billeting, rations and summer clothing for the troops, including the rental, reconditioning and maintenance of premises;

(*b*) Payment to each member of the Force of a daily overseas allowance, equivalent to 86 cents, in accordance with a decision by the Fifth Committee of the General Assembly at its 541st meeting on 3 December 1956;

(*c*) Costs of the rotation of contingents;

(*d*) Travel and subsistence allowances of military personnel proceeding on official business to points outside the area of operations;

(*e*) Operation and maintenance of a suitable leave centre and other welfare expenses, such as rental of films, periodic contracting for live shows for the entertainment of the troops, and postage for personal mail;

(*f*) Miscellaneous supplies and services such as cobbling, tailoring, laundering and hair-cutting;

(*g*) Motor transport and heavy mobile equipment;

(*h*) Miscellaneous non-expendable operational equipment such as barrack stores, tentage, workshop equipment, water and petroleum cans and generators;

(*i*) Spare parts, maintenance and petrol, oil and lubricants for motor transport and other mobile equipment;

(*j*) Stationery, photographic and other miscellaneous supplies;

(*k*) Payment for the use of Royal Canadian Air Force planes comprising the UNEF Squadron, at specified rates per flying hour.

Other costs assumed by the United Nations are:

(*a*) Salaries, travel and subsistence and other appropriate staff costs of international staff detailed from Headquarters or other United Nations offices, Field Service personnel, and locally recruited personnel;

(*b*) Communications services, costs of transporting and issuing supplies, and claims against the United Nations for personal injury, property damage and loss of income arising from traffic accidents and other effects of the operation of the Force;

(*c*) Costs of external auditors and assistants visiting the mission;

(*d*) Other miscellaneous supplies and services.

[A/3943, Summary study of the experience of UNEF.]

In 1960 the Secretary-General reported:

7. It will be recalled that in the 1960 budget estimates no specific dollar amount was provided in respect of section 9 of part B, which relates to compensation for equipment, *matériel* and supplies furnished by Governments to their contingents, but that the General Assembly decided in resolution 1441 (XIV) that if Member Governments do not avail themselves of credits, deriving from the $3,475,000 of special financial assistance which had been pledged voluntarily for the Force in 1960, the amounts involved would be credited to that section of the 1960 budget. Although several Member Governments have already indicated they would not avail themselves of the credits referred to above, it is not possible at this time to estimate realistically the total amount that may be credited to section 9 in 1960 since a number of Governments still have the matter under consideration.

8. Every effort is being made to keep the Organization's liabilities for such reimbursement to the lowest possible level by equipping and providing contingents in the Force to the maximum extent feasible with UNEF-owned rather than contingent-owned equipment and supplies; nevertheless, liabilities for reimbursements to Governments must continue to be incurred, principally in respect of contingents' clothing, small arms and ammunition.

9. In view of the fact that UNEF will soon be in its fifth year of operation, that substantial claims for loss or deterioration of Government-owned equipment and supplies have accrued during the past three and one-half years, and that increases in such claims must be expected so long as UNEF continues, I consider it would be appropriate for the General Assembly at its fifteenth session to reconsider the original reimbursement policy which it approved at its twelfth session (resolution 1151 (XII)), which defers reimbursements to the Governments concerned until the conclusion of the total period of service of its contingents in UNEF. Accordingly, I shall refer to this matter in the report on the Force which will be submitted to the General Assembly at its fifteenth session.   *[A/4396, 8 July 1960.]*

The Secretary-General advanced specific proposals, and the General Assembly, in Resolution 1575 (XV), paragraph 5, approved the new policy of reimbursing governments on a current basis for equipment, materials, and supplies furnished to their contingents.[14]

A third category of reimbursements was negotiated between the UN and the contributing states (and also approved by the Assembly in Resolution 1151 (XII) of 22 November 1957). This provided for the settlement of claims from participating governments relating to expenditures incurred in respect of pay and allowances over and above those costs which the governments concerned would have been obliged to meet. (The detailed annual cost of these three categories of reimbursement—in respect of death and disability awards, in respect of equipment, material, and supplies, and in respect of extra and extraordinary costs relating to pay allowances to contingents—is to be found in part B of the Annual Cost Estimates of UNEF.)

Both in relation to these particular matters, and in relation to the broader issues of the interplay of national contingents with an international Force, relations between the UN and the contributing states remained excellent throughout. Close co-ordination of views was maintained through the Advisory Committee, in which the contributing nations were represented.[15]

9

RELATIONS WITH HOST STATES

IN Resolution 998 (ES–I) the Assembly called for the placing of the UN Emergency Force along both sides of the armistice demarcation line. Israel did not accept this proposal, and hence never became a 'host' to UNEF. The relations between Israel and the UN accordingly are dealt with under Section 10 below.

Egypt was the 'host' to UNEF, and the very fact that UNEF was in that country with Egypt's consent led to the establishment of a relationship with the UN which was to serve as a precedent for subsequent UN peacekeeping. Indeed, it is difficult to exaggerate the degree to which the techniques evolved to meet the needs of the UN–Egypt relationship were to mould subsequent UN peacekeeping practice.

(a) The Question of Consent: Establishment, Stationing, and Withdrawal

The legal relationship established between UNEF and the UN remain, in spite of subsequent alterations of particular aspects, the classical statement of the line to be drawn between the right of the UN to act to fulfil its general peacekeeping role and a specific approved mandate, and the sovereign rights of

---

[14] A/4784, 13 July 1961.   [15] See s. 5 above.

a host country which is not being subjected to international enforcement action. The question of the consent of Egypt to UNEF was not directed to only one phase of the operation: it was at issue in respect of the establishment of UNEF, its stationing, its composition, its freedom of movement, its relationship with the civil and criminal system of the host country, and its ability to determine the appropriate moment for withdrawal.[1]

. . . the Force, if established, would be limited in its operations to the extent that consent of the parties concerned is required under generally recognized international law. While the General Assembly is enabled to *establish* the Force with the consent of those parties which contribute units to the Force, it could not request the Force to be *stationed* or *operate* on the territory of a given country without the consent of the Government of that country. [*A/3302, 2nd and final Report of the Secretary-General on the plan for an emergency international UN Force,*[2] *6 Nov. 1956,* para. 9.]

Both Resolutions 998 (ES–I) and 1001 (ES–I) had referred to the setting up of an international force being with the consent of the nations concerned. Egypt accepted, in a message to the Secretary-General,[3] the terms of the Assembly resolution of 5 November calling for an international force. The Secretary-General indicated that this 'may be considered as having accepted the establishment of an international Force under the terms fixed by the United Nations'.[4] The relationship obviously required formalizing, however:

1. After the adoption, 7 November 1956, by the General Assembly of resolution 1001 (ES–I) concerning the establishment of the United Nations Emergency Force, the Government of Egypt was immediately approached by the Secretary-General though the Commander of the Force, Major-General E. L. M. Burns, in order to prepare the ground for a prompt implementation of the resolution.

2. The Government of Egypt had, prior to the final decision of the General Assembly, accepted the Force in principle by formally accepting the preceding resolution 1000 (ES–I) on the establishment of a United Nations Command. Before consenting to the arrival of the Force, the Government of Egypt wished to have certain points in the resolutions of the General Assembly clarified. An exchange of views took place between the Secretary-General and the Government of Egypt in which the Secretary-General, in reply to questions addressed to him by the Government of Egypt, gave his inter pretations of the relevant General Assembly resolutions, in respect of the character and functions of the Force. . . .

3. On the basis of the resolutions, as interpreted by the Secretary-General, the Government of Egypt consented to the arrival of the United Nations Force in Egypt. The first transport of troops took place on 15 November 1956.

4. While the Secretary-General found that the exchange of views which had taken place was sufficient as a basis for the sending of the first units, he felt, on the other hand, that a firmer foundation had to be laid for the presence and functioning of the Force in Egypt and for the continued co-operation with the Egyptian authorities. For that reason, and also because he considered it essential personally to discuss with the Egyptian authorities certain questions which flowed from the decision to send the Force, after visiting the staging area of the Force

---

[1] On the overall problem of 'consent' in UN peacekeeping operations, see Bowett, pp. 412–22.

[2] The Philippines representative maintained that whereas 'consent' was needed for UNEF's operation on Egyptian territory, this did not extend to Gaza, which was under Egyptian administration but not sovereignty (see s. 10, p. 391). It may be noted that Egypt never expressly consented to UNEF's operations in the Gaza strip—though consent thereto was assumed by the Secretary-General (*GAOR*, 11th sess., 659th plen. mtg, pp. 1192–5). And see Bowett, p. 125, n. 8.

[3] A/3295, 5 Nov. 1956.   [4] A/3310, 7 Nov. 1956.

in Naples, he went to Cairo, where he stayed from 16 until 18 November. On his way to Cairo he stopped briefly at the first staging area in Egypt, at Abu Suweir.

5. In Cairo he discussed with the President and the Foreign Minister of Egypt basic points for the presence and functioning of the Force in Egypt. Time obviously did not permit a detailed study of the various legal, technical and administrative arrangements which would have to be made and the exchange of views was therefore related only to questions of principle.

6. The Secretary-General wishes to inform the General Assembly of the main results of these discussions. They are summarized in an '*Aide-mémoire* on the basis for presence and functioning of the United Nations Emergency Force in Egypt', submitted as an annex to this report.

7. The text of this *Aide-mémoire*, if noted with approval by the General Assembly, with the concurrence of Egypt, would establish an understanding between the United Nations and Egypt, on which the co-operation could be developed and necessary agreements on various details be elaborated. The text, as it stands, is presented on the responsibility of the Secretary-General. It has the approval of the Government of Egypt.

ANNEX

Aide-mémoire ON THE BASIS FOR THE PRESENCE AND FUNCTIONING OF THE UNITED NATIONS EMERGENCY FORCE IN EGYPT

Noting that by telegram of 5 November 1956 addressed to the Secretary-General the Government of Egypt, in exercise of its sovereign rights, accepted General Assembly resolution 1000 (ES–I) of the same date establishing 'a United Nations Command for an emergency international Force to secure and supervise the cessation of hostilities in accordance with all the terms of resolution 997 (ES–I) of the General Assembly of 2 November 1956';

Noting that the General Assembly in its resolution 1001 (ES–I) of 7 November 1956 approved the principle that it could not request the Force 'to be stationed or operate on the territory of a given country without the consent of the Government of that country' (A/3302, para. 9).

Having agreed on the arrival in Egypt of the United Nations Emergency Force (UNEF);

Noting that advance groups of UNEF have already been received in Egypt,

The Government of Egypt and the Secretary-General of the United Nations have stated their understanding on the basic points for the presence and functioning of UNEF as follows:

1. The Government of Egypt declares that, when exercising its sovereign rights on any matter concerning the presence and functioning of UNEF, it will be guided, in good faith, by its acceptance of General Assembly resolution 1000 (ES–I) of 5 November 1956.

2. The United Nations takes note of this declaration of the Government of Egypt and declares that the activities of UNEF will be guided, in good faith, by the task established for the Force in the aforementioned resolutions; in particular, the United Nations, understanding this to correspond to the wishes of the Government of Egypt, reaffirms its willingness to maintain UNEF until its task is completed.

3. The Government of Egypt and the Secretary-General declare that it is their intention to proceed forthwith, in the light of points 1 and 2 above, to explore jointly concrete aspects of the functioning of UNEF, including its stationing and the question of its lines of communication and supply; the Government of Egypt, confirming its intention to facilitate the functioning of UNEF, and the United Nations are agreed to expedite in co-operation the implementation of guiding principles arrived at as a result of that joint exploration on the basis of the resolutions of the General Assembly. [*A/3375, Report of Secretary-General on basic points for the presence and functioning in Egypt of UNEF, 20 Nov. 1956.*]

It was thus agreed that Egypt should exercise her sovereign rights in the light of good faith, and specifically her acceptance of Assembly Resolution 1000 (ES–I). Of this arrangement Israel commented: '. . . while the presence of this Force depends upon Israel's agreement, its functions cannot be subordinated to Egypt's desires. Its movements and its composition cannot be the subject of dictation by the host country.'[5]

Equally, in Israel's view, it was not for Egypt to decide when UNEF's mission was to be terminated.[6] This view received wide support—generally tacit, but explicit among those who were sympathetic to the Anglo-French-Israel position. Thus Sir Leslie Munro, speaking for New Zealand, urged that the interested delegations should declare:

(a) that the decision that the tasks of the United Nations Emergency Force have been completed should be a matter for the United Nations, not Egypt or any other country;
(b) that the decision to withdraw the Force should therefore also be a matter for the United Nations, not for Egypt or any other country. . . . [GAOR, 11th sess., 639th plen. mtg, para. 111.]

Australia bolstered this argument by contending that if there was any question about Egypt being allowed to withdraw her consent, or declare UNEF's mission terminated, then this power would run counter to the professed intention that UNEF was not to affect the power balance in the area.[7] The Secretary-General replied that

The proposition . . . according to which the use of military forces by the United Nations, other than that under Chapter VII of the Charter, requires the consent of the State in which the Force is to operate . . . [cannot] be challenged. . . .
111. However, I fully agree with the representative of Australia that, if this were the whole story, the situation would be most unsatisfactory. In practice, the consent obviously must be qualified in such a way as to provide a reasonable basis for the operations of the United Nations Force. That is exactly the reason why, in November 1956, an arrangement was agreed upon with the Government of Egypt, according to which the Government of Egypt declared that, when exercising its sovereign rights on any matter concerning the presence and functioning of the United Nations Emergency Force, it would be guided in good faith by its acceptance of the General Assembly resolution [1000 (ES–I)] of 5 November 1956. (A/3375, annex.)

The need to test the concept of consent arose in dramatic form in May 1967 when President Nasser asked UNEF to withdraw. The coming to power in 1966 of the new, militant régime of Premier Atassi had led to a sharp deterioration on the Israel–Syrian front during the previous nine months. Incursions by Syrian terrorists, had been followed by Israel government retaliation. In November 1966 the veto of the Soviet Union prevented the Security Council from adopting a resolution calling on both parties to heed their armistice obligations. When Syrian terrorists again attacked Israel from Jordanian territory, Israel struck back massively at Jordan: and she was condemned by the UN.[8] Within Israel, this was seen as entirely unjust, given the unwillingness or inability of the Security Council to condemn Syria. Under considerable domestic pressure in the face of continuing Syrian harassment, Prime Minister Eshkol warned on 12 May that Israel would strike back 'massively, at a time and place of our own choosing'. Premier Atassi now turned to Nasser, claiming that Egypt was

[5] GAOR, 11th sess., 592nd plen. mtg, para. 130.   [6] Ibid. para. 131.
[7] Ibid. 649th mtg, para. 79.   [8] For details of the events of this period, see pp. 193, 199–202.

dragging her feet on the Israel question, and sheltering behind UNEF. The Russians now circulated information that there was a heavy concentration of Israel armour on the Syrian front. (This aspect, at the time of writing, still remains something of a mystery: UNTSO observers reported that there were no such concentrations or troop movements.[9] Whether the Russian report was deliberate or in error is not certain.) Nasser now requested UNEF to move back from its established positions; and, when the Secretary-General indicated that it could not stay in Egypt if it was not allowed to fulfil its mandate, Nasser asked for UNEF's withdrawal.

On 18 May the Secretary-General issued a document showing the exchanges between himself and the Egyptian government:

Special report of the Secretary-General

1. This special report is submitted in accordance with paragraph 4 of General Assembly resolution 1125 (XI) of 2 February 1957.

2. On 18 May 1967, at 12 noon, I received through the Permanent Representative of the United Arab Republic to the United Nations the following message from Mr. Mahmoud Riad, Minister for Foreign Affairs of the United Arab Republic:

'The Government of the United Arab Republic has the honour to inform Your Excellency that it has decided to terminate the presence of the United Nations Emergency Force from the territory of the United Arab Republic and Gaza Strip.

'Therefore, I request that the necessary steps be taken for the withdrawal of the Force as soon as possible.

'I avail myself of this opportunity to express to Your Excellency my gratitude and warm regards.'

3. I replied to the above message in the early evening of 18 May as follows:

'I have the honour to acknowledge your letter to me of 18 May conveying the message from the Minister of Foreign Affairs of the United Arab Republic concerning the United Nations Emergency Force. Please be so kind as to transmit to the Foreign Minister the following message in reply:

' "Dear Mr Minister,

"Your message informing me that your Government no longer consents to the presence of the United Nations Emergency Force on the territory of the United Arab Republic, that is to say in Sinai, and in the Gaza Strip, and requesting that the necessary steps be taken for its withdrawal as soon as possible, was delivered to me by the Permanent Representative of the United Arab Republic at noon on 18 May.

"As I have indicated to your Permanent Representative on 16 May, the United Nations Emergency Force entered Egyptian territory with the consent of your Government and in fact can remain there only so long as that consent continues. In view of the message now received from you, therefore, your Government's request will be complied with and I am proceeding to issue instructions for the necessary arrangements to be put in train without delay for the orderly withdrawal of the Force, its vehicles and equipment and for the disposal of all properties pertaining to it. I am, of course, also bringing this development and my actions and intentions to the attention of the UNEF Advisory Committee and to all Governments providing contingents for the Force. A full report covering this development will be submitted promptly by me to the General Assembly, and I consider it necessary to report also to the Security Council about some aspects of the current situation in the area.

[9] S/7896, para. 9.

"Irrespective of the reasons for the action you have taken, in all frankness, may I advise you that I have serious misgivings about it for, as I have said each year in my annual reports to the General Assembly on UNEF, I believe that this Force has been an important factor in maintaining relative quiet in the area of its deployment during the past ten years and that its withdrawal may have grave implications for peace.

"With warm personal regards . . ."

6. The general considerations which I have had in mind and the sequence of events leading up to the present situation are set out in an *aide-mémoire* of 17 May which I handed to the Permanent Representative of the United Arab Republic at 5.30 p.m. on 17 May, the text of which reads as follows:

'1. The Secretary-General of the United Nations requests the Permanent Representative of the United Arab Republic to the United Nations to convey to his Government the Secretary-General's most serious concern over the situation that has arisen with regard to the United Nations Emergency Force in the past twenty-four hours as a result of the demands upon it made by United Arab Republic military authorities and of certain actions of United Arab Republic troops in the area.

'2. Before engaging in detail, the Secretary-General wishes to make the following general points entirely clear:

(*a*) He does not in any sense question the authority of the Government of the United Arab Republic to deploy its troops as it sees fit in United Arab Republic territory or territory under the control of the United Arab Republic.

(*b*) In the sectors of Gaza and Sinai, however, it must be recognized that the deployment of troops of the United Arab Republic in areas in which UNEF troops are stationed and carrying out their functions may have very serious implications for UNEF, its functioning and its continued presence in the area.

(*c*) The Commander of UNEF cannot comply with any requests affecting the disposition of UNEF troops emanating from any source other than United Nations Headquarters, and the orders delivered to General Rikhye on 16 May by military officers of the United Arab Republic were not right procedurally and quite rightly were disregarded by General Rikhye.

(*d*) UNEF has been deployed in Gaza and Sinai for more than ten years for the purpose of maintaining quiet along the Armistice Demarcation Line and the International Frontier. It has served this purpose with much distinction. It went into the area and has remained there with the full consent of the Government of the United Arab Republic. If that consent should be withdrawn or so qualified as to make it impossible for the Force to function effectively, the Force, of course, will be withdrawn.

'3. The following is the sequence of events which have given rise to the present crisis:

(*a*) At 22.00 hours LT on 16 May Brigadier Eiz-El-Din Mokhtar handed to General Rikhye, the Commander of UNEF, the following letter:

"To your information, I gave my instructions to all UAR Armed Forces to be ready for action against Israel the moment it might carry out any aggressive action against any Arab country. Due to these instructions our troops are already concentrated in Sinai on our eastern borders. For the sake of complete security of all UN troops which install OPs along our borders, I request that you issue your orders to withdraw all these troops immediately. I have given my instructions to our Commander of the eastern zone concerning this subject. Inform back the fulfilment of this request. Yours, Farik Awal: (M. Fawzy) COS of UAR Armed Forces."

(*b*) The Commander of UNEF replied that he had noted the contents of General Fawzy's letter and would report immediately to the Secretary-General for instructions, since he had no authority to withdraw any troops of UNEF, or in any other way to redeploy UNEF troops, except on instructions from the Secretary-General.

(*c*) On learning of the substance of General Fawzy's letter to General Rikhye, the

Secretary-General asked the Permanent Representative of the United Arab Republic to the United Nations to see him immediately. The Permanent Representative of the United Arab Republic came to the Secretary-General's office at 18.45 hours on 16 May. The Secretary-General requested him to communicate with his Government with the utmost urgency and to transmit to them his views, of which the following is a summary:

(i) The letter addressed to the Commander of UNEF was not right procedurally since the Commander of UNEF could not take orders affecting his command from a source other than the Secretary-General. General Rikhye was therefore correct in his insistence on taking no action until he received instructions from the Secretary-General.

(ii) The exact intent of General Fawzy's letter needed clarification. If it meant the temporary withdrawal of UNEF troops from the Line or from parts of it, it would be unacceptable because the purpose of the United Nations Force in Gaza and Sinai is to prevent a recurrence of fighting, and it cannot be asked to stand aside in order to enable the two sides to resume fighting. If it was intended to mean a general withdrawal of UNEF from Gaza and Sinai, the communication should have been addressed to the Secretary-General from the Government of the United Arab Republic and not to the Commander of UNEF from the Chief of Staff of the Armed Forces of the United Arab Republic.

(iii) If it was the intention of the Government of the United Arab Republic to withdraw the consent which it gave in 1956 for the stationing of UNEF on the territory of the United Arab Republic and in Gaza it was, of course, entitled to do so. Since, however, the basis for the presence of UNEF was an agreement made directly between President Nasser and Dag Hammarskjöld as Secretary-General of the United Nations, any request for the withdrawal of UNEF must come directly to the Secretary-General from the Government of the United Arab Republic. On receipt of such a request, the Secretary-General would order the withdrawal of all UNEF troops from Gaza and Sinai, simultaneously informing the General Assembly of what he was doing and why.

(iv) A request by the United Arab Republic authorities for a temporary withdrawal of UNEF from the Armistice Demarcation Line and the International Frontier, or from any parts of them, would be considered by the Secretary-General as tantamount to a request for the complete withdrawal of UNEF from Gaza and Sinai, since this would reduce UNEF to ineffectiveness.

(d) The Secretary-General informed the Commander of UNEF of the position as outlined above, as explained to the Permanent Representative of the United Arab Republic, and instructed him to do all that he reasonably could to maintain all UNEF positions pending further instructions.

(e) At 08.000 hours Z on 17 May, the Commander of UNEF reported that on the morning of 17 May, 30 soldiers of the Army of the United Arab Republic had occupied El Sabha in Sinai and that their troops were deployed in the immediate vicinity of the UNEF Observation Post there. Three armoured cars of the United Arab Republic were located near the Yugoslav UNEF camp at El Sabha and detachments of 15 soldiers each had taken up positions north and south of the Yugoslav camp at El Amr. All UNEF Observation Posts along the Armistice Demarcation Line and International Frontier were manned as usual.

(f) At 10.30 hours Z on 17 May, the Commander of UNEF reported that troops of the United Arab Republic had occupied the UNEF Observation Post on El Sabha and that the Yugoslav UNEF camps at El Quseima and El Sabha were now behind the positions of the Army of the United Arab Republic. The Commander of UNEF informed the Chief of the United Arab Republic Liaison Service of these developments, expressing his serious concern at them. The Chief of the United Arab Republic Liaison Service agreed to request the immediate vacation of the Observation Post at El Sabha by troops of the United Arab Republic and shortly thereafter reported that orders to this effect had been given by the United Arab Republic military authorities. He requested, however, that to avoid any future misunderstandings the Yugoslav Observation Post at El Sabha should be immediately withdrawn to El Quseima camp. The Commander replied that any such withdrawal would require the authorization of the Secretary-General.

(g) At 12.00 hours Z, the Chief of the United Arab Republic Liaison Service conveyed to the Commander of UNEF a request from General Mohd Fawzy, Chief of Staff of the Armed Forces of the United Arab Republic, for the withdrawal of UNEF Yugoslav detachments in the Sinai within twenty-four hours. He added that the Commander of UNEF might take forty-eight hours or so to withdraw the UNEF detachment from Sharm el Sheikh.

(h) At 13.30 hours Z, the Commander of UNEF reported that a sizable detachment of troops of the United Arab Republic was moving into the UNEF area at El Kuntilla.

'4. The Secretary-General is obliged to state that UNEF cannot remain in the field under the conditions described in the foregoing paragraphs. The function of UNEF has been to assist in maintaining quiet along the Line by acting as a deterrent to infiltration and as a buffer between the opposing forces. It can discharge neither of these functions if it is removed from the Line and finds itself stationed behind forces of the United Arab Republic. In other words, UNEF, which has contributed so greatly to the relative quiet which has prevailed in the area in which it has been deployed for more than ten years, cannot now be asked to stand aside in order to become a silent and helpless witness to an armed confrontation between the parties. If, therefore, the orders to the troops of the United Arab Republic referred to above are maintained, the Secretary-General will have no choice but to order the withdrawal of UNEF from Gaza and Sinai as expeditiously as possible.

'5. The Secretary-General wishes also to inform the Permanent Representative of the United Arab Republic that as of now, on the basis of the fully reliable reports received from the Chief of Staff of the United Nations Truce Supervision Organization in Palestine, there have been no recent indications of troop movements or concentrations along any of the Lines which should give rise to undue concern.

'6. The Secretary-General requests the Permanent Representative of the United Arab Republic to transmit the contents of this *aide-mémoire* with utmost urgency to his Government.'

7. At the same time the following *aide-mémoire* dated 17 May was handed by me to the Permanent Representative of the United Arab Republic:

'It will be recalled that in an *aide-mémoire* attached to the report of the Secretary-General on basic points for the presence and functioning in Egypt of the United Nations Emergency Force it was recorded that:

'1. The Government of Egypt declares that, when exercising its sovereign rights on any matter concerning the presence and functioning of UNEF, it will be guided, in good faith, by its acceptance of General Assembly resolution 1000 (ES-I) of 5 November 1956.'

The *aide-mémoire* also records that:

'2. The United Nations takes note of this declaration of the Government of Egypt and declares that the activities of UNEF will be guided, in good faith, by the task established for the Force in the aforementioned resolutions; in particular, the United Nations, understanding this to correspond to the wishes of the Government of Egypt, reaffirms its willingness to maintain UNEF until its task is completed.'

'The General Assembly, in resolution 1121 (XI) of 24 November 1956, noted with approval the contents of the *aide-mémoire* referred to above.

'The Minister for Foreign Affairs of Egypt, in concluding on behalf of the Government of Egypt the agreement of 8 February 1957 concerning the status of the United Nations Emergency Force in Egypt, recalled:

"... the declaration of the Government of Egypt that, when exercising its sovereign powers on any matter concerning the presence and functioning of the United Nations Emergency Force, it would be guided, in good faith, by its acceptance of the General Assembly resolution of 5 November 1956 . . ." '

8. As a result of the situation described above, I held an informal meeting with the representatives of the countries providing contingents to UNEF in the late afternoon of 17 May. I informed them of the situation as then known and there was an exchange of views.

9. Since the first *aide-mémoire* was written the following developments have been reported by the Commander of UNEF:

(*a*) Early on 18 May, the sentries of the UNEF Yugoslav detachment were forced out of their observation post on the International Frontier near El Kuntilla camp. At 12.20 hours GMT on 18 May 1967, soldiers of the United Arab Republic forced UNEF soldiers of the Yugoslav contingent to withdraw from the observation post on the International Frontier in front of El Amr camp, and later officers of the United Arab Republic visited El Amr camp and asked the UNEF Yugoslav platoon to withdraw within fifteen minutes.

(*b*) At 12.10 hours GMT on 18 May, officers of the United Arab Republic visited the Yugoslav camp at Sharm el Sheikh and informed the Commanding Officer that they had come to take over the camp and the UNEF observation post at Ras Nasrani, demanding a reply within fifteen minutes.

(*c*) At 14.30 hours GMT on 18 May, the UNEF Yugoslav detachment at El Quseima camp reported that two artillery shells, apparently ranging rounds from the United Arab Republic artillery, had burst between the UNEF Yugoslav camps at El Quseima and El Sabha.

(*d*) At 08.57 hours GMT on 18 May, a UNEF aircraft carrying Major-General Rikhye, the Commander of UNEF, on a flight from El Arish to Gaza was intercepted west of the Armistice Demarcation Line by two Israel military aircraft which tried to make the UNEF aircraft follow them to the Israel side of the Line to land, and went so far as to fire several warning shots. The pilot of the United Nations aircraft, on instructions from the UNEF Commander, ignored these efforts and proceeded to land at Gaza. I have strongly protested this incident to the Government of Israel through the Permanent Representative of Israel to the United Nations. The Chief of Staff of the Israel Defence Forces has since conveyed regrets for this incident to Major-General Rikhye.

10. Late in the afternoon of 18 May, I convened a meeting of the UNEF Advisory Committee, set up under the terms of paragraphs 6, 8 and 9 of resolution 1001 (ES–I) of 7 November 1956, and the representatives of three countries not members of the Advisory Committee but providing contingents to UNEF to inform them of developments and to consult them on the situation.

11. The exchange of notes between the Minister for Foreign Affairs of the United Arab Republic and the Secretary-General, quoted at the beginning of this report, explains the position which I have found myself compelled to adopt under the resolutions of the General Assembly and the agreements reached between the Secretary-General of the United Nations and the Egyptian authorities as the basis for the entry of UNEF into the territory of the United Arab Republic in November 1956, and its subsequent deployment in Gaza and Sinai in 1957.

12. I have taken this position for the following main reasons:

(*a*) The United Nations Emergency Force was introduced into the territory of the United Arab Republic on the basis of an agreement reached in Cairo between the Secretary-General of the United Nations and the President of Egypt, and it therefore has seemed fully clear to me that since United Arab Republic consent was withdrawn it was incumbent on the Secretary-General to give orders for the withdrawal of the Force. The consent of the host country is a basic principle which has applied to all United Nations peace-keeping operations.

(*b*) In practical fact, UNEF cannot remain or function without the continuing consent and co-operation of the host country.

(*c*) I have also been influenced by my deep concern to avoid any action which would either compromise or endanger the contingents which make up the Force. The United Nations Emergency Force is, after all, a peace-keeping and not an enforcement operation.

(*d*) In the face of the request for the withdrawal of the Force, there seemed to me to be no alternative course of action which could be taken by the Secretary-General without putting in question the sovereign authority of the Government of the United Arab Republic within its own territory.

13. I cannot conclude this report without expressing the deepest concern as to the possible implications of the latest developments for peace in the area. For more than ten years UNEF, acting as a buffer between the opposing forces of Israel and the United Arab Republic on the Armistice Demarcation Line in Gaza and the International Frontier in Sinai, has been the principal means of maintaining quiet in the area. Its removal inevitably restores the armed confrontation of the United Arab Republic and Israel and removes the stabilizing influence of an international force operating along the boundaries between the two nations. Much as I regret this development, I have no option but to respect and acquiesce in the request of the Government of the United Arab Republic. I can only express the hope that both sides will now exercise the utmost calm and restraint in this new situation, which otherwise will be fraught with danger. . . . [*A/6669, Spec. Report of the Secretary-General, 18 May 1967,* mimeo.]

The consequences of UNEF's withdrawal were so great—for the Big Powers, for the Middle East, for the UN itself—that it has been thought appropriate to reproduce in full the detailed sequence of events:

1. This report on the withdrawal of the United Nations Emergency Force (UNEF) is submitted because, as indicated in my statement on 20 June 1967 to the fifth emergency special session of the General Assembly (1527th plenary meeting), important questions have been raised concerning the actions taken on the withdrawal of UNEF. These questions merit careful consideration and comment. It is in the interest of the United Nations, I believe, that this report should be full and frank, in view of the questions involved and the numerous statements that have been made, both public and private, which continue to be very damaging to the United Nations and to its peace-keeping role in particular. Despite the explanations already given in the several reports on the subject which have been submitted to the General Assembly and to the Security Council, misunderstandings and what, I fear, are misrepresentations, persist, in official as well as unofficial circles, publicly and behind the scenes.

2. A report of this kind is not the place to try to explain why there has been so much and such persistent and grossly mistaken judgement about the withdrawal of UNEF. It suffices to say here that the shattering crisis in the Near East inevitably caused intense shock in many capitals and countries of the world, together with deep frustration over the inability to cope with it. It is, of course, not unusual in such situations to seek easy explanations and excuses. When, however, this tactic involves imputing responsibility for the unleashing of major hostilities, it is, and must be, a cause for sober concern. The objective of this report is to establish an authentic, factual record of actions and their causes.

3. It follows, therefore, that the emphasis here, therefore, will be upon facts. The report is intended to be neither a polemic nor an apologia. Its sole purpose is to present a factually accurate picture of what happened and why. It will serve well the interests of the United Nations, as well as of historical integrity, if this presentation of facts can help to dissipate some of the distortions of the record which, in some places, apparently have emanated from panic, emotion and political bias.

CHRONOLOGY OF RELEVANT ACTIONS

4. Not only events but dates, and even the time of day, have an important bearing on this exposition. The significant events and actions and their dates and times are therefore set forth below.

16 May 1967

5. *20.00 hours GMT (22.00 hours Gaza local time)*. A message from General Fawzy, Chief of Staff of the United Arab Republic Armed Forces, was received by the Commander of UNEF, Major-General Rikhye, requesting withdrawal of 'all UN troops which install OPs along our borders' (A/6730, para. 6, sub-para. 3 (a)). Brigadier Mokhtar, who handed General Fawzy's letter to the Commander of UNEF, told General Rikhye at the time that he must order the immediate withdrawal of United Nations troops from El Sabha and Sharm el Sheikh on the night of 16 May since United Arab Republic armed forces must gain control of these two places that very night. The UNEF Commander correctly replied that he did not have authority to withdraw his troops from these positions on such an order and could do so only on instructions from the Secretary-General; therefore, he must continue with UNEF operations in Sinai as hitherto. Brigadier Mokhtar told the Commander of UNEF that this might lead to conflict on that night (16 May) between United Arab Republic and UNEF troops, and insisted that the Commander issue orders to UNEF troops to remain confined to their camps at El Sabha and Sharm el Sheikh. General Rikhye replied that he could not comply with this request. He did, of course, inform the contingent commanders concerned of these developments. He also informed United Nations Headquarters that he proposed to continue with UNEF activities as established until he received fresh instructions from the Secretary-General.

6. *21.30 hours GMT (17.30 hours New York time)*. The Secretary-General received at this time the UNEF Commander's cable informing him of the above-mentioned message from General Fawzy. The UNEF Commander was immediately instructed to await further instructions from the Secretary-General and, pending this later word from him, to 'be firm in maintaining UNEF position while being as understanding and as diplomatic as possible in your relations with local UAR officials'.

7. *22.45 hours GMT (18.45 hours New York time)*. The Permanent Representative of the United Arab Republic visited the Secretary-General at this time at the latter's urgent request. The Secretary-General requested the Permanent Representative to communicate with his Government with the utmost urgency and to transmit to it his views (A/6730, para. 6, sub-para. 3 (c)). In particular, the Secretary-General requested the Permanent Representative to obtain his Government's clarification of the situation, pointing out that any request for the withdrawal of UNEF must come directly to the Secretary-General from the Government of the United Arab Republic.

8. *23.44 hours GMT*. The UNEF Commander further reported at this time that considerable military activity had been observed in the El Arish area since the afternoon of 16 May 1967.

17 May 1967

9. *08.00 hours GMT (04.00 hours New York time)*. The Commander of UNEF reported then that on the morning of 17 May, thirty soldiers of the Army of the United Arab Republic had occupied El Sabha in Sinai and that United Arab Republic troops were deployed in the immediate vicinity of the UNEF observation post there. Three armoured cars of the United Arab Republic were located near the Yugoslav UNEF camp at El Sabha and detachments of fifteen soldiers each had taken up positions north and south of the Yugoslav contingent's camp at El Amr. All UNEF observation posts along the armistice demarcation line and the international frontier were manned as usual, but in some places United Arab Republic troops were also at the line.

10. *10.30 hours GMT (06.30 hours New York time)*. The Commander of UNEF reported then that troops of the United Arab Republic had occupied the UNEF observation post at El Sabha and that the Yugoslav Arab Republic had occupied the UNEF observation post at the positions of the army of the United Arab Republic. The Commander of UNEF informed the Chief of the United Arab Republic Liaison Staff of these developments, expressing his serious concern at them. The Chief of the United Arab Republic Liaison Staff agreed to

request the immediate evacuation of the observation post at El Sabha by United Arab Republic troops and shortly thereafter reported that orders to this effect had been given by the United Arab Republic military authorities. He requested, however, that to avoid any future misunderstandings, the Yugoslav observation post at El Sabha should be withdrawn immediately to El Quseima camp. The Commander replied that any such withdrawal would require the authorization of the Secretary-General.

11. *12.00 hours GMT (08.00 hours New York time)*. The Chief of the United Arab Republic Liaison Staff at this time conveyed to the Commander of UNEF a request from General Mohd Fawzy, Chief of Staff of the Armed Forces of the United Arab Republic, for the withdrawal of the Yugoslav detachments of UNEF in the Sinai within twenty-four hours. He added that the UNEF Commander might take 'forty-eight hours or so' to withdraw the UNEF detachment from Sharm el Sheikh. The Commander of UNEF replied that any such move required instructions from the Secretary-General.

12. *13.30 hours GMT*. The Commander of UNEF then reported that a sizable detachment of troops of the United Arab Republic was moving into the UNEF area at El Kuntilla.

13. *20.00 hours GMT (16.00 hours New York time)*. The Secretary-General at this date held an informal meeting in his office with the representatives of countries providing contingents to UNEF to inform them of the situation as then known. There was an exchange of views. The Secretary-General gave his opinion on how he should and how he intended to proceed, observing that if a formal request for the withdrawal of UNEF were to be made by the Government of the United Arab Republic, the Secretary-General, in his view, would have to comply with it, since the Force was on United Arab Republic territory only with the consent of the Government and could not remain there without it. Two representatives expressed serious doubts about the consequences of agreeing to a peremptory request for the withdrawal of UNEF and raised the questions of consideration of such a request by the General Assembly and an appeal to the United Arab Republic not to request the withdrawal of UNEF. Two other representatives stated the view that the United Arab Republic was entitled to request the removal of UNEF at any moment and that that request would have to be respected regardless of what the General Assembly might have to say in the matter, since the agreement for UNEF's presence had been concluded between the then Secretary-General and the Government of Egypt. A clarification of the situation from the United Arab Republic should therefore be awaited.

14. *21.50 hours GMT (17.50 hours New York time)*. The Secretary-General at this time saw the Permanent Representative of the United Arab Republic and handed to him an *aide-mémoire*, the text of which is contained in paragraph 6 of document A/6730. The Secretary-General also gave to the Permanent Representative of the United Arab Republic an *aide-mémoire* calling to the attention of his Government the 'good faith' accord, the text of which is contained in paragraph 7 of document A/6730.

18 May 1967

15. *13.21 hours GMT (09.21 hours New York time)*. The Commander of UNEF reported at this time that his Liaison Officer in Cairo had been informed by an ambassador of one of the countries providing contingents to UNEF that the Foreign Minister of the United Arab Republic had summoned the representatives of nations with troops in UNEF to the Ministry for Foreign Affairs and informed them that UNEF had terminated its tasks in the United Arab Republic and in the Gaza Strip and must depart from the above territory forthwith. This information was confirmed by representatives of some of these countries at the United Nations.

16. Early on 18 May the UNEF sentries proceeding to man the normal observation post at El Sabha in Sinai were prevented from entering the post and from remaining in the area by United Arab Republic soldiers. The sentries were then forced to withdraw. They did not resist by use of force since they had no mandate to do so.

17. *11.00 hours GMT*. United Arab Republic soldiers at this time forced Yugoslav UNEF

sentries out of their observation post on the international frontier in front of El Kuntilla Camp. One hour later, United Arab Republic officers arrived at the water point and asked UNEF soldiers to withdraw the guard.

18. *12.00 hours GMT.* At this hour, United Arab Republic soldiers entered the UNEF observation post on the international frontier in front of El Amr Camp and forced the Yugoslav soldiers to withdraw. Later, two United Arab Republic officers visited El Amr Camp and asked the UNEF platoon to withdraw within fifteen minutes.

19. *12.10 hours GMT.* United Arab Republic officers then visited the Yugoslav camp at Sharm el Sheikh and informed the Commanding Officer that they had come to take over the camp and the UNEF observation post at Ras Nasrani, demanding a reply within fifteen minutes. The contingent commander replied that he had no instructions to hand over the positions.

20. *14.30 hours GMT.* The UNEF Yugoslav detachment at El Quseima camp reported that two artillery shells, apparently ranging rounds from the United Arab Republic artillery, had burst between the UNEF Yugoslav camps at El Quseima and El Sabha.

21. *10.30 hours New York time.* The Secretary-General met at this time with the Permanent Representative of Israel who gave his Government's views on the situation, emphasizing that the UNEF withdrawal should not be achieved by a unilateral United Arab Republic request alone and asserting Israel's right to a voice in the matter. The question of stationing UNEF on the Israel side of the line was raised by the Secretary-General and this was declared by the Permanent Representative of Israel to be entirely unacceptable to his Government.

22. *16.00 hours GMT (12 noon New York time).* At this hour the Secretary-General received through the Permanent Representative of the United Arab Republic the following message from Mr Mahmoud Riad, Minister of Foreign Affairs of the United Arab Republic:

> 'The Government of the United Arab Republic has the honour to inform Your Excellency that it has decided to terminate the presence of the United Nations Emergency Force from the territory of the United Arab Republic and Gaza Strip.
>
> 'Therefore, I request that the necessary steps be taken for the withdrawal of the Force as soon as possible.
>
> 'I avail myself of this opportunity to express to Your Excellency my gratitude and warm regards.'

At the same meeting the Permanent Representative of the United Arab Republic informed the Secretary-General of the strong feeling of resentment in Cairo at what was there considered to be attempts to exert pressure and to make UNEF an 'occupation force'. The Secretary-General expressed deep misgivings about the likely disastrous consequences of the withdrawal of UNEF and indicated his intention to appeal urgently to President Nasser to reconsider the decision. Later in the day, the representative of the United Arab Republic informed the Secretary-General that the Foreign Minister had asked the Permanent Representative by telephone from Cairo to convey to the Secretary-General his urgent advice that the Secretary-General should not make an appeal to President Nasser to reconsider the request for withdrawal of UNEF and that, if he did so, such a request would be sternly rebuffed. The Secretary-General raised the question of a possible visit by him to Cairo and was shortly thereafter informed that such a visit as soon as possible would be welcomed by the Government of the United Arab Republic.

23. *17.00 hours New York time.* The Secretary-General met with the UNEF Advisory Committee, set up under the terms of paragraphs 6, 8 and 9 of resolution 1001 (ES–I) of 7 November 1956, and the representatives of three countries not members of the Advisory Committee but providing contingents to UNEF, to inform them of developments and particularly the United Arab Republic's request for UNEF's withdrawal, and to consult them for their views on the situation. At this meeting, one of the views expressed was that the United Arab Republic's demand for the immediate withdrawal of UNEF from United Arab Republic territory was not acceptable and that the ultimate responsibility for the decision to withdraw rested with the United Nations acting through the Security Council or the General Assembly.

12*

The holder of this view therefore urged further discussion with the Government of the United Arab Republic as well as with other Governments involved. Another position was that the Secretary-General had no choice but to comply with the request of the Government of the United Arab Republic, one representative stating that the moment the request for the withdrawal of UNEF was known his Government would comply with it and withdraw its contingent. A similar position had been taken in Cairo by another Government providing a contingent. No proposal was made that the Advisory Committee should exercise the right vested in it by General Assembly resolution 1001 (ES–I) to request the convening of the General Assembly to take up the situation arising from the United Arab Republic communication. At the conclusion of the meeting, it was understood that the Secretary-General had no alternative other than to comply with the United Arab Republic's demand, although some representatives felt the Secretary-General should previously clarify with that Government the meaning in its request that withdrawal should take place 'as soon as possible'. The Secretary-General informed the Advisory Committee that he intended to reply promptly to the United Arab Republic, and to report to the General Assembly and to the Security Council on the action he had taken. It was for the Member States to decide whether the competent organs should or could take up the matter and to pursue it accordingly.

24. After the meeting of the Advisory Committee, at approximately 19.00 hours New York time on 18 May, the Secretary-General replied to the message from the Minister for Foreign Affairs of the United Arab Republic through that Government's Permanent Representative as follows:

'I have the honour to acknowledge your letter to me of 18 May conveying the message from the Minister of Foreign Affairs of the United Arab Republic concerning the United Nations Emergency Force. Please be so kind as to transmit to the Foreign Minister the following message in reply:

"Dear Mr Minister,

Your message informing me that your Government no longer consents to the presence of the United Nations Emergency Force on the territory of the United Arab Republic, that is to say in Sinai, and in the Gaza Strip, and requesting that the necessary steps be taken for its withdrawal as soon as possible, was delivered to me by the Permanent Representative of the United Arab Republic at noon on 18 May.

As I have indicated to your Permanent Representative on 16 May, the United Nations Emergency Force entered Egyptian territory with the consent of your Government and in fact can remain there only so long as that consent continues. In view of the message now received from you, therefore, your Government's request will be complied with and I am proceeding to issue instructions for the necessary arrangements to be put in train without delay for the orderly withdrawal of the Force, its vehicles and equipment and for the disposal of all properties pertaining to it. I am, of course, also bringing this development and my actions and intentions to the attention of the UNEF Advisory Committee and to all Governments providing contingents for the Force. A full report covering this development will be submitted promptly by me to the General Assembly, and I consider it necessary to report also to the Security Council about some aspects of the current situation in the area.

Irrespective of the reasons for the action you have taken, in all frankness, may I advise you that I have serious misgivings about it for, as I have said each year in my annual reports to the General Assembly on UNEF, I believe that this Force has been an important factor in maintaining relative quiet in the area of its deployment during the past ten years and that its withdrawal may have grave implications for peace.

With warm personal regards,

U THANT"

Please Accept, Sir, the assurances of my highest consideration.'

It is to be noted that the decision notified to the Government of the United Arab Republic in this letter was in compliance with the request to withdraw the Force. It did not, however, signify the actual withdrawal of the Force which, in fact, was to remain in the area for several more weeks.

25. Formal instructions relating to the withdrawal of UNEF were sent to the UNEF Commander by the Secretary-General on the night of 18 May (see annex).

26. Also on the evening of 18 May the Secretary-General submitted his special report to the General Assembly (A/6730).

27. On 19 May the Secretary-General issued his report to the Security Council on recent developments in the Near East (S/7896).

19 May 1967

28. *11.30 hours New York time*. The Secretary-General again received the Permanent Representative of Israel who gave him a statement from his Government concerning the withdrawal of UNEF, strongly urging the Secretary-General to avoid condoning any changes in the *status quo* pending the fullest and broadest international consultation.

29. On the afternoon of 22 May, the Secretary-General departed from New York, arriving in Cairo on the afternoon of 23 May. He left Cairo on the afternoon of 25 May, arriving back in New York on 26 May (see S/7906). While *en route* to Cairo during a stop in Paris, the Secretary-General learned that on this day President Nasser had announced his intention to reinstitute the blockade against Israel in the Strait of Tiran.

17 June 1967

30. The withdrawal of UNEF was completed. Details of the actual withdrawal and evacuation of UNEF are given in document A/6730/Add. 2.

Main Points at Issue

31. Comment is called for on some of the main points at issue even prior to the consideration of the background and basis for the stationing of UNEF on United Arab Republic territory.

The causes of the present crisis

32. It has been said rather often in one way or another that the withdrawal of UNEF is a primary cause of the present crisis in the Near East. This is, of course, a superficial and over-simplified approach. As the Secretary-General pointed out in his report of 26 May 1967 to the Security Council (S/7906), this view 'ignores the fact that the underlying basis for this and other crisis situations in the Near East is the continuing Arab–Israel conflict which has been present all along and of which the crisis situation created by the unexpected withdrawal of UNEF is the latest expression'. The Secretary-General's report to the Security Council of 19 May 1967 (S/7896) described the various elements of the increasingly dangerous situation in the Near East prior to the decision of the Government of the United Arab Republic to terminate its consent for the presence of UNEF on its territory.

33. The United Nations Emergency Force served for more than ten years as a highly valuable instrument in helping to maintain quiet along the line between Israel and the United Arab Republic. Its withdrawal revealed in all its depth and danger the undiminishing conflict between Israel and her Arab neighbours. The withdrawal also made immediately acute the problem of access for Israel to the Gulf of Aqaba through the Strait of Tiran—a problem which had been dormant for over ten years only because of the presence of UNEF. But the presence of UNEF did not touch the basic problem of the Arab–Israel conflict—it merely isolated, immobilized and covered up certain aspects of that conflict. At any time in the last ten years either of the parties could have reactivated the conflict and if they had been determined to do so UNEF's effectiveness would automatically have disappeared. When, in the context of the whole relationship of Israel with her Arab neighbours, the direct confrontation between Israel and the United Arab Republic was revived after a decade by the decision of the

United Arab Republic to move its forces up to the line, UNEF at once lost all usefulness. In fact, its effectiveness as a buffer and as a presence had already vanished, as can be seen from the chronology given above, even before the request for its withdrawal had been received by the Secretary-General from the Government of the United Arab Republic. In recognizing the extreme seriousness of the situation thus created, its true cause, the continuing Arab–Israel conflict, must also be recognized. It is entirely unrealistic to maintain that that conflict could have been solved, or its consequences prevented, if a greater effort had been made to maintain UNEF's presence in the area against the will of the Government of the United Arab Republic.

The decision on UNEF's withdrawal

34. The decision to withdraw UNEF has been frequently characterized in various quarters as 'hasty', 'precipitate', and the like, even, indeed, to the extent of suggesting that it took President Nasser by surprise. The question of the withdrawal of UNEF is by no means a new one. In fact, it was the negotiations on this very question with the Government of Egypt which, after the establishment of UNEF by the General Assembly, delayed its arrival while it waited in a staging area at Capodichino airbase, Naples, Italy, for several days in November 1956. The Government of Egypt, understandably, did not wish to give permission for the arrival on its soil of an international force, unless it was assured that its sovereignty would be respected and a request for withdrawal of the Force would be honoured. Over the years, in discussions with representatives of the United Arab Republic, the subject of the continued presence of UNEF has occasionally come up, and it was invariably taken for granted by United Arab Republic representatives that if their Government officially requested the withdrawal of UNEF the request would be honoured by the Secretary-General. There is no record to indicate that this assumption was ever questioned. Thus, although the request for the withdrawal of UNEF came as a surprise, there was nothing new about the question of principle nor about the procedure to be followed by the Secretary-General. It follows that the decision taken by him on 18 May 1967 to comply with the request for the withdrawal of the Force was seen by him as the only reasonable and sound action that could be taken. The actual withdrawal itself, it should be recalled, was to be carried out in an orderly, dignified, deliberate and not precipitate manner over a period of several weeks. The first troops in fact left the area only on 29 May.

The possibility of delay

35. Opinions have also been frequently expressed that the decision to withdraw UNEF should have been delayed pending consultations of various kinds, or that efforts should have been made to resist the United Arab Republic's request for UNEF's withdrawal, or to bring pressure to bear on the Government of the United Arab Republic to reconsider its decision in this matter. In fact, as the chronology given above makes clear, the effectiveness of UNEF, in the light of the movement of United Arab Republic troops up to the line and into Sharm el Sheikh, had already vanished before the request for withdrawal was received. Furthermore, the Government of the United Arab Republic had made it entirely clear to the Secretary-General that an appeal for reconsideration of the withdrawal decision would encounter a firm rebuff and would be considered as an attempt to impose UNEF as an 'army of occupation'. Such a reaction, combined with the fact that UNEF positions on the line had already been effectively taken over by United Arab Republic troops in pursuit of their full right to move up to the line in their own territory, and a deep anxiety for the security of UNEF personnel should an effort be made to keep UNEF in position after its withdrawal had been requested, were powerful arguments in favour of complying with the United Arab Republic request, even supposing there had not been other overriding reasons for accepting it.

36. It has been said that the decision to withdraw UNEF precipitated other consequences such as the reinstitution of the blockade against Israel in the Strait of Tiran. As can be seen from the chronology, the UNEF positions at Sharm el Sheikh on the Strait of Tiran (manned by thirty-two men in all) were in fact rendered ineffective by United Arab Republic troops before the request for withdrawal was received. It is also pertinent to note that in response to a

query from the Secretary-General as to why the United Arab Republic had announced its reinstitution of the blockade in the Strait of Tiran while the Secretary-General was actually *en route* to Cairo on 22 May, President Nasser explained that his Government's decision to resume the blockade had been taken some time before U Thant's departure and it was considered preferable to make the announcement before rather than after the Secretary-General's visit to Cairo.

The question of consultations

37. It has been said also that there was not adequate consultation with the organs of the United Nations concerned or with the Members before the decision was taken to withdraw the Force. The Secretary-General was, and is, firmly of the opinion that the decision for withdrawal of the Force, on the request of the host Government, rested with the Secretary-General after consultation with the Advisory Committee on UNEF, which is the organ established by the General Assembly for consultation regarding such matters. This was made clear by Secretary-General Hammarskjöld, who took the following position on 26 February 1957 in reply to a question about the withdrawal of the Force from Sharm el Sheikh:

'An indicated procedure would be for the Secretary-General to inform the Advisory Committee on the United Nations Emergency Force, which would determine whether the matter should be brought to the attention of the Assembly.'[10]

The Secretary-General consulted the Advisory Committee before replying to the letter of 18 May 1967 from the United Arab Republic requesting withdrawal. This consultation took place within a few hours after receipt of the United Arab Republic request, and the Advisory Committee was thus quickly informed of the decision which the Secretary-General had in mind to convey in his reply to the Foreign Minister of the United Arab Republic. As indicated in the report to the Security Council of 26 May 1967:

'The Committee did not move, as it was its right to do under the terms of paragraph 9 of General Assembly resolution 1001 (ES–I) to request the convening of the General Assembly on the situation which had arisen.' (S/7906, para. 4.)

38. Before consulting the Advisory Committee on UNEF, the Secretary-General had also consulted the Permanent Representatives of the seven countries providing the contingents of UNEF and informed them of his intentions. This, in fact, was more than was formally required of the Secretary-General in the way of consultation.

39. Obviously, many Governments were concerned about the presence and functioning of UNEF and about the general situation in the area, but it would have been physically impossible to consult all of the interested representatives within any reasonable time. This was an emergency requiring urgent action. Moreover, it was perfectly clear that such consultations were sure to produce sharply divided counsel, even if they were limited to the permanent members of the Security Council. Such sharply divided advice would have complicated and exacerbated the situation, and, far from relieving the Secretary-General of the responsibility for the decision to be taken, would have made the decision much more difficult to take.

40. It has been said that the final decision on the withdrawal of UNEF should have been taken only after consideration by the General Assembly. This position is not only incorrect but also unrealistic. In resolution 1000 (ES–I) the General Assembly established a United Nations command for an emergency international force. On the basis of that resolution the Force was quickly recruited and its forward elements flown to the staging area at Naples. Thus, though established, it had to await the permission of the Government of Egypt to enter Egyptian territory. That permission was subsequently given by the Government of Egypt as a result of direct discussions between Secretary-General Hammarskjöld and President Nasser of Egypt. There is no official United Nations document on the basis of which any case could be made that there was any limitation on the authority of the Government of Egypt to rescind that consent at its pleasure, or which would indicate that the United Arab

[10] A/3563.

Republic had in any way surrendered its right to ask for and obtain at any time the removal of UNEF from its territory. This point is elaborated later in this report (see paras 71–80 below).

41. As a practical matter, there would be little point in any case in taking such an issue to the General Assembly unless there would be reasonable certainty that that body could be expected expeditiously to reach a substantive decision. In the prevailing circumstances, the question could have been validly raised as to what decision other than the withdrawal of UNEF could have been reached by the Assembly once United Arab Republic consent for the continued presence of UNEF was withdrawn.

42. As regards the practical possibility of the Assembly considering the request for UNEF's withdrawal, it is relevant to observe that the next regular session of the General Assembly was some four months off at the time the withdrawal request was made. The special session of the General Assembly which was meeting at the time could have considered the question, according to rule 19 of the Assembly's rules of procedure, only if two-thirds or eighty-two members voted for the inclusion of the item in the agenda. It is questionable, to say the least, whether the necessary support could have been mustered for such a controversial item. There could have been no emergency special session since the issue was not then before the Security Council, and therefore the condition of lack of unanimity did not exist.

43. As far as consultation with or action by the Security Council was concerned, the Secretary-General reported to the Council on the situation leading up to and created by the withdrawal of UNEF on 19 May 1967 (S/7896). In that report he characterized the situation in the Near East as 'extremely menacing'. The Council met for the first time after this report on 24 May 1967, but took no action.

44. As has already been stated, the Advisory Committee did not make any move to bring the matter before the General Assembly, and no representative of any Member Government requested a meeting of either the Security Council or the General Assembly immediately following the Secretary-General's reports (A/6730 and S/7896). In this situation, the Secretary-General himself did not believe that any useful purpose would be served by his seeking a meeting of either organ, nor did he consider that there was basis for him to do so at that time. Furthermore, the information available to the Secretary-General did not lead him to believe that either the General Assembly or the Security Council would have decided that UNEF should remain on United Arab Republic territory, by force if necessary, despite the request of the Government of the United Arab Republic that it should leave.

Practical factors influencing the decision

45. Since it is still contended in some quarters that the UNEF operation should somehow have continued after the consent of the Government of the United Arab Republic to its presence was withdrawn, it is necessary to consider the factors, quite apart from constitutional and legal considerations, which would have made such a course of action entirely impracticable.

46. The consent and active co-operation of the host country is essential to the effective operation and, indeed, to the very existence, of any United Nations peace-keeping operation of the nature of UNEF. The fact is that UNEF had been deployed on Egyptian and Egyptian-controlled territory for over ten and a half years with the consent and co-operation of the Government of the United Arab Republic. Although it was envisaged in pursuance of General Assembly resolution 1125 (XI) of 2 February 1957 that the Force would be stationed on both sides of the line, Israel exercised its sovereign right to refuse the stationing of UNEF on its side, and the Force throughout its existence was stationed on the United Arab Republic side of the line only.

47. In these circumstances, the true basis for UNEF's effectiveness as a buffer and deterrent to infiltration was, throughout its existence, a voluntary undertaking by local United Arab Republic authorities with UNEF, that United Arab Republic troops would respect a defined buffer zone along the entire length of the line in which only UNEF would operate and from which United Arab Republic troops would be excluded. This undertaking was honoured for more than a decade, and this Egyptian co-operation extended also to Sharm el Sheikh, Ras

Nasrani and the Strait of Tiran. This undertaking was honoured although UNEF had no authority to challenge the right of United Arab Republic troops to be present anywhere on their own territory.

48. It may be pointed out in passing that over the years UNEF dealt with numerous infiltrators coming from the Israel as well as from the United Arab Republic side of the line. It would hardly be logical to take the position that because UNEF has successfully maintained quiet along the line for more than ten years, owing in large measure to the co-operation of the United Arab Republic authorities, that Government should then be told that it could not unilaterally seek the removal of the Force and thus in effect be penalized for the long co-operation with the international community it had extended in the interest of peace.

49. There are other practical factors relating to the above-mentioned arrangement which are highly relevant to the withdrawal of UNEF. First, once the United Arab Republic troops moved up to the line to place themselves in direct confrontation with the military forces of Israel, UNEF had, in fact, no further useful function. Secondly, if the Force was no longer welcome, it could not as a practical matter remain in the United Arab Republic, since the friction which would almost inevitably have arisen with that Government, its armed forces and with the local population would have made the situation of the Force both humiliating and untenable. It would even have been impossible to supply it. UNEF clearly had no mandate to try to stop United Arab Republic troops from moving freely about on their own territory. This was a peace-keeping force, not an enforcement action. Its effectivenesss was based entirely on voluntary co-operation.

50. Quite apart from its position in the United Arab Republic, the request of that Government for UNEF's withdrawal automatically set off a disintegration of the Force, since two of the Governments providing contingents quickly let the Secretary-General know that their contingents would be withdrawn, and there can be little doubt that other such notifications would not have been slow in coming if friction had been generated through an unwillingness to comply with the request for withdrawal.

51. For all the foregoing reasons, the operation, and even the continued existence of UNEF on United Arab Republic territory, after the withdrawal of United Arab Republic consent, would have been impossible, and any attempt to maintain the Force there would without question have had disastrous consequences.

LEGAL AND CONSTITUTIONAL CONSIDERATIONS AND THE QUESTION OF CONSENT FOR THE STATIONING OF UNEF ON UNITED ARAB REPUBLIC TERRITORY

52. Legal and constitutional considerations were, of course, of great importance in determining the Secretary-General's actions in relation to the request of the Government of the United Arab Republic for the withdrawal of UNEF. Here again, a chronology of the relevant actions in 1956 and 1957 may be helpful.

53. *4 November 1956.* The General Assembly, at its first emergency special session in resolution 998 (ES–I), requested 'the Secretary-General to submit to it within forty-eight hours a plan for setting up, with the consent of the nations concerned, of an emergency international United Nations Force to secure and supervise the cessation of hostilities . . .'

54. *5 November 1956.* The General Assembly, in its resolution 1000 (ES–I), established a United Nations Command for an emergency international Force, and, *inter alia*, invited the Secretary-General 'to take such administrative measures as may be necessary for the prompt execution of the actions envisaged in the present resolution'.

55. *7 November 1956.* The General Assembly, by its resolution 1001 (ES–I), *inter alia*, approved the guiding principles for the organization and functioning of the emergency international United Nations Force and authorized the Secretary-General 'to take all other necessary administrative and executive action'.

56. *10 November 1956.* Arrival of advance elements of UNEF at staging area in Naples.

57. *8–12 November 1956.* Negotiations between Secretary-General Hammarskjöld and the Government of Egypt on entry of UNEF into Egypt.

58. *12 November 1956*. Agreement on UNEF entry into Egypt announced and then postponed, pending clarification, until 14 November.

59. *15 November 1956*. Arrival of advance elements of UNEF in Abu Suweir, Egypt.

60. *16 November to 18 November 1956*. Negotiations between Secretary-General Hammarskjöld and President Nasser in Cairo on the presence and functioning of UNEF in Egypt and co-operation with Egyptian authorities, and conclusion of an '*aide-mémoire* on the basis for the presence and functioning of UNEF in Egypt' (the so-called 'good faith accord').[11]

61. *24 January 1957*. The Secretary-General in a report to the General Assembly[12] suggested that the Force should have units stationed on both sides of the armistice demarcation line and that certain measures should be taken in relation to Sharm el Sheikh. On *2 February 1957*, the General Assembly, by its resolution 1125 (XI), noted with appreciation the Secretary-General's report and considered that 'after full withdrawal of Israel from the Sharm el Sheikh and Gaza areas, the scrupulous maintenance of the Armistice Agreement required the placing of the United Nations Emergency Force on the Egyptian–Israel armistice demarcation line and the implementation of other measures as proposed in the Secretary-General's report, with due regard to the considerations set out therein with a view to assist in achieving situations conducive to the maintenance of peaceful conditions in the area'.

62. *7 March 1957*. Arrival of UNEF in Gaza.

63. *8 March 1957*. Arrival of UNEF elements at Sharm el Sheikh.

64. In general terms the consent of the host country to the presence and operation of the United Nations peace-keeping machinery is a basic prerequisite of all United Nations peace-keeping operations. The question has been raised whether the United Arab Republic had the right to request unilaterally the withdrawal 'as soon as possible' of UNEF from its territory or whether there were limitations on its rights in this respect. An examination of the records of the first emergency special session and the eleventh session of the General Assembly is relevant to this question.

65. It is clear that the General Assembly and the Secretary-General from the very beginning recognized, and in fact emphasized, the need for Egyptian consent in order that UNEF be stationed or operate on Egyptian territory. Thus, the initial resolution 998 (ES–I) of 4 November 1956 requested the Secretary-General to submit a plan for the setting up of an emergency force, 'with the consent of the nations concerned'. The 'nations concerned' obviously included Egypt (now the United Arab Republic), the three countries (France, Israel and the United Kingdom) whose armies were on Egyptian soil and the States contributing contingents to the Force.

66. The Secretary-General, in his report to the General Assembly of 6 November 1956, stated, *inter alia*:

> '9. Functioning, as it would, on the basis of a decision reached under the terms of the resolution 337 (V) "Uniting for peace", the Force, if established, would be limited in its operations to the extent that consent of the parties concerned is required under generally recognized international law. While the General Assembly is enabled to *establish* the Force with the consent of those parties which contribute units to the Force, it could not request the Force to be *stationed* or *operate* on the territory of a given country without the consent of the Government of that country.'[13]

67. He noted that the foregoing did not exclude the possibility that the Security Council could use such a Force within the wider margins provided under Chapter VII of the United Nations Charter. He pointed out, however, that it would not be necessary to elaborate this point further, since no use of the Force under Chapter VII, with the rights in relation to Member States that this would entail, had been envisaged.

68. The General Assembly in its resolution 1001 (ES–I) of 7 November 1956 expressed its approval of the guiding principles for the organization and functioning of the emergency

[11] A/3375. Ann.   [12] A/3512.   [13] A/3302, para. 9.

international United Nations Force as expounded in paragraphs 6 to 9 of the Secretary-General's report. This included the principle of consent embodied in paragraph 9.

69. The need for Egypt's consent was also stated as a condition or 'understanding' by some of the States offering to contribute contingents to the Force.

70. It was thus a basic legal principle arising from the nature of the Force, and clearly understood by all concerned, that the consent of Egypt was a prerequisite to the stationing of UNEF on Egyptian territory, and it was a practical necessity as well in acquiring contingents for the Force.

The 'good faith' aide-mémoire of 20 November 1956

71. There remains to be examined whether any commitments were made by Egypt which would limit its pre-existing right to withdraw its consent at any time that it chose to do so. The only basis for asserting such limitation could be the so-called 'good faith' aide-mémoire which was set out as an annex to a report of the Secretary-General submitted to the General Assembly on 20 November 1956.

72. The Secretary-General himself did not offer any interpretation of the 'good faith' aide-mémoire to the General Assembly or make any statement questioning the remarks made by the Foreign Minister of Egypt in the General Assembly the following week (see paragraph 74 below). It would appear, however, that in an exchange of cables he had sought to obtain the express acknowledgement from Egypt that its consent to the presence of the Force would not be withdrawn before the Force had completed its task. Egypt did not accept this interpretation but held to the view that if its consent was no longer maintained the Force should be withdrawn. Subsequent discussions between Mr Hammarskjöld and President Nasser resulted in the 'good faith' aide-mémoire.

73. An interpretative account of these negotiations made by Mr Hammarskjöld in a personal and private paper entitled 'aide-mémoire', dated 5 August 1957, some eight and a half months after the discussions, has recently been made public by a private person who has a copy. It is understood that Mr Hammarskjöld often prepared private notes concerning significant events under the heading 'aide-mémoire'. This memorandum is not in any official record of the United Nations nor is it in any of the official files. The General Assembly, the Advisory Committee on UNEF and the Government of Egypt were not informed of its contents or existence. It is not an official paper and has no standing beyond being a purely private memorandum of unknown purpose or value, in which Secretary-General Hammarskjöld seems to record his own impressions and interpretations of his discussions with President Nasser. This paper, therefore, cannot affect in any way the basis for the presence of UNEF on the soil of the United Arab Republic as set out in the official documents, much less supersede those documents.

Position of Egypt

74. It seems clear that Egypt did not understand the 'good faith' aide-mémoire to involve any limitation on its right to withdraw its consent to the continued stationing and operation of UNEF on its territory. The Foreign Minister of Egypt, speaking in the General Assembly on 27 November 1956, one week after the publication of the 'good faith' aide-mémoire and three days following its approval by the General Assembly, said:

'We still believe that the General Assembly resolution of 7 November 1956 still stands, together with its endorsement of the principle that the General Assembly could not request the United Nations Emergency Force to be stationed or to operate on the territory of a given country without the consent of the Government of the country. This is the proper basis on which we believe, together with the overwhelming majority of this Assembly, that the United Nations Emergency Force could be stationed or could operate in Egypt. It is the only basis on which Egypt has given its consent in this respect.'[14]

He then added:

[14] GAOR, 11th sess., 597th plen. mtg, para. 48.

'. . . as must be abundantly clear, this Force has gone to Egypt to help Egypt, with Egypt's consent; and no one here or elsewhere can reasonably or fairly say that a fire brigade, after putting out a fire, would be entitled or expected to claim the right of deciding not to leave the house'.[15]

Analysis of the 'task' of the Force

75. In the 'good faith' *aide-mémoire* the Government of Egypt declared that, 'when exercising its sovereign rights on any matters concerning the presence and functioning of UNEF, it will be guided, in good faith, by its acceptance of General Assembly resolution 1000 (ES–I) of 5 November 1956'.

76. The United Nations in turn declared 'that the activities of UNEF will be guided, in good faith, by the task established for the Force in the aforementioned resolutions (1000 (ES–I) and 997 (ES–I)), in particular, the United Nations, understanding this to correspond to the wishes of the Government of Egypt, reaffirms its willingness to maintain UNEF until its task is completed'.

77. It must be noted that, while Egypt undertook to be guided in *good faith* by its acceptance of General Assembly resolution 1000 (ES–I), the United Nations also undertook to be guided in *good faith* by the task established for the Force in resolutions 1000 (ES–I) and 997 (ES–I). Resolution 1000 (ES–I), to which the declaration of Egypt referred, established a United Nations Command for the Force 'to secure and supervise the cessation of hostilities in accordance with all the terms' of resolution 997 (ES–I). It must be recalled that at this time Israel forces had penetrated deeply into Egyptian territory and that forces of France and the United Kingdom were conducting military operations on Egyptian territory. Resolution 997 (ES–I) urged as a matter of priority that all parties agree to an immediate cease-fire, and halt the movement of military forces and arms into the area. It also urged the parties to the armistice agreements promptly to withdraw all forces behind the armistice lines, to desist from raids across the armistice lines, and to observe scrupulously the provisions of the armistice agreements. It further urged that, upon the cease-fire being effective, steps be taken to reopen the Suez Canal and restore secure freedom of navigation.

78. While the terms of resolution 997 (ES–I) cover a considerable area, the emphasis in resolution 1000 (ES–I) is on *securing and supervising the cessation of hostilities*. Moreover, on 6 November 1956 the Secretary-General, in his second and final report on the plan for an emergency international United Nations Force, noted that 'the Assembly intends that the Force should be of a temporary nature, the length of its assignment being determined by the needs arising out of the present conflict'.[16] Noting further the terms of resolution 997 (ES–I) he added that 'the functions of the United Nations Force would be, when a cease-fire is being established, to enter Egyptian territory with the consent of the Egyptian Government, in order to help maintain quiet during and after the withdrawal of non-Egyptian troops, and to secure compliance with the other terms established in the resolution of 2 November 1956' (997 (ES–I)).[17]

79. In a cable delivered to Foreign Minister Fawzi on 9 or 10 November 1956, in reply to a request for clarification as to how long it was contemplated that the Force should stay in the demarcation line area, the Secretary-General stated: 'A definite reply is at present impossible but the emergency character of the Force links it to the immediate crises envisaged in resolution 2 November [997 (ES–I)] and its liquidation.' This point was confirmed in a further exchange of cables between the Secretary-General and Dr Fawzi on 14 November 1956.

80. The Foreign Minister of Egypt (Dr Fawzi) gave his understanding of the task of the Force in a statement to the General Assembly on 27 November 1956:

'Our clear understanding—and I am sure it is the clear understanding of the Assembly— is that this Force is in Egypt only in relation to the present attack against Egypt by the United Kingdom, France and Israel, and for the purposes directly connected with the incursion of the invading forces into Egyptian territory. The United Nations Emergency

---

[15] Ibid. para. 50.   [16] A/3302, para. 8.   [17] Ibid. para. 12.

Force is in Egypt, not as an occupation force, not as a replacement for the invaders, not to clear the Canal of obstructions, not to resolve any question or settle any problem, be it in relation to the Suez Canal, to Palestine or to any other matter; it is not there to infringe upon Egyptian sovereignty in any fashion or to any extent, but, on the contrary, to give expression to the determination of the United Nations to put an end to the aggression committed against Egypt and to the presence of the invading forces in Egyptian territory.'[18]

81. In letters dated 3 November 1956 addressed to the Secretary-General, the representatives of both France and the United Kingdom had proposed very broad functions for UNEF, stating on behalf of their Governments that military action could be stopped if the following conditions were met:

'(*a*) Both the Egyptian and Israel Governments agree to accept a United Nations Force to keep the peace.

'(*b*) The United Nations decides to constitute and maintain such a Force until an Arab–Israel peace settlement is reached and until satisfactory arrangements have been agreed in regard to the Suez Canal, both agreements to be guaranteed by the United Nations.

'(*c*) In the meantime, until the United Nations Force is constituted, both combatants agree to accept forthwith limited detachments of Anglo-French troops to be stationed between the combatants.'[19]

These broad functions for the Force were not acceptable to the General Assembly, however, as was pointed out in telegrams dated 4 November 1956 from Secretary-General Dag Hammarskjöld to the Minister for Foreign Affairs of France and the Secretary of State for Foreign Affairs of the United Kingdom.[20]

82. Finally, it is obvious that the task referred to in the 'good faith' *aide-mémoire* could only be the task of the Force as it had been defined in November 1956 when the understanding was concluded. The 'good faith' undertaking by the United Nations would preclude it from claiming that the Egyptian agreement was relevant or applicable to functions which the Force was given at a much later date. The stationing of the Force on the armistice demarcation line and at Sharm el Sheikh was only determined in pursuance of General Assembly resolution 1125 (XI) of 2 February 1957. The Secretary-General, in his reports relating to this decision, made it clear that the further consent of Egypt was essential with respect to these new functions.[21] Consequently, the understanding recorded in the 'good faith' *aide-mémoire* of 20 November 1956 could not have been, itself, a commitment with respect to functions only determined in February and March 1957. It is only these later tasks that the Force had been performing during the last ten years—tasks of serving as a buffer and deterring infiltrators which went considerably beyond those of securing and supervising the cessation of hostilities provided in the General Assembly resolutions and referred to in the 'good faith' *aide-mémoire*.

The stationing of UNEF on the armistice demarcation line and at Sharm el Sheikh

83. There remains to examine whether Egypt made further commitments with respect to the stationing of the Force on the armistice demarcation line and at Sharm el Sheikh. Israel, of course, sought to obtain such commitments, particularly with respect to the area around Sharm el Sheikh.

84. For example, in an *aide-mémoire* of 4 February 1957,[22] the Government of Israel sought clarification as to whether units of the United Nations Emergency Force would be stationed along the western shore of the Gulf of Aqaba in order to act as a restraint against hostile acts, and would remain so deployed until another effective means was agreed upon between the parties concerned for ensuring permanent freedom of navigation and the absence of belligerent acts in the Strait of Tiran and the Gulf of Aqaba. The Secretary-General pointed out that such 'clarification' would require 'Egyptian consent'. He stated:

---

[18] *GAOR*, 11th sess., 597th plen. mtg, para. 49.   [19] A/3268 and A/3269.
[20] A/3284, anns 2 and 4.   [21] A/3512, para. 22; A/3527, para. 5.   [22] A/3527, ann. I.

'The second of the points in the Israel *aide-mémoire* requests a "clarification" which, in view of the position of the General Assembly, could go beyond what was stated in the last report only after negotiation with Egypt. This fol'ows from the statements in the debate in the General Assembly, and the report on which it was based, which make it clear that the stationing of the Force at Sharm el Sheikh, under such terms as those mentioned in the question posed by Israel, would require Egyptian consent.'[23]

85. It is clear from the record that Egypt did not give its consent to Israel's proposition. The Secretary-General's report of 8 March 1957[24] recorded 'arrangements for the complete and unconditional withdrawal of Israel in accordance with the decision of the General Assembly'. There is no agreement on the part of Egypt to forgo its rights with respect to the granting or withdrawing of its consent to the continued stationing of the Force on its territory. On the contrary, at the 667th plenary meeting of the General Assembly on 4 March 1957, the Foreign Minister of Egypt stated:

'At our previous meeting I stated that the Assembly was unanimous in expecting full and honest implementation of its resolutions calling for immediate and unconditional withdrawal by Israel. I continue to submit to the Assembly that this position—which is the only position the Assembly can possibly take—remains intact and entire. Nothing said by anyone here or elsewhere could shake this fact or detract from its reality and its validity, nor could it affect the fullness and the lawfulness of Egypt's rights and those of the Arab people of the Gaza Strip.'[25]

86. The Foreign Minister of Israel, in her statement at the 666th meeting of the General Assembly, on 1 March 1957, asserted that an assurance had been given that any proposal for the withdrawal of UNEF from the Gulf of Aqaba area would come first to the Advisory Committee on UNEF (see paragraphs 95–98 below).

Question of the stationing of UNEF on both sides of the armistice demarcation line

87. Another point having significance with respect to the undertakings of Egypt is the question of the stationing of UNEF on both sides of the armistice demarcation line. The Secretary-General, in his report of 24 January 1957 to the General Assembly,[26] suggested that the Force should have units stationed also on the Israel side of the armistice demarcation line. In particular, he suggested that units of the Force should at least be stationed in the El Auja demilitarized zone[27] which had been occupied by the armed forces of Israel. He indicated that if El Auja were demilitarized in accordance with the Armistice Agreement and units of UNEF were stationed there, a condition of reciprocity would be the Egyptian assurance that Egyptian forces would not take up positions in the area in contravention of the Armistice Agreement.[28] However, Israel forces were never withdrawn from El Auja and UNEF was not accepted at any point on the Israel side of the line.

88. Following the Secretary-General's report, the General Assembly on 2 February 1957 adopted resolution 1125 (XI), in which it noted the report with appreciation and considered:

'. . . that, after full withdrawal of Israel from the Sharm el Sheikh and Gaza areas, the scrupulous maintenance of the Armistice Agreement requires the placing of the United Nations Emergency Force on the Egyptian–Israel armistice demarcation line and the implementation of other measures as proposed in the Secretary-General's report, with due regard to the considerations set out therein with a view to assist in achieving situations conducive to the maintenance of peaceful conditions in the area.'

[23] Ibid. para. 5.   [24] A/3568.   [25] *GAOR*, 11th sess., 667th plen. mtg, para. 240.   [26] A/3512.
[27] Article VIII of the Egyptian–Israel General Armistice Agreement provides that an area comprising the village of El Auja and vicinity, as defined in the article, shall be demilitarized and with both Egyptian and Israel armed forces being totally excluded. The article further provides that on the Egyptian side of the frontier, facing the El Auja area, no Egyptian defensive positions shall be closer to El Auja than El Qouseima and Abou Aoueigila.   [28] A/3512, paras 15–22.

89. On 11 February 1957, the Secretary-General stated in a report to the General Assembly that, in the light of the implication of Israel's question concerning the stationing of UNEF at Sharm el Sheikh (see paragraph 84 above), he 'considered it important . . . to learn whether Israel itself, in principle, consents to a stationing of UNEF units on its territory in implementation of the functions established for the Force in the basic decisions and noted in resolution 1125 (XI) where it was indicated that the Force should be placed "on the Egyptian–Israel armistice demarcation line" '.[29] No affirmative response was ever received from Israel. In fact, already on 7 November 1956 the Prime Minister of Israel, Mr Ben-Gurion, in a speech to the Knesset, stated, *inter alia*, 'On no account will Israel agree to the stationing of a foreign force, no matter how called, in her territory or in any of the territories occupied by her.' In a note to correspondents of 12 April 1957 a 'United Nations spokesman' stated:

'Final arrangements for the UNEF will have to wait for the response of the Government of Israel to the request by the General Assembly that the Force be deployed also on the Israeli side of the Armistice Demarcation Line.'

90. In a report dated 9 October 1957 to the twelfth session of the General Assembly,[30] the Secretary-General stated:

'Resolution 1125 (XI) calls for placing the Force "on the Egyptian–Israel armistice demarcation line", but no stationing of UNEF on the Israel side has occurred to date through lack of consent by Israel.'

91. In the light of Israel's persistent refusal to consent to the stationing and operation of UNEF on its side of the line in spite of General Assembly resolution 1125 (XI) of 2 February 1957 and the efforts of the Secretary-General, it is even less possible to consider that Egypt's 'good faith' declaration made in November 1956 could constitute a limitation of its rights with respect to the continued stationing and operation of UNEF on Egyptian territory in accordance with the resolution of 2 February 1957.

92. The representative of Israel stated at the 592nd meeting of the General Assembly, on 23 November 1956:

'If we were to accept one of the proposals made here—namely, that the Force should separate Egyptian and Israel troops for as long as Egypt thought it convenient and should then be withdrawn on Egypt's unilateral request—we would reach a reduction to absurdity. Egypt would then be in a position to build up, behind the screen of this Force, its full military preparations and, when it felt that those military preparations had reached their desired climax, to dismiss the United Nations Emergency Force and to stand again in close contact and proximity with the territory of Israel. This reduction to absurdity proves how impossible it is to accept in any matter affecting the composition or the functions of the Force the policies of the Egyptian Government as the sole or even the decisive criterion.'[31]

93. The answer to this problem which is to be found in resolution 1125 (XI) of 2 February 1957 is not in the form of a binding commitment by Egypt which the record shows was never given, but in the proposal that the Force should be stationed on both sides of the line. Israel in the exercise of its sovereign right did not give its consent to the stationing of UNEF on its territory and Egypt did not forgo its sovereign right to withdraw its consent at any time.

Role of the UNEF Advisory Committee

94. General Assembly resolution 1001 (ES–I) of 7 November 1956, by which the Assembly approved the guiding principles for the organization and functioning of UNEF, established an Advisory Committee on UNEF under the chairmanship of the Secretary-General. The Assembly decided that the Advisory Committee, in the performance of its duties, should be empowered to request, through the usual procedures, the convening of the General Assembly

---

[29] A/3527, para. 5.   [30] A/3694, para. 15.
[31] *GAOR*, 11th sess., 592nd plen. mtg, para. 131.

and to report to the Assembly whenever matters arose which, in its opinion, were of such urgency and importance as to require consideration by the General Assembly itself.

95. The memorandum of important points in the discussion between the representative of Israel and the Secretary-General on 25 February 1957 recorded the following question raised by the representative of Israel:

> 'In connexion with the duration of UNEF's deployment in the Sharm el Sheikh area, would the Secretary-General give notice to the General Assembly of the United Nations before UNEF would be withdrawn from the area, with or without Egyptian insistence, or before the Secretary-General would agree to its withdrawal?'[32]

96. The response of the Secretary-General was recorded as follows:

> 'On the question of notification to the General Assembly, the Secretary-General wanted to state his view at a later meeting. An indicated procedure would be for the Secretary-General to inform the Advisory Committee on the United Nations Emergency Force, which would determine whether the matter should be brought to the attention of the Assembly.'[33]

97. On 1 March 1957 the Foreign Minister of Israel stated at the 666th plenary meeting of the General Assembly:

> 'My Government has noted the assurance embodied in the Secretary-General's note of 26 February 1957 (*A*/3363, annex) that any proposal for the withdrawal of the United Nations Emergency Force from the Gulf of Aqaba area would first come to the Advisory Committee on the United Nations Emergency Force, which represents the General Assembly in the implementation of its resolution 997 (ES–I) of 2 November 1956. This procedure will give the General Assembly an opportunity to ensure that no precipitate changes are made which would have the effect of increasing the possibility of belligerent acts.'[34]

98. In fact, the 25 February 1957 memorandum does not go as far as the interpretation given by the Foreign Minister of Israel. In any event, however, it gives no indication of any commitment by Egypt, and so far as the Secretary-General is concerned it only indicates that a procedure would be for the Secretary-General to inform the Advisory Committee which would determine whether the matter should be brought to the attention of the General Assembly. This was also the procedure provided in General Assembly resolution 1001 (ES–I). It was, furthermore, the procedure followed by the Secretary-General on the withdrawal of UNEF.

OBSERVATIONS

99. A partial explanation of the misunderstanding about the withdrawal of UNEF is an evident failure to appreciate the essentially fragile nature of the basis for UNEF's operation throughout its existence. UNEF in functioning depended completely on the voluntary co-operation of the host Government. Its basis of existence was the willingness of Governments to provide contingents to serve under an international command and at a minimum of cost to the United Nations. It was a symbolic force, small in size, with only 3,400 men, of whom 1,800 were available to police a line of 295 miles at the time of its withdrawal. It was equipped with light weapons only. It had no mandate of any kind to open fire except in the last resort in self-defence. It had no formal mandate to exercise any authority in the area in which it was stationed. In recent years it experienced an increasingly uncertain basis of financial support, which in turn gave rise to strong annual pressures for reduction in its strength. Its remarkable success for more than a decade, despite these practical weaknesses, may have led to wrong conclusions about its nature, but it has also pointed the way to a unique means of contributing significantly to international peace-keeping.

---

[32] A/3563, ann. I, A, 2.   [33] Ibid. ann. I, B, 2.
[34] *GAOR*, 11th sess., 666th plen. mtg, para. 8.

ANNEX

Cable containing instructions for the withdrawal of UNEF sent by the Secretary-General to the Commander of UNEF on 18 May 1967, at 22.30 hours New York time

The following instructions are to be put in effect by you as of date and time of their receipt and shall remain operative until and unless new instructions are sent by me.

1. UNEF is being withdrawn because the consent of the Government of the United Arab Republic for its continued deployment on United Arab Republic territory and United Arab Republic-controlled territory has been rescinded.

2. Date of the commencement of the withdrawal of UNEF will be 19 May when the Secretary-General's response to the request for withdrawal will be received in Cairo by the Government of the United Arab Republic, when also the General Assembly will be informed of the action taken and the action will become public knowledge.

3. The withdrawal of UNEF is to be orderly and must be carried out with dignity befitting a Force which has contributed greatly to the maintenance of quiet and peace in the area of its deployment and has earned widespread admiration.

4. The Force does not cease to exist or to lose its status or any of its entitlements, privileges and immunities until all of its elements have departed from the area of its operation.

5. It will be a practical fact that must be reckoned with by the Commander that as of the date of the announcement of its withdrawal the Force will no longer be able to carry out its established functions as a buffer and as a deterrent to infiltration. Its duties, therefore, after 19 May and until all elements have been withdrawn, will be entirely nominal and concerned primarily with devising arrangements and implementation of arrangements for withdrawal and the morale of the personnel.

6. The Force, of course, will remain under the exclusive command of its United Nations Commander and is to take no orders from any other source, whether United Arab Republic or national.

7. The Commander, his headquarters staff and the contingent commanders shall take every reasonable precaution to ensure the continuance of good relations with the local authorities and the local population.

8. In this regard, it should be made entirely clear by the Commander to the officers and other ranks in the Force that there is no discredit of the Force in this withdrawal and no humiliation involved for the reason that the Force has operated very successfully and with, on the whole, co-operation from the Government on the territory of an independent sovereign State for over ten years, which is a very long time; and, moreover, the reasons for the termination of the operation are of an overriding political nature, having no relation whatsoever to the performance of the Force in the discharge of its duties.

9. The Commander and subordinate officers must do their utmost to avoid any resort to the use of arms and any clash with the forces of the United Arab Republic or with the local civilian population.

10. A small working team will be sent from Headquarters by the Secretary-General to assist in the arrangements for, and effectuation of, the withdrawal.

11. The Commander shall take all necessary steps to protect United Nations installations, properties and stores during the period of withdrawal.

12. If necessary, a small detail of personnel of the Force or preferably of United Nations security officers will be maintained as long as necessary for the protection of United Nations properties pending their ultimate disposition.

13. UNEF aircraft will continue flights as necessary in connexion with the withdrawal arrangements but observation flights will be discontinued immediately.

14. Elements of the Force now deployed along the line will be first removed from the line, the IF and ADL, including Sharm el Sheikh to their camps and progressively to central staging.

15. The pace of the withdrawal will of course depend upon the availability of transport by

air, sea and ground to Port Said. The priority in withdrawal should of course be personnel and their personal arms and equipment first, followed by contingent stores and equipment.

16. We must proceed on the assumption that UNEF will have full co-operation of United Arab Republic authorities on all aspects of evacuation, and to this end a request will be made by me to the United Arab Republic Government through their Mission here.

17. As early as possible the Commander of UNEF should prepare and transmit to the Secretary-General a plan and schedule for the evacuation of troops and their equipment.

Preparation of the draft of the sections of the annual report by the Secretary-General to the General Assembly should be undertaken and, to the extent possible, completed during the period of the withdrawal.

19. In the interests of the Force itself and the United Nations, every possible measure should be taken to ensure against public comments or comments likely to become public on the withdrawal, the reasons for it and reactions to it. [*A/6730/Add. 3, Report of the Secretary-General on the withdrawal of the Emergency Force, 26 June 1967,* mimeo.]

This document summarized events which had earlier been reported in A/6669, 18 May 1967. The Secretary-General had also noted that the reason for the demand for the withdrawal of UNEF

. . . had nothing to do with the conduct of the Force itself or the way in which it was carrying out the mandate entrusted to it by the General Assembly and accepted by the Government of the United Arab Republic when it gave its consent for the deployment of the Force within its jurisdiction. There can be no doubt, in fact, that the Force has discharged its responsibilities with remarkable effectiveness and great distinction. No United Nations peace-keeping operation can be envisaged as permanent or semi-permanent. Each one must come to an end at some time or another. [UNEF] has been active for ten and a half years and that is a very long time for any country to have foreign troops, even under an international banner, operating autonomously on its soil. On the other hand, it can be said that the timing of the withdrawal of the Force leaves much to be desired because of the prevailing tensions and dangers throughout the area. It also adds one more frontier on which there is a direct confrontation between the military forces of Israel and those of her Arab neighbours. [*S/7896, Secretary-General's Report to the Security Council on the situation in the Near East, 19 May 1967,* para. 10.]

It will be seen that in several of the key positions, including that of Sharm el Sheikh, UNEF had already been rendered ineffective before the request for UNEF's withdrawal was transmitted. That factor, together with the attitude of India and Yugoslavia, placed U Thant in an exceedingly difficult situation. The question of whether he could have temporized, and whether he should have referred the matter to the General Assembly, are dealt with in Sections 5 and 4 respectively (pp. 276 and 250). In this section, which is devoted to an examination of the relations between the UN and Egypt, we have thought it useful to make certain observations on the legal aspects of the 'consent' principle in relation to withdrawal. Paragraphs 52–74 of another document[35] are directly relevant. That Egypt's consent was necessary before UNEF could be stationed there is clear beyond doubt. The real legal question that arose in May 1967 was whether Egypt's acceptance of resolution 1000 (ES–I), and her agreement to the *aide-mémoire* of 20 November 1956 (A/3302), operated to limit this principle. It is clear from paragraph 72 of A/6730/Add. 3 that Hammarskjöld believed that these two acts by Egypt must mean that the 'consent' principle did

[35] A/6730/Add. 3.

not give Egypt the freedom to demand UNEF's withdrawal before its task was completed. Hammarskjöld explained the significance of the *aide-mémoire* in his Summary Study of the experience of UNEF:

The consequence of such a bilateral declaration is that, were either side to act unilaterally in refusing continued presence or deciding on withdrawal, and were the other side to find that such action was contrary to a good-faith interpretation of the purposes of the operation, an exchange of views would be called for towards harmonizing the positions. This does not imply any infringement of the sovereign right of the host Government, nor any restriction of the right of the United Nations to decide on the termination of its own operation whenever it might see fit to do so. But it does mean a mutual recognition of the fact that the operation, being based on collaboration between the host Government and the United Nations, should be carried on in forms natural to such collaboration, and especially so with regard to questions of presence and maintenance. [*A/3943*, para. 158.]

On 5 August 1957 Hammarskjöld committed his understanding to paper in the form of a personal *aide-mémoire*, which has never been published as a UN document.[36] It has only the status of a private paper, and cannot as such bind Egypt. None the less, it is of very high evidentiary value. U Thant has now asserted that Egypt never understood UNEF's position in this way, and never gave her agreement not to ask for UNEF's withdrawal before its tasks were completed. This writer believes that a reading of the document does not lead to this conclusion and that the evidence cited by U Thant[37] does not support this view. The citation in paragraph 74 merely goes to emphasize that UNEF could never legally have entered or operated in Egypt without Egypt's consent. It does not address itself to Egypt's right to demand withdrawal before UNEF's tasks were complete. The published *aide-mémoire* of 20 November 1956 would seem to have afforded a basis at least to have temporized, and to have sought discussions with President Nasser *before* the withdrawal of UNEF was announced.

5 August 1957

AIDE-MÉMOIRE

As the decision on the UNEF was taken under Chapter VI, it was obvious from the beginning that the resolution did in no way limit the sovereignty of the host state. This was clear both from the resolution of the General Assembly and from the Second and final Report on the Emergency Force. Thus, neither the General Assembly nor the Secretary-General, acting for the General Assembly, created any right for Egypt, or gave any right to Egypt, in accepting consent as a condition for the presence and functioning of the UNEF on Egyptian territory. Egypt had the right, and the only problem was whether that right in this context should and could in some way be limited.

My starting point in the consideration of this last mentioned problem—the limitation of Egypt's sovereign right in the interest of political balance and stability in the UNEF operation—was the fact that Egypt had spontaneously endorsed the General Assembly resolution of 5 November and by endorsing that resolution had consented to the presence of the UNEF for certain tasks. They could thus not ask the UNEF to withdraw before the completion of the

---

[36] The text of the *aide-mémoire* was first published in *International Legal Materials: Current Documents*, May–June 1967, pp. 595–602.

[37] S/6930/Add. 3, para. 74.

tasks without running up against their own acceptance of the resolution on the Force and its tasks.

The question arose in relation to Egypt first in a cable received 9 November from Burns, covering an interview the same day with Fawzi. In that interview Egypt had requested clarification of the question how long it was contemplated that the Force would stay in the Demarcation Line area. To this I replied the same day: 'A definite reply is at present impossible, but the emergency character of the Force links it to the immediate crisis envisaged in the resolution of 2 November and its liquidation. In case of different views as to when the crisis does not any longer warrant the presence of the troops, the matter will have to be negotiated with the parties.' In a further cable to Burns the same day I said, however, also that 'as the United Nations Force would come with Egypt's consent, they cannot stay nor operate unless Egypt continues to consent'.

On 10 November Ambassador Loutfi, under instruction, asked me 'whether it was recognized that an agreement is necessary for their (UNEF's) remaining in the Canal area' once their task in the area had been completed. I replied that it was my view that such an agreement would then be necessary.

On 11 November Ambassador Loutfi saw me again. He then said that it must be agreed that when the Egyptian consent is no more valid, the UN Force should withdraw. To this I replied that I did not find that a withdrawal of consent could be made before the tasks which had justified the entry, had been completed; if, as might happen, different views on the degree of completion of the tasks prescribed proved to exist, the matter should be negotiated.

The view expressed by Loutfi was later embodied in an Aide Mémoire, dated the same day, where it was said: 'The Egyptian Government takes note of the following: A. It being agreed that consent of Egypt is indispensable for entry and presence of the UN Forces in any part of its territory. If such consent no longer persists, these forces shall withdraw.'

I replied to this in a memo dated 12 November in which I said: 'I have received your Aide Mémoire setting out the understanding on the basis of which the Egyptian Government accepts my announcing today that agreement on the arrival in Egypt of the United Nations Force has been reached. I wish to put on record my interpretation of two of these points. Regarding the point quoted above in the Egyptian Aide Mémoire, I then continued: 'I want to put on record that the conditions which motivate the consent to entry and presence, are the very conditions to which the tasks established for the Force in the General Assembly Resolution, 4 November, are directed. Therefore, I assume it to be recognized that as long as the task, thus prescribed, is not completed, the reasons for the consent of the Government remain valid, and that a withdrawal of this consent before completion of the task would run counter to the acceptance by Egypt of the decision of the General Assembly. I read the statement quoted in the light of these considerations. If a difference should develop, whether or not the reasons for the arrangements are still valid, the matter should be brought up for negotiation with the United Nations'.

This explanation of mine was sent to the Egyptian Mission after my telephone conversation in the morning of the 12th with Dr Fawzi where we agreed on publication of our agreement on the entry of the UNEF into Egypt. In view of the previous exchanges, I had no reason to believe that my statement would introduce any new difficulty. I also counted on the fact that Egypt probably by then was so committed as to be rather anxious not to reopen the discussion. However, I recognized to myself that there was an element of gambling involved which I felt I simply had to take in view of the danger that further delays might cause Egypt to change its mind, accept volunteers and throw our approaches overboard.

However, the next morning, 13 November, I received a message from Dr Fawzi to the effect that the Government of Egypt could not subscribe to my interpretation of the question of consent and withdrawal, as set out on 12 November, and therefore, in the light of my communication of that date, 'felt impelled to consider that the announced agreements should remain inoperative until all misunderstandings were cleared up'. The Government reiterated in this context its view that if its consent no longer persisted, the UNEF should withdraw.

I replied to this communication—which caused a further delay of the transportation of troops to Egypt by at least 24 hours—in a cable sent immediately on receipt of the communication. In drafting my reply I had a feeling that it now was a must to get the troops in and that I would be in a position to find a formula, saving the face of Egypt while protecting the UN stand, once I could discuss the matter personally with President Nasser.

In the official reply 13 November I said that my previous statement had put forward my personal opinion that 'the reasons' for consent remained valid as long as the task was not completed. I also said that for that reason a withdrawal of consent leading to the withdrawal of the Force before the task was completed (as previously stated) in my view, 'although within the rights of the Egyptian Government would go against its acceptance of the basic resolution of the General Assembly'. I continued by saying that my reference to negotiation was intended to indicate only that the question of withdrawal should be a matter of discussion to the extent that different views were held as to whether the task of the General Assembly was fulfilled or not. I referred in this respect to my stand as explained already in my message of 9 November, as quoted above.

I commented upon the official reply in a special personal message to Fawzi, sent at the same time, where I said that we 'both had to reserve our freedom of action, but that, all the same, we could go ahead, hoping that a controversial situation would not arise'. 'If arrangements would break down on this issue' (withdrawal only on completion of the tasks), 'I could not avoid going to the General Assembly' (with the conflict which had developed between us on this question of principle) 'putting it to their judgment to decide what could or could not be accepted as an understanding. This situation would be a most embarrasing one for all but I would fear the political repercussions, as obviously very few would find it reasonable that recognition of your freedom of action should mean that you, after having permitted the Force to come, might ask it to withdraw at a time when the very reasons which had previously prompted you to accept were still obviously valid'. I ended by saying that I trusted that Fawzi on the basis of this personal message could help me by 'putting the stand I had to take on my own rights, in the right perspective'. The letter to Fawzi thus made it clear that if the Government did not accept my stand on withdrawal as a precondition for further steps, the matter would be raised in the Assembly.

On the basis of these two final communications from me, Egypt gave green lights for the arrival of the troops, thus, in fact, accepting my stand and letting it supersede their own communication 13 November.

In my effort to follow up the situation, which prevailed after the exchange in which different stands had been maintained by Egypt and by me, I was guided by the consideration that Egypt constitutionally had an undisputed right to request the withdrawal of the troops, even if initial consent had been given, but that, on the other hand, it should be possible on the basis of my own stand as finally tacitly accepted, to force them into an agreement in which they limited their freedom of action as to withdrawal by making a request for withdrawal dependent upon the completion of the task—a question which, in the UN, obviously would have to be submitted to interpretation by the General Assembly.

The most desirable thing, of course, would have been to tie Egypt by an agreement in which they declared, that withdrawal should take place only if so decided by the General Assembly. Put in this naked form, however, the problem could never have been settled. I felt that the same was true of an agreement to the effect that withdrawal should take place upon 'agreement on withdrawal' between the UN and the Egyptian Government. However, I found it worthwhile to try a line, very close to the second one, according to which Egypt would declare to the United Nations that it would exert all its sovereign rights with regard to the troops on the basis of a good faith interpretation of the tasks of the Force. The United Nations should make a reciprocal commitment to maintain the Force as long as the task was not completed. If such a dual statement was introduced in an agreement between the parties, it would be obvious that the procedure in case of a request from Egypt for the withdrawal of UNEF would be as follows. The matter would at once be brought before the General Assembly. If the General Assembly found that the task was completed, everything would be all right. If they found that the task was not completed and Egypt, all the same, maintained its stand and enforced the withdrawal, Egypt would break the agreement with the United Nations. Of course Egypt's freedom of action could under no circumstances be limited but by some kind of agreement. The device I used meant only that instead of limiting their rights by a basic understanding requesting an agreement *directly concerning withdrawal*, we created an obligation to reach agreement on the fact that the tasks were completed, and, thus, *the conditions for a withdrawal established*.

I elaborated a draft text for an agreement along the lines I had in mind during the night between 15 and 16 November in Capodichino. I showed the text to Fawzi at our first talk on 16 November and I discussed practically only this issue with Nasser for 7 hours in the evening and night of 17 November. Nasser, in this final discussion, where the text I had proposed was approved with some amendments, showed that he very fully understood that, by limiting their freedom of action in the way I proposed, they would take a very serious step, as it would mean that the question of the extent of the task would become decisive for the relations between Egypt and the United Nations and would determine Egypt's political freedom of action. He felt, not without justification, that the definition given of the task in the UN texts was very loose and that, tying the freedom of action of Egypt to the concept of the task— which had to be interpreted also by the General Assembly—and doing so in a written agreement, meant that he accepted a far-reaching and unpredictable restriction. To shoot the text through in spite of Nasser's strong wish to avoid this, and his strong suspicion of the legal construction—especially of the possible consequences of differences of views regarding the task—I felt obliged, in the course of the discussion, to threaten three times, that unless an agreement of this type was made, I would have to propose the immediate withdrawal of the troops. If any proof would be necessary for how the text of the agreement was judged by President Nasser, this last mentioned fact tells the story.

It is obvious that, with a text of the content mentioned approved by Egypt, the whole previous exchange of views was superseded by a formal and explicit recognition by Egypt of the stand I had taken all through, in particular on 9 and 12 November. The previous exchange of cables cannot any longer have any interpretative value as only the text of the agreement was put before the General Assembly and approved by it with the concurrence of Egypt and as its text was self-contained and conclusive. All further discussion, therefore, has to start from the text of the agreement, which is to be found in Document A/3375. The interpretation of the text must be the one set out above.

This leads on to a discussion of what UNEF's tasks were. This question has been analysed by U Thant in paragraphs 75–82 of S/6730/Add. 3. It is the Secretary-General's view that the tasks of securing and supervising the cessation of hostilities are the tasks assigned to UNEF under Resolution 1000 (ES–I). As it is the acceptance of Resolution 1000 (ES–I) which is mentioned in the *aide-mémoire* of 20 November 1956, it is to these functions that the 'good faith' clause applies. U Thant contends that UNEF was given the further task of supervising the armistice only in Resolution 1125 (XI), on 2 February 1957; thus, says the Secretary-General (in para. 82), 'the understanding recorded in the "good faith" *aide-mémoire* of 20 November 1956 could not have been, itself, a commitment with respect to functions only determined in February and March 1957'.

This is a line of reasoning with which this Editor finds it hard to concur. In the first place, good faith is a general requirement of international law: Egypt is not free to act in bad faith in respect of commitments which have not been formalized in any *aide-mémoire*. But—and this is more central to our argument —most international lawyers have always taken the view that Resolution 1000

(ES–I) stipulated all UNEF's functions, including its contribution to the observance of the armistice. This is so even though only 'securing and supervising the cessation of hostilities' are mentioned explicitly in Resolution 1000 (ES–I), because that resolution refers back to the terms of Resolution 997 (ES–I).

Thus Resolution 1000 (ES–I) provided that a UN Command was established 'for an emergency international Force to secure and supervise the cessation of hostilities in accordance with all the terms of General Assembly resolution 997 (ES–I) of 2 November 1956. . . .' and Resolution 997 (ES–I) in turn contained several clauses, para. 2 of which urged 'the parties to the armistice agreements promptly to withdraw all forces behind the armistice lines, to desist from raids across the armistice lines into neighbouring territory, and to observe scrupulously the provisions of the armistice agreements'.

Any normal reading of these two documents therefore, gives UNEF a role in relation to the Armistice Agreement from November 1956. The resolution of 2 February 1957 represented an agreement on *where UNEF should be placed* in order to fulfil this task. This Editor therefore believes that the *aide-mémoire* of 20 November 1956 governed this aspect of UNEF's role, as well as its tasks relating to the supervising of the cessation of hostilities. Indeed, by the time the Assembly was presented with the *aide-mémoire* on 20 November 1956, hostilities were virtually at an end: if the agreement was to have meaning, it must have covered the continuing functions of securing the withdrawal of foreign troops and assisting in the scrupulous observation of the Armistice Agreements. One may go even further and note that Resolution 997 (to which the enabling Resolution 1000 referred) mentioned also that steps should be taken, once a cease-fire had occurred, 'to re-open the Suez Canal and restore secure freedom of navigation'.

It is therefore possible to agree with U Thant that (1) Israel bears some measure of blame in not allowing UNEF to be stationed on her own territory, (2) that Israel's withdrawal was not legally conditional upon the UN manning Sharm el Sheikh (no matter how much the Israelis viewed this as a *quid pro quo*), without agreeing further that Egypt was legally completely unfettered in demanding UNEF's withdrawal. There are strong grounds for arguing that Egypt voluntarily tempered reliance on 'sovereign consent' by acknowledging that good faith would be relevant if ever she wished UNEF to withdraw before its tasks were completed. Its tasks were not yet completed, and in May 1967 it would seem to have been legally appropriate to call the good faith of Egypt in question. All of this is not to deny the very real political factors which militated against engaging in an argument with Egypt: it is merely to point out that the legal requirements did not necessarily lead in the very same direction.

(b) The Question of Composition

So far as the composition is concerned, the Secretary-General has insisted that it is his right, and not that of the host state, to choose the nationalities to participate in a UN Force. At the same time the formula has been evolved whereby this right is exercised 'in consultation' with the host government, and any strong objections to a particular nationality will in fact be listened to. Thus the Secretary-General later said:

> The choice of contingents for the Force, while subject to the decision of the United Nations alone, is nevertheless of major concern also to the country in which the Force operates. Thus, the United Nations must give most serious consideration to the views of the host government on such matters without, however, surrendering its right to take a serious difference, should one develop, to the political level for resolution. [*A/3943*, *Summary Study*, para. 16.]

Egypt in fact raised objections to three Commonwealth states which volunteered units for UNEF. The offers of New Zealand and Pakistan were in the event declined.[38] In the case of Canada a compromise was reached—the contingent which she had offered was 'kept in reserve', though she was to provide logistic support and headquarters staff. Egypt's doubts about the Canadian contingents arose not from Canada's position on the Suez Canal dispute—as the originator of the idea of UNEF, her credentials were impeccable—but rather because Canadians might easily be mistaken by the Egyptian populace for Britons.

In 1967 however, after President Nasser had demanded UNEF's withdrawal, real problems did arise over the Canadian contingent, because Lester Pearson had both expressed great opposition to the immediate withdrawal of UNEF at Nasser's request, and his disapproval of the ensuing closure of the Straits of Tiran. It had been agreed that, the withdrawal of UNEF being accepted in principle, the withdrawal would take place in an orderly manner. However, the UAR demanded the immediate withdrawal of the Canadian contingent. The tragic irony was that the Canadians, having been required to leave in this hasty manner, were safe by the outbreak of war on 5 June. The Indian contingent—whose government had expressed support for Nasser—were still at their withdrawal locations, and suffered heavy loss of life.

67. On the morning of 27 May 1967 the Secretary-General received the following communication from the Minister for Foreign Affairs of the United Arab Republic:

> 'Sir,
>
> 'I have the honour to bring to your attention a serious and grave situation resulting from the regrettable attitude of the Government of Canada, in connexion with the United Nations forces, to the withdrawal of which you have agreed upon the request of the United Arab Republic Government. From the beginning the Canadian Government has persistently resorted to procrastination and delay in the departure of these forces. We noted from the outset that the Canadian Government took an unfriendly position towards my Government.
>
> 'Furthermore, the Government of Canada took certain military measures, on which we have received definite information that some Canadian destroyers have already sailed towards the Mediterranean, an act which enflamed the public opinion in my country, to an extent that I fear that it already reached the point of hatred against Canada.
>
> 'In view of these serious acts and in the light of the present situation in the Middle East, and desirous to prevent any probable reaction from the people of the United Arab Republic against the Canadian forces in UNEF, which may have undesirable reflection on the United Nations forces as a whole. I urge you to order the complete withdrawal and de-

---

[38] See L. Goodrich and G. Rosner, 'The United Nations Emergency Force', 11 *Int. Org.* (1957), p. 424.

parture of the Canadian forces immediately, and not later than forty-eight hours from the time my cable reaches you.

'I hasten to inform you that our forces are ready to provide all the necessary facilities for the transportation of the Canadian forces, to the nearest possible place, namely Cyprus.

'Please, Sir, accept the assurances of my highest considerations.

Mahmoud RIAD'

68. On the same day, after consultation with the Permanent Representative of Canada, the Secretary-General sent the following reply to Mr Mahmoud Riad, Minister for Foreign Affairs of the United Arab Republic:

'Excellency,

'I have the honour to acknowledge receipt of your cable of 27 May 1967 in which you urge me to order the complete withdrawal and departure of the Canadian contingent in UNEF immediately and not later than forty-eight hours from the time of the receipt of your cable. As you know, the Commander of UNEF and United Nations Headquarters have been working on plans for the expeditious evacuation of UNEF, and these plans, of course, included the speedy withdrawal of the Canadian contingent. I deeply regret the circumstances which have led to the request for the immediate withdrawal of the Canadian contingent as stated in your cable. To avoid any further aggravation of the situation, I have immediately instructed the Commander of UNEF to accelerate the evacuation of the Canadian contingent. I am sure you will understand that, while the Canadian Government and the Commander of UNEF will co-operate in implementing this evacuation as quickly as possible, it cannot be absolutely guaranteed that it will be fully completed within forty-eight hours of the receipt of your cable, although all concerned are agreed that the Canadian contingent shall be evacuated with the minimum delay possible. I note with appreciation your offer to provide transportation facilities if necessary to take the Canadian contingent to Cyprus. I do not believe, however, that Cyprus would be an appropriate destination for the Canadian contingent, and we are therefore arranging to evacuate it elsewhere. May I request you, Excellency, to take all possible measures to ensure that, for the very short period of time in which the Canadian contingent of UNEF remains on United Arab Republic territory, their status as members of UNEF will be fully respected and any unnecessary friction or unpleasantness avoided.

'Accept, Excellency, the assurances of my highest consideration.

U THANT'

69. The Secretary-General, also on 27 May, addressed the following note to the Permanent Representative of the United Arab Republic:

'The Secretary-General of the United Nations presents his compliments to the Permanent Representative of the United Arab Republic to the United Nations and has the honour to refer to the cable of 27 May 1967 addressed to the Secretary-General by the Foreign Minister of the United Arab Republic urging that an order be issued for the immediate and complete withdrawal of the Canadian contingent in UNEF. The Secretary-General in his cabled reply of the same date informed the Foreign Minister that the necessary instructions would be given.

'Reference is made to the statement in the message from the Foreign Minister to the effect that "From the beginning the Canadian Government has persistently resorted to procrastination and delay in the departure of these Forces". For the sake of clarification and accuracy it may be pointed out that, as indicated in the Secretary-General's reply, plans for the evacuation of the Canadian contingent were a part of the over-all plan and schedule for withdrawal of the Force formulated by the Commander of UNEF and United Nations Headquarters and that part of the schedule affecting Canadian troops had been accepted by the Canadian authorities and was being implemented without delay.

'However, in view of the warning in the communication from the Foreign Minister about a possible hostile reaction by the people of the United Arab Republic against the continued presence of Canadian troops in their territory, it was decided to abandon the original evacuation plan for the Canadian troops and to arrange for their immediate departure.

'The Secretary-General takes this opportunity to renew to the Permanent Representative of the United Arab Republic the assurances of his highest consideration.'

70. On 27 May, at 21.45 hours local time, Brigadier Eiz-el-din Mokhtar of the Armed Forces Headquarters in Cairo handed the following letter to the UNEF Commander:

'Major General Rikhye,
'Owing to the biased attitude of the Canadian Government towards Israel, the general feeling among the masses of the people and the Armed Forces became mobilized against Canadian policy, and being aware for the safety of the Canadian troops and for the reputation of the United Nations emergency forces, which have done their best in carrying out their task, we demand the immediate withdrawal of the Canadian troops from the United Arab Republic territory within 48 hours, and we are ready to give all facilities if required for their transport by air or any other means.

'With kind regards to yourself, I am,
'Yours respectfully,
(Mohamed Fawzy)
FARIK AWAL: Chief of General Staff
UAR Armed Forces.'

71. On 27 May, the Secretary-General addressed the following message to the Prime Minister of Canada through the Permanent Representative of Canada.

'The Secretary-General of the United Nations presents his compliments to the Permanent Representative of Canada to the United Nations and has the honour to request him to transmit the following message to the Prime Minister of Canada:
"In view of circumstances which have developed in relation to the Canadian contingent of UNEF, the possibility of accelerating the withdrawal of the Canadian contingent from the area was discussed with the Permanent Representative of Canada on 26 May 1967. On the morning of 27 May I received a message from Mr Mahmoud Riad, the Minister of Foreign Affairs of the United Arab Republic, on this same subject, the substance of which has already been communicated to you by the Permanent Representative of Canada. In the light of these developments and after consultations with the Permanent Representative of Canada, I have now given instructions to the Commander of UNEF that the Canadian contingent of UNEF should be evacuated from United Arab Republic territory as quickly as possible. I therefore request the Government of Canada to undertake urgently the necessary transportation arrangements to carry out this evacuation. I have made it clear in my reply to the message of the Minister of Foreign Affairs of the United Arab Republic that, while all possible efforts will be made to evacuate the Canadian contingent as soon as possible, it cannot be absolutely guaranteed that the evacuation can be completed within forty-eight hours. I have also asked him to take all possible measures to ensure that, for the short period of time in which the Canadian contingent of UNEF remain on United Arab Republic territory, their status as members of UNEF will be fully respected and any unnecessary friction and unpleasantness avoided."

'The Secretary-General takes this opportunity to renew to the Permanent Representative of Canada the assurances of his highest consideration.'

72. On 29 May the Secretary-General received the following reply from the Permanent Representative of Canada:

'The Permanent Representative of Canada to the United Nations presents his compliments to the Secretary-General of the United Nations and has the honour to refer to the Secretary-General's message of 27 May 1967 to the Prime Minister requesting that the Government of Canada undertake urgently the necessary transportation arrangements to evacuate the Canadian contingent from United Arab Republic territory as quickly as possible. The Secretary-General explained that this request stemmed both from the discussions initiated by the Permanent Representative of Canada on 26 May concerning the possibility of accelerating withdrawal of the Canadian contingent and the request of the Foreign Minister of the United Arab Republic of 27 May, the substance of which was communicated to the Permanent Representative of Canda.

'The Permanent Representative has been instructed to say that the Canadian Government has acted on the Secretary-General's request to provide transportation for the immediate withdrawal of the Canadian contingent. The Canadian Government is ready to commence the withdrawal as soon as the Secretary-General has concluded the necessary arrangements with the Government of the United Arab Republic for withdrawal operations.

'The Permanent Representative of Canada is also instructed to record with the Secretary-General that the Canadian Government does not accept the reasons advanced by the United Arab Republic authorities in justification of the request that the Secretary-General order immediate withdrawal of the Canadian contingent. The reasons advanced are without foundation in fact and are based on a regrettable misunderstanding by the United Arab Republic of Canadian policy. For example, timing of withdrawal of the Canadian contingent was part of the evacuation plans developed by the United Nations; as the Secretary-General has indicated in his note, the Canadian Government had already, on 26 May, questioned the timetable in these plans and had requested that the withdrawal of the Canadian contingent be expedited.

'While it is acknowledged that some of the considerations advanced by the United Arab Republic Government in support of their request for the withdrawal of the Canadian contingent are beyond the competence of the United Nations, the Canadian Government assumes that nothing which is or may have been said in the communications with the United Arab Republic authorities in this connexion could be construed as indicating that these reasons have been accepted by the Secretary-General.'

73. The Secretary-General replied to the Canadian note of 29 May on the same day as follows:

'The Secretary-General of the United Nations presents his compliments to the Permanent Representative of Canada to the United Nations and has the honour to acknowledge receipt of the Permanent Representative's message of 29 May 1967 concerning the withdrawal of the Canadian contingent of UNEF. The Secretary-General notes with appreciation that the Canadian Government has acted upon his request to provide transportation for the immediate withdrawal of the Canadian contingent.

'The Secretary-General wishes to emphasize what has been stated to the Permanent Representative orally by Dr Bunche, that the sole basis for his decision to accelerate the evacuation of the Canadian contingent of UNEF was the fear expressed by the Foreign Minister of the United Arab Republic of possible hostile reactions on the part of the population of his country to the continued presence of Canadian troops and the Secretary-General's unwillingness to expose the Canadian troops to this risk. The Permanent Representative of Canada has also already been informed of the position of the United Nations as conveyed to the authorities of the United Arab Republic concerning the over-all plan for the evacuation of UNEF, of which the evacuation of the Canadian contingent was a part. It has been pointed out to the authorities of the United Arab Republic that the part of the original United Nations plan affecting the Canadian contingent had been accepted by the Canadian authorities and was being implemented without delay, and that the present plan for the immediate evacuation of the Canadian contingent was decided upon only because of the warning from the Foreign Minister of the United Arab Republic mentioned above.

'The Secretary-General takes this opportunity to renew to the Permanent Representative of Canada the assurances of his highest consideration.'

74. The authorities of the United Arab Republic agreed to the use of El Arish airfield for the

evacuation of the Canadians. The Commander ordered immediate concentration of all Canadians in Camp Rafah. He also replaced the Canadian guards at El Arish airfield and Camp Marina, El Arish, with Yugoslav guards and the Canadian guard unit at Camp Rafah with two companies of infantry from the Brazilian battalion.

75. The Canadian contingent was evacuated by twenty-one Royal Canadian Air Force C–130 aircraft flights on 29 and 30 May. The Canadian Air Transport Unit (115 ATU), which continued to provide support to UNEF operations till the last hour, departed on 31 May from Gaza at 06.45 local time for Beirut on their final UNEF flight, completing the Canadian contingent's evacuation from the area.

76. With the early withdrawal of the Canadian contingent, UNEF was left without its logistics and air support. In accordance with the withdrawal plans described above, it had been arranged that Canadian service troops would be amongst the last to leave the area. It was intended that the Canadian contingent would complete stock-taking and packing and would prepare UNEF stores, vehicles, and equipment for removal or disposal before their departure from the area. They would in turn transfer the depots in Camp Rafah to the Chief Administrative Officer of UNEF and a group of international staff and Field Service personnel who would then be responsible for the orderly disposal of United Nations equipment and *matériel*. As all other contingents were also to withdraw in the next few days, the Chief Administrative Officer and his group assumed all responsibilities from the departing Canadian service troops. On an *ad hoc* basis personnel were found to take charge of the ordnance and supply depots, medical stores, the transport company, workshops, and engineering equipment and stores. In addition, personnel had to be found to continue to run camp installations such as the power house, water plant, fire brigade, petrol, oil and lubricant installations.

77. The departure of the Canadian contingent and the consequent unemployment of a large number of their local civilian staff resulted in the looting of billets, messes and barracks at Camp Rafah. This was firmly dealt with by Brazilian troops who brought the situation completely under control within two days. Furthermore, at UNEF's request, additional security outside the camp perimeter was provided by the authorities of the United Arab Republic. The departure of the Canadians had also caused an interruption in all work and duties in the camp, resulting in a serious hygiene and sanitary situation. This too was dealt with promptly.
[*A/6672, Report of the Secretary-General on UNEF, 12 July 1967*, mimeo.]

Although the Secretary-General clearly states that the sole basis for his decision to accelerate the evacuation of the Canadian contingent was his unwillingness to put the Canadians at risk in a hostile local population, it is perhaps unfortunate that the opportunity was not used clearly to state to Egypt that the Canadian contingent were serving the UN, and were subject to the orders of only the UN and not of the Canadian government.

(c) Status of Forces Agreement

Once UNEF was established and operational on Egyptian territory, it was obviously desirable that its status as an international Force should be worked out in detail and formalized. The resultant agreement between Egypt and the UN was the first UN Status of Forces Agreement; and it provides a pattern which has been followed, with variations to meet differing circumstances, in the Congo and Cyprus.

1. The General Assembly by resolution 1000 (ES–I) of 5 November 1956 established the United Nations Emergency Force. By resolution 1001 (ES–I) of 7 November 1956, the Assembly approved the guiding principles for the organization and functioning of the Force

as set forth in the second and final report of the Secretary-General on the plan for an emergency international United Nations Force (A/3302) and, *inter alia*, authorized the Secretary-General to take all administrative and executive actions which might be essential to the effective functioning of the Force.

2. In accordance with this authority, the Secretary-General, in consultation with the Advisory Committee established under General Assembly resolution 1001 (ES–I), has negotiated and concluded arrangements with the Government of Egypt concerning the status of the United Nations Emergency Force in Egypt.

3. On 8 February 1957, an exchange of letters constituting an agreement was signed by the Secretary-General on behalf of the United Nations and by the Minister for Foreign Affairs of Egypt on behalf of Egypt. This agreement is submitted to the General Assembly for its approval as an annex to the present report.

EXCHANGE OF LETTERS CONSTITUTING AN AGREEMENT BETWEEN THE UNITED NATIONS AND THE GOVERNMENT OF EGYPT CONCERNING THE STATUS OF THE UNITED NATIONS EMERGENCY FORCE IN EGYPT, WITH A SUMMARY OF THE ARRANGEMENTS

I

Summary of the arrangements concerning the status of the United Nations Emergency Force in Egypt contained in a letter dated 8 February 1957 from the Secretary-General, addressed to the Minister for Foreign Affairs of Egypt

	Paragraphs
Definitions	1–5
Respect for local law and conduct befitting international status	6
Entry and exit: Identification	7–9
Jurisdiction	10
Criminal jurisdiction	11
Civil jurisdiction	12
Notification: certification	13
Military police: arrest: transfer of custody and mutual assistance	14–18
Premises of the Force	19
United Nations flag	20
Uniform: Vehicle, vessel and aircraft markings and registration: Operating permits	21
Arms	22
Privileges and immunities of the Force	23
Privileges and immunities of officials and members of the Force	24–25
Members of the Force: taxation, customs and fiscal regulations	26–28
Communications and postal services	29–31
Freedom of movement	32
Use of roads, waterways, port facilities, airfields and railways	33
Water, electricity and other public utilities	34
Egyptian currency	35
Provisions, supplies and services	36
Locally recruited personnel	37
Settlement of disputes or claims	38–40
Liaison	41
Deceased members: disposition of personal property	42
Supplemental arrangements	43
Effective date and duration	44

II

Letter dated 8 February 1957 from the Secretary-General, addressed to the Minister for Foreign Affairs of Egypt

I have the honour to refer to the United Nations Emergency Force, an organ of the General Assembly of the United Nations established in accordance with Article 22 of the Charter. I have also the honour to refer to Article 105 of the Charter of the United Nations which provides that the Organization shall enjoy in the territory of its Members such privileges and immunities as are necessary for the fulfilment of its purposes, to the Convention on the Privileges and Immunities of the United Nations to which Egypt acceded on 17 September 1948, and to the resolutions of the General Assembly providing for the United Nations Emergency Force. Having in view the provisions of the Convention on the Privileges and Immunities of the United Nations, I wish to propose that the United Nations and Egypt should make the following *ad hoc* arrangements defining certain of the conditions necessary for the effective discharge of the functions of the United Nations Emergency Force while it remains in Egypt.

Definitions

1. The 'United Nations Emergency Force' (hereinafter referred to as 'the Force') consists of the United Nations Command established by General Assembly resolution 1000 (ES–I) of 5 November 1956 and all military personnel placed under the United Nations Command by a State Member of the United Nations. For the purpose of these arrangements the term 'member of the Force' refers to any person, other than a person resident in Egypt, belonging to the military service of a State serving under the Commander of the United Nations Emergency Force either on the United Nations Command (Headquarters Staff) or with a national contingent; to any civilian placed under the Commander by the State to which such civilian belongs.

2. The 'Commander' includes the Commander of the United Nations Emergency Force and other authorities of the Force designated by him. 'Egyptian authorities' include all national and local, civil and military authorities called upon to perform functions relating to the Force under the provisions of these arrangements, without prejudice to the ultimate responsibility of the Government of Egypt.

3. 'Egyptian citizen' includes a person of Egyptian citizenship and a person resident or present in the territory of Egypt other than one associated with the Force.

4. 'Participating State' means a Member of the United Nations that contributes military personnel to the Force.

5. 'Area of operations' includes areas where the Force is deployed in the performance of its functions as defined in paragraph 12 of the second and final report of the Secretary-General to the General Assembly (A/3302), concurred in by the General Assembly in paragraph 2 of resolution 1001 (ES–I); military installations or other premises referred to in paragraph 19 of these arrangements; and lines of communication and supply utilized by the Force pursuant to paragraphs 32 and 33 of these arrangements.

Respect for local law and conduct befitting international status

6. Members of the Force and United Nations officials serving with the Force shall respect the laws and regulations of Egypt and shall refrain from any activity of a political character in Egypt and from any action incompatible with the international nature of their duties or inconsistent with the spirit of the present arrangements. The Commander shall take all appropriate measures to ensure the observance of these obligations.

Entry and exit: Identification

7. Members of the Force shall be exempt from passport and visa regulations and immigration inspection and restrictions on entering or departing from Egyptian territory. They shall also be exempt from any regulations governing the residence of aliens in Egypt, including

registration, but shall not be considered as acquiring any right to permanent residence or domicile in the territory of Egypt. For the purpose of such entry or departure members of the Force will be required to have only (*a*) an individual or collective movement order issued by the Commander or an appropriate authority of the Participating State; and (*b*) a personal identity card issued by the Commander under the authority of the Secretary-General, except in the case of first entry, when the personal military identity card issued by the appropriate authorities of the Participating State will be accepted in lieu of the said Force identity card.

8. Members of the Force may be required to present, but not to surrender, their identity cards upon demand of an appropriate Egyptian authority. Except as provided in paragraph 7 of these arrangements the identity card will be the only document required for a member of the Force. If, however, it does not show the full name, date of birth, rank and number (if any), service and photograph of a member of the Force, such member may be required to present likewise the personal military identity card or similar document issued by the appropriate authorities of the Participating State to which he belongs.

9. If a member of the Force leaves the service of the Participating State to which he belongs and is not repatriated, the Commander shall immediately inform the Egyptian authorities, giving such particulars as may be required. The Commander shall similarly inform the Egyptian authorities of any member of the Force who has absented himself for more than twenty-one days. If an expulsion order against an ex-member of the Force has been made, the Commander shall be responsible for ensuring that the person concerned shall be received within the territory of the Participating State concerned.

Jurisdiction

10. The following arrangements respecting criminal and civil jurisdiction are made having regard to the special functions of the Force and to the interests of the United Nations, and not for the personal benefit of the members of the Force.

Criminal jurisdiction

11. Members of the Force shall be subject to the exclusive jurisdiction of their respective national States in respect of any criminal offences which may be committed by them in Egypt.

Civil jurisdiction

12. (*a*) Members of the Force shall not be subject to the civil jurisdiction of Egyptian courts or to other legal process in any matter relating to their official duties. In a case arising from a matter relating to the official duties of a member of the Force and which involves a member of the Force and an Egyptian citizen, and in other disputes as agreed, the procedure provided in paragraph 38 (*b*) shall apply to the settlement.

(*b*) In those cases where civil jurisdiction is exercised by Egyptian courts with respect to members of the Force, the Egyptian courts and authorities shall grant members of the Force sufficient opportunity to safeguard their rights. If the Commander certifies that a member of the Force is unable because of official duties or authorized absence to protect his interests in a civil proceeding in which he is a participant, the Egyptian court or authority shall at his request suspend the proceeding until the elimination of the disability, but for not more than ninety days. Property of a member of the Force which is certified by the Commander to be needed by him for the fulfilment of his official duties shall be free from seizure for the satisfaction of a judgement, decision or order, together with other property not subject thereto under Egyptian law. The personal liberty of a member of the Force shall not be restricted by an Egyptian court or authority in a civil proceeding, whether to enforce a judgement, decision or order, to compel an oath of disclosure, or for any other reason.

(*c*) In the cases provided for in sub-paragraph (*b*) above, the claimant may elect to have his claim dealt with in accordance with the procedure set out in paragraph 38 (*b*) of these arrangements. Where a claim adjudicated or an award made in favour of the claimant by an Egyptian court or the Claims Commission under paragraph 38 (*b*) of these arrangements has not been satisfied, the Egyptian authorities may, without prejudice to the claimant's rights, seek the good offices of the Secretary-General to obtain satisfaction.

Notification: certification

13. If any civil proceeding is instituted against a member of the Force before any Egyptian court having jurisdiction, notification shall be given to the Commander. The Commander shall certify to the court whether or not the proceeding is related to the official duties of such member.

Military police: arrest: transfer of custody and mutual assistance

14. The Commander shall take all appropriate measures to ensure maintenance of discipline and good order among members of the Force. To this end military police designated by the Commander shall police the premises referred to in paragraph 19 of these arrangements and such areas where the Force is deployed in the performance of its functions. Elsewhere such military police shall be employed only subject to arrangements with the Egyptian authorities and in liaison with them and in so far as such employment is necessary to maintain discipline and order among members of the Force. For the purpose of this paragraph the military police of the Force shall have the power of arrest over members of the Force.

15. Military police of the Force may take into custody any person on the premises referred to in paragraph 19 who is subject to Egyptian criminal jurisdiction, without subjecting him to the ordinary routine of arrest, in order immediately to deliver him to the nearest appropriate Egyptian authorities: (*a*) when so requested by the Egyptian authorities; or (*b*) for the purpose of dealing with any offence or disturbance on the premises.

16. The Egyptian authorities may take into custody a member of the Force, without subjecting him to the ordinary routine of arrest in order immediately to deliver him, together with any weapons or items seized, to the nearest appropriate authorities of the Force; (*a*) when so requested by the Commander; or (*b*) in cases in which the military police of the Force are unable to act with the necessary promptness when a member of the Force is apprehended in the commission or attempted commission of a criminal offence that results or might result in serious injury to persons or property, or serious impairment of other legally protected rights.

17. When a person is taken into custody under (*b*) of paragraphs 15 and 16, the Commander or the Egyptian authorities, as the case may be, may make a preliminary interrogation but may not delay the transfer of custody. Following the transfer of custody, the person concerned shall be made available upon request for further interrogation.

18. The Commander and the Egyptian authorities shall assist each other in the carrying out of all necessary investigations into offences in respect of which either or both have an interest, in the production of witnesses, and in the collection and production of evidence, including the seizure and, in proper cases, the handing over, of things connected with an offence. The handing over of any such things may be made subject to their return within the time specified by the authority delivering them. Each shall notify the other of the disposition of any case in the outcome of which the other may have an interest or in which there has been a transfer of custody under the provisions of paragraphs 15 and 16 of these arrangements. The Government of Egypt will ensure the prosecution of persons subject to its criminal jurisdiction who are accused of acts in relation to the Force or its members which, if committed in relation to the Egyptian forces or their members, would have rendered them liable to prosecution. The authorities of the Force will take the measures within their power with respect to crimes or offences committed against Egyptian citizens by members of the Force.

Premises of the Force

19. The Egyptian Government shall provide, in agreement with the Commander, such areas for headquarters, camps, or other premises as may be necessary for the accommodation and the fulfilment of the functions of the Force. Without prejudice to the fact that all such premises remain Egyptian territory, they shall be inviolable and subject to the exclusive

control and authority of the Commander, who alone may consent to the entry of officials to perform duties on such premises.

United Nations flag

20. The Egyptian Government recognizes the right of the Force to display within Egyptian territory the United Nations flag on its headquarters, camps, posts or other premises, vehicles, vessels and otherwise as decided by the Commander. Other flags or pennants may be displayed only in exceptional cases and in accordance with conditions prescribed by the Commander. Sympathetic consideration will be given to observations or requests of the Egyptian authorities concerning this last-mentioned matter.

Uniform: Vehicle, vessel and aircraft markings and registration: Operating permits

21. Members of the Force shall normally wear the uniform prescribed by the Commander. The conditions on which the wearing of civilian dress is authorized shall be notified by the Commander to the Egyptian authorities, and sympathetic consideration will be given to observations or requests of the Egyptian authorities concerning this matter. Service vehicles, vessels and aircraft shall carry a distinctive United Nations identification mark and licence which shall be notified by the Commander to the Egyptian authorities. Such vehicles, vessels and aircraft shall not be subject to registration and licensing under the laws and regulations of Egypt. Egyptian authorities shall accept as valid, without a test or fee, a permit or licence for the operation of service vehicles, vessels and aircraft issued by the Commander.

Arms

22. Members of the Force may possess and carry arms while on duty in accordance with their orders. The Commander shall give sympathetic consideration to requests from the Egyptian authorities concerning this matter.

Privileges and immunities of the Force

23. The United Nations Emergency Force, as a subsidiary organ of the United Nations established by the General Assembly, enjoys the status, privileges and immunities of the Organization in accordance with the Convention on the Privileges and Immunities of the United Nations. The provisions of article II of the Convention on the Privileges and Immunities of the United Nations shall also apply to the property, funds and assets of Participating States used in Egypt in connexion with the national contingents serving in the United Nations Emergency Force. Such Participating States may not acquire immovable property in Egypt without agreement with the Government of Egypt. The Government of Egypt recognizes that the right of the Force to import free of duty equipment for the Force and provisions, supplies and other goods for the exclusive use of members of the Force, members of the United Nations Secretariat detailed by the Secretary-General to serve with the Force, excluding locally recruited personnel, includes the right of the Force to establish, maintain and operate at headquarters, camps and posts, service institutes providing amenities for the persons aforesaid. The amenities that may be provided by service institutes shall be goods of a consumable nature (tobacco and tobacco products, beer, etc.), and other customary articles of small value. To the end that duty-free importation for the Force may be effected with the least possible delay, having regard to the interests of the Government of Egypt, a mutually satisfactory procedure, including documentation, shall be arranged between the appropriate authorities of the Force and the Egyptian customs authorities. The Commander shall take all necessary measures to prevent any abuse of the exemption and to prevent the sale or resale of such goods to persons other than those aforesaid. Sympathetic consideration shall be given by the Commander to observations or requests of the Egyptian authorities concerning the operation of service institutes.

Privileges and immunities of officials and members of the Force

24. Members of the United Nations Secretariat detailed by the Secretary-General to serve

with the Force remain officials of the United Nations entitled to the privileges and immunities of articles V and VII of the Convention on the Privileges and Immunities of the United Nations. With respect to the locally recruited personnel of the Force, however, the United Nations will assert its right only to the immunity concerning official acts provided in section 18 (a) of the Convention on the Privileges and Immunities of the United Nations.

25. The Commander shall be entitled to the privileges, immunities and facilities of sections 19 and 27 of the Convention on the Privileges and Immunities of the United Nations. Officers serving on the United Nations Command (the Commander's Headquarters Staff) are entitled to the privileges and immunities of article VI of the Convention on the Privileges and Immunities of the United Nations. Subject to the foregoing, the United Nations will claim with respect to members of the Force only those rights expressly provided in the present or supplemental arrangements.

Members of the Force: Taxation, customs and fiscal regulations

26. Members of the Force shall be exempt from taxation on the pay and emoluments received from their national Governments or from the United Nations. They shall also be exempt from all other direct taxes except municipal rates for services enjoyed, and from all registration fees, and charges.

27. Members of the Force shall have the right to import free of duty their personal effects in connexion with their first taking up their post in Egypt. They shall be subject to the Egyptian laws and regulations governing customs and foreign exchange with respect to personal property not required by them by reason of their presence in Egypt with the Force. Special facilities for entry or exit shall be granted by the Egyptian immigration, customs and fiscal authorities to regularly constituted units of the Force provided that the authorities concerned have been duly notified sufficiently in advance. Members of the Force on departure from Egypt may, notwithstanding the foreign exchange regulations, take with them such funds as the appropriate pay officer of the Force certifies were received in pay and emoluments from their respective national Governments or from the United Nations and are a reasonable residue thereof. Special arrangements between the Commander and the Egyptian authorities shall be made for the implementation of the foregoing provisions in the interests of the Egyptian Government and members of the Force.

28. The Commander will co-operate with customs and fiscal authorities of Egypt and will render all assistance within his power in ensuring the observance of the customs and fiscal laws and regulations of Egypt by the members of the Force in accordance with these or any relevant supplemental arrangements.

Communications and postal services

29. The Force enjoys the facilities in respect to communications provided in article III of the Convention on the Privileges and Immunities of the United Nations. The Commander shall have authority to install and operate a radio sending and receiving station or stations to connect at appropriate points and exchange traffic with the United Nations radio network, subject to the provisions of article 45 of the International Telecommunication Convention relating to harmful interference. The frequencies on which any such station may be operated will be duly communicated by the United Nations to the appropriate Egyptian authorities and to the International Frequency Registration Board. The right of the Commander is likewise recognized to enjoy the priorities of government telegrams and telephone calls as provided for the United Nations in article 37 and annex 3 of the latter Convention and in article 83 of the telegraph regulations annexed thereto.

30. The Force shall also enjoy, within its area of operations, the right of unrestricted communication by radio, telephone, telegraph or any other means, and of establishing the necessary facilities for maintaining such communications within and between premises of the Force, including the laying of cables and land lines and the establishment of fixed and mobile radio sending and receiving stations. It is understood that the telegraph and telephone cables and lines herein referred to will be situated within or directly between the premises of the

Force and the area of operations, and that connexion with the Egyptian system of telegraphs and telephones will be made in accordance with arrangements with the appropriate Egyptian authorities.

31. The Government of Egypt recognizes the right of the Force to make arrangements through its own facilities for the processing and transport of private mail addressed to or emanating from members of the Force. The Government of Egypt will be informed of the nature of such arrangements. No interference shall take place with, and no censorship shall be applied to, the mail of the Force by the Government of Egypt. In the event that postal arrangements applying to private mail of members of the Force are extended to operations involving transfer of currency, or transport of packages or parcels from Egypt, the conditions under which such operations shall be conducted in Egypt will be agreed upon between the Government of Egypt and the Commander.

Freedom of movement

32. The Force and its members shall enjoy together with service vehicles, vessels, aircraft and equipment, freedom of movement between Force headquarters, camps and other premises, within the area of operations, and to and from points of access to Egyptian territory agreed upon or to be agreed upon by the Egyptian Government and the Commander. The Commander will consult with the appropriate Egyptian authorities with respect to large movements of personnel, stores or vehicles on railways or roads used for general traffic. The Government of Egypt recognizes the right of the Force and its members to freedom of movement across armistice demarcation lines and other military lines in the performance of the functions of the Force and the official duties of its members. The Egyptian authorities will supply the Force with maps and other information, including locations of mine-fields and other dangers and impediments, which may be useful in facilitating its movements.

Use of roads, waterways, port facilities, airfields and railways

33. The Force shall have the right to the use of roads, bridges, canals and other waters, port facilities and airfields without the payment of dues, tolls or charges either by way of registration or otherwise, in the area of operations and the normal points of access, except for charges that are related directly to services rendered. The Egyptian authorities, subject to special arrangements, will give the most favourable consideration to requests for the grant to members of the Force of travelling facilities on its railways and of concessions with regard to fares.

Water, electricity and other public utilities

34. The Force shall have the right to the use of water, electricity and other public utilities at rates not less favourable to the Force than those to comparable consumers. The Egyptian authorities will, upon the request of the Commander, assist the Force in obtaining water, electricity and other utilities required, and in the case of interruption or threatened interruption of service, will give the same priority to the needs of the Force as to essential Government services. The Force shall have the right where necessary to generate, within the premises of the Force either on land or water, electricity for the use of the Force, and to transmit and distribute such electricity as required by the Force.

Egyptian currency

35. The Government of Egypt will, if requested by the Commander, make available to the Force, against reimbursement in US dollars, Swiss francs or other currency mutually acceptable, Egyptian currency required for the use of the Force, including the pay of the members of the national contingents, at the rate of exchange most favourable to the Force that is officially recognized by the Government of Egypt.

Provisions, supplies and services

36. The Egyptian authorities will, upon the request of the Commander, assist the Force in
13*

obtaining equipment, provisions, supplies and other goods and services required from local courses for its subsistence and operation. Sympathetic consideration will be given by the Commander in purchases on the local market to requests or observations of Egyptian authorities in order to avoid any adverse effect on the local economy. Members of the Force and United Nations officials may purchase locally goods necessary for their own consumption, and such services as they need, under conditions not less favourable than for Egyptian citizens. If members of the Force and United Nations officials should require medical or dental facilities beyond those available within the Force, arrangements shall be made with the appropriate Egyptian authorities under which such facilities may be made available. The Commander and the appropriate local authorities will co-operate with respect to sanitary services. The Commander and the Egyptian authorities shall extend to each other the fullest co-operation in matters concerning health, particularly with respect to the control of communicable diseases in accordance with international conventions; such co-operation shall extend to the exchange of relevant information and statistics.

Locally recruited personnel

37. The Force may recruit locally such personnel as required. The Egyptian authorities will, upon the request of the Commander, assist the Force in the recruitment of such personnel. Sympathetic consideration will be given by the Commander in the recruitment of local personnel to requests or observations of Egyptian authorities in order to avoid any adverse effect on the local economy. The terms and conditions of employment for locally recruited personnel shall be prescribed by the Commander and shall generally, to the extent practicable, follow the practice prevailing in the locality.

Settlement of disputes or claims

38. Disputes or claims of a private law character shall be settled in accordance with the following provisions:

(*a*) The United Nations shall make provisions for the appropriate modes of settlement of disputes or claims arising out of contract or other disputes or claims of a private law character to which the United Nations is a party other than those covered in subparagraphs (*b*) and (*c*) following.

(*b*) Any claim made by

(i) an Egyptian citizen in respect of any damages alleged to result from an act or omission of a member of the Force relating to his official duties;

(ii) the Government of Egypt against a member of the Force; or

(iii) the Force or the Government of Egypt against one another, that is not covered by paragraphs 39 or 40 of these arrangements,

shall be settled by a Claims Commission established for that purpose. One member of the Commission shall be appointed by the Secretary-General, one member by the Government of Egypt and a chairman jointly by the Secretary-General and the Government of Egypt. If the Secretary-General and the Government of Egypt fail to agree on the appointment of a chairman, the President of the International Court of Justice shall be asked by either to make the appointment. An award made by the Claims Commission against the Force or a member thereof or against the Government of Egypt shall be notified to the Commander or the Egyptian authorities, as the case may be, to make satisfaction thereof.

(*c*) Disputes concerning the terms of employment and conditions of service of locally recruited personnel shall be settled by administrative procedure to be established by the Commander.

39. All differences between the United Nations and Egypt arising out of the interpretation or application of these arrangements which involve a question of principle concerning the Convention on the Privileges and Immunities of the United Nations shall be dealt with in accordance with the procedure of Section 30 of the Convention.

40. All other disputes between the United Nations and Egypt concerning the interpreta-

tion or application of these arrangements which are not settled by negotiation or other agreed mode of settlement shall be referred for final settlement to a tribunal of three arbitrators, one to be named by the Secretary-General of the United Nations, one by the Government of Egypt, and an umpire to be chosen jointly by the Secretary-General and the Government of Egypt. If the two parties fail to agree on the appointment of the umpire within one month of the proposal of arbitration by one of the parties, the President of the International Court of Justice shall be asked by either party to appoint the umpire. Should a vacancy occur for any reason, the vacancy shall be filled within thirty days by the method laid down in this paragraph for the original appointment. The tribunal shall come into existence upon the appointment of the umpire and at least one of the other members of the tribunal. Two members of the tribunal shall constitute a quorum for the performance of its functions, and for all deliberations and decisions of the tribunal a favourable vote of two members shall be sufficient.

Liaison
41. The Commander and the Egyptian authorities shall take appropriate measures to ensure close and reciprocal liaison.

Deceased members: disposition of personal property
42. The Commander shall have the right to take charge of and dispose of the body of a member of the Force who dies in Egyptian territory, and may dispose of his personal property after the debts of the deceased person incurred in Egyptian territory and owing to Egyptian citizens have been settled.

Supplemental arrangements
43. Supplemental details for the carrying out of these arrangements shall be made as required between the Commander and appropriate Egyptian authorities designated by the Government of Egypt.

Effective date and duration
44. Upon acceptance of this proposal by your Government, the present letter and your reply will be considered as constituting an agreement between the United Nations and Egypt that shall be deemed to have taken effect as from the date of the arrival of the first element of the Force in Egypt, and shall remain in force until the departure of the Force from Egypt. The effective date that the departure has occurred shall be defined by the Secretary-General and the Government of Egypt. The provisions of paragraphs 38, 39 and 40 of these arrangements, relating to the settlement of disputes, however, shall remain in force until all claims arising prior to the date of termination of these arrangements, and submitted prior to or within three months following the date of termination, have been settled.

(*Signed*) Dag HAMMARSKJÖLD

III

Letter dated 8 February 1957 from the Minister for Foreign Affairs of Egypt, addressed to the Secretary-General

I have the honour to refer to your letter of 8 February 1957 in which you have proposed that Egypt and the United Nations should make the *ad hoc* arrangements contained therein which define certain of the conditions necessary for the effective discharge of the functions of the United Nations Emergency Force while it remains in Egypt. Recalling the declaration of the Government of Egypt that, when exercising its sovereign powers on any matter concerning the presence and functioning of the United Nations Emergency Force, it would be guided, in good faith, by its acceptance of the General Assembly resolution of 5 November 1956, I have the pleasure to advise you in the name of the Government of Egypt of its full agreement on, and its acceptance of, the terms of your letter.

The Government of Egypt agrees, furthermore, that your letter and this reply will be considered as constituting an agreement between Egypt and the United Nations.

(*Signed*) M. Fawzi

[A/3526, Report of the Secretary-General on arrangements concerning the status of the UN Emergency Force in Egypt, 8 Feb. 1957.]

This agreement was negotiated and concluded by the Secretary-General after consultation with the Advisory Committee.[39] Together with the 1946 General Convention on Privileges and Immunities of the UN (to which Egypt had acceded in September 1948) and the Regulations issued for UNEF,[40] it constituted the legal framework within which UNEF was to operate on Egyptian territory. The General Convention enumerates the privileges and immunities to which the UN and its subsidiary organs are entitled, under Article 105 of the Charter, to achieve their purposes in the territories of member states.[41] UNEF was, of course, a subsidiary organ of the UN.[42] Specifically, Article II, s.2 of the General Convention on Privileges and Immunities provides that the 'United Nations, its property and assets wherever located and by whomsoever held, shall enjoy immunity from every form of legal process except as in any particular case it has expressly waived its immunity'. While it was thus clear that members of the UNEF staff, including those seconded to it from the UN Secretariat, could claim the rights flowing from the Convention it was less clear that members of the national contingents serving in UNEF should be automatically covered by that Convention. Thus paragraph 25 of the Status Agreement, while indicating those prerogatives to which the commander and officers on the HQ staff are entitled under the Convention states that with regard to the members of UNEF the UN will claim 'only those rights expressly provided in the present or supplemental arrangements'. Further, it will be seen that, in so far as exemptions from civil and criminal jurisdiction were concerned, it would have been far from appropriate for the arrangements in the General Convention to apply to UNEF contingents, for this would have removed the originating state from fulfilling the role of ultimate disciplining authority.[43]

This Status of Forces Agreement was considered to be operative as from the date of entry of UNEF into Egyptian territory; and it was approved by the Assembly in Resolution 1126 (XI) of 22 February 1957. The Agreement represents a balance between the acknowledged sovereignty of Egypt, and the international character of UNEF. The status granted to UNEF was functional: that is to say, the arrangements were not for the personal benefit of members of the Force, but so that UNEF could carry out its agreed functions. (It may be

---

[39] See above, p. 275.   [40] See above, pp. 288–92.

[41] For the text of the Convention, see A/64, 1 July 1949, pp. 25–33; see also Rosner, p. 254 n. 5; and Josef Kunz, 'Privileges and Immunities of International Organizations', *AJIL* (1947), p. 850.

[42] See above, p. 271.

[43] This point is well observed by Seyersted, p. 58. He further observed that the military members of the UNEF staff have been accorded immunity in respect of official acts and immunity from arrest even in their home countries under UNEF regulation 19 (see above, p. 290); and that the UN will have to waive this immunity if their home state were to be called upon to prosecute them, unless UNEF Regulation 34 is considered as a general waiver.

noted that the immunities of the UN itself have followed the functional, rather than the broader traditional diplomatic, principle.)

To a certain extent the text of the Status of Forces Agreement speaks for itself. It nevertheless contains legal principles of major importance and which merit further comment. In so far as this study is directed primarily to making available the documentation, it has not been felt appropriate to provide here a detailed legal analysis. Moreover, such studies are readily available elsewhere.[44] Accordingly, mention is made only of some of the major points.

Articles 19–27 of the General Convention on Privileges and Immunities were made applicable to the Commander and his family, who thereby enjoy the same prerogatives as the Secretary-General, and all Under Secretaries-General. He is granted immunity from all acts of an official nature, as well as acts of his private life; and his person, effects, and papers are inviolable. He is exempt from taxation on his salary, and when travelling in pursuit of UN business is entitled to facilities granted to a diplomatic envoy. Officials of the Commander's Headquarters' staff, being entitled to the privileges and immunities of Article VI of the General Convention of 1946, were granted the status of experts on mission for the UN. They have immunity from personal arrest and from local jurisdiction in respect of their official acts. Their papers are inviolable. As these exemptions are not personal, but for the protection of the UN while carrying out of its duties, the Secretary-General may waive any of the exemptions if he sees fit. This is true also of Secretariat members serving with UNEF, who are entitled to the benefit of Articles V and VII of the General Convention, thus being immune from local jurisdiction in respect of their official acts, from taxation of their salaries, and from national military service. So far as locally-recruited personnel are concerned, they have immunity from local jurisdiction in respect of their official acts, as guaranteed in Article V, section 18 of the General Convention, but are not entitled to the financial privileges referred to in Article 26 of the Status of Forces Agreement.

The national contingent members of UNEF are exempt from Egyptian taxation, and the Agreement makes specific arrangements concerning customs and foreign exchange regulation. Members of UNEF are exempt from Egyptian civil jurisdiction in respect of official acts. They are not exempt in respect of non-official acts, though the local courts shall grant sufficient opportunity for the protection of their rights. It is for the Commander to certify whether the acts referred to were or were not done in the official exercise of a UNEF member's duty.

The exemption which the Status Agreement provides from criminal jurisdiction was thought necessary both to preserve 'the independent exercise of the functions of such a force' and because 'obviously, [it] makes easier the decision of states to contribute troops from their armed forces'.[45] In order that a jurisdictional and disciplinary vacuum should not exist, it was necessary to insert the corollary into the Agreements between the UN and the contributing states, whereby the latter agreed that the immunity of their troops from Egyptian criminal jurisdiction was based on the understanding that the authorities of the participating states would exercise the required jurisdiction for crimes or offences committed in Egypt by any of their own troops.[46]

The Philippine representative (whose thoughtful contribution to other aspects of the Suez question have been noted below, p. 391) noted that, even under this formula, several legal problems could still arise. An offence could, for example, be *civil* under Egyptian law but *criminal* under the law of the contributing state. Under his national law, a UNEF member might be entitled to call witnesses, but the case would be heard perhaps thousands of miles from where the witnesses were available. Equally, an act might be an indictable offence in Egypt, but no indictable offence at all in the home state. Further, there might be a major discrepancy between the punishments envisaged in the two countries for a particular offence.[47] Such problems remained unresolved: the Secretary-General, being aware of them, has requested the governments of the participating states to review the position under their respective domestic laws, and there the matter rests.[48]

It may be noted that the Secretary-General cannot waive the immunities of the UNEF national contingents: their immunity is thus of a more absolute nature than that of the Headquarters staff and Secretariat members.

UNEF's premises, though provided by Egypt, are inviolable and subject to the exclusive control of the Commander. Freedom of communication and freedom of movement is guaranteed to UNEF.

In the event, the Status of Forces Agreement proved a very satisfactory basis of UNEF's status in Egypt, for the duration of its stay. The operation of this Agreement was without major difficulties.

2. *Arrangements affecting the operation of the Force*

35. The co-operation of the Gaza administration and an awareness of the people in the area that the mission of UNEF is friendly and has the support of the administration are essential to the effective discharge by UNEF of its responsibilities.

36. Information from the Commander of the Force is to the effect that the population of the Gaza Strip has been made to know that Egyptian policy is opposed to infiltration across the demarcation line. Egyptian regulations against infiltration, including penalties, have been put into force, and the people of Gaza have been made aware of the role of UNEF in the prevention of infiltration. The Commander has been informed that the CID (police) in Gaza has been instructed to act vigorously with the object of finding persons responsible for mining and other serious incidents and to prevent recurrence. Moreover, Gaza inhabitants are forbidden to approach within 500 metres of the demarcation line during darkness, and the *mukhtars* (local headmen) have been warned that they are responsible for preventing infiltration in their areas. Severe sentences may be awarded against violators of regulations against infiltration.

[46] See above, p. 227. A/3943 ann. I, para. 5.

[47] See *GAOR*, 11th sess., 659th mtg, p. 1192.

[48] A/3943, para. 137. Gabriella Rosner (pp. 148–9) has correctly observed that the exclusive criminal jurisdiction granted to the contributing states in respect of UNEF differs substantially from certain other major Status of Forces Agreements, including Article VII of NATO Status of Forces Agreement, where a concurrent jurisdiction is established.

37. There is an understanding whereby a unit of the Palestine Police would be assigned specific duty in the prevention of infiltration and would co-operate closely with UNEF in such function, particularly in acting on UNEF requests relating to actual or apprehended infiltration and the free exchange of information concerning actual or potential infiltrators. In practice, thus far, this has meant mainly that the Palestine Police received from UNEF the persons apprehended in the zone near the demarcation line. Patrolling along the line is done by UNEF alone. The Commander is of the view that the absence of incidents, and, in recent months, particularly those with mines, reflects more effective local police and CID action. He also reports that a re-grouping of the Force, so that battalion boundaries will generally correspond to administrative sub-districts in the Strip, which are also the police sub-districts, may facilitate police co-operation with UNEF at the battalion level.

38. UNEF is authorized to apprehend infiltrators, and the Commander reports that accepted practice is for UNEF to take infiltrators into custody in a zone extending 500 metres from the demarcation line and hand them over to the local police.

39. No serious difficulties are reported with regard to (a) the enjoyment by personnel and vehicles of UNEF of full freedom of movement in the Gaza Strip, and in the Sinai Peninsula between the bases and headquarters of UNEF and the elements of its troops deployed along the demarcation line; (b) UNEF aircraft flying freely over the Sinai and the Gaza Strip; (c) the manning of the Gaza Airport by UNEF.

40. The relations between UNEF and the local population are said by the Commander to be good, generally speaking. He finds that the presence of UNEF under its existing terms of reference, despite occasional minor difficulties, is accepted as a good development by the majority of the inhabitants of the Gaza Strip. [*A/3665 Report of Secretary-General*, 9 *Oct.* 1957.]

In 1958 the Commander reported that

15. Readjustment of the boundaries of the battalions deployed along the armistice demarcation line, to conform to the local police district boundaries, has facilitated a closer liaison and co-operation. Joint meetings between UNEF representatives and the Governors of districts of the Gaza Strip have been held for the purpose of discussing and settling problems concerning the reporting of incidents, matters relating to security and minor labour problems.

16. The Commander of the Force reports that, in general, the relations between UNEF and the local population have been satisfactory. Except for occasional minor thefts and pilferage, there have been no difficulties or incidents. [*A/3899, Report of Secretary-General*, 27 *Aug. 1958.*]

This pattern continued.[49] Further details of UNEF's status, and its relationship to Egypt, are revealed in the Secretary-General's summary study, which is reproduced *in toto* in section 12.

IO

RELATIONS WITH OTHER STATES INVOLVED

(a) Israel

ISRAEL'S relations with the UN in respect of UNEF were dictated by a variety of factors. She had invaded Egyptian territory, and had been condemned by the

[49] A/4210, para. 34.

Assembly for it: but she pointed to the previous record of *fedayeen* raids from Egypt. Israel was also concerned at the failure of Egypt to uphold the Security Council resolution of August 1951, which denied that Egypt could exercise belligerent rights in the Suez Canal against Israel. And freedom of passage in the Straits of Tiran and Gulf of Aqaba were high on Israel's priorities, and she felt that she should not be required to withdraw from Egypt without any of her grievances having been resolved. As she was at pains to point out, the *status quo ante* could not reasonably be described as a *status juris*, and therefore a mere return to it was unsatisfactory. Reference should also be made to section 12, (pp. 464–69 below), for details of the attempts by Israel to exact conditions upon her withdrawal from Egyptian territory. The remaining major factor in Israel's relations with the UN in respect of UNEF was that she had denounced the Egyptian–Israel Armistice Agreement, declaring it no longer operable in the light of continuing Egyptian violations of it. (The details of this denunciation of the Armistice Agreement are recounted in Part I.) The Secretary-General never directly replied to this claim by Israel, but instead let it be known that he regarded the Armistice Agreement as still operative, at least in part; at the same time, UNEF came to assume many of UNTSO's supervisory functions in respect of this armistice.

In its Resolution 999 (ES–I) the Assembly authorized the Secretary-General to arrange with the parties concerned for the implementation of the cease-fire and the halting of the movement of military forces and arms into the area as requested in Resolution 997 (ES–I). Accordingly, the Secretary-General sent cables to the parties concerned, including the following one to Israel:

CABLEGRAM DATED 4 NOVEMBER 1956 FROM THE SECRETARY-GENERAL, ADDRESSED TO THE MINISTER OF FOREIGN AFFAIRS OF ISRAEL

1. The first emergency special session of the General Assembly at its meeting of 3–4 November 1956 adopted the following resolution:
(*For this text, see resolution 999 (ES–I) below.*)[1]
2. In this regard, I note the statement conveyed in the *aide-mémoire* of 4 November 1956 (A/3279) to the effect that 'Israel agrees to an immediate cease-fire provided a similar answer is forthcoming from Egypt.'
3. It is noted from the *aide-mémoire*, 4 November 1956, that the Government of Israel has not stated its acceptance of the implementation of operative paragraph 2 of the resolution (999 (ES–I)) of 2 November, urging the parties to the armistice agreements 'promptly to withdraw all forces behind the armistice lines, to desist from raids across the armistice lines into neighbouring territory, and to observe scrupulously the provisions of the armistice agreements.'
4. I may call to your attention that the Government of Egypt had, before the meeting of the Assembly of 3–4 November, accepted the resolution of 2 November, 'on the condition . . . it could not implement the resolution in case attacking armies continue their aggression.'
5. In connexion with my responsibilities under the above-mentioned resolution of 4 November, I trust that the statement by the Government of Israel concerning a cease-fire applies to the resolution of 4 November.
6. In pursuance of the provision in operative paragraph 2 of the resolution (999 (ES–I)) of 4 November authorizing the Secretary-General 'immediately to arrange with the parties

1 For text, see above, p. 232.

concerned for the implementation of the cease-fire and the halting of the movement of military forces and arms into the area. I am requesting all four parties, which of course includes Israel, to bring to a halt all hostile military actions in the area at 20.00 GMT, Sunday 4 November 1956. May I further request that your Government's decision in this matter be communicated to me at the earliest possible moment, and at all events so early as to render it possible to inform the other parties concerned about your decision prior to the said hour. The decisions of the other parties in this regard will be transmitted to the Government of Israel without delay.

7. In view of the urgency of the situation, which accounts for the short time-limit fixed in the resolution of 4 November, I request again that a definitive reply be given at the earliest possible hour.

8. In pursuance of the function entrusted to me by operative paragraph 2 of the resolution of 4 November, and in view of the provisions of operative paragraph 2 of the resolution of 4 November and operative paragraph 3 of the resolution of 4 November, I must inquire whether the Government of Israel will accept these provisions and accordingly will be willing to make arrangements with the Secretary-General, assisted by the Chief of Staff and the members of the United Nations Truce Supervision Organization, for the withdrawal of the armed forces of Israel behind the armistice lines.

Dag HAMMARSKJÖLD

(A/3287, Ann. 3, Report of the Secretary-General, 4 Nov. 1956.]

Israel agreed to the cease-fire,[2] requiring only that Egypt also agreed (A/2397). The withdrawal of Israel forces, and the suggestion of stationing UNEF on both sides of the armistice line, presented greater difficulties, however:

In this connexion I have to draw your attention to a statement made by Mr Ben Gurion, the Prime Minister of Israel, in his address to the Knesset on 7 November. According to a report received from the Chief of the United Nations Command, the Prime Minister stated in this address: 'the Armistice lines between Israel and Egypt have no validity', and 'on no account will Israel agree to the stationing of a foreign force, no matter how called, in her territory, or in any of the areas occupied by her'.

If maintained in violation of the resolutions of the General Assembly on these matters, this position, while not affecting the cease-fire arrangements, would seriously complicate the task of giving effect to the resolution of 2 November 1956. [*A/3313, Letter from the Secretary-General to the Foreign Minister of France, 7 Nov. 1956.*]

116. My Government has submitted to the Security Council (*S/3742*) the effective operation orders in which Egyptian officers in Sinai and the Gaza Strip were bidden by their superiors to regard their objective as being the destruction of the State of Israel by the most brutal and savage means of fighting. The deployment of Egyptian forces in the Sinai Peninsula and in the Gaza Strip was progressively increased, and at the time of the Suez crisis it had risen to three infantry divisions and two armoured brigades. By then, these forces, relying on supplies in advanced depots, were in a position to launch an attack on Israel, if necessary, within less than twenty-four hours. On Sharm el-Sheikh, on the southernmost tip of the Sinai Peninsula, a fortified military base was constructed sufficient to accommodate an infantry battalion. An airfield, jetties and shore batteries were also set up. All this, of course, was for the sole purpose of effectively blocking the Straits of Aqaba, the Straits of Elath, and to complete the maritime blockade, a base for torpedo boats was erected on the Red Sea south of the Suez Canal.

117. This, then, is the scene which was revealed to our eyes during the action in the Sinai

[2] A/3301. 5 Nov. 1956.

Peninsula. Here was a wilderness bristling with death, pushing up against Israel's populated centres, and across the other side of the frontier, in Israel's territory, could be seen the targets for this massive rearmament—isolated farm settlements populated by young pioneers with pathetically primitive watchtowers and small-arms defences. Therefore, everything that has come into our hands and into our knowledge since I last addressed the General Assembly has fortified our conviction that the disaster which we prevented was far greater and more drastic than any of the hazards or perils which our limited military action incurred. . . .

120. It is salutary that we should look carefully at the provisions of resolution 997 (*ES–I*) governing United Nations policy, which was adopted on 2 November 1956. That resolution begins by urging the parties, as a matter of priority, to establish an immediate cease-fire. The General Assembly will recall that my Government gave this recommendation its priority consideration and was amongst the first of the belligerents to grant its consent. . . .

124. Beyond the cease-fire, there are other elements in that resolution of 2 November. There is the withdrawal of forces. There is the cessation of raids. There is the provision against the introduction of new military forces. There is the obligation to open and restore secure freedom of navigation in the Suez Canal. There is the call for scrupulous observance of the general armistice system which, in the case of Jordan, Lebanon and Syria, in their relations with Israel, is now in full effect, and that system, of course, has provisions against all acts of hostility or all belligerent acts.

125. This, then, is the integral system of objectives which resolution 997 (*ES–I*) calls upon the parties to achieve. It is only if we carry out all these things without further reservation, if we carry them out in such a way as to vindicate the paramount objective of our Charter, namely, the prevention of a recurrence of hostility, that we will give serious implementation to the desire and the wishes of the international community.

126. The General Assembly will recall that, in response to the resolution of 2 November and the subsequent resolutions, the Government of Israel notified the Secretary-General on 8 November as follows:

'. . . the Government of Israel will willingly withdraw its forces from Egypt immediately upon the conclusion of satisfactory arrangements with the United Nations in connexion with the emergency international force'. (*A/3320.*)

127. My Government stands firmly and faithfully upon that declaration, which was rightly regarded at that time as an important contribution to the task of restoring peace and stability in the area. The General Assembly will observe that in our conception the process of withdrawing Israel troops from Egyptian soil is integrated with the plans for the United Nations Force. We believe that this is a legitimate interpretation. Indeed, if we study the jurisprudence under which the United Nations Force was established, we find that it had an accepted relationship to the procedure for effecting the withdrawals. This was clear from the address by the Secretary of State for External Affairs of Canada, who, as the author of the concept of the United Nations Force in this General Assembly, speaks with a special authority in this as in other matters. There is what he called 'a relationship . . . between the withdrawal of the forces . . . and the arrival and the functioning of the United Nations Force' (*567th meeting, para. 260*). . . .

132. I should like to tell the General Assembly quite frankly what is the philosophy which underlies our present approach to this problem of the withdrawal of Israel forces in accordance with our undertaking of 8 November. Many representatives have spoken as if, in their view, the only important consideration is when we withdraw. Of far greater moment is the question: How do we withdraw? What situation will that withdrawal create? What comes in its place? Will the withdrawal become an integral stage in the promotion of peaceful conditions? Or will it pave the way to a return to the previous state of siege and of anarchy? This is perhaps the most fateful practical question which the United Nations now faces in the conduct of its work.

133. There are two possible approaches to this problem of withdrawal. One is a system—which I am certain the General Assembly will instantaneously reject—under which we would carry out the withdrawal without any co-ordination with the movements of the United

Nations Force, without any care for the future and without any guarantee of Egypt's future conduct towards Israel. Sinai would then become again a base for Nasser to renew against Israel the deadly menace which I have but briefly described. . . .

137. But there is another system of withdrawal fully consistent not only with the resolutions of the General Assembly, but also with the purposes and objectives of the United Nations and its Charter. . . .

143. We shall carry out our undertaking of 8 November, but there is a way of carrying it out which might lead to war. There is a way of carrying it out which gives a chance of peace. . . .

146. . . . A nation claims and exercises a state of war against its neighbour and then complains about the absence of peace. Egypt behaves to Israel as though there is war. Israel is called upon to behave towards Egypt as though there is peace. . . .

148. . . . We cannot solve the long-term political issues in the process of the withdrawal of forces, but we can secure such practical undertakings and arrangements in co-operation with the United Nations as will preclude acts of war and belligerency by land and by sea. . . .

[*GAOR, 11th sess., 592nd plen. mtg.*]

This position was reiterated in a letter sent by Israel to the Secretary-General, in which it was stated:

1. There has been a withdrawal of Israel's forces for varying distances along the entire Egyptian front.

2. The Government of Israel reiterates the position conveyed to the Secretary-General on 8 November 1956. Israel will willingly withdraw its forces from Egypt immediately upon the conclusion of satisfactory arrangements with the United Nations in connexion with the emergency international Force. The 'satisfactory arrangements' which Israel seeks are such as will ensure Israel's security against the recurrence of the threat or danger of attack, and against acts of belligerency by land or sea.

3. The Government of Israel has not yet had an opportunity of discussing satisfactory arrangements with the United Nations in connexion with the emergency international Force. It awaits information on the proposed size, location and stationing arrangements of the United Nations Emergency Force, and on the method proposed for the discharge of all the functions laid down in the resolutions of 2, 5 and 7 November. It is noted that the resolution of 5 November requires the United Nations Emergency Force to secure the cessation of hostilities 'in accordance with all the terms of the resolution of 2 November 1956'. These terms include various provisions, in addition to those for the cease-fire and the withdrawal of forces. When the Government of Israel has studied the Secretary-General's report, which came into its hands a few hours ago, and elicits further information relating to the functions of the United Nations Emergency Force, it will be prepared to make its own observations and suggestions, with a view to implementing its undertaking of 8 November.

4. The Government of Israel also awaits a reply to the information sought from Egypt in a communication to the Secretary-General on 3 November. It is obvious that a knowledge of Egypt's policy and intention with respect to belligerency or peace with Israel must influence Israel's dispositions on matters affecting her security.

5. Israel is strictly observing the cease-fire. There have been attempted penetrations of the cease-fire by Egyptian forces within the past two days. These have been repelled.

The delegation of Israel is now ready to discuss with the Secretary-General, or his representatives, considerations which arise in connexion with the resolution of 2 November and the implementation of the Israel Government's declaration of 8 November. [*A/3384, ann. II, Report by the Secretary-General on compliance with General Assembly Res. 997 (ES–I) and 1002 (ES–I), 21 Nov. 1956.*]

While some—as has been shown above (pp. 254–6)—had some sympathy with Israel's belief in the need for a review of the overall situation at this juncture, others insisted that her 'conditions' were unacceptable. Thus the Lebanon stated that:

88. It would also be contrary to the interpretation that the Secretary-General himself placed on those resolutions in paragraph 8 of his report of 6 November (*A/3302*), a report which was endorsed by the General Assembly (*resolution 1001* (*ES–I*)). 'There is no intent in the establishment of the Force', writes the Secretary-General in that paragraph of his report, 'to influence the military balance in the present conflict and, thereby, the political balance affecting efforts to settle the conflict.' This precise definition of the functions of the international Force rules out any peace conditions put by Israel for the withdrawal of its forces, as it rules out any question of the settlement of the Suez Canal problem as a condition for the withdrawal of the invading forces. [*Per the Lebanon representative, GAOR, 11th sess., 595th plen. mtg.*]

Similarly, the Ceylonese representative emphasized that the Assembly call for the withdrawal of Israel forces behind the armistice lines was unqualified, and not subject to negotiation:

17. The Secretary-General can certainly hold discussions with the Government of Israel, and the Government of Israel has the fullest liberty of holding any talks it likes with the Secretary-General. But the mandate of the General Assembly is quite clear. . . .

18. The fact is that there has been an invasion of Egyptian territory. Before any fruitful discussions can take place, therefore, the *status quo ante* must be restored. . . . [*Ibid. 638th plen. mtg.*]

Others put this view more strongly, saying that it entailed accepting

. . . that Egypt's consent having been obtained for the admission of the United Nations Emergency Force for a specific purpose, the Force is entitled to stay there until the settlements desired by certain States, and particularly by certain interested circles, have been successfully imposed. Among these problems, the representative of Australia mentioned freedom of navigation in the Suez Canal. Since freedom of navigation may be interpreted differently in certain circles, freedom of navigation in the Canal could be regarded as ensured once the Canal was removed from Egyptian sovereignty and placed under the control and management of another Universal Suez Canal Company. It is therefore obvious to those circles, that UNEF should be required to remain in Egyptian territory until such a solution, namely, the internationalization of the Canal, can be imposed on Egypt. [*Per the Bulgarian representative, ibid. 651st plen. mtg, para. 94.*]

106. I should like further to say that the subject before this Assembly, from the beginning of the first emergency special session till now, is not the resolving of what has been known as the Arab–Israel question. We were faced with the issue of invasion, the issue of aggression, and that is what we were dealing with. As Governments engaged in the consideration of these questions, it is inevitable that we should look at other related matters, but that would not take away from the crucial fact that other progress may follow afterwards. So that does not mean that there is any condition attached to the withdrawal. Each one of these resolutions asks for unconditional withdrawal. [*Per the representative of India, ibid.*]

Yet others voiced the opinion that, while indeed the Secretary-General could not take note, in his negotiations with Israel, of these questions of Aqaba and the Straits of Tiran, nevertheless they were questions which should immediately be faced by the Assembly.[3]

A specific problem arose over the question of the occupation of Gaza. Under

[3] e.g. per Australia, *GAOR*, 11th sess., 538th mtg, para. 81.

the Assembly resolutions, Israeli troops were required to withdraw from Egyptian territory; Israel argued not only that the Gaza Strip was a base from which *fedayeen* raids were made, but also that Gaza was not 'Egyptian territory' in the legal sense of the term. Israel contended that Gaza was an area seized by Egypt during the fighting of 1948, and while it fell to Egypt under the Armistice Agreement of 1949 to administer this territory, this in no way conferred title upon Egypt. Israel thus urged that, given the history of border raids, she should now provide a civilian administration for Gaza. The response of the Secretary-General is indicated in the following statement by the Philippines:

. . . I would wish to refer to the part of the Secretary-General's report where he states that the Israel proposal for the continuation of Israel administration in the Gaza Strip, accompanied by suitable relationship with the United Nations, cannot be accepted. I have no doubt that the Secretary-General had in mind the definition of the functions of the Force which he set out in his report of 6 November 1956:

'It is further clear that the General Assembly, in its resolution of 5 November 1956, by the reference to its resolution of 2 November, has wished to reserve for itself the full determination of the tasks of this emergency Force, and of the legal basis on which it must function in fulfilment of its mission.' (*A/3302*, para. 8.)

In paragraph 9 he added:

'While the General Assembly is enabled to establish the Force with the consent of those parties which contribute units to the force, it could not request the force to be stationed or operate on the territory of a given country without the consent of the Government of that country.'

In my view, that was the part of the earlier report which the Secretary-General had in mind when he made the following statements in his present report:

'These considerations exclude the United Nations from accepting Israel control over the area'—meaning the Gaza Strip—'even if it were of a non-military character. They would also exclude the deployment of the UNEF necessary, in the absence of Israel troops, if such arrangements as those proposed by the Government of Israel were to be implemented.'

'Any broader function for it in that area, in view of the terms of the Armistice Agreement and a recognized principle of international law, would require the consent of Egypt . . .' (*A/3512*, paras 13 and 14.)

121. For the present, it should be noted that before the occupation of the Gaza Strip by Israel forces, Gaza was under the military control of Egypt, but was not therefore a part of the territory of Egypt. It was under the control of Egypt as a result of the Palestine war. If we are to interpret the words 'territory of a State' in the Secretary-General's report, we must in this connexion recall the partition. Under the partition, the Gaza Strip was a part of the Arab State and not of Israel. Necessarily, it was also not a part of Egypt.
122. Therefore, if the legal and juridical link is to be established by the Secretary-General between this report and his previous report of 6 January, with reference to the consent of the State of a territory wherein these units may be stationed, the basis is erroneous. With respect to Egypt, Gaza is not its territory, and the consent of Egypt is not necessary for the continuance of UNEF in that area. Neither is the consent of Israel necessary, because, under the partition, Gaza was a part of the Arab State and not a part of Israel or Egypt. In this respect, therefore, I am not quite in agreement with the conclusions arrived at by the Secretary-General. [*Per the Philippines representative, GAOR, 11th sess., vol. 2, 645th mtg, paras 119, 121-2.*]

That the Israeli standpoint would lead to difficulties in its relations with the UN was inevitable.

ANNEX IV

LETTER DATED 21 NOVEMBER 1956 FROM THE SECRETARY-GENERAL, ADDRESSED TO THE MINISTER FOR FOREIGN AFFAIRS OF ISRAEL

(Original text: English)

According to information received which I must consider as reliable, the situation in the Gaza strip, in particular in Rafah, has been one giving rise to great concern. I will not here go into the question of the reasons for this unrest, nor into the information we have on the casualties ensuing. I hope that the situation has improved, and I gather from you that according to your information that is the case. However, the situation remains one which I cannot disregard in the execution of my obligations under the relevant General Assembly resolutions.

The other day I addressed to you a request that observers from the United Nations Emergency Force be permitted to enter, to be stationed and to function within the Gaza area. I now wish to repeat this request. It seems to me that such an arrangement is the only way in which I can fulfil my obligation to assist in securing the cessation of all hostilities within the area, which, in the light of the stand taken by the General Assembly, is the area where the United Nations Emergency Force has to function in support of the cease-fire.

The steps you have taken concerning the representatives in Gaza of the United Nations Truce Supervision Organization, has seriously limited their possibilities to fulfil their functions. I will not now enter on a discussion of the questions to which this policy on your side gives rise, but I mentioned it as an added reason for my request.

I may remind you of the fact that already at an early stage British and French authorities permitted United Nations observers to enter Port Said where we have at present also units of the United Nations Emergency Force.

I would appreciate an immediate reply to this request. I would also appreciate receiving all information you can furnish about the present state of affairs in the Gaza area. I am sure that you agree that in face of the concern felt in the light of previous events, and the possibilities implicit in the situation, it should be in Israel's own interest to receive observers, even if quiet would now prevail.

(Signed) Dag HAMMARSKJÖLD

[*A/3384, Ann. IV, Report of the Secretary-General on compliance with General Assembly Res. 997 (ES–1) and 1002 (ES–I), 21 Nov. 1956.*]

LETTER DATED 26 NOVEMBER 1956 FROM THE MINISTER FOR FOREIGN AFFAIRS OF ISRAEL, ADDRESSED TO THE SECRETARY-GENERAL

On 8 November, I conveyed to you my Government's expression of willingness to withdraw its forces from Egyptian territory on the conclusion of satisfactory arrangements with the United Nations in connexion with the emergency international Force.

On 21 November, this policy was reiterated in an *aide-mémoire* addressed to you. I understood from you that you would appoint representatives to pursue our discussions on this subject.

In the plenary meeting of the General Assembly on 24 November [*594th meeting*] the Israel representative expressed the willingness of the Israel Government to continue to discuss with you the means of implementing its undertakings with respect to the withdrawal of forces from Egypt.

I presume that you are now in a position to resume the discussion on these matters. We are prepared to make specific proposals in connexion with the United Nations Emergency Force.

In view of the time which has elapsed since I first made this suggestion I should be grateful to hear when you are prepared to meet me and members of my delegation for this discussion.

(*Signed*) Golda MEIR

LETTER DATED 26 NOVEMBER 1956 FROM THE SECRETARY-GENERAL, ADDRESSED TO THE MINISTER FOR FOREIGN AFFAIRS OF ISRAEL

I have the honour to acknowledge receipt of your letter of 26 November in which you express the expectation that I may now be in a position to resume the discussion of matters raised by you in connexion with the withdrawal of Israel forces. You further declare that you are prepared to make specific proposals in connexion with the United Nations Emergency Force, and that, in view of the time which has elapsed since you first made the suggestion, you would like to hear when I am prepared to meet with you and members of your delegation.

You will remember that, in reply to your letter of 8 November in which you stated your willingness to withdraw the Israel forces on the conclusion of satisfactory arrangements with the United Nations in connexion with the emergency international Force, I asked you, by letter of 11 November, to take immediately the necessary steps for the discussion to which you now refer. In that context I expressed my expectation that, prior to such a discussion, you would wish first to give me a clarification of your views.

My position as reflected in the letter, 11 November, remains unchanged. If you would find it possible to put forward the specific proposals concerning the United Nations Emergency Force, to which you refer in your letter of today, so that I could give them consideration before we engage in a discussion, I believe that it would considerably facilitate our task. Obviously I would not permit this in any way to delay the withdrawal of Israel's forces in compliance with the unqualified and unconditional demand of the General Assembly.

(*Signed*) Dag HAMMARSKJÖLD

[*A/3395, Exchange of letters between the Minister of Foreign Affairs of Israel and the Secretary-General.*]

2. The Government of Israel is agreeable that General Burns be in touch with it in connexion with the location of units of the United Nations Emergency Force in the area between the Suez Canal and the western limits of the Israel positions. The Israel Government will offer whatever technical assistance is necessary to facilitate the implementation of this measure.
[*A/3410, Letter from the Permanent Representative of Israel to the Secretary-General, 1 Dec. 1956.*]

As late as December 1956 the continuation of Israeli demolition in the Sinai peninsula was still an open question.

The Secretary-General on 7 December 1956 addressed to the Government of Israel a communication concerning demolitions on the Sinai Peninsula. Following receipt of an initial reply to this communication the matter was discussed at a meeting between the Secretary-General and the Permanent Representative of Israel on 11 December 1956. The Secretary-General has now received the following letter, dated 12 December 1956, which he wishes to communicate to the Members of the General Assembly:

'At our meeting yesterday you asked me if there would be any further destruction of roads, railways and installations in Sinai, and if there would be any further laying of mines.

'I communicated your enquiries to my Government immediately, and am now in a position to inform you that orders have been issued to refrain from any demolition and destruction in Sinai.

'On the question of mines, I informed you yesterday that General Burns had been provided with maps of all Israel minefields. These minefields are fenced and sign-posted. No other laying of mines has taken place.

(*Signed*) Abba EBAN'

[*A/3453, Note by Secretary-General, 12 Dec. 1956.*]

In January 1957 the Israel government sent an *aide-mémoire* to the Secretary-General, explaining its continued presence in the Sharm el Sheikh area and the Gaza Strip:

A. *Background*

1. In conversations between the Secretary-General and the Israel delegation during December 1956 and January 1957 it was agreed that the discussion of the problems of Sharm el-Sheikh and the Gaza Strip belonged to the final stage of the withdrawal process. There is an international interest involved in the former; and the problems inherent in the latter are especially complex.

2. Israel's approach to these, as to other problems, is influenced primarily by the policy of belligerency maintained by Egypt for several years. This policy finds expression in the Egyptian doctrine of a 'state of war'; in Egypt's refusal to recognize Israel's Charter rights of sovereignty, independence and integrity; and in the organization by Egypt of hostile acts including raids; armed attacks; and blockade activities in the Suez Canal and the Gulf of Aqaba.

3. It is clear that Israel's policy towards Egypt must be influenced by Egypt's policy towards Israel, since the duties of Member States towards each other under the Charter are governed by the principle of reciprocity. For this reason the Government of Israel has attempted to elicit a definition of Egypt's basic policy towards Israel. On 4 November 1956 and thereafter Israel attempted to clarify whether Egypt intends to maintain a state of war against Israel; whether it agrees to recall *fedayeen* gangs under its control in other territories; whether it will suspend the economic boycott and blockade of Israel-bound shipping in the Suez Canal; and whether it will agree to enter into negotiations with Israel with a view to the establishment of peace. Egypt's lack of response to these questions can only be interpreted as signifying that Egypt intends to maintain its belligerent policy towards Israel on land, sea and in the air.

4. This consideration strengthens Israel's concern to ensure that the withdrawal of its forces from Egypt should not be undertaken in such manner as to strengthen the serious likelihood of warlike acts against it.

5. The position would be radically different if Egypt would agree to a policy of simultaneous liquidation of belligerent acts. Israel is willing at any time to sign a protocol or other instrument for the mutual and simultaneous liquidation of belligerency; or a non-aggression pact.

B. *The Sharm el-Sheikh area*

6. The aim is the simultaneous reconciliation of two objectives—the withdrawal of Israel forces, and the guaranteeing of permanent freedom of navigation, by the prevention of belligerent acts against shipping in the Straits of Tiran and the Gulf of Aqaba, which have the character of international waterways in which the right of innocent passage exists.

7. The need for accompanying any withdrawal of Israel forces by related measures for ensuring free navigation and the prevention of belligerency is dictated by the following considerations:

(*a*) For six years Egypt imposed illegal restrictions on the passage of shipping to Elath by the use and threat of force, through the establishment of gun positions at Sharm el-Sheikh.

(*b*) If Egypt were able to re-establish its gun positions and to exercise forcible restrictions on Israel-bound shipping, a grave danger would arise to peace and security. It is axiomatic that the General Assembly cannot intend its resolutions to lead, in the course of their implementation, to the restoration of an illegal situation with a consequent eruption of conflict.

(*c*) Egypt has not taken any steps to comply with the basic decision against belligerency and maritime restrictions adopted by the Security Council on 1 September 1951 (S/2322). This fact has a direct effect on the nature of Israel's obligations towards Egypt and on the need for Israel to be safeguarded against maritime blockade in other waterways.

(*d*) Many nations have a legitimate interest in the freedom of navigation in the Gulf of Aqaba; and in the recent discussion of the General Assembly a wide consensus of opinion was heard in favour of establishing suitable measures forthwith for ensuring freedom of navigation.

(*e*) The deprivations suffered in the past, and still being suffered by many nations, including Israel, through Egypt's refusal to comply with her international obligations in the Suez Canal make it imperative to ensure that the blockade is never restored to the Gulf of Aqaba.

8. Egyptian compliance with the decision of the Security Council of 1 September 1951 has legal and chronological priority over Israel's duty to fulfil recommendations in which Egypt has an interest. Accordingly, Israel formally requests the Secretary-General to ascertain Egypt's intentions with respect to the 1951 resolution of the Security Council. . . .

D. *The Gaza Strip*

13. Israel's approach to this question comprises the following considerations:

(*a*) The Egyptian occupation of Gaza arose out of acts of force committed in 1948 during an attempt to overthrow a recommendation of the General Assembly, and in defiance of successive cease-fire resolutions by the Security Council.

(*b*) The area has never been part of Egypt and its inhabitants are not Egyptian citizens.

(*c*) During eight years of occupation, Egypt used the Gaza Strip solely as a spring-board for assaults against Israel. The notorious *fedayeen* movement had its main centres and recruiting grounds in Gaza. As a result of this fact, Gaza was the source of constant threats to peace and tranquillity over a large proportion of Israel's territory.

(*d*) During the occupation, Egypt made no attempt to rehabilitate any of Gaza's refugee population or to develop the political freedom or economic welfare of the permanent residents of the zone.

(*e*) At the present time law and order prevail in Gaza. Its municipal institutions and public utilities are soundly established. Autonomous local government is being developed; and numerous economic advantages accrue to the zone from the association of its economic life with that of Israel. A report by a representative of the Secretary-General (A/3491) makes it clear that hardship and disorder would result from the disruption of this pattern of growing stability.

(*f*) Israel does not seek to annex Gaza or to maintain its military forces there. On the other hand, Israel is the only State which has a direct interest in a peaceful, orderly and prosperous Gaza Strip.

14. In the light of these considerations Israel offers the following programme for study and comment:

(*a*) No Israel military forces will remain in the area of the Gaza Strip.

(*b*) Israel will continue to supply administrative services including agriculture, education, health, industry, labour, welfare.

(*c*) Law and order will be maintained by the Israel police (including local police).

(*d*) Israel will continue to make available and to develop the public utilities such as electricity and water.

(*e*) Israel will continue to develop local administration in towns and villages.

(*f*) Israel will support the development of means of livelihood for the local population of about 80,000, two-thirds of whom were unemployed under Egyptian administration.

(*g*) The necessary functions of security and administration are all covered by the above proposals. An international military force would not be able effectively to undertake the police duties necessary to prevent a recrudescence of *fedayeen* activities. Nor would such a force be in a position to carry out measures of administration and of economic development for the civilian population. For these reasons the entry of the United Nations Emergency Force into the Gaza area is not envisaged under this plan.

(*h*) Israel will continue to co-operate with the United Nations Relief and Works Agency for Palestine Refugees in the Near East in connexion with the care and maintenance of the refugees.

(*i*) Israel will make its full contribution towards any United Nations plan for the permanent settlement of the refugees, including those in Gaza. Israel urges that such plans be formulated and implemented as soon as possible.

(*j*) In connexion with the above matters, Israel is ready to work out with the United Nations a suitable relationship with respect to the Gaza Strip. [*A/3511, 24 Jan. 1957.*]

These comments drew the following response from the Secretary-General:

B

9. In considering the situation in Gaza the following should be taken into account.

10. Article V of the General Armistice Agreement between Egypt and Israel of 24 February 1949 provides that the armistice line established in article VI 'is not to be construed in any sense as a political or territorial boundary, and is delineated without prejudice to rights, claims and positions of either Party to the Armistice as regards ultimate settlement of the Palestine question'. It goes on to say that 'The basic purpose of the Armistice Demarcation Line is to delineate the line beyond which the armed forces of the respective Parties shall not move . . .'.

11. Although the armistice line thus does not create any new rights for the parties on either side, it resulted in a *de facto* situation by leaving the 'control' (see article VII) of the territory in the hands of the Government, the military forces of which were there in accordance with the stipulations of the Armistice. Control in this case obviously must be considered as including administration and security.

12. In article IV it is recognized that rights, claims or interests of a non-military character in the area of Palestine covered by the agreement may be asserted by either party and that these, by mutual agreement being excluded from armistice negotiations, shall be, at the discretion of the parties, the subject of later settlement. It follows that the *de facto* administrative situation created under the Armistice may be challenged as contrary to the rights, claims or interests of one of the parties, but that it can be legally changed only through settlement between the parties.

13. The Armistice Agreement was signed by both parties and, according to article XII, remains in force until a peaceful settlement between them is achieved. It was approved by the Security Council. Whatever arrangements the United Nations may now wish to make in order to further progress toward peaceful conditions, the Agreement must be fully respected by it. Thus, the United Nations cannot recognize a change of the *de facto* situation created under article VI of the Agreement unless the change is brought about through settlement between the parties; nor, of course, can it lend its assistance to the maintenance of a *de facto* situation contrary to the one created by the Armistice Agreement. These considerations exclude the United Nations from accepting Israel control over the area, even if it were of a non-military character. They would also exclude the deployment of the United Nations Emergency Force necessary, in the absence of Israel troops, if arrangements such as those proposed by the Government of Israel were to be implemented.

14. Deployment of the Force in Gaza, under the resolutions of the General Assembly, would have to be on the same basis as its deployment along the armistice line in the Sinai peninsula. Any broader function for it in that area, in view of the terms of the Armistice Agreement and a recognized principle of international law, would require the consent of Egypt. A widening of the United Nations administrative responsibilities in the area, beyond its responsibilities for the refugees, would likewise have to be based on agreement with Egypt. It follows, therefore, that although the United Nations General Assembly would be entitled to recommend the establishment of a United Nations administration and to request negotiations in order to implement such an arrangement, it would lack authority in that recommendation, unilaterally, to require compliance. . . .

D

23. In connexion with the question of Israel withdrawal from the Sharm el-Sheikh area, attention has been directed to the situation in the Gulf of Aqaba and the Straits of Tiran. This matter is of longer duration and not directly related to the present crisis. The concern now evinced in it, however, calls for consideration of the legal aspects of the matter as a problem in its own right. It follows from principles guiding the United Nations that the Israel military action and its consequences should not be elements influencing the solution. . . .

[*A/3512, Report of the Secretary-General in pursuance of General Assembly Res. 1123 (XI), 24 Jan. 1957.*]

On 2 February the General Assembly adopted Resolutions 1124 (XI) and 1125 (XI). The former deplored Israel's failure to withdraw behind the armistice demarcation line, and called for immediate compliance; the latter, recognizing that withdrawal by Israel must be followed by action which would assure progress towards the creation of peaceful conditions, stated that it considered that, after full withdrawal of Israel from the Sharm el Sheikh and Gaza areas, various measures, as proposed in the Secretary-General's report, would be required for the scrupulous maintenance of the Armistice Agreement. The Secretary-General was requested to take steps, in consultation with the parties concerned, to carry out the measures. He asked the representative of Israel to meet with him on 4 February, and on that date the representative of Israel presented him with an *aide-mémoire*:

3. In the *aide-mémoire* the Government of Israel requests the Secretary-General 'to ask the Government of Egypt whether Egypt agrees to the mutual and full abstention from belligerent acts, by land, air and sea, on withdrawal of Israel troops'. In another point in the *aide-mémoire* clarification is sought by Israel as to whether, 'immediately on the withdrawal of Israel forces from the Sharm el-Sheikh area, units of the United Nations Emergency Force will be stationed along the western shore of the Gulf of Aqaba in order to act as a restraint against hostile acts; and will remain so deployed until another effective means is agreed upon between the parties concerned for ensuring permanent freedom of navigation and the absence of belligerent acts in the Straits of Tiran and the Gulf of Aqaba'.

4. The first of these two points in the Israel *aide-mémoire* must be understood as a request for action in implementation of resolution 1125 (XI), while the wording of the request leaves open the question whether it involves a willingness to comply with the demand for withdrawal in resolution 1124 (XI), even given a positive response by Egypt. The Secretary-General, at the meeting with the representative of Israel, asked whether, with regard to Gaza, it is understood by the Government of Israel that the withdrawal must cover elements of administration as well as military troops, forces and units. A clarification on this point appeared to be a prerequisite to further consideration of the Israel *aide-mémoire*. This point and the following one are related, as there is an unavoidable connexion between Israel's willingness to comply fully with resolution 1124 (XI) as concerns the Gaza Strip and what may be done toward maintaining quiet in the Sharm el-Sheikh area. It is unrealistic to assume that the latter question could be solved while Israel remains in Gaza.

5. The second of the points in the Israel *aide-mémoire* requests a 'clarification' which, in view of the position of the General Assembly, could go beyond what was stated in the last report only after negotiation with Egypt. This follows from the statements in the debate in the General Assembly, and the report on which it was based, which made it clear that the stationing of the Force at Sharm el-Sheikh, under such terms as those mentioned in the question posed by Israel, would require Egyptian consent. In the light of this implication of

Israel's question, the Secretary-General considered it important, as a basis for his consideration of the *aide-mémoire*, to learn whether Israel itself, in principle, consents to a stationing of
UNEF units on its territory in implementation of the functions established for the Force in
the basic decisions and noted in resolution 1125 (XI) where it was indicated that the Force
should be placed 'on the Egyptian–Israel armistice demarcation line'.

6. Concerning his two questions, the Secretary-General received on 5 February a letter
from the Permanent Representative of Israel. The letter is annexed to this report (annex II).
The answer of the Secretary-General to this communication was transmitted by his letter of
6 February (annex III).

7. A further meeting with the representative of Israel was held, on the invitation of the
Secretary-General, on 10 February. Following the meeting, the representative of Israel sent
the Secretary-General an additional letter, received on 11 February. This letter is likewise
annexed to the report (annex IV).

8. This latest communication received from the representative of Israel does not add any
new information. Thus it is still an open question whether Israel, under any circumstances,
accepts full implementation of resolution 1124 (XI), which, as pointed out above, requires
withdrawal from the Gaza Strip of Israel's civil administration and police as well as of its
armed forces. Further, it is still an open question whether Israel accepts the stationing of
units of the United Nations Emergency Force on its side of the armistice demarcation line
under resolution 1125 (XI), concerning which, in a similar respect, Israel has raised a question
which requires clarification of the Egyptian stand. In case Israel were to receive the assurance
from Egypt, which it has requested the Secretary-General to ask for as an action in implementation of resolution II, the representative of Israel in his latest communication has stated
only that his Government 'would formulate its position on all outstanding questions in the
light of Egypt's response'.

9. The fact that the Government of Israel has not found it possible to clarify elements
decisive for the consideration of its requests, has complicated the efforts to achieve implementation of the resolutions of the General Assembly. If this development has 'adversely
affected the time-schedule for the withdrawal' of Israel forces, about which the Secretary-
General had not been informed, an ultimate reason is that Israel's request for an assurance
from Egypt concerning the cessation of all belligerent acts had been put forward while Israel
itself, by continued occupation, maintains a state of belligerency which, in the case of Gaza, it
has not indicated its intention fully to liquidate.

10. The Secretary-General shares the view of the Government of Israel that his offices
may serve as a means for an interchange between Member States of 'proposals and ideas', but
wishes to draw attention to the fact that the action which the Government of Israel has requested cannot be regarded as properly described in such terms, as it would be an action
within the scope of resolution 1125 (XI) and in implementation of this resolution which,
although closely related to resolution 1124 (XI), has, at least, full and unconditional acceptance
of the demand in that resolution as its prerequisite.

11. The Secretary-General does not consider it necessary here to discuss other points in
the latest Israel communication, to which he will have to revert in forthcoming discussions
with the representative of Israel.

PART TWO

12. The General Assembly, in adopting resolutions 1124 (XI) and 1125 (XI), was guided by
the need to 'assure progress towards the creation of peaceful conditions' in the area. It was
recognized that this objective—which was also the theme of the Secretary-General's report
(A/3512) on which the debate in the General Assembly was based—required, as an initial
step, withdrawal of Israel behind the armistice demarcation line, to be followed by various
measures within the framework of the Armistice Agreement. These measures aimed at 'a
return to the state of affairs envisaged in the Armistice Agreement, and avoidance of the state
of affairs into which conditions, due to a lack of compliance with the Agreement, had pro-

gressively deteriorated' (A/3512, para. 15). With this in view, resolution 1125 (XI) in its operative paragraph 2 called for scrupulous observance of the Armistice Agreement, which, in its first article, establishes the right of each party to 'its security and freedom from fear of attack by the armed forces of the other'.

13. The position of the Secretary-General, in his efforts to secure implementation of the two resolutions, has been based on the following considerations. First, agreement was wide-spread in the General Assembly, as reflected in the sequence of the two resolutions, that like the cease-fire, withdrawal is a preliminary and essential phase in a development through which a stable basis may be laid for peaceful conditions in the area. Second, the principle which must guide the United Nations after a change in the *status juris* through military action con-trary to the Charter, as stated in the last report of the Secretary-General (A/3512, para. 5 (*a*)), is recognized as expressing a basic rule of the Charter, thus giving a high priority to requests based on that principle. The key significance of resolution 1124 (XI), as indicated by these two considerations, is confirmed by the fact that resolution 1125 (XI) explicitly states that the measures to which it refers are to be carried out 'after full withdrawal of Israel' behind the armistice demarcation line.

14. The Secretary-General has understood the General Assembly to see in resolution 1125 (XI) a formal undertaking with respect to measures to be effected upon withdrawal, in the light of which resolution 1124 (XI) should be implemented without delay. This is par-ticularly so, since the United Nations Emergency Force is deployed in the region with an assurance from the Government of Egypt that the Government, when exercising its sovereign rights on any matter concerning the presence and functioning of the Force, will be guided in good faith by its acceptance of the basic General Assembly resolution of 5 November 1956 concerning the Force and its functions [*resolution 1000 (ES–I)*].

15. Beginning with its initial resolution of 2 November 1956 (resolution 997 (ES–I)) concerning this question, and culminating in its resolution 1125 (XI) of 2 February 1957, the General Assembly has stressed the key importance it attaches to scrupulous observance by both parties of the terms of the Armistice Agreement between Egypt and Israel. In this re-gard, the Secretary-General is able to report that the Government of Egypt reaffirms its intent to observe fully the provisions of the Armistice Agreement to which it is a party, as indicated earlier in its acceptance (A/3266) of resolution 997 (ES–I) of 2 November 1956, on the assumption, of course, that observance will be reciprocal. Attention should be drawn, in this context, to the statement in paragraph 22 of the last report of the Secretary-General (A/3512) reporting the desire of the Government of Egypt to see an end to all raids and incursions across the armistice line, in both directions, with effective assistance from United Nations auxiliary organs to that effect.

16. The position of the Government of Israel on the Armistice Agreement, as reaffirmed by the representative of Israel in response to a question on the matter during his meeting with the Secretary-General on 10 February, was set forth in the letter of 25 January 1957 from the representative of Israel to the Secretary-General (annex V).

17. The relationship between the two resolutions on withdrawal and on measures to be carried out after withdrawal, affords the possibility of informal explorations of the whole field covered by the resolutions, preparatory to negotiations. Later, the results of such explora-tions may be used in negotiations through a constructive combination of measures, represent-ing for the two countries concerned parallel progress toward the peaceful conditions sought. However, such explorations cannot be permitted to invert the sequence between withdrawal and other measures, nor to disrupt the evolution of negotiations toward their goal. Progress toward peaceful conditions, following the general policy suggested in the last report to the General Assembly, on which its resolution 1125 (XI) is based, has to be achieved gradually. To disregard this would render the process more difficult and might seriously jeopardize the possibility of achieving desired results. In explorations and negotiations, which in this sense necessarily have to proceed step by step, the parties involved must time and again show willingness to accept some risks as a condition for progress.

18. Peaceful conditions in the Middle East must be created in the interest of all countries

in the region and of the world community. The basic principles of the Charter must be asserted and respected, in the very same interest. Neither one of these imperative demands can be met at the expense of the other. The fulfilment of one will make it easier to meet the other, but to have peace with justice, adherence to principle and law must be given priority and cannot be conditional. In the present case, efforts to meet the two requirements just stated have so far been frustrated. The United Nations must maintain its position on these requirements and, in doing so, should be entitled to count on the assistance, in the complex process of gradual and sensitive approach to the objectives, in particular of the two Member States directly concerned. If such assistance is not forthcoming, the efforts of the United Nations will be caused to fail, to the detriment of all. In an organization based on voluntary co-operation and respect for the general opinion to which the organization gives expression, the responsibility for such a failure would fall, not on the organization, but on those who had denied it the necessary co-operation. This responsibility extends beyond the immediate issue. It may also, in this case, well have to cover difficulties flowing from possible failure of the United Nations to fulfil its vital functions under the Armistice Agreements and of the parties to come to grips with the wider problems which call for such urgent attention. . . .

21. In the situation now facing the United Nations the General Assembly, as a matter of priority, may wish to indicate how it desires the Secretary-General to proceed with further steps to carry out the relevant decisions of the General Assembly.

ANNEX I

Aide-mémoire DATED 4 FEBRUARY 1957, TRANSMITTED BY THE PERMANENT REPRESENTATIVE OF ISRAEL TO THE SECRETARY-GENERAL

The Government of Israel takes note of the adoption by the General Assembly of two inter-related resolutions (*1124 (XI) and 1125 (XI)*).

Israel will co-operate with any United Nations effort designed to establish peace in the area, based on the principles of the United Nations Charter.

I am instructed urgently to request the Secretary-General to ask the Government of Egypt whether Egypt agrees to the mutual and full abstention from belligerent acts, by land, air and sea, on the withdrawal of Israel troops. This matter is of central importance to all the questions at issue.

In considering the withdrawal schedule, I am instructed to refer to the Sharm el-Sheikh area, and the related question of measures designed to prevent hostile acts, such as inter-ference with free navigation in the Straits of Tiran and in the Gulf of Aqaba. The General Assembly in its resolution 1125 (XI) has recognized 'that withdrawal by Israel must be followed by action which would assure progress towards the creation of peaceful conditions'.

A renewal of interference with shipping bound to and from Elath would clearly lead to hostilities and thus prejudice the declared objective of United Nations resolutions. Accordingly, I am instructed to obtain clarification without delay, whether immediately on the withdrawal of Israel forces from the Sharm el-Sheikh area, units of the United Nations Emergency Force will be stationed along the western shore of the Gulf of Aqaba in order to act as a restraint against hostile acts; and will remain so deployed until another effective means is agreed upon between the parties concerned for ensuring permanent freedom of navigation and the absence of belligerent acts in the Straits of Tiran and the Gulf of Aqaba.

A positive response to the above questions from all concerned would greatly facilitate the early fulfilment of United Nations objectives as set forth in the United Nations resolutions taken as a whole.

ANNEX II

LETTER DATED 5 FEBUARY 1957 FROM THE PERMANENT REPRESENTATIVE OF ISRAEL, ADDRESSED TO THE SECRETARY-GENERAL

I have been in touch with my Government on the subject of our conversation yesterday.

The Government of Israel attaches primary importance to the elucidation of the two questions which I presented to you in my *aide-mémoire*.

An affirmative response from Egypt to the first question, on belligerent acts, would affect my Government's policies on outstanding issues. A positive response to the second would greatly assist us to understand the potential role of the United Nations Emergency Force in the creation and maintenance of peaceful conditions.

Accordingly, on the clarification of these basic matters, a position would be created in which the other questions which you raised at yesterday's meeting could be considered in a more practical way.

(*Signed*) Abba EBAN

ANNEX III

LETTER DATED 6 FEBRUARY 1957 FROM THE SECRETARY-GENERAL, ADDRESSED TO THE PERMANENT REPRESENTATIVE OF ISRAEL

In our meeting of 4 February, as you will recall, I drew attention to two points on which you agreed to seek clarification from your Government 'immediately'. The two points were (1) whether with regard to Gaza it is understood by the Government of Israel that the withdrawal must cover elements of administration as well as military troops, forces and units; and (2) whether, as a question of principle, the Government of Israel agrees to the stationing of units of the United Nations Emergency Force on the Israel side of the armistice demarcation line.

Although undertaking to seek clarification from your Government, you indicated in our discussion and in response to an inquiry on the same matter made of you by Dr Bunche on 5 February, that the attitude of your Government on these two points is as set forth in your previous *aide-mémoire* (A/3511) and in your address to the General Assembly of 28 January. In these two documents, the answer to the first question concerning Gaza is that Israel does not intend to withdraw its civil administration from that territory, while there is no reference at all to the second question concerning stationing of UNEF on the Israel side of the line.

May I also point out that your communication to me of 5 February, although informing me that you have been in touch with your Government on the subject of our conversation on the previous days, has to say about the questions I raised, only that if 'affirmative' and 'positive' responses to the questions put by Israel were first obtained, then 'a position would be created' in which my questions 'could be considered in a more practical way'.

In the circumstances, I must assume, at least for the present, that the reply of your Government to my two questions is specifically negative in one instance and essentially so in the other.

(*Signed* Dag HAMMARSKJÖLD

ANNEX IV

LETTER DATED 10 FEBRUARY 1957 FROM THE PERMANENT REPRESENTATIVE OF ISRAEL, ADDRESSED TO THE SECRETARY-GENERAL

I refer to your letter of 6 February 1957.

My Government's position on the withdrawal of forces from the western coast of the Gulf of Aqaba and from Gaza has been set out in my *aide-mémoire* of 4 February and in my letter to you of 5 February.

The latter communication refers to the request which you made to me on 4 February for the clarification of two points bearing on matters other than the withdrawal of armed forces from the Gulf of Aqaba and Gaza. On learning from the Egyptian Government whether or not it will exercise belligerency by land, sea and air after the withdrawal of Israel forces, my Government would formulate its position on all outstanding questions in the light of the Egyptian Government's response.

A Government which anticipates that its neighbours will claim and exercise belligerency against it must clearly adopt a different view of its security problems than it might take if it could confidently assume full and mutual abstention from all belligerent acts. If the proposed affirmation of abstention from belligerent acts were made, Egypt and Israel could move forward to the establishment of agreed relations in the security and other spheres. I cannot predict what arrangements they might or might not then concert with respect to the disposition of their forces on each side of their frontier. The fact that I have not obtained assistance in receiving an official expression of Egypt's intentions on belligerency deprives my Government of an essential element for the consideration of a great variety of dependent problems.

I have similarly informed my Government that I have not been able to obtain clarification whether, immediately on the withdrawal of Israel forces from the Sharm el-Sheikh area, units of UNEF will be stationed along the western shore of the Gulf of Aqaba in order to act as a restraint against hostile acts, and will remain so deployed until another effective means is agreed upon between the parties concerned for ensuring permanent freedom of navigation and absence of belligerent acts in the Straits of Tiran and in the Gulf of Aqaba.

I have accordingly reported to Jerusalem that our conversations have thrown no light on the questions whether, on the withdrawal of Israel forces from the Sharm el-Sheikh area, there will be any effective guarantee for continued freedom of navigation in the waters of the Gulf of Aqaba. This freedom is a vital and legitimate national interest for Israel, and is also of international significance. The fact that we have not obtained a positive answer on this point has adversely affected the time-schedule for the withdrawal of forces.

I wish to explain why Israel attaches crucial importance to the questions set out in the *aide-mémoire* of 4 February.

In the light of past experience, and of recent Egyptian declarations, my Government must in all prudence hold the following assumptions unless evidence to the contrary becomes available:

First, that Egypt claims the withdrawal of Israel troops from its territory, while itself reserving belligerent rights to remain in effect after such withdrawal;

Second, that Egypt has not agreed that free navigation in the Gulf of Aqaba will be ensured after Israel's withdrawal, or that effective measures such as the stationing of units of UNEF should be instituted to ensure such continued freedom of navigation;

Third, that when the Suez Canal becomes physically opened for navigation Egypt will, as in the past, obstruct Israel's exercise of its rights in the Canal under the 1888 Convention;

Fourth, that the doctrine and practice of continuing belligerency will govern Egypt's relations towards Israel in such matters as frontier raids and the non-recognition of Israel's rights under the Charter.

These are sombre and disquieting assumptions. But nothing has yet happened to justify any contrary assumption on our part. I note, in particular, that you did not feel able to state today that Egypt's declaration of adherence to the 1949 Armistice Agreement includes the acceptance by that country of an obligation to abstain from the claim and exercise of belligerent rights in the Suez Canal, the Gulf of Aqaba or elsewhere.

Against this background, it has become clear to the Government of Israel that the withdrawal of troops, without simultaneous action to prevent the renewal of hostilities by land and sea, would in fact lead to the resumption of such conflict. It is noteworthy that in adopting resolutions calling respectively for the withdrawal of troops and for measures to ensure progress towards peaceful conditions, the General Assembly declined to separate its action under these two headings. It voted on the explicit assumption that action in one field without action in the other would jeopardize the prospects of peace.

In that spirit, my Government made an effort on 4 February to solve the deadlock by the clarification of the two points referred to in its *aide-mémoire*.

In the first place we sought a declaration by Egypt and Israel pledging themselves to full and mutual abstention from belligerent acts. Such an affirmation would set up an accepted principle for relations between the two countries, and bring those relations, for the first time, within the régime of the United Nations Charter. Abstention from belligerency would, of course, include the annulment of such practices as the restrictions on Israel-bound shipping in the Suez Canal and the Gulf of Aqaba, and of activities such as those of the *fedayeen*, which are incompatible with any policy of non-belligerency. On the basis of a mutual abstention from belligerent acts, Egypt and Israel could construct a coherent system of security relationships. The implementation of a non-belligerent agreement would still require certain measures and guarantees, but the conditions for progress in all fields would be automatically and radically transformed.

My Government feels that it is not equitable to ask it to discuss its attitude on any concrete question affecting its security unless it knows whether its answer must be based on the assumption of war, or on the assumption of progress to peace. Other Member States discussing this problem might reach more precise conclusions if they understood clearly whether or not Egypt, on securing the withdrawal of Israel forces, would renew its policy of blockade and raids.

A similar situation prevails with respect to my second request. I have enquired what arrangements for continued freedom of navigation on the Gulf of Aqaba and the Straits of Tiran would prevail on the withdrawal of Israel's forces from the Sharm el-Sheikh area. It is regrettable and puzzling that information so vital to our schedule for the withdrawal of troops should still be withheld from us. So long as this information is denied it, my Government must apprehend that the withdrawal of its forces would be followed by an immediate or early resumption of the illicit restrictions which effectively denied Israel the free use of its southern port and cut our country off from normal trading relations with a great part of the world during a period when the Suez Canal, too, has been effectively closed to essential Israel-bound commerce.

The priority of the Sharm el-Sheikh area in any discussion on the withdrawal of forces is justified by many considerations. The areas adjoining Sharm el-Sheikh have recently been evacuated. An important international interest is widely recognized in the adjoining waters. A wide consensus of opinion exists on the need to prevent blockades and maritime warfare. Withdrawal from this area would complete the evacuation of the territory of Egypt. In these circumstances my Government has felt justified in proposing that this problem be solved before others of greater complexity are broached. The solution which we seek is one that reconciles the withdrawal of forces with the maintenance of continued freedom of navigation.

My Government has studied your letter of 6 February and a published statement on that date. It does not agree that the solution of two other questions, not dealing directly with the withdrawal of forces, can justifiably be described as 'prerequisite' to the solution of the two basic problems of belligerency and withdrawal from the remaining area of Sinai. We hold that the two basic problems raised in the *aide-mémoire* of 4 February are objectively and intrinsically the most urgent of those still outstanding. My Government's position on this matter is set out in this letter, and it therefore does not agree that the formulation of the last paragraph of your letter of 6 February is an adequate description of its stand.

In the light of these considerations, and of my letter of 5 February, I am instructed to reiterate the request made through you in my *aide-mémoire* of 4 February for clarification by the Egyptian Government of its attitude to an affirmation of full and mutual abstention from belligerent acts; on the withdrawal of Israel troops; and for clarification of the guarantees to be established for continued freedom of navigation on the withdrawal of Israel forces from the Sharm el-Sheikh area.

My Government holds that it is one of the central functions of the high office of Secretary-General to serve as a means for the interchange of proposals and ideas between Member States, especially when normal methods of inter-State contact are not available. It hopes that in that spirit you will assist it to elucidate the two problems referred to in the 4 February *aide-mémoire*, in order that progress may be made in fulfilling the objectives of the General Assembly's recent resolutions.

(*Signed*) Abba Eban

ANNEX V

Letter dated 25 January 1957 from the Permanent Representative of Israel, addressed to the Secretary-General

In your letter of 6 December 1956, you asked me to ascertain the position of the Israel Government on the General Armistice Agreement between Israel and Egypt.

This question has also arisen on a number of occasions in our conversations, and, as you are no doubt aware, has formed the subject of public statements by the Prime Minister, and by other official Israel spokesmen.

Israel's view as outlined in these statements is, briefly, that the General Armistice Agreement has been consistently violated by Egypt both in letter and in spirit ever since it was signed on 24 February 1949. Its central purpose of non-belligerency and its character as a transition to a peaceful settlement have been constantly repudiated by Egypt. Egypt has even held, most incongruously, that the Agreement could coexist with a 'state of war' against Israel. This policy of Egypt and the actions flowing therefrom have brought the Agreement to nought, with the result that a new system of relationships must now be constructed. On the other hand, Israel does not consider that the relations between Israel and Egypt are those of a state of war: our mutual obligations are still defined by the Charter of the United Nations which rules out any concept of a 'state of war'. This was made clear by the Prime Minister of Israel in a speech in the Knesset on 23 January 1957. The relevant extract of this speech follows:

'As for the Armistice Agreement with Egypt, which was signed eight years ago (on 24 February 1949), as a transitional stage to permanent peace, the Egyptian dictator has violated its principles and purposes and by his repeated declarations that there is a state of war between Israel and Egypt, he has distorted the essence and aims of the Agreement. He exploited it as a smoke screen to cover up his murderous attacks against the people of Israel and his implacable blockade of Israel on land, at sea and in the air.

It was from the Gaza Strip that *fedayeen* units were dispatched to Israel and bands of murderers and saboteurs were organized in other Arab countries as well. Thus the Agreement was transformed into a harmful and dangerous fiction which only assisted the Egyptian ruling junta in its malevolent designs.

Any return to this Agreement means return to murder and sabotage. Israel does not claim that the absence of an armistice agreement means the existence of a state of war with Egypt even though Egypt insisted on the existence of a state of war even when the Agreement was in existence. Israel is prepared to confirm its position on this by signing immediately with Egypt an agreement of non-belligerency and mutual non-aggression, but the Armistice Agreement, violated and broken, is beyond repair.'

(*Signed*) Abba EBAN

[*A/3527, Report of the Secretary-General, 11 Feb. 1957.*]

Israel's position on Gaza did, however, soften. One month later the Secretary-General was able to report her full compliance with the call in Resolution 1124 (XI) to withdraw behind the armistice demarcation line. But the Israeli stand did not alter in respect of the denunciation of the Armistice Agreement, nor of her refusal to allow UNEF to be stationed on her side of the demarcation line:

2. The Foreign Minister of Israel, on 1 March, announced in the General Assembly the decision of the Government of Israel to act in compliance with the request in this resolution. The same day the Secretary-General instructed the Commander of the United Nations Emergency Force, as a matter of the utmost urgency, to arrange for a meeting with the Israel Commander-in-Chief, in order to agree with him on arrangements for the complete and unconditional withdrawal of Israel in accordance with the decision of the General Assembly.

3. On 4 March, the Foreign Minister of Israel confirmed to the General Assembly the Government of Israel's declaration of 1 March. The same day the Commander of the United Nations Emergency Force met at Lydda with the Israel Commander-in-Chief. Technical arrangements were agreed upon for the withdrawal of Israel and the entry of the United Nations Emergency Force in the Gaza Strip during the hours of curfew on the night of 6/7 March. Arrangements were made for a similar take-over of the Sharm el-Sheikh area on 8 March. . . .

6. The Secretary-General, thus, is now in a position to report full compliance with General Assembly resolution 1 of 2 February 1957 (1124 (XI)). [*A/3568, Second Report of the Secretary-General in pursuance of General Assembly Res. 1124 (XI) and 1125 (XI), 8 Mar. 1957.*]

Although UNEF's functions had officially terminated by the time fighting broke out in May 1967, UNEF personnel had not yet completed their withdrawal. In the event, they suffered considerable casualties. The measures taken by the Commander for the protection of UNEF personnel have been recounted elsewhere (pp. 295–300). However, the Commander had reason for direct protests to Israel over looting of UNEF property:

117. With the exception of small losses of Indian national stores caused by Israeli fire in Camp Delhi, no other damage or loss of contingent property occurred. Contingents were able to remove all national stores. With the exception of some barrack furniture which was uneconomical to transport, all UNEF property was removed from UNEF camps before they were abandoned. The water distillation and power plants in Sharm el Sheikh could not, however, be removed owing to the technical problems involved. Two UNEF installations were occupied by Israel forces, namely UNEF Headquarters in Gaza and UNEF depots in Camp Rafah.

118. When the Commander and his party returned to UNEF headquarters on the evening of 6 June, documents and office equipment were untouched. Some items, including radios, tape recorders and clocks, belonging to UNEF and to individuals had, however, been looted, presumably by Israel forces who occupied the building.

As it was no longer feasible to retain a UNEF guard at UNEF Headquarters owing to the presence of a large number of Israel troops, many of whom were inside the headquarters compound, the Israel Army authorities were requested to assume security responsibilities there in order to prevent further looting. Thus, from the evening of 7 June the Israel forces in Gaza were responsible for the security of UNEF Headquarters. A subsequent visit to the offices showed that most of the office furniture, typewriters, fans and other UNEF property had been removed by the Israel military personnel. In fact, UNEF representatives actually witnessed the removal of these items but were unable to secure any effective action by the responsible Israel authorities to prevent it. All of the United Nations vehicles in running condition had also been removed by Israel forces and were seen in use in the Gaza area.

119. When on 9 June representatives of UNEF paid their first visit to Camp Rafah the Israel forces were in occupation of the entire camp. UNEF representatives found that Israel forces had removed almost all UNEF vehicles in the park, barrack furniture, bedding and other portable property. Some pilfering by local civilians was also observed in the area. UNEF representatives called on local military authorities as well as the Israel military government of the Gaza Strip and protested the looting and removal of UNEF property. The Israel authorities gave every assurance that measures would be taken to prevent such looting and that orders would be issued for the return of all vehicles. A subsequent inspection of Camp Rafah indicated, however, that even more UNEF property had been removed since the initial appeal.

120. On 28 June, the Secretary-General addressed a note to the Permanent Representative of Israel to the United Nations in which he described the situation at Camp Rafah, protested against the looting and pilfering of UNEF property by soldiers of the armed forces of Israel and requested immediate remedial measures, including the return of vehicles and stores and

the ensuring of the unrestricted access to Camp Rafah for United Nations representatives. The Secretary-General pointed out that it was the intention to turn over to UNRWA all of the food and medical stores of UNEF, other suitable stores and vehicles which were appropriate for UNRWA use.

121. Since the note of 28 June was written, further reports received by the Secretary-General indicated that continued pilfering, vandalism, organized removal of UNEF property by members of the armed forces and disorderly conditions within the camp, including incursions by parties of the local population, had combined to make the task of the United Nations representatives extremely difficult, if not impossible. Consequently, in a further note to the Permanent Representative of Israel, the Secretary-General protested most strongly to the Government of Israel against the continuance of this situation and requested it most urgently to take the necessary measures to put a stop to looting, pilfering and the removal of UNEF property from Camp Rafah, so that the United Nations representatives in the area and the representatives of UNRWA could go about their task in an expeditious, orderly and effective manner.

122. On completion of the withdrawal of all military personnel of UNEF and after establishing a proper organization under United Nations international staff for the disposal of UNEF property, the Commander left the area on 17 June. Remaining on duty are about thirty civilian personnel under the supervision of the representative of United Nations Headquarters and the Chief Administrative Officer of UNEF. They have arranged for the transfer of some medical stores and some of the food still remaining in Camp Rafah to UNRWA. They are also arranging to transfer some vehicles and radio equipment to UNTSO or to ship them to the United Nations office in Pisa. Instructions have been issued to this group to compile detailed information on UNEF property which has been looted for purposes of record and of claiming compensation. [*A/6672, Report of the Secretary-General on UNEF, 12 July 1967*, pp. 39–41, mimeo.]

At the governmental level, Israel sought to punish such acts:

The Permanent Representative of Israel to the United Nations presents his compliments to the Secretary-General of the United Nations and in referring to the Secretary-General's Note Verbale of 28 June 1967 relative to recent acts in the UNEF Base Camp Rafah, has the honour to state as follows:

The Secretary-General's Note Verbale was immediately transmitted to the Ministry for Foreign Affairs which is giving it the closest attention.

At the same time the Secretary-General is informed that all cases of pilferage which come to notice are brought before an appropriate Court Martial or Military Court.

It is understood that free access to the Camp has been accorded to a representative of UNEF, Mr Seward, who visited the Camp on the morning of 30 June.

The Permanent Representative of Israel avails himself of this opportunity to express to the Secretary-General the assurances of his highest consideration. [*A/6672/Add. 1, Note Verbale dated 1 July from the Permanent Representative of Israel to the Secretary-General, 15 July 1967*.]

(b) The United Kingdom and France

Once UNEF had been established, the relations between the UN and the United Kingdom and France were fairly satisfactory. This was so notwithstanding public opinion in those countries, which was strongly divided and one part of which saw the UN Force as an instrument in their country's humiliation. We have already shown that the United Kingdom and France sought to portray UNEF as the kind of force which was needed to separate Egypt and Israel, and whose existence and effectiveness would make unnecessary the continued presence of British and French troops in Egypt.

I have the honour, on instructions from my Government, to communicate to you the following in response to resolution A/3256 adopted by the General Assembly on 2 November 1956 (resolution 997 (ES–I)), during its emergency special session:

'1. The British and French Governments have given careful consideration to the resolution adopted by the General Assembly of the United Nations on 2 November. They maintain their view that police action must be carried through urgently to stop the hostilities which are now threatening the Suez Canal, to prevent a resumption of those hostilities and to pave the way for a definite settlement of the Arab–Israel war which threatens the legitimate interests of so many countries.

'2. They would most willingly stop military action as soon as the following conditions could be satisfied:

'(*a*) Both the Egyptian and Israel Governments agree to accept a United Nations Force to keep the peace.

'(*b*) The United Nations decides to constitute and maintain such a Force until an Arab–Israel peace settlement is reached and until satisfactory arrangements have been agreed in regard to the Suez Canal, both agreements to be guaranteed by the United Nations.

'(*c*) In the meantime, until the United Nations Force is constituted, both combatants agree to accept forthwith limited detachments of Anglo-French troops to be stationed between the combatants.'

I request you to be so good as to circulate this note immediately to all Members of the United Nations.

(*Signed*) L. DE GUIRINCAUD
Alternate Permanent Representative of
France to the United Nations

[*A/3268, Letter of 3 Nov. 1956 to the Secretary-General.*]

A letter (A/3269) in identical terms was sent by the permanent representative of the United Kingdom. The Secretary-General sent identically-worded responses to the two governments:

1. The first emergency special session of the General Assembly at its meeting of 3–4 November 1956 adopted the following resolution. [999 (ES–I)].

2. In this regard, I note the information conveyed in the letter of 3 November addressed to the Secretary-General by the permanent representative of the United Kingdon of Great Britain and Northern Ireland to the United Nations (A/3269) and particularly the conditions under which military action would be stopped.

3. I wish to make the following comments on the three conditions established by your Government for a cessation of your action. (*a*) In the voting on the resolution contained in document A/3276 requesting the Secretary-General to submit within forty-eight hours a plan for the setting up of an emergency international United Nations Force, the delegations of Egypt and Israel abstained. (*b*) The request to which I have just referred, and which was approved by the Assembly, establishes that the Secretary-General should submit his proposal within forty-eight hours. In a separate resolution at the same meeting the Assembly established a time-limit of twelve hours for a report on the cease-fire. It thus follows that the General Assembly did not accept the decision on the establishment of a United Nations Force as a condition for the cease-fire. (*c*) The statements made prior to the adoption of the resolution on the United Nations Force made it clear that it was a widespread view that none of the parties engaged in the present operation in the area should participate in the Force. This has a direct and obvious bearing on any possibility of stationing Anglo-French troops between the combatants, pending the establishment of a United Nations Force. I must assume the

decision in question to have been taken on the basis of an interpretation which if maintained would exclude such an arrangement as a possible condition for a cease-fire.

4. In pursuance of the functions entrusted to me by operative paragraph 2 of the resolution of 4 November, quoted above; in view of the provision in paragraph 2 of the resolution of 2 November and operative paragraph 3 of the resolution of 4 November; and in view, further, of the Canadian-sponsored resolution, also adopted on 4 November, concerning the plan for a United Nations Force, and the indications it gives as to the attitude of the General Assembly to the three conditions established by your Government, I must inquire whether the Government of the United Kingdom will accept the provisions set forth in operative paragraphs 1 and 3 of the resolution of 2 November and will be willing to make arrangements with the Secretary-General for the implementation of the cease-fire and the halting of the movement of military forces and arms into the area, in accordance with operative paragraph 2 of the resolution of 4 November.

5. I wish to draw to your attention that the Government of Israel has accepted the cease-fire on the condition of reciprocal acceptance by Egypt, while Egypt has accepted the cease-fire provided that military actions against Egypt are stopped. With the stands thus taken by Israel and Egypt, it is obvious that the position of your Government and the Government of France will determine whether or not it will be possible to achieve a cease-fire between Egypt and Israel.

6. In pursuance of the provision in operative paragraph 2 of the resolution (999 (ES–I)) of 4 November authorizing the Secretary-General 'immediately to arrange with the parties concerned for the implementation of the cease-fire and the halting of the movement of military forces and arms into the area,' I am requesting all four parties, which of course includes the United Kingdom, to bring to a halt all hostile military actions in the area by 20.00 GMT, Sunday, 4 November 1956. May I further request that your Government's decision in this matter be communicated to me at the earliest possible moment, and at all events so early as to render it possible to inform the other parties concerned about your decision prior to the said hour. The decisions of the other parties in this regard will be transmitted to the Government of the United Kingdom without delay.

7. In view of the urgency of the situation, which accounts for the short time-limit fixed in the resolution of 4 November, I request again that a definitive reply be given at the earliest possible hour.

Dag HAMMARSKJÖLD

[A/3287, ann. 4, Cable of 4 Nov. 1956.][4]

The two governments responded in identical fashion:

I have the honour on instructions from Her Majesty's Government in the United Kingdom to transmit the following reply to your communication of 4 November 1956 (A/3287, annex 4).

1. The Governments of the United Kingdom and France have studied carefully the resolutions of the United Nations General Assembly passed on 4 November. They warmly welcome the idea, which seems to underlie the request to the Secretary-General in the resolution sponsored by Canada and adopted by the Assembly at its 563rd meeting, that an international Force should be interpolated as a shield between Israel and Egypt, pending a Palestine settlement and a settlement of the question of the Suez Canal. But, according to their information, neither the Israeli nor the Egyptian Government has accepted such a proposal. Nor has any plan for an international Force been accepted by the General Assembly or endorsed by the Security Council.

2. The composition of the staff and contingents of the international Force would be a matter for discussion.

3. The two Governments continue to believe that it is necessary to interpose an international Force to prevent the continuance of hostilities between Egypt and Israel, to secure

---

[4] See also A/3287, ann. 2, for cable to Government of France.

the speedy withdrawal of Israeli forces, to take the necessary measures to remove obstructions and restore traffic through the Suez Canal and to promote a settlement of the problems of the area.

4. Certain Anglo-French operations with strictly limited objectives are continuing. But as soon as the Israeli and Egyptian Governments signify acceptance of, and the United Nations endorses a plan for, an international Force with the above functions, the two Governments will cease all military action.

5. In thus stating their views, the United Kingdom and French Governments would like to express their firm conviction that their action is justified. To return deliberately to the system which has produced continuing deadlock and chaos in the Middle East is now not only undesirable but impossible. A new constructive solution is required. To this end they suggest that an early Security Council meeting at the ministerial level should be called in order to work out an international settlement which would be likely to endure, together with the means to enforce it.

I request you to be so good as to circulate this reply to all Members of the United Nations.

(*Signed*) Pierson DIXON

Permanent Representative of the United Kingdom
of Great Britain and Northern Ireland to the United Nations

[*A/3293, 5 Nov. 1956.*][5]

On 5 November the British announced that they had ordered a cease-fire at Port Said, and a cessation of bombing throughout Egypt—though the right was reserved to continue 'other forms of action as opposed to bombing [which] will be confined to the support of any necessary operation in the Canal area' (A/3299). The Egyptian government insisted that no such cease-fire at Port Said had been ordered.[6]

A further exchange between Britain and France on the one hand and the Secretary-General on the other, took place in which the former suggested that a Franco-British force was the appropriate one to clear the Suez Canal:

. . . I have been instructed to convey to you at once the following message from Her Majesty's Government:

'Her Majesty's Government welcome the Secretary-General's communication, while agreeing that a further clarification of certain points is necessary.

'If the Secretary-General can confirm that the Egyptian and Israeli Governments have accepted an unconditional cease-fire, and that the international Force to be set up will be competent to secure and supervise the attainment of the objectives set out in the operative paragraphs of the resolution passed by the General Assembly on November 2, Her Majesty's Government will agree to stop further military operations.

'They wish to point out however that the clearing of the obstructions in the Suez Canal and its approaches, which is in no sense a military operation, is a matter of great urgency in the interests of world shipping and trade. The Franco-British force is equipped to tackle this task. Her Majesty's Government therefore propose that the technicians accompanying the Franco-British force shall begin this work at once.

'Pending the confirmation of the above points, Her Majesty's Government are ordering their forces to cease fire at midnight GMT unless they are attacked.'

I request you to be so good as to circulate this reply to all Members of the United Nations.

(*Signed*) Pierson DIXON

[*A/3306, 6 Nov. 1956.*][7]

[5] See also A/3294, 5 Nov. 1956, for Letter from Government of France.

[6] A/3305, 6 Nov. 1956; A/3312, 7 Nov. 1956.

[7] See also A/3307 for letter in identical terms from France.

4. The Government of Egypt has, 4 November 1956, accepted the request of the Secretary-General for a cease-fire, without any attached conditions. It is to be assumed that this acceptance (A/3287, annex 6), although referring to the time-limit set in the request of the Secretary-General, is generally valid.

5. The Government of Israel has now, in a clarification (A/3297) of its first reply to the request of the Secretary-General for a cease-fire, stated that in the light of Egypt's declaration of willingness to a cease-fire Israel confirms its readiness to agree to a cease-fire.

6. The conditions for a general cease-fire would thus seem to be established and a new request warranted, provided that the Governments of France and the United Kingdom would recognize the decision of the General Assembly, establishing a United Nations Command, as meeting the condition they have made for a cessation of hostilities, and if, further, the Government of Israel were to endorse the same General Assembly decision.

7. In view of the urgent request from the General Assembly for a cease-fire, in view of the attitudes on a cease-fire taken by the Governments of Egypt and Israel, in view of the General Assembly decision to establish a United Nations Command and its acceptance by the Government of Egypt, and in pursuance of the General Assembly resolution (A/3275) adopted on 4 November 1956 (resolution 999 (ES–I) operative paragraph 2), I wish to ask the Governments of France and the United Kingdom whether they would recognize the decision of the General Assembly, establishing United Nations Command, as meeting their conditions for a cease-fire. I likewise wish to ask the Government of Israel if it finds itself in a position to accept the General Assembly resolution on the establishment of a United Nations Command.

8. In case of affirmative replies to the questions in paragraph 7 I intend to address again a proposal for an agreed cease-fire to the four Governments concerned. [*A/3310, Aide-Mémoire from the Secretary-General addressed to the Governments of France and the UK, 7 Nov. 1956.*]

A full statement of the British position and reasons for the delay in withdrawal, was made later in the month, at the 11th regular Assembly session, by Foreign Secretary Selwyn Lloyd:

87. I deny emphatically the allegation that Her Majesty's Government in the United Kingdom instigated the Israel attack or that there was agreement between the two countries about it. The United Kingdom and French Government decided to intervene and prevent the spread of hostilities, to stop the conflagration from spreading. We wished to put, as rapidly as possible, a protective shield between the combatants, and that was a situation which really brooked of no delay. And that, in fact, was what was achieved.

88. Whatever may be thought of our actions or our motives, out of the painful discussions regarding them there has come the idea of a United Nations Force, the idea that the United Nations should act through an international Force. The idea was first mooted by Sir Anthony Eden in his speech before the British Parliament on 1 November 1956, when he said that if the United Nations were willing to take over the physical task of maintaining peace in the area, then no one would be better pleased than the British. That statement of the Prime Minister's was immediately repeated in the General Assembly by Sir Pierson Dixon (*563rd meeting*). Mr Pearson, the Canadian Secretary of State for External Affairs, referred to it at the same session, and he introduced the draft resolution for establishing the Force (*A/3276*). After that, the concept of an international force gained rapid acceptance. Many nations have offered contingents. The Secretary-General and his staff have worked untiringly at the detailed arrangements, and a rapid start has been made in bringing in advance contingents of the Force to Egypt.

89. We are doing what we can to help. In response to requests made on behalf of the Secretary-General, arrangements were made for a Norwegian-Danish company to enter Port Said. We have agreed that the main body of the Yugoslav contingent should disembark at Port Said and be assisted in transit. We have agreed to provide, if wanted, military transport for the Indian infantry battalion which will form part of the Force, the necessary vehicles for the

Norwegian medical company, and some medical supplies and food for the Force itself. In other words, it is our declared purpose to co-operate to the best of our ability with the Force and with those who are seeking to make arrangements for it.

90. With regard to the tasks of the Force, we have noted the Secretary-General's report (*A/3375*) and, in particular, the annex to it. We understand this to mean that the Force will carry out all the tasks laid upon it in accordance with the resolutions of 2, 5 and 7 November. We have great confidence in the Secretary-General and we believe that he and the General Assembly will in good faith see to it that the Force is effective and competent to carry out those tasks. On that basis we have agreed to withdraw our forces.

91. The action we took was of a restricted, temporary character designed to meet an emergency. It was not directed against Egyptian sovereignty or Egyptian independence. Therefore we wish to withdraw as soon—I say again, as soon—as the United Nations Force is in a position to assume effectively the tasks assigned to it. One of those tasks, of course, is to ensure that hostilities are not resumed.

92. It is our desire that the Force should be in that position as soon as possible. However, it does take a little time to organize the command arrangements for the Force, to integrate a sufficient body of its units, to make the necessary arrangements for supply and command and control, so that it will be a Force and not just a hotchpotch of military units. It is my hope that this Force will be a credit to the United Nations. It will be under close scrutiny; and I say that unless you give General Burns and his officers time to organize it, you will bring the United Nations itself into disrepute. We do not want this Force to be laughed at.

93. When the word 'immediately' was put into resolution 1002 (ES–I), many representatives expressed the view that it did not mean 'instantaneously', that there had to be a relationship between the withdrawal of the forces referred to in the resolution and the arrival and functioning of the United Nations Force. I think that was recognized in many of the speeches which were made on 7 November. I shall quote from only two of them. The representative of the United States said:

> 'We understand that the withdrawal will be phased with the speedy arrival of the international United Nations Force. We hope that this phased operation, as contemplated by the resolution, will begin as soon as possible . . .' (*567th meeting, para. 305.*)

The representative of Canada said:

> '. . . we give the same interpretation to the word "immediately" that has been given by others, that is "as quickly as possible". In our minds, there is a relationship, implicit in the word "immediately", between the withdrawal of the forces referred to in the resolution and the arrival and the functioning of the United Nations Force.' (*Ibid., para. 260.*)

I think that others spoke in similar terms. I believe that to act otherwise would bring discredit rather than credit upon the United Nations. Nevertheless, as an indication of the sincerity of our intentions, we have given immediate orders that one battalion should be withdrawn as quickly as possible.

94. I hope that members of the Assembly will realize that in taking up this position on withdrawal, the United Kingdom Government has asked the British people to endorse an act of faith. We believe—and, whether you agree with us or not, we believe it sincerely—that we have stopped a small war from spreading into a larger war. We believe that we have created the conditions under which a United Nations Force is to be introduced into this troubled area to establish and maintain peace; and we believe that thereby we have given the Assembly and the world another opportunity to settle the problems of the area. We believe that we have brought matters to a head, to a crisis, that we have cast down a challenge to world statesmanship, the statesmanship of the Assembly, to achieve results. We think that there is in this a great test for the United Nations and for the Powers on whose continued support the United Nations ultimately depends.

95. We are, therefore, prepared to make this act of faith because we believe that the United Nations has the will to ensure that the United Nations Emergency Force will effectively and

honourably carry out all the functions laid down for it in the Assembly resolutions. But, should our faith prove to have been misplaced, should all this effort and disturbance have been for nothing, should the United Nations fail to show the necessary will-power to procure the lasting settlements required, then indeed there will be cause for alarm and despondency.

96. That is our position with regard to this question of withdrawal: it will take place as soon as possible, as the United Nations Force becomes effective and competent to discharge its functions.

97. My third point is with regard to clearance of the Suez Canal. This is an immediate and urgent task. It is in the interests of many nations, African, Asian and European alike.

98. I shall remind you in passing of the note sent by the United Kingdom Government to the Secretary-General on 11 November (*A/3382*). I do not want to dwell today on those actions or their relationship to international obligations. However, the task is to get the Canal cleared —and cleared without delay. The United Kingdom Government has formally expressed its full support for the efforts of the Secretary-General to organize a salvage team under the auspices of the United Nations. It has declared its willingness to release any salvage ships now under charter to the British Admiralty or to the United Kingdom Government. We shall do everything in our power to help, and we welcome the assumption of United Nations responsibility.

99. We ourselves have for some days been working to remove the twenty or so ships sunk in the harbour at Port Said. By the end of this week, we shall have cleared a channel which will enable 70 per cent of normal traffic to pass into the Canal, which will immediately allow the passage of salvage vessels urgently needed to clear the obstacles sunk further south. We are ready to lend our resources, to work in any way desired in this task of such concern to so many countries here represented.

100. We have begun our withdrawal, as I have stated. It seems to me reasonable that the clearance of the Canal should also begin. I can offer that, under United Nations auspices, a group can move within the next forty-eight hours or so down the Canal to the obstacles beyond those which we have cleared and can begin, under United Nations auspices, work upon these further obstacles. In this matter, upon which there is so much common interest even between those who are in bitter conflict on other matters, I would hope that practical considerations would apply, and I would refer in particular to the speech of the representative of Ceylon, a country much concerned with this matter, during the general debate at the 590th meeting. [*GAOR, 11th sess., plen. mtgs, vol. 1, 591st mtg*, pp. 258–9.]

Other nations however, pointed to the three weeks which had elapsed since the Assembly had for the second time called for British and French withdrawal from Egyptian territory, and found unacceptable the 'whole series of conditions . . . being put forward'.[8] They found Mr Lloyd's argument that delay was necessary, in order to ensure 'that the United Nations Force would be a credit to the United Nations . . . completely fallacious and . . . ridiculous'.[9]

Towards the end of November 1956 the following communications were sent by France and the United Kingdom respectively to the Secretary-General:

1. The disposition of the Anglo-French forces has been adapted to the new conditions created by the cease-fire. It has now been almost stabilized so as to be in a position to fulfil the task of defence, policing and repairs, which is incumbent on our forces. Approximately one-third of the French forces which were deployed on 7 November has been withdrawn.

2. We are studying plans for withdrawal, but it is difficult to make them final until the necessary contacts have been made between the Franco-British Command and the Command of the international emergency Force.

---

[8] e.g. *GAOR*, 11th sess., plen. mtgs, vol. 1, 592nd mtg, pp. 265–7.   [9] Ibid. para 51.

3. The French Government remains ready to proceed with the withdrawal of its forces as soon as the international Force which is being established is in a position to discharge the functions which have been entrusted to it under the General Assembly resolutions 997 (ES–I) of 2 November, 1000 (ES–I) of 5 November and 1002 (ES–I) of 7 November.

4. In particular it considers it essential that the Force be capable of seeing that, in the Port Said area, the cease-fire is strictly observed by the Egyptian authorities, ensuring that quiet is maintained and guaranteeing the protection of persons whatever their nationality during and after the withdrawal of the Franco-British forces. [*A/3384, ann. I, 21 Nov. 1956.*]

With regard to the withdrawal of British forces from Egypt, I have the honour to make the following communication on behalf of Her Majesty's Government in the United Kingdom.

1. No significant withdrawal has yet taken place. In response, however, to requests made to me on your behalf in New York, the following arrangements have been agreed to by the Anglo-French Command:

(*a*) A Norwegian-Danish company of the United Nations Emergency Force is to enter Port Said today;

(*b*) The main body of the Yugoslav contingent for UNEF will disembark at Port Said and will be assisted in transit;

(*c*) The Anglo-French Command will make provision for:

(i) The necessary vehicles for the Norwegian medical company;

(ii) Complete military transport for the Indian infantry battalion of some 800 men which will form part of UNEF;

(iii) Fuel, medical supplies and food for the use of the international Force.

Detailed arrangements for implementing these and similar requests will be concerted between the Anglo-French Command and the Command of the United Nations Emergency Force.

2. It will be recalled that the following statement was made on behalf of Her Majesty's Government in the letter from the permanent representative of the United Kingdom to Your Excellency dated 6 November (A/3306). 'If the Secretary-General can confirm that the Egyptian and Israel Governments have accepted an unconditional cease-fire, and the international Force to be set up will be competent to secure and supervise the attainment of the objectives set out in the operative paragraphs of the resolution passed by the General Assembly on 2 November, Her Majesty's Government will agree to stop further military operations.' As a consequence of satisfactory arrangements being made regarding the cease-fire and of the steps taken, pursuant to the Assembly's resolution of 7 November, to establish the international force, Her Majesty's Government ordered the cessation of all military operations.

3. As soon as Her Majesty's Government is satisfied that UNEF is in a position to assume effectively the tasks assigned to it under the Assembly resolutions, the Anglo-French forces will be withdrawn. At the present time, however, UNEF is still in the process of being built up and is not yet in a position to carry out effectively the functions assigned to it.

4. Nevertheless the United Kingdom Government, as an indication of its intentions, has decided to withdraw at once an infantry battalion from Port Said. The withdrawal of other units will proceed as the United Nations Force becomes effective.

5. The cease-fire has and is being strictly observed by the Anglo-French forces. Egyptian regular troops and non-military Egyptian elements, who have been supplied with arms, have on several occasions opened fire, without provocation, on Anglo-French units.

(*Signed*) Selwyn LLOYD

[*A/3384, ann. III, 21 Nov. 1956.*]

The Secretary-General stated:

6. As to the part of the letter from the Government of the United Kingdom which refers to the possibility of certain facilities being made available to the United Nations Emergency

Force, the Secretary-General finds it premature now to comment on questions which form part of the general problem of supplies and transport to be treated in a later report to the General Assembly. Solutions will be sought to that problem which are fully in line with the international character of the Force, as set up for the specific purposes defined in the relevant General Assembly resolutions. [*A/3384, 21 Nov. 1956,* para.6.]

By the beginning of December however, progress was made:

1. Her Majesty's Government and the French Government note that:

(*a*) An effective United Nations Force is now arriving in Egypt charged with the tasks assigned to it in the Assembly resolutions of 2, 5 and 7 November.

(*b*) The Secretary-General accepts the responsibility for organizing the task of clearing the Canal as expeditiously as possible.

(*c*) In accordance with the General Assembly resolution of 2 November free and secure transit will be re-established through the Canal when it is clear.

(*d*) The Secretary-General will promote as quickly as possible negotiations with regard to the future régime of the Canal on the basis of the six requirements set out in the Security Council resolution of 13 October.

2. Her Majesty's Government and the French Government confirm their decision to continue the withdrawal of their forces now in the Port Said area without delay.

3. They have accordingly instructed the Allied Commander, General KEIGHTLEY, to seek agreement with the United Nations Commander, General BURNS, on a time-table for the complete withdrawal, taking account of the military and practical questions involved. This time-table should be reported as quickly as possible to the Secretary-General of the United Nations.

4. In preparing these arrangements the Allied Commander will ensure:

(*a*) That the embarkations of personnel or material shall be carried out in an efficient and orderly manner;

(*b*) That proper regard will be had to the maintenance of public security in the area now under Allied control;

(*c*) That the United Nations Commander should make himself responsible for the safety of any French and British salvage resources left at the disposition of the United Nations salvage organization.

5. In communicating these conclusions Her Majesty's Government and the French Government recall the strong representations they have made regarding the treatment of their nationals in Egypt. They draw attention to the humane treatment accorded to Egyptian nationals in the United Kingdom and France. They feel entitled to demand that the position of British and French nationals in Egypt should be fully guaranteed. [*A/3415, Note by the Secretary-General, 3 Dec. 1956.*]

The French government transmitted a Note Verbale in virtually identical terms. The Secretary-General now instructed the Commander of UNEF, Major-General Burns, to get into immediate touch with the Anglo-French Commander with a view to working out with him arrangements for the complete withdrawal of Anglo-French forces.

The position was later admirably recounted by the Secretary-General in his summary study on UNEF:

Agreement to the cease-fire by the parties concerned and the withdrawal of troops

21. Agreement without conditions by the parties engaged in hostilities to the cease-fire called for by the General Assembly, in resolutions 997 (ES–I) of 2 November 1956 and 999 (ES–I) of 4 November 1956, so that the cease-fire could actually take effect, was a prerequisite to the operation of UNEF. Egypt, on 2 November (A/3266) and 4 November

(A/3287, annex 6), accepted the two calls of the Assembly for a cease-fire. Israel, which had announced on 3 November (A/3279) its agreement to an immediate cease-fire on condition that Egypt would do the same, confirmed its unconditional acceptance on 5 November (A/3301). The Governments of France and the United Kingdom, in identical replies of 5 November (A/3294 and A/3293) to the Secretary-General's communications of 4 November on arrangements for a cease-fire (A/3287, annexes 2 and 4), stated that they would cease all military action as soon as the Israel and Egyptian Governments accepted a United Nations plan for an international force with certain prescribed functions. In his *aide-mémoire* of 5 November 1956 to the Governments of France and the United Kingdom the Secretary-General informed these Governments that since on that date the General Assembly had taken a decisive step towards setting up the international force by establishing a United Nations Command, and since the Governments of Egypt and Israel had agreed, without conditions, to a cease-fire, 'the conditions for a general cease-fire would thus seem to be established' (A/3310, para. 6). In letters to the Secretary-General of 6 November (A/3307 and A/3306), replying to his *aide-mémoire* of the previous day, the Governments of France and the United Kingdom announced that their forces were being ordered to cease fire at midnight GMT of that day, pending confirmation that Egypt and Israel had accepted an unconditional cease-fire and that there would be a United Nations force competent to secure and supervise the attainment of the objectives of resolution 997 (ES-I). The Secretary-General promptly informed Egypt and Israel that the cease-fire would become effective on the hour of midnight and on this basis the cease-fire began at that time. It is to be noted that the General Assembly did not make the cease-fire dependent upon the creation or the functioning of UNEF. Its calls for a cease-fire and its decision to establish the Force were in separate resolutions (resolutions 997 (ES-I) and 999 (ES-I) on the one hand, and 998 (ES-I) on the other). [*A/3943, Summary Study of the experience derived from the establishment and operation of the Force: Report of the Secretary-General, 9 Oct. 1958.*]

I I

FINANCE[1]

Two major questions arose on the financing of UNEF, first, how would costs be apportioned as between the UN on the one hand, and the contributing states on the other? Second, how would those costs allotted to the UN be apportioned among its members?

The first question was answered more satisfactorily than the second.

(a) Apportionment as between the UN and the Contributing States
The Secretary-General initially proposed:

15. The question of how the Force should be financed likewise requires further study. A basic rule which, at least, could be applied provisionally, would be that a nation providing a unit would be responsible for all costs for equipment and salaries, while all other costs should

---

[1] There exist two very useful studies of UN finance as a whole, which put the problem of UNEF in a proper background and perspective: J. D. Singer, *Financing International Organizations: the UN Budgetary Process* (1961); and J. G. Stoessinger, *Financing the United Nations System* (1964).

be financed outside the normal budget of the United Nations. It is obviously impossible to make any estimate of the costs without a knowledge of the size of the corps and the length of its assignment. The only practical course, therefore, would be for the General Assembly to vote a general authorization for the cost of the Force on the basis of general principles such as those here suggested. [*A/3302, 2nd and final Report of the Secretary-General on the plan for an emergency international UN Force, 6 Nov. 1956.*]

On 6 November the Assembly gave its provisional approval: '*The General Assembly.* . . . 5. *Approves provisionally* the basic rule concerning the financing of the Force laid down in paragraph 15 of the Secretary-General's report . . .'.[2]

In December the Assembly passed a further resolution which was relevant to the apportionment as between the UN and the contributing states:

The General Assembly. . . .
1. *Decides* that the expenses of the United Nations Emergency Force, other than for such pay, equipment, supplies and services as may be furnished without charge by Governments of Member States, shall be borne by the United Nations and shall be apportioned among the Member States, to the extent of $10 million, in accordance with the scale of assessments adopted by the General Assembly for contributions to the annual budget of the Organization for the financial year 1957. . . . [*GA Res. 1089 (XI), 21 Dec. 1956.*][3]

Cost estimates were made of the expenditure on UNEF for the period November 1956 to December 1957[4] (which was the heaviest period, as many of the expenditures were not recurring). The Secretary-General made the following observations:

58. The estimates do not include the value of materials and services which have been provided without charge by Governments, including, of course, the substantial contribution, in the form of military personnel and equipment, which the ten member states furnishing national contingents have generously made available. Additionally, the following facilities and assistance have been furnished by Governments for the transportation of troops, equipment and supplies to the area of operations:

(i) Airlifts arranged by the United States, at a cost approximating $2,250,000, from the base countries of contingents to Naples or Beirut;

(ii) Transport of Canadian troops and equipment from Canada to Egypt by Canadian aircraft carrier, at a cost of $333,312, and by airlift, at a cost of $438,819;

(iii) Acceptance by the Government of Switzerland of charges approximating $390,000 for commercial air transportation of troops and equipment from Italy to Egypt in the initial stages;

(iv) Extensive airlift and staging facilities provided by Italy for troop and supply movements from Naples to Egypt;

(v) Airlifts arranged by Scandinavian Governments for regular transport service to and from Naples.

59. In addition, the Secretary-General is examining with the Government of Brazil the question whether costs which that Government incurred in transporting its first contingent to Egypt in one of its own naval vessels will, as was originally understood, represent a voluntary contribution to UNEF or whether the Government will seek reimbursement of those costs.

---

[2] Res. 1001 (ES–I).
[3] The Assembly based itself upon two reports of the Advisory Committee on Administrative and Budgetary Questions, A/3402 and A/3456.
[4] Totalling $23,920,500.

60. A variety of other supplies, services and facilities have also been furnished without charge. These have included the provision by Italy of labour for loading planes and ships, crating and carting services, local transport facilities, space and telephone services, billeting facilities, airport and hangar facilities, and service personnel. Egypt has contributed office and other accommodations, transport facilities, and general supplies. Several Governments are providing additional communications facilities and mailing privileges, and many of the contingents are being provided with recreational, welfare and other materials by their Governments and by private sources.

61. The fact should not be overlooked, therefore, that, had the United Nations been obliged to bear the entire costs of establishing and maintaining the Force, the financial burden on its membership as a whole would be substantially greater than is, in fact, the case.

62. The estimates also make no provision for the reimbursement to Governments of special allowances paid to their contingents as a direct result of their service in the area. Certain Governments have approached the Secretary-General in regard to the assumption of this obligation by the United Nations, and it is the Secretary-General's view that for the initial six-month period of service, such reimbursement would be a legitimate claim against the Special Account.

63. Further issues that have been raised with the Secretary-General by certain of the Governments providing contingents are: (a) the reimbursement of all identifiable additional costs incurred in making the contingents available; (b) compensation for depreciation or replacement of equipment provided by the Governments concerned. The Secretary-General has regarded it beyond the scope of his authority to make any commitment in regard to these issues and has, therefore, reserved them for the consideration of the Assembly. . . .

5. *Allocation of costs of the contingents of the Force between the United Nations and the Member States concerned*

79. The need has arisen for a clearer and more precise determination as to the principles in accordance with which the costs of national contingents comprising UNEF should be allocated between the United Nations, as a charge to the Special Account, and the Member States concerned. In presenting the observations and proposals which follow, the Secretary-General has sought to distinguish between arrangements which he believes to be within his present authority to implement, and those which, while not necessarily inconsistent with the resolutions adopted by the General Assembly at its eleventh session, would represent elaborations involving financial obligations that, in the Secretary-General's judgement, require the further consideration of the General Assembly as the only organ competent to decide whether another formula for more general distribution of the cost incurred in maintaining the Force might be adopted. To this end, regard should be had to the original intent of the General Assembly, as expressed in the relevant resolutions and debates, as well as to the position of Member States furnishing contingents, as explained in the course of subsequent consultations and negotiations with the Secretary-General.

80. Attention is called, in the first place, to the following fundamental elements of the prior decisions of the General Assembly, as summarized under section 1 above:

(i) The basic rule referred to in paragraph 5 of resolution 1001 (ES–I) of 7 November 1956, to the effect that a nation providing a unit would be responsible for any costs of equipment and salaries, while all other costs should be financed outside the normal budget of the United Nations;

(ii) Resolution 1089 (XI) of 21 December 1956 in which, after recalling the provisional decision of 7 November, and, while recognizing that the question of how the Force should be financed required further study, the General Assembly decided, *inter alia*, 'that the expenses of the United Nations Emergency Force, other than for such pay, equipment, supplies and services as may be furnished without charge by Governments of Member States', should be borne by the United Nations and apportioned to the extent of $10 million, in accordance with the scale of assessments for 1957.

81. In the opinion of the Secretary-General, resolution 1089 (XI) was intended to clarify and, in a sense, amplify the Assembly's earlier provisional decision without, however, necessarily detracting from the basic rule provisionally laid down in the latter resolution, as to the responsibility of Member States furnishing contingents for the relevant costs of salaries and equipment.

82. It is pertinent to note, however, that, prior to the adoption of the resolution, a number of participating Governments stressed the fact that their contributions and the allocation of costs resulting therefrom would be the subject of negotiations between themselves and the Secretary-General. Thus, paragraph 24 of the Fifth Committee's report (A/3560 and Add. 1) stated that 'some delegations . . . felt it was appropriate that arrangements should be agreed upon between the Secretary-General and the Governments regarding the reimbursement of the "extra costs" which contributing Governments might be obliged to incur in making troops available for service in the Emergency Force.'

83. In the course of such negotiations which subsequently took place, it became clear that certain of the Governments concerned considered that resolution 1089 (XI) superseded the basic rule provisionally adopted in resolution 1001 (ES–I) and that it had, in effect, been the intention of the General Assembly to alter the basic rule and to include the cost of salaries and equipment of contingents among the expenses to be borne by the United Nations, unless furnished without charge by Member Governments.

84. The Secretary-General has, however, felt bound to take into account the fact that, although the terms of resolution 1089 (XI) did not explicitly define the basis on which pay, equipment, supplies and services should, in fact, be furnished without charge to UNEF by contributing Governments, the view was widely expressed and is reflected in the records of the Fifth Committee, that countries which had supplied troops should continue to pay such expenses as they would normally have incurred in any event, and that any reimbursement obligation to be assumed by the United Nations should be limited to the additional expenditure which such countries might incur as a direct result of their having made contingents available for UNEF service.

85. The Secretary-General is also conscious of the fact that some Governments may have had in mind service of a much shorter duration for their contingents than developments have required. The need will be readily appreciated, furthermore, for ensuring that arrangements finally decided upon are uniformly applied to all participants and that the total financial burden is distributed as widely and as equitably as possible. These considerations suggest that, for the purpose of determining what costs should be reimbursed by the United Nations, a distinction might logically be drawn between the first six months of service of a national contingent and any subsequent period of such service.

86. It is the Secretary-General's considered view, as indicated earlier, that, for the first six months (i.e., during what might reasonably be regarded as the initial emergency period), it would be in keeping with the intent of the General Assembly, and, therefore, within the scope of his present financial authority, for the United Nations to reimburse participating Governments for any special allowances, as distinct from basic salaries, paid to members of their contingents as a direct result of their service with UNEF in its area of operations, provided that such allowances can be considered reasonable, having regard to the circumstances in which the troops have been made available and to legal and other obligations devolving upon the Government concerned. Unless it should be the view of the General Assembly that no adequate authority in fact exists, and that no element of 'extra costs' associated with pay and allowances can be accepted as a proper charge against the Special Account, the Secretary-General proposes to honour reimbursement claims presented in accordance with the foregoing formula and to adjust his budget estimates for UNEF accordingly.

87. On the basis of claims submitted and of data obtained directly from the field, it is estimated that for all contingents such 'special allowances' involved, during the initial six-month period, an expenditure on the part of the Governments concerned of approximately $330,000 per month. Reimbursement by the United Nations may thus be expected to result in an additional charge to the Special Account for the period in question of $2 million.

88. In the event, however, of a contingent serving beyond the initial six-month period or of a replacement contingent being made available, the Secretary-General holds that the United Nations should agree to assume financial responsibility for all extra and extraordinary costs which a Government is obliged to incur in making forces available for UNEF service. Apart from the costs of equipment referred to below, acceptance of this principle would mean, in effect, reimbursement by the United Nations of expenditure incurred in respect of pay and allowances over and above those costs which the Government concerned would, in any event, have been obliged to meet. It would not, of course, preclude any Government, who chose to do so, from voluntarily assuming all or part of such expenses.

89. In commending this general principle to the General Assembly, the Secretary-General is conscious of the fact that those Member States which have been maintaining UNEF contingents for more than ten months are finding it increasingly difficult to prolong the period of service of their troops, or to make replacements available in the absence of any firm assurance that identifiable direct expenses thereby incurred will be borne by the United Nations. It would seem to the Secretary-General, moreover, that beyond a limited emergency period, any arrangement under which a few Member States carry a disproportionately heavy financial burden does not represent a sound or equitable basis on which to discharge a collective United Nations responsibility.

90. Pending the receipt of more complete and documented statements from some of the participating Governments, it is difficult to furnish any reasonably exact estimate and analysis of the 'extra and extraordinary costs' which, under the proposed new formula, would fall to be reimbursed by the United Nations. Assuming, however, that, apart from equipment costs, they would relate almost exclusively to pay and allowance expenditures which would not otherwise have been incurred, it would appear from the data available that the approximate current level of such expenditures (i.e., during the remaining period of eight months) amounts to some $575,000 per month (inclusive of special allowances). This monthly estimate may be expected to be somewhat reduced, perhaps to a level of $545,000, consequent on the anticipated readjustment in the strength and composition of the Force, following the withdrawal of the Indonesian contingent during September 1957. Since the status of the various contingents and the conditions of their assignment differ very widely (e.g., in some cases, they are regular units of the country's armed forces, while in others, they are comprised of volunteers specially recruited for UNEF service) and since their rates of pay and other benefits are in accordance with national laws and regulations, which in themselves reflect wide variations, any subsequent changes in the composition of the Force could have a significant bearing on the future level of reimbursement costs. For the purposes of the first financial period, however (i.e., from November 1956–31 December 1957), the financial implications of the two reimbursement principles formulated above are tentatively and provisionally estimated as follows:

	United States dollars
For the first six months:	
Reimbursement of special allowances	2,000,000
For the remainder of the period:	
Extra and extraordinary costs relating to pay and allowances	4,500,000
TOTAL	6,500,000

91. It should also be pointed out that, because of the prolongation of the period of service, most of the participating Governments are faced with unforeseen costs in connexion with the equipment, material and supplies initially furnished to their contingents. The General Assembly has, therefore, also to consider whether the United Nations should assume financial responsibility for the replacement of equipment that is destroyed or worn-out and for such deterioration beyond that provided for under normal depreciation schedules as can be assessed at the conclusion of the total period of service of a Government's forces. In view of the fact

that the main burden of furnishing much of the heavy and expensive equipment needed for the operations of UNEF, as a whole, has fallen on a limited number of Member States, the Secretary-General believes that, in the interests of an equitable sharing of costs, some appropriate recognition by the United Nations of this obligation is called for. The task of estimating possible claims that may eventually be made in this regard presents obvious difficulties. Some indication of the maximum liability, which the United Nations would be assuming, will be possible when detailed schedules recently supplied by the Governments concerned have been analysed and costs estimated. [*A/3694, Report of the Secretary-General, 9 Oct. 1957.*]

The Secretary-General therefore requested Assembly action on his interpretation of his authority in the matter of reimbursement of special allowances paid by governments to members of their UNEF contingents for the first six months of their service; on the formula that in respect of any period subsequent to the first six months of service, the United Nations would assume financial responsibility for all 'extra and extraordinary' costs incurred by a member government as a direct result of furnishing a contingent to UNEF; and on the proposal that, in respect of equipment furnished by a participating government to its contingent, the UN should be financially responsible for its replacement in the event of its being destroyed or worn out, or for such depreciation as can be assessed at the conclusion of the total period of services of a government's forces.[5]

The Assembly gave its approval to all the Secretary-General's proposals in Resolution 1151 (XII) of 22 November 1957 (para. 2). Although these arrangements were to work fairly satisfactorily, they were not without their difficulties:

. . . It has been extremely difficult, in view of widely differing national practices, to define what may be reasonably regarded as a 'special allowance'. Furthermore, although it had been assumed that national contingents would be composed of regular army personnel who would, in any event, have been in the service of their country, certain Governments organized special volunteer units to serve with UNEF. This was done because national laws precluded the assignment of members of the regular armed forces to service overseas other than in defence of the homeland. In other cases, new units had to be organized within the contributing States to replace regular units dispatched for UNEF duty. In these circumstances, some Governments from the outset assumed additional financial liabilities which they believed should be compensated for by the United Nations. Experience indicates the validity of the view that the most equitable collective arrangement is one which distributes among the membership as a whole those costs which a participating Government would not otherwise have incurred.

119. According to the formula adopted by the General Assembly in resolution 1151 (XII), the United Nations would assume financial responsibility for the replacement of equipment destroyed or worn out and for such deterioration beyond that provided for under normal depreciation schedules as could be assessed at the conclusion of the total period of service of a Government's contingent. It is not specified, however, whether or not the word 'equipment' should be interpreted in the wider sense of 'equipment, *matériel* or supplies', and no qualification is made as to the terms under which the items had been made available, i.e. it is not indicated either that they should have been normal and necessary in the circumstances or that they should have saved the United Nations expenditure which it otherwise would have had to incur. Consequently, decisions must be based on interpretations of the formula in the light of the actual circumstances of each particular case. [*A/3943, Summary Study*, paras 118–19.][6]

---

[5] A/3694, para. iii. The Secretary-General also initiated proposals for payment of compensation in the event of injury or death attributable to service with the Force: see pp. 329–32 above.

[6] For the itemization of those expenses borne by the UN see s. 12, pp. 333–4.

(b) Apportionment of the UN's Expenses among its Members

i. *The method employed for appropriating UNEF expenses*

The annual resolutions of the General Assembly on the budget authorized the Secretary-General to raise up to $2 million for unforeseen and extraordinary expenses relating to the maintenance of peace. This sum, however, was obviously insufficient for UNEF, and an alternative method had to be devised. The device of increasing the annual overall expenses of the UN, in the authorizing resolutions, was thought not to meet the needs of the case, and the raising of UNEF's expenses on a separate and *ad hoc* basis seemed preferable because:

(*a*) the scope and duration of UNEF's assignment were uncertain; (*b*) cost estimates could not in the early stages be developed with any precision; (*c*) various offers of assistance without charge to the United Nations had been made, as well as promises of grants; (*d*) the initial basic rule for the sharing of costs, which was accepted by the General Assembly on 7 November 1956 (resolution 1001 (ES–I), para. 5), whereby a participating State would be responsible for all costs for the equipment and salaries of its contingent, had been submitted by the Secretary-General as provisional and subject to further study; (*e*) available balances in the Working Capital Fund were not sufficiently large to underwrite the expenses of even a relatively small Force for any appreciable period of time, in addition to financing other unavoidable United Nations requirements; and (*f*) the procedure adopted would avoid the virtually certain delay that would otherwise have resulted from the deep differences of opinion about who should be responsible for meeting the costs. [*A/3943*, para. 108.]

On 26 November 1956 the Assembly addressed itself to this question, and authorized the raising of an initial $10 million through a Special Account, outside of the regular budget. This amount was increased in subsequent resolutions ($16·5 million for the annual period ending 31 December 1957, and $30 million in November 1957), though it later dropped in amount. But a yearly authorization for a Special Account for UNEF continued throughout its stay in Egypt. The Secretary-General was also authorized to advance needed sums from the UN's Working Capital Fund, pending the receipt of funds into the Special Account. When this authority was renewed in 1957, the Secretary-General was also granted leave to arrange loans for the Special Account. This loan procedure 'was suggested and adopted as an extraordinary measure, designed to meet serious gaps in standard methods of providing for cash requirements of the Organization'.[7] The establishment of the Special-Account system, together with the backing of advances from the Working Capital Fund, and the arrangement of loans, may be seen from the following resolutions:

The General Assembly

Having decided, in resolutions 1000 (ES–I) and 1001 (ES–I) of 5 and 7 November 1956, to establish an emergency international United Nations Force (hereafter to be known as the United Nations Emergency Force) under a Chief of Command (hereafter to be known as the Commander),

Having considered and provisionally approved the recommendations made by the Secretary-General concerning the financing of the Force in paragraph 15 of his report of 6 November 1956 (A/3302),

[7] A/3943, para. 110.

1. *Authorizes* the Secretary-General to establish a United Nations Emergency Force Special Account to which funds received by the United Nations, outside the regular budget, for the purpose of meeting the expenses of the Force shall be credited, and from which payments for this purpose shall be made;

2. *Decides* that the Special Account shall be established in an initial amount of $10 million;

3. *Authorizes* the Secretary-General, pending the receipt of funds for the Special Account, to advance from the Working Capital Fund such sums as the Special Account may require to meet any expenses chargeable to it;

4. *Requests* the Secretary-General to establish such rules and procedures for the Special Account and make such administrative arrangements as he may consider necessary to ensure effective financial administration and control of that Account;

5. *Requests* the Fifth Committee and, as appropriate, the Advisory Committee on Administrative and Budgetary Questions, to consider and, as soon as possible, to report on further arrangements that need to be adopted regarding the costs of maintaining the Force. [*GA Res. 1122 (XI), 26 Nov. 1956.*]

The General Assembly,

Recalling its resolutions 1000 (ES–I) of 5 November 1956, 1001 (ES–I) of 7 November 1956, 1089 (XI) of 21 December 1956, 1125 (XI) of 2 February 1957 and 1090 (XI) of 27 February 1957 concerning the establishment, organization, functioning and financing of the United Nations Emergency Force,

Noting with appreciation the report of the Secretary-General on the Force, dated 9 October 1957 (*A*/3694), and the effective assistance rendered by the Advisory Committee on the United Nations Emergency Force,

Mindful of the contribution of the Force to the maintenance of quiet in the area,

1. *Expresses its appreciation* of the assistance rendered to the United Nations Emergency Force by Members of the United Nations which have contributed troops and other support and facilities, and expresses the hope that such assistance will be continued as necessary;

2. *Approves* the principles and proposals for the allocation of costs between the Organization and Members contributing troops as set forth in paragraphs 86, 88 and 91 of the report of the Secretary-General, and authorizes the Secretary-General in connexion therewith to to enter into such agreements as may be necessary for the reimbursement of appropriate extra and extraordinary costs to Members contributing troops;

3. *Authorizes* the Secretary-General to expend an additional amount for the Force, for the period ending 31 December 1957, up to a maximum of $13.5 million and, as necessary, an amount for the continuing operation of the Force beyond that date up to a maximum of $25 million, subject to any decisions taken on the basis of the review provided for in paragraph 5 below;

4. *Decides* that the expenses authorized in paragraph 3 above shall be borne by the Members of the United Nations in accordance with the scales of assessments adopted by the General Assembly for the financial years 1957 and 1958 respectively, such other resources as may have become available for the purpose in question being applied to reduce the expenses before the apportionment for the period ending 31 December 1957:

5. *Requests* the Fifth Committee to examine, with the assistance of the Advisory Committee on Administrative and Budgetary Questions and in the light of the present resolution, the cost estimates for maintaining the United Nations Emergency Force contained in the report of the Secretary-General, and to make such recommendations as it considers appropriate concerning the expenditure authorized under paragraph 3 above. [*GA Res. 1151 (XII), 13 Dec. 1957.*]

The General Assembly,

Takes note with approval of the observations and recommendations contained in the twenty-sixth report of the Advisory Committee on Administrative and Budgetary Questions to the 12th session of the General Assembly. [*GA Res. 1204 (XII), 13 Dec. 1957.*]

The General Assembly,

Having considered the progress report of the Secretary-General on the United Nations Emergency Force (A/3899),

Noting with satisfaction the effective way in which the Force continues to carry out its function,

Requests the Fifth Committee to recommend such action as may be necessary to finance the continuing operation of the United Nations Emergency Force. [*GA Res. 1263 (XIII)*, *14 Nov. 1958.*]

The General Assembly,

Recalling its resolutions 1151 (XII) of 22 November 1957 and 1204 (XII) of 13 December 1957 concerning the financing of the United Nations Emergency Force beyond 31 December 1957,

Recalling also its resolution 1263 (XIII) of 14 November 1958 requesting the Fifth Committee to recommend such action as may be necessary to finance the continuing operation of the Force,

Having examined the budget estimates for the Force submitted by the Secretary-General for the year 1958 (A/3823) and for the year 1959 (A/3984),

Having considered the observations and recommendations of the Advisory Committee on Administrative and Budgetary Questions on the estimates for the Force for 1958 in its second report to the thirteenth session of the General Assembly (A/3839), and on the estimates for 1959 in its twenty-fifth report to the thirteenth session of the General Assembly (A/4002),

1. *Confirms* its authorization to the Secretary-General to expend up to a maximum of $25 million for the operation of the United Nations Emergency Force during 1958;

2. *Authorizes* the Secretary-General to expend up to a maximum of $19 million for the continuing operation of the Force during 1959;

3. *Approves* the observations and recommendations contained in the second and twenty-fifth reports of the Advisory Committee on Administrative and Budgetary Questions to the thirteenth session of the General Assembly;

4. *Decides* that the expenses authorized in paragraph 2 above, less any amounts pledged or contributed by Governments of Member States as special assistance prior to 31 December 1958, shall be borne by the Members of the United Nations in accordance with the scale of assessments adopted by the General Assembly for the financial year 1959;

5. *Requests* the Secretary-General to consult with the Governments of Member States with respect to their views concerning the manner of financing the Force in the future, and to submit a report together with the replies to the General Assembly at its fourteenth session. [*GA Res. 1337 (XIII), 13 Dec. 1958.*]

The General Assembly,

Recalling its resolutions 1089 (XI) of 21 December 1956, 1151 (XII) of 22 November 1957 and 1337 (XIII) of 13 December 1958,

Having considered the observations made by Member States concerning the financing of the United Nations Emergency Force,

Having examined the budget estimates for the Force submitted by the Secretary-General for the year 1960 (A/4160, A/C.5/800) and the observations and recommendations of the Advisory Committee on Administrative and Budgetary Questions thereon in its eleventh (A/4171) and twenty-eighth (A/4284) reports to the General Assembly at its fourteenth session,

Having noted with satisfaction that special financial assistance in the amount of about $3,475,000 has been pledged voluntarily towards the expenditures for the Force in 1960,

Considering that it is desirable to apply voluntary contributions of special financial assistance in such a manner as to reduce the financial burden on those Governments which have the least capacity, as indicated by the regular scale of assessments, to contribute towards the expenditures for maintaining the Force,

1. *Authorizes* the Secretary-General to expend up to a maximum of $20 million for the continuing operation of the United Nations Emergency Force during 1960;

2. *Decides* to assess the amount of $20 million against all Members of the United Nations on the basis of the regular scale of assessments, subject to the provisions of paragraphs 3 and 4 below;

3. *Decides* that voluntary contributions pledged prior to 31 December 1959 towards expenditures for the Force in 1960 shall be applied as a credit to reduce by 50 per cent the contributions of as many Governments of Member States as possible, commencing with those Governments assessed at the minimum percentage of 0·04 per cent and then including, in order, those Governments assessed at the next highest percentages until the total amount of voluntary contributions has been fully applied;

4. *Decides* that, if Governments of Member States do not avail themselves of credits provided for in paragraph 3 above, then the amounts involved shall be credited to section 9 of the 1960 budget for the Force.   [*GA Res. 1441, (XIV), 5 Dec. 1959.*]

The General Assembly. . . .

Having examined the budget estimates for the Force submitted by the Secretary-General for the year 1961 [A/4396] and the observations and recommendations thereon of the Advisory Committee on Administrative and Budgetary Questions [A/4459]

Having noted with satisfaction that special financial assistance has been pledged voluntarily towards the expenditures of the Force in 1961. . . .

1. *Authorizes* the Secretary-General to expend up to a maximum of $19 million for the continuing operation of the United Nations Emergency Force during 1961. . . .   [*GA Res. 1575 (XV), 20 Dec. 1960.*]

The General Assembly. . . .

Having examined the budget estimates for the United Nations Emergency Force submitted by the Secretary-General for the year 1962 [A/4784] and the observations and recommendations thereon of the Advisory Committee on Administrative and Budgetary Questions [A/5812],

1. *Decides* to continue the Special Account for the expenses of the United Nations Emergency Force;

2. *Authorizes* the Secretary-General to expend, during 1962, at an average monthly rate not to exceed $1,625,000 for the continuing cost of the United Nations Emergency Force;

3. *Decides* to appropriate an amount of $9·75 million for the operations of the United Nations Emergency Force for the period 1 January to 30 June 1962. . . .   [*GA Res. 1733 (XVI), 20 Dec. 1961.*]

The General Assembly. . . .

Having considered the report of the Secretary-General on the cost estimates of the United Nations Emergency Force for the period 1 January 1963 to 31 December 1963 (*A/5187*), and the report of the Advisory Committee on Administrative and Budgetary Questions thereon (A/5274),

1. *Decides* to continue the Special Account for the expenses of the United Nations Emergency Force;

2. *Authorizes* the Secretary-General to expend up to 31 December 1963 at an average monthly rate not to exceed $1,580,000 for the continuing cost of the United Nations Emergency Force;

3. *Decides* to appropriate an amount of $9·5 million for the operations of the United Nations Emergency Force for the period 1 July to 31 December 1963. . . .   [*GA Res. 1875 (S-IV) 27 June 1963.*]

The General Assembly. . . .

Having considered the reports of the Secretary-General on the cost estimates of the United Nations Emergency Force for the period 1 January to 31 December 1964 [A/5495 A/C.5/1000] and the report of the Advisory Committee on Administrative and Budgetary Questions thereon [A/5642]. . . .

1. *Decides* to continue the Special Account for the United Nations Emergency Force;

2. *Decides* to appropriate an amount of $17,750,000 for the operations of the United Nations Emergency Force for 1964; . . . . [*GA Res. 1983* (XVIII), *17 Dec. 1963.*]

The General Assembly . . . .

1. *Authorizes* the Secretary-General, subject to statutory requirements, to enter into commitments and to make payments at levels not to exceed the corresponding commitments and payments for the year 1964; . . . . [*GA Res. 2004 (XIX), 18 Feb. 1965.*]

The General Assembly

Having considered the reports of the Secretary-General on the cost estimate of the United Nations Emergency Force for the period 1 January to 31 December 1965 [A/6059] and 1 January to 31 December 1966 [A/6060, A/C.5/1049] and the report of the Advisory Committee on Administrative and Budgetary Questions thereon [A/6171]. . . .

Decides to appropriate for the operation of the United Nations Emergency Force an amount of $18,911,000 for 1965 and an amount of $15 million for 1966. . . . [*GA Res. 2115 (XX), 21 Dec. 1965.*]

The General Assembly

Having considered the report of the Secretary-General on the cost estimates of the United Nations Emergency Force for the period 1 January to 31 December 1967 (A/6498) and the report of the Advisory Committee and Administrative and Budgetary Questions thereon (A/6542). . . .

Decides to appropriate for the operation of the United Nations Emergency Force an amount of $14 million for 1967. . . . [*GA Res. 2194 (XXI), 16 Dec. 1966.*]

While the provision of a Special Account for UNEF had many advantages, it also led to certain problems,[8] including the claim by certain nations that monies raised outside of the regular budget were all 'expenses' of the Organization within the meaning of Article 17 (2) of the Charter. Article 17 (2) provides that 'The expenses of the Organization shall be borne by the members as apportioned by the General Assembly'. Thus the question of the Special Account was in fact directly related to the question of apportionment.

ii. *The method of apportioning UNEF expenses*

UNEF's expenses have been met by monies coming from two major sources —apportionment among the members in accordance with the scale obtaining for the regular budget, and voluntary contributions. While the basic principle

[8] Gabriella Rosner (p. 182) has written that the Special Account system 'permitted States to default in their contributions to UNEF, without, at the same time, defaulting in their assessments for the regular budget. It permitted nations, in essence, to veto an important activity of the United Nations. Psychologically, the system of separate accounting obstructed any immediate financial benefits which might have been gained at the very start when UNEF was being given near-unanimous approval by the Assembly Members. It opened the way to doubts concerning the application of Article 17 of the Charter. Finally, it made more difficult a possible conversion of the Force into a permanent organ, as had been done with other operations in the past'. Another scholar has said of this: '. . . there remains a good deal of force in these criticisms. However, they are criticisms based on hindsight, and, at the inception of UNEF, the difficulties which the future held were not anticipated by the Secretary-General' (Bowett, p. 144).

was followed throughout of apportionment according to the regular budget scale, attempts were made, from 1957 onwards to alleviate this overall burden by the introduction of voluntary payments. Thus UNEF has never been, even before the financial crisis of the 1960s, financed solely by assessments over the entire membership. Instead, the Secretary-General was authorized to have an annual Special Account of x million; voluntary contributions were invited for y million; and the overall membership was apportioned, initially on the regular budget scale, to meet the balance between x and y.

That such apportionment should occur at all has been hotly disputed by many nations; while yet others, conceding the principle of collective financial responsibility, have thought that assessments should have been on a different scale from that used for the regular budget. The Soviet Union and her allies pressed the view, from the outset, that UNEF must be paid for not by the UN membership at large, but by the 'aggressors' who had rendered its existence necessary:

81. It is self evident that the cost of freeing the Canal, which has been immobilized by the British–French attack, as well as the other expenses linked with the return of the Near Eastern situation to normal, cannot be borne by all the Member States of the United Nations, but must be borne by the Governments which committed the aggression. [*Per Poland, GAOR, 11th sess., 592nd plen. mtg.*]

32. The delegation of the Byelorussian SSR yesterday (*596th meeting*) voted against the draft resolution proposed by the Secretary-General[9] for the allocation of a preliminary sum of $10 million for the maintenance of the United Nations Emergency Force. We consider that the United Kingdom, France and Israel, which perpetrated the aggression against Egypt, should bear the burden of any expenses arising from the maintenance of the Force. [*Ibid. 597th mtg.*]

Speaking of those nations which decided not to contribute towards UNEF's expenses, the Soviet Union was to say:

137. . . . The reason for this, as we see it, is quite plain. These States are aware that the establishment of a United Nations Emergency Force resulted from the armed attack of the United Kingdom, France and Israel on Egypt and consider that it would therefore be reasonable and fair if the cost of maintaining the Force were borne by the States responsible for the aggression. Such a method of financing the cost would correspond to one of the basic and most important principles of contemporary international law, under which a State that has committed aggression must bear both material and political responsibility for it.

138. It is therefore entirely legitimate that a number of Member States have announced that in principle they refuse to make any contribution towards financing the United Nations Emergency Force and at the same time that some other States, as the Secretary-General points out in his report, have declared that they cannot make any voluntary contributions towards the expenses of the Force.

139. The Soviet Union's position on the financing of the United Nations Emergency Force was defined at the eleventh session of the General Assembly (*592nd meeting*). The Soviet delegation continues to hold the view that the cost of maintaining the Force should be borne by the States which engaged in armed aggression against Egypt. The Soviet delegation considers that to relieve the United Kingdom, France and Israel of material responsibility for the expenditure arising out of their aggression against Egypt, including the cost of maintaining

[9] Adopted as Res. 1122 (XI).

the United Nations Emergency Force, and to place this responsibility on the shoulders of other States which resisted that aggression and themselves suffered loss from the prolonged obstruction of the Suez Canal, would be incompatible with elementary concepts of fairness and with the principles on which the United Nations is based. [*GAOR, 12th sess., 720th mtg.*]

The same point was made by the Czech delegate[10] and by the Romanian delegate.[11]

Other nations voiced similar, though not identical, misgivings. Thus Mr Krishna Menon said: 'We must also consider who is to cover such costs, whether the United Nations is to indemnify aggression, which, in my opinion, would mean that it would have to underwrite aggression to a certain extent.'[12]

The Latin American nations by and large shared the Soviet view in so far as the costs of clearing the Canal were concerned. With regard to the costs of UNEF, they wished to see members apportioned on a different basis from the one used in the regular budget:

32. My delegation considers that there are circumstances in which the United Nations collectively and its Members individually must assume financial responsibilities in connexion with a specific situation. But in this particular instance, where the situation was brought about through the deliberate action of certain Member States, the Government of El Salvador can hardly be expected to agree to contribute in any way towards the costs of clearing the Suez Canal of the obstructions which prevent it from operating normally.

33. It would like to refer in a general way to the theory of human responsibility. Within a given State, when an offence of any kind is committed, there is as we all know a twofold responsibility: criminal responsibility and civil responsibility. If we apply this to the case under discussion, we cannot but conclude that those responsible for the present situation in the Middle East should bear the responsibility for restoring the situation as it existed before the events which have taken place in Egypt since the end of last month. In any case, if there is to be any sharing of the costs involved in clearing the Suez Canal, then the users of the Canal, those who benefit from its use, should be the ones to bear the financial responsibility.

34. I am certain, and I should like to state emphatically and very clearly, that neither the Executive nor the Legislative Assembly of my country could agree to endorse any legislation under which El Salvador would contribute to the costs involved in the clearing operations. I should like our position on the question to be perfectly clear, because the solemn responsibility of the delegation of El Salvador towards the General Assembly is involved. This morning we learned that some countries are proposing to undertake the clearing of the Suez Canal on their own account. If that is so, what I said is superfluous. However, in any event, I must state that my delegation is very much concerned with this aspect of the question and wishes to place on record that it could not endorse any resolution to such an effect. [*Per El Salvador, GAOR, 11th sess., 596th mtg.*]

So far as UNEF itself was concerned, the view taken by Ecuador and Guatemala was typical of many of the Latin American nations. Unlike the Communist nations, they approved of UNEF and thought that the principle of collective responsibility was sound: but they rejected the view that apportionment on the regular budget scale was the best way to proceed:

62. This problem was taken into consideration when the United Nations was established. As we know, Article 43 lays the obligation on all members to make available to the Security Council, in accordance with special agreements, any assistance which may be necessary for the

---

[10] *GAOR*, 12th sess., 721st mtg, para. 13.   [11] Ibid. para. 54.
[12] *GAOR*, 11th sess., 596th mtg, para. 95.

purpose of maintaining international peace and security. Thus, the importance of equipping the United Nations with forces sufficient to secure respect for its decisions and to maintain peace and security was recognized, but it was recognized that a special agreement was necessary, an agreement negotiated directly between the United Nations and an individual State or group of States, so that each State could decide its contribution in the light of its economic strength and the land, sea and air forces at its disposal.

63. The obligation of Members to contribute to the general administrative expenses of the Organization is not the same as this additional obligation which may be larger in some cases and smaller in others than the contribution of the State concerned to the annual budget.

64. Realizing the difficulties that the negotiation of such agreements would involve owing to the position of the great Powers in the Security Council, and knowing that an armed force was urgently necessary to maintain peace in the Middle East, my country not only voted for resolution 1089 (XI) but also, despite its small size, was among the first nations to make a small contingent of its armed forces available to the Secretary-General.

65. My delegation's present position does not therefore imply any criticism of an innovation which was, we believe, absolutely necessary; it does indicate that we do not accept the principle in accordance with which the cost of the new body is being apportioned. This question should, as the Secretary-General has said, be thoroughly and attentively studied. It is not enough to say, as is now being said, that the costs should be apportioned in accordance with the scale of assessments for contribution to the annual budget. Although the offers of some Latin American countries, Colombia and Brazil, for example, have been accepted, so that one continent is well represented, we cannot accept this principle, under which the contribution required of us would be unfairly determined.

66. As I believe that the resolutions adopted by the Assembly in this case have legal as well as moral force, I wish, on behalf of my Government, to make two points perfectly clear: first, the Government of Ecuador believes the establishment of these armed forces to be absolutely necessary; secondly, it appreciates the work of the Emergency Force in the Middle East and the work of the Secretary-General, but it will vote against the twenty-one Power draft resolution, which accepts the principle that the expenses should be apportioned in accordance with the scale of assessments for contributions to the annual budget.   [*Per the representative of Ecuador, ibid. 721st mtg.*]

68. Our position may be summed up by the following three points: we are in favour of the maintenance of the Emergency Force as an institution which is necessary for peace in the Middle East and as a basis for the evolution of a permanent instrument of military action by the United Nations; we recognize the political expediency and the principle of equity which make it necessary for all Member States to contribute to the maintenance of the Force; we cannot, however, regard as either just or equitable an assessment system according to which the financial contributions to be made by Member States are in proportion to their contributions to the regular administrative budget of the United Nations.

69. Our arguments in support of the latter objection may be briefly stated as follows.

70. In the first place, we consider that, in the case of the Middle East, the Emergency Force became necessary owing to the individual action of certain Powers which, in our opinion, thus became primarily responsible for the crisis which compelled the United Nations to set up the Emergency Force. We consider also that this responsibility cannot and should not be limited to political matters, but must inevitably include financial liability.

71. Secondly, we believe that peace is a universal responsibility and that stability in the Middle East must therefore be a matter of international concern. Apart from these general interests, however, we also believe that there are material interests, which affect certain Powers and certain European and Asian geographical areas much more directly than others. I must point out that these material interests cannot fail to exercise an influence on the question of stability in the Middle East.

72. Thirdly, we consider that not only the nations outside these regions, but more particularly the peoples of the area, have a more direct responsibility, owing to the tensions and instability

prevailing among them, and that a more determined effort on the part of those peoples would decrease the risks which have made it necessary to establish and maintain the Emergency Force. This responsibility of causality and this direct interest in survival should entail not only political, but also financial responsibility.

73. Fourthly, Article 24 of the Charter establishes the primary responsibility of the members of the Security Council for the maintenance of peace and, in our opinion, this responsibility rests with the five great Powers who are permanent members and have the privilege of the veto, so often attacked by the Latin American countries. We firmly believe that the greater the privilege, the greater the responsibility, and that this responsibility is not limited to political matters. Our congratulations are due to the United States for the efforts it has made through voluntary contributions, over and above its regular contribution. We regret that another great Power has refused to make any contribution whatsoever, and hope that this will be remedied in the future. Finally, we are surprised that two other great countries have not made a greater effort.

74. Fifthly, we know that the defence budgets of the great Powers are reckoned in millions; that is not the case of the countries in my region. For these great Powers, the contribution to the Emergency Force is but a drop in the financial torrent of their military appropriations; but for the small countries of the United Nations, the increase of their contribution by 50 per cent—for that is what the effort demanded of us amounts to—entails extraordinary sacrifices. We realize that this effort must be international and we therefore do not refuse to contribute, but we should like to do so on a more equitable basis.

75. Sixthly, the financial sacrifice of the more highly developed countries would mean one more tax for their citizens and one luxury the less in their daily life; for the less-developed countries, however, where the level of living is very low and where constant effort is exerted to raise this level inch by inch, against tremendous odds, the financial sacrifice asked of us does indeed mean one more tax, but not one luxury the less. It means that we would have to dispense with something vitally necessary, some remedy for the ills that oppress our peoples. It would not be amiss to point out to public opinion outside this assembly hall that a Latin American citizen pays more to the United Nations than a citizen of the United States of America; and it is in this proportion that we are asked to contribute to the Emergency Force. We quite realize that the voluntary contributions of the United States of America exceeded its regular contribution in 1957. Would that that example were followed by other great Powers!

76. Seventhly and finally, it should be borne in mind that the Emergency Force paradoxically seems to relate to a permanent emergency and that, like so many other bodies established on a short-term basis by the United Nations, it shows every sign of continuing for years.

77. It is painful to present all these arguments, but my Government has obligations to its own people. In speaking of financial matters, in which selfish interests always tend to appear, it is usually forgotten that questions relating to contributions must always be based on an inexorable principle of justice and equity. There is no modern country which does not realize that in contributions justice lies in proportionality, but there seems to be a tendency at times to forget the criteria of judgement and the standards to which the proportions must be adjusted.

78. For these reasons, my delegation will be unable to support the draft resolution (*A/L.235 and Add. 1*) to which I have referred and, in explaining our position, I should like to submit my Government's formal reservation with regard to any obligations to which this draft resolution may give rise if it is adopted by the Assembly. I would also extend this reservation to the doubtful interpretation whereby a draft resolution such as that proposed may be held to place obligations upon Member States under Article 19 of the United Nations Charter.

79. I cannot and should not leave this rostrum without expressing on behalf of my Government our gratitude for the timely and generous effort of the Governments of Brazil, Canada, Colombia, Denmark, Finland, India, Indonesia, Norway, Sweden and Yugoslavia, countries which, at great sacrifice, have sent contingents to the United Nations Emergency Force. Our gratitude is also due to the United States for its exceptional financial effort. [*Ibid.*]

Similar opinions were advanced by Mexico[13] and Chile.[14] It is difficult to assess the precise position of all the Latin-American countries, because some of them indicated that a vote for the resolution should not be taken as approving the financial recommendations which it contained; while others abstained; and yet others voted against. It would seem, from its own statements,[15] that the Dominican Republic approved of apportionment on the scale of the regular budget. Bearing in mind the caveat above, it may be noted that the following South American nations voted in favour of Assembly Resolution 1511 (XII), which decided on the basic principle to govern the apportioning of UNEF expenses: Argentina, Bolivia, Brazil, Colombia, Dominican Republic, Haiti, Paraguay, Peru. Uruguay, and Venezuela. Ecuador voted against, and El Salvador, Guatemala, Mexico, and Panama abstained.

The Western nations took a different view, insisting on the collective responsibility of all members to finance a force brought into existence by a decision of the Assembly.[16] This view was to prevail, though later voluntary contributions were sought over and above the compulsory assessments.

For his part, the Secretary-General made plain what he sought from the Assembly in this matter:

223. I have accordingly considered it imperative to seek the concurrence of the General Assembly in the following matters: first, the establishment of a United Nations Emergency Force Special Account; secondly, the establishment of this Account in an initial amount of $10 million; thirdly, the authorization of advances from the Working Capital Fund for the purpose of interim financing of the Force; fourthly, authorization to establish necessary rules and procedures and to make necessary administrative arrangements for the purpose of ensuring effective financial administration and control of the Account so established.

224. First, let me make it abundantly clear that the draft resolution I have offered, both in its original and in its revised form, relates solely and exclusively to arrangements regarding the Emergency Force, and in no way to other responsibilities which the United Nations may acquire in the area.

225. Secondly, I wish to make it equally clear that while funds received and payments made with respect to the Force are to be considered as coming outside the regular budget of the Organization, the operation is essentially a United Nations responsibility, and the Special Account to be established must, therefore, be construed as coming within the meaning of Article 17 of the Charter. It follows from this that the Secretary-General will be obliged to follow to a maximum degree the regular financial rules and regulations of the Organization, as well as the machinery and processes that have been laid down by the General Assembly for the purpose of financial review and control.

226. Having regard to the scope and complexity of the financial operations involved, it is indeed my intention to make special arrangements for a continuing independent audit to be carried out of all financial transactions concerning the Force.

227. Thirdly, it has been my assumption in drafting the revised text that Member States, while recognizing the need for taking certain decisions without delay, will nevertheless wish to follow established procedures to the fullest extent practicable. Accordingly, I have felt it wise to suggest that such problems as allocation of costs among Member States should be deferred temporarily, pending an opportunity of their being properly and adequately considered and discussed in the appropriate committee of the Assembly, that is, the Fifth Committee. Such action as the Assembly may see fit to take here and now in plenary session would

---

[13] *GAOR*, 11th sess., 721st mtg, paras 81–89.   [14] Ibid. paras 90–94.   [15] Ibid. paras 11–19.
[16] e.g. per the UK, *GAOR*, 12th sess., 720th mtg, para. 83; per Australia, ibid., para. 150.

therefore be without prejudice to subsequent decisions on other complementary and supplementary financial arrangements that need to be made. I would, however, hope that the Fifth Committee and, as necessary, the Advisory Committee on Administrative Budgetary Questions, would give these matters priority consideration. [*GAOR, 11th sess., 596th mtg.*]

The General Assembly responded on 26 November 1956 by passing Resolution 1122 (XI) by 52 votes to 9, with 13 abstentions:

The General Assembly,

Having decided, in resolutions 1000 (ES–I) and 1001 (ES–I) of 5 and 7 November 1956, to establish an emergency international United Nations Force (hereafter to be known as the United Nations Emergency Force) under a Chief of Command (hereafter to be known as the Commander),

Having considered and provisionally approved the recommendations made by the Secretary-General concerning the financing of the Force in paragraph 15 of his report of 6 November 1956,

1. *Authorizes* the Secretary-General to establish a United Nations Emergency Force Special Account to which funds received by the United Nations, outside the regular budget, for the purpose of meeting the expenses of the Force shall be credited, and from which payments for this purpose shall be made;

2. *Decides* that the Special Account shall be established in an initial amount of $10 million;

3. *Authorizes* the Secretary-General, pending the receipt of funds for the Special Account, to advance from the Working Capital Fund such sums as the Special Account may require to meet any expenses chargeable to it;

4. *Requests* the Secretary-General to establish such rules and procedures for the Special Account and make such administrative arrangements as he may consider necessary to ensure effective financial administration and control of that Account;

5. *Requests* the Fifth Committee and, as appropriate, the Advisory Committee on Administrative and Budgetary Questions, to consider and, as soon as possible, to report on further arrangements that need to be adopted regarding the costs of maintaining the Force.

VOTING: In favour: Afghanistan, Argentina, Australia, Austria, Belgium, Bolivia, Brazil, Burma, Canada, Ceylon, Chile, China, Colombia, Denmark, Dominican Republic, Egypt, Ethiopia, Finland, France, Greece, Haiti, Iceland, India, Indonesia, Iran, Iraq, Ireland, Italy, Jordan, Liberia, Libya, Morocco, Nepal, Netherlands, New Zealand, Norway, Pakistan, Panama, Peru, Saudi Arabia, Spain, Sudan, Sweden, Syria, Thailand, Tunisia, United Kingdom of Great Britain and Northern Ireland, United States of America, Uruguay, Venezuela, Yemen, Yugoslavia.

Against: Albania, Bulgaria, Byelorussian Soviet Socialist Republic, Czechoslovakia, Hungary, Poland, Romania, Ukrainian Soviet Republic, Union of Soviet Socialist Republics,

Abstaining: Cambodia, Costa Rica, Cuba, Ecuador, El Salvador, Guatemala, Israel, Luxembourg, Mexico, Nicaragua, Paraguay, Turkey, Union of South Africa.

Other relevant resolutions were also adopted during the eleventh session;

The General Assembly,

Recalling its resolutions 1001 (ES–I) of 7 November 1956 and 1122 (XI) of 26 November 1956,

Emphasizing the fact that expenses incurred by the Secretary-General under the resolutions of the General Assembly are without prejudice to any subsequent determinations as to responsibilities for situations leading to the creation of the United Nations Emergency Force and to ultimate determination as to claims established as a result of expenses arising in connexion therewith,

Considering that the Secretary-General, in his report of 4 November 1956 (A/3302), particularly in paragraph 15, has stated that the question of how the Force should be financed requires further study,

Considering that the Secretary-General, in his reports dated 21 November and 3 December 1956 (A/3383, A/C.5/687), has recommended that the expenses relating to the Force should be apportioned in the same manner as the expenses of the Organization,

Considering further that several divergent views, not yet reconciled, have been held by various Member States on contributions or on the method suggested by the Secretary-General for obtaining such contributions,

Considering that the Secretary-General has already been authorized to enter into commitments for the expenses of the Force up to an amount of $10 million,

Considering further that the matter of allocation of the expenses of the Force beyond $10 million necessitates further study in all its aspects,

3. *Decides* to establish a Committee composed of Canada, Ceylon, Chile, El Salvador, India, Liberia, Sweden, the Union of Soviet Socialist Republics and the United States of America to examine the question of the apportionment of the expenses of the Force in excess of $10 million. This Committee shall take into consideration, among other things, the discussions on this matter at the General Assembly, and shall study the question in all its aspects, including the possibility of voluntary contributions, the fixing of maximum amounts for the expenses of the Emergency Force that, with prior approval by the General Assembly, could be established on each occasion, and the principle of the formulation of scales of contributions different from the scale of contributions by Member States to the ordinary budget for 1957. The Committee will present its report as soon as possible.

1. *Decides* that the expenses of the United Nations Emergency Force, other than for such pay, equipment, supplies and services as may be furnished without charge by Governments of Member States, shall be borne by the United Nations and shall be apportioned among the Member States, to the extent of $10 million, in accordance with the scale of assessments adopted by the General Assembly for contributions to the annual budget of the Organization for the financial year 1957;

2. *Decides further* that this decision shall be without prejudice to the subsequent apportionment of any expenses in excess of $10 million which may be incurred in connexion with the Force. [*GA Res. 1089 (XI), 21 Dec. 1956.*]

This resolution was adopted by 62 votes to 8, with 7 abstentions, but no breakdown of the voting is given in the records.

The General Assembly,

Recalling its resolution 1122 (XI) of 26 November 1956 authorizing the establishment of a United Nations Emergency Force Special Account in an initial amount of $10 million and its resolution 1089 (XI) of 21 December 1956 apportioning this initial $10 million among the Member States in accordance with the scale of assessments adopted by the General Assembly for contributions to the annual budget of the Organization for 1957,

Noting that the expenses of the Force already approved for 1957 represent a sizable increase in assessments placed on Member States, causing a grave unanticipated financial burden for many Governments,

Acknowledging that certain Governments have borne without charge certain of the expenses of the Force, such as pay, equipment, supplies and services,

Noting nevertheless that the Secretary-General estimates that the expenses of the Force for 1957 will exceed the $10 million previously assessed,

Noting the request of the Secretary-General for authority to enter into commitments for the Force up to a total of $16.5 million,

1. *Authorizes* the Secretary-General to incur expenses for the United Nations Emergency Force up to a total of $16.5 million in respect of the period of 31 December 1957,

2. *Invites* Member States to make voluntary contributions to meet the sum of $6.5 million so as to ease the financial burden for 1957 on the membership as a whole,

3. *Authorizes* the Secretary-General, pending receipt of contributions to the United Nations Emergency Force Special Account:

(*a*) To advance from the Working Capital Fund such sums as the Special Account may require to meet any expenses chargeable to it;

(*b*) Where necessary, to arrange for loans to the Special Account from appropriate sources, including other funds under the control of the Secretary-General, provided that the repayment of any such advances or loans to the Special Account shall constitute a first charge against contributions as they are received, and further provided that such loans shall not affect current operational programmes;

4. *Decides* that the General Assembly, at its twelfth session, shall consider the basis for financing any costs of the Force in excess of $10 million not covered by voluntary contributions. [*GA Res. 1090 (XI), 27 Feb. 1957.*]

At its twelfth session, this financial pattern was confirmed, the protests of the Communist nations, and the misgivings of certain Latin Americans, notwithstanding:

The General Assembly,

Recalling its resolutions 1000 (ES–I) of 5 November 1956, 1001 (ES–I) of 7 November 1956, 1089 (XI) of 21 December 1956, 1125 (XI) of 2 February 1957, and 1090 (XI) of 27 February 1957, concerning the establishment, organization, functioning and financing of the United Nations Emergency Force,

Noting with appreciation the report of the Secretary-General on the Force, dated 9 October 1957, and the effective assistance rendered by the Advisory Committee on the United Nations Emergency Force,

Mindful of the contribution of the Force to the maintenance of quiet in the area,

1. *Expresses its appreciation* of the assistance rendered to the United Nations Emergency Force by Members of the United Nations which have contributed troops and other support and facilities, and expresses the hope that such assistance will be continued as necessary;

2. *Approves* the principles and proposals for the allocation of costs between the organization and Members contributing troops as set forth in paragraphs 86, 88, and 91 of the report of the Secretary-General, and authorizes the Secretary-General in connexion therewith to enter into such agreements as may be necessary for the reimbursement of appropriate extra and extraordinary costs to Members contributing troops;

3. *Authorizes* the Secretary-General to expend an additional amount for the Force, for the period ending 31 December 1957, up to a maximum of $13.5 million and, as necessary, an amount for the continuing operation of the Force beyond that date up to a maximum of $25 million, subject to any decisions taken on the basis of the review provided for in paragraph 5 below;

4. *Decides* that the expenses authorized in paragraph 3 above shall be borne by the Members of the United Nations in accordance with the scales of assessments adopted by the General Assembly for the financial years 1957 and 1958 respectively, such other resources as may have become available for the purpose in question being applied to reduce the expenses before the apportionment for the period ending 31 December 1957;

5. *Requests* the Fifth Committee to examine, with the assistance of the Advisory Committee on Administrative and Budgetary Questions and in the light of the present resolution, the cost estimates for maintaining the United Nations Emergency Force contained in the report of the Secretary-General, and to make such recommendations as it considers appropriate concerning the expenditure authorized under paragraph 3 above. [*GA Res. 1151 (XII), 22 Nov. 1957.*]

This resolution was adopted by 51 votes to 11, with 19 abstentions. Chile and Ecuador had joined the dissenters, and the ranks of the abstainers had swollen from 7 on 21 December 1957, to 19:

In favour: Afghanistan, Argentina, Australia, Austria, Belgium, Bolivia, Brazil, Burma,

Canada, Ceylon, Colombia, Costa Rica, Cuba, Denmark, Dominican Republic, Finland, France, Ghana, Greece, Haiti, Honduras, Iceland, India, Indonesia, Iran, Ireland, Israel, Italy, Japan, Jordan,[17] Laos, Liberia, Luxembourg, Netherlands, New Zealand, Nicaragua, Norway, Pakistan, Paraguay, Peru, Philippines, Portugal, Spain, Sweden, Thailand, Turkey, UK, Uruguay, USA, Venezuela, Yugoslavia.

Against: Albania, Bulgaria, Byelorussian SSR, Chile, Czechoslovakia, Ecuador, Hungary, Poland, Romania, Ukrainian SSR, USSR.

Abstaining: Cambodia, China, Egypt, El Salvador, Ethiopia, Guatemala, Iraq, Lebanon, Libya, Malaya (Federation of), Mexico, Morocco, Nepal, Panama, Saudi Arabia, Sudan, Syria, Tunisia, Yemen.

Moreover, a gap had also begun to appear between votes and performance, for by November 1957 only thirty-three members had paid their contributions towards even the initial $10 million assessment under the terms of Resolution 1089 (XI), so that only $5·8 million of the $10 million was in hand. Further, Resolution 1090 (XI) had called for $6·5 million in voluntary contributions, and only $1·8 million had been received.[18]

In view of delays in the receipt of contributions to the UNEF Special Account, it has been continuously necessary for the Secretary-General, since the commencement of UNEF's operations and under the authority granted in resolution 1122 (XI) and confirmed in resolution 1090 (XI) to advance from the Working Capital Fund various sums required to meet the expenses chargeable to the Special Account. [*A/3694, Report of the Secretary-General*, para. 74.]

Certain nations, however, did respond to the call for voluntary contributions to meet the sum of $6·5 million: they included the United Kingdom and the United States, Austria, Burma, Ireland, Japan, and Liberia,[19] the Dominican Republic, Greece, New Zealand, Pakistan,[20] and France.[21]

69. The United Kingdom contribution has been treated as a reduction of its claim against the Special Account for equipment and supplies provided to the Force. The contribution pledged by the United States is subject to the condition that other Member States contribute an equal amount. The contributions by the Dominican Republic, New Zealand and the United Kingdom are based on a percentage of the $6·5 million corresponding to their percentage assessment for contributions to the regular budget for 1957. [*A/3694, Report of the Secretary-General.*]

Voluntary contributions also came from Australia, Ceylon, Mexico, the Netherlands.[22] Not all of these countries however, continued to make voluntary contributions throughout UNEF's life: after 1961 only the United States and the United Kingdom continued to make such contributions.

The Advisory Committee for Administrative and Budgetary Questions proposed:

(*a*) That a formal budget for the Force in respect of 1958 should be prepared and published at the earliest possible moment;

(*b*) That, initially, the budget should cover the first half-year, in effect reflecting the allotments made by the Secretary-General for that period;

[17] In a letter to the President of the General Assembly dated 26 November 1957, the delegation of Jordan stated that its affirmative vote should not be interpreted in any way as an acceptance by the Jordanian government of the financial commitment involved.
[18] *GAOR*, 12th sess., 720th plen. mtg, para. 147.   [19] Ibid. para 4.   [20] A/3694, para. 68.
[21] A/3694 and Add. 1.   [22] A/3826, *GAOR*, 13th sess., suppl. 6, schedule A.

(*c*) That, in view of the lower rate of expenditure foreseen for many items, the total for the first six months should not exceed $9 to $10 million, exclusive of extra and extraordinary expenses, as approved for reimbursement by the Organization in accordance with the terms of General Assembly resolution 1151 (XII);

(*d*) That estimates for the full year should subsequently be made available to the Advisory Committee in time for review during its first session of 1958, at which time the Committee, with the further aid of financial statements and an audit report for 1957, might give further suggestions to the Secretary-General and make recommendations for final action on the 1958 UNEF budget as a first item of business at the thirteenth session of the General Assembly. [*A/3761, 3 Dec. 1957*, para. 5.]

On 13 December 1957 the Assembly approved these proposals in its Resolution 1204 (XII). The recommendations were subsequently implemented. At its thirteenth session the Assembly, in addition to authorizing the Secretary-General to expend up to $25 million on UNEF during 1958, and up to $19 million during 1959,[23] also dealt with the vexed question of apportionment:

The General Assembly. . . .

4. *Decides* that the expenses authorized in paragraph 2 above, less any amounts pledged or contributed by Governments of Member States as special assistance prior to 31 December 1958, shall be borne by the Members of the United Nations in accordance with the scale of assessments adopted by the General Assembly for the financial year 1959;

5. *Requests* the Secretary-General to consult with the Governments of Member States with respect to their views concerning the manner of financing the Force in the future, and to submit a report together with the replies to the General Assembly at its fourteenth session. [*GA Res. 1337 (XIII), 13 Dec. 1958*.]

By September 1959 the Secretary-General was able to report on the consultations with member governments which this resolution had called for. Some 50 governments replied at this time. The ensuing observations of the Secretary-General related to 46 nations (Afghanistan, Australia, Austria, Belgium, Brazil, Bulgaria, Burma, Byelorussian SSR, Cambodia, Ceylon, Chile, Cuba, Denmark, Dominican Republic, Ecuador, Finland, France, Greece, Guatemala, Guinea, Hungary, India, Iran, Ireland, Italy, Japan, Jordan, Luxembourg, Malaya, Mexico, Netherlands, New Zealand, Norway, Pakistan, Poland, Portugal, Romania, Saudi Arabia, Spain, Sweden, Thailand, Ukraine SSR, USSR, USA, Venezuela, and Yugoslavia). Four further replies were subsequently attached as annexes (Canada, China, Laos, and the UK), and the Editor has taken these views into account in providing the figures footnoted.

(*a*) Thirty-four favour assessment of UNEF's expenses among all Members, of which

(i) Twenty-six[24] wish the basis of assessment to be the scale of assessments adopted for the United Nations budget, and

(ii) Eight[25] wish adoption of some scale of assessment different from that adopted for the United Nations budget;

(*b*) Eight Members expressed the opinion or referred to their earlier views that only the States which took the action resulting in the creation of the Force should pay its expenses;

(*c*) Two Members indicated merely their inability to pay for the Force, and one Member proposed that the costs be defrayed entirely by voluntary contribution. One Member stated

[23] For full text, see above, p. 422. [24] 29, with the addition of Canada, Laos, and the UK.
[25] 9, with the addition of China.

15

that it would prefer a thorough discussion of the matter at the fourteenth session of the General Assembly before taking a definite stand on the question.

3. The twenty-six Members referred to under paragraph 2 (*a*) (i) above are: Australia, Austria, Belgium, Brazil, Cambodia, Denmark, Dominican Republic, Ecuador, Federation of Malaya, Finland, France, India, Iran, Ireland, Italy, Japan, Luxembourg, Netherlands, New Zealand, Norway, Pakistan, Portugal, Sweden, Thailand, United States of America and Yugoslavia.[26]

4. The eight Members whose views are summarized under paragraph 2 (*a*) (ii) are; Burma, Ceylon, Cuba, Greece, Guatemala, Mexico, Spain and Venezuela.[27]

5. The eight Member States whose views are summarized under paragraph 2 (*b*) are: Bulgaria, Byelorussian Soviet Socialist Republic, Hungary, Poland, Romania, Saudi Arabia, Ukrainian Soviet Socialist Republic and Union of Soviet Socialist Republics.

6. The four Member States whose views are referred to under paragraph 2 (*c*) are: Afghanistan, Chile, Guinea and Jordan.

7. Seven Member States referred to the desirability of the continued acceptance of voluntary contributions as well as assessments on all Members. These Members are: Belgium, Cambodia, Federation of Malaya, Guatemala, Japan, Luxembourg and United States of America.

8. Three Members indicated either that they favoured or would not object to including the costs of UNEF in the regular budget of the Organization. These Members are: Australia, Japan and Netherlands.

9. The Secretary-General continues to hold the view which he has previously expressed that the costs for United Nations operations such as UNEF, based on decisions of the General Assembly or the Security Council, should be allocated among all Members on the normal scale of contributions to the budget of the Organization and that the United Nations should assume responsibility for all additional costs incurred by a contributing country because of its participation in the operation, on the basis of a cost assessment which, on the other hand, would not transfer to the United Nations any costs which would otherwise have been incurred by a contributing Government under its regular national policy. [*A/4176, 10 Sept. 1959.*]

The Assembly gave clear support both to the evidence of this exchange of views, and to the Secretary-General's own position, by passing Resolution 1441 (XIV), which provided that the amount of $20 million should be assessed 'against all Members of the United Nations on the basis of the regular scale of assessments'.[28] However, some concession was now made, for the first time, to the position of the less developed countries, because the resolution also provided that

3. . . . voluntary contributions pledged prior to 31 December 1959 towards expenditures for the Force in 1960 shall be applied as a credit to reduce by 50 per cent the contributions of as many Governments of Member States as possible, commencing with those Governments assessed at the minimum percentage of 0·04 per cent and then including, in order, those Governments assessed at the next highest percentages until the total amount of voluntary contributions has been fully applied;

4. *Decides that* if Governments of Member States do not avail themselves of credits provided for in paragraph 3 above, then the amounts involved shall be credited to section 9 of the 1960 budget for the Force.[29] [*GA Res. 1441 (XIV), 5 Dec. 1959.*]

[26] Canada, Laos, and the UK also fall within this category.

[27] China also falls in this category.

[28] For the complete text of Res. 1441 (XIV), see pp. 423–4.

[29] Certain governments, including Australia, Belgium, Netherlands, and Norway, announced their intention to forego the benefits of this clause (A/4486, para. 64).

In 1960 a further concession was made to the states with the least capacity to pay, though the device adopted enabled the principle of collective financial responsibility, based on regular budget assessments to remain-precariously-intact:

The General Assembly. . . .
Considering that it is desirable to apply voluntary contributions of special financial assistance in such a manner as to reduce the financial burden on those Governments which have the least capacity to contribute towards the expenditures for maintaining the Force,
1. *Authorizes* the Secretary-General to expend up to a maximum of $19 million for the continuing operation of the United Nations Emergency Force during 1961;
2. *Decides* to assess the amount of $19 million against all States members of the United Nations on the basis of the regular scale of assessments, subject to the provisions of paragraphs 3 and 4 below;
3. *Decides further* that the voluntary contributions pledged prior to 31 December 1960, including those already announced and referred to in the fourth preambular paragraph above, shall be applied, at a request of the Member State concerned made prior to 31 March 1961, to reduce by up to 50 per cent;

   (*a*) the assessment that the Member States which were admitted during the fifteenth session of the General Assembly are required to pay for the financial year 1961 in accordance with Assembly resolution 1552 (XV) of 18 December 1960;
   (*b*) the assessment of all other Member States receiving assistance during 1960 under the Expanded Programme of Technical Assistance, commencing with those States assessed at the minimum percentage of 0·04 per cent and then including, in order, those States assessed at the next highest percentages until the total amount of the voluntary contributions has been fully applied;

4. *Decides* that, if Member States do not avail themselves of credits provided for in paragraph 3 above, the amounts involved shall be credited to section 9 of the 1961 budget for the Force. . . . [*GA Res. 1575 (XV), 20 Dec. 1960.*]

By 1961, not only had the failure of a substantial number of nations to meet their contributions created a major problem, but the question of financing ONUC was now also before the UN. So far as finance was concerned, UNEF and ONUC were henceforth to be intertwined problems.[30] The Secretary-General indicated that the net cash deficit of the UN as on 31 December 1960 totalled $34·6 million in respect of those activities wholly or mainly financed by means of assessments on member states, and that

$21·6 million of this total was attributable to serious delays in payment, or to the unwillingness or refusal of some Governments to recognize their obligations, in the case of the UNEF Special Account. In addition to the cash deficit, the net amount of unliquidated obligations payable in respect of UNEF activities for which no cash was available at 31 December 1960, without resort to borrowing from trust and special funds, totalled approximately $19·9 million. [*A/4784, Report of the Secretary-General on the cost estimates for UNEF, 13 July 1961.*]

We have already shown that the response of the Assembly was to see if there were not ways of cutting down the size of UNEF—though the Commander had indicated time and again that he did not think the size of UNEF could be further reduced without impairing its effectiveness.[31] The Assembly passed the following resolutions:

---

[30] The Congo will be covered in Vol. III of the present study.   [31] See above, pp. 308–9.

The General Assembly,

Recalling its resolutions 1089 (XI), of 21 December 1956, 1151 (XII) of 22 November 1957, 1337 (XIII) of 13 December 1958, 1441 (XIV) of 5 December 1959 and 1575 (XV) of 20 December 1960,

Having examined the budget estimates for the United Nations Emergency Force submitted by the Secretary-General for the year 1962 (A/4784) and the observations and recommendations thereon of the Advisory Committee on Administrative and Budgetary Questions (A/4812),

1. *Decides* to continue the special account for the expenses of the United Nations Emergency Force;

2. *Authorizes* the Secretary-General to expend, during 1962, at an average monthly rate not to exceed $1,625,000 for the continuing cost of the United Nations Emergency Force;

3. *Decides* to appropriate an amount of $9.75 million for the operations of the United Nations Emergency Force for the period 1 January to 30 June 1962;

4. *Decides* to apportion the amount of $9.75 million among all States Members of the United Nations in accordance with the regular scale of assessments for 1962, subject to the provisions of paragraph 6 below;

5. *Appeals* to all Member States who are in a position to assist to make voluntary contributions to help defray the costs of the United Nations Emergency Force;

6. *Decides* to reduce:

(*a*) By 80 per cent the assessment of Member States whose contributions to the regular budget range from 0.04 per cent to 0.25 per cent inclusive;

(*b*) By 80 per cent the assessment of Member States receiving assistance during 1961 under the Expanded Programme of Tecnnical Assistance, whose contributions to the regular budget range from 0.26 per cent to 1.25 per cent inclusive;

(*c*) By 50 per cent the assessment of Member States receiving assistance during 1961 under the Expanded Programme of Technical Assistance, whose contributions to the regular budget are 1.26 per cent and above;

7. *Decides* to apply the voluntary contributions of Member States to offset the deficit resulting from the implementation of the provisions of paragraph 6 above. [*GA Res. 1733 (XVI), 20 Dec. 1961.*]

The Assembly also, in Resolution 1739 (XVI) of 20 December 1961, authorized the Secretary-General to issue bonds to the amount of $200 million at 2 per cent interest, with the principal repayable over twenty-five years.[32]

It was obvious, however, that while these measures might alleviate the difficulties of the poorest nations and the short-run liquidity of the UN, they would do nothing to solve the financial difficulties in which the UN found itself because of the failure to pay assessed contributions on UNEF and ONUC. It was now decided to seek legal guidance from the International Court:

The General Assembly,

Recognizing its need for authoritative legal guidance as to obligations of Member States under the Charter of the United Nations in the matter of financing the United Nations operations in the Congo and in the Middle East,

1. *Decides* to submit the following question to the International Court of Justice for an advisory opinion:

'Do the expenditures authorized in General Assembly resolutions 1583 (XV) and 1590 (XV) of 20 December 1960, 1595 (XV) of 3 April 1961, 1619 (XV) of 21 April 1961 and 1633 (XVI) of 30 October 1961 relating to the United Nations operations in the Congo under-

---

[32] For a full account of the various measures taken, see Terence Higgins, 'The Politics of UN Finance', *World Today*, Sept. 1963, pp. 380–9.

taken in pursuance of the Security Council resolutions of 14 July, 22 July, and 9 August 1960 and 21 February and 24 November 1961, and General Assembly resolutions 1474 (ES–IV) of 20 September 1960 and 1599 (XV), 1600 (XV) and 1601 (XV) of 15 April 1961, and the expenditures authorized in General Assembly resolutions 1122 (XI), of 26 November 1956, 1089 (XI) of 21 December 1956, 1090 (XI) of 27 February 1957, 1151 (XII) of 22 November 1957, 1204 (XII) of 13 December 1957, 1337 (XIII) of 13 December 1958, 1441 (XIV) of 5 December 1959 and 1575 (XV) of 20 December 1960 relating to the operations of the United Nations Emergency Force undertaken in pursuance of General Assembly resolutions 997 (ES–I) of 2 November 1956, 998 (ES–I) and 999 (ES–I) of 4 November 1956, 1000 (ES–I) of 5 November 1956, 1001 (ES–I) of 7 November 1956, 1121 (XI) of 24 November 1956 and 1263 (XIII) of 14 November 1958, constitute 'expenses of the Organization' within the meaning of Article 17, para. 2 of the Charter of the United Nations?'

2. *Requests* the Secretary-General, in accordance with Article 65 of the Statute of the International Court of Justice, to transmit the present resolution to the Court, accompanied by all documents, likely to throw light upon the question. [*GA Res. 1731 (XVI) 20 Dec. 1961.*]

The International Court moved with great speed, and, having examined the dossier transmitted by the Secretary-General, and written statements from Upper Volta, Italy, France, Denmark, Netherlands, Czechoslovakia, the United States, Canada, Japan, Portugal, Australia, the United Kingdom, Spain, Ireland, South Africa, the USSR, Byelorussia, Bulgaria, Ukraine, and Romania, and heard oral pleadings by Canada, Netherlands, Italy, the UK, Norway, Australia, Ireland, USSR and the United States,[33] handed down its Opinion on 20 July 1962 in good time for the next Assembly.

The Court was not asked to pronounce on the legality or otherwise of UNEF and ONUC: though it did in fact make many references to this question, which have been incorporated in Section 4 (pp. 267–71 above). Nor was the Court asked to pronounce directly on the major constitutional dilemma facing the UN namely, whether UNEF (or ONUC) assessments were part of those contributions to the Organization covered by Article 19:

A Member of the United Nations which is in arrears in the payment of its financial contributions to the Organization shall have no vote in the General Assembly if the amount of its arrears equals or exceeds the amount of the contributions due from it for the preceding two full years. . . . [*Art. 19, UN Charter.*]

Although the Assembly was acutely aware of this problem of vote-deprivation looming on the horizon,[34] it addressed itself instead to whether the expenditures authorized by the Assembly for UNEF (and ONUC) were 'expenses' under Article 17 (2): 'The expenses of the Organization shall be borne by the Members as apportioned by the General Assembly.' The Court found in the affirmative of the question asked of it, by 9 votes to 5:

Turning to the question which has been posed, the Court observes that it involves an interpretation of Article 17, paragraph 2, of the Charter. On the previous occasions when the Court has had to interpret the Charter of the United Nations, it has followed the principles and rules

---

[33] See *Expenses case, ICJ, Pleadings, Oral Arguments and Documents, 1962.*

[34] Certain writers have, because of this, criticized the Assembly for asking for an Opinion: 'if the submission is made in the face of strong objections from members of the political organ, the inference can only be that the motive for invoking the Court's jurisdiction was not to bring about a settlement acceptable to all sides, but to exert political pressure on the recalcitrant minority' (D. W. Grieg, 15 *ICLQ*, 1966, p. 327).

applicable in general to the interpretation of treaties, since it has recognized that the Charter is a multilateral treaty, albeit a treaty having certain special characteristics. In interpreting Article 4 of the Charter, the Court was led to consider 'the structure of the Charter' and 'the relations established by it between the General Assembly and the Security Council'; a comparable problem confronts the Court in the instant matter. The Court sustained its interpretation of Article 4 by considering the manner in which the organs concerned 'have consistently interpreted the text' in their practice (*Competence of the General Assembly for the Admission of a State to the United Nations, I.C.J. Reports 1950*, pp. 8–9).

The text of Article 17 is in part as follows:

'1. The General Assembly shall consider and approve the budget of the Organization.
2. The expenses of the Organization shall be borne by the Members as apportioned by the General Assembly.'

Although the Court will examine Article 17 in itself and in its relation to the rest of the Charter, it should be noted that at least three separate questions might arise in the interpretation of paragraph 2 of this Article. One question is that of identifying what are 'the expenses of the Organization'; a second question might concern apportionment by the General Assembly; while a third question might involve the interpretation of the phrase 'shall be borne by the Members'. It is the second and third questions which directly involve 'the financial obligations of the Members', but it is only the first question which is posed by the request for the advisory opinion. The question put to the Court has to do with a moment logically anterior to apportionment, just as a question of apportionment would be anterior to a question of Members' obligation to pay.

It is true that, as already noted, the preamble of the resolution containing the request refers to the General Assembly's 'need for authoritative legal guidance as to obligations of Member States', but it is to be assumed that in the understanding of the General Assembly, it would find such guidance in the advisory opinion which the Court would give on the question whether certain identified expenditures 'constitute "expenses of the Organization" within the meaning of Article 17, paragraph 2, of the Charter'. If the Court finds that the indicated expenditures are such 'expenses', it is not called upon to consider the manner in which, or the scale by which, they may be apportioned. The amount of what are unquestionably 'expenses of the Organization within the meaning of Article 17, paragraph 2' is not in its entirety apportioned by the General Assembly and paid for by the contributions of Member States, since the Organization has other sources of income. A Member State, accordingly, is under no obligation to pay more than the amount apportioned to it; the expenses of the Organization and the total amount in money of the obligations of the Member States may not, in practice, necessarily be identical.

The text of Article 17, paragraph 2, refers to 'the expenses of the Organization' without any further explicit definition of such expenses. It would be possible to begin with a general proposition to the effect that the 'expenses' of any organization are the amounts paid out to defray the costs of carrying out its purposes, in this case, the political, economic, social, humanitarian and other purposes of the United Nations. The next step would be to examine, as the Court will, whether the resolutions authorizing the operations here in question were intended to carry out the purposes of the United Nations and whether the expenditures were incurred in furthering these operations. Or, it might simply be said that the 'expenses' of an organization are those which are provided for in its budget. But the Court has not been asked to give an abstract definition of the words 'expenses of the Organization'. It has been asked to answer a specific question related to certain identified expenditures which have actually been made, but the Court would not adequately discharge the obligation incumbent on it unless it examined in some detail various problems raised by the question which the General Assembly has asked.

It is perhaps the simple identification of 'expenses' with the items included in a budget, which has led certain arguments to link the interpretation of the word 'expenses' in paragraph 2 of Article 17, with the word 'budget' in paragraph 1 of that Article; in both cases, it is contended, the qualifying adjective 'regular' or 'administrative' should be understood to be implied. Since no such qualification is expressed in the text of the Charter, it could be read in, only if such qualification must necessarily be implied from the provisions of the Charter considered as a whole, or from some particular provision thereof which makes it unavoidable to do so in order to give effect to the Charter.

In the first place, concerning the word 'budget' in paragraph 1 of Article 17, it is clear that the existence of the distinction between 'administrative budgets' and 'operational budgets' was not absent from the minds of the drafters of the Charter, nor from the consciousness of the Organization even in the early days of its history. In drafting Article 17, the drafters found it suitable to provide in paragraph 1 that 'The General Assembly shall consider and approve *the budget* of the Organization'. But in dealing with the function of the General Assembly in relation to the specialized agencies, they provided in paragraph 3 that the General Assembly 'shall examine the *administrative budgets* of such specialized agencies'. If it had been intended that paragraph 1 should be limited to the administrative budget of the United Nations organization itself, the word 'administrative' would have been inserted in paragraph 1 as it was in paragraph 3. Moreover, had it been contemplated that the Organization would also have had another budget, different from the one which was to be approved by the General Assembly, the Charter would have included some reference to such other budget and to the organ which was to approve it.

Similarly, at its first session, the General Assembly in drawing up and approving the Constitution of the International Refugee Organization, provided that the budget of that Organization was to be divided under the headings 'administrative', 'operational' and 'large-scale resettlement'; but no such distinctions were introduced into the Financial Regulations of the United Nations which were adopted by unanimous vote in 1950, and which, in this respect remained unchanged. These regulations speak only of 'the budget' and do not provide any distinction between 'administrative' and 'operational'.

In subsequent sessions of the General Assembly, including the sixteenth, there have been numerous references to the idea of distinguishing an 'operational' budget; some speakers have advocated such a distinction as a useful book-keeping device; some considered it in connection with the possibility of differing scales of assessment or apportionment; others believed it should mark a differentiation of activities to be financed by voluntary contributions. But these discussions have not resulted in the adoption of two separate budgets based upon such a distinction.

Actually, the practice of the Organization is entirely consistent with the plain meaning of the text. The budget of the Organization has from the outset included items which would not fall within any of the definitions of 'administrative budget' which have been advanced in this connection.

Thus, for example, prior to the establishment of, and now in addition to, the 'Expanded Programme of Technical Assistance' and the 'Special Fund', both of which are nourished by voluntary contributions, the annual budget of the Organization contains provision for funds for technical assistance; in the budget for the financial year 1962, the sum of $6,400,000 is included for the technical programmes of economic development, social activities, human rights activities, public administration and narcotic drugs control. Although during the Fifth Committe discussions there was a suggestion that all technical assistance costs should be excluded from the regular budget, the items under these heads were all adopted on second reading in the Fifth Committee without a dissenting vote. The 'operational' nature of such activities so budgeted is indicated by the explanations in the budget estimates, e.g. the requests 'for the continuation of the operational programme in the field of economic development contemplated in General Assembly resolutions 200 (III) of 4 December 1948 and 304 (IV) of 16 November 1949'; and 'for the continuation of the operational programme in the field of advisory social welfare services as contemplated in General Assembly resolution 418 (V) of 1 December 1950'.

It is a consistent practice of the General Assembly to include in the annual budget resolutions, provision for expenses relating to the maintenance of international peace and security. Annually, since 1947, the General Assembly has made anticipatory provision for 'unforeseen and extraordinary expenses' arising in relation to the 'maintenance of peace and security'. In a Note submitted to the Court by the Controller on the budgetary and financial practices of the United Nations, 'extraordinary expenses' are defined as 'obligations and expenditures arising as a result of the approval by a council, commission or other competent United Nations body of new programmes and activities not contemplated when the budget appropriations were approved'.

The annual resolution designed to provide for extraordinary expenses authorizes the Secretary-General to enter into commitments to meet such expenses with the prior concurrence of the Advisory Committee on Administrative and Budgetary Questions, except that such concurrence is not necessary if the Secretary-General certifies that such commitments relate to the subjects mentioned and the amount does not exceed $2 million. At its fifteenth and sixteenth sessions, the General Assembly resolved 'that if, as a result of a decision of the Security Council, commitments relating to the maintenance of peace and security should arise in an estimated total exceeding $10 million' before the General Assembly was due to meet again, a special session should be convened by the Secretary-General to consider the matter. The Secretary-General is regularly authorized to draw on the Working Capital Fund for such expenses but is required to submit supplementary budget estimates to cover amounts so advanced. These annual resolutions on unforeseen and extraordinary expenses were adopted without a dissenting vote in every year from 1947 through 1959, except for 1952, 1953 and 1954, when the adverse votes are attributable to the fact that the resolution included the specification of a controversial item—United Nations Korean war decorations.

It is notable that the 1961 Report of the Working Group of Fifteen on the Examination of the Administrative and Budgetary Procedures of the United Nations, while revealing wide differences of opinion on a variety of propositions, records that the following statement was adopted without opposition:

'22. *Investigations and observation operations undertaken by the Organization to prevent possible aggression should be financed as part of the regular budget of the United Nations.*'

In the light of what has been stated, the Court concludes that there is no justification for reading into the text of Article 17, paragraph 1, any limiting or qualifying word before the word 'budget'.

Turning to paragraph 2 of Article 17, the Court observes that, on its face, the term 'expenses of the Organization' means all the expenses and not just certain types of expenses which might be referred to as 'regular expenses'. An examination of other parts of the Charter shows the variety of expenses which must inevitably be included within the 'expenses of the Organization' just as much as the salaries of staff or the maintenance of buildings.

For example, the text of Chapters IX and X of the Charter with reference to international economic and social co-operation, especially the wording of those articles which specify the functions and powers of the Economic and Social Council, anticipated the numerous and varied circumstances under which expenses of the Organization could be incurred and which have indeed eventuated in practice.

Furthermore, by Article 98 of the Charter, the Secretary-General is obligated to perform such functions as are entrusted to him by the General Assembly, the Security Council, the Economic and Social Council, and the Trusteeship Council. Whether or not expenses incurred in his discharge of this obligation become 'expenses of the Organization' cannot depend on whether they be administrative or some other kind of expenses.

The Court does not perceive any basis for challenging the legality of the settled practice of including such expenses as these in the budgetary amounts which the General Assembly apportions among the Members in accordance with the authority which is given to it by Article 17, paragraph 2.

Passing from the text of Article 17 to its place in the general structure and scheme of the Charter, the Court will consider whether in that broad context one finds any basis for implying a limitation upon the budgetary authority of the General Assembly which in turn might limit the meaning of 'expenses' in paragraph 2 of that Article.

The general purposes of Article 17 are the vesting of control over the finances of the Organization, and the levying of apportioned amounts of the expenses of the Organization in order to enable it to carry out the functions of the Organization as a whole acting through its principal organs and such subsidiary organs as may be established under the authority of Article 22 or Article 29.

Article 17 is the only article in the Charter which refers to budgetary authority or to the power to apportion expenses, or otherwise to raise revenue, except for Articles 33 and 35, paragraph 3, of the Statute of the Court which have no bearing on the point here under discussion.

Nevertheless, it has been argued before the Court that one type of expenses, namely those resulting from operations for the maintenance of international peace and security, are not 'expenses of the Organization' within the meaning of Article 17, paragraph 2, of the Charter, inasmuch as they fall to be dealt with exclusively by the Security Council, and more especially through agreements negotiated in accordance with Article 43 of the Charter.

The argument rests in part upon the view that when the maintenance of international peace and security is involved, it is only the Security Council which is authorized to decide on any action relative thereto. It is argued further that since the General Assembly's power is limited to discussing, considering, studying and recommending, it cannot impose an obligation to pay the expenses which result from the implementation of its recommendations. This argument leads to an examination of the respective functions of the General Assembly and of the Security Council under the Charter, particularly with respect to the maintenance of international peace and security.

Article 24 of the Charter provides:

> 'In order to ensure prompt and effective action by the United Nations, its Members confer on the Security Council primary responsibility for the maintenance of international peace and security . . .'

The responsibility conferred is 'primary', not exclusive. This primary responsibility is conferred upon the Security Council, as stated in Article 24, 'in order to ensure prompt and effective action'. To this end, it is the Security Council which is given a power to impose an explicit obligation of compliance if for example it issues an order or command to an aggressor under Chapter VII. It is only the Security Council which can require enforcement by coercive action against an aggressor.

The Charter makes it abundantly clear, however, that the General Assembly is also to be concerned with international peace and security. Article 14 authorizes the General Assembly to 'recommend measures for the peaceful adjustment of any situation, regardless of origin, which it deems likely to impair the general welfare or friendly relations among nations, including situations resulting from a violation of the provisions of the present Charter setting forth the purposes and principles of the United Nations'. The word 'measures' implies some kind of action, and the only limitation which Article 14 imposes on the General Assembly is the restriction found in Article 12, namely, that the Assembly should not recommend measures while the Security Council is dealing with the same matter unless the Council requests it to do so. Thus while it is the Security Council which, exclusively, may order coercive action, the functions and powers conferred by the Charter on the General Assembly are not confined to discussion, consideration, the initiation of studies and the making of recommendations; they are not merely hortatory. Article 18 deals with '*decisions*' of the General Assembly 'on important questions'. These 'decisions' do indeed include certain recommendations, but others have dispositive force and effect. Among these latter decisions, Article 18 includes suspension of rights and privileges of membership, expulsion of Members, 'and budgetary questions'. In connection with the suspension of rights and privileges of membership and expulsion from

15*

membership under Articles 5 and 6, it is the Security Council which has only the power to recommend and it is the General Assembly which decides and whose decision determines status; but there is a close collaboration between the two organs. Moreover, these powers of decision of the General Assembly under Articles 5 and 6 are specifically related to preventive or enforcement measures.

By Article 17, paragraph 1, the General Assembly is given the power not only to 'consider' the budget of the Organization, but also to 'approve' it. The decision to 'approve' the budget has a close connection with paragraph 2 of Article 17, since thereunder the General Assembly is also given the power to apportion the expenses among the Members and the exercise of the power of apportionment creates the obligation, specifically stated in Article 17, paragraph 2, of each Member to bear that part of the expenses which is apportioned to it by the General Assembly. When those expenses include expenditures for the maintenance of peace and seeurity, which are not otherwise provided for, it is the General Assembly which has the authority to apportion the latter amounts among the Members. The provisions of the Charter which distribute functions and powers to the Security Council and to the General Assembly give no support to the view that such distribution excludes from the powers of the General Assembly the power to provide for the financing of measures designed to maintain peace and security.

The argument supporting a limitation on the budgetary authority of the General Assembly with respect to the maintenance of international peace and security relies especially on the reference to 'action' in the last sentence of Article 11, paragraph 2. This paragraph reads as follows:

'The General Assembly may discuss any questions relating to the maintenance of international peace and security brought before it by any Member of the United Nations, or by the Security Council, or by a State which is not a Member of the United Nations in accordance with Article 35, paragraph 2, and, except as provided in Article 12, may make recommendations with regard to any such question to the State or States concerned or to the Security Council, or to both. Any such question on which action is necessary shall be referred to the Security Council by the General Assembly either before or after discussion.'

The Court considers that the kind of action referred to in Article 11, paragraph 2, is coercive or enforcement action. . . .

Moreover, an argument which insists that all measures taken for the maintenance of international peace and security must be financed through agreements concluded under Article 43, would seem to exclude the possibility that the Security Council might act under some other Article of the Charter. The Court cannot accept so limited a view of the powers of the Security Council under the Charter. It cannot be said that the Charter has left the Security Council impotent in the face of an emergency situation when agreements under Article 43 have not been concluded.

Articles of Chapter VII and of the Charter speak of 'situations' as well as disputes, and it must lie within the power of the Security Council to police a situation even though it does not resort to enforcement action against a State. The costs of actions which the Security Council is authorized to take constitute 'expenses of the Organization within the meaning of Article 17, paragraph 2'.

The Court has considered the general problem of the interpretation of Article 17, paragraph 2, in the light of the general structure of the Charter and of the respective functions assigned by the Charter to the General Assembly and to the Security Council, with a view to determining the meaning of the phrase 'the expenses of the Organization'. The Court does not find it necessary to go further in giving a more detailed definition of such expenses. The Court will, therefore, proceed to examine the expenditures enumerated in the request for the advisory opinion. In determining whether the actual expenditures authorized constitute 'expenses of the Organization within the meaning of Article 17, paragraph 2, of the Charter', the Court agrees that such expenditures must be tested by their relationship to the purposes of the

United Nations in the sense that if an expenditure were made for a purpose which is not one of the purposes of the United Nations, it could not be considered an 'expense of the Organization'.

The purposes of the United Nations are set forth in Article 1 of the Charter. The first two purposes as stated in paragraphs 1 and 2, may be summarily described as pointing to the goal of international peace and security and friendly relations. The third purpose is the achievement of economic, social, cultural and humanitarian goals and respect for human rights. The fourth and last purpose is: 'To be a center for harmonizing the actions of nations in the attainment of these common ends.'

The primary place ascribed to international peace and security is natural, since the fulfilment of the other purposes will be dependent upon the attainment of that basic condition. These purposes are broad indeed, but neither they nor the powers conferred to effectuate them are unlimited. Save as they have entrusted the Organization with the attainment of these common ends, the Member States retain their freedom of action. But when the Organization takes action which warrants the assertion that it was appropriate for the fulfilment of one of the stated purposes of the United Nations, the presumption is that such action is not *ultra vires* the Organization.

If it is agreed that the action in question is within the scope of the functions of the Organization but it is alleged that it has been initiated or carried out in a manner not in conformity with the division of functions among the several organs which the Charter prescribes, one moves to the internal plane, to the internal structure of the Organization. If the action was taken by the wrong organ, it was irregular as a matter of that internal structure, but this would not necessarily mean that the expense incurred was not an expense of the Organization. Both national and international law contemplate cases in which the body corporate or politic may be bound, as to third parties, by an *ultra vires* act of an agent.

In the legal systems of States, there is often some procedure for determining the validity of even a legislative or governmental act, but no analogous procedure is to be found in the structure of the United Nations. Proposals made during the drafting of the Charter to place the ultimate authority to interpret the Charter in the International Court of Justice were not accepted; the opinion which the Court is in course of rendering is an *advisory* opinion. As anticipated in 1945, therefore, each organ must, in the first place at least, determine its own jurisdiction. If the Security Council, for example, adopts a resolution purportedly for the maintenance of international peace and security and if, in accordance with a mandate or authorization in such resolution, the Secretary-General incurs financial obligations, these amounts must be presumed to constitute 'expenses of the Organization'. . . .

The obligation is one thing: the way in which the obligation is met—that is from what source the funds are secured—is another. The General Assembly may follow any one of several alternatives: it may apportion the cost of the item according to the ordinary scale of assessment; it may apportion the cost according to some special scale of assessment; it may utilize funds which are voluntarily contributed to the Organization; or it may find some other method or combination of methods for providing the necessary funds. In this context, it is of no legal significance whether, as a matter of book-keeping or accounting, the General Assembly chooses to have the item in question included under one of the standard established sections of the 'regular' budget or whether it is separately listed in some special account or fund. The significant fact is that the item is an expense of the Organization and under Article 17, paragraph 2, the General Assembly therefore has authority to apportion it.

The reasoning which has just been developed, applied to the resolutions mentioned in the request for the advisory opinion, might suffice as a basis for the opinion of the Court. The Court finds it appropriate, however, to take into consideration other arguments which have been advanced.

The expenditures enumerated in the request for an advisory opinion may conveniently be examined first with reference to UNEF and then to ONUC. In each case, attention will be paid first to the operations and then to the financing of the operations.

In considering the operations in the Middle East, the Court must analyze the functions of UNEF as set forth in resolutions of the General Assembly. Resolution 998 (ES–I) of 4 November 1956 requested the Secretary-General to submit a plan 'for the setting up, with the consent of the nations concerned, of an emergency international United Nations Force to secure and supervise the cessation of hostilities in accordance with all the terms of' the General Assembly's previous resolution 997 (ES–I) of 2 November 1956. The verb 'secure' as applied to such matters as halting the movement of military forces and arms into the area and the conclusion of a cease-fire, might suggest measures of enforcement, were it not that the Force was to be set up 'with the consent of the nations concerned'.

In his first report on the plan for an emergency international Force the Secretary-General used the language of resolution 998 (ES–I) in submitting his proposals. The same terms are used in General Assembly resolution 1000 (ES–I) of 5 November in which operative paragraph 1 reads:

> '*Establishes* a United Nations Command for an emergency international Force to secure and supervise the cessation of hostilities in accordance with all the terms of General Assembly resolution 997 (ES–I) of 2 November 1956.'

This resolution was adopted without a dissenting vote. In his second and final report on the plan for an emergency international Force of 6 November, the Secretary-General, in paragraphs 9 and 10, stated:

> 'While the General Assembly is enabled to *establish* the Force with the consent of those parties which contribute units to the Force, it could not request the Force to be *stationed* or *operate* on the territory of a given country without the consent of the Government of that country. This does not exclude the possibility that the Security Council could use such a Force within the wider margins provided under Chapter VII of the United Nations Charter. I would not for the present consider it necessary to elaborate this point further, since no use of the Force under Chapter VII, with the rights in relation to Member States that this would entail, has been envisaged.
>
> 10. The point just made permits the conclusion that the setting up of the Force should not be guided by the needs which would have existed had the measure been considered as part of an enforcement action directed against a Member country. There is an obvious difference between establishing the Force in order to secure the cessation of hostilities, with a withdrawal of forces, and establishing such a Force with a view to enforcing a withdrawal of forces.'

Paragraph 12 of the Report is particularly important because in resolution 1001 (ES–I) the General Assembly, again without a dissenting vote, '*Concurs* in the definition of the functions of the Force as stated in paragraph 12 of the Secretary-General's report'. Paragraph 12 reads in part as follows:

> 'the functions of the United Nations Force would be, when a cease-fire is being established, to enter Egyptian territory with the consent of the Egyptian Government, in order to help maintain quiet during and after the withdrawal of non-Egyptian troops, and to secure compliance with the other terms established in the resolution of 2 November 1956. The Force obviously should have no rights other than those necessary for the execution of its functions, in co-operation with local authorities. It would be more than an observers' corps, but in no way a military force temporarily controlling the territory in which it is stationed; nor, moreover, should the Force have military functions exceeding those necessary to secure peaceful conditions on the assumption that the parties to the conflict take all necessary steps for compliance with the recommendations of the General Assembly.'

It is not possible to find in this description of the functions of UNEF, as outlined by the Secretary-General and concurred in by the General Assembly without a dissenting vote, any evidence that the Force was to be used for purposes of enforcement. Nor can such evidence be found in the subsequent operations of the Force, operations which did not exceed the scope of the functions ascribed to it.

It could not therefore have been patent on the face of the resolution that the establishment of UNEF was in effect 'enforcement action' under Chapter VII which, in accordance with the Charter, could be authorized only by the Security Council.

On the other hand, it is apparent that the operations were undertaken to fulfil a prime purpose of the United Nations, that is, to promote and to maintain a peaceful settlement of the situation. This being true, the Secretary-General properly exercised the authority given him to incur financial obligations of the Organization and expenses resulting from such obligations must be considered 'expenses of the Organization within the meaning of Article 17, paragraph 2'.

Apropos what has already been said about the meaning of the word 'action' in Article 11 of the Charter, attention may be called to the fact that resolution 997 (ES–I), which is chronologically the first of the resolutions concerning the operations in the Middle East mentioned in the request for the advisory opinion, provides in paragraph 5:

> '*Requests* the Secretary-General to observe and report promptly on the compliance with the present resolution to the Security Council *and* to the General Assembly, for such further *action as they may deem appropriate in accordance with the Charter.*"

The italicized words reveal an understanding that either of the two organs might take 'action' in the premises. Actually, as one knows, the 'action' was taken by the General Assembly in adopting two days later without a dissenting vote, resolution 998 (ES–I) and, also without a dissenting vote, within another three days, resolutions 1000 (ES–I) and 1001 (ES–I), all providing for UNEF.

The Court notes that these 'actions' may be considered 'measures' recommended under Article 14, rather than 'action' recommended under Article 11. The powers of the General Assembly stated in Article 14 are not made subject to the provisions of Article 11, but only of Article 12. Furthermore, as the Court has already noted, the word 'measures' implies some kind of action. So far as concerns the nature of the situations in the Middle East in 1956, they could be described as 'likely to impair . . . friendly relations among nations', just as well as they could be considered to involve 'the maintenance of international peace and security'. Since the resolutions of the General Assembly in question do not mention upon which article they are based, and since the language used in most of them might imply reference to either Article 14 or Article 11, it cannot be excluded that they were based upon the former rather than the latter article.

The financing of UNEF presented perplexing problems and the debates on these problems have even led to the view that the General Assembly never, either directly or indirectly, regarded the expenses of UNEF as 'expenses of the Organization within the meaning of Article 17, paragraph 2, of the Charter'. With this interpretation the Court cannot agree. In paragraph 15 of his second and final report on the plan for an emergency international Force of 6 November 1956, the Secretary-General said that this problem required further study. Provisionally, certain costs might be absorbed by a nation providing a unit, 'while all other costs should be financed outside the normal budget of the United Nations'. Since it was 'obviously impossible to make any estimate of the costs without a knowledge of the size of the corps and the length of its assignment', the 'only practical course . . . would be for the General Assembly to vote a general authorization for the cost of the Force on the basis of general principles such as those here suggested'.

Paragraph 5 of resolution 1001 (ES–I) of 7 November 1956 states that the General Assembly '*Approves provisionally* the basic rule concerning the financing of the Force laid down in paragraph 15 of the Secretary-General's report'.

In an oral statement to the plenary meeting of the General Assembly on 26 November 1956, the Secretary-General said:

'. . . I wish to make it equally clear that while funds received and payments made with respect to the Force are to be considered as coming outside the regular budget of the Organization, the operation is essentially a United Nations responsibility, and the Special Account to be established must, therefore, be construed as coming within the meaning of Article 17 of the Charter'.

At this same meeting, after hearing this statement, the General Assembly in resolution 1122 (XI) noted that it had '*provisionally approved* the recommendations made by the Secretary-General concerning the financing of the Force'. It then authorized the Secretary-General 'to establish a United Nations Emergency Force Special Account to which funds received by the United Nations, outside the regular budget, for the purpose of meeting the expenses of the Force shall be credited and from which payments for this purpose shall be made'. The resolution then provided that the initial amount in the Special Account should be $10 million and authorized the Secretary-General 'pending the receipt of funds for the Special Account, to advance from the Working Capital Fund such sums as the Special Account may require to meet any expenses chargeable to it'. The establishment of a Special Account does not necessarily mean that the funds in it are not to be derived from contributions of Members as apportioned by the General Assembly.

The next of the resolutions of the General Assembly to be considered is 1089 (XI) of 21 December 1956, which reflects the uncertainties and the conflicting views about financing UNEF. The divergencies are duly noted and there is ample reservation concerning possible future action, but operative paragraph 1 follows the recommendation of the Secretary-General 'that the expenses relating to the Force should be apportioned in the same manner as the expenses of the Organization'. The language of this paragraph is clearly drawn from Article 17:

'1. *Decides* that the expenses of the United Nations Emergency Force, other than for such pay, equipment, supplies and services as may be furnished without charge by Governments of Member States, shall be borne by the United Nations and shall be apportioned among the Member States, to the extent of $10 million, in accordance with the scale of assessments adopted by the General Assembly for contributions to the annual budget of the organization for the financial year 1957;'

This resolution, which was adopted by the requisite two-thirds majority, must have rested upon the conclusion that the expenses of UNEF were 'expenses of the Organization' since otherwise the General Assembly would have had no authority to decide that they 'shall be borne by the United Nations' or to apportion them among the Members. It is further significant that paragraph 3 of this resolution, which established a study committee, charges this committee with the task of examining 'the question of the *apportionment* of the expenses of the Force in excess of $10 million . . . and the principle or the formulation of *scales of contributions different from the scale of contributions* by Member States to the ordinary budget for 1957'. The italicized words show that it was not contemplated that the Committee would consider any method of meeting these expenses except through some form of apportionment although it was understood that a different *scale* might be suggested.

The report of this study committee again records differences of opinion but the draft resolution which it recommended authorized further expenditures and authorized the Secretary-General to advance funds from the Working Capital Fund and to borrow from other funds if necessary; it was adopted as resolution 1090 (XI) by the requisite two-thirds majority on 27 February 1957. In paragraph 4 or that resolution, the General Assembly decided that it would at its twelfth session 'consider the basis for financing any costs of the Force in excess of $10 million not covered by voluntary contributions'.

Resolution 1151 (XII) of 22 November 1957, while contemplating the receipt of more voluntary contributions, decided in paragraph 4 that the expenses authorized 'shall be borne by the Members of the United Nations in accordance with the scales of assessments adopted by the General Assembly for the financial years 1957 and 1958 respectively'.

Almost a year later, on 14 November 1958, in resolution 1263 (XIII) the General Assembly, while '*Noting with satisfaction* the effective way in which the Force continues to carry out its function', requested the Fifth Committee 'to recommend such action as may be necessary to finance this continuing operation of the United Nations Emergency Force'.

After further study, the provision contained in paragraph 4 of the resolution of 22 November 1957 was adopted in paragraph 4 of resolution 1337 (XIII) of 13 December 1958. Paragraph 5 of that resolution requested 'the Secretary-General to consult with the Governments of Member States with respect to their views concerning the manner of financing the Force in the future, and to submit a report together with the replies to the General Assembly at its fourteenth session'. Thereafter a new plan was worked out for the utilization of any voluntary contributions, but resolution 1441 (XIV) of 5 December 1959, in paragraph 2: '*Decides* to assess the amount of $20 million against all Members of the United Nations on the basis of the regular scale of assessments' subject to the use of credits drawn from voluntary contributions. Resolution 1575 (XV) of 20 December 1960 is practically identical.

The Court concludes that, from year to year, the expenses of UNEF have been treated by the General Assembly as expenses of the Organization within the meaning of Article 17, paragraph 2, of the Charter. . . .

The conclusion to be drawn from these paragraphs is that the General Assembly has twice decided that even though certain expenses are 'extraordinary' and 'essentially different' from those under the 'regular budget', they are none the less 'expenses of the Organization' to be apportioned in accordance with the power granted to the General Assembly by Article 17, paragraph 2. This conclusion is strengthened by the concluding clause of paragraph 4 of the two resolutions just cited which states that the decision therein to use the scale of assessment already adopted for the regular budget is made 'pending the establishment of a *different scale of assessment* to defray the extraordinary expenses'. The only alternative—and that means the 'different procedure'—contemplated was another *scale* of assessment and not some method other than assessment. 'Apportionment' and 'assessment' are terms which relate only to the General Assembly's authority under Article 17.

At the outset of this opinion, the Court pointed out that the text of Article 17, paragraph 2, of the Charter would lead to the simple conclusion that 'the expenses of the Organization' are the amounts paid out to defray the costs of carrying out the purposes of the Organization. It was further indicated that the Court would examine the resolutions authorizing the expenditures referred to in the request for the advisory opinion in order to ascertain whether they were incurred with that end in view. The Court has made such an examination and finds that they were so incurred. The Court has also analyzed the principal arguments which have been advanced against the conclusion that the expenditures in question should be considered as 'expenses of the Organization within the meaning of Article 17, paragraph 2, of the Charter of the United Nations', and has found that these arguments are unfounded. Consequently, the Court arrives at the conclusion that the question submitted to it in General Assembly resolution 1731 (XVI) must be answered in the affirmative. [*Case of Certain Expenses of the UN, Advisory Opinion, ICJ Reports 1962*, pp. 157–79.]

Meeting in the autumn of 1962, the Assembly rejected a Soviet proposal that it merely 'note' the Court's Opinion, and instead, by a large majority accepted 'the Opinion of the International Court of Justice on the question submitted to it'.[35] There was no improvement shown in the situation, however, for the recalcitrant nations refused to pay and the membership at large was extremely reluctant to invoke the sanction of Article 19 in respect of Russia and

[35] Res. 1854 (XVII), 19 Dec. 1962.

France.[36] The Soviet Union had indicated her intention to leave the UN if deprived of her vote in the Assembly. Thus the Assembly, while 'accepting' the Court's Opinion, now sought a way out, and

convinced of the necessity of establishing at the earliest possible opportunity different financing methods from those applied to the regular budget to cover, in the future, peace-keeping operations of the United Nations involving heavy expenditure, such as those for the Congo and Middle East,

1. *Decides* to re-establish the Working Group on the Examination of the Administrative and Budgetary procedures of the United Nations . . . to study . . . special methods for financing peacekeeping operations of the United Nations involving heavy expenditures, such as those for the Congo and the Middle East, including a possible special scale of assessments;

2. *Requests* the Working Group to take into account in its study the criteria for the sharing of the costs of peacekeeping operations mentioned in past resolutions of the General Assembly, giving particular attention to the following:

(*a*) The references to a special financial responsibility of members of the Security Council as indicated in General Assembly resolutions 1619 (XV) of 21 April 1961 and 1732 (XVI) of 20 December 1961;

(*b*) Such special factors relating to a particular peacekeeping operation as might be relevant to a variation in the sharing of the costs of the operation;

(*c*) The degree of economic development of each Member State and whether or not a developing State is in receipt of technical assistance from the United Nations;

(*d*) The collective financial responsibility of the Members of the United Nations:

3. *Further requests* the Working Group to take into account any criteria proposed by Member States at the seventeenth session of the General Assembly or submitted by them directly to the Working Group;

4. *Requests* the Working Group to study also the situation arising from the arrears of some Member States in their payment of contributions for financing peace-keeping operations and to recommend, within the letter and spirit of the Charter of the United Nations, arrangements designed to bring up to date such payments, having in mind the relative economic positions of such Members States; . . . [*GA Res. 1854 B (XVII), 19 Dec. 1962.*]

The 21-member[37] Working Group submitted its report, as a basis for dis-

---

[36] 'The reluctance of the majority to assert its authority . . . was probably due in part to a realization of the ethical weakness (whatever the legal soundness) of the majority's case against the non-paying Members who were vulnerable to Article 19 . . . Many of the small, new countries, who held the balance of voting power on this decision, and who had earlier voted with the overwhelming majority that had accepted the World Court's Opinion . . . had paid nothing . . . Yet they escaped the penalty of Article 19 because they had in recent years (by virtue of the same favourable balance of power) voted themselves rebates and reductions in peacekeeping assessments . . . Thus by continuing to pay only their regular budget assessments, those with reduced peacekeeping dues could hold their arrears below the critical point without even paying the reduced peacekeeping assessments'. C. S. Manno, 'Majority Decisions and Minority Responses', *J. of Conflict Resolution*, Mas. 1966, p. 2. For articles on the Court's Opinion, see L. Gross, 'Expenses of the UN Peacekeeping Operations, Advisory Opinion of the ICJ', *Int. Org.* (Winter 1963), pp. 1–35; W. H. Barton, 'Who will pay for Peace: the UN Crisis', *Canadian J. of Int. Affairs*, Apr. 1965; J. F. Hogg, 'Peacekeeping costs and charter obligations-implications of the ICJ decision' *Columbia Law R.*; (1962); J. Jackson, 'The Legal Framework of United Nations Financing: peacekeeping and penury' 51 *Calif. Law R.* (1963).

In May 1963 the Secretary-General stated that Haiti was two years in arrears, and the Assembly President replied that, had Haiti sought to participate in the Assembly voting, she would not have been permitted to do so. It will readily be seen that one did not have to pay the *full* backlog of one's dues on the UNEF and/or ONUC accounts in order to remove oneself from the position of being in arrears to the amount equivalent to the contributions due for the preceding two years.

[37] Argentina, Australia, Brazil, Bulgaria, Cameroun, Canada, China, France, India, Italy, Japan, Mexico, Mongolia, Netherlands, Nigeria, Pakistan, Sweden, UAR, UK, USA, USSR.

cussion, to a special session of the Assembly convened to discuss the UN's financial problems in 1963. The special session passed a cluster of resolutions; one reiterated the *mélange* of relevant and *prima facie* mutually incompatible factors (collective responsibility, limited capacity of developing nations, special Security Council responsibility, desirability of voluntary contributions), terming them 'general principles to serve as guidelines for the sharing of the costs of future peacekeeping operations'.[38] Another contained the authorization of the bond issue,[39] a third called for the establishment of a peace fund through voluntary contributions,[40] a fourth extended the existence of the Working Group. Resolution 1877 (S–IV) tried to provide a way out of the impasse on arrears:

The General Assembly. . . .

1. *Appeals* to Member States which continue to be in arrears in respect of their assessed contributions for payment to the United Nations Emergency Force Special Account and the *Ad Hoc* Account for the United Nations Operation in the Congo to pay their arrears, disregarding other factors, as soon as their respective constitutional and financial arrangements can be processed, and, pending such arrangements, to make an announcement of their intention to do so;

2. *Expresses its conviction* that Member States which are in arrears and object on political or juridical grounds to paying their assessments on these accounts nevertheless will, without prejudice to their respective positions, make a special effort towards solving the financial difficulties of the United Nations by making these payments. . . . [*GA Res. 1877 (S–IV)*, *27 June 1963.*]

Defaulting nations did not avail themselves of this proposed loophole: their objections—at least so far as the wealthier nations were concerned—were political and constitutional, and not financial.[41] So far as UNEF was concerned, the Assembly decided to appropriate $9·5 millions for the period 1 July–31 December 1963 and made the following arrangements:

The General Assembly,

Recalling its resolutions 1089 (XI) of 21 December 1956, 1090 (XI) of 27 February 1957, 1151 (XII) of 22 November 1957, 1337 (XIII), of 13 December 1958, 1441 (XIV) of 5 December 1959 1575 (XV) of 20 December 1960 and 1733 (XVI) of 20 December 1961.

Having considered the report of the Secretary-General on the cost estimates of the United Nations Emergency Force for the period 1 January 1963 to 31 December 1963, and the report of the Advisory Committee on Administrative and Budgetary Questions thereon,

1. *Decides* to continue the Special Account for the expenses of the United Nations Emergency Force;

2. *Authorizes* the Secretary-General to expend up to 31 December 1963 at an average monthly rate not to exceed $1,580,000 for the continuing cost of the United Nations Emergency Force;

3. *Decides* to appropriate an amount of $9·5 million for the operations of the United Nations Emergency Force for the period 1 July to 31 December 1963;

4. *Decides* to apportion:

(*a*) The amount of $2·5 million among all Member States in accordance with the regular scale of assessments for 1963;

[38] Res. 1874 (S–IV) 27 June 1963.   [39] Res. 1878 (S–IV).   [40] Res. 1879 (S–IV).

[41] For the substantive issues at stake in the financial crisis, and the viewpoints of the various protagonists, see Higgins, 'United Nations Peacekeeping—political and financial problems', *World Today* (1965), pp. 324–37.

(*b*) The $7 million balance of the amount appropriated in paragraph 3 above among all Member States in accordance with the regular scale of assessments for 1963, except that each economically less developed country shall be assessed an amount calculated at 45 per cent of its rate under the regular scale of assessments for 1963;

provided that this apportionment shall constitute an *ad hoc* arrangement for the present phase of this peacekeeping operation, and shall not constitute a precedent for the future;

5. *Decides* that, for the purpose of the present resolution, the term 'economically less developed countries' shall mean all Member States except Australia, Austria, Belgium, Byelorussian Soviet Socialist Republic, Canada, Czechoslovakia, Denmark, Finland, France, Hungary, Iceland, Ireland, Italy, Japan, Luxembourg, Netherlands, New Zealand, Norway, Poland, Romania, South Africa, Sweden, Ukrainian Soviet Socialist Republic, Union of Soviet Socialist Republics, United Kingdom of Great Britain and Northern Ireland and the United States of America;

6. *Recommends* that the Member States named in paragraph 5 above make voluntary contributions in addition to their assessments under the present resolution in order to finance authorized expenditures in excess of the total amount assessed under this resolution, such voluntary contributions to be credited to a special account by the Secretary-General and transferred to the United Nations Emergency Force Special Account as and when an economically less developed country has once paid to the credit of the latter account its assessment under paragraph 4 (*b*) above or an equal amount, the transfer to be of an amount which bears the same proportion to the total of such voluntary contributions as the amount of such payment bears to the total of the assessments on economically less developed countries under paragraph 4 (*b*); any amount left in such special account on 31 December 1965 shall revert to the Member States that made such voluntary contributions in proportion to their respective voluntary contributions;

7. *Appeals* to all other Member States which are in a position to assist to make similar voluntary contributions or alternatively to forgo having their assessments calculated at the rate mentioned in the exception contained in paragraph 4 (*b*) above;

8. *Decides* that the voluntary contributions referred to in paragraphs 6 and 7 above may be made by a Member State, at its option, in the form of services and supplies acceptable to the Secretary-General, furnished for use in connexion with the United Nations Emergency Force during the period 1 July to 31 December 1963, for which the Member State does not require reimbursement, the Member State to be credited with the fair value thereof as agreed upon by the Member State and by the Secretary-General. [*Res. 1875 (S–IV), 27 June 1963.*]

In December 1963 a further resolution was adopted:

The General Assembly

Recalling its resolutions 1089 (XI) of 21 December 1956, 1090 (XI) of 27 February 1957, 1151 (XII) of 22 November 1957, 1337 (XIII) of 13 December 1958, 1441 (XIV) of 5 December 1959, 1575 (XV) of 20 December 1960, 1733 (XVI) of 20 December 1961, and 1874 (S–IV) and 1875 (S–IV) of 27 June 1963,

Having considered the reports of the Secretary-General on the cost estimates of the United Nations Emergency Force for the period 1 January to 31 December 1964 (A/5495, A/C.5/1001) and the report of the Advisory Committee on Administrative and Budgetary Questions thereon (A/5642),

Expressing the hope that this *ad hoc* assessment will be the last one to be presented to the General Assembly and that the Working Group on the Examination of the Administrative and Budgetary Procedures of the United Nations will be able to recommend to the Assembly, at the nineteenth session, a special method for the equitable sharing of the costs of peacekeeping operations involving heavy expenditures,

Taking into account that the economically more developed countries are in a position to make relatively larger contributions and that the economically less developed countries have a relatively limited capacity to contribute towards peace-keeping operations involving heavy expenditures,

1. *Decides* to continue the Special Account for the United Nations Emergency Force;

2. *Decides* to appropriate an amount of $17,750,000 for the operations of the United Nations Emergency Force for 1964;

3. *Decides* to apportion:

(*a*) The amount of $2 million among all Member States in accordance with the regular scale of assessments for 1964,

(*b*) The $15,750,000 balance of the amount appropriated in paragraph 2 above among all Member States in accordance with the regular scale of assessments for 1964, except that each economically less developed country shall be assessed an amount calculated at 42·5 per cent of its rate under the regular scale of assessments for 1964,

provided that this apportionment shall constitute an *ad hoc* arrangement for the present phase of this peace-keeping operation and shall not constitute a precedent for the future;

4. *Decides* that, for the purpose of the present resolution, the term 'economically less developed countries' shall mean all Member States except Australia, Austria, Belgium, the Byelorussian Soviet Socialist Republic, Canada, Czechoslovakia, Denmark, Finland, France, Hungary, Iceland, Ireland, Italy, Japan, Luxembourg, the Netherlands, New Zealand, Norway, Poland, Romania, South Africa, Sweden, the Ukrainian Soviet Socialist Republic, the Union of Soviet Socialist Republics, the United Kingdom of Great Britain and Northern Ireland and the United States of America;

5. *Recommends* that the Member States named in paragraph 4 above make voluntary contributions in addition to their assessments under the present resolution in order to finance authorized expenditures in excess of the total amount assessed under this resolution, such voluntary contributions to be credited to a special account by the Secretary-General and transferred to the Special Account for the United Nations Emergency Force as and when an economically less developed country has once paid to the credit of the latter account its assessment under paragraph 3 (*b*) above or an equal amount, the transfer to be of an amount which bears the same proportion to the total of such voluntary contributions as the amount of such payment bears to the total of the assessments on economically less developed countries under paragraph 3 (*b*); any amount left in such special account on 31 December 1966 shall revert to the Member States that made such voluntary contributions in proportion to their respective voluntary contributions;

6. *Appeals* to all other Member States which are in a position to assist to make similar voluntary contributions or, alternatively, to forgo having their assessments calculated at the rate mentioned in the exception contained in paragraph 3 (*b*) above;

7. *Decides* that the voluntary contributions referred to in paragraphs 5 and 6 above may be made by a Member State, at its option, in the form of services and supplies acceptable to the Secretary-General, furnished for use in connexion with the United Nations Emergency Force during the period 1 January to 31 December 1964, for which the Member State does not require reimbursement, the Member State to be credited with the fair value thereof as agreed upon by the Member State and by the Secretary-General.   [*Res. 1983 (XVIII), 17 Dec. 1963.*]

By the nineteenth session however, France and Russia had reached the position of being sufficiently in arrears for Article 19 to become applicable. The Assembly, by common unspoken agreement, sought[42] to avoid a situation whereby these countries would seek to exercise their vote, and possibly be

---

[42] With the exception of Albania, who sought to force a vote (see *YBUN, 1964,* p. 41). A vote was taken (with the USSR participating, and voting against), on whether a vote should be taken.

denied it. Hence the only decisions taken were those on which there was unanimity, and approval was indicated by private notification to the Assembly President, and not through a vote. It was essentially an Assembly where no business was transacted[43] and it was widely felt that another such could spell the end of the UN.

At the twentieth session therefore, it was the nations in the majority which gave way: they removed the threat of applying Article 19, while reserving their legal position. The turning point came in a speech by the new US Ambassador to the UN. He said that the United States position

had never been an issue in the cold war: it would be identical regardless of which Member State or States happened to be in arrears. . . . The United States Government did not regard the issue as a 'confrontation' between major Powers . . . nor was it prepared to undo or revise the precedents established by the Assembly itself by overwhelming majorities. . . . The United States had regretfully concluded that, at the present stage in the development of the United Nations, the General Assembly was not prepared to carry out the relevant provisions of the Charter, that is, to apply the loss-of-vote sanction provided in Article 19. . . . The United States continued to maintain that Article 19 was applicable in present circumstances, it recognized that the consensus of opinion in the Assembly was against the application of the Article and in favour of having the Assembly proceed normally. The United States would not seek to frustrate that consensus, since it was not in the interests of the world to have the Assembly's work immobilized in view of present world tensions. It agreed that the Assembly must proceed with its work. At the same time, if any Member State could make an exception to the principle of collective financial responsibility with respect to certain United Nations activities, the United States reserved the same option to make exceptions if, in its view, there were compelling reasons to do so. There could be no double standard among the Members of the Organization. [*Per Ambassador Goldberg, UN Special Committee on Peace-keeping Operations, 16 Aug. 1965, A/AC. 121/SR.15, pp. 5–6.*]

It was possible once again to adopt a resolution on UNEF:

The General Assembly,

Having considered the reports of the Secretary-General on the cost estimates of the United Nations Emergency Force for the period 1 January to 31 December 1965 (A/6059) and 1 January to 31 December 1966 (A/6060, A/C.5/1049) and the report of the Advisory Committee on Administrative and Budgetary Questions thereon (A/6171),

Expressing the hope that the *ad hoc* arrangements provided in the present resolution will not need to be repeated in future years and that the Special Committee on Peace-keeping Operations will be able to recommend to the General Assembly at its twenty-first session an acceptable method for the equitable sharing of the cost of peace-keeping operations involving heavy expenditure, taking into account the principles affirmed as guidelines by the General Assembly in resolution 1874 (S–IV) of 27 June 1963,

Taking into account that the economically more developed countries are in a position to make relatively larger contributions and that the economically less developed countries have a relatively limited capacity to contribute towards peace-keeping operations involving heavy expenditures,

I

Decides to appropriate for the operation of the United Nations Emergency Force an amount of $18,911,000 for 1965 and an amount of $15 million for 1966;

---

[43] Though interim financial arrangements were approved, by the 'no voting' device (Res. 2004 (XIX)) as well as a decision to set up a Special Committee to examine all aspects of peacekeeping (Res. 2006 (XIX)). The Special Committee was able to produce no solutions acceptable to all. For a detailed review of the Committee's work, see *YBUN, 1964,* pp. 1–33.

II

1. *Decides* as an *ad hoc* arrangement, without prejudice to the positions of principle which may be taken by Member States on the eventual recommendations of the Special Committee on Peace-keeping Operations on this question:

(*a*) To credit against the appropriation for the United Nations Emergency Force for 1965 provided for in section I above, $3,911,000 from those funds already contributed as voluntary contributions to restore the solvency of the United Nations;

(*b*) To apportion an amount of $800,000 for 1965 among the economically less developed Member States in the proportions determined by the scale of assessments for 1965;

(*c*) To apportion an amount of $14·2 million for 1965 among the economically developed Member States in the proportions determined by the scale of assessments for 1965 plus—in order to meet reserve requirements—an additional amount from each contributor in this group equal to 25 per cent of its apportionment, such additional contributions to be reimbursable on a *pro rata* basis when the General Assembly shall determine that all or part of these additional contributions are no longer needed;

2. *Calls upon* States members of the specialized agencies and of the International Atomic Energy Agency which are not Members of the United Nations to make contributions appropriate to their circumstances;

3. *Decides* that the contributions called for in paragraph 1 above may be made by a Member State, at its option, in the form of services and supplies acceptable to the Secretary-General, furnished for use in connexion with the United Nations Emergency Force during the period 1 January to 31 December 1965 for which the Member State does not require reimbursement, the Member State to be credited with the fair value thereof as agreed upon by the Member State and by the Secretary-General;

4. *Decides* that such amounts as a Member State has advanced for the United Nations Emergency Force pursuant to General Assembly resolution 2004 (XIX) of 18 February 1965 shall be credited by the Secretary General to the amounts apportioned against such Member State in paragraph 1 above;

5. *Further decides* that such Member States as have made voluntary contributions to restore the solvency of the United Nations may request the Secretary-General to apply these contributions to the amounts apportioned against them in paragraph 1 above;

6. *Decides* that, for the purpose of the present resolution, the term 'economically less developed Member States' shall mean all Member States except Australia, Austria, Belgium, the Byelorussian Soviet Socialist Republic, Canada, Czechoslovakia, Denmark, Finland, France, Hungary, Iceland, Ireland, Italy, Japan, Luxembourg, the Netherlands, New Zealand, Norway, Poland, Romania, South Africa, Sweden, the Ukrainian Soviet Socialist Republic, the Union of Soviet Socialist Republics, the United Kingdom of Great Britain and Northern Ireland and the United States of America;

III

1. *Decides* as an *ad hoc* arrangement, without prejudice to the positions of principle which may be taken by Member States on the eventual recommendations of the Special Committee on Peace-keeping Operations on this question:

(*a*) To apportion an amount of $800,000 for 1966 among the economically less developed Member States in the proportions determined by the scale of assessment for 1966;

(*b*) To apportion an amount of $14·2 million for 1966 among the economically developed Member States in the proportions determined by the scale of assessments for 1966 plus—in order to meet reserve requirements—an additional amount from each contributor in this group equal to 25 per cent of its apportionment, such additional contributions to be reimbursable on a *pro rata* basis when the General Assembly shall determine that all or part of these additional contributions are no longer needed;

2. *Calls upon* States members of the specialized agencies and of the International Atomic Energy Agency which are not Members of the United Nations to make contributions appropriate to their circumstances;

3. *Decides* that the contributions called for in paragraph 1 of this section may be made by a Member State, at its option, in the form of services and supplies acceptable to the Secretary-General, furnished for use in connexion with the United Nations Emergency Force during the period 1 January to 31 December 1966, for which the Member State does not require reimbursement, the Member State to be credited with the fair value thereof as agreed upon by the Member State and by the Secretary-General;

4. *Decides* that, for the purpose of the present resolution, the term 'economically less developed Member States' shall mean all Member States except Australia, Austria, Belgium, the Byelorussian Soviet Socialist Republic, Canada, Czechoslovakia, Denmark, Finland, France, Hungary, Iceland, Ireland, Italy, Japan, Luxembourg, the Netherlands, New Zealand, Norway, Poland, Romania, South Africa, Sweden, the Ukrainian Soviet Socialist Republic, the Union of Soviet Socialist Republics, the United Kingdom of Great Britain and Northern Ireland and the United States of America.   [*Res. 2115 (XX), 21 Dec. 1965.*]

In 1966 an almost identical resolution was adopted. It contained the same hope that the present *ad hoc* arrangements would not need to be repeated; called for contributions from non-UN members who were members of the Specialized Agencies or the International Atomic Energy Authority; continued the crediting procedure; and listed the same 'developed' countries. The Assembly also

Decides to appropriate an amount of $14 million for the operation of the United Nations Emergency Force for 1967. . . .

(*a*) To apportion an amount of $740,000 for 1967 among the economically less developed Member States in the proportions determined by the scale of assessments for 1967;

(*b*) To apportion an amount of $13,260,000 for 1967 among the economically developed Member States in the proportions determined by the scale of assessments for 1967 plus—in order to meet recent requirements—an additional amount from each contributor in this group equal to 25 per cent of its apportionment, such additional contributions to be reimbursable on a *pro rata* basis when the General Assembly shall determine that all or part of these additional contributions are no longer needed. . . .   [*GA Res. 2194 (XXI) B, 16 Dec. 1966.*]

Thus UNEF's budget was further whittled away without any of the underlying problems being resolved. And thus it was when UNEF withdrew in May 1967.

12

IMPLEMENTATION

UNEF's mandate, as has been shown above, was multifold: to secure the cessation of hostilities and supervise the cease-fire; to ensure the orderly withdrawal of British, French, and Israel forces; to patrol the border areas; and to oversee the observance of the Egypt–Israel Armistice provisions.[1] It is con-

[1] See s. 2, pp. 250-60.

venient, when seeking to assess how successful UNEF was in implementing its mandate, to take each of these tasks separately.

(a) Securing the Cease-fire and Cessation of Hostilities

This was fairly rapidly achieved, though in the early stages there were Egyptian denials that British and French hostilities had actually terminated:

In the resolution adopted on 2 November 1956 the General Assembly urged, as a matter of priority, that all parties now involved in hostilities in this area agree to an immediate cease-fire. My Government has given priority consideration to this recommendation and it now empowers me to announce that Israel agrees to an immediate cease-fire provided a similar answer is forthcoming from Egypt. [*Per Mr Eban, Israel, 1st emerg. spec. sess., 563rd mtg*, para. 170.]

The Egyptian government indicated that it would accept the call for a cease-fire 'on the condition . . . that it could not implement the resolution in case attacking armies continue their aggression.'[2] The Secretary-General then notified the other three parties involved of the nature of Egypt's acceptance, and called upon all four nations to bring hostilities to an end.[3] He also addressed identical cables to France and the United Kingdom:

4. In pursuance of the functions entrusted to me by operative paragraph 2 of the resolution of 4 November, quoted above; in view of the provision in paragraph 2 of the resolution of 2 November and operative paragraph 3 of the resolution of 4 November; and in view, further, of the Canadian-sponsored resolution, also adopted on 4 November, concerning the plan for a United Nations Force, and the indications it gives as to the attitude of the General Assembly to the three conditions established by your Government, I must inquire whether the Government of France will accept the provisions set forth in operative paragraphs 1 and 3 of the resolution of 2 November and will be willing to make arrangements with the Secretary-General for the implementation of the cease-fire and the halting of the movement of military forces and arms into the area, in accordance with operative paragraph 2 of the resolution of 4 November.

5. I wish to draw to your attention that the Government of Israel has accepted the cease-fire on the condition of reciprocal acceptance by Egypt, while Egypt has accepted the cease-fire provided that military actions against Egypt are stopped. With the stands thus taken by Israel and Egypt, it is obvious that the position of your Government and the Government of Great Britain will determine whether or not it will be possible to achieve a cease-fire between Egypt and Israel.

6. In pursuance of the provision in operative paragraph 2 of the resolution (999 (ES–I)) of 4 November authorizing the Secretary-General 'immediately to arrange with the parties concerned for the implementation of the cease-fire and the halting of the movement of military forces and arms into the area', I am requesting all four parties, which of course includes France, to bring to a halt all hostile military actions in the area by 20.00 GMT Sunday, 4 November 1956. May I further request that your Government's decision in this matter be communicated to me at the earliest possible moment, and at all events so early as to render it possible to inform the other parties concerned about your decision prior to the said hour. The decisions of the other parties in this regard will be transmitted to the Government of France without delay.

7. In view of the urgency of the situation, which accounts for the short time-limit fixed in the resolution of 4 November, I request again that a definitive reply be given at the earliest possible hour.

Dag HAMMARSKJÖLD

[*A/3287, 4 Nov. 1956, ann. 2.*][4]

[2] A/3266, 2 Nov. 1956.   [3] A/3287, ann. 1.   [4] See ann. 4 for identical telegram to UK.

I have the honour, on instructions from Her Majesty's Government in the United Kingdom, to inform you of the following points:

1. Despite any reports to the contrary, bombing has been conducted with the utmost consideration for civilians. Photographs of results show that little civilian loss of life can have been caused. This is proved by the fact that Egyptian army units are known to be sheltering in towns and villages in the knowledge that they are there immune from air attacks;

2. At Port Said a cease-fire has been ordered today;

3. In consequence, orders have been given that all bombing should cease forthwith throughout Egypt. Any other form of air action as opposed to bombing will be confined to the support of any necessary operation in the Canal area.

(*Signed*) Pierson DIXON
*Permanent Representative of the United Kingdom of Great Britain
and Northern Ireland to the United Nations*

[*A/3299, Letter to the Secretary-General, 4 Nov. 1956.*]

I have received the following cable from my Government:

'6 November 01.46. Inform Secretary-General immediately that Israel agrees unconditionally to cease-fire. Since this morning, 5 November, all fighting has ceased between Israel and Egyptian forces on land, sea and air and full quiet prevails.'

(*Signed*) Abba EBAN
*Permanent Representative of Israel
to the United Nations*

[*A/3301, 5 Nov. 1956.*]

With reference to the letter delivered to you and contained in document A/3299, I have the honour to inform you that:

1. Port Said is still courageously fighting and no cease-fire 'has been ordered' as was alleged by the representative of the United Kingdom.

2. Cairo, Alexandria, Ismailia, Suez, Port Said and many other cities, as well as civilian population, have been and still are the subject of the severest bombardment, against the elementary rules of humanity, which inflicted since only yesterday lives of thousands of innocent civilians; and this contrary to 'orders have been given that all bombardment should cease forthwith throughout Egypt' as was alleged by the representative of the United Kingdom.

I have the honour to request that the contents of this letter be brought to the attention of the President of the General Assembly, the President of the Security Council, and all the Members of the United Nations.

(*Signed*) Omar LOUTFI
*Permanent Representative of Egypt
to the United Nations*

[*A/3305, 6 Nov. 1956.*]

NOTE BY THE SECRETARY-GENERAL: The Secretary-General circulates the following *aide-mémoire* which is the communication referred to in the first paragraph of the messages received by the Secretary-General on 6 November from the Government of France and the United Kingdom (A/3307, A/3306). The *aide-mémoire* was given to the delegations for immediate transmittal to their Governments in the late afternoon of 5 November, after receipt of the Israeli acceptance of a cease-fire (A/3297), later supplemented through a further communication (A/3301).

1. In replies received to the request for a cease-fire, effective 4 November 1956, 24.00 GMT the Governments of France and the United Kingdom informed the Secretary-General (A/3293, A/3294) that as soon as the Governments of Israel and Egypt signify acceptance of, and the United Nations endorses a plan for, an international Force with the functions prescribed, the two Governments would cease all military action.

2. By adoption of the resolution, 5 November 1956, providing for the establishment of a United Nations Command, the United Nations General Assembly has taken the first decisive step in implementation of its previous acceptance in principle of a United Nations Force to secure cessation of hostilities under all the terms established in its resolution on the subject of 2 November 1956.

3. The Government of Egypt has, through a message to the Secretary-General of 5 November 1956 (A/3295), accepted the resolution of the General Assembly of 5 November 1956, and may thus be considered as having accepted the establishment of an international Force under the terms fixed by the United Nations. No similar declaration is yet available from the Government of Israel.

4. The Government of Egypt has, 4 November 1956, accepted the request of the Secretary-General for a cease-fire, without any attached conditions. It is to be assumed that this acceptance (A/3287, annex 6), although referring to the time-limit set in the request of the Secretary-General, is generally valid.

5. The Government of Israel has now, in a clarification (A/3297) of its first reply to the request of the Secretary-General for a cease-fire, stated that in the light of Egypt's declaration of willingness to a cease-fire Israel confirms its readiness to agree to a cease-fire.

6. The conditions for a general cease-fire would thus seem to be established and a new request warranted, provided that the Governments of France and the United Kingdom would recognize the decision of the General Assembly, establishing a United Nations Command, as meeting the condition they have made for a cessation of hostilities, and if, further, the Government of Israel were to endorse the same General Assembly decision.

[*A/3310, Aide-mémoire from the Secretary-General to the governments of France and the U.K, 7 Nov. 1956.*]

I have the honour to inform you that the Government of Egypt has carried out the cease-fire since 02.00 local time today, 7 November 1956, according to the resolution adopted by the General Assembly of the United Nations, and following your request. Nevertheless, according to a communiqué issued by the Egyptian Army General Headquarters at 15.15 local time, the French and British armed forces are continuing their hostile military action and are firing at both military and civilians at Port Said. They have furthermore encircled the city and severed its communication from the rest of the country.

I shall be grateful if you order the circulation of this letter as United Nations document.

Mahmoud FAWZI
Minister of Foreign Affairs of Egypt

[*A/3312, Cable of 7 Nov. 1956.*]

France however, had occasion to claim that the Franco-British troops were upholding the cease-fire, but that it was being broken by incidents for which Egypt was responsible:

5. The cease-fire is being strictly observed by the Franco-British troops. It has nevertheless been disturbed by at least four incidents since the date on which it was ordered.

(*a*) On 7 November at noon an Egyptian patrol opened fire from the zone north of El Qantara on Franco-British advance posts. The firing lasted for some time.

(*b*) In the night of 10 to 11 November about ten Egyptian light machine guns opened fire on El Cap wounding one person in the English lines.

(*c*) In the night of 16 to 17 November an explosion breached the sweet water canal at the northern limits of the village of El Qantara. This breach resulted in the town of Port Said being deprived of a part of its water supply.

(*d*) On 18 November at noon a patrol of thirty-five Egyptians armed with a machine gun opened fire in the direction of the French positions. Firing continued regularly for half an hour and then became less frequent. The United Nations observers were informed of this.

[*A/3384, ann. I, aide-mémoire from the French Government, 21 Nov. 1956.*]

Apart from isolated incidents, however, the cease-fire was in fact rapidly achieved and maintained.

(b) Supervising the Withdrawal of Foreign Troops

The accomplishment of this task turned out to be a more lengthy process. The United Kingdom and France claimed that a premature withdrawal by their troops, before UNEF was seen to be fully operational and effective, could only be harmful.[5] Israel was reluctant to withdraw from the Gaza Strip (which had been the base of *fedayeen* raids) and from the positions she had captured on the two small islands in the Straits of Tiran and at Sharm el Sheikh which commanded the entrance to the Gulf of Aqaba. She had urged UN administration of the Gaza Strip, which she did not accomplish: but the presence of UNEF on this strip of border did much to meet her needs, and led to her eventual withdrawal. UNEF was placed in the key shore position at Sharm el Sheikh, and this factor, together with the public American guarantee that the US government regarded the Straits of Tiran as international waters, led to the pulling back of Israeli troops from here, too. Israel's views on these questions have been recounted above (pp. 385–406). They were far from acceptable to the Communist and Arab nations:

23. . . . Three weeks have elapsed since the United Nations adopted a resolution which for the second time called upon the United Kingdom and France to withdraw their troops immediately from Egyptian territory and upon Israel to withdraw its troops behind the armistice line previously established by a United Nations decision.

24. The impression is being given that the United Kingdom, France and Israel do not intend to withdraw their forces. What, in effect, is the significance of the replies, which have been circulated to us, of these three States to Mr Hammarskjöld's letter? They merely contain vague promises to effect a partial withdrawal of some military units as an indication of goodwill. Mr Lloyd touched on this today in vague terms, mentioning a single battalion.

25. In addition, a whole series of completely unacceptable conditions are being put forward, as if the United Kingdom, France and Israel are in Egypt by right and as if the United Nations was in the position of a petitioner. While this correspondence is in progress, the aggressors are strengthening the positions they have occupied in Egyptian territory. [*Per the representative of USSR. GAOR, 11th sess., 592nd mtg.*]

79. . . . It is clear from the report that every day's delay in complying with the United Nations decisions on the withdrawal of armed forces from Egyptian territory means a further delay in the restoration of this international waterway and thus causes serious damage to the economies of all countries.

80. To sum up, the Polish delegation considers that: first, the armed forces of the United Kingdom, France and Israel must be immediately withdrawn from Egyptian territory, for every day they remain in Egypt not only is an affront to the prestige of the United Nations and its decisions, but also increases tension in the Middle East and the world as a whole; secondly, with the consent and agreement of Egypt, the essential measures to free the Suez Canal must be undertaken, so that it can be reopened to navigation as early as possible; thirdly, the units of the United Nations Emergency Force must be withdrawn to the Israel–Egyptian frontier as soon as the British, French and Israel troops have left, staying there only during a transitional period sufficient to ensure a peaceful return to normal relations in that region, and in

[5] See above, p. 411.

any case leaving whenever the Egyptian Government so demands. [*Per the representative of Poland, ibid.*][6]

The Lebanese representative noted disapprovingly, on 26 November 1956, that withdrawal by the Franco–British forces had not yet taken place:

75. 'We are studying plans for withdrawal,' says the French Government in reply to Mr Hammarskjöld's query. 'The French Government,' continues the reply, 'remains ready to proceed with the withdrawal of its forces as soon as the international Force which is being established is in a position to discharge the functions which have been entrusted to it under the General Assembly resolutions of 2, 5 and 7 November.'

76. Now, who is to determine whether this international Force is in a position to discharge its functions? Why, of course, in the opinion of the aggressors, it is the aggressors themselves.

77. 'As soon as Her Majesty's Government is satisfied that the United Nations Emergency Force is in a position to assume effectively the tasks assigned to it under the Assembly resolutions, the Anglo-French forces will be withdrawn' (*A/3384, annex III*), says the United Kingdom Government in reply to Mr Hammarskjöld's inquiry about withdrawal.' [*Ibid. 595th mtg.*]

This view received the support of many countries, for reasons expressed by Mr Krishna Menon:

71. Therefore to suggest in any way that the withdrawal is dependent upon the judgement of the United Kingdom and French Governments as to the competence of the United Nations Emergency Force, is again to seek to usurp the powers of this Assembly. Who are these two Governments to make their own judgements? They can no more make judgements about the action of the Assembly by themselves than we can—and we do not claim that right. Therefore, whether this United Nations Emergency Force is competent, is a matter for General Burns on the one hand and the Secretary-General on the other. Constitutional responsibility for it rests in this Assembly, and my delegation denies the right of the Governments of the United Kingdom and France to appropriate to themselves the right to say that this Force is competent for any one purpose or another.

72. But the position becomes much worse when we go into the substance of this competence. Competence for what? Competence to perform the duties that the Anglo-French invaders were supposed to be attempting? In other words, the view expressed in the statement by Mr Lloyd before this Assembly is that the United Nations Emergency Force is a continuation of the invading forces. It is to perform the part of putting what is called a protective shield between the combatants, of staying there for the solution of various problems, of preventing conflicts in the sense they understood it—and therefore hallowing the aggression. . . .

82. I come next to the Israel position. So far as the General Assembly resolutions are concerned, the Assembly has called upon Israel to withdraw its forces behind the armistice lines. Speaking on the Belgian amendment, I said (*594th meeting*), on behalf of my delegation, that in view of the arguments that had been raised, we would be willing to reconsider the draft resolution (*A/3385/Rev. 1*) if it were pointed out to us that the Israel forces had withdrawn behind the armistice lines. Then the representative of Israel, in his intervention, went on to say that thousands of people from the Sinai peninsula had gone back to their homes, to their factories and to their farms. Well, soldiers going back home is not the withdrawal of forces behind the armistice line. But if the Secretary-General had been informed with particulars that Israel forces had been withdrawn behind the armistice line, my delegation would consider it the duty of the Assembly to have recorded that fact. However, that does not appear to be the position. As I said on 24 November, if an action of that kind had been taken, the Israel

---

[6] For the rejected offer of the UK to provide the technical personnel for the clearance of the Canal, and the Secretary-General's report on the measures taken, see A/3382, 21 Nov. 1956, A/3376, 20 Nov. 1956, A/3492, 10 Jan. 1957.

Government would not be loath to inform the Assembly about it, because it would be to its advantage. And even in the evening of that day my delegation reiterated that if there were such a communication before the Secretary-General, we would be prepared to refer to it and to make our own position clear in the course of the intervention today. We waited for it. 83. This afternoon, there was a communication from the Minister for Foreign Affairs of Israel to the Secretary-General (*A/3395*). I have read this document carefully, and the wording is just the same. There is no reference to withdrawing behind the armistice lines, merely to the withdrawal of forces from Egypt. This communication states the following:

'In the plenary meeting of the General Assembly on 24 November the Israel representative expressed the willingness of the Israel Government to continue to discuss with you the means of implementing its undertakings with respect to the withdrawal of forces from Egypt.'

It goes on to say that Israel is prepared to make specific proposals. The document also says:

'On 8 November, I conveyed to you my Government's expression of willingness to withdraw its forces from Egyptian territory on the conclusion of satisfactory arrangements with the United Nations.'

84. I wish to say, in order to be frank with the Assembly, that I have not seen any document so far, coming from the Government of Israel, which categorically informs the Secretary-General that any appreciable part of its troops has been withdrawn. By this is meant regiments, units of the army, and not soldiers going home for a holiday; that can take place even in the middle of a war; soldiers go home and that cannot be regarded as withdrawal. What is more, even in this latest Israel communication, there is a specific refusal to mention withdrawal behind the armistice lines. This matter is of very great importance. [*Ibid. 596th mtg.*)

On 8 November 1956 the Government of Israel conveyed to you its willingness to withdraw its forces from Egypt on the conclusion of satisfactory arrangements with the United Nations in connexion with the emergency international Force.

Since that date substantial withdrawals have taken place and information to that effect has been conveyed to you (A/3389 and A/3389/Add. 1).

I have had opportunities of discussing with you the kind of arrangements which, in our view, should be instituted in connexion with the agreed withdrawal of forces. We have also received relevant information from you on the progress made and envisaged in the arrival and functioning of the United Nations Emergency Force.

In the light of these discussions the Government of Israel is now taking the following additional steps in implementation of the General Assembly's recommendation of 2 November (*resolution 997 (ES–I)*), with particular reference to paragraph 4 providing for the reopening and restoration of secure freedom of navigation in the Suez Canal:

(1) As a result of the progressive withdrawal of our forces, in accordance with the undertaking conveyed to you on 8 November, there will be no Israel forces anywhere within a wide belt of territory (about 50 kilometres) in proximity to the Suez Canal along its entire length by the morning of 3 December.

(2) The Government of Israel is agreeable that General Burns be in touch with it in connexion with the location of units of the United Nations Emergency Force in the area between the Suez Canal and the western limits of the Israel positions. The Israel Government will offer whatever technical assistance is necessary to facilitate the implementation of this measure.

(3) As a result of this and of other troop movements carried out pursuant to a policy of progressive withdrawal, another infantry brigade has now been moved entirely out of Egyptian territory into the territory of Israel, and has been demobilized. This is in addition to the withdrawals announced on 24 November.

(*Signed* Abba EBAN
Permanent Representative of Israel to the United Nations
[*A/3410, Letter of 1 Dec. 1956.*]

Progress was now made with the withdrawal of French and British troops:

B. Note verbale dated 3 December 1956 from the Permanent Representative of France addressed to the Secretary-General

(Original text: French)

The Permanent Representative of France has the honour to make the following communication to the Secretary-General on behalf of his Government:

1. The Governments of France and the United Kingdom note that:

(*a*) An effective international Force is now arriving in Egypt charged with the tasks assigned to it in the resolutions of the United Nations General Assembly of 2, 5 and 7 November.

(*b*) The Secretary-General accepts the responsibility for organizing the task of clearing the Suez Canal as expeditiously as possible.

(*c*) In accordance with the resolution of the United Nations General Assembly of 2 November, free and secure transit will be re-established through the Canal when it is clear.

(*d*) The Secretary-General will promote as quickly as possible negotiations with regard to the future régime of the Canal on the basis of the six principles set out in the Security Council resolution of 13 October.

2. The Governments of France and the United Kingdom confirm their decision to continue the withdrawal of their forces in the Port Said area without delay.

3. They have accordingly instructed the Allied Commander, General Keightley, to seek agreement with the United Nations Commander, General Burns, on a time-table for the complete withdrawal of their forces, taking account of the military and practical questions involved. This time-table should be reported as quickly as possible to the Secretary-General of the United Nations.

4. In preparing this time-table, the Allied Commander will have regard to the following requirements:

(*a*) That the embarkations of personnel and material shall be carried out in an efficient and orderly manner.

(*b*) That steps will be taken to ensure the maintenance of public security in the area now under Allied control.

(*c*) That the Commander of the international Force should make himself responsible for the safety of any French and British salvage resources left at the disposition of the competent organization of the United Nations.

5. In communicating these conclusions, the two Governments nevertheless recall the strong representations they have made regarding the treatment of their nationals in Egypt. They draw attention to the humane and liberal treatment accorded to Egyptian nationals in their territory. They feel entitled to demand that the position of British and French nationals in Egypt should be fully guaranteed.

C. Instruction issued by the Secretary-General to the Commander of the United Nations Emergency Force

[Original text: English]

The Secretary-General has instructed the Commander of the United Nations Emergency Force, Major-General Burns, to get into immediate touch with the Anglo-French Commander with a view to working out with him arrangements for the complete withdrawal of Anglo-French forces without delay. General Burns has been further instructed to arrange for the earliest possible date for the completion of this programme, taking into account the military and practical questions involved and the need to maintain public security in the area. In view of the Secretary-General's understanding of the policy of the United Kingdom and French Governments regarding withdrawal, the attention of General Burns has been drawn to the need to ensure that the United Nations Emergency Force should be in a position to assume its responsibilities in the Port Said area by the middle of December. *[A/3415, 4 Dec. 1956.]*

On 21 December the Secretary-General provided the Assembly with further information:

7. On 1 December, the representative of Israel informed the Secretary-General by letter (*A/3410*) that, on the morning of 3 December, Israel forces would be removed from 'a wide belt of territory (about 50 kilometres) in proximity to the Suez Canal along its entire length . . .'. This withdrawal has been confirmed by General Burns, and elements of the United Nations Emergency Force immediately entered this area, although progress in it has been impeded because of minefields and destroyed roads.

8. On 11 December, the representative of Israel informed the Secretary-General that Israel was now ready to effect further withdrawals of Israel troops in the Sinai peninsula, in order to enable the United Nations Emergency Force to extend its occupation eastwards, and invited a meeting between the Commander of the United Nations Emergency Force and the Israel General Staff to discuss arrangements to this effect.

9. General Burns met with General Dayan, the Israel Commander, on the morning of 16 December. General Dayan informed General Burns that, according to his instructions, the Israel forces were to be withdrawn from the Sinai peninsula at the approximate rate of 25 kilometres per week during the 'next few weeks'. General Burns recalled to General Dayan that the Israelis were expected to withdraw behind the armistice lines as rapidly as possible. He felt sure that the rate mentioned would not be acceptable to the Secretary-General.

10. Specific arrangements presented at the same time provided for the withdrawal of Israel forces on 18 December to Misfaq on the El Qantar–El Arish road, and to Bir Gifgafa on the Ismailia–El Auja road. The Israelis stated that on the road from Suez to Elath they had already withdrawn to Sudr el-Heitan. In each such withdrawal, the United Nations Emergency Force contingents would advance to within 5 kilometres of the Israel positions. In the Suez Gulf coast region, the Israel forces were to withdraw from Sudr on the morning of 19 December, with a UNEF detachment moving promptly forward to take over the oil-well installations in that place.

11. The specific withdrawal arrangements for 18 and 19 December were accepted by General Burns.

12. Subject to further discussion, and in addition to the aforementioned withdrawals, it was assumed as a tentative arrangement that, within a week, the United Nations Emergency Force would move forward approximately another 25 kilometres on roads eastward from the Canal, and also to Wadi Feiran on the Suez Gulf coast. It was agreed that a 'reconnaissance party' of UNEF would proceed immediately to El Arish to obtain information regarding the billeting and other requirements of UNEF preparatory to its entry there.

13. It was estimated by my military adviser, General Martola, and his military aides, that the pace and schedule for the Israel withdrawal reported to General Burns by General Dayan on 16 December would mean that from four to six weeks might elapse before the withdrawal would bring Israel forces behind the armistice lines, as required by the resolutions of the General Assembly. The assumption by General Burns that the pace of withdrawal proposed by General Dayan would be unacceptable to me was confirmed to a member of the Israel delegation on 17 December.

14. Specific Israel proposals for the withdrawal of its forces beyond what had been agreed upon on 19 December were presented the same day to General Burns. In substance, they provided for a further withdrawal of only some 20 kilometres along the main roads. General Burns informed General Dayan that these proposals were inadequate. On 20 December, I informed the representative of Israel that this schedule of withdrawal, which had no completion date, was inconsistent with the intention of the resolutions of the General Assembly and unsatisfactory. The representative of Israel informed his Government to this effect.

15. Today the representative of Israel has presented a new withdrawal proposal which had been received from his Government and which supersedes the proposal of 19 December. This envisages that the remaining Israel withdrawal will take place in two phases. In the first phase, no Israel forces would be 'west of El Arish' after the first week in January, although

Israel occupation of Sharm El Sheikh and Tirana would continue. The details of this phase of the withdrawal are to be worked out in another meeting between General Burns and General Dayan. The second phase would involve full Israel withdrawal, understood to mean behind the armistice lines, at an unstated date.

16. Despite the difficulties encountered by the United Nations Emergency Force in its advance into the Sinai peninsula, resulting from minefields and destroyed roads, some limitations in communications and transport, and the nature of the terrain, the Force is prepared to move forward at whatever pace may be required by a rapid Israel withdrawal behind the armistice lines, as envisaged by the General Assembly.

17. The second question put to me this morning concerned the withdrawal of French and British troops from Egyptian territory. The Anglo-French withdrawal from Port Said is in a very late phase, and I do not feel that it calls for any specific comments from my side. [*SCOR, 11th yr, 632nd plen. mtg.*]

Three weeks later the Secretary-General prepared a further and more detailed report:

1. A report on compliance with the General Assembly resolutions 997 (ES–I) and 1002 (ES–I) of 2 and 7 November 1956, with particular reference to the withdrawal of forces, was submitted to the General Assembly by the Secretary-General on 21 November 1956, as document A/3384. At that time only limited withdrawals had taken place. On 22 December 1956, however, the withdrawal of the Anglo-French forces was completed, thus achieving full compliance with one aspect of the requirement defined in the four resolutions of the General Assembly relating to withdrawal of forces (resolution 997 (ES–I) of 2 November 1956, resolution 999 (ES–I) of 4 November 1956, resolution 1002 (ES–I) of 7 November 1956 and resolution 1120 (XI) of 24 November 1956). Thereafter, those aspects of compliance concerning withdrawal of forces have involved only Israel troops.

2. An oral report on the extent of the withdrawal of Israel forces at that time and the further withdrawal in prospect, was presented by the Secretary-General at the 632nd plenary meeting of the General Assembly on 21 December 1956.

3. On the basis of the several relevant resolutions, the Secretary-General has held extensive discussions with representatives of the Government of Israel, aiming at full compliance with the withdrawal requirements by the earliest possible date. In the course of these discussions, which have taken place since the letter of the Permanent Representative of Israel of 24 November 1956 reported the first Israel withdrawal (A/3389 and Add. 1), the Israel representatives have announced further withdrawals of Israel troops, which have occurred in phases as follows:

(*a*) On 3 December 1956, withdrawal from the Suez Canal area, along the length of the Canal, to a distance of some 50 kilometres;

(*b*) on 7–8 January 1957, withdrawal to a line roughly following meridian 33 degrees 44 minutes, leaving no Israel forces west of El Arish;

(*c*) On 15 January, withdrawal eastward another 25 to 30 kilometres, except in the area of Sharm el-Sheikh. This phase involved the entry into El Arish and St Catherine's Monastery of United Nations forces, which have closely followed the Israel withdrawals.

4. On 14 January, the Representative of Israel, on behalf of his Government, conveyed to the Secretary-General the following communication concerning an intended further withdrawal:

'By 22 January the Sinai desert will be entirely evacuated by Israel forces with the exception of the Sharm el-Sheikh area, that is, the strip on the western coast of the Gulf of Aqaba which at present ensures freedom of navigation through the Straits of Tiran and in the Gulf.

'In connexion with the evacuation of this strip the Government of Israel is prepared to enter forthwith into conversations with the Secretary-General.'

The Commander of UNEF is to meet with the Commander of the Israel forces to make arrangements for carrying out this latest phase of the withdrawal. At this meeting, the Israel Commander will be requested to define the precise meaning of 'the Sharm el-Sheikh area' and 'the strip on the western coast of the Gulf of Aqaba'.

5. The intentions of the Government of Israel concerning compliance with the resolutions by withdrawal of Israel forces from the Gaza Strip had not yet been made known to the Secretary-General. . . .

13. The communication of 14 January from the Government of Israel, in making an exception for the Sharm el-Sheikh area as 'the strip on the western coast of the Gulf of Aqaba which at present ensures freedom of navigation in the Straits of Tiran and in the Gulf', indicates that the evacuation of the strip is anticipated, although further conversations with the Secretary-General are suggested in connexion with this evacuation. The area referred to and the islands opposite Sharm el-Sheikh are Egyptian territory or territory under Egyptian jurisdiction on the basis of an agreement with Saudi Arabia. Under the terms of the General Assembly resolution, the forces should be withdrawn from these territories. The Israel declaration of 8 November stated that Israel would be willing to 'withdraw its forces from Egypt' (A/3320).

14. The international significance of the Gulf of Aqaba may be considered to justify the right of innocent passage through the Straits of Tiran and the Gulf in accordance with recognized rules of international law. The Secretary-General has not considered that a discussion of the various aspects of this matter, and its possible relation to the action requested in the General Assembly resolutions on the Middle East crisis, falls within the mandate established for him in the resolution of 4 November.

15. Like the cease-fire, withdrawal is a preliminary and essential phase in a development through which a stable basis may be laid for peaceful conditions in the area. When the General Assembly, in its various resolutions concerning the recent crisis in the Middle East, gave high priority to the cease-fire and the withdrawal, the position of the Assembly reflected both basic principles of the Charter and essential political considerations.

16. The Assembly, in taking this position, in no way disregarded all the other aims which must be achieved in order to create more satisfactory conditions than those prevailing during the period preceding the crisis. Some of these aims were mentioned by the Assembly. Others are to be found in previous decisions of the United Nations. All of them call for urgent attention. The basic function of the United Nations Emergency Force, to help maintain quiet, gives the Force great value as a background for efforts toward resolving such pending problems, although it is not in itself a means to that end. . . . [*A/3500 and Add. 1, Report by the Secretary-General on compliance with General Assembly resolutions, 15 Jan. 1957.*]

He further reported:

PART ONE

1. In resolution 1123 (XI) adopted on 19 January 1957, the General Assembly, after recalling its resolutions of 2, 4, 7 and 24 November 1956, requested the Secretary-General 'to continue his efforts for securing the complete withdrawal of Israel in pursuance of the above-mentioned resolutions, and to report on such completion to the General Assembly, within five days'.

2. In pursuance of the resolution of 19 January, the Secretary-General held further discussions on withdrawal with the representative of the Government of Israel on 20 and 23 January. On 23 January, the Government of Israel presented its views in an '*aide-mémoire* on the Israel position on the Sharm el-Sheikh area and the Gaza Strip'. This *aide-mémoire* has been circulated separately with a note by the Secretary-General (A/3511).

3. At the expiration of the time limit set by the resolution for the Secretary-General to report to the General Assembly, Israel has not fully complied with the requests of the General

Assembly for withdrawal. The present situation, following the latest phase in the withdrawal of Israel forces on 22 January 1957, is shown on the map in the attached annex.

4. The views of the Secretary-General on the urgency of the prompt conclusion of the first phases of implementation of the General Assembly resolutions, as expressed in the previous report (A/3500 and Add. 1), remain firm. The further comments he considers it desirable to make are presented in Part Two of the present report.

PART TWO

A

5. To help towards solutions of the pending problems in the area, United Nations actions must be governed by principle and must be in accordance with international law and valid international agreements. For his part, the Secretary-General, in carrying out the policies of the United Nations, must act with scrupulous regard for the decisions of the General Assembly, the Security Council and the other principal organs. It may be useful to note the implications of the foregoing for the actions of the United Nations and of the Secretary-General in the present situation. In this regard, it would seem that the following points are generally recognized as non-controversial in the determination of the limits within which the activities of the United Nations can be properly developed. Within their scope, positive United Nations measures in the present issue, rendered possible by full compliance with the General Assembly resolutions, can be and have to be developed, which would represent effective progress toward the creation of peaceful conditions in the region.

(*a*) The United Nations cannot condone a change of the *status juris* resulting from military action contrary to the provisions of the Charter. The Organization must, therefore, maintain that the *status juris* existing prior to such military action be re-established by a withdrawal of troops, and by the relinquishment or nullification of rights asserted in territories covered by the military action and depending upon it.

(*b*) The use of military force by the United Nations other than that under Chapter VII of the Charter requires the consent of the States in which the force is to operate. Moreover, such use must be undertaken and developed in a manner consistent with the principles mentioned under (*a*) above. It must, furthermore, be impartial, in the sense that it does not serve as a means to force settlement, in the interest of one party, of political conflicts or legal issues recognized as controversial.

(*c*) United Nations must respect fully the rights of Member States recognized in the Charter, and international agreements not contrary to the aims of the Charter, which are concluded in exercise of those rights.

6. Point 5 (*a*) above, in general terms, is clearly reflected in the various decisions of the General Assembly on withdrawal of troops behind the armistice lines. Its further consequences with respect to *de facto* situations of a non-military nature in various territories will require consideration in later parts of this report in connexion specifically with the bearing of point (*c*) above on the cases at issue.

7. Point (*b*) above finds expression in the second and final report on the United Nations Emergency Force from which the following passages may be quoted. 'It follows from its (UNEF's) terms of reference that there is no intent in the establishment of the Force to influence the military balance in the present conflict and thereby the political balance affecting efforts to settle the conflict' (A/3302, para. 8). Further 'nor, moreover, should the Force have military functions exceeding those necessary to secure peaceful conditions on the assumption that the parties to the conflict take all necessary steps for compliance with the recommendations of the General Assembly' (A/3302, para. 12).

8. Point (*c*) is reflected in General Assembly resolution 997 (ES–I) of 2 November 1956, wherein the parties are urged to observe scrupulously the Armistice Agreements. . . .

29. Israel troops, on their withdrawal from the Sharm el-Sheikh area, would be followed by
16

the United Nations Emergency Force in the same way as in other parts of Sinai. The duties of the Force in respect of the cease-fire and the withdrawal will determine its movements. However, if it is recognized that there is a need for such an arrangement, it may be agreed that units of the Force (or special representatives in the nature of observers) would assist in maintaining quiet in the area beyond what follows from this general principle. In accordance with the general legal principles recognized as decisive for the deployment of the United Nations Emergency Force, the Force should not be used so as to prejudge the solution of the controversial questions involved. The Force, thus, is not to be deployed in such a way as to protect any special position on these questions, although, at least transitionally, it may function in support of mutual restraint in accordance with the foregoing.

E

30. In the last report (A/3500 and Add. 1), it was stated as essential that through prompt conclusion of the first phases of implementation of the General Assembly resolutions, Member States should now be enabled to turn to the constructive tasks to which the establishment and the maintenance of the cease-fire, a full withdrawal of forces behind the armistice lines, a desisting from raids and scrupulous observance of the Armistice Agreements, should open the way.

31. The report paid special attention to the problem of raids. In the debate following its presentation, concern was expressed about the problems which might arise in connexion with the withdrawal of Israel forces from the residual areas held at Gaza and at Sharm el-Sheikh. These latter issues, and the Israel views on the manner in which they might be met, have been the subject of the communication of 23 January from the Government of Israel (A/3511).

32. In the present report to the General Assembly on the situation now prevailing, the Secretary-General has endeavoured to clarify both the limits on United Nations action set by considerations of principle and law, and the directions in which such action might be usefully developed in the case of the two last mentioned problems and related questions. The basis for doing so has been primarily the Armistice Agreement between Egypt and Israel, scrupulous observance of which was requested by the General Assembly in its resolution of 2 November 1956. The Secretary-General believes that the concern expressed in the General Assembly debate in connexion with the final withdrawal can be met in a satisfactory manner within the obligation resting on the United Nations to base its action on principle, on international law and international agreements. A development of United Nations action, as indicated, would represent a significant step in preparation of further constructive measures. [*A/3512, Report of the Secretary-General in pursuance of General Assembly Res. 1123 (XI), 24 Jan. 1957.*]

On 2 February 1957 the General Assembly adopted Resolution 1124 (XI)[7] which deplored Israel's failure to complete her withdrawal behind the armistice demarcation line. The ensuing resolution, 1125 (XI),[8] did much to reassure Israel about anxieties over the two areas where her troops remained, for it agreed with the Secretary-General that measures needed to be taken 'upon Israel's complete withdrawal' from the Sharm el Sheikh and Gaza areas, for the scrupulous maintenance of the Armistice Agreement. The Secretary-General's report, and this resolution, now moved the log-jam:

I

1. The General Assembly, on 2 February 1957, adopted resolution 1124 (XI) in which, after recalling its previous resolutions on the same subject, the Assembly called upon Israel to complete its withdrawal behind the armistice demarcation line without further delay.

[7] See s. 2, p. 240.   [8] See s. 2, p. 241.

2. The Foreign Minister of Israel, on 1 March, announced in the General Assembly the decision of the Government of Israel to act in compliance with the request in this resolution. The same day the Secretary-General instructed the Commander of the United Nations Emergency Force, as a matter of the utmost urgency, to arrange for a meeting with the Israel Commander-in-Chief, in order to agree with him on arrangements for the complete and unconditional withdrawal of Israel in accordance with the decision of the General Assembly.

3. On 4 March, the Foreign Minister of Israel confirmed to the General Assembly the Government of Israel's declaration of 1 March. The same day the Commander of the United Nations Emergency Force met at Lydda with the Israel Commander-in-Chief. Technical arrangements were agreed upon for the withdrawal of Israel and the entry of the United Nations Emergency Force in the Gaza Strip during the hours of curfew on the night of 6/7 March. Arrangements were made for a similar take-over of the Sharm el-Sheikh area on 8 March.

4. On 6 March, General Burns reported that the 'United Nations Emergency Force troops are now in position in all camps and centres of population in the Gaza Strip'. At that stage the operation had been carried out according to plan and without incidents. At 04.00 hours GMT 7 March all Israelis had withdrawn from the Gaza Strip with the exception of an Israel troop unit at Rafah camp. By agreement, that last Israel element was to be withdrawn by 16.00 hours GMT 8 March. Full withdrawal from the Sharm el-Sheikh area would be effected by the same time.

5. On 7 March, the Commander of the United Nations Emergency Force notified the population of Gaza that 'the United Nations Emergency Force, acting in fulfilment of its functions as determined by the General Assembly of the United Nations with the consent of the Government of Egypt, is being deployed in this area for the purpose of maintaining quiet during and after the withdrawal of the Israel defence forces. Until further arrangements are made, the United Nations Emergency Force has assumed responsibility for civil affairs in the Gaza Strip. . . . The United Nations Relief and Works Agency for Palestine Refugees in the Near East (UNRWA) will continue to carry out its responsibility and will continue to provide food and other services as in the past. UNEF and UNRWA will do their best to relieve pressing needs which may arise from the present situation.'

6. The Secretary-General, thus, is now in a position to report full compliance with General Assembly resolution 1 of 2 February 1957 (1124) (XI).)

II

7. On 2 February, the General Assembly adopted a second resolution (1125 (XI)) 'recognizing that withdrawal by Israel must be followed by action which would assure progress towards the creation of peaceful conditions' in the area. Under the terms of this resolution, the completion of withdrawal puts its operative paragraphs into full effect.

8. In the resolution on action to follow a withdrawal, the General Assembly requested the Secretary-General, in consultation with the parties concerned, to carry out measures referred to in the resolution and to report as appropriate to the General Assembly. The Secretary-General will now devote his attention to this task. The stand of the General Assembly in the resolution is to be interpreted in the light of the report of the Secretary-General of 24 January (A/3512), which the Assembly noted 'with appreciation'.

9. Specifically, the General Assembly called upon the Governments of Egypt and Israel scrupulously to observe the provisions of the General Armistice Agreement between Egypt and Israel of 24 February 1949 and stated that it considered that, after full withdrawal of Israel from the Sharm el-Sheikh and Gaza areas, the scrupulous maintenance of the Armistice Agreement 'requires a placing of the United Nations Emergency Force on the Egypt–Israel armistice demarcation line'.

10. The Assembly further stated that it considered that the maintenance of the Armistice Agreement requires the implementation of 'other measures as proposed in the Secretary-General's report', with due regard to the considerations set out therein, with a view to assist

in achieving situations conducive to the maintenance of peaceful conditions in the area. This statement, as it was formulated, read together with the request to the Secretary-General to consult with the parties, indicates that the General Assembly wished to leave the choice of these 'other measures' to be decided in the light of further study and consultations.

III

11. Arrangements made by the Commander of the United Nations Emergency Force provided for an initial take-over in Gaza by the Force. This was in accordance with the statement of the Secretary-General to the General Assembly on 22 February, that 'the take-over of Gaza from the military and civilian control of Israel . . . in the first instance would be exclusively by UNEF'. Instructions from the Secretary-General to the Commander of the United Nations Emergency Force reflected the position thus reported to the General Assembly. The notification by the Commander quoted in section I above indicates the basis for this initial take-over as well as its extent. The same statement indicates the importance of the role that UNRWA can play in the initial take-over.

12. In accordance with decisions of the General Assembly, UNRWA has important functions in relation to the refugees in Gaza, which constitute the major part of the population of the area. Because of these normal functions and of the additional contributions which that agency can make in aiding the non-refugee population, UNRWA is of essential assistance to the United Nations Emergency Force in its present operation. Therefore, and on the assumption that this course is in accordance with the General Assembly's wishes, the Director of UNRWA has agreed with the Secretary-General in this phase of the development to extend its immediate assistance beyond its normal functions. This would be done in fields which are related to those functions and in which a sharing of responsibilities devolving on the United Nations Emergency Force at the initial take-over seems indicated. The Secretary-General wishes to express his appreciation for this assistance, of which he feels he can avail himself within the terms established for the United Nations Emergency Force as they have to be applied in the present phase of its activities. To the extent that UNRWA in this context is incurring additional costs, the reason for which is within the sphere of the responsibilities of the United Nations Emergency Force, a question of compensation will arise for later consideration.

13. The United Nations may also incur other additional costs than those caused by the assistance rendered by UNRWA. The Emergency Force may be in need of expert advice that can properly be provided by the Secretariat. If members of the Secretariat are taken over by the United Nations Emergency Force on a secondment basis, the cost obviously will be finally provided for as UNEF expenditures under the relevant resolutions of the General Assembly. In other cases costs should be carried by the Secretariat in the normal way.

14. The Secretary-General finally wishes to inform the General Assembly that arrangements will be made through which, without any change of the legal structure or status of the United Nations Truce Supervision Organization, functions of UNTSO in the Gaza area will be placed under the operational control of the Force. A close co-operation between UNTSO and UNEF will be maintained. [*A/3568, 2nd Report of the Secretary-General in pursuance of General Assembly Res. 1124 (XI), and 1125 (IX), 8 Mar. 1957.*]

Thus by 8 March 1957 UNEF had played its role, with the Secretary-General, in achieving that aspect of its mandate which required it to oversee the withdrawal of all foreign troops from Egypt.

(c) Patrolling the Armistice Lines

It will be recalled that in 1956 Israel repudiated the Israel–Egypt Armistice, thus ending her representation at any further meetings of the Mixed Armistice

Commission.[9] Although a rump of UNTSO continued to operate on the Israel–Egypt armistice line, the greater part of the patrolling functions were now assigned to UNEF. The effective patrolling of the Gaza Strip and the frontier of Sinai was of paramount importance to Israel, and indeed, she had delayed her withdrawal from that area in the hope of getting some guarantees.

UNEF achieved a commendable success in this matter, and provided a very effective contribution to the cause of peace along both the Gaza Strip and the international frontier in the Sinai peninsula. In the first progress report on 6 October 1957, the Secretary-General noted that 8 March marked full compliance with Assembly Resolution 1124 (XI) as to withdrawal:

1. Prior to that date, the Force had been concerned mainly with taking over from the foreign troops, following the successive stages of their withdrawals from the Suez Canal area, the Sinai Peninsula, and the Gaza Strip. Since 6 March, the Force, interposed between the armed forces of Egypt and Israel, has concentrated on its basic function of maintaining quiet in the area through deployment and patrolling in the Gaza Strip, along the eastern border of the Sinai Peninsula and in the region of Sharm el Sheikh. . . .

3. Incidents

41. Since the Force was deployed along the Gaza line and to the south of it, there has been a steady reduction in both the number and the severity of incidents along that line. Indeed, as of 15 September, no report of any serious incident had been received since 14 July, when a UNEF patrol was fired at, without casualties. There have been no raids from either side, whether in retaliation or of the *fedayeen* type. Military elements of Egypt and Israel are never in sight of each other.

42. The monthly figures on numbers and types of incidents involving the Egyptian–Israel

Type of incident	OCCURRENCES BY MONTH*						
	March	April	May	June	July	August	September (1–15)
Involving mines	5	1	4	5	0	0	0
Crossings of ADL† involving firing	1	1	2	2	2	0	0
Firing across ADL	0	3	2	2	2	0	1
Crossings of ADL involving theft or, occasionally, kidnapping	10	12	21	39	10	2	2
Crossings, or attempted crossings, of ADL not involving firing, theft of kidnapping	6	18	13	6	8	3	1
TOTALS	22	35	42	54	22	5	4

Total incidents for the six and one half months: 184.

* Based on figures from UNEF headquarters, which include complaints presented by both parties as well as observations independently made by UNEF. Record for March is incomplete.
† Armistice demarcation line.

[9] See above, pp. 108–16.

line and UNEF, including the reports of incidents presented by Egypt and Israel, reveal the significant trend, particularly marked since June, towards fewer and less serious incidents. All nine incidents reported in August and September, for example, were of a minor nature.

43. As reported from all sources, the type and number of incidents of all kinds other than alleged violations of territorial waters (of which there have been only two—in May) and of air space (which are difficult to establish) are as shown in table [on p. 475].

44. UNEF was designed to meet a particular need in an acute emergency. The authority given to it was limited, as it could only be. The demands upon it which might arise from specific situations could not all be foreseen. The basic purposes and role, however, as defined by the General Assembly, have been clear enough from the beginning, and the orders and directives of its Commander on its functions and authority are precise. It often has had to move and act swiftly, but has done so always with the restraint required by the very nature of its status and role. In the course of its functioning, many issues have arisen, for most of which satisfactory solutions have been found. A few issues are unresolved, but still open. These include the completion of UNEF's deployment; authority for UNEF to fire during darkness at infiltrators approaching the line from either direction, which would be somewhat broader than its unquestioned right to fire in self-defence—a right which it has, on occasion, exercised; and the idea of a protective fence along a part or the whole of the demarcation line.

45. Despite its limited authority and some unsettled questions, there would seem to be no good reason to doubt that UNEF has been effective. It has earned acceptance as a significant pioneering effort in the evolution of methods of peace-making.

46. The prevailing quiet and generally satisfactory conditions along the line, so far as UNEF is concerned, should not, however, as the Commander of the Force has warned, be considered as obviating the need to find, when the time is propitious, satisfactory solutions for the main unresolved issues noted above. The line under present conditions is vulnerable and the quiet, at any moment, could be abruptly broken.

47. Looking back to November of last year, it may be recalled that UNEF was, in the first place, a pre-condition set by France, Israel and the United Kingdom for the cease-fire. Subsequently, it was a pre-condition for the withdrawals from Egypt of the Anglo-French and Israel forces. Upon completion of the withdrawals, it became, and undoubtedly continues to be today, one of the pre-conditions for the preservation of quiet along the line between Egypt and Israel. Such quiet, in turn, is indispensable to fruitful effort towards the removal of the major obstacles to peace in the Near East. [*A/3694 and Add. 1, Report of the Secretary-General, 9 Oct. 1957*.]

At the same time, it must be observed that General Assembly Resolution 1125 (XI) had called for the placing of UNEF on both sides of the armistice line, so in a technical sense all UNEF's achievements were in partial fulfilment of that resolution.

The following year the Secretary-General was able to report

2. The operation of UNEF throughout this year, in all aspects of its task, has continued to produce the same favourable results as those described in the previous report. During the period covered in this report, virtually unbroken quiet has prevailed along the entire line between Egypt and Israel. [*A/3899, Report of the Secretary-General, 27 Aug. 1958*.]

1. This report on the United Nations Emergency Force, submitted in pursuance of General Assembly resolution 1125 (XI), paragraph 4, covers the functioning of the Force since 27 August 1958. . . .

2. The period covered by this report has been, in general, one of continuing quiet along the entire line between Egypt and Israel—a condition attributable, in no small measure, to the presence of UNEF. Here is renewed testimony to the effectiveness in the performance of its task which the UNEF operation has demonstrated from the beginning. For there can be little

doubt that were it not for this peace force along the long line from the Mediterranean to the Red Sea, the likelihood of disturbances in that area would be greatly increased. It would follow, of course, that the cumulative effect of numerous incidents along the line would probably soon attain a seriousness far overshadowing the effort and expense now involved in the maintenance of the Force. The success of UNEF notwithstanding, the attention of the Assembly must be seriously called to the fact that the operation is now in a crucial stage, owing to several factors. In the first place, in present circumstances, it is difficult to foresee when UNEF might be withdrawn without inviting the risk of dangerous consequences. . . .

3. In the year under review, the operation of UNEF has continued to be directed at the maintenance of peace and quiet in the area. Few serious incidents have occurred in this period, although there have been situations which, in the absence of a restraining influence, could readily have assumed serious proportions. . . .

35. As reported from all sources, the type and number of incidents which occurred between 1 August 1958 and 31 July 1959, are shown in the table [not reproduced here].

36. The total of 137 incidents reported for the twelve months' period may be compared with the 95 which occurred in the ten and one-half months' period covered by the report for 1958. All but a very few of these later incidents, however, have been of a minor nature. Of this year's total, 125 were confirmed by UNEF; 5 were reported by the United Arab Republic, and investigated and confirmed by the Egypt–Israel Mixed Armistice Commission (EIMAC), and 7 were reported by the United Arab Republic but were not confirmed by either the Commission or UNEF.

37. Based on figures from UNEF headquarters, which include complaints presented by both parties as well as observations independently made by UNEF, a total of 452 violations of airspace by identified planes and a total of thirty-nine such violations by unidentified planes occurred in the period from 1 August 1958 to 31 July 1959. Of these, thirteen were by aircraft of the United Arab Republic (UAR) overflying on the Israel side of the line, the others involving Israel aircraft overflying Gaza and the Sinai Peninsula. All of the instances of unidentified aircraft also involved overflights on the UAR side. Of the identified planes, 410 were observed by UNEF, twenty-two were reported by the UAR and confirmed by UNEF, and twenty were reported by the UAR but not confirmed by UNEF. UNEF headquarters reports that 374 of the UNEF-observed violations by Israel aircraft involved overflights in the northeast corner of the Gaza Strip by aircraft coming from the Israel aerodrome of Wadi Sharia. It is added that this airfield is only some twenty kilometres south-east of Gaza and that the prevailing wind is such that jet aircraft in taking off head in a direction which may take them over the north-east corner of the Strip. Strong representations about such repeated violations have been made and in recent weeks a notable decrease in this type of activity has been observed.

38. In the same period, a total of 113 violations of territorial waters were observed by the Force, apparently by fishing boats for the most part. Of the total violations, sixty-nine were in UAR waters and forty-four in Israel waters. Following a United Nations protest, this type of activity has virtually ceased in recent months. [*A/4210 and Add. 1, Progress Report of Secretary-General, 10 Sept. 1959.*]

This encouraging pattern of effectiveness continued.[10]

1. Throughout the period covered by this report, quiet has prevailed in the area. Constant vigilance by UNEF sentries and patrols, by day and by night, continues to be, as in previous years, an effective influence in restraining infiltration activities across the Armistice Demarcation Line and in the prevention of incidents along the Line. The relatively few incidents that have occurred have been of a very minor nature. It may be noted that agricultural and grazing activities now take place without molestation on both sides of the Line and up to the Line itself. In general, there has been no resort to force by UNEF, the mere presence of

[10] See A/4486, 13 Sept. 1960.

armed personnel on the spot being adequate to prevent incidents. On one occasion, however, when an armed infiltrator fired at a patrol in order to resist apprehension, United Nations troops had to take appropriate action in self-defence. Air violations, on the other hand, have been numerous. On two occasions, interception developed into air combat, during one of which a fighter plane was shot down. . . .

10. UNEF continues to be deployed along the western side of the Egypt–Israel Armistice Demarcation line (ADL), and the International Frontier, covering a distance of 273 kilometres. The Sinai Coast from the northern end of the Gulf of Aqaba to the Straits of Tiran, a further distance of 187 kilometres, is kept under observation by UNEF air reconnaissance. . . .

11. By day, the entire length of the ADL is kept under observation from a series of seventy-two inter-visible observation posts (OP's). Each OP is manned during daylight hours by shifts of approximately six hours. By night, the sentries are withdrawn and replaced by patrols varying in strength from five to seven men. These patrols move on foot and cover the length of the ADL on an average of three times each night and give particular attention to routes likely to be used by infiltrators. Platoon camps, to the rear of the OP's, each hold a reserve detachment available to go to the aid of an OP or patrol should the need arise. Telephone communication by day, and a system of flare signals supplemented by wireless at night, ensure a speedy response to calls for assistance.

12. Along the IF, rough terrain and scattered, uncleared minefields continue to restrict the access routes for potential infiltrators and tend to confine their activities to certain areas. These sensitive areas are patrolled, as in the past, by the Canadian reconnaissance squadron and the Yugoslav reconnaissance battalion. The former has two outposts in its sector and the latter has six, each of approximately one platoon in strength. Motor patrols operating from these bases cover the areas between outposts and certain tracks leading to the frontier. In one particular sector where it was found that more patrolling was necessary, a special track was made by the UNEF Engineers. This operation included clearing of mines along the track. In addition to ground observation, the entire length of the IF is also patrolled at irregular intervals on an average of four times a week by Otter aircraft of 115 Air Transport Unit. While on these patrols the aircraft are linked by wireless communication to the Canadian reconnaissance squadron, the Yugoslav reconnaissance battalion and the Brazilian battalion on the adjacent portion of the ADL. Any suspicious activity seen from the air can, therefore, be checked by ground patrols dispatched from the reserves available in these units.

13. A detachment of approximately one and one-half platoons of the Swedish battalion, with Canadian administrative troops, is stationed at Sharm-el-Sheikh to keep the Straits of Tiran under constant observation. The detachment has been reduced in size to promote greater efficiency and economy and the task has been permanently allotted to the Swedish battalion instead of rotating detachments from different battalions.

14. Detailed deployment of units along the ADL and the IF is as follows:

(a) *Armistice Demarcation Line (ADL)*

(i) *Sector 1* (from the sea to Gaza–Beersheba road)—DANOR battalion. Battalion headquarters is located on Hill 88 approximately two kilometres east of Gaza. Four companies man twenty-three observation posts along this twenty-kilometre sector of the ADL and include in their task watching the seaward extension of the ADL for possible violations of territorial waters.

(ii) *Sector 2* (from Gaza–Beersheba road to Wadi Ghazza)—Swedish battalion. Battalion headquarters is in Gaza. One company mans six OP's along approximately six kilometres of the ADL. The sector on the ADL allotted to this battalion has been reduced, owing to the transfer of two companies to ONUC.

(iii) *Sector 3* (Deir-el-Balah)—Indian battalion. Battalion headquarters is at Deir-el-Balah. Four companies man twenty-two observation posts along approximately sixteen kilometres of the ADL. In addition, the company formerly held in reserve at Khan Yunis has taken over four kilometres of the sector allotted to the Swedish battalion (see (ii) above).

(iv) *Sector 4* (Khan Yunis, Rafah)—Brazilian battalion. Battalion headquarters is at Rafah. Three companies man eighteen observation posts along approximately twenty kilometres of the ADL to its junction with the IF.

(b) *International Frontier (IF)*

The Canadian reconnaissance squadron and the Yugoslav reconnaissance battalion are deployed along the 215 kilometres of the IF as follows:

(i) *Sector 1* (from ADL/IF junction to Abu Aweigila–El Auja road)—Canadian reconnaissance squadron. Mobile patrols operate from two outpost camps and cover the entire length of the IF in this sector twice by day. By night, patrols stand by, ready to move out should the need arise. Squadron headquarters is located in the UNEF Maintenance Area at Rafah.

(ii) *Sector 2* (from Abu Aweigila–El Auja road to the Gulf of Aqaba)—Yugoslav reconmaissance battalion. This area is kept under observation by mobile patrols operating from permanent outposts established at Taret Umm Basis, El Amr, El Quseima, El Saba, El Kuntilla and Ras el Naqb. Battalion headquarters is at El Arish.

(c) *Guards and detachments*

(i) *Headquarters UNEF and installations in Gaza.* One company (three platoons) from the Swedish battalion located in Gaza provides these guards.

(ii) *UNEF Maintenance Area, Rafah.* One company (four platoons) from the DANOR battalion guards the perimeter of the Maintenance Area by manning the searchlight towers as well as by patrolling on a twenty-four-hour basis.

(iii) *Port Said.* One platoon from the Indian battalion guards the UNEF port warehouse in Port Said.

(iv) *UNEF Air Station, El Arish.* The area of the El Arish airfield controlled by 115 Air Transport Unit and their camp at Marina are guarded by two platoons from the Yugoslav reconnaissance battalion. [*A/4857, Progress Report of the Secretary-General, 30 Aug. 1961.*]

1. During the period covered by this report, there has been no appreciable change in the relationship between the United Arab Republic and Israel pertaining to the operations of UNEF. Virtually uninterrupted peace and quiet have prevailed all along the ADL in the Gaza Strip and on the IF in the Sinai Peninsula, and UNEF has continued to be the decisive influence in the maintenance of these conditions.

2. The number of cases of infiltration and other incidents along the ADL and the IF between the United Arab Republic and Israel have been few and, as in previous years, of a very minor nature. There has been no case in which UNEF has had to employ its arms—the pattern of deployment of sentries and constant patrolling has proved to be sufficient in the accomplishment of its task. The confidence of the local population in the prevailing peaceful conditions continues to grow and this is reflected in the markedly increased agricultural development that is taking place, often up to the ADL on both sides. It is regretted, however, that there has been no appreciable reduction in the number of air violations, more particularly in the north-east area of the Gaza Strip. . . .

9. UNEF continues to be deployed along the western side of the Egypt–Israel ADL and the IF, covering a distance of 273 kilometres. The Sinai coast from the northern end of the Gulf of Aqaba to the Straits of Tiran, a further distance of 187 kilometres, is kept under observation, the entire length of the IF is also patrolled at irregular intervals on an average of four times a week by aircraft of ISATU. While on these patrols the aircraft is linked by wireless communication to the unit responsible for the particular sector. Any suspicious activity from the air can then be checked by ground patrols dispatched from the reserves available in these units. . . .

15. There is little change in the total number of ground incidents as reported in the

16*

previous report. It should, however, be noted that there has been a considerable reduction in incidents involving firing and thefts; the corresponding increase in attempted crossings has been mainly by Bedouins in the northern sector of the IF. Air space violations, however, showed a very considerable increase from 242 to 422. There has also been an increase in violations of territorial waters from 79 to 129. In both the latter cases UNEF could not exercise any control other than that of observing and informing the parties concerned.

16. The general well-being of the Force and its health situation has been very satisfactory. There has been a steady decrease in the number of cases of acute hepatitis. This fact may be due to the gamma globulin inoculations given to the Scandinavian contingents which have hitherto been the most affected by this serious disease. [*A/5172, Secretary-General's Progress Report, 22 Aug. 1962*].

In 1963

the total number of violations of the ADL and of the IF and of cases of infiltration were approximately the same as in the year 1961–1962. These violations, except for the very few cases which involved planned attempts on the part of individuals to enter the territory of the other side, were quite minor in nature, such as incursions of 10 to 50 metres, until the parties were warned off by UNEF patrols. . . .

16. The type and number of incidents observed by UNEF troops between 1 August 1962 and 31 July 1963 are indicated in the annexes to the present report. Incidents reported by Israel or United Arab Republic authorities which could not be investigated and which therefore were not confirmed have not been included in this report. It will be noted that the number of incidents involving firing both in the area of the ADL and the IF and on UNEF has slightly increased.

17. The incidents of firing across the ADL and the IF were of two categories: some were random shots heard by UNEF patrols; others were exchanges of fire between Israel patrols in territory controlled by Israel and local bedouin in territory controlled by the United Arab Republic which were observed from the OPs. The incidents of firing on UNEF troops occurred when infiltrators were challenged by night patrols from the Force. but it was not possible to locate or apprehend the culprits. These incidents caused no casualties.

18. The number of incidents of other types shows a decrease as compared with the year 1961–1962, except in the case of violations of the ADL by persons from territory controlled by Israel. These violations occurred most frequently between January and May 1963 and were due mainly to the fact that the Israelis were at that time constructing a road very close to and parallel with the IF for a distance of approximately 10 kilometres south of Rafah. [*A/5494, Report of Secretary-General, 12 Sept. 1963.*]

In 1964 the total number of violations remained the same, though air violations gave rise to come concern.[11]

1. The United Nations Emergency Force continued to serve effectively as a stabilizing influence in maintaining peace in the Gaza/Sinai area of operations.

2. The total number of violations of the ADL and the IF has shown a slight increase during the year under review, as compared with 1963–1964. There have been some incidents which were relatively more serious than any which occurred in 1963–1964, as, for example, in November 1964, the removal by Israel forces of a border pillar in the area of El Amer, on the plea that it was incorrectly positioned. In February 1965, the Israel Defence Force (IDF) complained of three mine incidents in which residents of the Gaza Strip were alleged to have crossed the ADL into Israel-controlled territory (ICT) and laid mines which, in one case, caused injuries among a patrol of the IDF. There have been no further incidents of this sort

[11] A/5736, Progress Report of Secretary-General, 29 Sept. 1964.

NUMBER OF OCCURRENCES

TYPE OF INCIDENT	Sept.–Sept. 1957–8	1958–9	1959–60	1960–1	1961–2	1962–3	1963–4	1964–5	Aug 1966–May 1967
Crossing of AD/IF involved firing	5	20		5	0	0	3	0	0
Firing across ADL/IF	4	4		4	4	8	8	5	3
Crossing of ADL/IF involving theft or kidnapping	34	32		28	0	0	37	0	4
Crossings or attempted crossings of ADL/IF involving none of above	49	80		81	122	113	48	82	51
Air violations by UAR				9	4	1	5	4	0
Air violations by Israel				205	394	318	285	382	447
Air violations by unidentified aircraft				28	24	57	42	33	63
Violations of Israel-controlled waters by UAR vessels				42	63	72	91	64	40
Violations of UAR-controlled waters by Israel vessels				36	66	30	77	49	44
Number of Incidents caused by persons from Israel-controlled territory					31	64	51	71	42
Number of Incidents caused by persons from UAR-controlled territory					95	57	45	22	19

Note: Tables compiled by the Editor

since February 1965. The number of violations of the Restricted Zone along the ADL by military groups and individuals has increased in 1965 as compared with previous years, and there have been cases in which a UNEF patrol has had to apprehend or disarm groups of armed people. Owing to good understanding and co-operation between UNEF and the local authorities, however, such incidents have not developed into anything more serious.

3. Air violations have continued to cause concern, both because of their increasing frequency and their deeper penetration. Many have occurred in the north-east corner of the Gaza Strip, and most of these may be attributed to the high speed of jet aircraft. [*A/5736*, *Progress Report of Secretary-General, 29 Sept. 1964.*]

The two tables on p. 477 show the nature and origin of incidents occurring in the areas falling within UNEF's mandate. The Editor has compiled the figures from official sources, but the tables are not themselves official documentation. Should the reader seek monthly details, as well as certain other aspects, and also the figures relating to incidents, he will find them in Annexes I–IV of the Secretary-General's annual reports on UNEF.

(d) Observation of the Armistice Agreement

Although Israel had in 1956 denounced the utility of the Armistice Agreement, she retained a major interest in ensuring that the agreed demarcation line was observed. Border patrol by UNEF was undoubtedly successful in bringing the 1955–6 *fedayeen* raids in the Gaza Strip down to a minimum, and in containing occasional border infringements by both parties. UNEF's presence thus brought about a great improvement over the pre-1956 situation, Israel's withdrawal from the MAC notwithstanding.[12]

The refusal of Egypt to allow Israeli ships through the Suez Canal continued;[13] and in so far as such a refusal is to be considered as incompatible with the Armistice Agreement of 1949,[14] UNEF was unable in this case to uphold its terms. Prior to 1956 Egypt had also refused passage to Israel ships through the Straits of Tiran into the Gulf of Aqaba. Here the situation did change after 1956, for during the Suez Canal intervention of that year Israeli troops occupied the installations at Sharm el Sheikh, and then handed them to UNEF when they withdrew. Thereafter—until the withdrawal of UNEF itself in May 1967 —the Straits were open for all shipping including ships bearing the Israeli flag, and ships bringing cargo to and from Israel. While the tonnage of Israeli ships using Aqaba was comparatively small, the Gulf did provide the outlet for

[12] See Part I, s. 9; and pp. 255–8 above.

[13] For incidents arising in respect of this see S/4173, 17 Mar. 1959; and S/4211, 31 Aug. 1949.

[14] In Res. S/2322 of 1 Sept. 1951 the Security Council found that the claim by Egypt to be exercising belligerent rights, or rights of self-defence was not compatible with the Armistice Agreement. Many of the questions raised were directly relevant to the dispute which arose in May 1967, when Egypt asked for UNEF's withdrawal, and then closed the Straits of Tiran to Israel or Israel-bound shipping. They will therefore be referred to in more detail below, p.481. But on the question of passage through the Suez Canal, see Higgins, *Development of International Law*, pp. 206–7, 213–15; and R. Baxter, *The Law of International Waterways* (1964), pp. 221–39. See also Dinitz, 'The Legal Aspects of the Egyptian Blockade of the Suez Canal', 45 *Geo. Law J.* (1956–7), and Gross, 'Passage through the Suez Canal of Israel-bound cargo and Israel ships', 51 *AJIL* (1950), p. 530. For detailed legal arguments by distinguished jurists from the two nations directly concerned compare M. el-Hefnaoui, *Les problèmes contemporains posés par le Canal de Suez* (1951), pp. 182–6, and S. Rosenne, *The Legal Status of the Armistice Agreements* (1951).

Israel's growing trade with Asia and Africa. Further, after 1956 an oil pipeline was built from Eilat, Israel's port on the Gulf. Her anxiety over her access in Aqaba was one of the major factors in the delay in Israel's withdrawal from Egyptian territory after the Suez intervention. It has already been noted that many western nations deemed it essential that UNEF should on the withdrawal of Israel forces from the Gaza Strip and the positions in the Gulf of Aqaba . . . ensure that those positions are not directly or indirectly occupied by Egyptian forces, thereby creating again a situation of imminent danger.

74. The positions relinquished by Israel troops must, we believe, be occupied effectively by elements of the United Nations Emergency Force, at least for so long as is necessary to establish procedures for the settlement of the problems existing in those areas. It is my understanding that the functions of the United Nations Emergency Force specifically include the occupation of areas relinquished by opposing parties, and I hope that my understanding in this respect will be confirmed. . . .

81. I should now like to refer briefly to the report of the Secretary-General (*A/3500 and Add. 1*). It is a factual and non-contentious account of his negotiations with the Government of Israel, and my Government finds itself largely in accord with the conclusions he has drawn. I observe with pleasure that the Secretary-General states, in paragraph 14, that:

> 'The international significance of the Gulf of Aqaba may be considered to justify the right of innocent passage through the Straits of Tiran and the gulf in accordance with recognized rules of international law.'

I agree that the discussion of this question does not fall within the mandate of the Secretary-General, but I do wish to reiterate that the question is one which must be faced by the General Assembly.   [*Per the Australian representative, GAOR, 11th sess., 638th mtg*, paras 73, 74, 81.]

At the same time, it was acknowledged that Israel could not

properly make the withdrawal of its troops from the Gaza Strip and from the vicinity of the Straits of Tiran conditional upon the prior provision of hard and fast guarantees by the United Nations. In the last resort, the withdrawal of Israel's forces, like that of British and French forces, must be an act of faith. But Israel is entitled to some assurance from those in whom faith is placed.

111. Such assurances might take various forms. For example, it would be reasonable that a resolution on this subject should provide that, following the completion of the Israel withdrawal, the questions of the Gaza Strip and the Gulf of Aqaba would be taken up by the Assembly. Alternatively, or additionally, leading delegations might make declarations to the effect, *inter alia*:

(*a*) That the decision that the tasks of the United Nations Emergency Force have been completed should be a matter for the United Nations, not for Egypt or any other country;

(*b*) That the decision to withdraw the Force should therefore also be a matter for the United Nations, not Egypt or any other country;

(*c*) That the Force, in the performance of its function of securing and supervising the cessation of hostilities, should remain in the area at least until the Suez and Aqaba issues are settled, and some progress is made towards an over-all settlement;

(*d*) That consideration should be given to the creation of a demilitarized zone between Israel and Egypt, and—in accordance with the suggestion of the Secretary-General in his report of 15 January 1957—to the possibility of transferring to UNEF responsibilities so far carried by the Truce Supervision Organization;

(*e*) That the Assembly has an obligation to ensure against the future use of the Gaza Strip for attacks on Israel, and should give consideration to ways and means of bringing the area under some form of United Nations supervision;

(*f*) That freedom of passage must be secured for shipping of all nationalities, including Israel;

(*g*) That the Assembly must proceed at an early stage to frame recommendations designed to bring about a general settlement of the Palestine question. [*Per the New Zealand representative, GAOR, 11th sess., 639th mtg.*]

Of the assurances here suggested, scarcely any came to be provided. Points (*a*) and (*b*) were deliberately left blurred, with the Secretary-General preferring to rely on the balance between the principle of 'consent' on the one hand, and on the terms of the Egypt–UN *aide-mémoire* on the other.[15] Certainly UNEF has withdrawn, at Egypt's request, prior to any solution of the Suez and Aqaba issues, as mentioned in (*c*). No demilitarized zone was established—(*d*)—but certain of UNTSO's functions were assigned to UNEF.[16] The Gaza Strip was not brought under UN supervision, though UNEF was very successful in limiting raids from that area (*e*). Point (*f*) was achieved in the Straits of Tiran while UNEF was there, but was not sustained beyond its departure. Point (*g*) has manifestly not been achieved.

In the event, Israel appears to have chosen to rely—in respect of her withdrawal from Sharm el Sheikh—on a United States declaration that she regarded the Straits of Tiran as an international waterway,[17] and that it was 'essential that units of the United Nations Emergency Force be stationed at the Straits of Tiran.'[18] Certainly some other nations saw the stationing of UNEF at Sharm el Sheikh as clearly falling within its mandate to prevent a breach of the 1956 cease-fire and to achieve stability in the area.[19] The Secretary-General referred, in paragraph 29 of his report of 24 January 1957 (A/3512), to the possible use of UNEF in the Sharm el Sheikh area. By contrast one may note the Soviet disapproval, and the disapproval expressed at the United States statement that UNEF was needed in the Straits of Tiran 'in order to achieve there the separation of Egyptian and Israel land and sea forces'. Mr Kuznetsov observed:

7. We cannot help asking what is meant here by the separation of Egyptian and Israel forces, for after the Israel forces have been withdrawn from this area where, incidentally, there is no demarcation line—there will be no one at all to separate. Consequently, the United States proposal for the placing of United Nations forces in the Sharm el Sheikh area must be seen as an attempt to bring about the illegal occupation of a part of Egyptian territory for its own far-reaching purposes. The additional explanations of the United States representative have shed no new light on the matter. [*GAOR, 11th sess., 652nd plen. mtg, 12 Feb. 1957.*]

UNEF was however, stationed on the Straits, and remained there till it was asked to withdraw in May 1967.

The speed with which UNEF was withdrawn was the object of some criticism in certain quarters,[20] and it was suggested that the failure of U Thant to play for time was itself a further cause of a deteriorating situation in the Middle

---

[15] See above, p. 337.   [16] See above, pp. 56–57.

[17] It has been suggested in some quarters that a secret undertaking was in fact given by Dulles to guarantee access to the Straits of Tiran.

[18] Per the US representative, *GAOR*, 11th sess., 650th mtg, para. 55.

[19] See e.g. Norway, *GAOR*, 11th yr, 652nd mtg, p. 1084, paras 92–96.

[20] For details of UNEF's withdrawal, see pp. 344–58 above.

East. Having announced the withdrawal of UNEF, U Thant then flew to Cairo on 23 May 1967, and learned *en route* of the Egyptian decision to restrict shipping in the Straits of Tiran.[21] A meeting of the Security Council was inconclusive.

UNEF's role in Egypt was thus at an end. It had had remarkable success in maintaining stability in Israel–Egyptian relations, and, for the duration of its stay in Egypt, there can be no doubt that it ranked among the most effective of all UN peacekeeping operations. But the manner and occasion of its withdrawal caused widespread doubt about the overall efficacy of UN peacekeeping. It had been shown that a state, basing itself on the principle of 'consent', could require a UN Force to withdraw, in order to be free to do precisely what the presence of the Force was meant to discourage. It is thus now clear that not only does the effectiveness of a UN Force depend (among other factors) upon the co-operation of the host country, but that that co-operation can be withdrawn even after a prolonged period of efficient work and cordial relations. That is to say, whether a UN Force does succeed in implementing its mandate may, in the long run, turn on factors completely extraneous to the integrity and competence of the Force itself.

When UNEF withdrew in May 1967 the Secretary-General issued certain

[21] The legal arguments were complex. Basically, the Egyptians claimed that (1) the Straits of Tiran fell within their own territorial waters, and under Art. XIV of the Territorial Seas Convention one might refuse passage to ships which were not 'innocent' or whose passage was prejudicial to the security of the coastal state, (2) that the Gulf of Aqaba was an 'internal' sea, in what had traditionally been an all-Arab bay; (3) that in Egyptian eyes Israel had no legal coastal egress on to the Gulf, because Eilat was seized by Israel afger the signature of the 1949 Armistice; (4) that Egypt is not a party to the 1958 High Seas Convention, which defines an international waterway as one connecting High Seas with other High Seas *or the territorial waters of a third state*; (5) that even if the Straits were an international waterway, Egypt is entitled to exercise belligerent rights against Israel, with whom there is only an Armistice, and not a final peace. Traditional international law has always recognized the compatibility of an armistice with the continued existence of belligerent rights; (6) that these belligerent rights were exercised in the Straits of Tiran from 1949–56, and therefore were not shown to be incompatible with the Armistice. And Western Powers have in effect acquiesced in similar Egyptian action in the Suez Canal; (7) that Israel has forfeited her rights by denouncing the Armistice in 1956.

The Israeli response rests on the following propositions: (1) that the 1958 Convention on the High Seas is authoritative, at least so far as descriptive matters are concerned, and that the definition of an international waterway makes it clear that the Straits of Tiran fall into this category; (2) to claim that it is an internal sea ignores the existence of Israel (and of Jordan); (3) that Eilat was disputed as between Jordan and Israel, and came under Israel control before the Armistice with Jordan was signed; further, it fell within the territory allotted to 'the Jewish State' under the 1948 Partition Plan; (4) that Israeli passage, which has been occurring for 10 years, is not contrary to the security of Egypt, and nothing has now occurred to make it so; (5) that the exercise of belligerent rights is contrary to the Armistice Agreement, which, unlike traditional armistices, was concluded under the auspices of the UN and envisaged a permanent return to peace. Further, Hammarskjöld, Ralph Bunche, and the Security Council (S/2322, 1 Sept. 1951) had each indicated the incompatibility of belligerent rights with the Armistice; (6) that it was made perfectly clear that the repudiation of the Armistice in 1956 did not entail the view that Israel was reverting to a state of war. She was at peace with Egypt, but did not think the Armistice Agreement an effective instrument for guaranteeing that peace. For legal arguments on the Gulf of Aqaba, see C. B. Selak, 'A Consideration of the Legal Status of the Gulf of Akaba', 52 *AJIL* (1958), pp. 660–7; Baxter, pp. 160–3, 209–16; L. M. Bloomfield, *Egypt, Israel and the Gulf of Aqaba in International Law* (1957); B. Hammad, 'The Right of Passage in the Gulf of Aqaba', 15 *R. égyptienne de droit international* (1959), pp. 118–40. For comment on all the above points, see Higgins, 'The June War: the United Nations and legal background', *J. of Contemp. History* (1968).

documents providing an assessment of UNEF's contribution to peace in the Middle East. He correctly observed that UNEF had played a considerable part in stabilizing Egyptian–Israel relations for ten years, and that the reasons for the request for withdrawal were in no way related to any charge of inadequate performance on UNEF's part. He continued:

11. It is well to bear in mind that United Nations peace-keeping operations such as UNEF, and this applies in fact to all peace-keeping operations thus far undertaken by the United Nations, depend for their presence and effectiveness not only on the consent of the authorities in the area of their deployment but on the co-operation and goodwill of those authorities. When, for example, the United Arab Republic decided to move its troops up to the line, which it had a perfect right to do, the buffer function which UNEF had been performing was eliminated. Its continued presence was thus rendered useless, its position untenable, and its withdrawal became virtually inevitable. This was the case even before the official request for the withdrawal had been received by me.

12. It is all too clear that there is widespread misunderstanding about the nature of United Nations peace-keeping operations in general and UNEF in particular. As I pointed out in my special report of 18 May 1967 to the General Assembly [A/6669, paragraph 12 (c),] 'The United Nations Emergency Force is, after all, a peace-keeping and not an enforcement operation'. This means, of course, that the operation is based entirely on its acceptance by the governing authority of the territory on which it operates and that it is not in any sense related to Chapter VII of the Charter. It is a fact beyond dispute that neither UNEF nor any other United Nations peace-keeping operation thus far undertaken would have been permitted to enter the territory involved if there had been any suggestion that it had the right to remain there against the will of the governing authority.

13. The order for the withdrawal of UNEF has been given. The actual process of withdrawal will be orderly, deliberate, and dignified and not precipitate.

14. I do not believe that any of the Governments concerned are so careless of the welfare of their own people or of the risks of a spreading conflict as to deliberately embark on military offensives across their borders, unless they become convinced, rightly or wrongly, that they are threatened. Nevertheless, there is good reason to fear that the withdrawal of UNEF will give rise to increased danger along the armistice demarcation line and the international frontier between Israel and the United Arab Republic. The presence of UNEF has been a deterrent and restraining influence along both lines. There are some particularly sensitive areas involved, notably Sharm el-Sheikh and Gaza. The former concerns the Strait of Tiran. In the Gaza Strip there are 307,000 refugees and the substantial Palestine Liberation Army must also be taken into account.

15. It is true to a considerable extent that UNEF has allowed us for ten years to ignore some of the hard realities of the underlying conflict. The Governments concerned, and the United Nations, are now confronted with a brutally realistic and dangerous situation.

16. The Egyptian–Israel Mixed Armistice Commission (EIMAC), established by the Egyptian–Israel General Armistice Agreement, remains in existence with its headquarters at Gaza, and could, as it did prior to the establishment of UNEF, provide a limited form of United Nations presence in the area, as in the case of the other Mixed Armistice Commissions which are served by UNTSO. The Government of Israel, however, has denounced the EIMAC and for some years has refused to have anything to do with it. The United Nations has never accepted as valid this unilateral action by the Government of Israel. It would most certainly be helpful in the present situation if the Government of Israel were to reconsider its position and resume its participation in EIMAC. [S/7896, *Secretary-General's report on the situation in the Near East, 19 May 1967.*]

It remains true that for ten years UNEF was remarkably successful in contributing to containment of Israeli-Egyptian hostility. In spite of the manner of its withdrawal, it is hard to see, given the jealous protection of their sovereign rights by UN members, that it will be possible in any future peace-keeping operations to provide any different basis for the presence of UN Forces. Those nations who complained in May 1967 that UNEF's withdrawal was 'taking away the umbrella when it began to rain' were the same nations who had in 1956 accepted as realistic the basis of UNEF's presence in Egypt. Nor would they be likely to accept a UN Force on their own territory with any lesser degree of ultimate control. These facts—and the ten-year success of UNEF before its abrupt termination—make it likely that it will still constitute an important precedent in UN peacekeeping. UN operations in the Lebanon (1958), the Congo (1960–2), and Cyprus (1964–) have already been closely based upon the UNEF precedent. For all these reasons, therefore, it has been thought useful to include here the complete text of the Summary Study which the Secretary-General prepared in 1958 on the experience of UNEF. It will readily be seen that certain sections of this Summary Study relate to matters falling under particular headings (e.g. composition, functions, etc.) which we have already covered. While extracts have therefore been used elsewhere, the historical importance of this particular document merits its reproduction here *in toto*:

(Note. *As the United Nations Emergency Force came into being before the establishment of the United Arab Republic, the pertinent resolutions of the General Assembly and earlier reports of the Secretary-General used the terms 'Egypt' and 'the Government of Egypt', and these terms have been retained throughout the present report for convenience of reference.*)

INTRODUCTION

1. In the almost two years of operation of the United Nations Emergency Force (herein-after referred to as 'UNEF' or 'the Force'), the United Nations has acquired considerable experience in the establishment, organization and functioning of such an international in-strument. UNEF represents a new and in many ways unique experiment by the United Nations in a type of operation which previously it had not been called upon to conduct.

2. The Force was created as a temporary measure, its characteristics were determined by the nature of its role, and its functions were defined and limited by decisions of the General Assembly applying to a particular set of circumstances.

3. This report presents a summary analysis of the organization and operation of the Force. It is neither a comprehensive account of the Force nor a historical chronicle of its develop-ment. There is, unavoidably, a limited amount of narrative description of the principal activities. The emphasis, however, is on those principles and conclusions which emerge from a study of the operation as a whole and which might afford useful guidance for any future efforts looking towards the establishment or use of international United Nations instruments serving purposes of the kind met by UNEF.

4. A list of relevant basic documents is appended in annex II.

CHAPTER I. POLITICAL AND CONSTITUTIONAL QUESTIONS

Establishment of the United Nations Emergency Force

5. The first resolution adopted by the General Assembly when it began consideration of the military operations against Egyptian territory (resolution 997 (ES–I) of 2 November 1956) was directed primarily and as a matter of priority toward obtaining an immediate cessation of hostilities, a halting of the movement of military forces and arms into the area, a full obser-vance of the provisions of the armistice agreements, and the re-opening of the Suez Canal.

6. The question of setting up an emergency international United Nations force followed closely upon the adoption of that resolution. It grew out of the increasing recognition by Members that extraordinary measures had to be taken in order to achieve all the objectives sought by the resolution.

7. The actual establishment of UNEF was accomplished rapidly. By resolutions 998 (ES–I), 1000 (ES–I) and 1001 (ES–I) of 4, 5 and 7 November 1956 respectively, the General Assembly, approving the recommendations of the Secretary-General in the latter two resolutions, set up a United Nations Command; appointed Lieutenant-General (then Major-General) E. L. M. Burns, Chief of Staff of the United Nations Truce Supervision Organization (UNTSO), as Chief of the Command; made provision for the establishment of an initial small staff of officers drawn from the ranks of military observers serving with UNTSO and for the recruitment of additional staff officers; and approved certain guiding principles concerning the role, composition, recruitment, organization, operation and financing of the Force, and the definition of its functions, as set forth by the Secretary-General in his report of 6 November 1956 (A/3302). The Assembly also invited the Secretary-General to continue his discussions with Governments of Member States concerning offers of participation in the Force. An Advisory Committee was created to assist the Secretary-General in developing certain aspects of the planning and operation of the Force not already dealt with by the Assembly and which did not fall within the area of direct responsibility of the Chief of the Command. Following these actions, the first units of the Force reached the staging area at Capodichino, Italy, on 10 November and its first elements, consisting of UNTSO officers, arrived in Egypt on 12 November, followed by advance units of troops on 15 November.

Role assigned to the Force by the General Assembly

8. The General Assembly, in its resolution 1000 (ES–I) of 5 November 1956, provided that the Force should 'secure and supervise the cessation of hostilities in accordance with all the terms' of resolution 997 (ES–I) of 2 November, which would include the withdrawal of non-Egyptian forces from Egyptian territory and the restoration of observance of the provisions of the General Armistice Agreement between Egypt and Israel. These objectives could not be achieved through an organization similar in kind to UNTSO or to the Egyptian–Israel Mixed Armistice Commission, which had been established in other and different circumstances and were designed to meet different and narrower needs. The role of UNTSO is to observe and maintain the cease-fire in Palestine ordered by the Security Council. The Mixed Armistice Commission, serviced by UNTSO, is the bilateral machinery established under the Egyptian–Israel General Armistice Agreement in connexion with the execution of the provisions of that Agreement, exercising such functions as the investigation of incidents and complaints.

9. Under the conditions prevailing in November 1956, it was clear that a new approach and a new type of operation were required in order to facilitate compliance with the recommendations of the General Assembly relating to the armed interventions in Egypt.

10. This new instrument was charged with a dual role: initially to secure and supervise the cease-fire and the withdrawal of armed forces from Egyptian territory, and later to maintain peaceful conditions in the area by its deployment along the Egyptian–Israel armistice demarcation line in the Gaza area and to the south along the international frontier. This dual role determined the size, organization, equipment and deployment of the Force.

11. The two reports submitted by the Secretary-General to the Assembly on 4 November (A/3289) and 6 November (A/3302) on the plan for an emergency United Nations Force dealt with these factors and their implications.

12. In the guiding principles set forth by the Secretary-General for the organization and functioning of the Force and approved by the Assembly, it was emphasized that there was 'no intent . . . to influence the military balance in the present conflict and, thereby, the political balance affecting efforts to settle the conflict' (A/3302, para. 8). Nor was the Force to be 'used so as to prejudge the solution of the controversial questions involved' (A/3512

para. 29). It was felt, moreover, that the creation of peaceful conditions in the area required avoidance of the state of affairs into which conditions had progressively deteriorated in the past as a result of the lack of full implementation of the clauses of the Armistice Agreement. The objective sought was to ensure strict compliance by Egypt and Israel with the letter and spirit of the General Armistice Agreement concluded between them. Towards this end, the General Assembly decided, on 2 February 1957, that:

> 'the scrupulous maintenance of the Armistice Agreement requires the placing of the United Nations Emergency Force on the Egyptian–Israel armistice demarcation line and the implementation of other measures as proposed in the Secretary-General's report [A/3512], with due regard to the considerations set out therein with a view to assist in achieving situations conducive to the maintenance of peaceful conditions in the area' resolution 1125 (XI), para. 3].

The deployment of the Force along the Israel–Egyptian armistice demarcation line and the international frontier south of Gaza, and in the Sharm el Sheikh area, was not meant to and could not effect any change in their prior *status juris*; its sole purpose was to maintain quiet and prevent the recurrence of incidents.

Essential characteristics of UNEF

13. In its resolution 1000 (ES–I) establishing the United Nations Command and in the recruitment procedure prescribed, the General Assembly indicated that the Force would be set up on the basis of principles reflected in the structure and Charter of the United Nations itself, in that its Commanding Officer would be appointed by and responsible to the United Nations, and that his authority would be so defined as to make him fully independent of the policies or control of any one nation. The status of the 'Chief of the Command' (later to be known as 'Commander') was illustrated by the authority given to him, in consultation with the Secretary-General, to recruit for the Force officers from Member States other than the permanent members of the Security Council. At the same time, an important principle was introduced regarding the composition of the Force. The concept of a force established on this basis is basically different from that by which the United Nations might entrust a country, or a group of countries, with the responsibility of providing independently for an international force serving purposes determined by the Organization, as in the case of the Unified Command in Korea. It is also different from the concept, for which there is no precedent in application, of an international force set up by agreement among a group of nations, later to be brought into some appropriate relationship with the United Nations.

14. The functions of the Force are exclusively international in character in that they relate to armed conflict among States, and since the purpose of the Force is to facilitate compliance with resolutions relating to that conflict adopted by the General Assembly, the Force, during its early stages, in some instances had to undertake limited responsibility for administrative and security functions, but this was entirely temporary and incidental to the main tasks assigned to it.

15. The first emergency special session of the General Assembly, at which it was decided to establish an emergency force, had been called into session under the terms of the 'Uniting for peace' resolution (resolution 377 (V) of 3 November 1950).Thus, UNEF has been necessarily limited in its operations to the extent that consent of the parties concerned is required under generally recognized international law. It followed that, while the General Assembly could establish the Force, subject only to the concurrence of the States providing contingents, the consent of the Government of the country concerned was required before the Assembly could request the Force to be stationed or to operate on the territory of that country. The Force has no rights other than those necessary for the execution of the functions assigned to it by the General Assembly and agreed to by the country or countries concerned. The Force is paramilitary in character and much more than an observer corps, but it is in no sense a military force exercising, through force of arms, even temporary control over the territory in

which it is stationed; nor does it have military objectives, or military functions exceeding those necessary to secure peaceful conditions on the assumption that the parties to the conflict will take all the necessary steps for compliance with the recommendations of the General Assembly.

16. The Force is composed of national contingents accepted for service by the Secretary-General from among those voluntarily offered by Member States. The question of the composition of a force based on national contingents offered for service is a fundamental one. In the case of UNEF, the policy has been to exclude military personnel belonging to any of the permanent members of the Security Council and from any country which for geographical or other reasons might have a special interest in the conflict. The choice of the contingents for the Force, while subject to the decision of the United Nations alone, is nevertheless of major concern also to the country in which the Force operates. Thus, the United Nations must give most serious consideration to the views of the host Government on such matters without, however, surrendering its right to take a serious difference, should one develop, to the political level for resolution. In the experience of UNEF, this latter course has not been necessary, since no impasse has ever developed in this area. A balanced composition was always sought in the selection of units.

17. The size of component units has been determined by two primary requirements. From the point of view of efficiency, it was necessary that Member States should provide units sufficiently large to be relatively self-contained. From the point of view of balance, it was desirable that the Force should include adequate support elements and that the differences in the size of units should not be so great as to lead to excessive dependence on any one State.

18. In practice, the UNEF operation is an example of fruitful military and civilian collaboration. Matters relating to its administration and finance, communications, maintenance and other services are taken care of within the framework of the United Nations Secretariat. The resolutions of the General Assembly authorize the Secretary-General to take all executive and administrative actions essential to the effective functioning of the Force.

19. The Regulations for the Force (ST/SGB/UNEF/I) affirm its international character as a subsidiary organ of the General Assembly. The Assembly intended that the Force should be a temporary arrangement, whose duration would be determined by the needs created by the emergency, and whose tasks and legal basis could be defined only by the Assembly.

Circumstances bearing upon the establishment of the Force

20. That the Force was established and began operating within a very few days was due to a number of circumstances, political and otherwise, which constitute a significant element in the over-all experience.

Agreement to the cease-fire by the parties concerned and the withdrawal of troops

21. Agreement without conditions by the parties engaged in hostilities to the cease-fire called for by the General Assembly, in resolutions 997 (ES–I) of 2 November 1956 and 999 (ES–I) of 4 November 1956, so that the cease-fire could actually take effect, was a prerequisite to the operation of UNEF. Egypt, on 2 November (A/3266) and 4 November (A/3287, annex 6), accepted the two calls of the Assembly for a cease-fire. Israel, which had announced on 3 November (A/3279) its agreement to an immediate cease-fire on condition that Egypt would do the same, confirmed its unconditional acceptance on 5 November (A/3301). The Governments of France and the United Kingdom, in identical replies of 5 November (A/2394 and A/3293) to the Secretary-General's communications of 4 November on arrangements for a cease-fire (A/3287, annexes 2 and 4), stated that they would cease all military action as soon as the Israel and Egyptian Governments accepted a United Nations plan for an international force with certain prescribed functions. In his *aide-mémoire* of 5 November 1956 to the Governments of France and the United Kingdom the Secretary-General informed these Governments that since on that date the General Assembly had taken a decisive step towards setting up the international force by establishing a United Nations Command, and since the

Governments of Egypt and Israel had agreed, without conditions, to a cease-fire, 'the conditions for a general cease-fire would thus seem to be established' (A/3310, para. 6). In letters to the Secretary-General of 6 November (A/3307 and A/3306), replying to his *aide-mémoire* of the previous day, the Governments of France and the United Kingdom announced that their forces were being ordered to cease fire at midnight GMT of that date, pending confirmation that Egypt and Israel had accepted an unconditional cease-fire and that there would be a United Nations force competent to secure and supervise the attainment of the objectives of resolution 997 (ES–I). The Secretary-General promptly informed Egypt and Israel that the cease-fire would become effective on the hour of midnight and on this basis the cease-fire began at that time. It is to be noted that the General Assembly did not make the cease-fire dependent upon the creation or the functioning of UNEF. Its calls for a cease-fire and its decision to establish the Force were in separate resolutions (resolutions 997 (ES–I) and 999 (ES–I) on the one hand, and 998 (ES–I) on the other).

22. The Force, the first elements of which landed in Egypt on 12 November 1956, was initially stationed between the Anglo-French and the Egyptian troops in the Suez Canal area and particularly in Port Said and Port Fuad, and remained largely in that area during the gradual withdrawal of the Anglo-French forces, which was completed on 22 December 1956. The Force, strengthened by the arrival of additional troops, was then gradually deployed in the Sinai Peninsula from the Suez Canal towards the armistice demarcation line, following the progressive withdrawals of the Israel troops. Israel troops withdrew in three stages from the Sinai Peninsula, which was entirely evacuated by 22 January 1957, with the exception of the Sharm el Sheikh area and the Gaza Strip. The evacuation of Israel troops from the Gaza Strip was completed on the night of 6–7 March, UNEF entering simultaneously. Arrangements were made on 8 March for the withdrawal from the Sharm el Sheikh area, which was begun on that date and completed on 12 March 1957 (see A/3568, paras. 3 and 4).

Concurrence of the parties engaged in hostilities in the establishment of an international force

23. UNEF as a practical operation was made possible only by the concurrence, in one form or another, of the parties to the conflict in its establishment by the General Assembly. France and the United Kingdom welcomed the idea of an international force to be interposed between Egypt and Israel, as a basis for the cessation of all military action in Egypt (A/3294 and A/3293). Egypt's acceptance of the resolution providing for the establishment of a United Nations Command was considered as acceptance of the establishment of an international force under the terms fixed by the United Nations (A/3310). As for Israel, the Secretary-General was informed on 8 November 1956 that Israel's forces would be withdrawn from Egypt immediately upon the conclusion of satisfactory arrangements with the United Nations in connexion with the emergency international force (A/3320).

Offers of participation by Governments in UNEF

24. When the Secretary-General submitted his first report to the General Assembly, on 4 November 1956, on a plan for an emergency international United Nations Force, he could state that, among the representatives until then consulted, three had accepted, on behalf of their Governments, participation in the projected force (A/3289). Within a month or so following the submission of the Secretary-General's second and final report on 6 November, a total of twenty-four Governments had offered contingents to the Force, while three other Governments had offered assistance in other forms (A/3302 and Add. 1–30). The Governments whose offers were accepted have been particularly helpful in trying to meet the specific needs of the Force with regard to number of troops, types of units, rotation plans and transportation arrangements.

Assistance from United Nations bodies in the area

25. Practical arrangements for the establishment of UNEF were facilitated by the presence

in the area in which the Force was to operate of the United Nations Truce Supervision Organization and the United Nations Relief and Works Agency for Palestine Refugees in the Near East (UNRWA), which, through their personnel, facilities and extensive experience in the region, were able to give valuable assistance. The immediate availability, for temporary transfer, of a corps of experienced military officers who had been serving as military observers in UNTSO was especially helpful. Most important, the Chief of Staff of UNTSO was able and willing to assume the post of Commander of the Force. Pending the re-establishment, following the withdrawal of Israel, of normal administrative machinery by the local authorities in the Gaza Strip, UNRWA, which exercises important functions among the refugees in that area, also gave substantial assistance through aid to the non-refugee population.

Responsibilities entrusted to the Secretary-General by the General Assembly

26. The resolutions of the General Assembly, involving decisions on various policy matters, required the Secretary-General to assume important additional responsibilities; he was requested to observe and report on compliance with certain Assembly resolutions, and to implement others by executive and administrative actions. For example, in addition to the general requests for reports on compliance, the Assembly authorized him to arrange with the parties concerned for the implementation of the cease-fire and the halting of the movement of military forces and arms into the area; he was also requested, with the assistance of the Chief of Staff and the military observers of UNTSO, to obtain the withdrawal of all forces behind the armistice lines (resolution 999 (ES–I)). In another resolution, the Secretary-General was requested to continue his efforts to secure the complete withdrawal of Israel forces and to report on such completion within five days (resolution 1123 (XI)).

27. In the first phase of the development of UNEF, the Secretary-General was requested to submit a plan for setting up, with the consent of the nations concerned, an international Force to fulfil certain indicated functions (resolution 998 (ES–I)). Having approved the plan, as formulated in his first two reports, the Assembly invited the Secretary-General to take all appropriate administrative measures for its execution (resolution 1000 (ES–I)). He was authorized to issue all regulations and instructions essential to the effective functioning of the Force and to take all other administrative and executive action which he might consider necessary for this purpose (resolution 1001 (ES–I)).

28. With regard to financing, the Secretary-General was authorized to establish a United Nations Emergency Force Special Account and to advance from the Working Capital Fund such sums as might be required pending the receipt of funds for the Special Account (resolution 1122 (XI)). In this connexion, the Secretary-General was requested to establish rules and procedures for the Special Account and to make the necessary arrangements for its effective administration and control.

29. In some resolutions, the Secretary-General was asked to discuss or to communicate with certain Members on particular matters. Thus, he was invited to continue discussions with Governments concerning offers of participation in the Force, toward the objective of its balanced composition (resolution 1001 (ES–I)). In two other instances, he was directed to communicate the text of a resolution to the parties concerned and to report without delay. In still other cases, the resolutions provided that authority given to the Chief of the Command should be exercised in consultation with the Secretary-General.

Advisory Committee on UNEF

30. In conjunction with the establishment of the Force, the General Assembly decided to create an Advisory Committee composed of seven representatives of Member States, under the chairmanship of the Secretary-General (resolution 1001 (ES–I)). In its advisory capacity, this Committee was to assist the Secretary-General in the planning and operation of the Force. It was empowered to request, through the usual procedures, the convening of the General Assembly and to report to the Assembly, if matters should arise which, in its opinion, were of such urgency and importance as to require consideration by the Assembly itself. It

has had no occasion to invoke this authority. Meetings of the Advisory Committee have been held whenever matters have arisen requiring discussion, or whenever the Secretary-General has sought advice, or, at times, only to keep the Committee informed on current developments. The Advisory Committee has been consulted particularly on those questions which the Assembly had indicated should be the subject of consultation between it and the Secretary-General, such as the Regulations for the Force, the policy of the Force with regard to self-defence and the issue of medals. The effective assistance rendered by the Committee was noted with appreciation by the Assembly at its twelfth session, in resolution 1151 (XII), and the Secretary-General, in the introduction to his annual report to that session,[22] paid tribute to the indispensable services performed by the Committee.

CHAPTER II. FORMATION AND COMPOSITION OF UNEF

Special co-operation by Governments

31. A number of delegations have given full co-operation in obtaining from their Governments indispensable assistance in the establishment and maintenance of the Force. Indeed, the entire history of the operation has been characterized by unusually close and effective co-operation between Governments and the United Nations. Invaluable assistance on military aspects of the initial planning was given by a group of military representatives of the countries contributing troops to UNEF, who sat as an informal military advisory committee at United Nations Headquarters during the early stages of the operation. This group, under the informal chairmanship of a Major-General, appointed temporarily as personal adviser to the Secretary-General on UNEF military matters, provided expert planning and advice on matters of military organization, transport, equipment and logistics, and also greatly expedited the dispatch of contingents by their Governments. Similar co-operation and assistance by delegations and Governments would be essential to the success of any future operations of this kind.

USE OF SECRETARIAT RESOURCES

32. At the outset, the Secretary-General directed that United Nations Secretariat personnel, procedures and facilities should be utilized to the maximum in organizing and maintaining the Force. This reduced substantially the degree of improvisation which would otherwise have been required for a project so large and so new in international experience as UNEF. Even so, there was much occasion to improvise in the early stages. The Secretariat, as a result of long and well-tested experience, could provide UNEF with efficient services and personnel in such necessary fields as administration, financial procedures, personnel recruitment, legal and political advice, public information, procurement and supply and communications. High-level responsibility for the organization and direction of the operation was facilitated by the principle of flexibility in the use of senior staff. From the beginning, the Secretary-General designated one of his Under-Secretaries without Department to be responsible for direct supervision of the organization and operation of the Force and the co-ordination of administrative actions relating to it (see A/AC.89/R.1). Most of the major units of the Secretariat were called upon to make their contribution to the total task in one way or another, with the Executive Office of the Secretary-General, the Office of General Services, the Office of the Controller, the Office of Legal Affairs and the Office of Personnel rendering especially important assistance.

33. The experience gained by the Secretariat over the years in the administration of missions in various parts of the world provided many well-tried procedures which were immediately put to good use in meeting the broad requirements of UNEF. Machinery for the necessary administrative co-ordination at United Nations Headquarters already existed and was readily adapted to the new emergency task. Certain mission facilities which had been found essential over a period of years were immediately available in the area: an aircraft

[22] A/3594/Add. 1.

permanently assigned to UNTSO provided emergency transportation locally, which was indispensable to the early planning; an independent United Nations network of low-powered radio receivers and transmitters, linking UNTSO offices in Cairo and Gaza with UNTSO headquarters in Jerusalem, gave United Nations personnel in the area an uninterrupted contact of their own with United Nations Headquarters in New York through the United Nations relay station in Geneva; an adequate code system and routine procedures for the handling of United Nations diplomatic pouches ensured security for United Nations communications. Arranging for such needs as identity cards, visas, passports and inoculations, and obtaining clearances for flying over the territory of numerous countries, were routine duties for the Secretariat.

INITIAL ASSESSMENT OF REQUIREMENTS

34. The Commander of UNEF estimated that, in order to perform the tasks assigned by the General Assembly, the Force would require the equivalent of two combat brigades, or about 6,000 men. The initial concept of military organization, later modified in the light of further clarification of the functions of the Force, was that it should be built around regimental combat teams. It would require an independent signals company expanded to provide all necessary communications facilities for Force headquarters and in the field. In addition, headquarters, engineer, transport, shop repair and medical personnel would be needed. It was decided that the infantry should be equipped with normal regimental weapons, that there should be a transport company sufficient to lift one infantry battalion, and that each battalion should be administratively self-contained. The Commander also stressed the desirability of an armoured car squadron for reconnaissance work, in view of the nature of the terrain and the task of the Force. It was further concluded at an early stage that a light air unit was essential for functions inside the UNEF operations area.

The first phase

35. There was urgent need to assemble a usable force, as rapidly as possible, and to land it in Egypt. While awaiting the conclusion of arrangements with Egypt for the entry of the Force into that country, it was decided that a staging area near the Mediterranean would be necessary, as it would expedite the flow of troops and *matériel* to Egypt. Arrangements were quickly made with the Government of Italy for the use of Capodichino airport, Naples, for this purpose. Most of the troops brought to Egypt by air were sent via Naples, others were flown in via Beirut, while others came by sea to Port Said. The small staff in charge of the staging area at Capodichino took care of the incoming (and later outgoing) contingents, dealt with the several authorities in Europe through whom major logistic support was obtained, supervised the air-lift to Egypt and arranged for the surface transport of heavy stores.

36. The initial movements of troops from their home bases to Italy were arranged through United Nations Headquarters. The problems were mainly transportation and co-ordination. The bulk of the transport to the staging area was provided by the United States Air Force. The representatives of the contributing countries supplied information to United Nations Headquarters concerning the numbers, equipment and state of readiness of their national units, and this was transmitted to the representatives of the United States Air Force designated for this purpose. The latter, in turn, gave notification concerning the precise arrangements for transporting the contingents named, which was transmitted to the appropriate Governments by their military representatives at United Nations Headquarters.

37. A selected group of United Nations military observers, who were detached temporarily from their duties with UNTSO and who commenced planning while still in Jerusalem, served at first as the nucleus of a UNEF headquarters staff. They arrived in Egypt on 12 November 1956, established a temporary headquarters in Cairo and, together with Secretariat officials, arranged for the reception and billeting of the first contingents, and the early procurement, storage and issue of the supplies and equipment required. Through negotiations with the Egyptian Government, an air base at Abu Suweir, near Ismailia, became the arrival depot

for the early contingents. As the contingents arrived, their officers took over the duties being performed by the military observers, who were then able to return to their UNTSO duties in Jerusalem.

38. Advance elements of UNEF were moved to Egypt at a time when hostilities had but recently ceased; there were restrictions on the times and lanes of flights, and aircraft transporting contingents had to be of suitable nationalities. The initial air-lift of troops to Abu Suweir was carried out by Swissair. The Naples to Egypt air-lift was subsequently taken over by the Royal Canadian Air Force with some assistance from the Italian Air Force in lifting supplies.

39. Speed was a major reason for initially moving some troops and equipment to Egypt by air, but as ships under some flags could not be used, and as ships proceeding to Port Said at that time were required to be self-sustaining, the immediatel possibilities of employing sea transport were in any case severely reduced. The Yugoslav reconnaissance battalion, with all its equipment, was brought to Port Said by sea on 28 November 1956, while the main elements of the Canadian and Brazilian contingents arrived in national naval vessels on 11 January and 2 February 1957, respectively. All heavy equipment for UNEF was brought in by ship.

40. One consequence of having to rely on air transport for the first units and their equipment was an immediate and severe shortage of transport vehicles. This difficulty was aggravated by the fact that several of the contingents had not contemplated bringing most of their vehicular transport with them in any event because of the desert conditions. The shortage was alleviated by obtaining vehicles from UNRWA, by local purchases and by rental. But, as requirements mounted, these sources became inadequate.

41. A preliminary understanding had been reached in New York on the purchase of vehicles and supplies in Port Said from the British forces as they withdrew, the details of the transaction being worked out on the spot. This procurement was very helpful in facilitating the rapid deployment of UNEF forces in the Sinai Peninsula and in equipping the two transportation platoons used for supplying the forces. Shortly after the formation of the Force, a large order for vehicles was placed with United States military authorities. These vehicles arrived in January 1957 and filled the additional transport requirements.

42. The need to transport UNEF units to positions evacuated by the Anglo-French and Israel forces, to keep them supplied and to provide replacements, required the immediate establishment at Abu Suweir of a dump of petrol, oil and lubricants. The necessary stocks and installations were obtained in the area. Additional storage facilities were obtained in Port Said, and further supply points were established as the operation moved forward.

43. The clear identification of UNEF personnel, beyond the customary United Nations armbands, was an immediate necessity for security and other reasons. Light blue helmet liners with United Nations markings were adopted for this purpose, and were later supplemented by blue berets and desert caps and UNEF badges and insignia. Vehicles and aircraft were painted white with United Nations markings.

National contingents and supporting units

44. On the basis of the position taken in the General Assembly resolutions—which reflects a principle that is both sound and practical—no units from any of the permanent members of the Security Council have been included in the Force. Nor have any been recruited from countries in the area or from countries which might, for other reasons, be thought to have a special interest in the conflict situation. In selecting contingents, weight was given to such factors as their suitability in terms of the needs of the Force, their size and availability, the extent to which they would be self-contained, the undesirability of too great a variation in ordnance and basic equipment, the problem of transportation, and the goal of balanced composition.

45. In the period November–December 1956, twenty-four Member States offered to provide units (see A/3302 and Ad. 1–30). A number of these countries also offered other forms of assistance, as did two other Member States and one non-member. Most of the offers of

assistance were of infantry units. The Force, at the peak of its strength totalling about 6,000 officers and men, consisted of contingents from the following countries: Brazil, Canada, Colombia, Denmark, Finland, India, Indonesia[23] Norway, Sweden and Yugoslavia.

46. The extent of the area to be covered by UNEF called for highly mobile reconnaissance. This need was met by Yugoslavia, which provided a complete reconnaissance battalion, and by Canada, which later provided a fully-equipped light armoured squadron.

47. Supporting units were obtained and assigned with the same urgency as those engaged in patrolling. Experience with the Force soon demonstrated the desirability of limiting the number of countries participating in it, particularly those providing support units, in view of the difficulties in co-ordinating and controlling a number of relatively small units having different arms and equipment, requiring varying diets and speaking different languages. Thus, to simplify the organization in the interest of efficiency, the Indian contingent was given responsibility for the Supply Depot and the Service Institute; Canada and India provided units for Transport, the Provost Marshal and Signals; Norway and Canada covered the medical needs. The Canadian contingent was also made responsible for the Ordnance Depot and Workshop, the Base Post Office, Engineering, the Dental Unit, Movement Control and Air Support.

48. When the contingents were being accepted, it was impossible to determine or to foresee the duration of the UNEF mission. National terms of military service, the nature of the mission, conditions of weather and terrain, and considerations of morale and efficiency, gave strong support to the principle and practice of rather frequent periodic rotation. The exact rotation policies adopted by contributing Governments, however, have varied somewhat, and in some cases the length of the period of service has been shorter than would be dictated exclusively by considerations of efficiency and economy. Full responsibility for the cost of transportation is accepted by the United Nations.

49. The schedules of rotation are fixed by the contributing countries in consultation with the Commander, in such a way as to ensure continuity of national participation in the Force and to protect it from being undermanned.

50. With regard to the withdrawal of contingents from the Force, the contributing Governments agreed with the Secretary-General that, in order to protect the organizational strength of the Force, participating Governments would inform the Secretary-General in advance of a decision to withdraw their contingents. In each of the two cases of withdrawal that have occurred to date, notice was given sufficiently in advance to enable the Force to obtain replacements through increasing the size of one or more of the existing contingents.

CHAPTER III. OPERATIONS IN THE FIELD

The stages

51. The operations of the Force in the field may be divided into three successive stages. The first lasted roughly from mid-November until the end of December 1956, and centred in the vicinity of the Suez Canal (mainly Port Said and Port Fuad); this stage was concluded with the withdrawal of the British and French troops. The second extended from late December 1956 to early March 1957. During that time, the activities of the Force covered the Sinai Peninsula following the phased withdrawal of the Israel forces. The third stage began on 8 March 1957, when Israel forces had fully withdrawn from the Gaza Strip and had begun their withdrawal from the Sharm el Sheikh area. The activities of the Force since that time have centred on the Egyptian–Israel armistice demarcation line and along the international frontier south of the Gaza Strip.

52. The technical arrangements for the withdrawals were negotiated, in consultation with the Secretary-General, by the Commander of UNEF with the Commanders of the British, French and Israel forces.

[23] The contingents from Finland and Indonesia have been withdrawn, so that the Force in September 1958 conisisted of contingents from the eight remaining countries.

Operations relating to the cessation of hostilities

(*a*) In the Suez Canal area

53. In the first stage, the objective of the Force was to secure and supervise the cessation of hostilities. The Force was immediately interposed between the Anglo-French and the Egyptian troops, occupying a buffer zone. Units of the Force also entered Port Said and Port Fuad and, by arrangement with the Anglo-French forces, took responsibility for maintaining order in certain areas, in co-operation with local authorities. The Force also undertook guard duty over some vulnerable installations and other points, but turned over all administrative and policing responsibilities to the Egyptian authorities the day following the Anglo-French evacuation.

54. In the period of transition when the British and French forces were preparing to leave and were actually leaving, the Force temporarily undertook certain essential administrative functions, such as security, with the co-operation of the Governor and the Police Inspector in Port Said. UNEF personnel took measures to protect civilian life and public and private property. With the sanction of local authorities, they also undertook administrative functions with respect to public services and utilities, arranged for the provisioning of the local population with food-stuffs, and exercised a limited power of detention. During this period, UNEF was called upon to investigate a number of incidents, such as violations of the cease-fire, missing personnel and smuggling. Incidents involving the cease-fire were reported to the proper authorities, who were urged to prevent any recurrence.

55. No provision having been made for the establishment of joint machinery whereby incidents could be examined and discussed, UNEF's role was limited to investigating, reporting and, if warranted, lodging protests with the proper authorities.

56. The Force cleared minefields in the Suez Canal area, and arranged and carried out exchanges of prisoners, detainees and internees between the Egyptian Government and the Anglo-French Command. It guarded the off-loading of UNEF stores and vehicles from ships at Port Said and, in the final stage of the withdrawal of British and French troops from Port Said and Port Fuad, the Force was stationed around the final perimeter of the zone occupied by Anglo-French forces, thus preventing clashes between them and the Egyptians.

(*b*) In the Sinai Peninsula

57. The original plan of operations assumed that, in compliance with General Assembly resolutions, Israel troops would, after the cease-fire, withdraw within a short time behind the armistice demarcation line and that the Force would then be deployed along the Egyptian-Israel armistice demarcation line and the international frontier south of the Gaza Strip.

58. Israel's forces withdrew from the Sinai Peninsula in three stages, on 3 December 1956, 7–8 January and 15–22 January 1957, with the exception of the Gaza Strip and of the Sharm el Sheikh area at the Gulf of Aqaba, which were evacuated on 6–7 March and 8–12 March 1957, respectively. The Force could not be effectively deployed along the Egyptian–Israel armistice demarcation line and the international frontier south of the Gaza Strip before completion of the withdrawal. The intention of the Government of Israel to withdraw from the Gaza Strip and Gulf of Aqaba areas was announced to the General Assembly by the Foreign Minister of Israel on 1 and 4 March 1957 and, on 8 March, the Secretary-General reported that no Israel troops were left in the Gaza Strip and that UNEF troops had entered Sharm el Sheikh.

59. On the whole, the functions performed by the Force in the Sinai Peninsula were similar to those undertaken in the Suez Canal area. It was interposed between the forces of Egypt and Israel from 3 December 1956 onwards; it undertook temporarily some local civic responsibilities, including security functions, in a few inhabited areas during the successive stages of the withdrawal of Israel, handing over all such responsibilities to the Egyptian authorities as soon as they returned to their posts; it arranged and carried out the exchange of prisoners of war between Egypt and Israel; it discharged certain investigatory functions; it cleared mine-

fields in the Sinai Peninsula; and it repaired temporarily portions of damaged roads and tracks crossing the Peninsula, necessary for the conduct of its operations.

Operations along the armistice demarcation line and the international frontier

60. Two local conditions were of special concern to the Force as it moved into the Gaza Strip. In the first place, it was across the Gaza Strip line that the greatest number of incidents, infiltrations and raids had occurred since the armistice. Secondly, there were a very large number of Palestine Arab refugees, who are assisted by the United Nations through UNRWA, living in the Gaza Strip. The United Nations took no action which in any way affected the *status juris* of the Armistice Agreement or the Gaza Strip, since these matters are subject only to agreement of the parties.

61. Following the completion of Israel's withdrawal, the functions of the Force were determined by a General Assembly resolution calling for 'the placing of the United Nations Emergency Force on the Egyptian–Israel armistice demarcation line and the implementation of other measures as proposed in the Secretary-General's report' (resolution 1125 (XI)). In partial implementation of that resolution, the Force was deployed on the Egyptian side, along the armistice demarcation line and along the international frontier to the south. The completion of its deployment remains an unresolved issue.

62. As regards the Sharm el Sheikh area, the Secretary-General in his report to the General Assembly of 24 January 1957 concluded that on the withdrawal of Israel troops UNEF would follow in the same way as it had in other parts of Sinai, its movements being determined by its duties in respect of the cease-fire and withdrawal (A/3512, para. 29). The Secretary-General further stated that, in accordance with the general legal principles recognized as decisive for the deployment of the Force, it should not be used in such a way as to prejudice the solution of the controversial questions involved; thus, it was not to be deployed in such a manner as to protect any special position on these questions.

Pending the re-establishment of local authority in the Gaza Strip

63. Within the Gaza Strip, the operations of the Force took place in two stages. The first covered the evacuation of the Strip by Israel troops and the simultaneous entry of UNEF. The second began after local authority had been re-established under the Egyptian Administrative Governor and the local administration was able to resume its duties.

64. As the first step, arrangements were made between the Commander of UNEF and the Chief of Staff of the Israel Defence Forces for the United Nations to take over its responsibilities in the Gaza Strip as Israel withdrew. Pending the re-establishment of local civilian authority in the Strip, and on the basis of a division of responsibilities suggested by the Secretary-General, UNEF and UNRWA co-operated in meeting local needs, as a purely temporary measure.

65. The operation of the Force at the time of its entry into Gaza was facilitated by the presence there of an important branch of UNRWA, which permitted a quick distribution of civil functions between UNEF and UNRWA to meet the immediate needs of the local population, and by the fact that the Egyptian–Israel Mixed Armistice Commission had its headquarters in Gaza, thus enabling the Force to enjoy the immediate use of the Commission's communications facilities and its personnel.

After the re-establishment of local authority in the Gaza Strip

66. After the local authorities had taken over administration and internal security, the Force was deployed along the armistice demarcation line and the international border south of the Gaza Strip, in patrol and reconnaissance activities designed to avert incidents and to maintain quiet along that entire sector.

67. The population of Gaza was officially informed that the Government of Egypt, as a matter of policy, is opposed to infiltration across the armistice demarcation line, UNEF's

purpose was explained, and the Administrative Governor-General of the Gaza Strip took other effective measures. Gaza inhabitants were notified that they were forbidden to approach the demarcation line within 50–100 metres by day and 500 metres by night. The CID (police) in Gaza were instructed to act vigorously with the object of finding persons responsible for mining and other incidents and to prevent recurrences. The local (Palestine) police co-operate with UNEF in preventing infiltration. In order to be as effective as possible in this sphere, the Force was regrouped so that its battalion boundaries now generally correspond to administrative sub-districts in the Strip. This facilitates police co-operation with UNEF at the battalion level.

68. The normal channel for contacts between the Force and the local administrative authorities, as well as with the Egyptian national authorities, has been the Egyptian liaison staff. This staff was constituted by the Government of Egypt at the time of the entry of UNEF into Egypt, and it has served continuously as the regular channel for communication between the Government and the Force. The Commander has also consulted directly, when necessary, with officials of the Government in Cairo. There are some direct contacts between UNEF lower echelons and the local administration. Close liaison has been maintained between commanding officers of units and the administrative governors and police officials in their respective sectors through periodic meetings, and direct contacts have also been maintained between the UNEF military police and the local police.

69. With only an occasional hitch, and this seldom more than minor, UNEF personnel and vehicles have enjoyed freedom of movement in the Gaza Strip and between the Sinai Peninsula posts, the headquarters of UNEF and the units deployed along the demarcation line. This includes freedom of flight over the Sinai Peninsula and the Gaza Strip for UNEF aircraft and the manning of the Gaza airport by UNEF.

70. UNEF troops have a right to fire in self-defence. They are never to take the initiative in the use of arms, but may respond with fire to an armed attack upon them, even though this may result from a refusal on their part to obey an order from the attacking party not to resist; a proper refusal, since they are to take orders only from the Commander. UNEF is authorized to apprehend infiltrators and persons approaching the demarcation line in suspicious circumstances. In practice, this applies to a zone extending up to 500 metres from the demarcation line; after interrogation, the persons apprehended are handed over to the local police.

71. The Force is deployed along the demarcation line and the international border, over a length of 273 kilometres in largely rugged terrain. The perimeter of the Gaza Strip (60 km) is covered by means of observation posts by day and patrols by night. There are seventy-six observation posts, the location of which varies according to the nature of the terrain. The primary purposes of the observation posts and patrols are to prevent any movements across the line and to observe and report incidents. All troops have received full briefing on their outpost and patrolling duties. In conjunction with the observation duties, reconnaissance flights by UNEF's light aircraft are carried out in the Sinai Peninsula in order to detect movements along the roads, or elsewhere in the area of the frontier. In view of the prevailing quiet all along the line, air reconnaissance, which had been carried out on a daily basis, was reduced in August 1957 to three days a week.

Investigation of incidents

72. The deployment of UNEF along the armistice demarcation line and the line south of Gaza raised the question of the respective responsibilities of UNEF and UNTSO. The Government of Israel took the position that the Egyptian–Israel General Armistice Agreement was no longer in effect. The United Nations, however, could not accept a unilateral decision on the Armistice Agreement, and therefore the Chairman of the Egyptian–Israel Mixed Armistice Commission and the UNTSO military observers have continued at their posts throughout the Israel occupation of the Gaza Strip, and since. The General Assembly called upon the parties to comply with all the provisions of the General Armistice Agreement between them.

73. Upon the withdrawal of the Israel forces, arrangements were made which, without any

change in its legal status, placed the Egyptian-Israel Mixed Armistice Commission under the operational control of the Commander of UNEF. Upon the appointment in March 1958 of a new Chief of Staff for UNTSO, the Secretary-General confirmed to the representatives of Egypt and Israel that the Commander of the Force would continue to exercise his functions as Chief of Staff in respect of the Egyptian–Israel General Armistice Agreement, i.e. as Chairman *ex officio* of the Mixed Armistice Commission, in accordance with article X of that Agreement.

74. In view of its position with respect to the Armistice Agreement, the Government of Israel has preferred to lodge its complaints with UNEF, but UNEF representatives have consistently maintained that official investigations of incidents can be carried out only through the Mixed Armistice Commission.

CHAPTER IV. ORGANIZATION AND ADMINISTRATION IN THE FIELD

Organizational structure

The Commander

75. The functioning of UNEF in the field is the direct responsibility of the Commander, who serves both as the director of operations and as the supervisor of all other activities of the Force.

76. The Commander holds office through appointment by the General Assembly. He operates under the instructions and guidance of the Secretary-General on the basis of executive responsibility for the operation entrusted to him by the Assembly. In practice, from the inception of the Force, the Commander has functioned as the principal agent of the Secretary-General in the area of operations, within the limits of his post.

77. The position of Commander combines leadership of the Force with the role of representative of the United Nations. Much the same qualities are called for in the Chief of Staff of UNTSO, although the military observers in UNTSO do not form a military organization in the UNEF sense and their functions are quite different. Both operations, however, combine political and administrative with military functions.

Military staff organization

78. The military staff organization of UNEF consists of officers selected from each of the contingents, and is headed by the Chief of Staff. The Chief of Staff acts for the Commander during his absence. The position of Deputy Commander was tried for a while but was found do be unnecessary. The Headquarters Staff comprises three sections—(1) Personnel, (2) Operations, and (3) Logistics—and a Special Staff composed of a number of specialized officers who advise and assist the Commander in particular fields and, in some cases, co-ordinate, supervise or carry out functional activities. The physical separation of UNEF headquarters in Gaza from the maintenance area at Rafah results in some inconvenience and perhaps a mild loss of efficiency, but it is unavoidable and there is no practical alternative.

79. The contingents receive their instructions and direction from the Commander, advised and assisted by his Staff. The commanding officers of the units are held responsible by the Commander for the proper functioning and discipline of their personnel. The contingent commanders are free to communicate with their home Governments on all matters affecting their units.

80. It is the practice of those contingents furnishing units for more than one functional task to designate a contingent commander, in addition to commanders for each functional activity. This contributes to clarification of responsibility in those matters affecting personnel which are subject to national authority.

81. Aside from the battalions with clearly defined missions of a military nature, normally involving patrol duties along the armistice demarcation line and the international frontier as well as guard duties, there are a number of units assigned to UNEF which perform administrative and other support tasks. Supporting elements for any force represent a special

problem in co-ordination and control. To weld together elements of several different nationalities having similar functions would be very difficult. For this reason, UNEF has tended to rely mainly upon two countries, Canada and India, for its supporting units other than the medical.

82. Some of the contributing Governments designated 'liaison officers' to represent their interests on the scene of operations of UNEF and to serve as points of contact for them. These liaison officers, not being under the authority of the Commander, are not members of UNEF. Their status, therefore, is rather anomalous. In practice, the liaison officer function has worked best when the officer concerned was one assigned to a UNEF post having important duties in its own right. Those liaison officers not combining functions in this manner have no direct responsibility to the Commander, yet can scarcely avoid becoming involved in matters of Force administration and operations. Moreover, it is difficult for the Commander and his staff, as well as for the commanders of operating units, to decide when and under what circumstances the liaison officers should be consulted and informed. However, in the early days of the organization of the Force, liaison officers for special purposes performed a useful and necessary function.

83. From the beginning of the Force, it was found useful, even essential, to maintain representation in Cairo for liaison with the appropriate authorities in the host Government. UNEF also has liaison representation in Tel Aviv. Military observers have been seconded from the staff of UNTSO for service with UNEF as its liaison officers. UNEF representation is also maintained at places outside the area of operations where UNEF activities and interests are involved, as in Beirut and Pisa (and earlier in Naples) in connexion with the airlift.

The Secretariat

84. Administratively, responsibility for UNEF rests with the Secretary-General, in order to ensure that the operation will be executed in a manner consistent with the established practices and administrative principles of the United Nations. The day-to-day responsibilities of administration are exercised by the Commander of the Force, assisted by the senior Secretariat officials assigned by the Secretary-General to the Force, and such military officers having important administrative functions as the Chiefs of Personnel and Logistics. Experience has demonstrated that, by and large, requirements for the administrative servicing of an operation such as UNEF, both at Headquarters and in the field, can be met through existing Secretariat services, modestly expanded in certain sections to permit the absorption of heavier work-loads, together with such administrative assistance from the military side as may be implicit in the nature of the organization.

85. Three categories of Secretariat staff have served and are serving with the Force:

(*a*) Officers, such as the Chief Administrative Officer, with responsibility for the financial affairs of the Force and for the application of United Nations administrative rules and procedures. The Chief Administrative Officer reports directly to the Commander and works closely with him, but also has a direct reporting link with United Nations Headquarters, as the senior Secretariat official who is designated by the Secretary-General and in that capacity is responsible to him. He is assisted by a Chief Procurement Officer, a Chief Finance Officer and a Personnel Officer;

(*b*) Officials such as the Legal Adviser and the Public Information Officer, both of whom belong to the staff of the Chief Administrative Officer, but who work directly with the Commander in view of the nature of their duties;

(*c*) Personnel providing services not readily available from military sources, or requiring special training and knowledge. The Field Operations Service, for example, which assists the operation in many ways, quickly sets up external communications service with skilled personnel, and also provides trained security personnel.

86. The main and most direct impact of staffing and control arrangements is, of course, felt in the field. With the continuing expansion of the administrative responsibilities of the United Nations in connexion with the growing number of operations in widely scattered places, it has become increasingly apparent that qualified administrative personnel within the regular

Secretariat do not exist in sufficient numbers adequately to cover all important tasks, particularly in the financial area. The addition of UNEF to existing responsibilities, and the possibility of other such operations in the future, has made it necessary to devise ways and means of augmenting the regular Secretariat in order to assure that financial administration in the field is properly carried out. To service these activities, accountants, auditors, procurement and property control specialists and supporting staff, of high calibre, are required for service in the field in substantial numbers. The fluctuating needs of the Organization argue against expanding the permanent Secretariat staff. Increasing attention, therefore, is being given to the development of additional sources of field assistance including, in particular, arrangements whereby specialist civilian personnel may be made available by Member Governments on a temporary secondment basis for service with UNEF as part of the Secretariat staff, following brief periods of training or briefing at Headquarters or at another United Nations office prior to taking up their field assignments.

Joint civilian-military organization

87. The fusion of military and civilian activities requires considerable understanding as well as knowledge on the part of the Commander, who is the only officer of the Force operating in both a military and a civilian capacity, as also on the part of the senior military and civilian officers. In practice, in the day-to-day activities, it falls mainly to the Chief of Staff to set the tone for civil-military relationships. The possibility of friction, stemming from differences in background, training and discipline, is always present and deserves special attention. There are some areas so clearly defined as to allow little occasion for military-civilian misunderstanding. Among them are military operations, air operations, health services, military police, legal affairs, public information, and relations with other United Nations agencies. Only slight difficulty has been experienced in some other areas where civilian-military responsibilities are mixed, such as personnel, maintenance and construction, welfare programmes, supervision of mess facilities and canteens, rotation of contingents and, finally, relations with Governments. On the other hand, although they have always been solved, problems of this kind have arisen in connexion with logistics, finance and accounting, radio communications, transportation and travel, and the issuance of directives and instructions covering the general administration of the Force. With regard to senior officers on the civilian side and staff officers on the military side, it may be said that too frequent rotation has been a hindrance to the development and consolidation of maximum efficiency in administration.

Public information

88. From the very beginning of the operation, the Secretariat has assigned public information officers to UNEF. They report directly to the Commander. Their principal function has been to assist in press relations with correspondents assigned to cover the Force. Correspondents have been accredited to UNEF on the same conditions as to all other United Nations missions. It has been necessary, in the best interests of the operation, to adhere strictly to a policy of accreditation which is similar to that applied in other United Nations missions, but which takes into account certain unusual problems arising out of conditions unique to UNEF. The main features of this policy are: (*a*) that only correspondents reaching Egypt on their own and applying personally to UNEF headquarters can be accredited, this accreditation being for the purpose of covering UNEF only and not entitling them to any other facilities or rights of movement in the country; (*b*) that accredited persons must be *bona fide* correspondents actively engaged in covering the work of the United Nations; and (*c*) that, as far as UNEF facilities are concerned, accredited correspondents of all nationalities must receive equal treatment.

89. The public information staff have also helped to provide Headquarters with general coverage of UNEF operations for its various information media, and special coverage for the Member States furnishing the contingents. UNEF's own weekly newspaper, *Sand Dune*, is edited and published under their guidance. One or more of the national contingents has always

included a public relations officer. These officers have been of great assistance in all matters relating to public information for UNEF.

Logistics and administrative problems

90. Unusual and perplexing administrative problems are constantly encountered by UNEF in many fields of activity, and the brief descriptions of some of the broader ones set forth below are intended only as selected examples of the novel difficulties faced.

Procurement

91. In military logistics work, it is customary for supply requirements to be met through requisitions prepared or screened against standard supply tables, and the procurement action is undertaken without further review. The heterogeneous composition of UNEF has precluded thus far the development of detailed and standardized supply tables, although these are in course of preparation. In the meantime, the Chief Procurement Officer must assure himself that each requisition covers only essential supplies for which there are no other alternatives, and differences sometimes tend to arise over the conclusions about proper purchase.

92. An important area of difficulty is the procurement and delivery of supplies and equipment, after agreement is reached on requirements. Four main sources of supply have been drawn upon by UNEF:

(a) A good part of the requirements is furnished by the participating Governments directly to their own troops;

(b) United Nations Headquarters procures and ships those supplies that can be economically secured through its own procurement channels;

(c) The UNEF supply office in Italy procures and ships other supplies from military sources in Europe, when authorized by United Nations Headquarters under standing arrangements with Governments of Member States;

(d) Supplies are purchased locally when the exigencies of the situation so demand or when price comparisons show that this is the most economical course.

93. In the early days of an operation such as UNEF it is imperative to have an assured source that can produce most of the supplies required by modern troops in the field. Once a 'pipeline' has been established, attention can be given to developing alternative sources that may be cheaper or more satisfactory in other ways. The provision of rations in sufficient quantity and appropriate variety for soldiers of differing nationalities and dietary habits is especially important and often difficult. The question of the most suitable ration scale for UNEF is kept under review. In the early stages, when UNEF was concentrated at Abu Suweir, the quantities of rations brought in by air-lift were inadequate, and procurement through the Egyptian Army was necessary for a brief period. This arrangement ceased when local contractors were able to deal directly with United Nations procurement officers. The necessity of bringing rations in by air greatly reduced the air-lift available for other purposes and caused much difficulty.

Transportation

94. Transportation within the area of operations when public and commercial facilties are limited is a burdensome problem. Major reliance has to be placed on the use of UNEF vehicles and aircraft, with a consequent strain on maintenance and repair facilities and supplies. The periodic movement of troops on rotation to and from the home country creates an administrative challenge, owing largely to the absence of scheduled air or shipping services from that country to the area of operations and the rapidity with which sizeable units of troops must be interchanged. Rotational movements of troops have required intensive planning and complex administrative arrangements. Use has been made of commercial and governmental aircraft and ships, the arrangements varying according to the demands of the particular situation.

95. It is apparent that a force in the circumstances of UNEF must be largely self-sufficient

17

as regards vehicular and aircraft maintenance, for outside facilities are largely unavailable and generally unsuitable when they do exist. The maintenance and repair facilities provided by the Royal Canadian Air Force have kept the UNEF aircraft up to a satisfactory operational standard. The situation has been far more difficult with regard to motor vehicles. The Ordnance Workshop facilities, also provided by Canada, are not designed for the repair of large components and, until contract arrangements were made for such repairs, many vehicles were out of action for long periods. Moreover, it has proved very difficult to obtain the necessary quantities of spare parts for obsolete vehicles.

Medical arrangements

96. While some contingents have limited health services of their own, the Force relies mainly on the central medical facilities in Rafah, under joint Canadian–Norwegian operation. Until late 1957, a Norwegian field hospital was maintained in Gaza while the Canadians operated a small hospital at Rafah. In practice, there was some duplication, and a consolidation was therefore arranged. The Rafah hospital is equipped and staffed to treat most of the disabilities occurring in UNEF, and its location is such that it can provide services to most contingents without undue delay.

97. Cases in need of advanced or specialized medical services require evacuation to hospitals outside the area. It has proved important to have ready access to such facilities, as emergency cases regularly occur. Working relationships for this purpose have been established in a number of countries.

Morale and welfare

98. The morale of UNEF has been consistently good, but local physical conditions are none too congenial and, therefore, both United Nations Headquarters in New York and UNEF headquarters in Gaza have from the beginning given special attention to the maintenance of morale. A United Nations Welfare Officer was appointed to supervise all welfare activities including the provision of reading material, films, PX facilities, sports equipment and, when possible, live entertainment. Inter-contingent sporting events are an important feature of the recreation programme. Units also organize their own entertainment from the very considerable talent available in their various national ranks. Leave centres were established in Beirut on 1 May 1957, in Cairo in November 1957 for the winter months, and again in Beirut and later Alexandria in 1958. Occasional tours to historic places have also been arranged.

Relations with the local population

99. The relations of UNEF with the local population have in general been good and no serious incidents have occurred, except for one on 10 March 1957. The Gaza Strip, with its large refugee population, is a sensitive area where particularly strict standards of behaviour and respect for local customs have been necessary and have been adhered to by members of the Force. The order issued in November 1957 that troops should carry arms only when on duty has been a factor in good relations. Along the international frontier, with its sparse and largely nomadic population, a tradition of goodwill and co-operation has also been built up, to the advantage of both parties. At the leave centres—whether in Beirut, Cairo or Alexandria —relations with the local populations have posed no serious problems.

Signals communications

100. Responsibility for UNEF's communications services is divided. The necessity at the outset for instant communications services within the area of operations dictated the use of a military signals system, while the heavy United Nations traffic to and from New York, Geneva and other points made it essential to establish a typical unit, although larger than usual, of United Nations radio officers. Thus, military personnel (largely Canadian, but in-

cluding a small Indian unit), under the Chief Signals Officer, have undertaken most of the communications functions involving operational requirements in the local area, while most traffic going beyond the area is handled by United Nations Field Service personnel. Telephonic service in UNEF has been provided satisfactorily by military signals personnel. Varying standards of performance and quite different types of equipment have made it difficult to achieve a cohesive communications pattern and full effectiveness on the part of available personnel. The entire radio communications service, including the military operational requirements, possibly could be performed satisfactorily by the United Nations Field Service, but only with increased staff resources. A fully integrated and cohesive external and internal communications service would then be possible.

Postal arrangements

101. One of the first arrangements for UNEF was the establishment of a base post office in Naples, Italy, in connexion with a franking privilege plan worked out with the Governments concerned through the Universal Postal Union. When UNEF was moved into the area of operations in Egypt, mail for its personnel was first flown to Naples. All Governments having troops in UNEF participate in the mail plan except Yugoslavia, which has a national airline operating between Cairo and Belgrade, the Yugoslav contingent being thus enabled to pick up and despatch its own mail. India, although participating in the plan, operates its own post office in Cairo. Subsequently, the only major change in the arrangements has been the transfer of the base post office to Beirut, with the closing of the UNEF base at Naples.

Property responsibility

102. The question of property responsibility and accountability in an organization such as UNEF has its complexities. The problems are due partly to the fact that the property may be either contingent-owned or UNEF-owned, and partly to the wide variations in practices and procedures among the different contingents. The lack of uniform ownership has meant that the personnel responsible for such matters have had to maintain two types of record and to engage in two different systems of recording. With regard to UNEF-owned property, a central authority is required to supervise and audit in detail the activities of contingents. Certain controls must also be exercised over contingent-owned equipment, in view of the possible ultimate UNEF responsibility for depreciation and replacement.

Financial administration

103. For the guidance of those concerned with financial administration, and in accordance with the General Assembly's request in resolution 1122 (XI), the Secretary-General, after consultation with the Advisory Committee on Administrative and Budgetary Questions, established in December 1956 provisional financial rules for UNEF (ST/SGB/UNEF/2). These rules and the procedures developed in connexion therewith are designed to ensure effective financial administration and control along the lines generally followed by the United Nations and, therefore, have been patterned to the maximum extent appropriate on established United Nations financial rules and procedures. Detailed field procedures are effected through Command orders and administrative instructions. In respect of audit arrangements, the provisions of the United Nations Financial Regulations as to external audit, and of the United Nations Financial Rules as to internal inspection, have been applied. The Advisory Committee on Administrative and Budgetary Questions and the Board of Auditors have expressed satisfaction with these arrangements.

104. Since 1 July 1957, the UNEF accounts have been operated on an imprest account basis.* This means that the cash needs of UNEF are provided as required from United

---

* The accounting system has been changed twice since November 1956. During the period prior to January 1957, the imprest account system was applied. Later, it was decided to make UNEF a self-accounting unit along the lines followed for the European Office of the United Nations at Geneva and

Nations Headquarters, and that all expenditures and commitments are reported to Headquarters for recording and auditing. Funds are made available for obligation or expenditure only through allotments by the Controller.

105. The United Nations has at its disposal various bank accounts in national currencies at centres of UNEF activity. A US dollar operations account is established with a bank at United Nations headquarters. All the accounts abroad are funded from United Nations Headquarters, mainly with US dollars.

106. Activities having broad financial implications, but falling outside the regular system of accounts, such as the administration of service institutes, messes and canteens, have required the development of thorough control procedures to protect fully the interests of the United Nations and of the participating States. Any such activity which involves an investment by the United Nations, either through advances of operating capital or some form of subsidy, is subject to thorough financial controls in the same manner as regular accounts.

107. Prior to December 1957, it was not considered possible to prepare a formal budget covering UNEF's operation during 1958, as the continuance of the Force could not be forecast beyond a period of a few months. In December 1957, it was agreed, on the recommendation of the Advisory Committee on Administrative and Budgetary Questions (A/3761), that a formal budget for the Force for the year 1958 should be prepared. Consequently, budget estimates for 1958 are being submitted to the thirteenth session of the General Assembly (A/3823). The budget consists of two parts, part A dealing with the operation of the Force and part B with the reimbursement to Governments of costs incurred in providing military contingents. Part B contains two sections, the first covering the extra and extraordinary costs relating to pay and allowances and the second covering compensation to be paid in respect of equipment, material and supplies.

CHAPTER V. FINANCIAL ARRANGEMENTS

Methods of financing

108. The task of financing an operation as large and as costly as UNEF has posed great and continuing problems. In financial terms, the expenses caused by UNEF's formation and operation have had to be considered as extraordinary, according to the definition generally applied by the General Assembly. The authority conferred on the Secretary-General by the annual General Assembly resolution relating to unforeseen and extraordinary expenses to finance commitments (up to a total of US $2 million) relating to the maintenance of international peace and security was not sufficient to cope with even the initial cost of so large an undertaking. In theory, it was possible for the General Assembly to increase the amount appearing in this annual resolution, and thereby to include UNEF's expenses in the normal budget of the United Nations. For the following reasons, however, it was deemed preferable to finance UNEF's initial expenses on an *ad hoc* and separate basis: (*a*) the scope and duration of UNEF's assignment were uncertain; (*b*) cost estimates could not in the early stages be developed with any precision; (*c*) various offers of assistance without charge to the United Nations had been made, as well as promises of grants; (*d*) the initial basic rule for the sharing of costs, which was accepted by the General Assembly on 7 November 1956 (resolution 1001 (ES–I), para. 5), whereby a participating State would be responsible for all costs for the equipment and salaries of its contingent, had been submitted by the Secretary-General as provisional and

---

for the International Court of Justice. With this decision, it was not possible to maintain at Headquarters a close check on UNEF field obligations and expenditures. In the same period, difficulties arose in the field in the maintenance of proper accounts and financial controls, and the Controller found himself severely handicapped, through lack of adequate accounting records, in the formulation of realistic budget estimates for UNEF's continuing needs. As a result of this experience, it was decided to revert to the imprest account system.

subject to further study; (*e*) available balances in the Working Capital Fund were not sufficiently large to underwrite the expenses of even a relatively small Force for any appreciable period of time, in addition to financing other unavoidable United Nations requirements; and (*f*) the procedure adopted would avoid the virtually certain delay that would otherwise have resulted from deep differences of opinion about who should be responsible for meeting the costs.

109. In view of the impossibility in the initial stages of making any firm estimate of costs, the General Assembly granted a general authorization for the cost of the Force. The first authorization, voted on 26 November 1956 (resolution 1122 (XI)), was for an amount of $10 million. This was increased, on 27 February 1957 (resolution 1090 (XI)), to $16·5 million in respect of the period ending 31 December 1957; then, on 22 November 1957 (resolution 1151 (XII)), it was increased to $30 million for the same period. For the continuing operation of the Force beyond 31 December 1957, the Assembly, by the last-mentioned resolution, authorized the Secretary-General to expend up to a maximum of $25 million, it being understood that budget estimates would be submitted to the Assembly in the course of 1958. These estimates (A/3823) indicated that normal running expenditures were expected to amount to $14·2 million and reimbursements to participating States (apart from any compensation to be paid for *matériel*) to $6 million. If the Force is to operate beyond the end of 1958, further Assembly action will be required to provide the necessary authority and financial support.

110. On 26 November 1956, the General Assembly, by resolution 1122 (XI), authorized the Secretary-General to establish a Special Account to which funds received by the United Nations for the express purpose of meeting the expenses of the Force should be credited and from which payments for this purpose should be made. At the same time, the Secretary-General was authorized, pending the receipt of funds for the Special Account, to advance from the Working Capital Fund such sums as the Special Account might require to meet any expenses chargeable to it. But even in normal circumstances the heaviest drain on the Working Capital Fund occurs in the first half of the year, and it was anticipated that by February 1957 there would be a very limited availability of cash or immediately realizable resources. The Secretary-General, therefore, suggested that the General Assembly authorize him, when necessary, to arrange for loans to the Special Account from appropriate sources, including Governments and international agencies, and from other funds under his custody or control (see resolution 1090 (XI), para. 3). The loan procedure was suggested and adopted as an extraordinary measure, designed to meet serious gaps in standard methods of providing for cash requirements of the Organization. The necessity to use this authority has been avoided to date, but only narrowly so. It was recognized, in any event, that such loans could only provide temporary relief in limited amounts and should not be relied on as a means of assuring financial solvency for UNEF's operations.

111. By resolution 1090 (XI), the General Assembly invited Member States to make voluntary contributions in order to ease the financial burden for 1957 on the membership as a whole.

112. When the Assembly revised the expenditures authorized for the period ending 31 December 1957 to a total of $30 million (resolution 1151 (XII)) it decided that these authorized expenses would be borne by Member States in accordance with the scale of assessments adopted by the General Assembly for the financial year 1957. However, grants of special assistance having been promised, the Assembly, in the same resolution, agreed that such other resources as might become available would be applied to reduce the expenses before the apportionment for the period ending 31 December 1957.

113. It thus became possible to arrange the financing of the $30 million expenditures in the following manner:

(*a*) To the extent of $1,841,700, by voluntary contributions made by Member States in response to the invitation to them extended in resolution 1090 (XI);

(*b*) To an additional extent of $13,129,312, by grants of special assistance made by a number of Governments in order to reduce the total of the amount to be assessed on all Members, on the basis of resolution 1151 (XII);

(*c*) The balance ($15,028,988), by assessments on Members in accordance with the approved scale of assessments for 1957.

114. UNEF's expenses for 1958 will also be borne by Member States in accordance with the scale of assessments of their contributions to the United Nations budget of 1958 (resolution 1151 (XII)).

115. A Special Account 'outside the regular budget' of the Organization was established by the General Assembly at its eleventh session (resolution 1122 (XI)). Although voluntary contributions in cash and services were received in substantial amounts during the first financial year of UNEF's operation, the progressive action of the Assembly in the matter of financing the Force, as noted above, clearly implies that contributions from Member States in accordance with an approved scale for apportioning the expenses should normally be relied upon as the principal source for continuing financial support for the Force.

116. Subject to this basic principle, the possibility will, of course, always exist of taking advantage of offers of special assistance in the form of voluntary cash contributions or of goods and services offered free of charge or at nominal prices.

Apportionment of costs between the United Nations and the participating States

Expenses incurred by the participating States

117. The following formulae for the sharing of costs in respect of troops between the Organization and the participating States were adopted by the General Assembly on 22 November 1957 (resolution 1151 (XII)) based on proposals submitted by the Secretary-General (A/2694, paras 86, 88 and 91) as a result of many difficulties which had earlier arisen in arriving at equitable and uniform reimbursement arrangements:

(*a*) For the first six months (i.e., during what might reasonably be regarded as the initial emergency period), the United Nations would reimburse to participating Governments any special allowances, as distinct from basic salaries, paid to members of their contingents as a direct result of their service with UNEF in its area of operations, provided that such allowances could be considered as reasonable.

(*b*) In the event of a contingent serving beyond the initial six-month period, or of a replacement contingent being made available, the United Nations would assume financial responsibility for all extra and extraordinary costs which a Government was obliged to incur in making such forces available for UNEF service. Apart from the costs of equipment referred to below, this means, in effect, reimbursement by the United Nations of expenditure incurred in respect of pay and allowances over and above those costs which the Government concerned would have been obliged to meet in any event.

118. These principles were designed to provide a generally equitable basis upon which a collective United Nations responsibility could be discharged and to avoid the possibility of a few Member States assuming a disproportionately heavy financial burden beyond a limited emergency period. But their application in practice has proved difficult. For example, in the case of the formula in sub-paragraph (*a*) of the preceding paragraph, it has been extremely difficult, in view of widely differing national practices, to define what may be reasonably regarded as a 'special allowance'. Furthermore, although it had been assumed that national contingents would be composed of regular army personnel who would, in any event, have been in the service of their country, certain Governments organized special volunteer units to serve with UNEF. This was done because national laws precluded the assignment of members of the regular armed forces to service overseas other than in defence of the homeland. In other cases, new units had to be organized within the contributing States to replace regular units dispatched for UNEF duty. In these circumstances, some Governments from the outset assumed additional financial liabilities which they believed should be compensated for by the United Nations. Experience indicates the validity of the view that the most equitable collective arrangement is one which distributes among the membership as a whole those costs which a participating Government would not otherwise have incurred.

119. According to the formula adopted by the General Assembly in resolution 1151 (XII),

the United Nations would assume financial responsibility for the replacement of equipment destroyed or worn out and for such deterioration beyond that provided for under normal depreciation schedules as could be assessed at the conclusion of the total period of service of a Government's contingent. It is not specified, however, whether or not the word 'equipment' should be interpreted in the wider sense of 'equipment, *matériel* or supplies', and no qualification is made as to the terms under which the items had been made available, i.e., it is not indicated either that they should have been normal and necessary in the circumstances or that they should have saved the United Nations expenditure which it otherwise would have had to incur. Consequently, decisions must be based on interpretations of the formula in the light of the actual circumstances of each particular case.

Expenses borne by the United Nations directly

120. On the basis of the relevant decisions of the General Assembly[24] the United Nations assumes the following direct costs, when they are not otherwise provided for:

(*a*) Billeting, rations and summer clothing for the troops including the rental, reconditioning and maintenance of premises;

(*b*) Payment to each member of the Force of a daily overseas allowance, equivalent to 86 cents, in accordance with a decision by the Fifth Committee of the General Assembly at its 541st meeting on 3 December 1956;

(*c*) Costs of the rotation of contingents;

(*d*) Travel and subsistence allowances of military personnel proceeding on official business to points outside the area of operations;

(*e*) Operation and maintenance of a suitable leave centre and other welfare expenses, such as rental of films, periodic contracting for live shows for the entertainment of the troops, and postage for personal mail;

(*f*) Miscellaneous supplies and services such as cobbling, tailoring, laundering and haircutting;

(*g*) Motor transport and heavy mobile equipment;

(*h*) Miscellaneous non-expendable operational equipment such as barrack stores, tentage, workshop equipment, water and petroleum cans and generators;

(*i*) Spare parts, maintenance and petrol, oil and lubricants for motor transport and other mobile equipment;

(*j*) Stationery, photographic and other miscellaneous supplies;

(*k*) Payment for the use of Royal Canadian Air Force planes comprising the UNEF Squadron, at specified rates per flying hour.

Other costs assumed by the United Nations are:

(*a*) Salaries, travel and subsistence and other appropriate staff costs of international staff detailed from Headquarters or other United Nations offices, Field Service personnel, and locally recruited personnel;

(*b*) Communications services, costs of transporting and issuing supplies, and claims against the United Nations for personal injury, property damage and loss of income arising from traffic accidents and other effects of the operation of the Force;

(*c*) Costs of external auditors and assistants visiting the mission;

(*d*) Other miscellaneous supplies and services.

Agreements with Governments relating to financial responsibilities

121. UNEF experience indicates that such an operation would be greatly facilitated by a standing provision that the costs falling to the United Nations, including the extra and extraordinary costs incurred by Governments furnishing troops, supplies and equipment, should be met by Member States collectively. Acceptance of this principle would facilitate the preparation and consideration of budget estimates and lead to improved financial and logistic arrangements for any new operation. Thereafter, once the nature and scope of an operation

[24] General Assembly res. 1001 (ES–I), 1089 (XI) and 1151 (XII). See above pp. 416–22.

were clearly established, agreements could be formulated between Governments providing military personnel and the United Nations, in the light of the particular circumstances, which should specify the types of services, accommodation and allowances which would be provided directly at United Nations expense.

122. With respect to extra costs incurred by Governments as a result of their participation in the operation, standard rates on a monthly, quarterly or annual basis could be negotiated for inclusion in an agreement, covering such items as:

(a) Reimbursement for governmental pay and allowances;

(b) Payment for personal equipment or governmental issues (clothing, arms, ammunition, etc.);

(c) Rental of equipment furnished at the request of the United Nations (with title to pass to the United Nations when full value has been paid as rent).

The agreement could also provide for straight reimbursement of governmental supplies furnished at United Nations request and costs of rotating units and transporting equipment. It would likewise be advisable to include in the agreement provision for the reimbursement to Governments of such costs as they might incur under their own legislation in connexion with compensation payable for the death or disability of their nationals while serving the United Nations.

123. Experience also warrants the assumption that once the nature of the operation is clear, a number of Member States would be prepared to provide assistance to the United Nations in the procurement of vital *matériel* and services quickly and economically, under arrangements similar to those entered into for the purpose of assuring logistic support to UNEF.

Summary of basic financial provisions

124. The foregoing review of the problems encountered and experience resulting therefrom in the financing of UNEF would seem to point to the conclusion that, while there is clearly scope for the development and application in similar situations of relatively standard principles, policies and procedures, detailed arrangements in this as in other essential respects must be tailored to a variety of circumstances which in most cases will not be predictable in advance. Thus, budgetary and related arrangements will be conditioned in each instance by personnel and equipment needs, which in turn will tend to be determined by a wide range of political, geographic and other circumstances.

CHAPTER VI. LEGAL ASPECTS

Means employed

125. It was natural, in view of the lack of precedents for UNEF as an international Force, that new legal questions should arise in each phase of its development. Most of these questions are settled on the basis of formal agreements or understandings, and others through mutually acceptable working procedures devised at the local level.

126. Written arrangements or understandings have been effected by means of bilateral agreements entered into by the United Nations, represented by the Secretary-General, on the one hand, and the State concerned, on the other; they have not required ratification, but are legally binding on the parties to them.

Legal character of UNEF; its Regulations[25]

127. The Force was recognized as a subsidiary organ of the General Assembly, established under the authority of Article 22 of the Charter of the United Nations (regulation 6). A problem of first importance, therefore, was that of harmonizing the international character of the Force with the fact of its being composed of national contingents. This was accomplished through the chain of command and through definition of the legal status of the Force and of its

---

[25] See s. 6, pp. 288–92.

members. Subject to the resolutions of the General Assembly, the Secretary-General has authority for all executive, administrative and financial matters affecting the Force (regulation 15).* The Commander has direct command authority over the Force and its operations. Acting in consultation with the Secretary-General in the exercise of this authority, he remains operationally responsible for the performance of all functions assigned to the Force by the United Nations, and for the deployment and assignment of troops placed at the disposal of the Force (regulations 11 and 16). By designating the chain of command for the Force, through which he is empowered to delegate his authority, the Commander in turn is able to make use of the commanding officers of the national contingents (regulation 12).

128. This effective marriage of national military service with international function is also reflected in the status of individual members of the Force. Although remaining in their national service, they are, during the period of their assignment with UNEF, international personnel under the authority of the United Nations and subject to the instructions only of the Commander and his chain of command. They discharge exclusively international functions (regulations 6, 29, 31 and 32).† The immunities necessary to assure their international character as members of the Force are developed in detail in the Agreement on the status of the Force, discussed below.

129. As a subsidiary organ, UNEF enjoys the status, privileges and immunities of the Organization as already established by the Convention on the Privileges and Immunities of the United Nations. The independent exercise of the functions of UNEF was thus assured in respect of property supplied by the United Nations, but it was necessary to make provision for supplies and equipment which were the property of the national contingents. It was accordingly established that the relevant terms of the Convention also applied to the property, funds and assets of the participating States used in connexion with UNEF (regulation 10).

Agreements and understandings concerning the formation and supply of the Force

130. The informal arrangements initially made by the Secretary-General, with the assistance of an Under-Secretary, the Military Adviser and the military advisory group, for the provision of national contingents to the Force, were formalized on 21 June 1957, in a letter addressed by the Secretary-General to each of the ten States contributing contingents (see Annex I). This letter referred to the guiding principles and the policies adopted by the General Assembly, as well as to the relevant provisions of the Agreement reached with Egypt on 8 February 1957 on the status of the Force. With the reply of each participating State, the letter constitutes an agreement between the United Nations and the particular State in question, which remains in force until the withdrawal of that national contingent from the Force.

131. Arrangements were also made with other Member States, concerning such matters as air-lift requirements, supplies and equipment, and right of air passage over natural territories.

Understanding on the presence and functioning of UNEF

132. The Government of Egypt had accepted the Force in principle by formally accepting resolution 1000 (ES–I) establishing a United Nations Command, but wished to have certain clarifications before the actual arrival of the Force. The Secretary-General had, therefore, given interpretations of the relevant General Assembly resolutions to the Government of Egypt, reporting in full to the Advisory Committee on the interpretations given. The Advisory Committee had approved these interpretations and recommended that the Secretary-General should start at once the transfer of the Force to Egypt, an action to which the Government of Egypt had consented on the basis of the interpretations given by the Secretary-General.

* See also regulation 4, which provides that Command orders issued by the Commander are subject to review by the Secretary-General.

† See also regulation 19 (*b*), which provides that members of the Secretariat detailed to UNEF remain subject to the authority of the Secretary-General.

17*

133. While this procedure was an adequate basis for the dispatch of the first units to Egypt, the Secretary-General, feeling that some firmer foundation was necessary for the presence and functioning of the Force in that country and for continued co-operation with the Egyptian authorities, visited Cairo from 16 to 18 November for personal discussions on these points with the Egyptian authorities. The questions of principle resolved in these talks were embodied in an '*Aide-mémoire* on the basis for the presence and functioning of the United Nations Emergency Force in Egypt', which was approved by the Government of Egypt. This *aide-mémoire* was submitted to the General Assembly on 20 November 1956 (A/3375) and, when noted with approval by that organ on 24 November 1956 (resolution 1121 (XI)), constituted an understanding between the United Nations and Egypt concerning the presence and functioning of UNEF in Egypt. The *aide-mémoire*, after noting the arrival of advance units of UNEF in Egypt, stated the understanding between the Government of Egypt and the Secretary-General on the basic points for the presence and functioning of UNEF as follows:

'1. The Government of Egypt declares that, when exercising its sovereign rights on any matter concerning the presence and functioning of UNEF, it will be guided, in good faith, by its acceptance of General Assembly resolution 1000 (ES–I) of 5 November 1956.

'2. The United Nations takes note of this declaration of the Government of Egypt and declares that the activities of UNEF will be guided, in good faith, by the task established for the Force in the aforementioned resolutions; in particular, the United Nations, understanding this to correspond to the wishes of the Government of Egypt, reaffirms its willingness to maintain UNEF until its task is completed.

'3. The Government of Egypt and the Secretary-General declare that it is their intention to proceed forthwith, in the light of points 1 and 2 above, to explore jointly concrete aspects of the functioning of UNEF, including its stationing and the question of its lines of communication and supply; the Government of Egypt, confirming its intention to facilitate the functioning of UNEF, and the United Nations are agreed to expedite in co-operation and implementation of guiding principles arrived at as a result of that joint exploration on the basis of the resolutions of the General Assembly.'

Agreement on the status of the Force

134. The Secretary-General, acting in consultation with the Advisory Committee, negotiated and concluded on 8 February 1957 with the Government of Egypt the Agreement on the status of the Force (hereinafter referred to as 'the Agreement'). The Agreement, concluded by an exchange of letters (see A/3526), was deemed to have taken effect as from the date of the arrival of the first element of UNEF in Egypt and to remain in force until the departure of UNEF from Egypt. On 22 February 1957, the General Assembly, by resolution 1126 (XI), noted with approval the Secretary-General's report which included the Agreement. Matters of principle dealt with in the Agreement are, to a large extent, reflected in the UNEF Regulations, and they are summarized below.

Legal aspects of the presence, functioning and operation of UNEF in Egypt

Presence of UNEF in Egypt

135. The presence of the Force was accepted in the 'area of operations', which is deemed to include areas where it is deployed, its installations and premises, as well as its lines of communication and supply (Agreement, paras 5, 19, 32 and 33). The United Nations, in turn, acknowledged the obligation of its personnel and of the members of the Force to respect the laws and regulations of Egypt and to refrain from actions incompatible with their international status (Agreement, para 6). To implement the exemption of members of the Force from passport, visa, and Egyptian immigration regulations, rules were issued authorizing their use of military movement orders and identity cards in lieu of passports and visas (Agreement, para. 7). Provision was made for appropriate display of the United Nations flag, for a prescribed uniform, for a distinctive identification of UNEF vehicles, for UNEF licences and operator's permits, and for the carrying of arms on duty (Agreement, paras 20, 21 and 22)

Jurisdiction

136. The question of criminal jurisdiction raised a number of points of basic policy in the establishment of UNEF. It is essential to the preservation of the independent exercise of the functions of such a force that its members should be immune from the criminal jurisdiction of the host State. The Agreement accordingly provided that members of the Force should be under the exclusive jurisdiction of their respective national States with regard to any criminal offences committed by them in Egypt (Agreement, para. 11). Such a policy, obviously, makes easier the decision of States to contribute troops from their armed forces. At the same time, it was important that this waiving of jurisdiction by the host State should not result in a jurisdictional vacuum, in which a given offence might be subject to prosecution by neither the host State nor the participating State. For this reason, the agreements between the United Nations and the participating States specify that this 'immunity from the jurisdiction of Egypt is based on the understanding that the authorities of the participating States would exercise such jurisdiction as might be necessary with respect to crimes or offences committed in Egypt by any members of the Force provided from their own military services'. The Secretary-General, therefore, sought assurance from each participating Government that it would be prepared to exercise this jurisdiction as to any crime or offence which might be committed by a member of its contingent.

137. Even so, it was probably inevitable that from time to time a number of difficult legal problems would arise in giving effect to these provisions, involving varied legal systems and terms of military law prevailing in participating States. Fortunately, the number of acts having possible implications under criminal law committed by members of UNEF have been very few. The Secretary-General has thought it desirable, none the less, to ask the Governments of participating States to review the position under their laws. As an indication of the type of problem that could arise, it may be noted that national laws differ in the extent to which they confer on courts martial jurisdiction over civil offences in peacetime, or confer on either military or civil courts jurisdiction over offences committed abroad. Some provide only for trial in the home country, thus posing practical questions about the submission of evidence.

138. As to civil jurisdiction, members of the Force enjoy immunity from legal process in any matter relating to their official duties; but the same machinery is available for settlement as in the case of claims against the United Nations. In other civil cases, where jurisdiction over a member of the Force might be exercised in Egypt, there are agreed measures to prevent the proceedings from interfering with the performance of his official duties (Agreement, paras 12 and 38 (*b*)).

Discipline

139. The disciplinary system in UNEF, from the strictly military point of view, is rather anomalous. Normally, the commander of a force has powers both of command and punishment, whereas the Commander of UNEF has powers only of command. Disciplinary authority resides in the commanding officer of each national contingent (regulation 13). To confer such authority upon the Commander would probably require specific legislation in most participating States.

140. The Agreement authorized the use of military police by the Commander to assure the maintenance of discipline and good order among members of the Force. They police UNEF premises, and perform functions elsewhere only in accordance with specific arrangements made with local police authorities. They have the power of arrest over members of the Force. The Agreement likewise sets out a mutual arrangement by which the UNEF military police can, in certain conditions, take other persons into custody for immediate delivery to the Egyptian authorities, or the Egyptian authorities can take into custody a member of the Force for immediate delivery to UNEF (Agreement, paras 14–18).

Claims

141. In accordance with the obligations established in the Convention on the Privileges

and Immunities of the United Nations, the Organization makes provision for the settlement of disputes or claims of a private law character to which it is a party. In addition, the Agreement authorizes the establishment of a Claims Commission for settlement of claims against a member of the Force, or by the Force or the Government of Egypt against one another (Agreement, para. 38), but, in practice, all settlements to date have been by a process of informal negotiation between the parties directly, or between UNEF and the Egyptian Liaison Office subject to the ratification of the claimant. In the relatively few cases of accidental death, UNEF has taken into account local levels of compensation as evidenced by the system of *diyet* used by the *Sharia* (Moslem religious) Courts, formulas stated in workmen's compensation laws, and other local practice.

142. The Egyptian Government has undertaken to provide the necessary areas for headquarters, camps, and other premises of the Force (Agreement, para. 19). Such of these properties as were Government-owned were provided free. With respect to privately-owned land, however, a large number of claims for compensation or rentals have been presented to UNEF through the Egyptian Liaison Office. UNEF agreed that it should pay for damages to real property arising out of negligence or other causes not related to the necessary functions of the Force, and that it should pay reasonable rentals for property utilized by UNEF for the comfort and convenience of the Force. The question of privately-owned land used because of operational necessity, and for that reason required to be provided under the Agreement, has been the subject of discussion between Egyptian authorities and the Secretary-General, resulting in a procedure whereby UNEF surveys the sites together with representatives of local authorities and, on that basis and on the assumption that it is established that the Egyptian Government would have honoured the claim, makes payment to the owners, reserving its rights under the Agreement and the possibility, in due course, of raising with the Government such demands for reimbursement as those rights warrant.

143. In addition to the types of claims noted above, consideration has been given to possible claims by participating States for equipment destroyed in the service of UNEF, or for increased costs resulting from compensation paid to members of the Force or their dependants for death or injury attributable to UNEF service (see A/3694, paras 91–98, and resolution 1151 (XII)).

Movement and communications

144. Provision is made for freedom of movement for the Force within its area of operations, to and from agreed points of access to Egyptian territory, and across the armistice demarcation line. This includes the use of roads and waterways, port facilities and airfields, without payment of fees except charges directly related to services rendered (Agreement, paras 32 and 33).

145. The Force also enjoys within its area of operations the right of unrestricted communication by radio, telephone, telegraph or other means, and the right to make its own postal arrangements free of censorship. The radio stations installed by UNEF connect with the United Nations network (Agreement, para. 29).

146. The Commander has authority under the Agreement to recruit local personnel as required, who enjoy immunity in respect of their official acts (Agreement, paras 24 and 37). As nationals or residents of Egypt, however, they are required to obtain permits to cross the frontier between Sinai and the Gaza Strip. UNEF requires that its locally recruited personnel have freedom of movement in connexion with their work, and in general they do, but there have been occasions when individual permits have been withdrawn for reasons of security.

Conclusions as to legal arrangements

147. Not a few of the specific legal arrangements under which UNEF operates might well require different treatment for a force operating under differing conditions in some other area, although precise variations cannot, of course, be foreseen. Questions of movement to some extent, and to a great extent the exercise of authority over premises, have been considerably simplified by the fact that much of the region in which UNEF has been deployed is sparsely

populated. A more populous area, or one offering greater opportunities for local procurement, might give rise to quite different claims procedures.

CHAPTER VII. CONCLUDING OBSERVATIONS AND PRINCIPLES

A. *Observations*

148. In the preceding pages of this report a summary has been given of the experience of the United Nations derived from the establishment and operation of the United Nations Emergency Force. In advance of the conclusions, certain observations are called for regarding the specific circumstances in which the experience with UNEF has been gained, since those circumstances definitely limit any detailed application of that experience to the general problem of United Nations operations of this character. It is useful, in this context, also to note and compare the subsequent experience with United Nations operations in relation to Lebanon and Jordan.

149. UNEF was brought into being to meet a particular situation in which a United Nations force could be interposed between regular, national military forces which were subject to a cease-fire agreed to by the opposing parties. UNEF has continued to function along the 'dividing line' between the national forces. It follows that in UNEF there has never been any need for rights and responsibilities other than those necessary for such an interposed force under cease-fire conditions. The Force was not used in any way to enforce withdrawals but, in the successive stages of the withdrawals, followed the withdrawing troops to the 'dividing line' of each stage. It is also to be noted that the Force has functioned under a clear-cut mandate which has entirely detached it from involvement in any internal or local problems, and also has enabled it to maintain its neutrality in relation to international political issues. The fact that UNEF was designed to meet the needs of this specific situation largely determined its military components, geographical composition, deployment and status, and also its effectiveness.

150. A further factor of significance in the evaluation of the UNEF experience is that in Gaza the Force is in an area having special status under the Armistice Agreement. In Gaza and elsewhere in its area of operations, UNEF has been able to function without any question arising of its presence infringing upon sovereign rights, on the basis that, at the invitation of the Egyptian Government and in accordance with the decision of the General Assembly, the United Nations assists in maintaining quiet on the armistice demarcation line around the Gaza Strip and along the international line to the south. The Government of Egypt has co-operated by taking the necessary steps to facilitate the functioning of UNEF in the Gaza area. The same is true of the position of the Egyptian Government in keeping its limited military units in the Sinai Peninsula away from the area in which the UNEF chiefly functions.

151. Obviously, some of the above-mentioned circumstances are of such a nature that it could not reasonably be expected that they would often be duplicated elsewhere. Nor can it be assumed that they provide a sufficient basis to warrant indiscriminate projection of the UNEF experience in planning for future United Nations operations of this kind. Indeed, the more recent experiences in Lebanon and Jordan serve only to emphasize the uniqueness of the UNEF setting, which, in part at least, explains the success of this pioneer venture. Neither in Lebanon nor in Jordan would it have been possible to interpose a United Nations force between conflicting parties. Nor would it have been possible in either of those situations to preserve a natural distinction between the presence and functions in various areas of any United Nations force and the presence and functions of government troops. In Lebanon, it is unlikely that a United Nations force could have operated without soon becoming a party to the internal conflicts among nationals of the country. In Jordan, the presence of a United Nations force has been regarded by the Government as difficult to reconcile with its own exercise of full sovereignty over the people and territory of the country. United Nations experience with these three Middle East operations justifies the assumption that, in each new conflict situation in which the United Nations might be called upon to intervene with military personnel, the

nature of the actual organization required and its paramilitary aspects would be determined by the particular needs of the situation and could not, therefore, be anticipated in advance. Thus, for example, stand-by arrangements for a force designed for a UNEF-type operation would not have been of practical value in either of the situations in Lebanon or Jordan, where conditions required an approach in all relevant aspects quite different from that employed in UNEF.

152. The foregoing leads to the obvious conclusion that, in considering general stand-by arrangements for United Nations operations of the kind envisaged in this report, a course should be followed which would afford a considerable degree of flexibility in approaching the varying needs that may arise. This could be achieved if stand-by arrangements were to consist of an approval of those general conclusions regarding principles which can be reached in the light of the UNEF experience, and which would provide a setting within which, with the necessary variations of approach, personnel in units or otherwise could be recruited and an operation organized without delay and with full adjustment to the specific situation requiring the action.

153. Further support for the position here taken is found in that the type and rank of military personnel required, the need for specialists and for supporting units, as well as the vehicle and equipment demands, as experience has shown, also vary so much from case to case that more far-reaching and firm arrangements—as, for example, the maintenance of a nucleus United Nations force of the type generally envisaged—would be without great practical value and certainly would not warrant the substantial sacrifices involved. By way of illustration of this point UNEF has been able to use enlisted men with short military experience under the command of experienced officers; the recruitment of personnel for the United Nations Observation Group in Lebanon (UNOGIL) has been limited largely to officers, who, however, with few exceptions, did not have to be rigorously screened for the mission; while the arrangements in relation to Jordan may involve, if any, only a very limited number of military personnel, all of officer rank but individually and carefully chosen for the purpose. Similar differences are apparent as regards the need for *matériel*, with UNEF being adequately served by, in military calculations, a quite modest number of aircraft and vehicles, while UNOGIL has had to have a considerably higher ratio of planes and vehicles to the men involved, because of the specific tasks with which it has been entrusted.

B. *Basic principles*

154. In view of the impossibility of determining beforehand the specific form of a United Nations presence of the type considered in this report, which would be necessary to meet adequately the requirements of a given situation, a broad decision by the General Assembly should attempt to do no more than endorse certain basic principles and rules which would provide an adaptable framework for later operations that might be found necessary. In a practical sense, it is not feasible in advance of a known situation to do more than to provide for some helpful stand-by arrangements for a force or similar forms of a United Nations presence. In the following paragraphs, certain principles and rules are laid down in the light of the experience gathered in the past years, which, if they were to meet with the approval of the General Assembly, would provide a continuing basis on which useful contacts in a stand-by context might be established with interested Governments, with the aim of being prepared for any requests which might arise from future decisions by the Assembly on a force or similar arrangement to deal with a specific case.

155. As the arrangements discussed in this report do not cover the type of force envisaged under Chapter VII of the Charter, it follows from international law and the Charter that the United Nations cannot undertake to implement them by stationing units on the territory of a Member State without the consent of the Government concerned. It similarly follows from the Charter that the consent of a Member nation is necessary for the United Nations to use its military personnel or *matériel*. These basic rules have been observed in the recent United

Nations operations in the Middle East. They naturally hold valid for all similar operations in the future.

156. The fact that a United Nations operation of the type envisaged requires the consent of the Government on whose territory it takes place creates a problem, as it is normally difficult for the United Nations to engage in such an operation without guarantees against unilateral actions by the host Government which might put the United Nations in a questionable position, either administratively or in relation to contributing Governments.

157. The formula employed in relation to the Government of Egypt for UNEF seems, in the light of experience, to provide an adequate solution to this problem. The Government of Egypt declared that, when exercising its sovereign right with regard to the presence of the Force, it would be guided by good faith in the interpretation of the purposes of the Force. This declaration was balanced by a declaration by the United Nations to the effect that the maintenance of the Force by the United Nations would be determined by similar good faith in the interpretation of the purposes.

158. The consequence of such a bilateral declaration is that, were either side to act unilaterally in refusing continued presence or deciding on withdrawal, and were the other side to find that such action was contrary to a good-faith interpretation of the purposes of the operation, an exchange of views would be called for towards harmonizing the positions. This does not imply any infringement of the sovereign right of the host Government, nor any restriction of the right of the United Nations to decide on the termination of its own operation whenever it might see fit to do so. But it does mean a mutual recognition of the fact that the operation, being based on collaboration between the host Government and the United Nations, should be carried on in forms natural to such collaboration, and especially so with regard to the questions of presence and maintenance.

159. It is unlikely that any Government in the future would be willing to go beyond the declaration of the Government of Egypt with regard to UNEF. Nor, in my view, should the United Nations commit itself beyond the point established for UNEF in relation to the Government of Egypt. In these circumstances, I consider it reasonable to regard the formula mentioned in paragraph 158 above as a valid basis for future arrangements of a similar kind.

160. Another point of principle which arises in relation to the question of consent refers to the composition of United Nations military elements stationed on the territory of a Member country. While the United Nations must reserve for itself the authority to decide on the composition of such elements, it is obvious that the host country, in giving its consent, cannot be indifferent to the composition of those elements. In order to limit the scope of possible difference of opinion, the United Nations in recent operations has followed two principles: not to include units from any of the permanent members of the Security Council; and not to include units from any country which, because of its geographical position or for other reasons, might be considered as possibly having a special interest in the situation which has called for the operation. I believe that these two principles also should be considered as essential to any stand-by arrangements.

161. Given the two principles mentioned in paragraph 160, in actual practice the area within which conflicting views may be expressed will in all probability be so reduced normally as to facilitate the harmonizing of the rights of the United Nations with the interests of the host country. It would seem desirable to accept the formula applied in the case of UNEF, which is to the effect that, while it is for the United Nations alone to decide on the composition of military elements sent to a country, the United Nations should, in deciding on composition, take fully into account the view of the host Government as one of the most serious factors which should guide the recruitment of the personnel. Usually, this is likely to mean that serious objections by the host country against participation by a specific contributing country in the United Nations operation will determine the action of the Organization. However, were the United Nations for good reasons to find that course inadvisable, it would remain free to pursue its own line, and any resulting conflict would have to be resolved on a political rather than on a legal basis. I would recommend that the basis thus laid in the case of

UNEF be considered as the formula on composition applicable to similar operations in the future.

162. The principles indicated in the four points discussed above (paragraphs 155–161 inclusive) were either established by the General Assembly itself, or elaborated in practice or in negotiations with the Government of Egypt. They have served as the basis for a status Agreement which applies to the United Nations personnel in the Force in Egypt. In its entirety, this status Agreement has stood up well to the test of experience. Its basic principles should be embodied in similar agreements in the future, and their recognition, therefore, would seem necessarily to form part of any stand-by arrangements for a force. The agreement regarding the presence of UNOGIL in Lebanon, although much less elaborate because of the modest size of the operation and the fact that normal immunity rules could be applied to the bulk of the personnel, also reflects the basic principles I have in mind.

163. The most important principle in the status Agreement ensures that UNEF personnel, when involved in criminal actions, come under the jurisdiction of the criminal courts of their home countries. The establishment of this principle for UNEF, in relation to Egypt, has set a most valuable precedent. Experience shows that this principle is essential to the successful recruitment by the United Nations of military personnel not otherwise under immunity rules, from its Member countries. The position established for UNEF should be maintained in future arrangements.

164. Another principle in the UNEF status Agreement which should be retained is that the United Nations activity should have freedom of movement within its area of operations and all such facilities regarding access to that area and communications as are necessary for successful completion of the task. This also obviously involves certain rights of over-flight over the territory of the host country. These principles have been maintained in the case of UNOGIL. Their application requires an agreement on what is to be considered as the area of operations and as to what facilities of access and communications are to be considered necessary. On the assumption that, like UNEF, any similar United Nations operation in the future would be of assistance to the nation on whose territory it is stationed, it is not to be expected that the necessary process of agreement will give rise to any serious complications in the interpretation of the principle.

165. Apart from the principles thus established in negotiated agreements or formal decisions, a series of basic rules has been developed in practice. Some of these rules would appear to merit general application. This is true especially of the precept that authority granted to the United Nations group cannot be exercised within a given territory either in competition with representatives of the host Government or in co-operation with them on the basis of any joint operation. Thus, a United Nations operation must be separate and distinct from activities by national authorities. UNEF experience indicates how this rule may apply in practice. A right of detention which normally would be exercised only by local authorities is extended to UNEF units. However, this is so only within a limited area where the local authorities voluntarily abstain from exercising similar rights, whether alone or in collaboration with the United Nations. Were the underlying principle of this example not to be applied, United Nations units might run the risk of getting involved in differences with the local authorities or public or in internal conflicts which would be highly detrimental to the effectiveness of the operation and to the relations between the United Nations and the host Government.

166. A rule closely related to the one last mentioned, and reflecting a basic Charter principle, precludes the employment of United Nations elements in situations of an essentially internal nature. As a matter of course, the United Nations personnel cannot be permitted in any sense to be a party to internal conflicts. Their role must be limited to external aspects of the political situation as, for example, infiltration or other activities affecting international boundaries.

167. Even in the case of UNEF, where the United Nations itself had taken a stand on decisive elements in the situation which gave rise to the creation of the Force, it was explicitly stated that the Force should not be used to enforce any specific political solution of pending

problems or to influence the political balance decisive to such a solution. This precept would clearly impose a serious limitation on the possible use of United Nations elements, were it to be given general application to them whenever they are not created under Chapter VII of the Charter, However, I believe its acceptance to be necessary, if the United Nations is to be in a position to draw on Member countries for contributions in men and *matériel* to United Nations operations of this kind.

168. Military personnel employed by the United Nations in paramilitary operations are, of course, not under the same formal obligations in relation to the Organization as staff members of the Secretariat. However, the position must be maintained that the basic rules of the United Nations for international service are applicable also to such personnel, particularly as regards full loyalty to the aims of the Organization and to abstention from acts in relation to their country of origin or to other countries which might deprive the operation of its international character and create a situation of dual loyalty. The observance of this rule is not only vital for good relations with the host country, it is also to the benefit of the contributing countries concerned, as any other attitude might involve them in responsibilities which would be undesirable in the light of the national policies pursued.

169. In setting up UNEF, the General Assembly appointed a Commander of the Force with the position of an international civil servant responsible for the discharge of his task to the Assembly, but administratively integrated with the United Nations organization, and under instructions from the Secretary-General on the basis of the executive authority for the operation vested in him by the Assembly.

170. A somewhat different procedure was followed in the case of UNOGIL, where the Security Council delegated to the Secretary-General the responsibility for constituting the Observation Group. However, basically the same principle employed in UNEF is applied to UNOGIL, for the Group is responsible for the conduct of its business to the Security Council, while administratively it is under the Secretary-General, who is charged with its organization. A basically similar pattern finds reflection also in the arrangements being made by the United Nations in relation to Jordan.

171. The innovation represented by the constitutional pattern thus followed in recent United Nations field operations has, in experience, proved to be highly practical and, especially, politically of decisive importance, as it has provided for an integration giving the operation all the advantages of administrative co-ordination with the Secretariat and of the fully internationalized status of the Secretariat. As pointed out in the 'Second and final report of the Secretary-General on the plan for an emergency international United Nations Force' (A/3302), on which the General Assembly based its decision to organize the Force, the appointment by the General Assembly of a Commander determined the legal status of the Force. The other arrangements, mentioned above, reflect the same basic concept.

172. In full recognition of the wide variety of forms which decisions on a United Nations operation may take in seeking to fit differing situations calling for such an operation, the underlying rule concerning command and authority which has been consistently applied in recent years, as set out above, should, in my view, be maintained for the future. Thus, a United Nations operation should always be under a leadership established by the General Assembly or the Security Council, or on the basis of delegated authority by the Secretary-General, so as to make it directly responsible to one of the main organs of the United Nations, while integrated with the Secretariat in an appropriate form.

173. Were soundings with Member Governments, based on the aforementioned legal and political principles and rules and on the regulations regarding financial responsibilities set out below, to show that a number of Governments in their planning would be willing to take into account the possibility of having to provide promptly—on an emergency basis, in response to a specific appeal from the United Nations—men and *matériel* to a United Nations operation of the kind envisaged in this report, a question would arise regarding the conditions under which such a desirable stand-by arrangement could be utilized.

174. Under the Charter, and under the 'Uniting for peace' resolution (General Assembly resolution 377 (V)), a formal decision on a United Nations operation must be taken by the

General Assembly or by the Security Council. It must be regarded as excluded that the right to take such a decision, in any general terms, could properly be considered as delegated to the Secretary-General. Short of an explicit decision by the General Assembly or the Security Council with a specific authorization, the Secretary-General, thus, cannot be considered as entitled to appeal to a Member nation for military personnel to be dispatched to another Member country in a United Nations operation.

175. The terms of the delegation in each operation thus far have set the limit of the Secretary-General's authority. Thus, for example, as apparent from the description of the new body, the decision relating to UNEF, which was to be implemented by the Secretary-General, qualified the operation as being one of a paramilitary nature, while the absence of an explicit authorization for the Force to take offensive action excluded the organization by the Secretary-General of units for such action, and consequently, the units generally were equipped only with weapons necessary for self-defence. Had there been any remaining doubts in this respect, the legal basis on which the General Assembly took its decision would have made this limitation clear.

176. Similarly, the Security Council decision on the United Nations Observation Group in Lebanon (S/4023) qualified the kind of operation that the Secretary-General was authorized to organize by the very name given to the unit to be established. That name excluded the creation of a paramilitary force and imposed, in fact, such limitations on the operation as to call for great restraint regarding the arming of the unit and its right of self-defence.

177. The General Assembly decision concerning the arrangements in relation to Jordan (resolution 1237 (ES–III)) was in such broad terms as to provide possibilities for the organization of any kind of operation, short of one possible only under Chapter VII of the Charter. In this case, however, as in the case of UNEF, a certain incompleteness in the terminology of the decision was covered by the conclusions following from the legal basis on which the decision was taken.

178. Confirmation by the Assembly of the interpretation of the question of authority given above would be useful. This interpretation would signify that a Member country, in deciding upon a contribution of men or *matériel* to a United Nations operation on the basis of such stand-by understandings as may have been reached, could reply upon the explicit terms of the executive authority delegated to the Secretary-General in determining the use which could be made of the units provided; it being understood, naturally, that in the types of operation with which this report is concerned this could never include combat activity. There will always remain, of course, a certain margin of freedom for judgement, as, for example, on the extent and nature of the arming of the units and of their right of self-defence. In the case of UNEF, such questions of interpretation have been solved in consultation with the contributing Governments and with the host Government. The Advisory Committee on UNEF set up by the General Assembly has in this context proved to be of especially great assistance.

179. In the preceding paragraph I have touched upon the extent to which a right of self-defence may be exercised by United Nations units of the type envisaged. It should be generally recognized that such a right exists. However, in certain cases this right should be exercised only under strictly defined conditions. A problem arises in this context because of the fact that a wide interpretation of the right of self-defence might well blur the distinction between operations of the character discussed in this report and combat operations, which would require a decision under Chapter VII of the Charter and an explicit, more far-reaching delegation of authority to the Secretary-General than would be required for any of the operations discussed here. A reasonable definition seems to have been established in the case of UNEF, where the rule is applied that men engaged in the operation may never take the initiative in the use of armed force, but are entitled to respond with force to an attack with arms, including attempts to use force to make them withdraw from positions which they occupy under orders from the Commander, acting under the authority of the Assembly and within the scope of its resolutions. The basic element involved is clearly the prohibition against any *initiative* in the use of armed force. This definition of the limit between self-defence, as permissible for

United Nations elements of the kind discussed, and offensive action, which is beyond the competence of such elements, should be approved for future guidance.

180. The clear delimitation of the right to use force which has been set out above as a basic rule for the type of operations discussed in this report should dissipate any objections to the suggested stand-by arrangements which would be based on the view that they go beyond the measures which the Charter permits the General Assembly to take and infringe upon prerogatives of the Security Council. The principles outlined above put UNEF on the same level, constitutionally, as UNOGIL, for example, qualifying it so as to make it an instrument of efforts at mediation and conciliation. It may be noted in this context that UNOGIL has not given rise to any constitutional objections; the fact that the Group was created by the Security Council is in this case irrelevant, as the Council acted entirely within the limits of Chapter VI of the Charter, and as a similar action obviously could have been taken by the General Assembly under Article 22.

181. In the case of UNEF, the General Assembly decided to organize an Advisory Committee, under the chairmanship of the Secretary-General, to assist the operation. In practice, this arrangement has proved highly useful. In principle, it should be accepted as a precedent for the future. Extensive operations with serious political implications, regarding which, for practical reasons, executive authority would need to be delegated to the Secretary-General, require close collaboration with authorized representatives of the General Assembly. However, it would be undesirable for this collaboration to be given such a form as to lead to divided responsibilities or to diminished efficiency in the operation. The method chosen by the General Assembly in the case of UNEF seems the most appropriate one if such risks are to be avoided. The Advisory Committee is fully informed by the Secretary-General and his associates. There is a free exchange of views in closed meetings where advice can be sought and given. But ultimate decisions rest with the Secretary-General, as the executive in charge of carrying out the operation. Dissenting views are not registered by vote, but are put on record in the proceedings of the Committee. It is useful for contributing countries to be represented on such an advisory committee, but if the contributing States are numerous the size of the committee might become so large as to make it ineffective. On the other hand, it is obviously excluded that any party to the conflict should be a member. Normally, I believe that the same basic rule regarding permanent members of the Security Council which has been applied to units and men in the recent operations should be applied also in the selection of members for a relevant advisory committee.

182. In the administration of UNEF at Headquarters, certain special arrangements were made on an *ad hoc* basis to provide expert military guidance. Thus, a senior Military Adviser and three officer assistants were attached to the Executive Office as consultants. The Military Adviser, and the Under-Secretary representing the Secretary-General on current matters relating to the Force, were assisted by a group of military representatives from the countries providing contingents, sitting as an informal military advisory committee. Once the operation was firmly established, these arrangements could be and were reduced and simplified, but in the initial stage they proved to be of great value organizationally and also as an added means of maintaining close contact with contributing Governments.

183. A parallel arrangement was that by which, for a period, a personal representative of the Secretary-General was stationed in the capital of the host country as a liaison officer directly in contact with the Government.

184. In view of the great diversity likely to characterize the experience in practice of using United Nations units within the scope of this report, it is impossible to enunciate any principles for organizational arrangements at Headquarters or in the host country that should be made in anticipation of each case. There will always be developed, as a matter of course, the forms of liaison for which there will be a clear need.

185. The question, however, is of interest in this context, as it has a bearing on the problem whether or not such stand-by arrangements as those for which the principles and rules set out here would provide, would call for any kind of nucleus of military experts at United Nations Headquarters. At some stage, a standing group of a few military experts might be useful in

order to keep under review such arrangements as may be made by Governments of Member States in preparation for meeting possible appeals for an operation. I would consider it premature, however, to take any decision of this kind at the present time, since the foreseeable tasks that might evolve for the Secretariat do not go beyond what it is now able to cope with unassisted by such special measures. Were a more far-reaching understanding than I have indicated to prove possible, the matter obviously would have to be reconsidered and submitted again in appropriate form to the General Assembly, which then might consider the organizational problem. Pending such a development later, the present working rule, in my view, should be that the Secretariat, while undertaking the soundings mentioned above and the necessary continuing contacts with the Governments, should not take any measures beyond keeping the situation under constant review, so as to be able to act expeditiously, if a decision by the General Assembly or the Security Council should call for prompt action.

186. It may be reiterated in passing that the United Nations Secretariat has by now had extensive experience in establishing and maintaining United Nations operations involving military personnel and, without improvising or augmenting unduly, can quickly provide any operation of that nature with efficient communications service in the field and with Headquarters, with transportation and vehicles for local transport, with well-tested administrative and accounting systems and expert personnel to man them, and with effective procurement and security arrangements.

187. The financial obligations of Member countries to the United Nations are of two kinds. On the one hand, there are such obligations as are covered by the scale of contributions established by the General Assembly; on the other, there are certain voluntary commitments outside that scale, such as United Nations technical assistance or the United Nations Children's Fund. While, of course, contributions from individual Member nations to United Nations units for field operations may always be made on a voluntary basis, thus being lifted outside the scale of contributions, the principle must be that, as flowing from decisions of one of the main organs of the United Nations, such contributions should be subordinated to the normal financial rules. Any other principle would seriously limit the possibility of recruiting the necessary personnel from the most appropriate countries and achieving the best geographical distribution, since most countries are not likely to be in a position to assume the additional financial burdens involved and since, unless otherwise agreed, all contributing countries should be treated on the same basis.

188. In the initial stages of UNEF, Member nations assumed certain additional burdens beyond those which would follow from the application of normal rules governing contributions to the United Nations. Later, financial relations were adjusted so as to be based on full compensation for extra and extraordinary costs, financed under the normal scale of contributions. The underlying rule is that a contributing country, by such action, should not be subjected to financial sacrifices beyond those obligations which would be incurred if it were not contributing directly to the operation. On the other hand, naturally, contributing countries should not shift to the United Nations any costs which they would in any case have had to meet under their normal domestic policy.

189. I believe that, as part of the stand-by arrangements, it should be established that the costs for United Nations operations of the type in question, based on decisions of the General Assembly or the Security Council, should be allocated in accordance with the normal scale of contributions. The United Nations in this way should assume responsibility for all additional costs incurred by a contributing country because of its participation in the operation, on the basis of a cost assessment which, on the other hand, would not transfer to the United Nations any costs which would otherwise have been incurred by a contributing Government under its regular national policy.

190. With relation to the men engaged in one of its operations, the United Nations should naturally assume all responsibilities necessary to safeguard the normal interest of those so employed. Thus, they should be fully compensated by the United Nations for any losses of earning power or social benefits which may be suffered because of their service with the United Nations. In view of the great variety of regulations applied by various countries, it is

impossible to go beyond this general statement of principle; the details would have to be worked out with each contributing Government, as appropriate.

191. With relation to a host Government, it should be the rule that as the United Nations units are dispatched to the country in the interest and with the consent and co-operation of the host Government, that Government should provide all necessary facilities for the operation. This, in principle, should be done without any compensation, in cases where such facilities are in the possession of the host Government itself. Thus, for example, contributions of government services or government-owned property placed at the disposal of the United Nations for its operation should not be subject to compensation.

192. Concerning the claims of private citizens in the host country, the applicable rule is that the United Nations should pay compensation for the use of their property or services, whenever the host Government would have been obligated to pay for similar services or uses. The question whether the United Nations, in its turn, should be reimbursed by the host Government for such outlays would properly be settled through negotiation, in the light of the circumstances in each separate case.

193. The approach indicated in this chapter suggests a way in which the United Nations, within the limits of the Charter, may seek the most practical method of mustering and using, as necessary, the resources—both of nations and its own—required for operations involving military personnel which may be conceived in response to the needs of specific conflict situations. The national resources likely to be available for such purposes, if our limited experience is a gauge, are no doubt substantial, but they cannot now be calculated or even estimated, and even their availability at any particular time would probably be subject to considerable fluctuation, for political and other reasons. Formalizing the principles and rules outlined above, however, would afford a strengthened basis on which to expedite the mobilization of voluntary aid towards meeting urgent need. Their approval by the Assembly, thus clarifying and regularizing important legal and practical issues, would also ensure a more efficient use of any aid extended to the Organization, were it again to have to appeal to Member nations for such assistance.

ANNEX I

TEXT OF LETTER DATED 21 JUNE 1957 FROM THE SECRETARY-GENERAL TO THE STATES PROVIDING CONTINGENTS

1. I have the honour to refer to the resolutions of the General Assembly relating to the United Nations Emergency Force (UNEF) and particularly to resolution 1000 (ES–I) of 5 November 1956 and resolution 1001 (ES–I) of 7 November 1956. I also have the honour to refer to our previous communications concerning the national contingent provided by your Government for service with UNEF.

2. It will be recalled that the guiding principles for the organization and functioning of the Force were set out in paragraphs 6 to 9 of the 'Second and final report of the Secretary-General on the plan for an emergency international United Nations Force' (A/3302). They were approved by the General Assembly in paragraph 1 of resolution 1001 (ES–I). By paragraph 2 of the same resolution the General Assembly concurred in the definition of the functions of the Force as stated in paragraph 12 of the Secretary-General's report.

3. Paragraph 7 of resolution 1001 (ES–I) authorized the Secretary-General to issue regulations and instructions which may be essential to the effective functioning of the Force, following consultation with the Advisory Committee established by the same resolution, and to take all other necessary administrative and executive actions. Pursuant to this resolution I have, on 8 February 1957, concluded by exchange of letters an Agreement between the United Nations and the Government of Egypt concerning the status of UNEF in Egypt. On the same date I submitted a report (A/3526) on this Agreement to the General Assembly which was noted with approval by resolution 1126(XI) adopted on 22 February 1957. Following consultation with the Advisory Committee, the participating States, and the Commander of the Force, I have also issued Regulations for the United Nations Emergency Force

(ST/SGB/UNEF/1) on 20 February 1957. Copies of these documents are attached as annexes I and II respectively.[26]

4. The Regulations referred to above affirm the international character of the Force as a subsidiary organ of the General Assembly and define the conditions of service for the members of the Force. National contingents provided for UNEF serve under these Regulations.

5. The Regulations and the Agreement referred to in paragraph 3 of this letter also secure to the Force and its individual members the privileges and immunities necessary for the independent exercise of its functions. I should like to direct your attention to the provisions of the Regulations and of the Agreement which provide these privileges and immunities and particularly to article 34 of the Regulations and to paragraphs 10, 11 and 12 of my letter to the Minister of Foreign Affairs of Egypt of 8 February 1957 (A/3526). It will be noted that paragraph 11 of this letter states that 'Members of the Force shall be subject to the exclusive jurisdiction of their respective national States in respect of any criminal offences which may be committed by them in Egypt'. This immunity from the jurisdiction of Egypt is based on the understanding that the authorities of the participating States would exercise such jurisdiction as might be necessary with respect to crimes or offences committed in Egypt by any members of the Force provided from their own military services. It is assumed that the participating States will act accordingly.

I should also like to direct your attention to article 13 of the UNEF Regulations concerning 'Good order and discipline'. This article provides:

'The Commander of the UNEF shall have general responsibility for the good order of the Force. Responsibility for disciplinary action in national contingents provided for the Force rests with the commanders of the national contingents. Reports concerning disciplinary action shall be communicated to the Commander of the UNEF who may consult with the commander of the national contingent and if necessary the authorities of the Participating State concerned.'

7. In view of the considerations set out in paragraphs 5 and 6 above, I should appreciate your assurance that the commander of the national contingent provided by your Government will be in a position to exercise the necessary disciplinary authority. I should also appreciate your assurance that your Government will be prepared to exercise jurisdiction with respect to any crime or offence which might be committed by a Member of such national contingent.

8. The effective functioning of the United Nations Emergency Force requires that some continuity of service of units with the Force be ensured in order that the UNEF Commander may be in a position to plan his operations with knowledge of what units will be available. I should, therefore, appreciate your assurance that the national contingent provided by your Government will not be withdrawn without adequate prior notification to the Secretary-General, so as to avoid the impairment of the ability of the Force to discharge its functions. Likewise, should circumstances render the service of your national contingent with the Force no longer necessary, the Secretary-General undertakes to consult with your Government and to give adequate prior notification concerning its withdrawal.

9. Reference is also made to articles 11 and 12 of the UNEF Regulations which deal with 'Command authority' and 'Chain of command and delegation of authority'. Article 12 provides, *inter alia*, that changes in commanders of national contingents which have been made available by participating Governments should be made in consultation between the Commander of the United Nations Emergency Force and the appropriate authorities of the participating Government.

10. Finally, I suggest that questions involving the allocation of expenses should be dealt with, in the light of relevant resolutions of the General Assembly, in a supplemental agreement. Such other supplementary arrangements concerning the service of your national contingents with the Force may be made as occasion requires.

11. It is the intention that this letter together with your reply accepting the proposals set

---

[26] These annexes are not reproduced here.

forth herein shall constitute an agreement between the United Nations and . . ., and shall be deemed to have taken effect from the date that the national contingent provided by your Government departed from its home country to assume duties with UNEF. It is also intended that it shall remain in force until such time as your national contingent may be withdrawn from the Force either in accordance with the terms of paragraph 8 above or in the light of developments affecting the functioning of the Force which may render its service no longer necessary. The provisions of paragraph 12 relating to the settlement of disputes should remain in force until all outstanding claims have been settled.

12. It is also proposed that all disputes between the United Nations and your Government concerning the interpretation or application of this agreement which are not settled by negotiation or other agreed mode of settlement shall be referred for final settlement to a tribunal of three arbitrators. One of the arbitrators shall be appointed by the Secretary-General of the United Nations, one by your Government, and the umpire shall be chosen jointly by the Secretary-General and your Government. If the two parties fail to agree on the appointment of the umpire within one month of the proposal of arbitration by one of the parties, the President of the International Court of Justice shall be asked by either party to appoint the umpire. Should a vacancy occur for any reason, the vacancy shall be filled within thirty days by the method laid down in this paragraph for the original appointment. The tribunal shall come into existence upon the appointment of the umpire and at least one of the other members of the tribunal. Two members of the tribunal shall constitute a quorum for the performance of its functions, and for all deliberations and decisions of the tribunal a favourable vote of two members shall be sufficient.

(*Signed*) Dag HAMMARSKJÖLD

[*A/3943, Summary Study of the experience derived from the establishment and operation of the Force: report of the Secretary-General, 9 Oct. 1958.*]

The Secretary-General's final Annual Report on UNEF also contains useful information for a re-assessment of the UNEF experience as it stood in 1958 with its experience viewed after the events of May–June 1967:

4. The Force was a highly successful peace-keeping operation, but it was costly enough by United Nations standards. In the period of its existence it suffered eighty-nine fatalities and many wounded and injured, a number of these occurring in the early period of the Force as a result of encounters with mines, often in poorly mapped minefields. Its total cost to the United Nations over its ten and one half years of deployment was approximately $213 million, which was, by normal military standards, quite inexpensive for a force of UNEF's size. Its peak strength was 6,073 in March 1957; it had been reduced to 3,378 at the time of its withdrawal. This was a small cost by comparison with the human and financial consequences of a resumption of war in the area. The financial cost of the Force to the United Nations was, of course, considerably reduced by the absorption by the countries providing contingents of varying amounts of the expenses involved.

5. The sudden outbreak of war in the Near East, the severe crisis in the United Nations and the disastrous shattering of peace in the area which soon followed the withdrawal of UNEF need be mentioned only in passing in this report on UNEF's final period of service. What would probably happen whenever UNEF might be withdrawn had been pointed out by the Secretary-General in his reports on UNEF in preceding years. This likelihood was why, despite the increasing difficulties of financing the Force and his belief that no United Nations peace-keeping operation should become relatively permanent, the Secretary-General never recommended the termination of UNEF or even its conversion into a large-scale observation operation. The risk implicit in any such action had always seemed to the Secretary-General to be much too great.

6. The recent tragic events in the Near East that followed UNEF's withdrawal, however—a withdrawal which in itself was a product of deep-seated and long-continuing Arab–Israel hostility—do not obscure, but rather underscore, the achievements of UNEF as a unique

peace-keeping venture. When, in March 1957, UNEF reached the International Frontier in Sinai and the Armistice Demarcation Line in the Gaza Strip as the military forces of Israel withdraw across the line, it was deployed along what had been only four months before one of the most troubled borders anywhere in the world. With UNEF's deployment there, that line became and remained almost completely quiet. The terrorizing raids of the 'fedayeen' across that line into Israel became a thing of the past. Infiltration across the line from either side was almost ended. Fields near the line on both sides, which for long had been left uncultivated because it was near suicidal to come into view in the open fields, were now being worked right up to the line itself and on both sides of it. Costly irrigation systems were extensively installed. Heavy investments in new citrus orchards and in other cash crops were made. A new prosperity came to the area in UNEF's decade. Above all, because of UNEF's effective buffer role, there was security as there was no longer a military confrontation between the armed forces of Israel and the United Arab Republic, and clashes between those forces practically ceased.

7. In consequence, there was throughout Gaza and Sinai an unaccustomed quiet for more than ten years. This was due, very largely, if not entirely, to the presence of UNEF.

8. It is very much to the credit of UNEF, to the wisdom and tact of its successive commanders and officers, to the understanding, the fine demeanour and the discipline of its men that throughout the years of its deployment in Sinai and the Gaza Strip its relations with the local population and with the local authorities continued excellent until the last few days of its presence. This was of crucial importance because otherwise it would be impossible for a United Nations peace-keeping operation to maintain itself and to function for very long. It is inconceivable that the personnel of such a United Nations operation could be maintained if hostile relations should develop between it and the local authorities and, particularly, between it and the local population.

9. The Force, in the sense of maintaining quiet and preventing incidents, was a most effective United Nations peace-keeping operation, although others have also enjoyed great success. Like the other peace forces—the United Nations Force in Cyprus and the United Nations Operation in the Congo—UNEF was, however, an international force in only a limited sense. Its troops were provided as national contingents which retained their identity as such and were seldom broken up. The officers and men wore their national uniforms except for the distinctive United Nations headgear: the helmet, fieldcap or beret of United Nations blue, and the United Nations insignia. The personal arms they carried for self-defence only were those employed and provided by their national armed forces. Each contingent marched according to its own national custom and cadence. Each contingent had its national commanding officer who gave his orders in his national language. Each contingent had its own national dishes and dietary practices. The Force as a whole, however, was under a Commander who was an international staff member, being appointed by the Secretary-General and responsible only to him. But the Governments providing the contingents retained the right to withdraw their units at their pleasure. It is surprising, in retrospect, how seldom this authority has been exercised.

10. It is relevant to note some of the features which are peculiar to United Nations peace-keeping forces in general and to UNEF in particular, as compared with normal military operations. The essentially *ad hoc* nature of United Nations peace-keeping operations affects their nature and functioning from the very outset. In these operations none of the planning and preparation which are expected of normal military procedures can be counted upon. UNEF, for example, was called for in mid-emergency by a resolution of the General Assembly and had to be quickly established out of nothing, without the benefit even of its anticipation. The process of organizing, dispatching, concentrating and deploying the Force, not to mention its logistical support, had to be telescoped into a few days. Such a procedure inevitably gives rise to all sort of problems—organizational, administrative, and military. It particularly causes some shock at first to well-trained military men and requires a considerable adjustment on their part to very unfamiliar ways.

11. The United Nations, unlike national Governments with military establishments, has no

permanent logistical services or military establishment. The logistical basis of a peace-keeping operation is therefore an *ad hoc* emergency arrangement organized by the Field Operations Service with the assistance of Governments and various private concerns throughout the world. Furthermore, the budgetary scale of United Nations peace-keeping operations is always at the minimum level and does not allow for logistical establishments, communications, depots, etc., of the kind which normally support national armies at home or serving abroad. Under rigid budgetary limitations, therefore, and subject to constant pressures for new economies, the Field Operations Service has to provide logistical support for such operations as best it can.

12. The circumstances of the setting up of such an *ad hoc* emergency operation make it inevitable that the Commander, his staff, his contingent commanders and the national contingents meet each other for the first time in the area of operations and when already fully committed to their tasks.

13. The *ad hoc* nature of United Nations peace-keeping operations has other consequences. There can be no initial standardization of stores and equipment, which leads to serious problems of administration and maintenance later on. There are no standard operating procedures to begin with, but these are soon formulated. The standard of training and method of operation of contingents vary widely. The rotation of some contingents every six months also militates against continuity and whatever common standards may be hoped for. Although there is no difficulty in obtaining infantry units, adequately trained technical support elements are far less easily available.

14. While the Force Commander exercises operational command and control of the Force as a whole, the national contingents exercise responsibility over their men for such matters as discipline, punishment, awards and promotions. Although this never caused any serious problem in UNEF, the relationship of the Force Commander with the contingents under his command was in fact quite different from, and potentially far weaker than, the relationship of the commander of a national army with the units under his command. On the other hand, the pride of national contingents and their officers and men in being part of a United Nations Force offsets, to a very large extent, the weakness in the link of command between national and international responsibilities and produced a remarkable solidarity, *esprit de corps* and high standard of discipline in UNEF throughout its existence.

15. Despite the excellent morale of UNEF, difficulties of communication among personnel and contingents did give rise to some serious problems and misunderstandings, especially when senior military officers and staff could not communicate in one or other of the United Nations working languages.

16. The UNEF military man was faced with a concept of soldiering which is entirely foreign to anything taught him in national service. The soldier is trained basically to fight. In UNEF, however, he was ordered to avoid fighting in all circumstances, and, indeed, to seek to prevent it. Though armed, he could use force only in the last resort in self-defence. He had no enemy. Under provocation he had to show discipline and restraint; his tasks had to be carried through by persuasion, tact, example, calm and soldierly bearing, but, if humanly possible, never by force. It is an immensely encouraging fact that the soldiers of UNEF, almost without exception, were able for over ten years to live up to these unaccustomed and exacting standards and to carry out their duties with extraordinary success and with a minimum of friction.

17. There are a number of circumstances peculiar to United Nations peace-keeping forces which can, and sometimes do, create considerable problems for the Commander of a force and also for the Secretary-General. In particular, they constitute potential weaknesses in the authority of the Force Commander. For example, most contingents in a United Nations force maintain direct communications with their home countries. These are supposed to be used only for domestic and national administrative matters. When, however, as does happen, they are used for direct communication with the home Government on matters which are strictly within the authority of the Force Commander or at times even on political matters, misunderstandings and confusion are very likely to arise.

18. It may be inevitable that, for reasons usually quite unconnected with the peace-keeping

force, some contingents of a force will come to be viewed with more favour than others by the host Government. This can also give rise to embarrassment and difficulty both in the relations among the contingents of the Force and in the task of the Commander in maintaining its unity and morale and even in its proper use and deployment.

19. On the administrative side, too, there are certain potential or actual problems. The relationship of civilian and military authorities is sometimes strained even in national establishments. In UNEF and other peace-keeping operations the entire financial and logistical set-up has to be under the supervision of a civilian, normally the ranking Secretariat member who usually is the chief administrative officer, and of United Nations Headquarters in New York. The Secretary-General has the responsibility to ensure co-ordination, sound administration, economy and accounting to the Advisory Committee on Administrative and Budgetary Questions and the Fifth Committee of the General Assembly. The disbursement of United Nations funds has to be kept under United Nations control. Inevitably this distribution of functions, administrative authority and responsibilities may lead to friction between the international Secretariat element and the Military Command and staff. In particular, the stringent economies which have to be practised in United Nations operations may be, and sometimes have been interpreted by the military as arbitrary and unjustified attitudes on the part of civilians which handicap the operation, while the civilians, in their turn, may feel that the military are showing little understanding for the particular administrative and other difficulties of United Nations operations. In only one United Nations operation, however, and in that only during one brief stage, has the misunderstanding between the military and civilian branches assumed an acute form. In that single instance, the relief of the Commander sooner than had been planned proved to be the necessary and adequate remedy.

20. Another potential source of unpleasantness on the administrative side is the difference in the reimbursable allowances stipulated by Governments for their contingents. This difference in the money actually paid to individual soldiers by the United Nations, which is determined by the varying pay and allowance scales among the Governments contributing the contingents, is in some cases very striking and does not fail to have an adverse effect on the relations among the contingents of the force and on its morale. All efforts to gain acceptance of an equitable scale of allowances common to all contingents have, however, so far been unsuccessful.

21. An operation such as UNEF is not an end in itself. It is, in fact, a practical adjunct to peace-making. It becomes necessary in a conflict situation, when fighting is stopped, because cease-fires, truces and armistices are seldom self-enforcing or self-policing. Some third presence is required at least to verify and report the breaches. The true function of a peace-keeping effort is to create a climate of quiet which is more congenial to efforts to solve the underlying problems that lead to conflict. It may achieve this better climate in a number of ways, such as averting military confrontations by acting as a buffer through patrolling and policing activities, and through providing an added assurance by its very presence. It is not an enforcement agent and can expect to exercise at best only a very limited degree of authority; an authority, moreover, which, unless explicitly defined in its mandate and the consequent agreements with the host country, automatically and instantly vanishes once it is challenged by the host Government.

22. It is only realistic to accept the fact that when a United Nations peace-keeping operation, whether it may be an observation mission or a peace force, is no longer welcome in a country and co-operation with it is withheld, it cannot hope to continue to perform any useful function, may well soon find itself defenceless and in grave danger, and thus had best be withdrawn as amicably as the prevailing circumstances will permit. If there should be serious doubt about the wisdom of this latter course, it would be advisable to abandon altogether the notion of a voluntary peace-keeping operation and turn to consideration of enforcement-type actions under Chapter VII of the Charter. The two cannot be mixed. It should be added, however, that it is extremely doubtful that any of the peace-keeping operations thus far mounted by the United Nations would have been acceptable to the Governments of the countries in which they have been stationed if they had been originally envisaged in the con-

text of Chapter VII of the Charter. There is no room at all for doubt about this as regards UNEF.

23. Some fundamental principles clearly applicable to any United Nations peace force have been forged in the long experience of UNEF. Such an operation is entirely voluntary: the full consent of the host country and any other parties directly concerned is the indispensable pre-condition for the stationing of the force. The contingents comprising the force are voluntarily provided by the Governments of Member States, subject to conditions of service and finance mutually agreed upon by the Governments and the United Nations. There must be a will on the part of the parties themselves for quiet in the area together with a recognition of the need for international assistance to this end, which is expressed in the extension of a reasonable degree of co-operation to the operation in the performance of its functions. The force must be always exclusively under United Nations command and neither the force as a whole nor any of its components shall take instructions from the host Government, from any other party directly concerned, or from a Government providing a contingent. The force must have assurance, by means of a formal agreement, of the rights, privileges and immunities essential to its effective functioning, such as freedom of movement on land and in the air and exemption from customs duties for its equipment and supplies.

24. United Nations experience with such operations, and this was notably so in the case of UNEF, indicates that the success of a peace-keeping operation may, in itself, induce a false sense of security. The ability of the operation to re-establish and maintain quiet for an extended period may come to be mistaken for a solution of the basic problem. This can only increase the sense of shock when, ultimately and inexorably, it is demonstrated that problems of conflict may lie dormant even for long periods but they do not necessarily solve themselves by the passage of time, and the day may come when they will explode anew. Peace-keeping operations can serve their purpose properly only if they are accompanied by serious and persistent efforts to find solutions to the problems which demanded the peace-keeping in the first place.

25. It merits emphasis that United Nations peace-keeping operations function within the wider framework of the United Nations as a whole. Many of the frustrations, the cross-currents, the pressures and particularly the political stresses of the Organization inevitably have a major impact on the original setting-up of a peace-keeping operation and on its day-to-day functioning as well. The present limitations of the United Nations in a world still dominated by rigid concepts of national sovereignty, by power politics and by acute nationalistic sentiments are also the inherent limitations of United Nations peace-keeping operations.

26. The recognition of the existence of these limitations should not lead to a passive acceptance of a situation which needs to be remedied. The Secretary-General interprets the shock and dismay produced by the withdrawal of UNEF and the renewed fighting in the Middle East as an expression of how much reliance, especially on the part of those directly concerned, had come to be placed upon the United Nations as an instrument for the maintenance of peace in some areas of the world. Clearly, an important lesson to be gained from this sobering experience is that the peace-keeping function of the United Nations should be strengthened so as better to serve the cause of world peace.

27. Before concluding these observations, the Secretary-General wishes once again to pay tribute to the Governments which have provided contingents for UNEF—those of Brazil, Canada, Denmark, India, Norway, Sweden and Yugoslavia, which provided contingents throughout the existence of the Force—and also those of Colombia, Finland and Indonesia which responded promptly to the initial requirement for troops for UNEF and whose contingents served in the early months of the Force. In taking part in such a novel operation, these Governments willingly accepted the risks and uncertainties as well as the varying financial burdens involved and showed in a most practical manner their support of a pioneering effort of the United Nations towards keeping the peace. The Secretary-General would also wish to express his admiration and gratitude to the many thousands of officers and men from these ten countries, without whose discipline, understanding and exemplary bearing UNEF's success would have been impossible. In addition, he wishes to express appreciation to those

Governments which, throughout the years, gave the financial and other support to UNEF which allowed it to continue its most valuable function for a far longer period of time than was originally foreseen.   [*A/6672, Secretary-General's Final Report on UNEF, 12 July 1967.* mimeo.]

13

ANNEXES

A. Checklist of Documents

1. *Meetings of the Security Council*
   SCOR 11th yr, mtgs 734–45, 748–51, 778–82. *SCOR* 21st yr mtgs

2. *Security Council Documents relating to nationalization of Suez Canal*

S/3645	12 Sept. 1956	S/3674	13 Oct. 1956
S/3649	15 Sept. 1956	S/3679	15 Oct. 1956
S/3650	17 Sept. 1956	S/3680	1 Oct. 1956
S/3654	24 Sept. 1956	S/3683	17 Oct. 1956
S/3656	24 Sept. 1956	S/3706	30 Oct. 1956
S/3665	5 Oct. 1956	S/3707	30 Oct. 1956
S/3668	8 Oct. 1956	S/3712	30 Oct. 1956
S/3666	5 Oct. 1956	S/3720	31 Oct. 1956
S/3671	13 Oct. 1956	S/3728	3 Nov. 1956
S/3673	13 Oct. 1956		

3. *General Assembly Resolutions relating to UNEF*

997 (ES–I)	1 Nov. 1956	1263 (XIII)	14 Nov. 1958
998 (ES–I)	4 Nov. 1956	1337 (XIII)	13 Dec. 1958
999 (ES–I)	4 Nov. 1956	1441 (XIV)	5 Dec. 1959
1000 (ES–I)	5 Nov. 1956	1442 (XIV)	5 Dec. 1959
1001 (ES–I)	7 Nov. 1956	1575 (XV)	20 Dec. 1959
1002 (ES–I)	7 Nov. 1956	1733 (XVI)	20 Dec. 1961
1003 (ES–I)	10 Nov. 1956	1854B (XVII)	19 Dec. 1961
1121 (XI)	24 Nov. 1956	1877 (S–IV)	27 June 1963
1122 (XI)	26 Nov. 1956	1875 (S–IV)	27 June 1963
1124 (XI)	2 Feb. 1957	1983 (XVIII)	17 Dec. 1963
1125 (XI)	2 Feb. 1957	2115 (XX)	21 Dec. 1965
1181 (XII)	22 Nov. 1957	2194 (XXI)	16 Dec. 1966
1204 (XII)	13 Dec. 1957		

4. *Meetings of the General Assembly (GAOR)*
   1st Emerg. Spec. sess., plen. mtgs 561–3, 565, 567, 572
   11th and 12th sessions
   13th sess. Spec. Political Cttee, mtgs 96–100; 5th Cttee mtgs 697–699, 705; plen. mtgs 780, 790
   14th sess. 5th Cttee, mtgs 749–753, 759; mtgs 846
   15th sess. 5th Cttee, mtgs 721–2, plen. 824; plen. mtg 960
   16th sess. 5th Cttee, mtgs 899, 901, 903, 905, 909; plen. mtg 1086

17th sess. 5th Cttee, mtgs 979, 982, 983; plen. mtg 1201
18th sess. 5th Cttee, mtgs 1052, 1053, 1055–8, 1060; plen. mtgs 1284–5
20th sess. 5th Cttee, mtgs 1112–3, 1116–7; plen. mtg 1407
5th Emerg. Spec. sess., plen. mtgs 1529, 1538, 1541, 1542, 1544–9

5. *Reports of the Secretary-General*

A/3267 3 Nov. 1956	Rep. under res. 997 (ES–I)
A/3284 4 Nov. 1956	Rep. under res. 997 (ES–I)
A/3289 4 Nov. 1956	1st Rep. on an emergency international Force
A/3296 5 Nov. 1956	Rep. under res. 997 (ES–I)
A/3302 & Add. 1–6 6 Nov. 1956	2nd & final rep. on an emergency international Force
A/3375 20 Nov. 1956	Rep. on presence and functioning of UNEF
A/3376 20 Nov. 1956	Rep. on clearance of Suez Canal
A/3392 24 Nov. 1956	Note on appointment of representative
A/3492 10 Jan. 1957	Second rep. on clearance of Suez Canal
A/3500 & Add. 1 15 Jan. 1957	Rep. on compliance with resolutions
A/3512 24 Jan. 1957	Rep. in pursuance of res. 1123 (XI)
A/3526 8 Feb. 1957	Rep. on status of UNEF
A/3568 8 Mar. 1957	2nd Rep. in pursuance of res. 1124 (XI) & 1125 (XI)
A/3694 & Add. 1 9 Oct. 1957	Rep. on UNEF
A/3745 17 Nov. 1957	Note by Secretary-General
A/3899 27 Aug. 1957	Rep. on UNEF
A/3943 9 Oct. 1958	Summary Study of the experience derived from UNEF
A/4176 & Adds. 1 & 2 10 Sept. 1957	Rep. on the manner of financing UNEF
A/4486 & Adds. 1 & 2 13 Sept. 1960	Rep. on UNEF
A/4857 30 Aug. 1961	Rep. on UNEF
A/5172 22 Aug. 1962	Rep. on UNEF
A/5494 12 Sept. 1963	Rep. on UNEF
A/C.5/1001 2 Sept. 1963	Rep. on redefining &c. UNEF's functions
A/5494 12 Sept. 1963	Rep. on UNEF
A/5736 29 Sept. 1964	Rep. on UNEF
A/5919 22 Sept. 1965	Rep. on UNEF
A/C.5/1049 13 Dec. 1965	Rep. on Survey of UNEF's functions
S/7896 19 May 1967	Rep.. on situation in the Near East
S/9906 26 May 1967	S–G's Rep. on reasons for UNEF's withdrawal
A/6672 12 July 1967	S–G's Annual Rep. on UNEF
A/6730/Add. 3 26 June 1967	S.-G's Rep. on the withdrawal of UNEF

6. *Financial Aspects: Reports of 5th Committee, Advisory Committee on Administrative and Budgetary Questions, and Cost Estimates*

A/3402	30 Nov. 1956	A/4002	19 Oct. 1958
A/3415	3 Dec. 1956	A/4072	11 Dec. 1958
A/3456	14 Dec. 1956	A/4160	23 July 1959
A/3560 & Add. 1	25 Feb. 1957	A/4176	10 Sept. 1959
A/3761	3 Dec. 1957	A/4284	17 Nov. 1959
A/3790	12 Dec. 1957	A/4335	4 Dec. 1959
A/3823	Suppl. 5A, 1958	A/4396	8 July 1960
A/3826	Suppl. 6, 1958	A/4409	21 July 1960

A/3839	3 July 1958	A/4674	19 Dec. 1960
A/4688	Suppl. 5B, 1961	A/6060	22 Oct. 1965
A/4786	13 July 1961	A/6171	15 Dec. 1965
A/4812	24 July 1961	A/6217	20 Dec. 1965
A/5065	19 Dec. 1961	A/6588	14 Dec. 1966
A/5187	13 Sept. 1962	A/6497	3 Nov. 1966
A/5274	2 Nov. 1962	A/6498	3 Nov. 1966
A/5495	16 Sept. 1963	A/6542	2 Dec. 1966
A/6737	3 Mar. 1965	ST/SGB/UNEF 2	
A/6059	22 Oct. 1965		

7. *Correspondence between the parties and the Secretary-General relating to the cease-fire and withdrawal of foreign troops*

A/3268	3 Nov. 1956	A/3305	6 Nov. 1956
A/3279	4 Nov. 1956	A/3306	6 Nov. 1956
A/3291	5 Nov. 1956	A/3307	6 Nov. 1956
A/3293	5 Nov. 1956	A/3310	7 Nov. 1956
A/3294	5 Nov. 1956	A/3313	7 Nov. 1956
A/3297	5 Nov. 1956	A/3414	7 Nov. 1956

8. *Status of UNEF*
ST/SGB/UNEF 1.
A/3302, Annex. 'Good faith' accord.

9. *Decision of UAR to terminate consent to UNEF's presence*

9. S/7896 and Corr. 1.   Rep. on situation in the Near East
           19 May 1967

B. Bibliography

Azeau, H. *Le piège de Suez*. Paris, 1964.

Benton, W. H. Who will pay for peace: the UN crisis. *J. Canadian Inst. of Int. Affairs*, Apr. 1965.

Baxter, Richard. *The Law of International Waterways*. Cambridge, Mass., 1964.

Bloomfield, Louis. *Egypt, Israel and the Gulf of Aqaba in International Law*. Toronto, 1957.

Bowett, D. W. *United Nations Forces*. London, 1964.

Burns, A. L. and Hathcote, Nina. *Peacekeeping by United Nations Forces*. London, 1963.

Burns, E. L. *Between Arab and Israeli*. London, 1962.

Cohen, Maxwell. The United Nations Emergency Force: a preliminary view. 12 *Int. J.*, Spring 1957.

Dayan, Moshe. *Diary of the Sinai Campaign*. London, 1966.

Dinitz, Y. The legal aspects of the Egyptian blockade of the Suez canal. 45 *Georgetown Law R.*, 1956–7.

Draper, G. I. A. D. United Nations forces: (1) UNEF. *R. de droit pénal militaire et de droit de la guerre*, v/1, 1966.

Epstein, Leon David. *British Politics in the Suez Crisis.* Urbana, Ill., 1964.

Goodrich, L., and Rosner, Gabriella. The United Nations Emergency Force. 11 *Int. Org.*, 1967.

Gross, Leo. Expenses of the United Nations peacekeeping operations; the Advisory Opinion of the International Court of Justice. *Int. Org.*, Winter 1963.

—— Passage through the Suez canal of Israel-bound cargo and Israel ships. 51 *AJIL*, 1957.

Hammad, B. The right of passage in the Gulf of Aqaba. 15 *R. égyptienne de droit international*, 1959.

el-Hefnaoui, Moustapha. *Les problèmes contemporains posés par le canal de Suez.* Paris, 1951.

Higgins, Rosalyn. The June War: the United Nations and legal background. *J. Contemp. History*, 1968.

—— United Nations peacekeeping; political and financial problems. *World Today*, Aug. 1965.

Hogg, J. F. Peacekeeping costs and Charter obligations; implications of the ICJ decision. *Columbia Law R.*, 1962.

Jackson, J. H. The legal framework of United Nations financing: peacekeeping and penury. 51 *Calif. Law R.*, 1962.

Jennings, R. Y. International Court of Justice: Advisory Opinion of 20 July 1962: certain expenses of the United Nations (Art. 17 (2)). 11 *ICLQ*, 1962.

Lauterpacht, Eli. *The United Nations Emergency Force: basic documents.* London, 1960.

Moncrieff, Anthony, ed. *Suez Ten Years After; Broadcasts from the BBC Third Programme [by] Peter Calvocoressi [and others].* London, BBC, 1967.

Nutting, Anthony. *No End of a Lesson.* London, 1967.

Poirier, Pierre. *La force internationale d'urgence.* Paris, 1962.

Robertson, T. *Crisis.* London, 1965.

Rosner, Gabriella. *The United Nations Emergency Force.* New York, 1963.

Sayegh, Fayez. The status of the Strait of Tiran. 10 *Middle East Econ. Survey*, 2 June 1967.

Selak, C. B. A consideration of the status of the Gulf of Aqaba. 52 *AJIL*, 1958.

Seyersted, F. *United Nations Forces in the Law of Peace and War.* Leyden, 1967.

Singer, J. D. *Financing International Organizations: the UN Budget Process.* The Hague, 1961.

Stoessinger, J. G. *Financing the United Nations System.* Washington, 1964.

Thomas, Hugh. *The Suez Affair.* London, 1967.

Part 3

THE UNITED NATIONS
OBSERVER GROUP IN LEBANON (UNOGIL),
1958

1. INTRODUCTION (p. 535)
PRESIDENT CHAMOUN seeks a second term of office and claims that the UAR is actively supporting the revolt in Lebanon; the Security Council meets, and the UN Observation Group
in Lebanon (UNOGIL) is established; fighting breaks out again in mid-June 1958; UNOGIL
denies major infiltration from the UAR; a military coup in Iraq; Lebanon and Jordan obtain
military aid from the United States and the United Kingdom; the Security Council recon-
venes; the matter is transferred to the Assembly; the evolution of an 'Arab solution'; the
role of Hammarskjöld and UNOGIL.

2. ENABLING RESOLUTION AND VOTING (p. 546)
Swedish resolution of 11 June 1958 and voting thereon.

3. FUNCTIONS AND MANDATE (p. 547)
UNOGIL's initial role in observing illegal traffic in arms and personnel; and, later, in facilitating the withdrawal of United States troops.

4. CONSTITUTIONAL BASIS (p. 549)
Subsidiary organ of the Security Council; constitutional limits to the authority of the Secretary-General; the enlargement of UNOGIL.

5. POLITICAL CONTROL (p. 551)
Relationship between the Security Council and the Secretary-General; the 3-man executive
authority in the field; and its liaison with observers.

6. ADMINISTRATIVE AND MILITARY CONTROL (p. 553)
Headquarters arrangements; Chief Military Observer and his Deputy Chief of Staff.

7. COMPOSITION AND SIZE (p. 555)
Twenty countries represented; numbers of UNOGIL; ground and air observers; a further
build-up.

8. RELATIONS WITH CONTRIBUTING STATES (p. 558)
Absence of formal agreements on major practical problems.

9. RELATIONS WITH THE HOST STATES (p. 558)
The request of the host state; non-intervention in internal affairs; freedom of movement;
exchange of letters concerning status of UNOGIL.

10. RELATIONS WITH OTHER STATES INVOLVED (p. 565)
Positions of the other Arab nations; the United States; the United Kingdom.

II. FINANCE (p. 566)
General Assembly resolution 1237 ES–II; expenses raised on the regular budget; increased allocations.

12. IMPLEMENTATION (p. 568)
Observation and reporting; contribution to improving relations sufficiently for the withdrawal of foreign troops; UNOGIL's first report and the Lebanese response; 2nd reports on particular regions; 3rd, 4th, and final reports; detailed arrangements for the withdrawal of American and British troops; the withdrawal of UNOGIL; special arrangements for Jordan.

13. ANNEXES (p. 602)
  A. Checklist of Documents (p. 602)
  B. Bibliography (p. 603)

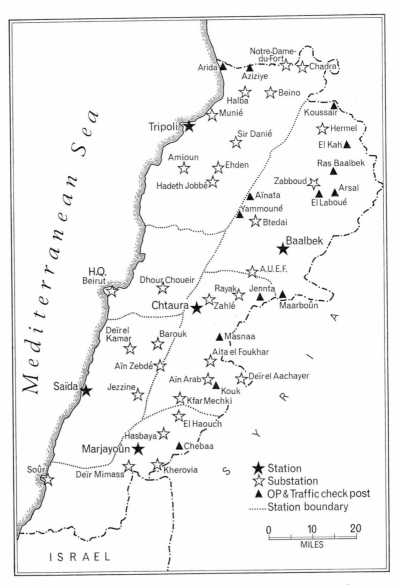

3. Operations of the UN Observation Group in Lebanon, 1958

Based on S/4040/Add.1, ann. III.

I

INTRODUCTION

THE clear establishment in the developing countries of nationalism as a genuine force, and the degree of understanding which has been achieved in the last few years over limits to Big Power interventions in the Middle East, makes it difficult to recall accurately the political assumptions of 1958. Yet the crisis in Lebanon (and the related events in Jordan and Iraq) which took place in the summer of 1958 occurred at a time when the ability of Arab nationalism to retain an identity distinct from those Communists who supported it was still in doubt; when the United States still believed in the necessity of 'filling the vacuum' in the Middle East; and when a direct Soviet military response in that region was by no means to be ruled out.

UNOGIL covered two phases of that turbulent summer, and its role changed accordingly. It was initially established, as we shall see, to observe to what extent the United Arab Republic was giving material support to rebels in Lebanon; later in the year, while continuing with this task, it became a UN body whose very presence would permit the otherwise impossible withdrawal of foreign powers who had become embroiled in the situation. We here seek to provide the background to both these phases.

In February of 1958 Egypt and Syria united, forming the United Arab Republic. By way of response, in mid-February Jordan and Iraq decided to form a federation, with the two nations as equal partners, but with King Faisal of Iraq as head of the federation. Cairo indicated in various ways its disapproval of this federation. In the spring, considerable disturbances occurred in the Lebanon, occasioned in large part by the intention of President Chamoun to alter the constitution so as to permit himself an otherwise unconstitutional second term in office. The government of President Chamoun was pro-Western and unacceptable to Cairo for many reasons, including its failure to break relations with Britain and France during the Suez crisis of 1956, and its acceptance of the 'Eisenhower Doctrine' on the Middle East.[1] When widespread revolt broke out in May 1958, President Chamoun declared that he had evidence of 'massive infiltration' from Syria, and that the rebellion was being fomented from outside by the UAR. The Lebanese army was quite small, and its Chief of Staff, General Chehab, was evidently reluctant for it to

---

[1] This 'doctrine', approved by Congress in January 1957, authorized the US to co-operate with any nation in the Middle East in economic development needed to maintain national independence, and to provide military assistance, when requested, against aggression emanating from any Communist-controlled nation. For the political and diplomatic history of the evolution of this doctrine, see Dwight Eisenhower, *The White House Years; Waging Peace* (1965), pp. 176–83.

be used for overt confrontation with the rebels, fearing that those soldiers who were Moslem would be sympathetic to pan-Arab Mohammedanism seeking the overthrow of Chamoun's Christian government.[2]

Chamoun appears to have inquired of the United States in early May if help would be forthcoming if requested, and Eisenhower apparently replied sympathetically, though laying down the conditions that there must be the concurrence of another Arab nation and that United States troops were not to be used to secure Chamoun a second term of office.[3] In fact, at this stage Chamoun made no formal request for aid to the United States; instead, on 22 May, he requested a meeting of the Security Council to consider his complaint that the UAR was instigating a rebellion in Lebanon (S/4007). The meeting was actually convened on 6 June 1958, after the Arab League, before whom Lebanon had put her complaint, had met for six days, without reaching agreement. Dr Malik, Lebanon's Foreign Minister, flew to New York for the debate.

The essence of Dr Malik's case before the UN was as follows:

11. The case which we have brought to the attention of the Security Council consists of three claims. The first is that there has been, and there still is, massive, illegal and unprovoked intervention in the affairs of Lebanon by the United Arab Republic. The second is that this intervention aims at undermining, and does in fact threaten, the independence of Lebanon. The third is that the situation created by this intervention which threatens the independence of Lebanon, is likely, if continued, to endanger the maintenance of international peace and security. I now proceed to the proof of these three claims.

12. The actuality of the intervention is proven by adducing six sets of facts concerning:

(a) The supply of arms on a large scale from the United Arab Republic to subversive elements in Lebanon;

(b) The training in subversion on the territory of the United Arab Republic of elements from Lebanon and the sending back of these elements to Lebanon to subvert their Government;

(c) The participation of United Arab Republic civilian nationals residing in or passing into Lebanon in subversive and terrorist activities in Lebanon;

(d) The participation of United Arab Republic governmental elements in subversive and terrorist activities and in the direction of rebellion in Lebanon;

(e) The violent and utterly unprecedented press campaign conducted by the United Arab Republic against the Government of Lebanon;

(f) The violent and utterly unprecedented radio campaign conducted by the United Arab Republic inciting the people of Lebanon to overthrow their Government. [SCOR, 13th yr, 824th mtg, pp. 3–4.]

He then offered various items of evidence to support these charges. Of the validity of charges (e) and (f) there was no doubt. The UAR however, categorically denied the charges listed under (a), (b), (c) and (d) above. Her representative, Mr Omar Loutfi, noted that virtually all the Lebanese claims were based on reports by the Lebanese police or *Deuxième Bureau*, and these he dismissed

[2] The motives ascribed to Gen. Chebab differ, varying from determination to preserve the unity of his army; to indecision; to opportunistic caution in waiting to see whether the President or the rebels would gain the upper hand. Cf. Eisenhower, pp. 265–6; C. W. Thayer, *Diplomat* (1960), pp. 54–87; and Robert Murphy, *Diplomat among Warriors* (1964), pp. 394–419.

[3] Eisenhower, p. 267. Though the United States greatly approved of Chamoun, she was considerably less enthusiastic about his anticipated attempt to alter the constitution in his own favour (ibid. p. 265); Murphy, pp. 407–8.

as of no probative value. How far the United States actually believed Lebanon's claims—other than the undeniable ones of hostile press and radio propaganda—is not entirely clear; the evidence is conflicting.[4]

The Security Council met again on 10 June, when a further series of accusations and denials took place between Dr Malik and Mr Loutfi. The Lebanese case was supported by Iraq, whose representatives spoke of the problems which 'Nasserism' was causing to Iraq, Lebanon and Jordan.[5] The United Kingdom representative indicated 'that my delegation considers that the Foreign Minister of Lebanon has fully made out and substantiated his contention that Lebanon had suffered, and is suffering, interference from the United Arab Republic by infiltrations of armed men, smuggling of arms, attack on frontier posts, incitements to revolt and other subversive methods'.[6] The French representative also felt that 'the very detailed factual information which [Dr Malik] cited in support of his complaint constitutes a significant, specific and convincing body of evidence'.[7]

The Soviet Union on the other hand, categorically supported the position of the UAR. She accused Lebanese leaders of 'speaking for the Western Powers'; of betraying Arab nationalism by supporting the Eisenhower Doctrine in the Middle East; and of causing a threat to the peace by preparing to invite intervention by the United Kingdom and the United States in what was purely an internal quarrel.[8] The smaller nations on the Security Council refrained from supporting either the Lebanon or the UAR, seeking only to find a solution acceptable to all parties. To that end, Sweden introduced a draft resolution (S/4022) authorizing a UN observation group to proceed to the Lebanon to ensure that there was no illegal infiltration across her borders. This resolution was adopted by 10 votes to 0, with the USSR abstaining.[9]

Thus UNOGIL was established. Until mid-June the situation was quieter, but on 14 June the rebels—who had been encircled in Basra—broke out from behind their barricades and fighting was renewed. Civil disorder in the Lebanon increased again. Hammarskjöld himself arrived in the Lebanon on 18 June, and an undeclared forty-eight-hour truce began. On 3 July 1958 UNOGIL submitted a report to the Security Council[10] which found that there was no major infiltration occurring from the United Arab Republic. This report was strongly criticized by President Chamoun's government;[11] and it is also fair to say that there was fairly widespread scepticism—among Western countries at least—of the ability of UNOGIL to ascertain the necessary information on which to base its report.[12] It now appears that during June President Chamoun several times endeavoured, unsuccessfully, to secure American intervention.[13] Interestingly, it was at this time that President Chamoun announced publicly, for

---

[4] Thayer speaks of the United States as being 'sceptical of the "massive infiltrations" claimed by Malik' (p. 75); while Eisenhower asserts, 'There was no doubt in our minds of the truth of the charge' (p. 267).
[5] *SCOR*, 13th yr, 824th mtg, pp. 35–44.   [6] Ibid. p. 50.   [7] Ibid. p. 45.
[8] Ibid. pp. 26–35.   [9] See below, pp. 546–7 and pp. 564–5.   [10] S/4040 and Corr. 1.
[11] S/4043; *SCOR*, 13th yr, 827th mtg, pp. 14–15, and below, pp. 572–5.
[12] Below, pp. 573–5.   [13] Thayer, p. 76.

the first time that he would leave office when his term expired on 23 September, and that he would not seek a second term under a revised constitution. The civil war now quietened down and 'in early July it appeared that the Lebanon crisis would pass without Western military assistance'.[14]

Developments from an unexpected quarter were to prevent this. On 14 July 1958 there was a military coup in Iraq. King Faisal and the Prime Minister Nuri es Said, both pro-Western, were murdered and a republic was proclaimed. The coup, led by Brigadier-General Kassim, was violent and brutal. There was a widespread belief at the time that Kassim was pro-Nasser, and Chamoun greatly feared that his success would further encourage the Moslem rebels in the Lebanon. At the same time, King Hussein's throne in Jordan was reported to be in danger. The king declared that the Jordan–Iraq Union still stood, and that, with King Faisal dead, he was now the head of the Union.[15] President Chamoun requested intervention by the United States, and Jordan requested intervention by the United Kingdom. Both requests were this time granted.[16] The United States and the United Kingdom each declared that they were acting under Article 51 of the UN Charter—helping a legitimate government, at its own request, to defend its country against external aggression. The other Arab states and the Soviet Union took the position that the situations existing in Iraq, Jordan, and the Lebanon revealed civil war, and civil war only; that this view had been upheld, so far as the Lebanon was concerned, by UNOGIL's first report; that no outside state could legitimately intervene; and that collective self-defence under Article 51 was only permitted until the Security Council could act—which it had already done by sending UNOGIL to Lebanon.[17]

On 15 July a meeting of the Security Council was convened. There was some initial confusion over the credentials of the representatives of Iraq, due to the fact that King Hussein, declaring himself the new head of the Jordan–Iraq Union, had confirmed the appointment of King Faisal's representative at the UN; while the new Foreign Secretary in Kassim's government had issued

---

[14] Eisenhower, p. 269.

[15] Art. 5 of the constitution, on which Hussein based his claim, stated: 'The King of Iraq shall be the Head of the Union, and, in his absence, the King of Jordan shall be Head.'

[16] The position of the US troops, in political terms, in Lebanon is interesting. Eisenhower issued a directive—over the recommendations of his military—that American troops should occupy only Beirut and the airport, for: 'If the Lebanese army were unable to subdue the rebels when we had secured their capital and protected their government, I felt, we were backing a government with so little popular support that we probably should not be there'(p. 275, n. 8). Eisenhower also observes 'the Lebanese along the beaches welcomed our troops' (p. 275), whereas an eye-witness from the US Embassy writes, 'The bathers on the beach watched silently and sullenly' (Thayer, p. 81). It was the reaction of the Lebanese army that was most in doubt, and ingenious means had hastily to be devised—sometimes in the face of the insensitivity of the US military—of assuaging their fears that the US Marines were an 'invading' force (Thayer, pp. 81–87).

[17] It is our purpose here merely to report the positions taken, and not to analyse the merits thereof: see however, Higgins, 'Legal Limits to the Use of Force by Sovereign States: UN Practice', 37 *BYIL* (1961), pp. 293–4, 304–5; and Pitman Potter, 'Legal Aspects of the Beirut Landing', 52 *AJIL* (1958), pp. 727–30.

credentials to a new representative.[18] Eventually, however, the Security Council began its debate. Ambassador Lodge of the United States said that although UNOGIL had helped to reduce interference across the border, arms and personnel were being infiltrated into the Lebanon at a greatly increased rate since the revolution in Iraq. He emphasized that the United States regarded her action as complementary to the work of UNOGIL, and would withdraw her forces as soon as the UN could effectively guarantee Lebanon's independence.[19] The Soviet Union, on the other hand, introduced a resolution (S/4047) which would have condemned the United States action as contrary to Article 2 (7) of the Charter, and as a serious threat to international peace, and which would call for the immediate withdrawal of American troops from the Lebanon. While the Security Council was still debating the question, a new Interim Report was cabled from UNOGIL, stating that it had met with success in negotiations for inspection all along the Lebanese border. The report also suggested that UNOGIL's size should be considerably increased. The United States introduced her own draft resolution (S/4050) which, while commending the work of UNOGIL, would also require

. . . the Secretary-General immediately to consult the Government of Lebanon and the Member States as appropriate with a view to making such additional arrangements, including the contribution and use of contingents as may be necessary to protect the territorial integrity and independence of Lebanon and to ensure that there is no illegal infiltration of personnel or supply of arms or other material across the Lebanese borders.

The Soviet representative opposed this on the grounds that the United States draft resolution, though commending UNOGIL, ignored its findings—namely, that no major infiltration was occurring. France thought that UNOGIL's own interim report made it clear that only in the last few days had it been able to carry out its tasks. Japan, announcing that she would vote for the American resolutions, did so with 'certain misgivings concerning the circumstances which have made the landing of the Marines necessary' and believing that 'the first operative paragraph of the United States draft resolution appears somehow not quite consonant with the report of the United Nations Observer Group in Lebanon'.[20] These misgivings were stated even more forcefully by the Japanese representative a day later.

So far the debate had proceeded much as expected. There was some surprise, however, when the Swedish representative suggested the activities of UNOGIL be suspended until further notice. The Swedish government rejected the United States argument that her troops were in the Lebanon under the terms of Article 51 of the Charter (i.e. providing collective self-defence); and thought

---

[18] Several fascinating legal problems were involved, though they are beyond the scope of this book. See *SCOR*, 13th yr, 827th and 834th mtgs and Higgins, *The Development of International Law through the Political Organs of the United Nations* (1963), pp. 159–61.

[19] *SCOR*, 13th yr, 827th mtg, pp. 6–11. This suggestion was repudiated by UNOGIL itself: *SCOR*, 13th yr, suppl. for July–Sept. 1958, S/4085, para. 4.

[20] *SCOR*, 13th yr, 829th mtg, p. 14, paras 67 and 68.

18*

that the United States presence made it impossible for UNOGIL to carry out the tasks assigned to it (S/4054).[21]

The next day—17 July 1958—the Security Council had an additional item on its agenda: a complaint by Jordan of interference in her domestic affairs by the UAR (S/4053); and with this came the news that the United Kingdom had sent troops to Jordan at King Hussein's request, to forestall an attempted coup. The arguments now heard ran closely parallel to those concerning the Lebanon; the United Kingdom asserted that she was helping Jordan to face an external threat;[22] while the Soviet Union and the UAR claimed that King Hussein faced no threat save his own discontented people, and that outside Powers had no right to intervene in a domestic quarrel.[23] The Soviet Union now revised her draft resolution to include a demand for the withdrawal of United Kingdom troops from Jordan.[24]

The debate was still in progress, and the draft resolutions still had to be voted upon, when the Second Interim Report of UNOGIL was published (S/4052). Once again the Lebanese delegate felt obliged to point out that the report was based on information which was very limited in certain particular respects.[25]

The voting on the draft resolutions was as follows:

(1) *Soviet Draft Resolution* (S/4047/rev.1)
> *For:* USSR
> *Against:* Canada, China, Colombia, France, Iraq, Panama, UK, USA
> *Abstaining:* Japan, Sweden.
>> *Rejected:* 1–8–2.

(2) *USA Draft Resolution* (S/4050/rev. 1)
> *For:* Canada, China, Colombia, France, Iraq, Japan, Panama, UK, USA
> *Against:* USSR
> *Abstaining:* Sweden.
>> *Rejected:* 9–1–1.
>> (The negative vote being that of a Permanent Member.)

(3) *Swedish Draft Resolution* (S/4054)
> *For:* Sweden, USSR
> *Against:* Canada, China, Colombia, France, Iraq, Japan, Panama, UK, USA.
>> *Rejected:* 2–9–0.

No draft having been adopted, a compromise resolution was now introduced by Japan[26] which, instead of asking the Secretary-General to create a police force in Lebanon, requested him in general terms 'to make the necessary

[21] Ibid. 830th mtg, p. 9, para. 48. The Editor, who was in the Council chamber at the time, remembers the widespread speculation that this suggestion was in fact a trial balloon floated at the request of the Secretary-General. However, this rumour took account neither of the fact that Hammarskjöld had already stated that he hoped UNOGIL would 'retain its key position' (829th mtg, p. 2), nor that the views of the Swedish government were on no account to be assumed necessarily to be those of its national who held the high office of Secretary-General.

[22] Harold Macmillan the Prime Minister stated that the request from Jordan had been received a few moments after the House of Commons had concluded its heated debate on the Near Eastern situation. It was thus, he said, not possible to consult parliament on the urgent decision to send troops to Jordan. According to Eisenhower, however, Macmillan told him that he had received a request from Hussein on July 14—some two days earlier (Eisenhower, p. 273).

[23] *SCOR* 13th yr, 831st mtg.   [24] S/4047/Rev. 1.   [25] *SCOR*, 13th yr, 833rd mtg, pp. 2–8.
[26] Ibid. 835 mtg, 21 July 1958.

arrangements which will enable the United Nations to fulfil the general purposes established in the resolution of 11 June 1958'.[27] This, too, was rejected by the Soviet veto; and Soviet amendments to the Japanese resolution were also not adopted:

(4) *Japanese Draft Resolution* (S/4055/rev. 1):
> *For:* Canada, China, Colombia, France, Iraq, Japan, Sweden, UK, USA.
> *Against:* USSR.
>> *Rejected:* 10–1–0.
>> (The negative vote being that of a Permanent Member.)

(5) *USSR Amendments* (S/4063)
> *For:* USSR
> *Against:* Canada, China, Colombia, France, Iraq, Panama, UK, USA
> *Abstaining:* Japan, Sweden.
>> *Rejected:* 1–8–2.

The Soviet Union and the United States both proposed now that the matter should be transferred to the General Assembly.[28] The Security Council was adjourned, but in fact no action was taken to call the Assembly into session until 7 August: the intervening time was used by the major Powers to engage in negotiations, by letter, between themselves. Khrushchev suggested to Eisenhower, Macmillan, de Gaulle, and Nehru that the recommendations of a summit meeting should be submitted to the Security Council.[29] The Secretary-General made it clear that he believed that any such meeting should be held under UN auspices.[30] Eisenhower was not at all enthusiastic about the idea of a 'summit' on the Middle East: he felt that foreign ministers, or even heads of state, could represent their countries on the Security Council, and that any 'summit' should be within the framework of that organ. He obviously also had doubts about the advisability of any 'summit' meeting on the Middle East at which Israel was not represented.[31] He and Macmillan (S/4071) replied in these terms to Khrushchev. Khrushchev indicated that a meeting of heads of government, within the framework of the Security Council, would be acceptable to the Soviet Union.[32] He emphasized that he thought it essential that India should be invited to attend the Security Council for this purpose. This letter, unlike the previous one, was very moderate in its terminology, and for a brief moment it looked as if an agreement to meet was drawing nearer. Eisenhower, however, now backed away, saying that the suggestion that India should be included was arrogating to the Soviet Union the privilege of determining who should participate in a Security Council discussion (S/4074). The prospect of a consensus was further dissipated when de Gaulle rejected the Macmillan–Eisenhower stand on the necessity of any meeting being held within the Security Council, and proposed that a heads of government meeting be held in Europe (S/4075). The Soviet Union thus turned once again to this idea, which tallied with her own original proposal (S/4067). After a further exchange of letters (S/4079) it became apparent that no agreement was going to be

---

[27] See above, p. 541. [28] S/4056, S/4057 respectively. [29] S/4059, 20 July 1958.
[30] S/4062, 22 July 1958. [31] Eisenhower, pp. 284–6. [32] S/4064, 23 July 1958.

reached; and, after a brief reconvening of the Security Council on 7 August, all the parties agreed that the matter should be transferred to the General Assembly.

Two events of importance—perhaps sufficient to break the deadlock—had occurred by the time that the Assembly met on 8 August; first, General Chehab, the widely respected and acceptable army leader, had been elected President of the Lebanon by a democratic vote, and thus the question of a second term for Chamoun had been irrevocably removed from the scene; and second, the new Iraq revolutionary government had been at pains to indicate that it regarded itself as bound by the UN Charter, and had now been officially recognized by both the United States and the United Kingdom. There was now a tacit agreement that the best solution to the problem would be an 'Arab solution'. It was clear that the Americans and British wished to withdraw from the Lebanon and Jordan respectively, and the task was to devise the UN role which would most facilitate this withdrawal. Many delegations[33] thought that some UN presence was required in Jordan, and suggested that this might be achieved by strengthening UNTSO within the framework of the Arab–Israeli Armistice Agreements. Jordan, however, made it quite clear that a force of the UNEF type, or an Observer Group of the UNOGIL type, was not welcome on Jordanian territory.[34] Some other form of UN presence would have to be found. This, as we shall see, is what the Secretary-General ultimately did. So far as the Lebanon was concerned, the question here was whether the mere enlargement of UNOGIL would facilitate a United States withdrawal, or whether its mandate and functions also needed to be changed. The choices before the Assembly were effectively summarized by a future Secretary-General, U Thant, then speaking as the representative of Burma; and his response to the choices reflected a widely shared view. There was little desire to see a force of the UNEF type established in the Lebanon:

. . . the only logical step for the United Nations is to find some suitable ways and means, whereby the foreign troops may be speedily withdrawn from Lebanon and Jordan and stability restored to the area.

104. There also appears to be a general agreement that some kind of United Nations presence in these two countries is necessary to ensure the speedy withdrawal of foreign troops. Only the nature of this 'presence' is in dispute. Some Member States favour the strengthening of the United Nations Observation Group in Lebanon in accordance with the plan presented by the Observation Group in its second report ($S/4069$), and to send a fresh United Nations observation group to Jordan to perform similar functions. The advocates of this action insist that the enlargement of the functions of the Observation Group is not warranted by the prevailing circumstances. The other school of thought, however, prefers to enlarge the functions of the United Nations force. It advocates some kind of international constabulary with police, if not strictly military, functions. The functions of this constabulary, recruited from among the small nations, if my interpretation is correct would fall short of the normal functions of a fighting force. It would be authorized to shoot, but would carry only small arms.

105. On the basis of all available information in the Middle East, my delegation cannot agree

[33] See e.g. M. Couve de Murville (France), *GAOR*, 3rd emerg. spec. sess., 742nd plen. mtg, p. 124, paras 104–5; and the Secretary-General himself, Ibid. 732nd plen. mtg, p. 4.

[34] Ibid. 738th plen. mtg, p. 59, paras 8–10.

to the substitution of the Observation Group with limited functions by an international police force that would be expected to enforce its authority by force of arms. [*GAOR, 3rd emerg. spec. sess., 740th plen. mtg,* p. 96.]

These were the essential issues before the Assembly, though inevitably the speeches ranged considerably wider. Eisenhower, for example, addressed the Assembly and made certain specific proposals, including a study on a UN stand-by force, and the establishment of a Middle Eastern regional economic plan involving an internationally-supported development institution.[35]

Further evidence that the UN could play a vital role in facilitating the withdrawal of British and American forces appeared in the following letters which were sent to the President of the Assembly while that body continued its discussions:

LETTER DATED 18 AUGUST 1958 FROM THE SECRETARY OF STATE OF THE
UNITED STATES OF AMERICA TO THE PRESIDENT OF THE GENERAL ASSEMBLY

(*Original text: English*)

United States forces are now in Lebanon in response to an appeal of the duly constituted Government of Lebanon for assistance in maintaining Lebanon's territorial integrity and political independence against danger from without. United States forces will be withdrawn from Lebanon whenever this is requested by the duly constituted Government of Lebanon or whenever, as a result of the further action of the United Nations or otherwise, their presence is no longer required. The United States will in any event abide by a determination of the United Nations General Assembly that action taken or assistance furnished by the United Nations makes the continued presence of United States forces in Lebanon unnecessary for the maintenance of international peace and security.

I would appreciate it if you would have this letter circulated to the Members of the General Assembly for their information.

(*Signed*) John Foster DULLES

[*A/3876.*]

LETTER DATED 18 AUGUST 1958 FROM THE SECRETARY OF STATE FOR FOREIGN AFFAIRS
OF THE UNITED KINGDOM OF GREAT BRITAIN AND NORTHERN IRELAND
TO THE PRESIDENT OF THE GENERAL ASSEMBLY

(*Original text: English*)

United Kingdom forces are now in Jordan in response to an appeal of the duly constituted Government of Jordan for assistance in maintaining Jordan's territorial integrity and political independence against danger from without. United Kingdom forces will be withdrawn from Jordan whenever this is requested by the duly constituted Government of Jordan or whenever, as a result of the further action of the United Nations or otherwise, their presence is no longer required. The United Kingdom will in any event abide by a determination of the United Nations General Assembly that action taken or assistance furnished by the United Nations makes the continued presence of United Kingdom forces in Jordan unnecessary for the maintenance of international peace and security.

I would appreciate it if you would have this letter circulated to the Members of the General Assembly for their information.

(*Signed*) Selwyn LLOYD

[*A/3877.*]

Three resolutions were put to the Assembly—one sponsored by the USSR, one by Norway, and one by the Arab states.

[35] Ibid. 733rd plen. mtg, pp. 7–10.

UNION OF SOVIET SOCIALIST REPUBLICS: DRAFT RESOLUTION

(Original text: Russian)
(12 August 1958)

The General Assembly,

Recognizing the necessity of adopting urgent measures for the relaxation of tension in the area of the Near and Middle East in the interests of preserving universal peace,

1. *Recommends* the Governments of the United States of America and the United Kingdom to withdraw their troops from the territory of Lebanon and Jordan without delay;

2. *Instructs* the Secretary-General to strengthen the United Nations Observation Group in Lebanon in accordance with the plan presented by the United Nations Observation Group in Lebanon in its second interim report (S/4052) and to send an observation group to Jordan with a view to the supervision of the withdrawal of United States and United Kingdom troops from Lebanon and Jordan, and of the situation along the frontiers of those countries.

[A/3870.]

CANADA, COLOMBIA, DENMARK, LIBERIA, NORWAY, PANAMA AND PARAGUAY: DRAFT RESOLUTION

(Original text: English)
(18 August 1958)

The General Assembly,

Having considered the item 'Questions discussed at the 838th meeting of the Security Council on 7 August 1958',

Noting the declarations addressed to the President of the General Assembly of 18 August 1958 by the United States regarding United States forces now in Lebanon and their withdrawal and by the United Kingdom regarding British forces now in Jordan and their withdrawal.

Noting the Charter aim that States should practise tolerance and live together in peace with one another as good neighbours,

I

1. *Reaffirms* that all Member States should refrain from any threats or acts, direct or indirect, aimed at impairing the freedom, independence or integrity of any State, or at fomenting civil strife and subverting the will of the people of any State;

2. *Calls upon* all Member States strictly to observe these obligations and to ensure that their conduct, by word and deed, in relation to the general area of the Near East, conforms to the above-mentioned policy;

II

Requests the Secretary-General, in accordance with the Charter, forthwith to make such practical arrangements as he, in consultation with the Governments concerned, may find would adequately serve to help in upholding the purposes and principles of the Charter in relation to Lebanon and Jordan in present circumstances, having in mind section I of the present resolution;

III

1. *Notes* that the Secretary-General has studies in preparation, for consideraton by the General Assembly at its thirteenth session, of the feasibility of establishing a stand-by United Nations peace force;

2. *Invites* the Secretary-General to continue his studies now under way and in this context to consult as appropriate with the Arab countries of the Near East with a view to possible assistance regarding an Arab development institution designed to further economic growth in these countries;

IV

1. *Requests* Member States to co-operate fully in carrying out this resolution;

2. *Invites* the Secretary-General to report hereunder, as appropriate, the first such report to be made not later than 30 September 1958. [*A/3878*.]

Neither the Russian nor the Norwegian drafts were put to the vote. With a sense of relief, the Assembly turned towards an 'Arab solution' and adopted unanimously the following resolution sponsored by Iraq, Jordan, Lebanon, Libya, Morocco, Saudi Arabia, Sudan, Tunisia, UAR, and Yemen:

The General Assembly,

Having considered the item entitled 'Questions considered by the Security Council at its 838th meeting on 7 August 1958',

Noting the Charter aim that States should practise tolerance and live together in peace with one another as good neighbours,

Noting that the Arab States have agreed, in the Pact of the League of Arab States, to strengthen the close relations and numerous ties which link the Arab States, and to support and stabilize these ties upon a basis of respect for the independence and sovereignty of these States, and to direct their efforts toward the common good of all the Arab countries, the improvement of their status, the security of their future and the realization of their aspirations and hopes,

Desiring to relieve international tension,

I

1. *Welcomes* the renewed assurances given by the Arab States to observe the provision of article 8 of the Pact of the League of Arab States that each member State shall respect the systems of government established in the other member States and regard them as exclusive concerns of these States, and that each shall pledge to abstain from any action calculated to change established systems of government;

2. *Calls upon* all states Members of the United Nations to act strictly in accordance with the principles of mutual respect for each other's territorial integrity and sovereignty, of non-aggression, of strict non-interference in each other's internal affairs, and of equal and mutual benefit, and to ensure that their conduct by word and deed conforms to these principles;

II

Requests the Secretary-General to make forthwith, in consultation with the Governments concerned and in accordance with the Charter, and having in mind section I of this resolution, such practical arrangements as would adequately help in upholding the purposes and principles of the Charter in relation to Lebanon and Jordan in the present circumstances, and thereby facilitate the early withdrawal of the foreign troops from the two countries;

III

Invites the Secretary-General to continue his studies now under way and in this context to consult as appropriate with the Arab countries of the Near East with a view to possible assistance regarding an Arab development institution designed to further economic growth in these countries;

IV

1. *Requests* Member States to co-operate fully in carrying out this resolution;

2. *Invites* the Secretary-General to report hereunder, as appropriate, the first such report to be made not later than 30 September 1958.

746th plenary meeting,
21 August 1958.

[*GA Res. 1237* (ES–III).]

The resolution placed enormous reliance on the discretion of the Secretary-General. All specific suggestions having failed, the Secretary-General was authorized to make 'such practical arrangements, as would adequately help. . . .' The practice of 'Leave it to Dag' perhaps at this moment reached its height. What Hammarskjöld in fact did was to follow UNOGIL's own suggestion, and greatly increase the strength of that group, while continuing to limit its mandate to observer functions. In other words, conditions had so modified, and confidence in the Secretary-General was at that time so great, that Hammarskjöld pursued a course of action which the Security Council had a month previously failed to agree upon.[36] The Secretary-General also secured Jordan's agreement

. . . to serve as host country for a United Nations representative, properly staffed, to serve 'as a Special Representative of the Secretary-General to assist in the implementation of the resolution, specifically with a view to help in upholding the purposes and principles of the Charter in relation to Jordan in the present circumstances'. The Governments of Lebanon and the United Arab Republic had both undertaken to grant all the facilities—including liaison offices in Beirut and Damascus—needed in support of the establishment of a United Nations organ in Jordan. Ambassador Spinelli, Under-Secretary in charge of the United Nations office in Geneva, had proceeded to Amman on 27 September to work out the necessary practical arrangements. He was to serve as Special Representative on a preliminary basis. [A/4132, *Annual Report of the Secretary-General on the Work of the Organization, 16 June 1958–15 June 1959, GAOR, 14th sess., suppl. 1*, p. 21.]

By 25 October the United States had withdrawn her troops from Lebanon, and by 2 November the United Kingdom had withdrawn her troops from Jordan. In mid-November the Lebanon requested her complaint against the UAR to be withdrawn from the agenda of the Security Council, and shortly thereafter the Secretary-General put into operation a plan for the termination of UNOGIL. By 9 December UNOGIL had left Lebanon, and normal relations between Lebanon and the UAR were resumed.[37]

2

ENABLING RESOLUTION AND VOTING

UNOGIL was established within the terms of the following resolution:

The Security Council,
Having heard the charges of the representative of Lebanon concerning interference by the United Arab Republic in the internal affairs of Lebanon and the reply of the representative of the United Arab Republic,

---

[36] See above, pp. 540.
[37] Details of the termination of UNOGIL, and an assessment of its success in implementing its mandate, will be found below, pp. 568–602.

1. *Decides* to dispatch urgently an observation group to proceed to Lebanon so as to ensure that there is no illegal infiltration of personnel or supply of arms or other *matériel* across the Lebanese borders;

2. *Authorizes* the Secretary-General to take the necessary steps to that end;

3. *Requests* the observation group to keep the Security Council currently informed through the Secretary-General. [*SC Res. S/4022, 11 June 1958.*]

(Proposed by Sweden)

VOTING
> *For:* Canada, China, Colombia, France, Iraq, Japan, Panama, Sweden, UK, USA.
> *Against:* ——
> *Abstaining:* USSR.

At its 746th plenary meeting, the General Assembly adopted Resolution 1237 (ES–III), by unanimous vote. Although this does not specifically refer to UNOGIL, its significance to the UN endeavour is discussed above (pp. 541–5).[1]

3

FUNCTIONS AND MANDATE

It will be recalled that UNOGIL was established on 11 June 1958, over one month before the United States landings in Lebanon. It was established in the context of a claim by Chamoun's government of interference by the UAR, in order: '. . . to ensure that there is no illegal infiltration of personnel or other *matériel* across the Lebanese borders.'[1]

The Secretary-General, at the very next meeting of the Security Council, made a statement giving his view on UNOGIL's tasks: 'The Security Council, in deciding to dispatch to Lebanon an "observation group", defined not only the character of the operation but also its scope. It did so by linking the observation to illegal traffic in arms and infiltration.'[2] UNOGIL's role was strictly limited to observing whether illegal infiltration was occurring; but it was at the same time hoped that its very presence on Lebanon's borders would contribute to the cessation of any such traffic: 'I have . . . considered myself free to take all steps necessary for an operation, covering illegal traffic in arms or infiltration, as effective as it could be made as a tool towards ensuring against such traffic or infiltration with its basic character of observation maintained.'[3] To this end:

5. The United Nations Observers, in vehicles painted white with United Nations insignia, began active reconnaissance on the morning of 18 June in Beirut and its environs . . . the initial purpose of the patrols and road reconnaissance was to have United Nations observers

---

[1] For the verbatim text, see p. 545, above.
[2] *SCOR*, 13th yr. 827th mtg, para. 62.

[1] S/4022; *SCOR*, 13th yr, 825th mtg.
[3] Ibid., para. 63.

and vehicles appear in as many areas as possible as soon as possible. [*S/4029, 1st Report by Secretary-General on the implementation of the resolution adopted by the Security Council on 11 June 1958, 16 June 1958.*]

10. It is evident that for the performance of the task assigned to it, the Observation Group's activities must be directed to the border region and to areas immediately adjacent to them. For that reason, the barest minimum of staff is maintained in Beirut, and the Observation Group Headquarters have only some 14 officers, whereas the rest of the entire force of officers, including air crews, is constantly out in the field. [*S/4052, 2nd Interim Report of UNOGIL, 17 July 1958.*]

It was *not* the task of UNOGIL to mediate, arbitrate, or forcefully to prohibit illegal infiltration, and it reported on occasion that it was being asked by the Lebanese authorities to do such things, which were not properly within its mandate.[4]

It has been explained above (p. 539) that there were some suggestions, after the events of mid-July, that the character and functions of UNOGIL should be changed. But these suggestions did not prevail: the general view was that it would not be desirable to empower 'the Secretary-General to create a United Nations emergency force in Lebanon, nor to create a type of United Nations force such as is now stationed in Korea, nor to create a police force of any kind.'[5] Instead, when the matter was transferred to the Assembly and a broadly-worded resolution resulted, UNOGIL's functions and character officially remained the same, though—at the decision of the Secretary-General—its size was increased. At the same time, realism requires the admission that, once it had been decided to continue UNOGIL's work in spite of the changed circumstances of the United States landings, it was tacitly hoped that the stabilizing influence of an enlarged UNOGIL would facilitate the speedy withdrawal of United States troops. Indeed, the United States (and the British *vis-à-vis* Jordan) had made it clear that if the UN could in some sense protect the governments from outside 'interference', they themselves would withdraw their troops. This dual role— never explicitly stated in a Security Council resolution—gradually became accepted:

21. The Secretary-General, in his report to the General Assembly under the terms of General Assembly resolution 1237 (ES–III) of 21 August 1958, has described the Group as presenting a practical arrangement in the sense of that resolution for upholding the purposes and principles of the Charter in relation to Lebanon in the present circumstances and for facilitating the withdrawal of foreign troops from the country. As has been noted, the withdrawal of foreign troops from Lebanon was completed before the end of October. As regards the more general task of fostering peaceful relations between Lebanon and other Arab States, the Group has made an effective contribution by carrying out as efficiently as possible its mandate under the Security Council resolution of 11 June 1958. [*S/4114, 5th Report of UNOGIL, 17 Nov. 1958.*]

This was spelled out further in a report made by the Secretary-General to the General Assembly, in accordance with the terms of the Assembly resolution of 21 August:

[4] See below, p. 559.   [5] Per the delegate of Japan (*SCOR*, 13th yr, 835th mtg., para. 7.)

13. It may be noted, further, that the resolution does not give the Secretary-General a mandate to negotiate with the Arab States regarding additional or more specific assurances with regard to their policies. This, obviously, does not exclude any action which may properly be his under the Charter, or that, in consultations with the Governments concerned, he would seek all the clarification, regarding their intentions with respect to the implementation of the good neighbour policy, which he would consider necessary as a background for decisions on practical arrangements. A clear distinction should, however, be made between such clarifications and any further assurances regarding intentions formally given by one Government to another.

14. While the resolution does not—as was the case in the Suez question—establish negotiations regarding withdrawals as a task of the Secretary-General, he is, under the resolution, to facilitate 'early withdrawal' by the practical arrangements he is requested to make. For that purpose he must inform himself about the intentions of the Governments concerned and consult with them with a view to clarifying the relationship between the practical arrangements to be made and the withdrawals. Likewise, he must maintain contact with Governments so as to be able to respond to the invitation of the General Assembly to him to report on the developments under the resolution also in this respect. These contacts or consultations, however, include responsibilities for him regarding the withdrawals only to the extent which follows from the relationship, established in the resolution, between the implementation of a good neighbour policy, the practical arrangements which the Secretary-General is in a position to make in its support, and the withdrawal.

15. What emerges as the task of the Secretary-General under the resolution is in the first instance to consult with the Arab Governments concerned regarding their views on the need for, and form of, practical arrangements as envisaged in the resolution. In the second place he has to see how he can relate the various governmental positions, as determined in the course of the consultations, so that they can best serve and support the implementation of a general good neighbour policy, especially in relation to Lebanon and Jordan. In doing so, he must be guided by the desirability of achieving the highest degree of efficiency which respect for the views of the Governments concerned and adherence to the rules of the Charter permit. Were he to consider the measures possible under those conditions to be inadequate, or were the Governments concerned to consider them insufficient, this naturally should be brought to the attention of the General Assembly.

16. In judging the adequacy of the practical arrangements possible, he must be guided by the interpretation of the resolution set out above. While it cannot be a question for him of evaluating the arrangements as substitutes for the presence of foreign troops, as the arrangements are clearly not intended to be, he should consider them in the context of the withdrawals. This factor forms a part of his general evaluation, which must take into account especially the degree to which the pledges to a good neighbour policy seem to have already been translated into live reality. [*A/3934/Rev.1, 29 Sept. 1958*, mimeo.]

4

CONSTITUTIONAL BASIS

THOUGH it is nowhere explicitly stated, it is reasonable to assume that UNOGIL was a subsidiary organ of the Security Council established within the terms of Article 29.[1]

[1] Art. 29 provides 'The Security Council may establish such subsidiary organs as it deems necessary for the performance of its functions.'

At the same time, the precedent of UNEF was followed in that UNOGIL was clearly regarded as needing the consent of the 'host government' before it could become operational. Indeed, one month later it was to prove impossible to extend this type of UN operation to Jordan in the face of the latter's opposition.[2]

Operative paragraph 2 authorized 'the Secretary-General to take all necessary steps' to establish an observation group capable of fulfilling its mandate; and accordingly it was the Secretary-General who negotiated with the Lebanese government for facilities for UNOGIL, and who entered into arrangements with various countries for contributions of personnel and materials. The Security Council was at this stage perfectly content to leave these matters to the Secretary-General. The constitutional limits to the authority of the Secretary-General were marked by the relation he had to maintain between his powers of discretion and the mandate laid down by the Council:

62. The Security Council, in deciding to dispatch to Lebanon an 'observation group', defined not only the character of the operation but also its scope. It did so by linking the observation to illegal traffic in arms and infiltration, requesting the Group to keep the Council currently informed of its findings. In taking this stand, the Council defined the limits for authority delegated to the Secretary-General in this case.

63. I have, in the light of the decision, considered myself free to take all steps necessary for an operation, covering illegal traffic in arms and infiltration, as effective as it could be made as a tool towards ensuring against such traffic or infiltration with its basic character of observation maintained. I have had a free hand as to the structure and organization of the operation but have considered myself as barred from an interpretation of the authority granted which would have implied that I changed the policy, laid down by the Council, by my decisions on the scope of the operation and the authority of the observers.

64. In fact, had I, by going beyond the reasonable limits of a 'group' charged with 'observation', or by deciding on terms of reference exceeding observation, changed the observation operation into some kind of police operation, not only would I have overstepped the resolution but I would also have faced a conflict with principles laid down in the Charter. In a police operation, the participants would in this case need the right, if necessary, to take the initiative in the use of force. Such use of force would, however, have belonged to the sphere of Chapter VII of the Charter and could have been granted only by the Security Council itself, directly or by explicit delegation, under conditions spelled out in that chapter.

65. As to the structure and organization of the observation group and its activities, I have at the initial stage acted in close consultation with members of the Security Council and the representative of Lebanon. My interpretation of the resolution, as presented to them before any action was taken, met with their full approval, including that of the representative of Lebanon. At later stages I have naturally, to a decisive extent, depended upon the judgement of the highly qualified military, political and diplomatic experts of the United Nations who are in the field. The present arrangements are in accordance with their suggestions and meet with their full approval.   [*Per the Secretary-General, SCOR, 13th yr, 827th mtg*, p. 12.]

The observation group was 'requested' to keep the Security Council informed through the Secretary-General. But it was made clear from the outset that the Secretary-General would feel free to determine the size of UNOGIL, at the request of the group itself: 'As I have already said in public, the Observation Group has and will have as many observers as it has asked or might ask for.'[3]

In July the Group announced that it would 'suggest to the Secretary-General that a force of unarmed non-commissioned personnel and men of other ranks should be assigned to it' to help in observation duties;[4] and the Secretary-General informed the Security Council that 'I fully endorse the plan here outlined by the Observation Group as representing adequate interpretation of the Security Council resolution of 11 June 1958 (S/4023), in the light of the needs and possibilities flowing from the progressive development of the operations of the Group.'[5]

It will be recalled that when American troops landed in the Lebanon, after the revolution of Iraq, Japan had entered a resolution which implicitly authorized the enlargement of UNOGIL by requesting the Secretary-General to make the necessary arrangements which will enable 'the United Nations to fulfil the general purposes established' in the resolution of 11 June 1958'.[6] This resolution was defeated by a Soviet veto. None the less, the Secretary-General on his own authority, did in fact meet UNOGIL's request for enlargement, thus confirming his views of his constitutional powers as he stated them on 15 July. The fact that the Japanese resolution was approved by ten Security Council members no doubt provided an additional moral justification as, later, did the broadly-worded mandate given to the Secretary-General by the General Assembly.[7]

5

POLITICAL CONTROL

WHEN the Security Council, by its resolution of 11 June 1958, authorized the Secretary-General to establish an observation group in the Lebanon, it requested him to keep the Council informed. No part of the day-to-day political or administrative handling of UNOGIL lay with the Security Council.

The Secretary-General made the necessary military and political appointments for the implementation of the resolution. Those in the field with senior executive authority were designated the 'Observation Group', while the men who carried out the Group's instructions were known as the observer teams.

The Observation Group consisted of three members, supplemented by two senior Secretariat posts:

2. The three members of the Observation Group have been appointed. They are: Mr Galo Plaza of Ecuador, Mr Rajeshwar Dayal of India and Major-General Odd Bull of Norway. The Observation Group will constitute itself and determine its own procedures. Military officers in the capacity of observers are assisting the Group. Major-General Bull has been designated as 'executive member of the Observation Group, in charge of military observers'.

---

[4] S/4052, p. 36, para. 7.   [5] Ibid. p. 34.   [6] S/4055/Rev. 1; and above, pp. 540-1.
[7] See above, p. 545

Major-General Bull arrived in Beirut early on the morning of the fifteenth, Mr Galo Plaza is scheduled to arrive on the seventeenth, and Mr Dayal is expected on the same day.

8. On 11 June, I appointed Mr David Blickenstaff as Secretary of the Observation Group, and Mr Shiv K. Shastri as Assistant Secretary. Mr Blickenstaff arrived in Beirut on 12 June and Mr Shastri on 14 June. In the days immediately following, the operation was provided with the secretariat staff required. The United Nations Relief and Works Agency for Palestine Refugees in the Near East, from the beginning, on an emergency and temporary basis, has readily afforded all necessary administrative assistance and other co-operation. This has in no way involved an association of UNRWA with the operation. [*S/4029, 1st Report by Secretary-General on the implementation of the resolution adopted by the Security Council on 11 June 1958, 16 June 1958.*]

Day-to-day decisions were made by this Group, assisted by a five-man commission set up by the Lebanese government to assist UNOGIL.[1] In order to get UNOGIL operative as soon as possible, Hammarskjöld decided that briefing and initial decision-taking should take place in Lebanon rather than New York:

In view of the urgency of the situation in Lebanon, I considered that it would involve an unwarranted loss of time to request the three members of the Observation Group to assemble in New York prior to their arrival in Lebanon. . . . I have decided that I should give assistance to the Group by being present when the three members assemble in Beirut and by attending the Group's first meetings there. [*Ibid.* para. 12.]

The *modus operandi* of this Group—in which the civilian and military elements of UNOGIL were integrated in the tripartite command which was jointly responsible to the Secretary-General—is indicated by the following arrangements:

2. . . . On that date [18 June], the Group met informally and was briefed by its secretary on developments since the arrival on 12 June in Beirut of the first secretariat members and military observers. At the same time, attention was also given to administrative arrangements and the activities of the military observers.

3. On 19 June, the Group held a further informal meeting, with the Secretary-General presiding. Later the same day, it held its first formal meeting and organized its work. At this meeting Mr Galo Plaza was designated Chairman of the Group. The first meetings of the Group were devoted to an exchange of views on the methods and procedures which it would follow in carrying out its mandate with regard to illegal infiltration of personnel or supply of arms or other *matériel* across the Lebanese borders, under the resolution of the Security Council, and in keeping the Security Council 'currently informed through the Secretary-General'. The Secretary-General was in close consultation with the Group throughout his stay in Beirut. [*S/4038, 2nd Report by the Secretary-General on the implementation of the resolution adopted by the Security Council on 11 June 1958, 28 June 1958.*]

It was by submitting periodic reports that UNOGIL kept the Security Council informed: 'However, the Group has been in daily contact with United Nations Headquarters in regard to its task.'[2]

Requests for the enlargement of UNOGIL came from the Group, were approved by the Secretary-General and immediately acted upon; the Security Council, though notified, was not called upon formally to play any part in these decisions. Further, since

---

[1] See below, p. 559.   [2] S/4040 and Add. 1, 1st Report of UNOGIL, 3 and 5 July 1958.

the Observation Group's activities have been established on a fully operational basis, the three members have been considerably relieved of the pressure of organizational work necessitating their presence at Headquarters and they have been able to undertake frequent visits to the outstations and border areas . . . [this] helped them greatly to acquire a fuller understanding of the situation. . . . [*S/4052, 2nd Interim Report of UNOGIL, 17 July 1958*, para. 11.]

The Group continued this practice of frequent visits to frontier posts and the maintenance of the close personal relations with its observers.[3]

6

ADMINISTRATIVE AND MILITARY CONTROL

MAJOR-GENERAL BULL of Norway was in charge of the military observers.[1] As one of the three members of the Observation Group, he was jointly responsible with his colleagues to the Secretary-General. He was aided at the outset by the secondment of a small number of seasoned men and an experienced officer from UNTSO:

4. On 11 June, I requested the Chief of Staff of the United Nations Truce Supervision Organization in Palestine, Major-General von Horn, to afford temporary assistance toward the execution of the Security Council's action by detaching ten United Nations military observers from Truce Supervision Organization duty to the Observation Group operation in Lebanon, five of whom were to arrive on the twelfth and another five not later than the fourteenth, under the command of an officer of sufficient rank. The first five military observers arrived in Beirut on the afternoon of the twelfth and a second group of five arrived there on the afternoon of the thirteenth. They were under the command of Lieutenant-Colonel W. M. Brown. On 14 June, the Chief of Staff in Jerusalem agreed to provide another five United Nations military observers. [*S/4029, 1st Report by the Secretary-General on the implementation of the resolution adopted by the Security Council on 11 June 1958*, 11 June 1958.]

UNOGIL, in a later report, provided details of the organization of the military staff:

III. ORGANIZATION OF THE MILITARY STAFF

18. In the initial stages of the mission, it was essential to send the maximum number of military observers into the field immediately after they arrived. Neither the time nor the personnel were available for a complete headquarters organization and emphasis was placed on the establishment of an operations branch, with a small staff of evaluation officers. As information started to flow in rapidly increasing quantities from the field, the evaluation branch was rapidly built up. Finally as the scale of operations steadily developed, the time came when it was necessary to divest the overburdened operations branch of responsibility for personnel and for supply, separate staff sections being provided for these matters. Thus, the Headquarters is now organized on full military lines, as shown in the chart forming annex 1 of the present report.

[3] See also, for example, S/4100, 4th Report of UNOGIL, para. 57, 29 Sept. 1958.
[1] S/4040 and Add. 1, 1st Report of UNOGIL, 3 and 5 July 1958, para. 3.

19. The headquarters organization now comprises a Chief Military Observer and a Deputy Chief of Staff, responsible to the Chief of Staff, and four section staffs consisting of G–1 Personnel; G–2 Evaluation; G–3 Operations (including ground and air components), and G–4 Logistics. While the civilian administrative staff provide administrative service in such fields as personnel, finance, supply, transportations and communications, the military counterparts, G–1 and G–4 working in close liaison with them, provide the necessary planning information and provide the link between the military observers in the field and the civilian staff.

20. More specifically, the duties allotted to the four staff sections are as follows:

G–1: Reception, allocation, posting and transfer of military observers between stations, also welfare, leave and morale;

G–2: Collection, collation, evaluation and dissemination of information from all sources;

G–3 (ground operations): All ground operations, training, liaison, staff procedures and organization; the allotment of operational resources such as vehicles and wireless sets; the issue of the necessary orders to meet the requests of G–2. G–3 ground works in close co-operation with G–3 air.

G–3 (air operations): All air operations, training, staff procedures and organization. G–3 air works in close liaison with G–2 and G–3 ground.

G–4: All logistical matters, including equipment, maintenance, accommodation and such transport matters as are not dealt with by the civilian side. [*S/4100, 4th Report of UNOGIL, 29 Sept. 1958.*]

UNOGIL MILITARY ORGANIZATION CHART

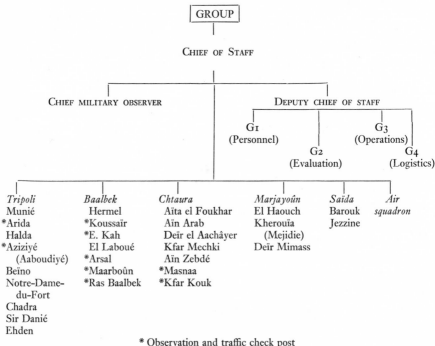

* Observation and traffic check post

[*Ibid. ann. 1.*, p. 170.)

7

COMPOSITION AND SIZE

UPON the adoption of the resolution establishing UNOGIL, the Secretary-General said:

I envisage an operation, so to say, on two levels: the observation group proper, mentioned in the resolution, which may not be on the spot tomorrow because it should be composed of highly qualified and experienced men who have to be collected from various corners of the globe; a second category which is, so to say, the group servicing the main group which can be recruited from the personnel we have at present in Jerusalem in the United Nations Truce Supervision Organization in Palestine. Some of them could be in Lebanon tomorrow.

There is, of course, a difficulty which arises in the planning of the activities of its personnel, but I do not believe that this will introduce any delay. [SCOR, 13th yr, 825th mtg., p. 18.]

As has been seen, the military observers in the Lebanon were directed by a triumvirate known collectively as the 'Observation Group'. This comprised Mr Galo Plaza of Ecuador, Mr Rajeshwar Dayal of India, and Major-General Odd Bull of Norway.[1] The military observers themselves were drawn from the following countries: Afghanistan, Argentina, Burma, Canada, Ceylon, Chile, Denmark, Ecuador, Finland, India, Indonesia, Ireland, Italy, Nepal, Netherlands, New Zealand, Norway, Peru, Portugal, Sweden.

The provision of Secretariat staff and administrative needs was facilitated by the presence of UNRWA in Beirut:

. . . The United Nations Relief and Works Agency for Palestine Refugees in the Near East, from the beginning, on an emergency and temporary basis, has readily afforded all necessary administrative assistance and other co-operation. This has in no way involved an association of UNRWA with the operation. The headquarters of the Group was established in a Beirut hotel, close to its telecommunications facilities, where all of the staff members, including the observers, are housed.

4. On 11 June, I requested the Chief of Staff of the United Nations Truce Supervision Organization in Palestine, Major-General von Horn, to afford temporary assistance toward the execution of the Security Council's action by detaching ten United Nations military observers from Truce Supervision Organization duty to the Observation Group operation in Lebanon, five of whom were to arrive on the twelfth and another five not later than the fourteenth, under the command of an officer of sufficient rank. The first five military observers arrived in Beirut on the afternoon of the twelfth and a second group of five arrived there on the afternoon of the thirteenth. They were under the command of Lieutenant-Colonel W. M. Brown. On 14 June, the Chief of Staff in Jerusalem agreed to provide another five United Nations military observers. [S/4029, 1st Report by the Secretary-General on the implementation of the resolution adopted by the Security Council on 11 June 1958 (S/4023), 16 June 1958, p. 70.]

So far as supporting equipment was concerned, the Secretary-General reported on 28 June that:

[1] S/4029, p. 70, para. 2.

7. The basic items of equipment for the observer teams are transport and communications. Arrangements have worked well for the delivery of jeeps and supporting transport at a rate compatible with the arrival in the area of military observers. Thus, as of 26 June, there were 74 vehicles to 94 observers. A fully operating radio communication system has been installed for contact between group headquarters, observer outstations and jeeps circulating within the areas assigned for observation.

8. At the request of the Group, United Nations Headquarters has obtained two small helicopters. The helicopters arrived in Beirut on 28 June and, with Norwegian pilots, are now in operation. Four light observation planes have also been requested and will be on hand soon. [*S/4038, 2nd Report of the Secretary-General on the implementation of the resolution adopted by the Security Council on 11 June 1958, 28 June 1958*, pp. 120–1.]

In its Second Interim Report of 17 July the Observer Group had obtained access to a greater number of regions, and consequently felt the need for additional personnel. It had already requested an additional 25 observers, and now reported:

A further 65 observers will now be required, raising the total observer force to a figure of some 200.

5. It should be borne in mind that while night watches had been kept at all existing posts, the new posts on the frontier will be required to function on a 24-hour basis. Furthermore, the Group should also be in a position to establish such additional posts as the situation may require.

6. The advance of the Observation Group's activities up to or close to the frontier will change to a considerable extent the character of the field operations. It has hitherto been possible to place observation stations in the great majority of cases in hotels or other public facilities and the auxiliary needs of the staff of observers has been met by local arrangement. Most of the new posts to be established will be placed near or on the frontier, where suitable accommodation is generally not available. It will, therefore, be necessary to establish tented camps for which some *matériel* was already requested on 12 July.

7. This raises the question of the need for providing additional support for the ground observers, in respect of the performance of their observation duties, as well as by way of relief from duties not strictly connected with the responsibility of observation. It would greatly help in the extension of the activities of the observers if they were assisted by a certain number of unarmed troops to be used for regular ground reconnaissance on foot, based on outposts. Patrols could consist of officers, accompanied by a small number of men of other ranks, patrolling on foot or by mule along the frontier areas, thus permitting wider and more profitable use of the force of observers at the Group's disposal. In addition, observers stationed at observation posts along the border would have men under their command to undertake the variety of duties required for the operation and maintenance of such posts, which in many cases would be located in isolated positions. Furthermore, the men of other ranks could be very usefully employed as guards; they could undertake the maintenance of transport, communications, supply and equipment and, in general, relieve military observers of other time-consuming and non-essential duties. The Group will, therefore, suggest to the Secretary-General that a force of unarmed non-commissioned personnel and men of other ranks should be assigned to it.

8. Experience with air reconnaissance since the Group's first report was submitted on 3 July 1958 has shown that this is a most valuable adjunct to the Group's ground observation. The aircraft and personnel at the disposal of the Group have been used to the maximum of their capabilities. Up to 15 July, 82 missions had been flown, totalling 150 flying hours. [*S/4052, 2nd Interim Report of UNOGIL*, pp. 35–36.]

After the settlement of the constitutional crisis in the Lebanon (General Chehab being elected as the next President on 31 July), the situation stabilized further, and UNOGIL obtained access to yet more opposition-held areas. In order to be able to carry out its mandate in these areas, it needed more personnel and equipment. This pattern continued: the more the situation stabilized—with UNOGIL itself playing a role in this process—the larger UNOGIL needed to become to take advantage of access. The following charts indicate the growth in the size and scope of UNOGIL throughout its stay in the Lebanon.

A. *Size and Scope of UNOGIL*

	S/4038 26.6.58	S/4040 3.7.58	S/4052 17.7.58	S/4085 14.8.58	S/4100 29.9.58	S/4113 17.11.58
Ground observers	} 94	No information given	113	166	214	501
Air observers			20	24	73	90
Manned outstations	6	8	150	22	34	49

B. *Air Observation by UNOGIL, per Month*

	Sorties	Flying Hours
June	15	23
July	160	360
August	210	494
September	221	515

Note: These charts are not official documents, but have been compiled by the Editor from information from the following sources: S/4052, paras 4, 7–9, 12; S/4085, para. 8; S/4100, paras 6–10, 58; S/4114, paras 7–11.

The build-up effectively occurred in two phases: first, to meet the requirements of the plan put forward by UNOGIL in its Second Interim Report;[2] and second, under the terms of a further plan announced publicly in its Fourth Report (S/4100):

8. The Group . . . came to the conclusion that a number of posts considerably in excess of the number proposed in the second interim report was needed. This had important implications on the number of observers and the amount of material required.

9. . . . . the Group feels that, in order to develop its operations to their full capacity, more than 50 fully manned posts will be required. It has therefore recently requested a considerable further increase in the number of observers. . . .

58. . . . . In this connexion, the following press release was issued by the Observation Group on 18 September 1958:

'On the basis of the resolution of the Security Council of 11 June 1958 (*S/4023*), the United Nations Observation Group in Lebanon submitted, in its second interim report to the Council (*S/4052*), a plan for the development of the operations of the Group to their full capacity. The implementation of this plan was slowed down pending the consideration of current problems of the region by the General Assembly. Its full implementation as envisaged by the

[2] S/4052, 17 July 1958.

Secretary-General of the United Nations when presenting his comments on the report in the Council has now been found consistent with the resolution adopted by the General Assembly, at the end of this consideration, on 21 August 1958 (*resolution 1237 (ES–III)*).

'The United Nations Observation Group in Lebanon, which at present employs 217 officer ground observers and 22 air officers and 46 air NCOs, will, in the next few weeks, be augmented. The augmentation will not involve any change in the terms of reference of the Group, or in its authority. It will be effected under the terms of the Council resolution of 11 June 1958.

'The plans are flexible. Any changes in them which may be called for by later developments can be worked out at that stage in consultation between the authorities of Lebanon, the members of the Observation Group and the Secretary-General.' [*S/4100, 4th Report of UNOGIL, 29 Sept. 1958.*]

8

RELATIONS WITH CONTRIBUTING STATES

SUCH agreements as the UN may have entered into with nations contributing men and equipment to UNOGIL have never been published. No practical problems were encountered.

9

RELATIONS WITH HOST STATES

THE status of UNOGIL was based upon a relationship with the host government that has become fairly typical in UN practice: UNOGIL was on Lebanese territory at the request of the government, but it was not to be a party to any internal dispute.

61. My actions have had no relation to developments which must be considered as the internal affairs of Lebanon. . . .

65. As to the structure and organization of the observation group and its activities, I have at the initial stage acted in close consultation with members of the Security Council and the representative of Lebanon. [*Per the Secretary-General, SCOR, 13th yr, 827th mtg.*]

Freedom of movement and access to all the border regions was regarded as essential; and in so far as the government was not able to guarantee this in rebel-held quarters, UNOGIL regarded it as quite in order to deal with the leaders of opposition forces for that purpose.[1]

---

[1] This practice never gave rise to the sort of bitterness that was felt by various parties in the Congo when ONUC dealt, on a day-to-day basis, with their opponents. The Lebanese government accepted the practical necessity of the UN having to make arrangements with opposition elements.

The relationship between UNOGIL and the government remained basically cordial, though the Observation Group obviously felt that the government was unreasonably asking it to investigate past complaints (rather than to observe and report daily); while the Lebanese government resented the view of UNOGIL that there was no substantial infiltration from the UAR, and thought that UNOGIL was in no position to be able to reach such a conclusion.

Officials of the Group in Beirut, from the beginning, requested of the Lebanese authorities that the United Nations observer teams be accorded complete freedom of movement throughout government-held areas. . . .

It is reported that so far the United Nations observers have generally met with a good reception, particularly in Beirut.

9. Immediately upon arrival in Beirut, the United Nations representatives in the operation, both civilian and military, established contact with the appropriate Lebanese authorities with a view to facilitating its work. The Lebanese Government has designated a minister to be in charge of relations between the Government and the Observation Group, and has set up a five-man commission to assist in this purpose, as indicated in the letter of 15 June from the Prime Minister of Lebanon to Major-General Bull (annex I).

10. The status of the United Nations Observation Group in Lebanon, its privileges and immunities, etc., have been defined in a letter of 18 June from the Secretary-General of the United Nations to the Foreign Minister of Lebanon (annex II).[2]

ANNEX I

LETTER DATED 15 JUNE 1958 FROM THE PRIME MINISTER OF LEBANON TO MAJOR-GENERAL ODD BULL

I have the honour to inform you that the Lebanese Government, at a meeting held on 12 June 1958, has taken a decision nominating His Excellency Dr Albert Moukheiber, Minister of Health, as Minister in charge of relations between the Government of Lebanon and the United Nations Observation Group.

A Commission has also been formed to assist Dr Moukheiber in the fulfilment of this mission, composed of: Emir Farid Chehab, Director-General of the Sûreté générale, Edward Chorra, Director of International Relations in the Ministry of Foreign Affairs, Captain François Ginadrh, Representative of the Lebanese Army Headquarters, Mr Raja Hamady, representative of the Ministry of Finance.

The mission of this Commission is to take all necessary measures to facilitate the task of the United Nations Observation Group, to supply said Group with all information coming to the knowledge of the Lebanese Government about the infiltration of arms and armed men and other material from across the Lebanese border, and to assure the contact between the various sections of the Lebanese administration and your Group.

The office of this Commission will be in the Ministry of Foreign Affairs. I would be very grateful if you would channel all communications with the various departments of the Lebanese Government through this Commission which stands ready at all times to answer your requests and to facilitate your work. [*S/4029, 1st Report by the Secretary-General on the implementation of the resolution adopted by the Security Council on 11 June 1958, 16 June 1958.*

9. Arrangements have been made by the Group for receiving from the ministry in charge of relations between the Government of Lebanon and the Group, written communications on cases which the Lebanese Government desires to bring to the attention of the Group. The Group in turn submits these to independent study through its own means and in the light of

[2] For text, see below, pp.563–5.

supporting evidence provided. The Group has received information concerning prisoners, said to be Syrians, taken by Lebanese authorities. Such prisoners, when made available to the Group, are being interrogated by the Executive Member of the Group, Major-General Bull, with the assistance of qualified military observers, concerning matters covered by the Security Council resolution. [*S/4038, 2nd Report by the Secretary-General on the implementation of the resolution adopted by the Security Council on 11 June 1958, 28 June 1958.*]

5. The Observation Group had been assured by the Lebanese Government that it would be accorded free access to the areas under Government control. No formal assurances from any quarter were offered to the Group with regard to access to territory not under Government control, nor were such assurances sought by the Group. . . .

9. The Observation Group has given its most careful consideration to another condition which has a bearing on its observation activities within Lebanon and particularly in the border areas referred to above. The existence of a state of conflict between opposing armed forces in a territory to which an independent body of observers seeks free access throughout imposes upon that body an attitude of discretion and restraint if the express or tacit acceptance of its presence is to be obtained from those exercising authority or effective control on different sides in the conflict. The Observation Group is fully conscious of the fact that its methods of observation and its use of the information it receives must duly reflect the independent character of its status and its complete objectivity and impartiality in relation to the present conflict. . . .

14 (*f*) A special procedure has been established in order to utilize the information which the Lebanese Government possesses about suspected infiltration. The Government thus sends frequent reports about such alleged infiltrations to the Group, which immediately deals with each case as conditions require. The majority of these communications contain statements regarding alleged infiltration incidents, routes and methods. Instructions have, wherever appropriate, been issued to the observers for the maintenance of special vigilance within the areas in question. In other cases the Group has requested, through the executive member of the Group, that the military observers inquire into the matter. Either final or preliminary reports have already been received from military observers or are awaited. In some cases the Observation Group has requested further clarification by the Government in order to determine whether useful action by the Observation Group may be taken. Some of the communications refer to events which are said to have taken place before the establishment of the Observation Group and which have no bearing on situations likely to become the object of the Group's proper concern. Others relate to events falling wholly within the framework of the internal conflict between the governmental authorities and opposition groups or supporters, and having no *prima facie* relationship to questions of infiltration. Information of a general character is contained in many of the communications. Though specific action on them is not possible, they constitute for the Group a possible source of background information. . . .

23. Observer teams have on occasion experienced difficulty in penetrating opposition-held territory, and there are cases where the local inhabitants have made it obvious that they do not welcome observers in the area. The teams have, by perseverance, managed to allay fears and gain the confidence of the local population by a strict display of independence and impartiality. However, two leaders, Mr Jumblatt of the Choûf area and Mr Haidar of central Bekaa have so far both politely indicated that they do not want observers acting in their official capacity. Both men stated that this was a matter of principle, since they were involved in an internal conflict with which the United Nations was not concerned. [*S/4040 and Add. 1, 1st Report of UNOGIL, 3 and 5 July 1958.*]

The degree to which the problems which UNOGIL faced prevented the implementation of its mandate is examined below (p. 569–78). It is appropriate, however, to draw attention here to the reaction of the Lebanese government to UNOGIL's conclusion in its First Report that it had not been possible to show massive infiltration from outside. UNOGIL, however, reiterated its general viewpoint in its next report.

4. In carrying out its task, an important source of information for the Group is contained in the communications received by it from a liaison committee established by the Lebanese Government. A preliminary analysis of the type of information thus provided appears in paragraph 14(*f*) of the Group's first report (*S/4040 and Add. 1*). This analysis remains broadly correct, but it seems appropriate in the second report to repeat it in somewhat greater detail and to deal with certain special problems raised by some of these communications.

5. In all, 102 communications had been received from the Lebanese Government by 15 July. Of these, 18 contained information relating to alleged subversion within Lebanon or to reports of alleged infiltration prior to the date of the Group's commencement of operations, while a further 21 referred to such matters as the destruction of bridges and buildings, the mining of roads, clashes between Government and opposition forces, news broadcasts from the United Arab Republic stations and the expulsion of certain United Arab Republic diplomats, etc. These reports were regarded by the Group as for information purposes only.

6. Thirty-three of these communications contained reports of alleged acts of infiltration, of the routes said to have been used for that purpose or of the presence of foreign nationals amongst the opposition forces. Three of these reports were urgent ones concerning infiltration said to be actually occurring at the time. Air patrols were dispatched as soon as possible, but when they arrived on the scene they found nothing to observe. The remainder of the communications were usually received several days after the events complained of. In these cases, the information was transmitted by the Group to the outstation in the area concerned for inquiry, and reports were requested. In no case was it possible to find explicit confirmation of specific allegations and only in a few cases was the information obtained of such a nature as to require further action by the Group. These cases are dealt with later in the present report. However, the information has also been used by the out-stations to maintain special vigilance along certain routes.

7. The thoroughness of the watch carried out by the United Nations observers is revealed by the following specific example. In its communication dated 11 July, the Lebanese Government liaison committee stated that on 4 July three Syrian trucks loaded with slaughtered cattle and ammunition, preceded by a pilot car with private Syrian licence No. 8445 passed by the intersection of the Damascus–Beirut road and the road south from Masnaa to Rachaya. This intersection is situated at a distance of six kilometres from the frontier and falls within the eighteen kilometres of the frontier which the Group was informed was under government control. The liaison committee inquired if the observer on duty had noticed this infiltrating convoy. A United Nations observation post is in fact stationed at this important point during the hours of daylight. The report of the observers on duty on 4 July, which is annexed to the present report (*annex I*) contains a full log of all vehicular movements on that day and shows that no such convoy passed by. It should be added that during the day, Lebanese forces were not present at this most strategic point of entry into the country, but were stationed some two kilometres to the north-west on the road towards Beirut.

8. In one of these communications, it is alleged that United Nations observers are not prepared to go out at night to investigate cases of possible infiltration. It is correct that regular ground patrols have not been carried out by night. The Group has given careful consideration to the question of checking, by means of night patrols, possible infiltration routes, but, in view of the harassments suffered by its observers in such areas even by day, it reluctantly came to the conclusion that night patrols would involve a degree of risk to the observers which it could not accept. It was confirmed in this view by the fact that well-armed Lebanese forces have established no control along the routes in question. Further confirmation was provided subsequent to the period covered by the present report, when a lighted United Nations jeep proceeding by night under a previously concluded arrangement to a village near an infiltration route came under heavy fire and was hit several times. The Group wishes to take this occasion of paying tribute to the courage and devotion to duty shown by its observers,

who have carried out their responsibilities with firmness and tact in areas where, in addition to the risks represented by actual hostilities, law and order are by no means ensured.

9. A further two of the communications received from the Lebanese Government liaison committee are unusual in that they contain inaccurate accounts of incidents in which observers were actually involved. One of these incidents, the finding of a group of armed men near Masnaa on 10 July is referred to later in the present report. The second incident turned out to be another case of firing on United Nations military observers by a band of armed men.

10. The remaining twenty-eight communications contained reports of alleged infiltration based on statements made to Lebanese authorities by persons said to have been arrested in the course of the commission of subversive acts. In all, 75 persons under arrest were involved, of whom 14 were said to be Syrian and 61 Lebanese. It was considered that the interrogation of such persons, provided it was obtained under conditions which would ensure that it was freely given, and that it would be relevant to the specific mandate of the Group, might provide a useful basis for observation purposes.

11. It may be recalled that at the specific request of the Lebanese Foreign Minister, conveyed through the Secretary-General, the Group carried out at an early stage of its operations the interrogation of two persons in Lebanese custody. Reference is made to this in paragraphs 27 to 29 of its first report. Subsequently the Group requested that persons in custody mentioned in other communications should be made available to it for interrogation and the Group adopted a suitable procedure for their interrogation. However, it will be seen from the subsequent paragraphs that the Group was unable to utilize this source of information, for the reasons clearly brought out in the correspondence.

12. In a letter dated 8 July, the Group informed the Lebanese authorities as follows:

'It is anxious that the procedure followed for the interrogation of these persons should permit them to be questioned as soon as possible. It feels that in order that the interrogation may have the greatest value it should take place at the headquarters of the Observation Group with only the United Nations interrogation team present. However, it should be pointed out that throughout the period of interrogation, the custody of the prisoners will remain the responsibility of the Lebanese authorities, and Lebanese guards, if so desired, may be stationed outside the room in which the interrogation is taking place.'

13. In a letter dated 10 July, the Lebanese Minister in charge of relations with the Group, Dr Albert Moukheiber, replied as follows:

'I have referred the letter to the Ministry of Justice for advice. The said Ministry informed me that the Lebanese laws do not permit that any interrogation of a person accused of a crime may be undertaken on Lebanese territory by any other authority than the Lebanese judicial authorities. Article 71 of Criminal Procedure provides that during the interrogation of an accused the following persons only may be present: the attorney-at-law of the accused, the plaintiff or his attorney-at-law. Nevertheless the Ministry of Justice is willing to provide you with certified copies of the interrogation records of the persons in whom you might be interested for the purposes of your investigation together with copies of the sentences rendered by the court.'

14. The Group gave careful consideration to the question and in a further letter dated 14 July it brought the following points to the Minister's attention:

'(a) The right to interrogate persons in a position to tender information relevant to their activities has been freely granted to other United Nations missions by the Government concerned.

'(b) It was at the specific request of the Lebanese Foreign Minister, conveyed through the Secretary-General, that two persons in Lebanese custody have already been interrogated by the Group.

'(c) You have yourself offered, in communications Nos. 4/50/42/57 and 76, to have the persons concerned produced for interrogation by the Group.'

In the light of these considerations, the Group inquired whether, without infringing Lebanese law, it would be possible for the Lebanese authorities to make persons in custody available to the Group upon its request for interrogation according to the procedure previously suggested by it. Up to the present, no reply to the letter of 14 July has been received. [*S/4069, 2nd Report of UNOGIL, 30 July 1958.*]

Although UNOGIL felt its position further undermined by the arrival of United States troops on 14 July,[3] the atmosphere gradually improved and the underlying tension disappeared in its relations with Lebanon:

6. The election of General Chehab as the next President of Lebanon took place on 31 July. Even before the election informal truces had taken effect in Saïda and Soûr; in fact, during the period immediately preceding the election there was a noticeable reduction in tension practically throughout the country and a comparative absence of armed clashes between Government and opposition forces. Since 31 July, there has been a further reduction in tension throughout the country, including the opposition-held areas. There has, in fact, been virtually a nation-wide truce since then with only occasional reports of sporadic fighting in some areas. [*S/4085, 3rd Report of UNOGIL, 14 Aug. 1958.*]

The above selection of documents shows something of the relationship between UNOGIL and the Lebanese government as it worked out in practical terms. On a more formal level, an agreement was reached between Lebanon and the UN concerning the status to be accorded to UNOGIL:

EXCHANGE OF LETTERS CONSTITUTING AN AGREEMENT BETWEEN THE UNITED NATIONS AND LEBANON CONCERNING THE STATUS OF THE UNITED NATIONS OBSERVATION GROUP IN LEBANON. NEW YORK, 13 JUNE 1958

I

13 June 1958

Sir,

I have the honour to refer to the resolution of 11 June 1958, by which the United Nations Security Council decided to dispatch urgently an 'observation group to proceed to Lebanon so as to ensure that there is no illegal infiltration of personnel or supply of arms or other material across the Lebanese borders', and authorized the Secretary-General to take the necessary steps to that end.

In view of the special importance and difficult nature of the functions which this Observation Group will perform, I would propose that, with the operation as now envisaged, your Government might agree to extend to the Observation Group consisting of three senior members, the United Nations military observers and the United Nations Secretariat—over and above the status which they enjoy under the Convention on the Privileges and Immunities of the United Nations—the privileges and immunities, exemptions and facilities which are enjoyed by diplomatic envoys in accordance with international law. The privileges and immunities necessary for the fulfilment of the functions of the Observation Group also include freedom of entry, without delay or hindrance, of property, equipment and spare parts; freedom of movement of personnel, equipment and transport; the use of United Nations vehicle registration plates; the right to fly the United Nations flag on premises, observation posts and vehicles; and the right of unrestricted communication by radio, both within the area of operations and to connect with the United Nations radio network, as well as by telephone, telegraph or other means.

It is my understanding that the Lebanese Government will provide at its own expense, in agreement with the Representative of the Secretariat, all such premises as may be necessary

---

[3] See below, p. 566.

for the accommodation and fulfilment of the functions of the Observation Group, including office space and areas for observation posts and field centres. All such premises shall be inviolable and subject to the exclusive control and authority of the Observation Group. I likewise understand that your Government will in consultation with the Observation Group provide for necessary means of transportation and communication.

If these proposals meet with your approval, I should like to suggest that this letter and your reply should constitute an agreement between the United Nations and Lebanon, to take effect from the date of the arrival of the first members of the Observation Group in Lebanon.

Accept, Sir, the assurances of my highest consideration.

Dag HAMMARSKJÖLD
Secretary-General

His Excellency Dr Charles Malik
Minister for Foreign Affairs

PERMANENT MISSION OF LEBANON TO THE UNITED NATIONS, NEW YORK

II

13 June 1958

Excellency,

I have the honour to refer to your letter of 13 June 1958 concerning certain privileges, immunities and facilities for the Observation Group established by Security Council Resolution of 11 June 1958. I am pleased to advise you in the name of my Government that, having in mind the difficult nature of the functions of the Observation Group, the Government of Lebanon fully agrees with and hereby expresses its acceptance of the terms of your letter.

The Government of Lebanon also agrees that your letter and this reply should constitute an agreement between the United Nations and Lebanon, effective from the date of the arrival of the first members of the Observation Group in Lebanon.

Please accept, Excellency, the assurances of my highest consideration.

Charles MALIK
Minister for Foreign Affairs
of the Republic of Lebanon

His Excellency Mr. Dag Hammarskjöld . . .

EXCHANGE OF LETTERS CONSTITUTING AN AMENDMENT TO THE AGREEMENT OF 13 JUNE 1958 BETWEEN THE UNITED NATIONS AND LEBANON CONCERNING THE STATUS OF THE UNITED NATIONS OBSERVATION GROUP IN LEBANON. NEW YORK, 26 AND 30 JUNE 1958

I

26 June 1958

Sir,

I have the honour to refer to our exchange of letters of 13 June 1958 determining the privileges and immunities to be enjoyed by the members of, and specified personnel associated with, the United Nations Observation Group in Lebanon established by the Security Council in its resolution of 11 June 1958.

In view of the various technical services and functions which may prove necessary in support of the work of the Observation Group in Lebanon, I should like to propose that the same privileges and immunities accorded to the categories of persons mentioned in our exchange of letters of 13 June should also be extended by your Government to experts sent to Lebanon to perform missions in connexion with the work of the United Nations Observation Group in Lebanon.

If this proposal meets with your approval, I would suggest that this letter and your reply might be treated as an amendment to the agreement effected by our exchange of letters of 13 June.

Accept, Sir, the assurances of my highest consideration.

Dag HAMMARSKJÖLD
Secretary-General

His Excellency Dr Charles Malik

PERMANENT MISSION OF LEBANON TO THE UNITED NATIONS, NEW YORK

II

30 June 1958

Sir,

I have the honour to refer to your letter of 26 June 1958, proposing an amendment to the agreement effected by our exchange of letters of 13 June 1958 establishing the privileges and immunities of the United Nations Observation Group in Lebanon.

Having in mind the necessity of providing the Observation Group with essential technical services, I am pleased to advise that the Government of Lebanon accepts your proposal and agrees to extend the same privileges and immunities as accorded in our exchange of letters of 13 June to such experts as may be sent to Lebanon to perform missions in connexion with the work of the United Nations Observation Group in Lebanon.

Accept, Sir, the assurances of my highest consideration.

Charles MALIK
Minister for Foreign Affairs

His Excellency Mr Dag Hammarskjöld

[*303 UNTS 271.*]

10

RELATIONS WITH OTHER STATES INVOLVED

THE functioning of UNOGIL created no major problems for the general membership of the UN. No obligations additional to those already in the Charter were placed upon members, and no directives were addressed to them. The countries directly involved in the two phases of the dispute—the UAR, Jordan, Lebanon, Iraq, the United States, and the United Kingdom—all presented their views in the Security Council, either as of right or by invitation; and they were all heard again in the Assembly. As a matter of prudence and courtesy 'the Governments of neighbouring countries have been notified by the Secretary-General of [UNOGIL's] observation flights over Lebanese territory in the proximity of the borders'.[1]

The relationship between the United States and the UN after the American landings was obviously a delicate one. On the one hand, at no time was any resolution passed condemning the United States for its action; on the other

[1] S/4038, 2nd Report by the Secretary-General on the implementation of the resolution adopted by the Security Council on 11 June 1958, 28 June 1958, para. 8.

hand, widespread misgivings had been expressed, and UNOGIL itself made no bones of the fact that it found its work impeded by the presence of American marines:

3. . . . the effect of the landing of United States armed forces on the inhabitants of opposition-held areas where observers were operating, occasioned difficulties and caused setbacks to the task of observation. Not only was the Group prevented from carrying out its plan to establish immediately the permanent posts in opposition-held areas for which it had made arrangements on 15 July, but also its observers had to resume the difficult task of gaining the confidence of the inhabitants of those areas in the impartiality and independence of the observers. [*S/4085, 3rd Report of UNOGIL, 14 Aug. 1958.*]

Particularly resented, it would seem, was the United States claim that her troops were in effect a supplement to UNOGIL, in the carrying out of its mandate:

4. With a view to emphasizing the independent nature of its task, the Group made the following announcement on 16 July:

The United Nations Observation Group in Lebanon wishes to clarify its position in regard to its relationship with the foreign forces on Lebanon soil. The United Nations Observation Group alone is in Lebanon in pursuance of the mandate contained in the Security Council resolution of 11 June 1958 (*S/4023*). The United Nations Observation Group represents the only action taken by the Security Council. There is, therefore, no basis for establishing any contact or working relationship, formal or informal, between the United Nations Observation Group and any non-Lebanese forces in Lebanon beyond what may be strictly required for the independent fulfilment of its mandate from the United Nations Security Council, which cannot be altered without further action by the Council. [*Ibid.*]

II

FINANCE

THE expenses of UNOGIL—together with expenses flowing from the implementation of General Assembly Resolution 1237 (ES–III) on the Middle East crisis—were apportioned as an integral part of the regular budget. These items fell within the section of the budget concerned with 'special missions and related activities'. In 1958 it was still customary for minor peacekeeping activities to be grouped in this part of the budget—UNTSO, the Observation Group in India and Pakistan, and the Commission on Korea for example, were all that time appearing under that heading. What is certain, however, is that UNOGIL, unlike UNMOGIP and UNTSO, never appeared in the detailed breakdown which customarily follows the bald itemization of the budget estimates. After UNOGIL ceased, however, and expenses arising from General Assembly

Resolution 1237 (ES–III)[1] began to appear as a separate item, this latter *was* included in the detailed breakdown of items.

The cost of UNOGIL was levied upon all UN members—a practice which was politically no longer possible by the time the financing of the UN Temporary Executive Authority for the Administration of West Irian (UNTEA) and the UN Observation Mission in Yemen (UNYOM) came to be considered.[2] There was a singular lack of debate or comment upon the financing of UNOGIL in the Security Council, the emergency General Assembly, or the official documentation on the Lebanon and Jordan cases. It was treated as an ordinary matter for the regular budget. UNOGIL, together with field services, amounted to 6 per cent of the 1958 budget.[3]

The 1958 appropriations for special missions and related activities had been $2,082,900.[4] Under the terms of General Assembly Resolution 1138 (XIII) a specific appropriation was made for UNOGIL:

Budget Appropriation for the Financial Year 1959

　The General Assembly

　Resolves that for the financial year 1959
　　1. Appropriations totalling $US 60,802,120 are hereby voted for the following purposes:

　　Pt. II. *Special Missions and Related Activities*
　　4a. Expenses arising from GA Res. 1237 (ES–III) and residual expenses of the United Nations Observation Group in Lebanon: $500,000　[*GA Res. 1338 (XIII)*.]

It proved necessary, however, to provide supplementary estimates:

　Supplementary Estimates for the Financial Year 1959

　The General Assembly

Resolves that for the financial year 1959 the amount of US $60,802,120 appropriated by its Resolution 1338 (XIII) of 13 December 1958 be increased by $854,980, as follows:

Pt. II. *Special Missions and Related Activities:*
4a. Expenses arising from GA Res. 1237 (ES–III) and residual expenses of the United Nations Observation Group in Lebanon:

Amount appropriated by Resolution *1338 (XIII)*	Supplementary appropriation	Revised amount of appropriation
$500,000	($164,000)	$336,000

[*GA Res. 1435 (XIV)*.][5]

The detailed breakdown for 1958's account in respect of UNOGIL became available in 1959:

---

[1] e.g. the expenses of the Secretary-General's Special Representative in Amman. See, for example, *GAOR*, 15th sess., suppl. 5, A/4370, p. 70.

[2] See below, pp. 645–52.

[3] J. G. Stoessinger, *Financing the United Nations System* (1964), p. 105.

[4] Budget Estimates for the financial year 1959, *GAOR*, 13th sess., A/3825, suppl. 5, p. xv.

[5] See also *GAOR*, 14th sess., suppl. 6, A/4116, p. 4.

Extract from Account for the year ended 31 December 1958

Special Missions and Related Activities

4a. *UN Observation Group in Lebanon and General Assembly resolution 1237 (ES–III)*

Original appropr	Suppltry appropr	Subseqt section transfer	Revised appropr	Liquidated by disbursmts	Unliqdtd total	Unobligated balance of revs approprtd
—	$3,700,000	—	$3,700,000	$2,998,027	$667,804	$34,169

[*GAOR, 14th sess., suppl. 6, A/4116*, pp. 8–9.]

Budget Estimates compared with 1959: Appropriations and 1958 Expenses, Table S–1

Special Missions and Related Activities

4a. *Expenses arising from UN Observation Group in Lebanon and General Assembly Resolution 1237 (ES–III):*

1960 Estimates	1959 Appropriation	1958 Expenses	Increase or decrease 1960 compared with 1959
—	$500,000	$3,665,831	$ (500,000)

[*GAOR, 14th sess., suppl. 5, A/4110*, p. xvii.]

Note: At the 15th session of the General Assembly, the section in the Estimates covering special missions and related activities includes, within a lump sum allocated to '1959–60 missions not provided for in 1961', some $120,778 for residual expenses for UNOGIL. [*GAOR, 15th sess., suppl. 5, A/4370*, p. 65.]

12

IMPLEMENTATION

ANY assessment of the extent to which UNOGIL succeeded in implementing its mandate first necessitates a clear understanding of what it was that the UN was meant to achieve in the Lebanon. This has been dealt with above (pp. 545–7), and we merely need to mention here, as a guide to the ensuing documents, that:

(*a*) (1) formally, UNOGIL was to 'ensure that there is no illegal infiltration of personnel or supply of arms or other *matériel* across the Lebanese borders'.[1]

    (2) after August, by tacit understanding it became generally accepted that UNOGIL was also to contribute, by its presence, to stabilizing the situation to such a degree that the United States should withdraw its troops.

(*b*)   UNOGIL was not in the Lebanon to end the civil war *per se*; but only to *observe and report*.

[1] S/4022, 11 June 1958.

(c)   Its success depended not only upon its own actions and administration, but also upon circumstances imposed by local conditions (such as the inability of the Lebanon government to guarantee freedom of movement and access to all border regions) and other events (such as the arrival of United States troops).

That UNOGIL observed and reported is beyond question; its detailed reports are testimony to this. Its contribution to an improvement in relations, permitting the withdrawal of foreign troops, is also clear, though it is a matter of conjecture to what extent the praise belongs to UNOGIL, the new government of General Chehab, or—if one takes a certain view—to United States intervention. What is more debatable is how far UNOGIL, given that it was forced to carry out (especially in the early stages) an operation limited in several respects, was competent in its findings that there was no adequate evidence of massive interference by the UAR. These various strands all run through the documentation included in this section:

Areas being regularly patrolled by the Observer teams are the following: around Tripoli and south of that city; the coastal road from Nakoura to Damour, and roads branching off toward the interior; the Marjayoun area; the Chtaura area and north-east beyond Baalbek; the area north and east of Beirut and south of the city, except in the vicinity of Beit el Dine. . . .

6. In visiting areas outside government control, the observers have met local leaders and have discussed with them freedom of movement in the Bekaa area north of Baalbek, the Chouf area south of Beit el Dine, and the area north of Tripoli. It was reported from the headquarters of the Group on 25 June that for the time being further efforts at moving deeper into such areas were deferred at the following main points: the area north and north-east of Tripoli (where firing is in close vicinity and the roads are mined), the Beit el Dine area, and the north Bekaa area. [*S/4038, 2nd Report by the Secretary-General on the implementation of the resolution adopted by the Security Council on 11 June 1958, 28 June 1958,* paras 4 and 6.]

5. It was learned that of the total land frontier with Syria, of some 324 kms in length, only 18, lying on either side of the main Beirut–Damascus road, remained under the control of the Government forces. The Observation Group had been assured by the Lebanese Government that it would be accorded free access to the areas under Government control. No formal assurances from any quarter were offered to the Group with regard to access to territory not under Government control, nor were such assurances sought by the Group. Inasmuch as the areas to be observed by the Group in accordance with the mandate from the Security Council would necessarily include the border zones, the question immediately arose as to how the Group could fulfil its functions in these zones where its right to engage in observation activities had not been formally or implicitly recognized.

6. Another major factor which would inevitably influence the means to be employed was the nature of the terrain in the frontier regions. The eastern frontier runs roughly from north north-east to south-west along the Anti-Lebanon and Hermon mountain formations, which attain heights of 2,400 to 2,800 metres respectively. Main roads of communication on the Lebanese side of this chain of mountains run parallel to it in the Bekaa valley, the sole exception being the Beirut–Damascus road, which crosses the Bekaa from the north-west and passes between the Hermon and the Anti-Lebanon highlands. Thus physical accessibility to the border by road is considerably restricted in the area lying between the frontier itself and the main roads running the length of the Bekaa valley. This is an area which ranges from approximately 10 to 25 kms in width.

7. The northern frontier lies in a broad plain. However, access by land from the Lebanese side is by the coastal highway running north-east from Tripoli towards Homs. There are no roads connecting this northern border area with the north Bekaa valley. Thus, the northern border can be reached only through the area north of Tripoli, an area now under the control of the opposition forces.

8. The remaining frontier of concern to the Observation Group is the sea coast of some 220 kms, along the full length of which runs a main highway from Arida in the north to Nakoura in the south. It will be seen, therefore, that the areas of primary concern to the Observation Group are those where the problems of accessibility are the greatest, both from the standpoint of topography and of obtaining freedom and security of movement.

10. In this connexion it would be relevant briefly to outline the situation in regard to the present state of the conflict, in so far as it concerns the functions of observation with which the Group is charged. In Beirut, Tripoli and Saida, sections of the city lie behind barricades, and are normally inaccessible to observation, except under previously negotiated arrangements. In all these towns, intermittent clashes have been occurring. The area to the north of Tripoli, stretching to the border, has been the scene of some hostilities, and a similar situation prevails in the region to the north of Baalbek. In the south and south-east, armed clashes are taking place, while the Chouf area, to the south-east of Beirut, is under the complete control of opposition elements.

11. An additional factor which the Observation Group feels it should take into account in its activities and in its reporting on observations concerns the nature and location of the populations which live along the border regions, particularly in the eastern zones, and the traditional freedom of association which has existed for centuries among certain peoples living in areas now lying on both sides of the frontier. Moreover, persons could move freely across the frontier merely on the presentation of identity cards and did not require passports and visas. In some areas a tribal structure of society is prevalent which creates bonds of identity within ethnic groups, the realities of which are in some cases not diminished by the existence of a political frontier which is, in some places, the subject of disagreement or uncertainty. The peoples of these areas have traditionally borne arms, and habits of mutual assistance in peaceful as well as in troubled times have been regarded as a normal expression of tribal solidarity. There are some other areas also where the border is not clearly demarcated or recognized. Furthermore, throughout the country the possession of arms is common practice, in spite of governmental efforts in the last few years to curb such habits through licensing, which has not been properly enforced. The methods employed by the Observation Group in carrying out the mandate from the Security Council must be directed toward the explicit purposes of observation and reporting for which the Observation Group was established. The Group is of the opinion that the above facts require it to pursue its activities with particular vigilance and care in order that its mandate may be fulfilled with accuracy and thoroughness.

18. From the descriptive account of the nature of the observers' task and the circumstances in which it has to be performed and from the methods that have been adopted to perform it, it will be evident that the task of the observation Group is one of considerable complexity.

19. The Group has received a large number of daily reports from its observer patrols; it has examined these reports most carefully and has made its evaluations. It would like here to record the result of this examination and evaluation.

20. The patrols of the Group have reported substantial movements of armed men within the country and concentrations at various places. For example, they have penetrated deep into the headquarters of one of the opposition leaders right up to the village of Deir el Aachâyer, close to the eastern border. They were escorted by armed men and they established contact with the opposition leader and met his followers. In the area of Rachaya, the patrols have frequently come across armed groups. In Baalbek and north of it, groups of armed men have been seen. South of Baalbek land mines have been found in territory not held by the opposition. North of Baalbek, observers have established contact with the local opposition leader and seen some 200 of his men. Still further north at Zghorta, observers have been on

the fringe of opposition-held territory and seen some arms and other material in use. In the Chouf region, one observation group has visited the headquarters of the opposition leader and established contact with him. In this region again, larger groups amounting to several hundred armed men were seen.

21. The arms that were seen consisted mostly of a varied assortment of rifles of British, French and Italian makes. Some hand-granades were also seen at various places. Occasionally, opposition elements have been found armed with machine-guns. Mines seen near the Baalbek area were of British and French makes. It has not been possible to establish where these arms were acquired; but, in this connexion the remarks contained in paragraph 11 of the present report should also be borne in mind. Nor was it possible to establish if any of the armed men observed had infiltrated from outside; there is little doubt, however, that the vast majority were in any case Lebanese. . . .

24. The observer teams have experienced difficulty in the following areas:

(*a*) North of Tripoli and south-west of Tripoli adjacent to Zghorta;
(*b*) The Bekaa valley north of El Laboué;
(*c*) Baalbek and areas to the east;
(*d*) The Rachaya and Saghbine areas in south Bekaa.

25. In all these instances the observer teams appear to have touched upon sensitive spots which are in areas claimed by government sources to be supply and infiltration routes. . . .

27. By a letter dated 18 June 1958, the Lebanese Government liaison committee communicated to the Group 'a preliminary report about the arrest of two Syrian subjects belonging to the Syrian armed forces'. They were accused of having participated in terrorist activities in Beirut, and were further alleged to have acted on behalf of a supposed terrorist organization, to have thrown bombs near the Rivoli cinema and in El Khouri Street, and to have participated in an attack on El Ramal prison on 15 June.

28. The Group immediately made a verbal request for the prisoners to be brought before it and confirmed the request on 21 June. The prisoners were produced on 23 June and the interrogation took place on that day and the following day. The first prisoner, Mahmoud Abboud Ibrahim, an illiterate 21 years of age, described himself as a deserter from the Syrian Army who had come to Lebanon in March 1958 to earn his living as a fisherman. He added that he had been coming to Lebanon since 1952 for the same purpose. He denied having visited Beirut after the troubles started in May 1958, and claimed that while he was returning to Syria on 16 June he was apprehended by the *gendarmerie* near Tripoli and forced, under pressure, to admit that he had participated in terrorist activities in Beirut. The second youth, Ibraham Muhamad Moussa Sulayman Haydar, aged 17, admitted that he was a Syrian and a friend of the first prisoner. He stated that he had accompanied his friend to Lebanon about three months ago and was earning his living as a fisherman about twenty miles from Beirut. He alleged that when the trouble started he was brought, under pressure, to Beirut and kept under surveillance at the house of a local opposition leader. He said that he was given two bombs which he placed as directed by a Lebanese organizer, but he said that he had been afraid to operate the firing mechanism. He admitted collaborating with his friend in the attack on the local prison, when he had had to carry a box of ammunition. He complained of having been beaten by the *gendarmerie* after his apprehension on 16 June.

29. The Group has carefully considered the testimony of the two youths, which, it is evident, is contradictory in material particulars. From such conflicting evidence, it is not possible to draw any firm conclusions in regard to the charges made against them. Not only are there numerous inconsistencies in the accounts of their movements given by the two youths, but there is also an absence of any supporting evidence. In the circumstances, the Group must conclude that the complicity of these two persons in terrorist activities or their participation in actions of rebellion as members of an organized foreign terrorist group has not been established beyond reasonable doubt.

[Annex I. List of out-stations omitted]
[Annex II. s. 1. List of opposition weapons omitted]

II. Armed opposition forces

1. *Choûf area*
    (*a*) Approximately 200 armed men observed at Moukhtara on 23 June;
    (*b*) On 28 June, United Nations military observers on patrol were escorted by armed opposition from Katermaya to 3 km south of Chhim.

2. *Akkar area*
    On 21 June, United Nations military observers were in contact with armed opposition (old rifles) at El Minié.

3. *Central Bekaa*
    United Nations military observers have observed armed opposition in the area of Baalbek.

4. *South Bekaa*
    On 25 June, United Nations military observers observed approximately one company of uniformed Syrian soldiers on both sides of the road leading from Deir el Aachâyer into Syria, in an area where the location of the border is under dispute and is not known to the local inhabitants. The opposition leader, however, proffered the information that the area concerned was generally considered Syrian.
    In the area of Deïr el Aachâyer, United Nations military observers also observed approximately 1,000 armed opposition soldiers. *[S/4040 and Add. 1, 1st Report of UNOGIL, 3 and 5 July 1958, paras 5–8, 10–11, 24–29, and ann. II, s. 11.*

The Lebanese government issued the following official comments:

1. The Government of Lebanon wishes to make the following formal comments on the first report of the United Nations Observation Group in Lebanon (document S/4040, of 3 July 1958). These comments seek to establish three theses which are the headings of each one of the three sections below.

I

First thesis: The positive conclusions drawn by the Observation Group in its first report are either inconclusive, misleading or unwarranted.
    2. The fundamental substantive conclusions are to be found in paragraph 21. They are three, and read as follows:
    (1) 'It has not been possible to establish from where these arms [namely, the arms seen by the Observation Group] were acquired';
    (2) 'Nor was it possible to establish if any of the armed men observed had infiltrated from outside';
    (3) 'There is little doubt, however, that the vast majority were in any case Lebanese.'
    3. The first and second conclusions are obviously misleading. To say that 'it has not been possible to establish where these arms were acquired' does not at all tell us either that the Group actually inquired into their origin and did not succeed in establishing it, or that it is sure they were not smuggled from Syria. The phrase 'it has not been possible' could mean only that the Group had no time to carry out the necessary investigation to establish the origin of the arms, or that it met with insurmountable difficulties, or any number of other logical possibilities; but from none of this can any positive conclusion be drawn as to the origin of these arms. The Government of Lebanon wishes to ask: where did these arms come from, and why did the Observation Group go out of its way to state that it could not establish their origin, when we know it made no attempt to do so? Furthermore, the arms the Group saw are, from the very report iself, a very small part of the ammunition at the disposal of the rebels. Consequently, nothing can be concluded from this as to the origin of all the arms used by the rebels.

4. Concerning the second conclusion above, three remarks are to be made. First, did the Observation Group really investigate every one of the armed men they 'observed' to determine whether they did or did not really infiltrate from outside? Why then this sweeping statement? It would thus seem that this negative statement of the Observation Group has no substantive, conclusive character. Secondly, as the report itself states, the Observation Group was able to 'observe' a very small number of the men fighting against the Government in Lebanon. Thus, even supposing that this 'observation' was most meticulous, which clearly it was not, nothing follows from this report as to the origin of all the men fighting against the Government in Lebanon. Thirdly, when the very charge of the Government of Lebanon is that there are infiltrators in Lebanon fighting with the rebels against the Government, and when the Observation Group was dispatched by the Security Council precisely 'to ensure that there is no illegal infiltration of personnel or supply of arms or other *matériel* across the Lebanese borders' [*S/4023*], is it not certain that when the rebel leaders take the Observation Group into their territory, they will see to it precisely that the Observation Group 'observe' no infiltrators? Thus, how does the Observation Group know that between its establishment by the Council and the moment it started 'observing'—and this was a matter of about ten days—the rebel leaders did not 'de-infiltrate' the infiltrators back into Syria or move them away from the areas to which the Observation Group was admitted? It would take about one day, not more, to send back to Syria several thousand infiltrators who had been fighting in Lebanon.

5. Concerning the third conclusion above, it is clear that this is both misleading and un- warranted. It is misleading because while it refers only to the armed men 'seen' by the Observation Group—and they are a very small fraction of the total number of men fighting in the rebellion—careless readers and commentators have taken it to refer to all the armed men fighting against the Government. Thus a false impression has been created by the world Press, both the tendentious and even some of the honest Press, that one of the findings of the Observation Group has been that 'the vast majority' of the men fighting the Government are Lebanese. This is of course not at all what the report says. And the third conclusion is un- warranted because the Observation Group does not tell us how it was able to establish that the 'vast majority' of the armed men it 'observed' 'were in any case Lebanese'. Did they in- vestigate each one of them? Is it not certain that the rebel leaders only showed them Lebanese fighters? How then can the Observation Group possibly justify this sweeping statement?

6. A more careful editing of the text of this report would unmistakably have drawn atten- tion to these most important distinctions.

7. It seems therefore that the positive conclusions drawn by the Observation Group in its report are clearly either inconclusive, misleading or unwarranted.

II

Second thesis: There are, on the other hand, warranted positive conclusions that can be drawn from this report but that have not been drawn explicitly or sufficiently by the Observation Group; all these warranted positive conclusions completely support, or at least do not at all weaken, the thesis of the Government of Lebanon concerning the existence of illegal infiltration of men and smuggling of arms.

Warranted positive conclusion No. 1: The Observation Group has not yet been able to carry out its mandate.

8. The mandate of the Observation Group is 'to ensure that there is no illegal infiltration of personnel or supply of arms or other *matériel* across the Lebanese borders'. But, in the first place, the report tells us that of the 324 km. of the total Lebanese–Syrian land frontier only 18 km are under the control of the Government forces, the rest being under the control of the rebels. With respect to this rebel-controlled territory the report explicitly says: 'No formal assurances from any quarter were offered to the Group with regard to access to territory not under government control, nor were such assurances sought by the Group' (para. 5). And the report further states (paras 23–25) that the observer teams 'have on occasion experienced

difficulty in penetrating opposition-held territory', especially with respect to four areas where they 'appear to have touched upon sensitive spots which are in areas claimed by government sources to be supply and infiltration routes'.

9. It is clear from all this that the mandate to 'observe' and 'ensure that there is no illegal infiltration of personnel or supply of arms or other *matériel* across the Lebanese borders' has not been fulfilled so far by the Observation Group. For only a small part of the frontier has to be shut off from the Observation Group to 'ensure' free infiltration from Syria into Lebanon; how much more so when practically all the frontiers are, as the report says, 'opposition-held'?

10. Again, the Observation Group complains that the difficult topography of the Syrian–Lebanese frontiers has impeded its task of observation, even along the Government-held short stretch of 18 km otherwise fully accessible to the Group (see especially paras 6, 7 and 8). But the inhabitants of these areas, on both sides of the frontier, are quite used to the rugged character of the topography and therefore can easily filter back and forth precisely at the points where the Observation Group would find it difficult to go and 'observe'. Difficulty of terrain could prevent the Observation Group from 'observing' and for that reason would be an ideal condition under which the infiltration could go on 'unobserved'.

11. The difficulty or inability of the Group, as it is at present conceived and constituted, to carry out the mandate of the Security Council is clearly recognized by the report when it says: 'It will be seen, therefore, that the areas of primary concern to the Observation Group are those where the problems of accessibility are the greatest, both from the standpoint of topography and of obtaining freedom and security of movement' (para. 8).

12. Again, the report recognizes that night observation has not yet started (paras 14 (*a*) and 17 (*d*)). But when the infiltrators know that the observers are not watching at night, even if they are otherwise watching all the borders, then they will choose precisely the night to carry out their movements. It follows that the Observation Group has not been able so far to carry out its mandate.

13. Again, aerial reconnaissance, which the report says 'will be employed in an increasing measure' with a view to patrolling 'the border areas', has not yet really begun so far as this first report is concerned (paras 14 (*e*) and 17 (*c*)). Thus, whatever information can be gathered by this device has not yet been gathered. But even if this aerial reconnaissance were fully operative, it would still have two limitations: it cannot spot all infiltration during the day, and it can hardly spot anything during the night. There is thus no substitute for on-the-spot physical land 'observation' at the borders themselves.

14. Concerning the cities, the report says: 'In Beirut, Tripoli and Saïda, sections of the city lie behind barricades, and are normally inaccessible to observers, except under previously negotiated arrangements' (para. 10). Such inaccessibility is also true of the Choûf area which, the report says, 'is under the complete control of opposition elements' (*ibid.*). The Government of Lebanon hold that in these cities and areas the rebels have been assisted by hundreds of Syrians, Egyptians and Palestinian refugees. The observers now recognize that they were unable to cross the barricades or penetrate areas into these pockets of rebellion and search them out thoroughly for infiltrator participants in the rebellion; thus they have not been able to observe and report on a very important aspect of the situation, and therefore in that extent have not carried out the mandate of the Security Council.

15. The report says that the preparations for the final stage of operation of the Observation Group are now 'virtually completed'; and that therefore this 'final stage—when the Group can operate at its planned strength—is about to commence' (para. 13). By stating that the preparations are 'virtually completed' and that the definitive stage of operation 'is about to commence', the Group clearly recognizes that it has not yet fulfilled the mandate of the Security Council.

16. It appears to the Government of Lebanon now that the interpretation given to the resolution of the Security Council of 11 June 1958 (*S/4023*) has been insufficient. The interpretation of the Secretary-General may have been a possible one, but it is no longer adequate to the present situation as revealed by the report of the Observation Group. Therefore, the Government of Lebanon wishes to register its strong reservations concerning this matter.

17. The report says: 'The methods employed by the Observation Group in carrying out the mandate from the Security Council must be directed toward the explicit purposes of observation and reporting for which the Observation Group was established' (para. 11). The Secretary-General in his Press releases stressed the matter of 'observation' as 'decisive'. In all this the clear tendency is to underline, in the resolution of 11 June 1958, the observing and reporting functions of the Group. The Government of Lebanon believes that 'observing' and 'reporting' are subordinate to the truly decisive part of the text of the resolution: 'so as to ensure that there is no illegal infiltration of personnel or supply of arms or other *matériel* across the Lebanese borders'. As the third thesis . . . will presently prove, the illegal infiltration of personnel or supply of arms or other *matériel* across the Lebanese borders still continues (not to mention the other phases of the massive intervention in Lebanon's internal affairs of which the Government of Lebanon complained to the Security Council, such as the training of Lebanese rebels on Syrian soil, the violent and utterly unprecedented Press and radio campaigns by the United Arab Republic against the Government of Lebanon and inciting the people of Lebanon to overthrow their Government by force); therefore to that extent the most important part of the Security Council resolution has not been implemented.

18. From all this, then, it appears to the Government of Lebanon that the most striking warranted positive conclusion of this report—a conclusion at the very surface of the report— is that the Observation Group has not yet been able to carry out the mandate entrusted to it by the Security Council, and that the resolution of the Security Council has not really been implemented. [*S/4043, 8 July 1958.*]

One may contrast paragraph 17 of the above document with the interpretation which the Lebanese government gave to the Security Council resolution.[2] The remainder of document S/4043 is given over to further 'warranted positive conclusions' based on the facts as given in UNOGIL's First Report. The Lebanese government found that 'the report of the Observation Group admits, either directly or indirectly, the existence of illegal infiltration of men and smuggling of arms' (paras 19–28); and that

The independent position of the Government of Lebanon remains today exactly what it was when the Government of Lebanon first presented and defended its case before the Security Council, namely:

(1) That there has been and there still is massive, illegal and unprovoked intervention in the affairs of Lebanon by the United Arab Republic;
(2) That this intervention aims at undermining and does in fact threaten the independence of Lebanon;
(3) That the situation created by this intervention is likely, if it continues, to endanger the maintenance of international peace and security. [*Ibid.* paras 29–35.]

In time, certain admitted limitations upon UNOGIL's efficiency—non-admittance to some opposition-held areas, insufficient personnel and equipment for night patrols—were removed:

1. The Group wishes to take the earliest opportunity to report to the Security Council that, on 15 July 1958, it completed the task of obtaining full freedom of access to all sections of the Lebanese frontier.

2. The first of these frontier areas held by the opposition—the Akkar plain—extends from Tripoli north and east to the Syrian border. On 2 July the Group was able to report that it had obtained freedom of access to this area. In the succeeding few days, some patrols penetrated into the area. From 9 July patrols began reaching the frontier at several points in the

[2] And cf. above, pp. 551–2.

roads leading to it from south to north. On the morning of 15 July, the Group received the fullest assurances of complete freedom to patrol throughout the area north of Tripoli, and to establish permanent observation posts anywhere in the area, and in particular, at the intersections of the north-bound roads and the frontier. At the same time arrangements were made for the inspection by military observers of all vehicles and cargoes entering Lebanon across the northern frontier. Again on the same day an outstation was established at the important road junction of Halba.

3. The second of the border areas held by opposition forces is that part of the Bekaa valley north and east of Baalbek. The northern frontier is crossed by a main road leading to Homs, Syria, and a minor road running north from Hermel. Until 11 July, patrols were not able to penetrate beyond El Laboué. On that day United Nations military observers, at a meeting with the local opposition leader, obtained freedom of movement to patrol up to the border by day, but were not yet enabled to establish permanent stations. On the morning of 15 July 1958, at a further meeting, arrangements were concluded to establish permanent stations at Koussair on the border and at Baalbek with effect from 16 July.

4. The next section of the border east of the centre of the Bekaa valley consists of hilly country, through which pass two main communication routes—the Beirut–Damascus railway east of Rayak and the Beirut–Damascus road of Masnaa. Further south, near Deïr el Aachâyer, two subsidiary roads provide a more difficult road connexion between Lebanon and Syria. The main centres of this region are under government control, but almost all of the border is under opposition control. This region is covered by Chtaura outstation and its network of sub-stations. This network had already been established at the time of the first report (S/4040 and Add. 1), but consistent success has been achieved in pushing eastwards from the main roads up to the frontier. Observation posts are manned by day on a regular basis at the following points on or close to the frontier: Yahfoû, near the Beirut–Damascus railway. Masnaa, on the Beirut–Damascus road, and Deïr el Aachâyer. The remaining section of the border with Syria is covered by an outstation at Marjayoûn, from which a good road leads to Kuneitra in Syria. This section of the frontier is held by opposition forces. Observers from Marjayoûn outstation finally penetrated into Chebaa, the main opposition village in this area, on 12 July.

5. The remainder of the land frontier of Lebanon and the sea frontier continue to be accessible to the Group. Thus the Group is able to report to the Security Council that it has, as of 15 July, access to all parts of the frontier. [*S/4051, Interim Report of UNOGIL, 15 July 1958.*]

2. As of 15 July the Group had established the following network of outstations, substations and permanently manned observation posts, the number of observers stationed in each of these posts being indicated:

Headquarters Beirut	14
Tripoli area	
Tripoli	7
Sir Danié	3
Ehden	4
Les Cèdres	4
Halba	4
Bekaa area	
Chtaura	17
Btedaï	6
American University Experimental Farm	6
Zahlé	6
Rachaya	6
Saghbine	6

South-east Lebanon
Marjayoûn   10

Saïda area
Saïda   13
Jezzine   3
Soûr   4

Total observers   113

3. As a result of this improved access to the frontier, the Group proposes to establish stations or permanent observation posts on or close to the frontier at the following points (manned by the number of observers indicated against each), which include all important road and rail frontier crossings:

Tripoli and the Akkar plain
Arida   8
Aziziyé   8
Braghite   8

North Bekaa
Baalbek Headquarters   8
Koussair   12
El Kah border customs post   8
Arsal   8
Yahfoû   8

Central Bekaa
Masnaa   8
Deïr el Aachâyer   8

South-east Lebanon
Chebaa   6
Kherouia   6

Total observers   96

[*Para. 4 omitted.*]

5. It should be borne in mind that while night watches had been kept at all existing posts, the new posts on the frontier will be required to function on a 24-hour basis. Furthermore, the Group should also be in a position to establish such additional posts as the situation may require. [*S/4052, 2nd Interim Report of UNOGIL, 17 July 1958.*]

6. In no case [of listed allegations presented by the Lebanon Government] was it possible to find explicit confirmation of specific allegations and only in a few cases was the information obtained of such a nature as to require further action by the Group. These cases are dealt with later in the present report. However, the information has also been used by the out-stations to maintain special vigilance along certain routes.

7. The thoroughness of the watch carried out by the United Nations observers is revealed by the following specific example. In its communication dated 11 July, the Lebanese Government liaison committee stated that on 4 July three Syrian trucks loaded with slaughtered cattle and ammunition, preceded by a pilot car with private Syrian licence No. 8445 passed by the intersection of the Damascus–Beirut road and the road south from Masnaa to Rachaya. This intersection is situated at a distance of six kilometres from the frontier and falls within

the eighteen kilometres of the frontier which the Group was informed was under government control. The liaison committee inquired if the observer on duty had noticed this infiltrating convoy. A United Nations observation post is in fact stationed at this important point during the hours of daylight. The report of the observers on duty on 4 July, which is annexed to the present report . . . contains a full log of all vehicular movements on that day and shows that no such convoy passed by. It should be added that during the day, Lebanese forces were not present at this most strategic point of entry into the country, but were stationed some two kilometres to the north-west on the road towards Beirut.

8. In one of these communications, it is alleged that United Nations observers are not prepared to go out at night to investigate cases of possible infiltration. It is correct that regular ground patrols have not been carried out by night. The Group has given careful consideration to the question of checking, by means of night patrols, possible infiltration routes, but, in view of the harassments suffered by its observers in such areas even by day, it reluctantly came to the conclusion that night patrols, would involve a degree of risk to the observers which it could not accept. It was confirmed in this view by the fact that well-armed Lebanese forces have established no control along the routes in question. Further confirmation was provided subsequent to the period covered by the present report, when a lighted United Nations jeep proceeding by night under a previously concluded arrangement to a village near an infiltration route came under heavy fire and was hit several times. The Group wishes to take this occasion of paying tribute to the courage and devotion to duty shown by its observers, who have carried out their responsibilities with firmness and tact in areas where, in addition to the risks represented by actual hostilities, law and order are by no means ensured. . . .

[*The report then considered progress made in specific areas.*]

1. *Akkar plain*

16. The first of the frontier areas held by the opposition—the Akkar plain—extends from Tripoli north and east to the Syrian border. The frontier on the north is flat and is crossed by the main Tripoli–Latakia road at Arida, by the main Tripoli–Homs road at Aziziyé and by a secondary road from Halba at Braghite. On the east, the area is bounded by the Lebanon range. . . .

18. In this area, air reconnaissance has been of particular importance because, until 9 July, ground patrols had not begun to reach the frontier regularly; jeep patrols of military observers had, however, been into the Akkar plain intermittently since 3 July when, for the first time, the frontiers at Arida and Aziziyé were visited. Military observers could not establish permanent observation posts in the Akkar plain, as the full freedom of movement demanded was not forthcoming.

19. Between 2 and 15 July 1958, thirty-nine reconnaissance sorties were flown, sixteen of which were by helicopter. The Akkar area was thus observed on thirty-five occasions, twenty times during the night.

20. The first air patrols by day revealed only sporadic traffic along the three roads crossing the frontier. At night, the traffic movements observed on the Arida–Tripoli road, as well as the Aziziyé–Abdé–Tripoli road, were insignificant. However, eight vehicles were observed actually crossing the border into Lebanon at 20.00 hours (local time) on 9 July. The greatest amount of traffic was observed on the Braghite–Halba road. On each of the nights of 5 to 11 July, 50, 5, 20, 10, 25 and 25 headlights were seen moving southwards, in what appeared to be convoys, at various times between 21.00 hours and 24.00 hours (local time).

21. It cannot be assumed that all the existing traffic has been observed by air. The traffic along the above three roads has proved to be heavier at night than during the daytime. A large majority of the vehicles observed were moving southwards and westwards.

22. It was observed that after the second night of aerial reconnaissance the lights of vehicles were switched off or dimmed when an aircraft was in the vicinity. What appeared to be a strong flashing light was observed on a hill-top, presumably to warn the vehicles on the

Braghite–Halba road of the approach of aircraft. Up to 6 July, the villages in this area were well illuminated at night. On successive nights, however, aerial observations have established that the villages along this road have been blacked out, except for a few odd lights.

23. This may perhaps be a normal reaction since the area has been subject to air attack in the past and even now the government air forces have been attacking the Jabal Terbol area. The people of the area have complained particularly against strafing and against shelling from the sea by government gun-boats at Abdé. The natural reaction of villages on hearing the sound of an aircraft in the air would be to black out as many lights as possible. The convoys returning from Syria might well have arranged a system of warning-lights for their safety.

24. Every effort was made to ascertain on the ground the nature of the traffic seen at night from the air, but since permission to establish permanent stations in the area had not been secured, no direct ground observation of it was possible. However, ground patrols at the border at Arida and Aziziyé and in the interior of the region have frequently seen lively vehicular and other traffic moving in both directions in the daytime and have observed nothing which would lead them to believe that it was anything but the normal movement of goods and passengers.

25. In default of direct ground observation at night, ground patrols during the day have paid close attention to the arms at the disposal of opposition forces in the Tripoli area. They have observed no change in the general character of the arms carried by these forces as indicated in the first report and, in particular, no evidence of the use of heavy weapons or their presence at strategic positions. There have been no such movements as might indicate a major build-up. The possibility of the infiltration of a certain amount of the type of arms and ammunition previously observed is not, however, excluded. . . .

2. *North Bekaa valley*

30. Access to the area was restricted at first, but subsequently our patrols were in a position to reach every part of it during the day. Until 11 July, patrols were being held up at El Laboué, 30 km from the border. Despite this, day observation of the North Bekaa valley was possible, to an extent limited by frequent poor visibility on account of fog and haze, from observation posts established on the Lebanon range and at Btedaï. Beginning on 11 July, day patrols from Chtaura out station began to reach the frontier in this area and on 15 July agreement was reached with the local opposition leaders to establish stations at Baalbek and near the northern frontier. Pending their establishment, however, air observation has also been of considerable importance in this area.

31. Day patrols have reported that the Lebanese customs post at El Kah on the main road is intact, but unmanned; there is a Syrian customs post on the other side of the frontier. Vehicles have been seen crossing the border on both the main and subsidiary roads, though traffic north of Baalbek has not seemed to be heavy. Air observations confirm this, except that on the nights of 5 and 6 July at about 22.00 hours, a considerable number of vehicles not in regular formation was seen proceeding south towards Baalbek. It may be noted that a similar number of vehicle lights in more regular formation was seen on the same nights in the government-controlled area south of Baalbek proceeding in both directions.

32. Since an unsuccessful attack by opposition forces on government positions near Baalbek on 17 June, in which, in addition to small arms, bazookas and mortars were said to have been used, and in which one government soldier was killed and five were wounded, there has been no major military activity in the area, but there has been at times considerable firing of small arms, to which the government forces have replied with small arms and mortar fire. The opposition forces, which are in part posted among the celebrated ruins of the town, have drawn the attention of observers to some damage done to the ruins by government fire.

3. *Central Bekaa valley*

35. Adequate ground observation of this area has been possible from Chtaura outstation

and substations at Btedaï, American University Experimental Farm and Zahle and observers have experienced no great difficulty in access to the frontier here, although they were fired at on two occasions and had to withdraw. Day observation posts have been established near the frontier at Masnaa on the main road and on occasion at Yahfoû on the railway. The log kept at the former post shows a considerable movement of traffic across the frontier in both directions, but there has been nothing to indicate that any infiltration of arms or ammunition has occurred. As noted above, government forces are in a position to control the important road junction at Masnaa on the Beirut–Damascus highway, although they have not done so due to the fact that they have not been stationed at the road junction during the hours of darkness and have only lately taken up position in daytime as far eastward. There are, however, no government posts from the Masnaa road crossing to the frontier.

4. South Bekaa valley

39. Opposition forces are in control of most of the area between the Masnaa–Rachaya road and the frontier and appear to have recently exercised control even in the daytime over the main road from Masnaa to Rachaya. When members of the Group visited the latter town on 9 July, they passed a notice placed in the centre of the road warning travellers that they proceeded further on their own responsibility. Many of the villages to the west of the road appear to contain opposition sympathizers and a number of armed men have been seen there regularly. Sporadic firing occurs between villages at night, but the only activity by government forces in the area was the recapture of the village of Aïha by a government armoured column which proceeded to Rachaya on 6 July, and occasional machine-gun and mortar fire from government forces in the citadel of Rachaya, mostly in the direction of Kfar Kouk. A government post has existed there throughout the disturbances, but it has been practically cut off from outside contact.

40. The ground observation in this area is carried out from a sub-station at Rachaya on the northern foothills of Mount Hermon and that of Saghbine at a point overlooking the Bekaa valley from the west. A subsidiary night observation post was established on 11 July near Kafraya on the Saghbine–Chtaura road. Access to the frontier areas near Deïr el Aachâyer has presented no particular difficulty and a day observation post has been established in the region on a regular basis. However, the observers have been allowed to use only the northern road into this area. Traffic on the road leading to Kfar Kouk has not been possible since 26 June, since the road is said to be mined. Opposition forces seen in this area have been considerably less than the thousand men noted in the first report (*S/4040 and Add.1, annex II*). It should be added that this area consists also of Druze tribesmen, whose homeland extends well across the border.

41. In its first report, the Group reported that its observers had noticed approximately one company of uniformed Syrian soldiers on both sides of a road leading from Deïr el Aachâyer into Syria in an area where the location of the border is under dispute (*ibid.*). This matter has received the further careful consideration of the Group. On 11 July the Executive Member of the Group personally visited the area and made an inspection tour there in order to check the findings of the observers as regards the exact location of the Syrian company's camp. The camp lies some $4\frac{1}{2}$ km. south-west of Deïr el Aachâyer along the road from that village leading towards Kfar Kouk, at a junction where a side road branches off to Rahle in Syria. It was verified that the company had remained in this position at least since 25 June. The road junction in question is only about $\frac{1}{2}$ kilometre from the border, as shown on the maps officially transmitted to the Group by the Lebanese authorities, and is well inside the area which, according to the Lebanese authorities, has been claimed by Syria and hence is subject to dispute. The Syrian company was found to be entirely within territory claimed to be Syrian; some further tents in indisputably Lebanese territory were found to be occupied by nomads. The Executive Member was of the impression that the company was an ordinary border patrol. . . .

43. The Government has in fact submitted to the Group several intelligence reports to the

effect that there is passage by night of caravans of armed men and munitions from the vicinity of Deïr el Aachâyer via Aïta el Foukhar, Joub Jannine, Aïn Zebdé over the Lebanon range to the Choûf area south-east of Beirut. It has even been alleged that such movements have taken place by vehicle as far as Joub Jannine, where the bridge over the Litani has been blown up by the opposition. Other routes north and south of the one mentioned above are also reported and in fact the terrain would offer no obstacle to the passage of mule traffic over a wide variety of routes. Observers have received several reports of such traffic from other sources.

44. The day patrols carried out by observers have revealed no significant movements in the area by day. Instances of interference with patrols, have, however, continued to occur. . . .

48. Finally, the arms which have been observed in the Choûf area and the nature of such military operations as have occurred would imply the existence of some source of supply, and it may therefore be presumed that arms and ammunition are entering the area long the route indicated, although it should be added that it has not been possible for observers to ascertain the exact nature of the cargo.

49. It remains to make some estimate of the scale of such infiltration as may be occurring. There is no evidence of substantial road traffic into the villages of the South Bekaa valley. The size of the mule caravans subsequently seen would set an upper limit on the scale of the operation. Previous negative observations would tend to suggest that any infiltration which has taken place has occurred in the recent dark nights and not in the previous period of moonlight. It can be assumed therefore that the operations have been on a limited scale sufficient perhaps to supply the Druze tribesmen and others of the Choûf with a certain amount of arms and ammunition, but scarcely sufficient to transform them into a force capable of operating effectively outside their own mountain fastnesses or against well-armed military forces. The observations recorded later in the report in the section on south-west Lebanon indicate this. . . .

5. *South-east Lebanon*

51. The remaining section of the frontier with Syria consists of the mountainous region of Mount Hermon (2,814 metres), but just before the Israel border it falls away into the upper Jordan valley and is traversed by a second-class road leading to Bâniâs and Kuneitra in Syria. The high ground along the frontier is controlled by opposition forces, which made themselves more secure by blowing up the bridges and mining the road leading up the hills. It was not until 12 July that observers proceeding on horseback were able to reach the opposition headquarters in this area, at Chebaa.

52. The main government force in this area is stationed at Marjayoûn, a town strategically situated on high ground between the Jordan and Litani rivers. This is also the outstation from which military observers patrol the main road north-east to Rachaya and southward along a section of the frontier with Israel. In its first report, the Group noted that Marjayoûn and Khiam had been fired at on several occasions from mortars in opposition-held territory near Halta within Lebanon (*S/4040 and Add. 1, para 22*). There have been no further reports of such fire during the period 2–15 July. The only action reported during the period was an attempt by the government forces to recover a number of its supporters, who had been ambushed and held prisoner near Hasbaya.

53. In certain of the communications received from the Lebanese Government, the area round Chebaa has been mentioned as the starting point of routes for the despatch of mule trains carrying arms to the Choûf and other opposition-held areas in the interior. The Group has made no direct observations, either from the ground or the air, tending to confirm this. In any case, it intends to establish sub-stations at Chebaa and Kherouia in the area in question.

6. *South-west Lebanon*

54. The Group's outstation at Saïda has direct access to the southern border with Israel and to the seacoast northward towards Beirut. Sub-stations have been established at Soûr

further south on the coast, and at Jezzine south of the opposition-held Choûf area. There are opposition-held sections in the towns of Saïda and Soûr.

55. A particular concern of the Group has been to guard against possible infiltration from the sea. In addition to ground patrols from Saïda and Soûr, air patrols have been ordered from time to time on this and other sections of the sea frontier. No significant observations have, however, been reported. Sea patrolling of the coast has been considered, but the Group felt that that was primarily the duty of the Lebanese authorities.

56. Another activity of observers has been to endeavour to ascertain if arms and ammunition are being moved to the opposition quarters of Saïda and Soûr and to the southern part of the Chouf from the eastern and south-eastern frontier. The sub-station at Jezzine is particularly well located to patrol roads and tracks which might be used for this purpose. Here again, however, no significant observations have been made.

57. The areas controlled by the opposition have been visited at frequent intervals with a view to ascertaining possible changes in the arms at their disposal. There has been considerable exchange of small arms fire at both Saïda and Soûr. The symbolic nature of much of it, is, however, revealed by the fact that there is a sort of informal truce at Saïda and Soûr each evening from 17.00 to 19.00 hours to enable shopping to be done. Members of the Group, while visiting Saïda on 3 July, were able to see government soldiers moving freely in an area commanded by houses fifty yards away where the opposition forces were standing guard on the roof tops.

58. Military observers from Saïda have also on several occasions visited Moukhtara, the opposition headquarters in the Choûf. These visits have revealed no particular change in the situation as described in the first report. It should be noted that in the first few days of July, Druzes from the Choûf advanced to Chamlane and other hill stations overlooking Beirut city and airport from the south-east. These attacks were observed by military observers from Headquarters at Beirut. The opposition forces, which were using only small arms, were repelled without undue difficulty by government forces with armoured cars, with the assistance of government partisans.

59. Since that time, opposition forces in the Choûf area have been quiescent.

60. Finally, it should be noted that the opposition-held quarter of Beirut has continued to be held behind barricades, although most of the civic services there are said to be functioning. There have been frequent bursts of firing on both sides as well as a certain number of acts of terrorism and sporadic firing in other quarters of the city. Observers have entered the opposition-held quarter in Beirut only for discussions concerned with arrangements for access to opposition-held frontier areas.

IV. CONCLUSIONS

61. It will be clear from the report that considerable progress has been made in extending and intensifying observation activities over most of the significant areas, both along the borders and in the areas adjacent to them. United Nations military observers have operated with skill and devotion and often in conditions of considerable danger and difficulty in areas where there is no effective governmental authority of any kind and where they have to depend for their safety largely on the good will of the inhabitants or on such influence as the local opposition leaders may exercise.

62. The extent of the infiltration of arms which may be taking place has been indicated in the report. It is clear that it cannot be on anything more than a limited scale, and is largely confined to small arms and ammunition. In conditions of civil conflict, when the frontier is open and unguarded practically throughout its length, some movement of this kind may well be expected.

63. As regards the question of the illegal infiltration of personnel, the nature of the frontier, the existence of traditional, tribal and other bonds on both sides of it, the free movement of produce in both directions, are among the factors which must be taken into account in making an evaluation. It must, however, be said that in no case have United Nations observers, who have been vigilantly patrolling the opposition-held areas and have frequently observed the

armed bands there, been able to detect the presence of persons who have indubitably entered from across the border for the purpose of fighting.

64. It must be emphasized that from the observations made of the arms and organization in the opposition-held areas, the fighting strength of opposition elements is not such as to be able successfully to cope with hostilities against a well-armed regular military force. There is no evidence of the existence of radio contact between the opposition forces scattered over different parts of the country nor of any co-ordinated military planning and control.

65. These observations are based upon the results of incessant patrolling both in the air and on the ground. Whatever information has been received, whether from the Lebanese Government liaison committee or from other sources or clues, has been followed up with great care. Intensive air patrolling has been carried out by day as well as by night, and the observations thus made have been closely checked against the results of ground patrolling and observation. All-night watches have been instituted at the outstations and sub-stations and occasionally, observers have patrolled at night.

66. In the report, everything of consequence or significance observed has been fully assessed and set out, irrespective of whether the results have been of a positive or negative nature. The observations therefore accurately reflect the situation in regard to the question of the 'illegal infiltration of personnel or smuggling of arms or other *matériel* across the Lebanese borders'. [*S/4069, 2nd Report of UNOGIL, 30 July 1958.*]

6. . . . Since 31 July, there has been a further reduction in tension throughout the country, including the opposition-held areas. There has, in fact, been virtually a nation-wide truce since then with only occasional reports of sporadic firing in some areas.

7. On the other hand, there appears to have been a decrease in some areas in the ability of opposition leaders to control their followers, and a noticeable increase in acts of lawlessness. The Group has received frequent reports of hold-ups, stealing of vehicles, shootings and other acts of terrorism and of kidnapping in pursuit of party feuds or personal vendettas. This breakdown of law and order has only once directly affected observers, as noted in paragraph 22 below, but has added appreciably to the difficulties of observers in carrying out their duties. . . .

By the redeployment of existing observers in positions closer to the frontier, it has been possible to bring the main possible infiltration routes under direct observation. Air operations have continued uninterrupted despite the fact that aircraft have frequently been fired at and have been hit on four occasions, fortunately without injury to the pilots or serious damage to the craft. Co-ordination between air and ground observation has been further intensified and improved. Air patrols have been closely checking the results of ground observations and *vice versa*, and direct radio contact between air patrols and stations has greatly increased the effectiveness of the combined operations.

11. In this section, the Group has set forth, in respect of each sector of the frontier, the progress achieved in expanding the scope of observation and the results of the patrols actually carried out.

1. *Tripoli and the Akkar plain*

12. The first sub-station in the Akkar plain had been established on the morning of 15 July at Halba. Because of the difficulty of supplying this station by road, it was intended that a United Nations plane should land with supplies at the airfield west of Klaïate on 16 July. Observers from Halba arriving at the airfield on the morning of that day found the runway covered with obstacles, some of which they removed. Armed men in the vicinity, in a state of agitation because of their fear that the airfield might be used by foreign military planes, stated that they would shoot at any plane which might try to land. The flight of the United Nations plane was therefore cancelled. Later in the day, because of the threatening attitude of armed bands near Halba, the sub-station was withdrawn to Tripoli.

13. On 17 July, a United Nations aircraft reported that the airfield had been damaged. Subsequent ground patrols confirmed that the runway had been blown up in places and mines

had been laid, making it unusable. This fact was also reported to the Group by the Lebanese Government liaison committee, which charged that the demolitions had been carried out with the help of a detachment of Syrian Army soldiers who had crossed the frontier in fourteen to sixteen jeeps on the evening of 16 July. While, for the reasons given earlier in the present report, there were no observers present in the area at the time the damage was done to the airfield, they subsequently inspected the damage and reported that the demolitions were not of such a nature as would suggest that they had been carried out by professionally trained personnel.

14. On the following days, repeated attempts were made to ensure the safe passage of observers through Munié and Abdé to the Akkar plain, but it was not until 21 July, and only after reassuring numerous groups of armed men, that a patrol accompanied by an opposition guide reached Halba once more. The sub-station there was re-established on 22 July, and patrols to the frontier were resumed. Priority was immediately given to patrolling the Halba–Braghite road, down which substantial traffic by night was reported in the period covered by the second report, and on 26 July a tented sub-station was opened at Mechta Hammoud near Braghite on the northern border. It was subsequently moved to a house in the neighbouring village of Chadra. A further sub-station was opened at Notre-Dame-du-Fort (half way between Braghite and the point where the Tripoli–Homs main road crosses the frontier) on 31 July.

15. While the reaction to the presidential election has been generally favourable in this area, the uncertainty about subsequent developments has caused some anxiety and restlessness. This has resulted in a less friendly attitude towards observers, who have been frequently stopped and on three occasions were even fired at. This change of attitude and the reluctance of local leaders, because of the changed circumstances, to carry out their earlier undertakings, delayed for a time the establishment of the proposed sub-stations on the frontier at Arida (on the Tripoli–Latakia road) and at Aziziyé (on the Tripoli–Homs road). These were established, however, on 11 August. In the meantime, on 4 August, the Halba sub-station was discontinued and replaced by more conveniently situated sub-stations at Beino (some 10 kilometres to the east) and Tell Abbas (some 5 kilometres to the north). Night patrolling has since been instituted along the roads near the frontier as necessary.

16. The difficult ground communications between Halba and Tripoli were interrupted by the outbreak of fighting near Mariata on 28 July and the sub-stations in the north were supplied on the following day by helicopter. Subsequently negotiations were carried on with the local army commander and opposition leaders, which resulted in the main road between Tripoli and the north being repaired and opened to United Nations traffic on 9 August. Civilians wishing to proceed across the lines are obliged to change vehicles.

17. Air patrolling had continued in spite of the fact that United planes have frequently been fired at from the ground in this area and hit on three occasions. Because of the large number of United States planes constantly flying over the area, the local population is excited and apparently fires indiscriminately at all planes.

18. The ground and air observations of traffic on the roads leading from the Syrian frontier into Lebanon have revealed a very different picture from that given in the second report. A certain amount of traffic has been observed on the main road south of Arida and Aziziyé, but very little on the Braghite–Halba secondary road. Motor traffic, particularly since 28 July, has moreover been less intense than previously and mule and camel traffic has been very limited. In fact, ground reconnaissance has shown that traffic with heavy loads is practicable only on the first two routes and that the Braghite–Halba road is passable by trucks only with difficulty, particularly near the Syrian border where in fact the road branches into two. Moreover, this road passes through the Christian villages of Koubayate and Andakat, which are strongly pro-Government and which themselves stop and inspect vehicles passing through. The sub-station located at Mechta Hammoud, and later at Chadra, has reported little or no traffic passing along the road since the date of its establishment. It should be noted that no further evidence has been found of the strong flashing light mentioned in the second report or of trucks or villages dimming or extinguishing lights on the approach of aircraft.

19. Following the landing of United States forces, opposition forces in the Tripoli area were reinforced from Halba and Sir Danié and there is some indication of a subsequent rotation of armed men between those areas. The arrival of reinforcements caused a temporary increase in fighting in the Tripoli–Mariata area until 25 July with another outbreak on 28 July, but since then fighting has generally quieted down in and around Tripoli; subsequent sporadic clashes seem to have been motivated by local feuds.

20. Government forces have informed observers that mortars have occasionally been fired by opposition forces in the Tripoli area. During the period observers have reported seeing some home-made muzzle-loading and breech-loading mortars of an unusual 64 mm calibre. No other heavy weapons have been observed.

21. The interference with the activities of observers noted above has so far prevented a complete check on road traffic. Nevertheless during the past two weeks, United Nations ground patrols have had a much better opportunity to assess the nature of the traffic crossing the frontier, which in any case has been much lighter than that reported in the second report. In the light of their observations, the Group feels that such traffic as is crossing the frontier is related to the normal economic life of the territory, but as the frontier is open and unguarded, the possibility of the infiltration on a limited scale of arms and ammunition cannot be wholly excluded.

2. North Bekaa valley

22. Arrangements had been made on 15 July to establish sub-stations at Koussair and at Baalbek. These plans could not be implemented at once due to the changed circumstances referred to earlier in the report and to the marked reluctance of opposition leaders to agree to the establishment of permanent posts. Reconnaissance patrols, however, pushed into the opposition-held town of Baalbek on 16 July, and as far as El Laboué on 19 July. Sub-stations were ultimately established at El Kah Customs Post in a village of Government sympathizers on 26 July, and at Hermel on 27 July. Observers at the latter station were held up by armed bandits and robbed of personal valuables in the early morning of 29 July, but assurances of safety were subsequently given by local leaders and the sub-station has functioned since without incident. A permanent observation post has also been established at Koussair just inside the Lebanese border. Finally, a sub-station was established in the opposition-held portion of Baalbek on 29 July. In view of the development of activities in the north Bekaa valley, the sub-stations there were removed from the control of Chtaura station, and Baalbek was established as the main station for that area on 8 August. The Group has thus been able to bring the possible infiltration routes in this area under direct observation.

23. Between 15 July and the establishment of these permanent posts, no less than 20 flights took place over the north Bekaa valley, several of them by night. Little traffic was reported and none of it appeared to be out of the ordinary. The reconnaissance patrols northward by day did not report any abnormal or significant movements.

24. Since the establishment of the new sub-stations, only normal day traffic and little night traffic has been reported by them, despite the fact that frequent patrols have been carried out by day and by night. Air patrols have reported the same observations in the valley, but have reported several large mule and camel caravans, as well as a few truck movements near the large village of Arsal, in the hills to the east of El Laboué. Firing at United Nations aircraft has twice occurred over Arsal, one plane having been hit in the wings, fuselage and tail.

25. Ground patrols sent from El Kah to Arsal have verified that there are large mule and donkey caravans employed in carrying water to Arsal, which has a population of 3,500 to 4,000 persons with no permanent water supply, from the nearest spring on the road to El Laboué. Parties of some sixty armed men have been seen undergoing training near Arsal on two occasions. The question of whether there is any further mule traffic which would need explanation is under investigation and it is intended to set up an observation post at Arsal based on a sub-station to be established at El Laboué.

3. *Central Bekaa valley*

26. There is little to report from this sector, where the main centres and roads are under the control of Government forces. The stations at Chtaura and the American University Experimental Farm have continued to operate, but the personnel at Zahle and Btedaï were moved up to the new stations established in the north Bekaa. The day observation post at Masnaa has continued to function and patrols have been carried out without difficulty both on the main roads and into villages in the hands of opposition forces on both sides of the valley. It is intended to establish sub-stations at Masnaa and Yahfoû in the immediate future.

4. *South Bekaa valley*

27. The sub-stations of Rachaya and Saghbine continued to operate in this sector with the support of a permanent observation post at Kafraya on the Saghbine–Chtaura road, of a night observation post in varying positions near Aïn Zebdé just north of Sighbine and of day observation posts at Yanta, Aïta el Foukhar and Kfar Kouh, all three of which are in the Deïr el Aachâyer salient. There has continued to be no particular difficulty in penetrating into this opposition-held area and arrangements have been made to establish a sub-station there. It may be noted that the Syrian company, which was mentioned in the second report (*S/4069, para. 41*) as being located near the road junction leading to Rahle, was found on 19 July to have withdrawn. . . .

30. In its second report (*S/4069*) the Group discussed at some length the question of the existence of an infiltration route from the frontier in the vicinity of Deïr el Aachâyer across the south Bekaa valley and thence by mule caravan across the mountains into the Choûf, and arrived at the presumption that arms and ammunition were being transported on a limited scale along the route in question. This question continued to receive the close attention of the Group and of its observers during the period covered by the present report.

31. The observations carried out in the period 15 to 28 July have provided much detailed information bearing on this subject. Both air and ground observations reveal the movement of a few vehicles usually in the evening from Yanta or Heloué in the vicinity of Deïr el Aachâyer via Aïta el Foukhar to the Joub Jannine area. On 19 July, two sacks of ammunition were seen in a jeep along this route. There is regular traffic on the main Damascus–Beirut road towards Masnaa. Since the road junction there is left unguarded by the Lebanese Army at night, vehicles could proceed unchecked into the south Bekaa.

32. More detailed observations have been made by patrols from Saghbine sub-station, in particular from a hidden observation post established, at considerable risk, in the vicinity of Aïn Zebdé. This observation post saw a caravan with fifteen–twenty loaded mules and about thirty armed men pass nearby from east to west on 22 July at 23.05 hours and another convoy of eighteen mules on 24 July, from 21.35 to 21.50 hours, also crossing the road at Aïn Zebdé westward. Moreover, Saghbine patrols have seen four similar caravans on 19, 20, 22 and 25 July pass unloaded in the neighbourhood of Aïn Zebdé from west to east. In addition to these direct observations, such indications as signal lights and shots, presence of armed guards on the roads, sounds of movement and reports of local inhabitants show that mule caravans passed on nearly every night between 15–28 July. There are also some indirect reports of the passage of armed men who were not escorting caravans.

33. The greater part of the information mentioned in the previous paragraphs was already at the disposal of the Group when it formulated the conclusions on this traffic which are contained in paragraphs 47 to 49 of its second report (*S/4069*). The conclusions apply with equal force to events up to 28 July and the essential points are given in the following remarks. In brief, the eastern frontier in the area is quite unguarded and the roads from there to the Joub Jannine area are open to passage and a few vehicles have been seen moving along them. The passage of mule caravans from the Joub Jannine area to the Choûf has been confirmed and although the cargo has not been inspected, the movement of a certain amount of arms and ammunition may be presumed. The size of the caravans sets an upper limit on the

scale of the operation, which can be assumed to have been on a limited scale and scarcely in sufficient quantity to transform the Druze tribesmen in the Choûf into a force capable of operating against well armed military forces.

34. The Group wishes to add that despite frequent night patrols, no further mule convoys have been observed in the south Bekaa since 28 July. On 10 August, the Saghbine sub-station and the Kafraya permanent observation post were closed down and the personnel were transferred to a sub-station established at Aïn Zebdé.

35. There have been no hostilities between Government armed forces and opposition elements in the south Bekaa. In fact on 29 July, when the Group paid a visit to Saghbine, Kafraya and Aïn Zebdé, it was able to verify that a Government column had passed right beside an outpost of Druze tribesmen from the Choüf, located in the same building as the United Nations post at Kafraya, without any interference. There is, however, growing evidence that there are armed bands intent on loot or pillage roaming about the South Bekaa area.

5. *South-east Lebanon*

36. In this sector, the opposition-held village of Chebaa in the south-western foothills of Mount Hermon had been one of the most inaccessible points in the period prior to 15 July covered by the second report and was visited for the first time only on 12 July. On 19 July arrangements were made with the opposition leader in Hasbaya to revisit Chebaa with a view to setting up a post. He insisted, however, on being given forty-eight hours' notice, and in fact when the patrol reached Chebaa on 21 July, it received a hostile reception from an excited crowd and was somewhat roughly handled. Opposition supporters there threatened to fire on United Nations planes unless they were given previous notice of their flights over the area. A further effort to reach Chebaa on 26 July was unsuccessful, since the opposition leader at Hasbaya declined to allow them to proceed, saying that he could not be sure of the safety of the observers if they went in without prior notice. The plan to establish a post at Chebaa cannot therefore be executed for the time being and an alternative site for a station, with better visibility, has been selected at Chouaya.

37. In its second interim report, the Group also stated that it intended to establish a sub-station near Kherouia (*S/4052, para. 3*), at a point where the road leading from Marjayoûn to Bâniâs and Kuneitra in Syria crosses the border. Patrols to the border in this area have continued without interference. A permanent observation post to cover the road was set up on 20 July and a permanent sub-station at Kherouia (Mejidie) on 29 July. Members of the mission personally visited the area on 9 August and made arrangements for the post at Chouaya to be established without delay. The road to the village was repaired by opposition forces on the following day and the station will be established shortly.

6. *South-west Lebanon*

38. Saïda outstation and Jezzine outstation have continued to operate along the lines indicated in the previous report, while a night watch was kept at Soûr until 31 July. No significant observations have been made. Arrangements were made on 28 July with the opposition leader in the Choûf for observers to patrol that region by day and night. This has been carried out for the most part by the Headquarters patrol from Beirut. A virtual truce exists in the area and, although both sides maintain their armed posture, comparative calm prevails.

IV. Conclusions

39. During the period under report, in spite of the set-back caused by the landing of United States troops on 15 July, which resulted in a sharp reaction in the opposition-held areas, the ground lost was steadily regained through the tact, patience and perseverance of the military observers. The extension of the Observation Group's activities therefore continued and posts have been established at most of the sensitive points along the borders and

in the areas immediately adjacent to them. This process is continuing and is being intensified as additional observers arrive on the scene.

40. Members of the Group have either separately or jointly toured over all parts of the country and have visited a large number of posts and acquainted themselves personally with the local conditions in each area. Their visits have had a good effect on the inhabitants of these areas and have conveyed a sense of reassurance to them. They have also given encouragement and support to the observers, who are often working in conditions of danger and difficulty. The members of the Group intend to continue these visits.

41. It should be recorded that the presence of the United Nations observers moving around in their white jeeps from village to village is welcomed both by Government supporters and by opposition elements. The independence and impartiality of the observers is universally recognized and appreciated, and they are regarded as the symbol of the United Nations presence in the area; they help to inspire feelings of calm and confidence in the areas patrolled by them. Sometimes local disputes and difficulties have been referred to them by different parties, and they have occasionally been instrumental in solving them.

42. As will be seen from the observations made in the report, the situation in regard to the possible infiltration of personnel and the smuggling of arms from across the border is that, while there may have been a limited importation of arms into some areas prior to the presidential election on 31 July, any such movement has since markedly diminished. A virtual truce has prevailed since about that time in most of the disturbed areas. However, acts of brigandage and lawlessness, unconnected with the political movement, are being increasingly reported. Many of these lawless acts are motivated by economic considerations, as normal life throughout the country has been severely disrupted by the prolonged state of civil strife.

43. It is evident that the nature and scope of the work of the observers will inevitably be conditioned by the progress made in dealing with the internal political aspects of the Lebanese problem and with the return to normal conditions both in the countryside and in the towns. [*S/4085, 3rd Report of UNOGIL, 14 Aug. 1958.*]

5. Despite the presence of a considerable number of men under arms, there have been no significant clashes between the Lebanese armed forces and organized opposition forces. This has facilitated the deployment of the observers at the disposal of the Group in the most strategic locations and has enabled the observers to obtain a much fuller knowledge of the frontier areas in which they are operating. With the establishment of its extended network of posts, the Group is confident that any infiltration which may still be occurring is on a very small scale indeed. It has no convincing reports of such infiltration and has, on the contrary, some detailed reports, which are mentioned below, that persons who had presumably entered Lebanon for illegal purposes have now left the country. . . .

1. *Tripoli and Akkar plain*

24. Interference with United Nations patrols has largely ceased during the period covered by the present report, although United Nations vehicles have been sporadically stopped between Tripoli and Munié, where a long detour from the main road along the railroad continues to be necessary. For this reason helicopters have been frequently used to maintain communications between Tripoli and the Akkar plain. It is to be regretted that there have been further cases of firing at United Nations aircraft by unknown persons. It may, however, be noted that an armed man who fired at a United Nations helicopter which was trying to land at Sir Danié on 31 August was severely beaten by the villagers.

25. The traffic pattern across the frontier revealed by the posts on the main road has conformed with that recorded in previous reports, mainly as a result of air observation, although it appears that traffic across the frontier increased after the coastal road between Tripoli and Munié was opened to traffic on 10 August. On the basis of vehicle logs kept, the heaviest traffic has been on the Tripoli–Homs road where there has been an average of some 160 vehicle movements a day across the frontier in both directions. At Arida the traffic has been

about half as much, while the traffic reported by the Chadra outpost is limited to some 2 to 4 vehicles a day. The most prevalent type of vehicles are buses and cars with civilian passengers. The remainder of the traffic consists almost entirely, as was presumed by the Group in its earlier reports, of trucks carrying agricultural products to Syria. . . .

2. *North Bekaa valley*

29. The eastern frontier with Syria consists of the difficult mountain country of the Anti-Lebanon range, which has an average height of 2,400 metres. During the period under review, detailed reconnaissances have been made of the numerous tracks in this area to see which, if any of them, are passable by vehicle. . . .

31. The Group has thus achieved coverage of all practicable roads leading into the country. There are also numerous mule tracks and other paths by means of which the frontier could be crossed. Considering, however, the difficulties of terrain in the east, the Group is confident that its air patrols would be able to bring any suspicious movements across the frontier to the attention of the ground observers in time to have them investigated. In fact, however, no such movements have been reported by them.

32. The only considerable traffic across the frontier has been reported by the post at El Kah where some twenty to twenty-five vehicles, mostly buses and private cars, have been reported moving daily in each direction. On the other roads and mule tracks, only a little incoming and outgoing traffic has been observed. Some families in north Bekaa seem, however, to own land well inside the Syrian territory, so there is a daily traffic of vehicles and camels across the northern border carrying mostly farm produce.

33. Military observers have on two occasions reported the presence of a white car with licence plates which has been noticed coming down the Homs–Baalbek road, driven by a man in Arab robes. Several local inhabitants have maintained that this person has been selling rifles and that he is a Syrian army officer in disguise. There is no confirmation of this.

34. Towards the close of the period, military observers have been able to carry out thorough inspections of almost all vehicles crossing the frontier. This inspection has revealed no sign of infiltration. On the other hand, it may be noticed that on 28 August fifty men, several of them armed, in six cars with Syrian licence plates, passed El Kah heading north. The cars have not been seen coming back.

35. A certain amount of traffic both by day and night consisting of cars and camel and mule caravans has been observed by the air patrols on a tableland some 12 to 15 kilometres west of Hermel. When this traffic was investigated from the ground, however, it was found to consist entirely in the transportation of crops from this locality towards Hermel.

36. Many armed men are still to be seen throughout the area, although both the government and opposition forces have ceased to man their positions on the south-west edge of Baalbek itself. Reference has already been made to the increased lawlessness in this region and to robberies which have occurred, of which United Nations observers on three occasions have been the victims. On one of these occasions, however, the stolen property was returned through the good offices of an opposition leader. There is still some fighting between the different villages in north Bekaa because of local feuds and rivalries. On one occasion, about 200 men in Arsal took up defensive positions around the village because they expected an attack from villages in the vicinity. The villagers even fired on a United Nations patrol on the road to the village. However, in general the attitude towards the military observers throughout the whole area, including Arsal itself, has become increasingly friendly and observers can move freely over the whole area.

37. The concern of the local leaders for the restoration of order in this part of the country has been shown not only by the establishment of local 'police' but also by the fact that certain villages have requested the Lebanese armed forces to move into this part of the country. Two strong army patrols have recently proceeded along the main road as far northwards as El Kah and returned south of Baalbek. Other villages have been discussing whether to invite the Army to visit them. These developments confirm the fact that no appreciable infiltration is occurring

3. Remainder of the Bekaa valley

39. To enable the railroad to operate it was first necessary for a blown culvert to be repaired. Three trains a day have been proceeding in each direction. Incoming trains are inspected by the Lebanese customs authorities at Rayak. The Group has arranged for observers to travel on these trains from time to time in order to make certain that they are not being used for the purpose of infiltration.

40. On 12 August, the day observation post at Masnaa was transformed into a permanent observation post with watches being kept on a 24-hour a day basis. Lebanese armed forces took up permanent positions there on the same day and the customs post was manned in the daytime from 19 August. In view of the fact that inspections were being carried out in the daytime by both the Lebanese Army and customs and in view of the need for observers in other locations, the observation post was maintained only at night from that date. Arrangements were, however, made with the Lebanese authorities to have observers on call at Chtaura, in case it was necessary to verify any case of infiltration.

41. Prior to the opening of the customs post, some 30 trucks laden with animals and other produce and some 15 cars or buses were arriving daily at Masnaa, while some 15 trucks and the same number of cars or buses were returning to Syria. Beginning on 23 August the traffic was increased, by agreement between the Governments concerned, by a considerable number of oil tankers proceeding loaded to Syria and returning empty.

42. South of Masnaa, the frontier consists of the Deïr el Aachâyer salient, which is crossed by a number of minor roads from which there is access to the main Lebanese road network. In previous reports, the Group had come to the conclusion that a certain amount of infiltration of arms and ammunition had been taking place in this area across the south Bekaa valley in the direction of the Choûf. It has been the concern of the Group to establish a network of stations on the roads along which this infiltration might have been taking place. To this end, the Rachaya sub-station, which was situated at some distance from the likely infiltration routes, was transferred on 19 August to Aïta el Foukhar which lies astride one of these routes. A second station was established at Aïn Arab on 24 August and a third at Kfar Mechki on 31 August. Finally, with the various routes thus covered, a permanent observation post was established at Deïr el Aachâyer itself on 16 September. Active night patrolling has been carried out between these various stations and also in the villages of Joub Jannine, Lela and Balloul further to the west near the Litani River. Finally, the sub-station at Aïn Zebdé on the eastern slopes of the Lebanon range has continued to observe whether there has been any traffic westward over the mountains into the Choûf.

43. The sub-station at Aïn Zebdé has received only infrequent reports of movements of caravans towards the Choûf. Such caravans as have been checked have been small ones carrying innocent cargo. From the above findings, there is every reason to conclude that the infiltration noted in July across the south Bekaa is no longer taking place.

44. There has been a considerable improvement over the period in the security situation in the south Bekaa area and in the attitude towards military observers. At the beginning of the period under review, the Lebanese armed forces began to patrol much more actively southward of the main Beirut–Damascus road, and during most of the period they have occupied a position in strength just north of Joub Jannine. Since that time, armed men have virtually disappeared from that area. East of the Masnaa–Rachaya road, the previously somewhat disorganized armed bands have been organized into a so-called national liberation army which appears to be well disciplined and paid and seems mainly concerned to keep order in the area. Further south near Rachaya, there have been a number of cases of brisk exchanges of firing and there have also been several cases in which United Nations patrols have been fired upon or halted at night. Otherwise, the attitude towards United Nations observers is friendly enough. The opposition forces at Aïta el Foukhar have been most co-operative in permitting inspections of vehicles passing through that place. In Deïr el Aachâyer there has been some reluctance in this respect, but the Kfar Kouk road, the only practicable route, has been well covered by standing patrols of observers. Such observations as have been made have re-

vealed comparatively heavy traffic, the most significant element of which has been buses apparently plying between the Joub Jannine area to and from Damascus; incoming truck traffic has been almost entirely laden with wheat. There have been no apparent infiltrations of armed men, arms or ammunition over the period in question.

45. It would seem probable that at least some of the persons moving across the frontier were returning to Syria after having entered Lebanon illegally. At about 02.00 hours on the morning of 3 September, a convoy of eight army lorries escorted by soldiers in jeeps was seen by United Nations observers at the Masnaa observation post passing eastward carrying some 240 persons who were being transported across the border and whose identity they were not able to establish. The Group, on receiving this report, contacted the Lebanese authorities with a view to getting the question of their identity and the circumstances of their departure clarified, but has not yet been provided with any official information. According to unofficial reports, the persons came from the opposition-held part of Beirut, but it has not been verified as to when and how they entered the city. The Group would, however, recall that, upon its arrival in Lebanon, the Lebanese Government alleged that there were several hundred non-Lebanese residing in the opposition-held area of Beirut and actively supporting the opposition.

4. South-east Lebanon

47. It is possible for persons on foot or by caravan to cross the frontier south of the road. A sub-station was established at Deïr Mimass on 14 August to guard against this possibility. Finally, non-vehicular traffic can proceed without difficulty across the foothills to the south-west of Mount Hermon towards opposition-held areas around Chebaa and Rachaya Foukhar. The roads leading up into the hills from the main Marjayoûn-Rachaya road have been demolished in places and, it is believed, mined, and it was not easy for United Nations observers to attain access to these areas, where the armed men had shown themselves in the past to be somewhat hostile. However, the Group noted in its last report that it had persuaded the local opposition leader to have the road cleared as far as the village of Chouaya, where it was hoped to establish a substation in the near future (S/4085, para. 37). Unfortunately, advantage was taken of the repairing of the road to Chouaya to send up a punitive army column to that village, which also mortared a number of villages in the vicinity. As a result, it was not possible to proceed with the plans to establish the post at Chouaya. A sub-station was, however, placed at El Haouch on the main Marjayoûn-Rachaya road on 24 August 1958. . . .

49. Very little traffic has been observed crossing the frontier in this region although some small-scale mule traffic has been observed in the Chebaa area along the mountain tracks leading to Syria. Such traffic as is observed appears to be normal.

50. In the main opposition-held areas there continues to be a considerable number of men still under arms and there has been a certain amount of tension. These armed men, however, have remained within their own area and do not appear to have received any supplies for, or to have any intention of carrying out, active operations outside their defensive positions.

5. South-west Lebanon

51. The United Nations military observers in this region have as their objectives to keep watch on any possible illegal infiltration of personnel or *matériel* from the sea and to observe closely the existing concentrations of armed men in order to ascertain whether they have been receiving additional reinforcements and supplies from elsewhere. The main station for the area is at Saïda, with sub-stations at Jezzine and Barouk. This last post, which was established on 25 August, is within the Choûf area held by well-organized Druze tribesmen, who constitute the principal opposition force in this region. There are also concentrations of opposition forces in certain parts of the towns of Saïda and Soûr. A considerable number of armed men have also been seen in Kana and other villages in southern Lebanon.

52. While there have been some reports of banditry in the area, in general the situation has been relatively calm and there have been no active military operations. There have been,

however, as verified by United Nations patrols, a number of minor clashes between opposition forces and armed partisans on the fringes of the Choûf.

53. The headquarters patrol stationed at Beirut has continued to observe the situation in the area towards the north of the Choûf and also to patrol from time to time the opposition-held area of Beirut. While frequent shootings and a considerable number of acts of terrorism occurred in the Beirut area at the beginning of the period under review, these incidents have gradually become less frequent, particularly since the beginning of September. The number of armed men visible in the opposition-held quarters of Beirut has much diminished. . . .

58. As has already been stated, the posts in the field have been somewhat thinly manned and have not always been organized in as much depth as might have been desirable. Moreover, the observers have been functioning up to the present time on an emergency basis with little regard being paid to hours of duty and normal periods of rest. It is therefore clear that if the Group is to operate at maximum efficiency, additional observers will be required. The Group has therefore requested an immediate increase in the number of its ground observers. [S/4100, *4th Report of UNOGIL, 29 Sept. 1958.*]

In its final report UNOGIL observed that organized opposition had now virtually ceased and the government was extending its authority. Sporadic disorders still continued, however, but did not seem evidence of illegal infiltration:

16. Thus, on 10 October 1958, a United Nations patrol proceeding from Chebaa towards the Syrian border came under heavy fire and withdrew only with great difficulty. On 22 October a United Nations plane flying over Arsal was fired at and the pilot suffered a wound in the shoulder which fortunately proved not to be serious. Ground patrols in the north Bekaa valley have also been shot at and there have been several additional cases of observers being held up and robbed in that area. Such incidents as these have, of course, been a matter of concern to the Group, which has, however, after due inquiry, found that they are to be interpreted not as a pattern of denying access to its observers to infiltration routes but rather as residual manifestations of the state of insecurity and disorder which has existed in Lebanon over the last six months.

17. The Group has, throughout its stay in Lebanon, directed its observers to pay close attention to all instances of the bearing of arms throughout the country with a view to determining by changes in the strength of such armed bands where additional *matériel* may have been brought into the country. The period covered by the present report has been remarkable for the steady decrease in the number of armed men visible throughout the country. This decrease has been even more marked since the unanimously accepted appointment of the new Government in the middle of October. [*S/4114, 5th Report of UNOGIL, 17 Nov. 1958.*]

UNOGIL now made this assessment of its attempts to implement the mandate with which it was charged:

20. The mandate of the Group under the Security Council resolution of 11 June 1958 (*S/4023*) has been to ensure that there is no illegal infiltration of personnel or the smuggling of arms or other *matériel* from across the Lebanese borders. In view of the absence for some time of any reports of infiltration of personnel or smuggling of arms and of the recent marked improvement in the general security situation in Lebanon, and in the relations between Lebanon and its eastern neighbour, the Group has come to the conclusion that its task under the 11 June resolution may now be regarded as completed.

21. The Secretary-General, in his report to the General Assembly under the terms of General Assembly resolution 1237 (ES–III) of 21 August 1958, has described the Group as presenting a practical arrangement in the sense of that resolution for upholding the purposes and principles of the Charter in relation to Lebanon in the present circumstances and for facilitating the withdrawal of foreign troops from the country. As has been noted, the withdrawal of foreign troops from Lebanon was completed before the end of October. As regards the more general task of fostering peaceful relations between Lebanon and other Arab States,

the Group has made an effective contribution by carrying out as efficiently as possible its mandate under the Security Council resolution of 11 June 1958.

22. Since the task assigned to it may now be regarded as completed, the Group is of the opinion that the withdrawal of the United Nations Observation Group in Lebanon, should now be undertaken and the Group accordingly submits its recommendation to that effect. It may be mentioned here that a substantial reduction in the force of observers is to take place as soon as necessary travel arrangements are made, involving those observers who have been with the Group since the earliest stages of the operation. For the complete withdrawal of the mission, it would be necessary for a detailed plan to be drawn up in consultation with the Lebanese Government, after which appropriate steps could be taken for its execution.

23. As this is perhaps the last substantive report of the mission, it would be proper to add some brief comments of a general nature on the work of the Group. These will of necessity be limited in scope, as the wider impact of the Group's endeavours on the general situation in the area can only be assessed in the light of history.

24. When the first few observers arrived in Lebanon some five months ago, they found an extremely complex situation, with large groups in different parts of the country in open and armed opposition to the Government, while practically the entire land frontier was open and outside the control of the Government. To enable the function of observation to be performed, it was first necessary to obtain physical access to the areas where such observation would be valuable, namely, along the borders. After patient and persistent efforts, the observers were able to gain access to one part, and then to another of the frontier, so that eventually a string of sub-stations and observation posts came to be established practically throughout the length of the frontier. From these posts and others to the rear, and by means of incessant patrolling, the observers were able to maintain constant vigilance.

25. During the five months, the situation in and around Lebanon has undergone big and sometimes dramatic changes, which have inevitably affected the task of observation. Without departing from the mandate of the Group, it has been necessary to vary the approach to the task from time to time. This has involved the taking of timely decisions, while keeping the standing instructions under constant review; what is more, these decisions have had to be communicated promptly to the observers in the field and their execution closely supervised. Considering the complex, and in many respects unprecedented, nature of the Observation Group's operations, it is a matter of some satisfaction that a proper balance was maintained throughout and that the Group's efforts at no point got out of contact with the realities of the changing situation.

26. In general, it may be stated that the United Nations Observation Group in Lebanon has been a symbol of the concern of the international community for the welfare and security of Lebanon. Apart from the effects of its mission of observation and reporting, its presence has had a reassuring effect on the population and has influenced the historic events which have taken place. By helping to free the Lebanese situation from its external complications, it has contributed to the creation of conditions under which the Lebanese people themselves could arrive at a peaceful solution of their internal problems.

27. In expressing these views, the Group feels it appropriate to pay tribute to the devotion to duty shown by the military observers under its control. The success of an operation such as the present one depends on the application of moral force to circumstances where otherwise only the use of arms would be effective. The military observers, armed only with the moral authority of the United Nations and their own determination and courage, have been able to fulfil their task of peace and have won for themselves the respect of the people in all areas in which they have operated. In doing so they have, even in the recent improved circumstances in Lebanon, repeatedly undergone hardship and dangers, which have been described in detail in this and previous reports.

28. The distinctions of national origin have proved to be superficial in relation to the deep significance of the common task which the observers were called upon to perform. Observers from twenty-one countries from different parts of the world have co-operated effectively and in a spirit of comradeship not only in circumstances of danger and under the stimulus of

urgent events, but also in the carrying out of routine duties and patrols. If, as it believes, the Group has been able to make a useful contribution to the restoration of more peaceful conditions in Lebanon, it is because it has been able to base its reports on the objective information faithfully supplied to it by its observers on the ground and in the air.

29. The Group wishes to express its appreciation to the Secretary-General for his co-operation and constant support in providing the Group with the necessary facilities for carrying out its task throughout the operation. The Group wishes also to thank the staff members of the United Nations Secretariat assigned to the mission, who at all levels have made a significant contribution to its success.

30. Finally, the Group wishes to express its appreciation to the Lebanese Government for its co-operation and for providing the necessary conditions for the Group to fulfil its mission in an independent and objective manner. The Group's appreciation is also due to the people of Lebanon from all walks of life for the many evidences of their courtesy, hospitality and friendship. [*Ibid.*]

It may be noted that the Observation Group itself suggested that its task was complete, and that UNOGIL should be disbanded. Some two days later the Lebanese government wrote to the President of the Security Council:

1. I have the honour to inform you as follows.

2. The Security Council, whose function in relation to the maintenance of international peace and security may consist principally of calling upon the parties to settle their disputes by peaceful and direct means of their own choice, will be pleased to learn that cordial and close relations between Lebanon and the United Arab Republic have resumed their normal course on the basis both of a long-standing tradition of brotherhood, friendship and mutual understanding and of respect for the provisions of the Pact of the League of Arab States and the Charter of the United Nations.

3. The Lebanese Government, conscious of the higher interests of the Lebanese people and the need to safeguard peace and security in the area, and in the spirit which led to the unanimous adoption of the decision taken by the United Nations General Assembly at its third emergency special session on 21 August 1958 (*resolution 1237 (ES–III)*), intends in the future to strengthen its co-operation with the United Arab Republic and other Arab States still further.

4. For this reason, and in order to dispel any misunderstanding which might hamper the development of such relations, the Lebanese Government requests the Security Council to be good enough to delete from the list of matters before it the Lebanese complaint submitted to it on 22 May 1958 which reads as follows:

'Complaint by Lebanon in respect of a situation arising from the intervention of the United Arab Republic in the internal affairs of Lebanon, the continuance of which is likely to endanger the maintenance of international peace and security.'

5. The Lebanese Government requests the Security Council to ask the Secretary-General to communicate its decision to the General Assembly.

6. The Lebanese Government takes this opportunity to acknowledge once again the important part played by the United Nations in relations between nations and the efforts made by its organs to bring about the harmony and co-operation necessary to the attainment of a better world. The Lebanese Government wishes to express its gratitude to all friendly nations, and in particular to its fellows of the Arab world, for the spirit of understanding and sympathy they have displayed towards Lebanon in this difficult period of its history.

(*Signed* Hussein EL OUEINI

[*S/4113, Letter from the Minister of Foreign Affairs of Lebanon to the President of the Security Council, 17 Nov. 1958.*]

The Secretary-General, Dag Hammarskjöld, in a letter to the President of the

Security Council (S/4115) referred to the jointly-held view by UNOGIL and the Lebanese government that the UN's task was completed, and instructed the group to prepare a plan for withdrawal. He added:

I have taken this step under the authorization given to the Secretary-General in the Security Council resolution of 11 June 1958 (S/4023) to take the necessary steps for implementation of the Security Council's decision. The instruction given to the Observation Group implies that I consider the task of the Group as completed and that my remaining duty under the resolution thus covers only the necessary measures for the liquidation of the operation. [S/4115, 17 Nov. 1958, para. 2.]

Such a plan was indeed drawn up, approved by the Secretary-General and by the Lebanese government.[3]

UNOGIL's duty to keep the Security Council informed, through the Secretary-General, stemmed from the Security Council resolution of 11 June 1958. It will be recalled, however, that the resolution on the Middle East problem which the General Assembly passed on 21 August invited the Secretary-General to report to the Assembly on developments. The role which the UN was to play under this Assembly resolution in promoting good relations in the Middle East went considerably further than the tasks assigned to UNOGIL. The Secretary-General's Reports are correspondingly wide-ranging (and are beyond the scope of this study), but there are items contained therein that are relevant to an assessment of UNOGIL's role. Noting that he had visited Amman on 27–28 August and again on 8–9 September, and that he had gone to Cairo on 3–5 September, Baghdad on 7–8 September, and Beirut on 10–12 September, the Secretary-General went on to discuss the particular arrangements he had made under General Assembly resolution 1237 (ES–III):

Practical Arrangements in relation to Jordan[4]

26. The representative of the Government of Jordan stated in the debate of the General Assembly at the Emergency Special Session that his Government did not accept the stationing of a United Nations force in Jordan nor the organization of a border observation group in the country for purposes similar to those served by UNOGIL in Lebanon. This view was re-stated to me in the consultations in Amman.

27. As from the beginning it had been also my view that neither a United Nations force nor a border observation group would adequately serve the purposes of the resolution in relation to Jordan, I accepted this stand of the Government of Jordan. Consequently the consultations in Jordan were limited to other forms of UN involvement, both sides being guided by the wish to see such an involvement developed in a form which would support the policies of co-operation to which all Arab States, in co-sponsoring the resolution, had pledged themselves. . . .

29. It was agreed that the most practical location of a United Nations organ, designed to keep under purview the adherence of all to the principles set out in part I of the resolution in relation to Jordan, would be Jordan itself. In recognition of this, Jordan stated its willingness to serve as host country for a United Nations representative, properly staffed, to serve 'as a special representative of the Secretary-General to assist in the implementation of the resolution, specifically with a view to help in upholding the purposes and principles of the Charter in relation to Jordan in the present circumstances'.

30. The stationing in Jordan of a United Nations organ, for the purposes mentioned, gave

[3] S/4116, 21 Nov. 1958.
[4] For the relationship of the Jordan problem to the Lebanon question, see above, pp. 537–40.
20

rise to a practical problem because the new organ with this location would require an established and guaranteed line of communication. For practical reasons this would involve also the Governments of Lebanon and the UAR. However, as both these Governments have undertaken to grant all the facilities, including liaison offices in Beirut and Damascus, needed in support of the establishment of a United Nations organ in Jordan, I have concluded that the practical problems can be resolved and that the new organ can be stationed in Amman.

31. In the light of this conclusion, based on the stands taken by the Governments of Jordan, Lebanon and the UAR, Ambassador Spinelli, Under-Secretary in charge of the European Office of the United Nations in Geneva, has been assigned to go to Amman in order to work out the necessary practical arrangements for the new operation with the Governments concerned. He proceeded to Amman on 27 September. In the course of his stay there he will also, on a preliminary basis, serve as special representative with the terms of reference mentioned above. When his duties in Geneva make a replacement necessary, a new representative will be appointed on a more definite basis. . . .

35. Were a local diplomatic representation to be established, it should obviously cover the whole area . . . the most satisfactory arrangement has seemed to me to be the assignment for the purpose of a special representative at Headquarters, who would proceed to the area and visit the various Governments on behalf of the Secretary-General, as need be. The Government of Jordan, recognizing the reasons for my conclusion, has accepted it while maintaining its stand that local diplomatic representation in all the capitals from its viewpoint would have been preferable. The other Governments concerned have assured me of their willingness to receive a diplomatic representative of the Secretary-General from Headquarters, as I might find it necessary.

36. Under the planned practical arrangements there will thus be two officials assigned to assist the Secretary-General, for purposes of the resolution: one keeping within his purview the implementation of the principles of the resolution by all nations in relation to Jordan; one serving as a special representative of the Secretary-General in such direct contacts of a diplomatic nature with the Governments concerned as the Secretary-General may find called for in the light of the findings of the representative charged with the purview. The last mentioned representative would for practical reasons be stationed in Jordan, while the diplomatic spokesman would be at Headquarters. . . .

Practical Arrangements in relation to Lebanon

39. During his stay in Lebanon, the Secretary-General had the privilege of getting the views of the Lebanese authorities on practical arrangements which, in their view, would adequately help in upholding the purposes of the Charter in relation to Lebanon. It was felt that the United Nations Observation Group, set up under a resolution of the Security Council, 11 June 1958, while continuing to serve the general purposes mentioned in that resolution, presents a practical arrangement in the sense of the resolution of the General Assembly, 21 August 1958, and in present circumstances, with the further development of it envisaged, adequately helps in upholding the purposes of the Charter in relation to Lebanon.

40. It was found unnecessary for the time being to consider any additional practical arrangements under the General Assembly resolution. Decisive significance was, in this context, attached to the successful implementation of part I of the resolution, that is, to the development of the good neighbour policy in the area, to which the Arab Governments have pledged themselves in the resolution. The United Nations operation, now organized in Lebanon, was considered as helpful in the development of such a policy. After the withdrawal of foreign troops from Lebanon, the question of the Observation Group and of alternative or additional practical arrangements under the resolution would have to be considered in the light of the degree of success with which the implementation of part I of the resolution of 21 August 1958 had met.

41. In the finding that no additional arrangements were needed in Lebanon, with the Observation Group to be developed as envisaged, it was recognized that the terms of reference of the

Group precluded it from reporting on all the possible departures from a satisfactory implementation by Arab States of the principles of the resolution in relation to Lebanon. This marks a basic difference between the Observation Group in Lebanon and the planned arrangement in relation to Jordan. The Observation Group must follow any infiltration and smuggling of arms, and its reports are public. The special representative in relation to Jordan should follow any departures from the principles of the resolution and report to the Secretary-General, for further action, but his findings would not be public unless their nature would seem to call for a circulation of a report in the United Nations. One reason why no additional arrangement in Lebanon, similar to the one organized in relation to Jordan, has been found to be necessary, is that in the cases not covered by the UNOGIL it is felt that the matters may be drawn directly to the attention of the Secretary-General, who can follow them up, using the official assigned to assist him with the diplomatic action necessary under the resolution. This stand may have to be reconsidered in the light of experience at a stage when the withdrawal has taken place.

Withdrawals of United States and British Forces

42. The Governments of Lebanon and of the United States have been fully informed about the conclusions drawn after my consultations in the region and about the arrangements made or planned regarding the United Nations Observation Group in Lebanon. In view of the information thus conveyed, the Government of Lebanon and the United States Government are at present discussing a schedule for the completion of the withdrawal of the United States forces. I am informed that it is the intention of the two Governments that the total withdrawal of the forces shall begin in the near future and be completed as expeditiously as possible, they hope by the end of October, provided the international security situation with respect to Lebanon continues to improve in the framework of a successful implementation of part I of the resolution of 21 August 1958. The two Governments concerned plan to announce their decision shortly. A memorandum received by me from the Government of the United States is annexed to this report (Annex I).

43. I have informed the Governments of Jordan and of the United Kingdom about these conclusions and the arrangement in relation to Jordan set out in this report, including the designation of a Special Representative who is now in Amman to elaborate, in consultation with the Government of Jordan, the organizational details of the arrangement. I have further informed them about the situation, as known to me, regarding the resumption of oil deliveries to Jordan and related matters. Taking this information into account, the Governments of Jordan and of the United Kingdom are discussing the fixing of dates for the beginning and the completion of the withdrawal of British forces. It is their intention that, provided satisfactory progress is being made, the withdrawal shall begin during the month of October and that it shall be completed as quickly as the situation in the area allows. . . .

MEMORANDUM: Annex I

In view of improvements in the international aspects of the Lebanese security situation owing to the steps which have been taken with respect to the situation in Lebanon, it has already been possible for the United States Government, in agreement with the Lebanese authorities, to withdraw a portion of its forces. The United States Government has now been informed by the Secretary-General of his view, shared by the Lebanese authorities, that the United Nations Observation Group set up under the resolution of the Security Council of 11 June 1958 presents a satisfactory practical arrangement within the meaning of the resolution of the General Assembly of 21 August 1958, and in present circumstances is, or can be made, adequate to uphold the purposes and principles of the Charter in relation to Lebanon. The United States Government has also been informed by the Secretary-General of the planned augmentation of the United Nations observation group in Lebanon and of his view, likewise shared by the Lebanese authorities, that for the time being it is unnecessary to consider any additional practical arrangements under the General Assembly resolution of 21 August with regard to Lebanon.

In view of the above information conveyed to the United States Government by the Secretary-General, the United States Government has informed the Secretary-General that it is discussing with the Government of Lebanon a schedule for the completion of the withdrawal of United States forces. It is the intention of the United States and Lebanese Governments that the total withdrawal of United States forces shall begin in the near future and be completed as expeditiously as possible, we hope by the end of October, provided the international security situation with respect to Lebanon continues to improve in the framework of successful implementation of part I of General Assembly resolution of 21 August 1958. The Governments of the United States and Lebanon plan to announce their decision shortly.

27 September 1958

MEMORANDUM: Annex II

1. Her Majesty's Government in the United Kingdom have taken note of the arrangements which the Secretary-General is making, in agreement with the Governments directly concerned, for the stationing of a United Nations Representative in Amman, for the establishment of Liaison Offices in Beirut and Damascus and for the appointment of a diplomatic agent to maintain such contact as may be necessary between the Secretary-General and the Arab capitals other than Amman. The United Kingdom Government understand that the object of these measures is to keep under continuous review the implementation of the Resolution of August 21 in relation to Jordan under present circumstances, and to provide means, in the event of a failure to implement the resolution, for the United Nations to take appropriate action.

2. The United Kingdom Government have been informed by the Secretary-General that the Governments concerned have again expressed their intention to conduct their relations with Jordan in accordance with the Resolution of August 21, and in particular have expressed their willingness to restore Jordan's normal communications by land and air across their territories.

3. The United Kingdom Government have accordingly informed the Secretary-General that, taking this information into account, they are discussing with the Government of Jordan the fixing of dates for the beginning and completion of the withdrawal of British forces. It is the intention of the United Kingdom and Jordanian Governments that, provided satisfactory progress is being made on the lines set out in paragraphs 1 and 2 above, the withdrawal shall begin during the month of October and that it shall be completed as quickly as the situation in the area allows. The Governments of the United Kingdom and Jordan hope to be able to announce their decision on October 1st.

28 September 1958

[A/3934/Rev. 1, 29 Sept. 1958, mimeo.]

Shortly afterwards the governments of the United States and United Kingdom issued the following statements:

I have the honour to inform you that as forecast in the memorandum annexed to your report of September 29 (A/3934) Her Majesty's Government in the United Kingdom together with the Jordan Government are today able to announce their decision with regard to the withdrawal of United Kingdom forces from Jordan. The two governments have reviewed together your report and the arrangements which you have made to assist in giving effect to the General Assembly's resolution of August 21. They have also taken note of the assurances received by you from other Arab Governments concerned that they intend to conduct their relations with Jordan in accordance with this resolution. Taking into account the above-factors and the confidence of the Jordan Government that the atmosphere will improve, Her Majesty's Government have agreed with the Jordan Government that the withdrawal of British troops will begin on October 20th. This withdrawal will be completed within a period not exceeding such time as may be required for the necessary arrangements for the movement of personnel, stores and equipment.

(*Signed*) PIERSON DIXON

[*A/3937, 1 Oct. 1968*, mimeo.]

MEMORANDUM

The Government of the United States announces that by agreement with the Government of the Republic of Lebanon it has now been decided to complete withdrawal of United States force from Lebanon. It is expected that, barring unforeseen developments, the forces will all be withdrawn by the end of October.

The United States sent forces to Lebanon in response to the urgent appeal of the then Government of that country for assistance in maintaining Lebanese independence and integrity. At the same time, the United States took steps in the United Nations with a view to having it take measures to preserve the independence and territorial integrity of Lebanon and thus facilitate the withdrawal of the United States forces. Subsequently, the United Nations General Assembly unanimously adopted a resolution developed by the Arab States and designed to ensure respect by States for the freedom, independence and integrity of other States, and to establish practical arrangements to uphold the purposes and principles of the Charter in relation to Lebanon.

The steps which have been taken with respect to the situation in Lebanon have led to a substantial improvement in the international aspects of the Lebanese security situation. The current unrest appears to have essentially domestic origins. In view of the progress made toward more stable international conditions in the area, it has been concluded that United States forces can now be totally withdrawn from Lebanon. It is the confident hope of the United States Government that the Republic of Lebanon, its sovereignty and independence strengthened, will move forward in unity, peace and prosperity. [*A/3942, 8 Oct. 1958*, mimeo.]

The United States and the United Kingdom later both sent confirmation that their troops had in fact withdrawn.[5] The means by which the UN was able to facilitate this process are of some interest:

Withdrawal by air of British troops from Jordan

1. At the request of the Government of the United Kingdom of Great Britain and Northern Ireland, the United Nations undertook to consult and to obtain agreement with the other Governments directly concerned on arrangements for United Nations assistance in the transportation by air of the British troops in Jordan from Amman to Nicosia during the period 25–29 October 1958.

2. The Secretary-General designated Major–General Odd Bull, who was granted leave of absence from his post as Executive Member of the United Nations Observation Group in Lebanon for the purpose, to organize the participation of United Nations personnel in the control arrangements for this movement by air. General Bull assembled the necessary staff by detaching from the UNOGIL air service men with the requisite training and experience to serve on the planning staff and to man the control posts required.

3. General Bull's mission was also assisted by the officials and technical personnel of the United Nations Truce Supervision Organization (UNTSO), the Israeli–Syrian Mixed Armistice Commission and UNOGIL for liaison, communication, transportation and secretarial work. The UNTSO transport aircraft was put at General Bull's disposal for the period of planning and negotiation and also during the period of the withdrawal operation, thus affording him the necessary mobility for rapid negotiations in several widely separated places.

[5] A/3986, ann. I and II, 6 Nov. 1958.

General Bull and his staff, for the purposes of this operation, were directly responsible to the Secretary-General.

4. The operation involved eighty-six round trip missions (Nicosia–Amman) by transport aircraft from Nicosia, and single flights from Jordan to Nicosia by six fighter aircraft and three Valetta transport aircraft. The total load carried included 2,168 passengers, 117 vehicles of various types, together with eighty-five trailers and seventy-four airborne trolleys, twenty-five guns and 230,500 lbs. of freight. The aircraft involved flew over the territories of Jordan, the United Arab Republic (Syria) and Lebanon and the operation had, therefore, to be cleared and co-ordinated among the Governments and air forces in Amman, Damascus and Beirut and the Middle East Air Force Headquarters in Cyprus, who were executing the operation. The Government of Israel, due to the proximity of the flights to Israel territory, was kept informed through UNTSO in Jerusalem.

5. The principal problems involved were routing, the clearance of flight plans and the establishment of the necessary control and navigational systems and communications.

6. Planning work began on 14 October. The UNOGIL Chief Communications Officer was charged with organizing an exclusive communications net with coding facilities connecting all the control stations. A preliminary routing plan for the aircraft was obtained from British sources on 16 October and this was discussed by General Bull at the Middle East Air Force Headquarters in Cyprus on 17 October. The major problem was to find a route which was operationally and politically acceptable to all parties concerned.

7. The tentative British flight plan was the basis of discussions by General Bull in Amman on 19 October and in Damascus on 20 October. Changes in the British plan were suggested in these discussions in order to avoid flying over prohibited or sensitive areas. In particular, it was proposed to route aircraft over United Arab Republic territory by Chahba and Saassa, instead of over Banias. These proposed changes were communicated to the Middle East Air Force Headquarters and to United Nations Headquarters in New York. Middle East Air Force Headquarters pointed out that certain technical difficulties would be involved by the changes proposed, which would considerably increase flying time and take the course closer to Mount Hermon. For this course to be acceptable, a radio beacon at Chahba would be required.

8. A further meeting was held at Damascus on 22 October, at which other details of the flight plan were discussed, based on the Chahba-Saassa route, including the width of the flight corridor, the spacing and timing of aircraft, the filing of flight plans, test flights by two transport aircraft on 24 October and the installation of a radio beacon at Chahba manned by United Nations radio officers. Since the British flight plan had to be submitted in Damascus on 23 October if the operation were to be able to start on 25 October, these proposals were cabled to Middle East Air Force Headquarters on the afternoon of 22 October.

9. General Bull and his staff, together with the two control officers to be stationed at Nicosia, went to the Middle East Air Force Headquarters at Nicosia on 23 October to reconcile the proposals of the United Arab Republic with the requirements of the Middle East Air Force Headquarters, the principal difficulty being the position of the United Arab Republic in favour of formation flying, which presented serious problems for transport aircraft. Middle East Air Force Headquarters then worked out a revised plan, taking into account the United Arab Republic position. This plan was handed by General Bull to the United Arab Republic Air Force in Damascus on the afternoon of 23 October and was accepted in principle, with a few details, including the procedure to be applied in case of forced landings at Damascus airport, to be agreed upon later. The final reconciled plan was signed in Damascus at 10.20 hours on 24 October, and by a Middle East Air Force representative in Beirut at 13.00 hours on the same day. The control officers for Beirut and Amman were then briefed on the final plan and proceeded to take up their posts; the Damascus control officers and the Chahba beacon operators were already in position. Two trial runs were made on 24 October, according to plan.

10. The route followed was a corridor ten nautical miles wide from Nicosia over Sidon (Lebanon), Saassa (UAR), Chahba (UAR) to Amman. Not more than six loaded and six un-

loaded aircraft were to be over United Arab Republic territory simultaneously. The six fighters and three Valetta transports were to be flown out in addition to these flights. Aircraft would not be over United Arab Republic territory on any day before 06.00 hours or after 17.00 hours, local time. All transport aircraft would fly at altitudes between 11,500 and 14,500 feet. Any changes of more than fifteen minutes in times given in the flight plan were to be notified to Damascus, Beirut and the terminal point. United Nations control officers had lists of registration numbers of all participating aircraft and spare aircraft for identification purposes. Aircraft reported on entering and leaving the territory of the countries overflown and over the Chahba beacon. Signals for United Arab Republic fighters intercepting for control purposes had also been agreed upon.

11. The main responsibility of the United Nations control officers was to see that the detailed flight plan was adhered to and to exercise their judgement in resolving any problems which might arise resulting from unforeseen delays or variations in the execution of the flight plan. Each control post reported to General Bull in Beirut at the end of each day's operations.

12. The withdrawal operation began on schedule on 25 October and proceeded on schedule until its termination on 29 October, when the last aircraft left United Arab Republic territory at 15.14 hours. The original flight plan had listed a full complement of the possible daily missions, thus leaving a margin for cancellations due to weather or other causes. Since there were, in any event, no cancellations because of weather or unserviceability, it was possible to dispense with some of the missions scheduled in the original flight plan. There were very few deviations from the time schedule and no incidents.

13. The successful conclusion of this operation is a tribute to the ready co-operation and technical skill of all parties concerned and to the effective efforts of Major General Bull and his staff.

14. On completion of the mission a message of thanks was addressed to the Secretary-General by the Government of the United Kingdom (annexed).

LETTER DATED 30 OCTOBER 1958 FROM THE PERMANENT REPRESENTATIVE OF THE UNITED KINGDOM OF GREAT BRITAIN AND NORTHERN IRELAND TO THE UNITED NATIONS, ADDRESSED TO THE SECRETARY-GENERAL

I have been instructed by Selwyn Lloyd to pass to you the following message from him:

'News of the successful completion of the air-lift of British troops from Amman to Cyprus has just reached me.

'My colleagues and I are most grateful to you personally for having made this whole operation possible. I understand from our Chiefs of Staff and our Commanders-in-Chief in the Middle East that they have the greatest admiration for the way in which General Bull and his staff made the practical arrangements and thereby ensured the smooth running of what was a highly technical and complicated matter. I am conveying my thanks to General Bull direct and the Chief of the Defence Staff is doing likewise. I should also like to thank you personally for having made the services of this distinguished officer and his staff available for the task.

'You will know that our decision to use the route via Syria was not an easy one. We foresaw many awkwardnesses and difficulties. I hoped, however, that a practical demonstration of co-operation between the United Arab Republic and us under United Nations auspices would be of some help to you in your task of furthering the fulfilment of the Arab resolution. I now hope that the successful outcome of this operation may augur well for the future.

'With warm regards.'

(*Signed*) Pierson DIXON

[*A/4056, Report of Secretary-General, 10 Dec. 1958*, mimeo.]

The Secretary-General summarized the situation one year later:

It should further be noted that the question of Lebanon and Jordan, which last year at this time were at the centre of the attention of the Members, have been wholly or partly resolved. As a consequence, the United Nations Observation Group in Lebanon was withdrawn at the end of 1958. The Office of the Special Representative of the Secretary-General, stationed in Amman under the terms of the Assembly resolution of 21 August 1958, is still maintained. The supporting communication offices in Beirut and Damascus, which were suggested in my report to the General Assembly in September of last year, and on which agreements were reached through exchanges of letters in the Spring, have been found unnecessary and have, therefore, not been established. [*A/4132/Add. 1, Introd. to Annual Report of Secretary-General, 16 June 1958–13 June 1959, suppl.* 1A, p. 4.]

13

ANNEXES

A. Checklist of Documents

Debates in UN Organs
SCOR, 13th yr, mtgs 823–5, 827–38, 6 June–7 Aug. 1958.
GAOR, 3rd Emerg. Spec. Sess., plen. mtgs 732–46, 8–21 Aug. 1958.

Reports to the Security Council by the Secretary-General on the implementation of the Council's resolution of 11 June 1958

S/4029	16 June 1958	S/4038	28 June 1958

Reports of UNOGIL

S/4040	3 July 1958	S/4085	14 Aug. 1958
S/4051	15 July 1958	S/4100	29 Sept. 1958
S/4052	17 July 1958	S/4114	14 Nov. 1958
S/4069	30 July 1958		

Other Documents

S/4007	23 May 1958	S/4071 S/4072 S/4074 S/4075	1 Aug. 1958
S/4018	2 June 1958		
S/4023	11 June 1958		
S/4043	8 July 1958		
S/4050	15 July 1958	S/4078 S/4079	5 Aug. 1958
S/4050 and rev. I S/4053 S/4054	17 July 1958	S/4080 S/4081	6 Aug. 1958
S/4055	21 July 1958	S/4083	7 Aug. 1958
S/4056/rev. I	7 Aug. 1958	S/4113	17 Nov. 1958
S/4057	18 July 1958	S/4115 S/4116	20 Nov. 1958
S/4059	20 July 1958	GA res. 1237 (ES–III)	
S/4060	21 July 1958	A/3934 rev. I	29 Sept. 1958
S/4062 S/4063	22 July 1958	A/3937	1 Oct. 1958
		A/3986	1 Nov. 1958
S/4064	23 July 1958	A/4056	10 Dec. 1958
S/4067	28 July 1958	A/4132 p. 15 ff.	16 June 1959

B. Bibliography

Agwani, M. S. The Lebanese crisis in retrospect. *Int. Studies*, Apr. 1963.
— *The Lebanese Crisis 1958: a Documentary Study*. London, 1965.
Bustani, Emile. *The Lebanon, a Dissection of the Current Situation*. Beirut, 1959.
Chamoun, Camille. *Crise au Moyen-Orient*. Paris, 1963.
Curtis, Gerald. The UN Observation Group in Lebanon. *Int. Org.*, Autumn 1964.
Eisenhower, Dwight D. *The White House Years: Waging Peace*. New York, 1965.
al-Maryati, A. UN Observation Group in Lebanon. *Foreign Affairs Reports*, Apr. and May 1967.
Meo, L. *Lebanon, Improbable Nation*. Bloomington, Ind., 1965.
Murphy, Robert. *Diplomat among Warriors*. New York, 1964.
Potter, Pitman. Legal aspects of the Beirut landings. 52 *AJIL*, 1958.
Qubain, Fahim. *Crisis in Lebanon*. Washington, DC, 1961.
Thayer, Charles W. *Diplomat*. London, 1960.
Wright, Quincy. United States intervention in the Lebanon. 53 *AJIL*, 1959.

Part 4

THE UNITED NATIONS
YEMEN OBSERVATION MISSION (UNYOM),
1963-4

1. INTRODUCTION (p. 609)
DEATH of Imam Ahmad; revolt in Yemen; proclamation of a Republican government; the arrival of Egyptian forces and experts; attempts by the United States to mediate in the civil war; the UN Credentials Committee faces a problem; Ralph Bunche's fact-finding mission; the parties talk to General von Horn about the role of UN observers in the disengagement agreement; deteriorating relations between Egypt and Saudi Arabia; the Yemen Arab Republic complains of United Kingdom bombing.

2. ENABLING RESOLUTION AND VOTING (p. 620)
Security Council resolution of 11 June 1963; American and Soviet attitudes.

3. FUNCTIONS AND MANDATE (p. 622)
Tasks under the disengagement agreement and Security Council resolution; limits to the narrow mandate.

4. CONSTITUTIONAL BASIS (p. 625)
Authority of the Secretary-General; Articles 98 and 99; objections by the Soviet Union; relationship to the Security Council; initiatives on financing UNYOM; the Secretary-General consults the Security Council informally; the authority to terminate UNYOM.

5. POLITICAL CONTROL (p. 635)
Effective control in hands of Secretary-General; designation of Major-General von Horn; the Secretary-General's special political representative becomes head of the entire mission in Yemen.

6. ADMINISTRATIVE AND MILITARY CONTROL (p. 637)
Differences between von Horn and the Secretariat; the Chief of Staff resigns; appointment of an acting Commander; designation of a Chief of Staff responsible to the civilian head of UNYOM.

7. COMPOSITION AND SIZE (p. 638)
Numbers and countries comprising UNYOM.

8. RELATIONS WITH CONTRIBUTING STATES (p. 641)
Absence of any formal agreements or major problems.

9. RELATIONS WITH THE HOST STATES (p. 641)
The parties to the disengagement agreement and the 'host states'; the stationing of UNYOM in Yemen and Saudi Arabia; the UN deals with the republican government; privileges and immunities agreement between the UN and Saudi Arabia; absence of a comparable agreement between the UN and Yemen; the legal situation.

10. RELATIONS WITH OTHER STATES INVOLVED (p. 645)
Questions concerning Saudi Arabia, the UAR, the Soviet Union.

11. FINANCE (p. 645)
General Assembly Resolution 1862 (XVII); estimates based on General von Horn's report; Soviet attitudes on financing; arrangements with Saudi Arabia and UAR; different views held in the Security Council; costs of UNYOM.

12. IMPLEMENTATION (p. 653)
Distinction between fulfilling the limited mandate and obtaining a settlement to the war; UNYOM's fulfilment of duties to report and certify; failure of the parties to implement the disengagement agreement; difficulties presented by the terrain; aerial activity; reappraisal of UNYOM's needs; UNYOM's findings on Saudi aid to royalists; problems on the northern frontier; formation of a new Yemen government in December 1963; the UAR does not withdraw her troops; the termination of UNYOM; events since September 1964; the continuing search for peace in Yemen.

13. ANNEXES (p. 669)
    A. Checklist of Documents (p. 669)
    B. Bibliography (p. 669)

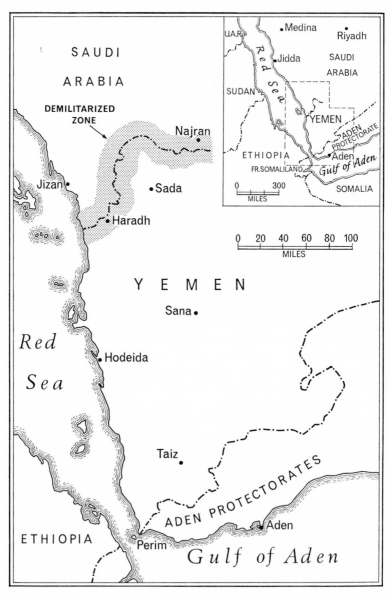

4. Yemen, showing Demilitarized Zone

I

INTRODUCTION

On 19 September 1962 the death was reported of King Ahmad, the Imam of Yemen. The obituaries in the press revealed an uncommon unanimity that his régime had been harsh and tyrannous. *The Times* (20 Sept. 1962) observed that the dead Imam 'will be remembered for his success in preserving his kingdom virtually intact against all the political and social ideas of the twentieth century'. A coup had been attempted—and suppressed—in 1955, after which the Imam's son, Badr, generally thought of as a moderate, was appointed Prime Minister and Crown Prince by his father. His appointment was believed to have been strongly resented by the Imam's brother Hassan, who had been led to believe that he would eventually succeed to the throne.

In March 1958 the Yemen joined the UAR in an association called the United Arab States. By 1961 this association had disintegrated, and the Imam became the target of hostile propaganda from Cairo.

Throughout his reign the Imam had asserted that the Aden Protectorate was legally part of southern Yemen, and that the British had no legal status there.

Upon the death of his father in September 1962, the new Imam publicly promised to pursue a policy of modern reform. He also emphasized his desire to have cordial relations with all his neighbours, and granted an amnesty to all political prisoners. He then established a Consultative Council of forty members, half to be elected and half to be appointed.

In just over a week, however, there was an army revolt in the Yemen, carried out with the purpose of establishing a republic. As the *Guardian* (28 Sept. 1962) observed: 'No Government is more in peril than one that tries to loosen the bonds of past tyranny.' The reports which ensued were conflicting as to the degree of control achieved by the armed forces. At first it was believed that the new Imam had been killed, though it was later to emerge that he was still alive. The situation was further confused at this point by the return to Yemen of Prince Hassan (the new Imam's uncle) from New York, where he had been leading the Yemeni delegation at the UN, to proclaim himself the new ruler.

Meanwhile it was announced from Sana by the rebel government that Brigadier Abdullah Sallal was the new Prime Minister. The Aden Trades Union Congress sent messages of support to the rebels, as did the Aden People's Socialist Party. On 29 September the UAR recognized the revolutionary government. While in Aden there was vociferous support for 'a greater Yemen', including the 'British-occupied South Yemen' (Aden and Aden Protectorate), the revolutionary government itself remained restrained in its statements on Aden. Soviet recognition was accorded to the republican government on 30 September.

By the first week in October there began to be reports of the arrival of Egyptian army and military experts in Yemen. At the same time the Republican government ordered the closure of its embassy in Saudi Arabia in protest against anti-republican radio broadcasts from that country. The accusation was also made that Saudi Arabia was harbouring and encouraging Yemeni royalists. It became clear that the new régime, which had undoubted control of Sana and Taiz (the twin capitals), was being resisted in the southern desert and the northern hills. The frontiers of Yemen were closed and messages censored— and the British government (which was soon to come under pressure on this point from the Opposition) insisted that no recognition of the Republican government could be considered while there was no free movement permitted. Nor had the United States yet recognized the new government.

By 8 October it was widely reported that Yemen and Egypt were considering a revival of the Union between them (though this was to come to nothing), and that a substantial number of UAR forces had landed in the territory. The Yemen charged that the British-controlled South Arabian Federation was aiding Yemeni royalist leaders to organize resistance to the Republican government. The British Foreign Office denied that assistance was being infiltrated from Aden to the royalists. Skirmishes and air attacks were continuing on Yemen's northern borders too. On 15 October Brigadier Sallal reported that his government was fighting Jordanian officers and Saudi irregulars in the north, and men from the State of Beihan (in the South Arabian Federation) in the east. Brigadier Sallal felt, however, that the United States was sympathetic to his cause and that relations with the British would soon improve. By 4 November, after accusations and counter-accusations between Saudi Arabia and Egypt, the Yemeni Republican government indicated that it might have to carry the fighting to Saudi Arabia because of provocation.[1] Such action seems to have been deterred in large part by the appearance of USAF Super Sabre jet fighters and bombers on demonstration flights over Saudi Arabian cities, and also of a United States warship at Jidda.

Soon after mid-November it became apparent that the United States was prepared to mediate to seek an end to the civil war in the Yemen. The United States was anxious to dissociate herself from the previously repressive royalist régime, and although she had not yet recognized Sallal's government, she was appreciative of the moderate tone employed by Brigadier Sallal towards the United States government. Moreover, the State Department was no doubt disturbed by the reports of the increasing members of Soviet technicians who were coming to Sana. The United States plan was reported as providing that Brigadier Sallal should declare that he was interested only in Yemen's welfare, and not in any territory outside her present borders; that President Nasser should be encouraged to a phased withdrawal from an increasingly unrewarding commitment in the Yemen; and that the United States would then recognize

[1] *The Times*, 5 Nov. 1962.

the Sallal government. Such a plan was hardly acceptable to Jordan and Saudi Arabia. Nor, it was to prove, was it acceptable to the Yemeni royalists, who felt that they had little to gain from it at a time when they were making some progress in the north and east.

The UN now gradually began to be drawn into the situation. The permanent mission in New York was still composed of Yemeni royalists, and on 27 November 1962 it urged that the UN should establish an inquiry as to whether the rebellion was or was not fostered from Cairo. The request was confined to a letter circulated to UN members, and was not taken to a competent UN organ for further action. The Yemeni republicans—who by now also had sent a delegation to the UN—let it be known that they would have no objections to such a UN on-site inquiry. On 11 December King Hussein of Jordan himself suggested that the presence of a UN team of observers might be useful in finding a solution (he apparently foresaw a plebiscite following upon the establishment of an impartial 'presence' in the Yemen). No doubt it was in the context of these developments that the Secretary-General decided to consult with the representatives of the interested parties: though first it was necessary to decide, from the UN point of view, which of the two rival delegations properly represented the Yemen.

The Credentials Committee of the General Assembly met, in fact, on the very last day of the Assembly's seventeenth session.[2] The Committee had had before it a Memorandum by the Secretary-General:

The Secretary-General said that on 27 September 1962 he had received credentials, dated 9 September, signed by the Imam of Yemen, and on 10 December he had received new credentials, dated 7 December, for the delegation of the Kingdom of Yemen, signed by the Minister for Foreign Affairs.

On 17 December, the Secretary-General had received credentials for the delegation of the Yemen Arab Republic, signed by the President of the Republic and dated 8 December.

The Credentials Committee, on 20 December, approved a proposal by Guinea, recommending that the Assembly accept the credentials submitted by the President of the Yemen Arab Republic. The vote was 6 to 0, with 3 abstentions.

The recommendation was contained in the Committee's report to the General Assembly, considered by the Assembly later the same day. After hearing statements by a number of representatives, the Assembly approved the Committee's report by a vote of 73 to 4, with 23 abstentions.[3]

During the debate in the Assembly, the Committee's recommendation for acceptance of the credentials of the representatives of the Yemen Arab Republic was opposed by the representatives of Saudi Arabia and the Kingdom of Yemen. The representative of Jordan expressed doubts that the Committee was competent to decide which government in Yemen was the legal one.

The Committee's recommendation was supported by the representatives of Algeria, Bolivia, Iraq, Mali, Somalia, Syria, the USSR and the United Arab Republic. Several other representatives said that their vote in favour of the report was without prejudice to their position on the Yemen representation question, on which their Governments had as yet taken no decision. Among these were the representatives of France, Japan, Venezuela and the Philippines. The

---

[2] On the practice of the Credentials Committee in meeting very late during the session for which it is purportedly approving credentials, see Higgins, *Development of International Law through the Political Organs of the UN*, pp. 158–66.   [3] Res. 1871 (XVII).

representative of Mexico said his delegation had abstained in the vote in the Credentials Committee because it felt that the Committee's decision could have very serious implications.

The representative of Jordan, in raising doubts about the Credentials Committee's competence to take a decision in the matter, observed, among other things, that what was indisputable was that there were two authorities in Yemen: one was 'the legitimate Government' of the Imam Al-Badr, who had succeeded his late father in September; the other authority was that of Brigadier Al-Sallal. He did not wish to touch on such questions as the implications of the present situation, or the prospects for the future; but in these circumstances, he asked, how could the Assembly decide at this stage which Yemen delegation should be seated?

In opposing the Committee's recommendation, the representative of Saudi Arabia declared that the Government of the Yemen Arab Republic was a 'self-proclaimed' régime, which would have virtually no chance of survival but for the presence of foreign troops. The representative of the Kingdom of Yemen charged that 'the so-called republican Government in Yemen' was only a front for the expansionist moves of the United Arab Republic, and lacking the support of the people of Yemen. The United Arab Republic, he declared, had committed an act of aggression against the people of Yemen which was an act of war, contrary to the principles of the United Nations Charter.

The representatives of Saudi Arabia and the Kingdom of Yemen both suggested that the Assembly should delay a decision on the credentials question pending an inquiry by the United Nations.

In reply, the representative of the United Arab Republic said that, 'since the emergence of the new and progressive revolution of the people of Yemen against the reactionary feudalist régime', the population of the country had been subjected to a brutal combination of the reactionary forces in the Arab world. As to the allegations that United Arab Republic forces in Yemen were interfering in the country's internal affairs, nothing could be more inconsistent, since the military forces dispatched by his Government at the request of the Yemen Arab Republic had been placed at the disposal of the supreme command of the Yemen army, with the sole purpose of enabling the people to practice their inherent right of self-defence in a war launched against them from outside by the enemies of the revolution. The United Arab Republic had been duty bound to come to the aid of the Yemen Arab Republic in defence of its sovereignty and territorial integrity; moreover, the United Arab Republic could not remain indifferent to reactionary aggressive conspiracies designed to re-impose the monarchy which for generations had isolated the Yemen people from the world and from civilization. The people of Yemen had chosen the Government of President Al-Sallal on 26 September; no one could challenge the authority of this Government, or the fact that it was the only Government in full control of the country.

Other representatives who supported acceptance of the credentials of the Yemen Arab Republic either pointed out that their Governments had already recognized the Republic or expressed the belief that events within Yemen were exclusively a domestic affair.

Expressing his gratification after the vote had been taken, the representative of the Yemen Arab Republic, described his Government as a democratic and progressive republic, dedicated to a policy of non-alignment and positive neutrality. [*YBUN*, *1962*, pp. 148–9.]

In April of the following year the Secretary-General reported that his consultations with the various interested parties had resulted in the acceptance of a disengagement agreement in the Yemen.[4] Ralph Bunche had gone, in February and March, on a fact-finding mission for the Secretary-General. The United States, in her search for a peaceful solution to the Yemen problem, had sent Mr Ellsworth Bunker to Saudi Arabia and Cairo for talks. U Thant was kept informed of this approach.

1. Since the fall of 1962 I have been consulting regularly with the representatives to the

4 For full details, see below, p. 622.

United Nations of the Governments of the Arab Republic of Yemen, Saudi Arabia and the United Arab Republic, about certain aspects of the situation in Yemen of external origin, with a view to making my Office available to the parties for such assistance as might be desired toward ensuring against any developments in that situation which might threaten the peace of the area. I have encountered from the beginning a sympathetic and co-operative attitude on the part of all three representatives and their Governments.

2. It was in this context that, after clearance with the respective Governments, I asked Mr Ralph J. Bunche to go to Yemen and the United Arab Republic in late February and early March on a fact-finding mission primarily devoted to talking with the Presidents of Yemen and the United Arab Republic, in that order, with the purpose of ascertaining their views on the situation and what steps might be taken to ease tension and restore conditions to normal. It was left open whether Mr Bunche would eventually go also to Saudi Arabia, but developments made this unnecessary. Mr Bunche carried out this mission and reported fully to me on his talks, which I found encouraging. Subsequently, I was informed that the United States Government, on its own initiative, sent Mr Ellsworth Bunker to Saudi Arabia on a somewhat similar but unconnected mission. Mr Bunker later visited Saudi Arabia on two other occasions and also had extensive talks in Cairo with President Nasser. Mr Bunker kept me informed on the results of his missions. These talks in the end proved fruitful and from them emerged the agreed terms of disengagement. Mr Bunker's efforts are much appreciated. [*S/5298, Report of the Secretary-General to the Security Council concerning developments relating to Yemen, 29 Apr. 1963*, p. 33.]

The Secretary-General further reported that:

I have asked Major-General Carl Carlson von Horn, Chief of Staff of the United Nations Truce Supervision Organization in Jerusalem, to proceed without delay to the three countries concerned for the purpose of consulting with the appropriate authorities on details relating to the nature and functioning of United Nations Observers in implementation of the terms of disengagement and to report to me with his recommendations as to the size of the set-up that might be required to discharge this responsibility. [*Ibid.* p. 34, para. 5.]

On 27 May the Secretary-General reported the results of General von Horn's talks:

2. The parties again confirmed to General von Horn their acceptance of the terms of disengagement in Yemen as set forth in paragraph 4 of my 29 April report, General von Horn's concern, of course, being primarily with the questions relating to the need for United Nations Observers and their functions in the proposed demilitarized zone and elsewhere, as provided in the terms of disengagement.

3. General von Horn held discussions with the appropriate authorities of the three parties in Cairo, Jeddah and San'a, obtaining the views of the parties on the role, functioning, scope and strength of the proposed United Nations observation operation. He also carried out ground and aerial reconnaissance on both sides of the Saudi Arabia–Yemen border, visiting Qizan, Najran, Sada and Hodeida, and covering the proposed demilitarized or buffer zone, totalling approximately 15,000 square kilometres.

4. On the basis of the information available to me, with particular reference to that provided by General von Horn, I have reached the following conclusions:

(*a*) United Nations Observers in the Saudi Arabia–Yemen area are vitally necessary and could well be the decisive factor in avoiding serious trouble in that area; their presence is desired by all parties concerned; moreover, as the need is urgent, they should be dispatched with the least possible delay;

(*b*) The terrain and climatic conditions in which the Observers will have to function in some sectors will be extremely difficult and even forbidding, and considerable danger may be encountered. Problems of movement and logistics will be great. But the provision and stationing of Observers is considered feasible and can be accomplished;

(*c*) The total personnel required for the observation mission would not exceed 200. This figure would include a small number of Officer-Observers; a ground patrol unit numbering about 100 men, in suitable vehicles, carrying arms for self-defence only; crews and ground crews for about eight small aircraft, fixed-wing and rotary, for reconnaissance and transport; and personnel for such essential supporting services as communications, logistics, medical aid, transportation and administration;

(*d*) It is estimated that the United Nations observation function would not be required for more than four months;

(*e*) It is expected that at least some of the personnel required for this short-term observation operation could be recruited from the United Nations Emergency Force (UNEF), the United Nations Truce Supervision Organization in Palestine (UNTSO), and possibly the United Nations Military Observers Group in India and Pakistan (UNMOGIP), subject to clearance with the Governments concerned. I plan to designate General von Horn as Chief of the Yemen Mission. [*S/5321, 2nd Report of the Secretary-General to the Security Council on developments relating to Yemen*, pp. 46–47.][5]

On 7 June 1963 the Secretary-General—having indicated that an agreement had been reached on the financial basis of a UN Mission in the Yemen to observe the disengagement,[6] announced that: 'It is now my intention, therefore, to proceed with the organization and dispatch of the mission without further delay, and I am instructing General von Horn to go to the area with a small advance party within a day or two.'[7]

At the request of the Soviet Union the Security Council was convened, and from 9 to 11 June 1963 it discussed the situation.[8] On 11 June it adopted Resolution S/5331, authorizing the establishment of UNYOM.[9] This began its operations on 4 July.

During the period that UNYOM was authorized to remain in the Yemen, complaints continued to be put to the Secretary-General and the Security Council which were relevant, directly or indirectly, to the situation in the Yemen. The positions of Saudi Arabia and the UAR are clearly laid out in the following exchange of complaints:

Upon instructions from my Government it is my painful duty to report a summary record of the recent air-raids carried out by Egyptian military aircraft on Saudi Arabian territory, thereby inflicting loss of life and causing injuries to peaceful inhabitants and destroying or damaging property including many dwellings, a mosque and a hospital.

In one of these raids on 8 June 1963 thirty lives were lost and twenty-two homes were demolished aside from wounding a good number of persons in the city of Qizan.

All these raids on Saudi Arabian territory by Egyptian planes constitute a violation of the rudiments of international law aside from ignoring all humanitarian principles. Indeed, such aggression might be considered an act of war.

Inasmuch as the Government of Saudi Arabia has exercised extreme self-restraint, having refrained from retaliatory action for no other reason than to avoid further bloodshed, my Government might be compelled in the future to take measures for self-defence which may lead to a regrettable situation in the Middle East and the possibility of world-wide repercussions.

Whilst the people of Saudi Arabia and their Government desire to live in peace and whereas

[5] For the financial estimates based upon this original assessment, see below, pp. 646–7.

[6] See below, p. 647.

[7] S/5325, Report of the Secretary-General to the Security Council on the latest developments concerning the proposal to send a UN Observation Mission to Yemen, 7 June 1963, p. 50, para. 3.

[8] See below, p. 619. [9] See below, p. 620.

my Government so far has consistently abided by the terms of the United Nations Charter which provide for the settlement of differences by peaceful means, the patience and self-restraint which my Government has manifested should not be misconstrued as a sign of weakness or helplessness. It is because of Saudi Arabia's deep desire for peace in order to carry out its extensive economic and social plans, instead of getting embroiled in a senseless bloody conflict, that my Government has put its confidence in the integrity of the Secretary-General in the hope that through his tact and wisdom, the recent agreement concluded with reference to the Yemen will be implemented in good faith by the parties concerned.

Since my Government wishes that the report of the recent Egyptian air-raids on Saudi Arabian territory be distributed, may I ask you to make it available to the members of the Security Council as well as to have it circulated among the States Members of the United Nations.

(*Signed*) Jamil M. BAROODY

ANNEX

SUMMARY REPORT OF RECENT EGYPTIAN AIR-RAIDS ON SAUDI-ARABIAN TERRITORY

1. On Thursday morning 6 June 1963 three Egyptian Ilyushin military aircraft carried out an air-raid on the town of Najran. They repeated the raid three hours later on the same day.

Also on the same date two Mig and one Ilyushin aircraft carried out another air-raid on Khamis Mushayt. These planes indiscriminately hit many peaceful inhabitants, inflicting some loss of life. Dwellings were either wholly or partly destroyed whilst a mosque and a hospital were damaged. Saudi-Arabian anti-aircraft guns opened fire and finally the planes were forced to withdraw.

2. On the morning of Saturday 8 June 1963 five Egyptian Mig and Ilyushin aircraft carried out an air-raid on the peaceful city of Qizan. During the raid these planes dropped a considerable number of bombs on homes and demolished part of the city's hospital. As a result of this raid, thirty persons were killed and seventeen others suffered injuries. In addition, twenty homes of the peaceful inhabitants were destroyed. Saudi-Arabian anti-aircraft guns opened fire and the planes were forced to withdraw.

Four aircraft, two Migs and two Ilyushins, carried out another air-raid on the city of Khamis Mushayt. One of these aircraft dropped eight bombs without causing any damage. Again Saudi-Arabian anti-aircraft fire drove them off.

In announcing this painful news, the Government of Saudi-Arabia wishes to state that by such aggression the Egyptian authorities have flouted the rudimentary principles of international law and human decency. Moreover, this aggression constitutes a flagrant violation of the United Nations Charter. [*S/5333, Letter dated 14 June 1963 from the representative of Saudi Arabia to the Secretary-General, 17 June 1963*, pp. 54–55.]

I have the honour to bring to your attention that, when the Security Council met on 10 June 1963 (1037th meeting) to discuss 'the reports of the Secretary-General concerning developments relating to Yemen', the delegation of the United Arab Republic, considering that the position of its Government with regard to foreign intervention against Yemen had been amply explained, refrained from participating in the discussion in order to avoid a lengthy and involved debate which could have hindered the speedy dispatch of a United Nations Observation Mission to the Saudi–Yemeni border area and in the hope that the United Nations presence would end the aggression against the people of Yemen.

The letter addressed to Your Excellency on 14 June 1963 (S/5333) by the delegation of Saudi Arabia has, however, made it incumbent upon the delegation of the United Arab Republic to state the following facts.

1. In his letter addressed to Your Excellency on 18 January 1963, the representative of the Yemen Arab Republic stated that on 26 September 1962 the Yemen people declared their determination to start a new era in their history and revolted against the corrupt medieval

régime, which immediately collapsed. He stated further that the new Republic extended a hand of friendship to its Arab sister countries, as well as to other countries, provided naturally that the independence and integrity of Yemen would be respected and that no interference in its internal affairs would be tolerated. However, the representative of the Yemen Arab Republic concluded that the Government of Saudi Arabia took an openly hostile attitude. Continuous, premeditated armed attacks were launched against the people of Yemen. Consequently, the Yemen Arab Republic requested assistance from the United Arab Republic, in accordance with the provisions of the Mutual Defence Pact concluded between the two Governments, in repelling this aggression.

2. Under such perilous circumstances facing the Yemeni people, the Government of the United Arab Republic, which gave its full support to the new Government of Yemen, could not but respond to its request. Military forces were dispatched and placed at the disposal of the Yemeni Supreme Command.

3. It is indeed most regrettable that Saudi Arabia was found to be actively engaged in playing a predominant role in the aggression against the people of Yemen. It is no secret that aggression against Yemeni territory emanated from inside Saudi Arabia, huge sums of money were tendered to incite mercenaries and provide them with arms to fight the people of Yemen, centres were established in Saudi Arabia to train those mercenaries in sabotage and laying mine fields. Furthermore, a flow of arms and ammunition were sent across the frontier to entice tribes to rise against their Government.

4. The armed forces of the Yemen Arab Republic and the United Arab Republic can undoubtedly deal with any military aggression against Yemen. Nevertheless, motivated by an earnest desire to avoid bloodshed and to restore peace to the area, the two Governments have, in good faith, accepted the terms of disengagement which provided for the establishment of a United Nations observation mission whose main aim is the termination of outside military intervention against Yemen.

5. Obviously, therefore, the Government of Saudi Arabia should be the last to complain or protest. Offensive action against a peaceful people is a flagrant violation of the United Nations Charter and constitutes a threat to international peace and security.

6. The restoration of peace and security in this part of the world requires that those who are vainly trying to re-impose a feudal and reactionary régime on the people of Yemen should cease their futile attempts.

I should be grateful if you would arrange for the circulation of this letter to the President and members of the Security Council as well as to the Members of the United Nations.

(*Signed*) Mahmoud RIAD

[*S/5336, Letter dated 20 June 1963 from the representative of the United Arab Republic to the Secretary-General, 21 June 1963*, pp. 56–57.]

There was also an exchange of accusations between Yemen and the United Kingdom. On the insistence of President Sallal, the British—who still had not recognized his government—closed their legation at Taiz in February 1963.

Then:

On 28 February 1963, the President of the Yemen Arab Republic, in a cable[10] to the President of the Security Council, complained that British forces, supported by tanks, had arrived in the Hareb area. British planes had dropped circulars on Yemeni forces, warning them to withdraw from the area or they would be bombed. This was characterized as aid to infiltrators coming from Saudi Arabia to help the dethroned Imam, and was described as flagrant aggression against the territory of the Yemen Arab Republic.

In a letter of 4 March[11] to the President of the Security Council, the Permanent Representative of the United Kingdom challenged the accuracy of the Yemeni complaint and described the sequence of events relating to the incursions by Republican Yemeni forces into the South

[10] S/5248.   [11] S/5250.

Arabian Federation. After suitable warning, he said, artillery fire had been opened up to evict Yemeni forces from Federal territory. No tanks were used and no bombs were dropped. The action taken by his Government was directed exclusively to the protection of the territory of the South Arabian Federation, to which his Government was committed by treaty. The United Kingdom's policy, he stressed, was one of strict non-involvement in the internal dispute in the Yemen and it was clearly unacceptable that either party in that dispute should be allowed to use Federal territory as a springboard for action against the other party.

On 22 June, a further communication[12] from the Yemen Arab Republic addressed to the President of the Security Council and the Secretary-General stated that British forces had been conducting continuous armed aggression on the borders of the Yemen Arab Republic since 11 June, resulting in heavy losses in lives and property. Urgent measures were sought to stop the aggression, so that the Yemen Arab Republic might not find itself obliged to take any retaliatory steps the result of which might threaten peace and security in the Middle East.

On 1 July, in a letter[13] to the President of the Security Council, the United Kingdom representative transmitted a list of incidents which had occurred on the frontier since the beginning of June and said that in each case Yemeni forces had been the first to open fire without provocation. His Government could not tolerate such open aggression and would take whatever action was necessary to defend the territory of the South Arabian Federation in accordance with its treaty obligations.

A letter from the representative of the Yemen Arab Republic[14] on 28 August contained a further list of what were termed British raids and severe attacks against Yemeni towns and villages. His Government, he said, would not hesitate to use all possible means to defend its territory against any aggressor.

In reply, the United Kingdom representative on 10 September[15] transmitted a list of incidents which had occurred on the frontier since 25 June. In every case, he said, Yemeni forces had been the first to open fire. His Government continued to hold the Yemeni Republican authorities responsible for casualties and damage caused in incidents provoked or initiated by their forces and would continue to observe its treaty obligations. [*YBUN, 1963*, p. 69.]

This situation was to continue well into 1964:

9. COMPLAINT BY YEMEN

On 1 April 1964, Yemen requested an urgent meeting of the Security Council to consider the 'situation resulting from the British continuous acts of aggression against the peaceful Yemeni citizens' culminating in an attack on 28 March in which, Yemen declared, twenty-five persons had been killed and several more injured. Yemen further charged that the United Kingdom had committed more than forty acts of aggression against Yemeni towns and villages since the establishment of the Yemen Arab Republic.

The Security Council had also received three latters, dated 20, 28 and 30 March 1964, in which the United Kingdom charged Yemen with violations of the air space of the South Arabian Federation in the area south and west of Harib and with air attacks with machine-guns and incendiary bombs on Bedouin in the territory of the Federation. In spite of warnings and protests, those violations had continued. Accordingly, after an attack on 27 March against a fort occupied by Federal Guard troops near Jabal Bulaig, British aircraft had been ordered to counter-attack on the following day, after dropping a warning message first, upon a Yemeni military fort just inside the Yemeni frontier about a mile from the township of Harib. The United Kingdom had taken that action strictly in exercise of its rights of defence against attacks on the Federation.

The Security Council included the item in its agenda on 2 April and invited the representative of the Yemen Arab Republic to participate without vote. The Council also acceded to the requests of Iraq, the United Arab Republic and the Syrian Arab Republic to participate in

[12] S/5338.   [13] S/5343.   [14] S/5408.   [15] S/5424.

the discussion without the right to vote. It discussed the matter at six meetings held between 2 and 9 April 1964.

Opening the discussion, the representative of Yemen stated that while the United Kingdom was carrying out its aggressive policy against his country, it was at the same time sending communications to the Security Council charging Yemen with aggressive actions. Those propagandistic letters and charges were merely a smoke-screen to cover its own plan of aggression. The United Kingdom considered that a progressive republic in the Arabian Peninsula endangered its own presence and interests in that region and had, therefore, carried out numerous acts of aggression to disrupt the progress of the Yemen Arab Republic. In the circumstance, the Council must condemn those acts, in particular that of 28 March, ensure just compensation for the Yemeni lives and property losses, ensure withdrawal of the British troops from the area, and recognize that the British presence in Aden and the Protectorates was a threat to the people and security of the whole region.

The United Kingdom representative stated that the British action of 28 March at Harib Fort was a defensive response, falling under Article 51, in order to preserve the territorial integrity of the Federation of South Arabia against further attacks by the forces of the Yemeni Republican authorities. While the United Kingdom Government regretted any loss of life as a result of the defensive act, it did not agree with the figure submitted by Yemen. The United Kingdom was primarily interested in seeing peaceful conditions established on the frontier and in the whole area. It was for that reason that it had already proposed the establishment of a demilitarized zone on the border in the Beihan area from which both sides could withdraw their military forces. Although there had not been a favourable response to that proposal, the United Kingdom was still prepared to see whether, on the basis of equal withdrawal on both sides of the frontier, a solution could be found to ease the tension in the area.

The representatives of Iraq, the United Arab Republic and the Syrian Arab Republic stated that the description of the attack on 28 March in the Harib area as a 'defensive response' was based on the theory of retaliation which the Security Council had rejected on a number of occasions when the representative of the United Kingdom himself had concurred. For the time being, the Council should limit itself to the consideration and condemnation of that action and should not be diverted into considering other political problems of the area.

The representative of the Union of Soviet Socialist Republics stated that if the United Kingdom had any justification for its action of 28 March, it should have submitted its case to the Security Council before carrying out the aggression unilaterally. The British action was a flagrant violation of the Charter and the Soviet Union would support the demand that the Council should condemn it as well as British intervention in the internal affairs of a Member State.

The United States representative said that it was clear that there had been deplorable incursions and attacks along the border in both directions for some time, which could quickly escalate into full-scale war. For that reason, the United States welcomed the proposal for the withdrawal of forces on both sides. Much of the trouble seemed to arise from the fact that the frontier had never been defined. The Security Council might ask the Secretary-General to consider appointing someone to use his good offices to bring the parties together and to finds ways and means of resolving the present dispute.

On 8 April, the Ivory Coast and Morocco introduced a draft resolution under the operative paragraphs of which the Security Council would: condemn reprisals as incompatible with the purposes and principles of the United Nations; deplore the British military action at Harib on 28 March 1964; deplore all attacks and incidents which had occurred in the area; call upon the Yemen Arab Republic and the United Kingdom to exercise the maximum restraint in order to avoid further incidents and to restore peace in the area; and request the Secretary-General to use his good offices to try to settle outstanding issues in agreement with the two parties.

The representative of Morocco stated that his delegation, along with other Arab representatives who had participated in the discussion, felt that the draft fell far short of the action that could have been justifiably expected from the Council in view of the United Kingdom aggression of 28 March.

The representative of the United States maintained that the Council should condemn not only reprisals, but also the attacks which had led to those reprisals. For that reason his delegation had suggested to the sponsors the modification of the first operative paragraph of the draft to read '*Condemns* both attacks and reprisals as incompatible with the purposes and principles of the United Nations'; and the substitution, for operative paragraphs 2 and 3, of a single paragraph reading: '*Deplores* the British military action in Harib on 28 March 1964 and all attacks and incidents which have occurred in the area.' Since those suggestions were unacceptable to the sponsors, the United States could not consider the draft resolution equitable and responsive to the realities of the situation, and accordingly could not vote for it. [*A/5801, Annual Report of the Secretary-General on the work of the Organization, 16 June 1963–15 June 1964, GAOR, 19th sess., suppl. 1,* pp. 18–19.]

A resolution was adopted 'recalling Article 2, paragraphs 3 and 4, of the Charter', and stating that the Security Council:

1. *Condemns* reprisals as incompatible with the purposes and principles of the United Nations.
2. *Deplores* the British military action at Harib on 28 March 1964;
3. *Deplores* all attacks and incidents which have occurred in this area;
4. *Calls upon* the Yemen Arab Republic and the United Kingdom to exercise the maximum restraint in order to avoid further incidents and to restore peace in the area;
5. *Requests* the Secretary-General to use his good offices to try to settle outstanding issues, in agreement with the two parties. [*SC Res. S/5650, 9 Apr. 1964.*]

The voting was 9 to nil, with the United Kingdom and the United States abstaining.[16]

UNYOM—which was operative at the time of these incidents—remained in existence until September 1964. Between April and September 1964 the relationship between the Yemen and the United Kingdom remained comparatively calm. On 28 April 1964, following upon a visit of President Nasser to Yemen, Mahmoud al-Jaifi was designated Prime Minister of the Yemen. He had previously been Yemen's ambassador to Cairo, and this move was widely regarded as an Egyptian curb on the power exercised by Sallal as President. Thus during the presence of UNYOM in the Yemen, there were two Republican governments—first that of the President, Sallal, and then that of the Prime Minister, Jaifi. UNYOM withdrew in September 1964.

Further observations of a 'background' nature, relating to the period since UNYOM's termination up to the present time, will be found below (pp. 665–8) in the section assessing the degree to which UNYOM was successful in discharging its tasks.

---

[16] A very detailed account of the British–Yemeni incidents and exchange of accusations is to be found in the Report of the Security Council, 16 July 1963–15 July 1964, A/5802, *GAOR*, 19th sess., suppl. 2, pp. 102–9.

2

ENABLING RESOLUTION AND VOTING

The Security Council,
Noting with satisfaction the initiative of the Secretary-General mentioned in his report of 24 April 1963 (S/5298) 'about certain aspects of the situation in Yemen of external origin', and aimed at achievement of a peaceful settlement and 'ensuring against any developments in that situation which might threaten the peace of the area',
Noting further the statement by the Secretary-General before the Security Council on 10 June 1963 (1073rd Mtg),
Noting further with satisfaction that the parties directly concerned with the situation affecting Yemen have confirmed their acceptance of identical terms of disengagement in Yemen, and that the Governments of Saudi Arabia and the United Arab Republic have agreed to defray the expenses over a period of two months of the United Nations observation function called for in the terms of disengagement,

1. Requests the Secretary-General to establish the observation operation as defined by him;
2. Urges the parties concerned to observe fully the terms of disengagement set out in the report of 29 April and to refrain from any action which would increase tension in the area;
3. Requests the Secretary-General to report to the Security Council on the implementation of this decision. [*SC Res. S/5331, 11 June 1963.*]

VOTING
    In favour: Brazil, China, France, Ghana, Morocco, Norway, Philippines, UK, USA, Venezuela.
    Against: ——
    Abstaining: USSR.

The adopted resolution was tabled jointly by Ghana and Morocco. The members of the Security Council were especially concerned with the financial arrangements[1] and with the proper distribution of authority between the Council and the Secretary-General.[2]

The following observations were made by delegates exercising their right to explain their vote:

8. Mr Stevenson (USA): I should like to explain very briefly the understanding of the United States in regard to the draft resolution we have just adopted, particularly in light of other statements that had been made to the Council. Frankly, it was our hope that the Secretary-General might have proceeded promptly and without objection on the basis of his reports to the Council, to the dispatch of the United Nations observation mission in compliance with the request of the parties.

9. Although the resultant delay was unfortunate, it is apparent that the resolution we have just adopted is generally satisfactory. I feel that I should emphasize, however, that the disengagement between the parties involved in the Yemen situation placed no limitation upon the duration of the United Nations operation to two months or any other time. The reference to two months arose solely because the Governments of Saudi Arabia and the United Arab

---

[1] See below, pp. 645–52.   [2] See below, pp. 635–7.

Republic agreed to finance the operation for two months, but without prejudice to the manner of financing thereafter if a longer operation should prove to be necessary.

10. As to the question of the duration of the operation, we consider that the Secretary-General's report deals with this matter sufficiently and satisfactorily and that the resolution we have adopted asks him to proceed in accordance with the plans set forth in these reports.

11. As to the financing of the observer operation, it is proper, in our opinion, that the Security Council resolution makes no provision therefor and merely notes that the parties have agreed between themselves to pay the costs for a limited time. Accordingly, the United States delegation voted for the resolution and will welcome the prompt dispatch of observers to the area as proposed by the Secretary-General. We wish to express our thanks to him for his prompt and effective initiative to avoid international conflict in this area. [*SCOR, 18th yr, 1039th mtg*, pp. 2–3.]

The Soviet delegate explained his abstention on grounds of dissatisfaction (*a*) with the financing arrangements[3] and (*b*) with the directions for the duration of UNYOM:

13. Mr FEDORENKO (USSR) (translated from Russian): The resolution on the United Nations Observation Mission which has just been adopted by the Security Council does not, in the view of the Soviet delegation, fully meet the requirements of the situation, and is therefore inadequate.

14. In the first place, the resolution gives no direct indication of the specific amount of time for which the Observation Mission is to serve in the region of the frontier between Yemen and Saudi Arabia. Yet, as we know from the statement made to the Council by the Secretary-General yesterday (1037th meeting), what is contemplated is to send United Nations observers for a specific, limited period of time.

15. In fact, no one in the Council has suggested sending the observers to the region for an indefinite period. But in general, can we adopt a serious decision if we fail to consider specific time-limits? There cannot be any question, after all, of the United Nations observers settling permanently in the region! How, we ask, can action be taken, if we disregard the time factor?

16. What is clearly contemplated under the agreement reached by the parties concerned during the talks in which the Secretary-General took part is a limited, completely definite period of time during which the observers are to be present. In view of these considerations, there seems to be no ground for the attempts of some members of the Council to bar from the Council's decision any reference to a specific period of time for which the United Nations observers would be sent. Such attempts were made before the adoption of the resolution, and are now being made retrospectively, as it were, after the resolution has been adopted.

17. As already stated, the Soviet delegation is not in principle opposed to the dispatch of United Nations observers to the region. However, this operation, like any other operation involving the use of armed forces under the auspices of the United Nations, must be limited in time. Otherwise, a difficult situation may arise. On the basis of the Secretary-General's statements, the Soviet delegation urged that the Council's decision should clearly specify that the United Nations observers were being sent for a period of two months. This is wholly in keeping with the agreement reached by the parties concerned.

18. The question of prolonging the observation mission's stay in the region of the frontier between Yemen and Saudi Arabia should be considered by the Security Council after the two months have elapsed, and the appropriate decision taken. We have naturally taken note of today's statement by the Secretary-General to the Council (1038th meeting), that 'in the event that more than two months should be required' he would 'certainly report this fact to the Council in advance'. [*Ibid.*, pp. 3–4.]

---

[3] See below, pp. 649–51.

3

FUNCTIONS AND MANDATE

THE resolution of 11 June 1963 (S/5331) authorizing UNYOM refers to 'the United Nations observation functions called for in the terms of disengagement'; and requests the Secretary-General to establish 'the observation operation as defined by him'.

The disengagement agreement has not been published as a separate, solemn agreement; however, the Secretary-General described it in his report to the Security Council in the following terms:

. . . it is now possible for me to inform the Security Council that I have received from each of the three Governments concerned, in separate communications, formal confirmation of their acceptance of identical terms of disengagement in Yemen. The will of all three of the interested parties to ease the situation has been the decisive factor, of course, and they are to be commended for their constructive attitude.

4. In substance these terms are the following: the Government of Saudi Arabia on its part will terminate all support and aid to the Royalists of Yemen and will prohibit the use of Saudi Arabian territory by Royalist leaders for the purpose of carrying on the struggle in Yemen. Simultaneously, with the suspension of aid from Saudi Arabia to the Royalists, the United Arab Republic undertakes to begin withdrawal from Yemen of the troops sent on request of the new Government, this withdrawal to be phased and to take place as soon as possible during which the forces would withdraw from field activities to their bases pending their departure. The United Arab Republic has also agreed not to take punitive action against the Royalists of Yemen for any resistance mounted by them prior to the beginning of their disengagement. There would likewise be an end to any actions on Saudi Arabian territory by United Arab Republic forces. A demilitarized zone to a distance of twenty kilometres on each side of the demarcated Saudi-Arabian–Yemen border is to be established from which military forces and equipment are to be excluded. In this zone, on both sides, impartial observers are to be stationed to check on the observance of the terms of disengagement and who would also have the responsibility of travelling beyond the demilitarized zone, as necessary, in order to certify the suspension of activities in support of the Royalists from Saudi Arabian territory and the outward movement of the United Arab Republic forces and equipment from the airports and seaports of Yemen. The United Arab Republic and Saudi Arabia have further undertaken to co-operate with the representative of the United Nations Secretary-General or some other mutually acceptable intermediary in reaching agreement on the modalities and verification of disengagement.   [*S/5298, 29 Apr. 1963*, pp. 33–34.]

There were thus three parties to the disengagement agreement, though the main duties thereunder fell upon the UAR and Saudi Arabia. UNYOM was to be stationed on the territory of two of the three parties—in the Yemen and Saudi Arabia. The details of the methods of functioning were not specified in either the authorizing resolutions or the disengagement agreement, but were to be worked out between the Secretary-General's representative and the parties concerned.

. . I have asked Major-General Carl Carlson von Horn, Chief of Staff of the United Nations

Truce Supervision Organization in Jerusalem, to proceed without delay to the three countries concerned for the purpose of consulting with the appropriate authorities on details relating to the nature and functioning of United Nations Observers in implementation of the terms of disengagement and to report to me with his recommendation as to the size of the set-up that might be required to discharge this responsibility. . . . [*Ibid.* p. 34.]

The limits to this very narrow mandate became apparent as UNYOM became operational:

6. . . . The function of the Mission is to check and certify on the observance by the two parties of the terms of the disengagement agreement. This entails ground patrolling in the buffer zone and surrounding areas by the units stationed in Jizan, Najran and Sa'da, and air patrolling in the mountainous central part of the buffer zone where land patrolling is impossible. The military observers stationed in Sana and Hodeida are primarily responsible for observing and certifying the withdrawal of troops.

7. It is to be noted particularly that by the provisions of the agreement on disengagement, UNYOM's functions are limited to observing, certifying and reporting. This operation has no peace-keeping role beyond this and therefore it has a more restricted range of activity than the United Nations Truce Supervision Organization in Palestine and the United Nations Military Observers Group in India and Pakistan, not to mention the United Nations Emergency Force and the United Nations Operation in the Congo. It could not, in fact, effectively undertake any broader functions with the personnel, equipment and funds now available to it. It bears emphasis, also, that the agreement on disengagement involves only Saudi Arabia and the United Arab Republic by the former's intention to end activities in support of the royalists from Saudi Arabian territory and the latter's intention to withdraw its troops from Yemen. UNYOM, therefore, is not concerned with Yemen's internal affairs generally, with actions of the Government of Yemen, or with that Government's relations with other Governments and bordering territories, nor does UNYOM have any authority to issue orders or directions. The parties themselves are solely responsible for fulfilling the terms of disengagement on which they have agreed. . . .

17. UNYOM, because of its limited size and function, can observe and certify only certain indications of the implementation of the disengagement agreement. It can, within limits, also serve as an intermediary and as endorser of good faith on behalf of the parties concerned, and it is my intention to have the Mission perform these roles to the maximum of its capability. . . . [*S/5412, 4 Sept. 1963*, pp. 153–4, 156.]

UNYOM's functions were expanded to include the investigations of alleged incidents 'where appropriate and possible'. These complaints generally fell into two categories:

(*a*) Allegations of offensive action by United Arab Republic forces against royalist positions in Yemen and on Saudi Arabian territory;

(*b*) Activities in support of the royalists emanating from Saudi Arabia.

It is to be expected that in a situation of the kind found in Yemen, there would be some spectacular allegations about the conduct of one side or the other. This has happened. UNYOM, where possible, has sought to investigate such allegations. . . . [*S/5412, 4 Sept. 1963*, p. 155, para. 14.]

Reference to the map on p. 608 will facilitate a more detailed explanation of UNYOM's functions, region by region.

12. The main function of the detachments stationed in Sada and Harad is to observe and report on disengagement and withdrawal of United Arab Republic forces from field activities in these areas, while the main function of the post at Hodeida is to observe and report on the departure of United Arab Republic forces from Yemen. . . .

14. The main function of the detachments stationed at Jizan and Najran is to check on the reduction or cessation of assistance from Saudi Arabia to the royalists. . . .

16. In Saudi Arabia territory, including the demilitarized zone on the Saudi Arabian side of the frontier, most United Nations patrols and check points are accompanied by Saudi Arabian liaison officials, who check cargoes as requested by United Nations observers. Some check points are manned for three to four days at a time and some for shorter periods. Gaps in between manning periods do not exceed two days and in the intervening period the areas are covered by patrolling. . . [*S/5447 and Add. 1, 2, Report by Secretary-General to Security Council on functioning of UNYOM and the implementation of the terms of disengagement, 28 Oct. 1963, pp. 46–48.*]

In virtually every one of his reports to the Security Council the Secretary-General found it necessary to reiterate the limited nature of UNYOM's mandate. He also came rapidly to believe that the mandate was unsatisfactory.

24. I pointed out in my last report that UNYOM, because of its limited size and function, can observe and certify only certain indications of the implementation of the disengagement agreement. . . .

25. I also said in my last report that UNYOM could, within limits, serve as an intermediary and as an endorser of good faith on behalf of the parties concerned. I believe that within its severe limitations it has fulfilled this role very well and that certain improvements in the situation have been the result. I do not, however, believe that the solution of the problem, or even the fundamental steps which must be taken to resolve it, can ever be within the potential of UNYOM alone—and most certainly not under its existing limited mandate.

29. In the course of my consultations with the parties I have made clear my own dissatisfaction with the mandate of UNYOM as now defined. That mandate, set forth in the disengagement agreement, is so limiting and restrictive as to make it virtually impossible for UNYOM to play a really helpful and constructive role in Yemen. Indeed, given the nature of the situation and of the terrain, it is not possible for UNYOM with its present personnel, or for that matter, with a much expanded establishment, to observe fully, let alone to certify to the satisfaction of both parties, what specifically is being done in the way of disengagement. I frankly see little prospect that the disengagement agreement could be so amended as to correct this deficiency. [*Ibid.* pp. 49, 51.]

. . . the implementation of the disengagement agreement . . . is the primary concern of the two parties to the disengagement agreement. The terms of that agreement give the United Nations no role beyond observation and reporting with regard to its implementation. The United Nations, therefore, cannot ensure that it will be carried out. . . . [*S/5794, 2 July 1964*, p. 2.]

The functions of UNYOM remained basically the same throughout its existence, though as time went by the need to perform specific tasks in certain regions became clearer. At the end of October 1963 it had been anticipated by the Secretary-General that its work would have to end because of Saudi-Arabian reluctance to pay for a new two-month period.[1] Arrangements were fairly far advanced for the withdrawal of military components of the Mission before Saudi Arabia reversed her position. This fact led to a military reappraisal of the functions being performed, with the ensuing results:

Because of the co-operation shown by the authorities on both sides of the Saudi Arabian–Yemen frontier and because of the peaceful and friendly attitude of the people in the area

[1] See below, p. 650.

covered by the Mission, irrespective of their political attitudes towards United Nations personnel, it was felt that it was no longer necessary to maintain a military unit in the demilitarized zone. The Yugoslav detachment at Najran continued, however, to carry out patrols in that area until 25 November, while the Observer personnel was being built up to full strength. During the same period, United Nations Military Observers at Jizan and Najran manned check-points on the frontier to the limit of their ability.

9. The functions of the observers at Najran and Jizan are to maintain permanent checkpoints at the main border crossings into Yemen and temporary checkpoints on an irregular basis at the more difficult crossings, as well as patrols, in order to observe the nature of the traffic across the border. Most United Nations patrols and checkpoints are accompanied by Saudi Arabian liaison officials, who check cargoes as requested by the observers. Occasionally, observers visit Royalist areas on the Yemeni side of the border in order to check on the extent to which arms and ammunition may be reaching them from abroad and the degree of fighting occurring between them and the forces of the United Arab Republic in Yemen. The observers in Sada, Sana and Hodeida observe the extent to which the United Arab Republic forces are being disengaged from Yemen. [*S/5501, 2 Jan. 1964*, pp. 4, 5.]

Not only was the state of the Yemen's relations with the United Kingdom not included in the disengagement agreement,[2] but nor was observation of the frontier with the South Arabian Federation. Accordingly, when UNYOM's investigations effectively caused a great decrease in the arms coming to the royalists across the northern frontier and supplies instead began entering from the Beihan area, UNYOM was not competent to investigate.

5. The nature and extent of the military operations carried out by the royalists during January and February would seem to indicate that arms and ammunition in appreciable amounts have been reaching them from some source, though not necessarily across the northern frontier. Yemen Arab Republic and United Arab Republic sources assert that such supplies are being introduced from the Beihan area across the frontier with the South Arabian Federation. This frontier is not included in the disengagement agreement, and United Nations Observers, therefore, do not operate in that area. . . . [*S/5572, 3 Mar. 1964*, p. 96.]

4

CONSTITUTIONAL BASIS

THE Security Council had been seized of complaints by Yemen of British aggression, of United Kingdom complaints of violations by Yemen of airspace over the South Arabian Federation, and of Saudi Arabian complaints of aggression by the UAR.[1] However, the actual question of Egyptian and Saudi Arabian involvement in the Yemen civil war had not been before the Security Council, and it was from U Thant's personal initiative that the services of the UN were offered to the parties.

[2] Although, as indicated above, pp. 616–19, they were a relevant political factor throughout.
[1] For the relevance of these to the ultimate establishment of UNYOM, see above, pp.614–16.

1. Since the fall of 1962 I have been consulting regularly with the representatives to the United Nations of the Governments of the Arab Republic of Yemen, Saudi Arabia and the United Arab Republic, about certain aspects of the situation in Yemen of external origin, with a view to making my Office available to the parties for such assistance as might be desired toward ensuring against any developments in that situation which might threaten the peace of the area. I have encountered from the beginning a sympathetic and co-operative attitude on the part of all three representatives and their Governments.

2. It was in this context that, after clearance with the respective Governments, I asked Mr Ralph J. Bunche to go to Yemen and the United Arab Republic in late February and early March on a fact-finding mission primarily devoted to talking with the Presidents of Yemen and the United Arab Republic, in that order, with the purpose of ascertaining their views on the situation and what steps might be taken to ease tension and restore conditions to normal. It was left open whether Mr Bunche would eventually go also to Saudi Arabia, but developments made this unnecessary. Mr Bunche carried out this mission and reported fully to me on his talks, which I found encouraging. Subsequently, I was informed that the United States Government, on its own initiative, sent Mr Ellsworth Bunker to Saudi Arabia on a somewhat similar but unconnected mission. Mr Bunker later visited Saudi Arabia on two other occasions and also had extensive talks in Cairo with President Nasser. Mr Bunker kept me informed on the results of his missions. These talks in the end proved fruitful and from them emerged the agreed terms of disengagement. Mr Bunker's efforts are much appreciated.

3. As a result of these activities, it is now possible for me to inform the Security Council that I have received from each of the three Governments concerned, in separate communications, formal confirmation of their acceptance of identical terms of disengagement in Yemen. The will of all three of the interested parties to ease the situation has been the decisive factor, of course, and they are to be commended for their constructive attitude. [*S/5298, Report of the Secretary-General to the Security Council concerning developments relating to Yemen, 29 Apr. 1963*, p. 33.]

The authority of the Secretary General to take this sort of initiative is not to be found in the Charter, but only in a liberal interpretation of his role as chief administrative officer of an organization dedicated to peace. The question is worth looking at more closely, for the diplomatic history of the establishment of UNYOM is instructive on the developing role of the Secretariat as well as about peacekeeping.

Under Article 98 of the Charter the Secretary-General 'shall perform such other [i.e. non-administrative] functions as are entrusted to him [by the Assembly, Security Council, ECOSOC or Trusteeship Council]'. Under Article 99 he 'may bring to the attention of the Security Council any matter which in his opinion may threaten the maintenance of international peace and security'. The Secretary-General's right of political initiative, in strict Charter terms, is thus limited to requesting the Security Council to place an item on its agenda. An ever-present problem in the context of peacekeeping has been the extent to which the Security Council should properly delegate authority to the Secretary-General; and the degree to which he should infer such delegation in the absence of explicit instructions. The problem of delegated powers does not concern us here, however, in the context of UNYOM.[2] What is here relevant is another question—namely, the right of the Secretary-General to take anticipatory diplomatic initiatives even before a dispute is placed before

[2] Though it is highly relevant in the Congo experience, details of which will appear in Vol. III of this study.

the Security Council (or, we may note, the General Assembly—as in the case of West Irian).[3]

It has been argued, in terms of law, that according to Article 99, the Secretary-General *may* bring a matter to the attention of the Security Council (but need not do so) if *in his opinion* it threatens the maintenance of international peace. Thus, it has been said, 'the Secretary-General, prior to forming an opinion, has an implicit right to collect information, to make investigations and even to engage in negotiations'.[4] It is perhaps easier to read into Article 99 the implied right to gather information than the right to enter negotiations. This Editor believes that the right to enter into negotiations prior to the Security Council being seized of a matter cannot objectively be read into Article 99. The truth of the matter seems to be that this is a practice which has developed partly due to political necessity and partly due to the personality of the various Secretaries-General, and that it finds its legal basis not in Article 99, but in a broad interpretation of the Charter which permits as valid every action within the purposes and principles of the Charter, and not expressly prohibited thereunder.

It would seem that Hammarskjöld had much the same view, for in August 1959 he wrote:

It should also be noted that in some recent cases of international conflict or other difficulties involving Member States the Secretary-General has dispatched personal representatives with the task of assisting the Governments in their efforts. This may be regarded as a further development of actions of a 'good offices' nature, with which the Secretary-General is now frequently charged. The steps to which I refer here have been taken with the consent or at the invitation of Governments concerned, but without formal decisions of other organs of the United Nations. Such actions by the Secretary-General fall within the competence of his Office and are, in my view, in other respects also in strict accordance with the Charter, when they serve its purpose. As a matter of course, the members of the appropriate organ of the United Nations have been informed about the action planned by the Secretary-General and were given an opportunity to express views on it. These cases also should not be considered as setting precedents, especially as it always remains open to the appropriate organs to request that such an action, before being taken by the Secretary-General, be submitted to them for formal decision. However, in these cases too, what has been tried may provide experiences on which, later, stable and agreed practices may usefully be developed.

The main significance of the evolution of the Office of the Secretary-General in the manner referred to above lies in the fact that it has provided means for smooth and fast action, which might otherwise not have been open to the Organization. This is of special value in situations in which prior public debate on a proposed course of action might increase the difficulties that such an action would encounter, or in which a vacuum might be feared because Members may prove hesitant, without fuller knowledge of the facts or for other reasons, to give explicit prior support in detail to an action which, however, they approve in general terms or are willing should be tried without formal commitment. [*A/4132/Add. 1, Introd. to the Annual Report of the Secretary-General, 16 June 1958–15 June 1959; GAOR, 14th sess., suppl. 1A*, p. 3.]

In any event, the practice of diplomatic action by the Secretary-General without delegation has undoubtedly grown. The negotiations concerning the

---

[3] This case is analysed in Vol. II of this study.
[4] Alexandrowicz, 'The Secretary-General of the UN', *ICLQ* (1962), p. 1115.

release of detained American airmen by Peking, the Netherlands–Indonesia Agreement on West Irian, and the Saudi Arabian–Egyptian Agreement may all be cited. Again, he has taken other actions without formally going to the Security Council, but after holding informal consultations with the members thereof: in this category fall the examples of his role in the Cambodia–Thailand border dispute, the sending of a representative to Laos in spite of Russian objections, and the method employed to renew the mandate of UNYOM beyond its initial two-month period. Although the Soviet Union, and to some extent France, continue to protest at this sort of action, it has by now become an effective usage in UN practice.

After the Secretary-General reported to the Security Council his proposals for setting up an observation mission to fulfil the functions envisaged in the disengagement agreement, and after the details and costs had been estimated, the Soviet Union indicated that she thought that the agreement of the parties directly concerned, their request to the UN, and their bearing of the financial burden did not remove the necessity for prior approval by the Security Council:

LETTER DATED 8 JUNE 1963 FROM THE REPRESENTATIVE OF THE UNION OF SOVIET SOCIALIST REPUBLICS TO THE PRESIDENT OF THE SECURITY COUNCIL

(Original text: Russian)

On instructions from the Government of the Union of Soviet Socialist Republics, I have the honour to request you to convene the Security Council in order to consider the reports of the Secretary-General to the Council on developments relating to Yemen (S/5298, S/5321, S/5323 and S/5325), since the reports contain proposals concerning possible measures by the United Nations to maintain international peace and security, on which, under the Charter, decisions are taken by the Security Council.

I request you to arrange for the distribution of this letter as an official document of the Security Council.

(Signed) N. FEDORENKO

[S/5326.]

Accordingly, the members of the Security Council met on 11 June 1963, following informal consultations among themselves. The Secretary-General referred only obliquely to the constitutional point here being discussed:

2. The SECRETARY-GENERAL: If I speak to you again so soon, it is because of my concern that the United Nations observation assistance called for under the terms of disengagement in Yemen, as agreed upon by the parties, should be provided with the least possible delay. I am naturally hopeful that the informal consultations that have been going on in an effort to achieve general agreement on the wording of the resolution relating to the Yemen observation mission will prove fruitful. I am compelled to say that I feel strongly that it would not be in the interest of peace in the Near East, and certainly not in the interest of this Organization, if it should for any reason fail to provide the observation assistance requested by the parties, or delay much longer in doing so.

3. From my informal talks with members of this Council, I am of the firm impression that everyone agrees that the observation function called for should be provided. This, in my view, is a key point, along with two other key points—namely, that the parties concerned are themselves agreed on the need for United Nations observation, and have asked for it; that the

parties also are prepared to bear the cost of the operation for a period of two months, and possibly for a total period of four months, should that prove necessary.

4. It is not, then, as I see it, the question of the establishment of the proposed observation mission that is really at issue now in the Council, since everyone agrees that this operation is necessary. Rather, it is the question of what and how much should go into a resolution about that matter.

5. I am prepared to commence the operation immediately. The Council is already aware that it will be a modest mission, not exceeding 200 people, including some carefully selected and experienced military officer observers and a small number of other ranks. Its duration should not exceed four months, and it could be concluded in two. In the event that more than two months should be required, I would certainly report this fact to the Council in advance. [*SCOR, 18th yr, 1038th mtg*, p. 1.]

Certain other states explicitly reserved their positions to the effect that the resolution which was passed should not be taken to mean that Security Council approval was legally required in every subsequent similar case:

33. However, we should like to state, as the representative of Morocco has said, that this is a unique situation calling for a unique solution, and that it should not, therefore, be considered as a precedent, particularly with regard to the assumption that only the Security Council can authorize peace-keeping operations or that it is the only body that can initiate action to keep the peace. [*Per the Philippines delegate, ibid. 1039th mtg*, p. 6.]

The Moroccan representative had said:

36. . . . In our opinion, the details of the solution cannot in any way effect the permanent principles of the Charter of the United Nations or the permanent means presented by it for the settlement of problems, methods of financing or the establishment of the periods during which the United Nations should be responsible for ensuring the maintenance of international peace and security everywhere. [*Ibid. 1038th mtg*, pp. 7–8.]

The protests by nations that their actions do not constitute precedents may excuse them legally at a later stage from following a different course; but such protests cannot prevent the weight of political precedent from being created in the minds of men. The Soviet Union was here successful in making the point that the establishment of an observation mission, for a limited period, at the request of the parties for the dispute, and paid for by them, required the formal consent of the Security Council.

However, the resolution which was adopted praised the Secretary-General for the initiative he had taken (as did the Soviet delegate in his speech); and the subsequent renewals of the mandate of the Mission were achieved by informal consultations and not by formal meetings on votes in the Security Council. The repeated renewal of the mandate was largely presented in terms of the continued provision by Saudi Arabia and Egypt of the necessary finances.[5]

In his reports to the Security Council—which were not made the subject of debate—the Secretary-General offered his personal view, based on information which he provided, as to whether the Mission should continue. In them he indicated whether financial support would be forthcoming, made the necessary preliminary arrangements, and made it fairly clear that the renewal of the life of UNYOM needed no formal approval of the Security Council.

[5] This is fully documented below, pp. 651–2.

19. The Security Council adopted its resolution of 11 June on the understanding that the Governments of Saudi Arabia and the United Arab Republic had agreed to defray the expenses, over a period of two months in the first instance, of the United Nations Yemen Observation Mission called for in the terms of disengagement. As indicated above, the Observation Mission became operational with the arrival of the main body of the Yugoslav reconnaissance unit on 4 July. The two months period, therefore, expires on 4 September. It is now obvious that the task of the Mission will not be completed by that date. Indeed, this possibility was foreseen in my report of 7 June, in which I pointed out that at the end of the first two months of the Mission, an appeal to the parties for additional financial assistance could be made. Accordingly, I have approached both parties through their representatives to the United Nations to defray the expenses of the Yemen operation for a further period of two months, as from 4 September. I have received oral assurances from the two representatives that their Governments agreed to do so. [*S/5412, Report by the Secretary-General to the Security Council on the functioning of UNYOM, 4 Sept. 1963, p. 157.*]

. . . On the grounds that the disengagement agreement had not been fulfilled and United Nations observation was therefore still required, these two Governments undertook to meet the expenses of UNYOM for a further period as from 4 September 1963, until 4 November 1963.

27. In anticipation of this date, in order to be prepared either to withdraw the Mission personnel, vehicles and equipment, or to maintain it beyond that date should this be desired, I have been conferring over the past fortnight with representatives of the Governments of Saudi Arabia, the United Arab Republic and Yemen. It emerges from these consultations that there is a general appreciation of the helpful assistance rendered by the United Nations Mission in Yemen and of the manner in which it has conducted itself. The view is also general among the parties that the continuation beyond 4 November of a United Nations presence in some form, although not necessarily including military components, would be desirable and useful. On the other hand, one of the two Governments concerned with financing UNYOM has indicated that it is not prepared, on the basis of the existing situation, to share the cost of UNYOM beyond the 4 November commitment. The position of the Government of Saudi Arabia on this question, as it has been communicated to me, is that any extension of UNYOM beyond 4 November would depend upon concrete evidence that the agreement on disengagement is to be implemented within a specified period of time, which in effect means a time schedule for the withdrawal of United Arab Republic troops. As of now, therefore, assuming no change in the situation as regards fulfilment of the disengagement agreement, the Government of Saudi Arabia has made it clear that it undertakes no commitment concerning an extension of UNYOM beyond 4 November.

28. In the light of this latter circumstance, it has been necessary for me to take the essential preparatory steps looking towards the complete withdrawal of UNYOM by 4 November, beyond which date there will be no financial support for it. [*S/5447, Report by the Secretary-General to the Security Council on the functioning of UNYOM, 28 Oct. 1963, p.50.*]

1. This report is supplemental to my report of 28 October 1963 (*S/5447*).

2. In the afternoon of 31 October, the Permanent Representative of the Government of Saudi Arabia communicated to me a new and urgent message from his Government on the subject of the extension of the United Nations Yemen Observation Mission (UNYOM), beyond 4 November. This message, in substance, stated that despite the fact that the other party to the disengagement agreement had not carried it out, the Government of Saudi Arabia, being desirous of helping the United Nations complete its mission of peace in the Yemen area, and desirous also of saving human lives, has decided to participate in the financing of UNYOM for a further period of two months as from 5 November.

3. In view of the fact that the Government of the United Arab Republic had previously expressed its view that UNYOM should be extended as well as its willingness to continue to

share in the expenses of UNYOM for a further period of one or two months, the problem of financing a continuing mission is thus removed.

4. The Representative of the Government of Yemen had also indicated that it was the view of his Government that the continued presence of UNYOM beyond 4 November would be desirable and helpful.

5. In the light of these circumstances, and particularly of the new development incident to the latest message from the Government of Saudi Arabia, I have ordered the cancellation of the preparations that were under way for the withdrawal of UNYOM by 4 November. Therefore, UNYOM, in approximately its present form and size, will continue from that date for a further period of two months and its expenses will be borne in equal shares by the Governments of Saudi Arabia and the United Arab Republic. [*S/5447/Add. 1, 31 Oct. 1964.*]

1. This report is a further supplement to my previous reports (*S/5447 and Add. 1*), and is submitted for the purpose of information and clarification.

2. In document S/5447/Add. 1, I informed the Security Council that the United Nations Yemen Observation Mission (UNYOM) would be continued from 4 November for a further period of two months, in pursuance of the wishes of the two parties to the disengagement agreement as indicated by their willingness to continue to share the cost of UNYOM for that additional period.

3. In my report to the Council on 27 May 1963, in which I communicated my intention to establish the mission in Yemen, I estimated that the observation function in Yemen would not be required for more than four months.

4. The continuation of UNYOM for another two months after 4 November, goes beyond that original estimate. Therefore, although believing that no meeting of the Council on the subject was required, I have consulted the Council members informally in order to ascertain that in the light of the circumstances as reported there would be no objection to the extension. There was none. [*S/5447/Add. 2, 11 Nov. 1963.*]

24. Accordingly on 23 December 1963, I addressed identical messages to the Prime Minister of Saudi Arabia and to the President of the United Arab Republic in which I informed them of my conclusion, which seemed to be generally shared, that the Mission continues to serve a useful purpose and that its extension would be conducive to further progress towards both disengagement and a peaceful solution in Yemen. It followed that I would be prepared to extend the United Nations Yemen Observation Mission in approximately its present strength and composition for a period of up to six months. In that case, I pointed out, Mr Spinelli would continue to serve as my Special Representative for Yemen and as Head of the Mission. I inquired, therefore, whether the two Governments would be agreeable to the continuation of the Mission for such a period under the prevailing arrangements for its financing. In this regard, I also indicated that in view of recent reductions in the size of the Mission, the operating expenses had been substantially reduced.

25. On 27 December 1963, I was informed by the Permanent Representative of the United Arab Republic that his Government was in agreement with the suggestions mentioned in my message. After I had answered a preliminary request for clarification from the Saudi Arabian Government, I was informed on 2 January 1964 that it agreed to the extension of the Mission from 4 January 1964 for a period of two months ending 4 March 1964.

26. Although this period is not, in my opinion, sufficiently long in which to anticipate a full solution of the problem, I welcome the decision of the two Governments to continue to support the United Nations operation in the Yemen area as an indication of their desire for the maintenance of peace and security in the region and for progress towards complete disengagement.

27. Having ascertained by means of informal consultations that there is no objection among the members of the Security Council to that course, I intend to maintain the Observation Mission in Yemen for at least another two months and beyond that if the need for it continues and the two Governments concerned are prepared to defray its costs. [*S/5501,*

Report by the Secretary-General to the Security Council on the functioning of UNYOM, 2 Jan. 1964, pp. 8–9.]

In paragraph 27 of my report to the Security Council of 2 January 1964 (S/5501), I indicated that it was my intention to maintain the United Nations Observation Mission in Yemen for at least another two months. That intention has been carried out and the Mission continues. In pursuance of the informal procedure followed last November, although believing that no meeting of the Council on the subject was required, I have consulted the Council members informally in order to ascertain that in the light of the circumstances as reported there would be no objection to the extension. There was none. *[S/5501/Add. 1, 10 Jan. 1964, p. 9.]*

11. I have ascertained from the Permanent Representatives of the Governments of Saudi Arabia and the United Arab Republic that their Governments concur in the suggestion that the United Nations Observation Mission in the Yemen be extended for another two months as from 4 March 1964, that is, until 4 May 1964. In pursuance of the informal procedure followed last November, although believing that no meeting of the Council on the subject was required, I have consulted the Council members informally in order to ascertain that in the light of the circumstances as reported there would be no objection to the extension. There was none. *[S/5572, Report by the Secretary-General to the Security Council on the functioning of UNYOM, 3 Mar. 1964, pp. 97–98.]*

With regard to paragraph 11 of my last report (S/5572), I wish to inform the Council that having consulted the Council members informally for the extension of the United Nations Observation Mission in Yemen for a further two months as from 4 March 1964 and finding that there was no objection, I have in fact extended the Mission until 4 May 1964. *[S/5572/Add. 1, 16 Mar. 1964, p. 98.]*

9. In view of the contribution made by the Mission to improving the situation on the northern frontier and of the prospective negotiations on the Yemen problem, I am definitely of the opinion that it would be useful and advisable to extend the Mission for another two months and I propose to do so.

10. I have ascertained from the Permanent Representatives of the Governments of Saudi Arabia and the United Arab Republic that their Governments concur in my suggestion that the United Nations Observation Mission in Yemen be extended for another two months as from 4 May 1964, that is, until 4 July 1964. In pursuance of the informal procedure followed last November [S/5447/Add. 2], although believing that no meeting of the Council on the subject was required, I have consulted the Council members informally in order to ascertain that in the light of the circumstances as reported there would be no objection to the extension. In the absence of any objection, I am therefore proposing to extend the Mission until 4 July 1964. *[S/5681, Report by the Secretary-General to the Security Council on the functioning of UNYOM, 4 May 1964, p. 113, mimeo.]*

With regard to my proposal in paragraph 10 of my last report (S/5681) to extend the United Nations Yemen Observation Mission until 4 July 1964, I wish to inform the Council that since the informal consultations with the Council revealed no objection, I have, in fact, extended the mission until 4 July 1964. *[S/5681/Add. 1, 23 May 1964, pp. 113–14.]*

8. I believe that the Yemen Observation Mission, despite its unusually limited function and authority, has helped towards removing the threat to international peace and security implicit in the Yemen problem and towards keeping open the possibilities for a final settlement. With a view to providing a further opportunity for negotiations, I consider it advisable to extend the Mission after 4 July for another two months. I take this position with some reluctance, however, in view of the fact that during its year of operation the Mission in Yemen has been able

to observe and report only a disappointing measure of disengagement, in particular as regards the withdrawal of UAR troops. I feel obliged, therefore, to appeal most urgently to the parties concerned to meet at the highest level in the near future with a view to achieving full and rapid implementation of the disengagement agreement. I also feel bound to advise the Council that if this new period of two months were to register no substantial progress toward fulfilment or the firm prospect of imminent fulfilment, I would find it difficult to envisage a further extension of the Mission in its present form, and with its present terms of reference and purpose.

9. I have ascertained from the Permanent Representative of the Governments of Saudi Arabia and the United Arab Republic that their Governments concur in my suggestion that the United Nations Yemen Observation Mission be extended for another two months as from 4 July 1964, that is, until 4 September 1964. In pursuance of the informal procedure that has been followed since last November (S/5447/Add. 2), and again believing that no meeting of the Council on the subject was required, I have consulted the Council members individually and informally in order to ascertain that in the light of the circumstances as reported there would be no objection to the extension. In the absence of any objection, I am therefore proposing to extend the Mission until 4 September 1964. [*S/5794, Report by the Secretary-General to the Security Council on the functioning of UNYOM, 2 July 1964*, pp. 19–20.

In paragraph 9 of my report of 2 July to the Security Council on Yemen (S/5794), I indicated my intention to extend the United Nations Yemen Observation Mission until 4 September 1964. I may now inform the Council that, in view of the fact that the informal consultations with the individual members of the Council revealed no objection to the extension, I have in fact extended the Mission until 4 September 1964. [*S/5794/Add. 1, 3 July 1964*, mimeo.]

In due course the Secretary-General felt it necessary, due to the limitations of UNYOM's mandate upon its ability effectively to scrutinize the implementation of the demilitarization agreement, to move to the question of termination. It is evident that he believed authority to terminate UNYOM's existence fell within the scope of his own duties:

10. In the light of these circumstances, I addressed on 19 August 1964 identical notes to the two Governments (annex I) in which, after recalling the remarks set forth in my previous report, I asked them to inform me of their wishes with regard to the termination of the Mission on 4 September 1964 or its extension beyond that date on the prevailing basis.

11. In a reply dated 26 August 1964 (annex II), the Saudi Arabian Government, after noting that it had carried out its responsibilities as set out in the agreement faithfully and honestly, but that the other part had not carried out its responsibilities, stated that it found itself unable to continue the payment of expenses resulting from the agreement and unable to abide by its terms after 4 September 1964. I was informed orally on 31 August that the Government of the United Arab Republic in response to my note, had no objection to the termination of UNYOM on 4 September.

12. In view of the expressed wishes of the parties to the agreement and in accordance with my own previously stated views, it is my intention to terminate the activities of the United Nations Observation Mission in Yemen on 4 September 1964.

Annex I

Notes dated 19 August 1964 from the Secretary-General addressed to the Governments of Saudi Arabia and of the United Arab Republic

The Secretary-General has the honour to approach the Government of Saudi Arabia (or the United Arab Republic) on the subject of the United Nations Observation Mission in Yemen.

The purpose of this communication is to determine the wishes of your Government with regard to the Yemen Mission, which will come to an end on 4 September 1964, unless specific action is taken to extend it once again. A communication identical to this one is being addressed to the Government of the United Arab Republic (or Saudi Arabia).

The Mission to Yemen was established in July 1963, in response to the agreement between Saudi Arabia and the United Arab Republic on disengagement in Yemen. The Mission, by the terms of reference defined for it in that agreement, has had a limited purpose and function, which it has discharged to the best of its ability for more than a year.

It will be recalled that the Secretary-General in his report to the Security Council of 2 July 1964 (S/5794), indicated that on the expiration on 4 September of the present two months' extension of the Mission, he would not be inclined to take the initiative in seeking a further extension in the absence of substantial progress in the fulfilment of the agreement between the two parties.

Clearly, the wishes of the two parties to the agreement should be a major determining factor in arriving at a final decision on the future of the Mission. It will be very much appreciated, therefore, if the Government of Saudi Arabia (or United Arab Republic) will inform the Secretary-General within the next ten days as to its wishes with regard to the United Nations Observation Mission in Yemen, that is to say, whether it wishes the Mission to come to an end on 4 September 1964, or to be extended beyond that date on the prevailing basis.

The Secretary-General takes this opportunity to express to the Government of Saudi Arabia (or United Arab Republic) his appreciation of the co-operation it has never failed to extend to the Mission.

Annex II

Note dated 26 August 1964 from the Chargé d'Affaires of the
Permanent Mission of Saudi Arabia to the United Nations addressed to the Secretary-General

The Chargé d'Affaires of the Permanent Mission of Saudi Arabia to the United Nations presents his compliments to the Secretary-General of the United Nations and with reference to His Excellency's note dated 19 August 1964, regarding the future of the United Nations Observation Mission in Yemen, has the honour, upon instructions received from his Government to convey the following:

The Kingdom of Saudi Arabia, bearing in mind the contents of His Excellency's last report on the situation to the Security Council indicating that he will not request a further extension of the Mission on the basis that the two parties have not progressed in implementing the disengagement agreement, and noting that at the same time His Excellency has declared that Saudi Arabia has, for its part, carried out its responsibilities as set out in the agreement for a period of twelve months faithfully and honestly, and noting further His Excellency's observance that the other party has not carried out its responsibilities, finds itself unable to continue the payment of expenses resulting from the agreement and unable to abide by its terms after 4 September 1964, and at the same time the Saudi Arabian Government expresses its gratitude in appreciation of His Excellency's good offices and unceasing goodwill.
[*S/5927, Report by the Secretary-General to the Security Council on the functioning of UNYOM*, 2 Sept. 1964, pp. 258–60, mimeo.]

1. In my report to the Security Council dated 2 September 1964, on the operation of the United Nations Observation Mission in Yemen, I announced my intention to terminate the activities of the Mission on 4 September 1964.
2. That decision has now been put into effect and the Mission ended its activities on that date.
3. Plans for the orderly and expeditious evacuation of the personnel of the Mission and withdrawal or disposal of its equipment are being carried out. All of the twenty-five Military Observers have left Yemen and all of the eighteen civilian staff members will have departed on completion of the disposal of the Mission's equipment in the latter half of September.
[*S/5959, Report by the Secretary-General to the Security Council on the termination of the United Nations Observation Mission in Yemen, 11 Sept. 1964.*]

It merely remains to note that UNYOM was established by the Security Council, to fulfil functions agreed upon by previously disputing parties in a disengagement agreement; and, given its limited observation functions,[6] it may be assumed to be based on Chapter VI of the Charter. No Charter basis is explicitly mentioned in any of the documentation.

5

POLITICAL CONTROL

POLITICAL control over UNYOM lay firmly in the hands of the Secretary-General. Although he reported to the Security Council, and obtained the informal approval of members of the Council for each extension of UNYOM's life,[1] there was not a single meeting of the Security Council between June 1963 and September 1964 to debate UNYOM's role or the way in which the instructions by the Secretary-General were to be implemented in the field.

So far as settling the detailed methods of verifying disengagement was concerned, the parties agreed at the outset 'to co-operate with the representative of the United Nations Secretary-General or some other mutually acceptable intermediary'[2] in this.

The Secretary-General appointed Major-General von Horn for this task, as well as for making recommendations to him on the optimum size for UNYOM. This appointment was not submitted to the Security Council for approval. The advance party under General von Horn arrived in the Yemen on 13 June, two days after the Security Council had authorized the setting up of UNYOM:

2. . . . The object of the advance party was to undertake preparations for the Mission to be set up and become operational in the shortest possible time, through making the necessary contacts, preliminary surveys, administrative arrangements, and establishing a communications system. The headquarters of the Mission was set up in Sana, and a liaison office was placed in Jidda. The United Nations Emergency Force (UNEF) Liaison Office in Cairo assists in maintaining liaison with the appropriate authorities of the United Arab Republic.
3. There is a small civilian staff, based at Sana, consisting of twenty-eight international staff members and twenty locally recruited employees. [*S/5412, Report by the Secretary-General to the Security Council on the functioning of UNYOM, 4 Sept. 1963*, p. 153.]

In October 1963 it was believed, for reasons explained elsewhere (pp. 624, 650), that the continuation of UNYOM would not be approved. The Secretary-General made the following statement in his report to the Security Council, and no opposition was raised:

30. I have no doubt, however, that a continuing United Nations presence in Yemen, of some kind but not necessarily having military attributes, would be most helpful and might even be

---

[6] See below, p. 623.   [1] See above, pp. 634–7.   [2] S/5298, 29 Apr. 1963, p. 34, para. 4.
21*

indispensable to an early settlement of the Yemen problem, which clearly is primarily political and will require a political solution.

31. It is my intention, therefore, to maintain a civilian United Nations presence in the area, given, of course, the necessary agreement of the parties directly concerned. The terms of reference of such a presence would need to be worked out in consultation with the States concerned. The cost of such a presence would be small and it could, in fact, be initially financed by the existing authorization to the Secretary-General to enter into commitments to meet unforeseen and extraordinary expenses relating to the maintenance of peace and security in the financial year 1963.[3] [*S/5447, Report by the Secretary-General to the Security Council on the functioning of UNYOM, 28 Oct. 1963, p. 51.*]

Even when it became known that UNYOM would, after all, remain in the Yemen, the Secretary-General reported:

3. I considered, however, that it was desirable that the mission of military observation with its limited mandate should be complemented by a United Nations political presence, which, by exploratory conversations with the parties concerned, might be able to play a more positive role in encouraging the implementation of the disengagement agreement and peace and security in the region.

4. I therefore on 4 November appointed Mr Pier P. Spinelli, Under-Secretary and Director of the United Nations European Office, to undertake an assignment as Special Representative of the Secretary-General for Yemen and Head of the Yemen Observation Mission, when Lieutenant-General Gyani, as previously agreed, would return to his post as Commander of the United Nations Emergency Force in Gaza and Sinai. Mr Spinelli arrived in Yemen on 9 November. Colonel Branko Pavlovic, who had previously held the post of Deputy Commander and who had twice been acting Commander, became Chief of Staff. [*S/5501, Report by the Secretary-General to the Security Council on the functioning of UNYOM, 2 Jan. 1964, pp. 4–5.*]

It may be noted that at this point the Secretary-General's special political representative became head of the entire Mission in the Yemen, including the military side. The chief military appointment was now that of Chief of Staff, responsible to Mr Spinelli, who was in turn responsible to the Secretary-General. Thus civil seniority was now established in the field as well as at UN headquarters. This pattern was to continue, though when Mr Spinelli was forced for a period to be absent through ill health, UNYOM operated until his return under the direction of the Chief of Staff.[4] The Secretary-General's Special Representative played an active part in seeking to facilitate further direct negotiations between President Nasser and Prince Faisal. During August 1964 for example, Mr Spinelli visited the UAR, Saudi Arabia, and the Yemen for this purpose.[5]

It was the Secretary-General himself who recommended the termination of the Mission, and this was implemented in September 1964 after consultation with Saudi Arabia and Egypt.

---

[3] General Assembly Res. 1862 (XVII), para. 1a.   [4] S/5794, p. 17, para. 1.
[5] S/5927, p. 258, para. 9.

6

ADMINISTRATIVE AND MILITARY CONTROL

IN May 1963—when reporting to the Security Council on developments in the Yemen, but before the 'approving' resolution of that body, the Secretary-General stated: 'I plan to designate General von Horn as Chief of the Yemen Mission'.[1]

General von Horn was so designated, and went to Yemen with an advance party[2] in order to advise the Secretary-General as to what would be needed. By mid-August 1963 considerable problems had arisen, however. It seems that UNYOM was experiencing some difficulties over rations, because of transportation delays, and the lack of all amenities was severe. Further, the terrain was proving unfamiliar and hostile, and to carry out even the limited duty of observing and reporting was no easy task. Some of the helicopters provided had turned out to be unsuitable, and the strain was further felt by demands by the parties that UNYOM should investigate various incidents not covered in its terms of reference.[3] To compound all these difficulties, UNYOM personnel were being subjected to gunfire and were in danger. General von Horn seems to have become exasperated by what he regarded as incompetence at UN headquarters in rectifying these grievances; while UN headquarters seems to have felt such difficulties were perhaps inevitable in the early days, and that with calm and patience the situation would improve. In any event, U Thant reported to the Security Council that:

9. On 20 August, I received a cable from General von Horn, firmly submitting, for urgent reasons, his resignation as Commander of the Mission. After very careful consideration, I accepted his resignation, effective as of 31 August 1963, in the belief that this would be in the best interest of the Mission and of General von Horn himself. At my request, the Deputy Commander of the Yemen Observation Mission, Colonel Branko Pavlović, agreed to serve for the time being as Acting Commander. Colonel Pavlović had served with distinction in this same capacity during General von Horn's three-week absence from the Mission on leave in July. [*S/5412, Report by the Secretary-General to the Security Council on the functioning of UNYOM, 4 Sept. 1963*, p. 154.]

At the same time, Major-General Rikhye, the Secretary-General's Military Adviser, was sent to the Yemen 'to inspect the Mission and assist it in solving its problems'.[4] Although problems concerning effective observation in such a hard terrain continued, other difficulties seem thereafter to have been eased.

In his next report the Secretary-General does not mention any change in the military command of UNYOM. However, one may deduce from the documents that Colonel Pavlović was replaced as Acting Commander by Lt-General

---

[1] S/5321, 27 May 1963, p. 47, para. 4 (c).   [2] S/5325, p. 50, para. 3.
[3] S/5412, 4 Sept. 1963, pp. 154–5.   [4] S/5412, para. 10.

Gyani (seconded from UNEF) who became head of the Mission. This arrangement ceased, however, when the Secretary-General decided to introduce a civilian presence into the Yemen, for his personal representative, Mr Spinelli, became head of UNYOM,[5] and the senior military officer (once again Colonel Pavlović, General Gyani having returned to UNEF) became Chief of Staff:

3. I considered, however, that it was desirable that the mission of military observation with its limited mandate should be complemented by a United Nations political presence, which, by exploratory conversations with the parties concerned, might be able to play a more positive role in encouraging the implementation of the disengagement agreement and peace and security in the region.

4. I therefore on 4 November appointed Mr Pier P. Spinelli, Under-Secretary and Director of the United Nations European Office, to undertake an assignment as Special Representative of the Secretary-General for Yemen and Head of the Yemen Observation Mission, when Lieutenant-General Gyani, as previously agreed, would return to his post as Commander of the United Nations Emergency Force in Gaza and Sinai. Mr Spinelli arrived in Yemen on 9 November. Colonel Branko Pavlovic, who had previously held the post of Deputy Commander and who had twice been acting Commander, became Chief of Staff. [*S/5501, Report by the Secretary-General to the Security Council on the functioning of UNYOM, 2 Jan. 1964*, pp. 1–2.]

There is, again, no mention in the official UN documentation of Colonel Pavlović's departure, but some six months (and three reports) later, U Thant informed the Security Council: 'The Mission has continued to operate over this latest period under the direction of Mr Pier P. Spinelli, my Special Representative for Yemen, and, during his absence from the area for health reasons, under that of the Chief of Staff of the Mission, Colonel S. S. Sabharwal.'[6]

No further changes occurred in the military/administrative direction of UNYOM during the remainder of its stay in the Yemen.

7

COMPOSITION AND SIZE

WHEN the Secretary-General first reported to the Security Council on his initiative in seeking a solution to the Yemen problem, he stated:

I have been thinking in terms of not more than 50 observers, with suitable transportation, aerial and ground, for patrol purposes. A few helicopters, possibly three or four, and a similar number of small aircraft such as 'Otters', together with the required jeeps and lorries, should suffice. [*S/5298, Report of the Secretary-General to the Security Council concerning developments relating to Yemen, 29 Apr. 1963*, p. 34, para. 5.]

[5] See above, p. 636.
[6] S/5794, Report by the Secretary-General to the Security Council on the functioning of UNYOM, 2 July 1964, p. 17, para. 1.

After General von Horn had gone with an advance party to the Yemen, however, and had reported back, the Secretary-General revised his estimates:

(*c*) The total personnel required for the observation mission would not exceed 200. This figure would include a small number of Officer-Observers; a ground patrol unit numbering about 100 men, in suitable vehicles, carrying arms for self defence only; crews and ground crews for about eight small aircraft, fixed-wing and rotary, for reconnaissance and transport; and personnel for such essential supporting services as communications, logistics, medical aid, transportation and administration;. . . .

(*e*) It is expected that at least some of the personnel required for this short-term observation operation could be recruited from the United Nations Emergency Force (UNEF), the United Nations Truce Supervision Organization in Palestine (UNTSO), and possibly the United Nations Military Observer Group in India and Pakistan (UNMOGIP), subject to clearance with the governments concerned. . . . [*S/5321, 2nd Report of the Secretary-General to the Security Council on developments relating to Yemen, 27 May 1963,* p. 47.]

There is no trace in the official documentation of any clearances with the governments concerned. UNYOM, in the early stages, was in fact slightly larger than this estimate, and composed largely of Yugoslavs and Canadians:

3. There is a small civilian staff, based at Sana, consisting of twenty-eight international staff members and twenty locally recruited employees.

4. On the military side, UNYOM has a reconnaissance and an air unit. The reconnaissance unit consists of 114 Yugoslav officers and other ranks who were transferred from the Yugoslav contingent serving with UNEF. It arrived by ship at Hodeida on 4 July. The unit was promptly deployed, with platoons being placed in Jizan and Najran, Saudi Arabia, and in Sa'da, Yemen. The air unit of about fifty officers and other ranks has been provided by the Royal Canadian Air Force, employing Caribou and Otter aircraft and H-19 helicopters. It is based in Sana, Jizan and Najran. In addition to these two units, there is a small military headquarters staff based in Sana and six military observers stationed in Hodeida and Sana. [*S/5412, Report by the Secretary-General to the Security Council of the functioning of UNYOM, 4 Sept.1963,* p. 153.]

This was the picture presented at the end of October 1963:

11. Mission personnel are deployed in the area as follows:

Yemen

San'a — Headquarters and headquarters of the 134 ATU with 2 Caribou aircraft.

Hodeida — 1 United Nations military observer and a logistics detachment.

Sada — 1 section of the Yugoslav Company.

Saudi Arabia

Jizan — 2 United Nations military observers and 1 detachment of the 134 ATU with 2 Otter aircraft.

Demilitarized zone

Harad — 1 platoon of the Yugoslav Reconnaissance Company and 2 United Nations military observers.

Najran — 2 platoons less 1 section of the Yugoslav Reconnaissance Company, 4 United Nations military observers and 1 detachment of the 134 ATU with 2 Otter aircraft.

[*S/5447, Report by the Secretary-General to the Security Council on the functioning of UNYOM, 28 Oct. 1963,* p. 46.]

U Thant reported in January 1964 that:

7. With the arrival of new observers in the latter half of November and early December, the main task of observation has been carried out by a staff of military observers deployed as follows:

Sana	HQ staff and 3 observers
Najran	10 observers
Jizan	5 observers
Sada	2 observers
Hodeida	1 observer
Jiddah	1 liaison officer

8. The observers, including staff come from the following countries: Denmark, Ghana, India, Italy, Netherlands, Norway, Pakistan, Sweden and Yugoslavia. [*S/5501, Report by the Secretary-General to the Security Council on the functioning of UNYOM, 2 Jan. 1964*, p. 5.]

The decision had been taken in principle no longer to maintain a military unit in the demilitarized zone,[1] once the observer personnel were built up to full strength.

10. The ground observations of the Mission are supplemented by an Air Transport Unit provided by Canada, with two Caribou aircraft stationed at Sana. The Otter aircraft stationed at Jizan and at Najran in order to perform patrols in the border region were withdrawn in mid-December, since it was found that, after the withdrawal of the Yugoslav Company, the Caribou aircraft were capable of carrying out the patrols in addition to providing logistic support. [*Ibid.* p. 6.]

3. The composition and deployment of the staff of twenty-five military observers assigned to UNYOM continued to be as described in the last report. The majority of the observers are stationed at the main border crossings from Saudi Arabia into Yemen to check on the nature of the frontier traffic, making patrols at irregular intervals, to the less frequented crossings, while a small number are stationed at Sada, Sana and Hodeida to observe the extent to which the United Arab Republic forces are withdrawn from Yemen. A Canadian air detachment with two Caribou aircraft provides logistic support as well as air observation. [*S/5572, Report by the Secretary-General to the Security Council on the functioning of UNYOM, 3 March 1964*, p. 95.]

The number of military observers dropped to twenty-three by May 1964; Caribou planes of the Royal Canadian Air Force continued to support the mission.[2]

Details concerning the nationality and appointment of Chief of the Mission have been dealt with in the proceeding section.

---

[1] See below, p. 655.　　[2] S/5681, 4 May 1964, para. 1.

8

RELATIONS WITH CONTRIBUTING STATES

NO FORMAL agreements appear to exist between the UN and the states which contributed personnel to UNYOM. Many of the personnel were seconded from service in other UN bodies, such as UNTSO and UNEF. In his Second Report to the Security Council on developments relating to the Yemen, the Secretary-General said: 'The military personnel in the Yemen operation would be employed under conditions similar to those applying to other United Nations operations of this nature.'[1]

No major political problems arose in respect of the UN's relationship with the contributing states.

9

RELATIONS WITH HOST STATES

THERE appears from the documentation to be some confusion as to how many of the interested states were actually party to the disengagement agreement. On 29 April 1963 U Thant noted: 'I have received from each of the three Governments concerned, in separate communications, formal confirmation of their acceptance of identical terms of disengagement in Yemen.'[1]

It seems, however, that all material rights and duties under the agreement[2] fell upon Egypt and Saudi Arabia, and the Yemen merely 'approved'. In his report of 27 May 1963[3] the Secretary-General again referred to 'the appropriate authorities of the three parties'. But in his report of 4 September 1963 the Secretary-General referred to 'the two parties'[4] and added 'the agreement on disengagement involves only Saudi Arabia and the United Arab Republic'.[5] In October 1963 the Secretary-General's report again referred to 'the two parties to the disengagement agreement'.[6]

This tendency reflected the factual situation—namely, that as the months went by the Republican government of the Yemen had little authority of its own, independent of Egypt. The essential 'parties' to the dispute (whatever may have been the strict legal position with regards to the disengagement agreement) were Egypt and Saudi Arabia. This reality was accentuated by the

---

[1] S/5321, p. 47, para. 4 (f). [1] S/5298, p. 33, para. 3. [2] Ibid. para 4.
[3] S/5321, para. 3. [4] S/5412, p. 153, para. 6. [5] Ibid. pp. 153-4, para. 7.
[6] S/5447, p. 45, para. 8.

fact that the Yemen was contributing nothing to UNYOM's expenses, which were being borne solely by Saudi Arabia and the UAR. Nor—though the Mission was stationed in part upon Yemeni territory—was the Yemen's consent for its continuation considered of much significance. It was—in practical if not in legal terms—Saudi-Egyptian consent that was relevant. On the question of extending UNYOM's operation, U Thant customarily made no mention of the issues of the Yemen, but confined himself to observing: 'I have ascertained from the Permanent Representatives of the Governments of Saudi Arabia and the United Arab Republic that their Governments concur in my suggestion that the United Nations Observation Mission in Yemen be extended for another two months. . . .'[7] While all the evidence is that the Yemen Republican government was perfectly content for UNYOM to remain, this none the less—given the UN's customary deference to a 'host state'—seems a striking example that he who pays the piper calls the tune.

UNYOM's task was, of course, to observe the implementation of disengagement by Saudi Arabia and the UAR. It had no more direct role to play in bringing about an end to the civil war: 'UNYOM, therefore, is not concerned with Yemen's internal affairs generally, with actions of the Government of Yemen, or with that Government's relations with other Governments and bordering territories. . . .'[8] Other UN experience has all too clearly shown that a prohibition on UN interest in internal affairs has not sufficed to prevent severe disagreements between the UN and its host government. UN relations with both the Yemen and Saudi Arabia were, however, cordial. In the UN operation in the Congo (ONUC) the very loyalty of various factions was at issue; and in the early days of the UN Force in Cyprus (UNFICYP) the status of a solely Greek Cypriot goverment presented the UN with some problems. Although there was a civil war in Yemen, none the less, the credentials of the republicans had been unequivocally approved at the UN; it was they who had approved the disengagement arrangements, and they who maintained control of Sana and Taiz. The royalists never sought to force the UN to deal with them as the only 'government' in the Yemen. On the Saudi side of the border, UNYOM, with its exceedingly limited powers, presented no threat to the internal freedom of the Saudi government, and relations were excellent. In January 1964 the Secretary-General was able to decide that it was no longer necessary to maintain a military unit in the demilitarized zone, 'because of the co-operation shown by the authorities on both sides of the Saudi Arabian–Yemen frontier. . . .'[9]

The UAR and Saudi Arabia agreed at the outset 'to co-operate with the representative of the United Nations Secretary-General or some other mutually acceptable intermediary in reaching agreement on the modalities and verification of disengagement'.[10] To this end General von Horn went to Yemen as well as to Saudi Arabia and the UAR to consult with the authorities. This was done considerably in advance of the Security Council resolution establishing

---

[7] S/5794, 3 July 1964, para. 9.   [8] S/5412, 4 Sept. 1963, p. 154, para. 7.
[9] S/5501, p. 5, para. 6.   [10] S/5298, 29 Apr. 1963, p. 34, para. 4.

UNYOM. General von Horn asked of all three governments their views on 'the role, functioning, scope and strength of the proposed United Nations observation operation'.[11]

It was agreed that:

A demilitarized zone to a distance of 20 kilometres on each side of the demarcated Saudi-Arabian–Yemen border is to be established from which military forces and equipment are to be excluded. In this zone, on both sides, impartial observers are to be stationed to check on the observance of the terms of disengagement and who would also have the responsibility of travelling beyond the demilitarized zone, as necessary. . . . [S/5298, p. 34, para. 4.]

So far as this Editor has been able to ascertain, there is nowhere in the official Security Council records any mention of agreements between the UN and the host countries concerning the status of UNYOM. None the less, some trace of such an agreement is to be found in the UN Treaty Series.

EXCHANGE OF LETTERS CONSTITUTING AN AGREEMENT* BETWEEN THE UNITED NATIONS AND SAUDI ARABIA RELATING TO PRIVILEGES, IMMUNITIES AND FACILITIES FOR THE OBSERVATION OPERATION ALONG THE SAUDI ARABIA–YEMEN BORDER ESTABLISHED PURSUANT TO THE SECURITY COUNCIL RESOLUTION OF 11 JUNE 1963.† NEW YORK, 23 AUGUST 1963

I

23 August 1963

Sir,

I have the honour to refer to the resolution of 11 June 1963†, by which the United Nations Security Council requested the Secretary-General to establish the Observation Operation along the Saudi Arabia–Yemen border as defined by him in his reports and statements to the Security Council.

In order to facilitate the Operation in the fulfilment of its purposes, I propose that your Government, pending its accession to the Convention on the Privileges and Immunities of the United Nations, might extend to the Operation, its property and assets the status, privileges and immunities provided therein. I would also propose, in view of the special importance and difficult nature of the functions which this Operation will perform, that your Government might extend to the Commander of the Operation and to all personnel serving under him including military observers, secretariat and experts—over and above the status provided under the Convention on the Privileges and Immunities of the United Nations the privileges and immunities, exceptions and facilities which are enjoyed by diplomatic envoys in accordance with international law. The privileges and immunities necessary for the fulfilment of the functions of the Operation also include freedom of entry, without delay or hindrance, of property, equipment and spare parts; freedom of movement of personnel, equipment and transport; the use of United Nations vehicle registration plates; the right to fly the United Nations flag on premises, observation posts and vehicles; and the right of unrestricted communication by radio, both within the area of operations and to connect with the United Nations radio network, as well as by telephone, telegraph or other means.

It is my understanding that the Saudi Arabian Government will provide at its own expense, in agreement with the Commander, all such premises as may be necessary for the accommodation and fulfilment of the functions of the Operation, including office space and areas for

[11] S/5298, p. 34, para. 4.

* Came into force on 23 Aug. 1963 by the exchange of the said letters and, in accordance with their terms, became effective retroactively from 13 June 1963.

† UN, *Decisions taken and resolutions adopted by the Security Council during the year 1963* (S/INF/18), p. 7.

observation posts and field centres. All such premises shall be inviolable and subject to the exclusive control and authority of the Operation. I likewise understand that your Government will in consultation with the Operation provide for necessary means of transportation and communication.

If these proposals meet with your approval, I should like to suggest that this letter and your reply should constitute an agreement between the United Nations and Saudi Arabia, to take effect from the date of the arrival of the first members of the Operation in Saudi Arabia.

Accept, Sir, the assurances of my highest consideration.

U THANT

Mr Zein A. Dabbagh

II

23 August 1963

Sir,

I have the honour to refer to your letter of today's date concerning certain privileges, immunities and facilities for the Observation Operation established by Security Council Resolution of 11 June 1963. I am pleased to advise you in the name of my Government that, having in mind the difficult nature of the functions of the Observation Operation, the Government of Saudi Arabia fully agrees with and hereby expresses its acceptance of the terms of your letter.

The Government of Saudi Arabia also agrees that your letter and this reply should constitute an agreement between the United Nations and Saudi Arabia, effective from the date of the arrival of the first members of the Observation Operation in Saudi Arabia.

Please accept, Sir, the assurances of my highest consideration.

Zein A. DABBAGH

His Excellency U Thant

[474 UNTS, 155.]

This exchange of letters raises some interesting points. It shows an agreement, pending Saudi Arabia's accession to the Convention on the Privileges and Immunities of the UN, to extend to UNYOM 'the status, privileges and immunities provided therein'.[12] These are to be found in the text of that Convention, published in I UNTS (1946) 15. It may be noted, however, that Saudi Arabia has never acceded to this Convention. By contrast, the Yemen acceded to the Convention on 23 July 1963. As this date was soon after UNYOM became operational, and as the Yemen had had some seventeen years in which she could previously have become a party, it is reasonable to conclude that her action was intimately concerned with the presence of UNYOM on her territory. However, there exists neither in the UN Treaty Series nor in UN official documentation any agreement between the UN and the Yemen of the sort made between the UN and Saudi Arabia. The Yemen was bound therefore to extend the privileges and immunities provided for in the Convention. Article 105 of the Charter (reiterated in the preamble to the Convention) provides that the UN shall enjoy in the territory of each of its members 'such privileges and immunities as are necessary for the fulfilment of its purposes'; and in the letter to the Saudi Arabian permanent representative U Thant made it clear that in this particular case this functional concept included freedom of entry for property, equipment and spares, freedom of movement, and freedom of communication.

---

[12] See also the similar arrangements made in the West Irian operation in the forthcoming Vol. II of this study.

We may therefore conclude that, substantively, the Yemen and Saudi Arabia were legally bound to extend the same privileges and immunities to UNYOM, though the nature of the agreement with the UN so to do differed in each case. The letter from U Thant to the Saudi Arabian permanent representative refers, apparently as an additional category, to 'exceptions and facilities which are enjoyed by diplomatic envoys in accordance with international law'. The identification of these, and their differentiation from rights accruing under Article 105 of the Charter and under the Convention on the Privileges and Immunities of the UN, is no easy matter. In April 1961 an attempt had been made to codify the traditional customary rules of international law on diplomatic immunities[13] at a Conference held in Vienna. Yemen did not attend the conference. Saudi Arabia attended, and voted for the adoption of the final text of the Convention.[14] She has, however, neither signed nor ratified that Convention.

10

RELATIONS WITH OTHER STATES INVOLVED

CLEARLY, Saudi Arabia and the UAR were the two states most directly involved in the Yemen civil war. Their relations with each other, and with the UN have been subsumed under Sections 9, 11, and 12. Mention is also made of the attitude of the Soviet Union in Section 4.

11

FINANCE

As to the financing of any such activity by the United Nations, I have it in mind to proceed under the provisions of General Assembly resolution 1862 (XVII).[1] [*S/5298, Report of the Secretary-General to the Security Council concerning developments relating to Yemen, 29 Apr. 1963*, p. 34, para. 7.]

[13] See E. Kerley, 'Some aspects of the Vienna Conference on diplomatic intercourse and immunities', 56 *AJIL* (1962), pp. 88–129.

[14] For the final text, see 55 *AJIL* (1961), p. 1062; and for comments thereon, Kerley, p. 88.

[1] This resolution authorized the Secretary General, subject to certain conditions and with the prior concurrence of the Advisory Committee on Administrative and Budgetary questions 'to enter into commitments to meet unforeseen and extraordinary expenses in the financial year of 1963. Res. 1862 (XVII) also provided that '. . . if, as a result of a decision of the Security Council, commitments relating to the maintenance of peace and security should arise in an estimated total exceeding $10 million before the eighteenth session of the Assembly shall be convened by the Secretary-General to consider the matter'.

(*g*) It is estimated that the total cost of the Yemen Observation Mission will be less than $1,000,000. It has been my hope that the two parties principally involved, namely Saudi Arabia and the United Arab Republic, would undertake to bear the costs of the Mission and discussions towards this end are under way. These parties, I am sure, will agree to bear at least part of the costs, in money or in other forms of assistance. If necessary, to cover part of the cost of the operation, I would proceed, as previously indicated, under the provisions of General Assembly resolution 1862 (XVII). [*S/5321, 2nd Report of the Secretary-General to the Security Council on developments relating to the Yemen, 27 May 1963*, p. 47, para. 4.]

The estimates given at this stage were based on General von Horn's report that:

(*c*) The total personnel required for the observation mission would not exceed 200. This figure would include a small number of Officer-Observers; a ground patrol unit numbering about 100 men, in suitable vehicles, carrying arms for self-defence only; crews and ground crews for about 8 small aircraft, fixed-wing and rotary, for reconnaissance and transport; and personnel for such essential supporting services as communications, logistics, medical aid, transportation and administration. [*Ibid.*]

The estimates based thereon were as follows:

The estimates are presented in two parts:

(1) Cost of the mission on the assumption that it will have a maximum duration of four months;

(2) Additional cost of the mission per month after the first four months in the event the mission should have to be extended.

ANNEX

UNITED NATIONS YEMEN OBSERVATION MISSION: ESTIMATE OF COSTS

Part I. Estimates based on a duration of four months

	US dollars
1. Salaries and common staff costs	58,620

The estimate covers the cost of salaries and related common staff costs of the Chief of Mission, 10 locally recruited staff (clerks, messengers, maintenance workers, etc.), and 16 staff members (4 professional and 12 Field Service) detailed from regular establishment.

2. Travel and subsistence — 76,200

Provision is made for the travel to and from the mission area of 17 military observers and 16 detailed staff members, as well as for their subsistence for the duration of the mission. Also included is the cost of one roundtrip travel from the mission area to New York (for consultations) by the Chief of Mission as well as his *per diem* for the duration of the mission.

3. Transportation and other costs of military personnel (other ranks) — 163,180

This estimate comprises: $100,000 for the transport to and from the mission of 180 military personnel (other ranks) together with their equipment by means of 3 'Yukon' flights; $60,480 for their daily allowance ($1·30 each), hardship allowance ($0·50 each daily), and daily ration ($1·00 each); and $2·700 being the estimated reimbursement to the Government concerned for the equipment, etc. used by the military personnel.

4. Rental and maintenance of premises — 4,000

Provision is intended to cover the rental and maintenance of office premises and installations.

5. Operation and maintenance of transportation equipment — 12,000

Cost of maintenance, spare parts, gasolene, etc., for 60 vehicles used by the mission is covered by this estimate.

	US dollars
6. Rental of aircraft	322,000

This estimate comprises the cost of chartering and ferrying to the mission area of 3 'Otter' aircraft, 3 helicopters and 2 'Caribou' aircraft. Ferrying charges are estimated at $45,000, $51,000 and $10,000 respectively. Charter charges are estimated at $48,000, $108,000 and $60,000 respectively for 4 months on the basis of an average of 80 hours actual flying time for each 'Otter' aircraft, of a flat rate for the helicopters and of an average of 60 hours of actual flying time for each 'Caribou' aircraft.

7. Communications and freight	15,000

The estimate provides for the freight charges on 19 vehicles to be purchased ($9,500), other freight charges ($4,500) and the cost of telephones and commercial cables ($1,000).

8. Miscellaneous supplies and services	9,000

Covers cost of stationery, office supplies, insurance, medicines, flags, hospitality, etc.

9. Permanent equipment	147,500

Includes costs of: radio equipment for one main and five field radio stations as well as for the field units ($80,000); generators for the radio stations ($3,000); 50 tents with equipment for the observers and staff ($12,500); office equipment such as typewriters, reproduction machines and calculating machines ($2,500); and 19 vehicles ($549,500). It is assumed the military personnel will bring with them some 40 vehicles.

TOTAL COST	807,500

Part II. Estimates per month after the first four months

1. Salaries and common staff costs	14,650
2. Travel and subsistence	10,350
3. Transportation and other costs of military personnel (other ranks)	15,800
4. Rental and maintenance of premises	1,000
5. Operation and maintenance of transportation equipment	3,000
6. Rental of aircraft	54,000
7. Communications and freight	1,350
8. Miscellaneous supplies and services	2,250
TOTAL COST	102,400

[*S/5323, 3 June 1963*, pp. 48–49.]

In paragraph 4 (*g*) of my report to the Security Council of 27 May 1963 (S/5321) reference was made to the possibility that the two parties principally involved, namely Saudi Arabia and the United Arab Republic, would undertake to defray the costs of the Yemen operation. I am now able to report that Saudi Arabia has agreed orally to accept 'a proportionate share' of the costs of the operation, while the United Arab Republic agrees in principle to provide assistance, in an amount equivalent to $200,000 for a period of two months, which would be roughly half of the cost of the operation over that period as indicated in my report on financial implications (S/5323). It is not precluded, of course, that an appeal to the United Arab Republic Government for additional assistance could be made at the end of the two months, should it be found necessary to extend the operation beyond that period. [*S/5325, Report of the Secretary-General on the latest developments concerning the proposal to send a United Nations observation mission to Yemen, 7 June 1963*, p. 50.]

When the Security Council met to consider establishing UNYOM, the question of finance was further discussed. Indeed, to a certain extent the voting pattern was determined by attitudes towards the method of financing UNYOM.[2] The Soviet Union stated her general principle and then excepted the present case therefrom:

19. As for the defrayal of the expenses involved in these operations and listed in the estimates submitted by the Secretary-General (S/5323), the Soviet Union in this instance takes the same stand as it does in regard to the maintenance of the so-called United Nations Emergency Force in the Middle East and the Organization's forces in the Congo. That position is based on a just and politically reasoned approach, namely that the aggressor nations should pay the cost of liquidating the consequences of their aggression.

20. It must of course be remembered that in this specific instance, as stated by the Secretary-General in his report of 7 June (S/5325), agreement on the method of meeting the expenses entailed by the dispatch of the United Nations observers has already been reached between the parties concerned. In these circumstances, there is obviously no reason to think that any member of the Council will object to this step, and it can be anticipated that the Council will decide the matter without a special discussion.

21. An important reason why the Security Council should be able to reach a decision on this question smoothly is the fact that, as the report given at the last meeting to the Council by the Secretary-General shows, the Council is about to decide on an operation the duration of which is limited by a specific agreement between the Governments of the United Arab Republic and Saudi Arabia, whereby these Governments have undertaken to pay the costs of the operation in question for a period of two months, and the United Nations is not committed to any financial expenditure in respect of the observer operation.

22. The Soviet delegation assumes that, given these considerations and circumstances, the Security Council will adopt a decision which takes due account of the useful initiative of the Secretary-General, aimed at a peaceful settlement; of the fact that the parties concerned have agreed to the sending of a limited number of United Nations observers to the area of the frontier between Yemen and Saudi Arabia for a period of two months; and finally of the fact that this operation will be financed as indicated in yesterday's statement by the Secretary-General to the Security Council. [*SCOR, 18th yr, 1038th mtg*, pp. *4–5*.]

The resolution passed by the Security Council[3] noted only that 'the Governments of Saudi Arabia and the United Arab Republic have agreed to defray the expenses over a period of two months of the United Nations observation function'. Ambassador Adlai Stevenson explained the position of the United States: 'as to the financing of the observer operation, it is proper, in our opinion, that the Security Council resolution makes no provision therefor and merely notes that the parties have agreed between themselves to pay the costs for a limited time.'[4]

The Soviet Union found the wording of the resolution on the matter of finance unacceptable, presumably because the renewal of UNYOM beyond a four-month period was left as an open option, while the mention of the source of finance referred only to the first two months. This seems to be the reasoning, though Mr Fedorenko's statement is perhaps not as clear as one would wish:

---

[2] See above, p. 621. On the relationship between the agreement on finance and the length of mandate of the Mission, see also pp. 630–3.

[3] See p. 620 above.

[4] *SCOR*, 18th yr, 1039th mtg, p. 3.

19. Limiting the duration of the United Nations observers' stay in the region is also important from the financial standpoint. We have in mind the Secretary-General's statement of yesterday that the parties concerned will defray the expense of the operation over a period of two months and that there are therefore no financial implications for the United Nations. Despite the justified urgings of the Soviet delegation, this latter position too, concerning sources of financing, has not been duly reflected in the resolution adopted.

20. In deciding to conduct an operation entailing the use of armed forces under United Nations auspices, by virtue of Articles 43, 48 and 50 of the Charter, the Security Council is bound to consider the question of sources of financing as well. In essence the Council has already done this, since it received from the Secretary-General an estimate of the costs involved in the operation and it also heard the Secretary-General's statement that the maintenance of the United Nations observers for a two-month period would not entail any financial expenditure by the United Nations.

21. Let me say that we have, of course, taken note of the Secretary-General's statement, made to the Security Council at the last meeting, that the parties concerned will bear the cost of the Observation Mission 'for a period of two months, and possibly for a total period of four months, should that prove necessary'. We have also noted the Secretary-General's statement that the Observation Mission 'will be a modest mission, not exceeding 200 people'. Nevertheless, because of the position adopted by some delegations, the question of sources of financing was still not included in the resolution in a direct way, as it should have been.

22. The Soviet delegation is quite deliberately drawing the Council's attention to the financial side of the problem. The Council is not called upon to adopt abstract decisions that have no connexion with existing possibilities and material circumstances. The decisions of the Security Council, which is the principal organ of the United Nations, are meant to be carried into effect and not simply to swell the files.

23. Can the Council fail, then, to take account of the material and financial aspects of the execution of its decisions? Can it fail to do so particularly under the present circumstances, ignoring our Organization's financial situation, which is already far too serious? Have we not had enough unhappy experience of decisions adopted by the Organization but doomed to remain dead letters because the financial side of the matter was neglected?

24. Any approach which fails to reckon with this factor cannot be considered sober and realistic. This is why the Soviet delegation has consistently taken and continues to take the view that the Security Council, in keeping with the letter and spirit of the Charter, should adopt decisions involving action on behalf of the United Nations for the maintenance of world peace and security only when all aspects of the matter, including the material and financial conditions for the execution of its decisions, have been duly examined.

25. It is these considerations which led the Soviet delegation to abstain in the vote on the draft resolution. [*Ibid. 1039th mtg.* pp. 4–5.]

France declared herself satisfied by the resolution:

39. Since the financing of this operation is assured for a period of two months, the decision of the Security Council, in our opinion, is valid for that period. Moreover, we understand from the information given by the Secretary-General that no new expenditure will be incurred by the United Nations in this connexion, and that if the observation operation undertaken by the United Nations were to exceed two months, he would inform the Security Council of that fact in good time. We therefore consider that if that proved to be the case, and if the payments made by the parties were to cease, the Council would have to re-examine the problem.

40. That is the understanding on which my delegation has voted for the draft resolutions before it, in the firm hope that by its decision the Security Council will have made the most effective possible contribution to the preservation of peace and security in the Middle East. [*Ibid.* p. 7.]

It fell to Ghana (a co-sponsor of the resolution, with Morocco), to remind the members of the Security Council of the consistency or otherwise of their own positions:

For example, we could mention the case of Cambodia and Thailand in 1958; and this year an observation team has been sent without reference to the Security Council, because the parties concerned had agreed to defray the costs involved. In the case of West Irian, because the parties concerned—that is to say, the Netherlands and Indonesia—agreed to pay the costs, there was no reference to the Security Council. But in this case the matter has come here because there is still some uncertainty as to whether the disengagement can take place within the period specified in the agreement, which is to the effect, that the two parties will defray the cost over two months. If the observation team had to continue its efforts in the area after the two-month period, then in our view the Security Council would have to approve of further action in the area.

47. The Ghana delegation feels that it is the primary responsibility of the Security Council to see that a peace-keeping operation takes place. But we feel that any position taken by the Council implies some financial obligation, and once a position has been taken, then the assessment of the costs will, of course, be the prerogative of the General Assembly. Here, however, we are concerned with an agreement between two parties who have agreed to defray the expenses over a period of two months. That is why we saw our way clear towards preparing a compromise draft and urging members of the Council to vote for it accordingly, in order to help the Secretary-General in his efforts. [*Ibid.* p. 8.]

UNYOM thus became operational upon the financial basis laid down in the Security Council resolution. When its mandate came to be renewed, the Secretary-General reported to the Security Council on all matters, including finance. It may be noted that, in spite of (or because of) these very full reports, no further meetings of the Security Council were held on the question of UNYOM, nor was the method of financing further debated in the Council.

The [first] two months' period, therefore, expires on 4 September. It is now obvious that the task of the Mission will not be completed by that date . . . Accordingly, I have approached both parties through their representatives to the United Nations to defray the expenses of the Yemen operation for a further period of two months, as from 4 September. I have received oral assurances from the two representatives that their Governments agree to do so. [*S/5412, Report by the Secretary-General to the Security Council on the functioning of UNYOM, 4 Sept. 1963*, p. 157.]

In anticipation of this date [4 Nov. 1963] . . . I have been conferring. . . . One of the two Governments concerned with financing UNYOM has indicated that it is not prepared, on the basis of the existing situation, to share the cost of UNYOM beyond the 4 November commitment . . . In the light of this latter circumstance, it has been necessary for me to take the essential preparatory steps looking towards the complete withdrawal of UNYOM by 4 Nov., beyond which date there will be no financial support for it. [*S/5447, Report by the Secretary-General to the Security Council on the functioning of UNYOM, 28 Oct. 1963*, p. 50.]

This party was Saudi Arabia. However:

In the afternoon of 31 October, the Permanent Representative of the Government of Saudi Arabia communicated to me a new and urgent message . . . [stating that his government] has decided to participate in the financing of UNYOM for a further period of two months . . . The problem of financing a continuing mission, is thus removed. [*Ibid. Add. 1*, pp. 51–54.]

. . . The mission ended its activities on [4 September 1964] . . . It will be recalled that the two parties to the disengagement agreement assured me at its inception that they were prepared to defray the expenses of the mission in equal shares. Those assurances were renewed on the several occasions when the Mission was extended. The total expenses of the Mission during the fourteen-month period of its operation have not been finally determined, but they are expected to reach a total of $2 million. Contributions already made by the two Governments amount to $800,000 each. [*S/5959, Report by the Secretary-General to the Security Council on the termination of UNYOM,*[5] *11 Sept. 1964.*]

The financial position concerning UNYOM, as it was on 31 December 1963, and then on 31 December 1964, is shown in the following documents:

STATUS OF FUNDS AS AT 31 DECEMBER 1963*

	$	$
Payments received:		
Saudi Arabia		400,000
United Arab Republic		161,000
Public contributions		5
		561,005
Less:		
Loss on currency exchange		3,368
		557,637
Less:		
Obligations incurred		
Liquidated by disbursements	539,773	
Unliquidated obligations	275,412	815,185
Excess of obligations incurred over payments received		257,548
Represented by:		
Due to United Nations General Fund	7,088	
Accounts payable	12,245	
Unliquidated obligations	275,412	294,745
Less:		
Cash at banks and on hand	19,885	
Accounts receivable	17,312	37,197
		257,548

[*A/5806, Schedule 11, GAOR, 19th sess., suppl. 6, p. 58.*]

---

[5] The Secretary-General's bi-monthly reports of 2 Jan. 1964 (S/5501), 3 Mar. 1964 (S/5572), 4 May 1964 (S/5681), and 2 July 1964 (S/5794) do not *explicitly* mention the question of finance—though agreement on the continuation of the financial arrangements may be inferred from the approval on each occasion by Saudi Arabia and the UAR of the continuation of UNYOM.

* In accordance with the financial arrangements ageed by the Governments of Saudi Arabia and the United Arab Republic and the United Nations in regard to the costs of the United Nations Yemen Observation Mission, as set forth in the reports of the Secretary-General to the Security Council, it was agreed that the expenses of the mission would be borne in equal shares by the two Governments.

STATUS OF FUNDS AS AT 31 DECEMBER 1964

	Saudi Arabia $	United Arab Republic $	Total $
Income:			
Contributions received	1,000,000	800,000	1,800,000
Public contributions	3	2	5
	1,000,003	800,002	1,800,005
Less:			
Loss on exchange	2,051	2,050	4,101
	997,052	797,952	1,795,904
Less:			
Obligations incurred (schedule 15)			
Liquidated by disbursements	744,476	744,476	1,488,952
Unliquidated obligations	169,545	169,545	339,090
Excess of obligations incurred over payments received	(83,931)	116,069	32,138
Represented by:			
Accounts payable and sundry credits		13,753	
Unliquidated obligations		339,090	352,843
Less:			
Accounts receivable		3,254	
Due from United Nations General Fund		317,451	320,705
			32,138

[*A/6006, Schedule 14, GAOR, 20th sess., suppl. 6*, p. 63.]

OBLIGATIONS INCURRED AS AT 31 DECEMBER 1964

	Obligations incurred		
	Disbursements $	Unliquidated obligations $	Total $
Salaries and wages	144,588	86	144,674
Common staff costs	140,153	—	140,153
Travel and transportation	203,264	4,510	207,774
Rental and maintenance of premises	92,906	—	92,906
Rental and maintenance of equipment	17,257	—	17,257
Rental—aircraft	647,651	2,668	650,319
Communications	5,353	—	5,353
Freight	7,876	5,000	12,876
Miscellaneous supplies and services	176,498	265,136	441,634
Recreational supplies	78	—	78
Films	10,250	—	10,250
Personal mail and postage	67	—	67
Stationery and office supplies	1,786	—	1,786
Furniture, fixtures and equipment	13,547	—	13,547
Transportation equipment	20,134	61,690	81,824
Miscellaneous equipment	7,544	—	7,544
	1,488,952	339,090	1,828,042

[*Ibid., Schedule 15*, p. 64.]

12

IMPLEMENTATION

WHEN one assesses the effectiveness of UNYOM, one is really looking at two aspects. First, there is the question of how far UNYOM was successful in carrying out its mandate; and second, how far the UN presence in Yemen contributed to a peaceful settlement of the war. UNYOM is invariably judged on the second point alone—a response which is perhaps politically inevitable, but not very helpful. There are lessons to be learned about the functions which it is reasonable to ask a UN group to perform in certain circumstances; and this can only be done by looking at UNYOM within the narrower framework of its mandate.

UNYOM's functions, it will be recalled (pp. 622–5), stemmed from the Saudi-Egyptian disengagement agreement and were limited to 'observing, certifying and reporting'[1] whether the parties were upholding that agreement. UNYOM's tasks were therefore very limited, and were considerably more restricted than those of UNTSO, UNMOGIP, UNEF, and ONUC. It had no authority to issue orders. Moreover, under the terms of the disengagement agreement the UN was in no way charged with ending the civil war in the Yemen: the agreement was directed to ending the encouragement of the royalists by Saudi Arabia and the support of the republicans by the UAR. And 'the parties themselves are solely responsible for fulfilling the terms of disengagement on which they have agreed'.[2] As we shall see, the Saudi-Egyptian involvement became so deep that ultimately it was impossible to employ the classical mode of settlement—namely, the withdrawal of foreign elements leaving the local population to solve its own disputes. It was to prove necessary for Saudi Arabia and Egypt to agree between them—with the Yemeni leaders not represented at the conference—to a lengthily-phased withdrawal and to the establishment of a certain kind of caretaker government in the Yemen. The contribution of the UN presence to what turned out to be a virtually bipartite, external solution to Yemen's civil war, was at most marginal. It can perhaps be said that U Thant, in facilitating the first disengagement agreement, set the pattern for consultations between Riyadh and Cairo, and for containment of the dispute.

So far as the fulfilment of UNYOM's limited mandate is concerned, it may fairly be said that the task of 'observing, certifying and reporting', when entrusted to a tiny group on a huge and unfamiliar territory, operating on limited equipment and funds, was hopeless from the start. Yet none of the parties was willing to enlarge the scope of UNYOM. It seems reasonable to suggest that the Secretary-General was misinformed when he was advised that the initial

---

[1] S/5412, p. 15, para. 7.   [2] Ibid. para. 7.

strength of UNYOM was sufficient to carry out even the tasks of observation and reporting. The difficulties which UNYOM encountered, and its own assessments on the implementation of the disengagement agreement, are summarized below:

8. The United Nations Yemen Observation Mission encounters unusual hardships. Physical conditions in Yemen are severe. The terrain is rugged. Local supplies and facilities are meagre. Funds are limited. UNYOM personnel and aircraft have been subjected to gunfire and are frequently in danger. . . .

10. . . . I had . . . directed Major-General Rikhye, my Military Adviser, to go to the area to inspect the Mission and assist it in solving its problems . . . [Colonel Pavlović and General Rikhye assured me] there is not and never has been any serious shortage of rations, though ration stocks reached a low level at one point owing to a temporary uncertainty as to the best means of transportation . . . The parties are making increased demands on UNYOM to undertake tasks, such as investigation of incidents, not covered in the Mission's terms of reference. . . .

12. UNYOM reports that it has no firm figures on the number of United Arab Republic troops actually withdrawn and the number of fresh United Arab Republic troops that have arrived as replacements. Although United Arab Republic sources in Yemen withhold exact information on grounds of security, they state that some 13,000 troops from the United Arab Republic have been withdrawn. The figure of 1,500 for new arrivals has been cited but has not been verified as accurate. UNYOM observers have noted departures of United Arab Republic troops in substantial numbers, but have also seen replacements arriving, though in apparently lesser numbers.

13. There has likewise been an indicated reduction in the extent of assistance from Saudi Arabian territory to royalist ranks and supporters in Yemen, but such traffic has certainly not come to an end. In fact, UNYOM air and ground patrols report a recent possible increase in vehicular and animal traffic across the border.

14. There have been various complaints presented to UNYOM by both parties.[8] Where appropriate and possible, these complaints have been investigated by UNYOM. In general, they fall into two main categories, as follows:

(*a*) Allegations of offensive action by United Arab Republic forces against royalist positions in Yemen and on Saudi Arabian territory;

(*b*) Activities in support of the royalists emanating from Saudi Arabia.

15. It is to be expected that in a situation of the kind found in Yemen, there would be some spectacular allegations about the conduct of one side or the other. This has happened. UNYOM, where possible, has sought to investigate such allegations.

16. Observations of the Mission to date indicate clearly enough that in some important respects the terms of the disengagement agreement have not been fulfilled by either of the parties. Some of the complaints about United Arab Republic air actions have been investigated by military observers, and on occasion UNYOM personnel have witnessed such actions. In recent weeks, United Nations patrols have also observed trucks and camels carrying weapons and ammunition as well as food and other stores. . . .

18. In sum, it cannot be said at this stage that encouraging progress has been made toward effective implementation of the disengagement agreement. Both parties have expressed a willingness to co-operate in good faith with the United Nations Observation Mission and on the whole they have done so, particularly in assisting it to function in the area. But with regard to carrying out the specific provisions of the disengagement agreement, the actual situation depends on the position mutually taken that fulfilment by one side is contingent on fulfilment by the other. UNYOM reports, for example, that on the Saudi Arabian side troops and equipment remain in the buffer zone and that vehicular and animal traffic carrying goods of undetermined nature continues between points on both sides of the border. Within Yemen,

---

[3] For an account of these (and subsequent cases) see above, pp. 614–16.

United Arab Republic troops remain in the buffer zone, and since royalists continue active, United Arab Republic air and ground actions against them continue. There have been two recent instances of United Arab Republic air and ground actions against targets in Saudi Arabian territory, alleged to be supply dumps for aid to the royalists. UNYOM has been lately advised, however, that such attacks across the border will cease. No plan for phased withdrawal of United Arab Republic troops has been received. The Saudi Arabian Government insists that its official aid to the royalists ceased long ago, and claims that the traffic in the buffer zone and across the border is 'normal commercial traffic', though it is not denied that there is a flow of aid to the royalists from private sources in Saudi Arabia, without Government sanction. As regards continuing illicit traffic in arms and ammunition, as distinguished from the normal trade which has been traditional for centuries, across the border by private sources, the Saudi Arabian Government now, advises of its willingness to co-operate with UNYOM in checking also that flow and to this end is willing to assign Saudi Arabian liaison officers to United Nations patrols and to set up the necessary number of check posts in Saudi Arabian territory where United Nations observers could be stationed to check on convoys with the assistance of Saudi national guardsmen. United Arab Republic authorities maintain that since assistance from Saudi Arabian territory continues, enabling the royalists to maintain their offensive capabilities, any step taken by the United Arab Republic in implementation of the agreement leads to an increase in royalist activity. United Arab Republic air action against the royalists within Yemen also continues. Recent UNYOM observations in the Sa'da area would indicate that there has been no decrease in fighting in that locality. In fact, the situation has deteriorated to such an extent that observation in that area may no longer be feasible. [*S/5412, Report of the Secretary-General to the Security Council on the functioning of UNYOM and the implementation of the terms of disengagement, 4 Sept. 1963,* pp. 154–7.]

At the end of October 1964 the Secretary-General informed the Security Council:

4. South Yemen, that is the area south of San'a and the coastal strip, is more or less firmly in the hands of forces supporting the republican Government. Marib, Harib and the surrounding area on the eastern frontier are under the military control of United Arab Republic/Yemeni forces. San'a is firmly under republican control but there are two pockets close to it where some sections of the tribes have at times been unfriendly or even hostile to the Government. These are, respectively, to the west of San'a immediately north of the Hodeida/San'a road and north-east and east of San'a.

5. In the north, allegiance to the republican Government is loose and uncertain. This is due partly to conflicting loyalties, and partly to the traditional attitude of the tribes towards a central authority. It is here that the Imam and other royalist leaders have their main area of influence and the United Arab Republic/Yemeni forces are conducting military operations to retain administrative control. Military conflict of varying intensity, consisting of harassment, guerrilla raids and attempts to cut the San'a–Sada road by the royalists, and reprisals from ground and air by the United Arab Republic/Yemeni forces, has continued in this area throughout the past year. In particular, the inaccessible and mountainous region running northward of Wash-Ha through the demilitarized zone to the border in which the Imam is said to have his headquarters, is not under the control of the Yemen Arab Republic and United Arab Republic forces. In the demilitarized zone the United Arab Republic still has forces in Harad to check on infiltration and assistance to the royalists across the passes south of El Kuba.

6. There is considerable traffic from Saudi Arabia into northern Yemen, and vehicles and animal convoys containing food, supplies and occasionally petrol are seen almost daily. It is said that this traffic is traditional since the people of northern Yemen have always relied on Saudi Arabian towns such as Jizan and Najran for their necessities. To reduce the possibilities of this trade covering traffic in arms and military supplies, a procedure has recently been

developed by which United Nations military observers in co-operation with Saudi Arabian officials check this traffic. Nevertheless, it could be claimed that even peaceful traffic could help those tribes which are resisting the republican Government.

7. The lack of allegiance of certain tribes, especially in the north, and the known presence and activity of the Imam and Prince Hassan among them, evidently with sizable stocks of ammunition (whatever their source may be) continues to be a serious problem for the Government of Yemen and, therefore, for the troops of the United Arab Republic. This problem is aggravated by the apparent fact that the Yemeni army has not yet reached that standard of training and competence which would enable it to cope with the situation without outside assistance, or, perhaps, even to defend republican controlled areas, should one or more of these areas be attacked by hostile tribes. This dependence on outside military aid, which in practice means aid from the United Arab Republic, which sees itself as committed to assist the Yemen Government in its time of need, inevitably impedes the improvement of relations both between the United Arab Republic and Saudi Arabia and between Saudi Arabia and the Yemen. The problem is further complicated by both religious and political factors in Yemen itself.

Position of the two parties

8. In so far as the two parties to the disengagement agreement—Saudi Arabia and United Arab Republic—are concerned, the position may perhaps be briefly summed up as follows. The Saudi Arabian Government maintains that, while it is complying with the agreement, is no longer supplying war material to the royalists and has co-operated with UNYOM in verifying this contention, the other party has not withdrawn the main part of its military forces from Yemen and continues military activities, including bombing of royalist areas and over-flying of Saudi Arabian territory. In this situation, the warning is issued that it might be difficult for the Saudi Arabian Government to continue to carry on indefinitely what it considers to be a unilateral implementation of the agreement . . .

. . . In the Harad and Sada areas there has been, so far, no withdrawal from field activities of United Arab Republic forces, although they are no longer in constant close contact with the royalists. In the Sada area, especially, fighting appears to have died down in recent weeks, apart from occasional ambushes and mine-laying by royalists, and shelling and occasional aerial bombing of hostile concentrations by the United Arab Republic forces. These activities also are on the decrease. The area east and north-east of Sada is also reliably reported to be quiet.

13. At Hodeida the embarkation of 4,000 United Arab Republic troops during the period 1 September to 12 October 1963 has been reported and observed by United Nations military observers. The arrival of 1,300 United Arab Republic troops was observed on 19 October. The Commander of the United Arab Republic forces in Yemen informed the Commander of UNYOM that between 4 July and 22 October, 12,000 officers and men of the United Arab Republic forces had left Yemen, of which half had been replaced by fresh troops. It was added that a further 2,000 officers and men would leave Yemen by 1 November. This information was confirmed to the Secretary-General by the Foreign Minister of the United Arab Republic. Since then, official word has been received to the effect that an additional 3,000 United Arab Republic troops will be withdrawn before the end of December 1963. That is to say, a total of 5,000 troops will leave between the end of October and the end of December. It is assumed that these would not be replaced, in whole or in part. . . .

14. The main function of the detachments stationed at Jizan and Najran is to check on the reduction or cessation of assistance from Saudi Arabia to the royalists. It has been found that vehicle and animal convoys, on account of terrain, water resources, population and communication centres, have been necessarily confined to certain routes. On this basis, a pattern of air and ground patrolling and check points has been established covering all main routes and tracks leading into north Yemen and the demilitarized zone. Air and ground patrols have been carried out daily on varied timings and routes, the patrol plan being planned and co-ordinated every evening by a senior observer.

15. Ground and air patrolling has proved, however, to have two main limitations, namely that traffic could be observed only by day while for climatic reasons travel during hours of darkness is customary in this area, and cargoes could not be checked. This problem has been met by periodically positioning United Nations military observers at various communications centres for forty-eight hours or more. Thus traffic could be observed by day and night and contents of cargoes could also be checked. Observers have also visited royalist areas more frequently in recent weeks. . . .

16. In Saudi Arabian territory, including the demilitarized zone on the Saudi Arabian side of the frontier, most United Nations patrols and check points are accompanied by Saudi Arabian liaison officials, who check cargoes as requested by United Nations observers. Some check points are manned for three to four days at a time and some for shorter periods. Gaps in between manning periods do not exceed two days and in the intervening period the areas are covered by patrolling.

17. By these methods UNYOM has been able, since 10 September 1963, to make a more reliable assessment of the cessation of assistance to the royalists from Saudi Arabia. This assessment leads to the following conclusions:

(a) That the traffic across the frontier is now relatively sparse (some 28 vehicles and 48 animals per week) and contains normal consumer goods;

(b) That no military vehicles or material have been seen nor military equipment or stores found in the cargoes checked by United Nations observers;

(c) That there were no signs of Saudi Arabian military assistance or heavy weapons in royalist areas visited by United Nations observers.

18. These conclusions indicate that in the period under review no military assistance of significance has been provided to the royalists from Saudi Arabia.

19. As regards aerial activity, two over-flights over Saudi Arabian territory from Yemen were observed by United Nations patrols and observers, one of an unidentified aircraft on 12 September and one of an aircraft reported as a United Arab Republic jet aircraft on 2 October. In addition, the Saudi Arabian authorities reported over-flights over Saudi Arabian territory by aircraft identified by them as of the United Arab Republic, on 10 September, 23 September and 20 October 1963. The Commander of United Arab Republic forces was informed of these complaints and stated in reply that the flights in question were not carried out by aircraft of the United Arab Republic.

20. United Nations observers verified as correct a report that the Nahuga area (in the demilitarized zone) had been bombed by United Arab Republic aircraft on 3 September. On 7 October a United Nations observer at El Kuba reported parachute flares in an easterly direction and, immediately afterward, the sound of a jet aircraft and two loud explosions from the same direction.

21. Royalist observers reported to United Nations observers attacks by United Arab Republic aircraft on the Wash-Ha area on 4 October, on the Al Hashiwz area on 5 October and on the Boyi area on 7 October 1963. These reports were delayed and could not be verified.

22. Thus, since my last report, air activity by the United Arab Republic has considerably decreased. Air attacks over Saudi Arabian territory and the demilitarized zone have ceased. The air attacks reported (mainly in the Sada area), are in a region where ground operations have also been reported.

23. In general, it may be said that in many areas, particularly in north and north-east Yemen, where there was active fighting in early July, the fighting has since almost entirely ceased. Military operations are at present confined to the Sada area and to the south-east of it. They too are of a sporadic nature—i.e. bursts of light automatic and artillery fire and isolated occasional air activity, although heavier activity by United Arab Republic forces in the Gof area in the period 18–21 October has been reported. These reports are now under investigation.

24. I pointed out in my last report that UNYOM, because of its limited size and function, can observe and certify only certain indications of the implementation of the disengagement agreement. I believe that in the period under review its capacity for this purpose had been increased and made more efficient, and that its observations show accurately certain trends

and developments in the situation. Although these developments are far short of the disengagement and regularization of the situation which had been hoped for, they are in their limited way encouraging, in that the scale of fighting has been reduced and conditions of temporary truce apply in most areas. . . .

25. I also said in my last report that UNYOM could, within limits, serve as an intermediary and as an endorser of good faith on behalf of the parties concerned. I believe that within its severe limitations it has fulfilled this role very well and that certain improvements in the situation have been the result. I do not, however, believe that the solution of the problem, or even the fundamental steps which must be taken to resolve it, can ever be within the potential of UNYOM alone—and most certainly not under its existing limited mandate. [*S/5447, Report by the Secretary-General to the Security Council on the functioning of UNYOM, 28 Oct. 1964, pp. 44, 47, 48 and 49.*]

The next report came after the initial decision to wind up UNYOM's operation had been rescinded, due to forthcoming financial support from the UAR and Saudi Arabia.[4]

6. When it was decided to maintain the military Mission, General Gyani and his staff undertook a reappraisal of the requirements in personnel and equipment. Because of the co-operation shown by the authorities on both sides of the Saudi-Arabian–Yemen frontier and because of the peaceful and friendly attitude of the people in the area covered by the Mission . . . it was felt that it was no longer necessary to maintain a military unit in the demilitarized zone. The Yugoslav detachment at Najran, continued, however, to carry out patrols in that area until 25 November, while the Observer personnel was being built up to full strength. During the same period, United Nations Military Observers at Jizan and Najran manned checkpoints on the frontier to the limit of their ability. . . .

9. . . . Most United Nations patrols are accompanied by Saudi Arabian liaison officials, who check cargoes as requested by the observers. Occasionally, observers visit Royalist areas on the Yemeni side of the border in order to check on the extent to which arms and ammunition may be reaching them from abroad and the degree of fighting occurring between them and the forces of the United Arab Republic. The observers in Sada, Sana and Hodeida observe the extent to which the United Arab Republic forces are being disengaged from Yemen.

10. The ground observations of the Mission are supplemented by an Air Transport Unit provided by Canada, with two Caribou aircraft stationed at Sana. The Otter aircraft stationed at Jizan and at Najran in order to perform patrols in the border region were withdrawn in mid-December, since it was found that, after the withdrawal of the Yugoslav Company, the Caribou aircraft were capable of carrying out the patrols in addition to providing logistic support.

OBSERVATIONS OF THE MISSION

11. In relation to the provision of the disengagement agreement calling for the cessation of aid and support by Saudi Arabia to the Royalists of Yemen, the situation remains as before, namely, that no military vehicles or material have been seen nor military equipment or stores found in the cargoes checked by United Nations observers. The relatively small amount of traffic across the frontier has contained normal consumer goods, including small quantities of kerosene and petrol. Commercial traffic appears, however, to have been reduced generally because of fear of air attack. Vehicle tracks, some of them recent, have been observed from the air crossing the desert in the direction of Yemen far to the east of the demilitarized zone. No vehicles have actually been sighted and due to the inaccessibility of the area it has not been possible to station checkposts there by night.

12. As regards the phased disengagement of United Arab Republic troops from Yemen, a total of more than 5,000 troops have been observed to embark at Hodeida over the period

[4] See above, pp. 650-1.

1 November to 17 December. During the same period approximately 1,000 troops were observed to arrive.

13. With regard to the withdrawal of the armed forces of Saudi Arabia and the United Arab Republic from the demilitarized zone extending 20 kilometres on either side of the frontier, United Arab Republic forces continue to maintain themselves at Harad and some 5 to 8 kilometres to the north-east, covering a main route of entry from Saudi Arabia into Yemen, although the extent of the zone held has been reduced. The Saudi Arabian Government continues to keep an anti-aircraft unit in Najran.

14. The United Arab Republic air force has carried out a number of air attacks in the Yemeni portion of the demilitarized zone. In addition, in mid-November a number of over-flights by United Arab Republic planes over Saudi Arabia occurred in the El Kuba region some 60 kilometres south-east of Jizan; on 10 November, two bombs were dropped in the Fefa mountain 8 to 10 kilometres inside Saudi Arabia killing one person; and on 21 November trucks in the market-place at El Kuba, 4 to 5 kilometres inside Saudi Arabia, were attacked with 8 rockets and with machine-gun fire, resulting in four deaths.

15. With regard to the question of punitive action taken by United Arab Republic forces against Royalist forces in Yemen, it seems clear that in the greater part of the country no military operations of importance have occurred during the past two months, including certain areas to the west and north-east of Sana where tribes had previously been reported as hostile to the Government of the Republic of Yemen. However, tribes in the mountainous areas Wash-Ha-Hajja and to the north-west and north-east of Sana continue to pursue a pro-Royalist attitude and from time to time actively harass United Arab Republic troops. Aircraft of the United Arab Republic have been observed frequently taking off on armed missions and have been observed occasionally bombing. On 15 November two United Arab Republic planes attacked a truck moving northwards in Yemen toward the Saudi frontier near El Kuba; the wreck was examined by a United Nations Observer and found to contain coffee. On 21 November, a village was observed burning some 30 kilometres north-west of Sana following considerable United Arab Republic activity in that area. On 1 December, an aircraft of the United Arab Republic was observed dropping bombs in the same area.

16. In addition to material obtained through direct observations, valuable information about the situation with regard to the implementation of the disengagement agreement and the position of the parties was obtained by my Special Representative in the course of his extensive consultations with the Governments concerned and with their representatives in the affected region.

FINDINGS AND CONCLUSIONS

17. The observations of UNYOM and the statements of the parties tend to confirm the conclusion expressed in my previous report that no military aid of significance has been provided to the Royalists from Saudi Arabia. However, there appears to be *prima facie* evidence that the Saudi Arabian authorities are providing some forms of encouragement to the Royalists. It is not possible, within the means of observation available to UNYOM, to determine whether this encouragement is purely moral or has material and financial aspects.

18. The observations of UNYOM tend to confirm that there has been a substantial net withdrawal of United Arab Republic troops from Yemen during the period under review, amounting to some 4,000 troops.

19. All indications point to the fact that ground operations in Yemen have further decreased in intensity. Active opposition to the United Arab Republic forces continues in the area Wash-Ha-Hajja. United Arab Republic air activity has recently increased and appears, at least in some instances, to be directed at targets which are not of tactical military significance.

20. With the exceptions noted in paragraph 14 above, which have been attributed by the UAR Command to navigational errors, the United Arab Republic has observed its pledge not to carry out operations over Saudi Arabian territory.

21. From these findings, I arrive at the same conclusion reached in my previous report, namely, that while developments are, in a limited way, encouraging in that the scale of the

22

fighting continues to decrease, they fall far short of fulfilment of the disengagement agreement and regularization of the situation which had been hoped for. I reiterate the belief that the solution of the problem lies beyond the potential of UNYOM under its original mandate.

22. On the other hand, I believe, on the basis of the experience of the Mission especially during the last two months, that it exercises a pacifying influence on the situation in the frontier region and is an important factor in such improvements in the situation in Yemen itself as have occurred. Its continued functioning after 4 January 1964 seems to me, therefore, to be highly desirable if the situation is not to deteriorate and if a climate is to be created in which political approaches towards a solution to the problem may be attempted.

23. My Special Representative in Yemen has held extensive discussions with the members of the three Governments concerned. These discussions have been of an exploratory character with a view to ascertaining whether there were areas of agreement between the parties which might, through bilateral discussions or otherwise, lead to further progress towards disengagement and towards a peaceful situation in Yemen. I do not wish to prejudice the results of these efforts, except to state that they have started in an encouraging manner, and that I intend to have them pursued. I believe also that the Governments concerned are anxious that they should continue.

24. Accordingly on 23 December 1963, I addressed identical messages to the Prime Minister of Saudi Arabia and to the President of the United Arab Republic in which I informed them of my conclusion, which seemed to be generally shared, that the Mission continues to serve a useful purpose and that its extension would be conducive to further progress towards both disengagement and a peaceful solution in Yemen. It followed that I would be prepared to extend the United Nations Yemen Observation Mission in approximately its present strength and composition for a period of up to six months. . . . I inquired . . . whether the two Governments would be agreeable to the continuation of the Mission for such a period under the prevailing arrangements for its financing. . . . I also indicated that in view of recent reductions in the size of the Mission, the operating expenses had been substantially reduced. [*S/5501, Report by the Secretary-General to the Security Council on the functioning of UNYOM*, *2 Jan. 1964*, pp. 5–8.]

3. The composition and deployment of the staff of twenty-five military observers assigned to UNYOM continued to be as described in the last report. The majority of the observers are stationed at the main border crossings from Saudi Arabia into Yemen to check on the nature of the frontier traffic, making patrols at irregular intervals, to the less frequented crossings, while a small number are stationed at Sada, Sana and Hodeida to observe the extent to which the United Arab Republic forces are withdrawn from Yemen. A Canadian air detachment with two Caribou aircraft provides logistic support as well as air observation.

4. The observers stationed on the northern frontier have reported during this period an appreciable traffic by truck and camel across the border. In none of the cargoes inspected by the observers, however, have arms or ammunition been found. It must be noted in this regard that the control exercised by the observers on a long frontier is necessarily far from complete. Moreover, local inhabitants crossing the border in either direction almost invariably carry rifles and a number of rounds of ammunition on their persons.

5. The nature and extent of the military operations carried out by the royalists during January and February would seem to indicate that arms and ammunition in appreciable amounts have been reaching them from some source, though not necessarily across the northern frontier. Yemen Arab Republic and United Arab Republic sources assert that such supplies are being introduced from the Beihan area across the frontier with the South Arabian Federation. This frontier is not included in the disengagement agreement and United Nations Observers therefore do not operate in that area. The royalists also appear to be well provided with money and have engaged a number of foreign experts to train and direct their forces in modern guerrilla tactics. Not only have exposed United Arab Republic units, particularly those in the Sada area, been subjected to repeated harassing actions, including widespread use of anti-vehicles mines, but in the latter part of January the royalists undertook extensive

and co-ordinated operations designed to cut the roads leading from Sana to Hodeida, Taiz, Marib and Sada. The road from Hodeida, which is the most important supply line for the United Arab Republic forces, was actually cut for a week, but after heavy fighting, in which Yemeni Republican forces also participated in large numbers, the road was reopened and the situation has been relatively calm since that time, though some fighting occurred in the eastern part of the country until mid-February.

6. The United Arab Republic forces in Yemen for the most part have stayed on the defensive during the period covered by the present report. They have, however, reacted to royalist attacks, particularly against their communications, not only with ground operations, but with retaliatory air attacks. During the latter half of January, air activities of the United Arab Republic were quite heavy, while frequent sorties directed towards the east took place in early February. Since then, air activity has been on a lesser scale. Bombing has been occasionally heard by United Nations Observers on the northern frontier and at Sada. No over-flights of Saudi Arabian territory have been reported since last November.

7. As regards the strength of the United Arab Republic forces in Yemen, the United Nations Observers at Hodeida have reported that more than 4,000 United Arab Republic troops arrived there by sea, from 3 January to 18 February, while more than a thousand departed. The majority of these arriving troops seemed to be composed of organized military formations with appropriate equipment and transport, but a considerable number apparently consisted of individual soldiers returning from leave. It is customary for the United Arab Republic command to send troops from Yemen on leave in military transport aircraft which have brought supplies to their forces. While an exact determination of the number of troops involved is not possible, it is estimated that more than a thousand troops left by plane. Thus the effective strength of the United Arab Republic forces in Yemen during the period of this report appears to have increased by some one to two thousand men.

8. My Special Representative drew urgently to the attention of the authorities of the United Arab Republic the unfortunate impression which would be created by this increase in their forces. They explained that their original intention had been to replace one brigade by rotation and to withdraw one brigade entirely during that period. The incoming troops had arrived on schedule, but the withdrawal of the two brigades had been suspended because of the heavy royalist attacks. It was hoped that the improved situation would permit the withdrawal to be resumed at the end of February. The authorities of the United Arab Republic, however, maintained their position that the phased disengagement of their troops from Yemen must be subject to the existence of reasonably secure conditions in the country.

9. From the foregoing, I have reached the conclusion that progress towards the implementation of the disengagement agreement has been very disappointing during the period under review. Moreover, a state of political and military stalemate exists inside the country which is unlikely to be changed as long as external intervention in its various forms continues from either side. Were it not for somewhat encouraging external factors, it would be doubtful whether it would be useful to continue the Yemen Observation Mission.

10. The encouraging factors are the increasing unity of feeling and purpose within the Arab world arising from the Conference of Arab Heads of State held in Cairo in mid-January 1964 and the improvement in relations between Saudi Arabia and the United Arab Republic which resulted therefrom. Both before and after the Conference, I and my Special Representative on my behalf, had been urging the two Governments concerned to hold direct conversations on the Yemen question. After the Cairo Conference, this task was also undertaken by a Mission composed of representatives of the Presidents of Algeria and Iraq. I was pleased to learn from a communiqué issued by the Saudi Arabian Government, after discussions with the Arab Mission, that it welcomed the resumption of political relations with the United Arab Republic provided a meeting would be held between the two parties in Saudi Arabia which would be attended also by the mediating delegates. It is my understanding that this high-level meeting in Riyadh will be related mainly to problems concerned with the resumption of diplomatic relations. Nevertheless, it is hoped that it will result in some progress towards the implementation of the disengagement agreement, and also towards an understanding

between the two Governments to co-operate in promoting political progress and stability in Yemen.   [*S/5572, Report by the Secretary-General to the Security Council on the functioning of UNYOM, 3 March 1964, pp. 95–97.*]

This document is of especial interest in that it clearly points out the limits to UNYOM's mandate. In paragraph 5 attention is drawn to the fact that the Beihan border with Yemen did not come within the scope of the disengagement agreement, and hence any arms coming through that area were not subject to UN scrutiny. The gradual increase of Egyptian troops referred to in paragraph 7 was to set the pattern for later months. And paragraph 10 underlines the reality of the belief that any final solution to the problem lay not in the hands of the UN, but through bilateral Saudi-Egyptian agreement.

In the report of 4 May 1964 the Secretary-General admitted that the control exercised over the northern frontier was far from complete. He repeated the difficulty that arose because 'Yemeni and UAR authorities no longer allege that arms are coming in quantity over the northern frontier, but now claim that they are being introduced from the Beihan area of South Arabia'.[5]

4. As regards the strength of the UAR forces in Yemen the Observers stationed at Hodeida have reported that more than 4,000 troops arrived there by sea, including a number of anti-aircraft units which arrived in mid-March, though the majority appeared to be soldiers returning from leave. During the same period more than 2,000 UAR troops were reported by Observers to have left Hodeida. Taking into account movements by air, in which there is usually a net balance of troops leaving the country, it may be concluded that there has been no reduction in UAR forces in Yemen, and there even may have been some small increase.

5. The military situation within Yemen appears to have been rather quiet during the period covered by this report. Some pro-royalist tribes not far north of Sanaa appear to be hard-pressed by famine conditions. Royalist tribes elsewhere remain strong in their mountain positions, but have confined their military activities to occasional attacks on lines of communications to such relatively isolated UAR posts as Sada, Hajjah and Naham.

6. Activity by the UAR Air Force appears to have been rather limited, but United Nations Observers have confirmed a number of attacks south of Saada in early April, apparently in connexion with a royalist attack on the route to the south as well as two attacks about the same period in the mountainous area east of Saada resulting in three civilian deaths. No overflights of Saudi Arabia have been reported.

7. The period covered by the report has thus been marked by no progress in troop reduction towards implementation of the disengagement agreement. Moreover, if the military situation appears to have become somewhat more favourable for the forces of the Government and of the United Arab Republic, no actual end of the fighting appears to be in sight.

8. In my previous report I expressed the hope that the high-level meeting then taking place in Riyadh between representatives of the Governments of Saudi Arabia and the United Arab Republic would result in some progress towards disengagement and toward an understanding between the two Governments to co-operate in promoting political progress and stability in Yemen. I have been informed that in the communiqué issued at the conclusion of the discussions on 3 March 1964, the two parties reported noticeable progress in discussions of a number of problems at issue between them, in particular the problem of Yemen, and decided to continue their discussions and to settle those problems in the course of meetings between President Nasser and Prince Feisal to be held in Cairo toward the end of April 1964. The two parties also declared that they had no ambitions in Yemen and unreservedly supported the independence of that country and the freedom of its people. I have endeavoured to encourage

[5] S/5681, p. 1.

the parties to pursue this course of action. At the time of issuance of this report, however, the date of the Cairo meeting has not yet been announced.

9. In view of the contribution made by the Mission to improving the situation on the northern frontier and of the prospective negotiations on the Yemen problem, I am definitely of the opinion that it would be useful and advisable to extend the Mission for another two months and I propose to do so.

10. I have ascertained from the Permanent Representatives of the Governments of Saudi Arabia and the United Arab Republic that their Governments concur in my suggestion that the United Nations Observation Mission in Yemen be extended for another two months as from 4 May 1964, that is, until 4 July 1964. In pursuance of the informal procedure followed last November (S/5447/Add. 2), although believing that no meeting of the Council on the subject was required, I have consulted the Council members informally in order to ascertain that in the light of the circumstances as reported there would be no objection to the extension. In the absence of any objection, I am therefore proposing to extend the Mission until 4 July 1964. [*S/5681, Report by the Secretary-General to the Security Council on the functioning of UNYOM, 4 May 1964*, pp. 112–13.]

The same pattern—only limited fighting, non-fulfilment of the disengagement agreement, and an enforced reliance on a direct Saudi-Egyptian settlement—emerged in the next report.

3. United Nations Observers stationed on the northern frontier have continued to observe traffic crossing the border by the main routes. There has been a steady, though small, traffic in civilian supplies, but no military supplies have been noted. From time to time, however, armed royalists in small numbers have crossed the border in either direction.

4. As to the strength of the UAR troops in Yemen, the Observers stationed at Hodeida have reported that some 2,800 troops arrived there by sea during the period of this report; about 1,000 of these, however, were thought to be troops of the Yemen Arab Republic returning to the country after undergoing training in Egypt. During the same period, some 3,000 UAR troops were reported by Observers to have left Hodeida. Taking into account movements by air, in which there is usually a net balance of troops leaving the country, it is estimated that there has been a reduction of some 3,000 troops in the total strength of the UAR force in Yemen.

5. The formation in Yemen, at the beginning of May, of a government of broader composition under General Hammoud Jaifi, as Prime Minister, gave promise of an improvement in the political stability and independence of the country. The new Government promptly assured me of its desire for good and peaceful relations with all of Yemen's neighbours. The formation of this Government, however, has not resulted to date in any accommodation with the Royalist leaders, who have continued to hold out in various mountainous areas in north Yemen.

6. On the whole, the military situation in Yemen has remained fairly quiet over the past two months. Royalist attacks on UAR positions in the Hajja and Sada area are reported to have been repulsed with a number of casualties in the latter half of May. UAR units are reported to have launched aerial bombing attacks on those and other occasions. The military stalemate appears to continue.

7. While no military aid by Saudi Arabia to the royalists of Yemen has been observed during the period of this report, and while some slight progress in UAR troop reduction appears to have occurred, the implementation of the disengagement agreement is still far from complete in so far as the UAR troops in Yemen are concerned. . . .

8. I believe that the Yemen Observation Mission, despite its unusually limited function and authority, has helped toward removing the threat to international peace and security implicit in the Yemen problem and toward keeping open the possibilities for a final settlement. With a view to providing a further opportunity for negotiations, I consider it advisable to extend the Mission after 4 July for another two months. I take this position with some reluctance,

however, in view of the fact that during its year of operation the Mission in Yemen has been able to observe and report only a disappointing measure of disengagement, in particular as regards the withdrawal of UAR troops. I feel obliged, therefore, to appeal most urgently to the parties concerned to meet at the highest level in the near future with a view to achieving full and rapid implementation of the disengagement agreement. I also feel bound to advise the Council that if this new period of two months were to register no substantial progress toward fulfilment or the firm prospect of imminent fulfilment of the agreement, I would find it difficult to envisage a further extension of the Mission in its present form, and with its present terms of reference and purpose. [*S/5794, Report by the Secretary-General to the Security Council on the functioning of UNYOM, 2 July 1964*, pp. 1–3.]

In his final report to the Security Council the Secretary-General again acknowledged both the failure of the parties to implement the disengagement agreement, and the difficulties which UNYOM had faced in observing and reporting on those matters:

3. United Nations Observers stationed on the northern frontier have continued to observe traffic crossing the border by the main routes, though with increasing difficulty because, *inter alia*, of less favourable climatic conditions and of problems of vehicle maintenance. Moreover, as indicated in previous reports, the control exercised by Observers on a long frontier is necessarily far from thorough. A small, though increasing, traffic has been observed, but no military supplies have been discovered. However, Observers have noted that royalists in one area not far from the frontier maintain a substantial dump of fuel, arms, ammunition and rations. UAR military authorities have shown United Nations Observers an appreciable quantity of weapons and ammunition allegedly provided to the royalists by Saudi Arabia and captured from them by UAR troops. It was observed that according to the markings on the boxes the ammunition appeared to have been made in the United States in 1963–1964 and delivered to Saudi Arabia. The Saudi Arabian authorities have emphatically denied that any such war material had been given by them to the royalists of Yemen.

4. As regards the disengagement of UAR troops from Yemen, the United Nations Observers stationed at Hodeida have reported that during the period of this report some 6,700 troops departed by sea, of whom the great majority were in regular formations and were embarked with trucks and anti-tank guns. During the same period, some 4,300 UAR troops were observed to land at Hodeida, of whom about one third appeared to be returning from leave and the remainder to be replacements. Taking into account movements by air, in which there is usually a net balance of troops leaving the country, it is estimated that there has been over the past two months a reduction of about 4,000 troops in the total strength of UAR troops.

5. Despite the reduction in UAR strength, there has been a substantial amount of military action directed against royalist strongpoints in north Yemen, in which Yemen republican troops, some of them trained in the UAR, and Yemeni tribesmen, have taken an increasing part. These operations seem to have met with some success and additional tribes appear to have rallied to the Government of the Yemen Arab Republic. The UAR authorities have, however, stated that the Yemeni units will continue to be supported by UAR ground troops and the UAR Air Force. United Nations Observers at Sada have reported that on several recent occasions operations in that vicinity were supported by aerial bombing and artillery fire.

6. The Saudi Arabian authorities have complained that on several occasions during August UAR military aircraft have flown over Saudi Arabian territory east of Gizan. One of those reports has been confirmed by UNYOM. Representations were made to the UAR commander, who reiterated that his pilots have standing instructions not to fly over Saudi Arabia. . . .

8. The observations of the past two months have been somewhat more encouraging in that there has been a substantial reduction in the strength of the UAR armed forces in Yemen. However, it seems that this withdrawal is a reflection of the improved military situation in Yemen from the point of view of the UAR and of the increased participation by Yemeni

republicans, many of them trained in the UAR, in the fight against the royalists, rather than the beginning of a phased withdrawal in the sense of the disengagement agreement. There are indications, moreover, that the Yemeni royalists have continued to receive military supplies from external sources.

9. My Special Representative visited the UAR, Saudi Arabia and Yemen in the first half of August and held discussions with the authorities on the Yemen problem. However, the hoped-for direct high-level discussions between Saudi Arabia and the UAR with a view to further progress towards disengagement have not taken place, and there is no certainty that they will. . . .

13. It is a matter of regret to me that the Mission has been able to observe only limited progress towards the implementation of the disengagement agreement. In this regard, I must reiterate that the terms of reference of the Mission were restricted to observation and report only, and that the responsibility for implementation lay with the two parties which had concluded the agreement and which had requested the establishment of the Mission. My regret, however, is tempered by reason of the fact that the potential threat to international peace and security represented by the Yemen question has greatly diminished during the existence of the Mission and, I believe, to a considerable extent because of its activities. The true measure of the Mission, of course, is to be found in how it has discharged the limited responsibility and authority entrusted to it. In this respect, I think it can be said without question that the Mission actually accomplished much more than could have been expected of it, in the circumstances; it certainly could have been much more useful, had the definition of its functions been broader and stronger. It is clear, however, that during the fourteen months of its presence in Yemen, the UN Mission exercised an important restraining influence on hostile activities in that area. [*S/5927, Report of the Secretary-General to the Security Council on the functioning of UNYOM, 2 Sept. 1964, pp. 2–4.*]

So much for UNYOM's ability to carry out its mandate. In addition, certain events have occurred in the Yemen since UNYOM's departure in September 1964 which place in better perspective the UN's attempt to contribute to a peaceful solution. It will be recalled that on 28 April 1964 al-Jaifi was made Prime Minister. In January 1965 he resigned (there had been a cease-fire agreement in December 1964 between the royalists and republicans, but this had failed to hold, still less to solidify into a national reconciliation) and President Sallal designated General al-Amri Prime Minister. By 20 April 1965, however, al-Amri had resigned, and the premiership passed to Ahmed No'man. No'man was a moderate who attracted a fairly wide base of support. However, after a constitutional dispute with President Sallal, No'man resigned at the beginning of July 1965. The President himself now formed a new government. On 18 July he called upon General al-Amri to form a new government. Many moderate republicans, supporters of No'man, resented the return to office of al-Amri, and went to Saudi Arabia for peace talks with King Faisal (King Saud had been replaced by Faisal on 2 November 1964). They claimed that Egyptian interference in the Yemen was now perverting the ¦republican cause.

At this stage Egypt charged Saudi Arabia with allowing the Saudi towns of Jizan and Najran to be used as 'bases of aggression' against Yemen, and an Egyptian air strike was feared. The continuing United States air 'umbrella', guaranteeing Saudi territory, again proved a sufficient deterrent. In early August republican and royalist Yemenis met at Taiz for discussions, and there were also behind-the-scenes talks between Faisal and Nasser. On 13 August 1965 the Yemeni royalists and republicans announced agreement on a programme to end the civil war. Nasser and Faisal now arranged a meeting at Jidda. The meeting of these two Arab leaders in Saudi Arabia was the occasion of considerable interest and curiosity on the part of Arabs and Westerners alike. The meeting was more successful than had been anticipated and, with a great display of mutual cordiality, they announced agreement on ending the war in Yemen. The agreement envisaged the setting up of a new caretaker government within three months, followed by the staged withdrawal of Egyptian troops, culminating in a plebiscite. The main points were summarized by Reuter, from Cairo and Mecca radio broadcasts, as follows:

The aim of President Gamal Abdel Nasser and King Faisal in their talks in Jiddah was to make it possible for the Yemeni people to exercise their free will so that it could provide an atmosphere of peace, in addition to the removal of every cause of the transient disagreement between the United Arab Republic and Saudi Arabia, and to consolidate the historic ties between their two peoples.

As regards the relation of the United Arab Republic and Saudi Arabia to the present situation in Yemen, King Faisal and President Abdel Nasser, having got in touch with all the representatives of the Yemeni people and their national forces, and having been acquainted with their wishes, consider that the just and safest in facing responsibiliity towards the Yemeni people is through:

1. Giving the Yemeni people the right to decide and affirm their view to the kind of Government they want in a popular plebiscite at a date not later than November 23, 1966.
2. The remaining period up to the date of the plebiscite shall be considered a transitional period to prepare for the plebiscite.
3. Saudi Arabia and the United Arab Republic will co-operate in forming a transitional conference of 50 members representing all the national forces and people of authority in Yemen, after consultation with the various Yemeni groups in accordance with the agreement to be reached. The conference will meet at Harad (in Yemen) on November 23, 1965, and will undertake: determination of the system of government during the transitional period and until the popular plebiscite is held; formation of a provisional Cabinet to be in charge of the Government during the transitional period; determination of the form and kind of the plebiscite which will be held by November 23, 1966, at the latest.

JOINT NEUTRALITY

4. The two Governments adopt the resolutions of the above-mentioned transitional Yemeni conference, support them, and co-operate to ensure their successful implementation. They declare from now their acceptance of a joint neutral follow-up committee of both to be in charge of the plebiscite should the conference decide the need for the presence of such a neutral committee.
5. Saudi Arabia will immediately stop military aid of all kinds and the use of Saudi Arabian territory for operations against Yemen.
6. The United Arab Republic will withdraw all its military forces from Yemen within 10 months beginning on November 23, 1965.
7. Armed fighting in Yemen will be stopped immediately and a joint peace commission from both sides will be formed to: supervise the cease-fire through a special supervisory commission; supervise the frontier and ports and stop all kinds of military aid. Food aid will continue under the supervision of the peace commission. The said supervisory commis-

sions will be entitled to use all the necessary travel facilities within Yemeni territory as well as use Saudi Arabian territory, if necessary.

8. Saudi Arabia and the United Arab Republic will co-operate and act positively to ensure the carrying out of this agreement and impose stability in Yemen until the proclamation of the result of the plebiscite, by forming a force of the two countries to be used by the commission when necessary to prevent any departure from this agreement or any action to obstruct it or provoke disorder against its success.

9. In order to promote co-operation between the United Arab Republic and Saudia Arabia and enable this co-operation to continue beyond the present phase to the normal phase which should prevail over relations between the two countries, there will be direct contact between President Abdel Nasser and King Faisal to avoid any difficulties in the way of carrying out this agreement.—*Reuter*. [*The Times, 25 Aug. 1965.*]

It was a measure of the degree to which control had moved out of Yemeni hands that neither Yemeni republicans nor royalists were represented during the preparation of this agreement. This was, it may be noted, the third agreement between Saudi Arabia and the UAR on the Yemen. The first was the disengagement agreement made under the good offices of the UN Secretary-General, the implementation of which it was UNYOM's task to observe; the second was the accord reached during the autumn of 1964, when the two leaders met in Egypt. Yemeni republicans were reported to be annoyed that Nasser had agreed with Faisal that members of the royal dynasty should be allowed to participate in the proposed caretaker government—Sallal had accepted that royalist supporters should play a part, but not the royal family itself. The Baathist régime in Syria also strongly attacked Nasser for 'betraying the revolution' in the terms of the settlement.

In early September there was evidence of a closing of the ranks between the various Yemen republican factions, and a new Council was formed which included ex-premier No'man. A conference of leading republicans held in October 1965 significantly confirmed the resolutions of the republican-royalist conference which had been held, at the instigation of No'man, the month after his dismissal from the premiership.

However, this apparent progress was to lead nowhere. In November 1965 a conference between republican and royalist Yemenis was held at Haradh, to seek a formula, under the Jidda Agreement, for a provisional coalition government which would organize the holding of a plebiscite. Deadlock was reached: the republicans' demand that the interim government operate within a republican framework was unacceptable to the royalists. The desire of both Nasser and Faisal to see a solution was evident: but the republicans rejected the suggestions made by an Egyptian envoy for ending the deadlock, and made bitter charges that Egypt's prime concern was to secure terms leading to a resumption of the shipment of wheat from the United States.

Nasser now sent a high-level team, led by Field Marshal Abd al-Hakim Amer and General Mortaga, to Yemen, and continued private consultations with Faisal. By March 1966, however, sporadic fighting had broken out again. This reality, together with the British announcement that she would be leaving South Arabia by January 1968, now made Nasser decide not to withdraw his troops as envisaged under the Jidda Agreement. A major interest now lay in retaining the physical power to put Arab nationalists in control in South Arabia (Aden) after the British withdrawal.

In August 1966 President Sallal returned to Yemen from Egypt for the first time in a year. There were immediate rumours of an alleged plot against him, foiled by the Egyptian military, by Prime Minister al-Amri. By 17 September al-Amri's resignation had been forced, and Sallal took over as Prime Minister. When Major-General al-Amri and some supporters went to Cairo to protest, they were apparently arrested. Sallal now began a substantial purge of the army, and in October and December trials and public executions occurred. Large numbers thought to be hostile to Egypt were arrested. Claims were now advanced—and eventually confirmed by the International Committee of the Red Cross in June 1967—that Egypt was using poison gas in attacks on Yemeni royalists.

A major alteration in the situation occurred with the advent of the Arab–Israeli war of June 1967. As tension grew with Israel, Egypt withdrew some ten thousand of the forty thousand troops in Yemen. By 17 June a further five thousand had been withdrawn. After the Egyptian defeat, Nasser was seeking a formula for withdrawing the balance.

In August 1967 both Egypt and Saudi Arabia—who had been united in their opposition to Israel—accepted a Sudanese proposal for ending the Yemen war. Under the terms of the Khartoum Agreement Egypt would withdraw her remaining 25,000 men. A transitional government would be set up in Sana, with Sallal as figurehead President with little executive power. This time, no provision was made for a plebiscite, and a three-nation committee—consisting of Iraq, Morocco, and Sudan—would supervise the execution of the agreement.

Sallal announced that he was not bound by the terms of this agreement, which he declared an inadmissible interference in Yemen's internal affairs. However, on 6 November, while he was in Baghdad, a coup was mounted against him by more moderate republicans, who indicated their intention of opening talks with the royalists. Abdul Rahman al-Iryani was the new provisional President, and Mohsen al-Aini the new provisional Prime Minister. No'man also joined the new government, but soon resigned and returned to Beirut.

On 13 November a cease-fire had been agreed, and by the beginning of December all Egyptian troops had left the territory. This withdrawal coincided with the speeding up of the British withdrawal from Aden, which was also completed during 1967.

However, with Egyptian troops gone, the Yemen republicans now found themselves hard pressed by the royalists, who advanced to Sana. A conference held on 12 January between republicans and royalists once more ended in deadlock, in spite of the efforts lent by Iraq, Morocco, and Sudan towards a domestic settlement.

13

ANNEXES

A. Checklist of Documents

Debates in UN organs:
  SCOR, 18th yr, mtgs 1037–9, 10–11 June 1963.

Reports to Security Council by Secretary-General on
developments relating to Yemen

S/5298	29 Apr. 1963	S/5235	7 June 1963
S/5321	27 May 1963		

Reports by Secretary-General to Security Council on
functioning of UNYOM and implementation of the terms of disengagement:

S/5412	4 Sept. 1963	S/5681 & Add.	4 May 1964
S/5447 & Add.	28 Oct. 1963	S/5794 & Add.	2 July 1964
S/5501 & Add.	2 Jan. 1964	S/5927 & Annexes	2 Sept. 1964
S/5572 & Add.	3 Mar. 1964	S/5959	11 Sept. 1964

Other documents:

S/5326	8 June 1963	S/5336	21 June 1963
S/5331	11 June 1963	A/5801	Suppl. 1, 1964
S/5333	17 June 1963	A/5802	Suppl. 2, 1964.

B. Bibliography

Brown, William R. The Yemeni dilemma. 17 *Middle East J.*, 1963.

Flory, M. La mission d'observation des Nations Unies au Yemen. 9 *Annuaire français de droit international, 1963.*

Guldescu, S. Yemen: the war and the Haradh conference. *R. of Politics* (Notre Dame), *1963.*

Horn, Carl von. *Soldiering for Peace.* London, 1966.

Hottinger, Arnold. The war in Yemen. *Swiss R. of World Affairs*, 1965.

Kapeliuk, A. Stalemate in Yemen. *New Outlook*, Oct. 1963.

Kapil, Menahem. Revolution in Yemen. *New Outlook*, Nov.–Dec. 1962.

McLean, Neil. The war in the Yemen. *J. Rl United Service Inst.*, Apr. 1964.

O'Ballance, Edgar. The Yemen. *Quarterly R.*, July 1967.

Schuman, L. O. Égypte en Jemen. *Internationale Spectator*, 22 Nov. 1965.

Smiley, D. de C. The war in Yemen. *J. Rl United Service Inst.*, Nov. 1963.

INDEX

Advisory Committee, for UNEF, 271–81, 288, 307, 326, 347 f., 351 f., 358, 359–60, 382–92, 397, 422, 484, 488–9, 508, 516, 519

Al-Sallal, *see* Sallal

Aqaba, Gulf of, 113 f., 199, 200–1, 221, 227, 243, 247 ff., 250 f., 253 ff., 258, 276, 349, 357 f., 387, 390, 397, 402, 404, 460, 466, 474, 478 f., 481 n. 21

Arab refugees, *see* Refugees.

Armistice Agreements, Arab-Israeli, 18, 25, 26–9, 32–52, 60 f., 63, 65, 68, 86–105, 108–17, 138–141, 144, 150, 160, 203, 221, 227, 236, 242, 255, 358, 367, 386, 391, 398–9, 404, 456, 478, 481 n. 21, 496, 542

Aswan Dam, 222

Atassi, N., 338

Australia: attitude to military action in Suez (1956), 227, 230, 233, 237, 338; voluntary financial contribution to UNEF, 434.

Azazme Bedouins, 147–9

Ben-Gurion, David, 359

Belligerency, compatibility with armistice, 156–9, 402–3, 478 n. 13

Bennike, Gen. Vagn, 70, 100, 120, 168–70, 189

Bernadotte, Count Folke, 14, 22, 24, 60, 64, 70, 78, 80, 84; *see also* UN Mediator for Palestine

Bull, Gen. Odd, 55 ff., 62, 71, 127 f., 131, 190, 202, 205 f., 208, 210, 296, 551–2, 553, 555, 560, 599, 600 f.

Bunche, Ralph, 60 f., 67, 69, 83, 87, 91–2, 93, 95, 97, 158, 371, 481 n. 21, 612 f., 626

Bunker, Ellsworth, 612 f., 626

Burns, Maj.-Gen. E. L. M., 70, 105, 110 f., 180, 233, 265, 274, 279, 293, 301, 364, 414, 462, 463 f., 484

Canada: resolutions to establish UNEF, 230; contribution to UNEF, 284, 286, 317, 368, 497, 500; attitude to withdrawal of UNEF (1967), 368–72; air transport contribution to UNYOM, 640

Central Truce Supervision Board (Palestine), 22

Certain Expenses of the United Nations, 261 n. 4, 267–71, 438–49

Chamoun, Pres., 535 ff., 542, 547

Chehab, Pres., 535, 542, 556, 563, 569

Chief of Command of UNEF, *see* Commander of UNEF

Chief of Staff of UNTSO, 22, 25 ff., 30 f., 38 f., 50, 53 f., 57 f., 61–2, 63 ff., 78 f., 83, 88, 89–93, 94 ff., 104 ff., 124, 128, 140–2, 144 f., 150 f., 154 f., 171, 180, 190, 193, 201, 205, 207, 209,

210, 226, 233, 242, 256, 263, 276, 342, 483, 496, 498

Commander of UNEF, 53 f., 233, 273, 277–8, 279, 281 f., 283–4, 289–90, 294, 298–9, 302, 307 f., 310, 315, 340, 361–2, 375, 385, 404 f., 463, 469, 485, 490, 496 ff.

Commonwealth, response to British action in Suez (1956), 227

Consent, to establishment of UN Forces, 264–5, 335–44, 353–7, 362–72, 550

Constantinople Convention (1888), 224, 402

Convention on privileges and immunities of UN, 382, 383, 644; *see also* Privileges and immunities

Credentials of Yemen representatives to UN, 611–12

Damascus, 207

Dayal, Rajeshwar, 551, 555

Demilitarized Zones, *see* Zones, demilitarized

Dixon, Sir Pierson, 229, 237, 410

Dulles, J. F., 223 ff.

Eban, Abba, 230

Eden, Sir A., 223–4, 225

Egypt: Armistice Agreement, 43–8; sinks *Eilat*, 62, 71; fails to pay compensation for injuries to UN personnel, 80–1; tripartite invasion of (1956), 109; asserts state of war with Israel, 109, 200; closes Suez Canal to Israel shipping, 154–60, 476–7; agrees to UN observers on Suez Canal, 210–11; claims rights of belligerency, 221, 247; nationalizes Suez Canal, 222–3; consent given to UNEF, 246, 264, 274, 277, 335–44, 353–7, 362–72, 507–9; requests withdrawal for UNEF, 271, 326, 338–9, 345–9; objects to certain countries, 367–72; blocks Aqaba to Israel shipping, 478–9; forms UAR with Syria, 535; accused by Lebanon of intervention, 536–7; resumes relations with Lebanon, 546; involvement in Yemen civil war, 610–11, 613, 614–15, 618, 622–4, 626, 629–35, 641–5, 649–51, 653–68

Eilat (Elath), 109, 160, 200 f., 400, 478, 481 n. 21

Eilat, sinking of, 211–12

Eisenhower, Dwight D., 223, 536, 538, 540 n. 22, 543

El Auja, 53, 108, 112, 154, 156–7, 222, 258, 358

Eshkol, Levi, 338

Expenses of UN Forces, 267–71, 333–4, 421–56, 504–5; *see also Certain Expenses of the United Nations*

671

Faisal, King, 538, 636, 662, 666
Fedayeen, 22, 225, 239, 251
France: military action in Suez, 224·7, 228, 459;
response to US draft resolution, 230; response
to establishment of UNEF, 234–6, 246, 261;
position on withdrawal, 407–15; falls into two
years' arrears, 453

Gaza: UNTSO's duties in, 53 f.; arrival of UN
military observers, 80; MAC suggestions for
prevention of incidents, 106; UNTSO headquarters in, 110–11, 490; Israeli conditions
for withdrawal (1957), 113–14, 243, 250, 387,
390–1, 394–6, 398, 401, 404 f., 460, 466, 468 ff.,
479; violations of armistice along Gaza Strip,
149 f., 221, 473, 475 f.; effectiveness of UNEF
along Gaza Strip, 151, 344; suggestions by
Chief of Staff in respect of, 152–4; Israeli
occupation (1967), 203; deployment of UN
observers (June 1967), 205; UNEF's tasks in,
258, 260, 280 ff., 485, 492, 493–5, 522; withdrawal of UNEF from Gaza (1967), 295 ff.,
342, 346 f.; Norwegian hospital in Gaza town,
304; Egyptian rights in, 358, 391; UN
relations with local inhabitants, 384–5; presence of refugees and Palestine Liberation
Army, 482; Israeli withdrawal (1957), 487;
permits required for Egyptian nationals, 510
Gaitskell, Hugh, 223–4
Geneva Convention on treatment of prisoners of
war, 51, 143
Government House, Jerusalem, 55 f., 127–31,
201, 205
Gyani, Maj.-Gen. P. S., 293, 309, 636, 638, 658

Hammarskjöld, Dag, 124, 221, 225, 272 f.,
353 ff., 363, 481 n. 21, 540 n. 21, 546, 594–5
Hussein, King, 203, 538, 540, 611
Huleh, compatibility of drainage with Arts II & V
of Syria-Israel Armistice, 87–105, 137–8, 140,
185
Imam of Yemen, 609, 611, 616
Immunities, *see under* Privileges and immunities
India: attitude towards role of UNEF, 245;
contribution to UNEF, 284, 325, 497; withdrawal of detachment, 294, 362, 368; casualties suffered in June 1967, 296, 299; view on
financing of UNEF, 427; contribution to
UNYOM, 640
International Court of Justice, 77–8, 136, 267–
271, 328, 438–9, 501–2
Iraq: membership of Jordan-Iraq Union, 535;
revolution of July 1958, 538
Israel: independence proclaimed, 14, 73;
armistice negotiations, 24; invades Egypt, 53,
226; holds Government House, 55–6, 127–31;
retaliates against Port Suez, 71, 211; reparation
to UN for death of Bernadotte and Sérot, 77–9,
80; attitude to demilitarized zone, 87–105;
views on presence of UN observers in El Auja,

108; denunciation of Egyptian armistice, 109–
110, 114, 170; withdrawal from Israel-Jordan
MAC, 125; statement on status of Armistice
Agreements (1967), 130–1; retaliates against
Syria, 142–3; arguments on freedom of shipping through Suez Canal, 154–60; retaliates
against Jordan, 164–202; plans for diversion of
river Jordan, 191–2; refusal to participate in
Israel-Syria MAC, 195–6; occupies Arab
territories (1967), 203; position on shipping in
Suez Canal (1967), 209–10; views on establishment of UNEF, 249–50; conditions for withdrawal, 249, 387–405, 460; failure to withdraw (1956), 466–8; ultimate withdrawal
(1957), 470; *see also* Armistice Agreements,
Arab–Israeli

Jerusalem, 20–1, 36, 38, 55, 74 f., 77, 82, 127, 129,
164, 167, 174, 203, 205, 281 f., 490, 555; *see
also* Government House
Jordan: Armistice Agreement, 32–7; refuses to pay
compensation for death of Baake, 79; responsibility for Scopus incident, 124–6; seeks to control civilian infiltration into Israel, 164; position
on Scorpion Pass incident, 172; used as base
for Syrian incursions into Israel, 197; declares
Jordan-Iraq Union still in existence (1958),
538; asks for UK assistance, 538; claims
interference by UAR, 540; agrees to receive
UN representative, 546, 595–6, 602; attitude
to Yemen civil war, 611, 612
Jordan, river, diversion of, 99–101, 181–2, 189, 192
Jurisdiction, over UN Forces, *see* Status of UN
Forces

Khrushchev, Nikita, 541
Kuneitra, 208

Leary, Col., 103, 185 f.
Lebanon: Armistice Agreement, 49–52; charges
Israel with violating armistice lines, 179; faced
with civil war, 538; asks for UNOGIL, 538;
asks for US assistance, 538; resumes relations
with UAR, 546; disagreement with UNOGIL
over its tasks, 559; disputes UNOGIL'S findings, 572–5; asks Security Council to arrange
for withdrawal of UNOGIL, 594
Lloyd, Selwyn, 225 f., 253, 410, 601

Macmillan, Harold, 227, 540 n. 22, 541
Mixed Armistice Commissions, 25 ff., 484, 494,
496, 599; Israel-Syria, 29 f., 40, 86–105, 138–
141, 142 ff., 187, 188–9; Israel-Jordan, 122–3,
125, 161 ff., 169 f.; Israel-Egypt, 147–50
151, 473; Israel-Lebanon, 51, 176; EIMAC
suggests arrangements to prevent Gaza
incidents, 106–7; continues to function (1967),
319, 470–1, 482; Israel withdrawal from
EIMAC, 319, 470–1, 478; EIMAC considers closure of Suez Canal to Israel shipping,

157; Israel withdraws from JIMAC, 125; JIMAC continues to function (1967), 127; ISMAC unable to hold regular sessions, 187, 188–9, 193, 194–5, 196
Mount Scopus, 75 f., 79, 117–21, 125–6, 164, 167, 174, 201–2

Nasser, Pres., 221 ff., 226 f., 271, 326, 338, 349, 354, 366, 368, 619, 626, 639, 662, 666 f.
New Zealand: attitude to military action in Suez (1956), 227, 229 f., 234, 236–7, 250 f., 338, 368
Nuri Es Said, Gen., 222, 538

Observation Group (of UNOGIL), 551–3, 555, 561–2
Odd Bull, see Bull
ONUC, 133 n. 1, 267, 269, 308, 372, 437 f., 445, 450 n. 36, 522, 558 n. 1, 623, 642

Palestine: Anglo-American Committee of Enquiry, 5; Balfour Declaration, 5; Bevin's attitude towards Jewish claims, 5; Haganah activities, 5; General Assembly asked to consider problem, 6; trusteeship proposals, 6; UN Special Committee on Palestine (UNSCOP), 7; partition plan, 8–10, 481 n. 25; UN Palestine Commission, 10–11; Security Council begins consideration, 11; Truce Commission established, 13; Bernadotte, 14; cease-fire ordered by Security Council, 14 f.; Mediator appointed, 14 f., 18–24, 29; observers authorized, 15 f.; Armistice Agreements, 18; UN Truce Supervision Organization, 18–212; hostilities upon proclamation of State of Israel, 19; Jerusalem, special measures ordered by Security Council, 20–1; refugees, UNTSO's role in respect of, 30
Palestine Land Development Co., 88, 90, 93, 95 ff., 102, 137
Palestine Liberation Army, 322, 482
Pearson, Lester, 221, 227 f., 242–3, 251, 410
Pineau, Christian, 22
Plaza, Galo, 551 f., 555
Privileges and immunities, 277, 287, 288–9, 377–378, 382–4, 563–5, 643–5

Red Cross, 132
Refugees in Palestine, 30, 147, 178
Regulations, of UNEF, 266, 275 f., 288–92, 326–327, 328, 486, 489, 506–7, 519–21
Reparations for Injuries case, 78
Reparations, UN attempts to secure, 78–83; UNEF arrangements, 292, 329–35
Reprisals, 203, 619
de Ridder, Col., 70, 96
Rikhye, Gen., 277, 293, 340, 343, 345, 637, 654
Riley, Gen., 70, 96, 98, 102, 124, 139, 141, 168 f.

Sallal, Abdullah, 609 f., 612, 616, 619

Saudi Arabia: involvement in Yemen civil war, 610, 612, 614–15, 622–4, 626, 629–35, 641–5, 649–51, 653–68
Scorpion Pass Incident, 121–2, 172
Secretary-General: authority to enlarge UNTSO personnel, 62–3; consults with Chief of Staff on organization of UNTSO, 69; provides good offices for talks between Fawzi and Selwyn Lloyd, 225; prepares plans for UNEF, 242; authority to terminate UNEF, 271–3; duty to consult with Advisory Committee, 271–3, 351–2; relations with UNEF Advisory Committee, 274–5; authorizes UNEF's withdrawal, 277; authority to determine UNEF's size and composition, 300–1; appoints team to study UNEF reductions, 313; aide-mémoire of 5 Aug. 1957, 363; position on apportionment of UNEF expenses, 418–20, 430–1, 436; negotiates for cease-fire and withdrawal of foreign troops from Egypt (1956–7), 458–9; summary study of UNEF, 483–521; explains UNOGIL's tasks, 548; authority under UNOGIL resolutions, 549–51; initiative of Yemen, 611, 620, 626–33; authority to initiate diplomacy, 626–8; authority to terminate UNYOM, 633 f.
Self-defence, 181–3, 185, 226, 538
Sharm el-Sheikh, 113, 199–200, 221, 227, 251, 294, 315, 317, 350, 352, 354, 357 ff., 360, 362, 367, 387, 394–5, 397, 400, 402, 405, 460, 465 f., 468 f., 474, 480, 482, 485, 487, 492 f.
Sinai, 203, 226, 230, 252, 259–60, 340, 342, 344, 346, 348, 393, 461, 471, 474, 476, 487, 493, 495, 510 f., 522
Spinelli, Pier, 631, 636, 638
Status of UN Forces and Observers Agreements: for UNEF, 287, 326, 328 f., 373–84, 508–11, 514; UNOGIL, 563–5; see also under Privileges and immunities
Straits of Tiran, see Tiran Straits
Soviet Union, see USSR
Suez, 228, 239, 242 ff., 390, 402, 408; placement of UN observers on Canal (1967), 18, 57–9, 62, 71, 136, 205, 208–11; drawing of 1967 cease-fire line, 63; Anglo-French intervention, 109–10, 409; Security Council resolution on freedom of passage for shipping, 113; Egyptian nationalization, 156, 222–7; closure to Israel shipping, 157–60, 199, 248, 250, 386, 404, 478; UNEF's functions in Suez sector, 259, 483, 493; cost of clearing Canal, 427; UK offer to clear, 461 n. 6; withdrawal of Israel (1956–7), 464
Suez Canal Users' Association, 224 f.
Syria: decision not to participate in Truce Commission, 17, 66; Armistice Agreement, 38–42; attitude to disputes over demilitarized zone, 87–105, 189–93; protected by Soviet veto, 103, 193; incidents on Lake Tiberias, 142–4; complaints to MAC against Israel, 145–7; position on diversion

Syria—*cont.*
of Jordan, 192; forms UAR with Egypt, 535; charged with harbouring infiltrators into Lebanon, 573, 575

Territorial Seas Convention (1958), 201, 221 n. 3, 481 n. 21
Thant, U, 126 f., 130, 271, 276, 362 f., 367, 481, 612, 644
Tiberias, 90, 99, 131, 142–7, 189, 192, 197, 203
Tiran Straits, 113 f., 199 f., 221, 247, 249, 252, 258, 349, 350 f., 353, 357, 386, 390, 400, 465, 474, 478 n. 13, 478 ff., 481 n. 21, 482

United Arab Republic, *see* Egypt
United Kingdom: mandate in Palestine, 5–16, 73; attitude towards stationing of observers on Suez Canal (1967), 62; military action in Suez, 228, 459; response to establishment of UNEF, 231, 232–3, 236, 246, 261; position on withdrawal, 407–15; financial contribution to UNEF, 434; responds to Hussein's request for help, 538; withdraws from Jordan, 546, 597–602; accused by Yemen, 616–19, 625
UN Charter: Article 1, 445; Articles 5 & 6, 444; Art. 2(7), 539; Art. 10, 262; Art. 11, 262, 270, 444, 447, 268; Art. 12, 268, 270; Art. 14, 262, 267 f., 270, 443; Art. 17(2), 267, 269, 425, 430, 440–9; Art. 18, 443; Art. 19, 449, 454; Art. 22, 262, 514; Art. 24, 267, 443; Art. 35(2), 268; Art. 38, 268; Art. 40, 60 f.; Art. 43, 268–9, 427, 443, 649; Art. 48, 649; Art. 50, 649; Art. 51, 538 f.; Art. 98, 626; Art. 99, 626–7; Art. 105, 644–5; Chapter VI, 261; Chapter VII, 18, 76, 261 f., 264, 268 ff., 550
UN Conciliation Commission for Palestine, 24, 29 f., 42, 133–4
UN Emergency Force (UNEF), 53 f., 107, 130, 156, 199–200, 221–531, 614, 636, 638 f., 641
UN Force in Cyprus (UNFICYP), 133, 372, 522, 642
UN Mediator for Palestine, 14 f., 18–24, 29, 52, 60, 62, 64, 73 ff., 78–80, 82, 84, 199
UN Observation Group in Lebanon (UNOGIL), 512, 514 f., 517, 535–602
UN Palestine Commission, 10–11
UN Commission for the Unification and Rehabilitation of Korea (UNCURK), 133
UN Military Observer Group in India and Pakistan (UNMOGIP), 319, 566, 614, 623, 639
UN Relief and Works Agency (UNRWA), 164, 260, 280 f., 283, 469, 470, 488, 494, 552, 555
UN Security Force in West Irian (UNSF), 133
UN Special Committee on Palestine (UNSCOP): functions, 7; composition, 7; boycotted by Arab community, 8; Partition Plan recommendations, 8–10
UN Temporary Executive Authority in West Irian (UNTEA), 567.

UN Truce Commission for Palestine, 13 ff., 19–24, 30, 60, 62, 68, 76, 78 f., 86 f.; relations with UN Mediator, 15 f.; Syrian decision not to participate as member, 17; allotted observers, 20
UN Truce Supervision Organization (UNTSO), 18–21, 226, 242, 256–8, 264, 276, 284, 305, 319, 330, 386, 392, 470, 482 ff., 490, 497, 542, 553, 566, 599 f., 614, 623, 639, 641
UN Yemen Observation Mission (UNYOM), 133, 308 f., 567, 613–69
United States of America: attitude towards stationing of observers on Suez Canal (1967), 62; opposes Israel invasion of Egypt (1956), 226 f.; draft resolutions on Suez intervention, 226–7; withdraws from confrontation over Article 19, 454; responds to Chamoun's request for help, 538, 563, 566, 587, 597–602; relations with Yemen republicans, 610–11; response to establishment of UNYOM, 620–1
Uniting for Peace Resolution, 227, 229, 261, 263, 266, 485, 515–16
USSR: views on Palestine Truce Commission, 17–18; desire to see UNTSO disbanded, 61; attitude to stationing observers on Suez Canal (1967), 62; casts first veto on Arab-Israel question, 103; vetoes resolution in 1966, 193, 338; agrees to cease-fire in June 1967, 203; protests at formation of SCUA, 225; abstains on establishment of UNEF, 235, 241, 244–5; views on role of UNEF, 253, 264; denies Secretary-General's authority to determine composition and size of UNEF, 300–1; reports Israel concentration on Syrian front, 339; views on financing UNEF, 426–7, 449; threatens to withdraw if deprived of Assembly vote, 450; response to US assistance to Chamoun, 539; demands withdrawal of US and UK troops from Lebanon and Jordan, 539; condemns British action at Fort Harib, 618; response to establishment of UNYOM, 621, 628–9, 648–9

Von Horn, Maj.-Gen., 70, 126, 553, 555, 613 f., 622, 637–8, 642, 646

West Irian, 627 f.

Yemen, 609–20, 641, 653–68
Yugoslavia: contributions to UNEF, 302 f.; position on Egypt's request for UNEF's withdrawal, 276, 295, 326; contribution to UNYOM, 630, 640

Zones, demilitarized, 37, 86–105, 108, 118 ff. 124–5, 138–47, 179, 185 ff., 194–5, 197–9, 640, 642–3, 655 f.

DATE DUE	
OCT 24 2004	